AMERICAN THEATRE:
A Chronicle of Comedy and Drama, 1869–1914

AMERICAN THEATRE:

A Chronicle of Comedy and Drama, 1869–1914

GERALD BORDMAN

New York   Oxford
OXFORD UNIVERSITY PRESS
1994

Oxford University Press

Oxford   New York   Toronto
Delhi   Bombay   Calcutta   Madras   Karachi
Kuala Lumpur   Singapore   Hong Kong   Tokyo
Nairobi   Dar es Salaam   Cape Town
Melbourne   Auckland   Madrid

and associated companies in
Berlin   Ibadan

Copyright © 1994 by Oxford University Press, Inc.

Published by Oxford University Press, Inc.,
200 Madison Avenue, New York, New York 10016

Oxford is a registered trademark of Oxford University Press

Library of Congress Cataloging-in-Publication Data
Bordman, Gerald Martin.
American theatre: A chronicle of comedy and drama,
1869–1914 / Gerald Bordman.
p. cm.   Includes index.
ISBN 0-19-503764-2
1. Theater—United States—History—19th century.
2. Theater—United States—History—20th century.
3. American drama—19th century—Stories, plots, etc.
4. American drama—20th century—
Stories, plots, etc.   I. Title.
PN2256.B6   1994
792'.0973'09034—dc20   92-16066

1 3 5 7 9 8 6 4 2

Printed in the United States of America
on acid-free paper

PREFACE

This book is the first of several projected volumes in which we hope to do for America's non-musical theatre what we did for song-and-dance entertainments in our earlier *American Musical Theatre: A Chronicle,* which Oxford University Press first published in 1978 and which has gone through several printings and several updated editions since that time. That single volume encompassed almost all of our musical shows; but since what we would now perceive as musicals came on the scene so much later and since in virtually all but the most recent times straight plays have far outnumbered musicals, several volumes are required for comedy and drama. Because we are least familiar with the Colonial and the pre-Civil War stage, we have left that volume for last and have begun with the earliest theatre that we believe still could have major relevancy for modern theatre-lovers. Therefore, this volume treats primarily New York's first-class houses from the start of the 1869–70 season until the eruption of World War I (with occasional looks at, by then decreasingly important, outlying theatrical centers).

In a way, dealing solely with first-class houses would be distressingly unfair. For the initial several decades covered in this book, American playwrights, producers, and more elite audiences were under the sway of foreign drama. Much of what we would find most intriguing today—plays about contemporary or historical America—was confined to lesser houses, which catered to the lowest classes. Since many of such plays were ignored by the newspapers and even by trade sheets of the day and are now lost, except for the final years of the vogue of cheap-priced theatre plays, we had no choice but to include only those readily accessible either in manuscript or as covered in contemporary reviews. But the numerous such plays we have detailed, among them such legendary hits as *The Phoenix* and *Bertha, the Sewing Machine Girl,* should fascinate readers as they once gripped audiences. Constraints of time and expense precluded our examining an additional handful of manuscripts known still to exist in out-of-the-way venues. In dealing with the melodramas and occasional comedies that played lower-class theatres, we usually have not included the players' names unless the players were the authors or went on to fame in first-class houses or in films.

The next volume, dealing with material from mid-1914 onward, is currently in the works.

There are a few caveats. For starters, we have ignored special matinees (an early form of tryouts) unless of outstanding interest. We have also passed over bills of one-act plays, again unless they hold particular interest. A few plays that were included in *American Musical Theatre* are also included in this book, since further consideration convinced us that they were not really musicals. It must be remembered that for most of the 19th century, the best playhouses, and numerous lesser ones, kept full orchestras on hand, with the result that not only was there an ongoing musical accompaniment throughout plays but dramatists and performers felt free to insert occasional songs and dances. Probably even contemporaries did not always distinguish between genres.

The flood of foreign plays has presented some problems. If an American title is distinct from an original we have mentioned the original, if we could determine it; but where a title was essentially a literal translation of its source and could not be mistaken, we usually have not listed both. (There are

Preface

some exceptions.) For brevity's sake we have sometimes spoken of Henri Bataille's *The Scandal*, although Bataille called it *Le Scandale*.

Within the texts of foreign plays, but more often of native plays set on foreign soil, other problems cropped up. For instance, in *The Song of the Sword* the program we have seen and all important reviews called a principal character, a Frenchmen, Egalite. Was it pronounced E-ga-lite, or was it given a correct French pronunciation? The central figure in *The Duke's Motto* was sometimes listed as Lagardere and sometimes as Lagardère. Similarly, the published text of *The Dictator* makes no distinction between "n" and "ñ," although some notices did employ the Spanish eñe, suggesting place names were properly pronounced in production. In two different dramas one famous historical figure was spelled variously as Santa Ana or Santa Anna. Nor were totally American names free from difficulty, a play dealing with Dolley Madison spelled her name Dolly, while a fictitious character in another play was Brinckerhoff in the manuscript but Brinkerhoff in surviving programs.

In a few instances character names were altered even more noticeably in the published text, in the manuscript, or in programs. For the most part—though not always—we have accepted the testimony of the programs.

To avoid a plethora of quotation marks we have regularly picked out adjectives from notices and quietly incorporated them into the text. Thus, if we call a farce's playing fast paced, that "fast paced" may well have been taken from a convincing review. Similarly to avoid what we deem unsightly [*sics*], obvious or seeming mistakes—such as the spelling "barring" in the quotation on the right-hand column of p. 17—have been quietly corrected.

In compliance with our fine copy editor's request, punctuation and capitalization in quotations have been brought in line with the most recently accepted modern procedure.

Special thanks must go to the excellent crew at the library of Millersville University, notably Ray Hacker, Leo Shelley, and Evelyn Lyons, to Geraldine Duclow and Elaine Ebo at the Theatre Collection of the Free Library of Philadelphia, to Robert Taylor at Lincoln Center's Library of the Performing Arts, to Sam Brylawski at the Library of Congress, to Ray Wemmlinger, librarian of The Players, to the courteous and efficient staff at the British Museum's manuscript collection (the lone repository for so many American texts), to the distinguished theatrical historians, Ian Bevan and Kurt Gänzl, and to Jacques Kelly. Of course, sincere thanks must also be conveyed to my friends and colleagues at Oxford University Press—to India Cooper, my copy editor, to Joellyn Ausanka, my typist and troubleshooter, and to my deeply admired, loyal editor, Sheldon Meyer.

Kirk's Mills, Pa.   Gerald Bordman
July 1993

Act Four, 1899–1906

The Growing
Americanization
of the American
Theatre

Act Five, 1906–1914

The Advance Guard
of the New Drama

ACT ONE
1869–1879

The Palmy Days of
Daly and Palmer

1869–1870

When the curtain rose on the 1869–70 season, the guns of the Civil War, that great watershed in American history, had been silent for more than four years. The victorious North's main goals—the preservation of national unity and the abolition of slavery—seemingly had been attained. How truly unified the nation was remained moot. Secession was now out of the question for the foreseeable future, but the South could and did pounce quickly on the issue of states' rights to constantly chip away at Washington's ever greedier grasp. And beyond the legalities and technicalities of a sometimes enforced unity, frustration and rancor festered. Similarly, while by any common definition slavery had become illegal, the South lost little time devising ways to keep down its often feared and detested blacks. In this, surprisingly, southerners found tacit and occasionally open support from onetime foes, the former abolitionists, many of whom had railed against the idea and practice of slavery while harboring no love or respect for the slaves themselves. The American Constitution and local laws might be amended in the name of civil rights, but for the most part the lot of blacks in American society, North and South, improved, if at all, far more in theory than in practice. Clearly, most Americans were all too happy to look away from wartime horrors and related national problems. In this respect the contemporary American theatre, so ruled by classic or escapist instincts, gladly catered to its public's clamor for traditional or unthinking entertainments. Even in so small and seemingly straightforward a matter as casting blacks to portray blacks, the theatre preferred to shun the possibility of controversy. Black roles, large or small, were still assumed by whites in blackface, while discussion of the day's most pressing issues—racial or regional—was reserved almost entirely for editorial pages. Not a single play in the 1869–70 season grappled with America's postwar problems.

In the South the war wrote a sad but effective finish to once great theatrical centers, most especially Charleston and New Orleans. The independent creativity (in particular at Charleston), the artistic elegance, the technical daring that had so frequently and so promisingly illumined southern stages flickered out with varying rapidity but dismaying permanence. Hereafter important southern cities would be merely touring stops at best.

On the other hand, some of the effects of the war could be seen as positive, albeit they involved American theatre more than American drama. In the North, increasing and spreading affluence meant more playgoers, more theatres, and more productions. This growth probably would have occurred even without war-fostered prosperity, but the relatively sudden expansion and redistribution of wealth provided an extra spur. Moreover, the development of industry encouraged technological advances, many of which found application sooner or later in the theatre. The first transcontinental rail line had been established in May 1869, just three months before the new season began. Rapidly developing rail transportation made it easier for stars to travel and within a decade or so would encourage the movement of whole companies—actors, scenery, and all—thereby ineluctably putting an end to the local stock ensembles that had been the mainstay of theatre all across the nation. This change would coincide with and impel the engulfing dominance of New York, removing one by one other major cities from the list of lively production centers.

The war had temporarily halted, or at least slowed markedly, the inpouring of aliens. Now, with peace restored, immigration swelled. Significantly, New York and those other northern cities that survived for a time as primary production centers were the very same cities that had welcomed and would continue to welcome the largest influx of newcomers. The first massive, important wave had been the Irish. By 1869, active in all fields of endeavor, they had not only started to consolidate their position but were watching a second, American-born generation of Irish mature. Theatre was one field they were to dominate speedily. The European revolutions of 1848 had prompted other, Continental figures to make a home in the New World. These arrivals included the German Jews who would eventually wrest control of the theatre from the Irish. (The influx of equally important Eastern European Jews did not begin in earnest until the 1880s.) These groups, and others, would put their stamps on

American theatre, pulling it out of its conservative lethargy and broadening its range of interest while, as some would add ruefully, weakening its respect for Shakespeare and other English classics.

Perhaps the most noteworthy development in the seasons immediately following the Civil War was the emergence of a popular musical theatre, beginning with the year-long success of an elaborate pastiche, *The Black Crook,* in 1866 and the subsequent rage of French opéra bouffe. A number of traditionalists, resorting to both aesthetic and moral arguments, spoke out loudly against the new genre. Since most of the Jeremiahs represented old American stock— many were leading Protestant ministers—they were implicitly challenging new foreign, Catholic, and, indirectly, Jewish influences on the theatre in general and the musical in particular. But musicals aside, unless the complainers were dead set against theatre itself, the 1869–70 season would give them little cause to be violently displeased. And most playgoers, regardless of ethnic origins, paid little heed anyway.

"A new era in New York theatricals begins in the year 1869." When the distinguished theatrical historian George C. D. Odell made that observation from the vantage point of nearly seventy years he was speaking of many things, none of which directly related to the Civil War or national trends. He referred, rather narrowly, to New York alone, although by then the city had become indisputably America's richest, biggest, and most vital theatrical center. Among other matters, he noted the recent passing of some once major playhouses as well as the death or retirement of beloved old performers. To balance these losses he recorded the debuts or rise to prominence of other soon to be famous players and one occasion of supreme interest to contemporaries, the opening of Booth's Theatre in February 1869. Less apparent as a theatrical milestone to 1869 playgoers, but in the long run the real justification for hailing the inauguration of a new era, were the first performances at Daly's Fifth Avenue Theatre.

So while few students would dispute Odell's conclusion, it could not have been all that obvious to patrons lining up at the box office or sauntering down the aisle to their seats. Indeed, at the time there must have been more to suggest to them an unshakable, fundamental continuity or at most a virtually imperceptible evolution. With Saturday matinees fast becoming standard, most plays now gave seven performances a week; midweek matinees were very rare. Ticket prices, which had been raised because of Civil War inflation, now held steady. In

first-class playhouses the $1.00 top was gone, more or less forever. A new top of $1.50 prevailed and, with some notable exceptions, would continue to prevail until the late nineties, when the Trust was able to establish at its best houses a $2.00 top that would obtain until World War I. With far more rapidity than in the less democratic theatres of England or the Continent, the infamous "pit," where for pennies poorer, rowdier loyalists could enjoy the play, had been dispensed with. The pit faithful were turned into "gallery gods," generally forced to use a separate side entrance and then to climb flight after flight of rickety stairs to their hard, cramping benches. Distance from the stage scarcely modified their often outlandish behavior—volubly cheering pet players and just as volubly hooting those they did not enjoy, or pelting the stage with fruit peels and nutshells. A few more elite houses managed to put an end to such behavior; other theatres attempted with varying degrees of sternness to restrain it. The entire lower level was now given over to expensive "orchestra" seats and, in a few old-fashioned houses, to parquet boxes at the rear and along the sides.

Moving from the lobby into the auditorium, more affluent patrons would be greeted not merely by the cacophonous chatter of other playgoers but by the more harmonious sounds of a fairly good-sized, well-rehearsed orchestra performing just below and in front of the stage. The best conductors were minor celebrities in their own right. When the curtain rose, audiences could be assured of a better view of their favorites than heretofore, since bright limelights, introduced only two or three years earlier, now focused on and followed prominent players. Prolonged applause always welcomed the entrance of those favorites and also rewarded their well-delivered speeches and well-played scenes. Performers acknowledged it by stepping out of character to take a bow. Nor, in a theatre still heavily presentational, were actors the only ones to shoulder aside the play for a time. At least on opening nights, superior examples of the scene painter's art usually elicited sufficient applause to prompt the designer to appear and take a bow—or two or three, if clapping warranted.

That designers were called scene painters was no accident. Scenery consisted largely of meticulously painted flats, affecting a studied realism. Since the 1840s the three-walled "box set" generally had been employed to depict drawing rooms or other relatively comfortable domestic settings, but the more ancient "wing-and-drop" style still prevailed when huge palaces or outdoor settings were required. For example, the drop curtain at the rear of the stage might depict a palace's staircase (if the action did not necessitate use of the stairs) or its great tapestries or windows, while flats depicting columns would be placed at the sides of the stage at regular intervals to further the illusion and to hide the wings. Most entrances and exits were made from behind these flats. On the stage's floor the regular intervals were grooved so that the flats could be slid on and off, usually in full view of the audience, with the stage carpenters not always carefully concealed. In *A Tramp Abroad* Mark Twain recalled seeing a "forest split itself in the middle and go shrieking away, with the accompanying disenchanting spectacle of hands and heels of the impelling impulse." Especially elaborate scene changes were glorified by the term "transformation scene." Entrances and exits were still sometimes made from doors on both sides of the proscenium, although newer theatres such as Booth's had started to omit these doors.

By modern standards acting styles remained broad. The fist-on-the-forehead-to-express-grief was still the accepted school; some idea of the style can be gotten from early silent films. Tradition, comparatively dim preelectric lighting, and the large size of so many of the period's theatres all militated against real change here. Lest audiences misunderstand the nature of a character, a crucial line, or an action, the orchestra was kept busy providing incidental music, not unlike background music of modern films or television. Soft romantic or vivacious music built to a crescendo for the hero or heroine's entrance, gay pizzicato underscored the ingenue, and ominous chords warned of villains and villainy.

All theatres signed on a basic company for each season, with actors generally hired to depict the "lines," or character types, they were best known for. Famous ensembles might confine their casting to their own members, but even in playhouses that relied on the comings and goings of stars, supporting players stayed on for the whole theatrical year.

Although the practice was slowly dying out, double bills were the order of many a night. Whether double or single bills, the plays presented were almost all foreign and almost all old. English plays more than dominated; they virtually monopolized the bills. And if a careful accounting could determine the average age of these plays, that average would surely put most of them in their teens and might well reveal a mellow maturity. Fewer than a quarter of the plays were new. The French would establish a beachhead that would be expanded noticeably in the years just ahead, but meanwhile the British hegemony persisted. Three playwrights—T. W. Robertson, Tom Taylor, and

Dion Boucicault—accounted for approximately a fourth of the newer attractions. True, Boucicault had spent most of the 1850s writing and acting in America and would return shortly to spend the rest of his life here, but with one exception the plays offered in the new season all represented the work of his London years. Just before the 1869–70 season began, William Dean Howells wrote in the *Atlantic Monthly*, with only slight exaggeration, "There is nothing American on the American stage." Only about half a dozen of the eighty-odd plays staged at New York's first-class houses during the 1869–70 season would be American works. These were hardly the glory years of American drama.

If a single word could characterize the plays of the time, especially the newer ones, that word could easily be "polite." Even the most rambunctious bumpkins and most arch evildoers were exceedingly well bred, particularly by later standards. "Chaste" was still an encomium often used by leading critics to describe a well-drawn character or a superior interpretation. There were rougher edges as well as dramatic examples of ugly violence, all hinting at things to come, but these were largely confined to sensation-dramas, such as those of Boucicault's school, and were seen far more at lesser houses catering to lower-class audiences than at those first-class theatres entertaining elite sophisticates. Even plays such as some of Robertson's, which might open on a disquieting note of genuine social turmoil, had a way of dwindling into escapist comedy by the second act.

Yet away from New York, except at such distinguished venues as Mrs. Drew's Arch Street Theatre in Philadelphia or the Boston Museum, many of these plays were dismissed as caviar to the general. Only a few larger cities had enough of a knowing, worldly clientele to permit their staging. In smaller cities and backwaters (and it must be remembered that towns of only a few thousand people supported a theatre at the time) there was little market for such plays. Audiences in those smaller cities may have dutifully trekked to the local playhouse to watch a famous touring star in Shakespeare and discovered to their surprise that they enjoyed the experience, but the mainstay of these theatres would be the likes of *Rip Van Winkle, Uncle Tom's Cabin,* and the soon to appear *Davy Crockett* or *Kit, the Arkansas Traveller,* along with homespun rustic comedies and dramas spelled by blood-and-thunder melodramas. To the extent that native American drama in these years was attempting to find itself, it was forced to look to playhouses and regions sneered at by citified highbrows.

The New York season opened on August 16. Precise dates of seasonal openings rarely matter much, even when, as happened in this case, a new theatrical year also marked the beginning of a fresh theatrical epoch. But in 1869, by a gratifying appropriateness, the curtain raiser was the very occasion that so affected American theatre and, to a somewhat lesser extent, American drama in coming decades—the relighting of the heretofore jinxed Fifth Avenue Theatre under the inspired management of Augustin Daly.

• • •

[John] **Augustin Daly** (1838–99) was born in Plymouth, N.C., the son of a sea captain and a soldier's daughter. He was only three when his father died and his mother moved her children to Norfolk, Va. It was there, watching James E. Murdoch in a performance of *Rookwood,* that his passion for theatre was kindled. A subsequent move to New York afforded additional opportunities to attend plays and further fired his enthusiasm. He soon became active in the amateur dramatic societies—usually named after celebrated performers—that flourished at the time. He also frequented the two quality companies that preceded his, Burton's and Wallack's. Shortly after he turned twenty-one he was appointed drama critic for the *Sunday Courier.* He earned national attention when his dramatization of S. H. von Mosenthal's *Deborah* was presented as *Leah, the Forsaken* in 1862 at the Boston Museum and on January 19 of the following year in New York. Hard on the heels of this success came his productions of his *Griffith Gaunt, Under the Gaslight,* and *A Flash of Lightning. Under the Gaslight* was famous for introducing the later overused device of a figure tied to railroad tracks and saved at the last moment from an oncoming train. Unlike most of his plays, it appears to be largely original, although the train-tracks scene may have been borrowed from a minor English melodrama. Reliance on European plays was to remain a Daly trait.

• • •

The seven-year-old Fifth Avenue Theatre stood on 24th Street at the rear of the then famous Fifth Avenue Hotel. Originally built as a stock exchange, it was not converted to theatrical uses until 1865. It was one of Broadway's smallest houses, with a seating capacity of approximately 900 plus additional room for standees. Whether Daly saw this as an advantage or disadvantage is unrecorded, but it certainly must have affected his thinking about the type of plays he would offer and the nature of their production. The yearly rent of $25,000 was a steep but not unreasonable figure at the time. Today a Broadway play can take in as much in a single performance, but in 1869 a capacity house at the Fifth Avenue probably grossed less than $1000. All Daly would promise his public was "the production of whatever is novel, entertaining and unobjectionable, and . . . the revival of whatever is rare and worthy in the legitimate drama." In no small measure Daly kept his promise.

However, Daly did have in mind one artistic innovation that he apparently chose not to broadcast. Type-casting of a peculiar sort had long been the rule on American stages. Actors specialized in what were then called "lines," such as "heavy lead," "first old man," or "walking lady." Thus the "heavy lead" was the principal villain and was portrayed by an actor who played almost nothing but blackguards. "First old man" was a principal character part, generally homey and kindly, and could be played by a very youthful, if heavily made up, actor, who moved from one similar assignment to the next. The absurdity of the practice often led to a relatively elderly player whose line was "leading man" or "leading lady" impersonating a teenager. (The "walking" lines were less problematic, covering minor roles and what we today call "walk-on" parts.) Daly determined to break free from this bondage and to cast people in whatever part most naturally seemed to suit them. His plan meant the actress who assumed the heroine's role in one play might be cast as a minor character in a second play and as a villainess in a third. He was to learn to his chagrin that many players and a hidebound public did not appreciate his novel idea (it was particularly difficult to demote a performer), and eventually he was obliged to modify it, so that in his later years, when many of his performers had earned widespread reputations and loyal followings, he was forced to find and even to write plays to accommodate expectations.

Daly also determined to mold his players into an ensemble as distinguished and permanent as Burton's had been and Wallack's still was. To this end he signed on an intriguing mixture of great oldtimers and unknowns. Oldsters included the venerable George Holland, William Davidge, E. L. Davenport, and one actress, still in her forties, who long since had established herself in the line of "first old lady," Mrs. G. H. Gilbert. All but Mrs. Gilbert and Davidge would soon resign from the company.

• • •

Mrs. [George Henry] **Gilbert** (1821–1904) Born Ann Hartley in England, she was trained there as a dancer. She married a fellow actor and dancer in 1846, and the two toured England and Ireland before coming to America. Here they played opposite many of the great stars of the time in the cities of the Midwest, where the couple first made their home. Mrs. Gilbert made her New York debut in 1864, and two years later her husband died. She first won major acclaim as the Marquise de St. Maur in the 1867 American premiere of Robertson's *Caste*. A homely woman with an angular, pinched face and heavy-lidded, protruding eyes, she so used her expressive, comic gifts that audiences overlooked her lack of beauty.

· · ·

Daly's less famous, younger players included a surprising recruit from contemporary burlesque, James Lewis, as well as some beautiful women who would soon generate their own special excitement, among them Fanny Davenport and Agnes Ethel.

For his opening attraction Daly decided on Robertson's **Play.** The selection is puzzling. The Bancrofts, English favorites who worked closely with Robertson in London, had first presented the comedy there early in 1868, and it had been only a modest success; among their Robertson productions it was one of only two they never attempted to revive. Doubts had apparently dissuaded Wallack, Robertson's principal New York producer, from bringing it to Broadway. Perhaps Daly concluded Robertson's prestigious name made the effort worth the risk. Nor do we know whether Robertson concurred in changes Daly made—introducing new characters, altering the names of others, rewriting whole scenes, and injecting melodrama at the expense of comedy. Changes of this sort would become standard practice with the producer.

Play's story was typical period frippery, set at a fashionable German spa. The Chevalier Browne (George Clarke) has deserted his actress wife, Amanda (Clara Jennings). When Browne learns that Rosie Farquhere (Agnes Ethel) is an heiress, he decides to keep the information to himself and to court her. Rosie, however, loves Frank Price (J. B. Polk), although her uncle and guardian, the Hon. Bruce Farquhere (E. L. Davenport), has long harbored a grudge against the whole Price family. Misunderstandings come between the lovers before a happy ending unites the pair as well as the chevalier and Amanda. Marriage also seems in order for a poor widow, Mrs. Kinpeck (Mrs. Gilbert), and a rich, hypochondriacal old bachelor, Bodmin Todder (George Holland).

Although the small opening-night audience, which filled less than half the house, was reported warmly welcoming, critics in their morning-after appraisals were not uniformly kind. Strong objections were voiced against the melodramatic elements

Daly had added, especially those for Amanda. Daly also transformed a harmless German count—originally the source of a running gag because his only English was "How do you do Illustrated London News"—into one of a pair of hotheaded Prussians. With regard to the acting, many felt that the stiff Davenport lacked the requisite lightness for such airy affairs. At least one critic among several who complimented Daly on the beauty and taste of his costumes and settings could not resist the barbed qualification that they bore no resemblance to anything German he had ever seen.

Play ran for a mere three weeks, an inauspicious start for the new enterprise.

On September 6, Niblo's Garden Theatre, popularly known simply as Niblo's, initiated its new season as it had closed its previous one—with a Boucicault play.

· · ·

Dion[ysius Lardner] **Boucicault** (1820?–90) was born in Dublin and named for his parents' friend Dr. Dionysius Lardner, who may have been his natural father and was known to have taken a paternal interest in the boy. He studied at several schools, including the College School of London University, and performed in amateur theatricals before turning professional in 1838. He made his London debut using the name Lee Moreton. However, he soon reverted to his real name, albeit the spelling he adopted departed from the traditional "Boursiquot." He won international renown with the production of his comedy *London Assurance* in 1841. The late 1840s were spent in France, where his first wife died under mysterious circumstances. When he returned to England he supposedly married Agnes Robertson, a marriage he would claim afterwards was not legal. His first American appearances were in 1854. He remained here until 1860, then came back, more or less permanently, in 1872. Among the plays he wrote during his first visit were *The Poor of New York* and *The Octoroon*. A small, dark, balding, round-faced man, he moved with ease from acting to writing to directing. His martinet ways earned him both the respect and fear of his associates.

· · ·

But whereas *Arrah na Pogue* had been a return engagement of a four-year-old success, the latest arrival was the American premiere of "a drama of modern life" that had first scored a palpable hit at London's Drury Lane only a month earlier. Most playgoers called it **Formosa,** but its full title was almost as complex as its plot—*Formosa: ("The Most Beautiful"); or, The Railroad to Ruin.* Some question remains whether or not the six-week New York run was forced. Unquestionably the stand was a disappointment.

Because capsulation is necessary for so lengthy a chronicle as this we normally might pass over the story by saying it described the downfall and, just possibly, the reformation of a not totally unprincipled courtesan, but a detailed look at the play spotlights many salient features both of contemporary plays and of their presentation.

The published text calls for an "Overture of nautical and English Country airs" and specifically suggests "Jolly Young Waterman" and "Lass of Richmond Hill." The first scene is set outside an inn with a view of the Thames. The inn is run by Sam Boker (Harry Pearson), a former prizefighter who now coaches the Oxford rowing team, and his wife (Annie Lonsdale). They are visited by their beautiful daughter, Jenny (Kate Newton), whom they believe to be living in London in the lap of luxury as companion to a rich widow. For some time Jenny has loved the team's stroke, Tom Burroughs (Charles Thorne, Jr.), but she quickly recognizes that his affections, if not all his attentions, have passed on to Nelly Doremus (Isabel Freeman). When Tom's young friend, the Earl of Eden (Ada Harland), who is the crew's coxswain, chides Tom for his fickleness, Tom insists he loves both women: "I love Nelly because she is an angel—but I love Jenny like the devil." Eden wishes he could infatuate women as Tom does, for he loves Tom's sister, Edith (Pattie Mackworth), who seems to favor Compton Kerr (A. Fitzgerald). However, Tom refuses to help the dissipated Kerr lead his sister to the altar. This presents a problem for Kerr and his cohort, Major Jorum (C. H. Morton), who are sorely in need of funds. Kerr had banked not only on Tom's favor but on his generosity. At this point Kerr and Jorum spot Jenny and realize that she is the London courtesan who maintains a villa at Fulham and who is known sometimes as Mrs. Lascalles, sometimes as Lady Arthur Pierpont, but more often among her high-living set merely as Formosa, the Most Beautiful. It takes just a little arm-twisting to persuade her to join their plan for ruining Tom. Kerr exults, "It's our profit, but your revenge."

The second scene takes place on a country road. Sam Boker encounters Bob Sanders (William Holston), a thieving roustabout who has served time in prison in Australia and who now returns to seek the daughter whom his wife had left as a baby in the charge of Dr. Doremus (A. D. Bradley). When Nelly, who believes Doremus is her father, passes by, Sanders attempts to steal her brooch, but Tom arrives in time to retrieve it and send Sanders

scurrying. Tom has come to ask Dr. Doremus for Nelly's hand. The embarrassed doctor takes Nelly aside to tell her that he cannot agree to the marriage since she is actually a penniless orphan left to his care years ago.

In the doctor's study Tom, Nelly, and the doctor are confronted by Sanders, who presents Doremus with a receipt the doctor had signed proving Nelly is Sanders's daughter. The doctor tells the stunned Tom, "Now, you know why she could never be your wife."

The second act opens in London, where Kerr has seen to it that Tom, thrown off balance by the shock he has received, has been frittering away his fortune at Formosa's gaming tables. Kerr's plan is to bet heavily on underdog Cambridge and then, moments before the race, have Tom arrested for debt, thus forcing Oxford to rely on a lesser stroke and lose the race. To compound Tom's problem, Kerr has forged additional IOUs, which Tom is supposed to have made out to Formosa's suitor, Spooner (H. Rendle). Kerr has also written to Edith, alerting her to Tom's misbehavior while naturally neglecting to mention his role in it. The grateful girl concludes everyone has misjudged Kerr and consents to marry him.

Meanwhile, the Bokers, who have come to London to surprise Jenny, discover that she does not live at the address she had given them. In Piccadilly they meet Nelly and Sanders. Nelly works for a bootmaker to support her worthless parent, and she has been helped on occasion by the still loyal Tom.

At Formosa's villa Tom continues his heedless gambling. Jenny is ashamed of her own behavior, but Kerr cunningly feeds her jealousy by telling her that Tom remains faithful to Nelly. All the remorseful Jenny can do to maintain her self-respect is to refuse Spooner's gift of jewels. "Fool!" she blurts out to him. "Can't you see that I want to preserve at least one love free from the taint of purchase."

The start of the third act finds Nelly housing the Bokers in her meager lodgings. She has learned that she must go to Fulham to deliver a pair of new boots to Lady Arthur Pierpont. Her father arrives, badly unnerved, to announce that he has been enlisted to arrest Tom at Lady Pierpont's villa. The Bokers decide to join Nelly and Sanders on their journey.

At the villa all the principals meet. Nelly begs Tom to escape, but Tom, believing himself betrayed on all sides, refuses. Jenny, overwhelmed with guilt, is prepared to give her whole estate to Spooner and go off to live a simple, repentant life with her grief-stricken parents.

The fourth act opens in Nelly's shabby room. Doremus, Edith, Nelly, and Mrs. Boker console each other, while Eden rushes about town attempting to raise bail for Tom. He even has prevailed on the Cambridge crew to help.

At the sponging house (a place where debtors initially were kept to give them time to work out arrangements with creditors) Kerr refuses Jenny's offer to pay off Tom's debts. But Spooner's revelation that Tom's IOUs were forged by Kerr gives Tom's friends the ammunition they need. The scene moves quickly to a rally in front of the sponging house, then to a street where Tom meets Jenny and forgives her. A contrite Jenny, having decided to go away to live with Spooner, replies, "I shall never cross your path again!" On the riverbank, as acrobats and Negro minstrels entertain, spectators watch Tom and his crew beat Cambridge.

Recountings of the story in New York reviews imply that during the sea crossing some interesting changes occurred that underscored Jenny's inherent goodness and final reformation. In the original Jenny hints at her unhappiness with her London life and her willingness to abandon it. In New York she was shown to have bought her parents their inn and went off to live with them, not with Spooner, in the end. This possibly happier ending suggests that in 1869 Americans enjoyed a far less vindictive morality than, say, the later Hays office legislated for Hollywood. The published text also noted, "In the United States, for season 1869–70, it will be at the manager's discretion to make [the] race, not one between the Oxford and Cambridge Eights, but one between the Oxford and Harvard Fours." Reviews indicate this change was not made.

Regardless of which version was used, plot was clearly the thing. Its convolutions and coincidences would defy acceptance a hundred years later. In its own day such writing, so occupied with story, left little time or room for characterization. For the most part, villains were the blackest villains, buffoons the personification of buffoonery, and heroes and heroines, if not snow-white pure, at least only momentarily misguided. Even Jenny, as her decent parentage and her adopted name of Formosa suggested, and as her decision to accept a life of exile (or with her parents) and repentance confirmed for audiences of the day, was simply a good girl gone wrong, whose goodness ultimately tells.

The writing and staging of such plays underscored the emphasis on story. The popular 19th-century device of the aside, which might well have been employed to bring to light unexpected nuances of character, rarely was. Instead it generally reinforced the obvious. For example, when Tom early on explains to Kerr why he cannot promote Kerr's courtship of Edith and asks Kerr to forgive his candor, Kerr smilingly acquiesces, then turns to the audience to snarl, "Hang his candor!" Even the choice of a name could be used to underline the restricted nature of character drawing, as Boucicault did with a bitter pun in the last act. When Mrs. Boker asks the conniver his name and he answers "Kerr," she responds, "(emphatically) How do you spell it?" Time and again, especially with dramatic turns that often concluded each act, tableaux reiterated the theatricality of the moment.

Even in a lesser play such as this, Boucicault's gifts emerged throughout. After the haughty Kerr has sneered at the lowly Bokers and dismissed them as dregs of society, Boker replies, "I dare say society has its impurities, like every other thing. Some of 'em float at the top and others settle at the bottom. If we are the dregs, you are the scum!" The artificiality of the whole entertainment was evident not only in the unnaturally clever speeches, the exaggerated turns of story, the stopping for bows, and the tableaux, but also in the casting of a woman to play a young man—in this instance, Ada Harland as Eden.

Two other plays opened on the same night as *Formosa*. **Dreams** (9-6-69, Fifth Ave.) was Daly's replacement for the failed *Play*. Its authorship has been ascribed variously to Robertson alone and to Robertson with substantial rewriting by Boucicault. The story centered on Rudolf (George Clarke), the composer of an opera called *Dreams*. He is loved by his foster sister, Lena (Agnes Ethel), but prefers his aristocratic pupil, Lady Clare Vere de Vere (Clara Jennings). When Clare learns of his passion, she is scornful. The cancellation of a performance of his opera, a duel, and his almost fatal illness follow before he and Lena are happily paired. James Lewis, in the comic relief role of John Hibbs, a commercial traveler, especially delighted audiences. But since each act was set in an interior represented by an elaborate box set, the scene changes required intermissions of twenty minutes or more and gave playgoers and critics time to dwell on the work's all too many inadequacies. Like *Play* before it, *Dreams* ran only three weeks.

The evening's third offering was the umpteenth revival of an old warhorse, *Uncle Tom's Cabin*. The first American play of the season, it addressed issues supposedly settled by the war, so scarcely had its former relevance. But its popularity was hardly diminished, especially when, as in this case, its cast included many of the 1853 stars. Mrs. G. C. Howard, sixteen years older, was still America's favorite Topsy, and the era's highest-paid star, the great pantomimist G. L. Fox, set aside his Humpty Dumpty to portray Deacon Perry. The revival enjoyed a month's stand at the Olympic.

Wallack's relit on September 15 with a company standby, *The School for Scandal.* John Gilbert was Sir Peter; Charles Fisher, Sir Oliver; J. W. Wallack, Joseph Surface; and a young man who had served as a doctor in the war and would soon become a London actor-manager, Charles Wyndham, played Charles Surface. Wallack's company was still as much a repertory theatre as it was a stock ensemble, so the revival ran uninterruptedly for two weeks and returned regularly for a performance or two through-out the season. While the troupe was unquestion-ably then the finest in New York, and its excellences prompted some loyalists to attend almost all its productions, the special attraction of its revivals of *The School for Scandal* was most certainly Gilbert's Sir Peter, considered generally as one of the era's greatest acting feats.

. . .

John Gilbert (1810–89) was born in Boston, where his next-door neighbor and childhood friend was Charlotte Cushman. After working for several years in a dry-goods store, he made his acting debut in 1828 at the Tremont Theatre as Jaffier in *Venice Preserved.* He next spent several years acting along the Mississippi River. His New York debut was in 1839 as Sir Edmund Mortimer in *The Iron Chest.* His somewhat portly build and round, sober-miened face led him to specialize in roles of older men. Stints in London, Paris, and Philadelphia followed before he joined Wallack's in 1862. Some sources give Gibbs as his middle name; others suggest it may have been his original surname.

. . .

Stars of the period, if they were lucky enough to find a great role they could make their own, often toured season after season in the play, only rarely, if ever, trying new parts. *Leah, the Forsaken,* which had catapulted Daly to fame, had done the same for Kate Bateman. She was not quite a one-play actress, but she did oblige her myriad fans by frequently returning to the role of the ill-starred Jewess. Her month-long stand as Leah at Booth's, beginning on the 20th, was a prelude to a new assignment. Like many great stars of the period she refused to perform on Saturday nights, so the house was often dark on the week's most popular evening unless some special attraction could be found.

Wallack's and Daly's, the old and the new, competed for attention on September 27. Perhaps a bit surprisingly, Wallack's offered the American premiere and Daly's the revival. Wallack chose the

season's third new Robertson work, **Progress,** a melodramatic play based on Victorien Sardou's *Les Ganaches.* Given Wallack's traditionalism, there was a certain irony in the selection, since the play's story pitted technological and social change against outmoded ways of life. The modern world was personified by John Ferne (J. W. Wallack), an engineer who has planned a railroad that must run right through the estates of Lord Mompesson (W. Hield) and his son, Arthur (Charles Fisher). The Mompessons are determined to make a stand against any innovation. (Curiously, the reason Robertson contrived for the Mompessons' bitter-ness and conservatism was the same he had offered in *Play* for Farquhere's disdain of Price—common-ers besting aristocrats in their political ambitions.) In the end, progress wins out and Ferne wins the hand of the Mompessons' niece, Eva (Louisa Moore), but not before the ailing Eva has at-tempted suicide by wandering out into the snow for a dramatic second-act curtain. The play was not a major success, only fitfully retaining its hold on the repertory.

Daly's revival, his first, was of a fast-aging comedy, *Old Heads and Young Hearts.* The piece was most admired for its drawing of a comical, incompetent clergyman, Jesse Rural, a role that gave Davidge one of his first chances to shine in the new group. Knowledgeable playgoers did not have to glance at their programs to learn the name of the playwright. They knew it was Boucicault.

It was Boucicault again two nights later when Daly offered the second in a nearly four-month-long series of rapid-fire revivals. This time it was the playwright's masterpiece, *London Assurance,* a bril-liant comedy of country life. What made the evening memorable for many was Daly's imaginative casting of Fanny Davenport. Her youth—she was only nineteen—intelligence, verve, and remarkable beauty made her the perfect Lady Gay Spanker. By contrast, the homely Charlotte Cushman had been thirty-five when she assumed the part at its Ameri-can premiere. Miss Davenport was to return to the role often and in her day came to be considered its best interpreter.

Yet another Boucicault opus was one of three reviv-als to raise their curtains on October 4. *The Streets of New York* (originally produced as *The Poor of New York)* followed *Uncle Tom's Cabin* into the Olympic, making that theatre the only one in New York to have offered American plays so far in the theatrical year. Of course, Boucicault had borrowed freely from a French work, so *Uncle Tom* remained the only purely Yankee work yet seen. A good cast kept this tale of financial treachery and retribution—with its cele-brated rescue from a burning building—alive for five weeks.

The other two October 4 revivals were Shake-spearean; as might be expected, neither came close to outrunning the popular melodrama. Actually, the mounting of *The Tempest* at the Grand Opera House was a return of a successful production from the preceding season and managed to chalk up a respectable two-week stay. It was typical of Shake-spearean revivals of the period at a certain order of popular playhouse such as the Grand Opera or Niblo's, a staging filled with elaborate, splashy scenery, huge ballets, and unexceptional players.

Far more interesting was Daly's first plunge into Shakespearean waters with his presentation of *Twelfth Night*. Dainty, singsong Mrs. [Mary Frances] Scott-Siddons was Viola. Clarke as Malvolio, Da-vidge as Sir Toby, Agnes Ethel as Olivia, and Fanny Davenport as Maria were all singled out for praise. Like the Grand Opera's *Tempest,* Daly's offering ran a fortnight.

The next week saw two openings, again revivals. They came one night apart as additions to Wallack's repertory. Tom Taylor's *An Unequal Match,* a comedy about a country girl who marries a lord and must assume his aloof airs, appeared on the 11th; the 12th saw the return of Robertson's *Caste,* with its ridicule of arbitrary, cruel class distinctions.

Because producers were anxious to pack in a full week's receipts, they regularly chose to open on Monday nights, frequently creating an unnecessary pileup and conflict. Newspapers' first-rank critics generally attended whichever show seemed most important, then caught up with the others on succeeding evenings, letting stringers write the morning-after notices. This meant lesser plays might not receive the most knowing treatment in reviews, but possibly this was what some producers wanted, hoping less knowing could mean less severe. They sometimes regretted their gamble. Mid-October saw the first of several Mondays when four plays opened simultaneously. In this instance the old and the new divided honors.

Tom Taylor's **Mary Warner** (10-18-69, Booth's) was brought in as a vehicle for Kate Bateman. The knavish Bob Levitt (Theodore Hamilton), an em-ployee at Dutton and Downes, robs the company's till and plants some of the bills and other incriminat-ing evidence at the home of his co-worker, George Warner (George Jordan), who is known to be dissatisfied with his job. Seeking a loan to help them emigrate, George and his wife, Mary (Miss Bate-man), have each separately visited the office of Mr.

Dutton (Augustus Pitou). When George is sus-pected of the theft, Mary states she committed the robbery. Her only intent is to spare George, whom she believes to be guilty. But when she is sent to prison, she discovers to her dismay that her husband accepts her confession. The truth is revealed in time for a happy ending.

The obvious absurdities of the story—such as Mr. Dutton conveniently leaving each of the three princi-pals alone in his office at one time or another in the first act—were passed over quickly, if scathingly, by the better critics. Patently the limelight was not on the play but on young Miss Bateman, an actress of excep-tional emotional power. She did not disappoint. The *Tribune* recorded, "In the opening scene she was gen-tle and winning to an extraordinary degree. In the prison-scene she expressed an extreme depth of devo-tion, the agony of an outraged heart, and the simple grandeur of magnanimous fortitude. Her acting in the later scenes, when Mary is a wandering outcast, showed a deep intuitive knowledge of real mimicry— the hopelessness and helplessness of poverty and de-spair. The parting with the wedding-ring, and the rec-ognition of the child, were points worthy of a true artist." The play ran six weeks, but critics and playgo-ers could not know this was their last chance to see the actress, who shortly would leave to spend the rest of her career in England. Augustus Pitou, who played Dutton, later became a major producer of plays for the road.

Charles O'Malley (10-8-69, Grand Opera) can be given shorter shrift. Edmund Falconer, an English playwright and actor whose brief, unsuccessful American visit was coming to an end, presented himself in his dramatization of Charles James Lever's 1840 swashbuckling novel about the Peninsu-lar War of 1808–14. The play's scenes shuttled between Ireland and Portugal and at one point featured "a troop of mounted dragoons." Falconer played not the title role but the jolly, wily servant, Mickey Free. The entertainment ran one month, after which the Grand's season was given over to musicals.

October 18's two revivals were *As You Like It* at Daly's and *East Lynne* at Niblo's. Daly's Forest of Arden was a romantic, melancholy place, and Mrs. Scott-Siddons's Rosalind was "like the carol of a bird." Audiences at Niblo's saw Lucille Western recreate the role of the unfaithful, doomed wife that she had played at *East Lynne*'s 1863 premiere. Her cast included James A. Herne, with whom she was romantically involved and who would soon become a major playwright.

As the parade of revivals continued, Wallack's

and Daly's again jousted for attention on the 22nd. The attraction at Wallack's was the younger George Colman's long-popular comedy *The Heir at Law*. The juicy plum role of Dr. Pangloss, the pompous, pedantic clergyman so proud of being an "L.L.D." and an "A double S," was assigned to one of the best low comedians of the time, J. H. Stoddart. Despite a fiery temperament that led to clashes with all his producers, the slim, gaunt-faced actor rarely failed to delight audiences.

At Daly's the lure was a double bill. Henrik Hertz's romance of a blind princess, *King René's Daughter,* featured Mrs. Scott-Siddons in the title role. Its mate was Sheridan Knowles's *The Love-Chase,* in which two comically complicated chases finally pair an old baronet with a widow (played by Davidge and Marie Wilkins) and the baronet's daughter with a young sportsman (played by Agnes Ethel and George Clarke).

On the 25th, for the second week of her brief engagement at Niblo's, Lucille Western turned to another favorite, *Oliver Twist.* From the time Charlotte Cushman assumed the role of Nancy Sykes at the Park Theatre, a month after the American premiere, the part became a standby for several leading actresses, no doubt altering the emphasis of Dickens's story in all of the period's subsequent dramatizations.

Daly's rapidly ballooning repertory grew by one more work when Colley Cibber's *She Would and She Would Not* was staged on the 27th. Mrs. Scott-Siddons was Dona Hypolita, who must resort to disguise to win the man she loves away from a rival.

Some idea of how the playgoing public was responding to the presentations offered can be gleaned from the monthly grosses reported in several newspapers. Booth's led the field with an October take of $34,000. Wallack's was a sizable distance behind in second place with $27,000. The Olympic registered $24,000 and Niblo's $21,000. Trailing was Daly's Fifth Avenue, which took in just under $18,000. How trustworthy the figures are cannot be determined. Daly's grosses are of special interest, since it has always been said his start was very shaky. These figures suggest that while the producer had little cause for jubilation, he was at least operating in the black. His house was the smallest of any of the major theatres, and $18,000 must have represented well over half-capacity business. Of course, it is generally recognized that Mrs. Scott-Siddons's engagement, which fell largely in this month, boosted his revenues. All in all, the reports indicate New York theatres were enjoying very comfortable returns.

Charlotte Crabtree, the tiny redhead with shimmering dark eyes who was known popularly as "Lotta" and was fast becoming the most beloved entertainer on the American stage, set up shop for a stand at Niblo's beginning November 1. Her first offering was *Little Nell and the Marchioness.* Dancing, singing, playing the banjo, and clowning in the dual title roles, she irresistibly enlivened John Brougham's theatricalization of Dickens's *Old Curiosity Shop,* bringing it to the border of musical theatre.

. . .

Charlotte [Mignon] **Crabtree** (1847–1924) was born in New York but taken to California at the age of six. There she was taught singing and dancing by the celebrated courtesan Lola Montez. Soon she was performing in mining camps and small-town variety theatres. Her San Francisco debut apparently came in 1858, and thereafter her career took off rapidly. New Yorkers first applauded her in 1864.

. . .

Competing with Lotta's opening was Wallack's remounting of Tom Taylor's melodramatic comedy *Still Waters Run Deep.* J. W. Wallack was the loyal, seemingly meek Mildmay, Charles Wyndham the blackmailing Hawksley, and Emily Mestayer the woman with an imprudent past, Mrs. Sternhold.

The still young season's most elegant turnout of first-nighters assembled to welcome back Lester Wallack from his summer vacation.

. . .

Lester [John Johnstone] **Wallack** (1819–88) was the son of James William Wallack and the only important member of the famous acting family born in America. However, his earliest theatrical training was obtained not in his native New York but in England, where he acted under the names of Allan Field and John Lester. He was still employing the latter name when he made his American debut in 1847 as Sir Charles Coldstream in *Used Up.* He performed for a while with Burton's ensemble, then joined his father's newly formed company, soon assuming its management. He had a fine figure, lively dark eyes, and jet black hair. The stockiness that beset him in his later years never diminished his grace and agility.

. . .

Audience and star alike were lucky in his choice of a new play, Robertson's **Home** (11-8-69, Wallack's). Supposedly conceived with Joseph Jefferson in mind, the main part had been assigned instead to E. A. Sothern in the London production the preceding January. Robertson based his story on Émile Augier's 1848 comedy *L'Aventurière.* In Robertson's version,

Alfred Dorrison (Wallack) returns from America, following a sixteen-year estrangement from his family, to learn that his elderly widowed father (John Gilbert) has decided to marry a woman known as Mrs. Pinchbeck (Madeline Henriques). The lady and her glib, unsavory brother, Captain Mountraffe (J. H. Stoddart), have seemingly taken over the household of the senescent old man. Deciding that his family will not recognize him, Alfred calls himself Colonel White. He lets slip that he is heir to an even richer estate than that of the elder Dorrison and, as he suspected he might, soon discovers Mrs. Pinchbeck is prepared to change her affections. The elder Dorrison stumbles in on the colonel and Mrs. Pinchbeck as they are embracing, but Mrs. Pinchbeck, still hedging her bets, convinces the old man that he has misconstrued the scene. However, White is able to unmask the mercenary pair, who are sent packing. To her brother's dismay, Mrs. Pinchbeck tears up the check she has been given to hasten her departure. With the intruders gone, White reveals his true identity. He brings together his sister, Lucy (Effie Germon), and her suitor, Bertie Thompson (B. T. Ringgold), and successfully concludes his own courtship of Dora Thornhaugh [Thornhough or Thornough in many programs] (Laura Phillips). One review noted that the family's happy reunion was underscored by the orchestra's playing "Home, Sweet Home." Although the villainous Mountraffe gave Stoddart a chance to portray the sort of heavy he eventually would turn to, Colonel White gave Wallack one of his greatest parts, one he would play virtually until his retirement. He portrayed White romantically, "with an air that was just a little more than natural . . . with a largeness of style and an inimitable richness of humor." He was not above making a tasteful burlesque out of White's groping attempt to tell Dora of his love. Wallack's Theatre usually gave its patrons value for money, and this occasion was no exception. *Home* was presented as part of a double bill, the other half featuring Lester Wallack as the debt-ridden Hugh De Brass trying to elude a bailiff in J. Maddison Morton's farce *A Regular Fix*.

Poor Humanity (11-8-69, Olympic), F. W. Robinson's dramatization of his popular novel about the seamier side of English life, was savaged by most critics as trashy and inept. Central to the story was the bedraggled figure of Nella Carr (Eliza Newton), a reformatory girl who would in fact reform, despite the sinister lures cast in her path by a cynical fence and thieves' den mother, Mrs. Wisby. Hurdling these obstacles, Nella helps exonerate her father, George (J. B. Studley), an ex-convict who has been falsely accused of a murder actually committed by the local clergyman, the Rev. Mr. Gifford (J. K. Mortimer). The character of Mrs. Wisby was made especially interesting to some reviewers by the fact that it was played by a man, William Holston, in drag. He played it not for laughs but seriously, with a restrained evil that won him applause from many playgoers. Scenery included the picturesque gypsy or tinkers' encampment that opened the show. To bolster attendance, Charles Mathews's comic afterpiece *A Bull in a China Shop* was added.

Opposing the two premieres was Daly's presentation of *Much Ado About Nothing* with Mrs. Scott-Siddons as Beatrice, D. H. Harkins as Benedick, Agnes Ethel as Hero, George Holland as Verges, and William Davidge as Dogberry. Although Mrs. Scott-Siddons's fragile charm was probably not quite right for Beatrice, the actress's box-office draw had helped Daly's struggling company. Unfortunately, prior commitments forced her withdrawal.

Another West End play, H. Leslie and J. S. Clarke's **London; or, Lights and Shadows of the Great City** (11-15-69, French) was waved away by critics almost as dismissively as *Poor Humanity*. It recounted the trials (literally) and tribulations of young Alice Heron (Clara Jennings); accused of theft by the man she believes to be her father, she finds the prosecuting attorney is her real father and eventually leaves for what she hopes will be a better life in Australia. Mediocre as the play undoubtedly was, its production was interesting on several counts. First, there was the presence of Clara Jennings in the leading role. At $100 per week she had been the highest-paid actress on Daly's original roster; her pay was nearly double that of the next-highest-paid actress, Mrs. Gilbert. But she had been the first to rebel against his new casting system and may thus have deprived herself of the opportunity for the major advancement so many felt she was entitled to. Second, while houses such as Wallack's and Daly's took pride in creating their own scenery, many productions, especially spectacles, still imported their scenery from London shops. This play was no exception. It prompted the *Times* to offer not only an extended description but also a discussion of the comparative virtues of wing-and-drop style (which it perceived as European) versus box sets (which it neglected to mention had come from England). The paper noted, "The scenes are not meaningless combinations of canvas and bright colors, but truthful, substantial, and skillfully executed views of the English metropolis, all appropriate, too, to the tale of the artists nightly unfold. London Bridge, with distant views of the tower, is the opening picture. Temple Bar is next seen, and afterward reproductions of the Charing Cross Railway Depot, of the Old Bailey Criminal Court, and of London Docks, with a dozen other panoramic tableaux, are shown. Some of the pictures are flats, only lowered after the European fashion, which, we are happy to note, prevents a constantly recurring exhibition of shifters' arms and carpenters' shoulders; but a few are box sets of the most massive kind. The Charing Cross Railway Depot is one of the best of the latter, and has certainly never been surpassed in accuracy and effect, while the one reproducing the London Docks is superior to it, and for local fidelity, deceptive power and richness of coloring, is quite unequaled." Possibly because of such striking scenery, *London* ran twice as long as *Poor Humanity*—one month.

Loopholes in the period's lax copyright laws occasionally allowed simultaneous mountings of a new play by competing houses. A famous instance had been W. J. Florence's use of a technicality to steal Wallack's thunder with the American premiere of *Caste*. Playgoers, however, rarely chafed at such tactics, for if scenery could overshadow a play, so could players' varying interpretations of a role. Again, the play was not entirely the thing. Much as today's audiences will willingly sit through an often seen opera, a familiar symphony, or an important Shakespearean play for the sake of a new interpretation, mid-19th-century playgoers were not at all loath to compare mountings of newer works. Thus few eyebrows were raised when on November 15 Daly brought out his own production of *Caste* to compete with the one still active in Wallack's repertory. In a way his production opened old wounds, for several of his principal performers were the very ones Florence had employed in his notorious premiere. Mrs. Chanfrau was again lowly Esther Eccles, Davidge her drunken father, and Mrs. Gilbert the hero's snobbish mother.

Daly's *Caste* ushered in another string of revivals to supplant the brief flurry of new plays. On the 20th Wallack's restaged its earlier hit *Henry Dunbar*, Tom Taylor's dramatization of M. E. Braddon's novel about a man who becomes wealthy by crooked means. Two nights later the Olympic offered a double bill of *The Lottery Ticket*, a farce celebrated for its principal figure of Wormwood (played on this occasion by William Holston), and *The Lost Will*. This second piece was merely a retitled version of an 1846 melodrama, *Susan Hopley*, which was long popular in minor houses and had for its heroine a servant girl who discovers she is an heiress. On the same evening at Niblo's, Lotta changed her bill to offer another of her popular vehicles, *The Firefly*,

Edmund Falconer's dramatization of Ouida's *Under Two Flags,* in which a camp follower falls in love with an exiled nobleman who is serving in disguise in the Foreign Legion. Her heroine, of course, was little more than a vaudevillian entertaining the troops.

Philip Massinger's *A New Way to Pay Old Debts,* with its fascinating figure of the doomed Sir Giles Overreach, was the only drama by Shakespeare's immediate successors to retain a firm hold on 19th-century audiences. It had proved a reliable vehicle for Edwin Forrest and Junius Brutus Booth and continued to loom importantly in Edwin Booth's repertory. But many, including Mrs. John Drew, who had seen all of these men as Sir Giles, insisted that E. L. Davenport's "masterly" rendition was unsurpassed. Davenport's known dissatisfaction with the parts Daly had so far assigned him (he had already resigned once from the company) may have prompted the producer to mount the revival on the 22nd. Both the production and Davenport won praise, although the actor was to leave the company permanently in just over a month.

Another addition to Daly's repertory came two nights later with a new mounting of Stirling Coyne's comedy focusing on the vain, eccentric Major Wellington de Boots, *Everybody's Friend.* Daly handed the rising James Lewis the star part.

Aging James H. Hackett made what proved to be his farewell New York appearances when he began a month-long stand at Booth's on November 29. Happily, the engagement gave his admirers a last chance to see him in his greatest Shakespearean impersonation, Falstaff, and even to see him portray the old fraud in two different plays. *Henry IV* came first. Critics were pleased, suggesting that while some of the bygone fire had disappeared, none of the sixty-nine-year-old Hackett's art was lost.

In his heyday Hackett had shuttled deftly between Shakespeare and popular American characters. The slightly younger "Yankee" Robinson—his given names were Fayette Lodawick—played Shakespeare only rarely, and then minor parts. He was far more popular playing American characters (and had also made a reputation proselytizing for religion and prohibition as well as serving as a tent show and circus proprietor). Never very welcome in larger cities, he made one of his infrequent ventures into New York when he appeared at the Olympic on the 29th in a double bill of *A Bull in a China Shop* (using the same scenery and supporting cast seen earlier at the theatre) and a stereotypical Yankee play, *Darius Dutton; or, The Yankee Farmer.* During his courtship of Sally Scribbins (Minnie Jackson), the farmer wins a fight with a bear and scares off a band of Indians by making them believe an empty whiskey bottle is a gun. Not even his boast that he can "beat any girl hoein' potatoes" discourages Sally.

Daly very briefly put aside revivals to offer a double bill of what hasty readers of his advertisements may have thought were two recent London hits by Andrew Halliday. They got only half of what they bargained for. The titular hero of Halliday's **Daddy Gray** (12-1-69, Fifth Avenue.) is an old man (E. L. Davenport) resolved to marry young, beautiful Jessie Bell (Agnes Ethel). He causes havoc and heartache before he is brought to realize his folly. The evening's second attraction was called *Checkmate*, the title of Halliday's delightful comedy of switched identities. But the *Checkmate* audiences at the Fifth Avenue saw a tale of a French lady and her niece vying for the love of a noble fugitive. More knowledgeable playgoers recognized it as the latest translation of Eugène Scribe and Ernest Legouvé's *Bataille de dames*. Fanny Davenport, Agnes Ethel, and George Clarke took the principal roles. The newer play left most critics cold, and many were displeased with the translation, too. What did please critics, and indeed had delighted them unceasingly since August, were the tastefulness and elegance of Daly's sets and costumes. Another cause for jubilation was the show-stopping clowning of James Lewis. In this instance he portrayed a lawyer, Augustus Jinks, making himself up to resemble a notoriously eccentric contemporary attorney.

. . .

James Lewis (1838–96) was born in Troy, N.Y., and served his theatrical apprenticeship touring western New York during his teens. He arrived in New York City in 1866. Almost at once he made a name for himself in Mrs. John Wood's burlesques at the Olympic and in similar pieces at Lina Edwin's Theatre. He was a small, slim man with blue pop-eyes and reddish-blond hair.

. . .

Another new play, and one that was to have a long life on American stages, was **The Little Detective** (12-6-69, Niblo's). Unlike Halliday's work it had not the slightest intrinsic worth. Its durability can be attributed solely to the incomparable star for whom it was written, Lotta Crabtree. The authorship is uncertain. (It is a curious fact that so many American plays of the time—if this is in fact one of them—survived only as vehicles for specific stars.) The play told of the adventures of Florence Langton (Crabtree), who resorts to all manner of disguises to solve a series of problems. She poses as Grizzie Gutteridge, a country girl; as Mrs. Gammage, an old crone; as Pat, a young Irish lad; as Jack (in some programs Harry) Racket, a wild man-about-town; and as a little "Dutch" (read German) girl, given to yodeling a "hoopty-dooden-do." In one guise or another she played her banjo, joked with her audience, and danced a "burlesque pas seni" (whatever that might have been). *An Object of Interest* served as afterpiece.

The evening of Lotta's premiere also welcomed three revivals. *The Wonder*, Susannah Centlivre's 1714 comedy whose subtitle, *A Woman Keeps a Secret*, gave away much of the plot, was unveiled at Wallack's. Mrs. Inchbald's *Wives as They Were and Maids as They Are* was the attraction at Daly's. Daly's own *Under the Gaslight* began a short stay at the Olympic.

The rest of December saw nothing but more revivals—a dozen of them. On the 7th Wallack's brought back one of the company's established favorites, Planché's droll *The Captain of the Watch*, with Lester Wallack recreating one of his most demanded roles, the quietly resourceful de Ligny. *Woodcock's Little Game*, in which a once wild man-about-town tries desperately to settle into a peaceful country life, was the afterpiece. Boucicault's *The Irish Heiress*, in which a sweet Irish lass is plunked down in snooty London society, came to Daly's on the 9th. Hackett wound up his stand at Booth's with two weeks of his Falstaff in *The Merry Wives of Windsor*, beginning on the 13th. That same busy night gave playgoers Daly's version of the long-voguish, swashbuckling *Don Caesar de Bazan*, while Wallack's coupled two more company standbys, *Ernestine; or, Wrong at Last* and William Brough's *Trying It On*, with its amusing figure of the unlucky Walsingham Potts.

The following Monday, the 20th, saw three more entries. John O'Keefe's raffish *Wild Oats* appeared for the first time in the season at Wallack's, with the fifty-year-old Lester Wallack, abetted by tradition and gas lighting, as the roistering young Rover. Daly's competed with a selection seemingly inappropriate for the company, John Brougham's blood-and-thunder melodrama *The Duke's Motto*. E. L. Davenport was the hero. Technically *Little Em'ly* nay not have been a revival, but it was one of many versions of Dickens's *David Copperfield*, long a drawing card at minor houses. The cast at Niblo's was good but unexceptional, and the work ran three weeks.

The last Monday in December, the 27th, brought in two more favorites. Emma Waller appeared at Booth's in a play and role usually identified with Charlotte Cushman, Meg Merrilies in *Guy Manner-*

ing. She emphasized the pathos of Walter Scott's bedraggled, doomed gypsy; while her performance was highly praised, she remained in the older tragedienne's shadow. At Wallack's the last offering for the fading year was Lester Wallack's own comedy *Central Park,* a look at love and jealousy, which concluded with a much publicized scene of skating in the park.

One new play arrived with the new year. **The Writing on the Wall** (1-3-70, Olympic) was by the same John Maddison Morton who had written *A Regular Fix.* According to contemporary commentators, it had been played originally in the West End as a serious melodrama about utopian aspirations. At the Olympic, with G. L. Fox as star, it was turned into a slapdash comedy. Fox mugged, took pratfalls, and did everything his legions of followers expected of him when he assumed the apparently greatly enlarged role of Ferguson Trotter, a city man determined to make a success of a model farm (with real chickens, pigeons, and pigs). He also helped solve a murder. Yet even his admirers must have sensed something was wrong, for the play struggled vainly and after two weeks gave up. The same evening, Daly ended his extended series of revivals with Susannah Centlivre's 1709 comedy about lovers, guardians, and an intrusive bungler, Marplot (James Lewis), *The Busybody.*

Of course, New York was not the sole center of theatrical production, for Philadelphia remained important. One interesting premiere there that season was **Champagne; or, Step by Step** (1-3-70, Chestnut St.), the story of a banker whose world falls apart after he takes to drink and who is redeemed by a loving wife. The play was the work of two great ladies of the American theatre, both of whose careers were cut short by tragedy. Laura Keene had never recovered from the stigma of starring at Ford's Theatre on the night of Lincoln's assassination; Matilda Heron, the greatest Camille of her day, was dying slowly of a wasting disease. Miss Keene at the time managed the Chestnut—indeed, it was briefly known as Laura Keene's—and assumed the role of the banker's wife. But neither good reviews nor the women's past fame brought further hearings for the play.

The most exalted American actor of the century, Edwin Booth, returned to his own theatre on the 5th with his great *Hamlet.*

. . .

Edwin [Thomas] **Booth** (1833–93), the son of Junius Brutus Booth and brother of John Wilkes Booth, was born in Belair, Md. He made his professional debut in 1849 at the Boston Museum playing Tressel opposite his father in *Richard III.* The following year he made an unpromising New York debut as Wilford in *The Iron Chest* but soon called attention to himself when he replaced his ailing father as Richard III. He then spent time in California and in the South Pacific, during which years he first essayed virtually all the roles for which he was afterwards acclaimed. He returned to New York as an important star in 1857. In 1862 he took over management of the Winter Garden, and it was there during the 1864–65 season that he mounted the first production of *Hamlet* to run for 100 consecutive performances in America. He retired temporarily after his brother's assassination of Lincoln, then, following the burning of the Winter Garden, built his own theatre. Booth was a slender man, about five feet six inches tall; his black hair, brown eyes, dark complexion, and somewhat sad or somber mien were said to reflect his Jewish ancestry. Despite critical sniping, which persisted throughout his career, he was generally acknowledged as the greatest American tragedian of the century.

. . .

Many critics felt his Dane was even better than it had been when he established his record run. The *Herald* reported, "He is . . . more moderate and natural in such passages of text as require a passionate delivery, but yet not too much so, and the result is that he is now nearer perfection than ever before. He has now a delicacy of touch and a finish of execution that betray in every line a thorough knowledge of the workings of the human mind." Of course, each generation had seen its actors as "more natural" than those of the past. Thomas Abthorpe Cooper seemed stiff-necked and preposterously formal to Forrest's admirers, and Forrest had been branded a ranter by advocates of Booth. Moreover, beneath such words as "more moderate and natural" contemporaries may have read a slight dig, since Booth, like his mad father before him, was often accused of an unevenness that led to great fire and vitality in major scenes but lifeless, indifferent playing in minor ones. Without motion pictures we can never fully know what Booth's Hamlet was like, although his few recordings, made shortly before he died, suggest a poetic voice with a surprising brogue. Yet for all the occasional cavils, to a man critics acknowledged he was the greatest Hamlet of the age. They were almost as unanimous in hailing Charles Witham's sumptuous, elaborate sets, which were said to have been archaeologically correct—a point modern archaeologists might dispute. To 20th-century eyes they seem like customary Victorian renderings of a suspiciously overbedecked Middle Ages.

On Saturday nights, when Booth refused to act, Emma Waller continued at Booth's with her Meg Merrilies and other roles.

Possibly only one other opening during the season excited expectations as much as Booth's return. That was the American debut of Charles Fechter at Niblo's on January 10.

. . .

Charles [Albert] **Fechter** (1824–79) was born in London, the son of a French father of German lineage and a Flemish mother of Italian background. He was raised in France, where he made his acting debut in 1844 and soon was much sought after. He won laurels as the original Armand Duval in *La Dame aux camélias*. In 1860 he returned to London, where for a decade he was acclaimed in a repertory that ranged from Shakespeare to contemporary melodrama. One of his greatest triumphs was as the hero in the world premiere of Brougham's *The Duke's Motto*. A short man, he was said to have been slim and strikingly handsome in his earlier years, but by the time of his American appearances he had grown stocky and bull-necked.

. . .

In a six-week stay at Niblo's and a briefer April return at the French Theatre, he brought out *Ruy Blas, The Duke's Motto, Hamlet, The Lady of Lyons, Don Caesar de Bazan,* and *The Corsican Brothers*. His robust style was seen as belonging to a passing school, but for the most part his heroes in modern pieces were well thought of. Sizzling controversy erupted after he offered his Hamlet. A fattish, blond-wigged, rough-hewn, and foreign-accented prince earned him numerous harsh notices. He himself is said to have believed his Dane was "natural" and "colloquial," in keeping with newer trends—a perception many critics found preposterous. Kate Field, his contemporary and biographer, dissented and in her detailed, adoring account of his performance left later generations a vivid picture of his acting. Describing the scene of the play within a play she recalled, "Throughout the play *Hamlet* had lain at *Ophelia's* feet. . . . Before him lay the text of the play, which he followed closely, thus anticipating it and watching the effect upon the royal pair. Discovery made and audience gone, Fechter tore the leaves from his play-book and scattered them in the air, as he rose and delivered the well-known quatrain. His utterance was rapid; excitement at last rendered it thick. The blood rushed to his head, he put his hand to his throat as if choking. 'Ah, ha!' became a gasp; he leaned upon *Horatio* and, for

relief, for solace, called for music. . . . It was perfect nature."

Far less controversial, indeed widely applauded, was Wallack's revival on the 10th of Robertson's *Ours,* a story of romance and class distinction set against a background of the Crimean War.

Surf; or, Summer Scenes at Long Branch (1-12-70, Fifth Ave.) was Daly's first attempt at new, totally American comedy. Its author was Olive Logan, daughter of Cornelius A. Logan, who had been a popular actor and playwright before his early death. The daughter was even more versatile than the father—an actress, playwright, essayist, lecturer, and public advocate of women's rights. Her "new and original local comedy" was a good-humored satire on the newly rich who gathered at a fashionable summer resort. The characters' names give some idea of her approach: Lothario Smasher (George Parkes), Barker Blunt (William Davidge), Mrs. Madison Noble (Fanny Davenport), Mrs. Fanny Flipaway (Marie Wilkins), and Mrs. Ogle (Mrs. Gilbert). James Lewis was Simon Schweinfleisch, a pork packer—a character soon to be a staple in American farces and musicals. A storm of applause was unleashed on opening night when an actor impersonating General Grant made a brief appearance. As always, Daly's beautiful mounting elicited special praise, notably "the view of the Stetson House—baring the large trees and the light blue sky out of doors and the lighted gas within." Daly's advertisements also promised "the down trip on the Jessie Hoyt, and the people one meets on a trip to 'The Branch,' " as well as "the Vivid Tableau, 'On The Beach at Long Branch!' The Bathers in Genuine Bathing Costumes! Beauty Unadorned!!!!" One scene included the "Children's Quadrille." The scenery must have been elaborate, for once again the long intermissions required to change the cumbersome settings evoked protests. The play had been done earlier in Boston and Philadelphia, where Long Branch had been replaced by Newport and Cape May respectively.

To replace the failed *The Writing on the Wall,* G. L. Fox offered a double bill of old favorites at the Olympic on the 17th and assumed the leading roles of the snooping hero in *Paul Pry* and the picaresque Jacques Strop in *Robert Macaire*. On the 31st he essayed two more roles, both long associated with William Burton. In *The Serious Family* he was Aminadab Sleek, the spouter of pious platitudes who is routed by young love; in *The Spitfire* he was Tobias Shortcut.

At Wallack's on February 7 another Robertson revival was given an airing. This time it was *School,* in which a waif at a ladies' seminary wins a rich man's hand.

Two of the season's biggest successes arrived one night apart in the following week. At the Olympic, G. L. Fox's burlesque *Hamlet* was so filled with musical numbers that it straddles the fence and probably ultimately falls into the musical field; the same applies to his later *Macbeth*.

"Sensation" was a pet catchword of the era, and certainly no play of the 1869–70 season caused quite the sensation **Frou-Frou** (2-15-70, Fifth Ave.) did. For many reasons the play was a landmark. First, it created, or at least revived, an interest in Parisian drama. Second, it put Daly's still uncertain new venture on the firmest of ground, almost singlehandedly ensuring future seasons at his theatre. Last, it made a star of Agnes Ethel.

· · ·

Agnes Ethel (1853–1903) was a somewhat frail blonde with piercing, questioning eyes. She trained under Matilda Heron and made her New York debut in 1868 in her tutor's most famous role, Camille. She is said to have spent the rest of the 1868–69 season with a touring company, then was enlisted by Daly.

· · ·

Henri Meilhac and Ludovic Halévy's drama had first been played at the Théâtre du Gymnase the preceding October. Monsieur Brigard (William Davidge) has two daughters, the staid, mature Louise (Kate Newton) and the irrepressible whirlwind Gilberte (Miss Ethel), who is known affectionately as Frou-Frou. It has long been assumed that Louise would marry one neighbor, Henri Sartorys (George Clarke), and Gilberte another, the Count de Valréas (George Parkes). To everyone's surprise Sartorys proposes to Gilberte, and her stunned sister urges her to accept, which she does. The young couple move to Paris, where Gilberte proves a feckless, spendthrift wife. She is not unloving but is uncaring—too absorbed in her rounds of pleasure to devote much time to her husband and young son. So when Brigard suggests that while he goes away for an extended trip Louise live with her sister and brother-in-law, everyone seems pleased. Without meaning to, Louise alienates Sartorys and his son from Gilberte by her quiet, thoughtful attention. Sartorys blurts out that he at last has a real wife. Gilberte recognizes that she has lost her family's affections, tries unsuccessfully to reclaim them, and then runs off with de Valréas, who still loves her and whom she realizes she has always loved. She returns Sartorys's two-million-franc dowry, and the couple move to Venice, where they are ostracized by those who knew them. Sartorys follows them and kills de Valréas in a duel. For a time

Gilberte works nursing the poor, but she contracts a fatal disease from one of her patients. Her only wish is to see her family one last time. At first Sartorys resists, but she comes anyway—gaunt and obviously dying. She asks to be buried not in her humble black dress but in a white gown covered with roses. Her last words are "You will pardon me, won't you—Frou-Frou, poor Frou-Frou!"

High and mighty moralists among the critics and playgoers (and there were still many of them) agreed with the *Tribune*'s William Winter, who dismissed the play as "pernicious to morality" and wailed, "Misconduct is extenuated." They missed the point. Gilberte was not an evil woman. She did not grossly and consciously misbehave and then repent as had Formosa earlier in the season. She was assuredly not a Marguerite Gautier. She was not even as worldly and knowing as Lady Isobel, whose desertion in *East Lynne* was less forgivable. Gilberte was simply an impetuous, spoiled child-wife, still too immature always to act responsibly. Her actions are neither black nor white but fall into a gray area that increasingly would occupy center stage in modern drama. In a way she could be seen as a precursor to Ibsen's door-slamming Nora in *A Doll's House*. The determined censurers aside, both the character and Miss Ethel's playing won over audiences who could understand that even her dying wish betrayed her innocence and still uncomprehending youthfulness. Olive Logan, recalling years later the "two handkerchief plays" of the period, wrote, "When Agnes Ethel played Frou-Frou you required two handkerchiefs for only the first act, and if one other sufficed you for the other acts, it was only because there were sweet gleams of girlish gladness in her acting where smiles and even laughter dried your tears." She also noted that when Miss Ethel wore "her hair down her back" in the play she started a brief fashion among impressionable young girls. Some critics complained that the new star had not totally caught fire on opening night, but she had plenty of time to do so, since *Frou-Frou* enjoyed the longest run of the season, 103 performances.

On the 21st Mr. and Mrs. Barney Williams (she was once Maria Pray) unpacked their sets and costumes and settled in for a six-week stand at Niblo's. Williams, whose real name was either Flaherty or O'Flaherty, long since had carved himself a comfortable niche in plays about Ireland and Irishmen, plays that regularly drew other loyal Irishmen to the theatres. The Williamses' opening bill was Edmund Falconer's **Innisfallen; or, The Men in the Gap**, set against the background of the Insurrection. The high-born Gerald O'Brien

(Charles Thorne, Jr.) and his rebels, who have hidden in a mountain gap, have been betrayed by two of their own men. It requires all the resourcefulness of the low-born Terence O'Ryan (Williams) and his fiancée, Katey Maguire (Mrs. Williams), to foil the duplicitous machinations of Buck Doran (J. B. Studley) and to save O'Brien. O'Brien eventually is pardoned, and the lovers prepare to wed. As with so many Irish pieces, room was found for one or two sentimental Irish ballads, which had to be encored. A much publicized panorama of the Lakes of Killarney was imported from London for the occasion. The rest of the highly praised scenery was by William T. Voegtlin, including "a bright, cheerful, lakeside scene, exquisitely painted" that opened the show. The idyllic setting seems to have gone hand in hand with a slow beginning, but once the exposition was accomplished according to the *Herald,* the play came "alive and tremulous with the element of suspense and the atmosphere of adventure."

Lost at Sea (2-28-70, Wallack's), a melodrama by H. J. (for Henry James) Byron and Boucicault, was one of the plays Boucicault wrote for London before his return to America. It had premiered in London the preceding October. The announcement that Walter Coram (J. W. Wallack) has been lost at sea seemingly spares Mr. Franklin (W. Hield) from bankruptcy and disgrace. Coram had lived for many years in India, made his fortune there, and placed all his monies in Franklin's bank. But highjinks within the bank have left it on a very shaky footing, and Coram's probable withdrawals would provide the final shove into disaster. Actually, the problems at the bank stem from the nefarious manipulations of Franklin's foolishly trusted assistant, Mr. Rawlings (Charles Fisher). Rawlings now plans to have a criminal friend of his, Joseph Jessop (J. H. Stoddart), pose as Coram, claim he took a different ship, and demand his money. Then Rawlings can insist he be made a full partner. What Rawlings does not know is that the real Coram has, in fact, taken another ship. Coram quickly perceives the problem and unmasks the treachery. So relatively simple a plot could hardly have satisfied Boucicault or those playgoers who relished his labyrinthine yarns. Thus Franklin's daughter, Laura (Laura Phillips), for a time is led to believe that her father's persecutor is her fiancé, Lord Alfred Colebrooke (Owen Marlowe), while Coram, when working under an alias, falls in love with Jessop's daughter, Katey (Madeline Henriques), and so eventually agrees to her father's exile rather then imprisonment. For good measure Boucicault also added a rescue from a burning building, much like a scene in *The Streets of New York.* The *Times* lamented, "Boucicault is not a very refreshing change after Robertson, even when he has the aid of so clever a constructor of stage dialogue as the present monarch of London burlesque. Beyond question the author of the 'Octoroon' and 'Formosa' is a consummate master of a certain kind of stage effect, and he has a talent for appropriation that sometimes soars almost to genius. But he is so tawdry, so stagy, and, except in his moments of highest inspiration, so intellectually commonplace, that his dramatic pabulum is apt to clog upon the taste and to make us wish in its serving up for more matter and less art." It may seem odd that New York's most prestigious house could present such shoddy goods, but Wallack's apparently knew what it was doing. The play's five-week run was the longest of the season at the theatre, giving the ensemble a much needed rest from incessant rehearsals and probably adding substantially to the till.

During March, Booth very briefly brought out such old reliables as *A New Way to Pay Old Debts* on the 22nd and *The Lady of Lyons* on the 24th, then suffered a major disappointment with an unsuccessful mounting of *Macbeth* on the 28th. The consensus was that Booth lacked the fiber and roughness required for the part. March's only other entry was Barney Williams's revival of a play John Brougham had written for him, *The Emerald Ring,* a melodrama set in Ireland—of course—telling of the search for a ring that will identify a young lady, and famous for its scene in which the villain attempts to wreck a vessel by sending false signals from a lighthouse.

Critics were quick to draw comparisons between Tom Taylor's **Men and Acres** (4-6-70, Wallack's) and Robertson's *Progress.* When the new play had been done in London the preceding autumn, it had been called *New Men and Old Acres*—the new men coming from the fast-rising middle class, the old acres belonging to a fading aristocracy. As in Robertson's comedy, an accommodation is reached, with the younger, feistier upstarts perhaps having a slight upper hand. In this instance the central romance involved a Liverpool merchant, Samuel Brown (J. W. Wallack), and the gay, spoiled Lillian Vavasour (Madeline Henriques). Wallack, like his cousin Lester, was in his fifties, but that hardly disqualified him from romantic leads, which some reviewers felt he played with fervor, charm, and understanding. Critics were also pleased that Stoddart had returned to the comic roles they perceived he excelled at, naturally unable to foresee his future turn. In *Men and Acres* he was the bumptious, snobbish Mr. Bunter. Although the play was made far more welcome than *Lost at Sea* and extolled in followup articles, it ran a mere two and a half weeks.

Booth's brother-in-law, tiny, elfin-faced John Sleeper Clarke, had been so embittered by his treatment at the hands of the authorities after Lincoln's assassination that he had moved more or less permanently to London. His 1869–70 American tour was the first of his very few subsequent returns to his homeland. He opened his New York engagement at Booth's on the 18th with two of his best-loved characterizations, Wellington de Boots in *Everybody's Friend* (which he retitled *The Widow Hunt*) and Timothy Toodle, whose wife is forever buying useless objects at auctions, in *The Toodles.*

Mrs. Cowley's ninety-year-old comedy *The Belle's Stratagem,* in which the wife of a cold husband stoops to reconquer, initiated another series of revivals at Wallack's on the 25th and was followed the next evening by the theatre's presentation of J. B. Buckstone's wry look at five disparate couples in *Married Life.* The very next night the theatre offered *The Love-Chase,* which Daly had produced several months earlier. For reasons now lost, none of the major critics chose to compare the two mountings. Instead several compared the comedy with other old comedies. One critic branded it inferior to *The School for Scandal* "by reason of its greater intricacy of plot"—a suggestion that the modern notion of "less is more" was creeping into contemporary thought. On May 9, the theatre mounted a revival of Leicester Vernon's romantic *The Lancers.*

That same night John Sleeper Clarke's new bill was headed by *The School for Reform,* Thomas Morton's curious mixture of comedy and melodrama It depicted a man's attempt to disclaim an earlier marriage and also told of the misdeeds and repentance of a kidnapper, Bob Tyke. Not everyone was happy with Clarke's assumption of the tricky role of Tyke, preferring his surefire clowning to his dramatic emoting. The other half of the bill was Brougham's comedietta *Among the Breakers* (called *Breakers Ahead* by the *Times*). This was apparently a new piece, but of so little merit that it was generally passed over in the press. Clarke's final bill, on the 16th, consisted of two plays new to America. **Fox Versus Goose,** by R. B. Brough and J. D. Stockton, had fun with problems arising from mistaken identity. A booby named Young Gosling (Clarke) meets the sharper Fox Fowler (W. E. Sheridan), who contrives to take Gosling's place at Gosling's wedding. This leads to a reluctant comic

duel between the men but delights Gosling's intended bride, Rose (Lizzie C. Winter), who uses the mixup as an excuse to marry the man she really loves. Frederic Hay's afterpiece, **Lost Ashore,** found Clarke impersonating Tom Tackle, a blundering sailor always "lost ashore" and "found at sea." Puns remained a staple of the era's comedy.

Although the season was fast drawing to a close, revivals at Wallack's proceeded apace. On the 23rd the stage was shared by Douglas Jerrold's warm domestic drama *The Rent Day* and Samuel Beazley's comic triangle *Is He Jealous?*

At Daly's on the 24th new life was breathed into Oliver Goldsmith's *The Good-Natured Man.* The opening fell just one month after the centennial of the first American performance, in Philadelphia on April 27, 1770. New York did not see the play until February 16, 1818, and this was its first revival since then. The title role of the all too generous and trusting Honeywood, who must be taught life's harsh realities, fell to George Clarke. But it was warm, vivacious Fanny Davenport as the heroine, Miss Richland, and droll Davidge as Croaker who stole the show.

Charles Gayler's **Taking the Chances** (5-30-70, Booth's) was the sort of Yankee comedy that still played to approving crowds around the country but was rejected by New York as old hat and backwater. Its booking at Booth's was attributable to its young star, James H. McVicker, being Booth's son-in-law. The play dumped the open, rustic Peter Pomeroy (McVicker) smack in the middle of nose-in-the-air New York society, where his gauche manners and homespun clothes are snickered at. But after Peter saves his cousin, Blanche (Blanche De Bar), from rushing headlong into a bigamous marriage with philandering Percy Bartlett (W. E. Sheridan), he is treated with a new respect. The same respect was not accorded the play; two weeks and it was gone.

Just how arduous a life in the theatre could be for even the most select performers was tellingly demonstrated by Wallack's closing week. With merely seven performances remaining to be given, the house nonetheless included three new revivals in the final week's bills. John Tobin's comedy about the taming of a shrew, *The Honeymoon,* appeared on the 30th, G. W. Lovell's *Love's Sacrifice* on June 1, and W. H. Hurlburt's look at travelers and expatriates, *Americans in Paris,* at the June 4 matinee for a single performance. That not everyone still subscribed to the idea of older men playing younger could be seen in the persistent digs at J. W. Wallack by the *Herald*'s critic, who condemned him as "too antiquated" for his part in the Tobin comedy and then turned the knife the next day by complaining, "He will insist on playing *rôles* which might legitimately fall to juvenile actors."

No sooner had Wallack's ensemble closed its season than John Brougham took over its stage for the hot weather months, enlisting several of the house's regular players in his company. His first offering was his adaptation of F. W. Robinson's novel *Annie Locke,* which he rechristened **The Red Light; or, The Signal of Danger** (6-6-70, Wallack's). Its central figures included the strange Paul Maynard (C. W. Barry), who can never be certain when he is suffering from one of his periodic bouts with insanity, and Anne Steele (Lizzie Price), the dutiful companion who is believed to be poor but is discovered in the end to be wealthy. Brougham, who took a comic role in the story, regaled patrons between each act with humorous remarks but could not get many reviewers to agree with the *Times* that the complicated, multiscened plot was filled with "effective climaxes."

Watts Phillips's London success **Not Guiilty** (6-6-70, Niblo's), which New Yorkers could have first seen the preceding November at the Bowery Theatre, was waved away when it finally reached a first-class Broadway house. It told one of the many tales of the era spotlighting a man falsely accused of a crime. At this far remove, it is hard to know whether its premiere at the déclassé Bowery had prejudiced critics and more sophisticated playgoers against it. It survived at Niblo's for a mere two weeks.

Having scored such a resounding hit with *Frou-Frou,* Augustin Daly reached over to France again for his closing production of the season. Probably the onset of summer heat prevented Victorien Sardou's **Fernande** (6-7-70, Fifth Ave.) from running as long as the earlier success. Its titular heroine (Agnes Ethel), forced by circumstances to become a courtesan, is determined to leave that life and live normally. Her chance comes when the Marquis André (George Clarke) falls in love with her and proposes. Fernande, determined to tell André her whole history but unable to do so face to face, writes about it in a letter to him. André's former fiancée, the vicious Clothide (Fanny Morant), manages to intercept the letter, keeps it from the groom, and sees to it that he indirectly learns the truth only after the wedding. André's reaction is to cast out the seemingly deceptive Fernande. The truth emerges, and a reconciliation follows before the final curtain. Although more than one paper found the play immoral, it was rightly perceived that this very trait would add to its

appeal. And then there were the superb performances. The *Times* wrote of Miss Ethel, "Her quiet pathos, her profound and touching horror over the shameful past[,] . . . her agony at the last when her husband turns upon her, are all natural, artistic and thoroughly satisfactory." However, for many it was the Clothide of Miss Morant—"magnetic in the highest degree"—that stole the show.

• • •

Fanny Morant (1821–1900) was an attractive if slightly mouse-faced actress who was born in London and acted there at Drury Lane before coming to America in 1853. From 1860 to 1868 she acted at Wallack's, leaving that company because she felt she was not assigned the best roles. Her years of renown, which were to last until she was an old woman, really began with her playing of Clothide.

• • •

Fernande ran until the company adjourned for the summer in early July, but it was to return to Daly's on several occasions. The adaptation was by N. Hart Jackson and Myron A. Cooney, neither of whom received billing.

The season at Booth's limped to a halt when Watts Phillips's *The Huguenot* was revived for a three-week engagement on June 14. The play, which recounted events leading up to the St. Bartholomew's Day massacre, had originally been known as *The Huguenot Captain.*

After the disappointing run of his *The Red Light,* an out-and-out melodrama, John Brougham turned to the sort of melodrama interlarded with songs and dances that Maggie Mitchell and, more especially, Lotta Crabtree had brought into vogue. His new piece was **Minnie's Luck; or, Ups and Downs of City Life** (6-27-70, Wallack's). Young Minnie (Leona Cavendish), the child of parents who have just been bitterly divorced, is kidnapped by her father. To be revenged on his ex-wife he rears their daughter in the meanest possible fashion until she is rescued by a newspaperman, Horatio Pryor (Brougham), who in the parlance of the time was called variously a "sensation reporter" or an "interviewist." Miss Cavendish was no Lotta, nor could Brougham find precisely the right combination of melody and drama, so the play was a quick flop.

As *Minnie's Luck* suggests, musicals were sneaking into the American theatre through the back door. The season's final offering is best treated as one, although it too hung its songs and jigs on a melodramatic frame, which coincidently was also premised on a young girl's abduction. Charles Gayler's **Fritz, Our Cousin German** (7-11-70,

Wallack's) recounted a man's search for his long-lost sister, who recognizes him when he sings an old family lullaby. The production's real attraction was the clowning, singing, and dancing of Joseph K. Emmet, and he played the role for as long as he lived. How interesting, though, that this important prototypical musical was housed at New York's most prestigious theatre.

A brief word has to be said about the historic old Bowery Theatre. By 1869–70 its sun was setting. Its bills were rarely advertised in major newspapers, and in return these papers rarely reviewed its offerings. It had become a workingman's theatre, increasingly a mecca for the growing immigrant community that surrounded it. Programs leaned heavily toward sensational melodrama, with dog dramas (plays in which trained dogs performed major roles), broad comedies, and spectacle for variety. Plays only infrequently ran more than a week and were often changed, repertory fashion, each night.

1870–1871

The tug between the past and the present (and, implicitly, the future), between foreign influences and native ones, continued throughout the new season. But whereas in the preceding theatrical year whatever was old or imported unmistakably had the upper hand, the new season brought with it some solid hope for the eventual triumph of fresh approaches and American writing.

Days after the season opened, Henry Wallack died. The brother of J. W. Wallack, who had founded Wallack's Theatre, he had retired sixteen years before. His passing removed virtually the last of the great figures of his generation. Henry's son, the *Herald*'s "too antiquated" J. W. Junior, was fast nearing his own retirement, which would leave the now fifty-one-year-old Lester to maintain the family traditions.

The season would also witness the farewell performances of the first real acting giant of the American stage, Edwin Forrest. Age and illness had subdued his former florid, ranting style to some extent, thus bringing him, possibly inadvertently, more in line with modern conceptions of interpretation. Years before, Forrest had pioneered in fostering native playwriting. The season's new American plays may not have represented the sort of high poetic tragedy

he had in mind, but at least four of them gave a new luster and excitement to American theatre.

Daly's *Horizon*, the work many observers considered the most intrinsically worthwhile, was a commercial disappointment. However, the well-written, hugely successful *Saratoga* earned an honored position in our theatrical history, while two rattlingly effective actor's vehicles, *Across the Continent* and *Kit, the Arkansas Traveller*, held the stage as long as their stars remained active. Yet not all theatregoers were pleased by what they saw. In his 1871 pamphlet *Democratic Vistas*, Walt Whitman complained, "Of what is called drama, or dramatic presentations in the United States, as now put forth at the theatres, I should say it deserves to be treated with the same gravity, and on a par with the questions of ornamental confectionery at public dinners, or the arrangement of curtains and hangings in a ball-room—nor more, nor less." Happily, many others were less censorious.

As if purposely to get the season off to the best of starts, differences were set aside for the moment and conflicting forces merged. Something old, something new, something borrowed from overseas, and something red, white, and blue could all be seen at Booth's on August 15. The play was the most popular American theatre piece of the era, *Rip Van Winkle*. Boucicault had redramatized Washington Irving's old story for Joseph Jefferson when both the playwright and the actor were in London, and it had been offered there first. Its American production in 1866 had won wide praise, but praise sprinkled with reservations about the play itself and Jefferson's interpretation. Jefferson had promptly set about revising both and now, four years later, offered essentially the version he would play right up to his retirement. Jefferson had been touring the country with the work, polishing it, winning for it and for himself the affection of playgoers and the commendations of not only local critics but national publications. The *Atlantic Monthly* informed its readers: "A worthy descendant of the noblest of the old players is before them. He leans lightly against a table, his disengaged hand holding his gun. Standing there, he is in himself the incarnation of the lazy, good-natured, dissipated, good-for-nothing Dutchman that Irving drew. Preponderance of humor is expressed in every feature, yea, in every limb and motion of the light, supple figure. The kindly, simple *insouciant* face, ruddy, smiling, lighted by the tender, humorous blue eyes, which look down upon his dress[;] . . . the lounging, careless grace of the figure; the low, musical voice, whose utterances are 'far above singing'; the sweet, rippling laughter—all combine to produce an effect which is rare in its simplicity. . . . The remarkable beauty of the performance arises from nothing so much as its entire repose and equality." A run of 149 performances was to remain not only the longest of its career but the longest for any play during the season.

• • •

Joseph Jefferson (1829–1905) The Philadelphia-born comedian came from an old theatrical family. He made his debut at the age of four, performing alongside and mimicking T. D. Rice, the popular creator of "Jim Crow." When he was thirteen his father died, and he embarked with his mother on a tour of theatrical backwaters. After later acting with Junius Brutus Booth and Edwin Forrest, he called attention to his comic abilities as a member of Laura Keene's troupe. Tallish and thin with a small head and long brown hair, Jefferson had a wizened face with a quizzical look, even in his youth.

• • •

Lawrence Barrett, a fast-rising actor with hauntingly burning eyes, was as interesting an artist as Jefferson, although he was never to approach the comedian's hold on the playgoing public. While no one questioned the intelligence he brought to every role, many considered him too mannered and stilted. New York audiences would have numerous chances this season to draw their own conclusions, beginning on the 16th at Niblo's when he appeared as Lagardere in *The Duke's Motto*. The choice was brave, possibly foolhardy, since it begged comparison with Fechter, who had offered it a few months earlier and whom many considered unrivaled in the part. Certainly the major critics felt Barrett came in second best.

He fared much better when he offered his Enoch Arden in **Under the Palm** (8-22-70, Niblo's), the latest of the period's many versions of Tennyson's poem. A week later he was seen in a third play, **True as Steel** (8-29-70, Niblo's). The new offering was derived from Paul Meurice's 1858 Parisian comedy *Fanfan la tulipe*. London had rejected several versions (including one with Fechter) that had emphasized melodrama at the expense of humor. Yet, surprisingly, this was precisely the approach James Schönberg adopted for his work, purportedly written with Barrett in mind. Fanfan (Barrett) is a naive soldier in the bodyguard of Mme de Pompadour (Louisa Moore). The tricky Baron de Alvera (F. C. Bangs) decides to use Fanfan to serve his own selfish ends, which include destroying the power of Pompadour and stealing the d'Armenierre estates. The baron's overreaching and Fanfan's true-as-steel loyalty save Pompadour. Fanfan's soldier buddy,

Gabriel (Charles Thorne, Jr.), proves to be the d'Armenierre heir and captures the hand of the baron's lovely niece, Alice (Lizzie Mahon). William T. Voegtlin's period scenery stole the show. Of Barrett the *Times* could say no more than that he was "manly" but lacked "vivacity" and "the halo of romance." Instead it singled out the "picturesqueness" of Bangs, concluding, "Picturesqueness in kindred productions is welcome almost at the expense of strict naturalness."

For his final week, beginning September 5, Barrett was joined by E. L. Davenport for a repertory of classics. *Othello,* with Davenport as the Moor and Barrett as Iago, and *London Assurance* were each given a single performance, but the main attraction was *Julius Caesar.* Davenport was Brutus; Barrett, Cassius; and Mme Ponisi, so long hailed as a fine Shakespearean actress and soon to be a fixture at Wallack's, Portia. Apparently a last-minute, unannounced change occurred in the casting of the title role, which some morning-after notices said was played by Theodore Hamilton and others by Bangs. The interpretation was praised for its reserve and its "absence of rant"—probably no small matter in a house as large as Niblo's, and a sign of a growing cry for more naturalistic acting that coincided with improved postwar lighting. Special laurels went to Walter Montgomery for his Antony. Montgomery was a young, very promising actor, American-born and London-trained. He was handsome, if somewhat heavy-set and balding. Shortly thereafter his unexplained suicide abruptly brought the curtain down on his career.

Tom Taylor's **'Twixt Axe and Crown** (9-5-70, Wood's Museum) portrays the conflicts between the Catholic Queen Mary (Henrietta Irving) and the Protestant Elizabeth (Mrs. Scott-Siddons). Mary realizes that if Edward Courtenay (Charles Thorne, Jr.) weds Elizabeth the marriage would further turn most Englishmen against her, so she frees Courtenay from the Tower and plies him with wealth and titles. Courtenay remains loyal to Elizabeth but is killed shortly before Elizabeth comes to the throne. Mrs. Scott-Siddons's best scene came early in the play, when Elizabeth is hounded by bloody visions of queens who had been put to death in the Tower. Thorne was admired for his virility and warmth. But all the fine acting could not keep the play on the boards for more than two weeks. Wood's, like many earlier houses, was really a combination of museum and theatre. By calling itself a museum, it allowed otherwise puritanical objectors to cross its threshold. To lure patrons to its exhibitions, its theatre offered not only evening performances of longer plays but afternoon performances of shorter burlesques and comedies.

Tiny, twenty-two-year-old Lotta, the era's Baby-Jane ancestor to Shirley Temple, took possession of the same stage where Barrett and Davenport had held forth when she opened as May Wyldrose in Edmund Falconer's **Heartsease** (9-12-70, Niblo's). May, the daughter of a California gold prospector, falls in love with a man who proves to be her long-lost cousin. She rescues him from danger after she uses a rope to swing across a gulch, and later she foils robbers who would steal a large nugget she has found. For a change of scene she travels to London, where she is lionized by society. In both settings Lotta unpacked her bag of stage tricks to delight her ever increasing following.

Lina Edwin's persistent determination to become an actress-manager briefly bore fruit when she converted what had been Kelly and Leon's minstrel house into a theatre carrying her own name. She appears to have been an odd woman. Some felt she was a pretty, light-headed creature whose ambitions far outran her abilities; others suggested she was a good, though not great, actress dogged by bad luck. In any case her forte was comedy, so she opened her house with a double bill including Frederick Phillips's **A Bird in the Hand Is Worth Two in the Bush** (9-12-70, Lina Edwin's) and a burlesque of Douglas Jerrold's famous nautical play of perfidy and love, *Black-Eyed Susan*, called *Black-Eyed Suzing; or, The Leetle Bill Which Was Taken Hup*. In the former, Capias Sharke (Harry Jackson), a scheming pettifogger, attempts to get the better of hefty Mrs. Prodigal (Amilie Harris) and her beautiful daughter, Ellen (Lillie Eldridge). The whole Prodigal family, joined by the resourceful Roderick Praiseworthy (Walter Grisdale), unite to unravel Sharke's cunningly knit plans. In the latter, Miss Edwin played Susan and was supported by the squeaky-voiced Stuart Robson, soon to be a major star in his own right.

The audience that congregated for Daly's reopening had little idea of the problems that had beset the producer over the exceedingly hot summer. He was determined to begin his season with a dramatization of Wilkie Collins's popular new novel *Man and Wife*, but on the day the adaptation was to be delivered to him the script was nowhere in sight. Daly spent a feverish night drawing up his own theatricalization. Then he discovered that Agnes Ethel, whom he had in mind for the leading role, adamantly refused to portray another fallen woman. His second choice proved inadequate, so he rushed in a new, totally untried young actress, Clara Morris.

Man and Wife (9-13-70, Fifth Ave.) told a grotesquely complicated story, much simplified here, which pivoted on some obscure Scottish laws. Its heroine, Anne Sylvester (Morris), is pregnant but unmarried. Her scoundrelly lover, Geoffrey Delamayn (D. H. Harkins), tricks his friend, Arnold Brinkworth (J. B. Polk), into a seemingly innocent declaration that under Scottish law allows Geoffrey to proclaim Arnold and Anne man and wife. This makes for several ugly situations since Arnold is already married to Blanche Lundie (Fanny Davenport), who had considered Anne her confidante. Luckily Blanche's uncle, Sir Patrick Lundie (James Lewis), knows his law even better than Geoffrey does and finds another technicality, which means that Geoffrey must be declared the groom. Furious, Geoffrey decides to murder Anne with the help of his supposedly deaf-mute cook, Hester Dethridge (Mrs. Gilbert), who, he has learned, had killed her brutal husband. His plan is to kill Anne by entering her bedroom through a secret passage while Anne is asleep. Hester, however, wakes Anne just in time. "Curses seize you both!" Geoffrey exclaims as her friends break down the bedroom door. Anne will wed the understanding Sir Patrick.

Each of the five acts built deftly to a dramatic climax underscored by music and a tableau, and this, coupled with the remarkably assured playing of Miss Morris and the rest of the company, gave Daly's season a superb sendoff. Unexpectedly, even William Winter, who so often rejected plays on moral grounds, wrote in the *Tribune* that "the drama proved to be exceedingly interesting and effective," adding it owed much of its success to "the refining influence of its spirit. Something of the debt, though, was due to its romantic interest, as the crystallization of a fine story." The play ran ten weeks.

On the 19th at Wood's Museum Daly's erstwhile star Mrs. Scott-Siddons appeared as Rosalind in *As You Like It,* with Charles Thorne, Jr., as her Orlando. A double bill of revivals on the 30th, *The Honeymoon* and *King René's Daughter,* closed out her stand.

Visits by great English stars had become increasingly commonplace since George Frederick Cooke's trailblazing appearances over half a century earlier. But visits of major Continental stars, who did not speak or perform in English, were still something of a rarity and were risky at that. Students continue to debate how commercially successful Rachel's engagements were. Ristori had better luck. Given the large German immigrant population of New York, the visit of Marie Seebach should have been less chancy, but the results, at least at the box office, seem to have been disappointing. Seebach was an actress of great delicacy and versatility. Her repertory, all in German, included *Faust,* Schiller's *Mary Stuart,* Scribe's *Valerie,* the comedy *Eine Tasse Thee, Jane Eyre, Kabale und Liebe* (which opera lovers know through Verdi's version, *Luisa Miller*), *Adrienne Lecouvreur,* and *The Taming of the Shrew.* Critics waxed ecstatic, the *Herald,* for example, proclaiming her Adrienne "equal to the best hour of Rachel." What remains uncertain is how many regulars of Niblo's or even Wallack's and Daly's trekked down to the 14th Street Theatre from the 22nd on, or to a later engagement in March.

Having watched the upstart Daly's launch its season so successfully with a new play, Wallack's held stubbornly to its established practice of inaugurating a season with an old favorite. Thus when the theatre relit on the 29th the attraction was *The Rivals.* Odell, reading between the lines of morning-after reviews, sensed "a feeling that perhaps the glory of the house was passing," but most of the notices, for all their minor cavils, seem to be what the trade calls "money" reviews—sufficiently enthusiastic to have patrons lining up for tickets. John Gilbert as Sir Anthony, George Clarke (lured away from Daly's) as Captain Absolute, J. H. Stoddart's broadly played Bob Acres, and the Irish-brogued Sir Lucius O'Trigger of John Brougham were all especially welcomed. The women fared slightly less well. Madeline Henriques's Lydia Languish was praised, but Emily Mestayer's "laughter-provoking" Mrs. Malaprop seemed overshadowed to some by memories of "the mingled pedantry and stately dignity" of the late Mrs. Vernon's characterization. The revival remained on the boards for three weeks while Wallack's prepared its first new offering of the season.

For the second offering of her season at Niblo's, Lotta came up with a surprising selection on October 3, Tom Taylor's study of the hounding of a parolee, *The Ticket-of-Leave Man.* Playing Bob Brierly, the central figure, was out of the question, but audiences remembering her success in *The Little Detective* would not have been too startled to find her essaying Hawkshaw. Wisely, she did not. Instead she portrayed the fourteen-year-old, sassy, street-smart Sam Willoughby, who provides so much of the comic relief and in the end rescues the detective from Dalton's murderous stranglehold. In both the London and New York premieres the part had been a trouser role. Most critics gave the evening short shrift, perhaps implying that Lotta's numerous vaudeville turns threw the play off balance. Her fans couldn't have cared less.

Versions of Dickens's *Barnaby Rudge* had maintained a fitful hold on the stage ever since one had been offered in September of 1841, but these dramatizations never approached the popularity of plays made from some other Dickens works. Now a new **Barnaby Rudge** (10-3-70, Lina Edwin's), written by H. A. Weaver and J. B. Bradford especially for Stuart Robson, cast its lot with theatregoers. The *Times* recorded Robson's personal triumph, noting, "His mock courage and real cowardice, his comic singing and his ingenious elaborations of comic business are keenly relished." Yet even Robson's quickly developing skills could not win a run for the piece.

Of the four openings competing for attention on Monday the 10th, two can be passed over quickly. At Lina Edwin's the failed *Barnaby Rudge* gave way to a double bill of *Everybody's Friend* and a musical burlesque. During the rest of the year these musical burlesques largely usurped the theatre's stage. Lotta returned to *Little Nell and the Marchioness* at Niblo's.

For many playgoers the most eagerly awaited new work of the season was James Albery's London hit **Two Roses** (10-10-70, Wallack's). Impoverished, money-mad Digby Grant (Charles Fisher) lives with his rose-loving daughters, Ida (Mrs. Thomas Barry) and Lottie (Effie Germon), in a quiet backwater and survives by condescendingly accepting charity and by not paying his bills. Suddenly he is advised that he has inherited a large fortune, although there is still one person, currently missing, who has first claim on the money if he can be found. Nevertheless, to tide him over until a final determination is made, the lawyer gives Grant a down payment of £2000 and a checkbook. In the play's most famous scene, the end of the first act, Grant, with the same comic condescension with which he had accepted gifts, now hands his creditors token installments on his debts. His line to each, "a little cheque," became a passing catchphrase. Grant assumes even lordlier airs until, to his dismay, the missing claimant is found: a young blind man, Caleb (Owen Marlowe), who has long loved Ida. Lottie is free to wed John Wyatt (George Clarke). Grant resigns himself to living condescendingly off the charity of his sons-in-law. In London the role of Grant had given Henry Irving a major leg up in his career, a leg up his playing of Kerr in *Formosa* had not given him. But in America something went wrong. Most reviews, both of the play and the acting, were tepid. Instead of the long run Wallack's undoubtedly had banked on, the play was withdrawn after three weeks.

On the same night, at the Academy of Music, Fanny Janauschek made her second debut. Her first had been in 1867, when she performed in German. In three years' time she had taught herself a fluent if markedly accented English.

. . .

Fanny Janauschek (1830–1904), whose given names were Francesca Romana Magdalena, had been an imposing star on European stages before venturing to America. She was a small, round-faced, stocky woman with heavy-lidded eyes.

. . .

Her sponsor was Augustin Daly, and though he had first won fame by translating her great vehicle, *Deborah,* as *Leah, the Forsaken,* he agreed to her appearing in another translation that hewed more closely to the original than his redaction had. The *Tribune*'s William Winter called her "superb," adding, "Janauschek has the vital fire of genius that can melt the heart and electrify the mind. She knows what love is. She knows what passion is. She knows what hate is. She has splendid intuitions." Her other assignments included the title role in *Mary Stuart* and the interpretation many critics considered her best, Lady Macbeth. The *Herald* observed, "In the scene where she welcomes her rude warrior, returning victorious from the wars, her sanguine, unscrupulous, irresponsible ambition was expressed with an eagerness and command that would have aroused the veriest craven." Some nights were given over to a brief dramatic sketch, *Come Here,* in which she played a young actress showing the range of her dramatic skills to a producer. This tour de force was paired with *The Lady of Lyons,* in which Agnes Ethel and Walter Montgomery assumed the leading roles.

Beginning on the 22nd, Lotta's ever changing lures were exhibited in a double bill. An old French vaudeville, *Captain Charlotte,* in which the heroine disguises herself as a naval officer, was coupled with an afterpiece, Boucicault's *Andy Blake,* the story of a young scamp who wangles the marriage of his sister to a soldier who was courting her in disguise.

Compelled to fill the stage left vacant by the disappointment of *Two Roses,* the anglophilic Wallack's embarked on a series of revivals, starting on the 31st with the younger Colman's affectionate parody of English stereotypes, *John Bull.* The juiciest roles, Dennis Brulgruddery and Job Thornberry, fell to Brougham and Gilbert, but even their superior clowning could not hide the fact that the old play seemed "stilted" and "dull."

That same night Mrs. Lander began a month-long stay at the 14th Street Theatre. Many playgoers remembered the petite, attractive actress as Jean Davenport. She had retired from the stage after marrying

in 1860 but reemerged following the death of her husband during the Civil War. She was an accomplished technician, with a "clarity and sweetness of elocution," who had started as a child prodigy, although she never truly reached the very front ranks as a performer. Her repertory consisted of *Elizabeth, Queen of England; Mary Stuart; Charlotte Corday; Frou-Frou;* and *Adrienne Lecouvreur.* The *Times* wrote approvingly of her Corday, reporting that she presented "a soft and finished picture of an historical character, who is scarcely remembered by her excessive tenderness. Her chanting of the 'Marseillaise,' it is true, is exceedingly spirited and forceful, but the pathos of the final scenes . . . is particularly to be admired."

The Serious Family was brought out at Wallack's on November 2 and replaced on the 14th by *The Road to Ruin,* Thomas Holcroft's story of a spendthrift son forced into marrying an absurd widow to recoup his fortune.

The Rapparee; or, The Treaty of Limerick (11-14-70, Niblo's) was the latest in the outlandishly convoluted sensation-melodramas of Dion Boucicault. Its hero, guerrilla leader Roderick O'Malley (Frank Mayo), loves Grace (Clara Jennings), daughter of the leading Connaught politician, Colonel O'Hara (Alexander Fitzgerald). When a truce and amnesty are signed, O'Malley is specifically excluded. The treacherous Ulrich McMurragh (L. R. Shewell) is also in love with Grace and is set on destroying his rival. O'Malley is forced to flee from troops searching for him and hides in a ruined castle that can be reached only at low tide. The searchers learn his whereabouts, come just as the tide is rising, and are saved from drowning by the generous hero. As he goes in search of help, Grace swims across the bay to join him, swoons as she reaches the castle, and is discovered there by Ulrich, who locks her in an upstairs room. The soldiers O'Malley has saved prove ungrateful. O'Malley sets fire to the castle, hoping to escape in the confusion. He then learns that Grace is locked in a room and braves the flames to rescue her. Caught, he is sentenced to death. Ulrich tells Grace that if she will marry him he can arrange for O'Malley's pardon, knowing all the while that a pardon is on the way. Grace consents. O'Malley, now free, encounters the pair and provokes Ulrich into a duel. Killing him with two bold thrusts, O'Malley exclaims, "That for my love, and that for myself." Boucicault enthusiasts, never tiring of his often repeated gimmicks, could rejoice at another spectacular fire scene, which even the *Times* allowed "has never been equaled." But the *Times*'s high praise for the play and its theatrical effects was not mirrored in other papers. The *Tribune* waved it away as another of Boucicault's "tinseled, tawdry stage carpenter dramas." It lasted a mere two weeks.

Billiards; or, Business Before Pleasure (11-14-70, Lina Edwin's) injected a bit of farce among the bills of burlesque at the house. It recounted the doings of Sam Sample (M. W. Leffingwell), a fast-living dandy and billiard sharp whose antics create problems for all his friends and relatives.

A rash of revivals ensued. On the 21st Daly's replaced the highly successful *Man and Wife* with Sheridan Knowles's long-popular tale of a country girl temporarily led astray by the lures of a big city, *The Hunchback.* Wallack's countered with *The School for Scandal.* The next night Daly mounted *The Heir at Law,* and one night later he brought back the preceding season's *Fernande.* On the 28th, while Wallack's added *Caste* to its repertory for the season, Mrs. Scott-Siddons, E. L. Davenport, Walter Montgomery, and Mme Ponisi began a short stand at Niblo's, offering *Hamlet, As You Like It, Othello, The Lady of Lyons,* and *Romeo and Juliet.*

Far downtown, the increasingly woebegone Bowery had offered its stage all season long to a rapid succession of new touring plays interspersed with occasional revivals. Then one novelty managed to halt the turnover and linger a whole month. The play was Charles Foster's **Neck and Neck; or, The Hangman's Noose** (11-28-70, Bowery), in which Walter Wilmarth clears himself of the false charge of defalcation. A drunken witness, Jim Johnson, figured prominently in the story. So, according to advertisements, did a "thrilling execution scene, surpassing anything of the kind that had ever been introduced upon the stage" and a "locomotive, tender and train of cars, elaborate and complete," onto which Wilmarth must jump from a roof. His characterization of Wilmarth propelled E. T. Stetson into stardom. For half a dozen seasons he played little else.

Coquettes; or, The Two Joneses (12-7-70, Wallack's) was by the same James Albery who had written *Two Roses.* Although finished before that play, it had languished until after the later one had succeeded, then had been mounted in the West End as *The Two Thorns* to capitalize on the earlier hit. The new play was not a success in London, and why Wallack's elected to attempt it is puzzling. The story centered on a snobbish member of Parliament, Arthur Minton (John Brougham), whose flirtatious wife (Madeline Henriques), a former actress, is forever embroiling him in unwelcome complications. More often than not, Brougham was an actor who loved to

ham it up, but even his remarkably restrained, understanding portrayal of Minton could not save the play, which struggled along for three weeks.

Meanwhile, Daly mounted two more revivals, *London Assurance* on the 9th and *Twelfth Night* on the 12th, before turning to a new American play. That play was to give him one of his most fondly remembered successes. **Saratoga; or, Pistols for Seven** (12-21-70, Fifth Ave.) was the work of Bronson Howard.

• • •

Bronson [Crocker] **Howard** (1842–1908) came from old American stock and was born in Detroit, where his father, a successful merchant, served a term as mayor. After eye problems forced him to leave Yale, he became drama critic for the *Detroit Free Press.* At the same time, he wrote *Fantine,* a play based on Hugo's *Les Misérables,* which was produced in Detroit in 1864. Shortly afterward he moved to New York, taking work first with the *Tribune* and then with the *Post.* Once he became convinced that he could support himself by playwriting, he abandoned newspaper work. As a result he is sometimes said to have been the first American to earn a living entirely by playwriting, although this palm is often awarded to Bartley Campbell. Later he was called "the dean of American drama."

• • •

The central figure of *Saratoga* is an irrepressible ladies' man, Bob Sackett (James Lewis), who insists to a friend, "You have never loved as I love!" Indeed, the program forewarned playgoers that he has "loved not wisely but four well." Actually, at the beginning of the play he is only engaged to three women: the progressive-thinking, self-reliant Effie Remington (Fanny Davenport), the flirtatious Virginia Vanderpool (Linda Dietz), and the lovely widow Olivia Alston (Fanny Morant). He has a narrow squeak when he comes across all three in rapid-fire succession at an art opening. The encounters leave him shaken, so he rushes off to the freedom of Saratoga, not knowing all three ladies also have decided to pack off to the spa. Meeting them there proves too much, prompting him to rush off again for a time. When he returns he tells his friend, Jack Benedict (D. H. Harkins), that a carriage accident flung into his arms the girl to end all girls, "the fairy of my dreams." That dream soon turns out to be Lucy Carter (Clara Morris), the young bride of an old man. Before long Mr. Carter (D. Whiting) and the other ladies' suitors have all issued demands for duels. They are cheered on by the elder Vanderpools (William Davidge and Mrs. Gilbert). Sackett invites them all to Jack's rooms, where he manages to defuse the situation. Virginia and the widow find attractive replacements, while Sackett settles for marrying Effie. The play's humor is exemplified by the opening, where two minor figures are examining a painting of a white cat.

—Ah! I was wondering if that was "Nemesis"— Nemesis is such a pretty subject to illustrate.
—Y-e-s, that is—ah—yes—very pretty subject indeed—a-h—by-the-way—what is a "Nemesis," Miss Ogden? Do you know if the catalogue didn't say this was a picture of—a-h—"Nemesis"—I should have taken it for a—cat— watching a—a-h—mouse—and a—chair—and— a-h—a big piece of cheese on the table.
—Why "Nemesis" is the name of the cat, I suppose.

Howard had fun, too, with society's eternal perception of the servant problem, and in this case perhaps with the attitude of newly emancipated blacks. When one character sends a servant on an errand, the servant responds:

—Beg pardon, sah, but we culled gemmen at Saratoga have made a new rule, sah—we always take it [the tip] in advance now, sah.
—Oh, you always take it in advance now (*gives him currency*).
—Beg pardon, sah, but this is a ragged one, sah; we culled gemmen of Saratoga have made a new rule, sah!

Later, when the servant delivers a letter from one guest to another he demands tips from both, once more citing new rules.

Programs put audiences in a properly happy mood for things to come with thumbnail descriptions of other colorful characters, such as Sir Mortimer Muttonleg (George Parkes), set down as "the familiar English Tourist, who comes to Hunt the Wild Buffalo on the wilds of Broadway," and Major Luddington Whist (A. Matthison), exposed as "the 'Swell' of the 'Wells,' a gentleman rather more familiar with horses than heraldry, and better acquainted with dice than delicacy." As always, Daly's stage pictures were magnificent, more often than not the best offered New York in those days. The *Herald* was especially taken with two of James Roberts's settings, suggesting that "the opening scene of the lake, terrace and mall of our Central Park from the cedar walk gives us the scene itself in the soft balmy atmosphere of a sweet summer day" and also calling attention to the depiction of the Congress Hotel and to Saratoga Lake with picnickers in the foreground. This implies that Daly may have scrapped the setting of the art exhibition, and

with it the "Nemesis" dialogue. Critics were virtually unanimous in conceding how uproarious the fun was. Nor were there many cries of overstepping moral bounds. But the *Times*'s slightly snide review addressed another matter that reviewers increasingly would harp on—the use of bad grammar by characters who should know better, and the employment, heaven forbid, of slang. Obviously the growing interest in realism or naturalism had its limits. Given the *Times*'s earlier bewailing of stilted speech in older plays, the paper's idea of realism seems to have been polite, contemporary drawing-room conversation. But quibbles aside, only *Rip Van Winkle* surpassed *Saratoga* among nonmusicals in popularity during the season. At one point in the 101-performance run, demand for seats was so great that Daly exiled his orchestra to behind the scenes and seated willing patrons in what had been the orchestra pit, raised by a temporary floor.

The 27th brought *The Heir at Law* back into the repertory at Wallack's, thereby allowing those playgoers who wished to do so to compare that house's version with the one Daly had offered in November.

The new year began with two new plays. First came **Kind to a Fault** (1-2-71, Lina Edwin's), a slight comedy by William Brough, reminiscent of *Everybody's Friend* and that play's Wellington de Boots. The more good deeds Frank Goldworthy (M. W. Leffingwell) attempts, the more trouble he creates.

Robertson's **War** (1-3-71, Wallack's) proved another casualty of Wallack's rocky season. Wallack's production preceded the English premiere by two weeks, but even that novelty could not shield the play from devastating notices by critics who found it clumsy and humorless. The dying Robertson (he died exactly a month after the American opening) had not intended it to be a comedy, but what had been perceived as his sure hand was missing. In its simple story, war breaks out between France and Germany just before a young Frenchman, Oscar (George Clarke), and a German girl, Lottie (Madeline Henriques), are to be married. Oscar is called to the front. He is seriously wounded and twice reported dead, but Lottie remains faithful and is finally able to marry him. The play's view of war was not typically romantic, and Wallack underlined this with a battlefield scene filled with gory human corpses and the badly mangled bodies of horses. Many critics and playgoers felt this carried theatrical realism too far, especially with recollections of our own bloody Civil War so fresh in many minds. The play was quickly withdrawn.

At Booth's *Rip Van Winkle* had finally come to the end of its long run, and Booth himself took the stage on the 9th in one of his most popular roles, the title part of Bulwer-Lytton's *Richelieu.* As they had the preceding season with his Hamlet, critics saw Booth as the best living American interpreter of the role, growing better with each passing year, but still given to a certain unevenness and to withholding his full resources from many scenes. And once again all critics joined in extolling the richly painted, historically accurate settings of Charles Witham. Lawrence Barrett played de Mauprat, and since Booth continued to refuse to perform on Saturday nights, Barrett was given an extra evening to show his stuff. Venturesome artist that he was, he elected on several occasions to try relatively obscure older plays, such as *Love and Loyalty,* in which the hero loves the daughter of a man he knows to be a traitor, and *The King of the Commons,* a tale of rebellion in which James V wrongly suspects his most loyal friend.

Having struck out with three new plays, Wallack's fell back to the safety of revivals. One assurance of better box office was Lester Wallack's first appearance of the season. On the 16th he essayed two diametrically distinct roles—the bold, impassioned Ruy Gomez, who wins over a reluctant duchess from the faint-hearted man she is supposed to wed, in Planché's *Faint Heart Never Won Fair Lady,* and the blasé, worldly Charles Coldstream, who accepts employment in the service of a farmer and courts a poor girl, in Boucicault's *Used Up.* On the 19th Robertson's *Ours* rejoined the repertory.

Although space limitations preclude listing benefits, so common at the time, the review of one deserves attention. The occasion was a benefit for the family of George Holland, long a favorite at Wallack's and briefly at Daly's. His death prompted one of the most famous of all American theatrical stories. Joseph Jefferson and one of Holland's sons had gone to an Episcopal minister to arrange for burial. The minister refused on the grounds that Holland was an actor and sniffed, "There is a little church around the corner where they do that sort of thing." Thus the Church of the Transfiguration gained a special place in actors' affections. Most benefits for Holland had been held on the 14th, but the 14th Street Theatre waited until the 25th. The play chosen was *The Lady of Lyons,* and for the occasion Fechter made his only major New York appearance of the season to play the hero, Claude Melnotte. The *Times* gave a vivid description of his acting, remarking, "Those who have heard of people loving the ground some woman treads on, without realizing it, may see the idea enforced throughout Mr. Fechter's impersonation. His eyes are fastened

to his mistress as though he would devour her. Her every movement is watched with worship, her lips are gazed at as if each word that fell from them would be garnished, like the girl's in the fairy tale, with diamonds and pearls. Every turn of his person, every glance, every breath, betokens perennial love and adoration."

Also on the 25th, at Lina Edwin's, the beleaguered Laura Keene began a stand in what had been one of her most admired characterizations, Mary Leigh, a remarried woman who is blackmailed by a husband she had believed to be dead, in Boucicault's *Hunted Down.* To many the star looked careworn, but those who continued to admire her felt her faded beauty added an extra touch of pathos to her performance. Playing opposite her in the role of young Willie Leigh—and passed over by the major reviewers—was "Little" Minnie Maddern, the magnificent Mrs. Fiske of later years. The younger Colman's *The Poor Gentleman,* famous for its character of Dr. Ollapod, was given a rehearing on the 28th at Wallack's, with Stoddart as the doctor.

Gilbert a' Beckett's **Red Hands** (1-30-71, Wood's) was written as a vehicle for Lucy Rushton, an English actress. Her attempts to achieve stardom in America all came up short. The present occasion was no exception. She portrayed Rachel Harmon, whose muderous second husband, Walter (C. W. Barry), kidnaps her child. Comic relief was provided by L. J. Mestayer as Crockett, the detective.

At Wallack's the parade of revivals went on. *The Clandestine Marriage* appeared on February 4, and two nights later came Bulwer-Lytton's *Money,* with its tale of a newly rich man who learns who really loves him when he pretends he has squandered his fortune. The role was a favorite of Lester Wallack's, and one paper noted, "He walks and speaks like a gentleman in polished society, whose life has been soured by early misfortune, but who is entirely versed in the *convenances.*"

Perhaps the saddest event of the season was the return of Edwin Forrest, in what proved to be his last New York appearance.

. . .

Edwin Forrest (1806–72) Customarily regarded as the first great American tragedian, the Philadelphian made an unexpected stage debut in 1817, when a local manager, noting his good looks, drafted him to substitute for an ailing actress. A more studied debut came in 1820 as Norval in *Douglas.* A dark-haired, coldly handsome, muscular man with a powerful voice, he rose swiftly to stardom. At his peak he promoted native drama as well as the classics and was admired by the elite as much as by the lower orders, but in later years his behavior cost him favor, especially among more well-to-do playgoers.

. . .

Old, ailing, and regarded in many quarters as exemplifying outmoded traditions, he was not even awarded one of the better playhouses but had to perform at the less desirable 14th Street Theatre. Quite probably he was all too aware of his position, and this may have prompted his selection for his first appearance, on the 6th—*King Lear.* Just as Laura Keene's personal problems and loss of her youthful beauty added to the pathos of her Mary Leigh, so Forrest's age and fragility gave his aging king a new poignancy. Critics said as much, albeit careful to couch their observations in the kindest terms. Moreover, the *Times* added, "Mr. Forrest also appears to have mellowed intellectually. There is a reserve and refinement of touch about him in this part which certainly were less conspicuous before." When, two weeks later, he boldly challenged Booth's still flourishing Richelieu with his own reading (he had been the original American interpreter of the part), the same paper advised, "In spite of some defects of exaggerated emphasis and undue prolongation of delivery, this embodiment . . . has bettered and not deteriorated with time." For all the critics' kindnesses, audiences were not large, and the engagement ended after three weeks. On Saturday nights, when, like Booth, Forrest would not perform, the theatre offered *Fanchon, the Cricket,* but without America's favorite Fanchon, Maggie Mitchell.

Wallack's list of plays for the season swelled during the ensuing weeks. On the 13th last year's hit, *Home,* was paired with the younger Colman's comedy about hypochondria, *Blue Devils.* The following Monday, the 20th, brought back *Woodcock's Little Game* coupled with *A Morning Call.*

This last bill vied with a revival of *Monte Cristo* at Wood's. Scene-chewing Edward Eddy, once the favorite of Bowery gallery gods but now nearing the end of his career, was the star.

March came in like a frolicsome lamb with Wallack's restaging on the 2nd of Brougham's *Romance and Reality,* a satire on prewar society. For the occasion Brougham recreated the role of the comically devious Jack Swift. Time and changing mores had taken the edge off much of the humor, but many could still relish the portrait of an early militant advocate of women's rights, with the telling name of Barbara "Barbary" Manly (Emily Mestayer).

Three openings lured first-nighters on the 6th. Booth supplanted his *Richelieu* with *Much Ado About Nothing,* not one of his happier achieve-

ments. Barrett was Don Pedro; Bella Pateman, Beatrice. J. H. McVicker, who was Booth's son-in-law, and Augustus Pitou, the future producer of cheap touring attractions, assumed lesser roles. The attraction at Wood's was Watts Phillips's *The Dead Heart,* a revenge tragedy set during the French Revolution. William Horace Lingard and his wife, Alice Dunning Lingard, took over Lina Edwin's for a five-week stand. Lingard had been an English music hall player before coming to America in 1868. His bills were a mixed bag of comic sketches, musical numbers, farces such as *A Silent Protector,* and comedies such as Robertson's *David Garrick* (which Lingard rechristened *Davy's Love*). In a later era Lingard might well have been a star of musical comedy or revue instead of the hodgepodges he was known for.

Across the Continent (3-13-71, Wood's) was the sort of exaggerated melodrama critics loved to tear to shreds; they seemed to save their most scathing adjectives and expressions for the time when they could review just this kind of play. After all, it was a sitting duck. Its characters were drawn in shadeless blacks and whites; its breathless progression of thumpingly dramatic incidents renounced all claim to probability and time and again wrenched the long arm of coincidence. Yet while critics railed, playgoers roared with delight, for *Across the Continent* unquestionably was what the next generation would call "an audience show."

James J. McCloskey had first written the play several years earlier as *New York in 1837; or, The Overland Route,* but he withdrew it and stored it away after a test performance demonstrated its inadequacies. McCloskey was an interesting figure. Born in Montreal in 1825, he migrated to New York when he was sixteen. Eight years later he joined gold seekers trekking to California. To support himself there he turned to acting. For the next thirty or so years he realized a haphazard career playing small roles in support of many of the era's great stars, managing theatres, and writing dozens of short-lived plays, mostly rough-and-tumble melodramas. His last years were spent as a court clerk. But shortly before his death he granted an interview in which he let slip some idea of how low his sights or tastes were. He ranked Edward Eddy far above E. H. Sothern and insisted a second-string, totally forgotten actor, Eddie Raynor, was America's greatest Shakespearean.

Just why or when McCloskey sold his play to Oliver Doud Byron is unknown; nor can it be ascertained which man added the two scenes that probably secured the play's success. What is certain is that *Across the Continent* gave Byron a meal ticket for the rest of his long career and entered him in theatrical annals as one of many 19th-century actors largely sustained by and remembered for a single role.

* * *

Oliver Doud Byron (1842–1920) was born in Frederick, Md., and made his debut at Baltimore's famed Holliday Street Theatre in 1856, playing opposite Joseph Jefferson in *Nicholas Nickleby*. Early in his career he acted under the name Oliver B. Doud. Later he performed with ensembles as far south as New Orleans, became a member of Wallack's for a time, and alternated with Edwin Booth as Othello and Iago.

* * *

The play opens on a snowy night in the heart of New York's worst slum, Five Points. Agnes Constance (Lizzie Safford), a bedraggled widow, approaches cold-hearted, tight-fisted barroom owner John Adderly (Charles Waverly), telling him her husband has spent their last cent at Adderly's gin mill and begging for pennies to feed her starving children. Adderly brushes her aside, so she curses him and his heirs, then goes out to die in the snow. Twenty years pass. Adderly has framed an easygoing gambler, Joe Ferris or "the Ferrit" (Byron), unaware that Joe is the dead widow's son. Adderly is also trying to destroy a rich merchant, Thomas Goodwin (Joseph Sefton), all the while courting Goodwin's daughter, Louise (Annie Firmin). Joe escapes from prison, entraps Adderly, and sees him sent to prison in return. Five more years pass, by which time Joe has left city life behind and becomes a stationmaster for the Union Pacific in Indian territory. The Goodwins detrain on the way to visit a ranch. But Adderly, who has also escaped from jail, has goaded the Indians into attacking the station. Joe sends an urgent telegram asking for a trainload of soldiers. With the help of others in the station, Joe keeps the attackers at bay until the "train comes on . . . and stops, and soldiers from the train fire at the Chief and Adderly, both of whom fall. Louise rushes into Joe's arms."

If critics tripped over themselves to denigrate the play, most were not much happier with Byron. The *Spirit of the Times* described him as "a gentleman who possesses many natural advantages for a player, such as a good voice, a not ungraceful figure, and considerable ease of deportment, but who, for some reason best known to himself, has a habit of playing with rather than for his audience, of addressing many of his speeches to them, instead of to the actors upon the stage."

Richard Moody, the play's modern editor, has suggested another reason for its success: its utilization of two comparatively new American achievements. The first telegraph message flashed across the continent was sent from San Francisco by California's Chief Justice Field to President Lincoln in 1861; transcontinental train service began in 1869. Moreover, a western setting and a look, however indirect, at postwar Indian problems gave the play a certain freshness and contemporaneousness.

Across the Continent held the boards for more than a quarter of a century, although its appeal at first-class houses was considerably shorter. Byron later confessed that as a result he played "first to the kid-gloved audiences, then to the woolen mittened." But in this premiere season the play ran six weeks at Wood's and returned for another month at Niblo's, in the face of a heat wave, beginning July 17.

At Booth's on the 20th the season's third staging of *Othello* raised its curtain, this time with Booth and Barrett alternating as hero and antagonist.

Despite the raging popularity of G. L. Fox, the out-of-the-way Olympic apparently was having problems drawing audiences and showing a decent profit. To complicate matters, John A. Duff, who believed he owned the theatre, found himself embroiled in a cynical, vicious lawsuit brought against him by the heirs of the house's architect, John Trimble, who sought repossession on a technicality. Although Duff had done little to help Augustin Daly, his son-in-law, when Daly had embarked on his own, he now turned to him for aid. Daly's generous response was his own new play and the loan of his troublesome beauty, Agnes Ethel.

Daly called his play **Horizon** (3-21-71, Olympic). Alleyn Van Dorp (Hart Conway), "just from West Point with his first commission, dispatched to the Far West," comes to the luxurious Waverly Place home of the woman who adopted and raised him to say farewell before heading for his new post. For years Mrs. Van Dorp (Mrs. J. J. Prior) has refused to change her will, hoping against hope that the failed husband she threw out long ago and who returned only once, to steal their daughter, will reappear along with the girl. Alleyn brings several guests. Most important is Sundown Rowse (G. L. Fox), "a distinguished member of the *Third House* [read lobbyist] at Washington. Owning a slice of every Territory, and bound for the Far West to survey his new Congressional Land Grant, which lies just this side of the Horizon." Mrs. Van Dorp gathers from Rowse that ne'er-do-wells such as her husband often gravitate west, so she asks Alleyn and her guests to be on the lookout for him. On their way to Fort

Jackson the travelers stop at the town of Rogue's Rest, a collection of rundown wooden buildings. There they meet a hunted criminal, John Loder (J. K. Mortimer), whom posses and vigilantes have dubbed "Panther Loder" or "the White Panther"; a hopeless drunkard, Wolf (J. B. Studley); and Wolf's charming daughter, Med (Agnes Ethel), whom the Indians have named "White Flower of the Plains." When Wolf is shot dead, Loder takes Med under his wing. For all his cruelty, he loves her and treats her kindly. Along with Rowse, Loder and Med take passage on a flatboat heading up Big Run River. The trip was depicted by means of a panorama, which gave way to a scene showing a woods. Indians lurk in wait, then attack, and their chief, Wannamucka (Charles Wheatleigh), kidnaps Med. Van Dorp rescues her, and Loder kills the chief. Loder gives Alleyn papers he found on Wolf's body that prove Med is Alleyn's lost stepsister. Recognizing that he cannot offer Med the advantages that Alleyn can, Loder relinquishes his claim on her.

Several critics complained that the play was much too long and repetitive, especially the first act, which, while presenting an elegant scene that contrasted with the untamed settings of the rest of the play, served little purpose. (Daly immediately obliged them with some sharp pruning but did not delete the first act.) Yet they were also in accord regarding the play's merits. First of all, they saw it as a reasonably realistic picture of the contemporary West, portraying, as the *Times* observed, "its Arcadian romance and its frantic dissipation, its wild adventure and its vivid contrasts of civilization and barbarism." Then there was Daly's sober honesty in drawing his major figures, finding virtues in villains and flaws in his heroes and heroines. A high point was the interview between a short-tempered, untrusting Alleyn and a gruff but well-intentioned Loder, in which Loder tries to find a better place for Med.

Loder: You mean to tell me you don't love her yourself, then! Why you've just confessed it to her.

Alleyn: (*Annoyed*) She told you—

Loder: Yes, and you're ashamed of it. You think it good sport to fool a friendless creature like her. You're deceiving her, and you know it!

Alleyn: Whatever you please.

Loder: Captain! I beg pardon again if I'm insulting. But if you only knew all. If I thought you really loved her, I'd be content.

Alleyn: I'm much obliged, I'm sure.

Last, there was a rich collection of minor characters such as an English aristocrat, a black, a Chinese laborer, Rowse's daughter, a lively Irishwoman, and a variety of Indians, all briefly but memorably limned. So many colorful figures and incidents should have won over audiences, but *Horizon* had at best a satisfactory run of eight weeks and never was given a major revival.

At Wallack's, while a new play was actively in rehearsal, the troupe returned Buckstone's *Married Life* to the repertory on the 23rd for the second season in a row. That new play was Robertson's **Birth** (3-27-71, Wallack's)—an ironic title in view of the author's recent death. *Birth* took a lighthearted look at a favorite Robertson theme, class distinction. In this instance, an energetic if meddlesome playwright, Jack Randall (Lester Wallack), attempts to make matings come out as happily in real life as they do in his plays. Before he is finished, the Earl of Eagleclyffe (Charles Fisher) is slated to wed Sarah Hewitt (Mrs. Barry), a rich ironmonger's daughter, and Lady Adeliza (Helen Tracy) looks to marry Sarah's father, Paul (B. T. Ringgold). After all, as Jack finally remarks, "It's a comedy—it's not a drama—it's a comedy." Unfortunately, audiences found the comedy had all too little substance and humor, so *Birth* went down as another disappointment for Wallack's season.

Some audiences took umbrage at Daly's advertising Boucicault's **Jezebel** (3-28-71, Fifth Ave.) as a comedy, and "an original and significant dramatic comedy" at that. It was not. Based loosely on Lessière's *La Fille du sud,* it was rather another of his defiantly complicated sensation-melodramas. In the simplest terms, it recounted the history of a Brazilian adventuress (Clara Morris). On a voyage to Europe she is shipwrecked and uses the opportunity to change identities with a drowned passenger. Once in France she marries George d'Artigues (D. H. Harkins), but her roving eye soon prompts her to take a lover. The lover is killed, and when she is caught attempting to poison her husband she is forced to flee. She returns to Brazil. Years later d'Artigues, believing her dead, remarries. Word of this reaches her, and she returns to France to blackmail her husband as a bigamist. Her efforts come to naught when it is learned she herself had been married at the time she wed d'Artigues. What little comedy the play had derived apparently from Daly's own additions. The evening's principal attraction was Miss Morris's acting. One critic noted, "To unusual ease and grace of action, a mixture of suppleness and languor in admirable harmony with the tropical nature to be depicted, Miss Morris adds an intensity and a variety of physiognomical expressions rarely seen."

By standards of the time, Miss Morris may well have been underacting—something Daly's tiny house would readily encourage. But Daly also encouraged another comparative rarity on contemporary stages. He insisted that even the smallest action be made more believable by being reasonably motivated. In her autobiography Miss Morris recalled an incident from *Jezebel*'s rehearsals. She was required to move across the stage to be out of hearing of two other characters. Most stage directors, she noted, "would simply have said: 'Cross to the Right,' and you would have crossed" because you had been told to. Not Daly. He and Miss Morris spent time proposing and rejecting numerous rationales. "There was no guest for me to cross to in welcoming pantomime; no piano on that side of the room for me to cross to and play on softly; ah, the fireplace! and the pretty warming of one foot? But no, it was summer-time, that would not do. The ancient fancy-work, perhaps? No, she was a human panther, utterly incapable of so domestic an occupation. The fan forgotten on the mantel-piece? Ah, yes, that was it! you cross the room for that—and then suddenly I reminded Mr. Daly that he had, but a moment before, made a point of having me strike a gentleman sharply on the cheek with my fan." In the end Daly inserted a few lines calling attention to the lady's smelling-bottle, and this allowed her to cross over in order to retrieve it.

The play allowed the scene painter to move from lush, palmy Brazil to Alpine views and elegant French interiors, and, as always with Daly, the scenery was praised. Nonetheless, this *Jezebel* was a quick flop.

Yet the very presence of such a play on Daly's stage, or the production of *Lost at Sea* at Wallack's the preceding season, is illuminating. Daly's was rapidly earning a reputation much like Wallack's. Both were perceived as theatres upholding the loftiest and most elegant standards, as houses where high comedy flourished. So such plunges from high comedy to Boucicault's low drama—perhaps some would have said high melodrama—were remarkable. But neither house was condemned for the change itself. Condemnation came only when the play in question was seen as inferior. Perhaps Daly's and Wallack's willingness to include such offerings, and the public's acceptance of them as not necessarily unworthy of its most elite houses, stem from one fact often ignored. The 19th century, at least in England and America, was a lean time for great tragedy. Nothing approaching the nobility of Greek or Shakespearean tragedy came from the pens of contemporary dramatists. The absence of good

modern tragedy and the perennial attraction the genre holds for some part of the playgoing audience may explain the relative frequency of Shakespearean revivals during the period and the vogue of stars such as Edwin Booth. Curiously, neither Daly's nor Wallack's gave much attention to Shakespearean drama—as opposed to Shakespearean comedy. Quite possibly both felt they could not compete with the reigning specialists. Their acceptance, then, of Boucicault's works and similar plays may have been their reluctant way of filling a void, reluctant at least artistically. In time the rise of the well-made problem play would provide something of an answer, eschewing at its best the outrageous theatrical excesses and stereotypically drawn characters of melodrama. Daly's production of *Frou-Frou* in his first season had hinted at things to come.

On April 1, Wallack's rushed in a double bill of revivals, pairing Bayle Bernard's *The Nervous Man* with *The Unfinished Gentleman*. John Gilbert had a field day in Bernard's play as the jittery Aspen confronted by the comically threatening McShane of Brougham.

Booth brought his own season to an end when, on the 3rd, he returned to one of his best non-Shakespearean roles, the hunchbacked jester, Bertuccio, in *The Fool's Revenge*, Tom Taylor's rendition of *Le Roi s'amuse* (the source of Verdi's *Rigoletto*).

Perhaps caught empty-handed by the failure of *Jezebel*, Daly did a rare thing: he enlisted the services of a visiting star for a prolonged engagement, beginning on the 10th. That star was the great English favorite Charles Mathews, whom Odell later wrote was at that time "still the most finished comedian ever seen on the New York stage." Contemporaries might not have gone quite that far but certainly agreed he was uncommonly gifted. His taste and charm, his liveliness and ease, his celebrated rapid speech—these had seemingly not diminished one iota since his visits in 1838 and 1857. Indeed, to show how little things had changed he opened with the same bill that had introduced his 1857 season, *Married for Money* and *Patter Versus Clatter*, and in the former impersonated a twenty-five-year-old man to everyone's satisfaction. The latter, a short piece, virtually a monologue, allowed the star to switch rapidly, in the protean fashion of the time, from one distinctive comic character to another. Subsequent bills included *If I'd a Thousand a Year; The Critic; Out of Sight, Out of Mind; Used Up;* and *Not Such a Fool as He Looks.*

The same night saw an even more interesting revival at Niblo's. Following a successful revival of the musical *The Black Crook,* the management brought in *Richard III.* Of course, the play had been on American stages from the earliest days of American theatre. What was unusual about this mounting was that it discarded Colley Cibber's redaction, so long employed as the standard text, and returned to Shakespeare's original. Cibber had reduced the number of scenes, rearranged their order, simplified the historical background of the play, and cut characters to focus more attention on and give more time to Richard. Moreover, Richard's soliloquies had been rewritten, with the result that they probed less deeply into his evil, warped character but instead placed his thinking in the context of the increasingly moral tone of Cibber's— and, later, Victorian—stages. For all the additional attention given Richard, he no longer opened the play but first appeared in the second scene (allowing expectations to build for the star's entrance), and his soliloquy started not with the famous "Now is the winter of our discontent" (although most stars restored this) but with "Now are our brows bound with victorious wreaths." Less discriminating playgoers had also appropriated such Cibber additions as "Richard's himself again" and "Off with his head!" For once, traditionalists and purists found themselves in opposition. Traditionalists—and that included almost all the newspaper critics—insisted Cibber's version was by far the more stageworthy. And playgoers apparently agreed. The meticulously detailed, historically correct costumes and scenery had been brought over in toto from Charles Calvert's Manchester theatre, and so had the bloodless, monotoned James Bennett in the title role. The physical production earned lavish praise, but Bennett only acted in the disservice of Shakespeare. After a week he was replaced and Cibber's version restored. The play continued for the rest of the month to good business.

Business was not so good farther uptown, where a lately unlucky actress took over a supposedly unlucky house. Laura Keene continued to serve as her own director and producer. For her latest appearance she offered a leading man long popular in Boston and London, William Creswick, in a play new to New York, Watts Phillips's **Nobody's Child** (4-11-71, 14th St.) Its central figure's history seemed too much like a watered-down version of Rip Van Winkle's to have novelty or appeal. The reception was icy, the play quickly taken off, and Miss Keene left to eke out the remainder of her stay by resurrecting *Hunted Down.*

For its next double bill Wallack's reached way back to revive Samuel Foote's 1762 comedy *The Liar.* The work, whose hero, Young Wilding, is a habitual prevaricator unflustered by constant exposure, was first done by British troops in New York in February 20, 1786, and had not been given a major revival since 1847. Neither age nor a sable mustache, which he adamantly refused to shave off even in the name of historical accuracy, deterred Lester Wallack from assuming the title role. For contemporary audiences an even greater hurdle was Foote's penchant for sly topical references, now beyond their ken. The companion play was Bayle Bernard's *His Last Legs,* which allowed Brougham to shine as O'Callaghan, a scapegrace who impersonates a doctor to earn some money and a dinner. Despite drawbacks, the bill won immediate popularity.

Not so A. W. Young's **Jonquil** (4-15-71, Booth's), which Barrett presented on one of those Saturday nights when Booth rested. (At least one notice called the play *Only a Heart* and listed its author as W. W. Young. Was this a twentyish William Young, a writer Barrett would promote in later years?) Its hero is a Parisian painter, Jonquil (Barrett), who joins the army to earn enough to support his wife, Faustine (Bella Pateman), who is an opera singer, and their young son. But his wife proves faithless, and after her lover is slain, Jonquil confronts her, weeping at the man's grave, with their dead child. One or two more performances, and the work was consigned to oblivion. To replace it Barrett brought out *The Winter's Tale* on the 25th, acting a Leontes that was full of poetic promise if not yet totally realized.

T. C. De Leon's **Pluck** (4-17-71, Lina Edwin's) was accorded an equally sour reception. A stalwart mining engineer, Ernest Sterling (George Clarke), stands by the falsely accused Kate Moore (Ione Burke) through thick and thin, even though his adversary, Egbert van Kraupt (G. C. Boniface), attempts to construe that loyalty in such a manner as to make Sterling's fiancée, Agnes Dodd (Lillie Eldridge), wonder about Sterling's affection for her. An explosion in a coal mine provided an end-of-act "sensation." The play's quick closing meant another "new American comedy" had bitten the dust. Sadly indicative of the period was the play's need to identify itself as a native effort.

Revivals held sway elsewhere. The night before the unveiling of Barrett's *The Winter's Tale,* Wood's offered an undistinguished mounting of *The Streets of New York;* on May 1, it gave its stage over to *Uncle Tom's Cabin.* That same evening Wallack's raised its curtain on *Americans in Paris,* one of several plays held over from the preceding season's list, while E. L. Davenport began a week's engagement at Niblo's in which he presented *A New Way to Pay Old Debts, Twelfth Night,* and *The Merchant of Venice.* On the 2nd Wood's produced Boucicault's romance about a poor girl and an impoverished aristocrat, *The Colleen Bawn.*

Four plays opened on May 8, and in a coincidence rare at the time, all four were new. One was English, one was of uncertain authorship, and two were American. The English play was William Schwenck Gilbert's **Randall's Thumb** (5-8-71, Wallack's). Like many other contemporary works, it employed a melodramatic frame filled with comic characters. In its basic story Buckthorpe (B. T. Ringgold), who has technically committed a murder for which he is not really guilty, attempts to conceal his act but is blackmailed by a finagling rascal, Randall (Charles Fisher). Two comic couples, the Scantleburys (John Gilbert and Mrs. John Sefton) and the Flamboys (Owen Marlowe and Effie Germon), and a pair of lovers, Joe Bangles (J. H. Stoddart) and Miss Spinn (Emily Mestayer), scamper through the story before Buckthorpe can exculpate himself. A picnic among the rocks at the shore was a highlight of the entertainment, with a clever depiction of the havoc created by an incoming tide winning special applause.

No author was credited with **Rank** (5-8-71, Lina Edwin's), which contemporary scuttlebutt suggested was an American adaptation of an English novel. It centered on Miles Hubb (George Clarke), whose wiles and determination sooner or later best his haughty, high-born adversaries.

The two American plays were basically vehicles for specific stars—too often the only way native playwrights could get hearings for their efforts. **Help** (5-8-71, Wood's) was the work of Frederick G. Maeder—son of the once famous actress Clara Fisher—a sometime actor who supplemented his income by writing just such vehicles. On this occasion his star was the Irish-American favorite Joseph Murphy. Murphy portrayed Ned Daly, who loves Lillie Waldro (Annie Firmin). Unfortunately, his criminal brother-in-law, Tracy Randall (T. W. Keene)—the second villainous Randall of the evening—is willing to kill his own wife to marry Lillie. Daly dons such disguises as a slow-witted Irish servant, a blind fiddler, and a German glazier ("a glass pudin man") to thwart Randall, and at one point he rescues his sister-in-law from a burning bed. Murphy also delighted his audiences with several songs and dances, including a blackface minstrel routine.

Although some critics predicted *Randall's Thumb* would run out the season, neither it nor *Rank* nor *Help* survived for long. The play that chalked up

season after season, surviving as long as its star was alive to play it, was T. B. De Walden and Edward Spencer's **Kit, the Arkansas Traveller** (5-8-71, Niblo's), and the star was Frank Chanfrau. The hulky, dark-haired, dark-eyed Chanfrau had rocketed to fame as the resourceful fireman, Mose, in *A Glance at New York in 1848.* For years he had played the part in revivals of the original and in sequels. In 1865 *Sam* had served him as a bridge between one enduring vehicle and another. Now he was Kit Redding, an Arkansas farmer whose wife and child are kidnapped by his wife's former suitor, Manuel Bond (George C. Boniface). For years Kit, who has grown wealthy, searches for his family. At last he encounters his grown daughter, Alice (Rose Evans), and Bond, who now calls himself Hastings, on a Mississippi River steamboat. Hastings sets fire to the boat, hoping to pull off a robbery in the confusion. The passengers are shipwrecked on an island, where Kit kills Hastings and convinces Alice of his own paternity. William Voegtlin's superb scenery enhanced the original production. His views of the levee at St. Louis, the ornate salon of the steamboat, and the boat's spacious decks all elicited sufficient response to prompt him to come forth and take bows. To create some idea of genetic verisimilitude Rose Evans played Kit's wife in the first act, while the very young Annie was portrayed by Minnie Maddern, whom the *Herald* declared "a wonder."

For the third time in the season the American West had provided the setting for a native melodrama. That *Kit* and *Across the Continent* became far more popular than *Horizon* can be attributed to their stars' appeal, to the more sensational elements in their stories, and to their principal characters being depicted in primary colors instead of Daly's more subtle shadings. *Kit,* in fact, outlived Chanfrau, drawing patrons in lesser theatres and in backwaters well into the 1890s.

On the next Monday night, *Horizon* was replaced by another new play, **Jack Sheppard** (5-15-71, Olympic). Of course, the story was old; only the version was new—and unattributed. Ada Harland, who had assumed the trouser role of the Earl of Eden in last season's *Formosa,* now had the title part of the famous highwayman. G. L. Fox, J. K. Mortimer, J. B. Studley, and all the other well-liked members of the Olympic's company offered her solid support.

Then the parade of revivals resumed. With *Randall's Thumb* unable to draw in ample business, on the 22nd Wallack's brought back Brougham's *Playing with Fire,* in which long-married couples are encouraged to try a little flirtation in order to rekindle their love. A week later, on the 29th, the house restored *Rosedale*, Lester Wallack's story of a cruel uncle who attempts to prevent his niece's remarrying.

On June 5, Lucille Western returned to the Olympic for a two-week engagement in her inevitable *East Lynne*. But first-nighters were more interested in a new play, W. G. Wills's **The Man o'Airlie** (6-5-71, Booth's), which secured Barrett a firm foothold on stardom.

. . .

Lawrence [Patrick] Barrett (1838–91), the son of a poor tailor, was born in Paterson, N.J., but raised in Detroit. Although Barrett persistently denied it, his real surname was believed to be Brannigan. He made his Detroit debut in 1853 in *The French Spy* and his New York debut three years later as Sir Thomas Clifford in *The Hunchback*. Beginning with the 1862–63 season he played opposite Edwin Booth, taking over Booth's Richard III when Booth left to be with his dying wife. After serving in the Civil War he joined John McCullough in managing San Francisco's California Theatre, then returned to New York. He was an attractive man with deep-set, burning eyes. Especially in his early years, some critics found his acting too formal.

. . .

The play spanned a period of over twenty years and centered on a poet, James Harebell (Barrett), who is generally unappreciated and suffers moments of incipient derangement. A gambler, George Brandon (J. J. Howson), persuades the poet to give over his life savings of $500 in hopes of Brandon's securing a London publisher for him. Of course, Brandon simply gambles away the money. The loss of his savings drives the poet over the brink, and in his madness he wanders off, not returning until he is a much older man. By then his work has come to be admired, and his fellow villagers, believing him dead, have erected a statue of him in the town center. Just as the statue is about to be unveiled, Harebell appears. While the shock of recognition seems to clear his mind, it strains his heart beyond endurance, and he dies.

William Winter saw Barrett's Harebell as at once "noble and pathetic," a sentiment the *Times* echoed, calling it "manly, athletic and forcible." The play ran a month, and Barrett returned to it in several revivals.

Two more new plays followed. **No Name** (6-7-71, Fifth Ave.) was Daly's version of Wilkie Collins's dramatization of his own novel. Daly no doubt hoped to repeat the success of his dramatization of Collins's *Man and Wife*. Any such hopes soon were dashed.

Like some other Collins stories, the plot hinged on a legal quirk, in this instance two sisters being left legally with "no name," or technically illegitimate, because of their father's early death. The feistier of the sisters, Magdalen Vanstone (Clara Morris), determines to fight for their rights and reputation but is opposed by their "consumptive, cross-grained" cousin, Noel (George Parkes). Magdalen wins. For many the most interesting event of the evening was the appearance of Fanny Davenport, who hid her youthful beauty to impersonate "the frowsy, chalk-faced, slipshod and half-cracked" Mrs. Wragge.

Perhaps eyeing the relative success of *Jack Sheppard* at the Olympic, on the 12th Niblo's breathed new life into one of the era's many dramatizations of Bulwer-Lytton's *Paul Clifford*, which had delighted American audiences since Louisa Medina had offered her redaction in 1830. Once again the gallant highwayman learns he is of good blood, reforms, and heads for a fresh start in America. Another revival was Charles Gayler's *Atonement; or, The Child Stealer*—this time only the thrill-promising subtitle was advertised—at the Olympic, for a week beginning on the 19th.

Delmonico's; or, Larks up the Hudson (6-20-71; Fifth Ave.) was not exactly the "new local comedy" that Daly claimed it to be. Seven years before, Daly had seen his earlier version of Sardou's *La Papillonne* brought to the stage as *Taming a Butterfly*. His original version had retained its French settings, hewed close to the original—and failed. Now more confident, Daly reset the action in America—though no scene showed the famed Delmonico's restaurant—and added characters and business. The birds who dominated the new version were not the producer's fine actresses but his menfolk, for the story really focused on a variety of men out for some not always licit fun. Spence Sherman (D. H. Harkins) was a philandering spouse, Dred Dandrey (George Parkes) a novice at the game, Brandywine Bowles (James Lewis) a doddering but determined roué, and Bottles (William Davidge) a reluctant model of a homebody. But whether the changes were inadequate or the play arrived too late in the season, an audience could not be found.

June closed with three revivals. *The Long Strike*, Boucicault's sensationalized view of early labor-management strife, went on view at Wallack's on the 21st. Five nights later Rose and Harry Watkins appeared at the Olympic in Watkins's tale of romance and intrigue, *Kathleen Mavourneen*, while at Niblo's playgoers could attend the season's second *Colleen Bawn*. (Watkins, by the by, left a fascinating if soured diary, which Otis and Maud Skinner later edited.)

Continuing prosperity saw to it that the season lingered on, although the major ensembles were preparing to close shop. The first Monday in July, the 3rd, presented theatregoers with the Watkinses in their drama of Irish rebellion, *Under Two Flags,* at the Olympic and, far uptown at Broadway and 30th, a new play by the original author of *Across the Continent.* James J. McCloskey's ripsnorting **Through by Daylight** (7-3-71, Wood's) had a plot so complex that it defied recounting even by contemporary critics accustomed to relating long, involved yarns. They contented themselves with itemizing salient incidents and sneering. The *Herald* reported, in part, "A young woman is saved from the wheels of a rail car; another one falls from a stupendous cliff, and hangs by a branch; counterfeiters are displayed at work; a girl is poisoned and dies[;] . . . the hero makes a perilous descent upon a cord, saves a young woman, and then marries her." The *Times* compiled a similar list, then added, "The performance was so brisk that it quite drew away attention from the mad story," which it characterized as "a very *olla podrida* of all that is sensational and all that is absurd." After two weeks the play joined the long catalogue of McCloskey's failures.

Yet the difference between sensationalism and absurdity that was unacceptable, and that which was, continued to be one of degree, not kind. Witness one newspaper's recapitulation of the story of Boucicault's **Elfie; or, the Cherry Tree Inn** (7-8-71, Wallack's), which wrote *finis* to the ensemble's lackluster season, lackluster at least with regard to new plays. And note the opening and closing remarks: "Briefly told, the story of 'Elfie' runs thus: *Dr. Aircastle* [Charles Wheatleigh], a village physician, imagining that he has discovered the science of transmuting pebbles into gems, sells a worthless stone to *Filey* [B. T. Ringgold], landlord of the Cherry Tree Inn. Like the honest doctor himself, *Filey* is deceived by appearances, and, made aware of the mistake, he threatens to imprison *Dr. Aircastle* unless the money advanced, and already expended in good deeds, is returned. *Sedley Deepcar* [Charles Rockwell], a clever and unscrupulous personage, promises to restore the amount claimed, hoping that for so doing the doctor, in gratitude, will bestow upon him the hand of his daughter, *Rose* [Lizzie Price]. To procure the sum needed, *Deepcar* and *Sadlove* [J. H. Stoddart], a rascally showman, plan the robbery of *Filey,* and with a view toward warding off suspicion, which might else attach to his movements, *Deepcar* attires

himself like *Bob Evans* [Mr. Teesdale], a worthy sailor, and his own happy rival in the affections of the maid he covets. Toward midnight the inn is entered, and *Filey* is stricken down by the semblance of *Bob Evans. Elfie* [Effie Germon], a vivacious barmaid, sees enough of the deed to warrant an accusation against this person, but soon convinced of his innocence, she investigates the circumstances surrounding the crime, and with better results. Accompanied by *Joe Chirrup* [Charles Fisher], a blind sailor, for whom *Bob* had cared in late years, *Elfie* becomes a *dea ex machina* in the last act, goes to London, and overhears *Sadlove's* denunciation of *Deepcar,* the sight of whose downfall ends the piece. We do not intimate that this recapitulation of incidents does justice to the interest of *Mr. Boucicault's* tale." Nearly a dozen tableaux and a striking setting showing both floors of the Cherry Tree Inn gave the work added visual excitement. *Elfie* ran for five weeks.

Daly's closing offering was novel, if not entirely a novelty. The main attraction on the 10th was his resurrection of William Mitchell's once esteemed burlesque *The Savage and the Maiden,* taken loosely from incidents in Dickens's *Nicholas Nickleby.* Mrs. Gilbert, wearing a low-necked white muslin frock with pantalettes and ankle-ties, and with two long plaits of hair down her back, stole the show as Ninetta Crummles, the infant phenomenon. Coupled with this revival was a new work, **An Angel,** an unattributed comedy based on an unspecified French play and, like *Delmonico's* before it, spoofing contemporary society.

McCloskey's third sensation-drama of the season was **Schneider; or, Dot House von de Rhine** (7-17-71, Olympic), which some critics saw as a blatant attempt to capitalize on the success of Gayler's *Fritz, Our Cousin German.* The plot centered on the kidnapping of Schneider's adopted daughter. The chase and rescue took the hero over a broken bridge and down a deep well. But the play's star, Johnny Allen, was no match for the beguiling Emmet, although he went Emmet two better by assuming not only the role of the fat, beer-swilling, garrulous hero but the roles of Frau Schneider and the Schneiders' young son as well. Music, of course, heightened all the action, the *Tribune* recording that "a groan from the bassoon always precedes the moment of danger and a crash of brass instruments always attends and emphasizes the climax." But the reviewer thought the production's scenery so poor that he was not certain when the action was taking place in Minnesota and when it was set on Division Street. *Schneider* hurriedly went the way of most McCloskey plays—into minor houses or into oblivion. The same night also saw a revival of *Les Misérables* at Wood's, and a week later the theatre offered a flamboyant old melodrama, *The Idiot of the Mountain*. After another week Wood's brought out its own version of *The Ticket-of-Leave Man*, which Lotta had also played during the season.

By now theatres had shuttered for the hot weather or turned their stages over to light musical offerings. Even the august Wallack's played host to a summer season of burlesque and opéra bouffe. The lone drama to brave the heat was the last of the season's innumerable sensation-dramas. Maeder's **Lola** (8-21-71, Wood's) told of Evelyn Blair (George C. Boniface), a man forever in trouble and forever rescued by the "will o' the wisp" Lola (Ada Harland), a resourceful young lady who effects these rescues by disguising herself as a sailor, an Indian squaw, a "billiard sport," and a demimondaine called "La Belle Inconnue." Among the vivid scenic contrivances were the sinking of a ship hit by an iceberg and a guillotining. The piece ran two weeks.

1871–1872

The 1871–72 theatrical season was a weird one, at least in New York. By 1871 the city finally could claim a population of more than one million, yet there was many a night when only three playhouses offered those carefully varnished dramas and comedies guaranteed to please most sophisticated playgoers. A curious potpourri of events and trends conspired to create this pinched situation. Except for a few weeks at the very end of the season, the Olympic was given over entirely to a hugely popular revival of the musical pantomime *Humpty Dumpty*, with G. L. Fox cavorting in the leading role. Opéra bouffe and minstrelsy usurped most of the season at Lina Edwin's. *The Black Crook* and other musicals, or prototypical musicals, occupied Niblo's stage for much of the time, until the theatre burned to the ground in May. The January shooting of James Fisk, Jr., owner of the Grand Opera House, left that theatre's bookings in a shambles for several months. One of the oddest changes occurred at Wood's Museum, as that busy house regularly offered different attractions at its daily matinees and evening performances. For all practical purposes, Wood's had become an uptown mirror of the Bowery, generally changing bills on a weekly or fortnightly basis and sometimes exchanging attrac-

tions with its downtown competitor. As a result, only three playhouses—Booth's, Daly's Fifth Avenue, and Wallack's—were primarily responsible for major theatrical news during the season. A second result was that all three houses frequently enjoyed exceptional business week in, week out.

Away from the artificialities of the stage, the fall of the Tweed Ring and the burning of Chicago presented real-life sensation-drama of universal appeal.

Indefatigable little Lotta launched the new season when she began a six-week engagement at Booth's on August 14. Her opening attraction was *Little Nell and the Marchioness*. Critics, especially the more brahmin reviewers, quickly had become sated with her cuteness, but her growing coterie of fans ignored them. On the 21st Niblo's relit with a revival of *Fritz, Our Cousin German*.

Revivals continued to be the order of the night when the Grand Opera House came alive again on September 2. On this occasion the play was Tom Taylor's translation of Albert Brachvogel's 1857 *Narcisse*, the tragedy of a husband deserted by Mme de Pompadour on her rise to power who returns to kill her and is himself killed. Daniel Bandmann played the title role. Bandmann was a German-born actor who began his American career performing at German-language theatres while in his teens. Since 1863 he had been performing in English. He was a superior emotional actor—albeit slightly pedantic in approach—who brought just the requisite bitterness and anger to the part. But his revival was merely a brief prelude to his appearance in a new play. T. C. De Leon's **Jasper** (9-4-71, Grand Opera) was an attempt to dramatize and solve Dickens's unfinished *The Mystery of Edwin Drood*. In the novel Drood disappears and is believed murdered. Suspicion falls on Edwin's guardian uncle, John Jasper, who has loved the girl to whom Edwin supposedly was betrothed. De Leon's explanation was that Edwin (E. F. Thorne) has not died but has become a drug addict, and that Jasper (Bandmann) is guiltless. The play was "big with murder, with the ravings of opium-eaters, with rambles in grave-yards, and with somnambulistic walks." De Leon's solution proved no more satisfying than many others, so Bandmann soon brought back *Narcisse*.

Another opening on the 4th was Lucille Western's engagement at Wood's, beginning with her customary *East Lynne*.

Apart from the revival of *Humpty Dumpty*, the season's biggest hit was Daly's **Divorce** (9-5-71, Fifth Ave.), which the multitalented producer based loosely on Anthony Trollope's *He Knew He Was*

Right. Lu Ten Eyck (Fanny Davenport) is about to marry the much older De Wolf De Witt (William Davidge). Lu's sister, Fanny (Clara Morris), has long loved Alfred Adrianse (D. H. Harkins), but he had been sent away several years earlier by Mrs. Ten Eyck (Fanny Morant) on the grounds that Fanny was too young to marry. When Adrianse now returns, a double wedding takes place. Both marriages quickly find themselves shaky. Adrianse proves all too eager to be suspicious, particularly of his wife's innocent relations with Captain Lynde (Louis James). Conversely, Lu finds De Witt exasperatingly obliging: "He says I may do what I like. I may buy all New York up, and beggar him—says all he can do is submit to my whims. Did you ever hear such outrageous language?" Her lawyer, Templeton Jitt (James Lewis), is left almost speechless by her plaint (which resembles one by Lady Gay Spanker, another famous Davenport role). Fanny's problems are more serious, for the mercurial Adrianse kidnaps their child, and Fanny must follow him to Florida to reclaim the youngster and effect a reconciliation. Lu is also brought to her senses.

Forever snatching opportunities to moralize, the *Tribune*'s William Winter questioned "whether art ought to invite public attention to minute vivisection of matrimonial infelicities." He then cut off debate by contending that the subject had in any case been handled, "with less prolixity, in other and better plays." Brushing aside textual concerns, he praised Daly's invariably superb settings, especially "views of Long Island Sound, the Hudson, and the ruins of St. Augustine," and concluded, "Mr. Daly's company proved very strong, and did everything needful for the success of the piece." That success included a New York run of 200 performances—the longest run for any comedy up to its day—and immediate productions in Boston, Buffalo, Philadelphia, St. Louis, and Chicago, where it became the first play mounted as the city recovered from the carelessness of Mrs. O'Leary's cow.

At Booth's on the 11th, Lotta brought out two more plays that had been staples in her repertory, *Family Jars* and *The Pet of the Petticoats*. Five nights later at Wood's, Lucille Western resorted to her version of another old favorite, *Lucretia Borgia.* Both ladies changed their bills again on the 18th, with Lotta starring in *The Little Detective* and Miss Western in *Leah, the Forsaken.*

A new play was Charles Gayler's **Carl, the Fiddler** (9-18-71, Niblo's), written as a successor to his *Fritz, Our Cousin German.* One more of the era's prototypical musicals, like *Fritz* it starred J. K. Emmet. Unlike *Fritz,* it failed.

Another new play with a German-dialect character was Edwin G. De Nyse's **Oofty Gooft** (9-18-71, Grand Opera), which starred Gus Phillips, supported by such superior performers as Mme Ponisi, Ione Burke, and J. B. Studley. The piece exemplified a peculiarity of the era's tastes, its appetite for sensational melodrama even in its comedies. The most famous example would probably be *The Gilded Age,* a few seasons hence, but it could be argued in that instance that Colonel Sellers was conceived originally as mere comedy relief for a more melodramatic yarn. There was no question but that *Oofty Gooft* was designed as a vehicle for a rising dialect comedian. Nonetheless the comedy was framed in a plot telling of a woman who murders the new wife of a lover who has deserted her. An unscrupulous lawyer, a blackmailer, and other stock melodramatic figures all cast their ominous shadows on the action. Yet the center of attention clearly was Hans (Phillips), a man who runs away from the army into which he has been conscripted, comes to New York, takes employment as a servant, and soon works his way up to become the owner of a brewery. He is a lovable cuss, never missing an opportunity to expound some homely philosophy in his fractured English, and he is known to one and all as Oofty Gooft.

Lucille Western's next offering was also a new play, **La Mendiante** (9-25-71, Wood's). It could be seen simply as *East Lynne* with a happy ending, for Marguerite Berghen (Western) deserts her husband, Jean Paul (James A. Herne), and child, repents, and this time lives to rejoin her welcoming family.

Miss Western's opening coincided with the return of a greater, more durable actress. By 1871, Charlotte Cushman had been on the stage for over thirty-five years and was nearing the end of her career.

• • •

Charlotte [Saunders] **Cushman** (1816–76), the first great American tragedienne, was born in Boston into an old New England family. Her early years were nonetheless hard, and she was forced to give up her ambition to sing in opera when her voice gave out. Turning to drama, she gained fame in 1837 as Meg Merrilies in *Guy Mannering.* Relatively tall and quite homely, she soon excelled in a long line of tragic figures, although she also created the part of Lady Gay Spanker in America. She was also dismayingly mannish. This led her not only into essaying such roles as Romeo and Hamlet but into fisticuffs with players who annoyed her.

• • •

Some critics said she seemed to have shrunk physically, but no one disputed her emotional force. What did lift eyebrows were her periodic announcements that she was making "farewell" appearances, which seemed to be made on revolving stages that soon brought her back. For her opening role in this "farewell" stand at Booth's, she offered her Queen Katharine in *Henry VIII*. The *Times* found hers a "masculine" interpretation filled with "cold power," but the *Herald* lamented that the aging actress, known to be in failing health, lacked the vocal fiber she had once enjoyed.

Wallack's rather late opening closed out the month on the 30th. The opening bill was the same as the preceding season's, *The Rivals*.

October 2nd raised the curtain on two revivals and one new play. Boucicault's *The Streets of New York* began a three-week stand at Niblo's with a solid cast that included Frank Mayo as Badger, while Lucille Western moved on to her version of Nancy Sykes in the still popular *Oliver Twist*.

The novelty was Edmund Falconer's London success **Eileen Oge** (10-2-71, Grand Opera). Ensuring it a reasonable welcome was the presence of a well-liked acting couple, Mr. and Mrs. W. J. Florence, although their followers would be surprised to learn they did not play the principal roles. Both rich, haughty Henry Loftus (J. W. Brutone) and poor farmer Patrick O'Donnell (George Clarke) love Ellen Moriarty (Rose Evans), who is known as "Young Ellen" or "Eileen Oge." When she agrees to marry Patrick, Henry vows to wreck her plans. Falsely accusing Patrick of a crime, Henry and the police arrest the groom on the church steps and cart him off to jail. Some years pass, during which Henry continues to woo Ellen. His own courtship is interrupted by the appearance of a mysterious stranger who has a bushy beard and wears an outsized coat. Knowing that Patrick has escaped from prison, Henry concludes, correctly, that this is Patrick in disguise. He arranges for Patrick to be waylaid in an old mill, chloroformed, and dumped into the millrace. The arrival of a peasant saves Patrick, who again disappears. By now Henry has convinced Ellen to marry him. But Patrick's revenge is sweet. He has Henry arrested—on the same church steps—just before the wedding and claims Ellen for his own. Florence portrayed Byron O'Farrell, whose life is spent "fighting, frisking and lovemaking," while Mrs Florence was the exuberant Bridget Maguire, given to singing and dancing. If one review is to be believed, a scene in a hayfield utilized "two hundred supernumeraries"; if true, they would have cluttered the stage for the next seven weeks.

Wallack's autumn procession of revivals moved on

with *The Heir at Law* on the 3rd, *The Serious Family* on the 4th, and, on the 9th, the elder Colman's comedy about a woman who henpecks her husband and drives her daughter into eloping, *The Jealous Wife*. The 9th also saw Lucille Western enter into the last week of her stand at Wood's with Gayler's *The Child Stealer*.

After she left, the house slid into a lower order of bookings. Space limitations again preclude any detailed study of these, although a separate study should certainly be done. There would be problems, of course. Many of these pieces were little more than expanded variety sketches or other ephemera. If they were ever published, copies are all but impossible to come by. Moreover, most newspapers of the day either gave them the shortest shrift or totally ignored them. Their stars, too, were not of the first rank, even if many of them had long careers in lesser houses and in theatrical backwaters.

What is sad about their omission here and about their apparent loss is that the plays often addressed contemporary American issues still passed over in dramas and comedies presented at truly first-class houses. For example, the afternoon attraction when Miss Western first opened her stand was a play whose name at least has given it a small niche in our theatrical history, **Bertha, the Sewing Machine Girl.** Bertha's harrowing adventures had first been serialized in the late 1860s in the *New York Weekly*. Like later movie serials or soap operas, each episode ended with a cliff-hanger. The version at Wood's was by Charles Foster, who also took a major role. While different versions gave the characters different names and subjected the heroine to different crises, all told basically the same story. A poor girl comes to New York and takes work in a clothing factory. She is persecuted by her employer, sometimes sent to prison on trumped-up charges, sometimes kidnapped, sometimes thrown in a lake, but whatever indignities she suffers she eventually finds a true love and happiness. In one form or another the play remained a staple at lesser theatres for forty years. Few of Bertha's classier companions were so long-lived.

On the 12th Wallack's produced Tom Taylor and Charles Reade's *Masks and Faces,* a dramatization of incidents in the life of the famous actress Peg Woffington. Four nights later Lester Wallack took a page from Daly's book and hired Charles Mathews for a prolonged visit. But Wallack announced Mathews would be a member of the company, not a special star. True or not, Mathews's engagement began with two old favorites, *A Curious Case* and *A Game of Speculation*. The same evening at Booth's,

Charlotte Cushman switched to her Lady Macbeth. Some papers, such as the *Herald,* were ecstatic, but the *Times* suggested all was not well, noting, "The house was moderately filled by a not very enthusiastic audience, and it was only after the sleep-walking scene that a feeble call brought Miss Cushman before the curtain." The paper, which earlier had taken note of her masculine approach, twisted the knife by faintly praising the lady it called "the greatest tragic actress—we might almost say the greatest tragic actor—that America has produced." A week later, on the 23rd, she turned to her most demanded role, Meg Merrilies, the doomed witch in Scott's *Guy Mannering.* The *Herald* observed, "So intense a representation of the mingled feelings of joy, hope and surprise, struggling with the memories of wrongs done and suffered, we have never seen. Her acting . . . without any forced effects revealed a depth of passion which froze the very soul." Even the *Times* joined in the huzzas.

E. A. Sothern returned from an extended sojourn in England to begin an engagement at Niblo's on the 23rd.

· · ·

E[dward] A[skew] **Sothern** (1829–81) was born in Liverpool and first performed in England using the name Douglas Stewart. The tall, lanky, eccentric comedian made his American debut in Boston in 1852 as Dr. Pangloss in *The Heir at Law.* Two years later he joined Wallack's company, where he began using his real name. However, it was only after he became a member of Laura Keene's ensemble and portrayed the silly, lisping Lord Dundreary in Tom Taylor's *Our American Cousin* in 1858 that he was propelled into the limelight.

· · ·

He marked his reappearance before New York footlights by again assuming the role of Dundreary. In Taylor's play, the story originally had centered on Asa Trenchard's attempts to rescue his English relatives from a greedy family counselor, but over the years Sothern had expanded his role to make it the center of attraction. The *Herald* rejoiced, "There is not an inflection, not a movement of muscle or eyebrow—and more especially of eyeglass—but adds another touch to the portrait and strengthens its effects. Every little detail of dress—even the glaring bad taste which so naturally clings to an imbecile like Dundreary—has been worked up with conscientious care." The now unrewarding role of Trenchard was awarded to deadpan John T. Raymond, who would soon become a star on his own.

The 23rd also saw a new double bill of oldies at Wallack's. Mathews shone as the difficult Samuel Naggins in *Aggravating Sam,* while Brougham and Gilbert were featured in *The Nervous Man.* The next Monday, the 30th, Wallack's brought out *The Busybody* with Mathews as Marplot.

These plays harked back to a time when infant prodigies had been a phenomenon—and often an embarrassment or nuisance—on American and European stages. Only his parents' putting their foot down had prevented John Howard Payne from becoming one; and Kate Bateman, along with her sister, had started her career in this manner. These earlier young geniuses had usually attempted to show their mettle by assuming roles such as Richard III or Hamlet. A sign of changing times was the appearance of little Percy Roselle at Wood's on the 30th. His vehicle was not a Shakespearean play but a specially written modern sensation-melodrama, **The Boy Detective,** in which the title character assists often thick-headed police in capturing a bevy of dangerous criminals. One newspaper reported, "The numberless hairbreadth 'scapes and daring feats of the boy detective were followed by uproarious demonstrations of delight."

November was given over almost entirely to revivals. *Dot,* Boucicault's dramatization of Dickens's short story *The Cricket on the Hearth,* was the offering at Booth's on the 6th. Just as Dundreary had come to dominate *Our American Cousin,* so the lovable toymaker, Caleb Plummer, and not the misunderstood young wife, Dot, had become the starring part in this theatricalization. John E. Owens was among the era's great comedians, and this was considered one of his two finest parts, although he emphasized Caleb's gentle humor and pathos. At Wallack's *The Critic* was the attraction that same night, coupled at first with *A Curious Case* and on some later nights with Tom Taylor's *A Nice Firm.* The next Monday, the 13th, Lester Wallack himself reappeared in his own *Rosedale,* which ran for a month with only occasional intrusions by other plays from the repertory.

Owens concluded his stand with a double bill, beginning on the 20th. Tom Taylor's look at life's odd justice and uncaring spouses, *Victims,* in which Owens was Joshua Butterby, was coupled with Owens's most celebrated role, the title part of the fuzzy Yankee preoccupied with his "barrel of applesarse" in *Solon Shingle* (first done in 1842 as *The People's Lawyer*). In her biography of her husband, Mrs. Owens claims the engagement was a major commercial and artistic success. Contemporary notices do not bear out her recollections, nor did Booth himself while the engagement was still fresh in his mind. He wrote to his friend Barrett, "My expenses are fearful. I have only made $49 dollars this season—losing *all* & more on Owens than I made on Cushman." For some reason he does not mention Lotta. Yet Mrs. Owens, who attributes what problems did arise to the fact that the theatre's ensemble was hired with an eye toward tragedy and that these actors looked down on modern comedy and comedians, states that Lotta encountered similar disappointments with Booth's players. In any case, Booth's financial difficulties were a small omen of large troubles ahead. The 20th also saw the Florences change their bill to *The Ticket-of-Leave Man,* a play they had introduced to New York.

The month's novelties appeared only in its last week. **Clairvoyance; or, The Man with the Wax Figures** (11-27-71, Wood's) was a translation of a French sensation-melodrama in which the evil Rodille (J. B. Studley) uses his black magic in an attempt to undo the Vaubrons (J. W. Albaugh and Susan Denin). T. C. De Leon's **Paris; or, Days of the Commune** (11-27-71, Grand Opera), was intolerably complex, even in light of contemporary practice, set in the turmoil of the French Revolution and spanning eighteen years. American diplomat Philip Livingston (Joseph Wheelock), defending the honor of Adèle Dupré (Ada Gray), is killed in a duel. Years later his son, Paul (also played by Wheelock), succeeds in his courtship of Adèle's daughter Theresa (again Miss Gray). Father and son have the sympathy of Emile de Roule (C. W. Barry), who rises from captain to general in the course of the action, but all these men must deal with a troublemaking turncoat and spy, Baudre (J. F. Hagan). Critics savaged the piece. By December 4, both houses had other plays: Wood's a low-grade melodrama, **Life in the Streets,** and the Grand Opera a version of *The Three Musketeers* called **The Three Guardsmen.** But on that evening critics and knowing theatregoers had flocked to Booth's for Edwin Booth's own return, which began with his Hamlet. Although Booth continued to refuse to perform on Saturday nights, he varied his bill with other plays for his Saturday matinee, giving, for example, his Claude Melnotte in *The Lady of Lyons* on the first two Saturdays of his stand.

Lester Wallack finally ventured into new waters with Brougham's **John Garth** (12-11-71, Wallack's), a dramatization of the novel *True to Herself.* Its hero, Garth (Lester Wallack), had been known to his Welsh neighbors as "Mad" Garth before he deserted his family and took off for South America, where he briefly rose to be president of a Latin republic. Now, years later, he returns to Wales to seek out his daughter. He encounters his old enemy, Gregory Deerham (John Gilbert), and also discovers he has been pursued by his Latin adversary, Paulo Barretti (Charles Fisher). Barretti attempts to murder Garth by opening a drawbridge over which Garth must pass in the dark of night. Instead Deerham uses the bridge and is drowned. Garth is suspected, tried, and acquitted. Eventually he engineers a rapprochement with his child.

The title role presented Lester Wallack with an exciting challenge, since Garth, from the viewpoint of the other characters in the play, is not particularly likable. He is distant, self-involved, and misanthropic—"warped by the world in disappointment's school"—yet all the while he must enlist the audience's sympathy. By general agreement, the skillful Wallack was able to have it both ways. And he framed his artistry in superb settings. "Of the *mise en scene* used in this play," one critic wrote eagerly, "we would particularly note that which pictures 'The Home of the Garths on the Coast of Wales, near Abergavenny.' Seldom is anything seen more realistic from the scene-painter's brush and stage-carpenter's skill, than the yacht Minnie as she rides at anchor in the harbor; the rise and fall of the picturesque little craft upon the undulating waters being exceedingly cleverly managed."

Of the play itself the *Times* commented, " 'John Garth' is a melodrama in the literal sense. It is full of startling situations, of mysterious mutterings, of bitter hatreds, and of anomalous juxtapositions. People come and go off to music, and patter love and fury to the *staccato* and hurry in the orchestra. . . . It is . . . full of life and 'go.' The incidents are well conceived or well chosen, they follow each other with tact and rapidity, the climaxes are bold and significant." Enough playgoers agreed to give the play a two-month run.

On the same night, versions of *The Streets of New York* competed for patronage at Wood's and the Grand Opera, while the forlorn Lucy Rushton, plummeting from favor, began a brief stay at the Bowery in *Red Hands.*

Edwin Booth's major offering of the season was his revival of *Julius Caesar* at his theatre on Christmas night. The original distribution included Booth as Brutus, Barrett as Cassius, and F. C. Bangs as Antony. William Winter recalled the production as "one of the highest achievements and one of the most imposing spectacles of the modern stage," but that was later, when he came to write Booth's biography. Contemporary criticism was quite captious, if not truly damning. Booth's Brutus was seen as too stagy or too nervous and pliable, and Barrett's gloomy, combative Cassius as too choleric or, conversely, too unfelt. Of Bangs, who suffered from hoarseness on opening night, criticism ran from merely "efficient" to "dashing." However, there were universal paeans for Witham's sumptuous settings. His spacious forum was magnificent with blue sky and white marble, while his design for the senate chamber used a curving backdrop to recreate Gérôme's famous painting of Caesar's assassination, with tier upon tier of stone benches rising from the center. Despite carpings, the production enjoyed a run of eighty-five nights—no mean achievement. At times during the run, Booth gave over Brutus to other players and essayed Cassius or Antony. Laura Keene praised Booth's reading of Antony's noted harangue for "its art, its elocution, tact and subtle management of the crowd, with the quicker and quicker delivery, till it swelled to a torrent of words; finally, the leap from the tribune (a trick, but a clever trick), and his thunderous denunciation of the traitors. . . . The house was swept away."

Christmas night also saw the Florences return to the Grand Opera, resuming where they had left off, with *The Ticket-of-Leave Man.* Weekly changes took them into 1872, when they offered *The Colleen Bawn* on New Year's Day and then on the 8th revived their version of Dickens and Collins's *No Thoroughfare,* a saga of intrigue in England and Switzerland, with Florence as the crafty, treacherous Obenreizer. After the Florences left, the theater was given over to a circus and then to something rare for the Grand Opera House—opera.

The preceding April, twenty-nine-year-old James Steele MacKaye had given a lecture advocating a new style of acting, the Delsartean school, which stumped for less ranting, fewer exaggerated, traditional gestures, and more naturalism. Of course, this was a cry heard throughout the 19th century, so to some extent the new movement was simply another generational reassessment of values. Acting, while tame by Forrest's standards, still was extremely broad. Moreover, the aim of the new school was not as objectively and spontaneously naturalistic as might first appear, for it proposed to supplant many of the traditional bombastic stage movements with new traditions of more restrained mannerisms. Every little meaning was still to have a movement of its own. If the fist would no longer be flung against the forehead to signify grief, some less violent gesture would take its place in an actor's catalogue of stock responses. As always, such proposals for change met with determined opposition. Some critics, actors, and playgoers fell back on easy ridicule; others were more considerate and

willing to give this "emotionally gentle manner" an opportunity to prove itself.

All through his life MacKaye would rush to put his principles into practice, and even at this early age that policy goaded him into action. On January 8, 1872, a vaudeville house at 28th and Broadway was rechristened the St. James Theatre and reopened with MacKaye starring in his own play, **Monaldi.** The work was based on a novel by Washington Allston. Since Allston was one of our most famous romantic painters and his novel a more or less traditional Gothic romance, MacKaye's choice was a little offbeat. After all, Robertson and his followers had begun to inject a new naturalism into theatrical writing, so it seems that his sort of play would have best showcased the new theory of acting; perhaps MacKaye set out to demonstrate that even the most florid dramas were amenable to a more reserved style of playing. He himself portrayed his titular hero, an artist who marries Rosina (Mary Griswold), the daughter of a patrician family. Monaldi's dear friend, Madwin (A. H. Davenport), is actually nothing of the sort, but rather a malevolent schemer who poisons the artist's mind with doubts about Rosina's fidelity. Driven to a fury, Monaldi kills his wife and then goes insane.

The results of MacKaye's demonstration were equivocal. Critics felt that players acquitted themselves adequately but were too inexperienced and too subject to first-night jitters to prove or disprove Delsartean ideas beyond question. The *Herald* also suggested the mounting was too much in the manner of a 14th-century morality play to appeal to 19th-century audiences. The play itself was greeted respectfully, but more as one showing a certain integrity and promise than as a triumphant accomplishment. Not exactly money notices, but *Monaldi* survived for six weeks.

. . .

[James Morrison] **Steele MacKaye** (1842–94) Born in Buffalo, where his father was a successful attorney and an art connoisseur, he studied painting while still in his teens with William Hunt, then continued his studies at the École des Beaux Arts under Gérôme. He returned to America to fight in the Civil War and had risen to become a major before illness forced his retirement. He then moved back to Paris, this time transferring his interests to the theatre and falling under the spell of François Delsarte's teachings.

. . .

With Booth's, Daly's, and Wallack's all occupied by hits, first-nighters had no occasions to visit these leading playhouses until Wallack's changed its bill on February 12. The revival on that occasion was *The Veteran,* a play set in India and purportedly by Lester Wallack. It was in this play that his father, J. W. Wallack, had made his last important appearance in a new role, that of Colonel Delmar, who would turn his home into an armed camp. John Gilbert now assumed the role. Lester Wallack was back as the colonel's son, but much of the laughter and applause was brought on by Brougham, who recreated his role of Ofl-an-agan, the Irishman who has become an Indian wazir.

The two new plays that opened on the 12th had to be content with second-string critics or to wait for later reviews. T. B. De Walden's **Darling; or, Woman and Her Master** (2-12-72, Wood's), filled with songs and dances, was another of those plays that walked a narrow line between musical and straight play. Its protean heroine resorts to a variety of disguises to achieve a happy ending.

Albeit belatedly, MacKaye's **Marriage** (2-12-72, St. James), an adaptation of Octave Feuillet's *Julie,* received more respectful attention. Marguerite Brooks (Mary Griswold) is almost lured away from her indifferent husband (A. H. Davenport) by the loving, well-meaning Col. Carroll Gray (MacKaye). The strictures of the time prevent her from actually abandoning her husband, and she dies of a broken heart. It was a relatively intimate play for the era, with only the three central figures having major roles, so it should have offered an even better stage for MacKaye's theories than had *Monaldi.* Once again, however, the results were equivocal, although the *Times* sniped that new ideas of naturalism did not excuse MacKaye's pronouncing "duty" as if it were "dooty." A five-week run was followed by a brief return of *Monaldi,* after which minstrels took over the theatre.

Another of the period's short-lived attractions, half musical and half serious drama, was Charles E. Newton's **Out at Sea** (2-28-72, Wood's), in which, amid "clog-dancers, vocalists and major soloists," a rich young man is kidnapped in an attempt to deprive him of his fortune. Its star was bantam Charles T. Parlsoe, Jr., most of whose better roles were still in the future.

Mrs. Wood swept into Niblo's on March 4 for a season of burlesques, again as much musicals as comedies. On the 18th, having come to the end of his long stay in *Julius Caesar,* Booth closed his stand by acting Sir Edward Mortimer in *The Iron Chest* and, later in the week, Bertuccio in *The Fool's Revenge.* Thomas Moore's latter-day Arabian Nights, *Lalla Rookh,* filled the stage at the Grand Opera on the 18th with scenery that was "the acme of glittering iridescence," a huge cast in elaborate Oriental costumes, and a large, classic corps de ballet. The spectacle was so successful that it was slated to move to Niblo's on May 6, but the fire there destroyed the transferred scenery. On the 19th Daly's embarked on a brief season of revivals. *Old Heads and Young Hearts* was followed in rapid succession by *Fernande, Wives as They Were and Maids as They Are, The Provoked Husband, London Assurance,* and *Frou-Frou.*

The talented Carlotta Leclercq, who for a time had been closely linked with Charles Fechter both on the stage and off, began a month's stay at Booth's on the 25th. She altered her bill almost weekly, switching from *As You Like It* to *The Hunchback,* then to a double bill of Tom Taylor's comedy of political intrigue, *Plot and Passion,* accompanied by *The Rough Diamond* (first done as *Cousin Joe* in 1849 and telling of a country girl who refuses to adopt fashionable follies), and closing with the double bill of *A Sheep in Wolf's Clothing* and *The Honeymoon.*

April began on a down note when Laura Keene opened a brief engagement at Wood's on the 1st, reviving *Hunted Down* for two weeks, after which she played a fortnight in *The Sea of Ice,* assuming the part of a white girl raised by Indians. Nothing was said about this being a farewell appearance, although that is what it turned out to be. Her most steadfast admirers must have sensed something of the sort. They braved a buffeting storm to pack Wood's for the first night of *The Sea of Ice.* Critics, less sensitive to the passing scene, gave the opening the same short notices they had given all of Wood's openings during the season, thus missing the chance to honor a great actress passing from the scene.

Most critics gave equally skimpy attention to a new play at a failing theatre, and in doing so they missed another opportunity, this time one to explore the future. The play was W. S. Gilbert's blank-verse comedy **The Palace of Truth** (4-1-72, Lina Edwin's), and it offered some of the soon to be lionized author's most fey situations and dialogue. The scene was set in an imaginary kingdom whose ruler, disgusted with his courtiers' hypocritical fawning and blatant dishonesty, moves his whole court to a fairy palace where a spell requires everyone to tell the truth. Unfortunately, American actors were unversed in the polished artificialities necessary to put across such charming nonsense. One week and it was gone.

The flurry of revivals at Daly's served as a lively intermission between his two successful premieres of the season. The second was **Article 47** (4-2-72, Fifth Ave.), and its reception made a star of Clara Morris.

* * *

Clara Morris (1848–1925), whose real last name was LaMontagne but who was raised as Clara Morrison, was born in Toronto but grew up primarily in Cleveland. Her childhood was marked by extreme poverty. Her first professional work was as a child ballerina, although she soon graduated into ever larger acting assignments, frequently playing in support of the greatest stars during their Cleveland and Cincinnati visits. She left Ohio to join Daly's company. Her face was heart-shaped, its features piquant and dominated by her large, expressive eyes.

* * *

Miss Morris played the Creole, Cora, who has been shot and scarred by her mercurial lover, Georges Duhamel (Henry Crisp). The drama begins with his trial and sentencing, under Article 47, to exile. Eight years pass, and Georges returns to France. He hides in the home of his mother (Mrs. Gilbert) and marries the innocent Marcelle (Linda Dietz). All this is illegal since his parole requires he advise authorities of his whereabouts and remain unattached. He now lives in fear that Cora will learn where he is and seek revenge. Cora does discover the truth but comes to him at first only to beg him to resume their liaison. Gazing at her scarred face, he shudders and refuses, screaming, "You are mad!" So Cora does determine to be revenged, but her jealousy of Marcelle and hatred of Georges become an obsession, ultimately fulfilling Georges's accusation by driving her over the brink into wild-eyed insanity.

Miss Morris's triumph was dramatic for several reasons. First of all, she appeared, in rather subdued fashion, for a mere ten minutes in the trial scene, which occupied the whole of the hour-long first act, and did not appear at all in the second act. Moreover, she went against then accepted practice by insisting that the scar be so large and hideous it would horrify even playgoers at the rear of the balcony. (When Adolphe Belot's original French version had been performed in Paris, its star, Mme Rousseil, had refused to allow a blemish to mar her features. She used a large scarf to suggest she was hiding her defacement.) Miss Morris made herself up with "white welts with angry red spaces painted between; and attached strong sticking plaster to her eyelid to draw it from its natural position." Sixty-five years later Odell recalled "the scene of oncoming madness, the rocking figure, the staring eyes, the muttered ravings, increasing in intensity until, as

Cora tore the covering from her ghastly-scarred cheek, that last frightful maniacal shriek rang through the house and simply chilled to the marrow all who heard." The *Herald* compared her death scene to Kate Bateman's in *Leah, the Forsaken* and Charlotte Cushman's in *Guy Mannering*, and playgoers flocked to the Fifth Avenue until heat forced a mid-June closing.

Always foresighted and adventuresome, Daly launched another effort during the run of *Article 47* that had a marked influence on the future of American theatre. He removed Fanny Davenport from the play's cast and set her up as star of a touring company of *Divorce,* using the New York sets and a complete complement of supporting players. Heretofore only stars had toured, accepting whatever ensemble and scenery they found in road theatres. (Daly earlier had sent the complete New York company of *Divorce*—with scenery—to Philadelphia for a special matinee and brought them back in time for the evening's performance. But that was obviously less practical and may have been done simply for the tremendous publicity it provoked.)

Wallack's continued to play it closer to the vest— and a very tweedy English vest at that—thereby allowing Lester Wallack to minimize his risks but also depriving him of the huge rewards Daly increasingly was to reap. This was manifested again when Wallack's replaced *The Veteran* with yet another safe standby, *London Assurance* on the 18th. Yet Wallack's conservatism was more and more met with a certain rueful condemnation by even the most respectful critics. A major problem was Lester Wallack's apparent refusal to take on a superior young actor who might steal his applause or limelight. And like him, his ensemble was aging— some almost absurdly so. Thus his Dazzle, Charles Mathews, was sixty-nine; his Harcourt Courtly, John Gilbert, was sixty-two; and he himself was playing young Charles at fifty-two. The younger women who were assigned major roles—since they obviously represented no threat—probably made for a striking if unspoken contrast. Nonetheless, Wallack's comedians were so talented and so experienced that their performances could have been enjoyed simply as lessons in technique. Whatever the reasons, enough playgoers were found to allow the play to run until the end of May.

In some ways the most interesting new play of the season was **Black Friday** (4-22-72, Niblo's). Never mind that it was a two-week fiasco. It was the only drama that dealt with matters of truly contemporary interest to play a first-class house in the 1871–72 season. If these issues were more related to lurid headlines than to the burning problems discussed on editorial pages, that was small matter in an era whose theatricals studiously avoided modern developments. The hero of *Black Friday* was a transparently disguised James Fisk, the successful financier and producer who had owned the Grand Opera House and had been assassinated the preceding January by his onetime associate and friend E. S. Stokes. The play dealt with Fisk's rise to power (aided by Daniel Drew), his machinations leading to the stock market collapse in September of 1869 that became known as Black Friday, and his affair with Mrs. Mansfield, as well as her later relations with Stokes and their attempts to blackmail Fisk. Theatre folk knew he had a soft spot for them; typically, the great comedian Eddie Foy remembered Fisk's aid to his family with gratitude and affection in his autobiography. So it was not too astonishing to see theatre people presenting him in the kindest light.

Indeed, although he was called Rob King (J. W. Collier) in the play, he was portrayed as generous and misunderstood. The villain in this version was unmistakably the playboy Stokes, who was renamed Dash Hoffman (Charles Thorne, Jr.), an allusion to his connection with the roistering Hoffman House, a favorite hangout of the era's "beautiful people." Mrs. Mansfield became Mrs. Spearheart (Lizzie Price); Daniel Drew, Sam Simms (J. K. Mortimer). Many critics were outraged at the very idea of dramatizing such scandal and felt the play added insult to injury with such scenes as one in which respectable ladies talk politely to ladies of the evening. Apparently newspaper stories long since had given the public its surfeit of these incidents, so audiences were small. Or was it all just too hot to handle? The show had no sooner closed than the theatre became New York's ninth playhouse to burn in seven years.

Booth returned to his own theatre on the 22nd for a second stand during the season, first bringing back his earlier mountings of *The Iron Chest* and *The Fool's Revenge*. On May 1, he revived *Richard III*—Cibber's version—which lingered for two and a half weeks, varied at matinees with such plays as *The Lady of Lyons, The Stranger,* and *Don Caesar de Bazan.* When Booth finally packed it in for the season, his stage was handed over to Edwin Adams, a former associate.

Looking back it is easy to picture the older Booth offering to allow the younger Adams the opportunity of closing out the theatrical year. But most theatre lovers' images of Booth come from John

Singer Sargent's famous portrait (now at the Players, the famous club Booth helped found), which was painted relatively late in the actor's life, or from similarly late photographs, while the best-known photographs of Adams were taken while he was in his late thirties or early forties, a few years before his untimely death. Moreover, Booth is identified with a number of older character parts; Adams is largely remembered for a single role. In fact, Adams was only a year younger than Booth. His most famous role, which did allow him to grow older, was the title part in Julie de Margueritte's version of Tennyson's *Enoch Arden,* and it was this interpretation that he brought to Booth's on the 20th and continued to play until the house shuttered at the end of June. Critics were happy to report that Adams had brought his sometimes excessive gesturing under control and had truly made the part his own.

The traffic among the lesser theatres was illustrated with the opening of Philip Stoner's **Woodleigh** (5-27-72, Lina Edwin's). Lizzie Safford had starred briefly in this saga of love disrupted by war earlier in the month at the Bowery. It was passed over by most reviewers until it moved to Lina Edwin's, which still clung precariously to the sort of reputation the Bowery had forfeited some seasons back. Even then, however, it was treated curtly and quickly disappeared.

The 27th also welcomed a revival of *Home* at Wallack's, coupled with *The Critic.* Two more revivals followed on June 1: *The Captain of the Watch* and H. J. Byron's *Not Such a Fool as He Looks,* which served as Mathews's farewell. *The Long Strike* was brought back on the 3rd, and two weeks later the company offered a new play, Watts Phillips's **On the Jury** (6-17-72, Wallack's). Dexter Sanderson (John Brougham) had once served on a jury that had convicted Mr. Tibbetts (Charles Fisher) of embezzlement. Tibbetts was actually innocent, but Sanderson could not know that, so when Sanderson learns that his son, Robert (B. T. Ringgold), proposes to marry Tibbett's daughter, he strenuously opposes the match. Belatedly Tibbetts must unearth the real criminal to prove his own innocence and secure his daughter's happiness. Even at a house so careful of its dignity, the sensational stage effects and dramatically heightened tableaux that closed each act elicited storms of applause. A collision of two boats on the Thames won loud approval, and the curtain had to be raised repeatedly on some of the closing pictures. Yet the play was a failure.

On the morning that the *Herald* issued a rather short notice of *On the Jury,* it devoted a full, tightly printed column to another play that had opened a week earlier, a play virtually every other paper failed to give any review—and thereby hangs a tale. For some while the *Herald* had been publishing stories about a group of North Carolina outlaws, the Lowerys. Although they were considered dangerous, a *Herald* reporter had won their confidence. In a series of articles he not only documented some of their bloodiest feats but, no doubt to the surprise of many readers, attempted to explain the injustices that had led them into their antisocial ways. The Lowerys were a mixed-breed family, part white, part black, and part Indian. They were united in their hatred of white aristocrats they felt had persecuted them, and they used the upheavals of the Civil War and the postwar era to secure themselves a base in the Carolina swamps. So Charles Foster's new melodrama, "before which the 'Corsican Brothers' or 'Six Degrees of Crime' must pale the splendors of their ineffectual fires," was called **The Swamp Angels; or, The Outlaws of Carolina** (6-10-72, Bowery). Unlike *Black Friday,* it suffered the fate of most native drama—consignment to the least desirable New York houses and to the road. A shorter, earlier version had been offered at the Comique as part of a triple bill in April. But this expanded version held the stage fitfully for several seasons, which is more than can be said for some of Wallack's or Daly's failures. If the *Herald*'s review was self-serving and, at least to modern readers, unwittingly humorous, it presented one of the most vividly written pictures of a contemporary production, affording not only a remarkable sense of the play but a memorable glimpse, which was probably only slightly tongue-in-cheek, at audience response.

"It was nine o'clock, and the great curtain arose to the slow and mournful music from the numberous musicians who have manfully stood out against the eight-hour strike. The lights burn dimly in the cabin of old Pop Strong, in the mulatto-peopled village of Scuffleton, in North Carolina. There is a dialogue between the aristocratic slave-holder Barnes and his fellow villain Harris, of slave-driving and slave-lashing proclivities. Old Pop Strong, who seems to be an *amicus curiae* of the Lowery family, has a ticket for a prize in the Havana lottery. By a fortuitous stroke of villainy the venerable Old Pop, who is only brought on stage to be killed, loses his life and his beloved $10,000 lottery ticket at the same moment. Instrumental in this deed of blood are the high-toned Barnes and the too profane Harris. Miss Rhody Lowery, who is the amalgamated affinity of Henry Berry Lowery, chief of the bandits, descends upon the scene and is hailed with a rapture of applause by the audience. The cold, damp and unpleasant body of Old Pop Strong is discovered, and Rhody Lowery, unduly exercised thereat, and being under the delusion that she is his daughter, takes a harrowing vow of vengeance. (Tremendous cheering.) Enter Henry Berry Lowery, As hard a looking, teeth-gnashing villain as ever appeared before a Bowery audience. Another vow of vengeance. Wild applause. Then there is a coroner's inquest, and such a coroner's inquest as this is. Twelve young gentlemen from the Bowery, who act as a North Carolina coroner's jury, lift their hands to heaven and swear impressively to the verdict, 'Shot by some person or persons unknown,' &c., &c., as in the fashion with all coroner's juries. Slow music.

"Act second (slow music)—The Lowerys have killed Barnes by 'blowing a hole in his roof,' as they kindly expressed it. They are now in jail, and a Yankee drummer from Boston, an agent for indelible ink, who has no business to neglect his employer's interest for such a purpose, inspired by a feed of baked beans, rescues the Loweries from jail. And now appears, amid the thunders of applause that proceed from an overheated and excited audience, Allen Lowery, father of the band of outlaws, with a make-up half Indian half mulatto. Slow music again. He is set upon by a group of North Carolina constables, among whom is the fiend Harris.

"But here is another wild cheer of deep import, as a young gentleman, in splendid clothes, and wearing a drab caster hat, descends the steps of the station at Moss Neck, with a rattan in his hand and a handsome fifteen dollar leathern satchel thrown carelessly over his shoulders. Inspiring and joyous music now. Hurriedly taking in the situation, he runs at the vile constables who have beaten old Allen Lowery badly, and, in the style of the London Prize Ring, he knocks two of the assailants down and kicks five or six others around the stage among the greatest cheering from the audience. 'Who are you?' shout the discomfited ruffians on the ground. 'I am the correspondent of the NEW YORK HERALD, the most fearless and independent journal in America or the world. I am here to protect innocence and virtue and get the earliest news for the NEW YORK HERALD.' The theatre rose as a man at the gallant correspondent and a halo of glory and enthusiasm surrounded his noble head and fell softly on his handsome features. The excitement became more intense among the audience as the correspondent, raising his cast-iron beaver, solemnly pronounced the word 'I must tell the truth—the public exact a faithful report.'

"The next scene is really an excellent one and well placed on the stage. We are introduced to the log cabin of the notorious Lowery gang—father, mother, sons, with lots of frolicsome mulatto girls, all being present. Every mother's son of the Lowerys is armed to the teeth. The HERALD correspondent, eager for news, visits the cabin while the negro festival is at its height. Sour looks and threats greet him, and his life is in danger. 'Why don't you shoot?' he says; 'I am only one unarmed man among five, but the HERALD has no cowards on its staff! Do your worst!' and he folded his arms like Washington at the battle of Brandywine. Slow music and a storm of cheers for the HERALD from the audience. The five rifles are cocked and drawn, and Rhody Lowery, moved by a deep, devoted sisterly affection (although she does not know it), dashes between the rifle of her darling and tender husband and the correspondent of the HERALD. More cheers and very slow music. At this moment, as fate and the author had ordered it, the State soldiery dash in, and a fierce fight ensues between the outlaws; the stage is bathed in smoke and red fire, although but a few moments before the entire company were dancing a country jig to the melodious tune of 'Felix Larkin,' and a hired negro had just finished 'Babylon is Fallen.' The curtain descends, the HERALD correspondent blessing Rhody Lowery, his savior, with one hand and taking notes with the other, while he looks with upturned eyes into the depths of the flies, rapturous cheering for the HERALD and its correspondent by the entire audience joining in.

"In the third act we have a railroad scene in Lumberton, with the outlaws drawn up across the track and their rifles pointed like a band of savage Indians. Rhody, the good angel of the 'Swamp Angels,' emerges from the brush and slime of the swamp with the HERALD correspondent. The outlaws threaten his life, and seize his details and letters of credit, causing much anguish to the correspondent. He is sentenced to die and tied to a tree. His documents being captured, the outlaws endeavor to read them; but, alas! the schoolmaster has not been abroad in Scuffletown. And here is shown the triumph of the pen over the rifle. They are compelled to release the correspondent in order that he may read his credentials. . . . The audience now became frantic with enthusiasm. . . . The correspondent is saved for the time being. . . .

"And now we are brought to the fourth act. Rhody saves the life of the correspondent. . . . She snatches the poison from his hand, which Tom and Andrew Lowery had given him, and the correspondent, grabbing two revolvers, keeps the villains at bay. 'Hi, hi, hi!' shout the audience and again he is saved to slow music.

"The correspondent discovers that Rhody Lowery is his sister, and protects her just as Henry Berry Lowery is about to take her life. . . . The soldiers burst in, Harris kills Lowery and Lowery kills Harris with poetic justice, and the curtain falls with a scene at the HERALD office, the correspondent, with his sister and her child, receiving the congratulations of the HERALD employers."

On the same night, the Olympic, which had been occupied all season by *Humpty Dumpty,* housed a return of *Schneider,* booked in for four weeks.

Wallack's final offering of the season was Palgrave Simpson's **The Last Trump** (7-1-72, Wallack's). The drama had the misfortune to open on a night of "insufferable heat," which wilted playgoers' enthusiasm. The scheming Vicomte de Noirmont (Charles Fisher), abetted by a greedy Jewish money-lender, Jabez Jubal (J. H. Stoddart), attempts to alienate the affections of Alice Walsingham (Ella Burns) away from a young naval officer, Cecil Seagift (B. T. Ringgold). Alice's friend, Cecilia Thornton (Mrs. Thomas Barry), tricks de Noirmont into showing his true colors when she makes it seem that Alice has lost her fortune. Perhaps because Wallack's was a house that shone most brightly in comedy, the comic side of the story was emphasized, or at least critics thought so. Stoddart turned Jubal into a not unlikable figure, one always sitting on or otherwise destroying someone else's hat, while Sir Slingsby Sorrell (H. W. Montgomery), a "turfite" who speaks largely in racing patois, and Mr. Sykes (Charles Rockwell), a henpecked lawyer, won a handsome share of laughs. Yet heat and the play's weaknesses combined to remove the show after a fortnight.

With *Schneider*'s departure the Olympic gave its stage over to Charlotte Thompson, who presented the senior Dumas's *La Princesse Georges* as **One Wife** (7-29-72, Olympic). Mrs. Vandyke (Thompson) learns from her maid that Mr. Vandyke (L. R. Shewell) is an adulterer. She confronts him, and a reconciliation follows his promise to reform. But before long she discovers he has reneged on his pledge. Her plans to confront him again and to leave him are forestalled when he is shot by the husband of the woman with whom he has had his affair. Cries of outrage were everywhere. The *Herald* called the play "detestable," while the *Times* condemned it as one "which no pure-minded woman can listen to, which not even any pure-minded man should care to hear." Although the play was hustled off after two weeks so that the

Lingards could play a short engagement, it returned as soon as the Lingards left. Afterwards, Miss Thompson moved on to *The Hunchback,* then moved out.

Meanwhile, Wood's pursued its policy of fast-changing bills, with different plays for afternoon and evening. Most of these plays were as forgettable as they are forgotten, but the important point is that they represented, for all their ineptness and cheapness, attempts to provide American playgoers with plays on American themes written by American dramatists—something first-class and even second-class Broadway houses generally eschewed.

Take four late-season examples. Vaudevillian Johnny Thompson donned blackface to star in his **Our Colored Brother** (6-3-72, Wood's), in which he played Dixie, "a sort of dark-hued knight errant, who rescues forlorn damsels, raises the oppressed and punishes the oppressor." For all the equality implied in the title, black roles were still performed by white actors. Albert W. Aiken's **The Red Mazeppa; or, The Madman of the Plains** (6-17-72, Wood's) was a thumping melodrama filled with "hair-breadth escapes and hand-to-hand combats," featuring an Indian hero, Silver Spear (Jennie Arnott), who makes a dashing ride to the rescue, and a deranged wanderer (Aiken). A week later **Escaped from Sing Sing** (6-24-72, Wood's) used a then still famous real-life escape from prison to create a romanticized story in which English Bill (Dominick Murray) assumes the name Eph Bloodsworth, joins a criminal band, is captured, jailed, and escapes, after which he lives the life of a playboy as Claude Livingstone until he is killed. On July 8, J. J. McCloskey appeared in his own sensation-melodrama *Pomp; or, Way Down South,* which had been presented first with great success at the Bowery in February of 1871 and dealt with a faithful black servant who extricates his master from a variety of dangers. Spectacular incidents included a Mississippi steamboat's boilers exploding and a voodoo rite.

At this far remove, the fluctuations at Wood's—between being a good second-class house, possibly even a first-class house, and sinking into a Bowery-like miasma—are hard to fathom. Certainly at the very end of the season it briefly recouped its renown when Frank Chanfrau came in for a summer stand on July 29. He opened with *Kit, the Arkansas Traveller,* changed over to *Sam* on August 12 and to *The Ticket-of-Leave Man* on the 19th, then brought out *The Octoroon* on the 26th before reverting to a final week of *Kit.*

1872–1873

Although contemporary observers might not have agreed with the conclusion, the 1872–73 season seems one of transition. Of course, the view comes from the vantage of more than one hundred years, and the transition was quiet if steady. Yet change was everywhere. That ever present terror of the era, fire, which had destroyed Niblo's late in the preceding season, blazed anew this year, removing forever the failing Lina Edwin's Theatre (recently converted to minstrelsy) and gutting Daly's Fifth Avenue (scarcely daunting the intrepid Daly and his determined band). The other side of the coin was the opening of a major new home for drama. And for several seasons to come, much of that drama would be of French origin. The floodgates that Daly had unlocked earlier with *Frou-Frou* were now to be opened wide. Of course, English drama continued to be a mainstay at all the first-class theatres, and its allure would be potent for seasons ahead. Nonetheless its heretofore incontestable dominance would be slowly eroded. Only crusaders for native writing might find the season cheerless, even if one new American play garnered long-lasting acceptance. Theatregoers who relished repertories of old comedies and dramas probably also were dismayed, since increasingly long runs allowed producers to put aside such comparatively unprofitable series. Nowhere was this to be more evident than at that most traditional of all houses, Wallack's.

The season's opener was **The Bells** (8-19-72, Booth's). Its production the preceding November at London's Lyceum Theatre had been a huge success and had propelled Henry Irving into the very front rank of English actors, opening the first door to his eventual knighthood. Its initial New York production, coming in the wake of high expectations, was anticlimactic. The story is exceedingly simple and straightforward. Some years before the action begins, Mathias (J. W. Wallack), an Alsatian innkeeper, had murdered a Jewish traveler, burned his body, and stolen his money. Over time, guilt feelings have haunted him and chipped away at his sanity. He is forever hearing the bells of his victim's sleigh. The murder has also become something of a legend in his small village and has intrigued a young gendarme, Fritz (F. Percy), who is in love with Mathias's daughter, Margaret (Bella Pateman).

Mathias presses the youngsters to marry, hoping that a son-in-law would not pursue the matter. The dowry he offers consists in large measure of the dead Jew's gold. He also learns that a mesmerist can force subjects to reveal the most hidden truths. This last news finally unhinges the innkeeper. In a dream, he is hailed into court, mesmerized, and made to divulge the whole story. The shock of his nightmare kills him.

Several reasons were bandied about to account for the disappointing New York reception. *The Bells* was derived from Émile Erckmann and Alexandre Chatrian's *Le Juif polonais,* but by general assent Leopold Lewis's London version had heightened and intensified its effectiveness. The American version was unattributed, used different character names (in London the lovers were Christian and Annette), and apparently lacked some of Lewis's striking theatricality. Moreover, Irving, a younger, more vital and imaginative performer than Wallack, had given an impassioned performance. Conversely, Wallack's Mathias was "a subtle study of the morbid anatomy of a haunted mind," according to William Winter. Reading between the lines of other notices, it would appear that Wallack had substituted careful technique for dramatic fervor. To compound problems, the supporting company at Booth's was embarrassingly weak. Complaints about this, which had surfaced almost as soon as the theatre opened, reached a crescendo during the new season and unquestionably aggravated Booth's mounting managerial problems.

The play ran five weeks, and after it closed another version, called *The Polish Jew,* was offered briefly at the Bowery with J. B. Studley in the leading role. But *The Bells* was never as popular in America as it was in England, and even here received its best reception when Henry Irving himself brought it over in later years.

French stages were also the source of **The Red Pocket-Book** (9-2-72, Olympic), another melodrama as jam-packed with a succession of cliff-hangers as any early movie serial. Films also inherited the teasing, alluring advertisements typical in the period. Unlike concise, terse modern play advertisements, late 19-century theatre ones were as overflowing as the plays they ballyhooed. They regularly provided synopses and other details, such as a complete cast of characters, offering potential playgoers a reasonable sense of the entertainment without giving too much away. A good instance was the synopsis provided in advertisements for this new play:

PROLOGUE

ANTE ROOM OF CHATEAU—The banker's private party. The forged note. The gambling debt paid. The family jewels. The unknown artist. The banker's bargain. "Any sacrifice for honor."

The assassin's work.

THE RED POCKETBOOK

DRAMA. ACT 1.—The good ship Minerva, after the storm and battle, disabled, in mid-ocean, introducing mechanical effects never before produced. Final terrific explosion. All the business of this act transpires on board the ship, which sinks and disappears in full view of the audience, without gauzes or artificial appliances.

A REAL SHIP WITH THE CHARACTERS ON BOARD,

SINKS! SINKS! ENGULFED IN MID OCEAN.

ACT 2.—Coast of Africa. The shipwrecked lovers. The "Wild Man of the Woods." The father and child. The convict. The caravan; living camels. Tableau.

ACT 3.—Interior of country chateau. The dead alive. Two poor, wounded hearts. A brave man's sacrifice. Separation of the lovers. Farewell!

ACT 4.—Interior of the Admiral's mansion, with the gardens of the chateau by moonlight. The bridal gift. The unexpected guest. The odious contract signed. Death the price. The wedding jewels. The family motto—"Heaven alone can save us." A startling revelation. The madman. The star of love lights the path of danger. The motto—"Heaven alone has saved us." The proof of innocence.

With all this before them, patrons need not have been surprised by the tale they sat through. Its hounded hero, Maurice (Neil Warner), sells some family jewels to a banker. Immediately thereafter the banker is murdered. Maurice is accused of the crime, tried, convicted, and sentenced to serve on a galley. He escapes but is captured at sea by the father of the girl to whom he is secretly betrothed. The admiral, who does not know the truth, will have nothing to do with Maurice, even after they are all shipwrecked and Maurice saves the life of his own beloved Helen (Laura Phillips). Luckily, the real killer is unmasked when he drops a red purse that had belonged to the banker and the purse is found to contain the jewels Maurice had sold.

Two weeks and the play was gone, at least from the Olympic. But just as *The Bells* quickly found its way to the Bowery and other lesser houses, so *The Red Pocket-Book,* or at least other versions of the

French play on which it was based, soon did the same, abetted by the loose copyright laws and freewheeling ethics of the day. If any Olympic patrons had meandered uptown in mid-October they could have seen, and probably recognized, **The Gambler's Crime; or, Murder on the Hudson** (10-14-72, Wood's). However, now Maurice had become Murty McNally (Dominick Murray), a young man from Mulberry Street's Irish ghetto. Other character names were also Americanized, although the heroine was still called Helen (Gussie De Forrest).

The intermittent cry for more American plays was given an unsatisfactory answer when Daly opened his season with Bronson Howard's comedy of manners **Diamonds** (9-3-72, Fifth Ave). Part of the problem was Daly himself, for the excellences of the costumes and scenery he provided had become such as to distract even the most dedicated critics when weaker plays were mounted. No less than the *Tribune*'s austere, high-minded Winter gave more detailed attention to the scenery than he did to the play, prattling on, "There is no scene painter whose brush is more delicate in touch than that of Mr. James Roberts. . . . A tendency toward gaudiness in metropolitan interiors—very common to the stage—was perceptible in some of the sets, but the touches of landscape and the sea-view at Fort Wadworth were sweet and charming." The *Herald* complained, "The toilets of the walking ladies ["walking men and women" were bit players] are of more importance than the clothing of the plot." That plot, laid in Manhattan and at a Staten Island villa, centered on several romances and marriages, especially one marriage in which the young husband is led to question his wife's faithfulness.

Like so many of the period's comedies, the play had a surprising share of melodramatic violence, and in this instance one scene elicited some vociferous condemnation. The scene included a shooting that patently had been staged to recall Stoke's killing of Fisk—the victim, like Fisk, being shot on a staircase and falling backward down the whole flight. Not only did the scene strike many as unwarranted sensationalism, but the more discerning critics recognized that it intruded into the comic tone of much of the play. Critics also took amazed note of Daly's continuing practice of alternating members of his ensemble in large and small parts; for instance, last year's vigorously applauded leading lady, Clara Morris, was consigned to a minor role. For all the critical harrumphs, *Diamonds* ran six weeks, testimony to Daly's growing reputation.

On September 9, an obscure and largely unwel-comed actress named Mrs. Macready began a stand at the Academy of Music. Like Charlotte Cushman or the earlier Josephine Clifton, she appears to have been a woman with a scarcely repressed masculine bent who insisted on assuming men's roles, for which one reviewer found her "palpably unfit." In her short engagement she offered her versions of Shylock and Richelieu. Something about her reviews suggests she was way out in left field.

More exciting news, of lasting interest to the American theatre, was made six nights later. The Union Square Theatre had been built in 1871 as yet another outlet for the fast-burgeoning variety, the early term for vaudeville. Luckily for our legitimate theatre, the policy did not sit well with patrons, so owner Sheridan Shook rather daringly appointed a man with virtually no theatrical background to manage the playhouse as a home of serious drama. That man was A. M. Palmer.

. . .

A[lbert] M[arshall] **Palmer** (1838–1905) was born in North Stonington, Conn., and studied law in New York City. He never entered practice, instead becoming active in politics, where he met Shook, who was collector of internal revenue for New York. He worked as a librarian and accountant until Shook appointed him head bookkeeper for the new theatre. When the new policy was established Palmer was promoted.

. . .

Palmer has been called "the first modern producer," an epithet based on the fact that, unlike Wallack, Daly, or most of their predecessors, he was not also an actor, director, or playwright. Indeed, all his previous theatrical experiences seem to have been on the dark side of the footlights. Throughout his managerial career he delegated most creative and interpretive chores to skilled associates, confining his contribution to handling business matters, determining basic policy, and offering occasional suggestions to increase box office or for other practical considerations. Of course, much the same could have been said of Stephen Price, who had guided the fortunes of the old Park Theatre half a century or so before, and of some managers elsewhere. But the theatre of their day was quite different. Because of Palmer's businesslike approach and his eventual advocacy of American drama and dramatists, many students believe his emergence rather than Daly's signals the real beginning of a new era.

More than any other contemporary playhouse, the new theatre was to be an American showcase for

French plays. The very first attraction was Victorien Sardou's **Agnes** (9-17-72, Union Square), purportedly written expressly for an unhappy defector from Daly's ranks, Agnes Ethel, who had, in any case, purchased the American rights. It was the biggest hit of the season. Despite a fine supporting cast, it was essentially a one-woman show. Agnes (Miss Ethel) is a modern wife, who has agreed with her husband, the Viscount de Thomery (D. H. Harkins), that both of them are entitled to a certain freedom in marriage. But the viscount oversteps these liberal limits when he falls in love with Mme Stella (Phyllis Glover), the prima ballerina at the opera. Agnes goes to the theatre, disguised as a dressmaker, expecting to confront her rival, only to overhear her husband propose elopement to the dancer. When she asks the police to prevent the pair's flight, she is told a husband has a right to love whomever he chooses. In desperation she obtains a medical certificate of insanity and uses it to have the viscount arrested. To her horror, he claims that she is having him committed so that she can elope with an unspecified lover. Agnes's brother eventually appears and restores a sense of balance to the marriage. For many the star (in gowns by Worth), not the play, was the thing. The *Times* stated, "Always intensely feminine, and delicate even to fragility, Miss Ethel wins the sympathy of the audience even before she has the time to conquer it by histrionic passion." The drama ran for 100 nights, after which the star toured with it and returned briefly in the spring.

The extent to which Palmer interjected himself into artistic decisions could be seen in two major changes. The adaptation by N. Hart Jackson and, possibly, Col. H. S. Olcott had retained both a "sensation" scene in which the viscount escapes from the asylum by climbing over rooftops and Sardou's original unhappy ending. Palmer persuaded his adaptors to delete the risky escape and had Miss Ethel's friend Charles Fechter write a new, happy conclusion. The latter change clearly had public acceptance in mind. Settings were based on drawings provided by Sardou. William Sanders and Richard Marston, the house's scene painters, rushed them to completion in three weeks' time and won accolades for their efforts. The *Sun* gushed, "The curtain rose upon a drawing-room 'set' that has probably never been equalled, for exquisite taste and richness, on the local stage. Hangings of real satin and lace, furniture of graceful shape and harmonious colors, rich carpets, consoles, bronzes, a carved fireplace, an abundance of flowers—the whole presented the appearance of an elegant drawing room in a private house." A quick transition from the dressing-room scene to a setting showing the stage and interior of the opera house earned loud applause. From the start Palmer insisted on box sets, virtually never employing obsolescent wing-and-drop scenery.

On the 23rd at Booth's, *Arrah na Pogue*, Boucicault's tale of an Irish girl who jeopardizes her freedom and forthcoming marriage by sheltering a fugitive, was revived. The occasion was Boucicault's own return to America. With him was his wife, Agnes Robertson. They played the lovers, Arrah and Shaun the Post. Their naturalness won applause, although the evening was almost stolen from them by the treacherous Michael Feeny of Sheil Barry. However, Booth's multiplying difficulties were apparently reflected in complaints about the scenery, which was said to be below that house's high standards.

Departing from its usual custom of beginning with a revival, Wallack's unveiled W. S. Gilbert's **Pygmalion and Galatea** (10-1-72, Wallack's) for its opening bill, initiating a season in the house in which new plays and carefully selected revivals would dispense with the need for repertory. The American production was directed by E. A. Sothern. Of course, the story was familiar, particularly to Wallack's more sophisticated clientele. But Gilbert's jaundiced, misanthropic slant infused it with a certain sharp freshness. In his version Pygmalion (George C. Boniface) is married to the shrewish Cynisca (Edith Challis), and when she discovers that her husband has fallen in love with his new statue and brought it to life, her response is to invoke a spell (accompanied on stage by lightning and thunder) by which Pygmalion is blinded whenever he thinks unchaste thoughts. The unworldly Galatea (Katherine Rogers) is puzzled by such harridan behavior, insisting she means no harm. After all, she was "only born yesterday." Of course, in her unworldly innocence Galatea blunders into shocking or offending almost everyone she meets. Before long she is happy to return to stone. Not everyone felt Miss Rogers possessed the requisite beauty for the role, but this unkind thought did not deter playgoers, who kept the comedy on the boards for a month and a half— not a bad run at Wallack's.

On the 22nd the Boucicaults changed their bill at Booth's, offering two plays for the price of one. **Kerry** was Boucicault's version of *La Joie fait peur*. The "comedy drama" told an Enoch Arden story with a happy ending. The main point of the play was how to break the news to a wife who has been wasting away in grief for her apparently lost husband. The center of interest, however, was not the young couple but their resourceful servant. Naturally Boucicault himself assumed this title part. Agnes Robertson shone in the companion piece, *Jessie Brown*, recreating the title role of the young girl whose hopefulness bolsters the morale of the English trapped in the siege of Lucknow, which she had played in the original 1858 production.

The closing of *Diamonds* prompted Daly to launch into the season's first spate of quickly turned-over revivals. An important addition to the producer's roster was a former Wallack's stalwart Charles Fisher, whose first assignment, on the 28th, was Old Dornton in *The Road to Ruin*. Two nights later the house was home to *The Belle's Stratagem*. *Everybody's Friend* was mounted on November 4, and George Farquhar's 1702 comedy *The Inconstant* entered the repertory on the 6th.

Having served as director for Wallack's seasonal opener, Sothern now returned to the greasepaint on the 11th to embark on what developed into a virtual six-month stand as that rarity at the house, a star heading a great, stable company. No doubt Wallack, possibly reluctantly, was bowing to changing patterns. Far less surprising was Sothern's choice of a debut—his beloved Dundreary in *Our American Cousin*.

The evening of the 18th introduced New York to one of the greatest and most beautiful English actresses of the decade, the tragically short-lived Adelaide Neilson. She scored an electrifying triumph at Booth's in her very first role there, Juliet. There was some mild dissent, especially in the *Herald*, but most critics and playgoers seemingly tripped over themselves in seeking out laudatory adjectives. First glance revealed a ravishingly beautiful young woman with abundant, rich, chestnut hair (later sometimes bleached blonde), dark, limpid eyes, slightly irregular features that gave her face a becoming piquancy, and a comely figure. Miraculously, at just twenty-four she possessed that blend of experienced talent and a genuinely youthful freshness so precious and hard to come by in Juliet. The *Times* suggested she might well be the best Juliet "ever seen in New York." William Winter was more specific: "The keynote of Miss Neilson's Juliet was struck in her solemn utterance of the words 'Too early seen unknown, and known—*too late!*' and from that moment onward the magic of her passionate sincerity never faltered. Her identification with the character was complete. Her movement, in the minuet, was exquisitely graceful. Her startled, bewildered gaze, at Romeo, subtly but completely expressed the effect of first love. In

saying 'If he be married, my grave is like to be my wedding bed' there was a thrilling tremor of her voice that enhanced the pathos of the words, and as her riveted glance followed the vanishing Romeo she suddenly raised her left hand and kissed the spot that he, a moment earlier, had kissed, in parting from her. . . . It was in the Potion Scene and the Tomb Scene, however, that she exerted all her power, showing an intensity of feeling and an artistic control and employment of it possible only to an exceedingly deep nature and great actress." Her scenery, of course, was Booth's—the same settings he had used when he opened the theatre in 1869. Unfortunately, her supporting players were also Booth's, but they were passed over curtly in the majority of notices.

So that Shakespeare need not vie with Shakespeare, Daly withheld unveiling his *The Merry Wives of Windsor* until the next night, the 19th. The merits of Fisher's Falstaff were hashed over in lively disputes, but the ladies—notably Mrs. Gilbert as Mistress Quickly, Fanny Davenport as Mistress Ford, and Sara Jewett as Anne Page—were soundly applauded.

But in fact Shakespeare did compete with himself on the 19th, for Edwin Forrest, no longer able to sustain a full-blown performance, gave a sedate reading of *Hamlet* that night at Steinway Hall; three nights later he sat down to read *Othello*. Yet a fifth Shakespeare play could have been seen when Adelaide Neilson broke the monotony of repeating *Romeo and Juliet* with a few performances of *As You Like It*. On December 9, she added several performances of *The Lady of Lyons* to her closing week schedule.

The 9th also saw Daly mount a disappointing revival of *The School for Scandal*. But the very next evening he suffered a greater disappointment with a new play and a new actress. The actress was the socially prominent Mrs. C. D. Abbott, hellbent for her hour in another sort of limelight. The drama was T. B. De Walden's **The Baroness** (12-10-72, Fifth Ave.), an adaptation, made especially for the debutante, of a French play. The Baroness Vaubrey (Mrs. Abbott) marries the aged Count de Savenay (G. H. Griffiths) for his money. When her mercenary motives are exposed, the count goes mad and kills her. Critics were kinder to Mrs. Abbott than they were to the play, although both soon disappeared from the theatrical scene. Whether Mr. Abbott helped reimburse Daly for his losses remains unrecorded. The next week Daly rushed in two revivals, *Married Life* on the 16th and Mrs. Cowley's *A Bold Stroke for a Husband* on the 17th. Odell has pointed out that by now Daly's company was so large and so diverse that he was able to employ totally different performers for each of the two plays.

Another new actress and another new play met with disfavor when the curtain came down on Helen Temple in Brougham's treatment of the St. Joan story, **The Lily of France** (12-17-72, Booth's), although in this instance reviewers thought better of the play than of the star.

There were no Wallacks on the stage of the family's theater when Sothern appeared in the American premiere of John Oxenford's **Brother Sam** (12-21-72, Wallack's). Regular playgoers could have guessed in advance that this was the same Brother Sam to whom Lord Dundreary had so often alluded in *Our American Cousin.* But Sam (Sothern) turned out to be as brash and purposeful as Dundreary was shy and bumbling. Indeed, the impecunious Sam's determination to wheedle a huge check from his uncle, Jonathan Rumbelow (John Gilbert), leads him to concoct a story about his imaginary marriage. The check is forthcoming, but so is Uncle Jonathan, forcing Sam to scurry about to round up a temporary wife and child. It takes the rest of the evening for Sam to extricate himself from the complications that immediately ensue. Just as letters from the absent Sam had provided laughs in *Our American Cousin,* telegrams from Dundreary provided some of the new play's mirth. And, of course, the tour de force allowed Sothern to show his versatility.

However, two nights later, on the 23rd, a Wallack was seen at Booth's. Although no one knew it, J. W. Wallack, Jr., in the title role of *Henry Dunbar,* was making his final appearances in New York. After a week's run the actor headed south to recruit his failing health, but died before he could return north.

Nor could playgoers have known they were saying good-bye to a theatre when they attended the opening night of Frank Marshall's **New Year's Eve; or, False Shame** (12-23-72, Fifth Ave.). The play centered on Lord Chilton (George Clarke), a basically decent chap who affects an idle foppery. He loves Magdalen Atherly (Clara Morris), but the romantic young lady disdains any man who is not dashingly brave. Chilton's opportunity comes when he rescues Magdalen from drowning. Still, he is reluctant to drop his mask, so he hies away before she regains consciousness, leaving only his ring on her finger in place of one of hers as a clue to his identity. His rival, Captain Bragleigh (C. H. Rockwell), claims the ring is his and also steals her ring from Chilton. Appearances lead Magdalen to accept Bragleigh's proposal of marriage, but the true

story comes out in time for a happy ending. Contemporary critics were usually infuriatingly silent on details of a production. Luckily, Miss Morris provided some glimpses in her autobiography. Recalling that for one scene Daly provided her with a beautiful gown, "a combination of sapphire-blue velvet and Pompadour brocade," she continued:

"In a lovely old English interior, all draped in Christmas greens, filled with carved-wood furniture, big logs burning in an enormous fireplace, wax candles in brass sconces, two girls are at the organ in dinner dress, who, nervously anxious about a New Year carol, with which they are going to surprise their guests at mid-night, seize the moment before dinner to try said carol over.

"Miss Davenport, regal in satin, stood, music in hand, the fire-light on her handsome face. I, seated at the organ in my precious blue and brocade, played the accompaniment, and sang alto."

But good notices and all Daly's expense went for little. With a certain irony, considering the title, the interior of the theatre was destroyed by fire on New Year's Day.

The third opening on the evening of the 23rd was at the Union Square, where Palmer began a brief repertory of revivals, starting with *London Assurance* and moving on to *The School for Scandal* on the 25th and *Money* on the 27th. All three plays failed to draw, and the experience persuaded Palmer such series were not for him.

The old year's last major production was Booth's revival at his own theatre on the 30th of *Richard III.*

The new year was rung in with a lone double bill, half old, half new. Herman Merivale's loose adaptation of François Ponsard's *Le Lion amoureux,* entitled **A Son of the Soil** (1-1-73, Union Square), was coupled with J. P. Woolner's afterpiece *Orange Blossoms,* in which a confirmed bachelor is led to the altar. The story of the main attraction told of the troubles that pile on Louis Martel (D. H. Harkins), a man of low birth who has been elevated to membership in the Committee of Safety under the Directoire, when he loses his heart to the high-born Beatrice, Duchess d'Armine (Clara Jennings). That a surfeit of French plays, particularly those set in this period, was developing could be gleaned from the *Tribune*'s calling the French Revolution and its aftermath "dramatically tedious." That an older order of acting was still very much alive, if increasingly deprecated, could be read in a review that wailed, "Mr. Harkins rants too much in the character, and speaks his side speeches as if he were hailing the topgallant yard from the quarterdeck. More light and shade and less cast-iron asperity would make his Martel at once more agreeable and more natural." The bill ran less than a week before being withdrawn in favor of Brougham's **Atherley Court** (1-6-73, Union Square), in which the Earl (F. F. Mackay) and Countess (Emily Mestayer) of Atherley are threatened with social ruin by a blackmailer, provoking the countess into plotting the malefactor's death. Only after her plans have succeeded does she learn the dead man was her long-lost illegitimate son.

Although the work, derived from T. W. Robinson's *A Bridge of Glass,* proved more satisfactory than its predecessors, it was not a real success. Highest praise seems to have gone to the house's young scene painter, Richard Marston, whose third-act drawing room and fourth-act exterior brought him onstage to accept the applause. In coming years many commentators would suggest he was possibly the finest painter of exterior scenes in New York. In his unpublished memoirs, Palmer asserted that it was with his work on this play that "Marston declared his supremacy" and recalled, "One scene was a reproduction of Haddon Hall, in Derbyshire, England. It had an impressive appearance of solidity, with its great panels of oak and massive carvings, the whole sustaining a graceful relief in the glow of color that belonged to the decoration, and was heightened by the light that came through the antique windows. A scene from the castle on its crag with a wide expanse of [moonlit] sea at its base, was an extraordinary triumph of his brush."

Booth received some of his best notices when he assumed the title role in John Howard Payne's *Brutus* on the 20th. The play was something of a rarity for Booth—a work by an American author—but he caught all the vengeful bitterness and pathos of the deposed noble who must eventually sentence his own son to death. While the settings were praised, his supporting company once again was either condemned or ignored. One wonders why Booth remained so loyal to apparently colorless performers when criticism was so constant. Had ego triumphed over idealism?

The loss of his theatre could hardly have been expected to slow the intrepid Daly. Earlier in the season he had taken over the Grand Opera House, mounting a series of productions best viewed as musical spectacles. Even his revival on the 20th of Moncrieff's long-popular *The Cataract of the Ganges* had its musical moments. For the occasion Brougham rewrote the text to include a part for his co-star, the great queen of burlesque, Mrs. John Wood. But it was the glittering pageantry and the heroine's celebrated ride on a "snow-white charger" from footlights to flies, leaping over the waterfall, that still provided the biggest thrills. The *Times* listed some of the spectacle: "In act the second comes an endless procession of men and horses, attired and caparisoned with all the picturesqueness and splendor of the Orient; in act the third are a pleasing and brief ballet, and a succession of wonder-provoking and amusing feats by a troupe of Bedouin Arabs; and throughout the evening are many sword-combats, carried on with rare spirit and endurance."

However, Daly's most pressing problem was his main company. He had sent them out on a hastily devised tour immediately after the fire and, at the same time, leased a darkened auditorium at 728 Broadway. In a mere three weeks he had completely refurbished the place and rehearsed a new show. The night after opening *The Cataract of the Ganges* he was ready to resume where he had left off. His new work was **Alixe** (1-21-73, New Fifth Ave.), his freewheeling translation of the Baroness de Prevois's *La Comtesse de Somerive* (some suggest her son-in-law, Théodore Barrière, had a large hand in the original). Although the woman known as Mme Valory (Fanny Morant) long ago deserted her husband, the Count de Somerive (Charles Fisher), and her two daughters, the elder, illegitimate Alixe (Clara Morris) and the younger, legitimate Lucienne (Linda Dietz), she is not so cold-blooded that she does not attempt to offer Alixe some of the affection the unhappy girl longs for. However, her attempts are awkward and unavailing. Moreover, Alixe loves rich, handsome Henry de Kerdran (George Clarke) and he loves her, but he is too weak to break his engagement to Lucienne and publicly acknowledge his feelings. When the lustful if kindly Duke de Miradol (Louis James) offers to make Alixe his mistress, she realizes the sort of future in store for her and so drowns herself. While the *Herald* chafed at "the social infelicities of the married state so necessary in a French play," it joined other papers in applauding the work's theatrical effectiveness and Miss Morris's moving performance. She somehow elicited tears and applause even in the final moments when she was brought onstage wet and lifeless. The play gave Daly his biggest hit of the season and confirmed Miss Morris's reputation as a powerful emotional actress. It ran until mid-March, when Daly brought back *New Year's Eve* to play in repertory with it for several more weeks.

The wavering fortunes of Wood's received a boost when Frank Chanfrau began a month-long stand on the 27th. He began with *Kit, the Arkansas Traveller,* later switching to *Sam* and concluding, from February 17 on, with a double bill that paired *The Toodles* and his old warhorse *A Glance at New York in 1848.* He was followed on the 26th by Oliver Doud Byron, now playing to woolen mittens, in *Across the Continent.*

Yet another play from the French was **One Hundred Years Old** (1-29-73, Union Square), which N. Hart Jackson derived Adolphe d'Ennery and Édouard Plouvier's *Le Centenaire.* The action takes place on the hundredth birthday of Jacques Fauvel (Mark Smith). By rights it should be a happy occasion, with the family celebrating and the youngsters playing merrily. Unfortunately, one married granddaughter, Juliette (Mary Griswold), has had a child out of wedlock. Matters are resolved when her sister, Camille (Clara Jennings), takes the child. Critics agreed that Smith was too forceful and active for a man of Fauvel's age, but the actor won over reviewers and playgoers alike in a scene in which the villainous Max de Maugars (George Parkes) attempts to cause Fauvel to have a heart attack by badgering him and Fauvel responds with such serenity that he drives Max to distraction.

W. J. Florence returned to Booth's for a month and a half beginning on February 3. Most of the time he played his ever dependable *The Ticket-of Leave Man,* but for the final fortnight, beginning on March 3, he offered *No Thoroughfare.*

Although New Yorkers had been given a fleeting opportunity to see an unauthorized, mediocre mounting of T. W. Robertson's *David Garrick* in 1869, they could now attend a first-rate production with a cast headed by the actor for whom Robertson had written the play. That production was at Wallack's on the 8th, and its Garrick was Sothern. Once again he could demonstrate his broad range, moving from the inept Dundreary to the brazen Sam to the considerate, high-minded old English idol. In Robertson's story Garrick has fallen in love with Ada (Katherine Rogers), a beautiful lady whom he has spotted in his audience. He has not attempted to pursue her, but when he is invited to the home of a rich London merchant, Simon Ingot (John Gilbert), he discovers that Ingot is her father and that he is distressed to find his daughter has, in turn, fallen in love with the actor. Ingot offers Garrick far more than he could ever earn in the theatre if he will leave the country. Garrick refuses but makes a counterproposal. If Ingot will invite him to dinner, he will behave so disgracefully that Ada will be disenchanted. Ingot accepts. Although Garrick feigns drunkenness, rips down a curtain, and otherwise acts the part of a boor, the plan somehow misfires. In the end Garrick and Ada do wed.

Garrick's real wife was named Eva, and her marriage to him had been opposed by her guardians. But the playwright is said to have taken his story not from real life but from a French drama, Mèlesville's *Sullivan.* Sothern apparently sometimes used an unhappy ending. Either way, the production was another feather in Sothern's and Wallack's caps. The theatre reportedly scoured the city to provide correct period furnishings for the play, but since so many of its offerings were set in Garrick's time, the claim smacks of publicity.

As we've seen, Olive Logan was a lady with fingers in several pies, among them advocacy of women's rights. She herself put her theories into theatrical form in **A Business Woman** (3-13-73, Union Square). Fanny Ingraham (Clara Jennings) despairs of the men in her life. Her father, Palissy [read Palsy?] Ingraham (F. F. Mackay), has wasted away the family fortune building preposterous inventions. The man she loves, Col. Collins Woods (D. H. Harkins), stubbornly clings to the glove of another woman, one who has time and again rejected him. Of course, by the final curtain Fanny has recouped the family bank account and won the colonel.

Miss Logan garnished the comedy with other oddball characters. Take the untutored, dottily smug Mrs. Hooker Wood (Emily Mestayer), whose own militancy prompts her to stump not for feminine causes but for the promotion of ignorance. Critics to a man, as indeed they all were, found little to like in such outrageous goings-on. The play lasted less than two weeks, so no one blamed the appalling idea of women advancing in business for the stock market crash that shook the nation six months later.

The theatre's contract for this play survives and shows Miss Logan's abilities as a businesswoman, if not as an authoress. It reveals that her husband, Wirt Sykes, was actually her collaborator. It also discloses that while the work was advertised as original, it was actually derived from two French plays. Miss Logan insisted this not be made public but did insist that her name appear prominently in all advertisements and bills. For her efforts she was to receive $40 for each evening performance and $25 for each matinee. In April Palmer sent her a check for $375.

Equally absurd, at the same time it reflected the Francomania engulfing American stages, was **Uncle Sam** (3-17-73, Grand Opera). Its original title had been *L'Oncle Sam,* and its author was Victorien Sardou. French authorities had denied a permit for the play's Paris production, reportedly out of fear of offending American sensibilities. Daly, hoping to profit from the headlines about the banning, had grabbed the rights and made a translation. The principal story in the play was a romance, begun on shipboard, between the Marquis de Rochemore (Henry Crisp), who is coming to visit America and to be amused by its uncouth natives, and Sarah Tapplebot (Mrs. John Wood), an orphan who has been raised by her rich uncle, Sam (John Brougham). Sarah is an interesting girl, an aggressive flirt who makes men woo her then breaks their hearts by deserting them for the next victim. One later commentator has observed, "She is presented as an early edition of Anne Whitefield of *Man and Superman*. Sardou has almost completely anticipated Shaw's reversal of the love chase." Caught in her snares, the Marquis bewails that he has been "sent skipping from icebergs to flames, from red pepper to snowballs, exasperated at beholding the fruit almost at my lips and unable to clutch it." In time Sarah recognizes that she, too, is caught in her own snares. She attempts to flee, but de Rochemore will not let her. She begs, "Leave me—oh, leave me—Robert, I am afraid!" Naturally, Robert does not leave.

But the love interest was merely a frame for some remarkable French ideas about American life. One lady tells of having bought a home that, she later learns, straddles state lines. She takes her case into the states' courts. Connecticut awards her her dining room, but Massachusetts disallows her claim to her parlor. She immediately appeals, and both judgments are reversed. She is no better off than she was before. Similarly, Sardou had fun with American political contests. The wealthy Republican candidate, who has risen from being a lowly cobbler, campaigns by making shoes for the poor. The Democrats, who also have no real issue to run on, seek votes by parading around a seal who can smoke a pipe. And then there is Uncle Sam Tapplebot, who is described as a man "who had sold brooms at the age of twelve, was a pork-packer at seventeen, manufacturer of shoe-polish at twenty, made a fortune in cocoa, lost it in tobacco, rose again with indigo, fell with salt pork, rebounded with cotton and settled definitely upon guano. He rises at six, rushes to his office in an omnibus, is greedy, extravagant, cunning and credulous, without scruples, yet a good fellow; will throw you overboard for a hundred dollars and spend two hundred to fish you out; a perfect type of the American whom nothing discourages, always at the front, his eyes fixed upon three beacons—wealth for an end, cunning for the means, and as for morals—success!" Even critics who held reservations about the play admitted first-nighters enjoyed themselves thoroughly. Yet after a month *Uncle Sam* disappeared, although its American production did prompt French censors finally to allow Parisians to see it.

Boucicault scored a success and provided himself with a future meal ticket when he brought out **Daddy O'Dowd; or, Turn About Is Fair Play** (3-17-73, Booth's). Michael O'Dowd (Boucicault) has a loving, fundamentally good son, who nevertheless leaves his Galway home and heads for London, where he is soon calling himself Percy Walsingham (Joseph Wheelock) and allowing himself to be led into dissolute behavior by Lady Gwendoline (Bella Pateman). Michael hopes the young man will return and stand for Parliament, but his hopes are dashed when a money-lender, Romsey Leake (Sheil Barry), appears and demands he pay his son's staggering debts. Michael does, is left penniless, and becomes a porter. Percy flees overseas in shame. Years later he comes back, but he is now a wealthy, sober man. He repays his father and marries the contrite Gwendoline. Reviewers heaped praise on Boucicault's finely modulated performance and on his fellow players as well. A careful production enhanced the evening, with a snowy Galway street scene evoking special applause. The play was based on Eugène Cormon and Eugène Grangé's *Les Crochets du Père Martin* and so was, in effect, yet one more French contribution to the season. It played six weeks, with a two-week interruption beginning April 21 for a revival of *Arrah na Pogue*.

On the same night as these two premieres, older playgoers may well have trekked to Steinway Hall for more readings, this time not by Forrest but by Charlotte Cushman. Except on the first night, when she read *Henry VIII,* she did not follow the actor's practice of confining an evening to a single play. Instead she read scenes from various plays and also recited 19th-century poems.

Some playgoers were disturbed by the similarity of **Cousin Jack** (3-22-73, Union Square) to *John Garth.* Certainly the likeness was striking, although the earlier play had been taken by Brougham from a well-known novel, while the new work was W. J. Florence's translation of Louis Leroy's French play. Where Leroy or the novelist got his plot is moot. In both stories a man leaves home under a cloud, goes to South America, where he becomes an important political figure, and later returns home to clear his name and become a local benefactor. Florence set the action in France and called the hero Jack Valdent (D. H. Harkins). Harkins's acting style constantly seemed to rub the *Times* the wrong way. The paper once more condemned "his preposterous habit of speaking his side speeches at the top of his voice, like an officer hailing the mast-head." For whatever reason the play was not a success, so to bolster attendance during the last week, starting April 9, one more play was added to the bill. **Micawber** was yet another version of Dickens's *David Copperfield* and served as a vehicle for George Fawcett Rowe's much admired interpretation. The piece was a cut-down version of Rowe's full-length *Little Em'ly,* which was later to make heaps of money, but not for Palmer. F. F. Mackay's unctuous Uriah Heep also won an ovation.

While Maeder's *Buffalo Bill* was circulating among lesser houses, the real-life hero, William F. Cody, appeared in another saga of his exploits at the resurrected Niblo's on the 31st. One of his co-stars was the then equally celebrated, if now forgotten, gunslinger John "Texas Jack" B. Omo-hundro. The production also featured twenty—count 'em, twenty—"honest injuns," some of whom had to play dishonest Indians. To top it off, a third star and author of the bill was the notorious Ned Buntline.

Buntline's real name was Edward Zane Carroll Judson. He had served as an adventurer and soldier in the West but was better known for other exploits, some highly unsavory. He had been a founder of the bigoted Know-Nothing party, an instigator of the Astor Place riots, and the originator—and an active scribbler—of the dime novel. Like many dangerous flag-wavers, he trafficked in a macho image. His latest works were **The Scouts of the Prairie** and a short, farcical curtain raiser, **The Broken Bank.** The comedy was quickly dismissed, since critics, like playgoers, were anxious to get on to the shootin'. The *Herald* did take time and space to allow that it was "probably the worst written and certainly the worst acted atrocity ever." That was far more attention than other papers accorded it, or than it probably deserved. With the curtain raiser put aside, the eagerly awaited shooting began in earnest. "In fact," one reviewer commented, "the unmitigated bloodshed that ends every act and almost every scene of this unique composition, were so satisfactory to the public, that the management might be forgiven for hereafter assuming that the key to success must lie in the exhibition of cataracts of gore."

In the first act the hero, Cale Durg (Buntline), "in a buckskin suit and long ringlets of supernaturally black hair," is captured by Indians, who "make speeches about the dew, the morning cloud and the badness of the white man" and tie Cale to a tree. He is rescued from imminent roasting by Dove Eye (Mlle. Morlacchi), the lovable daughter of a hostile chief, in conjunction with Bill and Jack. They also save Hazel Eye (Eloe Carfano), a second Indian maiden. The manly Cale is apparently more inter-ested in lecturing on the virtues of temperance than in protecting himself, for in the following acts his buddies regularly have to come to his aid. In the end he is fatally wounded while saving the lives of Dove Eye and Hazel Eye. To avenge him Bill and Jack massacre the redskins; then they marry Dove Eye and Hazel Eye. Not surprisingly, given Buntline's known hatreds, a secondary villain was the renegade Mormon Ben (Harry Wentworth), who, when not seeking a fiftieth wife, is goading on the Indians. The leading comic figures were Carl Pretzel (Walter Fletcher), a "Dutchman" who wants to be pals with "Beefalo Bull" and "Jackass (or Shackas) Tex," and Phelim (C. C. Davenport), an Irishman always in search of a drink. Largely unexpected are the marriages just before the final curtain. The cast included supposedly genuine Indians with names such as Grassi Chief, Prairie Dog, Big Elk, and Great River, but the roster of supernumeraries was seemingly insufficient. An amused critic observed, "We counted sixteen times that one poor 'supe' was killed during the play." The *Herald*'s critic, left in an especially dyspeptic mood by the whole evening, called Cody "ridiculous as an actor" and added that Buntline represented his part "as badly as it is possible for any human being to represent it." The public couldn't have cared less, so the show packed the huge theatre for two weeks, when previously made bookings forced it to move on.

The common practice of adding a second attrac-tion to a faltering bill could be observed again on April 3, when H. J. Byron's short, farcical afterpiece **Dundreary Married and Settled** accompanied *David Garrick* at Wallack's. It took less than half an hour to show that the ludicrous lord might marry but would forever remain unsettled, or at least unset-tling. All Lady Dundreary's friends come to sponge off him, so he calls on Asa Trenchard (J. B. Polk) to come to his assistance. Typical of Dundreary's bumbling drolleries was his solicitous "Speaking of bunions, how is your mother?" The title, by the way, was not a novel one for a sequel. To cite one earlier example, there had been a *Paul Pry Married and Settled.* Lady Dundreary was played by a lovely, promising young actress, Rose Coghlan. The double bill continued on for another month.

Genuine native works were still rare at first-class houses but increasingly on the bills at lesser theatres. The inconsistent Wood's offered an example on the 8th when squeaky-voiced Stuart Robson starred in a curious vehicle, **Law in New York.** Contemporaries may have seen its melodramatic frame as deriving from such headline-making scandals as the fall of the Tweed Ring and the Credit Mobilier, for the main story recounted the tricky manipulations of a convict turned alderman, who is heading once again for prison by the play's end. But the center of attraction was really Robson as John Beat, an absurdly obese policeman (with Robson no doubt wearing scads of padding) who is made jittery by the slightest noise or shadow. On the same night, Daly restaged *Old Heads and Young Hearts* for a week's worth of performances.

The next week belonged to Daly. Modern publicists might well have termed it a "Daly Festival." On the 14th at the Grand Opera he revived his *Under the Gaslight*, a production notable in retrospect for marking Mrs. John Wood's last New York appearance. Melodrama of this sort was not her forte, and she played only the minor role of Peachblossom, so the great lady's farewell was notably downbeat. On the same night, Daly's translation of *Frou-Frou* was to be seen at the rival Union Square Theatre, with Agnes Ethel and George Parkes in their original roles. The next evening Daly featured his principal company at the New Fifth Avenue in a return of his *Divorce*.

Virtually from the start of his career Daly had earned himself the reputation as one of the most understanding and generous of American theatrical figures. Learning of Fechter's frustrating attempts to take over the shuttered 14th Street Theatre, he offered the actor the use of his Grand Opera House. Fechter moved in on the 28th. His repertory of three plays, all vehicles his admirers expected of him, begain with *Monte Cristo,* followed by *The Corsican Brothers* on June 1 and *Ruy Blas* on the 9th. In a sense Fechter was playing it doubly safe, for the contemporary pieces did not suffer from his accent, his warm but sometimes uneven playing, or comparison—as, say, his Hamlet might have—with more exalted favorites. In his heart, despite his vaulting ambitions, Fechter must have known where he excelled.

May burst forth with a flowering of new plays. H. J. Byron's **The Squire's Last Shilling** (5-3-73, Wallack's) served as Sothern's final new offering for the season. Byron's story was straightforward but hardly novel. Sothern probably took it on to offer yet a further display of his remarkable versatility, since it allowed him to play a rustic, and a pathetic one at that. Charles Chuckles (Sothern) learns he has inherited a vast estate. His joy turns sour, however, when three men forge a will that suggests he is not the rightful heir after all. The men attempt to blackmail him with it. To their dismay he accepts the will as genuine and insists the property be turned over to the apparent heir. He himself returns to his former, relatively impoverished life, snubbed by the crooks, the new heir, and all the others who were prepared to fawn on him. Only Polly Greville (Effie Germon) remains loyal and loving. The fraud is finally exposed, so Chuckles, having the last laugh, can look forward to a comfortable life with her.

When Adelaide Neilson returned for her second visit of the season, she brought with her a new play, **Amy Robsart** (5-12-73, Booth's), Andrew J. Halliday's dramatization of Scott's *Kenilworth.* The story of the heroine's secret marriage to Leicester (F. C. Bangs), the attempts to keep news of the marriage from the jealous Queen Elizabeth (Bella Pateman), the meeting of Amy and Elizabeth, and Amy's murder by the duplicitous Varney (Neil Warner) were recounted with a deftness and knowing theatricality that earned the work general acceptance. But it was really Miss Neilson's performance that elevated the evening into art; the role became one of her most lauded interpretations. The *Herald* lavished a flood of praise on her "nobly portrayed" heroine, citing her ability to exhibit "the beauty and force of true womanhood" and her skill at depicting "love and constancy without degenerating into sentiment." One of the few dissenters was the *Times* critic. He not only rued that the drama displayed the shallowness of most such stage versions of novels but felt that the role was beneath Miss Neilson and, more damningly, that her performing in "the provinces" allowed her polish to tarnish. This had become and would remain a chauvinistic cry of many New Yorkers, who probably never had seen performances at Mrs. Drew's Arch Street Theatre in Philadelphia, at the Boston Museum, or at any number of artistically superb houses around the country. Mrs. Gilbert and others spoke of it, often bitterly, in their reminiscences. Happily, most playgoers ignored such silly carping. Except for a couple of performances of *As You Like It* during the final week, *Amy Robsart* was all Miss Neilson needed to sustain her month's engagement.

With his translation of **Madelein Morel** (5-20-73, New Fifth Ave.), Daly again borrowed from the same S. H. von Mosenthal whose *Deborah* had been the source of his first success, *Leah, the Forsaken.* Madelein (Clara Morris) is an unstable, suicidal actress. When she was a child her father had been steward to old Count Dalberg, but Dalberg had come to believe him a thief and had driven father and daughter from his home. The father soon died, and the young girl was taken in by performers. Like so many players of the time, they disdained a strict morality, and Madelein became for a while the mistress of the cold, haughty Frederick von Arnim (Louis James). The actors are hired to impersonate society figures at a ball to be given in honor of the new Count Dalberg, young Julian (George Clarke). At the ball Julian finds himself falling in love with Madelein, whom he does not recognize. He tells her that he has discovered the innocence of his father's old steward and is seeking to find him and his daughter in order to make some sort of restitution. Still ignorant of her history, he courts her and proposes marriage. But von Arnim turns out to be Julian's brother-in-law, and he threatens Madelein with exposure. She flees, eventually entering a convent. Time passes. Just before Madelein is about to take the veil, she enters a church where a wedding is in progress. She sees that Julian is the groom. Unhinged, she rips off her veil, flings her cross to the ground, and dies. Although Daly was a devout Catholic and had obtained his church's grudging approval of the production in advance, howls of outrage came from all corners. Moralists in high dudgeon accused Daly and theatre folk in general of condoning onstage what they would condemn off-stage. Such noisy protests only whetted the appetites of many playgoers, so the drama ran until the end of Daly's season in late June.

Nepotism reared its embarrassing head with the production of **Without a Heart** (5-21-73, Union Square), a play by the theatre owner's wife, Mrs. Sheridan Shook. Martha Dobson (Maude Granger) is a heartless adventuress who wheedles her way into the best society. She spurns the love of young Robert Marston (D. H. Harkins) and instead attempts to set her claws into Sir William Broughton (F. F. Mackay). An outbreak of smallpox thwarts her. She then sees the newly married Marston in a fresh light, but her plans to come between him and his wife are also frustrated. Critics were tactful but dismissive. They reserved their best adjectives for Maude Granger, who was making her debut in the leading role. Her beauty alone might have made critics susceptible, but from the start she displayed impressive talents. Her reading of the part was intelligent and mature. Even when she was not the center of action she paid interested attention to the other performers onstage—a practice not always observed by some egocentric performers, and one that caught the equally interested attention of several critics. However, she was still so unknown, and the play was so awkward, that Palmer changed his bill after a single week.

A month that began with a spate of new plays ended with revivals of productions from earlier in the season. Sothern wrapped up his engagement with *Our American Cousin* and a double bill of *Brother Sam* and *Dundreary Married and Settled,* on the 22nd and 29th respectively, while Agnes Ethel reappeared at the Union Square in *Agnes* on the latter Monday.

Frank Murdoch's **Davy Crockett; or, Be Sure You're Right, Then Go Ahead** (6-2-73, Wood's) was passed over slightly by most critics but went on to enjoy a longer, more active life than any other new play of the season. Murdoch did not live to profit from its success. A nephew of actor James E. Murdoch, whose surname he adopted, he was a minor actor and playwright before his death at twenty-nine in 1872. So the play served mainly to enrich its star, Frank Mayo, who had first performed in it the preceding September and had then toured with it while whipping it into shape.

. . .

Frank Mayo (1839–96) was a Boston native whose debut occurred on the other side of the country, in San Francisco, in 1856. In a very short time he earned a reputation as a promising Shakespearean, but after finding *Davy Crockett* he apparently decided that he could look forward to an easier and steadier income by joining the list of players who toured incessantly in a single starring role. He only rarely returned to Shakespeare in afteryears.

. . .

Although its modern editors have called it "probably the best-known of the American frontier dramas," the play is more like a drawing-room melodrama set incongruously in the wilderness. Davy Crockett (Mayo) comes back to his forest cabin carrying a buck he has shot and happy in the thought that his childhood sweetheart, Little Nell, is returning from a long stay abroad. By now, of course, she is a grown beauty and calls herself by her real name, Eleanor Vaughn (Rosa Rand). She is accompanied by her guardian, Major Hector Royston (T. W. Keene), and her fiancé, Neil Crampton (Harry Stewart). The trio are headed for the estate of Neil's uncle, Oscar Crampton (J. J. Wallace). Crockett suspects something is not right. With the snow starting to fall, he offers the travelers the shelter of his cabin. Noticing that Crampton is bleeding, Crockett fears more trouble ahead. To Miss Vaughn's expression of gratitude he responds, "Don't say that, miss, for what I did for you I'd have did for any living soul that came to my door in a storm like that. But you are safe, and I thank the Etarnal for that." Crockett's worst fears are realized when wolves, drawn by Crampton's blood, surround the cabin and he discovers the door bar is gone. Miss

Vaughn attempts to allay her terror by reading from *Lochinvar*, but the howling of the wolves leads her to cry out, "Nothing can save us!" Crockett replies that "the strong arm of a backwoodsman" can. The second-act curtain falls as *Davy bars [the] door with his arm. The wolves attack the house. Heads seen [at] opening in the hut and under the door.*" The party at last reaches old Crampton's estate, where Crockett discovers that the uncle is blackmailing Royston with forged papers and forcing his nephew to marry Miss Vaughn for her money. Crockett destroys the uncle's papers and takes Miss Vaughn home, to marry her himself.

Laurence Hutton, a contemporary critic and early theatrical historian, called *Davy Crockett* "almost the best American play ever written" and added that "Mayo's performance of his backwoods hero is a gem in its way. He is quiet and subdued, he looks and walks and talks the trapper to the life, never overacts, and never forgets the character he represents." Mayo continued to perform the role until just days before his death, and lesser actors took over after he died. But Hutton, writing in 1890, noted, "The play has never been properly appreciated by metropolitan audiences. Free from tomahawking and gun-firing; utterly devoid of emotional and harrowing elements, it does not appeal to the admirers of the morbid on the stage; and, giving no scope for richness of toilet, it has no charms for the habitual attendants upon matinée entertainments." More succinctly, Arthur Hobson Quinn has called it "an idyll . . . of the pioneer life."

It was becoming fashionable to compare Boucicault's newest efforts unfavorably with his earlier plays, while still acknowledging that in many cases his theatrical gifts were abundant. Such was the response to **Mora; or, The Golden Fetters** (6-3-73, Wallack's). Assuredly one had not deserted him— the gift for concocting byzantinely involved plots. In simplest terms, Paul Schuyler (Mr. Allerton), a banker from an old established family, has allowed his failing bank to be rescued by a kindly upstart, Philo Guffy (A. D. Bradley), on the promise that Schuyler will marry Guffy's daughter, Bella (Effie Germon). However, Schuyler secretly marries Mora Vansyke (Katherine Rogers). A group of unscrupulous Wall Street promoters, who are called the Modocs after an Indian tribe that had recently waged a violent war against encroaching Americans, force Schuyler to hand over Guffy's stocks in a railroad they hope to control. Guffy learns of Schuyler's actions and rushes to his office, where he is shot and the shooting made to look like a suicide attempt. Mora is suspicious. She hurries Guffy to a doctor, who discovers the wounds are not fatal, and sets out to convict the promoters. She finally succeeds and tells a contrite Schuyler the good news that Bella loves another man. So all ends happily. Although most of Wallack's own company had scattered for their summer vacation, Boucicault was able to assemble a competent cast. Some complaints were registered about the villains being too villainous and coarse, but whatever its shortcomings, *Mora* ran a full month.

On the 4th Palmer closed out his season at the Union Square with a revival of *Fernande* starring Agnes Ethel.

Inevitably the resounding success of Lotta spawned imitators, none of whom ever approached her popularity. Two such young aspirants were sisters, Louise and Clara Coleman, who portrayed a pair of resourceful waifs in **Driven from Home** (6-9-73, Olympic). On the road to reclaiming their rightful fortune they clog-danced and played banjos, a harmonica, and a cornet. Whether playgoers were deterred by the lateness of the season or by some cautioning instincts, the critic for the *World* could count only eighty-two neighbors in the orchestra seats on opening night. Nor did business improve much. A week later the sisters were replaced by a youngster billed as "Little Nell, the California Diamond," a blatant attempt to capitalize on Lotta's California background and on one of her most famous characterizations. Little Nell's vehicle was **Fidelia, the Fire Waif** (6-16-73, Olympic). She played the mascot of the Phoenix Hose Company and her problems elicited unsuspected streaks of paternalism and heroism in her roughneck buddies. While resorting to seven disguises, she, too, employed a variety of talents better suited to the vaudeville stage to reap a reward at the final curtain. Possibly some obscure obituary can tell what happened to Clara Coleman. Her sister went on to become a minor supporting actress. Little Nell, on the other hand, would become Helen Dauvray, an actress and producer of some repute.

Koomer (6-16-73, Niblo's) starred Gus "Oofty Gooft" Phillips, with his plastered-down hair, slightly crossed eyes, and fractured German-English, as Peter Koomer, an immigrant shoemaker who suddenly inherits a fortune. He attempts to put on airs, but his social gaucheries, such as slurping soup from a tureen and wiping his mouth with the tablecloth, make him an object of ridicule and nearly cost him his unpretentious fiancée.

One major late spring opening was **Jane Eyre** (6-18-73, Union Square). This was not Brougham's 1849 adaptation, which Laura Keene was wont to play, but a newer, fuller version. Charlotte Thompson used those Union Square players who elected not to take summer recesses, notably the ranting D. H. Harkins as Rochester. For all her limited abilities, the role fit the star like a glove, and it remained identified with her for the rest of her career. Sensation seekers could thrill to the fire at Rochester's home, which brought down the curtain of the second act.

Cigarette, the Little Leopard of France (6-30-73, Olympic) was yet another of the many touring versions of Ouida's *Under Two Flags.* Apart from Lotta's vaudevillized version, *The Firefly,* it would be several decades before Broadway would see a truly successful treatment. This one disappeared after two weeks.

Another instance of how loose copyright laws allowed adaptors to play free and easy with a famous work occurred when two dramatizations of Henri Murger's *Scènes de la vie de Bohème* appeared back to back. The first had a startlingly 1960-ish title, **The Beats of New York** (6-30-73, Niblo's). Its author was its leading man, J. J. Wallace. He changed the settings to the artistic slums of New York, but beyond that seemed to be less sure of himself. Reading between the lines of reviews, it appears that he discarded its potent sentimentality, playing the early scenes for laughs and then emphasizing black-and-white melodrama.

A surer hand, Boucicault, had better luck with his **Mimi** (7-1-73, Wallack's), with the author as the enamored poet, Maurice (not Rodolphe as in the original), and Katherine Rogers as the doomed seamstress. While there was praise for Boucicault's "felicitous dialogue," disagreements surfaced regarding just how theatrical the "shreds and patches" of Murger's scenes truly were and just how right Boucicault himself was in the role of a straightforward lover, instead of the rich character types he usually portrayed. The play ran throughout the summer heat, giving way in late August and early September to revivals of *Used Up, Kerry,* and *The Colleen Bawn.* By this time it was becoming common knowledge that Miss Rogers was Boucicault's mistress.

Sheil Barry, whom Boucicault had brought back with him from Europe, completed the stand without Boucicault when he starred in Charles Gayler's comic **Dust and Diamonds** (9-20-73, Wallack's), an adaptation of *La Fille du chiffonier.* Barry was Mooney Mick, an incredibly unkempt but good-hearted ragpicker who takes under his wing an unloved orphan, Maggie (Kitty Blanchard). Maggie has been cruelly abused by a haughty demimon-daine, Bianca (Fanny Foster). Matters turn out for the best after it is learned that Maggie is a long-sought heiress. She marries the sympathetic young doctor, Herman Leroy (George Becks), but does not forget to share some of her newfound wealth with Mooney. Despite satisfactory reviews, the play had to be withdrawn almost at once so that Wallack's could begin its new season. It never returned to a first-class house.

1873–1874

If the new season offered playgoers a few exceptionally exciting evenings, it brought with it far more disappointments. Only the most incorrigible Pangloss would have given the theatrical year a good rating. Most commentators pegged it as somewhere between drab and disastrous. Acceptable new plays seemed especially scarce, so once again revivals proliferated. This in itself would not have bothered playgoers, who welcomed fresh writing but who also embraced, far more than later audiences ever would, a repetitive repertory of old pieces. Yet all too many of these resurrections during the season seemed jerry-built or dispirited. One unhappy observer, Henry Dickinson Stone, called special attention to the proliferation of musicals featuring the buxom beauties of the time in revealing costumes when he lamented in his curious 1873 *Theatrical Reminiscences,* "There appears in these latter days so much of the il-*leg*-itimate drama, so much of the flashy, trashy, sensational afloat and tolerated, that the true, solid, intellectual old tragedies, comedies and sterling melodramas are wholly ignored, and made to 'take a back seat.' " Such qualitative letdowns led to increasing turnovers, pushing up slightly the number of productions. But another, external matter exacerbated the situation. The economic upheavals stemming from the late war—massive debt, persistent inflation, a continuing splurge in the often speculative development of land, manufacturing, and, most of all, railroads—came together, or perhaps more accurately came apart, on September 18, shortly after the new season had begun, with the failure of Jay Cooke, financier of the Northern Pacific Railroad. The nation was plunged abruptly into the Panic of 1873, one of the deepest, ugliest, and most prolonged of American financial depressions. Its effect on the theatre was instant and sometimes damaging. No major legitimate playhouses closed, although some sought refuge in vaudeville or musicals. After all, patrons did not have many cheaper or free alternatives of more recent eras. But newspapers chronicled numerous heartsickening dips in attendance. A few new enterprises were nipped in the bud, and some shaky managements, such as Booth's, were forced to step aside in favor of less idealistic, hardnosed successors. Always compassionate and generous, theatre owners and performers time and again gave special entertainments to benefit the poor. In their own way these charities reflected a genuine, personal connection that existed between theatre folk and audiences, a unique rapport that would fade away forever within a decade or so, as more impersonal managements took over and the country began to grow too large for such intimacy.

Some lower-class playgoers may not have found much real comfort in the cramped auditorium that was Wood's, but they remained so loyal that, in effect, Wood's had no season. It not only operated year-round but usually gave two performances a day, with the matinee selection differing from the evening one. Sometimes a play ran a week, sometimes less. As a rule newspapers took little or no notice of what went on there. More's the pity, since it would have been interesting to see how critics responded to many of the plays. What would first-stringers have said about young Bartley Campbell's **Watch and Wait** (8-11-73, Wood's)? Campbell's hero, Bert, is a bank clerk in love with Grace, his boss's daughter. But he loses his job after two scoundrels accuse him of a theft they themselves have committed. Bert spends the remaining four acts trying to clear himself and nail his accusers. This effort takes him to the plains, where he is called "Wild Nat," and then to California, where he is thrown off a cliff. Love and virtue triumph just before eleven o'clock. Bert and Grace were played by J. W. Albaugh and his wife, performers who would become most important in later Baltimore theatricals. The play had been done earlier in Pittsburgh and Chicago as *Through Fire.* Critics in those towns were kind, dismissing the drama as clumsy but seeing promise in its author.

What for most playgoers was the season's opener was indicative of the shortcomings that cropped up throughout the year. On August 19, Daly relit the Grand Opera House with a revival of *A Midsummer's Night Dream.* No one, of course, could foresee the brilliant revival Daly would mount in 1888, but critics and oldtimers could compare this production with those of Burton in 1854 and Laura Keene in 1859, and even the less artistic but longer-run Olympic Theatre version in 1867, with G. L. Fox as

Bottom. Fox was also Daly's Bottom, but most supporting players were not of the highest caliber. A later generation was intrigued that "Little" Fay Templeton played Puck. However, most morning-after reviews took no notice of her. In fact, they gave far more space to a band of fifty other youngsters, who comprised a special corps de ballet. Scene painter George Heister, a veteran of Burton's fondly remembered production, was singled out for the excellences of his settings. His Athenian woods seemed refreshingly cool even on a sweltering August night, and his panorama, which moved the characters out of the forest at the end of the second act, was widely extolled. But the revival's laudable virtues were insufficient to propel it beyond three weeks, even though afterpieces were offered as an additional lure on many evenings.

In an attempt to keep his theatre within the family, Edwin Booth had reliquished control of it to his brother Junius Brutus Junior. Junius had never demonstrated the undeniable acting talents with which his father and brothers had been gifted, so had increasingly withdrawn from performing in favor of business management. At least in theory he could devote far more time to salvaging the playhouse's precarious fortunes than his busier brother could. But theory could not take into account the economic crunch just ahead. The theatre's opening attraction on September 1 gave no cause for alarm. It was as safe and sound a booking as any theatre might want—ever popular Joseph Jefferson in his reliable *Rip Van Winkle.* The warmhearted story ran five weeks. On Saturday nights, when Jefferson, like so many of the era's stars, refused to perform, the company offered Wilkie Collins's *The New Magdalen,* a work that would be given a more important mounting later in the season.

The Wandering Jew (9-9-73, Grand Opera) was a fresh dramatization of Eugène Sue's *Le Juif errant.* The redaction was by Leopold Lewis, whose most famous English transcription was *The Bells,* and had first been seen in London the preceding April. Although nominally the story centered on a Jew (J. W. Jennings) who had mocked Christ and was condemned to roam the world until the second coming, it really told of attempts by Jesuits to secure a fortune to which they are not entitled. The monks arrange to kidnap the girls who are the rightful heiresses and to proffer a false claimant. Samuel (Cyril Searle), "the faithful Jew" to whom the fortune has been entrusted, has hidden the money in a casket. He manages to withhold the wealth from the fraudulent grabbers. When the girls who should have had the money die of cholera, the casket miraculously catches fire, destroying the fortune. Samuel and the Wandering Jew prove one and the same, and Samuel's loyal husbanding of the money releases the Jew from his eighteen-hundred-year curse. Almost nothing could be mounted at the Grand Opera without the injection of spectacle. Typical were a third-act bacchanal, with the same youthful corps de ballet that had danced in *A Midsummer Night's Dream,* and the burning of the casket in the last act. Afterpieces were included in the fortnight's run.

Andrew Halliday's stage version of **Notre Dame** (9-11-73, Lyceum) had been a major London success and now was the choice to open a "new" theatre. Actually the Lyceum was anything but new, having been known earlier as the French Theatre and the 14th Street Theatre. Two years earlier Charles Fechter had taken it over with grandiose plans to make it into a national theatre, but his elaborate schemes came to naught. He lost his fortune and was elbowed out by more level headed, commercial interests. Victorian excesses were evident both in the redecorated playhouse and in the production. The *Times,* calling the auditorium "the most elegant playhouse in the City," described "its beautiful proscenium, on which tropical vegetation is beheld stretching to the skies" and "its masses of lace overhanging the boxes; its rich crimson seats." Halliday's story hewed closely to the original. Quasimodo was played by an English favorite, Thomas C. King, and Claude Frollo by Charles Wheatleigh, while another debutante, Jeffreys Lewis, was Esmeralda. According to the *Herald,* she was "a pretty and slender brunette" who evinced "cool intelligence and correct training rather than a flow of natural emotion." Two settings were singled out by the *Times:* "The cathedral is literally put before the foot-lights in all its massiveness and architectural detail, as well as the final tableau, in which the twin towers rise into the heavens with the grandeur, almost, of the cloud-capped structures themselves." Critics were also pleased with the large number of extras, who turned a mob into a genuine mob, and with the intrusive ballets, including in the first act alone "a carnival ballet, a chorus of *zingari,* and a bacchanalian dance." The drama fell far short of repeating its London success but, despite its out-of-the-way theatre and sudden hard times, ran a month and a half.

Two momentous events followed in quick succession. The happier of the two was the American debut of forty-four-year-old Tommaso Salvini. The Italian tragedian was a majestic figure whose mobile face featured a prominent forehead, an aquiline nose, and dark, striking eyes. His voice was "one of the most powerful, flexible and mellifluous" ever heard onstage. For his debut on September 16 at the Academy of Music he chose his greatest role, Othello. Critics were awesome in tribute, even though they immediately understood his was no typical Othello but a violently impassioned, totally Mediterranean Moor. Indeed, his killing of Desdemona was so violent that many actresses reputedly refused to play opposite him. Throughout the season, supported by his own company of fellow Italians, he moved from one theatre to another offering a variegated, intriguing repertory: Giacometti's *Elizabeth* (in which he was Essex), Pellico's *Francesca da Rimini,* Saumet's *The Gladiator, Hamlet, Ingomar,* Giacometti's *La Morte Civile, The Romance of a Poor Young Man,* d'Aste's *Samson,* Alfieri's *Saul, Sullivan* (source of Robertson's *David Garrick*), and Voltaire's *Zaira.* Reviewers agreed that playgoers did not need to understand Italian to grasp any nuance this consummate performer elected to convey.

The Manhattan premiere of **Ben McCullough; or, The Wanderer's Divorce** (9-16-73, Wood's) was of considerably less importance. Billed as the "gigantic California success," it starred Oliver Doud Byron, who undoubtedly hoped to turn it into an alternate vehicle to *Across the Continent.* His hero was a hot-tempered gunslinger who is led to believe his mother-in-law has engineered false charges of theft against him. The charges are particularly galling since not only has he married her daughter, but earlier—at the end of Act I—he had saved her family from a blazing inferno. A wild shootout ends the second act, after which Ben is carted off to prison. He languishes there for years, until an earthquake helps him escape. More years of wandering follow, then Ben is able to learn the true story and set matters right in time for a happy ending. Although the play proved no match for *Across the Continent,* Byron was able to return to it off and on for several seasons.

Two days later the American economy went into a tailspin.

Ettie Henderson, a young actress and future playwright, took a chance by commissioning Bartley Campbell, then also largely unknown, to dramatize a novel that had been appearing in the *New York Weekly.* The result was **Little Sunshine** (9-22-73, Bowery). The star played Lilly (or Lily or Lillie) Davis, who is fondly known as "Little Sunshine." Lilly herself seems unaware that she is an heiress who long ago was abducted and raised in poverty. She is put to work in a sweatshop and gets caught up in a strike, a robbery, and all other manner of complications before she learns her true history and marries the man of her dreams. Critics marked the play's similarity to *Bertha, the Sewing Machine Girl,* but most felt that would not hamper its appeal.

A pair of Daly productions followed. Both failed. H. J. Byron's **Haunted Houses; or Labyrinths of Life: A Story of London and the Bush** (9-23-73, Grand Opera) was as absurd and labyrinthine as its title. Its central figure was Guy Mardyke (D. H. Harkins), the era's umpteenth victim of false accusations. Guy's nemesis is Daniel Blake (Frank Hardenberg), his rival for the hand of Alice (Mrs. C. M. Walcot). The hero flees certain imprisonment and takes a ship for Australia. On board he discovers a Jewish dealer in old clothes, Moss Morris (G. L. Fox), who has papers that reveal Alice's parentage. The vessel is shipwrecked, but Guy manages to survive this and other vicissitudes and to return to England, where he unmasks Blake's treachery, clears his own name, and marries Alice. Spectacle included the wrecking of the ship *Eclipse,* which gave Fox a chance to offer comic relief as he clung to a spar above the waves. Later Blake pushes Morris over a cliff, but Morris takes his revenge by pulling out the underpinnings from a dilapidated house in which the villain had decided to kill Alice, so it is Blake who dies instead. A short comedy preceded the main work.

Bertie Vyse's London failure **About Town, a Riverside Story** (9-29-73, Broadway) had even less luck. The theatre was the one at 728 Broadway that Daly had hastily employed after his Fifth Avenue had burned. He renamed it when the planned opening of his new Fifth Avenue was scheduled for early autumn. Delays set back the new house's unveiling, but Daly obviously wanted no confusion. What did confuse audiences was why the producer bothered to mount such a slipshod work. Its story told how Mr. Dixon (G. H. Griffiths) must erase the onus of a false accusation of forgery before he can arrange a suitable marriage for his daughter, Violet (Minnie Walton). The happy ending was no more of a surprise than was the stock device of the phony charge.

A double bill of comedies, H. T. Craven's **Barwise's Book** and J. Maddison Morton and A. W. Young's **Burrampooter** (9-30-73, Wallack's), was the season's opener at what most playgoers still looked upon as New York's most distinguished theatre. Craven's comedy got its laughs at the expense of human greed. Charles Mulcraft (E. A. Sothern), "a gentleman by profession," married Mrs. Mulcraft (Mrs. John Sefton), "a lady by inference," in the belief that she is rich—in fact, that she is the Barwise heir. Of course, Mrs. Mulcraft accepted his proposal in the belief that Mulcraft himself is rich—in fact, the Barwise heir. After complications in which a fraudulent will plays a prominent part, the Barwise heir turns out to be Ellen Petworth (Dora Goldthwaite), the very girl Mulcraft had jilted in his desperate search for an easy berth. Sothern portrayed Mulcraft as a lugubrious fool, always grabbing someone else's handkerchief whenever he was about to have a good cry. The *Herald* saw his costumes and makeup, including his slightly outlandish whiskers, as "being after the true fashion of the English swell of doubtful pursuits." In the shorter piece, Sothern was the nervous Augustus Thrillington, who must rid himself of a she-dragon of a mother-in-law, Mrs. Major Pucker (Mme Ponisi), especially after she gets it into her head that Augustus is philandering. He is not—though he would like to.

The season's first new hit was **The Geneva Cross** (10-1-73, Union Square), a play written by George Fawcett Rowe at Palmer's behest after Rowe had outlined the story for the producer. Rowe's plot was uncomplicated. Gabrielle LeBrun (Rose Eytinge) wins her father's consent to her marrying Riel de Bourg (Charles Thorne, Jr.), although LeBrun (John Parselle) had preferred she marry his overseer, Mathew Moineau (F. F. Mackay). Bitterly disappointed, Moineau determines to be revenged. The Franco-Prussian War gives him his opportunity, for while Riel has revealed he is of noble birth, he has concealed the fact that he is a Prussian. Moineau claims that Riel is a Prussian spy and has Gabrielle and her father arrested for concealing him. Taken to a fort to await execution, Gabrielle is confronted by Moineau, who offers to effect her release if she will divorce Riel and marry him. She refuses. Just as she is being led to her death, Prussian forces break through and rescue her. The *Times* hailed the play as "a melodrama of a superior kind" with "more coherency in the development of the plot than we usually see in such productions." Praise was also awarded to Richard Marston's excellent settings, including LeBrun's luxurious home and the grim fortress. And for Rose Eytinge, back on Broadway after years of traveling in Europe and the Orient, the show was a turning point.

· · ·

Rose Eytinge (1835–1911) was born in Philadelphia and raised there and in Brooklyn. She made her acting debut in Syracuse in 1852, then spent ten years in stock before first appearing in New York. In 1864, she became leading lady to Edwin Booth. Later she played opposite J. W. Wallack, E. L.

Davenport, and John Sleeper Clarke. Before returning to Wallack's ensemble she created the role of the maligned wife in Daly's 1866 *Griffith Gaunt.* She left Wallack's briefly to originate the role of Laura Courtlandt in Daly's 1867 *Under the Gaslight.* Black-eyed and black-haired, with facial features that hinted at her Jewish background, she was a temperamental performer who sometimes chided audiences or walked off the stage if playgoers were not properly responsive.

. . .

The Geneva Cross (an old name for the Red Cross organization) ran until mid-November, initiating a series of hits at the Union Square that allowed the theatre to ride out the economic turmoil far more successfully than any other Broadway playhouse. Clara Morris headed a touring company, while licensed mountings were quickly unveiled at the Boston Museum and in San Francisco.

Max; or, The Merry Swiss Boy (10-6-73, Broadway), by England's prolific H. J. Byron, was a vehicle for J. K. Emmet. It was essentially another of the period's prototypical musicals, with another of the plots turning on a recognition scene so favored by the star. It was also another failed attempt to capitalize on the success of *Fritz, Our Cousin German,* so when box-office sales languished, Fritz himself was rushed back in two weeks later. At Booth's on the same night, the 6th, Joseph Jefferson gave way to the equally popular Maggie Mitchell. Like her predecessor, the petite, curly-haired gamine offered only one play, her established vehicle, *Fanchon, the Cricket,* with its story of a wild, slightly mysterious country girl whose goodness wins over the family of the man she loves.

Whatever its faults, Wood's, no doubt reflecting the inherent nativism of less elitist houses, was virtually alone among Broadway's major theatres in persisting to try out new American plays. **The Life and Death of Natty Bumppo** (10-13-73, Wood's), a fresh theatricalization of Cooper's Leatherstocking tales, survived only one week, but it did wave the flag and give the aging Edward Eddy his last significant new lead.

Competing revivals drew playgoers on the 18th. Wallack's again hauled out *Our American Cousin* for Sothern, while Daly, increasingly desperate to keep the Grand Opera open, brought back his own *Under the Gaslight.* In good measure because of the panic, business had slumped markedly, prompting Daly to reduce prices to fifty cents for all seats. Yet nine nights later, on the 27th, he replaced his melodrama with his semimusical *Round the Clock.*

The 27th also summoned forth the season's ritziest gathering of first-nighters to welcome back Lester Wallack, so long absent from his own stage. His return was as Charles Marlow in *She Stoops to Conquer.* Unlike the *Herald,* which often continued to bewail older men's playing younger parts, the *Times* observed, "We do not know where to look for any younger actor who promises to place before us so complete a picture," going on to explain its satisfaction: "His bashfulness in the first scene with *Miss Hardcastle* is an instance of the method by which an artist may keep his audience in roars of laughter without once verging on the borders of buffoonery. His one touch of nature, when *Hastings* is about to leave him alone with *Miss Hardcastle* and he implores him to remain in a tone which very nearly becomes affecting in its intensity, would alone stamp him as a true artist. All his 'business,' too, is exquisitely finished—observe his by-play with his riding-whip and his hat."

The busy night saw a third interesting revival. The Olympic presented *Rip Van Winkle* without Jefferson. In his stead was Robert McWade. As far as Broadway playgoers were concerned, McWade was scarcely the renowned, increasingly endearing figure that Jefferson was. But critics and his fellow professionals knew that he was a superb actor who toured indefatigably along routes rarely traveled by his more illustrious rival. His New York notices were highly favorable. Reviewers suggested he leaned more strongly than Jefferson on the immediate humor and pathos of the character, but most agreed his was an intelligently independent interpretation. His reward was a month's engagement, an excellent showing all things considered.

Edwin Booth returned to his failing home on November 3. He began with *Hamlet,* and his production included some interesting departures from tradition. For one, in the scene in which Polonius hides to eavesdrop on Hamlet's conversation with Ophelia, Booth had Polonius attempt to slink stealthily across the stage. Hamlet spies him out of the corner of his eye. He pretends not to notice, but the action confirms Hamlet's suspicions. In the four-week stand Booth also appeared in *The Lady of Lyons, Richelieu, Much Ado About Nothing, Brutus, Don Caesar de Bazan, Othello, The Merchant of Venice,* and a double bill of *The Stranger* and *Katherine and Petruchio* (the standard contemporary version of *The Taming of the Shrew*).

With three theatres to manage, Daly had probably bitten off more than he could chew, especially with economic hard times at hand. On the same night Booth returned, Daly mounted *Under the Gaslight* at the Broadway. This was not the same production he had mounted a few weeks before at the Grand Opera. After all, each theatre had its own company to be kept active, and the sets at the huge opera house were probably too large for the smaller stage at the Broadway. So everything had to be done over—and all for a single week's run.

Roped In; or, Lost in New York (11-3-73, Wood's) was yet one more example of how domestic drama continued to find an outlet away from the fancier theatres. The play was by Dominick Murray, a favorite at the house, and he also assumed a leading role. His story, filled with dramatic curtains, centered on Rose Ransome, an heiress who is hounded by a vicious guardian uncle. When he attempts to make his son, Paul (Murray), marry her for her money, she flees to New York. There she is protected by "an exceedingly ubiquitous street Arab," until she discovers that Paul truly loves her. In the end the uncle is literally roped in and carted off to jail. Scenes depicted places familiar to New Yorkers, including Vanderbilt's railway terminal, a popular dry-goods store, a pawnshop, and, most tantalizing, "a bird's-eye view of Union Square." The play returned for a second week later in the season, then faded from view.

On the 10th another Daly revival vied for attention with a revival at Wallack's. The attraction at the Grand Opera was Daly's *A Flash of Lightning*, his sensation-melodrama revolving around a jewel theft. At Wallack's the play was the always dependable *Ours*. More interesting was Daly's offering of **The New Magdalen** (11-10-73, Broadway). Technically this was not a new play. Another version of the novel had been presented briefly at Wood's the preceding June, and Bella Pateman had been featured in a few special performances earlier in the season at Booth's. But this was Wilkie Collins's own dramatization of his book, a dramatization he wrote for the very leading lady heading the cast, and he personally directed the production. (He took bows from a stage box at the ends of the acts.) The basic story was not all that complex. Believing Grace Roseberry to be dead, Mercy Merrick (Carlotta Leclercq) assumes her name and place. What Mercy does not know is that a delicate operation has saved Grace (Bella Golden). Grace returns to confront the impostor. But while Mercy is genuinely contrite, Grace is cruel and unforgiving. It is Mercy who must come to Grace's aid when Grace's behavior becomes so violent that she is to be committed to an insane asylum. Mercy prepares to leave the home where she has been welcomed under false pretenses, but she is followed by Julian Gray (H. H. Wood), a young curate who perceives her fundamental goodness.

Miss Leclercq overwhelmed patrons. One reviewer reported that in the interview between the women, "at every fresh insult her face and her whole body acted, though she spoke no word, and the short dry sobs, the gasps of anguish that came from her overladen bosom, found a response everywhere throughout the audience. But when her rival has gone too far; when . . . she has sneered at her remorse, and denied her penitence as all a pretense to enlist the sympathies of the charming curate— then the crouching, bending form, bowed in the very agony of shame, became erect and queenly, and the hunted becoming the hunter, spurns away the idea of penitence and defies the true *Grace Roseberry* to prove her identity or to wrest from her the hold which she had won in the feelings of the inmates of the house, then the audience, electrified by the passion and force of the actress, found a vent for their excited feelings in stormy and tumultuous applause." Despite such high praise the play lingered only three weeks, but its fitful start on American stages hardly mirrored the years of success ahead for it.

W. S. Gilbert's fantastic blank-verse comedy **The Wicked World** (11-17-73, Union Square) provided a refreshing change from the period's standard theatrical fare and was welcomed accordingly. Its action takes place in an idyllic fairyland floating somewhere in the clouds. This obviously make-believe world is dominated by women, who in turn are ruled by Queen Selene (Clara Morris). Their tranquil ways are disrupted when a male fairy, Lutin (Stuart Robson), returns from a visit to Earth—a place so shockingly wicked that he is left almost speechless. The disbelieving ladies decide to bring two mortals to fairyland to see for themselves. They interrupt a duel between Ethais (Charles Thorne, Jr.) and Phyllon (McKee Rankin) and transport the men to their domain. Selene falls madly in love with Ethais and gives him her ring as a token of her affection. But another fairy, Darine (Maude Granger), also falls in love with Ethais. She wangles Selene's ring from him and confronts the queen with her coup. For a time the idyll seems shattered, until the men are sent back to Earth. Most critics admired the play, but many held reservations about American actors' abilities to cope with the stylized techniques required to display Gilbert at his best. Writing of the men, the often querulous *Herald* snapped, "They dressed their hair like young butchers and swaggered more outrageously than a New York politician or a Washington lobbyist." There were no such reservations about Marston's superb single setting, which conveyed precisely the requisite unworldliness and spaciousness. The play, which may have been a stopgap mounting, lingered only three weeks. A shorter, noisier, more earthbound comedy, **Conjugal Tactics,** served as a curtain raiser.

Opposed to the opening at the Union Square was John E. Owens's return to New York, rather surprisingly at Wood's, where he unquestionably elevated that house's somewhat questionable standards. His repertory, on the other hand, included no surprises, consisting entirely of such old standbys as *Solon Shingle, Victims, Everybody's Friend, Forty Winks, The Heir at Law, The Poor Gentleman, The Toodles,* and *Married Life.* His wife, not always the most reliable historian, recorded that he did excellent business for a whole month. One point in his favor was that he traveled with his own company of actors and did not use the theatre's roster of regulars, whom one critic branded "the worst that ever permanently took up its quarters in this City."

Although Bartley Campbell's New York fame lay in the not too distant future, he had begun to make a name for himself in Chicago. His **Hearts** (10-20-73, Hooley's, Chicago) was deemed by one Chicago paper his "best effort" and praised by another for its "situations of real power" and its "vivacious dialogue." What reviewers could not see was that Campbell would cling for all of his career to the tawdry, if then still effective, melodramatic devices he employed in it. Agnes is engaged to, and later married to, George Gartney, who keeps entering whenever Dr. Thorne appears to be wooing her. Of course, George always miscontrues what he sees and grows increasingly angry. So when Thorne is found murdered, George is suspected. Agnes goes mad but is restored to good health and an exonerated George after a tramp is shown to be the killer. The play did not prove popular, although it was performed in South Dakota as late as 1879. Thorne was originally played by Nate Salsbury, later so important to America's early musical theatre and circuses.

For all the respect still showered on old comedies, most of these plays, like all of Shakespeare's at the time, were rarely presented in the original versions. Thus when Wallack's revived Foote's *The Liar* on the 22nd, it was not Foote's unadulterated text that was employed but rather Charles Mathews's truncated version. Few critics complained, since that practice was so common and, more important, Wallack's mountings so exceedingly fine. Lester Wallack as Young Wilding, "the unapproachable" John Gilbert as Old Wilding, and Jeffreys Lewis as Miss Grantham walked away with the notices. But these same reviews revealed that Wallack was not above employing contemporary ideas of what a

20th-century writer might term "production values." The play's first act was set in St. James's Park. Comparatively cheap labor allowed the producer to include a fashionable promenade, all in correct period costumes, and a scene showing the changing of the guard. If these discreet spectacles affected the comedy's pacing, no one remarked on it. Filling out the bill was Tom Taylor's delightful comedietta *To Oblige Benson,* in which a couple attempt to cover up their friend's wife's imprudent flirtation.

Edwin Adams began a month's stand at the Olympic on the 24th, opening with his widely acclaimed Enoch Arden, then moving on to *The Marble Heart.* This story of a woman who gives up everything for wealth had long been a favorite vehicle for Laura Keene and other emotive actresses, but Adams had shown hidden riches in the role of the self-sacrificing artist, Raphael, and successfully readjusted the play's balance. He also offered *Richard III* and *The Dead Heart.* When Adams closed his engagement, the Olympic responded to economic turmoil by abandoning the legitimate fold and converting for a time to a vaudeville house.

December 1 saw two well-liked couples take up residence. The Florences came into Booth's for a fortnight, offering *The Ticket-of-Leave Man* and *Eileen Oge,* while at the Broadway the Lingards presented their customary grab-bag of comedies, dramas, sketches, and variety turns. Their major efforts were *A Life's Dream* on the opening bill and a week later a freewheeling version of Dumas's **Diane,** which told of a woman's doomed love for an artist. Interestingly, their company was billed as the Lingard-Dunning Combination Troupe. The term "combination" was only then coming into standard usage to indicate a group of actors touring together with their own scenery—the 20th-century "road company"—and reflected the change away from stars touring on their own, a change brought about by improving railroad service. Dunning, of course, was Alice Lingard's maiden name.

The trouble Daly was encountering in his attempts to keep the Grand Opera and Broadway on an even keel had been compounded for many months by a third difficulty. Throughout the summer and autumn Daly had been watching his new Fifth Avenue Theatre take shape at 28th and Broadway. In those preunion days theatres had been restored after devastating fires or built from the ground up at speeds that would shame modern malingerers. However, the Fifth Avenue had been beset by a series of frustrating delays. Daly had hoped to open it by late September or early October. Instead the gala first night took place several months later and proved anything but gala. The evening began with Fanny Morant reciting a special greeting composed by Oliver Wendell Holmes and moved on to the principal attraction, a work written for the occasion by London's James Albery and titled, ironically, **Fortune** (12-3-73, Fifth Ave.). Its heroine, Kitty Compton (Fanny Davenport), is housekeeper to the snobbish Major Hawley (Charles Fisher). When his artist son, Tom (George Clarke), falls in love with Kitty, the major fires the girl. Happily, Kitty's discharge coincides with her learning that she has come into a large inheritance. She buys all of Tom's paintings and marries him. So chilling was the reception that before the final curtain the producer posted a backstage notice announcing next-day rehearsals of a replacement.

Salt was rubbed into Daly's wounds when, immediately thereafter, an upstart rival house scored the season's biggest hit. The success proved a first-rate theatre piece could triumph over a panic. **Led Astray** (12-6-73, Union Square) was Boucicault's adaptation of Octave Feuillet's *La Tentation*. Its heroine, Armande (Rose Eytinge), has grown fond of poet George de Lesparre (McKee Rankin), but, considering herself happily married to Count Rudolphe Chandoce (Charles Thorne, Jr.), she resists the poet's overtures. Then she learns of Chandoce's affair with Suzanne O'Hara (Eliza Weathersby). The poet, playing on Armande's shocked sensibilities, calls on her and begs her to become his mistress, at which point Chandoce suddenly enters the room. He challenges the poet to a duel. However, Chandoce has recognized his wife's determined loyalty, so he purposely shoots to miss. His honor satisfied, he promises he, too, will be faithful ever after.

Typical of Marston's effective sets was the "Park and Grounds of Chateau Chandoce" for the first act. Using only part of the stage's depth and resorting to wing-and-drop construction, a relative rarity at the Union Square, he flanked his picture with "tree wings" and furnished flower pedestals, tables, and chairs downstage. Three steps led to a small terrace at the rear. More stairways and a view of the handsome grounds were all painted on a flat, the theatre's raked stage accentuating Marston's careful perspective. Yet Marston worked mainly with material from the storeroom, so, according to Palmer, the cost of scenery was only $300. Believable situations, taut writing, fine acting, and an elegant mounting combined to earn a run of 161 performances.

Of course, even the greatest successes fail to please some people. In this instance one detractor was none other than Miss Eytinge, who thought the heroine, particularly in the last act, "so replete with 'sweetness and light' " and so bathed in "a spirit of humility and submission, that I found it rather insipid." In her autobiography she asserts that she took it on herself one evening to change the heroine's last major speech into a more fiery, liberated one—and received a justified reprimand for her audacity.

Palmer agreed to pay Boucicault 5 percent of the first $2500 of the weekly gross and 15 percent of everything above that figure, but when he learned that the greedy, duplicitous Boucicault had not paid a penny to Feuillet, although the production had averaged $1000 a performance during its run, the producer wrote the French playwright offering to deal with him directly thereafter. This sort of behavior won Palmer the respect of playwrights worldwide and brought him scripts he might not otherwise have been given.

On the 8th Daly restored *Old Heads and Young Hearts* and had three more plays ready on three of the four succeeding evenings at his new Fifth Avenue—*New Year's Eve, Alixe,* and *London Assurance*. He did all this while rehearsing yet another new play.

The night of Daly's first revival, Wallack's returned *Home* to its more leisurely repertory, coupling it with J. J. Williams's farce *Ici on Parle Français*, in which owners of a boardinghouse must take over for their disgruntled help. The struggling Lyceum offered a revival of *The Lady of Lyons* on the 11th. A certain bitterness must have eddied around the production, for its star was Charles Fechter, who had conceived the refurbishing of the theatre and then been forced out. But audiences had no cause for concern. His performance of Claude Melnotte was as effective as ever. Still, the mounting survived a mere two weeks.

Just over a month earlier, Wilkie Collins had directed his own dramatization of *The New Magdalen* for Daly. Now the men had a second and seemingly even more promising production to offer, Collins's theatricalization of his best-selling **The Woman in White** (12-15-73, Broadway). Sir Percival Clyde (Charles J. Fyffe), in league with Count Fosco (Wybert Reeve), attempts to acquire the wealth of his wife, Laura (Helen Tracy). To this end he buries a mysterious, demented woman in white who remarkably resembles Laura, claims it is Laura he has buried, and has Laura committed to an insane asylum under the dead woman's name. His scheme is exposed and, in a change from the novel, he drowns attempting to escape. The count is murdered by a secret society. Laura, released, is free to marry another man. Reeve, a cool, calculating actor who had performed his part many times in England, dominated the evening. However, he was not famous enough to lure American patrons. Daly lowered prices as he had before at the Grand Opera. When this failed he closed the show and abandoned management of the theatre, which went over to musicals and then to vaudeville.

Meanwhile, at Booth's, Chanfrau came in on the same night with his hardy perennial, *Kit, the Arkansas Traveller,* enjoying a month of good business.

Daly came a cropper again with his second new offering at his new house, **The Parricide** (12-17-73, Fifth Ave.), taken from a French play, *Les Saltimbanques.* Two traveling mountebanks, Daccolard (Charles Fisher) and Lubin (William Davidge), murder a woman and frame her gadabout son, Laurent (George Clarke), for the deed. He is acquitted at his trial but ostracized by society. Determined to prove his innocence convincingly, he enlists the support of a detective, Roulé (Frank Hardenberg). The pair use a series of disguises to help unearth the necessary evidence. Critics divided on the merits of the play but were in accord about Daly's excellent mounting. A setting depicting a provincial circus, complete with acrobats and animals, drew particular praise. By no means the failure that *Fortune* had been, the play nonetheless ran only two and a half weeks.

The busy Boucicault had another translation from the French ready with **A Man of Honor** (12-23-73, Wallack's). His source was the younger Dumas's *Le fils naturel.* Jacques de Sanlieu (Lester Wallack) learns he was born out of wedlock, a blot that may preclude his marrying his beloved Renée (Jeffreys Lewis). Happily, the kindhearted Marquis de Rosny Latour (John Gilbert) takes him under his wing and secures him a post in Egypt, where he earns numerous honors. He returns home to marry Renée and to convince his father to marry his mother. The work was played skillfully as high comedy, although some may have snickered at the fifty-four-year-old Wallack portraying yet one more twenty-year-old. As always, the mounting was impeccable. One reviewer proclaimed the fourth-act setting—the library at Villa Rosny—"the most exquisitely artistic thing of the kind ever presented in the City."

E. L. Davenport, his reputation sagging and apparently unable to find a better berth, came into Wood's for two weeks beginning on the 23rd. Wood's mediocre supporting company and its stock scenery probably did little to help, although by and large critics handed the star very favorable notices.

His programs consisted of *Hamlet, A New Way to Pay Old Debts, Black-Eyed Susan, Jack Cade, Wild Oats, Oliver Twist, The Merchant of Venice,* and *Damon and Pythias.*

Theatrically, 1874 was ushered in with Daly's revival at the Fifth Avenue of another Wilkie Collins work, *Man and Wife,* on January 3. Daly used the occasion to introduce American audiences to an English actress, Ada Dyas. The response was disappointing, in part because the role of Anne Sylvester did not show off the intelligent, refined actress's virtues to best advantage. She would perform to more acclaim later and elsewhere. A week afterwards, on the 10th, *Saratoga* rejoined the repertory.

Agnes Booth, who was the wife of Junius Brutus Junior and had won prominence as an actress in Boston, opened in Adolphe Belot's **La Femme de Feu** (1-12-74, Booth's), which retained its French title (but with English capitalization).

· · ·

Agnes Booth [née Marian Agnes Land Rookes] (1846–1910) was born in Sydney, Australia. She made her American debut as a child dancer in San Francisco in 1858 and subsequently spent several seasons playing small parts at Maguire's Opera House, using the name Agnes Land. She had changed her stage name to Mrs. H. A. Perry by the time she first appeared in New York in 1865, when she portrayed Florence Trenchard in *Our American Cousin.* Shortly thereafter she played opposite Edwin Forrest. She married Booth in 1867 and followed him to Boston when he became manager of a theatre there. A small, attractive if not beautiful woman, she was noted for the clarity of her speech and, at a time when actresses still provided their own costumes, for her stylish dresses.

· · ·

Mrs. Booth played Diane Bérard, who loves the impoverished Lucien D'Aubier (Joseph Wheelock) but marries the rich, decrepit Baron de Séry (H. A. Weaver) for his money, hoping he will die soon. When he does not, she poisons him. She marries Lucien, who has risen to become a prosecuting attorney, and when she learns he is not totally faithful to her, she reveals her crime. Lucien must decide whether to bring her to trial or ignore what he has discovered. His problem is solved when Diane's would-be lover, Lami (H. F. Daly), also learns the truth and attempts to blackmail her. She rebuffs him, so he kills her, then kills himself. The *News* welcomed Mrs. Booth as "the most finished and effective emotional actress at present on the metropolitan stage," a sentiment echoed by many other reviews, most of which also assailed her supporting company as beneath her. One paper also complained of the "exasperating" musical accompaniment, noting that each of Diane's entrances and exits was underscored by a repetitive motif always played by a single clarinet. The play described Diane as a woman who loved to bathe in the sea at night, so one tableau showed her, with discreetly dim lighting, doing just that in a "phosphorescent sea." Not yet the renowned star she would eventually become, Mrs. Booth could sustain a run of only three weeks.

On the 17th Wallack's resurrected *Money.* It was hardly a rarity at the house, but for reasons now lost it proved the biggest success of that theatre's season, running through the first week in March without the injection of other plays from the ensemble's large roster. Of course, Alfred Evelyn was considered one of Lester Wallack's best interpretations. Yet Wallack's regulars were quite familiar with it, and the rest of the cast was unexceptional. Is it preposterous to wonder if the title was some sort of inexplicable lure at a time of economic hardship?

Money—and all the joys or headaches it brings—was also the subject of **Folline** (1-27-74, Fifth Ave.) adapted by Daly and his brother Joseph (who often worked as an uncredited co-adaptor) from Sardou's *Maison neuve!* Success in business has turned the heads of Folline (Ada Dyas) and her husband, René (D. H. Harkins). They take a grand apartment, start pushing their way into society, and look about for pleasant liaisons on the side. But difficulties arise when René's cashier absconds with funds and when bankruptcy threatens. To make matters worse, Folline's little affair with Count de Marsille (Louis James) takes on a frightening aspect after the count attempts some very drunken advances and Folline gives him a narcotic that will calm him. Instead he collapses just as René arrives with friends. Folline believes the count is dead and must hastily hide the supposed body. Happily, René's thoughtful uncle, Genevoix (Charles Fisher), appears on the scene to bring matters to a satisfying ending. Her acting of the title role allowed Miss Dyas to counterbalance the disappointing impression she had made at her debut. The *Herald* reported, "Miss Dyas gave culture, refinement, and the natural impression of highly wrought passion to the *rôle* of Folline, and was powerfully emotional in the ingenious situation in the last act, where the wretched wife is in agony lest her husband shall discover the concealed body of the count." The comedy was rewarded with a month's run.

At the end of January, Charlotte Cushman de-

lighted oldtimers with a series of readings, returning in April for a second series.

Agnes Booth abandoned one Belot drama for another with **Elene** (2-3-74, Booth's). This time she was the wife of a banker, Georges Montant (Joseph Wheelock). Elene's father, Count de Seran (H. A. Weaver), steals a large sum of money an American, Mr. Markett (Shirley France), has entrusted to Georges. Elene determines to make up the loss by going to Spa and trusting her luck at the gaming tables. She has won back almost every franc when a final turn of the wheel loses all for her. In despair she confronts Markett with the whole story. Touched by her bravery and candor, and confessing that he loves her sister, Markett destroys the receipt Georges had given him. The best act was the third, set in a glittering, bustling reproduction of the gaming room at Spa and enlivened by the comic carryings-on of one Mme Trebizonde (Mary Wells), a regular at the tables. The curtain fell with the last, fatal turn of the wheel and rose on two succeeding tableaux, showing Elene's increasingly despairing response. The *Times* confirmed earlier appraisals of the star when it noted, "She has grace and tenderness, exceptional experience, and a knowledge of her powers which guards her against exaggerations in delivery." At the very end of the play's three-week stand, Mrs. Booth offered single performances of *The Lady of Lyons* and *Romeo and Juliet,* both of which earned her long, laudatory reviews in the better papers.

For the second time in the season, Cooper's tales of Hawkeye and the Indians he dealt with were set onstage. This version was by its star, George Fawcett Rowe, and was called **Leatherstocking; or, The Last of the Mohicans** (2-16-74, Niblo's). Critics complained Rowe overreached his grasp, one reviewer observing that a plot summary provided with the program ran for six pages. As always at Niblo's the spectacle was excellent, with a retreat by a waterfall and the massacre at Fort William Henry eliciting loud applause. Many of the supporting players garnered high praise, especially J. B. Studley for his malevolent Magua; F. F. Mackay, who had done such fine work at the Union Square, for his General Montcalm; and petite, hoydenish Fanny Herring, darling of the gallery gods at the Bowery and other working-class theatres, as the heroic Uncas. The show ran three weeks before making way for a better American play.

A hint of the luxuriant Shakespearean revivals that would become a Daly trademark was offered at the Fifth Avenue on the 21st, when the producer mounted a "most graceful, most studious, and most ornamental presentation" of *Love's Labours Lost.* It was all the more interesting for being the first professional production of the play in New York. The cast included Ada Dyas as the Princess, Fanny Davenport as Rosaline, D. H. Harkins as the King, George Clarke as Biron, Charles Fisher as Don Adriano, and William Davidge as Holofernes. The playing was superb, and what flaws there were in the acting were glossed over by Daly's sumptuous costumes and settings. The *Herald* reported, "The skill with which the sense of atmosphere and expanse was given to the forest scenes was delightful. The tableau of winter showed an ice-hung scene, in the midst of which a snow-clad figure sang the strongly picturesque lines beginning, 'When icicles hang.' Spring was indicated by a Watteau tableau of great brilliancy. Cunning shepherds and shepherdesses sat on mossy elevations, fountains gurgled, arbors twined, gloomily green vistas opened, dazzling flowers and foliage spread seeming fragrance and rich growth, and over all fell a shower of changing lights." The production ran only one week, but it shored up Daly's reputation, which had begun to crack in recent months.

Some felt that star and play were mismatched when Fanny Janauschek, now performing in a thickly accented English, appeared in **Chesney Wold** (2-23-74, Booth's), a dramatization of Dickens's *Bleak House.* Her appearance was all the more remarkable for her assuming two roles: Lady Dedlock, who long before her marriage had a child, and Hortense, the coquettish yet vicious maid who had once served Lady Dedlock and knew her secret. Dissenters felt that Miss Janauschek was better at high tragedy than in such comparatively subdued melodrama, but the star and her admirers disagreed, so the play remained part of her permanent repertory, although it was often called simply *Bleak House.* After performing the work for three weeks she turned to other plays in that repertory, in two weeks' time offering *Deborah, Mary Stuart, Medea, Come Here, Macbeth,* and *Henry VIII.*

The artistic success of Daly's *Love's Labours Lost* was followed by the most commercially successful new offering of his shaky season, W. S. Gilbert's **Charity** (3-3-74, Fifth Ave.). It was another courageous venture on the part of the producer, for Daly was well aware that the play had not been well received at its London premiere six weeks before. The play spotlights the problems of Mrs. Vanbrugh (Ada Dyas), who years ago had given birth to a child out of wedlock but who has genuinely repented and become an exemplar of one who does good deeds for their own sake. Jonas Smailey (Frank Harden-berg), by contrast, is an ostentatious churchgoer and spouter of pious platitudes. He is also a hypocrite, a cheat, and a forger. He attempts to expose Mrs. Vanbrugh's past in order to gain a fortune she is slated to inherit. His own vileness is exposed in time for a happy ending, but not before Gilbert has shown society's uncharitable response to Mrs. Vanbrugh when her old sin is disclosed. Many playgoers thought Fanny Davenport virtually stole the evening. This gorgeous clotheshorse abandoned, as she had in 1871's *No Name,* her customary stylish elegance to assume the minor role of the tawdrily dressed Ruth Tredgett "with matted, straggling hair and furtive, hunted eyes." Daly and his cast were rewarded with a six-week run, toward the end of which, on April 6, was added Theyre Smith's short comedy **My Uncle's Will,** in which two youngsters must marry or lose an inheritance. Davidge walked away with honors in this one as the crotchety Barker, whose animal hospital benefits if the couple refuse to wed.

Davy Crockett, which had been seen earlier in the season at Wood's, came into Niblo's on March 9 with Mayo heading the cast, and it launched a brief spate of revivals. The same night Wallack's brought out *The Heir at Law,* with *The Rivals* added once again to the program a week later. The 16th also saw Boucicault start a fortnight's stand at Booth's in his *The Colleen Bawn.* On the 23rd Wallack's dusted off *Central Park.*

Frederick Marsden's **Zip; or, Point Lynde Light** (3-30-74, Booth's) was the latest in Lotta's specially tailored vehicles. Little Zip is raised in a fishing village near Anglesey and led to believe she is the daughter of a lighthouse keeper. He is murdered by men who are determined to sink a passing ship and who attempt to black out the light and set up a false beacon. Zip thwarts them, then learns one of the passengers she has saved is her mother. She also discovers she is an heiress. Taken into society, she is courted by yet another villain, who threatens to reveal she was born out of wedlock. Zip unearths a birth certificate and marriage certificate, proving him a liar. She eventually finds the man of her dreams. Replete with all of Lotta's dances, banjo playing, and other stock in trade, the piece enjoyed three weeks of good business and entered into the star's permanent repertory.

April's first offering was a revival of *The Veteran* at Wallack's on the 4th. Like *Money* before it, its nearly month-long stand was uninterrupted by other plays.

If there was an irony to so many new or refurbished theatres opening in the depths of a ghastly economic slump, there were additional ironies for anyone familiar with the playhouses' histories. The Lyceum had been planned by and taken away from Fechter, who nevertheless played there briefly. Now Fechter was the star at the unveiling of another new house, the Park, at Broadway and 22nd—which was supposed to have belonged to Boucicault but which he had lost. The theatre opened on April 13 with **Love's Penance,** Fechter's own transcription of d'Ennery's *Le Médecin des enfants.* Dr. Karl (Fechter) has married and had a daughter by a girl he loves, who believes her first husband, Count Rockland (J. B. Studley), is dead. The count suddenly appears. The shock kills the wife; the count, insisting that in law the child is his, takes the baby girl away. Years pass. Clarissa (Geraldine Stuart) is now grown to a marriageable age and has fallen in love with a young artist, Frank Maube (Henry Dalton), but the count, who has otherwise neglected her, insists she make a better marriage. Karl, now calling himself Hartreck, appears on the scene and quickly realizes that Clarissa is his long-lost daughter. He attempts to persuade the count to let the girl marry whomever she chooses and challenges him to a duel when he refuses. Karl is mortally wounded. Returning to the house, they find Clarissa apparently dead from shock. Her dying father sees a flicker of life in her and manages to bring her back to consciousness. The remorseful count agrees to honor the doctor's last wish—that Clarissa marry Frank. One critic wrote of Fechter, "We have had many occasions to point out his emotional power in depicting the passions of youthful, enthusiastic love, but never until last night did we see him in a character in which he could manifest the still higher passion of lofty, self-sacrificing, almost sublime paternal love. . . . Fechter paints this emotion with a master hand. . . . [His] electricity is marvelous." The physical production was also praised, particularly a library scene and a farm setting with a half-reaped field and mountains in the background. For all the high praise, the play ran less than a month.

Children born out of wedlock were getting to be almost as common a motif as false accusations, but the device was used with careful charm and skill in Dumas's **Monsieur Alphonse** (4-14-74, Fifth Ave.). Monsieur Octave (George Clarke), determined to wed a shrewish, nouveau riche ex-waitress, Mme Guichard (Fanny Davenport), decides to dump his illegitimate young daughter, Adrienne (Bijou Heron), on her mother. That woman is now Raymonde Montaglin (Ada Dyas), the wife of a well-to-do, loving French naval officer, Captain Montaglin

(Charles Fisher). Adrienne is not aware Octave is her father, knowing him only as Monsieur Alphonse, but she has been told Raymonde is her mother—at the same time she has been warned not to acknowledge the fact. The Montaglins are so taken with Adrienne that they have adoption papers prepared. Meanwhile, Mme Guichard has learned the truth, and to keep Octave under her thumb she also prepares adoption papers. A tug-of-war for possession of the child seems imminent until Adrienne has a bad fall and Mme Guichard, seeing Raymonde's concern, has a change of heart. Little Bijou Heron, daughter of Matilda Heron, all but walked away with the audience's affections. The *Times* noted, "This little girl is a marvel of precocity; her delivery is not a succession of words learned by rote, but the thoughtful utterances of feeling, and her looks and bearing seem touched by the sweet sad spell of an overclouded childhood." The single setting of the Montaglin drawing room reflected the new craze for everything Japanese in its low furniture, hangings, and vases. The play chalked up forty-six performances, a decent run considering the times.

The Lyceum was rescued for a time from musicals and variety bills with the presentation on April 20 of **La Marjolaine.** The titular heroine (Fanny Foster), the illegitimate, abandoned daughter of a French marquis, is the rival of her half-sister, Antoinette de St. Ramon (Phillis Glover) for the hand of Desir Henrion (Eben Plympton). Desir marries Antoinette, but when the Revolution comes both are sentenced to death. The self-sacrificing Marjolaine contrives their escape and takes her half-sister's place at the guillotine. F. F. Mackay, still not needed at the Union Square because of the long run of *Led Astray,* received approving notices for his subtle but cold portrayal of Robespierre.

Even more ecstatic notices greeted Adelaide Neilson when she began a two-week engagement at Booth's on the 20th. New York had seen her in all three plays before—*Romeo and Juliet, As You Like It,* and *The Hunchback*—but in her case familiarity bred admiration. The *Herald* said simply, "The actress walks the stage the incarnation of the poet's thought."

Daly, having relinquished control of the Broadway earlier in the season, gave over his management of the Grand Opera House at the end of March. The first new bill under the new operators was the return of the Florences at the beginning of April. Their initial offerings were the same plays they had performed in December, but for the final week, beginning on the 21st, they offered a double bill of revivals: *Inshavogue,* a tale of an outlaw's attempt to find his lost daughter, and *The Returned Volunteer,* a blackface comedy.

They left to make way for **Donald McKay, the Hero of the Modoc War** (4-27-74, Grand Opera). The play was yet one more vehicle for Oliver Doud Byron, already celebrated for his part in *Across the Continent,* although the *Times* seemed to think he was making his debut. Less than a year earlier the *Times* and every other major newspaper had devoted columns to the uprising of the Modoc tribe in the Northwest, their bloody attempt to reclaim lands ceded to the American government, their initial victories, and the final long siege with the Indians hiding in the area's lava beds. The new play was a semi-fictional, naturally somewhat romanticized account of the war. Its final scene was played out in an eerily lighted recreation of the lava beds that won loud applause. Acknowledging that the play would appeal to the working-class audiences for whom it was designed, the *Herald* added that it nonetheless had "the usual fault of the Western drama—a perfectly astonishing quantity of bowie knife and pistol eloquence."

April's last offering was a revival of *School* at Wallack's on the 30th.

John McCullough, generally acknowledged as heir to the traditions, and even some of the roles, of Edwin Forrest, returned to New York after a spell as manager in San Francisco.

. . .

John [Edward] **McCullough** (1832–85) was born in Ireland but was sent to live with relatives in Philadelphia after the death of his mother, when he was fifteen. He quickly took an interest in local amateur theatricals, then came to the attention of Edwin Forrest. The great actor adopted the youngster as a protégé, thereby determining both his pupil's style of acting and his repertory. For many years he played second leads to Forrest. Later he assumed the management of San Francisco's California Theatre, in conjunction with Lawrence Barrett. Apart from an appearance as Othello to Booth's Iago at a benefit in September of 1869, this was his first New York engagement in nearly a decade.

. . .

Starting with *The Gladiator* at Booth's on May 4, he moved on to *Richelieu, Hamlet, Damon and Pythias,* and *The Stranger.* The *Tribune* alluded to his inheritance when it spoke of his acting "under the shadow of such a reminiscence of past renown," but it joined other papers in praising his "vitality" and "uncommon force."

With one minor exception, May was given over entirely to revivals. The mounting of *The School for Scandal* at the Lyceum on the 4th starred Jane Coombs. Critics admired her often lusty but knowing Lady Teazle. New Yorkers, however, barely knew her, for her fame rested largely on the road. So she was able to chalk up only one week of disappointing business before returning to the hinterlands. On the 12th Daly brought out *Divorce* at the Fifth Avenue.

Perhaps the most interesting revival was the Union Square's restoration on the 14th of Matilda Heron's version of *Camille* as a showcase for Clara Morris. She had played it for one performance earlier in the season at a charity benefit, and her interpretation had caused alarm. She refused to see Camille as a vulgar or harshly cynical or cruel woman—the way the role had so often been depicted before. Instead she played her as an intelligent but misguided girl, far more to be pitied than censured. She played not to convey a moral lesson but to tug at heartstrings. And her success was total. The performance was a triumph, abetted by a superb, understanding cast that included Charles Thorne, Jr., as Armand and John Parselle as M. Duval.

The only novelty of the month was Martha Lafitte Johnson's **Justice** (5-18-74, Wood's), dealing with a man's attempt to avenge his sister's dishonor. The play was of little value, but it gave New Yorkers an opportunity to see the rising Louis Aldrich in the leading role. Curiously, the matinee bills that the house offered daily featured Aldrich in another of Mrs. Johnson's plays, **Fun,** a work most critics chose to overlook.

To capitalize on the recent successes of Bijou Heron and Fanny Davenport, Daly closed out his season at the Fifth Avenue with a production of *Oliver Twist* on the 20th. Young Bijou played the title role to Miss Davenport's Nancy. Davidge as Bumble, Fisher as Fagin, James Lewis as the Artful Dodger, and Louis James as Bill Sykes were among the strong cast.

Two nights later Wallack's won applause for its revival of *The Clandestine Marriage.*

After McCullough completed his solo engagement at Booth's, he lingered on for one additional week to join in a special production of *King John* on the 25th. McCullough was Faulconbridge; Agnes Booth, Constance; and Junius Brutus Booth, Jr., the King. Reviews were courteous rather than genuinely warm, although there was high praise for the settings, which again were hailed, in the popular fashion of the day, as historically accurate. The mounting served as a valediction, for when it closed the Booth family signed over control of their theatre to a more commercially minded management.

The failure of Booth's Theatre to become the "temple of drama" Edwin Booth had envisioned was not the first notable failure of such a dream in Broadway history. As it still is, Broadway was first and always more interested in good theatre than in great art. It would welcome high purpose and salute it when it succeeded, but it could not or would not sustain it. The washing-out of Fechter's hopes for a "national theatre" at the Lyceum had underscored this truism, as would the fate of the New Theatre, the Civic Repertory Theatre, the American Repertory Theatre, the Lincoln Center Repertory, and other such Olympian enterprises in ensuing decades. Certainly any house given over primarily to classic tragedy could not survive. Wallack's, which flourished for over thirty years, did so by emphasizing the great old comedies, interspersed with polite modern dramas, but even this lively theatrical museum—for that is what it was in its heyday—shied away from Shakespearean and other high drama. The more venturesome Daly was steadily putting distance between himself and tragedy and would eventually prosper on a brilliant mixture of modern and Shakespearean comedy. For the time being, the Union Square was home to the best modern drama, usually from the French. Other houses seemed to make do with whatever was available. High art and high drama became the province hereafter of a handful of dedicated theatre folk who would take bookings as they could find them. For all practical purposes the palmiest days of Shakespearean drama in America began an unyielding decline with the passing of Booth's Theatre from family hands. And history would show that this decline eventually led to a general rejection of all older plays. In the nineties "up-to-date" became a popular catchphrase whose vogue would be reflected in most theatrical production.

Meanwhile, two more revivals ended the month. Charles Thorne, Sr., who was father to the handsome matinee idol and who spent most of his long theatrical career traveling the hinterlands, produced a series of lushly mounted dramas at Niblo's, beginning on the 25th with *The Lady of the Lake.* Fading Edward Eddy must have been happily surprised to find himself at so major a house playing Roderick Dhu. Wheelock was Fitz James; Ione Burke, Ellen; and Edith Challis, Blanche. The version was probably not the same dramatization of Scott's poem that New Yorkers had first seen over seventy years before, but its drama and spectacle—with a complete ballet and highland drills—pleased

Niblo's regulars. On the 26th Wallack's raised its curtain on a double bill of standbys: *Woodcock's Little Game* and *The Nervous Man.* These were the final offerings of Wallack's own season, but the theatre was soon home to a new play.

That play, **Fate** (6-1-74, Wallack's), was the first of two to brave Broadway in June that were written by the same young playwright, Bartley Campbell.

* * *

Bartley [Thomas] **Campbell** (1843–88) was born in Pittsburgh, where he began his career as a newspaperman. He later worked for newspapers in Louisville and Cincinnati before founding the *Southern Monthly Magazine* in New Orleans in 1869. With the success of an 1871 Pittsburgh production of *Through Fire,* he abandoned journalism and attempted to earn his livelihood solely by playwriting, albeit he also served as a producer and director. As a result he often contends with Bronson Howard for the honor of being our first totally professional dramatist. In 1872 he moved to Chicago, there helping R. M. Hooley convert a theatre from minstrelsy to drama and writing plays for the theatre.

* * *

Fate was one of the dramas Campbell had written for Hooley's Theatre, and it had been presented there in January 1873, after which the author sold the rights to Carlotta Leclercq. It was she who brought it to New York, playing Helen Faraday, a loving but suspicious wife who divorces her husband, Frank (Theodore Hamilton), after she discovers he has fallen for the gold-digging June Temple (Miss Lillie). But when Frank's business and health both fail, June proves callous and uncaring. Helen returns to nurse Frank, and a reconciliation follows. The *Tribune* saw the work as "a play of slender merit—whether on the score of invention or that of intellectual treatment of character, emotion, and significance of thought—but it is commended by the domestic sentiment and by the interest of the domestic story." Although Miss Leclercq never achieved the broad-based acclaim most discerning critics felt she was entitled to—she was neither strikingly beautiful nor excessively emotive, but a finely disciplined artist—her coterie of admirers saw her through a three-week run.

The Cryptogram; or, Lost and Won (6-15-74, Niblo's), a dramatization of James DeMille's best-selling Canadian novel, was Thorne's next mounting. Hilda Krieff (Rosa St. Clair) is obsessed with her jealousy and hatred of Zillah (Ione Burke), the part-Indian daughter of an English officer, especially after Zillah weds Lord Chetwynde (Joseph Wheelock), the very man Hilda had hoped to marry. She comes upon a coded letter, which she attempts to decipher and which, according to her reading, besmirches the name of Zillah's father. She also intercepts letters that Zillah and Lord Chetwynde send each other and substitutes forged ones that lead to a breach in the marriage. Only when the forgery is exposed and a correct decoding is made is Hilda exposed. The twists of plot include a dramatic rescue and, with echoes of *East Lynne*, a deathbed scene in which the lady Lord Chetwynde has always assumed was his father's housekeeper confesses she is his mother, who years after deserting her husband and child returned unrecognized under another name. A panorama of the Mediterranean coast was a scenic high point. Critics felt the dramatization was as confusing and unsatisfactory as Hilda's decoding, so the production was withdrawn after a week, whereupon Thorne attempted to produce **The Two Sisters; or, The Deformed** (6-22-74, Niblo's). Palmer went to court and succeeded in obtaining an injunction after the first performance, since he held the American rights to the French original. As *The Two Orphans*, his transcription would be one of the smash hits of the coming season.

Two other plays opened the same night. For her final week, Carlotta Leclercq offered her version of *East Lynne*, a version in which the villain is exiled for life. The third opening was Campbell's other play, **Peril; or, Love at Long Branch** (6-22-74, Union Square). Its plot reverses the essentials of *Fate*, for here a husband, Ralph Hayden (M. A. Kennedy), becomes upset when his wife, Laura (Maude Granger), flirts with an adventurer, Lord Hagar (H. W. Mitchell). Ralph's friend, Dick Rothley (McKee Rankin), advises Ralph to give Laura a taste of her own medicine. But Ralph's flirtation only prompts Laura to attempt to elope with Hagar. Dick's intervention eventually sets matters aright. The *Graphic*, echoing the *Tribune*'s comments about *Fate*, observed, "There is some good dialogue, and the situations are sufficiently inspiring to draw applause from the audience; but there is a want of motive, or rather a lack of dignity of motive in the working out of the plot which prevents any active exercise of sympathy." Despite an initial run of only two weeks, *Peril*, in one form or another, held the stage for many years. It had first been produced at Philadelphia's Chestnut Street Theatre in early 1872 and thereafter, with frequent revisions, was produced elsewhere before New York saw it. Later it remained popular on the road, sometimes under its original title, sometimes as *Flirtation*. Campbell made more drastic revisions and revived the play in 1880 as *Matrimony*. *Fate* also was produced with

some regularity until the end of the century, although more fitfully in America than in England.

At Niblo's the elder Thorne continued with two more short-lived spectacles. *Ivanhoe; or Rebecca, the Jewess*, on July 1, was the latest of numerous uncredited versions that had been staged in New York since 1820. Variant versions of *Faustus; or, The Demon of the Dragonfels*, which appeared on the 13th, had been seen as far back as 1827. Although all the principals garnered attractive notices—Wheelock for his athletically agile heroes, Eddy for his unusually subdued Isaac of York and Mephistopheles, Ione Burke for her Rebecca and Aldine (read Marguerite), and Ida Vernon for her Rowena—it was the elaborateness of the mountings, so expected at Niblo's, that was awarded most space. The lively and colorful tournament and trial by combat in the dramatization of Scott's novel and the vividly graphic hellfire in *Faustus* were singled out for particular mention.

Charles Gayler's **With the Tide** (7-29-74, Union Square) was a vehicle written for Katie Mayhew, one of the many young ladies attempting with varying success to dance in Lotta's footsteps. The play's heroine is an orphan girl, Jennie Markland (Miss Mayhew), who is adopted by a rich Virginia family and selflessly assumes the blame for her adopted sister's indiscretions. Either the play was too good for the slapdash treatment Lotta and her ilk imposed on their vehicles, or else Miss Mayhew, as future events would suggest, had more ambition than flair. The *Times* slapped her wrist for being "prone to introduce character sketches and songs which . . . interfere a little with the continuity of the play." Still, without competition from major stars, she managed to keep the show before the footlights for four weeks.

Thorne wrote *finis* to the season with a pair of August productions at Niblo's. (The interim between these and his earlier mountings at the house had been given over to the New York premiere of the long-popular musical burlesque *Evangeline*.) On the 10th he presented a dramatization of Reade's *Griffith Gaunt*—not Daly's version—and on the 24th raised the curtain on *The Bride of Adydos;, or, The Pirate of the Isles*, which in one version or another had been bringing Byron's poem alive since 1818. This version was credited to William Diamond. The banks of the Hellespont, Hero's Tower, and numerous Oriental settings all contributed to making the show a visual treat, although one paper registered an interesting though hardly new complaint about "placing tediously prolonged front scenes on stage, with the view of allowing time to make the elaborate sets ready."

1874–1875

The 1874–75 season proved to be an exceedingly rewarding one, brimming over with an enlivening variety of superior plays and productions. If fewer dramas and comedies appeared before the footlights than in preceding seasons, that mattered little and was easily explained. First of all, with hard times persisting a demand for totally escapist entertainments grew, so many stages were turned over to less intellectually exhausting musicals and vaudevilles. Second, the season enjoyed more long runs than any previous theatrical year. The result was that playhouses had less need for rapid turnovers. Indeed, for all practical purposes New York had only five first-class auditoriums devoted to nonmusicals, although such lesser houses as the Bowery and Wood's Museum continued to offer patrons a steady program of works that would have instant appeal to less particular playgoers.

The season's opener, Boucicault's **Belle Lamar** (8-10-74, Booth's), was a harbinger of the excitement. It was produced with advance ballyhoo unusual for the time, promoted as an initial step in establishing a national drama. The ballyhoo, according to one paper, had "the effect of setting expectation on tip-toe." Quite probably, expectations were raised too high and a tumbling down was inevitable. Nevertheless, to paraphrase a modern critic, *Belle Lamar* was the sort of play that gives failure a good name. What Boucicault attempted was a serious drama about the Civil War—and to some extent he succeeded. Many scholars consider this, despite its flaws, the first important work dealing with the war. What tripped up Boucicault was the inescapable fact that he was too much a man of his own day and own theatre. His drama remained melodrama, replete with too many subordinate characters and twists of plot or subplots to deal earnestly and deeply with his principal story and figures.

Isabel Lamar (Katherine Rogers Randolph), a Virginia belle, has divorced her husband, Colonel Philip Bligh (John McCullough), a Union officer, in order that she might help the Confederacy. She returns north, allows another Union officer, Captain Marston Pike (Frederick Warde), to fall in love with her, and induces him to give her the army's plans, which she forwards to Stonewall Jackson (F. F. Mackay). She is caught and brought before a tribunal headed by Bligh, but she staunchly refuses to divulge the source of her information. To save her, Pike admits his guilt. Pike is sentenced to death, but through the pleadings of Jackson and another southern officer, Belle is spared and given a pass to return south. She contrives to give the pass to Pike, allowing his escape. But he also warns Bligh of an impending Confederate attack. Bligh holds out until relief comes. In time, he and Belle are reconciled.

Probably the play's cardboard heroism and facile happy ending contributed less to its failure than did disappointing performances, especially that of McCullough, for whom Boucicault is said to have written the piece. McCullough was so ensnared in the old Forrest school of acting that he could not handle the relatively quiet, realistic style required by the part. The English-born Warde, who was just embarking on an American career and who received many of the best notices, also recalled that either Boucicault or McCullough insisted on McCullough's appearing in a glitteringly new uniform even though Bligh was supposed to have been battle-weary. Of course, there were compensatory touches in both the writing and presentation. Boucicault was careful to balance rights and wrongs on both sides. The play opened with an effective scene on the banks of the Black Adder River, with soldiers from opposing forces waiting for a battle to begin and passing time by singing. The play had a decent run of five weeks but never entered into Boucicault's most popular canon.

Another interesting disappointment was the debut of the celebrated English comedian John Lawrence Toole on August 17 at Wallack's. His main offering was James Albery's **Wig and Gown,** coupled with *The Weavers,* his version of Thomas Haynes Bayley's *The Spitalfields Weaver.* In *Wig and Gown* Toole portrayed Hammond Coote, an addlepated barrister so impecunious that he is in danger of losing his most beloved possessions—his wig and gown. While trying a case dealing with a huge inheritance, he accidentally discovers that he is the rightful heir. Toole's reception was qualified. He was clearly a gifted comedian, but not one whose gifts were so exceptional as to propel him into the very front ranks in America. Moreover, many of the plays he chose seemed too English for American audiences. Although his engagement was interrupted by an injurious fall, he quickly returned and eventually won a grudging acceptance.

The Union Square relit on the 19th with the return of Charlotte Thompson in *Jane Eyre.* She had clearly honed her art in this most celebrated of her roles. By now the *Times* could report, "She has caught all the traits of the character with wonderful fidelity. The intense inner life of the helpless orphan, her fervent nature, her womanly pride, all are vividly presented in Miss Thompson's portraiture. . . . She produces effects without any semblance of striving after them; and when the deeper feelings of her nature come into play, their action is spontaneous and real."

Daly, not yet having hit upon the line that would bring him real fame or fortune, began his season with his brother's disastrous dramatization of Edmond About's novel *Germaine*, reset in England and called **What Should She Do?; or, Jealousy** (8-25-74, Fifth Ave.). Its morbid, grotesquely involved plot centered on the two marriages of Lord Basil Clavering (George Clarke). His first had been to Dianthe de Marec (Fanny Davenport), whose first husband was believed lost at sea but later was reported still alive. Clavering has his union with Dianthe annulled, and to protect the child of the marriage from the taint of illegitimacy, he marries Lady Elaine (Sara Jewett), the supposedly dying daughter of an impoverished earl. In the hope of recruiting her health, he takes her and their child to Jamaica. At this point Dianthe learns that her first husband finally has died. In order to be able to remarry Clavering, she sends a servant to Jamaica to poison Elaine. The small doses prove tonic rather than deadly. Dianthe sails over to see what she can do but soon realizes that she has lost not only her murderous gamble but her husband and child. The *World*'s famous critic Nym Crinkle summed up many an observer's ambivalence about the evening, calling the dramatization "a bad version of M. About's story" but continuing, "The demerits of the play belong to literature; its excellences to the stage. . . . But the playwright [Daly, as usual, took public credit for his brother's work] proves himself a good stage manager, and if he has not produced a play he has at least trotted out all his people. This, so far as he is concerned, then is exhibition, not execution." In fact, although Fanny Davenport was showing increasing talents as an emotive actress, Daly's company was not well suited for this sort of piece, as a better-acted, more morbid play shortly would show. Daly quickly withdrew it.

With Toole temporarily indisposed because of his accident, Wallack's hurried in the great minstrel Dan Bryant in two famous Irish vehicles. Beginning on the 27th, he cavorted in *Handy Andy* and *The Irish Emigrant*. By the 31st Toole had recovered enough to appear in a second double bill, consisting of the aging

Paul Pry and a new vehicle written for the comedian, **Off the Line,** the story of a railroad engineer who inadvertently makes his wife jealous of him.

In the wake of his opening failure, Daly fell back on revivals, bringing out *The Fast Family*, Benjamin Webster's translation of Sardou's comedy of manners *La Famille Benoîton*, on September 5. Bandying first nights back and forth at Wallack's on the 7th Toole, while retaining *Off the Line*, replaced *Paul Pry* with *Ici on Parle Français* and Tom Taylor's farcical sketch *Our Clerks*, in which the comedian shone as John Puddicombe, a solicitor's bumbling apprentice.

The ball bounced back to the Fifth Avenue on the 12th with Daly's presentation of *The School for Scandal*. Daly retained virtually all of the original dialogue but reordered it so that each act could be performed in a single setting. The practice of revamping classics was so common that complaints were few and muted. The increasing strength and experience of the company was now such that it could give Wallack's a run for its money in mounting comedies that had been considered for a time the province of the older theatre. Their excellent interpretations included Fisher's Sir Peter, Davidge's Oliver, Louis James's Joseph, George Clarke's Charles, Fanny Davenport's Lady Teazle, Mrs. Gilbert's Mrs. Candour, and James Lewis's scene-stealing Moses.

If classics still in the standard repertory were tampered with as a matter of course, long-neglected masterpieces were sometimes more drastically revised when they were dusted off. Otway's *Venice Preserved* had held the boards steadily well into the 19th century, only to all but disappear in recent decades. The revival at Booth's on the 14th was taken in hand by Boucicault, who deleted the subplot of the conspiratorial Pierre's affair with Aquilina and inserted a whole speech from Byron's *Marino Faliero* for the troublemaker. McCullough played Pierre with "a rough straightforwardness." Warde was Jaffier, and Fanny Brough, in her debut, was Belvidera. The old tragedy, perceived as damagingly dated, ran one week.

The first of the season's major successes was **The Gilded Age** (9-16-74, Park). George Densmore had made an unauthorized dramatization of Charles Dudley Warner and Mark Twain's novel and had presented it in San Francisco the preceding year. Clemens threatened suit, forced Densmore to waive his royalties, and then rewrote the piece. The play's principal story focused originally on the seduction of Laura Hawkins (Gertrude Kellogg) by Col. George Selby (Milnes Levick) and on her killing of him. It was typical period melodrama, and not very good at that. But the story found comic relief in the person of Col. Mulberry Sellers (John T. Raymond), an impoverished visionary forever concocting grandiose scheme after grandiose scheme and always certain "there's *millions* in it!" For example, he devises a plan to corner corn, and if that fails he will corner hogs—and feed them the corn. All the while he lives in abject, comically genteel poverty, offering his guest raw turnips and water and asking gravely, "Do you like the fruit?" William Winter wrote, "He had exceptional command over composure of countenance. He could deceive an observer by the sapient gravity of his visage, and he exerted that faculty with extraordinary comic effect. . . . Personality was the potent charm of Raymond's embodiment of *Colonel Sellers,*—a personality compounded of vigorous animal spirits, quaintness, rich humor, recklessness, a chronic propensity for sport, a sensitive temperament, and an ingenuous mind. The actor made the character lovable not less than amusing, by the spontaneous suggestion of innate goodness and by various scarcely definable sweetly winning traits and ways."

The characterization was immediately recognized as one of the most masterful and memorable of the era, so Twain and Raymond, possibly with Warner's assistance, further revised the work to minimize the melodrama and spotlight Sellers. Although Twain publicly implied he had been generous in dealing with Densmore and Raymond, who may have had a hand in the original dramatization, Palmer's private memoirs reveal that his terms actually were so stringent that Raymond's weekly draw was slight and that after a year of playing the part he was "utterly impecunious." Nonetheless, Raymond recognized the vehicle's other values to his career. As a result, the play, which chalked up 119 performances in its initial stand, served as a vehicle for the star for the rest of his career, sometimes offered under its original title but just as often as *Colonel Sellers.*

The 16th also witnessed a change in Toole's bills at Wallack's, the latest offering being H. J. Byron's *Dearer than Life,* in which Toole played a father who assumes blame for his son's misdeeds.

The Sphinx (9-21-74, Union Square) was the opening attraction when Palmer's company reassembled for the season. George Fawcett Rowe had done the translation of Octave Feuillet's original. The production suggested that great acting could overcome a play's ugliness, something Daly had failed to accomplish with his own season opener. A restless woman, Blanche (Clara Morris), whose husband is

away in the navy, lives at the home of her father-in-law in the company of her married friend, Berthe de Savigny (Charlotte Thompson). Berthe's husband, Henri (McKee Rankin), is alarmed by what he believes is Blanche's baleful influence on his wife and decides to take Berthe away. Blanche confronts Henri, tells him of her own love for him, and realizes that he loves her but will never admit it. She concludes the only way to happiness is to poison Berthe, but at the last moment her compunction gets the better of her, so she swallows the poisoned drink she has prepared. The magnificent settings, showing the elegant chateau's rooms and its nearby woods, were much admired. But Clara Morris's performance was the electrifying centerpiece of the evening. The *Times* critic, George Edgar Montgomery, noted, "Miss Morris' hurried declaration and strange intonations [she never totally lost her midwestern accent] and abrupt transitions are . . . in keeping with the part, while her genuine force has full scope for display." However, it was her horridly vivid death scene which became the talk of the town. The *Times,* which did not approve of such ghastliness, described her "eyes upturned, pallid face, foaming mouth, and hands clutching at her bosom— the waist of her dress being torn open in the agony of the moment." Her performance kept the play alive for five weeks and could have kept it on the boards longer, but the actress's growing displeasure with the role made her demand that Palmer withdraw it.

The 21st also saw the return to Booth's of Mr. and Mrs. Barney Williams, a couple long welcomed in typical Irish plays of the time. Their month-long stand began with three weeks of one of their most demanded vehicles, *Connie Soogah,* and concluded, in the week of October 12, with a double bill of *The Fairy Circle* and *The Custom of the Country.*

Toole wound up his engagement at Wallack's when he acted in H. J. Byron's **Uncle Dick's Darling,** beginning on the 26th. Its story told of a kindly peddler's problems with his adopted "niece."

When Toole departed, Wallack's opened its regular season with another new Byron play, **Partners for Life** (10-6-74, Wallack's). The trivial piece begins with the arrival of Fanny Smith (Jeffreys Lewis) at the home of Horace Mervyn (John Gilbert), where she promptly steals the heart of Ernest (J. B. Polk), who is engaged to Mervyn's niece, Emily (Dora Goldthwaite). Mervyn's nephew, the young lawyer Tom Gilroy (Henry J. Montague), appears on the scene and just as quickly winds both ladies around his finger. However, "Miss" Smith turns out to be Gilroy's ex-wife, whom he had left in a pique when he discovered she was wealthier than he. A servant precipitates some complications before the youngsters are properly partnered, this time for life. The play quickly disappeared, but for many playgoers—especially the more impressionable ladies in the audience—it served to introduce them to Henry J. Montague, an Englishman whose astonishing good looks, charm, and suavity made him an instant matinee idol. His accomplished acting, most smooth in lighter contemporary pieces, also impressed critics. No doubt he was hired by Lester Wallack in reluctant acceptance of the critical sniping about Wallack's own assumption of roles he was too old to play. His very early death was to cut short his career, but for years his legend survived, much like that of Valentino or James Dean in later times.

On the 10th Daly brought out an unusual triple bill at the Fifth Avenue. The first piece could hardly be called a play. Rather, **The Hanging of the Crane** was a recitation of Longfellow's poem, backed by a series of tableaux illustrating the story. It was followed by **The Two Widows**, a translation of Félicien Mallefille's comedietta. When Edgar de Brenne (George Clarke) meets Celine (Sara Jewett) and Francine (Fanny Davenport), two widows who share a country house, he falls in love with the former. Celine demurs, so Francine and Edgar stage a love scene to awaken Celine's jealousy. The ruse works. The lively Miss Davenport, dressed in pearl gray, and the birdlike Miss Jewett, dressed in black and playing with "her wonted simplicity and elegance," made a striking contrast. The evening concluded with *The Critic*.

A week later Daly had a new offering ready, Bronson Howard's **Moorcroft** (10-17-74, Fifth Ave.). Howard, who based his work loosely on John Hay's short story *The Foster Brothers*, outdid Boucicault in complexity. Reduced to its most basic elements, the story recounted how Russell Moorcroft (Louis James), a Georgia plantation owner in 1840, forges a will that indicates his adopted brother, Cyril (D. H. Harkins), is the son of an octoroon and therefore actually his "black" slave. When Russell encounters financial difficulties he puts Cyril on the block. Katherine Mordaunt (Annie Graham), who loves Cyril, purchases him and offers to set him free but then learns that he, in turn, loves Virginia St. Johns (Sara Jewett). Katherine becomes so vindictive that Cyril and Virginia flee to France. Eighteen years elapse. During that time Cyril has become a distinguished French lawyer under the name Alfred Lavergne. Virginia has died, and Alfred has raised their daughter, Marie (Emily Rigl). Now Alfred brings Marie to America, where the girl falls in love with Russell's son, John (B. T. Ringgold). Katherine learns of Alfred's presence and confronts him with the fact that under American law he is still her slave. Luckily, Marie's innocent sweetness melts Katherine's resolve. However, just as Marie and John's wedding is to begin, Russell appears. He is persuaded to confess his old crime, and, to the strains of Mendelssohn's "Wedding March," the wedding proceeds.

For many the success of the evening was little Emily Rigl, who had first come to America as a ballerina and still bore marked traces of her European accent. But even sumptuous settings and beautiful costumes—"too beautiful to be worn in real life"—could not provide sufficient sparks to kindle the convoluted drama. The play ran just two weeks, and its savage treatment in the press provoked Daly to write the *Herald* to complain that American playwrights were not given a proper chance to develop their art. He concluded, "American press writers are proud of everything American except other American writers."

On the 19th, while Wallack's returned *The Rivals* to its repertory, two great ladies of the theatre began engagements. At the Lyceum, Adelaide Neilson offered her Beatrice in *Much Ado About Nothing* and suffered one of her few failures, which she redeemed with a few performances as Juliet. Perhaps she was fortunate that most eyes were on Booth's, where Charlotte Cushman began what was really her farewell stand. Indeed, everyone knew that this time she was not bluffing. Supported by George Vandenhoff, another figure out of the fast-receding past, she opened with *Henry VIII*. The *Times* called her Katharine "little short of perfection. The ease and naturalness of her enunciation—which almost conceals the fact that she is speaking in blank verse, while she never loses the fine rhythmical effect of verse, never steps down into that common-place level of speech which some actors mistake for naturalness—cannot be too much commended." In subsequent evenings she moved on to her Lady Macbeth and her Meg Merrilies. For the final night tickets were raised to $2, but even that could not deter playgoers. Unlike her contemporary Edwin Forrest, Miss Cushman ended her long Broadway career in a blaze of glory. She gave some performances and readings in other cities and died early in 1876.

Wallack's revival on the 21st of *The Romance of a Poor Young Man* gave Montague a better chance to demonstrate his excellences than his debut had, and the mounting prospered accordingly. Five nights later, on the 26th, Clara Morris was starred in the

Union Square's restoration of *The Hunchback,* which had served as a showy vehicle for actresses ever since the days of Fanny Kemble. Critics divided on Miss Morris's ability to tackle this older-style melodrama, but her loyalists kept it onstage for three weeks, which Palmer claimed was an American record for the bewhiskered drama.

Another of Bartley Campbell's Chicago premieres was **The Virginian** (10-26-74, Hooley's, Chicago), a play that raised some hackles and eyebrows but went on to have an interesting history. In the early days of the Civil War, Vandyke Vernon is staying at an inn when the innkeeper's daughter-in-law, Kate Calvert, is told her husband has been killed in action. By the time the war is over, the loving, thoughtful Van has married Kate and they have had a daughter. But Kate's first husband, Richard, suddenly appears, saying he was only wounded and spent the war in a prison camp. In contrast to Van, he is hard and cruel. He demands that Kate never see Van or her daughter again. When she tries to leave to see the child, Richard catches her and tells her she is to be kept as a prisoner in his house. One Christmas, when Richard is away, Kate does manage to sneak out to the home of a warmhearted if boozy lawyer, Ananias Jingle, where Van has left his daughter in hopes that Richard will relent once he knows Van is not around. The effort is too much for Kate, and she dies. In London the play was mounted with a "happy ending," which had Richard dying and Kate surviving. The change brought charges of immorality, so the play failed. In the States it toured profitably for twenty years. Yet while it made two visits to Brooklyn, it never bothered to cross the river into Manhattan. In the initial Chicago production James O'Neill was Vandyke, and Nate Salsbury was Richard; William H. Crane, not yet a star, assumed the role of Ananias. Frank Mayo spent a season touring in the drama, which was sometimes called *Van, the Virginian.*

With the failure of *Moorcroft,* Daly brought back *The School for Scandal* for a couple of performances, then revived *The Belle's Stratagem* on November 4.

On the 9th Joseph Jefferson opened at Booth's in *Rip Van Winkle* and beguiled audiences for three weeks. The next evening Daly ushered in *Masks and Faces* at the Fifth Avenue, with Fanny Davenport as a lusty Peg Woffington.

Having taken bad tumbles with his attempt at native American drama and his try at resuscitating an old classic, Boucicault returned to the Irish themes that so often had served him well and scored one of the biggest hits not only of the season but of the era with **The Shaughraun** (11-14-74, Wallack's). While Robert Ffolliott (J. B. Polk) is under sentence of death for his Fenian sympathies, his sister, Claire (Ada Dyas), and his fiancée, Arte O'Neal (Jeffreys Lewis), live with him on his estate. Corry Kinchela (Edward Arnott), who covets the estate, plans to have Robert captured. Although Ffolliott is caught, Captain Molyneaux (H. J. Montague), the officer sent to arrest him, falls in love with Claire. Kinchela then learns that a pardon is at hand, so he attempts to persuade Ffolliott to escape, hoping to kill him as he does. Conn, the Shaughraun (Boucicault), a vagabond who is "the soul of every fair, the life of every funeral, the first fiddle at all weddings and parties," helps Robert make good his dash for freedom. Kinchela shoots Conn, leaves him for dead, and takes the girls captive. They are rescued, Kinchela is jailed, and the two pairs of lovers are free to wed.

Although there was praise for the excellent supporting cast, in particular Harry Beckett as the craven informer, Harvey Duff, and Montague's sturdy Captain Molyneaux, there was little dispute that Boucicault carried the play, and carried it handsomely, with what the *Herald* called his "intense good humor and ready wit." The *Times* acquiesced and then went on to extol the work, exclaiming, "A wittier play, a drama more replete with brilliant dialogue, as well as absorbing interest, has not been produced during the past fifteen years." Settings for the prison and the ruins of St. Bridget's Abbey were singled out for applause, as was the staging of a wake. A run of 143 performances grossed a then whopping $220,000 (less than many Broadway shows now gross in a single week), and the play remained a revival favorite for years to come. The show was written thirty-five years after Boucicault's first success, *London Assurance,* and though his career would continue for another ten years or more, *The Shaughraun* was his last play to enjoy universally enthusiastic endorsement. A highly praised 1988 London revival proved the work had lost none of its theatrical punch.

Time and again genuinely native drama—American plays on American themes—first saw the limelight at lesser theatres. More often than not they quickly vanished from the stage; a lucky handful found some life moving from one minor theatre to another. Those native works that did move up into first- and second-class theatres were dismayingly few and far between, although it cannot always be gauged with any certainty whether the pretensions of more affluent, knowing playgoers or the works' inherent weaknesses were mostly to blame. (Of course, it should also be noted that these same minor play-houses frequently welcomed once admired works long after they had been dismissed as "dated" by voguish playgoers.) **Wild Cat Ned** (11-16-74, Niblo's), which Barrett Sylvester had adapted from a story in the *New York Weekly,* had been seen two seasons earlier at the Bowery; now it was allotted a week's stand at the faltering old playhouse on lower Broadway. A treacherous British deserter turns the Indians against a true red-white-and-blue western scout. His cabin is burned, and he must fell a tree to make a bridge over a chasm and escape his pursuers. The mounting at Niblo's featured twenty Warm Spring Indians in the cast. Broadway would not buy the play. "To the boys in the gallery," the *Herald* recorded, "the play was perfectly glorious, to the more critical spectators below it was amusing." Ned could fight treachery, but sneering sophisticates confounded him, so he quickly returned to his old haunts, where he survived for several more seasons.

On the 16th Charlotte Thompson, who had starred at the Union Square for a month in *Jane Eyre* before the official season began, played it again there for three weeks in midseason. Revivals also continued apace at the Fifth Avenue, with *Everybody's Friend* reappearing on the 20th, followed one night later by *The Heart of Midlothian,* in a version by the ubiquitous Boucicault that had been mounted years earlier as *Jeanie Deans* and as *The Trial of Effie Deans.* On the 23rd Edward Eddy began a week's starring engagement at Niblo's, recalling from bygone days such works as *Metamora, Pizarro,* and *William Tell.* At Booth's on the 30th, John Sleeper Clarke opened a fortnight's stand offering his interpretation of *Everybody's Friend* along with Byron's short **Red Tape,** in which he played Redmond Tape, a shrewd village lawyer who frustrates a false claimant's attempt to win an inheritance. Niblo's was equally frustrated in its attempt to reclaim its former glory. Increasingly far away from newer theatres and unimaginatively managed, it resurrected *Norman Leslie,* telling of a mysterious murder. After a week of poor business the play and the house closed while management attempted to work out future bookings.

Always looking for fresh fields, Daly decided to buck the ballooning vogue for French drama, the intermittent cry for more native works, and the still potent spell of the West End. He threw in his lot with a play that had become a raging success in Spain, Manuel Tamayo y Baus's *Un Drama Nuevo,* presenting it as **Yorick: A New Play** (12-5-74, Fifth Ave.). It put flesh on and breathed life into Hamlet's poor Yorick (Louis James), who is about to offer a new play dealing with the infidelity of its hero's wife. Walton (Frank Hardenberg), the company's tragedian, hates Yorick and uses the performance to alert Yorick to the infidelity of Yorick's own wife, Alison (Sara Jewett). Yorick kills her paramour, Edmund (B. T. Ringgold), then kills himself. Charles Fisher, made up to resemble Chandos's famous portrait, portrayed Shakespeare. The play sharply divided critics; some found it artful and moving, but more thought it artificial and leaden. Daly, who withdrew it after a single week of dismal attendance, was especially bitter about its failure. He never again tried a Spanish work and moved still further away from tragedy. A few years later, Lawrence Barrett would score a major triumph in William Dean Howells's translation.

While rehearsing its own new production, the company at the Union Square revived *Love's Sacrifice* for a fortnight beginning December 7. On the 11th the dismayed Daly sought the standard refuge of the era, beginning a series of revivals with *London Assurance,* featuring Fanny Davenport in her by then classic Lady Gay Spanker.

Booth's also fared poorly, with a cape-and-sword melodrama that announcements claimed had been written expressly for the theatre by Paul Feval and translated by George Fawcett Rowe. The work was called **The Hero of the Hour** (12-14-74, Booth's) and dealt with the attempt by the Duchess of Maine (Maude Granger) to overthrow the Regent of France. A fine French actor, Henri Stuart, was brought over to play the dual roles of Richelieu and the Cavalier Fortune. The management clearly had the highest hopes for the play and had spared no expense in mounting it, and critics were indeed flattering in their appraisal of the scenery. Matt Morgan's colorful recreation of the Place St. Antoine won high praise, as did a moving panorama of old Paris, which halted its progress long enough to depict a murder on a bridge while conspirators huddle in a boat under its arch. But the expense went for naught; the play was not so well liked and disappeared after two weeks.

The Fifth Avenue plodded on with its revivals, bringing out *She Stoops to Conquer* the same night the new play premiered, and *Man and Wife* two nights later, on the 16th.

The season's biggest success was **The Two Orphans** (12-21-74, Union Square). Odell, writing in 1937, went further, calling it "one of the greatest theatrical successes of all time in America." A few playgoers had attended an unauthorized version of Eugène Cormon and Adolphe d'Ennery's *Les Deux Orphelines* the preceding season at Niblo's, but

Palmer's injunction had brought that production to a swift halt. The two apparent orphans, Henriette (Kitty Blanchard) and her blind sister, Louise (Kate Claxton), are wandering the streets of Paris when they are seized upon and cruelly separated. Henriette is carried off to the chateau of a cynical nobleman, while Louise is forcibly brought under the wing of La Frochard (Marie Wilkins) and her son Jacques (McKee Rankin), who live by thievery and make Louise beg for coins, even in the snowiest weather, on the porch of the church at the Place St. Sulpice. Fortunately, both girls find protectors who save them from the most sordid debasement. Henriette is rescued by the handsome Chevalier de Vaudrey (Charles Thorne, Jr.), who helps her flee the chateau; Louise is aided by the Frochards' kind, crippled son, Pierre (F. F. Mackay). But when the chevalier's family learn of his affection for Henriette, they conspire to have her imprisoned at La Salpetrière and sentenced to exile. At the last minute a sympathetic fellow prisoner takes her place. Pierre stops his brother from seducing Louise and turns him over to the police. In the end the girls are discovered to be the long-lost daughters of the Countess de Linières (Fanny Morant).

By common consent the high point of the evening was the scene in the prison's courtyard. One by one prisoners are called forth to be hustled off to a waiting ship. An ascetic but warmhearted nun, Sister Geneviève (Ida Vernon), who has said that no circumstance ever justifies telling a lie, must identify each prisoner. The last name to be called is Henriette's, but it is not Henriette who steps forth. Rather it is the outcast, Marianne (Rose Eytinge). She glances pleadingly at the nun, who hesitates but then identifies the deceiver as Henriette. When the prisoners have gone, the sister tells the doctor she has spoken her first untruth, but he responds that heaven will mark it down to her credit. By coincidence, it was this scene that led Palmer to produce the play. His adaptor, N. Hart Jackson, who had originally bargained for the rights before losing his fortune in the crash, and who apparently worked from a literal translation by A. R. Cazauran, had thought the play better suited to a lesser theatre—though he tried peddling it unsuccessfully to Booth, of all people. After reading the prison scene, Palmer disagreed, but he did suggest some alterations to make the play more palatable to American audiences. Thus Hart minimized the role of the countess and fudged on her unsavory past. He also spared Pierre from having to kill Jacques, instead allowing the heroic de Vaudrey to rescue Pierre from Jacques's clutches and to arrest the brother. For

various reasons not every newspaper reviewed the play; the *Herald,* for example, was at odds with Palmer and studiously avoided all his productions. Yet those critics who did offer notices, and subsequent playgoers, shared Palmer's opinion, which deemed the cast near perfect. Mackay's compassionate cripple and Miss Eytinge's touching cameo role won rave notices, but the star of the show was clearly Kate Claxton.

. . .

Kate Claxton (1848–1924) was born in Sommerville, N.J., granddaughter of a minister and daughter of a lawyer, both of whom opposed her becoming an actress. She made her debut in Chicago in 1869, then played for a while opposite Charlotte Crabtree. She joined Daly's troupe in 1870, but dissatisfaction with her advancement there prompted her to leave. She was a small, slightly chubby, round-faced woman with a face of remarkably childlike innocence.

. . .

In later interviews Miss Claxton claimed to have traded some of her own clothes for the rags worn by an old applewoman and her daughter, had them boiled for sanitary reasons, and used them to poignant effect in the role. After the Union Square production she bought the rights to the play from Palmer and toured with it off and on until her retirement.

The production was as outstanding as the acting. There were seven settings in all, the most striking being the scene at the chateau with players in gorgeous pre-Revolutionary period costumes, although it was the snowy scene on the church porch that most playgoers remembered. The waits occasioned by changing from one elaborate, cumbersome setting to the next caused the play to run until nearly one in the morning, at least on opening night. (One reason for them seems to have been that the logistics of moving scenery was not Marston's forte, and William Sanders, who had handled such matters, died while the play was in preparation.) Critics complained, but not too strenuously, for such delays were regular occurrences in the theatre of the time. Atrocious weather hurt business the first few nights, but good notices and excellent word of mouth quickly pulled in patrons. So did an interesting editorial in the *Daily Graphic* that observed, "Were some of the clergymen who denounce the theater to witness a play as that of the 'Two Orphans,' they could not avoid modifying their opinions. Though French in its origin the play is so thoroughly wholesome in its tone and preaches so powerful a sermon against vice that its influence must be altogether good." In its original run the play grossed $192,896 and netted the theatre a profit of $90,000, enormous figures at the time. With or without Miss Claxton, the play held the boards for a half a century, a major revival coming in the late 1920s. It was also the source of D. W. Griffith's famous silent film *Orphans of the Storm*, though the producer made numerous changes in the story.

Meanwhile, Daly struggled along with revivals, *A New Way to Pay Old Debts* joining his list on the evening *The Two Orphans* premiered. On the 26th at Booth's, Matilda Heron and George Vandenhoff brought out *Macbeth* for two performances; they were followed on the 28th by a highly successful revival of George Fawcett Rowe's *Little Em'ly*, with Rowe himself as Micawber. That same night Daly offered *Monsieur Alphonse*, and the next evening he presented *Pygmalion and Galatea*.

Not all foreign performers were welcomed with open arms, as an English favorite, Mrs. [Clara] Rousby, discovered when she opened an engagement at the Lyceum on January 4, 1875. Her beauty was acknowledged, one critic remarking on her "fine *spirituelle* Marie Stuart face, full eyes, regular features." Nor was her acting seriously deprecated. But her gifts were not the sort to rival the best American actresses' or set new high standards, as many other foreigners did. Her bills consisted of *'Twixt Axe and Crown, As You Like It,* and *Camille.*

Daly's discouraging turnovers continued into the new year, with *The Palace of Truth* on the 4th and *The Merchant of Venice* on the 11th. That latter evening also saw the relit Niblo's venture a revival of *Uncle Tom's Cabin*. Some critics asked openly why the play was brought back after the issues it had espoused supposedly were settled, but the recent massacre of seventy-five blacks in Mississippi and attempts by carpetbaggers to seize state governments suggested those issues were not yet entirely laid to rest. Daly closed out his revival series with *Charity* on the 18th.

The producer had seen Charles Morton's **Women of the Day** (1-20-75, Fifth Ave.) done earlier at Mrs. Drew's Arch Street Theatre in Philadelphia and had liked what he had seen. In this "comedy of the period" Adelaide Livingston (Annie Graham), having been jilted by the man she loved, determines to poison the mind of his new sweetheart, Clara Hoffman (Sara Jewett). Clara's loyal friend, Mrs. Meta Mestayer (Fanny Davenport), moves swiftly to open Clara's eyes. New York did not fully share Daly's enthusiasm, but the play chalked up a profitable month's run.

On the 25th Niblo's dragged out Harry Watkins's Irish drama *Trodden Down,* with the perennially touring author and his wife as stars. It was replaced on February 1 with what could have been seen as either a highly daring or utterly desperate revival, the 1823 *Tom and Jerry,* and when this could not survive a whole week, *The Ticket-of-Leave Man* was offered. All through February Niblo's continued to mount old warhorses, sometimes hauling in cheap touring companies to fill the stage and sometimes adding vaudeville turns to the bill. By the end of March the management threw in the towel, and this once great theatre went dark for a year and a half.

On February 1, Bartley Campbell's **Grana Uaile** opened at Chicago's Academy of Music. Dan Kelley and Ann Murray, each for his or her own nefarious ends, conspire to make it seem that sweet little Mary Clare is unfaithful to Conner Kennedy, the young heir to Tullyrush. Eventually they imprison her in a ruined castle. Conner is arrested on suspicion of having murdered her. It takes Ryman O'Reilly, a wandering minstrel, to exculpate the hero and unite him with the heroine. Critics felt that the character of O'Reilly and many of the incidents were ripoffs of Boucicault. When the show was taken on tour it was rechristened *O'Reilly's Risks.* It played Brooklyn briefly, but Manhattanites were to see it only a decade hence in, ironically, a plagarized version under yet another title.

Carlotta Leclercq came back to the Lyceum on February 8 in *The New Magdalen,* but that return was overshadowed by another revival. Almost imperceptibly Shakespeare's hold on American stages had been weakening, although by 20th-century standards it remained amazingly strong. No better example could be given than the revival on the 8th, ironically at Booth's, of *Henry V.* The production was an interesting Anglo-American venture. It had been presented first by the great actor-manager Charles Calvert at his Prince's Theatre in Manchester. At the time, the theatre was considered the finest producer of plays in England outside of London; though Calvert had complete artistic control, it was owned and underwritten by an American with the rather Runyonesque name of Boston Brown. Mountings there were exceptionally elaborate and, in keeping with the vogue of the period, always laid claim to the most careful historical accuracy. Because Calvert himself was too ill to perform nightly, he hired the dashingly handsome George Rignold to play the title part. Indeed, Rignold's looks were such that a member of the supporting cast, Frederick Warde, still remembered him years later as "the perfection . . . of heroic manhood, a veritable Greek god in his regal robes." Several other members of the English company also came over, including Mrs. Calvert, who played Rumor. While not well, Calvert was able to recreate his original staging.

Yet the opening night came close to being a debacle, for Rignold was so nervous that he forgot his lines and "completely lost his self-control." Several critics surmised he, too, was ill. Good luck had it that the rest of the cast was in fine fettle and the scenery was a knockout. One critic insisted, "Nothing surpassing it—if anything equalling it—in historical accuracy, minuteness and refinement of color, has ever been looked upon in this country, the crowds painted upon canvas sometimes seeming to mingle, so deceptive the art, with the living masses in front of it." A recreation of Westminster Abbey; the Boar's Head at Eastcheap; the beach at Southampton with the English fleet riding in the background; the dauphin's pavilion with its embroidery of gold fleur-de-lis; a tableau of the battle of Agincourt; the entry into London; the cathedral scene in which Henry weds Princess Katharine—all were applauded loudly. A second critic wrote of the tableau, "Although not so much as a finger is moved, the waves of war seem to the excited imagination to rise and fall as fortune favors one side or the other. In the foreground, *Henry,* on foot, fights with the *Duc D'Alençon,* whose sword is falling from his unnerved hand." Reviews were generally so laudatory that playgoers were prepared to overlook Rignold's lapses, and by the second night he had fully recovered. The production ran three months.

On the 15th Toole returned, this time to the Lyceum and for only two weeks. His bills included several plays each night and were changed almost nightly in the second week. Works presented for the first time included **The Dodger** (taken from Dickens's *Oliver Twist*), Mark Lemon's farce **Domestic Economy,** and **That Blessed Baby.** All were comic vehicles created with Toole in mind, and none had an afterlife on American stages once he departed.

Daly finally hit paydirt with the appropriately titled **The Big Bonanza** (2-17-75, Fifth Ave.). Its success not only restored Daly's faltering fortunes but pointed the way for him to take toward future hits, for the play was based on a German comedy, Gustav von Moser's *Ultimo,* and it was to Germany that the producer would look for many of his subsequent adaptations. Of course, Daly was careful to "Americanize" this and later translations in order to increase their acceptance.

His version was set in New York, opening at the Cadwalladers' luxurious home on Madison Avenue. Lucretia Cadwallader (Annie Graham) is a stuffy, domineering wife, provoked because her husband "insists on doing what he calls enjoying his own home." But for the moment her main concern is her daughter, Eugenia (Fanny Davenport), who is returning home from school and is at an eminently marriageable age. Lucretia is alarmed to learn that Eugenia was escorted from the train station by a shabbily dressed young man. However, her chagrin is deflected by the arrival of her husband's cousin, Professor Agassiz Cadwallader (James Lewis). Lucretia has warned her husband, Jonathan (Charles Fisher), not to argue with Agassiz, but her plea is unheeded. The men are soon disputing the merits of their respective livelihoods, and Jonathan is goaded into presenting his cousin with $30,000 and betting him that he cannot invest it successfully. Agassiz's efforts to learn the ways of bulls and bears are interrupted by the arrival of Bob Ruggles (John Drew), a dapper young man fresh from the western mines, who is a nephew of Agassiz's wife, Caroline (Mrs. G. H. Gilbert). When the professor's buying and selling come to naught, he is relieved to discover that Jonathan's clerk had paid no attention to his orders and he actually has lost nothing. At the same time, Eugenia and Bob, who was the shabbily dressed man who had escorted her home, have fallen in love, and the Cadwalladers have agreed to their marrying.

William Winter wrote in the *Tribune* that the play "has no claim to consideration. The dialogue drivels through four acts of hopeless commonplace in which there is not one spark of wit, not one bright thought, not even a gleam of smartness." By contrast, the critic for the *Daily Graphic* noted, "The play abounds in humorous situations, and is constantly moving the audience to merriment. It is well mounted, the costumes are superb, and it is very admirably represented by the members of Mr. Daly's company." Playgoers chose to heed this and other similar reviews. In retrospect, the turnaround in Daly's fortunes aside, the main significance of the evening was the debut of John Drew, whom Daly had spotted acting in *Women of the Day* with his mother's company. It was an unexceptional debut, although Drew hinted at his gifts as a farceur in the scene in which Bob and Eugenia first confess their romantic feelings to each other. They have been left alone by Lucretia and told to light the candles. The directions read, "*They are so agitated and preoccupied that they do not light the candles, but light and extinguish matches repeat-*

edly." One neglected match burns down and scorches Eugenia's fingers, which Bob promptly kisses. The play was the final smash hit of the season, running for 138 performances.

Daly's hefty profits from *The Big Bonanza* came primarily from its New York run, for the producer, like most of the era's theatrical entrepreneurs, continued to be bedeviled by weak copyright laws. Thus when the troupe made a postseason cross-country tour, the play was poorly attended in San Francisco, where Bartley Campbell's version, *Bulls and Bears,* had succeeded a few weeks earlier. Similarly, Boston had seen the play, with Sol Smith Russell, as *The Two Bonanzas.* Daly wanted to sue to prevent these and other versions from being staged but was discouraged by his lawyers. In one form or another, the play remained popular, especially on the road, for about twenty-five years.

One odd result of all the hits—*The Gilded Age* had closed, but *The Shaughraun, The Two Orphans, Henry V,* and *The Big Bonanza* were running profitably—was that none of Broadway's four most prestigious houses needed to bring out a new play in March. The month's most newsworthy event was the second American visit, at the Lyceum, of the Italian tragedienne Adelaide Ristori. Her first visit had been in 1866. As before, she displayed little delicacy or poetry but brought forceful grandeur to all her roles. She opened with her most famous part, the title role in Giacometti's *Elizabeth, Queen of England,* then appeared in Schiller's *Mary Stuart,* Legouvé's *Medea,* Giacometti's *Marie Antoinette, Macbeth,* and Hugo's *Lucretia Borgia.* When she returned briefly in May she also brought out Giacometti's *Renata da Francia* and two short pieces that she added to other bills, *Les Adieux de Jeanne d'Arc* (which she performed in French instead of her usual Italian) and De Cosenza's comic *I Pazzi per Progetto.*

The only other major March opening, on the 22nd at the Park, was yet one more seasonal stopover of Frank Mayo in his inevitable *Davy Crockett.*

When *The Shaughraun* finally closed, Wallack's turned once again to revivals. On April 10, the house offered **Rafael,** which was simply a new translation of *The Marble Heart.* Edwin Adams had shown how the play's balance could be tilted in favor of the hero rather than the heroine, and this version was probably brought out to capitalize on Montague's popularity. It failed, so a week later *The Romance of a Poor Young Man* was hurried back, and a week after that, on the 24th, *The Road to Ruin* took over. Some indication of Wallack's

approach to such "classics" could be gleaned from newspaper advertisements, which advised the play had been "altered and adapted to the present stage."

The incomparable Adelaide Neilson came into Booth's for a fortnight beginning on the 26th but offered nothing new. Her repertory consisted of *Amy Robsart, The Hunchback,* and *The Lady of Lyons,* this last coupled with the balcony scene from *Romeo and Juliet,* with Montague as her Romeo.

Meanwhile, Wallack's and Booth's alternated in offering revivals all through May, when their seasons ended. On the 8th Wallack's presentation of *The Rivals* was coupled with a new comedietta, **The Happy Pair,** in which a bride learns vinegar wins more than honey. *The Irish Heiress* returned on the 12th, and the season's final offering, *The Lady of Lyons,* raised its curtain on the 22nd. All these presentations displayed the company's self-assured polish and were received with general satisfaction.

The revivals at Booth's were another matter, for they were Clara Morris's first attempt to break away from the era's stock companies and appear as an independent star. It was a risky move and immediately embroiled the actress in controversy. Critics had long registered their dismay at her inability to overcome her midwestern burr, and at her failure to fully master all the theatrical techniques or tricks that secured an interpretation, which produced unevenness in even her best performances. Where she shone was in emotional scenes, in eliciting an audience's sympathy or condemnation for the character she was playing. In modern times she might well have become a Stanislavskian or "method" actress who triumphed only when she could get inside a character and bring to the surface the deepest passions of the moment.

The prosaic, melodramatic works in which she won her fame, backed by sturdy ensembles and fine productions, had covered her faults and spotlighted her virtues. Now she distanced herself from the comparative safety of such plays and milieus. Her first offering was Richard Sheil's *Evadne* on the 10th. Ever since this blank-verse tragedy had premiered it had been compared to *The Maid's Tragedy.* In both works the heroine is named Evadne, and in both she is compelled to marry a man she does not love, with disastrous results. By consensus Miss Morris's Evadne had its stirring moments but was too erratically performed to be wholly effective.

It was her next interpretation, Lady Macbeth, that set off fireworks when *Macbeth* followed on the 17th. Never one to blindly accept tradition—and perhaps recognizing her limitations up to a point—

she took the line "Look the innocent flower, but be the serpent under it" as her cue. Hers was no outwardly cold, steely, dominating wife, but a girlish mate, cajoling, humoring, lightheartedly egging on. More hidebound critics were outraged; more liberal ones, puzzled. They sensed there might be a certain theatrical validity in her novel approach, one that might serve in more skilled hands, but they were not sure Miss Morris had made it work. Rignold's unsteady Macbeth was no help. She turned to Rowe's 1754 tragedy *Jane Shore* on the 24th, then began her final week on the 31st with her more admired, if controversial, *Camille.*

The season's finale came at Wallack's after that house's company had dispersed for their summer vacations. Ostensibly **The Donovans** (5-31-75, Wallack's) was a contemporary, localized melodrama whose story was suggested by one of the most sensational front-page headlines of the time, the kidnapping of little Charley Ross. But the play was the work of Edward Harrigan, half of the tremendously popular variety team of Harrigan and Hart. The team was starred in the principal roles of Michael and Norah Donovan, with Tony Hart performing in drag, so inevitably some of the plot's serious aspects were given a comic tinge. Their onstage tour of New York and a Kentucky plantation was larded with songs, dances, and other variety turns, including the Peak Bell Ringers and Baby Bindley. Yet the rescue of a woman from a burning building and of the kidnapped child from the path of an oncoming train had long been stock dramatic motifs. The production was exceptionally fine, including a view of three stories of a Manhattan tenement, all the apartments bustling with activity. In a sense, combining so potentially frightening an adventure with lighthearted vaudeville had to produce even more of a clash of style and tone than had the melodramatic story that included Colonel Sellers as its comic relief. Within a very few seasons Harrigan would find precisely the right blend of essentially comic plot and divertissement, but most of those works belong more appropriately to America's early musical stage. Perhaps the public sensed the mixture in *The Donovans* was uncomfortable, for despite the well-publicized addition of new variety acts, the play survived a bare three weeks.

Of course, week in, week out lesser theatres had been busy supplying entertainments to their regular patrons. This was especially true of the lowly old Bowery and the newer, seesawing Wood's Museum. Both depended on revivals of aging comedies and melodramas considered passé by more sophisticated

audiences, cheap new comedies and melodramas— including some still popular "dog dramas," in which trained dogs helped heroes and heroines—and versions of foreign plays unable to find a home in better theatres. A few American examples from Wood's will illustrate.

An old actor, Philadelphia's Charles Morton— who also wrote *Women of the Day,* which Daly mounted—was the author of **Poor and Proud** (8-10-74, Wood's). Alice Russell (Sophie Miles), who works as a shop assistant for Allan Gregory (Louis Aldrich), is framed by her jealous rival, Ellen Vandyke (Nellie Sanford), for the theft of a diamond brooch; Alice is vindicated and wins Allan's hand. Aldrich also played the idealistic rescuer in **Quits** (12-14-74, Wood's), in which a shady broker and lawyer attempt to defraud a woman of her inheritance. However, the central role was that of Ebenezer Longbow (J. H. Vinson), a comically befuddled Yankee who alternately hinders and helps in the pursuit of justice. J. J. McCloskey's **Smoke** (1-4-75, Wood's) was an affectionate look at its title figure, a loyal black servant who helps his employer, the owner of a large plantation, out of all manner of scrapes. The title figure was played by W. T. Melville, a white actor in blackface. Of course, except for plays such as *Uncle Tom's Cabin,* major Broadway offerings shied away from works in which blacks were central figures. Upper- and middle-class audiences clearly had little interest in such stories. **Kidnapped** (3-1-75, Wood's) had been done earlier in Brooklyn as *The Orphans* and appears to have been a very loosely Americanized redaction of *The Two Orphans,* with the sisters of the original transformed into a younger brother and sister. Bartley Campbell was given credit for its authorship, although his modern editors suggest he had only a small hand in it. The title was changed not only to avoid a local lawsuit, which Palmer probably would have won, but to capitalize on the headline-grabbing kidnapping of young Charley Ross.

As these examples suggest, the major difference between such plays and those done at first-class houses seems to have been one of quality. These were the equivalent of the "B pictures" of sixty years later. On occasion, the house did rise above such second-rate drama. The most notable instance was E. L. Davenport's two-week stand in a repertory that offered *Richelieu, Othello, Macbeth, The Stranger, Hamlet,* and *Damon and Pythias* (with John McCullough in a guest appearance as Pythias). But then, Davenport was an unusual case—an actor much admired by his colleagues, but considered too aloof and formal to appeal to the most commercial audiences in Manhattan. So, although he toured as a star with some success, he often found himself shunted to such lesser theatres when playing New York.

1875–1876

The preceding season had been so diverse, so generally excellent, and, not infrequently, so astonishingly successful that knowledgeable theatrical circles could not expect the new season to repeat the pleasant surprises of the old. But in what may have been the biggest and happiest surprise of all, it almost did. Still, there was a slight falling-off. With one notable exception, long runs were not quite as long. Good plays were not quite as good. The uncertain drift toward more genuinely native theatre was even a little less certain. And the prolonged depression that had begun in 1873 seemed at last to be taking its toll. Niblo's, each year farther away from the northward-moving theatrical hubbub, remained dark for the entire season, while other houses continued to turn their stages over to variety or musicals. Practically speaking, only five first-class theatres were devoted to comedy and drama. Wallack's, with no new *Shaughraun* to offer, reverted to its obsolescent tradition of new English plays intermingled with older plays revived in classic repertory style. Booth's, with Booth himself nowhere in sight, spent most of the season holding the fort for Shakespeare and a few other dramas that predated even Wallack's programs. Only Daly's, the Union Square, and the Park catered primarily to the best in new works, although, of course, lesser houses continued to play host to new plays and, in their own way, to encourage native drama far more than did first-class theatres. Playgoers and theatre folk around the country assuredly never heard of a twenty-two-year-old man named Elihu Thomson, who was tinkering with the rudiments of a new invention that would not be perfected for many decades but that fifty years hence would become one of another century's many technological marvels to lure patrons away from live theatre—the radio. But even in the short run, as the seasons that immediately followed were to demonstrate, the American theatre could not sustain the excitement and glow that these two seasons, at their best, had offered. In no small measure its inherent weakness stemmed

from its failure to develop and encourage high-quality native dramaturgy.

Nevertheless there was a modest American tinge to the new season's opening weeks, albeit they also offered a not very edifying instance of American chauvinism. Revivals of *The Gilded Age* at the Union Square on August 16 and of *The Big Bonanza* at Daly's Fifth Avenue on the 23rd got the season merrily under way. Then, on the 30th, an unpleasant and unnecessary contretemps developed.

This theatrical squall came about because two actors, one foreign and one American, opened that night in theatres just two blocks apart, and both had announced not merely identical repertories but, at least for the first week, had opted to bring out the same plays on the same nights. A nasty echo of the circumstances that had led to the Astor Place riots just over twenty-six years before was not lost on more knowing playgoers. The foreigner was the Irish-born English favorite Barry Sullivan, who was booked into Booth's; the American was E. L. Davenport, who came into the Grand Opera House. A curious similarity marked the two men's histories—each had won the respect of the most discerning critics in their countries, but neither had ever captured the affection of a larger public.

The rugged, pock-faced Sullivan had first appeared in America in 1858, when he had received widespread critical acceptance but, except in free-wheeling San Francisco, had played largely to unprofitable houses. Admirers saw in him a reflective, forceful actor not given to pandering to popular tastes (albeit his English reputation was as something of a barnstormer). But actors who worked with him in this country found him arrogant, sarcastic, and tactlessly anti-American. In an oddball way his egotism put him in the still very small vanguard advocating new ideas of set design. Although Booth was no longer associated with the theatre that carried his name, the house had retained the excellent, elaborate scenery Witham had created for Booth's productions there. As a matter of course, use of the sets was offered to Sullivan, but he retorted that such heavy, ornate scenery distracted playgoers from the play and, more important, from him. He used only bits and pieces of Witham's work, relying wherever he could on suggestive fragments and drapes. By modern standards the results were probably still very old-school, and contemporary critics who commented on them found them wanting rather than helpful.

Both men opened with *Hamlet*. Just how much the critical reception was influenced by the noisy international rivalry is hard to gauge at this distance—and the *Times* suggested in one of its notices that the rivalry may have been nothing more than an agreed-upon publicity stunt. Yet critics differed as sharply as transatlantic accents. The *Herald* praised Sullivan's "thoroughly thoughtful and intellectual Hamlet"; the *Times* berated his "aged and stagey Prince." Conversely, while admitting that age had deprived Davenport of some of his former physical force, the *Times* concluded his performance brought the tragedy "into that realm of dreamy speculative inaction to which it properly belongs." The *Herald*, albeit respectful, felt Davenport offered no refreshing insights. When *Richelieu* and *Richard III* followed, most reviewers simply offered variations on the themes heard in their notices of *Hamlet*. Later, with any potential ugliness apparently defused, Sullivan moved on to *The Lady of Lyons* and, rather daringly, to Edward Moore's "realistic" prose tragedy of a gambler's downfall, *The Gamester;* Davenport brought out *Macbeth, Othello, The Merchant of Venice,* and *Oliver Twist.* Looking back, Odell remarked that neither actor "gathered many laurels in this contest."

Theatrical flag-wavers did have some cause for glee with the arrival of the season's first hit, Benjamin E. Woolf's **The Mighty Dollar** (9-6-75, Park). Granted, this dollar was rather shaky. In a Washington salon called Grabmoor, wheelers and dealers put aside their grasping ways long enough to assist newly married Clara Dart (Maude Granger) when an old suitor attempts to make trouble for her. However, as was the case in so many of the period's plays that were written as star vehicles, the plot was little more than a frame for some richly drawn character portraits. In this instance the stars were William J. and Malvina Florence. To Mrs. Florence fell the role of Mrs. General Gilflory, a pretentious upstart who betrays her lack of real education with such pet phrases as "from Alpha to Omaha."

But it was Florence's portrayal of an unethical legislator that contemporaries immediately set down as one of the richest, most memorable of American theatrical creations. Winter wrote in the *Tribune,* "The *Hon. Bardwell Slote,* acted by Mr. Florence, is a personage not unlike, in his effect, certain of the caricatures delineated by Dickens. He is portly, grizzled, slightly bald, red nosed, bright-eyed, addicted to black satin waistcoats and big bosom pins, voluble, grasping, unprincipled, saturated with greed and with an odd kind of smirking humor, and very absurd; and he is presented as a politician, resident in Washington, and engaged in trying to feather his nest by taking bribes for lobbying railway bills through Congress. . . . Mr. Florence exhibits artistic instinct in making *Slote* grotesque and amusing, without making him unsympathetic and contemptible." Loving the sound of his own voice, Slote was given to spouting long monologues and to peppering his speech with such abbreviations as "k.k." for "cruel cuss," "b.o.t." for "bully old time," and "p.d.q." for "pretty darn quick." Florence, considered a master at makeup, punctuated his physical portrait with a huge, rising curl at the front of what was left of his hair and a large goatee on his chin. Whatever failings and vulgarities the play displayed, the Florences' brilliant acting won the original production a three-month run—plus a brief revival later in the season—and kept it on the boards with some regularity for another decade.

Daly followed his revival of *The Big Bonanza* by opening a one-week revival of *Saratoga* on the 13th, then offered what promised to be another major new hit, H. J. Byron's London success **Our Boys** (9-18-75, Fifth Ave.). At this time Byron, who was a cousin of the famed poet, was London's most prolific and diverse playwright, pouring out a slew of popular pantomimes, burlesques, melodramas, librettos, and comedies. *Our Boys* had opened in the West End the preceding January, so it was still too early for anyone to realize that it would become the first play in London history to run over 500 performances, chalking up a remarkable 1362. However, even by mid-September it was evident that the comedy was on the way to approaching and probably surpassing all former records, so Daly had every cause for optimism. The play's modern editor has pointed out certain similarities among previous long-run comedies or at least comedies that enjoyed decades of revivals, noting in particular of such works as *The Road to Ruin, Paul Pry,* and *London Assurance,* "All had a slightly dated feel, even for the time for which they were written, and all dealt with marriage, money and class, concluding with some sort of reconciliation between estranged father and son or uncle and nephew."

Father and son conflict was at the heart of *Our Boys.* Charles Middlewick (D. H. Harkins), son of a crude but good-natured tradesman who has made a fortune in butter, and Talbot Champneys (Maurice Barrymore), son of a snobbish aristocrat, have met and become friends while on a Cook's tour of Europe. They return home to learn that their fathers have planned marriages for them. By theatrical coincidence each father has in mind the very girl the other man's son loves. Charles wants rich Violet Melrose (Jeffreys Lewis); Talbot her poor cousin, Mary (Fanny Davenport). When the boys rebel, their fathers throw them out, and they are forced to scrape for a living in a London garret until the eventual reconciliation.

The play was simpleminded and more good-humored than witty, but it did have a certain warmth and charm. In London David James had scored a coup as the butterman, Perkyn Middlewick. For all his comic excellences, James Lewis could not repeat that success, perhaps because so many local nuances were lost on American playgoers. Charles Fisher was the lordly Sir Geoffrey Champneys, but Mrs. Gilbert walked off with honors in the small, juicy role of the maiden aunt, Miss Champneys—"an elderly young lady." The play ran for five weeks and was later sent on tour; no failure, but far from the enormous success many had expected it to be.

For a short while, Booth's abandoned older classics to give over its stage to more modern, although not new, pieces. On the 20th the curtain rose on a revival of Boucicault's *Flying Scud,* in which an old jockey comes out of retirement to race a poorly regarded horse to victory in the Derby. For the occasion George Belmore, the star of the original London production, came to New York. Critics were divided on his performance, although those who had complaints accepted reports he was ill on opening night. They still saw the play as claptrap but effective theatre. It ran three weeks before the playhouse was host to an opera company.

October's first offering, on the 4th, was a revival of *Led Astray* at the Union Square, with many of the original performers repeating the roles they had created—Rose Eytinge, Kate Claxton, Charles Thorne, Jr., and Claude Burroughs among them.

On the 5th Wallack's relit for the new season with Tom Taylor's old comedy *The Overland Route,* describing the misadventures of passengers on a voyage from India to England. Heading the cast during the month-long run were H. J. Montague, John Gilbert, Ada Dyas, and Effie Germon.

With opera reigning at his old home, Booth had worked out an agreement to appear in his by then ossified repertory with Daly's company in support. Special interest attached to the fact that Booth, who had broken an arm the preceding August in a carriage accident, was forced to perform with his arm in a sling when he appeared on the 25th. His list of plays ran to *Hamlet,* Sheil's tragedy *The Apostate,* in which he was the malevolent Pescara, *Richelieu, Othello, The Merchant of Venice, King Lear, The Lady of Lyons, The Stranger,* and *Katherine and Petruchio.* The only novelty—novel at least as far as Booth was concerned—was his *Richard II.* By now critics had taken sides on Booth's artistry and rarely deviated from them.

Thus the *Times* man found cause for carping almost everywhere, while Winter felt the actor virtually could do no wrong. There was more of a consensus, and not too favorable at that, about the ability of Daly's comedians to give proper support. But then Booth rarely had proper support. Winter noted that on opening night "the gentleman who played Rosencrantz evidently had an engagement with a friend after the performance, so hurried was his speech and so evident his desire to get through with the part." The gentleman was John Drew.

On November 8, Wallack's restored *Caste* to its stage, and on the 22nd Daly reached back to his earliest years to revive *Leah, the Forsaken* under the title *The New Leah.* Clara Morris assumed the role so identified with Kate Bateman. The reception was surprisingly savage, critics seeing the play as old hat and Miss Morris as an actress who stubbornly had refused to develop her art.

Daly's gloom must have deepened when his competition brought out **Rose Michel** (11-23-75, Union Square), Steele MacKaye's adaptation of Ernest Blum's Parisian success. The season had been especially litigious for Daly. Required to answer Wallack's suit over the rights to *Our Boys,* he had won, but when he charged in another suit that he held the rights to Blum's play, he lost. The story was all the more moving for being simple. Rose Michel (Rose Eytinge) knows that her husband, Pierre (J. H. Stoddart), has murdered the not very likable Baron de Bellevie (Frederic Robinson) and allowed suspicion to fall on the Count de Vernay (Charles Thorne, Jr.), the son of a woman who often has helped her. Yet when the count is condemned to death for the crime, she remains silent for fear the stigma of having a murderer for a father will prevent her daughter, Louise (Nina Varian), from making a highly desirable marriage. However, her guilty secret weighs so heavily on her that she finally forces Pierre to help arrange for the count to escape. While pretending to assist her, Pierre informs the gendarmes of the plans. The count is seized, leaving Rose no further choice but to denounce Pierre. He is shot trying to flee. "May Heaven forgive the sins of my maternal love!" Rose exclaims. The count and Louise's suitor both understand Rose's dilemma and do forgive her.

Part of the play's appealing simplicity could be credited to Palmer, who had rejected versions by Hart Jackson and George Fawcett Rowe, which he felt were, like the original, too confused. For example, Blum had Rose Michel steal money from Pierre in order to buy dresses for her daughter, and this led to complications. These scenes were omitted in MacKaye's redaction. Not only was the play powerful, but the performances and production were outstanding. The opening scene of a quay on the Seine, showing the entrance to the count's palace with the river and Notre Dame in the background, and the last act's setting of a gallery at Little Chatelet prison with a moonlit Paris and its bridges in the distance were cited with special approval.

Stoddart's performance as the murderous Pierre was so brutally convincing that he was forced thereafter largely to surrender the sort of comic roles on which he made his reputation. On opening night his costumes were delivered by mistake to the Union Square Hotel, and he retrieved them in the nick of time. These costumes included a huge overcoat that he had dragged through the mud of his Jersey farm to obtain just the right effect—to "look old, moldy and weather-beaten, such as was necessary for the miser *Pierre Michel.*" In the play Pierre drugs the baron and goes to get a dagger with which to kill him. "Before committing the murder," Stoddart continued in his autobiography, "I threw it [the coat] from my shoulders, and it slipped down to the ground and lay at my feet like a bundle of old rags." Miss Eytinge, still bristling on opening night from what she considered the absurdities of MacKaye's Delsartean direction, gave a performance many critics considered the finest of her career. The *Times* praised her "intensity and force." Even lesser roles were beautifully done. Stuart Robson played the comic Moulinet, Pierre's servant, who spends much of his time in conversation with his pet terrier and has a sneezing fit whenever he is startled. The character was original with MacKaye.

In the *Tribune* Winter, while taking exception to "the allusions to the Deity," predicted the drama "may run until the kitten of the first act becomes an old cat." Although the stand fell short of that, the four-month run gave the Union Square Theatre one of its greatest hits (two performances on November 25 grossed a record $3165) and most memorable triumphs. Possibly thanks to Palmer's suggested changes, it surpassed the original Paris run. In London, where a more literal translation was employed, the work was a failure.

At the end of the run of *Flying Scud*, George Belmore had taken his benefit not in that play but in a specially mounted production of George Fawcett Rowe's adaptation of *Nicholas Nickleby*. Now, with musicals out of the way, *Little Em'ly*, Rowe's adaptation of *David Copperfield*, was brought back on the 29th at Booth's with Rowe himself in his much acclaimed role of Micawber. The production had been mounted hurriedly after G. L. Fox had become violently insane and his final week in *Humpty Dumpty* had to be canceled. Then, on December 6, Emma Waller came in as Meg Merrilies in *Guy Mannering*. She had "spirit, variety and power" and indeed was a fine actress, but she could not compete with the memory of Charlotte Cushman's interpretation.

Wallack's next revival was *Bosom Friends,* an adaptation of Sardou's *Nos Intimes,* in which a kindly man is beset by fair-weather hangers-on. Even critics who slighted the play once again agreed that Wallack's company made it appear eminently stageworthy when it was offered on the 9th.

On the same night, Mr. and Mrs. Barney Williams opened a two-week stand at Booth's in their old favorite, *Connie Soogah.*

C. J. Smith, a minor, overreaching playwright and producer, took over Dan Bryant's old minstrel house and promised playgoers "one of the most brilliant and sparkling comedies ever put on the stage." His play, **The Flatterer** (12-13-75, 23rd St.), failed to live up to his immodest claims. An ambitious mother, Mrs. Huntman (Annie Deland), sets out to find a rich catch for her daughter, Alice (Adelaide Lennox). Their paths cross that of Colonel Flatterme (M. V. Lingham), an adventurer. The only person not susceptible to the hypocritical flatteries bandied back and forth is Mr. Huntman (J. W. Jennings), but then he is totally deaf. Two weeks, and Smith's self-advertised "tremendous hit" was withdrawn.

Daly did not need to brood very long over his bitter loss of *Rose Michel* in the courts or its subsequent success at the Union Square, for his own play **Pique** (12-14-75, Fifth Ave.), became the biggest hit of the season and one of America's biggest theatrical successes up to its time. This "play of today" was in five acts, the story of the first three taken loosely from Florence Marryat Lean's religious novel *Her Lord and Master* and the incidents in the last two acts suggested by young Charley Ross's kidnapping. Although the upright if somewhat stiff naval captain, Arthur Standish (D. H. Harkins), fervently loves Mabel Renfrew (Fanny Davenport), she coldly rejects him, preferring the attentions of handsome Raymond Lessing (Maurice Barrymore), a man whom kindly Doctor Gossitt (John Brougham) brands "as dishonorable and double-faced a fellow as ever made love to two women at once." Indeed, as soon as Raymond realizes how wealthy is Mabel's widowed stepmother, Lucille (Emily Rigl), he switches allegiances. Mabel overhears and, in a fury, suddenly accepts Standish's offer of marriage. The couple return from an unhappy honeymoon in Europe to live with Standish's puritanical father, Matthew (Charles Fisher), in Massachusetts. Mabel remains icy, and when she blurts out that she only married him in pique, Arthur goes back to sea, leaving Mabel and the child she is expecting in his father's care. However stern Matthew is, he is also loving and thoughtful, but Mabel cannot see that, blinded by her longing for the glittering life she once enjoyed in New York. To escape she arranges to stage a kidnapping of her young son, yet when she relents she is unable to stop the kidnappers. The child is hidden in a thieves' den in New York, where old Matthew bravely goes to retrieve him. Mabel and the returned Arthur follow. With her child restored to her, Mabel finally recognizes Matthew's goodness and even understands that she has come to love Arthur. Raymond and Lucille announce their wedding plans.

A careful reading of the play is revealing, for despite its highly melodramatic plot, most of the time is given over to comedy—a not really surprising circumstance, considering that Daly's ensemble excelled at comedy. Two gay blades, Sammy Dymple (James Lewis) and Thorsby Gyll (John Drew), both of whom at one time toyed with ideas of marrying Mabel themselves, romp through the action. And then there is the comic figure of Padder (William Davidge). When the play opens he is a waiter at the ball under way: "I wouldn't be paid to dance on such a night. Hot enough carrying these ices and iced sherries. [*Looks around*] Glass o' wine, Padder? [*Same business*] Thank'ee, if nobody's looking, I will! [*Same business*] He, he. [*Empties one of the glasses*] If I've took one of them, tonight, I've smouched a dozen. [*Dr. Gossitt enters . . . Padder sees him and is embarrassed, with glass in hand, which he puts in his pocket*]." Later Dymple recognizes Padder as his former valet:

Dym.: . . . a drunken rascal with a wife and eight children, who stole my shirts, got drunk, got arrested, and gave my name at the station-house, so at least once a week I had the gratification of reading in the morning papers that I had been severely reprimanded by the magistrate and fined ten dollars, which I paid on the spot.
Thors.: You mean he paid.
Dym.: No—I paid. He always stole enough out of my pockets to keep me out of jail.

Eventually Padder becomes one of the kidnappers, although in the end he does help retrieve the baby and is let off scot-free.

However large the comedy loomed, it was so skillfully blended that it somehow enhanced the tensions of the melodrama. Even critics who saw little enduring merit in the play conceded it would delight playgoers. Its New York run was 237 performances. These included a rarity for the time, midweek matinees, added to meet the demand for tickets. On the road it established new records in several cities. Yet the play never had a major revival, although it was brought back sporadically in lesser New York houses and elsewhere for the rest of the century.

More than any other play she had heretofore appeared in, *Pique* raised the already high stock of Fanny Davenport.

. . .

Fanny [Lily Gypsy] **Davenport** (1850–98) was born in London while her father, E. L. Davenport, was appearing there. She was still a youngster when she made her debut in a Boston mounting of *Metamora*. Her first New York appearance came when she played Charles II to her father's Ruy Gomez in *Faint Heart Never Won Fair Lady* in 1862. When Daly organized his first troupe he quickly enlisted her. Daly's brother noted, "What Daly saw in her, besides her dazzling beauty, splendid presence, and blooming health were confidence and self-possession." Some critics complained that she was too boisterous and given to unconscionable mugging, but playgoers adored her. In this respect she enjoyed the opposite reception of her father.

. . .

Daly's day in court was not over. Newspapers picked up on several suits brought in the wake of *Pique*'s production, the most notorious stemming from a charge by A. C. Wheeler (Nym Crinkle), critic for the *World*, that Daly had stolen the play from one by Eleanor Kirk Ames. Daly won all these cases, and he also grabbed some free publicity when he invited the supposed widow of the man who allegedly kidnapped Charley Ross to see the play in the hope she would disclose Ross's fate. She did not.

Daly's lawyer in many of his most dramatic court battles was A. Oakey Hall, who had served New York City as district attorney and mayor before being dragged down in the Tweed scandal. Now, as author, producer, and star of **The Crucible** (12-18-75, Park), he attempted what was perceived variously as a public shriving or a rather transparent self-justification. Right at the start Hall found himself embroiled anew in controversy, for some newspapers, such as the *Tribune,* questioned how genuinely original his play was, suggesting it bore an incriminating similarity to a recent story, *File No. 113.* In the play Wilmot Keirton, a London bank clerk, is accused of a theft that the audience knows has been committed by a man dressed to resemble him. An unenlightened, prejudiced, and pilable jury, with the actual thief as one of the jurors, is manipulated by a self-righteous prosecutor. A young deaf-mute who witnessed the crime testifies against Wilmot in pantomime. Conviction and a brutally demeaning imprisonment follow before the protagonist's innocence is brought to light. Some critics were astonished that the play was not all that badly written and wondered aloud if Hall had received professional assistance. They also were surprised by his excellent reading of the leading role; his musical voice brought out all manner of subtle undercurrents, even if his stance was wooden. But New Yorkers apparently had been surfeited with local scandal, so the play had to be withdrawn after three weeks of poor business.

Two revivals on the 27th closed out the year. Wallack's restaged *The Romance of a Poor Young Man,* which lingered only briefly in the repertory, while at Booth's *Julius Caesar* enjoyed a success that even the management probably had not dreamed of. Sixty years later Odell could still call it one of America's "most notable Shakesperian productions." The production was sumptuously mounted, probably employing much of the scenery Witham had designed for earlier revivals of the play at the house. Milnes Levick was Caesar, Bangs an always excellent Antony, and E. L. Davenport a most noble Brutus, but the triumph of the evening was Lawrence Barrett's Cassius. With his burning eyes and truly lean and hungry look, he was the era's definitive interpreter of the part. The mounting ran until the end of March and returned again in late May.

Since three theatres were occupied by long-running hits, 1876 got off to a slow start. On January 3, Wallack himself returned to his own theatre to assume the leading role in yet another of his revivals of Robertson's *Home.* Coupled with this was William Suter's old farce *A Quiet Family.* The actor-manager supplanted this double bill with H. J. Byron's second new play of the season, **Married in Haste** (1-12-76, Wallack's). The precipitous newlyweds, both painters, are Augustus (A. C. Stevenson) and Ethel (Ada Dyas) Vere. Their nuptials alienate Augustus's uncle, Percy Pendragon (John Gilbert). To compound their problems, Ethel's father, Josiah (J. W. Shannon), suffers business

reversals so can be of no help. Moreover, Vere is jealous that his wife's paintings sell while his do not. He refuses to allow her to make further sales. Reduced to poverty—much as the young men in *Our Boys*—the lovers fall to quarreling until a friendly man-about-town, Gibson Greene (Lester Wallack), sets matters aright. The play was even slighter than *Our Boys* and was held together, at least as far as New Yorkers were concerned, by Wallack's performance as the deus ex machina. Although he had just celebrated his fifty-sixth birthday, Wallack could still portray a relatively young gadabout with enough flair to make him credible to most onlookers. The *Times* observed, "No comedian now before the English public can compete with Mr. Wallack in an effort of this kind. His manner is charmingly picturesque and yet perfectly natural; he does not miss a single point in his lines, and yet anything like premeditation in any one passage of his part is never discernible." Unfortunately for him, Wallack's followers were aging and fading away, so *Married in Haste* ran less than a month. On February 7, he changed his bill to *John Garth.*

George Fawcett Rowe's **Brass** (2-16-76, Park) won critical applause and a three-month run. Its principal plot concerned the attempt by Philip Markson (W. J. Cogswell) to avenge what he believes is the despoiling and desertion of his daughter, Mary (Rose Lisle), by wealthy Mr. Wyvern (Lewis Morrison). He is delighted to set aside his plan when Mary reveals that she is Mrs. Wyvern and willing to forgive Wyvern's running away. But like so many other plays of the time, this one readily intermingled a healthy serving of comedy with its melodrama. In this instance the comedy came in a subplot recounting how a loving Sybil Hawker (Rose Wood) cures Waifton Stray (Rowe) of his habitual roving and prevaricating. Rowe, with his "total lack of self-consciousness, the warmth of his delivery, the beaming cheerfulness of his face," turned his latter-day Munchausen into a gleeful tour de force. He gave each inquirer a different, increasingly preposterous history of a ring he wore conspicuously on his finger (his "See this ring? Fact, sir, I assure you!" became a popular catchphrase); he posed as a doddering servant to escape his irate uncle and later reveled in a fake mad scene. The *Times,* in a curiously snobbish query, asked if a play with so many excellences were not "too good for a miscellaneous public."

The month faded away with a revival on the 21st at Wallack's of another of that house's standbys, *She Stoops to Conquer,* with, unbelievably to modern playgoers, Wallack still cavorting as young Marlow. He was the same age as the actor who played his father and only nine years younger than the great John Gilbert, who played Hardcastle and had been specializing in old men for innumerable seasons.

If Wallack represented the very best in Anglo-Saxon theatrical traditions, another group, the Jews, were slowly making their presence felt. In her autobiography Clara Morris insisted that even in these years, before the most massive Jewish immigration had occurred, Jews were among the most devoted and appreciative playgoers. Jewish actresses such as Rachel and Rose Eytinge had been welcomed onstage, while such playwrights as Mordecai Manuel Noah, Isaac Herby, and Jonas B. Phillips had seen their works mounted successfully. The prolific Benjamin E. Woolf was still enjoying the rewards of his *The Mighty Dollar*. But plays about Jews continued to echo *The Merchant of Venice* and *The Jewess*. E. W. Tullidge's **Ben Israel; or, Under the Curse** (3-6-76, Grand Opera) was no exception, telling yet one more tale of the agony of a Jewish father whose granddaughter—named, not unexpectedly, Rachel—loves a Christian. The play was a quick failure. No doubt Christians were as bored with the theme as were Jews. When it closed, the Grand Opera, having suffered through several uncertain months, closed for the season.

On the 13th Wallack's presented *The Wonder* for the amusement of its faithful clientele.

The francophilia that flourished on 14th Street continued when *Rose Michel* was replaced with John Parselle's adaptation of Sardou's **Ferreol** (3-21-76, Union Square). It presented fresh variations on old themes, all the while throwing complications into an essentially elementary story. An army officer, Ferreol de Meyran (Charles Thorne, Jr.), pays what is actually a very innocent courtesy call on his former flame, Roberte (Kate Claxton), who is now the wife of the Marquis Dumartel (John Parselle), a prominent judge. In the course of the visit they witness a murder across the street. Though horrified, they assume the police will handle the affair correctly. Yet Ferreol is no sooner at his new post overseas when he learns that the brother of his fiancée has been accused erroneously of the crime. He rushes back to France first to attempt to bribe, then to scare, the real murderer, a drunken gamekeeper, Martial (J. H. Stoddart), into admitting his guilt. Martial, realizing that he can place Ferreol and Roberte in a compromising position, refuses. This prompts Ferreol to go to Dumartel and claim he himself is the murderer, a claim Dumartel quickly dismisses. The police then discover the real culprit. Martial, learn-

ing that Ferreol had nothing to do with his arrest, keeps silent. Unfortunately, a slip of the tongue by Roberte alerts her husband. He feels he must call both her and Ferreol as witnesses, despite the ghastly social consequences of his marriage. Martial's suicide puts the problem to rest.

The dramatic interview in the fourth act between the judge, his wife, and her erstwhile suitor was considered one of the most electrifying climaxes in contemporary theatre. As always, Marston's scenery also elicited laudatory comments, especially the magnificent salon of the second and third acts, hung with the huge, heroic paintings so stylish at the time. The verdict of the *Sportsman* was that "Mr. Marston has excelled himself; the attempt to represent the works (historical portraits) of the old masters in distemper-painting is something entirely new to the stage." Productions of the play sprang up all across the country, but for some reason the work proved more acceptable to critics than to patrons. The original New York run was a disappointing fifty performances.

While other playhouses were enjoying runs of longer or shorter duration, Wallack's plodded on doggedly with revivals, bringing down the curtain on March with a double bill of *The Captain of the Watch* and *Woodcock's Little Game,* then getting April under way on the 3rd by returning *The Rivals* to its repertory. On the 8th the ensemble offered an almost new play, Clement Scott's **Tears, Idle Tears,** which had been given one performance in a benefit the preceding season. The work proved an excellent vehicle for young Henry Montague. He portrayed Wilfred Cumberledge, who goes insane after accidentally killing his son. In his madness he does not realize that his wife has given birth to a second son. When that child reaches the same age at which the first one died, the family leads Wilfred to believe that no time has passed and that this is really the son he thought had been killed. His sanity is restored, and he clings to it even when a servant unwittingly exposes the hoax.

On the 10th Booth's again mounted its success of the preceding season, *Henry V,* with Rignold once more as the king. A month's run followed.

Wallack's departed from its custom of relying on English works when it offered A. C. Wheeler and Steele MacKaye's **Twins** (4-12-76, Wallack's). Lester Wallack impersonated twin brothers. One, Chester Delafield, is weak and imprudent, so the second, Mark must use his own good sense and drive to save his brother from ruin. At one point this means he must pose as Chester to discomfit a blackmailer who has been hounding Chester's wife. Wallack's production, which included bringing a horse-drawn cab onstage, was magnificent. The critic for the *Sportsman* gave over much of one notice to describing the settings: "The home of Chester Delafield, situated on the Connecticut shore, with a view of Long Island in the distance, is one of the most beautiful and realistic stage effects it has ever been our pleasure to witness. The water view is superb, one almost thinking, when looking upon it, that he can inhale the fresh and invigorating breeze from the ocean. Then the lawns and cliffs at the rear, with grand imposing trees at the right, the sunlight flickering through their branches playing hide-and-seek upon the piazza of the villa at the left, and the creeping vines entwining themselves so naturally around the columns, form . . . one of the most charmingly natural and pleasing stage deceptions ever presented in this city."

The critic was less happy with the vivid colors employed in Delafield's townhouse drawing room, scene of the second and third acts, but the fourth act's moonlit view of Delafield's grounds restored his satisfaction. Unfortunately, scenery could not save a tedious work. Percy MacKaye later wrote that the damning notices the play received stemmed from some reviewers' dislike of their fellow critic Wheeler, and their desire to put him down, but a reading of some morning-after notices shows that a few critics credited whatever was good in the play to the very same Wheeler. In any case, it was quickly withdrawn, and on the 26th the theatre revived *London Assurance*.

Another falsely accused, wrongly imprisoned young man was at the center of a new American play, A. E. Lancaster and Julian Magnus's **Conscience** (5-9-76, Union Square). Although their motifs were scarcely original, the authors, undoubtedly without realizing it, walked a borderline between older melodrama and later mystery-thrillers. It is midnight at the Hackensack summer home of a rich Wall Street broker, Nathaniel Harwood (Frederic Robinson). Harwood's daughter, Constance (Kate Claxton), is courted by three men: Harwood's nephew, Cyril (Charles A. Stevenson), Harwood's secretary, Eustace Lawton (Charles Thorne, Jr.), and old Judge Van Cort (John Parselle). Harwood has turned a deaf ear to Cyril's request for his daughter's hand and shortly thereafter discovers a large acceptance has been forged on his company. Suspicion falls on Cyril, so Harwood has invited the judge to visit him at his home and discreetly question his nephew. A scream is heard. Constance, Eustace, and the judge rush into the room and find that Harwood is dying of stab wounds. Cyril, seemingly shocked, is standing over him with a

bloody knife in his hand. As the music from a midnight mass comes through the open windows, Harwood dies. His last words are "Cyril, revenge." Cyril is tried and sent to prison, but Constance is certain of his innocence and persuades the judge to recreate the murder evening as precisely as possible, even to having the music of the mass sung. The recapitulation discloses that Eustace is a sleepwalker and that he had committed both the forgery and murder. In his *Tribune* notice Winter rued that the play "does not anywhere rise above the level of elegant mediocrity." More than anything else, capital acting, particularly by Thorne, kept the play alive for what remained of the season.

One curiosity competed for attention the same night. An obviously deranged Philadelphian, Dr. S. M. Landis, had won notoriety in his hometown by his behavior—taking to the stump for unpopular and mostly weird causes, writing preachy plays that largely went unproduced, and, to cap everything, proclaiming himself the incarnation of Hamlet. The best Philadelphia theatres had refused him a stage for performance, so he had sometimes played at lesser variety houses. Now he brought his Dane to Tammany Hall. He was a husky-voiced, flabby man with a long brown beard. As an actor he failed to follow Hamlet's advice. Instead he tore passions to shreds, wildly rolling his eyes, flailing his arms, virtually dancing with his legs. Critics and audiences alike howled with laughter, but this seemed not to bother him. Legend has it that when he returned to vaudeville a transparent screen had to be placed before him so that he would not be pelted with the overripe fruit and nutshells thrown on stage. If this is true, then he was years in the vanguard of vaudeville's famed Cherry Sisters.

On the 16th Wallack's introduced its last offering of the season, Boucicault's Restoration-like comedy *How She Loves Him*. Something of the company's remarkable stability was demonstrated by the number of performers who recreated the roles they had assumed in the play's 1864 American premiere. Among others, Lester Wallack was once again the stammering Dick Vacil and John Gilbert the blustering but good-hearted Sir Richard English.

For "Centennial Week," the celebration of the hundredth anniversary of American independence, the Park brought back the indestructible *Uncle Tom's Cabin* on the 22nd. Mrs. G. C. Howard once more was Topsy, a role she had been playing tirelessly for twenty-three years. Bijou Heron was Little Eva. A minstrel troupe was injected into the play for added appeal. The revival left to make way for the season's last opening, Fred Marsden's **The**

Kerry Gow (6-12-76, Park), yet another vehicle set in Ireland for another of the era's popular Irish entertainers. The star was Joseph Murphy, who played Dan O'Hara, a blacksmith, and who thus could show his ability to shoe a horse onstage. Dan loves Norah Drew (May Nunez), but his rival, Valentine Hay (W. J. Cogswell), frames him for forgery, and he flees into hiding until the truth is exposed. He returns just as Hay is about to switch horses before a big race. Not recognizing Dan, Hay brings him his horse for shoeing, and Dan sees to it the horse does not win the race. Although its initial run was less than a month, *The Kerry Gow* remained a favorite with Murphy and his Irish followers for well over a decade.

Away from the more glittering, swank first-class houses, lesser theatres remained active, often changing bills weekly and frequently giving two performances every day, with one play at the matinee and another play in the evening. Older standbys reappeared regularly, sometimes with stars who were equally at home on better stages. Chanfrau brought in *Kit* and *The Ticket-of-Leave Man; Lucille Western, *East Lynne* and *The Child Stealer. Around the World, The Spy,* and similar hits of bygone seasons remained attractions. But newer plays were even more numerous, and presumably even more popular. Most apparently were by native playwrights, although not all were set in America. Kate Fisher and her celebrated horse, Wonder, besides bringing a seemingly timeless Mazeppa back to life, offered **Schamyl; or, The Black Horse of the Caucasus** (2-28-76, Wood's), a saga of the Russian backwaters replete with "assassinations, massacres, hairbreadth 'scapes, and feats of human and animal daring." **Suil Gair** (3-13-76, Wood's) began unfolding in Ireland, where its titular hero assumes a succession of disguises to rout a devious Lothario who is scheming to steal another man's wife. But its action soon moved to New York, allowing its protean hero to appear first as an Irish landlady and then as a politically savvy immigrant. Another disguise-prone detective got his man—who was based on a real-life killer—in **Sharkey; or, The Shadow Detective** (2-21-76, Wood's). But this time all the action took place in New York. Famous sites were depicted "with considerable accuracy," while a concert-saloon setting allowed the action to stop long enough for some vaudevillians to do their turns. The play was sometimes listed as *Sharkey and the Shadow Detective.* Oliver Doud Byron, who at one time or another during the season offered all his old favorites, also brought in two new vehicles, both set in America. **Thoroughbred** (1-31-76,

Wood's) was listed as a "political society drama." **Rebel to the Core** (4-17-76, Wood's) found its star playing a British officer sent to teach American colonists a lesson. Before long he has switched allegiances. Sensation scenes included the burning of a mill and a military engagement in a snowstorm. Much more recent military matters were also theatricalized. Less than two months after Custer and his men had been slaughtered at Little Big Horn and thereby entered American legend, audiences were applauding Harry Seymour's **Sitting Bull; or, Custer's Last Charge** (8-14-76, Wood's). At a fort's trading post, the Peace Commissioner and representatives of the Indian Bureau are attempting to work out a fair settlement with the "Red Men." Ranger Rob has other ideas. His attempt to abduct Constance Pierpont is foiled by Sitting Bull (Seymour) and Metara (played by the author's wife, Carrie). But Rob does seize the Indians' land, thus setting off rebellion. A sign of which newspaper most playwrights for lesser theatres still agreed was tops in clout could be seen in the character of Kellogg, a reporter for the *Herald,* who was given such gallery-rousing lines as "We never desert out posts or shirk our duty either amidst the malignant pestilence of crowded cities, or in the face of our Country's Foes." Three weeks later a second play on the same theme, **Custer and His Avengers,** was also on the circuits. Whatever their setting or subject, the titles of plays at these lesser theatres time and again promised thrills—**Face to Face, Marked for Life, Parted.**

However, for most less affluent, less demanding audiences the most important premiere of the season occured at a far less fashionable house than the faltering Wood's. That premiere was **The Phoenix** (1-17-76, Bowery), with Milton Nobles as star. He played Carrol Graves, a bohemian New Yorker given too much to drink and guilt-ridden because he once inadvertently committed a forgery. The villain of the piece has gained possession of the incriminating papers. But Graves in turn has papers the villain needs. The villain visits Graves in his shabby Baxter Street tenement, drugs his brandy, steals the papers he wants, murders a man who may have overheard him, and sets fire to the place. One critic reported, "The fire scene . . . is one of the most horribly real-looking fires that ever burned on any stage; and if the jubilant gallery gods called the curtain up on it three times, the jubilant dress-circle lent a very helping hand." Luckily, Graves's sweetheart, a flower vendor, is nearby and pulls him from the building. He vows vengeance on the villain. When he reappears he goes by the name of Jim Bludsoe, claims he is a rich miner, and employs disguise within disguise to hound the villain into rushing off into the wings and shooting himself. The triumphant hero, standing on a table covered with $20,000 worth of coins and jewels, rips off his wig and proclaims his real identity.

Many a critic, his or her funny bone tickled, delighted to broadcast the play's absurdities. The heroine, for example, was described as "an exceedingly moral young woman, who goes about delivering verbal tracts." These seem to have an effect on the other characters, since "every time this young woman makes an exit, whoever is left upon the stage pronounces a eulogy upon her virtue and innocence." Sadly, her memory is not as remarkable as her virtue or innocence, for at one point she forgets her rescue of the hero and, "in a high treble, [proclaims] that her heart is buried in the ashes of Carrol Graves in the Baxter Street tenement." Nor was Nobles immune from ridicule. One reviewer, allowing he was "almost an actor," spoke of his "low growling monotone" and "high-flown style of speech," continuing, "His comedy is a nervous, impetuous, startling, dialectic affair. Grammar, and final consonants, and all that sort of thing, go to the wall." Even the costume he wore as Bludsoe was sneered at: "a *café au lait* suit, with long swinging coat-tails flapping about his heels[;] . . . add to this a broad slouch hat of the same peculiar hue, and yards of glittering watch chain outside of everything else." Some years later a critic described Nobles as "a slender gentleman . . . [with] a high forehead, a small, comic nose, and a dry voice, all in the middle register. In his lively moods he talks smoothly and glibly. In sentimental passages he makes use of the nasal whine of the camp-meeting exhorter." Whatever commentators thought of the star and his vehicle, lower-class audiences loved both. The play's initial one-week New York stand signified little. For several seasons Nobles, who was twenty-nine in 1876, played nothing else, and thirty years later *The Phoenix* remained the most prominent part of his repertory. One turn-of-the-century article claimed he played in the drama more than 5000 times.

1876–1877

It was certainly not the best of times. Nationally the outgoing Grant administration had reeled from one damning exposure of corruption after another. Now, in the new year, the next president, Rutherford B. Hayes, would enter the White House already under a cloud, for he had lost the popular ballot to Samuel J. Tilden by a sizable 250,000 votes only to win in an electoral count many felt was tainted. New York City, still wrestling with the debris left by Tweed's skullduggery, seemed awash in a miasma of unsteady idealism, incompetence, and continuing chicanery. And, of course, effects of the 1873 panic continued to haunt the nation.

At the same time, the American theatre, after a pair of interesting seasons, suddenly appeared to have exhausted some of the promising drive of those two years. A sense of déjà vu, once so comfortable to many critics and playgoers, returned, but now it brought less a feeling of well-being and security than one of staleness. Theatre lovers had been given an exciting taste of the future and hungered for more. Worst of all, at the very height of the season, on December 5, the Brooklyn Theatre caught fire during a performance of *The Two Orphans*. In the ensuing pandemonium 198 patrons died; it was the worst theatre fire so far in American history. The disaster scared away many playgoers for the rest of the season and for months beyond.

Yet outside of New York American playgoers were increasingly receiving and welcoming another taste of the future—combinations or road companies. These touring troupes had begun to multiply swiftly, and in 1877 Palmer became the first major producer to establish a policy of regularly sending out touring versions of his New York hits. In April the *Herald* reported there were 3500 theatres across the country and 500 traveling companies, giving employment to 40,000 people. The figures cannot be verified, yet they cannot be too far out of line, even for a nation whose population was then just under 50,000,000.

A respected graduate of the old school, E. A. Sothern, launched the new season happily enough when he unpacked his bags at the Fifth Avenue on July 31 to begin a six-week engagement. He offered nothing new, riding out the heat with his classic Dundreary in *Our American Cousin* and in the title role of *David Garrick*.

Newspapers reported that a veritable theatrical who's who turned out for the opening of **Sardanapalus** (8-14-76, Booth's). This redaction of Byron's work was by Charles Calvert, who had been responsible two seasons before for the successful *Henry V* revival. It clearly demonstrated that the thirst for such gargantuan spectacle remained unquenched. Calvert, according to one notice, grabbed every opportunity "to thrust in grand processions, gorgeous dresses and voluptuous pictures." He compressed Byron's original into four acts and added a corps de ballet and a number of brilliantly posed "living pictures" or tableaux, including one showing Sardanapalus coasting down the Tigris in a multihued barge. In this "barbarous splendor," King Sardanapalus (F. C. Bangs) discards his queen, Zarina (Dora Goldthwaite), in favor of a beautiful Ionian slave, Myrrha (Agnes Booth). The queen's infuriated brother, Salamenes (Louis Aldrich), enlists a band of supporters to overthrow the king. When they see all is lost, Sardanapalus and Myrrha throw themselves on a blazing funeral pyre. The blaze was created by a man listed in programs as pyrotechnist to the Queen of England. Although many of the fine players in the cast garnered appreciative notices, the most fervent encomiums were lavished on Ernesto Mascagno. The *Times* hailed him as "the best male dancer ever seen on our boards," while the *Herald,* in a more facetious vein, identified him as "a tragedian from the Italian theatres" and singled out "one fine tragic burst when standing on his toes he pirouetted across the stage and jumped at least four feet in the air, which drew forth thunders of applause from admirers of Byron's immortal genius." Such sarcasm could not dissuade playgoers, who kept the box office busy for nearly four months.

But the sarcasm became contagious, spreading like wildfire to any number of other newspapers, when the first American play of the season arrived. Bret Harte's **Two Men of Sandy Bar** (8-28-76), Union Square), the basic idea of which he took from his short story *Mr. Thompson's Prodigal,* was viewed as a serious setback to the cause of native drama. The *Herald* fulminated, "As an 'American drama' it is an absolute outrage upon the intellectual reputation of the country. . . . Ever since he left California, Mr. Harte has lived on his reputation and failed in his performances." The *Times,* picking the play to pieces scene by scene, wondered aloud how a father could mistake a black-haired man for his own redheaded son (actually a reflection on casting more than writing) and continued, "Every one has a long story to tell in the Old Bowery melodrama style, which always provided that two of the characters should bring two chairs down to the footlights, and sitting thereon one should detail to the other what the other already knew—the past action of the plot—beginning invariably 'Tis now some twenty years ago,' &c." It also made mincemeat of the role of a schoolmarm who "delivers sermons by the yard, in soliloquy, to the wretched audience."

The play had been commissioned by Stuart Robson for $3000 in advance and another $50 per performance ($25 for each matinee) until a figure of $6000 had been reached. (Leonard Grover was called in to make uncredited revisions.) Robson's growing band of followers were flabbergasted when he initially assumed the relatively minor role of a comic attorney. In Harte's story old Alexander Morton (H. F. Daly) mistakes John Oakhurst (Theodore Hamilton) for the long-lost son he had once disowned. Oakhurst has eloped with Donna Jovita (Laura Don), but Morton now is prepared to forget and forgive and to bring Oakhurst into his business. Watching all this is the dissolute man known both as Diego Smith and as Sandy (H. S. Murdoch), whose illegitimate child the garrulous schoolmarm, Mary Morris (Mary Cary), has consented to adopt. In the end the lawyer, Culpepper Starbottle (Robson), reveals that Sandy is really the long-lost son. Oakhurst is shamed by the revelation of his deception and proposes to leave, but Jovita loves him and Morton has come to respect him. So the old man embraces both Oakhurst and Sandy and changes the name of his company to Morton and Sons. Sandy and Mary agree to marry.

Unfortunately, the play was everything the critics said it was—clumsy (endless asides, even in an era that loved them, were ineptly handled), tedious, and prolix. While playgoers might read the equally prolix reviews of the time with some tolerance, they were reluctant to sit through such speeches as the one old Morton delivered on his first entrance: "As a God-fearing and forgiving Christian, Mr. Castro, I trust you will overlook the habitual profanity of the erring but well-meaning man [Starbottle], who, by the necessities of my situation, accompanies me. I am the person—a helpless sinner—mentioned in the letters which I believe have preceded me. As a professing member of the Cumberland Presbyterian Church, I have ventured, in the interest of works rather than faith, to overlook the plain doctrines of the church in claiming sympathy of a superstitious papist." Morton's speech was undoubtedly meant to show his blindness and tactlessness with a little humor, but it was not the rough-and-tumble talk playgoers expected from the Wild West—and the talk of the more rough-and-tumble characters was little more colloquial. An open letter from Harte to New York's critics, accusing them of demanding bribes for favorable reviews, apparently had no effect at the box office. The play ran a month in New York, and Robson later toured with it, assuming the role of Sandy, for which he was all wrong.

One of the peculiarities of ensembles such as Wallack's or Daly's was that they frequently opened their season with a revival of an old play meant to "reintroduce" the company to regular patrons. The first important new offering or major revival would follow a week or so later. Thus Daly inaugurated his new season with a remounting of Bulwer-Lytton's *Money* on September 12, announcing at the same time that a new play would be premiered the very next week. But in this instance the opener did more than just bring all the holdovers back from vacation. It served as the American debut of Charles Coghlan, who Daly's brother acknowledged had been hired "to strengthen the company where it had sometimes been found weak, that is, with regard to a masculine actor who possessed the authority of Wallack, the charm of Montague or Rignold, or the force of Thorne." Coghlan made an immediate impression. Several papers talked of the "expressive" eyes and "mobile" face of the tall, handsome actor. Many also found his acting somewhat cold—Mrs. Gilbert called him "curiously self-controlled, passionless"—but even detractors acknowledged he balanced this with his seeming spontaneity. All in all, his Evelyn bespoke well for his future. His notices may also have been the reason Daly set back the succeeding offering for an additional week.

That postponement meant the next new play first-nighters could attend was the prolific Fred Marsden's **Clouds** (9-18-76, Park). The clouds of the title temporarily darken the life of Stella Gordon (Rose Wood), who has secretly wed Ralph Randall (Cyril Searle) and watches in dismay as he packs his bags after his very rich father insists he marry Cora Adair (Ida Jeffreys). Just why Stella would want such an irresolute weakling is unclear, even given the tight social strictures of the time, but she does. So she makes it her business to prove that Cora is a money-hungry adventuress and by that means keeps Ralph. The play ran a month.

Having allowed his curtain raiser to serve as Charles Coghlan's American debut, when he presented his first new play of the season Daly brought forward another young player who had won acclaim in London. Her name was Amy Fawsitt, and she was a winsome-faced, remarkably promising actress. Yet the behind-the-scenes dramas that both she and Coghlan played out were as intriguing as the roles they performed before the footlights. Coghlan would die relatively early, under mysterious circumstances; Miss Fawsitt's history was far shorter and more ghastly. The new play had scarcely opened when she began absenting herself. Daly quickly recognized she was an alcoholic and otherwise alarmingly unstable. The producer dismissed her, giving her money for a return passage to England.

Instead of returning home, she took rooms in a shabby boardinghouse, where she was found robbed and fatally beaten shortly after the new play had closed. So it was doubly ironic that the new play, which came close to being an out-and-out failure, was called **Life** (9-27-76, Fifth Ave.).

Daly derived this largely unsatisfying medley of motifs and incidents from several sources, primarily a French play, Alfred Hennequin's and Alfred Delacour's *Le Procès Veauradieux*. If it had any plot at all to give it spine, it concerned a carefree, rich widow, Mrs. Masham Mallory (Fawsitt), whose pursuers include the philandering Schuyler Samples (Coghlan), the sporting Pony Mutuel (James Lewis), and the handsome, resourceful Frank Dodge (Maurice Barrymore). Samples in turn is relentlessly hounded by his battle-axe mother-in-law, Mrs. Brown Boston (Mrs. Gilbert). (Many playgoers knew that Boston Brown was an American with theatrical interests on both sides of the Atlantic.)

The characters assemble in the third and best act to attend the rehearsal of a spectacle. At this point, as the *Sportsman* informed its readers, "the audience are allowed to witness the drilling of a ballet preparatory to the rising of the curtain, then as the green baize slowly ascends, a fine view is afforded, showing the exact appearance of 'the front of the house' . . . as it looks from behind the footlights." For the performance of the spectacle, the view returned to normal. Like almost all such contemporary spectacles, it included a ballet and a transformation scene (one in which the scene is changed while the audience watches). This ballet featured two of the most famous ballerinas of the time, Marie Bonfanti and Augusta Sohlke, Miss Sohlke dancing to Offenbach music as the Spirit of the Snow in a gorgeous winter scene until being chased away by Miss Bonfanti's Spirit of the Sun. Matters go comically awry in the transformation scene when the sun evokes not a verdant spring but a golden and red blaze of autumn foliage; to add to the confusion Pony Mutuel somehow is recruited among the swirling, leaping dancers. Although *Life* did not add up to a completely successful evening, it was diverting enough to run until mid-November.

That was a longer run than Boucicault's **Forbidden Fruit** (10-3-76, Wallack's) could achieve. Yet *Forbidden Fruit*, which began Wallack's new season, was a far more accomplished play, a brilliant, hilarious Feydeau-like farce written years before Feydeau raced across Parisian stages. Junior Counsel Cato Dove (H. J. Montague) is meek and happily married, so he is flummoxed when a luscious little sexpot, Zulu (Effie Germon), who as "the Female

Cartridge" is nightly shot from a cannon at the Cremorne Gardens, appears at his office, offering to be a witness in a case he is conducting. He realizes that she has more in mind than just taking the witness stand. Dove's partner, Sergeant Buster (Harry Beckett), is a philanderer married to a dominating termagant, so when Dove lets slip that his own wife is showing signs of thoroughly unjustified jealousy, Buster sets about enlisting the younger man in his illicit escapades. He advises, "Justify her suspicion and spare her your reproaches by taking her sin on your shoulders. The fact is, she finds you so perfect that she is impatient to discover a fault in you; be generous—gratify her!" The men arrange to meet Zulu and another lady at the Cremorne Gardens that night. Buster helps Dove write a letter to Mrs. Dove telling her he has been called away to Nottingham for the evening, but Mrs. Dove (Ada Dyas) and Mrs. Buster (Mme Ponisi) appear at the office and mistakenly are handed the letter early. Mrs. Dove decides to see her husband off. This, of course, will force him to take a Nottingham-bound train, get off at the first stop, and take a train back. At the station all the other characters appear, each for his or her own good reason, to further complicate matters. Independently Captain Derringer (Edward Arnott), Mrs. Dove's brother, who is just returning from a long stint overseas and has never met her husband, also arrives. After Dove has started on the first leg of his journey, Derringer spots Mrs. Dove, and they agree to spend his first night home by taking in a show, then dining at a private suite in the Cremorne Hotel—the very place Buster has arranged for his and Dove's rendezvous. At the Cremorne Hotel confusion soon runs riot, with everyone misinterpreting each other's actions. At one point Dove poses as a waiter, with a bandaged eye and a fake nose, to spy on his wife and the young officer she is dining with. In the end explanations are forthcoming and everyone is pleased—even Buster, who has no intention of giving up his illicit wanderings. By all accounts the farce was brilliantly performed. Wallack's production included yet another horse-drawn cab onstage, perhaps the very same trotted out in last season's *Twins*. Newspapers reported the play did good business, but it was taken off after a month's stay, although it later was restored briefly.

The night before *Forbidden Fruit* opened, the Union Square revived *The Two Orphans*. The production had been promised from the start of the season but apparently had to be brought forward hurriedly when *Two Men of Sandy Bar* failed. It kept the house lit for nearly two months, until a new play

was ready. A pair of additional revivals came into the Lyceum for the week of October 16. They were occasioned by the attempt of Louise M. Pomery to raise herself to stardom. Both her *Romeo and Juliet* and her *The Lady of Lyons,* later in the week, were greeted politely but unenthusiastically.

A double bill of short plays by W. S. Gilbert, **Sweethearts** and **Tom Cobb** (10-17-76, Park), received much the same welcome. The former was a charming little play, essentially a bittersweet two-character study (two additional characters in the play, servants, hardly counted). Before Harry Spreadbow (Cyril Searle) leaves to assume a post in India, he comes to say good-bye to Jenny Northcote (May Howard). He has sent in advance a sycamore sapling for her to plant as a memento in her garden and has brought her a rose. Angry that Harry has chosen duty over love, Jenny tells him the sycamore will probably grow up to be a nuisance, and she peevishly discards the rose. She gives Harry an unwieldly flowerpot as her parting gesture. Thirty years pass. An older Harry and a very proper Miss Northcote meet again, under the now large tree. She shows him the rose, which she had retrieved and pressed after he had left, but Harry has long since forgotten both his gifts to her. It turns out that though Miss Northcote has cherished Harry's memory all these years, he has virtually forgotten her.

Tom Cobb recounted the plight of a struggling doctor (Thomas Whiffen) who cannot afford to wed until he suddenly comes into a huge inheritance. His tricky rival unintentionally brings about the happy ending. At the end of the month, a non-Gilbertian piece, **Adam and Eve,** was added to the bill to perk attendance.

Having picked forbidden fruit and fared somewhat disappointingly for doing so, Wallack's gave Boucicault's *The Shaughraun* its first major revival on November 9, using most of the original cast of two seasons earlier, including Boucicault himself. Even Wallack's aristocratic playgoers apparently still preferred this sort of highly colored melodrama to slambang farce, so the play ran until early January, when Wallack brought back *Forbidden Fruit* for a brief rehearing.

A more interesting revival was Daly's mounting of *As You Like It* at the Fifth Avenue on the 18th. Daly always was hailed for the excellence of his physical productions, and this one was no exception, with its "leafy vistas, continually changing, and sunset colors softening into dusk." The producer also was commended regularly for the taste and scholarship he displayed in treating the classics, and this time he apparently eschewed the drastic rewriting and reordering that later became his wont. What failed to totally please many of the critics were the interpretations of the leading roles. Fanny Davenport's Rosalind was seen as all life and little heart, while Coghlan's Orlando seemed too pensive and downbeat.

Two nights later yet another Shakespearean revival was at hand, this time *Hamlet,* with Edwin Booth in the title role. As usual the *Times* could find little to admire, carping that "not only every scene, and every speech in every scene, but every sentence in every speech and every word in every sentence is racked for a point and tortured for an effect," while the loyal *Tribune* found the interpretation "perfect." Most critics took a middle ground but clearly tilted in Booth's favor. Nor did they complain that once again his repertory offered nothing novel. Booth followed his opener with *The Lady of Lyons, The Fool's Revenge, Richard II, Othello, Don Caesar de Bazan, The Merchant of Venice, Richelieu, Much Ado About Nothing, Richard III, Ruy Blas, Brutus, King Lear, Katherine and Petruchio,* and *The Stranger*—virtually his complete standard repertory. The successful engagement lasted ten weeks at the Lyceum, even though some of his admirers were complaining that he had lost his oldtime fire and was becoming too studied and predictable in his performances. Booth responded privately to James E. Russell, a critic for the *Sun,* "I can't paint with big brushes—the fine touches come in spite of me. . . . I'm too damned genteel and exquisite."

If critics continued to take sharply opposing stances over Booth's acting, for the past several seasons they had mostly agreed in their growing disappointment with Clara Morris. Even the more tenderhearted regretted that she never quite lived up to the incandescent promise of her first years. Somehow she could not cast off her midwestern accent (an atrocious crime to unaccented New Yorkers), and she briefly became overambitious, especially in the light of her stunted artistic development. In fact, she was a fine if very limited actress. But when Palmer cast her in the title role of **Miss Multon** (11-20-76, Union Square), she once more had the sort of role in which she was incomparable, and she again tasted the triumph and adulation that many had despaired of her ever winning anew. Palmer's adaptor, A. R. Cazauran, took the work from a French play by Eugène Nus and Adolphe Belot, which some said had been derived in turn from *East Lynne.*

Having learned that the wife who long ago deserted him has died, Maurice de la Tour (James O'Neill) marries Mathilde (Sara Jewett). To make life easier for her, he sets about securing a governess for his children by his first wife. The woman selected is Miss Multon, a gray-haired lady with white at the temples, who arrives in a dark red dress that might be seen as hinting at long-banked passions. At first only an old servant recognizes her as Fernande, Maurice's supposedly dead wife. She so wins over the children's affections that Mathilde becomes jealous, and in a confrontation Miss Multon blurts out the truth. Maurice had come to suspect this, and when he overhears his suspicions confirmed he demands that Miss Multon tell her children her story. She refuses and leaves, returning to the home of crotchety but kindly Dr. Osborne (J. H. Stoddart), who had secured her the position. There, her weak heart strained by her ordeal, she dies, but not before Maurice and her children rush to forgive her.

Changes and additions Palmer suggested to Cazauran indicated his astute grasp of American tastes. The French play ended with Miss Multon's departure from the de la Tour home. Palmer had his adaptor tack on the death scene, subscribing to Daly's belief that audiences relished a heroine's death throes. He also ordered Cazauran to emphasize "the tremendous passion of maternity" since "sexual love alone" was not enough. In both versions the play demonstrated how modern notions of drama were creeping into the theatre. Its cast was comparatively small and its story acted out in just two settings, the doctor's office and Maurice's home. Unlike *East Lynne,* which dramatized the whole story of its heroine's departure and return, *Miss Multon* concentrated on a few final weeks. *East Lynne* was a melodrama in which the story was primary; *Miss Multon* moved much closer to a modern character study, with the plot's motifs pushed into the background.

Years later Palmer told Miss Morris that *Miss Multon* profited from the finest ensemble acting he had ever been able to offer, and she agreed. She recalled that O'Neill's Maurice "bore his wound with a patient dignity that made his one outbreak into hot passion tremendously effective, through force of contrast; while his sympathetic voice gave great value to the last tender words of pardon." Of Stoddart she wrote, "I never expect to find another *Dr. Osborne* so capable of contradicting a savage growl with a tender caress."

But, of course, she herself was the center of attention. The *Times*'s immediate impression was highly favorable: "In plays, lighted up here and there by expressions of purely human passions, and

101

rendered terribly impressive by pictures of acute physical pain which this actress paints with dreadful realism, no actress in this country can rival her. . . . Miss Morris' acting was as full of intensity, emotion and vigor as the story or audience would bear with." After watching her in several performances, William Winter recalled, "Contortions of the body, convulsions of the face, disproportionate attitudes, extravagant gestures, spasmodic starts and changes, and indescribable wild moans and cries were commingled in that singular embodiment with moments of sweet dignity, lovely tenderness, and exalted fortitude. Over the whole effort there was the lawlessness of a genius that was a law to itself; and the effect of the effort was that of deep pathos." Only reaction to the Brooklyn Theatre fire and the star's illness cut short the run after ten weeks.

There was little intrinsic merit in Fred Marsden's **Musette; or, Little Bright Eyes** (11-27-76, Park), but since it was written as a vehicle for its exuberant star, Lotta, it was assured a hearty welcome. Her fans remained as legion as they were loyal. This excuse for all of the petite actress's expected turns—her banjo playing, her breakdowns, her chatting with and winking to her audience—recounted the adventures of a gypsy girl who is pursued all across the map of England by the lecherous Sir Hugh Tracy (J. W. Carroll). When it is finally learned that she had been kidnapped as a baby by the gypsy band and is really an heiress, she can settle down with her own true love, the yokelish Billy Bokus (Thomas Whiffen). Although *Musette* quickly became one of the most popular plays in her repertory, Lotta played it for only the first three weeks of her stand. Perhaps boredom with such patent drivel prompted her frequent turnover of bills. It almost certainly caused her to make constant "improvements," even if this so infuriated the initially compliant Marsden that he eventually refused to attend performances of the play.

On December 4, two more fine stars, Lawrence Barrett and E. L. Davenport, returned to New York at Booth's. Unfortunately, the men had quarreled on the road, and after the first week Davenport withdrew. As it turned out, these were to be his last New York appearances, for he died the following summer. Their opening bill was *King Lear,* which was also on Edwin Booth's program at the Lyceum. Critics admired Barrett for his willingness to attempt new plays and in such roles as Cassius, but he was grossly miscast as Lear. His Edmund, Frederick Warde, remembered that "he lacked dignity and grandeur in the earlier scenes, his passion was petulance and his grief fretful rather

than pathetic." Most contemporary critics, while not quite so harsh, agreed. Davenport's Edgar was singled out for praise, one reviewer noting he "endowed with wonderful variety of accent the vagaries of 'Poor Tom.' "

On the 5th Daly introduced a revival of *The School for Scandal* at the Fifth Avenue, with Coghlan as "a miracle of elegance, dress, and distinction" in the part of Charles Surface and Fanny Davenport glowing with vitality as Lady Teazle. However, first-nighters emerging from the performance heard newsboys shouting the horrendous headlines of the extras they were peddling—the earliest gruesome tidings of the Brooklyn Theatre fire. The full horror became public by the next morning, and for the following weeks attendance at all theatres fell sickeningly, not totally recovering for the remainder of the season.

Despite plummeting patronage Broadway plodded on. On the 16th Barrett brought out *Richard III,* still using Colley Cibber's version. This time his hard, seemingly passionless acting was just right. Barrett had planned to offer *Julius Caesar,* but its scenery had been stored at the Brooklyn Theatre and was another casualty of the blaze. On the 18th Lotta cavorted through *Little Nell and the Marchioness* at the Park.

The American (12-20-76, Fifth Ave.) was Daly's title for *L'Étrangère,* the Parisian hit by Dumas fils. In a way his choice of title was curious, for Daly's adaptation had minimized the roles of the mysterious American (played in Paris by Sarah Bernhardt) and her husband and, with Coghlan in mind, centered on the self-serving Duke de Septmonts. His duchess (Fanny Davenport) has come to the bitter realization that he married her for her money and that he is openly and callously unfaithful. Mrs. Clarkson (Jeffreys Lewis), a pushy American of questionable reputation, offers to give a huge sum to charity in return for the privilege of having tea with the duchess. The duchess consents but at the same time discovers that the duke is one of the lady's lovers. This and his other infidelities drive her back into the arms of Gerard (Maurice Barrymore), whom she had loved and been prevented from marrying by her ambitious parents. Since Mrs. Clarkson herself has her eye on Gerard, she and the duke use a letter that has passed between Gerard and the duchess to discomfit the duchess. The whole matter is in danger of exploding publicly to everyone's scandal when the sensible Mr. Clarkson (James Lewis) quietly persuades all the parties to behave decorously. Coghlan was superb as the dissolute duke, injecting just the right measure of dignity and warmth to make his characterization acceptable, and the rest of the cast, especially James Lewis, won high praise. But the play, or at least its attitudes, proved simply too French for American audiences, so it ran less than a month.

Always willing to explore the best possibilities of contemporary drama, Barrett abandoned Shakespeare to bring out W. S. Gilbert's **Dan'l Druce, Blacksmith** (12-25-76, Booth's). Druce once had been successful, but after his wife deserted him and took their baby daughter with her, he became a confirmed miser living in an isolated hut. Sir Jasper Combe (W. E. Sheridan), fleeing defeat in battle, comes upon the hut. He has in hand a four-year-old girl whom he is taking to his wife. Combe forces himself on the miser, but when he discovers that Druce has gone to inform the local soldiery, he runs off, taking the miser's hoard of gold and leaving behind the child. Fourteen years go by. Druce has come to love the girl, whom he has raised and whom he calls Dorothy (Minnie Palmer). Then he learns that Combe has returned, this time as landlord of his village. Combe is attracted by the girl but does not associate her with the girl he left behind. He proposes to take her to his own estate. Druce protests, and in the ensuing argument Druce learns that she is his real daughter. The repentant Combe joins Druce in acquiescing to Dorothy's marriage to the neighbor she has come to love, Geoffrey Wynyard (Frederick Warde). While this highly sentimental play was not what most playgoers might expect from Gilbert, it was precisely the sort of work in which Barrett, with his gaunt appearance and stylistic peculiarities, could shine. The play ran a month and might have run longer but for the dismal slump in theatrical business everywhere.

The new year began with a change in Lotta's bills at the Park. On January 8, for the concluding week of her engagement, she brought back *Zip*. That Saturday, the 13th, Daly featured Coghlan and Fanny Davenport in a pair of performances of *The Lady of Lyons*, then brought forward his next new play. For **Lemons** (1-15-77, Fifth Ave.) the producer again turned to Germany, which would become increasingly his source for hits, taking this play from Julius Rosen's *Zitronen*. Perhaps because of her given names, Mrs. Elizabeth Victoria Stark (Mrs. Gilbert) insists that women were meant to rule—but only certain women. Her philosophy is: "Mankind is divided into classes:—Lemons and lemon squeezers! People are either lemons—to be squeezed by others! or they are squeezers of lemons themselves." She has summoned home to Lemon Lodge one lemon, her son Benny (Henry Crisp), in order to have him marry

another lemon, Margie (Sydney Cowell), daughter of a third squeezable, the rich, boozy widower Major Gooseberry (James Lewis). She also plans to tie the knot for two more lemons, her daughter Mary (Fanny Davenport) and Lord Loftus (John Brougham). Events conspire hilariously against her. Gooseberry and Loftus have come to Lemon Lodge to make arrangements for their very young orphaned niece to stay there. She arrives with her governess, Bertha (Emily Rigl). When Benny appears he is accompanied by his fellow lawyer Jack Perryn (Charles Coghlan). Benny has longed dreamed about a beautiful woman he saw briefly years before on a train, and Jack has loved Mary since they were children. Benny recognizes Bertha as the lady on the train. Jack himself is a consummate lemon squeezer and quietly sets about turning Mrs. Stark's stratagems inside out. He is helped immeasurably by Mrs. Stark, who is led to believe that both the Major and the Lord are madly in love with her and who vacillates ditheringly about which of their proposals to accept—although neither man has any intention of proposing. Jack proves victorious. Everyone is mated properly, and Mrs. Stark must confess she has been reduced to lemonade.

With his brother Joseph, who continued to labor as his uncredited collaborator, Daly contrived a lively adaptation. Although the young men are called barristers and one character specifically mentions that the action takes place in England, the play was essentially Americanized. With a few changes of lines there was no reason not to accept that the story was unfolding almost anywhere on this side of the North Atlantic. The entire action took place in a single setting, itself a novelty, but Daly managed to make matters more interesting by showing the drawing room from different angles in different acts. While Mrs. Gilbert had been with Daly from his first days at the burned-down Fifth Avenue, this play, probably more than any earlier one, catapulted her into the limelight. Her earnest incompetence and eventual fluttering helplessness were comic joys. So were the drolleries of the rest of the cast, including the sixty-six-year-old Brougham as the fortyish Loftus. The play ran two months, making it Daly's biggest hit of the season, and like several other plays it might have run longer but for the aftereffects of the Brooklyn fire. In Daly's and other versions, it was produced around the country off and on for the rest of the century.

Because *Miss Multon* required so small a cast, Palmer found himself with a large band of unemployed players under contract. His answer was to mount a two-week season of revivals at the Park, beginning on the 15th. The first offering was *The Marble Heart,* which gave way to *Led Astray* and *The Geneva Cross.*

Lester Wallack returned to the stage of his own playhouse when he assumed the leading role in Palgrave Simpson and Herman Merivale's London success **All for Her** (1-22-77, Wallack's). He mis-stepped on two counts. To contemporary critics Wallack was an even more dependable actor than Booth—though, of course, their repertories rarely overlapped. Yet while one paper proclaimed that "Wallack has absolutely no rival in romantic melo-drama" and noted that he was called before the curtain "again and again," others questioned the depth of his performance and, once more, his assuming a role belonging rightly to a younger man. They were less kind still to the play. Plagiarism was a common cry in these days of lax copyrights, but it was particularly painful when it was inept. Critics could not understand the play's West End acclaim and saw in it heavy-handed borrowings from *Don Caesar de Bazan, Marie Tudor,* and, most flagrantly, *A Tale of Two Cities.* Wallack portrayed Hugh Trevor, who loves Lady Marsden (Ada Dyas). But she loves Lord Edendale (Charles A. Stevenson), a man who has deprived Trevor of his inheritance and undercut him in many other ways. His affections unreturned and his own life a shambles, Trevor, for the sake of Lady Marsden, takes Edendale's place when the lord is condemned to death. The play was a short-lived failure.

Even theatrical doldrums could scarcely dampen the success of the next new entry, Leonard Grover's **Our Boarding House** (1-29-77, Park). At a time when critics had pen in hand to issue accusations of plagiary, they were apparently too busy laughing to see how closely the work paralleled *The Mighty Dollar.* If one was set in a salon, the other was set in a boardinghouse, at most suggesting perhaps a slightly less lofty social level. Both were comedies framed in a melodramatic story of a put-upon woman. And both relied for their laughs primarily on eccentrics whose carryings-on touched only gingerly on the main plot. In this instance the wronged lady was Beatrice Manheim (Maud Harrison), a music teacher who resides at the Bon Ton Boarding House in Chicago. Her supposed brother-in-law, Joseph Fioretti (W. E. Sheridan), a mean-spirited man who kicks little newsboys, arrives to take a room there and informs Beatrice and the other boarders that her marriage was a sham and her child is illegitimate. Many of the boarders are outraged and demand she leave. But she finds a staunch defender in Walter Dalrymple (A. H.

Stuart). At the last moment (just one page of dialogue remaining) a New York detective, Jack Hardy (W. J. Cogswell), appears to announce that her marriage was, in fact, legal and that her husband has died and left her an heiress. He arrests Fioretti. Beatrice and Walter are free to wed.

Even the play's stabs at humor often echoed *The Mighty Dollar.* Thus just as Mrs. General Gilflory had scattered malapropisms wherever she went, so does the Bon Ton's proprietress, Mrs. Colville (Alexina Fisher Baker). Only, at least to modern ears, they are not as funny. She confuses anarchy with arnica (then a popular herbal stimulant) and calls a gourmand "a gore man." The comedy's success stemmed entirely from the characterizations of two feuding guests, Col. M. T. Elevator (William H. Crane), an impecunious speculator always dreaming of making a killing in the commodities market (shades of Colonel Sellers), and Professor Gregarious Gillypod (Stuart Robson), an inventor determined to devise the great flying machine. He has had seventeen failures, but since the seventeenth was such a successful failure, he is determined to persevere. The brash, somewhat pompous and emotive Crane was the perfect foil for Robson, with his handsome but wooden face, squeaky voice, and uniquely staccato delivery. They performed so deliciously in tandem that for the next decade they were America's most popular comedy team.

• • •

Stuart Robson (1836–1903) was born Henry Robson Stuart in Annapolis, Md., and made his acting debut in Baltimore in 1852. After many years in stock he joined Laura Keene's company in New York in 1862, then spent time with Mrs. Drew in Philadelphia and playing opposite William Warren in Boston.

William H[enry] Crane (1845–1928) was born in Leicester, Mass. Unlike his slightly shorter, lighter partner's, his training was almost entirely in musical theatre. He made his debut in 1863 in a small role in *The Daughter of the Regiment* with Harriet Holman's touring company and remained with the group for eight seasons before moving on to play low comedian roles with Alice Oates's famous ensemble. In 1874, he created the role of Le Blanc, the notary, in the original New York production of *Evangeline.*

• • •

If the scampish Grover had shoplifted many ideas for the play, he had pulled an even more unethical trick in selling the rights to the play independently to at least three men, A. M. Palmer, T. H. French (the play publisher), and Henry Abbey (who owned the Park). When the men learned of the scam they hastily joined forces to produce the comedy, hoping to forestall anyone else to whom Grover might have sold the rights. Robson and Crane later purchased the rights from the producers.

Thanks in no small measure to Crane and Robson, *Our Boarding House* ran three months, a run surpassed only by *Sardanapalus* and equaled only by **The Danicheffs** (2-5-77, Union Square), Parselle and Cazauran's translation of Pierre Newsky and the younger Dumas's play. Like many of the best contemporary melodramas, this one avoided the older, spectacular "sensations," such as blazing buildings and sinking ships, and depended for its interest and tensions on its character studies and the dramatic interaction of its characters. The Countess Danicheff (Fanny Morant) is determined that her son, Vladimir (James O'Neill), shall not marry his beloved serf girl, Anna (Sara Jewett). Since Vladimir must spend some months in Moscow, the countess devises a ploy. She agrees that if he is still of the same mind on his return, she will give her consent. But he is no sooner gone than she frees another serf, Osip (Charles Thorne, Jr.), a close friend of the liberal Vladimir, on the condition that he marry Anna. Osip is forced to consent. Vladimir hears of the marriage and returns to confront Osip. He does, whip in hand, but Osip stares him down and, once Vladimir is calm, assures him the marriage has never been consummated. Despite further machinations by the countess and others, a divorce is obtained. The self-sacrificing Osip enters the church. What made the play so gripping was one stunningly acted confrontation after another. The duel of words between Vladimir and his mother, the painful encounter between the countess and Osip, and, most of all, the meeting of Vladimir and Osip on Vladimir's hurried return provided thrills more moving than any scene painter and carpenter's fake fire could ever do and allowed the drama to run until early May.

The very sort of old-fashioned contrivances that *The Danicheffs* wisely had cast aside were much in evidence in a play that opened the same night, **Fifth Avenue** (2-5-77, Booth's). George Fawcett Rowe had written the play, which was set in Civil War times, with Thorne and Henry Montague in mind but had to settle for George Rignold and Frederick Warde. With his very English accent Rignold played the American Richard Blake, who falls in love with Olivia Schuyler (Maude Granger) after rescuing her from a sinking ship. He is not dissuaded from courting Olivia even when he learns she has been promised to a languid English snob, Graham Liddesdale (Warde). Blake also saves Olivia's father,

Simon Schuyler (James H. Taylor), from bankruptcy, but after Schuyler is murdered, Blake is falsely accused of the crime. Inevitably all ends happily.

The settings were striking, including the sinking of the ocean liner; Wall Street and the uproar in the boardroom of a failing company; Fifth Avenue, just off Madison Square, by night; the launching of the *Monitor;* and the riots of 1863. But the real show-stoppers were three performers still known better as vaudeville entertainers than as legitimate players. In the Fifth Avenue scene Johnny Wild, in blackface, sang Negro songs, George S. Knight imitated an immigrant having a fit, and Charles Parsloe was a Bowery street arab. The *Express,* calling them "heroes of the hour," noted, "The boys in the gallery seemed to go wild in a frenzy of seeing their old friends, and applause almost shook the building." Yet the play was hardly a hit, running only a month, although it was immediately taken on the road.

The abruptly curtailed run of *All for Her* forced Wallack's to hustle up a parade of revivals. Pressed back into the repertory were a double bill of *A Morning Call* and *Married Life* on the 7th, *Wild Oats* on the 12th, *She Stoops to Conquer* on the 16th, and *The Rivals* on March 6. Whatever rehearsals were required to bring these pieces to the boards, the ensemble was also busy working on a new offering. Charles Mathews's **My Awful Dad** (3-10-77, Wallack's) was a slight enough and simple enough thing, but it proved the most popular of any of the house's premieres during the season. Perhaps one small point in its favor was that Lester Wallack for a change consented to play the older father of a younger son. His Adonis Evergreen was an aging cut-up and roué, but one whose seeming carelessness and irresponsibility hid a heart of gold. Evergreen's antics drive his proper albeit mean-minded son, Dick (Harry Beckett), a barrister, to distraction, until Adonis is able to bring home to his offspring that being fun-loving and thoughtful is neither impossible nor sinful. If Wallack, like most of his contemporaries, regularly rewrote the works of long-dead playwrights to make them more palatable to modern audiences, he was also quick to bring even current West End plays in line with American tastes by substantial revampings. In his autobiography he itemized several of the changes he incorporated into *My Awful Dad,* such as breaking up two long acts into three shorter ones and adding a scene in which, disguised as his own son, he addresses a jury. (He did not mention that this last change gave him the opportunity to pass once again as a younger man.) With an interruption caused by the star's illness, the play ran until mid-May.

Following the success of *Lemons,* Daly met with disastrous failure when he presented **Blue Glass** (3-12-77, Fifth Ave.), the Daly brothers' redaction of J. B. von Schweitzer's *Epidemisch.* Against the strictures of Colonel Howitzer (Charles Fisher), his wife, Sophie (Emily Rigl), invests heavily in a company that claims the sun's rays are therapeutic when filtered through blue glass and is manufacturing a product to take advantage of this amazing discovery. The Howitzers' niece, Estie (Fanny Davenport), has also gone against her uncle's grain by falling in love with a navy man, Lieutenant Tom Havens (Charles Coghlan). Preposterous complications follow when Estie's love note is delivered by mistake to Howitzer's aide, Lieutenant Reginald Havens (John Drew), and Sophie's order for more stock is sent in error to Tom.

Critics found the play unfunny and said it stretched credulity even beyond normal farcical limits. But most enjoyed the performance of Mrs. Gilbert as the hardnosed lady stockbroker, Mrs. Fletcher Bull, and James Lewis as the curbside hawker of stocks, Julius Popheimer. One week of poor business goaded Daly into closing the show and bringing out *London Assurance* on the 19th.

On the same evening, the widow of James H. Hackett played the title role of *Medea* at the Broadway. Productions of Greek tragedies were rare enough, even if, as in this case, they came through French retellings. But Mrs. Hackett's mounting stood little chance, since she was embarrassingly inadequate for the part and everything that could go wrong during the performance seemingly did. Typically, when one of her supporting actresses fainted onstage there was no understudy waiting in the wings, so someone was urgently enlisted to read the fallen player's role.

Effie Ellsler was a young actress looking for stardom. Although she had not yet caught the brass ring, she would eventually seize it and move on to a long if unsteady career. But even during her apprenticeship in Cleveland, where her father was a major theatre manager, she called attention to her skills. These prompted Bartley Campbell to write **A Heroine in Rags** (3-28-77, Euclid Avenue Opera House, Cleveland) for her and give her the role of Jeanette Brashear, a gamine Parisian flower vendor and street singer whose happy little world turns almost tragic until she feigns insanity to save her lover's life. Stock figures among the other characters included "a villain, a heavy father [foreshadowing her first big hit], a humorous man, and a jealous woman." When the work subsequently played Philadelphia, Miss Ellsler was advertised as the "charm-ing actress and vocalist." The *Evening Bulletin* agreed, seeing her as "a bright, vivacious little person, who seems completely at ease on stage," but it added skeptically, "Whether she has reserved power or not remains to be seen." The play, often with her in the lead, was performed on and off in various cities for more than a decade.

Just who turned *L'Officier de fortune* into **The Princess Royal** (3-31-77, Fifth Ave.) for Daly is open to some conjecture. Certainly Bronson Howard made a stab at it, but whether his version was as bad as Daly's brother claimed it was and thus was rejected, or whether the producer simply took credit for it, is unclear. The play centered on the romance of Baron Frederick Trenck (Charles Coghlan) and Princess Amalie of Prussia (Fanny Davenport), recounting how Frederick's scheming look-alike cousin, Francis (also Coghlan), throws all manner of obstacles in Frederick's path. At one point Frederick is even found guilty of misdeeds actually committed by Francis and is sentenced to death. Ten lavish sets and Miss Davenport's ability to wear gorgeous costumes to striking effect glossed over whatever shortcomings the drama had. In many ways the play was a glimpse of the Ruritanian sagas that would soon inundate the stage and would later serve so well and so long as bases for operetta plots. Apparently Daly had not expected the play to be quite the draw it was. A previous booking forced him to move it to the Grand Opera House in early May for a few additional weeks.

On April 2, John McCullough came into Booth's, still dutifully waving the tattered banners of Edwin Forrest's best traditions. His schedule ran to such Forrest standbys as *Virginius, Richelieu, Othello, The Gladiator,* and *King Lear* (the third major *Lear* of the season). Frederick Warde was a member of the theatre's company and so played in support. In his autobiography Warde remembered, "There was little subtlety in McCullough's acting—it was not in his nature, but in the impersonation of the elemental conditions and passions of the human heart he was admirable. His Virginius was a splendid presentation of the Roman patriot and father. The tender love of the earlier scenes, the indignation at the outrage of his child, the horror of the dreadful alternative in the Forum and the bereaved and distracted father in the later scenes were finely portrayed."

Niblo's Garden Theatre, which all season long had been moving from spectacle to variety to combination attractions, returned to the legitimate fold as a first-class house on the 2nd with a two-week revival of Shakespeare's rarely done *Antony and*

Cleopatra. Critics thought that Joseph Wheelock and Agnes Booth were believable if unexciting as the doomed lovers, but they saved most of their warmest adjectives for old George Heister, who probably had been the most respected scene painter of the 1850s and who for this occasion created a magnificent panorama moving Pompey's galley from the open sea to the Egyptian shore and then down the Nile.

The Eagle, another theatre with a vacillating policy much like Niblo's, drew most of the important critics and faithful first-nighters on April 4 when it offered the homely, determined Anna Dickinson in her own **A Crown of Thorns; or, Anne Boleyn.** Miss Dickinson was a lecturer, sometime actress, and playwright who could not accept that in the last two pursuits she was woefully deficient. She was at best barely competent as a writer, and not even that could be said of her acting. Her Anne went to her death after her love for Lord Henry Percy (Louis Aldrich) was discovered and used to deadly purpose by Cardinal Wolsey (W. H. Leake). One critic wrote, "Her delivery was monotonous, her tone nasal, her pathetic passages were sometimes whined and sometimes bleated." Her critical drubbing could not convince her to retire, and though this play's run was short she would be heard from again.

Another woman anxious for the world to recognize her acting abilities was Adelaide Lennox. On the 21st at the Lyceum she offered what she believed was incontestable proof of them by giving her interpretation of *Camille.* Her reception may have been even more unkind than that accorded Anna Dickinson. She huffily closed the show and wrote letters to the newspapers blaming the debacle on the critics, her producer, her supporting players, and anyone else who came to mind.

Another aspirant, hefty Bessie Darling, followed Miss Dickinson into the Eagle on the 24th. She survived for a single week, during which time she managed to display herself in *The Hunchback, Macbeth,* and *The Lady of Lyons.*

A far more welcome revival was that of *The Gilded Age,* which brought back John T. Raymond's Colonel Sellers to the Park on the 30th. Some newspaper advertisements imply the title had been changed to *There's Millions in It!*

Good things did not come in threes for A. M. Palmer. Following on the successes of *Miss Multon* and *The Danicheffs* he turned to **Smike** (5-7-77, Union Square), Andrew Halliday's dramatization of *Nicholas Nickleby.* The play, which had to pick and choose from Dickens's varied parade of incidents, seemed much too disjointed, and the players could

not instill the requisite touch of caricature with which the novelist had imbued almost all his characters. Young Bijou Heron had the title role, and C. A. Stevenson was Nicholas, but J. H. Stoddart walked away with acting honors for his Newman Noggs.

Competing with the new play at the Union Square was the return of Adelaide Neilson at the Fifth Avenue. She was a joyous tonic after all the unattractive, talentless women who had been bedeviling New York's stages. Many believed she was the finest actress on the boards at the time. To make her return even more exciting she began with two roles she had not played before in New York. Of her opening Viola, in *Twelfth Night,* Winter wrote in the *Tribune,* "Miss Neilson has added to the pantheon of the stage a figure that must long live in memory as exquisite in proportion, delicate in line and color, soft and dreamy in character, and very bright and tender in presence and emotion, an actual human being, entirely beautiful, and never to be forgotten." When, for her second week, she offered her Imogen in *Cymbeline* the *Times* exclaimed, "In no previous endeavor to illustrate the varied emotions of love-lorn womanhood has the achievement been more thoroughly poetical and marked by more delicate gradations of tone. The great scene with *Iachimo,* when she repels the Italian's brutal proposals, but afterward, in the goodness and gentleness of her nature, is wooed to forgiveness by recollections of her absent lord, was an admirable specimen of Miss Neilson's skill . . . and the interview with *Pisanio,* when the latter is about to kill her, was carried on with a tearful pathos and a power so genuine as to call forth a unanimous demonstration." For her final week she offered her incomparable Juliet.

Wallack's ensemble revived a less ancient play, the manager's own *Rosedale,* for its final production of the season, beginning on May 4.

George Rignold and some of his associates took over Booth's for a season that could best be called a mixed bag. The opener was a double bill of *Black-Eyed Susan* and a new play (although it had been given once the preceding season in a benefit performance), Palgrave Simpson and Herman Merivale's **Alone** (5-14-77, Booth's). Rignold portrayed Colonel Challice, a blind old man who believes he has been deserted by his wife and child. Rignold also played Romeo, first to Marie Wainwright's Juliet then to Minnie Cumming's. Near the end of the stand he also essayed a Romeo who made love to a different Juliet in each scene. Another of his "new" plays, Watts Phillips's **Amos Clarke** (5-21-77, Booth's), actually had first been offered, like *Alone,* at a benefit the preceding season. The play was set against the background of the Duke of Monmouth's rebellion. As its hero, Rignold found himself pitted against an uncle in the opposing forces and ultimately forced to sacrifice his own life to save his brother's. For all his good looks and talents there was something dissuadingly erratic about Rignold, who ended his stay by returning to his admired Henry V.

Daly's season ended on a down note with **Vesta** (5-28-77, Fifth Ave.), taken from Alexandre Parodi's French success *Rome vaincue*. Daly advertised the play from the start as being offered for only a single week, but beyond doubt he would have extended the run or returned it the following season if its reception had not precluded this. The story had an almost classic simplicity. With Hannibal at the gates of Rome, the Romans look for a scapegoat and find one in the vestal virgin Opimia (Jeffreys Lewis), who has broken her vows by taking a lover, Lentulus (Frederick Warde). Lentulus urges her to save her life by fleeing, but she refuses. Rather than see her granddaughter die a shameful death, Opimia's cronish grandmother, the blind Posthumia (Fanny Davenport), kills her, cursing Romans and their absurd beliefs as she does. Whether or not those beliefs are truly absurd, Opimia is no sooner dead than news of Hannibal's retreat reaches the city. Once again the beautiful Miss Davenport abandoned her modish dresses and fashionable makeup to turn herself into an aged hag with a puffed, wrinkled face, straggly white hair, and a ragged, formless black costume. She, not Miss Lewis, was the center of attention, although critics felt her acting was not up to her earlier playing of similar roles in *No Name* and *Charity*. The play's failure was an ominous hint of bad times just ahead for Daly.

At various periods in the history of our theatre, producers, writers, and press agents, perceiving a type of play is coming to seem outmoded, will attempt to inject new life into the form not by substantive changes but by suggesting a new name for the old genre. This may have been the case with Major Charles G. Mayers's **Waves** (6-11-77, Wallack's), which was advertised as a "comedy-drama" but was simply an old-fashioned sensation-melodrama. Edna Gordon (Lettie Allen) is told her husband, Leonard (Walter A. Eytinge), has been drowned in a ship's sinking and is hounded by his rejected rival, Captain Walton (Theodore Hamilton). Steeled by a dream in which she sees her husband, surrounded by icebergs, clinging for dear life to a bobbing funnel and eventually rescued by a lifeboat sent from "a shaky vessel in the distance,"

Edna endures the captain's persecutions until her husband reappears and metes out justice. In one scene she breaks the glass in a bow window to rescue her kidnapped child. If the melodrama was stale, so was much of the comedy, depending as it did on yet another Malaprop, this time called Mrs. Brightless (Mrs. A. F. Baker). The most refreshing character may have been Jerry Timkins (Thomas Whiffen), a reformed thief whose self-inflicted penitence is to commit further thefts. The work survived two weeks.

Nor could **Cross and Crescent** (6-18-77, Niblo's) run longer. The play reached back to the First Crusade to pit the Christian Bohemund (Frank Roche) against the mysterious infidel Hasan, the Old Man of the Mountain (Frank Mordaunt), whose murderous band gave us the word *assassin*. Although critics seldom complained about crowds painted on canvas, at least one critic railed against stuffed mannequins thrown over the ramparts in a scene depicting the siege of Jerusalem.

Lettie Allen, who had received favorable notices in *Waves*, was the star of its successor, Henry Morford's **Crabbed Age** (6-28-77, Wallack's), which earlier in the season had toured the area's combination houses. She played Hélène Volmier, yet one more victim of a false accusation. Hélène is falsely accused of having murdered her husband, and it takes the brilliant forensics of her lawyer, René Latrobe (J. B. Atwater), to secure her acquittal and release from prison. A subplot spotlighted the tribulations of Mme Dumoulin (May Roberts) caused by the unfounded jealously of her senescent husband, General Dumoulin (Theodore Hamilton). When this play failed to please, the company had another ready on the following Monday. In Philip Stoner's *Woodleigh* (7-2-77, Wallack's) the beauty and charms of Amy Winthrope (Lettie Allen) lead two brothers, Robert (Theodore Hamilton) and Maurice (Cyril Searle), to fall in love with her. The brothers also fall to fighting, and when Robert knocks Maurice into the water, he assumes he has murdered his brother, his mind snaps, and he flees. He later returns to find Amy has loved him and remained faithful.

That same night *The Three Guardsmen* was revived at Niblo's, followed on the 16th by the return of Boucicault's still popular *The Poor of New York*, which spanned the rest of the summer. The season ended, not with a bang or a whimper but with a thud, when still another aspiring lady, Anna Boyle, cast her lot with *Romeo and Juliet* at Booth's on the 30th. The heat and poor notices prompted her to cancel her stay after the second performance.

Away from the mainstream, lesser theatres remained busy, offering revivals of old plays, returns of not so old plays, chances for fading stars to find an audience, and, most of all, new American plays. While Broadway put up with *Two Men of Sandy Bar* for a month, lower-class houses welcomed a number of westerns. A pair of examples will have to suffice. Just as the Harte play was winding down its Broadway stand, blue-collar audiences began cheering **Wild Bill, King of the Border Men** (9-18-76, Wood's). (The play was also listed as *Wild Bill; or, Life on the Border.*). It starred a touring actor named Julian Kent and his trained bear, Julia. The play required Julia to impersonate a villain or villainess and be killed by Kent. Kent played a fictitious hero, but the celebrated Texas Jack portrayed himself in **Texas Jack (in the Black Hills)** (4-2-77, Bowery). Of course, plays of interest to American audiences were not necessarily westerns. Numerous pieces had New York City for a setting, and at least one focused on the Jewish immigrants beginning to make a name for themselves. **Moses, a Dealer in Second Hand Clothing** (9-11-76, Bowery) was given varying names in other programs and in other cities: sometimes *Moses Abraham, the Old Clothes Man,* sometimes *Moses, the Old Clothes Man,* and at least once *Abraham, the Old Clothes Man.* In outline the plot is melodramatic. Moses, robbed and separated from his daughter (another Rachel), must find her, then find her a husband. The action moved from a Bowery beer garden to Moses's second-hand clothing store off Union Square to a rich man's home. But audiences neither wanted nor got undiluted melodrama. Moses drowned his sorrow in music, playing a violin, a clarinet, a banjo, and a "Lilliputian fiddle." Ads promised "Laughable, Uproarious, Thrilling, Startling Situations and Sensations."

1877–1878

Two hugely successful foreign plays and a cadre of luminous stars provided the happiest theatrical news in this largely lackluster season, although several American plays were not without merit or interest. But the good news was interwoven with bad. Just as the effects of the 1873 panic finally seemed to be disappearing, newly organized labor decided to flex its muscles, and railroad strikes spread across the country. If New York City theatres were not as dependent on tourists as they would be in later years, business nonetheless had to be hurt. More important, railroads carried scenery and actors from place to place in days when every city and town of any real size had one or more legitimate theatres.

An even bigger shock was in store for New Yorkers when Augustin Daly abruptly withdrew from management of the Fifth Avenue early in the new season. His withdrawal marked the beginning of a series of historically important transitions during the next three seasons that would change the whole tone of American theatre and push it, however imperceptibly at the time, into a more recognizably modern era. In the 1879–80 season Daly himself would help complete that transition by introducing another great ensemble. Of course, 1877 playgoers could have no inkling of all this.

The new theatrical year got off to an appropriately youthful start with an adaptation of a French farce, Alfred Hennequin and Émile de Najac's *Bébé,* translated simply as **Baby** (7-16-77, Park). The baby in question is Willie St. Paul (Edwin F. Thorne), whose parents steadfastly have refused to acknowledge that he has long since reached puberty. Fortunately for Willie, his wily tutor, Tracy Coach (W. J. LeMoyne), also has an eye for a pretty girl. Together they contrive to bring Willie's parents to an acceptance of the facts of life. The farce, a far cry from its naughtier, more cynical French source, distracted playgoers from the summer's problems and returned for a second stand during the winter.

Benjamin E. Woolf's mediocre adaptation of Dicken's *Bleak House,* called **Poor Jo** (7-23-77, Union Square), met with a discouraging reception. Many in the cast, including Mary Cary, who assumed the title role, were popular Boston players. New Yorkers, however, traditionally felt they had a monopoly on the finest performers, and these artists did nothing to convince them that their beliefs were wrong. The production was short-lived.

Despite the hot weather, the next opening brought out an elite congregation of first-nighters. The play's co-author, dressed in summery white, assured them that the work was "intended rather for instruction than amusement," pointing out as an instance, "For the instruction of the young we have introduced a game of poker." Unfortunately for the speaker, Mark Twain, few playgoers were amused by **Ah Sin** (7-31-77, Fifth Ave.), which he had written with Bret Harte. Broderick (Edmund K. Collier), a "knave through circumstances over which he ought to have control," assaults and leaves for dead "the Champion Liar of Calaveras," Uncle Billy Plunkett (P. A. Anderson). Broderick manages to hang the crime on York (Henry Crisp), "the Gentleman Miner and Owner of the '40 Mill." A lynch mob would hang York, but that clever "Heathen Chinee," Ah Sin (Charles T. Parsloe), implicates Broderick by a telltale coat. Many contemporaries suggested that Harte injected much of the humor, but Arthur Hobson Quinn and other modern scholars have countered that Harte may have written most of the men's dialogue and Twain the women's. If so, Twain was not in top form. Mrs. Plunkett (Mrs. Gilbert), "the too apparent cause of Mr. Plunkett's absence from home," was simply the latest variation on Mrs. Malaprop, given to such statements as "I cannot think of him without going into ecstasies of sensibility, perfect ruptures of emotion." The play struggled through a forced run of thirty-five performances, long enough to confirm Parsloe as the era's best interpreter of amusing Chinese figures.

For many of New York's morally censorious critics—and they were plentiful at the time—a superb cast, all in top form, was the only reason for seeing **Pink Dominos** (8-16-77, Union Square), James Albery's adaptation of Alfred Hennequin and Alfred Delacour's *Les Dominos roses.* Lady Maggie Wagstaff (Agnes Booth) and Mrs. Greythorne (Linda Dietz) are as flirtatious as they are suspicious of their husbands, Sir Percy (Charles Stevenson) and Mr. Greythorne (Charles Coghlan). They arrange to meet the men and change partners in private rooms at a celebrated restaurant, with the inevitable farcical complications. Gentleman critics who might bend a little bit when husbands cheated, as in the preceding season's *Forbidden Fruit,* were outraged at a comedy that even suggested wives might play around. One exception was R. F. G. Haggard, who, writing in the *Tribune* in lieu of the sermonizing Winter, found it "brisk and lively . . . and ingeniously planned." Previous bookings forced the play's removal after a month's run, but it returned later for additional performances.

Although the initial run of Joaquin Miller's **The Danites; or, The Heart of the Sierras** (8-22-77, Broadway) was only thirty performances, it remained popular for many years and carved for itself a significant niche in the history of American drama. More than any other contemporary piece, it is credited with opening first-class American stages to sagas of our Wild West, heretofore largely the province of lesser, working-class theatres. Miller took his drama from his own stories *The First Woman in the Forks* and *The Last Man in the Camp.* His first version was made in England in collaboration with an unidentified English actor. A Philadel-

phia actor, Alexander Fitzgerald, revised it as a vehicle for McKee Rankin and Rankin's wife, Kitty Blanchard. Its adventures begin when a pair of youngsters escape from the vengeance wreaked upon the Williams family by a band of Danites, members of a Mormon secret society. One of the youngsters is Nancy Williams (Miss Blanchard), who fears the Mormons will pursue her and so disguises herself as a boy and adopts the name Billy Piper. She seeks refuge in a mining camp, where the comely schoolmarm, Huldah Brown (Lillie Eldridge), falls in love with the supposed young man. After Huldah accepts that Billy will not have her, she agrees to marry Alexander "Sandy" McGee (Rankin). Huldah then learns the truth about Billy and so feels no qualms about inviting him into the privacy of her rooms. Naturally, Sandy misconstrues this and becomes furious. When the Danites, who indeed have sought out Nancy, come to the camp and attempt to incite a lynch mob, Sandy at first is willing to join them. But Huldah reveals the whole story, and Sandy then turns the fury of the mob against the Mormons.

One character quickly usurping an important supporting role in western plays was the sly, impish "Chinee." In *The Danites* he was called Washee-Washee, since Chinese, unless they were building railroads, were looked on first and foremost as laundrymen. Harry Pratt originated the role, but he was eventually replaced by Parsloe, who made the part his own.

The drama helped secure a place for such tales on our best stages; at the same time it helped codify in theatrical terms the era's widespread disdain for Mormons. For nearly half a century afterwards Mormons would be portrayed either as the blackest villains or, at best, as unsavory comic figures. The *Times* in its review thought nothing of gratuitously branding the Mormons "an organized body [who] combine religion, murder, and rapine in their everyday life." The play, sometimes called *The Danites in the Sierras,* also secured McKee Rankin his long-lasting stardom.

. . .

[Arthur] **McKee Rankin** (1841–1914) was born in Sandwich, Canada, and first acted professionally in Rochester, N.Y., in 1861, using the name George Henley. After spending time in London, he made his New York debut in 1866 as Hugh De Brass in *A Regular Fix.* He became a leading man at the Union Square in 1872, scoring hits in such plays as *Led Astray* and *The Two Orphans.* In his earlier years he was a slim, handsome, round-faced, curly-headed man, but he grew portly with time and was never able to abandon the rather fustian style of acting that was already falling out of fashion in the 1870s.

. . .

The first of the season's major stars, E. A. Sothern, marched in the forefront of September's entries. His appearance as **The Crushed Tragedian** (9-3-77, Park) may have sent playgoers' memories scurrying back over the years to the earliest days of *Our American Cousin* in which the actor had assumed the then relatively unimportant role of Dundreary; for the vehicle he was now offering had been written by H. J. Byron as *The Prompter's Box*, and the character Sothern was portraying, De Lacy Fitzaltamont, originally had been quite secondary. Byron's plot had centered on the love story of Florence Bristowe (Ida B. Savory), a young actress and a prompter's daughter, and Ernest Glendenning (Henry Crisp), a barrister turned playwright. Florence, needing money to get her dissolute brother out a jam, accepts a large sum from Ernest's father in return for rejecting Ernest's marriage proposal. Several years pass before Ernest learns the whole story and the lovers are reconciled.

Through this romance wanders a decrepit old actor, a would-be tragedian, who eventually finds fame and fortune as "Maximilian, the Mammoth Comique" in music halls. As he had with Dundreary, Sothern made a theatrical mountain out of the playwright's molehill. His Fitzaltamont was a consummate blending of sharp-edged humor and pathos, while his touching acting was abetted by excellent costuming. Sothern's son, E. H. Sothern, recalled in his autobiography how his father had obtained the tatterdemalion outfit for his first appearance by getting his manager to wangle some seedy clothing from a demented Madison Square derelict in exchange for a new suit. (A number of great stars, including Kate Claxton after the opening of *The Two Orphans*, recounted similar instances. Thus the story is suspect, even if the son's highly circumstantial recounting of this case is uncommonly interesting.) In the third act, when he finally tastes success, Fitzaltamont appears, with long, shaggy hair and drooping mustache, in a shiny, silken new suit, complete with bejeweled chestpin, boutonniere, and huge gold fob watch. The outfit had just the right degree of outlandishness and brought down the house, at which point Fitzaltamont remarked, "You don't fancy that I got it out of the legitimate drama, do you?" Sothern had added one more gem to his collection of characterizations.

Sothern's success was followed by Daly's disaster. The producer's season began and ended with the short run of **The Dark City and Its Bright Side** (9-4-77, Fifth Ave.), a patently old-fashioned melodrama he and his brother Joseph had adapted from Théodore Cogniard and Clairville's *Les Compagnons de la truelle*. (Clairville was a nom de plume for Louis François Nicolae.) This time the men plainly had not done their work well or sufficiently. Opening night the play ran from 8:00 until about 1:00 a.m. Pruning after a first night was a common practice at a time when tryouts were still rare, but this sort of excess was totally unacceptable. Moreover, Daly had lost two of his brightest players, Charles Coghlan and Fanny Davenport. The story focuses on Sibyl Chase (Ada Dyas), whose vicious uncle, Nicholas Vannart (Frank Hardenberg), burns the will that would give her a fortune. The charred remains of the will, with just enough left to convict Vannart, are found in a chimney. Before this denouement, the loyal Dudley Arden (Maurice Barrymore) and others travel all across New York City in an attempt to right the wrong.

Most critics treated the play brutally. One surprising exception was William Winter in the *Tribune*, who admitted "the play was not received with the usual eclat" but suggested the trouble could be blamed simply on "an oversight on the part of the gifted author [again, only Augustin Daly was credited in programs] in endeavoring to avail himself of too much material." Reviewers were unanimous only in extolling the physical production, which included one set showing City Hall, its park, and Newspaper Row by gaslight; another of adjoining rooftops with a view of the city; and others depicting the Jefferson Market and the East River Bridge. Coming after other disappointments, the failure was so costly that Daly was forced to give up his lease and disband his great ensemble, bringing to an end one small era of American theatre. While it seems doubtful that Daly's first troupe had offered any new plays of lasting value, they had, unlike Wallack's, offered more American plays, or at least foreign plays that had been Americanized. Moreover, the players had a more distinctly American tinge than those at the anglophilic Wallack's. It had been a measured but significant move toward a more modern American theatre.

If Daly could not discard a predilection toward a dying school of melodrama, he was far from alone. Yet another French melodrama, *La Comtesse de Faverolles*, was offered as **Under the Willows** (9-4-77, Lyceum). The villainous Antoine Thibaut (D. W. Waller) attempts to blackmail the countess (Emma Waller) and murder her husband but eventually is slain himself. The evening's chief attraction was Mrs. Waller, a buxom, matronly actress who excelled at emotive, pathetic roles and whom many felt never achieved the renown she deserved. By this time she was nearing the end of her career. As usual her reviews were highly favorable, but they did not lure playgoers, so the piece was quickly withdrawn.

A man whose career had not yet hit full stride was J. C. Williamson. Although he would strike real gold by abandoning acting and becoming Australia's leading theatre magnate, at this time he was a highly admired actor who stopped off in New York, as part of an extended world tour, with his equally popular wife, Maggie Moore, to appear in **Struck Oil** (9-17-77, Union Square). The action, set in western Pennsylvania, then a source of much of America's oil, began at the time of the Civil War. Deacon Skinner (H. A. Weaver), who lusts after the property and wife of a Pennsylvania "Dutchman," John Stofel (Williamson), persuades him to act as his substitute in the war. Later John is reported missing and presumed dead. But he is not. Instead he has lost his mind and wandered hopelessly about the country. Coming to Oilsville, he is mocked and chased by a band of callous hoodlums. To escape he climbs an oil derrick. At the top he slips and falls twenty feet. The fall restores his senses, allowing him to be reunited with his family and put the deacon in his place. Critics dismissed the play as trifling and preposterous, but the stars were praised. Williamson was lauded for his comedy in the first act and for his pathos in succeeding ones; Miss Moore for her singing of several songs, in a manner that reminded some of Lotta. Marston's scenery also was singled out, including a night view of Pittsburgh and, most of all, the setting of the oil field, with derricks pumping away.

Beginning October 20, for the last week of the run, the Williamsons added a second play to the bill, Clay M. Greene's **The Chinese Question.** Set in Greene's native San Francisco, the play had fun with a burning issue of the day, Chinese immigration. A family falls to arguing over the merits of Irish versus Oriental servants. The father is a staunch proponent of the Chinese, while the rest of the family prefer Irish help. To win their case they persuade their Irish serving girl, Kitty McShane (Miss Moore), and her butcher swain, Billy (Williamson), to masquerade as voluble, inept Orientals. One newspaper reported that every suggestion of excluding Chinese from the country met with enthusiastic applause.

On the night of *Struck Oil*'s premiere another new play with an American setting opened at a theatre usually given over to road companies of older pieces. **Secret Service; or, McParlan, the Detective** (9-17-77, Grand Opera) was based on Allen

Pinkerton's *The Molly Maguires*. Its hero, under the alias McKenna, infiltrates this early terrorist organization and foils its attempt to pull off a bloody bombing. The play clearly pleased the gallery gods, provoking "a good deal of the old fashioned 'hi hi' [the cry of approval] of the east side." A touring production, it remained at the Grand Opera for a single week and moved on.

The Florences had begun a six-week stand at the Eagle in late August with a roster of plays composed almost entirely of old favorites. Their lone novelty was Ernst and Fred Williams's **That Wife of Mine** (9-24-77, Eagle), a French farce duly scrubbed clean for American audiences. Harry Granville makes the silly mistake of courting and proposing to two ladies whose gardens adjoin one another. He hustles back and forth across the separating fence until he is exposed and hauled into court, where two fathers in morning suits try to give away two appropriately dressed brides to the same man. For all the bowdlerizing, the play displeased patrons and quickly disappeared.

M. V. Lingham's **Michael Strogoff** (9-24-77, Lyceum), a hastily contrived adaptation of a Jules Verne story, was ignored by some newspapers and waved away by others. It quickly closed, but further versions of this patriot's retreat from Moscow would threaten to deluge New York stages a few seasons hence. Two nights later at the Broadway, McKee Rankin, Kitty Blanchard, and their company supplanted *The Danites* with a revival of *Oliver Twist* for the final week of their stand. Rankin was Fagin; Miss Blanchard, Nancy.

Whether Lester Wallack or Dion Boucicault was responsible for the hyperbolic publicity that preceded the opening of **Marriage** (10-1-77, Wallack's) is uncertain, but most likely the flamboyant, self-advertising playwright and not the more reserved producer was its source. In any case, it backfired noisily. Not a single critic could be found to support the claim that the new comedy was Boucicault's best since *London Assurance*. Instead of painting a vivid, hilarious picture of rural society and its colorful types, as he had in his earliest triumph, Boucicault attempted to make a farcical evening out of a single, rather tired motif. Walter Auldjo (Eben Plympton), fearful of telling his father, Silas (John Gilbert), of his marriage, persuades his friend, Archibald Meek (H. J. Montague), to pose as his wife's husband. Naturally, Archibald's fiancée, Fannie Tarbox (Stella Boniface), misconstrues matters. Bad notices, especially Winter's scathing rejection in the *Tribune*, prompted Boucicault to write to the newspapers, assailing the incompetency of contemporary criticism and critics and blaming the reviewers for the sorry state of contemporary dramaturgy. Winter responded, leading to an often intemperate debate between the two men. The debate intrigued potential playgoers but did not induce them to patronize the piece, which was withdrawn after six weeks. The play was by no means a failure, since six weeks was not a bad run at the time and Wallack certainly would have removed it sooner rather than play to empty houses. Boucicault's biographer may be correct in stating it was afterwards sent on tour.

The Law of the Land (10-1-77, Niblo's) was an Americanization of "a European success." One critic reported, "Robbery, supplemented by murder, is the chief ingredient in the drama, but it has other motives as, for instance, love, both paternal and filial, and that other love, which is of a more ardent, but possibly more short-lived quality." The play's two-week stand was a long run compared with the record of A. F. Leiss's "American comedy" **Married or Not Married** (10-13-77, Academy of Music). Reviewers savaged a company in which one of the leading ladies was patently drunk and several of the other players had not learned their lines. But then this "glimpse of our native society" was probably no inspiration to the performers; it was waved away as "jejune," "monotonous," and "ridiculous." Many playgoers left early; those who remained hooted and jeered. There was no second performance.

Most likely Bartley Campbell's **My Foolish Wife; or, A Night at Niagara** (10-15-77, Chestnut St., Philadelphia) was meant eventually to please New York audiences. It recounted the misadventures of a young wife who, because of her husband's opposition to the theatre, brushes up her acting abilities in secret. When friends and family come across these rehearsals unexpectedly and misinterpret what they see and hear, all manner of confusion results. Neither Philadelphia nor Chicago, where the farce next moved, apparently cared for it, and it seems to disappear from the records before ever playing New York.

If old plays continued to retain a hold on large audiences, they frequently did so away from the most elite playhouses. Among those that had claimed the boards at lesser houses for brief times during the still young season were *The Mighty Dollar* with the Florences; *Kit, the Arkansas Traveller* with Chanfrau; *The Sea of Ice*, done as *The Wild Flower of Mexico*; *Nick of the Woods*, still, after forty years, with its original star, Joseph Proctor; and *The French Spy*. But when Joseph Jefferson was doing *Rip Van Winkle*, he and his vehicle always

were assured a first-class berth. He opened at Booth's on the 29th. His producer was Augustin Daly, who was hoping to recover some of his earlier losses. However, it was not to be Daly's lucky season. The month-long stand was plagued by disappointing business, which was blamed on the violence connected with the railroad strike. On Saturday nights, when Jefferson did not perform, Daly brought out his *Under the Gaslight*.

As if to underscore the durability of older works, D. H. Harkins, now a star heading his own company, opened an engagement the same night at the Eagle, a theatre far down on the pecking order. His bills included such Forrest favorites as *Metamora* and *Jack Cade* as well as *Othello* and *Richard III*. His selection of plays goes a long way toward confirming contemporary complaints about his stiffness and overacting, since a predilection for several such obsolescent plays does imply a predilection for equally obsolescent acting styles.

On November 5, a greater player, Fanny Janauschek, began a three-week season at a more fashionable house, the Broadway. But her plays, too, were ones her followers had seen her perform before—*Brunhild, Chesney Wold,* and *Mary Stuart*. Despite her irrevocable accent, critics felt she was at the height of her powers, a fact that only called attention to the inadequacies of some of the supporting players in the Broadway's resident company.

The old—old plays—and the new—a new star—were brought together at the Fifth Avenue on November 12. The new star was Mary Anderson.

· · ·

Mary [Antoinette] **Anderson** (1859–1940), who was considered by many to be the most beautiful of all 19th-century American actresses, was born in Sacramento, Calif., but raised in Louisville, Ky. After watching Edwin Adams perform there, she decided to go on the stage and received encouragement from Charlotte Cushman and George Vandenhoff. She made her hometown debut at the age of sixteen as Juliet, subsequently touring the South and West. In the *Herald*'s description she was pictured as "tall, willowy and young, [with] a fresh, fair face, short and rounded, a small, finely chiselled mouth, large almond eyes of dark gray or blue, hair of a light brown, a long white throat."

· · ·

For all her youthfulness, she was an advocate of an older, almost moribund school of drama—as her program demonstrated. Starting with *The Lady of Lyons* she moved on to *Romeo and Juliet, Evadne, Guy Mannering, Ingomar,* and *Fazio*. The *Times*, after seeing her Pauline, suggested she would be more comfortable in tragedy than in domestic melodrama; nevertheless it was generous in praise, noting, "Her voice is deep and powerful, and her delivery and gestures are characterized by the measured grace associated, as a rule, with verse and heroic action." Witnessing her Juliet confirmed the *Time*'s opinion, although, in line with most other newspapers, it felt she was a diamond requiring further polishing. Her engagement quickly became one of the most excitedly talked about theatrical events in many seasons. Almost lost in the excitement was the fact that her handsome leading man was the rising Eben Plympton.

On the night of Miss Anderson's first appearance Wallack's brought out *False Shame,* the same play Daly initially had offered to New Yorkers in 1872 as *New Year's Eve.*

The Mother's Secret (11-15-77, Union Square) was the first major "new" play presented at a first-class New York theatre in more than a month, but even it was not truly new, since it was taken by Cazauran from Sardou's Parisian hit of the 1860s *Séraphine*. It was the very sort of French domestic-melodrama at which the Union Square company was unmatched, and it offered a subtle, powerful attack on religious hypocrisy in the bargain. Seraphine, Marquise de Jasmin (Katherine Rogers), has become something of a religious fanatic, and her newfound religiosity only has increased her private shame at being the mother of an illegitimate daughter, Elise (Sara Jewett). The marquis (John Parselle) has accepted the girl as his, but her real father is Henri Le Pont (Charles Coghlan). Seraphine decides to force Elise to become a nun, hoping thereby to somehow shrive herself of her old sin. Le Pont learns of Seraphine's action, and a seesaw battle of wills ensues, with Elise a puzzled, innocent bystander. Le Pont finally prevails, allowing Elise to go her own way. For all its dramatic tensions and excellent acting, the play was only a modest success.

Even that eluded Sothern when he replaced *The Crushed Tragedian* with H. J. Byron's **A Hornet's Nest** (11-20-77, Park). The central figure of this comedy "in three buzzes and a stinger" was a very rich, seeming simpleton, Sydney Spoonbill (Sothern). Mrs. Mandrake (Nellie Mortimer), a fortune-hunting widow, Straight Tipper (W. H. Lytell), a "turfite," and Hall Marks (G. F. DeVere), a financial "sharper," are among a large group of acquaintances who believe that they can gull Spoonbill, but of course, Spoonbill quietly turns the tables on all of them. The brummagen humor of the piece was too shoddy for even Sothern's sharply honed skills to save.

On her world trip Rose Eytinge had visited Egypt, possibly the first major American actress to do so. Now some years later she came to New York in Shakespeare's *Antony and Cleopatra,* which opened at the Broadway on November 26. She had performed it to great acclaim in San Francisco earlier and acted it to further good notices with various companies as she returned east. In her autobiography she insisted with a certain pride that her costumes were historically correct. But something must have happened en route, for the critics felt that, as someone would later say of another actress, she barged down the Nile only to sink. Her Antony, Frederick Warde, disagreed, recalling, "Her dark complexion and physical charms gave her an ideal appearance . . . and her splendid acting fully realized the 'Glorious serpent of the Nile.' " The role remained her personal favorite. Her run of three weeks cannot be put down as a complete failure, since the play rarely appealed to theatregoers.

But the complete failure of *A Hornet's Nest* prompted Sothern to briefly resurrect *The Crushed Tragedian* and then to seek refuge in his most popular vehicle, *Our American Cousin,* beginning on December 3 at the Park. Curiously, he changed the title to *Lord Dundreary.* Under one name or the other, the play held the boards through Christmas.

Possibly the best American play of the season was Steele MacKaye's **Won at Last** (12-10-77, Wallack's). The work, which had originally been called *John Fleming's Wife,* begins with the marriage of Fleming (H. J. Montague) to Grace Loring (Rose Coghlan). No sooner are the nuptials over than Grace overhears John confess to a friend that he has never found loving a woman rewarding and has only married "because my father's dying words, recorded in his will, besought me to marry without delay, and in America—a mere notion of his, but sacred under the circumstances." When the friend accuses him of having no heart, he responds, "But if I have, it is a heart of ashes." To make matters worse, Grace also overhears John's conversation with a former mistress, Sophie Bunker (Gabrielle du Sauld), and Sophie later leads Grace to assume the affair is far from finished. As a result, Grace is driven into the arms of her former love, William Tracy (Eben Plympton), an attractive young sea captain and the son of the family who adopted Grace when she became an orphan. She tells her husband, "I recoil with horror from a loveless marriage—because my love and hopes, John Fleming, are like your heart—ashes—ashes—ashes!" For all his professed cynicism and indifference, Fleming recognizes that he does love Grace and, concluding that he stands in

1877–1878

the way of her happiness, attempts suicide by drowning. However, Tracy has realized that Grace still loves Fleming. He rescues him from the waters and watches as husband and wife at last are reunited. Grace assures Fleming, "Ah! It is not your death, but your life—and your love that sets me free." And Fleming can now see "the dawn of a new and happy life" for the two of them.

Rather pretentiously, MacKaye labeled each act: Act I—Ashes, Act II—Embers, Act III—Fire, Act IV—Flame, Act V—Fireside. Winter may have had these headings in mind when he wrote in his review, "The Wallack audience is usually cool; last night it was full of flame. *Won at Last* is a thorough and really brilliant success. There are reasons for believing this verdict will remain the verdict of the best judgment of the time." The *Dramatic News* seconded this opinion, observing, "It is unquestionably the best of all the American comedies thus far produced, and the author has risen at one bound to front rank. It is the most original play produced in New York for many years." Not everyone concurred. The *Times,* for example, found the play uneven and the dialogue very ordinary.

Given the generally enthusiastic notices, the play's failure to catch hold is puzzling. It ran only a month. Perhaps the juxtaposition of an American author, already know for his advocacy of a new naturalism, and a theatre and ensemble noted for anglophilic traditionalism was dissuading to many. Time has shown that MacKaye really was not as advanced as the perceptions of his contemporaries and his own carefully orchestrated ballyhoo suggested; his writings were firmly rooted in the melodramatics of his own day, and he was unable in most important respects to transcend them. Yet the play's critical reception could only encourage those who in turn were anxious to encourage a modern native drama. The play was soon performed across the country and was briefly revived on several occasions for about a decade before slipping into obscurity.

While MacKaye was still at the beginning of his career, Charles Fechter was closing his. Only in his mid-fifties, he was now ponderously obese, terminally ill, and relying on drugs to see him through what proved to be his last New York engagement, which began at the Broadway on December 17. His bills started with a month-long stand in *The Count of Monte Cristo,* then moved on to *No Thoroughfare, Hamlet,* and *Ruy Blas.* Considering his difficulties, his swordsplay remained lively and elegant, and his controversial blond-wigged, bearded, and mustachioed Hamlet was an emotional tour de force "drowned in tears."

Two great actresses vied for attention on the 22nd: Helena Modjeska at the Fifth Avenue and Fanny Davenport at Booth's. For most critics the younger Miss Davenport was the lesser of the two. They had often chided her for relying too much on her ravishing beauty and an ability to display "the floss of satin and the sheen of jewels" rather than on probing deeply into her characters. On this occasion, her first real starring engagement, she muted such carping by appearing only in three comedies, all of which she had performed before. She went from Rosalind to Viola to Lady Gay Spanker. Maurice Barrymore was her leading man, adding his glamor and skill to the productions.

The critics devoted far more space to evaluating Modjeska.

. . .

Helena Modjeska (1840–1909) was born in Cracow, the daughter of a teacher and minor musician. Her family name was Opid. Since her half-brother was already a popular actor there, she was able to obtain parts while still quite young. She married Gustave Sinnmayer Modrejewski, a man twenty years her senior. Although the marriage did not last long, it gave her, with minor changes, the stage name she used thereafter. She next married a radical Polish aristocrat, Karol Bozenta Chlapowski, whose outspoken views forced the couple to flee their homeland. They settled in California, where a need for money forced her to learn English and resume acting. Her American debut was in San Francisco in *Adrienne Lecouvreur.* Even at thirty-seven she retained the slender figure and pensive beauty that had marked her earlier years. Like Miss Davenport, she was famous for her beautiful costumes.

. . .

The biggest problem confronting many critics was her still heavy accent. Beyond that her Adrienne divided the reviewers. The *Times* insisted, "Mme. Modjeska must be accounted a great actress," only to be contradicted by the *Herald,* which concluded, "She is not a great actress." However, the *Herald* did allow that "she combines rare intelligence with perfect refinement and correct study." But when she followed with her Marguerite Gautier in *Camille* on January 14, all reservations were hurled aside and she was firmly established in the theatrical pantheon. The *Sun* wrote, "Modjeska's representation of the part is unlike any other we have had here. It lacks the forceful physical agony that Miss Morris threw into it, and it never rose to the heights of delirium when Heron in her prime was at her best. But it is far more poetic in its passion, more effeminate in its pathos, and far more

115

beautiful in its many exquisite shades of tenderness and grief."

Another tremendous personal success was that scored by Charles Coghlan when he assumed the title role in **The Man of Success** (12-26-77, Union Square), the busy, dependable Cazauran's adaptation of Feuillet's *Montjoye*. Raoul Montjoye's ambition knows neither bounds nor scruples. He has driven his partner to suicide, reneged on his promise to marry the woman he has lived with, and forced her and his children to flee his house. His behavior finally alienates all his associates and threatens to destroy his hopes. At this point George (James O'Neill), the son of his dead partner, learns of his treachery and challenges him to a duel. George is seriously wounded. Montjoye's daughter, Cécile (Sara Jewett), has loved George, and his predicament drives her to the brink of madness and death. Only this brings Montjoye to his senses. He agrees to change his ways and to marry the children's mother, Henriette (Agnes Booth). Coghlan's cold, knifelike precision in the earlier acts and his gripping pathos at the end stole the show. But possibly because even his acting could not mask the absurdly manipulated ending, or perhaps because the whole plot was somehow unlikable, the play itself had only a small success.

On the same night, Sothern brought out *David Garrick* at the Park, playing it in conjunction with *A Regular Fix* until the end of his highly profitable four-month engagement.

Two more stars returned on January 7 to welcome in 1878. The leading critics and more dedicated playgoers attended Booth's opening, his first at the house that bore his name since he lost the theatre. His choice of play, *Richard III,* was not surprising, but he injected a note of novelty by using neither Cibber's standard version nor the original Shakespeare. Instead he employed a new one by William Winter, which attempted to have the best of both worlds. A third hat was thus tossed into the arena, although a consensus was slowly moving toward further purity. And once more, while extolling his hunchback, critics still found grounds for sniping. The *Herald* reported Booth blew many lines, while the *Times,* acknowledging his theatrical effectiveness and intelligent study, lamented his Richard was "destitute of 'human feeling.' " Later in the engagement he offered his Cardinal Wolsey, Petruchio, Othello, Iago, Shylock, Bertuccio, Richelieu, Richard II, and Ruy Blas.

Booth's competition was John T. Raymond, who began his stand with his beloved Colonel Sellers. After a single week he offered something new,

Bartley Campbell's **Risks; or, Insure Your Life** (1-14-78, Park). When the play had first been mounted five years before in Chicago, its main plot revealed how a man-about-town, Paul Varney, secretly marries Bella Newton, a farmer's daughter. Secrecy is necessary since Paul fears his rich aunt will disinherit him if she learns about the wedding. Paul receives a letter from his niece, Hester, signed teasingly "your little wife." Paul uses the letter to light his cigar, but it is not totally burned and Bella discovers it. Believing Paul is a bigamist, she attempts to drown herself in the East River but is rescued by an old flame, Luke Loring, who still loves her. However, the truth comes out, so husband and wife are reconciled. Through these misadventures wanders Pennington Pembroke, a doggedly persistent insurance salesman dressed in a white hat and striped linen suit, who drives potential clients up walls by his obtuse, single-minded determination to sell a policy to everyone he meets. In the New York mounting, Paul was played by J. G. Saville; Bella by Minnie Palmer; Hester by Lillie Eldridge; and Luke by Lewis Baker.

The devices of the melodrama were nothing new. Even in this half-finished season playgoers had seen them utilized in such plays as *The Dark City* and *Won at Last.* But Raymond, who had seen the play in Chicago, hoped to repeat the success of *The Gilded Age* by deemphasizing the principal story and building up the role of Pembroke for himself. He bought the play and made his own revisions, apparently not noticing that the character was scarcely as well woven into the frame as Colonel Sellers had been. The result was that Pembroke stood out like a sore thumb. Unhappy critics misplaced the blame and agreed with the *Graphic,* which wrote, "In developing the comedy rôle, the author has sacrificed both sense and probability." But a highly impressed Brander Matthews told his readers in the *Library Table,* "The part of the insurance agent is cheaply written and is largely made up of odds and ends from *Paul Pry* and *Mark Meddle* and their kin. The actor combines these heterogeneous elements into a harmonious whole. . . . He gives full effect to the volubility, the assurance, the impossible impudence of the part, while he reveals beneath these characteristics the true character of the man, his sincere good feeling, capable of self-sacrifice, if need be, and accomplishing it with the same unconscious humor with which he has just before seized an unsuspecting victim to insist on the advantage of life insurance." Despite such praise and an excellent production, including a highly lauded picture of New York and the East River by twilight, the play was dropped by Raymond before the season was over.

Vying for attention with Campbell's new play was Wallack's revival of *My Awful Dad.*

The season's biggest hit was yet another melodrama by the authors of *The Two Orphans.* D'Ennery and Cormon's **A Celebrated Case** (1-23-78, Union Square) furthered the theatre's fame as the American home of French drama during the decade. The play had been hurried into production when Palmer ascertained that Wallack had unwittingly put into rehearsals a pirated version by the devious Boucicault. The gentlemanly Wallack immediately abandoned his mounting, a move that earned him Boucicault's publicly expressed venom. At its most simple, the dizzyingly convoluted plot showed how a French soldier, Jean Renaud (Charles Coghlan), takes French leave to visit his child and his wife, who is murdered shortly after his visit. In court the word of his young daughter, who does not really understand what she is saying, is used to convict him of the crime and send him to prison. When the daughter, Adrienne (Sara Jewett), reaches maturity she meets her father, comprehends his innocence, and sets about helping him clear his name. The wife's jewels and jewel box, stolen at the time of her murder, finally lead to the real culprit. Marston's gorgeous scenery and Lanouette's sumptuous costumes, both mirroring 18th-century elegance, combined to make the evening all the more memorable. Yet not everyone was pleased. Winter complained, "At its best it is little more than a singularity, while at its worst it is the common blood and thunder of wild and whirling story-papers and stage of our ancestors. . . . There are persons who like to sup full of horrors, and who can defy intellectual nightmare: to them we commend it." Enough people liked such theatrical meat to allow the original production to record 111 performances.

Revivals followed, with Wallack's, having desperately scuttled its own new mounting, leading the way with *School* on the 25th. On the 28th at the Fifth Avenue, Boucicault's *Jezebel* came back under the new title *The Dead Secret.* Katherine Rogers, however, was no Clara Morris, so even with the added attraction of the comic curtain raiser *My Precious Betsey* the bill lasted less than two weeks. No more successful, but in a way more interesting, was a revival of Charles Reade's *The Courier of Lyons,* a tale of an innocent man condemned by his resemblance to a highwayman. The play had fallen from the repertory until Henry Irving had revised it and revived it in London as **The Lyons Mail,** and it was this redaction that Harkins brought out at the

Eagle on the 28th. Just as Miss Rogers could not duplicate Clara Morris's vivid portrayal, Harkins possessed none of Irving's singular charisma. A competing production at the Broadway featured the Australian actor Alfred Dampier. It was no more successful. Playgoers had to wait until Irving himself brought his own production to America to learn what all the London excitement was about.

In order to bolster disappointing attendance, Dampier added a second play to his bill, **Helen's Babies** (2-4-78, Broadway). The play was a dramatization of John Habberton's best-seller, which had already been offered as a burlesque in the previous season. The star's daughters assumed the roles of Budge (Lily Dampier) and Toddie (Rose Dampier), who, in their mother's absence, take charge of their home and their Uncle Henry (B. T. Ringgold), even though Henry has assumed he was to be in charge.

A series of very strange revivals began at the troubled Lyceum on the same night. No one could fault the repertory of plays, which included *Romeo and Juliet, Richard III,* and *Hamlet.* What caused even otherwise decorous playgoers to drop their reserve and to join the gallery gods and well-heeled undergraduates in hooting, waving handkerchiefs, pelting the stage with food remnants, and generally creating such mayhem that critics reported the production onstage seemed to be acted out in dumbshow was the presence of the star, the sixty-seven-year-old Count Joannes. The Count of Sertorii of the Holy Roman Empire of the First Commander of the Imperial Order of Golden Knight and Count Palatine had first acted in Boston in 1828 under his real name, George Jones, and had later become a respected performer at the old Bowery, when that theatre was still in its heyday. He had been received with acclaim and gave promise of a great career. But his eccentricities soon began to surface. For example, he started to acknowledge applause meant for other players. In time his peculiarities overwhelmed his art, and he became simply a figure of ridicule. The opening-night audiences grew so boisterous that the count called out the police. At first his houses were packed with people come to jeer, but by the end of his three-week stand he was playing to a half-empty auditorium.

The Dead Secret's poor reception prompted Katherine Rogers to rush forward a second production, **Sidonie** (2-9-78, Fifth Ave.), Frederick A. Schwab's dramatization of Alphonse Daudet's *Fromont jeune et Risler aîné.* Its protagonist was a female counterpart of the central figure in *The Man of Success,* a morally repulsive, reptilian climber, but unlike

Montjoye, and in fact, unlike Daudet's Sidonie, she came to an unhappy end. In the stage version Sidonie (Miss Rogers) throws over her suitor, Franz (George Clarke), when she learns his older brother, Risler (C. W. Couldock), has inherited a large business. She quickly sets about having an affair with the unsuspecting, loving Risler's partner, George Fromont (J. L. Gossin). However, after the business fails she deserts both men and attempts to run away with Franz, who has since become wealthy. Risler intercepts a revealing letter and kills both Sidonie and himself. Despite many good notices that praised the play, the performances, and the mounting, the work survived only a single week.

If Katherine Rogers was proving no match for Clara Morris, the erratic Miss Morris herself again was making many playgoers and critics question how enduring her artistry was. She had met with some success on the more accepting road in **The Governess** (2-11-78, Broadway), yet another theatricalization of *Jane Eyre,* but New Yorkers were coming to perceive her as burnt out. Two weeks and she returned to the road.

A fortnight's run was also all that J. W. Shannon's **Champagne and Oysters** (2-13-78, Park) could muster at first, even with a superior cast headed by James Lewis, Maude Granger, and W. J. LeMoyne. Lewis provoked most of the laughs as Godfrey Grahame, a rector who innocently finds himself dining with a lady of dubious repute in a restaurant of equally dubious fame. Flustered by meeting acquaintants there, he blurts out that the woman is his wife. It takes the rest of the evening to untangle the complications and misunderstandings. Although the *Herald* predicted that the play presented "too many suggestions of immorality to make it popular among church going young ladies," the comedy proved sufficiently attractive to enjoy a few subsequent revivals.

The flurry of new plays continued with **The Diaoulmaugh** (2-18-78, Fifth Ave.), which the *Times* deemed typical "Irish romantic drama, with its inevitable complement of spirited action, stirring incidents, and picturesque 'situations.' " The paper noted the play was rumored to be based on an unidentified French work but added that its humor, as it stood, would have been "inconceivable to a Frenchman." The title was Gaelic for "the good devil," personified in the figure of dashing Neil D'Orsay (George Clarke), who returns to his homeland to rescue a countess and her daughters from the treachery of Dugald Boyne (Harry Dalton) and his cohorts. These men have questioned the legitimacy of the countess's inheritance and of her

marriage and have seized her castle. At a masked ball there, Neil appears disguised as none other than the scarlet-clad devil himself and tricks the men into disclosing where they have cached the stolen will and marriage certificate. Another version, by N. Hart Jackson and called **The Craiga Dhoul,** played Niblo's in March.

Two revivals opened that same February night. At Wallack's the house's latest presentation of *Money,* with a remarkable if overaged cast, demonstrated the greatness and stability of the ensemble. Lester Wallack as Alfred Evelyn was supported by H. J. Montague, John Gilbert, John Brougham, Harry Beckett, W. R. Floyd, Henry Crisp, Rose Coghlan, Mme Ponisi, and Stella Boniface. Probably no other house in the country could so readily call on the service of so distinguished a company.

At Booth's the offering was a tune-filled production of the all but indestructible *Uncle Tom's Cabin.* Somewhat surprisingly, given the prejudices of the time, a large number of blacks were recruited to perform traditional black songs and dances. There was even, according to the newspapers, "a chorus of several hundred men and women, boys and girls." The encores they received caused the entertainment—was it now almost a musical?—to run over four hours. The theatre was packed on opening night and, apparently, for most of the limited three-week engagement.

On February 20, the Eagle Theatre was renamed the Standard. Its opening attraction was a revival of *Our Boarding House.* At first the theatre continued simply as another of the many combination houses in the city, though it would soon move on to more illustrious evenings. However, this revival did not include the play's original stars, Stuart Robson and W. H. Crane. They were occupied with a new comedy, Joseph Bradford's **Our Bachelors** (2-25-78, Park), based on the German *Der Weiberfeind.* Honors were not quite so carefully divided as they had been in the earlier play, for although Crane assumed what originally had been the title role, in the American version his part, Judge Joseph Jowler, a gruff man resolutely opposed to marriage, seems to have been cut from smaller cloth. Instead the spotlight fell on Robson as Juan Bangle, a music teacher who comes into a fortune and decides to wed. He loves Clara Courtney (Alicia Robson), ward of the rich, widowed Mrs. Clinton (Maude Granger), but is also pursued by another widow, Mrs. Mouser (Mrs. A. F. Baker), on behalf of her niece, Bella (Jennie Murdoch). Excitable and obliging, Bangle soon finds himself engaged not only to Clara but to Bella and Mrs. Clinton. His problems are solved when other men agree to marry his surplus fiancées. Jowler finds himself preparing to lead Mrs. Mouser down the aisle. Many playgoers looked on the piece as a hand-me-down copy of *Saratoga,* produced without the cachet Daly had brought to that mounting and relying largely on the piping-voiced Robson ("the same squeaking clarinet of a man as ever") and the assertive Crane for its pleasures. Although the play had a disappointing run of just over a month, it remained in the pair's repertory for several seasons.

Plays with Russian settings were becoming stylish—witness *The Danicheffs* and *Michael Strogoff.* The newest addition to the list was **The Exiles** (3-2-78, Broadway), George Fawcett Rowe's adaptation of Eugène Nus and Prince Lubomirski's French hit. A headline-grabbing legal battle over the rights, which no one won, whetted interest in the piece, even if it was seen as a partial throwback to the fading sensation-melodramas. The story recounted the travails of Tatiana, Countess Lanine (Jeffreys Lewis), and her family after she rebuffs the lewd advances of the head of the secret police, Schlem (Milnes Levick). He contrives to have them exiled to Siberia. There he still pursues the countess until a rebellion traps him in a castle, where he is burned to death. The production was graphic, not only including the spectacular blaze but depicting the hut-strewn Siberian wastes and featuring sleds drawn by dogs and other animals. One reviewer said the other animals were elks, but Frederick Warde, who was in the cast, says in his autobiography that they were reindeer and that on opening night one bolted loose, jumped over the orchestra pit, and shot through the aisles. The production ran until the end of April, although the inconclusive hearings allowed a company from Boston, in another version, to compete at Booth's for a while. Their New York engagements concluded, both groups took to the road.

The increasingly desperate Lyceum, ever farther away from the northward-moving theatrical hub, offered another freakish attraction when it gave its stage over to **Gold Mad** (3-4-78, Lyceum). Albeit some not unknown professionals were in the cast, the affair bordered on gross amateurism, especially the text, which was written by a playwright identified only as "a gentleman of Harvard College." One paper assumed that the author was, at best, a freshman. His hero leaves his family to hunt for gold and goes mad when he does not find any. Meanwhile, at home a villain threatens to kill his wife and kidnap his children. All ended happily, except for audiences who had to sit through the play. Scheduled to run a week, it apparently did not make it.

Contrasting talents—two mature, one immature—provided the next theatrical interest. On the 9th at the Fifth Avenue the bantam, gnomish John Sleeper Clarke made one of his infrequent returns from England. Like Booth, his brother-in-law, Clarke rarely ventured away from the safety of a rather unchanging repertory. His vehicles this time included such expected favorites as *The Toodles, The Widow Hunt,* and *The Heir at Law.* The 9th also saw John E. Owens begin a week's stay at the Standard, also with old favorites, a double bill of *Solon Shingle* and *Victims.* Theatregoers had a rare chance to compare two master comedians, almost side by side. Who was the better probably was a matter of taste, but Clarke clearly leaned closer to pure farce while Owens performed characters who elicited a touch of pathos or sympathy from audiences. At Booth's on the 11th the attraction was one of a blessedly disappearing kind, the child prodigy. This precocious pretender was named N. S. Wood. After offering his Poor Jo in yet another version of *Bleak House,* now called **Tom-All-Alone's,** he attempted nothing less than *Hamlet.* Unlike most of his ilk, he strutted and fretted his preposterous hour upon the stage, then reappeared season after season for decades, eventually even writing some of his own vehicles. But his career was confined largely to lesser theatres.

Far down on Broadway, Niblo's was making a valiant and seemingly successsful attempt to keep its head above water, even if that meant abandoning its claim to being a first-class theatre. But all season long its stock company had supplied its less elite, less demanding audiences with the sort of oldtime theatre they relished. That many of these productions ran three or more weeks suggests the management knew what it was doing. A new management took over in March and began its term with a new play, **The Serpent and the Dove** (3-11-78, Niblo's). Elsie Elliott (Gussie De Forrest) and her mother sail for England; Elsie marries the ship's captain (Samuel Piercy); her mother's death and burial at sea drive Elsie to attempt suicide, and she is rescued by her husband. Later, in England, Captain Barton must disentangle her from the snare of a malevolent nobleman. Basically the play was little different from those being performed uptown; in quality it was an ocean away.

Mignon (3-18-78, Standard), J. B. Runnion's dramatization of Goethe's *Wilhelm Meister,* brought Maggie Mitchell back to Broadway after a long absence. She played the title role of a girl who had been stolen by gypsies while she was still a young child. She is rescued by a handsome young student who, she learns to her dismay, is in love with an actress. Eventually she is returned to the castle from which she was abducted and, in a departure from the conclusion of Goethe's novel, settles down happily with her rescuer. For audiences, neither the play nor the supporting players mattered. What they wanted was the star. Although she was nearly forty-six, critics found her "as young as ever." The *Spirit of the Times* observed, "Her quaint coaxing tones, her mocking, elf-like gaiety, her gentleness in moments of feeling, and . . . the variety and altogether original charm of a distinct individuality, fitted the type which Mignon is universally held to represent. . . . Hers is the wayward child whose love is her life, and whose nature is as uncaged as that of the swallows, whose flight she yearns to follow." She played the part for only the first week of her month's engagement, moving on to two weeks of her most demanded *Fanchon* and then to the bucolic *Little Barefoot* and to *The Pearl of Savoy,* in which yet another farm girl wins the hand of a rich nobleman.

Miss Mitchell's reappearance coincided with a revival of *London Assurance* at Wallack's. This was the third standard play in a row to be revived at the house, but it soon gave way to a new play that allowed the great ensemble to end its season with a major success, one continuing the growing fascination with Russian matters. **Diplomacy** (4-1-78, Wallack's), was taken from Sardou's *Dora* by Clement Scott and B. C. Stephenson, writing as Saville and Bolton Rowe. The Countess Zicka (Rose Coghlan), a Russian spy who has had a passionate affair with Julian Beauclerc (H. J. Montague), turns furious and vengeful when she learns Julian has dropped her to marry Dora de Rio Zares (Maude Granger), a woman of very modest means. She steals a secret document in Julian's possession and plants it in a letter that Dora has sent innocently to another informer, her mother's friend, the German diplomat Baron Stein (J. W. Shannon). Exacerbating the suspicions thrown on Dora are the fact that her mother is rumored to be a spy and that a photograph of Count Orloff (Frederic Robinson), which the count had once given to Dora, is the very photograph used to identify and arrest him. Orloff, not aware that Julian has married Dora, reveals all this to his friend and then, learning of the marriage, attempts gallantly to exculpate the wife. Julian and his brother, Henry (Lester Wallack), browbeat the German into returning the correspondence, and Countess Zicka's guilt is brought to light. The taut writing and the polished ensemble playing were framed in superb settings, including a Monte Carlo apartment with a view of the shimmering Mediterranean in the distance. So excellent were the sets that,

as often happened at the time, the scene painters were called forth to take bows of their own. The play ran until Wallack's season ended in mid-June. It held the stage regularly until World War I and was given a major revival on Broadway in 1928.

February's presentation of *Uncle Tom's Cabin* clearly had not exhausted that warhorse's still potent appeal. If the version at Booth's had minimized the work's pleas for freedom and tolerance by flooding the stage with musical extravaganza, the production that came into the Fifth Avenue on April 1 hewed more closely to the original, so closely in fact that two of its perennial stars, Mr. and Mrs. G. C. Howard, remained at the head of the cast. By now Mrs. Howard had probably lost count of how many thousands of times she had performed little Topsy. She probably also lost track of the fact that, at just one year away from her fiftieth birthday, she was a mite old for the role. Certainly her loyalists did not give it a thought. The production also employed some black musical acts, albeit not with the largesse of the earlier mounting.

This play provided some of the few occasions that allowed the races to commingle on American stages. But on April 8th at the usually neglected Lyric Hall, an all-black cast offered its version of *Richard III* to a small audience, "four-fifths of whom were colored." Rare black mountings, when they were acknowledged at all by major newspapers, were always treated condescendingly, and this was no exception. The *Times* called the whole affair "laughable," going on to report, "All the actors were colored, and no two of them were of the same hue. Their costumes were typical of every period known in connection with the costumer's art, and combinations of green and crimson and scarlet and orange were among the quietest resorted to. The scenery was in keeping with the dresses. A room with green wall-paper, a single door and no window, did duty for the apartments in the palace, and *Clarence* lay in duress in a cell pictured by the ground floor of an Italian villa, with lovely gardens and dancing waters just across the threshold." Only B. J. Ford, who played the title role, was given even stinting praise, albeit his style reminded the critic of the burlesque muggings of the famous minstrel Charles Backus.

Possessive titles were enjoying a small vogue; J. B. Runnion called his second play of the season **Our Aldermen** (4-10-78, Park). His comedy reflected the growing reaction against corrupt city bosses and their cynical political machines, and the frustration of contemporary reformers. Runnion's heart was in the right place, but his dramatic skills were minimal, so he had to rely on some more highly skilled comedians to put over his material. They were unable to do it. Nor did a highly publicized visit to City Hall by the company a day before the opening whet interest. The cast was headed by droll James Lewis as the hypochondriacal and starry-eyed Lyman Drake, a retired merchant who is elected alderman. To his chagrin he discovers his only ally is Dr. Bernard Clancy (Ben Maginley). The rest of the aldermen are led by the nose by "Boss" Birney (W. J. LeMoyne), who sees to it that Drake is overwhelmed with petty requests for favors while the machine pushes through a bill to erect a new, unneeded dome on the local courthouse. Admitting he is not the right man at the right time, Drake leaves, hoping a better man will replace him and make the time right. Possibly the comedy's downbeat ending drove the final nail in its coffin. Two weeks and it was gone.

At the Fifth Avenue on the 22nd J. B. Studley came in as star of *The Bells*. Studley, an old Bowery favorite, had performed in another version of the play at about the same time James Wallack was introducing it to uptown audiences. He was a vigorous, unsubtle actor, but he was allowed to shine for only a week—possibly in a stopgap booking.

George C. Boniface, an actor of the same age and school as Studley, opened the same night in a new version of d'Ennery's *Le Vieux Caporal*, **The Soldier's Trust** (4-22-78, Broadway). He played Corporal Antoine, a man who returns home after being held for many years as a prisoner of war, only to find his property has been claimed by Peter Frochard (C. L. Graves). Frochard also is determined to marry the corporal's daughter, and when he discovers that Antoine is bent upon retrieving the property and preventing the marriage, he implicates him in a robbery. Antoine finally sets matters aright. The play lasted only a week at the Broadway, but Boniface toured lesser houses with it for several seasons. Oddly enough, the very next week another version, **The Old Corporal,** was offered at the Fifth Avenue. What little interest was shown in it came from the presence in the title role of Signor Majeroni, who had won praise here when he had appeared with Ristori and who had since learned English. Most critics admired his work but could not persuade the public to join in their huzzas.

A more popular player, J. K. Emmet, also greeted playgoers the same night, with a revised version at the Standard of his *Fritz, Our Cousin German*. He announced further revisions several times during the two-month engagement.

Two nights later many of the players who had performed in *Our Aldermen* were seen in its hastily got up replacement, a revival of *The Big Bonanza,* which this time proved no bonanza at all.

When Majeroni's version of *Le Vieux Caporal* was removed as quickly as Boniface's had been, the Italian joined his wife in a new play, **Husband and Wife** (5-6-78, Fifth Ave.), in which a husband murders a wife's lover, then slowly teaches her to accommodate to his otherwise quiet ways. This, too, lasted but a single week, after which the couple bowed out with a week of *Camille.*

A week was all **Magnolia** (5-6-78, Broadway) could manage. Unwisely, the producers made matters difficult for themselves by mounting a play with a troublesome theme in an unintentionally comic manner. The story's heroine, performed by Minnie Doyle, is an ex-slave's daughter whose light skin allows her to pass in white society until she is unmasked. A steamboat explosion—a tired enough device in itself—sounded to one critic like "a pop-gun report"; a duel by moonlight saw the two opponents seemingly running from each other on a stage lit as if it were high noon; and a "modern" ship looked suspiciously like some 18th-century hulk. For the rest of the season the Broadway struggled along with frequently changing bills of undistinguished, often creakily aging attractions. Not until new management took over in the fall could it again be judged a first-class house.

Another theatre that had fallen on hard times brought out two new works to end its uncertain season. **The Gascon** (5-20-78, Niblo's) was a swashbuckler, based on a Parisian hit by Louis Davyl and Théodore Barrière. Like several other later entries, it lasted a single week. Although **Love and Labor** (6-3-78, Niblo's) lasted no longer, at least it attempted to confront a modern domestic problem, using as background the violent railroad strike of the preceding summer. But the basic story itself was just the usual melodramatic claptrap. Her rich father having been killed by strikers, Annie Dean (Marie Prescott) finds she is being deprived of her rightful inheritance by the machinations of the unsavory Ernest Arnold (J. F. Peters) and his crony, Jonathan Green (J. V. Melton), who steals her father's will. At the same time, she falls in love with Harry Hinton (Edwin F. Kowles), who helped organize the strikes but deplored the violence they bred. However, Harry walks out on her when it appears she has had an affair with Arnold. Green overhears the argument, follows her, grabs her, and throws her over a bridge, leaving her for dead. He then announces that he has seen Harry kill her. Harry is brought to trial, but at the last minute Annie, who has fled to

New York, returns to help him win acquittal. Arnold shoots Green and then himself. So much for addressing important contemporary issues.

The season began to peter out with some would-be stars offering themselves in old plays. Two young ladies came forth in competing versions of *The Lady of Lyons,* while a gentleman offered his *Richelieu.* None of the three was heard from again. A better choice for playgoers was the bills presented by the Lingards at the Park. In their customary practice, they mixed small musical numbers, sketches, and playlets, with established comedies, this time including *Sweethearts* and *Our Boys.*

One final, interesting play seemed to sneak in and out virtually unnoticed. Bartley Campbell's **The Vigilantes; or, The Heart of the Sierras** (7-1-78, Grand Opera) was a rewriting of his *How Women Love,* which had first been presented by Mrs. Drew at her Arch Street Theatre in Philadelphia in 1877. The story now centered on Violette Varnett (Rosa Rand) and her foster brother, Frank Ransome (Harry Colton). Violette loves Frank, so is disappointed when he marries another women. In turn Violette is loved by Joe Comstock (W. H. Leake), an old miner who once had saved her life. But Violette does not return his affection. When Frank's wife deserts him and runs off to San Francisco with another man, he follows them and shoots the seducer. Vigilantes would hang him, but Violette and Joe come to town and Joe offers himself in Frank's stead. Violette manages to secure a pardon. The three take a coach headed east, only to have a snowstorm isolate them without any provisions. Just before they are rescued, Frank's wife, who has been similarly stranded, appears and begs his forgiveness. Although Campbell acknowledged that the idea for his last act came from Bret Harte's *Outcasts of Poker Flat,* and many of his other motifs were simply old ones set in a comparatively new background, those few critics who judged the play liked what they saw and heard. Still, the show ran only a week. It returned briefly during the next season and toured for a year or so before disappearing from the records.

1878–1879

Allowing the 1878–79 season to bring down the curtain on "Act I" may be giving it an undeserved importance. By theatrical standards of the late

1870s, and indeed by those of virtually all later good theatre except for what Max Beerbohm called the most "adramatic," such a curtain is weakly anticlimactic. Historians taking a long view of our stage's history might justify it by citing the Bowery Theatre, which at season's end left the lists of New York playhouses offering drama in English. By that time, however, the fifty-three-year-old house long had ceased being a first-class house, sinking ever lower in appearance and in the caliber of its audiences and of its plays. When its name was changed in the summer of 1879 and it began catering to the immigrants whose tenements surrounded it, it was truly venerable only in memory.

Conversely, the 1878–79 season marked a most important beginning. Smack in the middle of the theatrical year, Gilbert and Sullivan's *H.M.S. Pinafore* sailed into port, setting off what contemporaries called the "Pinafore craze" and, far more than any other single show, initiating the vogue for musical theatre in America. The concurrent appearance of *The Brook* and *The Mulligan Guards' Ball,* two historically significant prototypical native musicals, helped propel the momentum. But for all the telling effects musicals would soon have for American stages, these plays lie outside our present concerns.

Perhaps the main reason that this season must close an act is that the next season so unmistakably begins a new one. By rights, then, the 1878–79 season could be seen as a brief intermission, or perhaps the momentary lowering of the curtain to permit a scene change.

Yet if in historical terms the season was an anticlimactic ending to an interesting decade, it was not in itself uninteresting. No fewer than four new plays first offered in this year went on to enjoy long theatrical careers. That the two foreign works outlasted the two American ones could only reflect the still uncertain maturity of American dramaturgy.

Olivia (8-14-78, Union Square), W. G. Wills's dramatization of *The Vicar of Wakefield,* in which Ellen Terry had scored a pronounced success in London, got the season off to a very satisfactory start. Wills's change of title suggested his approach. Beloved characters such as the simple Moses Primrose were given short shrift, and the celebrated scene of his exchanging a horse for a gross of green spectacles was totally excised. Even the vicar, Dr. Primrose (Charles Fisher), was relegated to a supporting role, while the spotlight focused on his beautiful daughter, Olivia (Fanny Davenport), who runs away and is seduced after a seemingly sham marriage by Squire Thornhill (C. A. Stevenson). A subplot told of a second romance between Olivia's sister, Sophie (Linda Dietz), and Mr. Burchell (Edwin Rice), who turns out to be Thornhill's benevolent uncle and who helps make Thornhill repent his erring ways. At the close, the couples are happily united, kneeling before the vicar as carolers sing on the snowy lawn outside the vicarage. Most critics took for granted Miss Davenport's gift for modeling gorgeous period costumes, so they spent their time extolling her performance. Her teary farewell to her family, her fury at her apparent betrayal, and the warmth of the final reconciliation delighted everyone. She lingered at the Union Square for six weeks before embarking on a national tour.

Possibly an even more beautiful actress, but one dedicated to the highest spheres of what was still called by many "the legitimate," beckoned first-nighters to the Fifth Avenue on the 29th. In a single session Mary Anderson's artistry had grown appreciably, thanks in no small measure to a hurried trip to Europe to study the great performers there. But any alteration in her art went unmatched by any change of repertory. Once again *Ingomar*, *Evadne*, *Romeo and Juliet*, *Fazio*, and *The Lady of Lyons* served as vehicles. Her only novelty, at least as far as New Yorkers were concerned, was another old play, *The Hunchback*, a work long associated with Fanny Kemble and other bygone actresses.

Playgoers preferring new American plays did not have to wait much longer, for they soon had a double bill by the rising Bronson Howard: **Hurricane** and **Old Love Letters** (8-31-78, Park). The first, a three-act "comic drama," begins with the arrival of Mrs. Stonehenge Tuttle (Mrs. Gilbert) at the New Rochelle home of her married daughter, Lucy Batterson (Agnes Booth). There is no mistaking Mrs. Tuttle's character as she instantly launches into a series of complaints: "The railroad men were all so very uncivil. They didn't answer more than six questions in every hundred I asked them, and the baggage men growled at the baggage as if they expected extra compensation besides the wages they get from the company, and the air in the cars was simply abominable. Two old ladies in the seat before me insisted on having their window shut. They didn't like the dust, they said. I accidentally stuck my umbrella through the glass. That settled the question." So when she learns that her son-in-law, Alfred Batterson (Frank Hardenberg), and three other men spent the evening in New York on "business," her suspicions are aroused and she prepares her daughter and the other men's wives and sweethearts for battle. Unfortunately for the

men, her suspicions are justified. They have been cavorting at a masked ball. But they pretend to have been secretly preparing an anniversary vaudeville for Mrs. Batterson at the home of Mrs. Dalrymple McNamara (Sydney Cowell). Mrs. McNamara's untimely arrival bursts that bubble, and she finally persuades them to tell the truth. The men are forgiven, but Batterson has a way of preventing further difficulties of this sort. He sends his mother-in-law packing.

Many of the critics who condemned the play did so because, as they quite rightly saw, it fell apart after the first act. Howard could not sustain the joke successfully. But some newspapers, such as the *Times*, also jumped on the play on moral grounds, accusing the author of pandering "to the low taste of those who imagine themselves separated from vice when they are seated this side of the foot-lights."

The one-act curtain raiser fared much better, for it was a small gem. The Hon. Edward Warburton (Joseph E. Whiting) comes to the home of the widowed Mrs. Florence Brownlee (Agnes Booth) to return a packet of love letters she had written him many years earlier. Their reminiscences on this rainy afternoon lead to a rekindling of their former affections. In one of its many nice touches, Mrs. Brownlee sends her servant to look for the very letters she holds in her hand, so that she and Warburton will not be interrupted. The double bill ran until October.

A new American play and a new English work premiered on the same early September evening. Persisting snobbery led the major critics to review the English play, but it was the homespun Yankee entertainment that held our stages longer. **Joshua Whitcomb** (9-2-78, Lyceum) featured a character that Denman Thompson had been playing in vaudeville for several seasons. Stocky, balding, and jowly, Thompson dressed his New Hampshire farmer in baggy pants, an ill-fitting vest, thick glasses, and an outsized straw hat. In this extended character sketch Josh visits Boston, where he encounters a drunken derelict and the derelict's dying wife, a hoydenish street cleaner, a bootblack, and other assorted figures, most of whom accept his invitation to pay a call on his farm. The last act describes the simple joys he offers his guests at his homestead. Thompson eschewed the broad characterization, verging on caricature, of so many earlier stage Yankees. His was a warm, totally believable New Englander, albeit one not without a few flaws, such as occasional irascibility and a penchant for spitting. He played in *Joshua Whitcomb* steadily for almost a decade before devising a new and better play for the same character.

If many playgoers enjoyed a nodding acquaintance with Josh even before encountering him at the Lyceum, they were most likely still more familiar with the heroine of Wills's **Jane Shore** (9-2-78, Booth's). A real figure out of England's tempestuous past, she also had been the heroine of Nicholas Rowe's tragedy, which had been ragingly popular for generations and, while fading from the stage, had been revived on Broadway as recently as 1875. Except for tacking on a happy ending, Wills hewed as closely to the record as dramatic necessity allowed. But critics and playgoers were drawn to Booth's primarily to see the play's star, Genevieve Ward, an American who had learned her art in Europe and subsequently carved out a distinguished career there. She was not especially attractive; even calling her handsome might be stretching a point. Nor would her French style with its studied mannerisms and carefully regulated movements appeal to those playgoers who sought only flailingly impassioned playing. Rather, her appeal was to the most knowing audiences, who could appreciate the intelligence and the cultivated skills she brought to any role she assumed. Although many critics, including those of the *Herald* and the *Times,* insisted Wills's play was superior to Rowe's, she was not able to pack houses until she turned to Shakespeare later in the engagement, and then only with reduced prices.

Another European-trained actress was the much admired Ada Cavendish, who made her New York debut at the Broadway on the 9th in a revival of *The New Magdalen.* Still only in her early thirties, she had won high praise from critics in her native England, praise some American critics begrudged her. Although the *Herald* was laudatory and reported "the house positively rose at her," the *Times,* less impressed, insisted that "her acting shows an extraordinary combination of genuine fire, keen intelligence, and lack of artistic perception," citing as instances of this last her inexpressive gestures, her monotonous voice, and her "abrupt and unnatural" transitions from one mood to another. Her engagement, limited to a fortnight and including one performance of *The Lady of Lyons,* was not extended. However, she did return later in the season to try again.

Some scathing notices greeted **Clarissa Harlowe** (9-10-78, Wallack's), which Boucicault adapted from Richardson's famous novel and which inaugurated the season at New York's most prestigious playhouse. Whether his treatment was as grossly inept as some critics suggested or whether he was merely paying the price for baiting reviewers during the preceding year is uncertain. However, his resort to what was by then one of the most overused of all sensation-melodrama devices hints that his once fresh inspiration and assurance had become stale and unsteady. In outline his story was not unlike that Wills had drawn from Goldsmith's novel, except for the fate of the heroine. Clarissa (Rose Coghlan) runs away from home with the handsome Lovelace (Charles Coghlan), who attempts to trick her into a sham marriage and then seduce her. She locks herself in her room and sets fire to the building. Although she is rescued by Lovelace, she dies of shame, leaving Lovelace to repent alone. Apparently even Wallack's brilliant ensemble could do nothing with the piece, which was quickly withdrawn.

If such a distinguished company, working with an experienced playwright, could come a cropper, it was hardly surprising that lesser hands might blunder. But the unidentified author of **The Open Verdict** (9-2-78, Standard) received morning-after reviews every bit as devastating as Boucicault's, though he, too, had some fine players attempting to bring his drama to life. Two southern plantation owners, Neil Delafield (Eben Plympton) and Godfrey Pope (Frank Evans), are rivals for the affection of Edith (Rose Osborne). Despite the mysterious warnings of Hester Stanhope (Emma Waller), "a gypsy-looking creature," Edith marries Pope. Hester then incites a mob to attack Pope, who is protected by his ex-rival, Delafield. Later Edith divorces Pope and marries Delafield. At the wedding party Pope suddenly appears, bent on making trouble, but a shot kills him. Hester is tried and acquitted. Only after her acquittal does she confess to the murder. She reveals that she is Pope's half-sister, daughter of his father and a slave, and that Pope attempted to have her treated as a slave. In one effective bit of staging, the third act ended with the scene of the quarrel and shooting played out in a dumb show, supposedly from inside a mansion, while the action was seen through a window from outside the house, where a snowstorm raged. The fourth act began with the same scene, this time set totally inside the house and with spoken dialogue.

Brutal notices prompted the theatre's owner to show the play the stage door, but the work hustled in as a replacement fared no better. Frederic Clark's **A False Title** (9-21-78, Standard) told of two Englishmen, both operating under aliases, who court the same American, Florence Whittier (Rose Osborne). One of the Englishmen is Lord Kensington (Eben Plympton), who left home thinking his father was a forger who had irreparably shamed his whole family. In America Kensington discards his title and calls himself simply Victor Temple. The other Englishman, supposedly one Lord Towercourt, is in fact none other than the scoundrelly gambler Tom Tilbrook (Gustavus Levick). Tom attempts to blackmail Kensington and thus remove him as a rival. But when it is shown that Tom perpetrated the forgery for which Kensington's father had been convicted, Kensington and Florence are free to wed. The play could not make up its mind whether it wanted to be a social satire or a melodrama. For all the work's faults, several critics discerned nuggets of promise in its young American author, but he was apparently too discouraged ever to try for a second hearing.

Just as *A False Title* had been pressed into service to replace a prior failure, so Wallack's supplanted the disliked *Clarissa Harlowe* with *The School for Scandal* on the same night. By the late 1870s Lester Wallack was lamenting that his classic revivals often made no money for his house, yet with rare exceptions his choice of new and potentially profitable plays fared little better. His anglophilia was so ingrained that he only reluctantly turned to the French and occasional American plays that might have brought his programs more in line with changing tastes. Thus, whether Wallack acted out of duty or desperation, or simply for personal satisfaction, his remounting of *The School for Scandal* initiated yet another series of such revivals as once had been the glory of his theatre. He followed Sheridan's comedy with *The Road to Ruin* on October 7, *The Jealous Wife* on the 21st, and *The Rivals* on the 28th.

Niblo's was also given over largely to revivals, but of a different nature. Its offerings were old standards that still pleased its less fashionable clientele. It had opened its season with *Mazeppa* and later in the season presented such dependable attractions as *The Corsican Brothers, Nick of the Woods,* Oliver Doud Byron in *Across the Continent* and *Ben McCullough,* Frank Mayo in *Davy Crockett,* and Lotta's favorites, *Little Nell and the Marchioness* and *The Little Detective,* both without their most popular star. Occasionally, however, it ventured into new territory.

Its latest novelty, **M'liss** (9-23-78, Niblo's), was to remain an attraction, especially in backwater areas, for the rest of the century, but its Manhattan premiere was embroiled in controversy and prevented New Yorkers, at least initially, from seeing it performed by the actress who soon made the title part her own. That beguiling gamine was Annie Pixley, and she had been announced to bring the play into the Grand Opera in early September. Kate Mayhew went to court, insisting she held New York rights to the play, and her claim was upheld by a local tribunal. So it was she whom New Yorkers saw as the hoydenish waif of the Sierras, a bright, spunky girl neglected by her drunken father. Her spunkiness provokes her into battling a band of ruffians besetting the man she loves, and she later wins the susceptible young man away from Clytie (Lottie Murray), "the pink and white thing" who has been her rival.

The story was taken from Bret Harte, although it is uncertain if Niblo's used the dramatization by Clay Greene that Miss Pixley was to employ for so many years. Indeed, how much of the original story beyond its basic theme was retained in any version is uncertain. Reviews and programs list a cast of characters far larger than the spare handful Harte so carefully brought to life in his little tale. In Harte's telling, M'liss's mother is apparently dead and her father, Old Bummer Smith, appears only as a dead body after his suicide. Yet playbills carry not only the father's name but a "Mrs. Smith." At the same time, only Miss Mayhew's version gives Clytie the surname she had in Harte, Morpher. Miss Pixley's programs often list the character as "Clytie Smith." Her later programs, in fact, do not have the same cast of characters as earlier ones, so the play must have been subject to constant revision. A special attraction at Niblo's was Charles J. Edmonds, who had won a certain fame as a California stagecoach driver and who drove a coach and team of horses onstage in his role of Yuba Bill. The New York premiere lasted only two weeks, but the mounting was brought back later in the season, again with Miss Mayhew.

Two other attractions opened the same night to far more critical attention. Both offered leading actresses in older, foreign plays. Rose Eytinge was the star of **A Woman of the People** (9-23-78, Broadway), a new redaction of d'Ennery and Cormon's *Marie-Jeanne,* which had been seen years before in several other versions under several other titles. Its central figure, Marie, is forced to give up her child because her worthless husband will not support his family, and when she later tries to reclaim it she is declared insane. At Booth's, Genevieve Ward presented her Queen Katharine in Shakespeare's *Henry VIII*. Her stern, disciplined Katharine was caviar to the general public; though in her autobiography she remarks that she finally was playing to packed houses, she neglects to mention that reduced ticket prices probably filled many of the seats with bargain hunters. Shortly before concluding her engagement in mid-October, she brought out her Lady Macbeth and also gave a single performance of *The Honeymoon.*

Mother and Son (9-24-78, Union Square), derived

by Cazauran from Victorien Sardou's *Les Bourgeois de Pont-Arcy,* continued Shook and Palmer's tradition of providing their regulars with exciting mountings of contemporary French drama. It was the real opening of the playhouse's season, since *Olivia* had been rather a star's touring vehicle. Fabrice, Baron de St. André (Charles Thorne, Jr.), and his mother, the baroness (Fanny Morant), have been scrupulous about their family's honor, so it comes as a shock to the young man when Marcelle Aubrey (Linda Dietz) reveals to him privately that his late father had once tricked her into a marriage while he was married to Fabrice's mother. Fabrice decides to keep this disgraceful history secret, but his intention is frustrated when Marcelle is accused of theft as she is leaving his house. The accusation is seized upon by Clarisse Trabaud (Sara Jewett), the vicious wife of the town mayor, to uncover the secret interview, and she promotes the rumor that Marcelle is Fabrice's mistress. Although Fabrice is engaged to Gabrielle de Léry (Nina Varian), his mother's canons of rectitude make her insist on his marrying Marcelle. Reluctantly he apprises his mother of the true story. Torn between blemishing the family's heretofore good name and standing in the way of her son's future happiness, the baroness elects to acknowledge the truth. Some critics and playgoers were shaken by several bits of unusual casting, departing from the still common practice of confining performers to their expected "line." Linda Dietz was cast in the role of a hard if basically good woman; even more surprisingly, the delicate Sara Jewett was handed the role of the bitchy Clarisse. All in all, however, the reception was enthusiastic enough to give the Union Square another hit, which ran for over two months. During this period Palmer bought out Shook's interest in the theatre.

Great ladies of the theatre continued to hold sway over the still young season. Their ranks were augmented by the entry of Modjeska at the Fifth Avenue on the 30th, offering her *Camille, Romeo and Juliet,* and *Frou-Frou.*

Could a play with the ridiculous title of **Bouquets and Bombshells** (10-1-78, Park) find happiness on Broadway? The answer was no, but the title was not the only deterrent. J. W. Shannon adapted the piece from an unidentified German work, and he either could not overcome problems inherent in the original or created them in his own redaction. Comedy and melodrama were frequently intermingled in successful plays. A sense of consistent tone was never as important as a sense of theatrical effectiveness. Many of the best dramas had bright comic moments early on before the meat of the melodrama

thoroughly gripped playgoers. Some, like *Pique,* mixed the two knowingly from beginning to end. Several long-popular plays, such as *The Gilded Age,* had used a melodramatic frame to contain the central portrait of an essentially comic figure. But *Bouquets and Bombshells* provided a melodramatic first act that set up situations for comedy in the remaining acts. (Perhaps that was why the *Times* twisted the title, reviewing the play as *Bombshells and Bouquets.*) In the first act the impetuous Captain Victor Violet (George Clarke) defends a lady in a duel, wounds his opponent, and is sent to prison for his actions. But Victor was not defending his beloved Lady Sophia Grant (Agnes Booth). Rather he was merely fighting for the honor of Sophia's friend. Is Sophia grateful? Not really, for she still looks upon Victor as an irresponsible playboy. In subsequent acts all the characters, including several pairs of lovers, come together under one roof, where they are seemingly no match for Victor's matchmaking aunt, Lady Violet (Mrs. Gilbert). Mistaken identities, misconstrued actions, and all the other accoutrements of farce follow apace before everyone is properly paired. Once again, a fine cast could not save a weak play.

Failures of new plays continued to prompt revivals of old ones. Rose Eytinge withdrew her failure and substituted *Oliver Twist* on the 7th. A week later the bill at the Broadway was changed to Boucicault's *Louis XI,* with J. W. Albaugh as star. It was the last of his infrequent appearances in New York, for even at this date he had found a more congenial occupation in building and running theatres, including ones soon to be famous in Washington and Baltimore. At the Park a repertory of *Hurricane, Old Love Letters,* and last season's *Baby* and *Champagne and Oysters* succeeded the burst bombshells, beginning on the 15th.

Just as this flurry of revivals petered out, another actress of some repute on Continental stages challenged reigning American favorites. Mme Elizabeth von Stamwitz's reception was cordial but little more. Her unfortunate choice of plays may have given rise to the muted disappointment expressed in so many of her notices. **Messalina, the Roman Empress** (10-21-78, Broadway), an English adaptation of a German drama, detailed the downfall of the emperor Claudius's terrifying, lecherous consort. While Claudius is away, she forces a handsome young man to abandon his wife and become her lover. The emperor is alerted to the situation and orders her brutally murdered. Critics admired Mme von Stamwitz's regal bearing and stately mannerisms but found her voice cacophonous and her romantic moments coldly unconvincing. In the middle of her second week she brought out *Leah, the Forsaken,* but all too many playgoers felt that Kate Bateman, although she had long since left America for England, still held a virtual patent on the role and that even Miss Bateman's successors were a cut above the newcomer.

Incomparable, irrepressible Lotta cavorted in a new vehicle when she started in **La Cigale** (10-26-78, Park), Olive Logan's transcription of Henri Meilhac and Ludovic Halévy's play of the same name. The tiny star portrayed a circus performer who wins the man of her dreams away from a scheming noblewoman. The circus background injected a rainbow of colors, perhaps superfluous whenever Lotta was center stage, which was most of the time. Her fans really came to see her and little else and were in no way put out when she persisted in twitting her material. She punctuated every action with "a wink or a kick," one critic sighed, continuing, "Her natural step is a waltz *pas,* and her most comfortable movement is a jump in some unexpected direction. . . . Her voice is somewhat rasping, it is true, but it has sweet tones, and she uses it to good effect—when she is not singing." She was, in a sense, a musical comedy star before anything we would recognize as musical comedy existed. Lotta treated her following to the play for nearly a month, then left after giving a few performances of *Musette.*

Two more entertainers who might have drifted into musical comedy had there been any to drift into also enjoyed a month's run in their offering. Mr. and Mrs. George S. Knight were the entertainers, and their vehicle was Fred Marsden's **Otto, a German** (11-4-78, Broadway). Knight had made his mark both in vaudeville and on the legitimate stage; his wife, Sophie, had been one of the famous Worrell sisters, who had been among the first to present opéra bouffe in English. But their new comedy was simply the latest of many attempting to follow in the wake of *Fritz, Our Cousin German,* and its story of a kindhearted immigrant who saves his employer from treachery and is rewarded with the hand of the employer's daughter was sprinkled with innumerable songs, dances, and other variety turns.

If "comic opera" would soon be added to the theatrical lexicon, along with "opéra bouffe," to denote the first musical genres to reach maturity on popular stages, their lineal descendant, operetta, like their cousins, musical comedy and revue, was still years away from fulfillment. In the nonmusical theatre, new genres also were struggling to achieve a proper form. Tom Taylor's *The Ticket-of-Leave Man* had already pioneered, with conspicuous success,

one of those related types that would soon be called the "crook-play," the "detective-play," and the "mystery-thriller." But other isolated, early examples were forthcoming occasionally.

One was Ettie Henderson's **Almost a Life** (11-9-78, Standard). Mrs. Henderson was the wife of the Standard's manager, and she took her tale from a novel by Émile Gaboriau, who has been called the father of the French *roman policier.* The story suggests how naturally the crook-detective-mystery-thriller evolved by utilizing stock devices from traditional melodrama. In this case the stock device was the frequently overused false accusation. When Jules de Bonneval (Eben Plympton) is charged with shooting the haughty Count Clairnot (Harry Eytinge), his imprisonment brings about some strange bedfellows. United in his defense are his fiancée, Alvisie Doranche (Maude Granger), and his discarded mistress, Mélanie, Countess Clairnot (Rose Osborne), although at one point the countess threatens to turn against him if he does not elope with her. The wounded count, bent on getting even for being cuckolded, swears that Jules was his assailant, and his story is corroborated by Colinet (Charles Leclercq), who secretly covets the countess. Matters appear gloomy for Jules until Dr. Saumaise (H. A. Weaver) persuades a young friend, Philippe (Ben Maginley), to disguise himself and ingratiate himself with Colinet. He exposes Colinet's feelings and pins the shooting on him. The count has no choice but to retract his own accusations.

The *Times,* not seeing much hope for detective-plays, nonetheless put its finger on a characteristic of many later, successful examples when it observed, "The detective, in fact, is a necessary figure in his dramas, while the real actors are treated . . . like so many puppets." The big scene, the reviewer felt, was the one in which the two women put aside their differences in a common cause. Future works might be more clever in their characterizations and development, but Mrs. Henderson unmistakably put her own finger on a still weak theatrical pulse and was rewarded with a two-month run for her play—far longer than Mrs. Shook's *Without a Heart* had run.

Of course, not everyone could look ahead, and some persisted in peering steadily rearward. For all his many excellences, Edwin Booth most certainly subscribed to this more conservative approach, so when he announced his program for an engagement to begin on the 11th at the Fifth Avenue, playgoers expected no novelties and got none. His five-week stand offered *Hamlet, Othello, Richelieu, The Fool's Revenge, Ruy Blas, King Lear, The Merchant of Venice, Richard II,* and *Richard III.*

At heart Lester Wallack probably shared Booth's philosophy, but the reality of theatrical economics, even in these comparatively easygoing times, compelled him to seek out new works. Of course, whenever possible, new works meant to him new English works.

Thus it was that another glittering array of first-nighters assembled to enjoy F. C. Burnand's **Our Club** (11-16-78, Wallack's). Londoners probably saw the comedy in part as a telling sendup of club life and clubmen, but Americans could not be expected to savor many of those nuances. Instead they had to look upon it as simply another farce trafficking in mistaken identities. And there was no mistaking that mistaken identities abounded. Indeed, they all but defy recounting, or just plain counting. On Ladies' Day at the Eccentric Club, two feuding members, Stanislaus Radetzki (W. R. Floyd), an artist, and Henry Lennard (Charles Baron), an actor, both find themselves invited to the home of Mrs. Wray (Mrs. Lindsey). Mrs. Wray herself has invited Radetzki to discuss some decorations, while Lennard has been asked by his fiancée, Lady Ethel Crawford (Rose Coghlan), who lives with Mrs. Wray. Mrs. Wray also invites the club's secretary, Alphonse Dubuisson (Charles Coghlan), in order to inquire about a servant she hopes to hire—a man whose first name, so conveniently for farce purposes, is the same as Lennard's. Lennard's sister, Nellie (Stella Boniface), will be there to add to the confusion. Radetzki confuses Nellie with Lady Crawford, Lady Crawford thinks Dubuisson is Radetzki, and so on down the line. High comedy, not farce, was actually Wallack's forte, but the play nonetheless was a modest success. For what it is worth, in 1890 London artists and actors established a real Eccentric Club.

A more militant sort of English eccentric was the subject of **That Lass o' Lowrie's** (11-25-78, Booth's), which Frances Hodgson Burnett and Julian Magnus derived from Mrs. Burnett's popular novel. Joan Lowrie (Marie Gordon), a "pit girl" in the mines, protects a pregnant, unmarried friend from jeering co-workers, thwarts her own vindictive father's attempt to assault the mining engineer, Fergus Derrick (Harry Dalton), and later rescues Fergus from a mine explosion and restores him to health. The play was too episodic to be totally effective, but it had its exciting moments, most notably the vividly depicted explosion in the belly of the mine.

From the hard world of English coal mines to the not dissimilar rough and tumble of our own Wild West could have been only a short hop for playgoers wanting to see **Yulie; or, Kindes-Liebe** (11-25-78, Grand Opera). The story depicted the search by Franz Weber (J. C. Williamson) for his young daughter, who had been taken by his wife when she ran off with another man. The final curtain saw Franz cradling his dying, unrepentant wife in his arms and the youngster saying a prayer for her mother. The play was sometimes known as *Julie*.

One of the era's most interesting Shakespearean revivals opened in competition with the two new plays when Robson and Crane brought out *The Comedy of Errors* at the Park. They spared little effort or expense on the mounting. For the sumptuous and, by modern standards, excessively realistic scenery they hired the venerable George Heister, and to direct the production they imported Charles Webb. He and his recently deceased brother Henry had been London's most celebrated Dromios, reputedly playing the roles over 1500 times. Webb assumed the role of Aegeon, while Robson was Dromio of Syracuse and Crane was Dromio of Ephesus. Their masters were played by Frank Evans and Frank E. Aiken. Many critics agreed that the real challenge of the evening fell to Crane, who had to, in some manner or other, mimic Robson's singularly squeaky voice and deadpan expression. The same critics disagreed on just how well he met the challenge. The play ran nearly a month, then the team departed after a few performances of *Our Bachelors*. Shortly before the team split they would return to the Shakespeare work in an even more spectacular mounting.

Although the Union Square had made and sustained its reputation largely on its presentations of French drama, it scored the season's biggest hit when it turned to a native writer and offered Bronson Howard's **The Banker's Daughter** (11-30-78, Union Square). The play had originally been performed in Chicago in 1873 as *Lilian's Last Love*. Subsequently Cazauran helped Howard revamp the piece, adding, among other things, what many saw as the all-important happy ending. Lilian Westbrook (Sara Jewett) is a thoughtless, selfish young lady. She sneers openly at a friend who is about to marry a much older man and flirts just as openly with Count de Carojac (M. V. Lingham), although she is virtually engaged to Harold Routledge (Walden Ramsay). Then she learns her father is threatened with bankruptcy, so she throws over Harold to marry a richer—and much older—man, John Strebelow (Charles Thorne, Jr.). She comes as close as she can to confessing she has really loved Harold when she cries out to her Aunt Fanny (Mrs. E. J. Phillips), "Mr. Strebelow is to be my husband. Oh, Aunt Fanny, my heart is broken!" Seven years later, her life has come to revolve around her young daughter, but she still loves Harold and still sees both him and the count. The men fall out over her and fight a duel in which the count mortally wounds Routledge. In her shock at the news Lilian blurts out to Strebelow that she has never loved him. Strebelow blames himself for the failure of the marriage and leaves his wife. But Lilian soon realizes that she has acted cruelly and immaturely. A reconciliation is effected by letters sent to Strebelow by their daughter but dictated by Lilian.

Moving as the play was, it was made all the more powerful by an outstanding production. Sara Jewett gave what many felt was the best performance of her career, catching just the right degree of youthful naivete and its unthinking brutality in earlier scenes, then quietly maturing emotionally. Thorne, in a role quite unlike the more forceful, dashing heroes he was wont to play, excelled in a difficult, often thankless part. And the settings, which included several rich domestic interiors, the spacious vestibule and stairway at the American embassy in Paris, and an icy woods near a ruined chateau (site of the duel), were hailed for their "rare artistic beauty." The original production ran for 137 performances, bringing Palmer a profit of $45,000. The play was later done in England as *The Old Love and the New*, and in America it was revived with some regularity until the early years of the new century. Even then it remained popular in stock up to World War I.

Howard, like Bartley Campbell, was among the earliest American playwrights who attempted to support themselves solely by their playwriting. Not quite such an original conception, but still a relative rarity in American theatre, was the actress-manager. Actors who thought they could serve as their own producers were not uncommon. A few, such as Burton and Wallack, had been very successful; most had been failures or had gotten through by the skin of their teeth. By far the most successful actress-manager of the era was Mrs. Drew, but she was still confining her activity to Philadelphia. So some theatre buffs watched with interest Kate Claxton's entry into the arena. She was still quite young, having just turned thirty—or, if some biographical notices are to be believed, twenty-eight.

For her producing debut she offered Charles Reade's **The Double Marriage** (12-3-78, Lyceum), and she immediately ran into trouble. The play's claim to be new and original was greeted in some quarters with raised eyebrows. Scoffers suggested that Reade must have had at his elbow Auguste Macquet's old melodrama *Le Château de Grantier*, from which, it was charged further, he also had cribbed for his novel *White Lies*. Turning the knife

these same critics protested that Reade was no dramatist, however dramatically effective his novels were. Yet the heroine's dilemma, absurd though it might seem to our notions, was the very stuff of contemporary domestic-melodrama. As a young girl Josephine (Alice Dunning Lingard) had agreed to marry an officer, Dugardin (C. A. Stevenson), in order to save her family chateau. Later she is told that Dugardin had been killed in battle, so she marries the man she has long loved, another officer, Émile Raynal (Frederic Robinson), and has a child by him. When Dugardin suddenly reappears, his first reaction is one of outrage at her infidelity. Josephine's sister, Rose (Miss Claxton), hastily steps in to claim the baby as her own, even if this will jeopardize her forthcoming marriage to a nobleman. Of course, Dugardin sees through so transparent a lie, but he also comes to understand the fundamental goodness of the sisters, and he quietly walks out of their lives.

Casting Mrs. Lingard, best known for her vaudevilles and comedy, was a brave gesture on Miss Claxton's part. Critics judged this new attempt misguided, one reviewer complaining that Mrs. Lingard "acted the emotional Josephine as though she mistook her for *Lady Macbeth*." (New Yorkers probably did not know Mrs. Lingard had scored handsomely as Louise, Miss Claxton's great role, in a San Francisco production of *The Two Orphans*.) Another critic upbraided Miss Claxton for playing Rose with the "mincing ways of a little school girl."

The play's five-week run apparently was forced, and Miss Claxton was beset, both during it and afterwards, by lawsuits. The Society for the Prevention of Cruelty to Children—the infamous Gerry Society—denounced her for using an honest-to-goodness baby onstage, instead of a doll, and wondered out loud whether the infant had been drugged to keep it quiet. Later, charges were brought claiming Miss Claxton had not paid many of the Lyceum's staff. Such public failure in no way daunted her. She was to persist in producing plays over the years without ever discovering the major commercial success that her spunkiness, if nothing else, should have earned her.

Lester Wallack, perhaps less enthusiastically, also persisted in trying to find good, new, money-making plays. He may have made a small profit with Dr. F. Harris and Fred Williams's **My Son** (12-4-78, Wallack's), which the authors took from a long-popular German play, Adolf L'Arronge's *Mein Leopold*, and which ran for four weeks. Certainly reviews were encouraging, despite the play's unpleasant story. Herr Weigel (John Gilbert), a cobbler who has risen to become a rich shoe manufacturer, disowns his loving daughter, Clara (Rose Coghlan), when she disobeys him and marries his foreman, Rudolph (Charles Barron). His infuriated son-in-law warns him, "Never beneath my roof shall you taste bread or drink water, until I find you at my feet, kneeling before me, as your daughter is now kneeling before you." Weigel chooses not to heed this admonition and instead blindly squanders his affection on his worthless, totally ungrateful son, Leopold (Charles Rockwell), who soon bankrupts his father and then deserts him. Reduced once more to a cobbler, Weigel must decide if he is willing to abase himself and ask his son-in-law's help.

The play's good reviews were followed immediately by some singular publicity that could only have helped at the box office, for the day after the opening John Gilbert celebrated his fiftieth anniversary as an actor. Attached to or nearby the notices in many newspapers were articles recounting the actor's history and extolling his great artistry. The oddity of an actor considered by many his era's finest high comedian, the day's unsurpassed Sir Peter Teazle or Sir Anthony Absolute, celebrating his anniversary by assuming an essentially tragic role was not lost on many commentators.

Yet the starchy formality and clichés of his morning-after notices, however laudatory, were typical of the time and illustrate how difficult it remains for later generations fully to recreate Gilbert's obvious excellences. Thus the *Times* reflected, "To Mr. John Gilbert's impersonation of *Herr Weigel* the highest praise is due. A more beautiful and natural embodiment of fatherhood we have never seen. Mr. Gilbert conceives the part in the most sympathetic spirit, and he presents it with all the strength of feeling, graceful finish, and variety of proportion, which are its characteristics. His acting throughout the play—from the moment when, chasing his own daughter from his house, he proclaims to the world that his son is the only hope of his life, until he returns poor and broken-hearted to that same daughter—was marked by deep sincerity and touching pathos." Nary a telling gesture or revealing grimace is described, nor any hint whether Gilbert employed some slight German accent. To many Americans who could not travel to New York, another actor personified Herr Weigel, for on the road John T. Raymond took to spelling his Colonel Sellers with his interpretation of the role, receiving many flattering notices for his version.

An even bigger success, one that endured for many seasons, although the play is now totally forgotten, was E. A. Locke's **A Messenger from**

Jarvis Section (12-9-78, Broadway). It bore a striking resemblance to *Joshua Whitcomb* and, to the extent that its story was dramatically more gripping than the earlier play's, may have inspired Thompson's eventual replacement of *Josh* by a better play that told a story practically identical to Locke's. Like Josh, Uncle Dan'l is a New Englander, this time from Maine, who makes a visit to Boston. His visit, however, is not quite as purposeless as Josh's, since he goes seeking a long-lost brother. At Keppler's dingy saloon he encounters a grab-bag of lowly city types, including Clip (Katie Wilson), a street arab, whose grammar is a source of bewilderment to the Yankee. In turn Uncle Dan'l delights the city folk with his inventions, most notably a "crow annihilator." Before returning home Dan'l learns that his brother has been murdered and sees the murderer brought to justice. The hero was played by an amiable teddy bear of a man who was then calling himself Bernard Macauley. Shortly after this he announced that "family difficulties" forced him to change his name to McAuley. His quiet, docile Yankee stood in some contrast to the more irascible, expectorating Josh. He played Dan'l for the half-dozen or so years in which he remained on the stage, sometimes, according to Odell, offering the work either as *Uncle Dan'l, the Messenger from Jarvis Section* or simply as *Uncle Dan'l.*

On the night of McAuley's premiere, *Our American Cousin* was performed at Booth's, but without Sothern. George Parkes was Dundreary, and Frank Hardenberg was Asa Trenchard. The production was a limited one-week stand, and there was no call for any extension.

Few critics bothered to take note of William E. Barnes's **Only a Farmer's Daughter** (12-14-78, Globe), but then the Globe was a shabby, long-disused theatre, and its ticket scale—from fifteen cents to a top of fifty cents—suggested the sort of patronage it sought. Yet several good young actresses were in the cast. Mme Laurent (Laura Don), an adventuress, attempts to use an innocent farm girl, Justine (Lillie Eldridge), to further her own selfish plans. But it is Mme Laurent who comes in the end to a pauper's grave. The *Herald,* one of the few newspapers to review the piece, saw it as a pasted-together collection of theatrical clichés.

The coming holidays were made more cheerful by the return of Joseph Jefferson in *Rip Van Winkle*, which began its stand at the Fifth Avenue on the 16th.

Niblo's, which all season long had been given over to spectacles and to touring productions of ancient warhorses, was briefly host to a new play when

George Fawcett Rowe brought in his own combination in **New York and London** (12-23-78, Niblo's), a rather old-style melodrama Rowe had written with Paul Merritt. Hiram Maltby (F. A. Tannehill), a onetime mill hand who has become a rich, international gambler, saves Belle Lorimer (Annie Ward Tiffany) from being abused at a New York gaming house. He takes her to London, where he discovers that she is actually his own daughter, whom his wife long ago had sold to another gambler, John Ramirez (Richard C. White). Settings depicted Tattersall's, the notorious Cremorne Gardens, and the Goodwood Races. Clearly conceived as a touring production, catering to the more atavistic propensities of less sophisticated towns, the play remained only one week before moving on.

Merritt was also the author of **At Last** (12-30-78, Wallack's), with which that most illustrious house rang out the old year. To add to the hoped-for excitement Lester Wallack returned to his own stage, albeit in a minor, supporting role. The story centered on a married couple, the Roxbys, played by brother and sister Charles and Rose Coghlan, who must properly pair several initially ill-matched lovers. Notices provided little joy for the new year. The play was one of the worst failures of Wallack's recent seasons and struggled along for a mere two weeks, when it was supplanted by a revival of *Ours* on January 13.

But before that change of bill, another revival had appeared, this one at Niblo's. As we have noted, Niblo's, along with such other theatres as the Grand Opera House, was now devoted primarily to circulating productions of timeworn standbys. Most of these revivals were given short shrift in the press. Not *Davy Crockett*, which returned on the 7th with Frank Mayo still in his original role. In the slightly more than five years since its New York premiere it had come to occupy an almost hallowed place in the ranks of American drama, with only *Rip Van Winkle* approaching it in many critics' eyes as a landmark of truly native dramaturgy. The *Times* devoted a long essay to examining its merits, noting that Davy "draws his metaphors from the trickling streams and the companionable trees, and, with a burst of poetry which seems to most persons foreign to such a nature, he pictures the eyes of the woman he worships as entering within the heaven of his life by the same law which set the polar star in its eternal resting-place. It is because *Davy* is such a perfectly consistent and natural character, and withal such a simple one, that we regard it as a type worthy of attention and study." The essay concluded, "The success of 'Davy Crockett' . . . teaches us that a

pure and elevated purpose in the drama is akin to all human sympathies." While hardly modern standards of judgment, the sentiments undoubtedly express ideals held by many contemporary critics and probably by numerous playgoers of the time, suggesting the attitudes they brought with them to a play. That they leave many other aspects unaddressed was not considered; an idyllic play such as *Davy Crockett*—and the *Times* complained too many contemporary plays were called "idyllic" unjustly—did not call for discussing these other issues.

These sometimes too lofty, puritanical ideals may have been behind the critical displeasure with H. Dalziel's adaptation of Émile Augier's **Les Fourchambault** (1-13-79, Broadway). Certainly it was an unusual opening bill for the Lingards, who customarily reveled in comedy. Alice Dunning Lingard's taste of serious drama earlier with *The Double Marriage* may have prompted the surprising choice. Retention of the original French title reflected the ongoing cachet of Parisian craftsmanship. Mrs. Lingard played Marie Le Tellier, who is adopted by a cynical bourgeois family; one of the sons is encouraged by his father to despoil the innocent girl. A subsequent bill, headed by *Our Boys*, was probably more to the liking of many of the Lingards' loyalists.

One of the great touring comedians, John E. Owens, unpacked his bags for a month's engagement at the Park, beginning on the 20th. His opening vehicle was Boucicault's *Dot,* with Owens as Caleb Plummer. Boucicault's "fairy prologue" in blank verse, so often omitted, was restored and embellished with a ballet featuring Augusta Sohlke in a shadow dance. After two weeks *Dot* made way for the double bill of *Victims* and *Solon Shingle*.

Actor D. H. Harkins turned theatre manager and producer and met with a quick failure when he presented **Dr. Clyde** (1-25-79, Fifth Ave.), based on Adolf L'Arronge's German success *Dr. Klaus.* Sydney Rosenfeld, a highly talented but often erratic gadfly, made the translation, moving the setting from Germany to England. The pedantic, dry-as-dust Dr. Clyde (George D. Chaplin) seems an unlikely hero, but in his quiet way he helps the dissolute Lord Hammond (Henry Lee) patch up his failing marriage by making it seem that Samuel Meeker (Charles Fisher), father of Lady Hammond (Laura Don), is on the verge of bankruptcy and having Hammond come to the rescue. He also brings about the wedding of his own daughter, Emily (Ellie Wilson), to Totbury Simms (Owen Fawcett).

Another failure came when George Edgar, manager of the Broadway, turned actor to offer his *King*

Lear there on the 27th. Like some of his more famous brethren, he refused to act more than six times a week, so matinees were given over to *Enoch Arden,* with Joseph Wheelock in the role long associated with Edwin Adams. Later in the three-week stand Edgar offered *Othello.* Also high on the list of revivals was *The Danites* at Booth's on the 27th, with the Rankins and Louis Aldrich in their original assignments and Charles Parsloe now as Washee-Washee. Although the company had already appeared in the work during the season at several of New York's combination houses, they recorded good business at Booth's.

Interest in the next revivals at Booth's was whetted by offstage as well as onstage matters. Boucicault had long since left Agnes Robertson, claiming they had never really been married and thus making all their children illegitimate. Moreover, his affair with Katherine Rogers was an open secret. So when Agnes Robertson, along with the children, came to America in hope of effecting a reconciliation, his callous response was to have her agree to a week's engagement with him in their old favorites. Although she had grown conspicuously matronly and some of her former fire was missing, she had not been forgotten. The couple played to capacity business and realized a gross of $12,000 in a one-week engagement, beginning February 10, which brought back *The Colleen Bawn, Arrah na Pogue, Kerry,* and *The Shaughraun.* That was far more than Boucicault had taken in when he appeared without his wife earlier at the Grand Opera, but it seems not to have changed his feelings.

With *H.M.S. Pinafore* the season's runaway success, it was not unexpected that Broadway would enjoy a major mounting of W. S. Gilbert's **Engaged** (2-17-79, Park). And enjoy it it did! The play was one of the season's outstanding hits, running until the beginning of May, and returned for numerous subsequent revivals. Belinda Treherne (Agnes Booth), leaving her groom, Major Macgillicuddy (George Stoddart), waiting for her on the church steps, has eloped with Belvawney (Joseph E. Whiting). They take refuge from a train accident at a cottage on the English-Scottish border. Belvawney derives his income from the father of Cheviot Hill (James Lewis), on the condition that he keep Cheviot from marrying. If he fails, the income goes to Cheviot's uncle, Mr. Simperson (W. F. Owen). Cheviot and Simperson are on the same train, where Simperson has been persuading his nephew to marry his daughter, Minnie (Minnie Palmer). But Cheviot is a most susceptible bachelor, so when they arrive at the very cottage to which Belinda and Belvawney have come, Cheviot promptly falls in love with both the cottager's daughter and Belinda and proposes to both of them. The arrival of Macgillicuddy goads the protective Cheviot into claiming publicly that Belinda is his wife, which, under Scottish law, she automatically becomes. Back in London, Cheviot has forgotten the whole incident and is preparing to marry Minnie. Belinda is a friend of Minnie's and arrives at the wedding dressed in black, for she has lost track of Cheviot, doesn't know who he is, and, for all she does know, she may be a widow. The last two acts are spent untangling the mess.

The title of the play was a double entendre, since not only were many of the principal figures engaged to be married to each other (and sometimes to more than one at a time), but they were all relentlessly engaged in feathering their own nests. Every profession of love was coupled with a question of financial considerations. Much of the fun came from the fact that the play was performed in dead earnest, with the laughs arising from Gilbert's biting wit and preposterous situations. Although Cheviot Hill was the central figure, not all critics felt Lewis was right for the part. He was too much the comic to put on the pseudo-serious mask required. But the other players did, especially Agnes Booth, who stole the show. A highlight was the scene in which she ravenously gobbled up wedding tarts, all the while wondering, "Am I single? Am I married? Am I a widow? Can I marry? Have I married? May I marry? Who am I? Where am I? What am I?"

Comedy and drama were intermingled—this time unintentionally—when another of the era's determined aspirants debuted on February 17 at the Lyceum. The debutant was Frederick Paulding, a not unattractive young man of about twenty, but as an actor scarcely ready for the lofty roles he assigned himself. Whatever imagination he brought to his interpretations—and most critics felt that was precious little—he showed no imagination in selecting his repertory. Like all too many starry-eyed young players, he culled his pieces from the narrowest list of "legitimate" standards. In selecting a program consisting of *The Fool's Revenge, Hamlet,* and *The Lady of Lyons,* all of which Booth had recently offered, he unthinkingly invited comparison with the greatest and most experienced of players.

Across the continent, the program for **Within an Inch of His Life** (2-17-79, Grand Opera, San Francisco) was filled with still relatively unknown names that would soon be famous. The play's authors were James A. Herne and David Belasco. Its leading player was James O'Neill, supported by Herne, Herne's wife, Katharine Corcoran, and

William Seymour (later a famous director). The authors based their play on one of Émile Gaboriau's early novels of crime and detection, *La Corde au cou*—the source of *Almost a Life*. But they missed an opportunity to become pioneers in the detective-play by minimizing the role of the detective. Instead they centered attention on Jules de Dareville, who is arrested and condemned for the murder of the Count de Clairnot. He had been the countess's lover. Jules himself believes the countess actually murdered her husband after Jules told her he was breaking up their liaison to marry a young woman his family selected for him. At the very last minute a demented servant of the late count confesses.

If young, inexperienced hands were coming a cropper on both coasts, some of the greatest and most experienced artists were not always faring better, as the premiere of **Spell-bound** (2-24-79, Wallack's) demonstrated. Lester Wallack produced and starred in Boucicault's latest endeavor, and both were soundly excoriated for their efforts. The plot harked back to the Gothic horror stories so relished by an earlier generation (although Odell suggested it prefigured the later crook-play). Gabrielle (Rose Coghlan) falls in love with Count Raoul de Beaupré (Wallack) after watching him kill an infuriated tigress with his hands at night in a mountain pass in Hindustan and after he has saved her friend from a wild boar. But once they are married she begins to harbor suspicions about her husband. There are strange carryings-on in his eerie castle. Exploring the place, she comes across what appear to be torture chambers and a room in which a woman is being held captive. Her husband, she discovers, heads a gang of murderers. She saves the woman, and the two escape. The *Herald* reported snickers in the audience during the ineptly staged fight with the tigress (obviously an actor in costume). The *Times* chastised Wallack for being "merely stilted, affected, and theatrical." But almost all critics condemned the play itself as hopelessly dated. Actually, the story was not new. Boucicault had taken it from Dumas and used it in 1853 for *Pauline*. In a sense, the young, ambitious Paulding and the much older, established Boucicault and Wallack represented theatrical schools that subscribed to passing traditions, traditions coming under increasing fire from a new generation with different ideas.

Yet the replacement that Wallack's rushed in for the failed *Spell-bound* suggested just how viable much of the older school was, and indeed would long remain. The play was Sardou's 1860 success *Les Pattes de mouche*, which had been translated the following year by J. Palgrave Simpson as **A Scrap of Paper** (3-10-79, Wallack's) and, somewhat inexplicably, was only now being given its first New York performance in English. The scrap of paper is a love note Louise (Stella Boniface) wrote to Prosper Couramont (Wallack) before she married Baron de la Glacière (Charles Rockwell). Now Prosper is forced by his uncle's will to marry, so he attempts to use the old letter to make Louise help him in his courtship of her sister, Mathilde (Kate Bartlett). Louise enlists her cousin, Suzanne de Russeville (Rose Coghlan), to aid her in retrieving the letter, since she knows Mathilde loves someone else. Suzanne succeeds in her mission but at the same time falls in love with Prosper. Played with romantic dash by Wallack's superb ensemble, the comedy gave the theatre its biggest hit of the season.

Through the Dark (3-10-79, Fifth Ave.) was far less popular with playgoers, although many commentators felt it provided further evidence of Steele MacKaye's growing sureness. A prologue depicted the early years of several figures whose later history was recounted in the rest of the play. An incorrigible gambler, Harry Graham (G. D. Chaplin), having lost all his money and property, offers his young son, Arthur (Master Burnett), as stakes in a bet with Peter Van Slink (Frank Hardenberg), a notorious usurer and breeder of juvenile thieves. Naturally the ill-starred Harry loses, but before he can deliver his son to Van Slink, his wife, Sarah (Henrietta Irving), hides the boy. To force her to disclose his whereabouts Harry dangles their daughter over a balcony, threatening to throw her into the river below. A struggle ensues in which Harry himself slips, falls into the water, and is presumed drowned. Years pass. Arthur (now played by Joseph Wheelock) has been adopted by his uncle, John Allston (James G. Peakes), and has assumed both his uncle's surname and his trade as an engraver. Kate Mortimer (Ellie Wilton), niece of Sir Philip Mortimer (Charles Fisher), falls in love with Arthur, despite his patent poverty. But Sir Philip is outraged by their marriage, disowns Kate, and makes his debauched nephew, Robert (Arthur C. Dacre), his heir. In expectation of a fortune, Robert borrows greedily from none other than Van Slink, who goads him into killing his uncle before the old man can change his mind. Meanwhile, Arthur has struggled along as an engraver. Knowing Arthur's wife is dangerously ill, Billy Kloot (D. H. Harkins), a counterfeiter, asks Arthur to fake some bonds, assuring him the money Arthur will earn will pay for all of Kate's medical bills. Arthur refuses. At the same time, he is accused of Sir Philip's murder. Impressed by Arthur's high ethics, Kloot repents his ways and goes so far as to claim he murdered Sir Philip. Robert's suicide, however, intervenes to bring about a happy ending.

The *Herald*'s critic was not alone in suggesting that the prologue might have been dispensed with and its story told in a few lines of dialogue instead. Even the play's sometime excessively melodramatic incidents were dismissed as dated. But reviewers were pleased with MacKaye's quietly modern delineation of his leading figures and, especially in light of the moral strictures so many still brought with them to the theatre, with his compassionate, high-minded picture of loyalty and devotion in the face of dire poverty. The *Times* hailed the play's "force and significance" but, noting its many scenes of unalloyed impoverishment, bewailed the drift to "intolerable realism." Apparently playgoers shared this reservation. *Through the Dark* ran just two weeks.

Many playgoers may also have shared the *Times*'s rejection of a basic premise of the play that took the place of *Through the Dark*. This was **Whims** (3-27-79, Fifth Ave.), Stanley McKenna's Americanization of a German farce. That premise, according to the newspaper, reflected "the foolish desire among certain women to be emancipated, to exercise the noble and lofty prerogatives of manhood." The men who serve as comic exemplars or adversaries for the ladies include Dr. Kylman Slaughter (Henry Lee), inventor of a miraculous pill (did it make women more manly?); Dr. Sadeye (W. J. Gilbert), an editor; Maulstick Varnish (F. C. Hughner), an artist; Emanuel Bonds (Charles Fisher), a banker; Roger Shoutloud (T. Jefferson), a man-about-town; and Huntington Sleuth (A. S. Lipman), a detective. The characters' names suggest the author's idea of wit. *Whims* lasted one week.

By contrast, **The Lost Children** (4-17-79, Union Square) held the boards, although not without a struggle, for a month, despite an equally merciless critical drubbing. Taken by A. R. Cazauran from Michel Masson and Auguste Anicet-Bourgeois's *Les Orphelines du Pont Notre Dame*, it unfolded the saga of two abandoned children, Philip St. Val (Mabel Leonard) and Stephen Fournier (Hattie Anderson). The saintly Vincent de Paul (John Parselle) takes them under his wing until their missing mothers can be found. A "proscribed Italian statesman," Duc de Savelli (M. V. Lingham), plots against the youngsters and their benefactor until he is slain by Guy de Courci (Charles Thorne, Jr.). The story purported to describe the founding of one of France's most famous orphanages. What few kind words critics could muster were reserved for Richard Marston, who was called forth three times on opening night to accept applause for his magnificent scenery. These

settings included a snowy view of the Notre Dame bridge with the cathedral in the background, a chateau's salon with the Rhine seen through its windows, and a view of old Paris and the Seine by moonlight. The play's harsh reception did not deter a copycat version from being mounted for a week beginning May 26 at the Broadway under the title **The Foundlings.**

On April 23, the doors of a new theatre opened. Built on the site of Daly's first Fifth Avenue Theatre, it was called the Madison Square and was the brainchild of Steele MacKaye. Whatever might be said for the real or perceived modernity of MacKaye's writing, his new playhouse unmistakably prodded theatre construction into a new era. Several of his innovations would not be incorporated into its design until the following year, but one major change was there from the start. MacKaye intentionally made the house seem even smaller than its tiny predecessor. By lowering the stage, by further foreshortening the small apron between the proscenium and the audience, and by moving the orchestra from a pit between the stage and audience and placing it above the proscenium, he created an intimacy all but unknown previously. Such changes were designed to promote the new theatrical naturalism MacKaye was advocating, and some commentators suggested the effect was like inviting guests into a drawing room. If that drawing room sat nearly 700 playgoers, it was still far smaller than any other Broadway house and pointed the way to intimate theatres of the future. Not everyone was pleased, probably to some extent because actors trained in older, more demonstrative traditions could not readily modulate their styles and therefore appeared to be overacting. The very intimacy between player and playgoers was seen by some conservatives as "artistically disagreeable."

Imagination failed MacKaye when it came to selecting an opening bill. He merely revived *Won at Last*, albeit under the title of *Aftermath*. The play ran a month, following which the house joined the long list of theatres bringing out *H.M.S. Pinafore*. Not until the next season would the Madison Square Theatre start to make its mark on theatrical history.

Sydney Grundy's **The Snowball** (4-28-79, Wallack's), based on a French farce, was hardly more successful. Just why Wallack's regular audiences, which accepted all manner of melodrama and comedy, rarely accepted the house's mountings of farce, even when, as in this case, they were well received, can no longer be ascertained. Yet the reviews in general found the play not only funny but, again so important to contemporary playgoers, morally unquestionable. Indeed, the play derived some of its fun from twitting the very dubious French theatre that often raised American or English hackles. And, of course, it was beautifully performed. When Felix Featherstone (Charles Coghlan) sneaks off to see *Les Dominos roses,* one of those same French plays that no decent husband would take his wife to, he is horrified to discover his wife, Arabella (Rose Coghlan), sitting in a box with their ward, Ethel (Stella Boniface), and Ethel's beau. Rather than openly rebuke his wife, he decides to play a trick upon her. He sends her a letter suggesting a tryst and signed "Pink Dominos." Arabella contrives to send her maid, Penelope (Effie Germon), in her place. Uncle John (John Gilbert) walks in on Featherstone just as he is down on his knees to Penelope, and his price for keeping quiet about the matter is that Ethel marry his son. Naturally, Arabella has also "learned" of the incident, and her price for family peace is that Ethel be allowed to marry whomever she chooses. Charles Coghlan's comparatively reserved style of acting may not have been quite right for such a farce but nonetheless was praised, and he was seen to even greater advantage as the wise, patient revolutionary who wins back his wife from the cajolings of her old sweetheart, a weak-willed royalist, in the accompanying comedietta, Charles Dance's *Delicate Ground.*

One play Featherstone would certainly not have taken his wife to was **L'Assommoir** (4-30-79, Olympic). This dramatization of Émile Zola's novel had become the most talked-about success of the current Paris season, and hurried translations had been rushed onto stages at other theatrical capitals. Augustin Daly, visiting Europe, had seen the Paris mounting, borrowed money from his father-in-law to obtain the rights, and drafted Olive Logan to turn it into a suitable piece for New York audiences. From that point on, almost everything that could go wrong did go wrong. The production at the Théâtre Ambigu had been hailed immediately as a milestone in the drive toward theatrical realism, both in story and staging. Yet Daly, sharing contemporary American sensibilities, was offended. He wrote to his brother that the play was "disgusting" and, more important, wrote to Miss Logan, "Realism can scarcely go further; for the sensation scene of Coupeau's fall there is a real scaffolding & real ladders; real hot water for the lavoir scene, and the 2 rival washwomen drench each other, & stand with hair, face, & clothes dripping before the audience, while the stage is positively a puddle. But the whole affair is revolting." Miss Logan, for all her advanced views, acquiesced and proceeded to modify much of the harshest realism. Thus producer and translator

failed to respect the work, a dangerous beginning. Nor could Daly obtain a choice playhouse. He was forced to settle for the out-of-the-way, déclassé Olympic.

In the play New Yorkers saw, Gervaise (Maude Granger) is abandoned by the idle, selfish Lantier (B. T. Ringgold) and takes up with Coupeau (Harry Meredith), a roofer. But after he is crippled by a fall, he becomes a drunkard and Gervaise accepts work in a laundry. She, too, begins to drink heavily. Goujet (Clinton Hall), a poor but good-hearted blacksmith, falls in love with her and attempts to offer her a better life, only to have her ignore him. Totally besotted, Coupeau dies after a violent bout with delirium tremens, and Gervaise starves to death. As staged by Daly, Coupeau's fall used a dummy dropped from a patently painted scene, thereby destroying the shock value of the original. The battle between Gervaise and her vicious rival laundrywoman, Virginie (Emily Rigl), became simply a scratching and hair-pulling contest, although even that outraged many playgoers. However, the strongest objections of many critics were directed not to the staging but to the story, which even in its watered-down form struck them as morally unpalatable and unworthy of being dramatized. The play survived a mere three weeks. Virtually its only successful American mounting came in freewheeling San Francisco a few months later, in a version written and directed with stunning realism by young David Belasco and featuring Rose Coghlan, Lillian Andrews, and James O'Neill.

In May, Ada Cavendish made a second, largely futile attempt to win over New York playgoers. After appearing as the heroines of *As You Like It* on the 19th and *The Hunchback* on June 2, she closed her engagement in the title role of **Miss Gwilt** (6-5-79, Wallack's), which Wilkie Collins had dramatized for her from his novel *Armadale.* She received her best notices as the weak-willed woman who comes under the spell of a subtle troublemaker, Dr. Downward (H. A. Weaver). The twists and coincidences so favored by period writers see to it that before the final, happy curtain her path crosses those of two unrecognized cousins; one of them, Midwinter (Joseph Wheelock), rescues her from drowning, and the other, Armadale (Henry Lee), hires her as a governess for his children.

It had been an interesting, frequently tumultuous decade. But then, most decades are, if you know where to look.

Contemporaries had to look overseas for the bloodiest turmoil. The Franco-Prussian War had led to the downfall of Napoleon III and the siege of Paris, when French gourmets found themselves dining on odd cuts of meat from zoo animals and some Parisians were reduced to eating rats. By way of dessert the Third Republic was established to allow Frenchmen to taste again the fruits of soi-disant democracy along with their cheeses. The Ottoman Empire was also falling to pieces, unable to confront insurrections on all sides. Some of those flanks were effectively menaced by Great Britain's armed might, and it was in this period that the Union Jack was forcibly imposed on foreign nations around the globe. Queen Victoria added Empress of India to her titles, and her troops were engaged in subduing everyone from Afghans to Zulus. But the goriest war of all, between Paraguay and Bolivia, seemed too far away and prompted little concern among North Americans. In 1872 the Three Emperors' League, uniting Germany, Austria-Hungary, and Russia against France, was established and set the stage for even bloodier battles four decades hence.

Was the domestic front more peaceful? That depends on your point of view. This was the era when our Western gunslingers began to move from real-life showdowns into the pages of history and legend. In the South the count of lynchings of blacks grew shamefully. On a more official level, the American army was often deployed against American Indians, technically independent nations. Politically, bloodshed was avoided when courts and newspapers often put to rest endemic corruption, as in the Grant administration and Tweed Ring scandals. Political chicanery continued, of course, but President Rutherford B. Hayes and his teetotaling wife—the water flowed like wine at the White House—at least provided a comforting veneer of probity and quiet.

Through all this the American theatre gradually evolved. A growing population and, despite occasional setbacks, a growing national affluence saw to it that more and more theatres sprang up. And the plays they harbored also slowly changed.

This decade gave the first indisputable indication that many of the older comedies and plays, some of which had been drawing cards since virtually the earliest days of American theatre, were losing their appeal. Age alone may have worn thin their welcome. The changing ethnic makeup of audiences, especially in larger cities, may have also diminished their acceptance. At the same time, these growing, changing audiences precluded the need for a true repertory style of mounting, which sometimes had allowed fading plays to retain the stage, however fitfully.

On the other hand, changing tastes may have precipitated the decline of the excessively involved plots and reliance on pyrotechnical stage effects that still had been so popular at the opening of the decade but now were being increasingly waved away as dated. A surfeit of Boucicault-like tricks and stories had jaded audiences and critics alike. By the end of the seventies, domestic-melodrama, itself not really all that new, had nudged aside the vogue for sensation-melodrama. But the domestic-melodrama of the era, while distancing itself from older plot contrivances, had begun to delve more probingly into character. If its examination of character was still frequently cliché-ridden and shallow by later standards, it was a major move that would have lasting effect not only on dramaturgy but on acting and even on the building of theatres. Of course, cause and effect are often hard to determine, so whether the cry of Steele MacKaye and others for a more naturalistic acting style was encouraged by this trend or whether the trend was responding to these newer playing methods is open to debate. Similarly, when bold turns of story, which could be projected in the largest auditoriums, gave way to nuances of personality, which could not, smaller playhouses became desirable. This shift to smaller houses, promoted by other considerations as well, would start to gather steam at the very onset of the next era.

Much of the impetus for changing dramatic styles had come from the French, who provided some of the decade's biggest hits. French influences would continue to be felt, although French plays and ideas would rarely be the *dernier cri* that they had been in the seventies. Within a few seasons the avant-garde would be turning to a heretofore unexplored source, the Scandinavian stage, setting off possibly the most explosive debates in theatrical history. But the examples of August Strindberg and, more significantly, Henrik Ibsen, would also serve to begin the final emancipation of American playwriting.

Meanwhile, American drama was still mired in uncertainty and adolescence. Most of the more successful native plays of this period had remained claptrap vehicles, written for box-office stars who cared little about the quality of the works they appeared in, so long as they were stageworthy. The shopworn stage Yankee, so beloved since the days of *The Contrast*'s Jonathan, continued to find eagerly accepted exemplars in Josh Whitcomb and Uncle Dan'l and in similar, if non–New England, figures such as Bardwell Slote and Colonel Sellers, not to mention the older Rip. Whatever merits many critics discerned in *Davy Crockett,* the figure of Davy and not the play remained the unquestioned attraction for many playgoers. Yet *Davy Crockett,* along with a few other plays of its kind, helped open a new, major frontier and thus also contributed to the release of American playwriting from European shackles, for besides focusing on an interesting character such plays necessarily had to examine a new region and its often inherently theatrical way of life. Bucolic Yankees could do little but offer a contrast between rural solidity and citified pretensions. On the other hand, western pioneers, however intriguing in themselves, were thoroughly caught up in the hard, often dangerous life of still largely unsettled territories. Thus plays such as *Davy Crockett* opened our stages to vistas alien to Europeans, to genuinely American scenes and themes.

However, as we have noted, that opening at first was painfully narrow. Very few plays by American authors on American subjects graced first-class stages, especially in the earliest years of the seventies. The opening grew wider and more welcoming as the decade progressed, but lesser theatres in outlying neighborhoods still shamed their more elegant rivals. Yet even these theatres, at least by later standards, were derelict in promoting truly native theatre, and while tales of our Wild West were popular, other domestic concerns were studiously ignored. We have seen European plays deal with the Franco-Prussian War and other European battles, with labor strife and the determination of the middle class to have its place in the sun. How few American plays touched on similar themes.

The next ten years would bring some striking changes.

ACT TWO
1879–1892

The Passing of the Old Order

1879–1880

In 1877 the last Federal troops had been removed from the South, and carpetbaggers, deprived of their protection, scurried northward in their wake. As much as was politically possible, the Civil War had been relegated to history books. During the decade and a half since the shooting had ended, America had begun to flex its industrial muscle and had prospered accordingly. The 1880s and the very earliest years of the 1890s, then, were times of a steady if somewhat stolid consolidation. These years were certainly not uninteresting—politically, socially, or in the field of technological invention—but one would be hard put to refute a charge that they were colorless and undramatic compared to some previous or later epochs.

The same does not hold true for American theatre, for the next thirteen seasons were as exciting as they were productive. This "second act" saw the American theatre—its plays, its playhouses, its artists and entrepreneurs and audiences—begin to assume the shapes and attitudes that would characterize it throughout its years as a major source of American entertainment. Although American plays would still not dominate seasonal rosters, they became increasingly numerous and, more telling, increasingly identifiable as genuinely native efforts. No American work of this new period has retained a firm footing on our stages. Indeed, almost none is ever revived, even on collegiate stages. Yet this neglect is no real reflection on the merits of the best of them. Rather it probably stems from the sad truth that late 19th-century American drama has so far not enjoyed the unbiased reexamination we have accorded other contemporary art forms.

The season's opener was satisfyingly American. George Fawcett Rowe's **Wolfert's Roost; or, A Legend of Sleepy Hollow** (8-18-79, Wallack's) was a theatricalization of tales by America's first great storyteller, Washington Irving, and was written as a vehicle for a highly admired delineator of comic American types, John T. Raymond. Rowe's play, which borrowed some of its material from Irving works not mentioned in the title, begins with Dolph Haverstraw (Henry Lee), heir to the dilapidated Wolfert's Roost and suitor to Katrina Van Tassel (Kate Forsyth), going to sea, leaving his rival, the cocky butcher Brom Van Brunt (Frank Hardenberg), free to pursue his own courtship of Katrina. At the same time, Wolfert's "grimly ghost" rises up from a well beside the Van Tassel farmhouse and beseeches a terrified Ichabod Crane (Raymond), the local schoolmaster, to hunt for Wolfert's long-buried treasure. When Dolph is later reported lost at sea, Ichabod attempts to console Katrina and finds himself falling in love with her, but Brom, sensing another rival in the making, tells Ichabod that the region is haunted by more than Wolfert's ghost. There is, he assures the credulous Ichabod, a headless horseman who rides about at night. Sure enough, that same evening Ichabod is confronted by the apparition, which throws a very real pumpkin at him, knocking him down the well. Just then Dolph returns to claim Katrina. Ichabod emerges from the well with some of Wolfert's missing treasure in hand. And though Katrina is not to be his, he finds a sweetheart in Emma Haverstraw (Courtney Barnes).

While the headless horseman apparently was never seen by audiences, only his horse's hoofbeats and neighing being heard offstage, the meetings with Wolfert's ghost, bathed in an eerie greenish-blue light, were staged effectively. The entertainment was enhanced by George Heister's excellent settings of the Van Tassel farm and orchard, first in autumn and later in a snowy winter. Wallack's chief scene painter, Joseph Clare, designed the remaining settings, which included a view of Ichabod's school and the Dutch church at Sleepy Hollow, and an interior on the farm.

No doubt the exceptional, ongoing popularity of *Rip Van Winkle* was a consideration in prompting this dramatization. On the surface, in fact, the incidents with which Rowe was tinkering seemed even more amenable to theatrical adaptation, despite the difficulties inherent in bringing ghosts and, especially, a headless horseman and his horse on stage. But critics split sharply over the results, although a helpful majority reported favorably. A few dissenters complained about the continuing practice of using novels and short stories as a crutch, but most who were unhappy with the piece balked at the liberties Rowe had taken with plot details and characterization. On the other hand, the powerful

William Winter came down squarely in its corner, writing, "Rowe's play is pure drama, not comedy. There is no attempt in it to paint manners or to enliven artificial talk with the sheen of equivoke. Customs, indeed, are suggested—as when, in Act Third, the characters assemble in the 'living-room' of the farm-house on All-Hallow E'en. The fragrance of old-time civilization in what was still Dutch New York is made to saturate the texture of the piece. But manifestly the work was made for its own sake,—for its story, character, and vehicular utility in acting,—and not for the illumination of its epoch: and it was made well. There are a few defects in it of forced incident and untrue character. The fibre of the piece is slender, and, by reason more of the subject of the drama than the author's treatment of it, the play lacks that vitality which comes of everlasting applicability to common experience, that universality of interest which alone can give permanence to the creations of the human mind; but it is a charming play." Of course Ichabod could not dominate the story or the stage the way Rip could; nor, for all his acknowledged talents, could Raymond compare with Joseph Jefferson, generally considered the finest of all American comedians. But Raymond was no slouch, and Winter observed of his Ichabod, "He infused into it a sweet spirit, and he treated it with a delicacy of touch." The production ran until the end of September, after which Raymond took it on a cross-country tour.

Vying for attention with Raymond was one of the era's many tradition-bound debutantes. The latest was Adele Belgarde, who opened at Haverly's Lyceum Theatre. She seems to have occupied a middle ground, neither displeasing nor exciting most reviewers with her Rosalind, her Julia (*The Hunchback*), and her Parthenia (*Ingomar*).

Another debutante was less successful, although she did have the virtue of coming forth in an untried novelty. Her name was Marion Darcy, and her vehicle was **A Living Statue** (8-25-79, Park), reputedly taken from an Italian drama. Naomi Keller (Darcy) bears such a remarkable resemblance to a dead girl named Julia that Julia's pining fiancé, Count Paul (Joseph Wheelock), becomes obsessed with her. However, Naomi realizes that Julia's memory and not she herself is all that the count can think of. She falls in love with him, so sets about trying to change matters. One week and the play was gone.

Nearing his fifty-ninth birthday, Dion Boucicault was, of course, anything but a newcomer. He had been on the stage for forty years, yet of late all his experience seemed to have counted for little. The unerring theatrical instinct that had served him so well and so long apparently had deserted him, and he was left with not much more than his always inexhaustible energies. Over the summer he had signed a lease taking over Booth's theatre and planned a gala season, which was to include the debut of his son, Dion or Dot. Overflowing with optimism, he brazenly announced a $2 top for his first night. His opening attraction was his newest play, **Rescued; or, A Girl's Romance** (9-4-79, Booth's). A onetime train robber, who is now passing as a Russian count, Ruskov (George Clarke), forges a will. When the forgery is exposed, he attempts to kill off the heirs. At one point several characters were supposed to jump across a drawbridge that was swinging open, but on the first night the bridge would not swing and the characters had to walk across in obvious safety. Critics were harsh in their condemnation, assailing the play not only as "mechanical" and "lifeless" but perhaps more damningly as "old-fashioned" and "exceedingly complicated." One critic likened it to bygone Bowery melodrama. Yet Boucicault and his better-known players were well enough esteemed to give the piece a six-week run, albeit with a bit of forcing.

Another, only slightly younger veteran, E. A. Sothern, fared better by playing it safe with a repertory of established vehicles. His welcome was all the warmer because just months earlier he had been reported at death's door. During his two-month stand at the Park, beginning on September 8, he regaled audiences in *Brother Sam, The Crushed Tragedian, Our American Cousin, David Garrick, A Regular Fix,* and *Dundreary Married and Settled.* However, these were his last major New York appearances, for his recovery apparently had not been as complete as he and his followers had hoped, and he died less than two years later.

Almost lost in the attention accorded Sothern's return was the premiere of **Mitt; or, Life in California** (9-18-79, Olympic). The play's pedigree apparently was uncertain, but some critics, seeing it as the product of the unruly, unsophisticated West Coast theatre, dismissed it out of hand. To a man they ignored the accompanying curtain raiser, a comedietta called *The Young Widow,* which may or may not have been a novelty. But then the Olympic, far down on Broadway, was no longer in the front ranks of New York theatres and itself could have been advertising "last weeks." The plays survived for a fortnight.

On September 10, Daniel Bandmann began a six-week engagement at the Standard. Bandmann was a legitimate star—legitimate in both senses of the word—but also a study in contradictions. He was at once idealistic yet pedestrian, adventuresomely peripatetic (he would shortly begin a years-long world tour) yet stodgily conservative in his repertory. Except for his opening bill, *Narcisse,* which was translated from a play he had first performed in his native Germany, his schedule consisted entirely of English plays, mostly Shakespearean, which he performed with his still heavy accent. This time around that schedule included *Hamlet* and *The Merchant of Venice.*

The Criterion Comedy Company was, at least on a domestic level, as peripatetic as Bandmann. Unlike Bandmann, these strolling troupers usually performed newer, lighter plays, with only occasional forays into more serious classics. Probably very few playgoers knew or cared about its internal politics. The organization's business manager and driving force was Jacob Gosche, a man better known in musical circles; its artistic director was F. F. Mackay, who not long before had been a pillar of the Union Square's stock ensemble. But the group's financing came from a rich, young, aspiring actor, who was content to learn his trade by playing a variety of roles. He was De Wolf Hopper, and his glory days lay ahead—in musicals. However, he received no more than passing mention when the company presented New York with **Our Daughters** (9-15-79, Haverly's Lyceum), taken from Adolf L'Arronge's *Wohltätige Frauen.* Those daughters are the married Emily (Emma Fellman), the engaged Rose (Louise Sylvester), and the eligible Fanny (Helen Gardner). Their father, Jacob Van Dale (Mackay), has stood by while their permissive mother has spoiled them, but when their thoughtless behavior comes to jeopardize their happiness, he quietly but forcefully takes command and teaches them all the benefits of selflessness and consideration. The comedy was warm and homey, albeit too bland for some tastes. Mackay walked away with acting honors, moving skillfully from moments of quiet, sly humor to a touching scene in which Van Dale loses his composure and weeps on his wife's shoulder. The comedians remained in New York for three weeks before again taking to the road.

Severe as New York critics often might be on western-bred actors and plays, they could be giddily enthusiastic when a good play about western life appeared, especially one as grippingly engaging as Bartley Campbell's **My Partner** (9-16-79, Union Square). The *Herald* recorded, "Bartley Campbell has written several excellent plays—none better, however, than *My Partner.* . . . Keeping, as he does, the tide of interest always at the flood, in happily

commingling rough humor and homely pathos—the author appears to have succeeded in giving us a purely American drama, based on incidents that are possible and presented by characters not extravagant." The *Tribune* was even more laudatory about this "very strong piece," insisting, "It makes a very valuable addition to dramatic literature—and one strictly American. . . . It is a better piece of its class than has hitherto been produced in America."

The story that provoked all this excitement centered on two prospectors who have been the closest of friends for ten years, despite their markedly disparate natures. Joe Saunders (Louis Aldrich) is a gruff but warm idealist. Ned Singleton (Henry Crisp), younger and handsomer, is cynical and self-serving, though not, as developments show, totally conscienceless. Both love Mary Brandon (Maude Granger), daughter of Mathew Brandon (Harry Edwards), the financially plagued owner of the Golden Gate Hotel, which sits in the shadow of Mt. Shasta. Years earlier Brandon had won his late wife away from another suitor, the malicious Josiah Scraggs (J. W. Hague), and had horsewhipped Scraggs when he misbehaved. Now Scraggs lurks about the hotel, feigning forgiveness and repentance but plotting revenge. Joe discovers that Ned has violated Mary, and he demands his partner marry the girl, though he himself still loves her deeply. In their cabin they quarrel violently and loudly, but when Joe recognizes that Ned is genuinely conscience-stricken and will marry Mary, he prepares to go away, leaving his share of their claims and other properties to Ned and Mary. After he has departed, Scraggs comes in. Another argument ensues, and Scraggs kills Ned with Joe's knife. He runs off, first discarding his bloodstained cuff. Joe is arrested and charged with Ned's murder, in large measure on the report by Scraggs of Joe and Ned's quarrel, which Joe does not deny. Six months later Joe is placed on trial. During that time Mary has disappeared, and so has Wing Lee (Charles T. Parsloe), a Chinese employee at the hotel. They return while the jury is out, and even though everyone is sure that Joe will be convicted and hanged, Mary talks Joe into marrying her. Joe is such an honorable man that he is released on his own parole so the wedding can take place. But just as the men come to lead Joe to the gallows, Wing Lee springs a surprise. He pulls out a shirt with a missing cuff. The shirt has Scraggs's name on it and is all that is needed to finger the real murderer.

By the standards of a hundred or so years later, the play could be faulted. Some of the dialogue now sounds preposterously florid. The speech with which

Joe closes the play runs, "The night has been long and dark. But on the heights of happiness, where we are standing now, our love will illuminate our lives forever." Even stronger objections probably would be raised to Wing Lee's insistently comic portrayal and assuredly would be leveled against his chop-chop chatter on the order of "Me no likee fightee. Me no likee kickee. Kickee hurtee Chinaman samee Melican man! No difflence. No difflence." And the silence about Mary's true condition—certainly she was pregnant by Ned—might seem absurd today. Yet much of the dialogue is crisp and natural and frequently funny, intentionally funny. The depiction of Wing Lee, while admittedly drawn in the stereotypical caricature-lines of the era, is in no way malicious. Wing Lee is not only always likable, he is, after all, the deus ex machina who brings the play to its happy conclusion.

Then there are the play's patent virtues. The work is filled with all manner of memorable minor characters, such as the lovelorn spinster, Posie Pentland, and the loquacious, frustrated politician, Major Henry Clay Britt. Minor or major, all the characters are flesh-and-blood figures, with flaws beneath their kindly exteriors or, except for Scraggs, some goodness to ameliorate their weaknesses. Equally important, the story, set in a California where the first accoutrements of civilization are crowding in on older, freewheeling ways, is told with a galloping fervor and makes for rattling, thumping theatre. Allowing for period differences, it is much like the best Hollywood "oaters" that John Wayne and his ilk brought to life on the screen. Of course, some things, still standard in films and on television, would be lost in today's theatres. Those theatres rarely provide constant incidental music, so modern playgoers would not hear the "*Music, Agitato*" that accompanies Ned and Scraggs's fight or, following Joe's realization that Ned is dead, "*A pause during which there is utter silence save the plaintive music which continues for 12 bars after Joe speaks last word.*"

The original production ran just over a month and returned in the spring for a brief stay. Shortly after the play opened Campbell sold Aldrich the rights for a paltry $10 per performance, up to a total of $3000, and a little later Parsloe briefly became co-owner. The two men toured in the play steadily for four years. Following Parsloe's departure Aldrich continued to perform his role as late as 1887 and subsequently allowed others to produce the play, which remained on the boards actively until about 1907. A silent film version appeared in 1909. Although *My Partner* was not Campbell's most successful play, it has always, since its premiere, been considered his masterpiece.

The same night as *My Partner*'s opening, Augustin Daly launched his second great ensemble. In coming seasons Daniel and Charles Frohman were among the noted producers who established ensembles at playhouses they ran or owned, and some of these companies were hailed by knowing critics and theatregoers. But Daly's troupe, which would survive for two whole decades and win international renown, is generally looked back on as the last truly great stock company formed for a first-class theatre in America, an exemplar of its kind. Daly had taken over the theatre on the southwest corner of Broadway and 30th, which had been known as Wood's Museum and then as the Broadway, redecorating it lavishly and slightly decreasing its capacity. While it was larger than his first theatre, its seating capacity of about 1100 made it one of New York's smaller houses and reflected the movement toward more intimate theatres. This movement in turn reflected the growing class consciousness that had sprung up in America following the Civil War. Vaudeville and neighborhood houses had begun to open in large numbers to draw away less affluent, less demanding, and, perhaps, less faddist audiences. Increasingly throughout this period, first-class houses would lose and even discourage patronage by the raffish, unruly gallery gods who had so often enlivened and sometimes disrupted performances in not very bygone nights. More and more the best theatres would cater solely to middle-class notions of good theatre and drama.

By 1879 those notions demanded a generous sprinkling of musicals, or at least what the times perceived as musicals. So Daly's opening double bill, **Love's Young Dream** and **Newport** (9-17-79, Daly's), were in line with many of the prototypical musicals of the time, larded with uninspired songs and dances and boasting a colorful chorus. All through his career Daly retained a fascination with musicals, but he quickly came to understand that his new house and company were not ideally suited for these. It did not take him long to adjust his thinking and set his new theatre on the path to theatrical fame.

Benighted (9-22-79, Olympic) was derived from B. L. Farjeon's novel *Grif* and had first been presented under that name in western theatres, which again predisposed many New York critics against it. In this old-school melodrama, Grif (Isidore Davidson), an untutored but good-hearted man, rises above the chivings of rich hypocrites and the authorities. One week was all New York would give it. On the 29th it was replaced by a revival of *The French Spy.*

On the 30th Daly supplanted his failed opening bill with a revival of *Divorce.* The cast may not have seemed as illustrious as his first one had been, but it did include two of the four players who would serve so long as luminous mainstays of his new company: Ada Rehan in the role of Lu Ten Eyck and, in the far more subsidiary part of the Rev. Harry Duncan, John Drew. Both at the time were receiving the same pay—$35 per week.

Lester Wallack's company began its season with another new Boucicault play, **Contempt of Court** (10-4-79, Wallack's). The title promised melodrama, but the play was a farce, taken, as Boucicault confessed, from two French pieces. At the time some critics were unable to identify them, but modern audiences would have little trouble pinpointing one, Ludovic Halévy and Henri Meilhac's *Le Reveillon,* the inspiration for Strauss's *Die Fledermaus.* Parenthetically, that operetta would have its American premiere exactly two weeks later at the theatre that had long been known as the Bowery and was devoted in 1879, as the Thalia, to German language productions.

In Boucicault's version Clicquot (Harry Beckett), out on bail before serving his sentence for contempt, elects to attend a masked ball without telling his wife, Fanny (Ada Dyas). She, meanwhile, has a visit from an old friend, Lalouette (E. M. Holland), and it is he the bailiff hauls off to jail when he calls at the Clicquot home. Fanny, learning of her husband's caprice, goes off in disguise to the same ball, where Clicquot courts her, not realizing who she is.

The priggish response of all too many critics and playgoers to such carryings-on sealed the play's fate. Typical of this attitude was the review in the *Times,* whose man asserted, "If amusement which is obtained at the expense of one's sense of refinement, (provided one has such a sense, for many people undoubtedly lack it), is only worthy of censure, then 'Contempt of Court' must come in for its share— and a very large share it will be." He earned a few small credits by recognizing Boucicault's principal source, but then went on to use his knowledge solely to continue his whipping, for he immediately cited Gilbert's redaction, *On Bail,* as an exemplary instance of how this very same French offensiveness could be rendered at once funny and chaste. Wallack's kept the play on the boards for a month.

Boucicault himself returned to the footlights at Booth's on the 11th and immediately gave rise to a minor theatrical legend. For many years he had professed his desire to appear in New York in the

title role of his *Louis XI,* and of late, as mentioned, he had become eager to participate in his son's debut. Now he was to realize both ambitions simultaneously. Unfortunately, he came down with an appalling case of first-night jitters and had to be made up by one of his fellow actors. Onstage, matters went from bad to worse. The star and many of his associates had Irish brogues, which they came by naturally but had usually modified as occasion demanded. In a play set in France, these brogues came out in all their lush glory. Possibly Boucicault's nervousness made him forget himself, but John Brougham, Dominick Murray, and others took their cue from him and followed suit. The result, turning a drama into a comedy, was a debacle, although not all morning-after reviews took note of it. For example, the *Herald* ignored the accents, while the *Times* called them "a very malign influence, exciting laughter where tears should have flowed." The fiasco, coming on top of sniping notices for his two new plays and other problems, led to Boucicault's canceling his lease and having a nervous breakdown. Sadly, the play was also John Brougham's last New York appearance. He died in late spring.

Daly was having only slightly better luck in trying to find just the right policy for his new house. He had encouraged Bronson Howard to merge two Molière comedies, *L'École des femmes* and *L'École des maris.* The result was **Wives** (10-18-79, Daly's). Since both plays dealt with rearing young ladies for womanhood and wifehood, the blending was easily achieved. The girls who were foolishly reined in or foolishly kept in ignorance turn out far differently than their menfolk had hoped, but the girl raised with understanding and respect becomes an excellent wife. However, Daly's sights were still uncertain, so Howard was dismayed to learn that his comedy suddenly was sporting a chorus of twenty attractive ladies and that songs and dances had been interpolated. As presented, *Wives* had become yet another prototypical musical. With midweek matinees given over to a revival of *Fernande,* the work was played seven times a week for a month and a half, although surviving records show several of those weeks produced no profit.

How about another *Uncle Tom's Cabin?* For two weeks beginning on the 20th, playgoers still interested in sitting through the sturdy warhorse could hustle down to the fast-sinking Olympic to see a version in which the title role was played by J. B. Studley, an old Bowery favorite.

French Flats (10-21-79, Union Square) was far more up-to-date and escapist, and it got the theatre's regular company off to a surprisingly successful start. The success, in fact, was doubly surprising since the Union Square hardly was thought of as a theatre given to slambang farce, and word of mouth had bruited it about that the dress rehearsal had been disastrous. Happily, everything fell into place on opening night. A. R. Cazauran's translation of Henri Chivot's *Les Locataires de M. Blondeau* had been skillfully made, deftly obliging American tastes by removing all possible suggestiveness. Moreover, it addressed, however tangentially, a spanking new city consideration—apartment living. Apartment houses were just then beginning to replace boarding-houses and larger single homes as a way of life. But changing life-styles were not the crux of the play, eternal pretensions were. And as in many a good farce, a simple statement of truth early on would have prevented all the ensuing complications. In this case Monsieur Blondeau's determination to bury his lowly past sets off the comedy, for though Blondeau (John Parselle) is now the owner of a grand, modern apartment house, he once had earned a living as a barber and wig maker. His tenants include a stuffy lawyer, Bonay (J. H. Stoddart), a mercurial opera tenor, Signor Rifflardini (J. B. Polk), and the scampish Martin (M. V. Lingham). When Martin, who had worked with Blondeau in his wig-making days, makes the connection between his oh-so-proper landlord and his humble friend of old, the farcical domino effects begin. The helter-skelter antics found characters sequestered in closets, hiding under tables, and running madly in and out of doors, and in the biggest laugh of the evening, the usually reserved, immaculate Bonay was propelled in disarray into an astonished Rifflardini's arms. The entertainment's immediacy was underscored by the makeup several of the characters employed. Thus Polk was got up to resemble a popular opera singer. Theodore Wachtel, while Walden Ramsay, who portrayed a vacuously theorizing poet and play-wright, bore a telling resemblance to Steele Mac-Kaye. Although the Union Square's allegiance to French theatre remained obvious, its refreshing change of pace had playgoers lining up at the box office for three months.

Possessive titles continued to be insistently voguish, and a new one was added to the list with the arrival of H. J. Byron's **Our Girls** (7-5-79, Wallack's). This title clearly was meant to capitalize on Byron's earlier *Our Boys,* which had established a London long-run record. But even in London the new play had failed to find a large audience. The piece was not as farcical as *Our Boys* but was closer in style to L'Arronge's often sentimental domestic-comedy *Our Daughters,* which New Yorkers had seen a few weeks before. In Byron's story two half-sisters marry totally opposite types of men: one a nouveau-riche vulgarian, the other a poor but high-minded sculptor. Wallack's loyalists kept the play alive for four weeks in the face of respectful if cool notices.

A double bill of vanity productions, **The Picture** and **La Sociétaire** (11-10-79, Fifth Ave.), so irritated many critics that they pushed aside their inkwells to dip their pens in undiluted venom. The vanity belonged to Ion Perdicaris, a Greek-born American dilettante who was adept at publicizing his dabblings in artistic waters. He had painted a huge, allegorical canvas entitled *The Triumph of Immortality* and now attempted to bring the canvas to life onstage in the story of an artist who finds immortality by rejecting material pursuits. The *Tribune* called the hero a "small beer Raphael" and branded the play the "triumph of dullness." A short accompanying piece, which Perdicaris wrote with Townsend Percy, spoofed Sarah Bernhardt and the publicity that surrounded her. The irony of the self-publicizing Perdicaris satirizing the attention accorded to a great artist was not lost on the reviewers. Ineptly written and woodenly acted, the bill was swept away after a single week.

Nor was the playing any better in a lackluster revival of Boucicault's *The Octoroon,* which opened a brief stand at Haverly's Lyceum on the 17th. On the next night the undiscouraged Perdicaris tried to retrieve some of his tarnished reputation with **Self-Conquest** (11-18-79, Fifth Ave.), a dramatization of Wilkie Collins's *The Frozen Deep,* of which he was co-adaptor with Percy. Reviews for this tale of spiritualism and self-sacrifice were not as venomous as those handed Perdicaris a week earlier, but they were unwelcoming enough to prompt him to throw in his towel.

By contrast, Daly scored a hit and touched on the key to his future success when he introduced **An Arabian Night; or, Haroun al Raschid and His Mother-in-Law** (11-29-79, Daly's), derived from Gustav von Moser's *Haroun al Raschid*. Actually, he had touched on that key long ago when he achieved his first major success by using the German *Deborah* for his *Leah, the Forsaken.* In the ensuing years German immigration to New York had not abated, and while many Germans, still not fluent in English, patronized German-language productions downtown, others had mastered their new language well enough to enjoy outings at Broadway's best theatres. At the same time, Daly appealed to the widest possible audience by Americanizing these shows. His latest centered on Alexander Sprinkle (John Drew), a young married man and up-and-coming stockbroker given to daydreaming about Arabian Night glories. The closest he can come to realizing these dreams is at P. T. Boom's "Greatest Show on the Planet and under the Heavens," where he is instantly smitten by a bareback rider, Rosie Maybloom (Catherine Lewis), "the Wild Rose of Yucatan." His attempt to introduce her to his wife, Louise (Margaret Lanner), and his harridan mother-in-law, Mrs. Weebles (Mrs. Poole), as his long-lost niece backfires when, immediately thereafter, his real niece appears. Comic misunderstandings pile quickly on one another before Mrs. Weebles is tamed and marital bliss restored.

Because Catherine Lewis was known primarily as a musical star, some songs and dances were added, but not enough to nudge critics into considering this a musical. Most critics also passed over Ada Rehan, as the puzzled niece who is forever seeking attention and sympathy by feigning toothaches. The reviewers gave much of their heartiest praise to Drew, and in his biography of the actor Edward A. Dithmar noted that with his playing of Sprinkle "John Drew's hour of triumph had struck at last."

• • •

John Drew (1853–1927), the son of two famous performers, was born in Philadelphia and made his acting debut there at his mother's Arch Street Theatre in 1873, after first trying and rejecting a career with a department store. Daly spotted him and brought him to New York in 1875 to create the role of Bob Ruggles in *The Big Bonanza*. Drew was not a good-looking man. He had bulging, heavy-lidded eyes and a slightly bulbous nose, but he carried himself with grace, and his studied insouciance fitted him perfectly for the career of farceur that lay ahead.

• • •

An Arabian Night chalked up a two-month run, then embarked on a tour, which included a brief return to New York in March.

While critics persisted in hailing *My Partner* as Bartley Campbell's finest effort, the playgoing public was to show a marked preference for **The Galley Slave** (12-1-79, Haverly's Lyceum). True, one paper in Philadelphia, where it had been mounted the preceding September, called it "one of the best, if not the very best, of plays ever written by an American." But the paper also noted it was not without its faults, and it was these faults on which New York critics pounced. The *Herald* suggested, "It contains materials that should make any play succeed, but the author has not used all of them to the best advantage. There is too much talk that amounts to nothing, and the opportunities to explain

the misunderstandings upon which the whole plot hangs are so numerous that the audience can hardly help wondering that the dénouement escaped the second or third acts."

That plot, so wrapped in contemporary canons of behavior, described the beleaguered romance of Cicely Blaine (Maude Granger), a young American living in Europe, and Sidney Norcott (Frank Evans). The treacherous Baron Le Bois (J. J. Sullivan) tells Cicely that Norcott is unfaithful, but when Norcott later is found in Cicely's apartment he shows his mettle by claiming he is a thief, rather than compromise her position. He is sent to prison, where Cicely, followed by the baron, goes to visit him. At the prison they are confronted by a destitute girl named Francesca (Emily Rigl), who turns out to be the wife the baron had deserted. Her revelations help clear up matters, so Cicely and Norcott are free to wed. The play was indisputably an audience-pleaser. When a previous booking forced it out of the Lyceum after a month, it was moved to Niblo's and continued there until mid-February. A second company was sent out simultaneously. The play remained a favorite for a quarter of a century and was made into an early Theda Bara film.

The romance of an American girl in Europe was also the subject of A. E. Lancaster's **Estelle; or, False and True** (12-6-79, Wallack's), which was derived in part from Victor Cherbuliez's novel *Samuel Brohl and Company*. Estelle (Ada Dyas) lives in Rome and finds herself torn between the flattering attentions of Count Petrovsky (Gerald Eyre) and her affectionate memories of her American beau, Arthur Morton (Frederic Robinson). Although she recognizes that the count's love for her is genuine, she learns that he is no count at all, so when Morton sails over she is happy to accept his marriage proposal. Many critics liked the play, but, unexpectedly for what was generally considered the finest ensemble in New York, some had serious reservations about the performance. The *Times* rued, "Mr. Wallack's actors went through their parts like puppets—not like men and women; they played as though they had milk and water in their veins, not blood. The finest climaxes were toned down to drawing-room gentility, and situations requiring force and action were handled like languid effects in a Robertsonian comedy."

Tales of Irish rebellion against British rule could be expected to find support especially in those houses catering to immigrant playgoers. Taking into account the first night of Edmund Falconer's **Hearts of Steel** (12-15-79, Niblo's) and the consequent reception, the drama's three-week stand must testify

147

to such audiences' loyalty. Actors blew their lines, and scenery would not hold in place, causing untoward delays. But the crowning ignominy came at the end of the second act, in the climactic scene when Red Donohoe (James Cooke) must ride off on Crispin to alert his countrymen of their danger. Rider and horse had to jump a chasm created when the British destroyed the only bridge. Cooke was a celebrated rider, but on opening night he and Crispin came to the edge of the chasm (one paper reported it was only ten feet) and Crispin balked. Nothing Cooke or anyone could do would move the horse, so the curtain fell on gales of laughter and hooting.

Having suffered disappointments with three new plays, Wallack's reverted to an interlude of trusted revivals. John Gilbert, who had been ill, and Lester Wallack himself rejoined the ensemble, which brought out *Old Heads and Young Hearts* on the 24th and *She Stoops to Conquer* five nights later. The series continued into 1880, with *A Scrap of Paper* returning to the repertory on January 5, *London Assurance* on the 12th, and *My Awful Dad* on the 26th.

Meanwhile, the old year was ushered out just after the arrival of Bartley Campbell's third new play of the season, **Fairfax; or, Life in the Sunny South** (12-29-79, Park). Campbell had originally written the piece with the understanding that Lester Wallack would mount it, but some disagreement apparently scuttled the production. The play's first act, essentially a long prologue, takes place in a hut on the banks of the Mississippi. There the drunken James Marigold (Louis F. Barrett) attempts to take money that Dr. Guy Gaylord (Frederic Robinson) has given Mrs. Marigold (Agnes Booth) to buy medicine for her dying baby. When his wife refuses to hand over the bill, Marigold pulls a gun. A struggle follows, the gun goes off, and Marigold dies. Webster Winne (W. J. Ferguson), a tramp, witnesses the shooting. The rest of the play unfolds on the Florida plantation of Edwin Fairfax (J. E. Whiting), a widower who has hired a woman he knows only as Gladys Deane to take care of his younger daughter. Of course, Gladys is Mrs. Marigold. In the few months she has been there, she and Fairfax have fallen in love. The sudden arrival of Gaylord, an old friend of Fairfax, threatens the romance, for at first the doctor believes that Gladys might still be married, and even after he has learned her whole sad story he demands she tell it to his old pal. She refuses, but the appearance of the tramp, intent on blackmailing her by claiming she killed her husband, brings

matters to a head. When the tramp recants, affairs are concluded happily.

The *Dramatic Mirror* reported, "*Fairfax* is in many respects the best piece of work Mr. Campbell has thus far offered us. In it he has departed from the methods employed in his other most successful dramas . . . and has produced a piece which possesses the intrinsic merits of brilliancy, strong dramatic interest and broad bold reaches of thought and poetic imagination." Unfortunately for Campbell, the *Dramatic Mirror*'s was a minority report. To most contemporaries what strength the evening offered was imparted by Agnes Booth's warm, luminous performance. Read a hundred or so years later, the drama seems more convincing and therefore more touching than *The Galley Slave,* perhaps because the latter's European setting gives it a faintly Ruritanian odor that makes it seem distant and musty. Of course, Campbell's turns of plot pull out many of the melodramatic stops so common at the time, and most modern audiences would not find "poetic imagination" in Mrs. Marigold's musing about her dead child, "Ah, the little graves, the little graves that hold the jewels of so many desolate homes. They need no monuments for the names of their hushed inhabitants have been written by the fingers of love upon our hearts." *Fairfax* ran a little over a month and almost never was revived.

The few playgoers who saw **Our Candidate** (1-19-80, Standard) during its fortnight's stand may have been reminded of another play, if they had been among the few to see *Our Aldermen* during its equally short stay two seasons back. Both plays attempted to take a tongue-in-cheek look at the dark side of local politics, although the newer play tacked on a more optimistic ending. A scheming political boss, Col. Jim Dexter (I. N. Drew), enlists the seemingly gullible and pliant Josephus Grimwig (Harry G. Richmond) to run as a candidate for office. After Grimwig wins, Dexter discovers his man is not such a fool as he looks. The *Sun* called the whole affair absurd, noting derisively that a Chinese character called Shang Hi talked and danced like a black.

American dramaturgy received another small boost with the presentation of Edgar Fawcett's **The False Friend** (1-21-80, Union Square). Still in his early thirties, Fawcett already had made a name for himself as a poet and novelist. His first play to reach Broadway was testimony to the breadth of his talent. Lucien Gleyre (Charles Thorne, Jr.), hearing news from Australia of the death of his friend, Cuthbert Fielding, decides to take his place and thus enjoy all the comforts of an aristocratic life. Since both men have long been out of England and since acquaintances often have remarked on their startling resemblance, Lucien is sure he can pull off the imposture. He quickly convinces Cuthbert's sister, Edith (Sara Jewett), of his legitimacy. Only Cuthbert's shrewd old aunt, Lady Ogden (Mrs. E. J. Phillips), is not taken in. She determines to unmask him, but her exertions lead to a fatal stroke, and even her dying warning appears unheeded. Then the real Cuthbert (Harry Courtaine) turns up, very much alive. Lucien convinces everyone that Cuthbert is a fraud and has him imprisoned. However, the dead aunt's warnings and the real Cuthbert's pleadings have given Edith cause to question her acceptance of Lucien. Suspecting correctly that Lucien has fallen in love with her, she is able to cajole him into confessing.

Critics bandied about any number of possible sources for Fawcett's basic story, including the recent *Estelle* and its own inspiration, *Samuel Brohl and Company, The New Magdalen,* and, most of all, the recent Tichborne affair. However, the consensus was that Fawcett had handled his material artfully—constructing his scenes soundly, drawing truly three-dimensional characters, and giving them pungent dialogue. Not many critics knew that Cazauran quietly had helped Fawcett "patch" the play.

What bothered some reviewers, and apparently some playgoers, was a problem that shed light on strict 19th-century morality. They found themselves liking and rooting for Lucien. Fawcett had refused to make him an out-and-out villain, imbuing him with a compelling charm. Thorne accentuated this appeal with his ingratiating portrayal. Here, then, was an instance of genuinely modern characterization for which 1880 audiences were not totally prepared. Nevertheless, the play was a success, compiling a profitable two-month run.

W. S. Gilbert's **The Wedding March** (1-31-80, Park), his anglicization of Marc-Michel and Eugène Labiche's *Un Chapeau de paille d'Italie,* was presented in conjunction with a revival of his *Sweethearts.* The story detailed the mishaps that pursue a bridegroom after his pony eats the straw hat of a girl who had been flirting with a secret lover and the groom attempts to replace the hat. Gilbert himself, here for the world premiere of *The Pirates of Penzance,* staged the production. Neither good reviews nor Gilbert's fame could whet interest, but then neither could a novel convenience designed to facilitate ticket buying. The Park became the first Broadway theatre to install a telephone in its box office. Of course, just four years after its introduction, few New Yorkers owned a phone.

On the same night, Frank Mayo opened an eleven-week engagement at the Olympic, commencing his stand with his biggest money-maker, *Davy Crockett.* His other revivals would be *The Streets of New York, Man and Wife, The Ticket-of-Leave Man, The Robbers, Ingomar,* and, for those who might have forgotten that Mayo early on had been considered a promising Shakespearean, *Richard III.* Laura Don was his leading lady. Late in his engagement he essayed a new play, **Cadet la Perle; or, The Beggars of Pontarme** (3-29-80, Olympic), in which he played Count Henri d'Arcourt, who has loved a lowborn German girl, Hilda (Don), ever since she saved his life when he was wounded in battle. But after he is led to believe that Hilda has died, he turns to a life of dissipation. Hilda's reappearance brings him back to his senses. Mayo's last curtain also marked the final curtain for the Olympic, where Laura Keene had shone so brightly, where Joseph Jefferson and E. A. Sothern had risen to fame in her mounting of *Our American Cousin,* and where G. L. Fox had cavorted for so long in *Humpty Dumpty.* The theatre was demolished a few weeks later. It was too far downtown to cope with the city's seemingly inexorable move northward.

Wreckers down on Broadway between Bleecker and West Houston streets and a phone jangling away in a box office at Broadway and 22nd were only two signs of the era's swift progress. A more important indication of change, certainly a far more historical one, occurred on February 4 when Steele MacKaye's new Madison Square Theatre opened its doors for the first time. This was not the new Madison Square Theatre that had opened at precisely the same location the preceding April. In the late 20th century Broadway's aging, decaying playhouses are refurbished all too infrequently and often look it. Not so a century before. Then the better, more successful theatres, such as Wallack's or Daly's, were repainted or totally redecorated and even reseated every third or fourth year. They were almost always refreshingly inviting. When MacKaye had opened his theatre in the unseasonably hot spring of 1879, he had been deluged with complaints about poor ventilation. While mulling over ways to rectify the problem, he apparently also toyed with solutions to other widespread complaints of the time, such as achingly long waits during scene changes. His answer to the first problem was hundreds of huge tubes that shot hot or cold air as needed into the auditorium from the basement. When necessary, vents drew the unwanted heat of the gaslights to exhausts. To facilitate quick changes of settings, he devised a double stage, one on top of the other, so that a stage with a fully placed set could be lowered or raised rapidly. Both these technological innovations, however primitive, essentially addressed the matter of audience comfort. His more fundamental improvement, the house's virtually unprecedented intimacy, remained unaltered.

And this intimacy played a large part in the astonishing success of his first offering, his own play **Hazel Kirke** (2-4-80, Madison Square). MacKaye had hoped to open it, along with the theatre, in the fall, when the play was known as *An Iron Will.* But the building's renovations being incomplete, he took the drama on the road for an extended tour. Early on in the play, Pittacus Green (Thomas Whiffen), a minor comic character who has just misquoted some lines from *Othello,* uses this misquotation to summarize the events that have led up to the drama: "A certain rich Squire saves a certain poor father from ruin, and spends a little fortune in having the daughter taught to become his wife—that is the taking of the purse. . . . Before the wedding's had, and the purse is paid for, a good-for-nothing young fellow tumbles into a ditch, is fished out by the father, nursed by the daughter, and that is the stealing of the heart." The rich squire is Aaron Rodney (Dominick Murray), who years before had lent a hot-tempered miller, Dunstan Kirke (C. W. Couldock), the money to save his mill from bankruptcy. In return Rodney asked that when Kirke's daughter, Hazel (Effie Ellsler), comes of age he be allowed to marry her.

During the interim, Rodney offers to pay for the girl's education. But just before Hazel does come of age, Kirke rescues a handsome young hunter from drowning in a stream and sets his daughter to overseeing the man's recovery. The Kirkes know the man as Arthur Carrington (Eben Plympton), but they eventually learn he is actually Lord Travers. Rodney realizes that Hazel has fallen in love with Carrington. He also accepts that at fifty he is too old for Hazel, while Carrington is just the right age. He is generous enough to relinquish all claims on the girl, but Dunstan will not allow it. When Hazel admits to wanting to marry Carrington, he casts her out of his house and life: "Begone! Thou misbegotten bairn. I cast thee out adrift, adrift forever from thy feyther's love, and may my eyes no more behold thee." A year later Hazel's belief that she is happily married is shattered by the appearance of Carrington's mother, Lady Travers (Mrs. Cecil Rush), who informs her that since they were wed in a Scottish ceremony on English soil the wedding is illegal. Thinking herself deceived, Hazel runs away. On a snowy night some time later, Hazel returns wearily to her father's home. Rodney is

there, willing to receive and marry her, but Dunstan, who has become blind, remains adamant. He will not have his daughter in his house ever again. In despair Hazel rushes out and attempts to drown herself. Seemingly too late, Dunstan appreciates how foolishly obstinate he has been: "Oh, God! this is thy punishment! I was blind when I drove her out—and, now, when I could save her—I cannot see—I cannot see—I cannot see!" She is rescued in the nick of time by Carrington, who has come seeking her.

Quite possibly MacKaye had originally opened his theatre with a revival in order to ensure the new playhouse the lion's share of attention. But this time he clearly expected his new drama to command the spotlight. He was in for a disappointment—at least in the short run. Descriptions and comments on his technological experiments predominated in most reviews. To some extent MacKaye himself unwittingly was to blame. His play provided for only one setting in each act, so it offered no chance to demonstrate the remarkable double stage. To compensate, he kept his audience after school: when the final curtain calls had been taken he did not lower the curtain but instead, in full view of everyone, replaced the last act's setting of the mill's kitchen with the first-act setting of the exterior of the mill.

Of the play itself, the *Times* spoke for all too many other newspapers when it observed, "Its merits are not so great either in quantity or quality as to demand long discussion." But the paper did touch gingerly on one salient failing of the work, namely that Hazel may be the least interesting figure in the play. The menfolk steal the show. By contrast, theatrical historian Arthur Hobson Quinn has singled out the virtues for which the piece came to be admired: "the quiet natural dialogue, and the absence of the usual stage villain." Neither was totally novel, but *Hazel Kirke*'s subsequent success gave the play a special niche in the rise of naturalistic American drama.

MacKaye had three potential villains in the play—Dunstan, Rodney, and Lady Travers. Although Rodney earlier had tied his financial help to the right to marry Hazel, he is the first to comprehend her sentiments and to compassionately offer to withdraw. Lady Travers might have been depicted as a callous snob, but instead MacKaye shows her sympathizing with Hazel from the start, although concerned about her son's apparently illegal marriage and her own earlier promise of him to someone else. Dunstan is the most vividly drawn figure in the play. He is intemperate, obdurate, and fatuously unyielding in his sense of obligation. Yet his good deeds are catalogued early in the play, and at heart he is clearly loving.

It is harder now to perceive how "quiet" and "natural" much of the dialogue must have sounded to contemporary ears, for naturalism has evolved radically since 1880. Moreover, the dialogue is framed in a chain of obsolescent melodramatic clichés—the dramatic resues, the imposing promises, the expulsion from home, even the tricky Scottish marriage laws that more than one fine dramatist of the time conveniently fell back on. Despite his noisy proclamations of modernity, MacKaye remained the most tradition-bound of the newer major playwrights. Yet *Hazel Kirke* spoke tellingly to 1880 audiences. After a slow start—so slow, in fact, that another play was put into rehearsals—the work caught on. Helped no doubt by the intimacy of the theatre, it became the first nonmusical play in American history to run over a year, playing for 486 performances. Writing in 1917, Quinn noted, "It has continued on the stage for thirty years and in America has been acted at the same time by ten companies."

On the same night as *Hazel Kirke*'s premiere, Boucicault, recovered from his breakdown, began an engagement with Wallack's ensemble, appearing in *The Shaughraun, The Colleen Bawn,* and *Kerry.* Following a week's respite in which Lester Wallack appeared, on March 8, in a double bill of *The Liar* and Thomas Egerton Wilkes's *My Wife's Dentist,* Boucicault and Wallack co-starred in another revival of a Boucicault play. Its last performance almost did not come off, for as he sat down to dinner Boucicault was arrested at the behest of his neglected wife, Agnes Robertson. Wallack put up bail, and the men were able to end their run in the play with the suddenly ironic title of *How She Loves Him.*

John A. Stevens's **The Unknown** (2-9-80, Haverly's Lyceum) typified the sort of old-fashioned melodrama that continued to delight backwater audiences but only rarely played a better New York house, and then at its own peril as well as its heroine's. In this case the imperiled heroine is Bessie Merribright (Lottie Church), who is loved by the upright Albert Storming (A. H. Stuart) but whose future is endangered by the nefarious plans of her guardian, Dr. Richard Brinckton(Ralph Delmore)—he of the "triple-ply scowl"—and his unscrupulous lawyer, Arnold Tyson (George Sprague). Brinckton hopes to marry Bessie for her money, and when it appears he cannot, he attempts to poison her. Tyson substitutes a narcotic so that everyone will think Bessie dead, then kidnaps her, hoping to marry her himself. When his plans also go awry, he tries to stab her. He is thwarted by the appearance of the Unknown (Stevens), a seeming madman whom Bessie had befriended. The Unknown kills Tyson, then reveals he is Bessie's longlost brother, Harold.

If critics were only infrequently graphic in describing productions and performances they admired, they often coupled their sneering with enlightening detail. Thus one paper described the end of the first act, when the villains join forces to keep Harold from meeting his sister: "The East River—The bridge is ably represented by two black posts holding several dozen gray fiddle-strings. A dozen small boys in a free fight under a green speckled cloth enact the wild and heaving waves. The scene-shifter yanks a visible rope and pulls a pasteboard ferryboat across, amid great enthusiasm. Enter a strip of green canvas 7 feet long, supposed to be a boat. Behind it are Tyson, Villain, Harold, and Desperate Character. Strip of canvas stops. Harold wants it to go on. Tyson asks him for papers. Harold says he hasn't got any. Villian fires a pistol in air, and Harold, with three grunts, a yell, and a handspring, falls overboard, the fiddles scrape themselves into hysterics, and the curtain comes down on a tremendous scuffle among the riotous boys who play waves. Then there is an encore, of course, and when the curtain rises the villains have fled, and the Old Sailor is seen lifting Harold over another strip of blue canvas, also supposed to be a boat." After a fortnight the Unknown stalked back into the hinterlands, where he survived into the 1890s.

On February 16, Gilbert's double bill at the Park gave way to a revival of his *Engaged,* with its original New York cast largely intact. It stayed only a week, giving way in turn to H. J. Byron's **Chawles; or, A Fool and His Money** (2-24-80, Park). Critics took the occasion to compare Byron and Gilbert, and Bryon came out the loser, seen as lacking Gilbert's biting wit and keen sense of theatre. Byron's story recounted the comic misadventures of "Chawles" Liquorpound (James Lewis), a footman who inherits his employer's vast riches and begins to put on airs. Even the growing popularity of Lewis could not keep the play profitable for a full month.

But another rising comedian had better luck. Neil Burgess had been making his mark in variety as a female impersonator. Unlike most female impersonators, then and since, he refused to traffic in grotesque exaggeration. His ladies—always older and always ladies—were homey, affectionate characterizations that may have gently touched on caricature, but no more. For his first starring vehicle he appeared in the title role of **Widow Bedott** (3-15-80,

Haverly's Lyceum), a theatricalization of Frances Miriam Whitcher's *Widow Bedott Papers* by David Ross Locke, alias Petroleum Vesuvius Nasby. Nasby was said to have been Lincoln's favorite humorist. His story was simple. Widow Bedott is a small-town busybody who can chat and meddle all the while she is occupied baking her pies. Resolved to remarry, she sets her sights on the unsuspecting Elder Shadrack Sniffles (George Stoddart) and steals him away from a would-be rival, Widow Jenkins (Nellie Peck). The production was something of a family affair, since Stoddart was Burgess's father-in-law. But there was no question that without Burgess the play would not have been worth the trouble of mounting.

. . .

Neil Burgess (1846–1910) A native of Boston, he was nineteen when he made his variety debut with Spalding's Bell Ringers. His first New York appearance came as a blackface comedian at Tony Pastor's in 1872. New Yorkers initially saw his female inpersonations when he played on Harrigan and Hart's olio bill as "the Coming Woman" in 1877.

. . .

Widow Bedott delighted patrons until the beginning of May and remained in Burgess's repertory for a decade.

Revivals of two other plays on their way to proving their durability were the only lures for first-nighters on the 22nd. The Union Square brought out *The Two Orphans*, and while Charles Thorne, Jr., Marie Wilkins, and a few other members of the original cast were back, the replacements for many of the others left critics shaking their heads dejectedly. Nevertheless the play's popularity kept it going for three weeks. By contrast, there were huzzas that New Yorkers at last could see Annie Pixley in *M'liss*. She opened her five-week engagement at the Standard to a packed house that included a number of happy critics who would report admiringly on her "rollicking boisterousness" and "affecting pathos." California-trained artists were not often made welcome in New York, but Miss Pixley demonstrated just the right flair in just the right role to become a joyous exception.

The next Monday night saw another California product receive a more typical eastern cold shoulder, although time would show the opening was yet one more of the season's important landmarks. The play was **Hearts of Oak** (3-29-80, Fifth Ave.), by James A. Herne and David Belasco. The young authors, who had first presented their work on the West Coast as *Chums*, admitted to pirating the plot from Henry J. Leslie's *The Mariner's Compass*.

Although they adhered to Leslie's fundamental story, they emended the play significantly, all in the name of "modernization," deleting a comic subplot, cutting out such melodramatic excesses as the heroine's attempted suicide and her rescue from the millwheel, and tempering the florid dialogue. In their version Terry Dennison (Herne), an old sailor, has raised two orphans, Chrystal (Katharine Corcoran) and Ruby Darrel (H. Mainhall). Ruby follows in his adopted father's footsteps and goes off to sea. Terry, despite the differences in their ages, has come to love Chrystal, so he proposes marriage. Chrystal loves Ruby but, feeling a deep obligation to Terry, consents. Shortly before Ruby returns, the couple have a baby daughter. When Ruby reappears he is shocked and furious and confronts Chrystal with what he considers her infidelity. Chrystal confesses to still loving Ruby. Terry overhears all this, so goes off to sea again in despair. Years pass. Word has come that Terry had died, allowing Chrystal and Ruby to wed. They set up a small stone in Terry's memory. A blind, white-haired old man arrives at the house. By the tombstone that Chrystal and Ruby have erected, he encounters a little girl of about six or seven.

Little Chrystal: (A pitying look crossing her face.) Oh! I know, you're an orphan, ain't you?
Terry: (Holding out his hand.) Come here—little one—take my hand—(*She draws a little away.*) Don't be frightened. I won't harm you, my child. (*She gains courage and slowly crosses to him.*) I'm very fond of little children—come—take my hand, won't you? (*She draws closer and closer and finally takes his hand.*)

Terry dies contentedly after he hears Little Chrystal call him father. Only when he is dead does Chrystal appear to recognize him.

The play had met with poor receptions in San Francisco and on a subsequent western tour. Not until it reached Chicago, where it was given its final title, did it succeed, and there its success was so pronounced that others quickly pirated Belasco and Herne's piracy. In court the men learned they had no exclusive right to the story, only to their title. New York failed to share Chicago's enthusiasm, echoing instead the earlier displeasure. The *Times* condemned it as "a dull, long-winded, ultra-sentimental drama." Nor was the acting admired. William Winter in his *Tribune* notice dismissed Herne as a "phlegmatic and monotonous actor, neither brilliant in quality nor fine in touch." Only William T. Voegtlin's scenery impressed him favorably. He granted, "The flying-scud, in the first act, is exceedingly well managed, and the subsequent view of the quiet seaside is dreamy, poetical, and uncommonly strong." The play ran less than a month but eventually caught the public's fancy and was revived several times in ensuing seasons.

One reason for its eventual success was that it clearly represented the wave of future drama. Herne has been called Ibsen's first American disciple, although, of course, in 1880 Ibsen was still unknown here. But naturalistic drama was in the air. Like *Hazel Kirke, Hearts of Oak* had no old-fashioned villain, in fact no real villain at all. And its dialogue, especially by later standards, seems even more lifelike. In a way, it moved further still—toward the sort of theatrical realism that Belasco would soon master. In one scene a real dinner of freshly steamed potatoes, baked beans, buckwheat cakes, and meat pie was served onstage. The audience could sometimes see the steam rising from the hot food, and some may have even smelled aromas wafted across the footlights. And like Kate Claxton before them, the authors used a real baby in one scene, although this time the Gerry Society seems not to have noticed. (A wag would later write, "No Herne play is complete without a baby and a good dinner.")

If the new play marked a tentative lurch into the future, two other openings in the same week offered more certain entertainment, and they contrasted the ridiculous and the sublime. The ridiculous came first, on the 29th, in the tiny person of Lotta, who arrived at the Park with a pair of her most beloved vehicles, *The Little Detective* and *Zip*. The next night Booth played again at what had once been his own theatre. As usual, he offered no novelties as he hawked such standards as *Macbeth, Richelieu, Much Ado About Nothing, Richard III, Othello, Hamlet, The Merchant of Venice, The Taming of the Shrew (Katherine and Petruchio), The Fool's Revenge,* and *Ruy Blas*.

Lester Wallack, ignoring the occasional lack of profitability, was as fiercely proud of his loyalty to what were called "old comedies" as Booth was to his largely Elizabethan repertory. On April 5, he reached way back to revive Mrs. Inchbald's *To Marry or Not to Marry,* a curious choice. The play had never been particularly popular in either England or America. It was perceived as a not completely satisfactory attempt to write 18th-century comedy in the early 19th century. Perhaps wisely in this instance, Wallack's loyalty was not matched by his fidelity. He drastically rewrote the play, cutting out its subplot and more serious and sentimental moments. Of course, such pruning served to highlight his own leading role, that of Sir

Oswin Mortland, an avowed woman-hater who is eventually led to the altar. His daring was rewarded with a modestly remunerative run of two weeks, during which the play was coupled with *To Oblige Benson*.

If Booth and Wallack preferred to go back in time for their plays, Daly was increasingly happy to bring out contemporary works. More and more these would be German comedies, which he and his brother would then Americanize. Their latest offering was **The Way We Live** (4-10-80, Daly's), announced as being an adaptation of L'Arronge's *Wohltätige Frauen*. Since that same play had been announced as the source of *Our Daughters* earlier in the season, critics might have been eager to draw comparisons. Instead they simply panned the new production. Daly's redaction seems to have concentrated more on the farcical than on the sentimental aspects that the earlier offering had emphasized. His had fun with women so preoccupied with charitable concerns they have no time to look after their family life properly. One of the couples who find their marriage in difficulty are Clyde and Cherry Monograme (John Drew and Ada Rehan). When Cherry goes out of an evening to raise funds for the conversion of savages, the servants also decide to take the night off, leaving Clyde to lull their little boy to sleep by playing a music box for him. In his biography of the producer, Judge Daly wrote of the production, "In it Mr. Drew and Miss Rehan were cast for the first time in comedy parts of the kind they afterwards made famous."

• • •

Ada Rehan (1860–1916) Born in Limerick, Ireland, she was brought to America while still a child. Her family settled in Brooklyn. She made her stage debut in 1873 in *Across the Continent,* the starring vehicle for Oliver Doud Byron, her brother-in-law. She later moved on to Mrs. John Drew's Arch Street Theatre in Philadelphia. There a printer's error misspelled her real name, Crehan, inadvertently giving her the stage name she was to adopt. Following stints in Albany and Louisville she returned to New York, where she appeared in a revival of Daly's *Pique* and then in his mounting of *L'Assommoir*. She was one of the earliest recruits for his second company. With gray-blue eyes and brown hair, she had a regal beauty that reminded many of Romney and Gainsborough portraits.

• • •

Negative reviews spoke more loudly than superior acting and sumptuous staging, so the play ran for only two and a half weeks.

Lester Wallack also turned to a novelty for his

final new offering of the season. **A Child of the State** (4-21-80, Wallack's) was George Hoey's adaptation of d'Ennery's *Les Orphelines de la Charité*. In it, a man seduces an orphan, then learns to his distress that orphans are special wards of the state and that he is liable to forceful prosecution. The play received respectful though hardly jubilant notices, but Wallack managed to keep it alive for a month.

While still young and ravishingly beautiful, Adelaide Neilson was not in the best of health, but she had decided on a farewell American tour before retiring. On April 26, she began a month-long stand at Booth's, offering *Cymbeline, Twelfth Night, Romeo and Juliet, The Hunchback, As You Like It,* and *The Lady of Lyons*. Whatever her ailments, critics saw no dimunution in her captivating artistry, and her fans no doubt hoped that once her health improved she would reconsider her decision to retire. Sadly, her health worsened, and she died during the summer. She was only thirty-four. Legend has a way of romanticizing beauty and artistry that die early on, but contemporary reviews suggest that Miss Neilson was every bit as magnificent as her posthumous fame has claimed. However, her staunch devotion to a very limited repertory, much of which was going slowly out of style, leaves unanswered a question about what her future might have been like. Within two decades even so devoted a Shakespearean as Julia Marlowe would have to resort to sometimes shoddy modern vehicles to earn enough to allow her to perform her Shakespearean roles.

After Lotta scampered away, Denman Thompson sauntered into the Park on the 26th, once again in *Joshua Whitcomb*. His popular Yankee settled in for a run that lasted until mid-June.

As the nation expanded geographically and industrially, the rustic stage Yankee, such as Thompson's Josh, inevitably gave way to other recognizable regional types. J. B. Polk had won laughs and applause in *The Banker's Daughter* in the minor role of George Washington Phipps, a bustling traveling salesman for a stationery firm. His success was sufficient to prompt George H. Jessop to write a starring vehicle for him, featuring a similar character. In **A Gentleman from Nevada** (4-27-80, Fifth Ave.) Polk portrayed Christopher Columbus Gall, a miner who has struck it rich but whose wealth has never goaded him to put on airs or erase the crudities of his former life. He is plunked down into a lordly English estate, where his candor and bluntness prove as irritating as they are helpful. The play had scored a major success at the Boston Museum, but something hand-me-down in both

Jessop's writing and Polk's acting displeased New York critics, so play and star moved on after three weeks.

Plays about Irishmen and Irish life continued to be popular, too—if they were well written and well played. *The Kerry Gow,* which toured season after season with Joseph Murphy as the shrewd blacksmith, was welcomed on its return to Niblo's on May 10, while a new work, **The Croothawn** (5-25-80, Booth's), was slapped with some of the season's most damning notices and closed ignominiously after three nights. All one critic could say in its favor was that it eschewed some stock figures on many Irish or Irish-American plays, such as the kindly but bibulous priest and the evil Englishman.

If Murphy, like most actors of his ilk, played out virtually all of his career in second-rank theatres, Chanfrau frequently had been accorded the most fashionable stages. Of late, however, he had been relegated to lesser houses. His return to Wallack's on June 5 confirmed that he still could compete with the best. Even the *Times,* noting all this, recorded that prime theatres on the road usually remained available to him. His play was his ever dependable *Kit, the Arkansas Traveller,* and he apparently was awarded good business until the house closed for the summer at the end of June.

A revival of *The Child Stealer* began a two-week stand at Niblo's on the 7th.

Denizens of *Our Boarding House* took up lodgings at Niblo's on the 21st to write *finis* to the season.

1880–1881

Stars illuminated Broadway's nights all during the season. One blazing-red ball of fire held theatrical stargazers in particular thrall, kindling an excitement rare in American stage annals. She was, of course, Sarah Bernhardt. But she was not alone, even if for a time she threatened to dim all other stars' glow. As a result, dramaturgy took a back seat to histrionics for much of the season. But then contemporary playwrights were of little help; so many of their plays that did succeed were written expressly as vehicles for leading actors and actresses. A performer's theatre held sway on Broadway.

The season began quietly enough with **Our Gentlemen Friends** (8-14-80, Standard), a comedy that its star, George Holland, had helped adapt from a German work by Julius Rosen. Holland cast himself as Joseph Moorhouse, who has been henpecked so long and so completely that it takes his friends (Mrs. J. J. Prior) to allow him to smoke his pipe in his own home. That small taste of freedom proves provocative, and before long he is lording it over his household. Now it becomes Mrs. Moorhouse's turn to rebel, until an amicable truce is reached. This innocuous pleasantry lasted two weeks, then moved on to tour.

A more substantial work followed. Archibald Clavering Gunter's **Two Nights in Rome** (8-16-80, Union Square) served as a vehicle for Maude Granger, newly raised to stardom. In it she played the cold-blooded adventuress Antonia, who makes no bones about having married Gerald Massey (Joseph Wheelock) for his money. What she has not told Gerald is that she has fled from a Corsican husband, Louis Benedetti (J. B. Studley), who has sworn to find her and kill her. Learning that Benedetti has discovered her whereabouts, she runs away. When her hat and shawl are fished out of the Tiber, she is presumed to have drowned. This news allows Gerald to marry again, but Antonia soon reappears, hoping to blackmail Gerald by charging him with bigamy. Fortunately, Gerald now knows of her prior marriage and counters by threatening to inform Benedetti. Antonia walks away to face an uncertain, frightening future.

Despite generally favorable notices, the beautiful star found the role uncongenial and soon relinquished it to Laura Don. Thereafter her hold on stardom proved precarious, though she was regularly billed above the title when she toured. In her later years she became a respected character actress. The play itself, produced by the author "at his own risk and expenses," remained at the Union Square for a month. Before the season had run its course New Yorkers would see two versions of a London hit that utilized many of the same crucial motifs. Had Gunter read *Forget-Me-Not* (or at least a synopsis of it) and, in an era of loose copyright laws, felt no qualms about filching much of it? Or was the similarity merely a remarkable coincidence?

Daly relit his theatre with **Tiote** (8-18-80, Daly's), derived from Maurice Drach's *La P'tiote*. Although the producer, as was his custom, took credit for the adaptation, it was actually yet another work of his brother Joseph, who in turn employed a third man's translation. The story combined elegant high life with the colorful (at least onstage) world of roving gypsies. When Gwendolyn (Emily Rigl) mistakenly comes to believe that her father was murdered by her mother, Lady Normant (Fanny Morant), she attempts suicide but is rescued and adopted by some passing gypsies. Finally convinced of her mother's innocence, she returns home.

Although the story was slight, Daly filled the entertainment with superb settings—a richly decorated bedroom, a gypsy encampment, an artist's studio—and with an interesting assortment of subsidiary characters, all excellently cast. Tiny, winsome Miss Rigl, her speech still noticeably accented, gave an impassioned performance that contrasted powerfully with Miss Morant's dignified but distant mother. Ada Rehan was a gypsy queen; John Drew, a mysterious gentleman who has cast his lot with the wanderers. Many critics singled out Charles Leclercq's Daddy Cadvan, a slightly deranged sexton and gravedigger, as the hit of the evening, especially for his melodramatic recounting of an old murder. Possibly deterred by a blistering heat wave, playgoers came in discouraging numbers. Daly forced a run of one month.

The next entry also chalked up a month's run, but J. E. Brown's **Edgewood Folks** (8-23-90, Park) went on to enjoy a long afterlife, particularly on the road. First-nighters at the refurbished theatre may have been attracted by the reputation lanky, bright-eyed Sol Smith Russell had won on lecture circuits as a comic monologist. Now he was starred as a village ne'er-do-well, Tom Dilloway, an overgrown boy who spends his time beguiling children with his singing and clowning. The appearance in Edgewood of shady Mr. Ferguson (J. W. Lanergan), who would overthrow a will benefiting sweet Faith Hardewick (Carrie McHenry), brings out Tom's latent strength. He thwarts the schemer by a series of disguises, masquerading as a boozy German, a tramp, a possible confederate of Ferguson, and the deacon's spinster sister. When Ferguson is bested, Tom's neighbors look on the young man with a new respect. Whatever New Yorkers thought, this "pastoral-comedy-drama" was one small-town audiences could identify with and delight in.

J. W. Shannon's **The Golden Game; or, Spider and Fly** (8-30-80), Standard) marked an attempt by the author to provide himself with a starring vehicle. Two lecherous aristocrats enlist Max Strauss (Shannon) in their plot to seduce a young lady named Clara (Cora Tanner), unaware that Max is Clara's father. Again some good notices could not prevail over the uncomfortable heat, so the play was withdrawn after a fortnight.

Actresses commanded the spotlight in three plays opening on the same Monday night. Fanny Davenport and her wardrobe, reputedly by Worth, were the attraction in Anna Dickinson's **An American Girl** (9-20-80, Fifth Ave.). Miss Davenport portrayed Kate Vivian, daughter of a prosperous merchant. Kate falls in love with Allyn Cromarty (Henry Lee) but, believing him poor, hesitates to marry him. With time she determines to sacrifice her high life. Audiences could quickly guess the ending. The obviousness of the plot was coupled with a paleness in character delineation. Nor was the supporting cast particularly strong. At least one of the aisle-sitters also bridled at the star's fashion show, dismissing diamonds and satins in a Long Branch garden walk or a Hudson River cottage as "hardly being appropriate." Wives who cajoled their husbands into buying tickets clearly held no such reservations. Thanks to its glamorous star's appeal, the play ran six weeks.

A. C. Gunter's second play of the still young season was **The Soul of an Actress** (9-20-80, Grand Opera). Originally written as a vehicle for Clara Morris, it was offered to Broadway with Ada Cavendish in the lead. She played Josephine Clairon, an actress who loves the Chevalier de Crevecoeur (G. C. Boniface) but insists he marry another girl whom he had promised to wed. After a single week, she took the play on tour.

A dramatization of Charles Reade's **Christie Johnstone** (9-20-80, Windsor) was the offering at a house given over mainly to Buffalo Bill, Oliver Doud Byron, and other touring luminaries. Its star was Mrs. F. S. [Henrietta] Chanfrau in the title role of a Scottish fishergirl who wins over both the weak-willed artist, Charles Gatty (H. D. Gale), and his surly mother (Victoria Cameron). A week-long stand was merely one stop on a national tour.

The most joyous news on the next night was that Mrs. Gilbert and James Lewis were back in Daly's fold. The occasion was the premiere of Edgar Fawcett's **Our First Families** (9-21-80, Daly's). Mrs. Van Rensellaer Manhattan (Mrs. Gilbert) determines that her daughter, Eva (Ada Rehan), should marry Geoffrey Knickerbocker (John Drew). Geoffrey would prefer to enjoy himself sailing his yacht, but his uncle, Van Horn Knickerbocker (Charles Fisher), threatens to disinherit him if he demurs. Eva loves Leonardo Tompkyns (James Lewis), so her friend, Hebe Joscelyn (Laura Joyce), who has her own heart set on Geoffrey, helps Eva and Leonardo elope. Love triumphs. The *Times* review suggested that such plays, funny as they might be, did not bode well for American comedy and added, "The age of real comedy was the age of aristocracy, when such an enormity as a popular level of intelligence was unknown . . . [and] when morality

was not boring the world." The public, concerned only with a good time, kept the play on the boards for seven weeks.

American plays had dominated the season so far, and even the playhouse most identified with French melodrama succumbed to the trend when, prior to opening its regular season, it gave its stage over to another American play, John Habberton's **Deacon Crankett** (9-27-80, Union Square). Habberton was the author of the best-selling *Helen's Babies,* which had been dramatized several seasons earlier, but the new play represented his first attempt to write directly for the stage. The piece had been hailed by its producers as a "domestic comedy-drama containing the purest evidences of the artless simplicity of New England life ever uttered to the world by any dramatic littérateur," a claim that set the *Times* off on another generalizing discourse about theatre. Placing itself squarely in the vanguard of changing tastes, it condemned the piling on of melodramatic "situations," so often absurdly coincidental and untrue to life, in too many modern plays and held up as a model of how such a "heresy" could be eradicated Zola's *Thérèse Raquin,* which New Yorkers had yet to see. It particularly chafed at the inclusion of such plot contrivances in a rural play like *Deacon Crankett,* whose hero, Joe Thatcher (Joseph Wheelock), bests a swindling villain before he can win the hand of a young heiress, Eleanor Heatherton (Helen Sedgwick). A happy resolution is brought about by the help of the big-hearted, henpecked Deacon (Ben Maginley), "a jolly old fellow, who understands a good many things besides religion."

Not unexpectedly, the string of new plays—and mostly new American plays, at that—was broken by Wallack's, which inaugurated its new season with an old play on the 30th. What was surprising was that the old play was of a kind rarely seen in this most prestigious of New York theaters—a Shakespearean comedy, *As You Like It.* Critics were pleased that Wallack had restored much of Shakespeare's original text, which had traditionally been deleted or amended, and that Rose Coghlan as Rosalind, in her scenes when she was disguised as a man, attempted to be genuinely mannish, something many of her predecessors had shunned. The *Star* noted "the romping spirits, the delicious bandinage, the artful coyness, the romantic exuberance, the assumption of hoydenish simplicity, the vim of excited passion, the naturalness of assumed manhood . . . sketched in bold, masterly lines by this gifted lady."

Beginning on October 4, Niblo's housed a series of revivals. The first was *Hamlet,* with last season's determined debutante, Adele Belgarde, in the title role. A week later W. E. Sheridan, more popular in Philadelphia and San Francisco, performed in *The Duke's Motto,* after which *My Partner* settled in for a month's run.

Townsend Percy, a writer of guidebooks, whose *La Sociétaire* and *Self-Conquest* had been hissed off the stage less than a year before, adapted Frank Lee Benedict's novel *Her Friend Lawrence* as a vehicle for the temperamental Rose Eytinge and called it **A Baffled Beauty** (10-6-80, Park). The original story had told how the romance of Lawrence Aylmer (Mark Pendleton) and Violet Cameron (Ellie Wilton) almost had been derailed by the machinations of "a female Iago," the Duchess of Rimini. Since Miss Eytinge was assuming the role of the duchess, Percy had to alter the story's balance; in so doing, he apparently threw everything askew. Poor reviews led to more of Miss Eytinge's tantrums and to her walking out, leaving her place to be filled for the final week of the play's short run by Emily Rigl, who was probably totally unsuited for the part.

Boucicault's *The Snow Flower,* which originally had been done in 1858 as *Pauvrette* and had been taken from d'Ennery's *Le Bergère des Alpes,* was revived at the Bijou on the 13th with Kate Claxton in the starring role. A well-staged avalanche forced the seeming orphan to wander around the snowy mountains until reunited with her real parents. Miss Claxton's popularity earned the play a month's stand, at the end of which she offered a few performances of *The Two Orphans.*

More French drama came before the footlights with the production of Sardou's **Daniel Rochat** (10-16-80, Union Square). Once again Cazauran served as adaptor. The play pitted atheism against deep religious feeling and immediately stirred controversy, much as it had in France, but also gave the Union Square the season's biggest hit to date. Daniel Rochat (Charles Thorne, Jr.) is a rising politician who has no time for religion, which he sees as no better than superstition. He falls in love with Lea Henderson (Sare Jewett), who is as devout as he is unbelieving. They are married in a civil ceremony, but when she insists on a second, religious service, he adamantly refuses. An impassioned scene ensues in which Daniel attempts to argue that their love should overcome all differences. Lea will not bend, so Daniel reluctantly agrees to a second wedding. But Lea, recognizing that Daniel would only be going through the motions, concludes they must go their separate ways. Critics felt Thorne was forceful if not subtle and handed the palm for the fine acting to Miss Jewett, observing she was able to combine fervor with sweetness and delicacy. In Chicago, during the post-Broadway tour, Palmer unsuccessfully experimented with a happy ending.

Ever the ardent anglophile, Lester Wallack mounted his first new play of the season when he brought out E. G. Lankester's London hit **The Guv'nor** (10-19-80, Wallack's). The central figure is pig-headed Mr. Butterscotch (John Gilbert), who throws his family and friends into turmoil by always making mountains of jealousy out of molehills of suspicion. His outbursts nearly destroy the romances of his two children: his stuttering, monocled, athletic son, Freddy (Osmond Tearle), a rowing enthusiast, woos the coquettish Carrie Macclesfield (Adelaide Detchon); his daughter, Kate (Stella Boniface), loves Carrie's brother, Theodore (H. M. Pitt). Although Gilbert dominated the play, one comic highlight was an interview between Freddy and Carrie's boat-builder father (William Elton); since the kilted, dour Mr. Macclesfield senior is deaf and must read lips, Freddy's stutterings complicate matters. The practical Mrs. Macclesfield helps right the affairs. In 1880, the apron, although disappearing in newer theatres, still isolated playgoers. Actors and playwrights still made an attempt to reach out of the proscenium frame and touch, at least verbally, their audiences. Thus the play ends with the characters tying things up prettily in couplets. Old Macclesfield had the last word:

> . . . there never was no fear,
> 'Cos all along our sailing was so clear.
> (*to audience*) *My* course was *definite,* you
>   understand—
> I've come to square THE GOVERNOR—YOUR
>   'and!!

The comedy gave Wallack's a two-month success.

Probably no major American actress of the period elicited at one and the same time so much applause and headshaking as Clara Morris did. She must have been a compelling, exasperating performer. On the 26th she began a short season at the Park, where she appeared in two old favorites, *Alixe* and *Article 47.* Once again she was the doomed, illegitimate daughter and the brutally scarred, scorned lover. And once again reviewers, to use one of their own pet verbs, commingled awed compliments and angry complaints. Typically, the *Times* expended a long paragraph itemizing her faults—her coarseness, her lack of humor, her lamentable midwestern accent—then concluded, "But how wonderful, nevertheless, is her power—the power of absolute realism, it is true, but not less deep and sincere on that account. . . . It goes straight to its mark, and it throbs with a penetrating life."

Much farther up on Broadway, French opéra bouffe made way for French drama with the presentation of Heron and Belot's **The Upper Crust** (10-28-80, Standard). Marie Hagar (Annie Graham), an actress with the Comédie Française, suffers an unrequited love for the Count de Rives (Lewis Morrison). Although she loyally tends him through a near-fatal illness, he never reciprocates her affections and marries another girl. Marie pines away and dies.

Ladies remained front and center in early November. At the outset an aspiring young actress, deep-voiced Lillian Spencer, opened in a play by an aspiring playwright, Emma Schiff. **Norah's Vow** (11-1-80, Fifth Ave.) must have set a low for ineptness. No critic deigned to detail its plot, which one discouraged reviewer branded "improbable and incoherent." A second man, facetiously calling it "unique," complained it demonstrated "a lofty disdain for the ordinary canons of the playwrights' art," while a third observed, "When a heroine cries out: 'O God! I shall go mad,' one's confidence in the author . . . is considerably shaken." Lillian Spencer was soon heading a road company of *Hazel Kirke* and went on to a protracted if unimportant career. Emma Schiff was not heard from again.

But if their names have long since slipped into oblivion, Sarah Bernhardt's still conjures up a special magic. Even in 1880 her name had become a household word to American theatregoers, for the era's best newspapers regularly devoted extensive notices to Parisian plays and players, and so she had gobbled up many a column with her onstage triumphs and her backstage bickerings. Shortly before her American debut she had fought with and departed noisily from the august Comédie Française. By the time the curtain arose at Booth's on the 8th, excitement was feverish. The official top ticket price was $3, twice the going rate, but scalpers were said to be asking for and getting $5 or more. Three large electric lamps—a rarity then—lit up the theatre's facade, "flooding the junction of the two streets [Sixth Avenue and 23rd Street] with a radiance equal to hundreds of gas-jets." When she made her entrance New Yorkers saw a frail, attractive but not beautiful woman with a thin, exceedingly pale face, sharp eyes, and frizzy red-gold hair. Her first speech revealed a voice likened variously to a "golden bell" and the "silver sound of running water." Depending on whether her birth year was accepted as 1844 or 1845, she had just turned thirty-six or thirty-five.

For her opening bill she assumed the title role of *Adrienne Lecouvreur*. The *Tribune*'s William Winter rejoiced, "Throughout all that she does and says and is, there runs a glow of strange vitality and passionate abandonment, such as always, in its contact, must arouse and set free the deep soul of humanity. Quickened by this magnetic spell the frozen torrents of feeling flow once more; the tides of past experience surge up, bright and gleaming; the eyes fill with tears; and the mind is fervid with a keen and splendid perception at once of the dread reality and the still more awful perpetuity of the drama of human life." But Winter also attributed her power to "the genius of a woman who is strange rather then great, bizarre rather than glorious." Similarly, the *Herald* noted, "In depicting human suffering she seems to absolutely control every organ of her body—her cheek blanches, tears come at her bidding, and in the famous death scene there is a ghastly resemblance to the real in the feigned dissolution," only to conclude, "Mlle. Bernhardt lacked breadth, force and passion." Clearly hers was the carefully governed artistry of the French stage, arguably more showy than heartfelt, but nonetheless stunningly effective. Following *Adrienne Lecouvreur* she and her company brought out *Frou-Frou*, *La Dame aux camélias*, *Hernani*, *Phèdre*, and *Le Sphinx*. She then left to tour, returning for a second stand in April.

Almost lost in the Bernhardt furor was the opening of **Sharps and Flats** (11-8-80, Standard), the latest comic vehicle for Robson and Crane. Crane was Dullstone Flat, a former preacher turned hotel man, who is lured into the society of get-rich-quick speculators by Robson's brazen young stockbroker, Cutler Sharp. Flat's timidly anxious attempts to become a sporting "blood," even if it means furtively sipping some beer, were a high point of the comedy. For a while it looks as if Flat stands to lose all his money, but then a balloon stock takes off and all is well. The piece ran a month on the strength of its stars' performances.

The next night Daly enjoyed a smash hit with **Needles and Pins** (11-9-80, Daly's), taken from Rosen's *Starke Mitteln*. As Daly's biographer brother noted, this was the production "in which Miss Rehan, Mr. Drew, Mrs. Gilbert, and Mr. Lewis were first recognized as the famous quartet which for so many seasons endeared Daly's Theatre to the public." However, at the time critics felt Mrs. Gilbert all but stole the show as a Baby-Jane spinster, cavorting in long yellow pigtails and a short green dress much too youthful for her obvious years. Although Mrs. Vandusen (Fanny Morant) knows that her weak-willed son, Kit (John Brand), loves Mary Forrest (May Fielding), a poor piano teacher, she is resolved to have him wed a richer lady. She also has plans to marry off her absurd spinster sister, Dosie Heffron (Mrs. Gilbert), to anyone who will take her so that Silena Vandusen (Ada Rehan), Kit's sister, can then be married off as well. Mrs. Vandusen long has bristled because Mr. Vandusen (Charles Fisher), when he was Kit's age, also had loved a poor piano teacher. Her name was Silena, and Mr. Vandusen had insisted their daughter be named after her. Miss Forrest, who suddenly comes into a sizable inheritance, has learned of this old romance and so instructs her young attorney, Tom Versus (John Drew), to make Vandusen and Silena rich enough to marry, unaware that both have wed others. Since Kit had been named for his father and since his sister bears Silena's name, a series of mistaken identities ensues, and these are complicated further at a masked ball. Learning of Mary's newfound wealth, Mrs. Vandusen agrees to her marriage to Kit. Tom and young Silena also fall in love. And there is a good chance that Dosie can be foisted off on an elderly collector of bric-a-brac, Nicholas Geagle (James Lewis). The highly applauded scene at the masked ball, which swelled an already enormous cast with extras, typified Daly's sumptuous mounting. Yet Daly's huge outlays were amply rewarded when, in two slightly separated runs, the comedy compiled more than 100 showings.

Samuel W. Piercy was an actor and sometime playwright whose interpretations of a broad range of domestic characters were widely admired on the road. He rarely performed in New York. But his success across the country in his own play, originally called *Deception,* prompted him to venture a New York hearing for the work, now retitled **The Legion of Honor** (11-9-80, Park). His drama was derived from an unspecified French play. Raoul de Lignières (Piercy) is led by the treacherous Count de Maubraye (Lewis Morrison) to believe his own son, Gaston (Mark Pendleton), is not really his. He causes himself, his wife, Elise (Agnes Booth), and Gaston considerable grief until he wheedles the truth from the count and, in a striking scene in the court's opulent apartment, forestalls a duel between Gaston and the count. A Gallic Paul Pry, Viscount Distrait (Harry Courtaine), provided comic relief and additional complications. Good notices for both the play and the performers kept the play before the footlights until mid-December, but Piercy's career was cut short in 1882 in a Boston smallpox epidemic.

John McCullough did not have much longer to live than did Piercy, but he still appeared in fine fettle when he began a month-long stand at the Fifth Avenue on the 15th. His virile, vigorous manner breathed special strength into an aging repertory that started with *Virginius,* then brought forth *The Gladiator, Brutus, The Lady of Lyons,* and such Shakespearean standards as *Othello, King Lear, Richard III,* and *Katherine and Petruchio.* But just as Garrick's reworking of *The Taming of the Shrew* was wearing thin in many eyes, so was McCullough's rugged style. While most critics still found much to commend in his interpretations, some younger critics and playgoers felt he already belonged to history.

A few not so old plays ushered in December. For a fortnight at the Standard, beginning on the 6th, playgoers could assess Bartley Campbell's "modernization" of his *Peril,* revived under the new title *Matrimony.* Campbell's changes ranged from superficial ones, such as giving his principals new surnames, to more drastic alterations, such as attempting to turn a melodrama into a comedy. The *Dramatic Mirror* scolded him for falling into "the error of giving stage room to his earlier productions, which are crude, rough-edged, and wholly unfit for practical performance." The *Times,* equally unhappy, used its review for another digressive discourse, this time on the futility of being kind to native dramatists who did not approach their work with sufficient seriousness. On the same night, *A Celebrated Case* opened a week's run at Booth's, after public protests prevented a mounting there of Salmi Morse's *Passion Play.*

The following Monday, the 13th, two great artists vied for attention: Tommaso Salvini at Booth's and Mary Anderson at the Fifth Avenue. As great a performer as he was, Salvini disconcerted many observers by playing in Italian while the rest of the cast (mostly recruited from Boston actors) performed in English. *Othello, Hamlet, La Morte Civile, Sullivan,* and Saumet's *The Gladiator* comprised the bills. Salvini would act only four times a week, so the house remained dark the rest of the time. When he returned for another engagement in late January, he added *Ingomar* and *Macbeth* to his programs, but on this occasion alternate nights were given over to *Enoch Arden,* with James O'Neill and Agnes Booth starring. For some reason, the Americans drew dismayingly poor attendance.

Mary Anderson's bills consisted of *Ingomar, Evadne, The Hunchback,* Sir Thomas Talfourd's hoary, stiffly classical *Ion,* in which she assumed the trouser role of the foundling who wins a place for himself in society before his death, and Sheridan Knowles's rarely done *Love,* in which a countess becomes enamored of her father's slave and so is torn between pride and affection. Although she continued to fall far short of being a fully accomplished actress, her patent, superior talents were continually being polished, and her classic beauty excused any number of youthful flaws.

On the 15th the Union Square revived *The Banker's Daughter* for a month-long run. During the stand Palmer began an unusual series of matinees on Tuesdays and Thursdays. Prompted by the success of Clara Morris's return earlier in the season at the Park, he initiated a parade of revivals of her old favorites, starting with *Miss Multon*, then turning to *Camille*, and finally to *Conscience*, in which the actress had originally been slated to appear in 1876 when illness forced her withdrawal. By coincidence she was again ill, but her health did not stop her performing twice a week until March. Naturally her *Camille* prompted comparisons with Bernhardt's, allowing critics and audiences to choose between the American's often uneven if frequently dynamic interpretation and the Parisian's consistently studied, elegant, yet equally touching portrayal.

Expectations ran high for **Forget-Me-Not** (12-18-80, Wallack's). In London Genevieve Ward had scored a resounding triumph in Herman Merivale and F. C. Grove's play. The story centered on Stéphanie, Marquise de Mohrivart (Rose Coghlan), who in her younger years had lured patrons into her husband's gambling house. One night a patron whom she had betrayed, a volatile Corsican named Barrato (Gerald Eyre), had entered the couple's bedroom, killing the husband and leaving the Marquise for dead. The play opens after Stéphanie has recovered from her wounds and has decided to push her way into English society. To this end she goes to Rome, where she attempts to enlist the aid of two expatriates by blackmailing them, since one of these ladies had married Stéphanie's son without his parent's consent and, in law, the marriage is illegal unless Stéphanie now publicly agrees to it. The ladies' friend, Sir Horace Welby (Osmond Tearle), discovers her history and by a happy coincidence is able to draw aside the curtains and show Stéphanie the still vengeful Barrato lurking in the moonlit garden. Stéphanie has no choice but to abandon her ambitions and flee.

The action took place in a single setting, a richly appointed Roman palace, beautifully represented on Wallack's stage. The performances matched the physical production. Miss Coghlan's Stéphanie was surprisingly volatile, sensuous, and insinuatingly mischievous. Tearle's Sir Horace was courtly, manly, and forceful, yet not without some sins in his own

past, which Stéphanie attempts to invoke to counter his own charges. The reviews gave promise of a long run, but Miss Ward, who owned the American rights, won an injunction that forced Wallack to withdraw the production after four weeks.

Lawrence Barrett returned after a long absence to star in **Yorick's Love** (12-20-80, Park), William Dean Howells's version of the same Spanish drama that Daly's had offered in 1873 as *Yorick*. Barrett had been touring for several seasons with the work, which had originally been brought forth under a literal translation of its Spanish title, *A New Play*. Howells's adaptation was freer than Daly's had been, shuttling back and forth between prose and blank verse. At one point Yorick remembers a walk with "Master Shakespeare" and Shakespeare's odd example of tragedy:

. . . as we went, we talked of tragedy.
And "Pray thee, what is tragedy?" I cried.
We had stopped to hear a strolling mountebank
Making the crowd roar with his caps and bells
When, on a sudden, there arose a shriek
And a wild mother caught her dead child up
From under flying wheels. The fool who noted not
Capered and babbled on. But the great Master
Seized on my arm and pointed "There! There!"
'Twas all he said.

The character of Shakespeare, who had earlier been given the curtain speech, was eliminated and the closing spotlight allowed to fall on the dying hero's words, although Howells could not resist having one figure then exclaim, "Alas! Poor Yorick!" Barrett, in a curly blond or gray wig and sporting a conspicuous goatee, made Yorick resemble physically the popular image of Shakespeare. In *The Wallet of Time* Winter recalled, "The gentle humility of a fine nature was expressed by him with sweet and natural self-deprecation, so that *Yorick* was made wistful, and he would have been almost forlorn but for his guileless trust and blithe, eager, childlike spirit." Not all critics enjoyed the production, albeit they disagreed widely on what they thought was wrong, so that the public responded enthusiastically, so that Barrett's engagement, initially announced for two weeks, was soon extended for an additional fortnight. Barrett kept the play in his repertory for the rest of his career.

Many reviewers questioned how Irish Bartley Campbell's new Irish drama, **My Geraldine** (12-21-80, Standard), was, with the *Tribune* insisting, "It is called Irish because the scene is laid in Ireland and for no other reason." Nor, according to critics, was that the play's only problem. The *Dramatic Mirror* observed, "In many respects Mr. Campbell's play is worthy of commendation; in many others it deserves severe criticism. The story is interesting though improbable, the language is less didactic than that to which this particular author has accustomed us. On the other hand the story is tedious . . . and spread out. The scene in the ruined abbey, in which Geraldine goes into hysterics over some imaginary rats, might be properly curtailed. Many of the incidents are too lurid to coincide with the intense interest of the quiet portions of the play. These rugged faults may assume the guise of virtues to the gallery, but they form no bid to the favor of the downstairs people."

The story the paper alluded to tells how Squire Arden (John Jack) assumes his brother's estate after the brother is killed in battle. What the squire does not know is that his brother had been secretly married and a daughter had been born to the marriage. When this daughter, Geraldine (Louise Muldener), now a grown woman, appears on the scene she falls in love with the squire's son, Maurice (E. F. Thorne). However, her dead father's treacherous servant, Mike McShane (Frank Lawlor), kidnaps her. Maurice comes to the rescue, throwing Mike over a cliff. But Mike is not killed. Instead he returns, attempting to slay Geraldine. Once again Maurice must save her. Disguised in the moonlight as McShane's hunchbacked accomplice, he fatally stabs Mike and frees the heroine. One much applauded transformation scene saw a woods rolled offstage to reveal the ruined abbey. Despite critical reservations, the play ran a month, toured successfully, and was revived on and off for a decade.

Sandwiched in between Salvini's two visits to Booth's was a month-long revival of *Uncle Tom's Cabin.* It arrived on the 27th with a solid but unexceptional cast and boasting of a "gorgeous" transformation scene designed by Henry E. Hoyt, who was to rise quickly among the ranks of contemporary scene painters. The work's amazing, unbending popularity was attested to not only by the production's doing better business than Salvini had done but by its packing the theatre in the face of a competing version, which followed in the wake of the opera season at the prestigious Academy of Music.

One of the first new plays of 1881 was not offered at one of the leading theatres. Instead, **Our German Senator** (1-10-81, Grand Opera) debuted at a theatre that, since the departure of *The Soul of an Actress,* had been given over to vaudeville, operetta, and some perennial touring attractions such as Jefferson's *Rip Van Winkle* and Maggie Mitchell's

Fanchon the Cricket. The play was advertised as the first to utilize a telephone onstage. It starred the comic Gus Williams in the role of J. Adolph Dinkel, a retired brewer whom land speculators promote for an appointment to the Senate. Although his backers become embroiled in scandal, Dinkel wins the appointment.

That same night a better theatre offered a worse play, **Salviati; or, The Silent Man** (1-10-81, Fifth Ave.). Taken by William Seymour from an unnamed French work, the production was yet another attempt by youthful, incorrigible Frederick Paulding to assert his right to an obviously undeserved stardom. Raphael Salviati, (Paulding), the last surviving brother in a vendetta, is drugged and imprisoned. After many years he escapes, disguises himself as a herdsman, and wreaks vengeance on his opponents. The *Herald* wailed, "Almost everybody is disguised as somebody else, and discoveries of long lost mothers, brothers, cutthroats and cousins are incessant." The debacle survived one week.

The following Monday night saw the premiere of two more duds. **The Creole** (1-17-81, Union Square) was A. R. Cazauran's adaptation of d'Ennery's *Diana,* which Parisians had applauded in October. Its leading figure was hardly a heroine but was, like *Forget-Me-Not*'s marquise or *Two Nights in Rome*'s Antonia, a blackmailing adventuress. The West Indies–born Creole, Diana (Eleanor Carey), has learned that Armand de Maillepré (Walden Ramsay) apparently deserted a ship under his command during a naval battle off the coast of India; she attempts to use the charge against him. Armand's father, Count de Maillepré (Charles Thorne, Jr.), is so upset by these accusations that he takes to sleepwalking, and while asleep he walks right into Diana's bedroom and stabs her to death. To spare his father an unpleasant trial and his family the ignominy of airing Diana's story, Armand claims to be the girl's killer. All concludes happily when Diana is revealed to have been the vindictive daughter of a man executed for piracy and when Armand admits he was away from his ship helping to quash a slave insurrection at his fiancée's plantation. Critics ridiculed the story, asking why Armand had not told this story in the first act or how the count could so suddenly and conveniently become a somnambulist. Like so many French plays of the time, this one was set in the 18th century. But even lovely costumes and Marston's beautiful, evocative sets could not save the day.

A still less satisfactory evening was in store for first-nighters who elected to attend the opening of Ettie Henderson and Fannie Aymar Mathews's

Bigamy (1-17-81, Standard). Mrs. Henderson, the theatre manager's wife, had received encouraging notices two seasons earlier for her *Almost a Life*. Not so this time. The ladies' story was no more absurd or contrived than most that sufficed for the era's melodramas. Indeed, up to a point it had the virtue of relative simplicity. Yet critics would not buy. Its heroine, Miriam Strafford (Ada Dyas), had been so grasping in her younger days that she had married a man solely for his money. The marriage had not worked. Now she has married Philip Dacron (Eben Plympton) for love. Her cousin, Adele Delville (Louise Sylvester), had hoped to marry Philip herself, and her fury at learning of Miriam's marriage prompts her to charge her cousin with bigamy, since Miriam apparently never secured a divorce. But another happy ending ensues, since somehow Miriam had failed to notice that the man she once had married for his money and the man she now has married for love are one and the same. The play survived for two weeks, probably because of Mr. Henderson's forbearance.

Hardly a season passed without a staging of *The School for Scandal* at Wallack's. The court-ordered shuttering of *Forget-Me-Not* prompted the house to return it to the repertory on the 22nd. Naturally Gilbert was on hand for his incomparable Sir Peter, and his brilliant supporting cast included Rose Coghlan, Mme Ponisi, Osmond Tearle, and Gerald Eyre.

At the Standard on the 31st, Rose Eytinge headed the cast of *Drink*, Charles Reade's carefully laundered translation of the same *L'Assommoir* that Daly had presented unsuccessfully in 1879. The play ran two weeks, with Saturday matinees given over to *East Lynne*.

Where's the Cat? (2-5-81, Wallack's), James Albery's reworking of a Franz von Schönthan farce, *Sodom und Gomorrha,* was still doing well in London but failed to please finicky New Yorkers. Ten years before the action begins three men, Percival Gay (H. M. Pitt), George Smith (William Elton), and Scott Ramsay (Horatio Saker), are left a cat to care for. The cat dies, and the men have it stuffed and use it for a piggy, or more accurately a kitty, bank. They agree to contribute to it regularly and meet in ten years. When they do meet, along with their womenfolk, mistaken identities complicate the reunion, and at one time or another Sir Garroway Fawn (Osmond Tearle) is believed to be each of the threesome.

A. C. Gunter's **Fresh, the American** (2-7-81, Park) was no better as a play, and probably not as good. However, with John T. Raymond cavorting in the title role it tickled American risibilities and gave everyone concerned with it a tremendous hit. Raymond's Ferdinand Nervy Fresh had more than a touch of Colonel Sellers in him. Having failed to corner the market on Wall Street and in other grandiose schemes, he has taken to globe-trotting in search of fame and fortune. His roamings bring him to Egypt, where he falls in love with a harem beauty, Erema Almi (Laura Don). Achmet Pacha (G. F. DeVere) refuses to part with her—even after Fresh has offered to pitch pennies with him for the lady. The lovers manage to elope and elude their pursuers. Critics complained about the "Wall Street slang" employed throughout the piece but felt that nonetheless Raymond's "admirable fooling" made it work with what the *Critic* called "his well-known dash and bounce." The comedy ran two months and returned on several later occasions as part of its cross-country tours.

Even though it was fairly well received in its Chicago premiere and does not seem to have been a failure, Bartley Campbell's **Government Bonds** (2-7-81, Grand, Chicago) never made it to New York. Its star was George Knight, a popular comedian, albeit by no means in Raymond's league. Knight played Leopold Lander, a reformed revolutionist now employed in a bank. He absentmindedly stuffs some bonds into an oversized hat. When their loss is discovered he is arrested and convicted. By good fortune, the bonds are located before he can be sent to jail.

The failure of *The Creole* goaded the Union Square into reviving *The Danicheffs* on the 8th as a stopgap booking.

Two Chicago newspapermen, one Colonel Pierce and J. B. Runnion, were the authors of **One Hundred Wives** (2-14-81, Booth's), which the Gosche-Hopper Company, a reorganization of the Criterion Comedy Company and still bankrolled by young De Wolf Hopper, brought into New York as part of a long but apparently unprofitable tour. The play was another of the combinations of melodrama and comedy so popular at the time. In this case the melodrama focused on Elsie Bradford (Georgiana Drew Barrymore), who comes from Europe with her little girl and is almost entrapped into a bigamous Mormon marriage. To prevent this, Confucius McGinley (Hopper) marries her until her real husband can come to claim her. Never mind that McGinley is also married. Yet once more the *Times* used its review for digression, seeing an opportunity to assail the Mormons much as it had in its review of *The Danites*. It called Mormonism, among other things, "the flagrant evil which is allowed to thrive, weed-like, in our free land." But it found the play "a worthy addition to American drama." When the play's tour closed, Hopper, his inheritance exhausted, threw in the towel and looked to others for employment, thus starting on his real rise to stardom.

Despite his bad luck with so many recent London hits, several of them by H. J. Byron, Lester Wallack persevered, bringing out Byron's **The Upper Crust** (2-23-81, Wallack's) and again suffering a quick failure. This was not the same play as one with the same title produced earlier in the season. Its bourgeois gentleman, cockney Barnaby Doublechick (William Elton), has made a fortune with Doublechick's Diaphanous Soap and is resolved to use his wealth to buy a place in high society.

A better reception greeted **Felicia; or, Woman's Love** (2-28-81, Union Square), A. R. Cazauran's adaptation of Delpit and Belot's *Le Fils de Coralie*. The woman in question is Mme Dumont (Rose Eytinge), who years earlier, shamed by having given birth to a son out of wedlock, fled to the seclusion of a farm. She has raised her child to believe she is his aunt. Now that son, Captain John (Charles Thorne, Jr.), proposes to marry Dolores Mornoy (Sara Jewett). But Mr. Mornay (John Parselle), discovering that Mme Dumont's sister had been his brother's mistress, fears the marriage may be consanguineous. Mme Dumont is forced to reveal the truth. Indicative of how stories had to be cleansed to please American tastes was the fact that in the original the woman had been a notorious prostitute. Critics recognized such changes weakened the story but still breathed a sigh of relief at not having to confront such French unpleasantness.

For months the Bijou had been occupied with musicals and such touring shows as *Our Boarding House* and *Widow Bedott*. One of the season's rare novelties at the house was Edgar Fawcett's "comedy of dilemmas and delusion," **Sixes and Sevens** (3-1-81, Bijou). The play's awkwardly situated hero, Julian Suydam (Herbert Archer), is an artist who refuses to paint "badly enough to sell well" and has secretly married Isabel (Jeffreys Lewis). When a rich old aunt, Mrs. Vandervoort (Henrietta Irving), whom he had not seen for years, suddenly appears, he blurts out that Isabel is his sister. The aunt promptly sets about trying to marry off her nephew and "niece" to others. At heart another touring show, the comedy lingered two weeks, then headed out.

Fanny Janauschek came into Booth's for a fortnight beginning March 7. Besides revivals of *Brunhild*, *Medea*, *Macbeth*, *Bleak House*, and *Debo-*

rah, she introduced one new play, **Mother and Son** (3-8-81, Booth's), Janet Tucker's dramatization of Frederika Bremer's Swedish novel *The Neighbors*. The imperious Countess of Mansfield (Janauschek) casts out of her life a son she believes guilty of theft. The rupture eventually destroys her health, and only as she is dying does she discover her son's innocence. The star's performance inspired one critic to write, "Greater acting, in the best sense, has seldom been witnessed upon our stage."

Great acting—and old plays—were all Wallack's had to fall back on following its failure with *The Upper Crust*. On the 11th *The Rivals* raised its curtain; it was joined in the repertory by *Old Heads and Young Hearts* on the 24th and *A Scrap of Paper* on the 29th.

On the 18th playgoers who had seen Wallack's *Forget-Me-Not* could compare that house's version with Genevieve Ward's presentation at the Fifth Avenue. The contrast was striking, at least as far as the leading ladies were concerned. Remembering Rose Coghlan's youthful piquancy, Winter embarked on another of his beloved catalogues when he noted, "The point of assimilation between the present actress and the part arise in an imperial force of character, intellect, brilliancy, audacity of mind, iron will, perfect elegance of manners, a profound self-knowledge, and unerring intuition. . . . [The character] is cold as snow, implacable as the grave, remorseless, wicked, but beneath all this depravity capable at last of self-pity, capable of momentary regret, capable of a little bit of human tenderness, aware of the glory of the innocence she has lost, and thus not altogether beyond the pale of compassion." Others saw her more mature heroine not as an adventuress but as a creature of unfortunate circumstance. Odell, looking back over the years, was more graphic: "Who can forget her icy sarcasm, in the earlier scenes, her magnificent style, and the cry of fear as she recognised the enemy face, seen in the garden, by moonlight? I can still see her clutching the curtains that shut her in from that mortal terror." Oddly enough, while Wallack's production had held the boards for a month and could have run longer, Miss Ward could only remain in New York for two weeks as part of a prearranged tour. But she and the play would return.

The age-old conflict between country virtues and city wiles cropped up again in Piercy Wilsons's **That Man from Cattaraugus** (3-28-81, Fifth Ave.). In setting and tone the play seemed apple-pie American, even though Wilson had taken much of it from a German comedy, Friedrich Kaiser's *Stadt und Land*. He underscored American influence by having his disparate brothers come from the same town as had Adam Trueman in Anna Cora Mowatt's 1845 success *Fashion.* Wilson's brothers were also named Trueman, and the good-hearted country brother, Allan, a cattle dealer, was impersonated by the production's star, John E. Owens. His citified brother, Adolphus (F. S. Hartshorn), and Adolphus's family are given to putting on airs, but Allan and his daughter win everyone over with their simplicity and decency. Allan also saves Adolphus from misfortune by using his native generosity and shrewdness. Critics came down harshly on the play ("a sad exhibition") and suggested that Owens had failed to find a durable vehicle. In her biography of her husband, Mrs. Owens attributed the play's failure in New York to casting and backstage quarrels, which on one evening spilled out into the theatre lobby during a performance. She insists that away from Manhattan the show played to "standing room only" and that Owens's performance was one of his best: "The character was replete with bluff humor, and yet had its affectionate side. In light and shade it was an exquisite creation; and general opinion gave the verdict that 'it fitted Owens like a glove,' and was to him another leaf of laurel."

There was almost always disagreement when Lotta came to town, as she did on April 11 at the Park. But the disagreement pitted critics, who generally found her limited and cloying, against her adoring public. Neither side was ever swayed. This time she offered nothing new, filling out her four-week stand with revivals of *Little Nell and the Marchioness, Musette,* and *La Cigale.*

Scenery stole the show at Augustus Harris, Henry Pettitt, and Paul Merritt's Drury Lane sensation-melodrama **The World** (4-12-81, Wallack's). The *Herald* reported, "The harbor at the Cape with its shipping; the explosion of the dynamite machine on the ship at sea, followed by the bursting of flame through numerous traps in the stage, which is realistically set as the saloon deck of a steamer; the raft, with its living and dead cargo, floating on the 'boundless sea,' which is the most perfect scenic illusion of its kind ever seen within a theatre—the private Insane Asylum and the River Thames, with its panoramic effects; the Great Hotel, with its realistic passenger elevator, and many other details, are all such masterpieces of the stage carpenter's and scene painter's art that whenever they claim the attention of the audience they do so thoroughly and completely." Such distraction was fortunate, for the paper dismissed the play as "dramatic rot" that was "beneath serious criticism," though it no doubt unintentionally whetted many an appetite when it

characterized the work as "spasmodic, sensational drama in five horrors and eight shocks."

Most of those horrors and shocks befall Sir Clement Huntingford (Osmond Tearle), who is in the Cape Colony under an assumed name and encounters diamond thieves determined to prevent his returning home to claim a fortune. His ship is blown up, and he nearly dies while floating on a raft. Finally rescued and back in London, he must dodge the murderous schemes of his brother, Harry (H. M. Pitt), who has him committed to a mental institution. He fights off eight warders and breaks down an iron gate to escape. Sir Clement finally has the satisfaction of seeing the villain hurled down an elevator shaft. The play was a success, running until the beginning of July and initiating a brief vogue for English sensation-melodrama, but it was an odd piece to select for the final production at this highly respected playhouse. When the last curtain descended the theatre was handed over to Germans, who would employ it for foreign-language productions. Next season's Wallack's ensemble would perform at a new Wallack's, farther uptown at 30th Street.

On the 18th the Bijou was home to a revival of MacKaye's *Won at Last,* which lingered two weeks. MacKaye was forced to rent the Bijou after he had been shouldered out of his Madison Square Theatre by the treacherous Mallory brothers, publishers of religious books, who had backed the venture financially and promised to support MacKaye.

When Sarah Bernhardt returned to Booth's on the 18th she brought with her two productions she had not offered New Yorkers before. The first was Dumas's *La Princesse Georges,* which Americans had seen Charlotte Thompson do in 1872 as *One Wife.* Of course, when Miss Thompson played it the drama had been reset in America, and the original ending, which so many American critics had fulminated against, had been changed to allow the faithless husband to die. Bernhardt angered some moralistic reviewers when she restored the original French ending, in which the loyal, betrayed wife learns that the husband of her own husband's mistress has killed the wrong man and that her husband and his mistress have run off, leaving her bankrupt and alone. But Bernhardt's acting mollified most critics, the *Times*'s George Edgar Montgomery suggesting that her Séverine (Mrs. Vandyke in Thompson's version) was her finest achievement "in depth of passion and truthfulness. Her transitions were astonishing for their vigor and fire; her manner of combining delicacy, tenderness, and passion was full of knowledge and discrimination."

She also appeared as the pushy Mrs. Clarkson in *L'Étrangère,* which Daly had offered in 1876 as *The American.*

Daly had also first presented *Monsieur Alphonse* to New Yorkers in 1874, but its latest revival came at the Union Square on the 25th under the title *Raymonde.* The closing bill of the house's official season, it starred Clara Morris and ran a single week.

Meanwhile, Daly had concluded his own season (with a musical) and rented his theatre to producer J. M. Hill, who brought in W. D. Eaton's **All the Rage** (5-2-81, Daly's). A journalist named Will Goodwin (A. Z. Chipman) has gone off for a vacation at Long Branch after writing a column denouncing congressional candidate DeWitt C. Briggs (William Davidge). The infuriated Briggs heads for Long Branch to administer a thrashing to the newsman, but there confuses him with a "corn doctor," another Will Goodwin (Frank Hardenberg), who has written a book that is "all the rage" with young ladies. One reviewer noted a song from *The Pirates of Penzance* was interpolated and had to be encored on opening night. The farce had been playing prosperously around the country all season, and, though most critics made short work of it, did good business all month at Daly's before transferring to Niblo's for an extra week.

At a somewhat out-of-the-way, unfashionable theatre, another play that had prospered on the road was given equally short shrift by critics, but it would go on to more than a dozen years of popularity. Contemporary scuttlebutt suggested that **Sam'l of Posen; or, The Commercial Drummer** (5-16-81, 14th St.) was written by George H. Jessop at the behest of M[aurice] B[ertram] Curtis (his real surname was Strelinger), who wanted a play that did not depict a Jew as a villain or a ludicrously comic figure. Continuing Jewish immigration and growing Jewish theatrical patronage had made the time ripe for just such a vehicle. Whatever its dramaturgical faults, the new play filled the bill handsomely. Hereafter, along with the classic Yankee and more recent western characters, the shrewd, industrious, kindly Jew would become a stock figure in American plays. Samuel Plastrick (Curtis), a Polish immigrant, tired of his backbreaking work as an itinerant peddler, longs to settle down and marry Rebecca (Gertie Granville), whose uncle had been a family friend in the old country. Rebecca's buddy, Jack Cheviot (Nelson Decker), is the nephew of Mr. Winslow (Welsh Edwards), owner of a jewelry store, and Jack obtains work there for Samuel. Jack leads a dissipated life, though he swears he will reform and marry Ellen (Carrie Wyatt). But his

dissipation allows another Winslow nephew, Frank Kilday (Frank Losee), to implicate Jack in a crime Frank himself has committed. When the furious Winslow fires Jack and Samuel, Samuel takes it upon himself to get the goods on Frank. He soon does. Frank stalks out, cursing the lovers as he goes. Jack and Samuel embrace their sweethearts, and Samuel approaches the footlights to address the audience, as so many other characters had in seasons past and would continue to do for a while: "Now, as you are all happy, Rebecca and I will be married, and if any of our friends in front wish to buy diamonds, call on Sam'l Plastrick and he will sell you some as large as this [*Holding up big piece of cut glass*] for a half dollar." On its first New York visit, despite the summer heat, the play ran until the beginning of August. Curtis later rewrote the play, along with his fellow actor Ed Marble, took credit for it, and toured with it as long as the public wanted it.

If any theatre established a pattern for modern long runs, it was probably the Madison Square. Following the record-shattering run of *Hazel Kirke,* **The Professor** (6-1-81, Madison Square) took over its stage and bucked the heat to chalk up a stand of 151 performances. The play's author and star was William Gillette.

. . .

William Gillette (1855–1937) A lean, haughtily handsome man with bright blue eyes and an aquiline nose, he was born in Hartford, Conn., son of a U.S. senator. Early biographies say he studied at New York University and Boston University; later ones, at Harvard and Yale. In any case, he graduated from none. He first acted for no pay with a stock company in New Orleans in 1875, but that same year he made his professional debut as Guzman in *Faint Heart Never Won Fair Lady.* After appearing at the Boston Museum and elsewhere, he braved New York as the prosecuting attorney in *The Gilded Age* (Mark Twain was a neighbor and old acquaintance) in 1877. His acting style was subdued, his delivery quick and staccato. Other actors often spoke glowingly of his infallible sense of timing.

. . .

Although Gillette called his work "a character study," it was actually little more than lightweight summer comedy. His Professor Hopkins, bookish and seemingly unworldly, has gone to a vacation retreat in the White Mountains only to find himself pursued there by a group of ardent young ladies, who in turn are followed by the young men from Yale who have been courting them. The scholar must also deal with a kidnapper and the girl he has kidnapped and must help reunite a long-separated brother and sister.

All through the season, lesser theatres had played host to touring attractions and visiting stars, some of great note. Lester Wallack had played for a time at the Grand Opera House, and Fanny Davenport had brought her touring company of *Pique* into the same theatre. At one time a company of *Hazel Kirke* was playing at Niblo's while another troupe was continuing the long run at the Madison Square. And we have seen *All the Rage* move to Niblo's briefly after its stand at Daly's. Now Niblo's brought the season to a close when a sturdy old favorite—already seen at several playhouses—came in for a fortnight beginning June 20th. The drama was *Uncle Tom's Cabin*.

1881–1882

The last months of 1881 and the first of 1882 found most of the fine and lively arts just that. Distinguished American writers as diverse as Mark Twain and Henry James were issuing works still admired more than a century later. Proper Bostonians were sitting back to soak in the sounds of their new symphony orchestra. Tony Pastor was reshaping and sanitizing vaudeville with remarkable swiftness; although not everyone would consider vaudeville a fine art, it was a lively one.

Certainly the legitimate theatre was busy enough. How fine it was, or even how engagingly lively, was another matter. The new season offered its quota of successful productions. At least in retrospect, however, the theatrical year seems all too often stale and flat, if not always unprofitable. Perhaps the theatre is forever in transition, yet the 1881–82 season gives a feeling of being frequently lost in uncertainty. The rapid growth of touring productions—then still called combinations—was eroding the stability of the old stock companies. More slowly, primitive attempts at electric lighting were changing the complexion of productions as well. Moreover, although New Yorkers had yet to see many of his plays, uneasy reports had begun to circulate from the Midwest about the disturbingly written dramas by a new writer, a Norwegian named Henrik Ibsen. New commercial ideas, new technologies, and new intellectual currents were surely hurtling the American stage into a new era.

The winds of change could be felt briefly when the

season opened with George F. McDonald's **Coney Island; or, Little Ethel's Prayer** (8-8-81, Union Square). The play was produced by James W. Collier, who in a few seasons would take over the playhouse with Palmer's former partner, Sheridan Shook, and start it on its precipitous decline. His mounting was a hint of things to come there. The play was obviously unready, running on opening night until nearly one in the morning. Reviewers reported that by the end of Act III at eleven o'clock an exodus of playgoers had begun. Little Ethel (Fanchon Campbell) was not the central figure, for the play focused on the unhappy plight of her father, John (Cyril Searle), one of the era's many victims of a false accusation and of a hard-hearted father who casts out his son, daughter-in-law, and little granddaughter. The wanderings of the Oakburns took them from their Illinois homestead (exterior view), to Coney Island (with a panorama moving from the Oriental Hotel to the Iron Pier), to a New York City tenement garret, to the park fronting on City Hall and Printing House Row (in which the beleaguered wife, Adele, played by Laura Wallace, is caught in a "pitiless stage storm of thunder, lightning and sheeted rain"), to the final joyous resolution on a farm near Harlem. The tour survived for three weeks.

Edward Holst and Herman Lee's **Room for Rent** (8-15-81, Bijou) was no better and no more successful. Set in a boardinghouse catering to bohemian types, the farce intermingled several paper-thin stories. These included the misadventures of Henry Huccleman (W. J. Ferguson), a hack "penny-a-liner"; of Albert Raymond (Clarence Gibson), an artist who seemingly misplaces his wife, Mlle. Rosavilla (Genevieve Reynolds), only to find she has taken a room in the same establishment; and of the jabbering Mrs. Cutter (Mina Crolius), whose husband walks in on her as she is rehearsing a scene from *Othello* and misconstrues what he sees. The farce milked laughs from a lady's hiding in a trunk supposedly filled with dynamite and from a man's hiding under a dining-room table during a meal. Co-author Holst won a hand for his playing Frederick Dahl, a Danish dancing master who flutters in and out of the action. One or two songs embellished the evening.

There were even more songs, supplemented with a few vaudeville turns, in Theodore H. Sayre's **The Strategists** (8-15-81, 14 St.), yet reviewers perceived the evening as a regular farce and not as one of those farce-comedies just beginning to evolve into musical comedy. Although its initial engagement was only for a fortnight, it returned in the fall and toured all season.

On the same night, *The Banker's Daughter*

opened a fortnight's stand at the Grand Opera, *My Geraldine* came into Niblo's, and *The Galley Slave* began at the Windsor. Throughout the season houses such as these regularly served as hosts to such touring revivals. Even more important houses increasingly filled in weeks that otherwise might have remained dark with such combination bookings. Thus on the 20th *A Messenger from Jarvis Section*—with McAuley in the lead, of course—returned for a month to the Standard.

George Fawcett Rowe added no laurels to his record with his short-lived **Smiff** (8-22-81, Fifth Ave.), another farce punctuated with occasional musical numbers. In fact, it was billed as a "spectacular musical comedy," although its spectacle was more closely in keeping with the clichés of sensation-melodrama than what we would later consider musical comedy glitter. Its plot concerned the adventures of Philander Smiff (Rowe) and his family, all down-at-the-heel players, who leave England for America. A dramatic second-act curtain saw their ship struck and sunk by an iceberg. Rowe, who either flunked his geography course in school or relished Gilbertian absurdities, set the next act on a deserted tropical island. By the final curtain the Smiffs have found their niche, and the Smiff daughters have accepted the proposals of two young men who have followed them from England.

R. G. Morris's **Up Salt Creek** (8-29-81, Windsor) starred two comedians who had made a name for themselves in variety, P. F. Baker and T. J. Farron. Herman Krauss (Baker) and John Shay (Farron) are two immigrants who room at a boardinghouse run by the Hon. Patrick Myers (R. C. Hudson), an ambitious politician. Krauss and Shay also harbor political ambitions, but when ethnic differences arise after Krauss falls in love with Shay's sister, Bridget (Ettie K. Henry), and Shay with Krauss's sister, Ottile (Ada Boshell), Myers sees a way to further his own plans at their expense.

The comedy competed for first-nighters with J. P. Burnett's **Jo** (8-29-81, 14th St.), one of the era's many theatricalizations of *Bleak House*. The title role fell to Jennie Lee, a popular and respected burlesque comedienne who had made the part her own in England, where she was known as "the Vital Spark."

A third opening was *Michael Strogoff*, which was coupled with a variety bill at Aberle's, a house normally given over exclusively to vaudeville. New Yorkers had seen a version in 1877, but now they were abruptly to have a choice of three productions. The more spectacular were those that followed, on the 31st at Booth's and on September 3 at the Academy of Music (this last adaptation by

Cazauran). Too much of a not very good thing resulted in poor box office at all the versions.

Disappointments also plagued the early months of Daly's season. Despite high expectations, **Quits; or, A Game of Tit for Tat** (9-7-81, Daly's), his brother's translation of Julius Rosen's comedy, received a critical drubbing and a forced run of four weeks. Even on opening night that strange instinct that often governs playgoers kept the house small. What loyalists saw was a comedy about Col. Horatio Hickory (W. J. LeMoyne), a retired officer who is married to a rich widow. He opts to change places with his valet, Buttles (James Lewis), in order to enjoy a night on the town. Naturally Buttles also decides to have a fling, in the guise of his boss. Complications follow.

A season that had already been dismissed as "feeble and trivial" burst into brief bloom on the 12th when the Union Square Theatre's curtain rose on Sheridan's *The Rivals*. This restoration, one of the most ballyhooed and admired of the century, was the brainchild of Joseph Jefferson, who longed for escape from incessant Rip Van Winkles. Purists bridled at the revisions he made: deleting such characters as Julia and virtually all the more sentimental moments, and emphasizing his own part of Bob Acres and that of Mrs. Malaprop at the expense of the Absolutes. But most critics and the public at large loved the results. The play had first been mounted the preceding season at Philadelphia's Arch Street Theatre, and the duenna of that house, Mrs. John Drew, was enlisted as co-star. The company toured the entire season, with a cast that included Maurice Barrymore as Captain Absolute, playing to packed auditoriums. By the time it reached New York, Barrymore and several other players had retired, but Jefferson and Mrs. Drew remained.

. . .

Mrs. John Drew [née Louisa Lane] (1820–97) Born in the Lambeth district of London into a family that had been employed in theatricals since Elizabethan times, she was brought by her mother to America after her father's death and made her debut in Philadelphia in 1827, playing the Duke of York to Junius Brutus Booth's Richard III. Although she continued to act for the rest of her life, she was best known as the brilliant manager of Philadelphia's Arch Street Theatre from 1861 to 1892. A short, wispy woman with large eyes, she was the mother of the then famous comedian John Drew and grandmother to the later famous Barrymores.

. . .

Jefferson and Mrs. Drew's performances were the signal for much jubilation. William Winter gushed,

"For the first time it seemed as if *Mrs. Malaprop* might truly exist. The part has before now been greatly acted; but never till now, in our time, has it seemed to be actually lived." One bit of business added by the actress won special applause. Intending to hand Sir Anthony one of Ensign Beverley's intercepted letters, Mrs. Malaprop inadvertently gives him a love note from Sir Lucius O'Trigger. With a "simper and an antique blush that were irresistible" she hastily retrieves the note, murmuring, "There has been a slight mistake." Winter, writing from the Philadelphia premiere, noted, "It is worth the journey to this place merely to hear her say, 'He has enveloped the plot to me, and he will give you the perpendiculars.'" Jefferson had a field day, in one scene bowing and practicing deportment in front of a mirror, unaware of Sir Lucius watching, and in another trifling with Captain Absolute's gold-laced hat, considering how he would look in it. Winter found, "The interior spirit of Jefferson's impersonation, then, is humanity and sweet good nature, and the traits that he has especially emphasized are ludicrous vanity and comic trepidation." The two-week engagement was completely sold out.

Overshadowed by the opening of *The Rivals* was the premiere of Bronson Howard's **Baron Rudolph** (9-12-81, Grand Opera). The play had been conceived originally as a vehicle for the Florences, and called *Only a Tramp*, but it had never been produced by them. Instead Howard rewrote it, apparently to bring out the comedy underlining its melodramatic story, and it was first presented in England by Mr. and Mrs. George S. Knight. Tellingly, Mrs. Knight, the former Sophie Worrell, did not play the female lead but rather the comic part of Mrs. Dashwood, the rich widow seeking another husband. The lady is perspicacious enough to realize that Rhoda Lawrence (Charlotte Cobbe) is not truly happy in her own second marriage to the stern, corrupt Whitworth Lawrence (W. J. Cogswell), owner of a large iron foundry. Lawrence had helped impoverish Rhoda's first husband, the reckless, generous Rudolph (Knight). Now Rudolph is reduced to working as a laborer in the foundry, but a strike promises to wipe out what little remains to him. When the workers decide not only to strike but to rob the Lawrence mansion and, if she interferes, kill young Ernestine Lawrence (who is really Rudolph's daughter), Rudolph joins them in the burglary. The robbery is thwarted, but at the same time Lawrence is arrested for his own crimes. Rhoda, Ernestine (Josie Wilmere), and Rudolph are reunited, and Rudolph is found to have inherited a new fortune

and a baronetcy. Part of a prearranged national tour, the stand at the Grand Opera was limited to two weeks, but the play remained in the Knights' repertory for most of the decade.

Another popular touring couple, Mr. and Mrs. McKee Rankin, brought in W. G. Wills's **William and Susan** (9-19-81, 14th St.). The play was not really new, being a rewriting of an old favorite, *Black-Eyed Susan*. However, the appeal of the Rankins saw to it that business was good.

Before playgoers began streaming out of this latest opening President Garfield died; he had been shot in July but had clung to life for eleven weeks. Most theatres closed the next evening and on the night of his funeral, adding more gloom to a rather gloomy young season.

On the 27th Genevieve Ward returned in *Forget-Me-Not*, giving patrons at the Union Square a further chance to assess her interpretation.

The Rankins found another serviceable vehicle, one they performed on and off for several seasons, in **'49** (10-1-81, 14 St.). The work's authorship was uncertain, with some saying it was from the pen of Joaquin Miller. The wife and child of "Old '49" (Rankin), a relic of bygone days, were kidnapped by Mormons during a massacre carried out by the same Mormons. He has wandered aimlessly for years, finally settling in California. There he meets a spunky waif, Carrots (Mrs. Rankin). In time Carrots finds a husband, "Old '49" finds that Carrots is his long-lost daughter, and he also finds a valuable lode of gold on his land. The play's reception by audiences proved it was clearly stageworthy, but critics saw it merely as an assemblage of Wild West clichés. Disappointed by its failure to move beyond the immediacy of its lowly characters and their lowly way of life, the *Herald* condemned the play as "an unrefined and vulgar piece of dramatic writing." The newspaper's critic seemed especially incensed by a long scene in the third act in which several of the characters attempted to cook and eat a raccoon, with oldtimers at the table holding their noses.

Two friends, sometimes associates, sometimes competitors, opened engagements on the 3rd. Booth took over the stage of the theatre that bore his name; Barrett appeared at the much smaller Fifth Avenue. Probably by coincidence, they both elected to open with *Richelieu*. Booth's cardinal, while offering no more surprises than did anything in his repertory, was admired for its poetry and consistency. Barrett was assailed for his occasional overemphasis, angular movements, and often shrill, weak, "fish-horn" voice but at the same time was commended for touches of fire that made his interpretation seem more original and dramatic than Booth's. Except for his opener and *The Fool's Revenge,* Booth's repertory was entirely culled from his expected Shakespearean canon; Barrett gave his Hamlet and Cassius but also played Yorick and David Garrick. Some less responsible papers took the occasion of Booth's return (he had been in England) to bruit rumors of drunkenness and bankruptcy, but these reports seem not to have deterred his admirers. Both men returned for second visits later in the season.

Daly's ill luck continued with Edgar Fawcett's **Americans Abroad** (10-5-81, Daly's) spotlighting the family of Silas K. Wilks (James Lewis), who has made a fortune selling stove polish. The snobbish Mrs. Wilks (Mrs. Gilbert) breaks the engagement of her daughter, Lucy (May Fielding), to a clean-cut American boy and hustles the clan overseas to France, where she attempts to marry Lucy to Count de Beausejour (G. Vandenhoff, Jr.). Only after the count is exposed as a fortune hunter is Mrs. Wilks made to see the light. Critics were coming to the conclusion that Fawcett, for all his respected skills as a poet and novelist, could not grasp the tricks required for successful stage pieces. Within the month the more intuitively theatrical William Gillette would employ a similar story to greater effect.

Critics had only to attend the various offerings by Booth and Barrett and a return engagement on the 17th at the Fifth Avenue of Robson and Crane in *Our Bachelors* before trekking again to Daly's. This time the attraction was a French play, the elder Dumas's *La Jeunesse de Louis XIV,* which the producer brought out as **Royal Youth** (10-22-81, Daly's). The love affair between young Louis (John Drew) and Marie de Mancini (Ada Rehan), which the king must abandon for reasons of state, did not appeal to Americans. Even sumptuous period costumes and settings depicting the forest at Fontainebleau, the Orangerie, and a colorful hunt could not whet appetites.

Always an impressive actress, Fanny Janauschek began a three-week stand at the Union Square on the 24th with her Lady Dedlock and Hortense in *Bleak House,* then moved on to her even more admired Mary Stuart in *Mary, Queen of Scots.*

The limited stand of *The Rivals* aside, the season's first major success was Frances Hodgson Burnett and William Gillette's **Esmeralda** (10-29-81, Madison Square). When Esmeralda Rogers (Annie Russell), a sweet, carefree North Carolina farm girl, falls in love with her virile, handsome neighbor, Dave Hardy (Eben Plympton), her ambitious

mother, Lydia Ann (Kate Denin Wilson), determines to prevent their marriage. Overjoyed after gold is said to lie under the Rogers' land, she promptly hustles Esmeralda off to Paris, where a marriage is to be arranged with the Marquis de Montessin (Davenport Bebus). Her meek husband, Elbert (Leslie Allen), acquiesces reluctantly. Happily for the girl, the biting but good-hearted Mr. Estabrook (Thomas Whiffen) finds ways to delay the wedding until it is learned the gold is actually on Hardy's land. Esmeralda is allowed to marry the man she wants.

Some critics complained that the play lacked enough sustaining incidents and was, for all practical purposes, over at the end of the second act, when Dave is informed that the ore lies on his property. They missed the point. The last three acts take place in Paris (at an artist's studio and in a room at the Rogers' apartment). Dave, broke and ignorant of the fact that he is suddenly a wealthy man, has followed Esmeralda there, hoping for one last chance. The Paris acts were cleverly devised to display each principal's reaction to the news. Dave's response is manly determination to confirm his newfound wealth and assert his right to Esmeralda. In the third act, father and daughter learn the news. Mr. Rogers's reaction is quiet satisfaction and vindication; Esmeralda collapses in hysterics for a dramatic curtain. The last act is saved for Mrs. Rogers's humiliation. As bits of the news are broken to her, accompanied by a basso ostinato of Mr. Rogers's attempts of reassurance with his simple "Mother" and "Now Mother,' Lydia Ann becomes increasingly angry and explosive until she is finally and totally deflated. (Gallery gods must have yelled and stomped with glee.)

The play was filled with homey touches. Early on, Mr. Rogers explains Mrs. Rogers's eagerness to see the trickster who comes to buy the property and why she has always resented being immured on an isolated farm: "Lor', how tickled mother wud be ter see ye. She hain't never been ter New York, but Lizbethville—that ye know, whar she was raised—it kinder made her feel like she knowed suthin' of how New York was. Thar's three churches in Lizbethville, an' four stores, an' a post office." Paris friends are amused at Mrs. Rogers's extravagance. Each time she buys Esmeralda a new dress, she has her daughter's photograph taken—"eighteen times since we've known her, and we've known her only two months."

Whatever reservations critics held, audiences found the whole evening enchanting. Miss Russell played no small part in that enchantment. Years later Odell recalled "her charm, her grace, her exquisite voice, her genuine dramatic power." The play, which remained popular for the rest of the century, chalked up 350 performances, thereby continuing the chain of long runs at the little Madison Square and confirming the house's position as the cradle of modern long runs.

October faded away on the 31st with Robson and Crane mounting *Twelfth Night* at the Fifth Avenue and an Italian actor, Ernesto Rossi, making his debut at Booth's. Any *Twelfth Night* in which the stars are Aguecheek (Robson) and Belch (Crane) and in which the lovers are assigned to minor players is almost certainly out of whack. Even elaborate scenery could not save the ill-conceived production. The following week the pair revived *Sharps and Flats*. Rossi's reception was different: largely favorable, if peppered with reservations that varied from reviewer to reviewer. However, all agreed he could not compare to his countryman Salvini, a comparison he courted not only because of his nationality but because he opened with Salvini's great role, Othello. The *Times* found him "less graceful, less expressive, though more violently eloquent" than his compatriot; the *Herald* observed, "His was a laughing, buoyant, good-natured, almost happy-go-lucky soldier of fortune." Like Salvini in the preceding season, Rossi performed in Italian with an English-speaking supporting cast. He followed his Othello with his Romeo, Hamlet, and Lear. In essence he seems to have sacrificed poetry for a realism that many found displeasing. For example, his detailed, graphic murder to Desdemona had him "strangling her with his hands after twisting her long hair about her neck, as he shook her violently and then dragged her about the bed and finally tossed her down upon the pillows." Rossi's visit was part of his first and last American tour.

For the final week of her engagement, beginning on November 7, Fanny Janauschek essayed a new role. She was often applauded for her risk-taking, but her latest venture brought her only a good measure of ridicule, for her vehicle was a singularly inept, misguided effort by a controversial, misguided author. Salmi Morse's *Passion Play* had been forced to close at its San Francisco premiere, and he was still seeking a New York hearing for it. Meanwhile, he had convinced Miss Janauschek to star in his **The Doctor of Lima** (11-7-81, Union Square). Morse set his scene among the English colony in Lima, Peru. There the ghoulish Dr. James Austin (Alexander H. Stuart) buys corpses from body snatchers and performs electrical experiments on them. He succeeds in bringing back to life a dead

woman, with whom he falls in love and whom he marries. For eight years the doctor and Mrs. Austin (Janauschek) lead a happy life. Then her long-lost first husband, Mr. Babcock (James H. Taylor), abruptly reappears. He is not a nice man and seems bent on making trouble, but his suicide allows the Austins to resume their quiet ways. Some idea of Morse's strange humor comes in a story one of the characters tells of a man who has a leg amputated so that he will be on equal footing with a crippled sweetheart. A play about a woman brought back from the dead is oddball at best, but given Victorian sensibilities and Morse's want of dramatic skills, the production invited the headshaking it received.

Happily, headshaking gave way to handclapping when Daly broke his string of failures with a pronounced success, **The Passing Regiment** (11-10-81, Daly's). In von Moser and Franz von Schönthan's German original, *Krieg im Frieden,* a troop of soldiers is forcibly billeted in a small town. In Daly's Americanization members of the Excelsior Regiment of the National Guard of New York, on their way to Newport, are housed briefly at the Narragansett Pier. During their short stopover several romances spring up, most notably that between Adjutant Paul Dexter (John Drew) and a Russian heiress, Telka Essipoff (Ada Rehan). The suave, manly Dexter's rival is Lt. Thorpe Suydam (H. M. Pitt), "a New York exquisite of the 'lardy dah,' well combed poodle type." Guess who wins. Additional fun came from a mute burglar (Mr. Milton). The play's run of 103 performances helped Daly erase his earlier losses.

Another theatrical giant, the majestic, virile McCullough, began a six-week stand at the Fifth Avenue on the 11th. If Booth was an incorrigible traditionalist and Barrett an experimenting intellectual, McCullough remained an echo of an earlier era, sticking doggedly to his Forrest-like repertory. His bills this time offered *Virginius, Ingomar, King Lear, Richard III, The Gladiator, The Lady of Lyons,* and *Brutus.* One "new" play, Lewis Wingfield's **The Bondman,** was hardly all that new, being a rewriting of another Forrest favorite, Conrad's *Jack Cade.* His opening coincided with the return of the Union Square Theatre's company from an extended national tour and its revival at the house of *Daniel Rochat.*

Mlle. Rhéa, a French actress who had won accolades in Russia, was coolly received when she began a week's visit at Booth's on the 24th, giving first *Adrienne Lecouvreur* and then *Camille.* Far more to playgoers' liking during the same week was Clara Morris's performance in the latter play at the Union Square. (Later in the season she appeared there in revivals of other plays at midweek matinees.)

The theatre's two revivals were but prelude to its first new production—and its biggest success—of the season, G. R. Sims's West End hit **The Lights o' London** (12-5-81, Union Square). Despite Sims's piling one tired melodramatic cliché on another, the play proved gripping theatre. Its hero, Harold Armytage (Charles Thorne, Jr.), is accused by his villainous cousin, Clifford (F. de Belleville), of stealing money and valuable papers from his own father. The father is all too ready to believe the charges, and Harold is condemned to prison. He escapes, rejoins his wife, and lives in poverty until he can expose Clifford's treachery. Sims filled his piece with colorful minor characters such as the ham actor Joseph Jarvis (John Parselle) "of Jarvis' Temple of the Legitimate" and the actor's young son, Shakespeare Jarvis, a trouser role played by Maud Harrison. J. H. Stoddart played Seth Preene, Clifford's accomplice, whom Clifford eventually turns against and attempts to drown. He recalled, "It was anything but a pleasant situation being hurled backward from the rail of the bridge, a distance of possibly fifteen or twenty feet from the level of stage. The supposed water consisted of gauze set pieces running across the stage, between the lines of which was an open trap with a feather-bed at the bottom of it to receive me as I fell." He also had to endure "the additional discomfort of occasionally having my eyes and mouth full of salt (which they threw from beneath the stage as I fell, to indicate the spray of water)." Besides the setting of London Bridge, Marston's scenery—the most massive at the house since *The Two Orphans*—included the park and grounds at Armytage Hall, a snowy, moonlit road on the way to London, a London police station, a workhouse, and Jarvis's rooms.

The *Times* was delighted with the work, finding "something in it deeper than the external realism of melodrama. It leans rightly toward the realistic drama, toward the drama of truth and impressive fact, the tragedy of our present and complex life." But then the reviewer continued, "The man has not yet appeared who shall write—with courage and conviction and profound insight—such a drama: he will be a genius, for he will force us to see that life as it is has manifold aspects that have never been uncovered on the stage." That man and that drama were nearer at hand than the reviewer imagined.

First-nighters seeking comedy rather than melodrama could have attended the return of the Florences in *The Mighty Dollar* at Booth's. They could also have sampled Sims's versatility three nights later at **The Mother-in-Law** (12-8-81, Park). Talfourd Twigg (W. J. Ferguson) is going to produce a play about his prospective mother-in-law, Mrs. McTurtle (Nellie Mortimer), but he is given additional material when one of his cast members, Topsy Grey (Laura Don), recognizes the henpecked Major McTurtle (E. M. Holland) and Twigg's equally henpecked attorney, John Pownceby (John Dillon), as old suitors. The play ran successfully for five weeks, a run that fell far short of that accorded the playwright's melodrama.

Hardly any actress of the period could resist trying her hand at *Camille*. Unfortunately, Fanny Davenport was not one of the exceptions, and she opened her stand at the Fifth Avenue on the 26th with the play. She "draped it in some beautiful dresses," but her costumes could not hide her inadequacies. So she soon moved on to more congenial roles in *London Assurance, Oliver Twist, As You Like It,* and, probably less congenially, *Leah, the Forsaken.* She also gave, on January 6, one performance of the younger Dumas's *The Princess of Bagdad,* in which she played a virtuous countess caught between a persistent but unwanted suitor and a jealous husband. This play sometimes was called *Lionette.*

On the night of her opening, Chanfrau returned in his staple, *Kit, the Arkansas Traveller,* at the 14th Street Theatre, and Kate Claxton brought *The Two Orphans* to Booth's.

Mary Anderson ushered in 1882, opening on January 2 at Booth's. Her repertory consisted of *Romeo and Juliet, The Hunchback, Ingomar,* and *The Lady of Lyons.* In the course of her month-long visit she also introduced two plays new to her repertory. However, the first of these was preceded by another major opening, for on January 4 Lester Wallack unveiled his new theatre at Broadway and 30th Street to a posh audience, many of whom sauntered in rudely late. But then, if they had been regulars at the old Wallack's, they must have known the play by heart: *The School for Scandal,* with Gilbert as Sir Peter, Osmond Tearle as Charles, Gerald Eyre as Joseph, Rose Coghlan as Lady Teazle, and Mme Ponisi as Mrs. Candour. Whatever the excellences of the production—and critics agreed it was finished to a high polish—such conservatism did not bode well for the future of the new Wallack's.

At least at first, no such high gloss embellished Mary Anderson's performance in W. S. Gilbert's *Pygmalion and Galatea,* beginning on the 7th at Booth's, but within a few seasons the role of the statue brought to life and later returned to stone came to be considered by many her finest achievement. It was certainly the one for which she was most fondly remembered. Her most famous picture shows her on a pedestal, with a high Grecian hairdo and drapey Greek garments, looking down demurely on the world. In *The Wallet of Time* Winter recalled, "The charm which she diffused through the character was that of angelic innocence pervading a sinless though human and passionate love and expressing itself in artless words and ways, which sometimes brought a smile to the lips and sometimes smote the heart with a sudden sense of desolate grief. . . . Her horror at [the] sight of the dead fawn and her terror at [the] sight of its destroyer were so entirely earnest and seemingly natural that they created a distinct illusion and impressed as much as they amused. . . . Her pathos in the closing scene had the cruel reality of pain . . . the utter woe of a broken heart." For him her return to stone was a symbol not of defeat but of triumph. Her next offering was Count Henri de Bournier's **The Daughter of Roland** (1-14-82, Booth's). Berthe, the dead Roland's daughter (Anderson), falls in love with Gerald (William Harris), son of Count Amaury (J. B. Studley), who had once been known as Ganelon and had betrayed Berthe's father. Her love for Gerald allows her to forgive the past.

Now the spotlight swung back to Lester Wallack— not on the stage of his new theatre, but as star of F. C. Burnand's **The Colonel** (1-16-82, Park). Like Gilbert and Sullivan's *Patience,* which had reached Broadway in September, the play mocked the "aesthetic" movement of Oscar Wilde and his epicene coterie. Richard Forrester (Eric Bayley) believes an Englishman's home is his mother-in-law's castle. Unfortunately for him, his mother-in-law, Lady Tompkins (Maria Davis), worships at the feet of the limp-wristed, pretentious Lambert Streyke (C. P. Flockton), who prevails on her to redecorate Forrester's home, turning it into a gloomy medieval fortress. To make matters worse, Mrs. Forrester (Minda Bayley) falls under his spell. Enter a clear-eyed, forceful American, Col. Woothweel W. Woodd (Wallack) of the U.S. Cavalry to set matters aright. Many of the players had been recruited from the original London cast, but reviewers felt it was Wallack's knowing high-comedy touches—they were called "points" then—that made the evening worthwhile. The play was moderately successful, running until the end of February. It might have been better played and had an even longer run had Wallack used it to open his new playhouse—as earlier he had announced he would. Odell points out that the comedy gave contemporaries a fresh catchphrase, "Why cert'nly."

The next evening Rossi opened a second stand, this time at the huge Academy of Music. His bills consisted of *King Lear, Othello,* and a premiere, the elder Dumas's **Edmund Kean,** given initially on the 18th and advertised as the play's first American hearing. Its story found the actor battling with the Prince of Wales and torn between his affection for two women.

Having opened with a dutiful obeisance to its most beloved theatrical classic, Wallack's turned to a new play for its second attraction. The play had a squeak-through run of a month, to some extent because it had been carelessly rewritten (a new act was added for America), to an even greater extent because Wallack's skilled players somehow could not capture the requisite tone, and finally because New Yorkers may not have been ready for its newer, cynical realism. This was not the realism of a writer of "courage and conviction and profound insight," which the *Times* had earlier said was needed, but the work of an adept, clever, and not unthoughtful new dramatist, a dramatist whose writings would illumine the theatre for decades ahead—Arthur Wing Pinero.

The Money Spinner (1-21-82, Wallack's) tells how Millicent (Rose Coghlan), daughter of the unsavory gambling-house owner, Baron Croodle (William Elton), jilts a wealthy, good-natured idler, Lord Kengussie (Osmond Tearle), to marry Harold Boycott (Gerald Eyre). Kengussie transfers his affections to Millicent's sister, Dorinda (Stella Boniface). Shortly after their engagement is announced, Millicent discovers that her husband has stolen a considerable sum and will go to prison if the money is not returned. Using the knowledge she acquired at her father's gaming tables, she offers to play Kengussie for such high stakes that she will retrieve the amount needed. When Kengussie appears to be winning, Millicent resorts to cheating and is caught. She reveals her problem, so her understanding old suitor agrees to lend her the money. However melodramatic and contrived the story appears to modern tastes, in its day it seemed a marked stride away from the high coloring of a more obsolescent school of melodrama and presaged the nature of much dramatic writing for years to come.

Something rare and something freakish were coupled in the presentation of *Oedipus Tyrannus* at Booth's on the 30th. The rarity was a real Greek classic on American stages. The freakishness, not such a rarity on New York stages of the era, was an Oedipus performing in ancient Greek while the rest of the cast spoke English. Rossi, Salvini, and others had acted in their native tongues opposite Americans playing in theirs. But this Oedipus, George Riddle, was not an ancient Greek, or even a contemporary one, and he was more of a scholar than an actor. (Young Georgia Cayvan was Jocasta.) The whole affair had a discernible whiff of academia about it, understandably so since it had originated at Harvard. Some critics compared the audience to churchgoers, always dutiful, often attentive, occasionally bored. They also wondered aloud how viable, for all his blood and gore, Sophocles was for modern times. The play's producers were E. H. Ober, founder of the famed Boston Ideal Opera Company, and youthful, ambitious Daniel Frohman, who recalled in his memoirs that a cast of over 100 helped ensure that the tour would not make money.

Sardou's **Odette** (2-6-82, Daly's) gave the producer his second hit of the season and gave Ada Rehan one of her infrequent opportunities to essay an emotional role. She portrayed the title part of a wayward wife who long ago had been driven from home by her disgusted husband, Count Clermont-Latour (H. M. Pitt). When their daughter, Berangère (Hélène Stoepel), reaches marriageable age the count attempts to force Odette to move far away, so no hint of early scandal will mar the girl's chances for a happy alliance. At first she refuses, but a heart-tugging reunion with Berangère finally prompts her to enter a convent. (In Sardou's original, Odette commits suicide.) A majority of critics were pleasantly surprised by Miss Rehan's emotive gifts. The *Times* praised her "considerable feeling and force," and the *Evening Post* spoke of her "tearless grief which was genuinely pathetic." Praise was also showered on Miss Stoepel, who earlier had garnered raves as the child prodigy Bijou Heron but soon left the stage after marrying another young member of the cast, Henry Miller. There may have been a touch of nepotism in her casting, since she was the daughter not only of Matilda Heron but of Daly's musical director, Robert Stoepel.

Lawrence Barrett's second visit of the season gave renewed proof of his resolute willingness to explore fresh territory. For his first two weeks he offered an American novelty, William Young's blank-verse tragedy **Pendragon; or, The Knights of the Round Table** (2-13-82, Fifth Ave.), assuming the role of King Arthur to the Guinever of Marie Wainwright and the Sir Launcelot of Louis James. Cast in lesser roles were such rising artists as Otis Skinner as Sir Pelleas and Kate Meek as Vivien. There were critical complaints about the quality of Young's verse and the ability of many of the actors to handle it. The *Herald* observed, "Such language as 'What do you take me for' in the mouth of a king at the climax of his passion sounds strange upon the ear." (Curi-

ously, the paper's reviewer singled out for praise the thunderclap that accompanied Modred's presenting Arthur with a key that incriminated Guinever.) There were also questions raised about Young's conception of a charmless, shrewish queen and a pompous, pontificating king. However, on the whole, critics leaned over backwards to support what they saw to be a flawed but worthy effort, an attempt to lift American dramaturgy out of its turgid doldrums. When attendance fell, Barrett replaced the work with some of the productions he had offered in the fall and added evenings of *The Man o' Airlie, The Merchant of Venice, The Marble Heart,* and *Richard III.*

Lester Wallack found a major hit for his new theatre with Paul Merritt and Augustus Harris's London success **Youth** (2-20-82, Wallack's). Frank Darlington (Osmond Tearle) is disowned by his parents, the Rev. and Mrs. Darlington (John Gilbert and Mme Ponisi), for marrying Eve Malvoisie (Rose Coghlan). This time the parents are in the right, for Eve proves treacherous, and she and her lover, Major Reckley (Gerald Eyre), frame Frank for forgery and bring about his dismissal from his regiment. He reenlists as a private, goes to the Sudan, and there distinguishes himself. Eventually he also exonerates himself, and when he discovers that Eve was already wed at the time she married him, he is free to marry a better woman, Alice Wenlock (Stella Boniface), and once again receive his parents' blessings. Spectacular scenes included the sailing of a troop ship and some vividly staged battles. This was not the sort of thing highbrows expected of Wallack's, but coming in the wake of the preceding season's success with *The World* it apparently confirmed for the anglophilic producer that a lesser genre was acceptable so long as it was English. His competitor A. M. Palmer was later to say that Wallack's "foundered with its English melodramatic colors flying."

The prolific G. R. Sims was represented by a third play during the season, **The Member for Slocum** (2-27-82, Park), which starred Nat C. Goodwin and his wife at the time, Eliza Weathersby, and interjected some songs and vaudeville turns into the English farce. Although the title hinted at a political comedy, the play proved merely the latest in the season's rash of mother-in-law comedies. Onesimus Epps (Goodwin) is a young man wheedled by a pretty wife, Madelin (Emie Weathersby), and cowed by her intimidating mother, Mrs. Jeffs (Jennie Reiffarth). Mrs. Jeffs hits the ceiling when she discovers Onesimus is being pursued by Arathusa Smith (Eliza Weathersby), the wife of his best friend. Critical complaints about Goodwin's overacting had little effect at the box office.

Boucicault, confined for several seasons to less convenient houses, returned to a major stage in what was advertised as his latest play, **Suil-a-Mor; or, Life in Galway** (3-6-82, Booth's), but most observers dismissed it simply as a rewriting of his 1873 *Daddy O'Dowd*. His gifts as a playwright may have been waning, but this in no way diminished his ability to charm an audience with his histrionics.

Sardou and Émile de Najac's **Divorçons** (3-14-82, Park) was a better play and retained its popularity with American audiences at least until World War I. The flighty wife who insists "let's get a divorce" is Cyprienne (Alice Dunning Lingard), and the man she would marry is her own vacuous cousin, Adhémar (Charles B. Welles). Cyprienne's loving husband, Henri de Prunelles (Frederic Robinson), is naturally dismayed but calmly sets about having his way. He immediately agrees to divorce his wife and settle an annuity on Adhémar, quietly hinting that in being rid of her he will be able to marry a more beautiful, more intelligent woman. The ruse works. Cyprienne remains Mme de Prunelles.

Undaunted by ridicule and failure, and probably swayed by some minor success on the road, Anna Dickinson once again braved New York, opening at the Fifth Avenue on the 20th in nothing less than *Hamlet*. Their patience exhausted, critics were savage in damning her shrill, thin voice and clumsy, restricted gestures. Nor were they any more lenient when she switched to *A Crown of Thorns*. Somehow their message finally sank in. Hereafter Miss Dickinson confined her appearances to the lecture circuit, at least in New York.

Bartley Campbell's **The White Slave** (4-3-82, 14th St.) was allotted only two weeks for its initial New York run—its first performances anywhere—but the press at the box office caused it to be kept on for additional three weeks. It quickly became Campbell's most popular play, holding the boards with surprising regularity until that great watershed in American theatrical history, World War I. From the start critics dismissed the play as artistically worthless, all the while recognizing its appeal to a less demanding public. The *Dramatic Mirror* promised not to "draw and quarter the poor *White Slave*" since "Mr. Campbell's play was written to please the public, and this by catering to the appetite of the moment." In a similar vein the *Herald* recorded, "Bartley Campbell is in for another popular success. It is not as well written as *My Partner* and *The Galley Slave* but is full of effects pathetic, melodramatic,

and scenic, that are sure to please the people who buy theater tickets."

More than one critic remarked on the story's resemblance to Boucicault's *The Octoroon*. Although Judge Hardin (Welsh Edwards) has willed that when he dies his housekeeper, Nance (Etelka Wardell), and her quadroon daughter, Lisa (Georgia Cayvan), are to be set free, Hardin's adopted son, Clay Britton (Gustavus Levick), who has served as the judge's manager, has squandered his foster father's estate and so must reluctantly sell everything and everyone to William Lacy (Frank Roberts). The villainous Lacy, a man who boasts that he never deals in anything "except horses and niggers," has been secretly manipulating Britton's downfall. Too late, Britton realizes this and attempts to save Lisa. Lacy contrives to have Britton jailed. He also threatens that unless Lisa becomes his mistress he will reduce her to the lowliest of slaves, with "a hoe in your hand, rags upon your back." Lisa's answer is "Rags are royal raiment when worn for virtue's sake." In time, Lisa is proved to be the white child of Judge Hardin's long-dead daughter. With Lacy imprisoned for a murder he committed, Lisa and a reformed Britton are free to wed.

Memorable stage effects included a Mississippi River steamboat's nighttime explosion and its aftermath, for which the directions read: *"Red glare of burning boat fades out and deepens in the darkness. Music. Cotton bale, burning, floats [across stage]. When it is fairly off stage, a spar with Lisa lashed to it, her face upturned, and Clay with one arm thrown around spar, while with the other he holds up Nance, floats [across stage]. Only the blue flashes of lightning lighting up their faces when 2/3 across stage."* With such "a perfect terror of sensations," the *Dramatic Mirror* said, "the nervous spectator alternately jumps from his seat or rubs his chin against the big hat of the lady one row ahead." All this, coupled with Lisa's alliterative response, which soon was a national catchphrase, ensured packed houses for seasons to come.

The vogue for melodrama was attested to by openings on the same night at other playhouses, with James O'Neill starring in *A Celebrated Case* at the Fifth Avenue and the Florences in *The Ticket-of-Leave Man* at Booth's.

Cazauran's dramatization of Thomas Hardy's idyllic **Far from the Madding Crowd** (4-17-82, Union Square) was a two-week failure, in good measure because Clara Morris could not convey Bathsheba's simple goodness and open sentimentality. Its premiere coincided with a return of *Hazel Kirke*, this time housed at the Fifth Avenue, and of Booth's second visit of the season, again at Booth's and again with his standard compliment of plays.

When *Divorçons* had run its course, Alice Dunning Lingard and her company turned to A. C. Gunter's **After the Opera** (4-22-82, Park). Mrs. Lingard was Mrs. Alice Montague Marvin, "the most beautiful widow in New York." Along with her friend, Maria Pierson (Louise Dillon), a sophisticated "Connecticut floweret," they agree to attend the opera and a ball that is slated to follow in the company of a young bachelor, Jack De Lacy (J. G. Saville), and his boss, the prominent banker Harvey Kelsey (Charles Walcot). However, what should have been an evening of harmless fun for the foursome turns complicated when their innocent actions are misinterpreted by theologian Professor Probity Pierson (E. M. Holland) and Lavinia Backsetter (Elizabeth Andrews), a lady "devoted to religion and the keyhole."

The breakdown of the stock system and the concurrent rise of the policy of casting at large for every production continued to push some performers into premature stardom. A disastrous instance was the mounting of George Darrell's **Solange** (5-1-82, Union Square), which began the supplementary season at the fading playhouse. The author was co-starred with a new leading lady, Eugénie Legrand. His involved, often preposterous story moved from London to New York and spanned many years. At heart, it depicted the bravery of a young woman who is wrongly believed to have poisoned her husband, takes to the stage to support herself, and eventually finds happiness in a second marriage. Both Darrell's playwriting and his acting were soundly derided, although the critics saw a glimmer of promise in Miss Legrand. Perhaps because of their encouragement she moved on to *Camille* and *The Lady of Lyons* when *Solange* was hurriedly withdrawn. But both their careers were downhill thereafter.

By contrast, a name soon to make a towering mark on Broadway was first seen alone on a New York playbill at the opening of **La Belle Russe** (5-8-82, Wallack's). The play's author was David Belasco.

. . .

David Belasco (1853–1931) was born in San Francisco, the son of parents of Portuguese-Jewish origin whose name had originally been Velasco. Much of his youth was spent in Victoria, British Columbia. Even as a young child he apparently played infants and juveniles on stages there, but his earliest recorded appearance came in 1864 when he was cast as the Duke of York opposite Charles Kean's Richard III. He began writing plays while still in his early teens. When his family returned to San Francisco he increased his theatrical activities, not only acting and writing but directing as well. He soon became a major figure in West Coast theatricals, especially at the Baldwin Theatre, where *La Belle Russe* was first mounted. At the time New Yorkers knew him only as co-author of *Hearts of Oak*.

. . .

In keeping with the common practice of the day the play was hardly original, being advertised as "from the French" but in reality lifted largely from two popular successes Belasco had staged in California, *Forget-Me-Not* and *The New Magdalen*. Beatrice (Rose Coghlan), although a clergyman's daughter, has led a dissolute life, working as a shill in a gambling house, where she was known as "La Belle Russe," and apparently murdering her husband, Captain Brand. Her twin sister, Geraldine, married Sir Philip Calthorpe (Gerald Eyre), who deserted her when he encountered financial difficulties and joined the army. Beatrice has been reduced to poverty and has gone to live in Italy, but when she hears that her brother-in-law has been reported killed, she returns to America. She also has been given reason to believe that her sister is dead, so she appears at the offices of the Calthorpes' attorney, with her own young daughter, and claims to be Geraldine. Her claims are accepted and she is made welcome, but her comfortable new world begins to crumble when Sir Philip immediately appears. The reports of his death were erroneous. Philip is ready to accept Beatrice as Geraldine, and all might have gone well had not he been accompanied by none other than Captain Brand (Osmond Tearle), who did not die from Beatrice's bullets. Beatrice attempts to poison Brand, but he again survives and has a delicious revenge. Calling the whole family together in one room, he opens a door and shows them the real Geraldine in the next room. Beatrice is made to depart, leaving her daughter with Brand.

It was a tribute to Wallack's fine ensemble that a play overflowing with preposterous coincidences—three principal figures returning from the dead, the arrival of Calthorpe and Brand at the lawyer's office just after Beatrice has left—could be given credence, and testimony as well to how even the most sophisticated playgoers had been conditioned to outlandish dramatic conventions. Yet the play retained acceptance in ensuing years and was made into silent films at least twice, including a 1919 version starring Theda Bara. The drama's opening fell the same night that *The Professor* came into the 14th Street Theatre for a second visit.

Vast amounts of publicity about the teenager who played the lead in Charles E. Callahan's **Fogg's Ferry** (5-15-82, Park) ran the risk of building expectations too high. For once the buildup did not exaggerate, and critics immediately joined in to sing her praises. In fact, many of them had been doing just that for several seasons when she had played small roles in plays such as *Fritz, Our Cousin German* and *Kit, the Arkansas Traveller*. Yet it would still be a few years before Minnie Maddern would change her billing to Mrs. Fiske and move on to become one of the giants of the American theatre. Meanwhile, she used all her developing skills in a futile attempt to bolster a dismal vehicle. She played the part of the teenaged Chip, who has been raised to believe she is a ferryman's daughter. She is courted openly by warm, candid Gerald White (Atkins Lawrence) and more furtively by oily, sneering Bruce Rawdon (C. Russell Blake). Rawdon's evasiveness stems from the fact that he already is engaged to proud, haughty Blanche (Miss M. L. Young), daughter of Judge Norwood (R. C. Wilson). Blanche is the sort who proclaims, "I want action, society, amusement, the *world*. Farm hands and milk-maids—I rank them below my horse." Nor does she deign to notice "the presence of a menial," even if that menial is Chip, recently appointed by the judge as Blanche's governess. But she does notice Chip when she later finds her on her knees before Rawdon: "What is my affianced husband doing with this girl? Why on your knees, my lady? Is he pouring into willing ears his blazing passion?" Rawdon's response is a one-word aside to the audience, "Damnation!" Rawdon tries to steal important papers in the judge's possession and then incriminates Chip in the scheme. Her world collapsing around her, Chip rushes to the river, contemplating suicide. White stops her. She turns despairingly to him: "Gerald White, you are a man that any girl would gladly trust. But I am snared, helpless, wretched. What is to become of me?" His answer is a firm proposal, and though she has just been suicidal, he leaves her with a revolver. Chip learns that Rawdon has planted a mine in the river, hoping to destroy a steamer on which the judge is sailing: "The steamboat is coming and they've put that thing in the channel to blow her up. Merciful Heaven, what can I do. If I could but reach it. Any shock would burst it and save the boat. But I can do nothing. Oh, Heavenly Father, am I to idle here while innocent lives are butchered? Ah, the pistol!" She fires a pistol into the water, and the mine explodes. Then it is discovered that she, and not Blanche, is the judge's real daughter. Blanche is sent packing, and Chip accepts Gerald's proposal. The curtain falls, as did so

many curtains of the period, to the orchestra playing "Home, Sweet Home."

Not only was the play absurd when it was not obvious, but little else seemed right about the production. The *Herald* complained that "in a landscape stretching off apparently hundreds of miles, the artist has not provided a sign of the presence of man, woman, child, or beast, or a place of habitation" and went on to note that the star's costumes—"dresses cut to the knees"—befitted a girl younger than Chip was supposed to be. (Photographs dispute this, showing Miss Maddern in ankle-length skirts.) Only Maddern's art and vitality—her "abundance of animal spirits" and "a merriment that is charming"—kept the play's brief New York visit from being even briefer.

According to the *Times*, A. Z. Chipman's **A Checkered Life** (5-15-82, Fifth Ave.) was termed as "original domestic drama" because "its continued performance will tend to make persons of ordinary understanding cling to the comforts of home rather than trust themselves to the temptations of the playhouse." Through the machinations of its villain, its hero, Ernest Lenwood (Chipman), is condemned as an embezzler and murderer of a policeman and so becomes a bearded outcast until the tables can be turned and the manacled troublemaker led off to jail. Critics felt many of the subordinate characters were lifted from older plays—the aged, blind father, for example, coming straight out of *Hazel Kirke*—and they also questioned the need for intruding numerous songs. *A Checkered Life*'s own life was short but not sweet.

Robert G. Morris, drama critic for the *Evening Telegram* and reputedly an old sea hand, was the author of **Old Shipmates** (5-22-82, 14th St.). His central figures were contrasting types: Captain Weathergage (Frank Mordaunt), a warmhearted whaler, and the scheming Captain Witham (J. F. Hagan). Witham has gambled away monies entrusted to him by Weathergage and also has dipped into the inheritance of his ward, Harriet Lane (Georgia Cayvan), daughter of another seaman. When Weathergage comes for a visit he brings with him Dan Denny (Charles B. Waite), who had witnessed the contract between Witham and Harriet's father and carries a copy of it. Witham, albeit accidently, kills Denny and, grasping the opportunity, appropriates the incriminating contract. Eventually Weathergage is able to expose his old friend and in so doing wins the affection of Harriet. The play had been touring successfully all season, and, perhaps because Morris was a respected colleague, his fellow critics treated it with kid gloves. The work, like his earlier *Up Salt Creek,* seems to have been uninspired but competent. Whatever its faults, it pleased enough playgoers to enjoy a reasonably prosperous month's stand. That same night, at Niblo's, other theatregoers could watch one of the several companies of *Uncle Tom's Cabin* to visit New York during the season.

Another play that had enjoyed some acclaim on the road was Sydney Rosenfeld's **Florinel** (5-29-82, Park). This time New York was not so welcoming, either to the play or to the debutante who assumed the title role. Florinel (Julia A. Hunt) has been attending an elite, strict seminary. When one of her friends sneaks out to an encounter with a young man, Florinel attempts to shield the friend by claiming she was the culprit. She is expelled. The young man in question, René de Runières (Charles B. Welles), meets her, and the two fall in love. Naturally a happy ending comes in for the final curtain, made all the happier by the discovery that Florinel is actually the granddaughter of the wealthy Duchess d'Arolles (Alice Grey). Miss Hunt abruptly faded from the theatrical scene, but Rosenfeld, who had written the 1879 *Dr. Clyde,* was on the threshold of a long, variegated, and often controversial career.

Another fledgling playwright came dreadfully a cropper with his "American Pictorial Melodrama," **The Living Age** (5-30-82, Union Square). The author was Frederick Bock, a member of Lawrence Barrett's acting company (he had been Modred in *Pendragon*). Bock doubled in brass by taking on the role of Adam Peterson, a resolute detective who hounds a peripatetic villain determined to steal $100,000 in bonds belonging to the beautiful orphan, Marie Durant (Ellie Wilton), even if he has to marry her to get them. Colorful settings seemed to have been the real reason for the shabbily assembled story, and one critic insisted the villain must have owned a marvelous invisible balloon to move as far and as fast as he did. The action took sleuth and felon from the French Market in New Orleans (scene of a bread riot during a yellow fever epidemic), to the Great Snowball Chamber at Mammoth Cave in Kentucky (complete with a shooting), to the famed Horseshoe Curve on the Pennsylvania Railroad (where the villain blows up Locomotive 317), to a New York City opium den, to a Brooklyn Heights library. Since Marston did the settings, the last offered a vista of New York by moonlight, one of the scene painter's favorite devices for eliciting applause. Sure enough, the scene got it from the hardy patrons who had toughed out the "painfully degrading" evening.

There seemed little chance that the season could

get any worse, but several of the plays that followed took that chance—and won or lost as the case may be. Three driveling pieces opened on the same night.

The best of the three was probably **Alvin Joslyn** (6-5-82, Windsor), a play clearly out of the same mold as *Joshua Whitcomb* and *A Messenger from Jarvis Section.* Once again a New England farmer finds occasion to come to New York, to be amazed at the cold ways of city slickers, and to amuse them in turn by his rural gaucheries. Of course, he bests the most devious of the slickers before heading back. Its star was Charles L. Davis, who found a more cordial reception in the very backwaters he purported to represent.

J. J. McCloskey and P. F. Baker's **Max Müller** (6-5-82, Standard) was another piece written, according to one reviewer, "for the benefit of our innocent rural friends," this time in the tradition of *Fritz, Our Cousin German* and other similar works.

And then there was **Mardo; or, The Nihilists of St. Petersburg** (6-5-82, Niblo's), ostensibly starring Frank I. Frayne. Its forebears seemingly were the dog dramas of a generation earlier. At least the *Times* reported, "The principal characters are assumed by a dog, Jack, a bear, Bruno, and four hyenas, who take the place of a lion with a black mane, which is advertised in the bills, but did not appear last night." Jack was obviously the star, such "a remarkably sensational artist" that he was called to take special bows at the close of the first and third acts. Since no major critic deigned to retail the plot, we can only guess how such characters, taken from real life, as Czar Alexander I, John Quincy Adams, and Moses Rothschild wove their way in and out of the action, or what sort of comic relief Mrs. Titus Andronicus Snakeroot provided. Perhaps playgoers were too intrigued by several effectively staged fires and a huge snowstorm to care. The *Times* concluded the play was "the worst dramatic effort which the Summer season has thus far produced, but who can tell what the morrow will bring forth?"

It brought forth *East Lynne,* which opened at the Fifth Avenue on the 10th with Ada Gray. Miss Gray was a touring star who had, according to advertisements, performed the play on the road "over 2000 times." Still grumpy, the *Times* concluded that she at least had had "the wisdom to act in obscure places," then turned the knife by allowing, "But this is Summer and Miss Gray is one of the evils of the time." She kept the house lit for nearly a month.

Joseph Bradford, who had written *Our Bachelors,* was the author of **One of the Finest** (6-19-82, 14th St.), a vehicle for the German-dialect comedian Gus

Williams. As Patrolman John Mishler, Williams spouted homey philosophy and bungled his way into correcting a number of wrongs, bringing the miscreant Hugh Hickman to task and helping some lovers on the rocky road to the altar.

Louis F. Baum's **The Maid of Arran** (6-19-82, Windsor) was a dramatization of William Black's novel *A Princess of Thule*. Second-rate players, including the dramatist, attempted to bring to life this tale of the troubled marriage of a simple, pragmatic, and unspoiled Scottish girl, who has been raised on a remote island, and a complex, romantic, and pampered Londoner. Black's pictures of wild Scottish backlands and their rugged inhabitants were tremendously popular but were at heart too cinematographic to be adapted to the restricted environs of the stage. The play disappeared from the records after a short tour, of which its lone week in Manhattan was part. Its actor-author did not; as L. Frank Baum he wrote *The Wizard of Oz*. But he is listed as having written several other plays before that—*Matches* (1882), *Kilmore* (1884), and *The Queen of Killarney* (1885)—all of which reportedly were produced, although none seems to have reached New York. Baum's real first name was Lyman, but he used numerous pen names during his career.

Maggie Weston's **The Boy Scout of the Sierras** (7-3-82, Windsor) starred N. S. Wood, the child prodigy of a few seasons back. The *Herald* reported, "The play is of the regular 'dime novel' type, and Lightning Lew [Wood] had little else to do but appear at very opportune moments to point a pistol at one of several of the villains. A good deal of gunpowder and red fire were used." The grand finale employed four prancing horses. Something called **Nan, the Good-for-Nothing** served as a curtain raiser.

1882–1883

For dedicated playgoers the new season, like the one just gone by, must have been not uninteresting, even if it was largely undistinguished. The incessant winds of change blew more forcefully and, for careful observers, more noticeably. Several inescapable landmarks signaled evolving tastes and the American theatre's timely response to this evolution. In October New York's Casino Theatre opened its doors for the first time. New theatres had been springing up with some regularity in New York and elsewhere, but the Casino was the first American playhouse built expressly to present popular musical shows. (Only the Tivoli Opera House in San Fancisco could be cited as a forerunner, but that auditorium still clung to its beer-garden adjuncts.) A few days after the Casino opened, the Park Theatre burned down. Possibly New York's first major theatre erected to house touring shows as opposed to a resident stock company, and certainly the first to install a phone in its box office, the playhouse nevertheless was of only small historical significance. The loss of a second playhouse was more momentous. Late in the season, the financially unsteady Booth's was sold and demolished to make way for a department store. The theatre had survived for little more than fourteen years. It had been built with the highest hopes as a "temple of the drama," a home for the loftiest examples of dramatic art. Mismanagement and the city's northward surge both had played a part in its demise, but so did unrealistic aspirations. (Broadway was to forget that lesson a quarter of a century later, with much the same results.) One other major theatre was also affected. For some time Palmer had been giving interviews in which he stated his aim to leave the Union Square. He made good his threat at the end of the season, bringing to an end that theatre's heyday and with it the end of the reign of its school of French melodrama. English and, oh so slowly, American writers moved into the foreground. Palmer's move also was the beginning of the end of both his noteworthy career and the primacy of the Union Square as New York's Rialto, although that would become obvious only with hindsight.

The ursurpation of new stages by musicals (mostly operettas) and the disappearance or changing policies of theatres were not the sole omens of an altering theatrical scene. With accelerating speed the old repertory—the reliance on revivals of classic and less eminent, aging favorites—was also giving way to productions of new works. As late as Thanksgiving, setting aside the visits of a few touring stars, at most two major revivals had been offered at first-class houses, although lesser theatres continued to provide homes for combinations presenting the likes of the Rankins and Lotta performing their standards.

The Passing Regiment passed through Daly's as a summer filler, beginning August 9. Other major houses began a parade of new entries several weeks later.

That parade got under way in earnest with Henry Pettitt's **The Black Flag** (8-21-82, Union Square), another in the new wave of London melodramas sparked by the success of *The World.* Its hero is Harry Glyndon (E. F. Thorne), whose worthless half-brother, Jack (T. J. Martin), attempts to murder their father, Owen Glyndon (Edwin Varrey), and have Harry imprisoned for the deed. Jack is abetted by a villainous if comic Jew, Sim Lazarus (Nat Goodwin). Of course, the truth prevails, so Harry can wed his father's ward, Naomi (Agnes Proctor). Thorne and Goodwin produced the show, and Goodwin's wife took on the trouser role of Ned. If a trouser role flew in the face of realism, other touches attempted to compensate. Red-coated soldiers engaged in an impressive changing of the guard, convicts were shown at work with picks, a dovecote contained real pigeons, and a newfangled bicycle was pedaled across the stage. The play ran for a month and subsequently toured successfully.

Its premiere coincided with that of Harry Meredith's **Ranch 10** (8-21-82, 14th St.), a new American work mingling sensation-melodrama with the growing appeal of western settings. Meredith was the star of his own work, playing twin brothers, Al and Tom McClelland. When Tom arrives to attend his brother's wedding to Annie Smalley (Emma Vaders), the ward of ranch owner Miss Coriander Lucretia Smalley (Annie Douglass), he learns that Al has been framed by a treacherous Indian, Joseph Kebook (Harry Clifton), for the murder of another ward, the Indian Silver Bud (Marie Acosta). Al has fled, so Tom takes his place both at the wedding and at the trial, where a verdict of not guilty is brought in. Al dies soon after, but Annie sees no reason to annul the marriage to Tom. Once more a curtain fell to the strains of "Home, Sweet Home" from the orchestra.

Realistic touches included live pigeons on the roof of the ranch; striking stage effects depicted the wedding taking place outdoors during a blizzard, and the ranch's destruction by fire. However, the *Herald* carped that the cowboys looked like "Italian ragpickers," a complaint echoed in the *Times,* which found that their "demeanor and attire were evidently borrowed from the tramps who lounge on park benches after nightfall."

George L. Stout's **The Blackbird** (8-26-82, Theatre Comique) was something of an oddity. A melodrama set in Ireland and recounting how Colonel Raymond Darcy (De Wolf Hopper) eludes his pursuers after the rout at Culloden, it was presented by Harrigan and Hart as the season opener at their playhouse. Both took supporting comic roles, and Harrigan joined his father-in-law, Dave Braham, to write a few songs for the work. Their fine scene painter, Charles W. Witham, abandoned the cityscapes so standard on their stage

for splendid outdoors sets that included a moonlit cascade and whirlpool. But such relatively serious matter was not their patrons' cup of tea—or glass of beer.

Maggie Mitchell may well have appealed to many of Harrigan and Hart's regulars, but she, too, tripped up when she opened her visit with **Elsa** (9-2-82, Park), C. T. Dazey's dramatization of Wilhelmine von Hillern's *Geier-Wally.* She portrayed a Tyrolean herder who comes into a fine estate but must deflect the petty cruelties and jealousies of her neighbors. When this failed to please, she hurried in a mounting of *Jane Eyre* (a startling vehicle for her, and one in which Charlotte Thompson recently had been seen at a combination house), then concluded her month-long engagement with her always welcome *Fanchon.*

A touch of the hoyden ran through most of Maggie Mitchell's roles and performances, as it did in those of such contemporaries as Lotta and Annie Pixley. It also seems to have been part and parcel of the heroine's character in the increasingly numerous plays about western life. Thus Miss Mitchell inevitably was called to mind when another play premiered two nights after her own return. So was M'liss, the heroine of an earlier play by one of the new work's co-authors. Clay M. Greene and Slason Thompkins's **Chispa** (9-4-82, 14th St.) was another saga of western life, one that had won popularity at home in California—a point certain to prejudice some New York critics against it. Marion Elmore, who had first come to America's attention as one of Lydia Thompson's British blonde burlesquers, was starred. A group of travelers, including a young couple with a baby, are stranded in the desert. When the young couple die, James Downey (W. N. Griffith) and an accomplice steal their papers, while Jake Stevens (Frank Losee) takes the baby in hand. Years later at Bachelor's Gulch, where Jake has raised the now grown Chispa, Downey returns, acting like a rich San Francisco swell. Chispa falls in love with him, but he is killed and Jake is blamed. The shock drives Chispa mad, and she wanders deliriously across the desert. Papers found on Downey make Chispa a wealthy girl, and she is soon restored to health.

The season's second example of the "Surrey school" of London melodrama was Paul Merritt and George Conquest's **Mankind** (9-5-82, Daly's), which the producer offered as part of his own "prefatory season." None of his best-loved performers was in his cast, but the play nonetheless proved interesting enough to chalk up a five-week run. Several critics remained undecided whether the play was to be taken seriously or was a superb sendup of a dubious tradition. Daly's biographer brother suggested why such uncertainty might arise with his description of the plot: "The chief miscreant in this play was *Groodge* [Charles Leclercq], a money-lender, aged 101, who strangles his old associate *Sharpley* [W. J. LeMoyne], a stripling of 73, with a silk pocket-handkerchief. The principal occupation of the characters, good and bad, consists in endeavoring to get possession of a will; that document is stolen by A, recovered by B, cribbed by C, and rescued by D in a wild scramble on the Thames embankment." Spectacular scenes included a view of Ramsgate Pier, Leicester Square, a London tenement during a riot, and a channel steamer enveloped in fog (thus allowing the hero to make an escape).

Laura Don, an actress more accepted in the Midwest than in New York, was the star of her own play **A Daughter of the Nile** (9-6-82, Standard). A sloppily plotted, weakly motivated story seemed designed as an excuse for changes of scene and costume. The heroine, a New York belle, after rejecting the hero, marries an Egyptian prince. Following his death, she moves to Paris, where she dresses in Oriental splendor while living in French luxury. The hero marries her half-sister. After the half-sister's death the hero, who turns out to be an English lord, and heroine finally tie the knot. Since Miss Don once had been Raymond's leading lady in *Fresh, the American,* in which she portrayed an Egyptian odalisque, she may have derived many of her ideas from the older play. But whereas Raymond had made a hit of the earlier comedy, the new one quickly disappeared.

Whatever its merits, or lack of them, it provided a breather from the continuing onslaught of English melodrama. Exasperated critics, not a few of whom pointed condemningly at Wallack's mounting of *The World* as the fountainhead of the deluge, were particularly scathing when that august house brought forth yet another example. Pettitt's **Taken from Life** (9-9-82, Wallack's) told the story of the secret marriage of Kate Denby (Rose Coghlan) and of the abduction of her child by its uncle, all set against a background of socialist and nihilist agitation. The *Times* angrily waved away the work as "stupid rubbish," then, surveying the Broadway scene, added forlornly, "There is not at this moment upon our stage a play seriously worth seeing." Buffeted by similar rejections and a series of lawsuits, Lester Wallack withdrew the work at the end of the month.

But the spate of melodramas continued, enlisting even the once vaunted "temple of the drama" as a home for Sims's **The Romany Rye** (9-18-82, Booth's). Years before the action of the play begins,

the master of Craig's Nest secretly had married a gypsy and had a son by her. Later he disowned them and married a more respectable lady. Gypsy and child were both rumored to have died. Now the estate is home to a son of the second marriage, Philip Royston (Charles Rockwell). His serene life comes crashing down with the arrival of Jack Hearne (John W. Morton), the Romany Rye, who announces that he is the supposedly dead son and knows the whereabouts of the marriage certificate that would substantiate his claim and make Philip illegitimate. Philip has Jack kidnapped and taken to a London slum, where Philip contrives to have an old hag drug Jack so that he can be taken out to the Thames and drowned. The hag, however, takes pity on Jack and helps him escape. Philip is arrested for attempted murder, and Jack is declared the rightful heir. William Voegtlin's elaborate sets depicted the palatial estate, the slums of London, a boat on the Thames (where Jack uses life preservers and oars to subdue his would-be drowners and then jumps overboard to freedom), and a shipwreck. Despite a critical drubbing, playgoers decided this melodrama was one of the best of the lot. It ran through November and toured for several seasons.

Vying for attention that same night were two other openings. One was William Gill's **My Sweetheart** (9-18-82, 14th St.), which straddled the line between comedy and musical in telling how an openhearted innocent wins her sweetheart away from the wiles of a more cynical rival. With it Minnie Palmer found a vehicle that served her well in both America and England for the rest of the decade. At the Union Square, Joseph Jefferson and Mrs. Drew began a six-week stopover in *The Rivals.*

Leonard Grover's **Viva** (9-25-82, Niblo's) was a melodrama lightened by song and dance. Its story of an Italian street-singer seduced by a lecherous aristocrat proves to be its heroine's dream. Since its stars were Alice and Louis Harrison, two well-liked comics, no one took the melodrama seriously anyway.

In many eyes Lester Wallack atoned for his recent sins with his offering of G. W. Godfrey's "sparkling" English comedy **The Parvenu** (9-30-82, Wallack's). The impoverished Sir Fulke Pettigrew (Harry Edwards) and his pushy, vulgar wife (Effie Germon) have decided that their attractive daughter, Gwendolen (Ellie Wilton), should marry a rich upstart, Joseph Ledger, M.P. (William Elton), especially since Ledger holds the mortgage on Pettigrew's estate. They are appalled when Gwendolen announces her preference for a poor young artist, Claude Glynne (William Herbert). Talk suggests

Claude may actually be a wealthy peer, so the Pettigrews do an about-face, but when the talk proves only talk they do a second 180-degree turn. Through all this Ledger watches with a quiet compassion. His wedding gift to Gwendolen and Claude is the Pettigrews' mortgage. For all the critical applause, the comedy ran no longer than the lambasted melodrama that preceded it—one month.

On October 2, Raymond came into the Park with *Fresh, the American,* giving those playgoers who might want to do so a chance to compare it with *A Daughter of the Nile.* Later in his month's engagement he offered his Colonel Sellers. Immediately after his visit closed, the Park burned down.

For theatre buffs following the slow, uncertain development of American playwriting, October's first entry was a milestone. Bronson Howard's **Young Mrs. Winthrop** (10-9-82, Madison Square) was one of the first significant American dramas to take a serious look at materialism and social climbing. While Douglas Winthrop (George Clarke) is totally absorbed in his business, his wife, Constance (Carrie Turner), is equally preoccupied with her social life. One night, pleading an important business matter, Douglas asks his wife to remain home with their sick child while he goes out. She agrees, but during the evening a visit by a scatter-brained, garrulous gossip, Mrs. Chetwyn (Agnes Booth), triggers a suspicion that Douglas may be unfaithful. Constance rushes out to spy on her husband. In fact, Douglas does have legitimate business concerns at the same home where a ball is being held. While the Winthrops are away, their child dies. Its death brings recriminations and a separation until a kindly family lawyer, Buxton Scott (Thomas Whiffen), effects a reconciliation and forces both Douglas and Constance to face the nature of their own obsessions.

For all its seriousness, the play presented clever and pertinent comic relief in the character of Mrs. Chetwyn, who can never remember which of her husbands figures in any story she is telling. But in his use of asides Howard still demonstrated allegiance to a tradition soon to be swept away. The nature of the play and its subdued performance were precisely right for the tiny Madison Square's intimacy, so the drama became the fourth in a row to record a long run—190 performances. It remained a favorite in stock until World War I.

In London Pinero's **The Squire** (10-10-82, Daly's) had become entangled in controversy when Thomas Hardy accused the playwright of plagiarizing *Far from the Madding Crowd.* Most reviewers sided with the novelist, despite Pinero's unequivocal assertion that he had never read the book. Certainly the characters and adventures of Kate Verity (Ada Rehan), Lieutenant Throndyke (John Drew), and Gilbert Hythe (Yorke Stephens) paralleled those of Bathsheba, Sergeant Troy, and Gabriel. Yet even in his early years Pinero was a superior craftsman, something acknowledged dramatizers of the novel, even Cazauran, often were not. Moreover, Daly's production seems to have been cast more felicitously than had the earlier one at the Union Square, with Miss Rehan again showing remarkable range and skill. A pleasant "surprise of the performance" was James Lewis as a shepherd in his nineties. Long afterward Odell could still hear his recurrent plaint, "I'm an old man I yam, I yaven't got a tooth in my yed." Stolen goods or not, the mounting ran for nearly two months.

Bartley Campbell's **Friend or Foe** (10-16-82, Windsor) was a reworking of his 1875 *On the Rhine,* which had been played in San Francisco but never in New York. Campbell rewrote the play as a vehicle for W. J. Scanlan, then just embarking on a career as a singing actor specializing in Irish parts. Refreshingly, the story did not dredge up the standard Irish-English conflict. Carrol Moore (Scanlan) is taken into the home of an educated Frenchman and falls in love with his host's daughter, Andrea (Florine Arnold). Their romance is obstructed by the host's landlord, who covets Andrea for himself. However, the Franco-Prussian War intervenes. The landlord is conscripted but offers 15,000 francs for a substitute. Carrol accepts the offer and gives the money to Andrea and her father so they can buy their property. Carrol is later captured by the Germans and sentenced to death. Andrea assists in his escape, and the curtain falls as they are planning their wedding. Even before it opened, the *Herald* predicted it should have "a great go on the bowery." Several days later the *Mirror* reported, "The play is deserving of the success it has attained, for it furnishes a very delightful evening's amusement." It also furnished Scanlan with a role he played for several years. His opening night was the same as that of a revival of *Only a Farmer's Daughter* at the 14th Street Theatre.

New theatres continued to crop up to meet the demands of a growing and spreading city. The Mount Morris Theatre had opened a few weeks earlier on 131st Street in Harlem, joining the list of the city's outlying combination houses. On October 24, it offered the Manhattan premiere of Robert G. Morris's **The Irish-American,** a play that had toured earlier but never before braved even the outer reaches of the island. Quite possibly last season's success of *Old Shipmates* had spurred the venture. Once again the drama critic–playwright gave evidence of his theatrical know-how, if not of any higher abilities. Edward O'Donohue returns to his native Ireland to marry the girl he left behind when he went to America to seek his fortune. He discovers that his beloved Norah Kiely and her father are being pressed (shades of *Friend and Foe*) by their unscrupulous landlord, Daniel Macfarland, who is refused Norah's hand and so attempts to frame his tenants and Edward for treason. Macfarland is eventually shot, and the lovers sail for a better life in America.

On the 26th Salvini began a visit at the Fifth Avenue, presenting such expected favorites as *Othello, The Gladiator,* and *La Morte Civile.* Also unchanged were the rave notices he had grown accustomed to. Since the great star would only perform four times weekly, his English-speaking supporting cast filled in the other nights with *Rose Michel.*

The month ended with the first visit by Charles Wyndham and his Criterion Theatre company from London. Their initial offering was a double bill. A three-character curtain raiser, F. W. Boughton's **Ruth's Romance,** was coupled with H. J. Byron's adaptation of Edmond Gondinet and Alexandre Bisson's *Un Voyage d'agrément,* now called **Fourteen Days** (10-31-82, Union Square). In the latter Wyndham assumed the role of the glib, philandering Peregrine Porter. After a night on the town with a lady who was definitely not his wife, he misses a portrait of his wife that he has carried about with him, and, suspecting the lady has lifted it, runs after her. In his hurry he knocks down a policeman and earns a jail sentence of fourteen days for his disorderly conduct. Porter's attempts to avoid explaining matters to his wife constitute much of the fun.

For the most part critics and playgoers responded favorably, perhaps giving the edge to the men in the company. Wyndham, despite what some heard as his unpleasant voice, was a master farceur. The leading lady provoked gasps when she smoked a cigarette onstage. But some reviewers had curiously unkind reservations about all the women, with the *Spirit of the Times* remarking chauvinistically, "None of the ladies is a professional beauty. All are good looking and will become beautiful after a few month's stay in America has taught them how to make up and how to dress," then adding, "There is one thing in the performance that could be advantageously cut, and that is the stay-laces. English women are far too fond of the corset."

Out of courtesy to his compatriot Lillie Langtry, Wyndham had delayed his opening for a night to avoid a conflict. His generosity went for naught when just before her opening night at the Park the theatre was destroyed by fire. The actress was left without a stage until Lester Wallack postponed his next production and gave over his theatre to the English star. She debuted on November 6. Theatrical circles had been buzzing with excitement ever since her visit had been announced. Her chestnut-haired, grey-eyed beauty was renowned, her position in English high society added an extra cachet, but, most of all, gossip about her private love affairs, especially with the Prince of Wales, had whetted interest. Her program was variegated if not novel, beginning with Tom Taylor's *An Unequal Match,* then turning to *As You Like It* and *The Honeymoon.* Inevitably all the advance puffery led to some disappointment. The Jersey Lily was seen as good-looking but not truly an exceptional beauty, and as a skillful, intelligent but not inspiring actress. However, there was no disappointment about her ability to pack a theatre. She grossed nearly $62,000 in her four-week stand. When she returned in April for an equally profitable fortnight at the Fifth Avenue, she added Gilbert's *Pygmalion and Galatea* to her repertory.

But for now the Fifth Avenue, having played host to Salvini, turned its stage over to an American, McCullough, on the 13th. Perhaps more than any other major American tragedian of the time except Booth, he had firmly fixed his repertory. As usual, he brought out *Virginius,* Bird's *The Gladiator, The Hunchback, The Lady of Lyons, Brutus, Ingomar,* and *Damon and Pythias,* plus three Shakespearean offerings: *King Lear, Hamlet,* and *Othello.* At fifty-one he still appeared to be a fine specimen of a man and in full control of his acting skills, although privately he had begun to manifest signs of the insanity that would soon drive him from the stage.

For their second bill, Wyndham and his players presented an only partially new play at the Union Square on the 20th. *Brighton* was merely Bronson Howard's 1870 hit *Saratoga,* reset and retailored to please West End audiences. New Yorkers were unperturbed by the changes and delighted with the brisk ensemble playing, but when the company's tour later reached San Francisco it was met with howls of outrage for tampering with an American work.

Of course, Americans were all the while Americanizing foreign plays, such as von Moser's *Reif von Reiflingen,* which playgoers could enjoy as **Our English Friend** (11-25-82, Daly's). The visitor from overseas is Digby de Rigby (James Lewis), whose well-intentioned if impetuous actions at the home where he is staying lead the occupants to believe he is courting every young lady under its roof. Lewis deftly reined in his somewhat rambunctious style to win over many playgoers and critics, but some thought the role should have gone to John Drew, who was reportedly miffed at being passed over. A single elegant setting, which at one point served to house a cotillion in which all the principals danced away merrily, helped keep Daly's costs down and allowed him to wind up with a nice profit for the play's eight-week run.

Financially Palmer's next mounting brought him little if any profit, but it did earn him some praise. **The Rantzaus** (11-28-82, Union Square) was Cazauran's adaptation of the Émile Erckmann-Alexandre Chatrian play known variously as *Les Rantzaus* and *Les Deux Frères*. Two brothers, John (J. H. Stoddard) and James Rantzau (F. de Belleville), have had a bitter falling-out over their father's will but learn to their chagrin that their own children have come to love each other. John's response is to beat and attempt to kill his daughter, Louise (Maud Harrison); the cooler James merely disowns his son, Philip (Walden Ramsey). Shocked by John's brutal treatment of Louise, the quiet, humane Father Florence (John Parselle) gradually succeeds in making John see the virtues of compassion. In turn John humbles himself before his brother to beg that they both let the past be forgotten and allow their children to wed.

Stoddard's dramatic, emotive performance received many of the best notices. His hurling Louise about the room and kneeling abjectly before James elicited appreciative applause. The curious theatrical cliché of first cousins in love seemed to bother no one. But other matters did. The *Times* was disturbed by the increasingly short season the Union Square stock company now played in New York. (This late November production was the first of its "regular season.") It noted how the amazingly rapid growth of touring companies was prompting Palmer and other managers to cut costs by renting out their theatres and taking their own companies on the road, where larger theatres and a New York reputation ensured bigger returns. It also lamented the steady unraveling of the once steadfast Union Square ensemble, insisting, "Mr. Palmer's company is losing something of its fine prestige." Even before Palmer threw in the towel at season's end, a highly publicized disagreement would hasten the unraveling.

While Palmer was nearing the end of his decade-long allegiance to French drama and Daly was consolidating his hold on Americanized German comedy, Wallack clung to his English loyalties. Yet he was paying a price for it. In recent seasons only his mountings of new melodramas (along with outside bookings) had made much money for him, though the fattened tills were accompanied by critical drubbings and probably some defections among regular playgoers. High comedy mingled with revivals of classic English comedy had been the glory of this venerable ensemble. But now, even in his fine, new, conveniently located playhouse, these failed to draw as once they had. A disappointingly small first-night audience was followed by many later evenings of unfilled seats for G. W. Godfrey's **The Queen's Shilling** (12-4-82, Wallack's). After Kate Greville (Rose Coghlan) is caught in the rain while riding, she exchanges her wet habit for a serving girl's frock. Both Frank Esmonde (William Herbert), a young trooper, and his superior, Colonel Daunt (C. P. Flockton), fall in love with the supposed barmaid. A duel and near court-martial ensue before Daunt concedes that Esmonde is the better man for Kate. Despite largely laudatory reviews, Wallack was forced to close the show after two weeks.

On the 11th the resplendent Modjeska arrived for a month's visit, with Maurice Barrymore as her leading man. Her repertory consisted of *As You Like It*, *Twelfth Night*, *Camille*, *Frou-Frou*, and *Odette*. All of the plays had been seen before in New York, some many times, but, except for *Camille* and *Frou-Frou*, they were recent additions to the star's roster. Of the supporting cast, only Barrymore aroused any enthusiasm. And there were jibes aplenty at the wrinkled, unclean scenery.

On the other hand, allowing for her accent and newness to the roles, her interpretations were greeted with huzzas. The *Times*'s critic fell back on another of those catalogues so irresistible to contemporary reviewers to describe the ideal Rosalind, "a rare buoyancy of fancy and feeling, a lightness which is rapid as sun-play, a spontaneity that flows like a fountain[,] . . . [a] full, complex nature—simple enough, however, in its first impulse—the whole tenderness and sweetness of amorous womanhood," and concluded that in describing his ideal heroine he had described the star. Writing in the *Century* magazine, J. Ranken Towse particularly admired her love scenes with Orlando, "in which by an infinite variety of subtle touches, she suggests to the audience the archness and coquetry of women, while to her lover she is nothing but a wayward boy." The feminine, rich brocades and silks of the doublets she wore as the supposedly impoverished Ganymede contrasted with her tight-fitting, over-the-knees boots to underscore the duality. Towse said of her Viola, "At Booth's Theatre, [the] coast scene was a marvel of shabbiness and grotesque unfitness; yet the actress, by her power of pantomime, created a vivid impression of cold and storm, of suffering, fatigue, and fear."

Until this late date midway in the season, revivals had been exceedingly rare, apart from those offered by such stars as Salvini, Langtry, and Modjeska or those regularly moving in and out of the lesser combination houses. A rash of them began with Robson and Crane's presentation of Boucicault's slambang *Forbidden Fruit* at the Fifth Avenue on the 11th. On the 20th Wallack's brought out *Old Heads and Young Hearts* with John Gilbert as Jesse Rural. Christmas night saw Kate Claxton in *The Two Orphans* replacing Boucicault's farce; more than one Broadway critic, as faddist as ever, already was dismissing the eight-year-old success as crude and shopworn.

Wallack's greeted 1883 on January 3 with a revival of *Ours* in which the aging Lester Wallack appeared for the first time on his new stage. Five nights later Booth's was home to a revival of *The Corsican Brothers,* a production meant to inaugurate the career of Charles Thorne, Jr., as a major touring star. But Thorne was a dying man and had to relinquish the leading role of the twins after the second performance. F. C. Bangs assumed the dual parts, and the mounting struggled through a month's stand.

For all practical purposes Palmer closed the books on his management of the Union Square with the second production of his "regular" season, Feuillet's **A Parisian Romance** (1-10-83, Union Square), as adapted by the faithful Cazauran. Its hero is the high-principled if naive Henri de Targy (F. de Belleville). Learning that his late father had squandered three million francs that he held in trust for a young girl until her wedding, Henri determines that he and his wife, Marcelle (Sara Jewett), must sacrifice everything in order to repay what he deems a debt of honor. Never mind that the young girl is now the rich Baroness Chevrial (Eleanor Carey) and generously agrees to forget the matter. Her greedy, conniving husband, a dissipated voluptuary, demands full payment with interest. Indeed, some of the interest he hopes to receive would shock Henri, who does not hear the baron murmur aloud, "I wonder how his pretty little wife will bear poverty? H'm! We shall see." While turning Marcelle's head, the baron still finds time for his affair with Rosa Guerin (Maud Harrison), a beautiful ballerina. Rosa, unlike Marcelle, is clever enough to see through the baron. Aware that he hopes to bankrupt

her, too, so that she will be totally beholden to him, she asks his advice on financial matters and quietly succeeds by doing the opposite of what he tells her. To dazzle Rosa, he holds a sumptuous banquet, which he calls a "petit souper," for her in his magnificent frescoed and domed hall. The dome rests on huge Corinthian-capped marble pillars with bronzed and plated bases. Between these the baron has had a large table set with crystal, silver, snowy linen, palms, flowers, and candelabra. Before the guests arrive, the baron saunters down a staircase at the rear and looks out for a moment on a blue-black panorama of Paris with the Arc de Triomphe lit only by the moon. But his poor state of health is betrayed by his palsied movements as he attempts to adjust his monocle. When his guests come and begin to dance he joins in, until exhaustion forces him to seek a chair. Determined to brave out matters, he rises to propose a toast, only to collapse and shatter the glass he held so high. Attempting then to return upstairs, he loses his balance and tumbles down dead. Marcelle, shamed by having capitulated to the baron's entreaties, commits suicide, leaving Henri and the baroness with the possibility of making a happy marriage.

A disagreement before the opening led to one of Broadway's most memorable first nights and to a long run for the play. The role of the baron had been assigned to J. H. Stoddart, who begged off. Cazauran then attempted to enlist Nat Goodwin, who also declined. As a result Palmer took a chance on a twenty-nine-year-old newcomer, Richard Mansfield, who woke up the next morning to find himself famous.

• • •

Richard Mansfield (1854–1907) was born in Berlin. His mother was Erminia Rudersdorff, a celebrated prima donna; his father was an English merchant. He was first brought to America by his mother in 1872, and before returning to England he performed in amateur theatricals. He came back permanently in 1882. For about a year he performed mostly in musicals. Small and scholarly in appearance, he was a punctilious artist and proved venturesome and often foresighted in selecting his plays. Unfortunately, he was also exceptionally arrogant and duplicitous, thus earning the hatred of many associates.

• • •

William Winter described Mansfield's careful makeup and stance: "The face was wonderfully expressive—hard, crafty, wrinkled; the hair was thin, dark, and here and there slightly touched with copper-red; the jaws were partially relaxed, but were drawn together, at crucial moments, by a semi-conscious effort; the hands were a little tremulous, the eyes a little bleared and partially closed; the limbs a little frail, the condition and demeanor in general expressive of physical lassitude but unabated appetite; the person was richly and elegantly attired, though in somewhat gaudy style, and the manners were invariably those of the successful man of the world." In addition, photographs show Mansfield's Baron sporting a neatly twirled, curved mustache and a hint of a goatee. Many photographs of Mansfield in this and other roles also suggest he may have suffered from esotropia (semi-crossed eyes), which no doubt gripped the attention of patrons close enough to notice it.

Antiquarians could take comfort in Daly's revival on the 13th of *She Would and She Would Not,* its first New York mounting since the producer last offered it in 1869. No doubt many of these same playgoers applauded Mary Anderson in her four-week stand that began at the Fifth Avenue on January 15 and offered nothing new but fell back on *The Lady of Lyons, The Daughter of Roland, Pygmalion and Galatea, The Hunchback, Romeo and Juliet,* and *Ingomar.* She reappeared briefly in April. Shortly after she concluded her second visit she left for London. Her seasons there would have remarkable effect on her art.

John T. Raymond's sunny, humorous art needed no London polishing. His time-honed skills glossed over flaws in even a mediocre vehicle such as George H. Jessop and William Gill's **In Paradise** (1-15-83, Grand Opera). At a mining camp in Idaho, Francis Rawdon (G. F. DeVere) threatens to expose the criminal past of Boozy Old Joe (J. F. Dean) if Joe's daughter, Melia (Stella Boniface), refuses to marry him. Melia would prefer to marry Stephen Dallas (O. H. Barr), a young prospector. Only when Major Bob Belter (Raymond), a sometime editor, sometime lawyer, discovers that Rawdon is still legally married to a wife whom he deserted are matters concluded satisfactorily. The *Times*'s review hinted at increasing postwar class distinctions when it noted disdainfully the play's frequent resort to "street slang" and commented that such speech might please the gallery but not patrons in more expensive seats. Still, most plays and players had to be careful to strike a balance that would lure all manner of playgoers. Not for another quarter of a century and the coming of films would the gallery trade be seduced away and a new concept of theatre emerge. Meanwhile, Raymond had found one more play that would serve him profitably in ensuing seasons.

On the 17th Wallack's brought out a house favorite, *She Stoops to Conquer,* which occupied the stage for only a few nights until a new offering was ready. The new play was Henry Arthur Jones and Henry Herman's London success **The Silver King** (1-27-83, Wallack's). Its three-month New York run was a season record, matched only by *A Parisian Romance.* Wilfred Denver (Osmond Tearle) is an alcoholic failure whose lack of enterprise has reduced him, his wife, Nellie (Rose Coghlan), and his children to the direst poverty. For this failure he is reviled by Nellie's former suitor, Geoffrey Ware (Harry Bell). He goes to the old rival's home to confront him, but there he is met and chloroformed by a gang of thieves headed by the suave Captain Skinner, alias Spider (Herbert Kelcey). Skinner kills the rival, and when Denver regains consciousness he discovers the body and surmises he himself is the murderer. He flees to America, leaving his family to fend for itself. In America he turns over a new leaf and strikes it rich in Nevada. With his newfound wealth he returns to England to make amends to Nellie and the children and to unmask Captain Skinner. One of the best of contemporary melodramas, the play remained a strong attraction at Wallack's and elsewhere for the rest of the decade.

"A stunning play" was how Augustin Daly had characterized Georges Ohnet's **Serge Panine** (2-1-83, Daly's) when he had sent the French text to his brother Joseph to adapt. Parisians obviously had agreed, for they had accorded the original French production a long run. To Daly's profound dismay, New York's reception was frigid. The play revolved around the money-hungry Prince Serge Panine (John Drew), who throws over Jeanne de Cernay (Ada Rehan), the girl he loves, to marry young Lottie Belyew (Mary Shaw) at the urging of her rich, title-mad mother (Fanny Morant). Some of the problem may have arisen from Joseph's viewing the play as a "comedy of manners" even though it ended with the death of the prince. (In the original he was shot by his mother-in-law; at Daly's he killed himself with a large horse pistol.) But whatever its shortcomings, it gave playgoers a chance to welcome to Daly's Fanny Morant, so long of the now crumbling Union Square Theatre ensemble, and to assess the early work of Mary Shaw, an actress of intellectual brilliance if little real fire.

Plump blonde Annie Pixley also suffered a major disappointment when she attempted to break away from her popular *M'liss* and try Fred Marsden's **Zara** (2-5-83, Grand Opera). This spunky heroine, "a romping girl with gypsy blood in her veins," thwarts an attempt by several villains to foist a false heiress on Sir Godfrey Moslyn (M. C. Daly), retrieving the telltale papers at pistol point. Somehow occasion was found for her to sing Gilbert and Sullivan's "The Magnet and the Churn."

Nor could critics find much to admire in Anson Pond's **Her Atonement** (2-12-83, 14th St.), but the public ate up its spectacle and tear-jerking melodrama, so the play remained a lively attraction, especially on the road, for the rest of the century. The play was set against the background of the Civil War, with a regiment of country recruits trooping to the Courtland Street ferry to embark on the first leg of their trip to the front. Among them is James Morton (Myron Leffingwell), who is suspected of having murdered the unfaithful lover of Martha West (Emily Rigl). Four years later the regiment returns in triumph with Morton a hero. But he is promptly arrested and brought to trial. When it looks as if he will be hanged for a crime he did not commit, the real murderer confesses: none other than Martha, who swallows a fatal dose of poison after saving Morton's neck. Comedy relief was provided by Patrolman Mulligan (M. J. Gallagher), who would "rather be a live policeman than a dead hero" and whose principal duty seems to be to keep chasing a small newsboy, Johnny (Little Gracie Foster). A panorama showed the ferry crossing the Hudson and the troops reassembling at the New Jersey railroad station. Later a brass band and drum corps accompanying the returning troops as they paraded by Printing House Square won a rousing ovation when they blared out "Marching Through Georgia."

Most newspapers paid no more attention to a revival that opened at Booth's on the same night, even though it was produced by a major producer of the time, John Stetson, and had excellent scenery by two of the era's leading scene painters, Joseph Clare and William Voegtlin. After all, it was only the old warhorse *Monte Cristo*—Fechter's version, without the now dead Fechter to play the lead. Instead its star was a thirty-five-year-old actor who had appeared only intermittently in New York and was better known in Chicago and San Francisco. James O'Neill was a handsome man with a florid face dominated by brilliant brown eyes and with a deeptoned, musical voice. He had begun to earn respect as a performer of the newer, more subdued and realistic school of acting. Several critics implied such acting was all wrong for this sort of melodramatic work, so O'Neill soon changed to the more ornate style of the older romantic school. Before long the public was eating out of his hand.

Several supercharged moments quickly became identified with his performance. The first closed the second act, when Dantès, changing places with a dead fellow prisoner who had told him the whereabouts of a vast treasure, is dumped in the sea, rises from the waters, and exclaims, "Saved! Mine, the treasures of Monte Cristo! The world is mine!" Then came the counting up as he avenged himself on the three men who engineered his unjust imprisonment. The third-act curtain falls with Dantès pointing to the dead Villefort and shouting "One!" In the fifth and final act the other malefactors perish to his "Two!" and "Three!" Eventually, knowing audiences joined the hero in crying out the score. Thereafter, until late in his career, O'Neill played little else.

A third play that would enjoy revivals for the rest of the century was **7-20-8; or, Casting the Boomerang** (2-24-83, Daly's), taken from Franz von Schönthan's *Die Schwabenstreich*. By returning to the German stage, which had served him so well in the past, Daly scored one of his biggest and most enduring hits. After *Portrait of a Lady*, depicting a beautiful woman and her huge dog, is hung as picture #728 at the Academy's annual exhibition, a handsome young man-about-town, Courtney Corliss (John Drew), determines to find out who the mysterious subject is and marry her. His search brings him to the country estate of Launcelot Bargiss (James Lewis), where he discovers that Launcelot's daughter, Flos (Ada Rehan), is the sitter. He also meets Signor Tamborini (William Gilbert), who apparently had been engaged in the same search at the behest of Lord Lawntennis. Flos is bored cooped up so far from the city and fears she will "die of the blues," so Courtney suggests she try a little adventure, assuring her that if youthful follies boomerang they return only to amuse us in retrospect. Meanwhile, Mrs. Bargiss (Mrs. Gilbert) has arranged for the publication of poems her husband had sent her when they were courting, unaware that he had cribbed them from Shakespeare and elsewhere. To celebrate the publication and give Flos a chance for some fun, Courtney prevails on the Bargisses to come to New York. The trip is no fun for Launcelot, who is caught having a little fling of his own and must spend a sizable sum to buy up all the copies of his supposed works. Matters end happily for Courtney when he determines that Lork Lawntennis is not his rival but is seeking merely to buy Flos's dog.

The play ran only until late April, at which time commitments to tour forced Daly to take it on the road. But he revived it regularly thereafter. Its success erased the problems and losses that had plagued Daly since he inaugurated his second company, and it confirmed for playgoers the supremacy of his four capital farceurs. Daly took his title from the theatre at 728 Broadway, which he had used after his first house burned and which by 1883 was Harrigan and Hart's Theatre Comique.

Not many of his colleagues agreed with the critic of the *Dramatic Mirror* when he wrote, "With the dual exceptions of *The Ticket-of-Leave-Man* and *The Silver King,* no modern British drama will stand comparison with *Siberia.*" They found it episodic, filled with cardboard characters, and riddled with trite dialogue. Of course, Bartley Campbell's **Siberia** (2-26-83, 14th St.) was an American play. It was also the fourth major opening in a row that would find an audience for years to come. Albeit it quickly disappeared from better stages, it was welcomed in neighborhood and other lesser houses until World War I. Campbell's story undoubtedly was suggested by articles that filled newspapers after the assassination of Czar Alexander II. Its heroines, Sara (Georgia Cayvan) and Marie (Blanche Mortimer), are daughters of a Christian mother and Jewish father. In the midst of the pogroms and persecutions that followed the czar's death, the cynical, libertine governor, Jaracoff (George Hoey), attempts to seduce Marie and is stabbed to death by Sara for his pains. She is condemned as a nihilist and sent, with her sister, to Siberia. On their way there and in the prison camp they encounter real nihilists, bigots, lovers, and other assorted figures. A prison revolt allows them to escape, and at the last curtain they would seem to be heading for a ship that will take them to America.

A month elapsed before another nonmusical play opened at a major New York theatre. Of course, all that while playgoers enjoyed a rich choice of entertainments. Besides the newly arrived pieces, *The Silver King* and *A Parisian Romance* continued to flourish, as did several musicals. Salvini gave some performances at the Academy of Music. Barrett brought his repertory into the Grand Opera on the heels of Frank Mayo's appearance there in *The Streets of New York.* Another old Boucicault work, *The Long Strike,* could be viewed at the Windsor. It is difficult, almost impossible at this far remove, to judge just how playgoers approached the entertainments at the peripheral combination houses, or just precisely which playgoers went to them. Reviews continue to suggest that the gallery gods were far more vocal at such houses than they dared be at the first-class theatres. Did this dissuade more well-bred patrons from troubling themselves to go there? Did

Mayo or Barrett act more broadly for these audiences? Time and again critics complained that stars who spent too much time away from New York coarsened their art. Was this local chauvinism, or did it imply a knowing flexibility in performance? And if, indeed, the road was coarsening, did the neighborhood theatres of a large metropolis provide a sort of middle ground?

Boucicault himself was star and author of the play that probably lured most inveterate first-nighters back into the theatre, **Vice Versa** (3-26-83, Star). The playhouse with a name new to Broadway was actually the old Wallack's at Broadway and 13th. It had served briefly as a home to German-language plays before returning to the ranks of regular Broadway playhouses. As such it was attempting to enter the lists in an area that had surrendered its primacy to Madison Square, so its career, while distinguished at first, would just as often be uncertain. A hint of that could be seen in the opening attraction, for Boucicault, although still popular with the public, clearly was written out. Playing the role of the lordly Phoenix O'Flattery, Boucicault made his first appearance in a scarlet satin dressing gown, sea-green trousers, and yellow "Dundreary" whiskers. O'Flattery's main concern is how to avoid being ensnared by an aggressively insistent widow, Mrs. Clingstone Peach (Sadie Martinot). He decides the best way is to change places with his valet (shades of the previous season's *Quits*), hoping the lady is too starry-eyed to notice the difference. She is not. Instead she changes places with her maid and stoops to conquer. Although the *Tribune* thought that "much of the mood in which Mr. Boucicault wrote 'London Assurance' has survived in him—the impatient aversion to dullness, the relish of sensuousness, the disposition to satire," the play was a quick failure, so Boucicault filled the rest of his engagement with revivals of *The Shaughraun* and *The Colleen Bawn,* and one other new play in May.

Never Too Late to Mend (3-26-83, Booth's) was a dramatization of Charles Reade's 1856 propagandistic novel. Set in Australia, it meshed the saga of a young man who must earn a sum of money to win a father's consent to marry his daughter with a harrowing account of a criminal transported for thievery. Neither story caught critics' attention as commandingly as did the scenery. Clare's farm, with real animals, and model prison both were praised, along with Voegtlin's "view of Gold Stream," showing a waterfall, with real water, at sunrise. But these artists exerted themselves to no avail. The production was announced cautiously as a limited engagement and was withdrawn after two weeks.

Critics and playgoers went their separate ways when it came to **Vim; or, A Visit to Puffy Farm** (3-26-83, Bijou). This new vehicle for the famous female impersonator Neil Burgess was advertised as being "In Three Acts and a NIGHTMARE" and as offering a "Patented Revolving Stage." But critics saw only an uninspired, hand-me-down comedy, whose central figure, Tryphena Puffy, was "a character very like the Widow Bedott," "hardly more than an imitation of Widow Bedott," or the "twin sister of the famous widow." Like the widow, Tryphena is "a lady mighty in her own opinion and content to act wholly on her own judgment." There were some differences. She lives in Maine and, more important, has a husband. That poor man is so thrown off balance by his wife that even his dreams become weird. In the nightmare scene that takes up much of the last act he finds himself at a circus, where he watches Tryphena, "in fairy garb," ride bareback on a gaudily bedecked steed. In earlier farm scenes, real livestock was onstage. Despite critical disapproval, audiences apparently relished the fare. So *Vim* had a relatively long, prosperous career.

Some future doctoral candidate might care to ponder what relation *Vim* had with *My Opinions,* which Burgess had tried out the previous November in Brooklyn and which was taken from Marietta Holley's *Josiah Allen's Wife.* Tryphena's husband was also called Josiah, and many other characters had similar or identical names in both plays and were often interpreted by the same performers. Thus Clara Stoneall played Betsy Sonnet in *Vim* and Betsy Bobbitt in *My Opinions,* while May Taylor was Mattie Sommers in one and Maggie Snow in the other. Both plays have a character named Frank Thornton, although different actors took the part in Manhattan and Brooklyn.

Few if any American plays had created as much controversy as Salmi Morse's **The Passion Play,** sometimes called simply *The Passion* (3-30-83, Temple of the Passion). Its original production in San Francisco in 1879, when James O'Neill had portrayed Christ, had provoked protests, parades, court hearings, and a police raid. Denied a regular New York stage, Morse, who was described at the time variously as a Jew and an apostate Jew, as devoutly dedicated and deranged, was forced to set up his own auditorium and become his own producer. Morse carefully called the performance "private," and admission seems to have been by invitation. Morse's guests included not only religious figures of all faiths and a cross-section of theatrical names but

the district attorney and police commissioner. Nonetheless, word of mouth had spread, and the crush in front of the theatre turned into a melee. Clothing was torn, a woman fainted, and at least one aggressive crasher had to be turned away by force. Apparently the whole play, reputedly twenty-four full-length acts, was much too long for presentation in a single evening, so only six representative acts were given—and these six ran nearly four hours. Morse said he had written the work not in imitation of the Oberammergau spectacle, which he saw as virulently anti-Semitic, but out of respect for the life of a man he deemed an exemplar for everyone.

The performance began with the presentation by Jewish mothers of their infants to the high priest. When Mary attempts to present Jesus, the priest averts his eyes. Simeon cries out that the baby shall sit on David's throne, and this prompts the priest to notify Herod. From there the story follows the New Testament to the last, short act, which shows a view of Golgotha flanked by high mountains and with Jerusalem in the distance. The women are keening until a huge cross begins to shine, at which point a chorus of adoration concluded the evening. Those in the audience who were not moved (and some were said to cry) were at least respectful. But, according to William Winter, Judge George C. Barrett of the New York Supreme Court, bowing to Protestant pressure, prevented additional performances. Although he produced at least one more drama, within a year the despondent playwright committed suicide by drowning in the Hudson. However, he left behind a monument that endured for many years, since his Temple of the Passion was converted into the 23rd Street Theatre.

Increasingly Maude Granger was a more important star on the road than she was in New York. For some time she had been touring successfully in J. K. Tillotson's **The Planter's Wife** (4-2-83, 14th St.), in which she portrayed Edith Gray, a northerner who marries a southern planter and Confederate officer, Albert Graham (Harry Lacy). Unwisely, she does not tell him of her earlier unsuccessful marriage and of her trial and acquittal on trumped-up charges. That first marriage was to a scoundrel named Daniel Barton (Michael A. Kennedy), who was actually guilty of the crime for which she was brought to trial. He suddenly reappears, now using the name Harry Livingston, and he is bent on making more trouble.

Edith: Daniel Barton! The dead alive.
Livingston: Yes, resurrected; ain't you glad to see me?
Edith: I thought you dead.

Livingston: Oh, no! That was a little dodge of mine;
   I wanted to see if you would mourn the loss.
Edith: Villain!

Of course, matters are resolved satisfactorily. Even after Miss Granger relinquished the role, the play continued to tour for several years.

A Russian Honeymoon (4-9-83, Madison Square) was the work of a society woman, Mrs. Burton N. Harrison, who based her comedy on Scribe's *La Lune de miel*. But she might well have used any number of older plays, for the plot was simply another taming of a shrew. In this case the shrew is Poleska (Agnes Booth), who consents to wed Alexis (Frederic Bryton) in the belief that he is a nobleman but finds him working as a shoemaker. Her response is to sneer, break furniture, and eventually have Alexis arrested. It takes Count Woroffski to put her in her place, but then the count is her husband, Alexis. The play ran prosperously for two months, a relatively short run for the Madison Square Theatre. However, in that time it made theatrical history. After one evening's performance producer Daniel Frohman assembled the cast onstage, on the set showing a wooden but spacious shoemaker's home, and recreated the scene in which Poleska, standing by an old spinning wheel, demands that soldiers with their long-barreled rifles arrest the protesting Alexis. The theatrical photographer, Benjamin Joseph Falk, who, like his colleagues, until then had photographed players and small bits of scenes in his studio, took a picture of the entire, fully peopled stage—the first onstage theatrical photograph, at least in America. Once again the Madison Square had played the modern pioneer.

A Russian Honeymoon's opening night also brought back two admired luminaries: Modjeska (for her second visit of the season) to the Fifth Avenue and McCullough, who was relegated to the out-of-the-way Niblo's. Neither offered any additions to their standard programs. The same busy night was the occasion of Mary Anderson's brief return at the Grand Opera and of a revival of *The Banker's Daughter* at Booth's.

When the Bronson Howard revival departed, Booth's hosted its last major offering. Clara Morris and Salvini were co-starred, at $3 top (twice the going price), in presentations of *The Outlaw* (*La Morte Civile*) and *Othello*. Several critics thought Miss Morris outshone her leading man. When she became ill, Katherine Rogers had to take over several performances. After these stars left, Modjeska and Maurice Barrymore gave a single, special performance of *Romeo and Juliet* on the 30th to ring down

the curtain on the unlucky playhouse. Clara Fisher Maeder, who had played Juliet in New York in 1827, was the Nurse. The performance was listed as a benefit for the theatre's janitor.

The Bijou, usually given over to musicals, played host, beginning on April 17, to Henry M. Pitt, an English comedian who had worked briefly at Wallack's, and his company of American actors. He started his season with revivals of *Caste* and *Two Roses*, supported by the up-and-coming Eben Plympton and the old veteran William Davidge.

Leonard Grover's **Cad, the Tomboy** (4-23-83, Daly's) was a vehicle for Carrie Swain, one of the many touring performers of the day specializing in hoydens. The play, which the *Herald* found "well freighted with slang and boisterous fun," saw its heroine give up her roughneck ways for the more respectable ups and downs of young love.

A double bill coupled a revival of Grundy's *The Snowball* with Clement Scott's **The Cape Mail** (4-30-83, Wallack's). During the Zulu War, the family and friends of blind, aging Mrs. Preston (Mme Ponisi) read to her fictitious letters from her son, to spare her the news that he has been reported killed in action. Actually, he has been taken prisoner, so all ends happily. The play received fair enough reviews but failed to draw. Wallack's elite audience had apparently tired of comedy and even light drama, joining the rush for punching melodramas.

Clement Scott was also co-author, with Arthur Matthison, of **The Great Divorce Case** (5-1-83, Union Square), presented in conjuction with *Ruth's Romance*. Charles Wyndham and his Criterion Theatre ensemble had returned on April 9, first reviving *Brighton*. In the new play, two pitiable men are hounded by battle-axe mothers-in-law. To get away they write each other letters suggesting they meet to discuss "the great divorce case." In true farce fashion the letters fall into the wrong hands, and the fun begins. Previous commitments allowed the play to run only two weeks on this, its first New York hearing.

Etelka Borry, an Eastern European actress, offered *Camille* and *Adrienne Lecouvreur* in her week-long, unavailing bid for American acclaim, starting May 7 at the Fifth Avenue.

The failure of his double bill prodded Wallack into reviving *La Belle Russe* on the 12th.

At least as far as her adoring American public was concerned, Lotta had precious few if any failures. But just before she sailed for what proved a disastrous English visit, she came scarily close to displeasing all but her most uncritical admirers when she appeared in Fred Marsden's **Bob** (5-14-83, Fifth

Ave.). Her songs, dances, and banjo turns were desperately needed to cover up the holes and hack writing in Marsden's tale of a wildly uncontrollable schoolgirl up to every manner of mischief, whose self-inflicted troubles are compounded by villainous Victor Delpuis (Ralph Delmore).

Although Tom Taylor had been dead for several years, his ten-year-old play **Arkwright's Wife** (5-14-83, Union Square) was given its first New York presentation as a vehicle for an eye-catching English actress, Helen Barry, making her American debut. There were hints in its story of Ibsenite tragedy to come, but not in its treatment. When a mob of laborers threatens Richard Arkwright (Henry Holland) after he invents a spinning jenny that will deprive them of work, his wife, Margaret (Miss Barry), destroys the machine. Her behavior so infuriates Arkwright that he casts her out, so she and her aging father wander aimlessly. Their wanderings are made all the more bitter because they know that the father, Peter Hayes (Harry St. Maur), had been the actual inventor and that Arkwright had stolen his idea. Years later, when Arkwright has become a rich if hated manufacturer and a baronet, Margaret again has occasion to save him from an irate mob. Her action brings about a reconciliation. Given the unpleasantness of Arkwright's character, some critics wondered aloud about the weakly happy ending. Moreover, they found the tall, attractive, if somewhat masculine star had mastered technique without plumbing any depths. Miss Barry was not deterred.

Nor was Boucicault, although success had eluded him of late, except as a performer. His new play was **The Amadan** (5-15-83, Star), and in it he took the role of the vulgar, drunken contractor, Michael O'Leary, who insists that only if Elfie Carew (Lillian Cleves) marries him can she save her father from ruin, her brother from prison, and her lover from the gallows. Of course, O'Leary had had no small hand in seeing to it that these men are in a fix. But Elfie has befriended a dimwitted boy—the Irish term for such a boy supplied the title—Colley (Dion Boucicault, Jr.). Time and again his instinctive goodness and native common sense come to Elfie's rescue, though he is eventually shot for his pains.

Once again Boucicault resorted to the same old devices for sensational effects: Colley jumps into a river to retrieve papers O'Leary had thrown there; a man is pushed from a high cliff; an escape is made by breaking through a solid wall. Only now his effects were greeted with unwonted, unwanted laughter. The star's son stole the show, eliciting the sympathy of the audience and earning curtain calls at the end of each act, which he took hand in hand with his hopelessly vain father.

Harry Pitt reached back nearly a dozen years to offer New York a play London had seen with the late Harry Montague in the leading role in 1872. In Albery's **Forgiven** (5-16-83, Bijou) Claude Redruth (Pitt) deserts his wife, Rose (Bessie Robbins), a gardener's daughter, to woo Lady Maud (Cora Tanner). Lady Maud, in disguise, teaches Rose how to win back her man, so the curtain falls with everyone forgiving everyone else.

The pathetic Salmi Morse had become a figure of ridicule, supplanting, in a way, the late Count Joannes. He was rumored to sleep beneath a gem-encrusted quilt and to have written as many as forty unproduced plays, most in a marked Shakespearean manner. Once again he was forced to become his own producer with **A Bustle Among the Petticoats** (5-21-83, 23rd St.). The *Herald* called the work a play in six short acts and five long intermissions, so long, in fact, that playgoers had time to wander about, checking on who had registered into nearby hotels. Morse's shopkeeper hero, Blondin (Frederick Paulding), loves Floretta but is deflected in his courtship by Count Andrassi (Theodore Hamilton), who apparently leads him to a magical forest and there casts a spell on him. Blondin suddenly finds himself richly appareled and supposedly married to a duchess. He cannot resume his suit until the spell wears off. At least that is what critics thought the play was about, although they were not certain.

To cap matters, mishaps marred the opening. For one, the horses pulling the carriage in which the count took the young man into the forest had minds of their own and became entangled in the scenery. On the other hand, there was a graceful ballet, even if no one could figure its connection with the story. The *Herald* dished up its critique with malicious relish, repeatedly coming back to the audience response, reporting that patrons "laughed till tears came," that there had been "an insane asylum completeness about the performance that kept the house in an uproar," that the whole evening was "delirium tremens dramatized," and that when poor Paulding bemoaned all was not well "the audience yelled for dear life." The play closed quickly—its befuddled author's swan song.

A longer life was in store for John A. Stevens's **Her Second Love** (5-21-83, Windsor), with which Maude Granger toured for several seasons. She portrayed the voluptuous Countess Olga Demidorf, who is married to the debt-ridden, gambling Count Ivan (G. C. Boniface). In a desperate attempt to stave off bankruptcy, Ivan wagers 100,000 rubles that Olga is the world's most beautiful woman. He forces her to pose as Venus in a tableau vivant. She is made to stand on a pedestal, draped from neck to feet in white tulle with only her arms revealed. But the tulle is so arranged to show her shapely curves. Ivan wins the bet. Olga takes the money, hurls it at his feet, and walks out on him. Just how the title was related to the plot was something of a mystery.

Helen Barry won favorable notices when she switched to comedy on the 23rd and revived Robertson's version of Scribe's *The Ladies' Battle*, in which she assumed the role of a lovelorn countess who goes to preposterous lengths to win the hand of a young man, only to find he prefers her niece. The next evening Wallack's unveiled its last production of the season, a revival of *The Romance of a Poor Young Man*.

Roland Reed, the father of Florence Reed, tasted stardom in Marsden's **Cheek** (5-28-83, 14th St.). He played Dick Smythe, a newspaperman who tries to get people to pay him for putting articles about them in the paper. Like so many comedies devoted primarily to touring and consigned in New York to outlying theatres, this one offered songs and a few dances to prop up a fragile plot. Whether or not it was prototypical musical comedy, it caught the public's fancy, so toured prosperously for several seasons.

Although **The Thunderbolt** (6-4-83, Union Square) was set in America, it was unusual in that it was the work of a French-Canadian, Louis Frechette. Its hero, Paul Rodette (J. Newton Gotthold), returns to his Louisiana plantation after twenty years in Europe, where he had fled following a duel in which he killed his Creole brother-in-law. He had left his estate in the hands of a man he trusted, Joseph Renard (Lewis Morrison), but he finds his trust was misplaced. Renard now claims to be the owner, and unless Rodette can find a missing deed he will have no claim on the land. Renard tries to kill Rodette, but when the deed at last is unearthed Renard jumps in the Mississippi and drowns. The production was the first mounted at the theatre since Shook and his new partner, J. W. Collier, had taken over its management from Palmer. The quality of both the writing and the acting signaled a decline in the playhouse's standards that was to become increasingly apparent over the next few seasons.

Other changes were in the offing, with the Madison Square Theatre again in the vanguard. Its photograph of a scene from *A Russian Honeymoon* had caused such a stir that as soon as its latest offering was ready it distributed new photographs, which were featured in pictorial sections then

starting to appear in newspapers. This original, impressive publicity helped William Young's **The Rajah; or, Wyncot's Ward** (6-2-83, Madison Square) chalk up a seven-month run, another in the theatre's unbroken string of lengthy stands. But then the play was an ingratiating comedy by a playwright who, at the time, promised to become a leading light in American theatre. While Young was an American, his play was set in England. In India Harold Wyncot (George Clarke) had been branded "the Rajah" by his fellow officers for his indolence and hauteur. He returns home when his uncle's death makes him not only a rich man's heir but guardian to his uncle's adopted daughter, Gladys (Rillie Deaves). He arrives, as one photograph showed, dapperly dressed and monocled, protecting himself from the sun not only with his top hat but with a huge parasol, and he is greeted with cheers by the assembled staff. Gladys and her friends bristle at his pomposity and stern discipline. He even assigns Buttons (Alfred Klein), his housekeeper's pudgy son, to watch their every move, so that, in the most famous of all pictures from the play, when they arrive at a waterfall in a glade, there is Buttons seated on the bridge, keeping an eye on them. Of course, Harold has good reason for his vigilance since there are dangerous labor agitators, including an escaped convict, in the area. Before long—or at least before the final curtain—Gladys comes to understand Harold's behavior and to fall in love with him. Captions were careful to point out that the water in the fall was real.

The last new play of the season, A. C. Gunter's **Strictly Business** (6-25-83, 14th St.), was also a comedy. Its hero is a traveling salesman, P. P. Philkins (C. B. Bishop), whose wanderings in order to sell American canned goods and preserved meats take him as far as Russia. His ample girth is a strong selling point, since he obviously has sampled his own merchandise frequently and with relish. Nor is his obesity a stumbling block to romance. In Geneva he rescues a Russian countess (Emma Pierce), who is also a czarist spy, from nihilists and czarist intriguers and thus wins her hand.

1883–1884

As it had in so many recent seasons, the American theatre provided its patrons with a more or less continuous stream of passable entertainment, which, after all, is the primary purpose of theatre. Intermittently, it also offered evenings of exhilarating excitement and noteworthy distinction, which is the theatre's highest ambition. If that excitement and distinction reflected the players' art far more than it did the dramatists', contemporary playgoers expected little else. Nor would they have been surprised when the season's greatest excitement was generated by the first American appearances of two foreigners—Henry Irving and Ellen Terry. A hundred years later, although the stream had dried up alarmingly and Terry and Irving were long dead, much the same generalities could have been applied to late 20th-century American theatre. There were other similarities.

In the 1880s many leading intellectuals often embraced radical movements. Some had earlier attempted to justify the bloody behavior of the Communards in France. With the suppression of the Commune, socialism and nihilism had come to be perceived as the most ominous menaces to established society and frequently had won the support, qualified or not, of those who thought themselves rejected by or above the mainstream. So it was not too shocking to learn that Oscar Wilde was the author of **Vera; or, The Nihilists** (8-20-83, Union Square), a play sometimes called *Vera, the Nihilist* in this country. When her brother, Dmitri (Fred Lotto), is sent into exile for his anticzarist activities, he makes Vera (Marie Prescott) take an oath: "To strangle whatever nature is in me, neither to love nor be loved; neither to pity nor be pitied . . . till the end is come." She joins the nihilists, where, despite her oath, she finds herself falling in love with a young man known as Alexis (Lewis Morrison). The group's meeting is broken up by the czar's troops. As the conspirators are being hauled off to jail, Alexis reveals he is none other than the czarevitch. The muddleheaded, reactionary czar (G. C. Boniface) confronts his son, determined to change his thinking. But before he can do that he is assassinated. Alexis becomes czar and attempts to implement liberal reforms. This infuriates the nihilists, who really want power more than justice. They decide to kill Alexis, too. Their choice for assassin is Vera. Dutifully she goes to the palace. The czar is asleep, but her movements awaken him. He pours out his love for her and his plans for a better world. Grief-stricken, Vera stabs herself instead of Alexis, then, in a prearranged signal, throws the dagger out the window. When the czar asks what she has done, she answers equivocally, "I have saved Russia," and falls dead.

More than one critic, rather than expound on the play and its production, used his review to extol democracy and denigrate revolutionaries. What excellences reviewers did see in the play were not those of its political immediacy (though the action was set nearly a century in the past) but its effective bits of traditional dramaturgy: the dramatic confrontation between father and son; the pathetic, doomed last dialogue of the lovers who had never had the chance to love. Although a long list of distinguished theatrical figures attended the opening and apparently enjoyed themselves, the gallery was vociferous in hooting the play and Wilde himself when he took curtain calls. Their disdain prevailed, so the work was hurriedly withdrawn.

The revival of a twenty-eight-year-old American play by an American actor at the Star on August 27 was recognized instantly as a landmark in American theatrics. The play was George H. Boker's *Francesca da Rimini;* the star, Lawrence Barrett. Boker's drama had not been successful at its premiere, and by 1883 its pseudo-Shakespearean construction and blank verse represented an obsolete manner of playwriting. With William Winter's help Barrett had revised the play and tested it in the previous season at Philadelphia. Their changes deleted some of Boker's weaker passages and slightly reordered the action, but otherwise remained faithful to the story of a princess married to a deformed prince and of her tragic love for her husband's handsome brother. The play was beautifully mounted and to some extent consciously used colorful settings and costumes of Renaissance Italy to embellish the work's darker moments.

Several critics felt that Barrett still was given to overplaying and to unnecessarily underscoring important points with what Otis Skinner, who played the brother, Paolo, called his "volcanic elocution," but on the whole they felt that his deformed Lanciotto was a masterful blend of "heroic and tender, daring and enduring, savage and docile, violent and loving, morbid and yet just, true and generous." Winter himself had heard few finer readings than Barrett's response to Paolo's exhortation to Lanciotto to be hopeful: "I cannot, brother:—God has bowed me down."

In his autobiography Skinner presented a marvelous picture of Barrett's staging. At first he had Paolo and Francesca kiss and embrace during their secret tryst, but then decided that was too immodest and suggestive. Instead Paolo wandered off to pluck a rose while Francesca moved center stage to pick up a book she had been reading. As Paolo backed off the stage he held out the rose, and Francesca "limply followed after the extended arm as if hypnotized."

Skinner reported that jeers from the audience forced Barrett to restage the scene again. Louis James won applause as the villainous jester, Beppo Pepe, while Marie Wainwright's Francesca met a more divided reaction. However, several critics took the occasion to chide Booth, Jefferson, the dying McCullough, and others for lacking Barrett's willingness to enlarge his repertory. The revival enjoyed a remarkable stand of nine weeks.

Jefferson gave ammunition to those who decried his reliance on essentially one show when he opened a brand new playhouse—the Third Avenue Theatre—on September 3 with his sturdy *Rip Van Winkle.* However, even those who were unhappy with this virtually unvarying repertory granted his Rip retained all its "lightness, grace and humor."

The expression "dude," suggesting an overly fastidious, upholstered man-about-town, had recently been coined and had become the rage, so a play spoofing such a dude soon made its way in front of the footlights. The play was J. H. Farrell's **A Friendly Tip** (9-3-83, 23rd St.), and William J. Ferguson, who had been hailed as a highly promising actor, hoped to use it as a springboard to stardom. Farrell's yarn centered on the exploits of the dudish Sir Chauncey Trip and his misbegotten attempts to court a featherbrained heiress. Critics found themselves at odds; some claimed that Ferguson could not distinguish between a modern dude and a Restoration fop, while others suggested the whole point of the comedy was that Sir Chauncey was so empty upstairs that he himself didn't know how to act like a true dude. Whichever was the case, the critics united to pan the play. It soon disappeared. Ferguson spent most of his remaining years not as a star but as a respected supporting player.

E. A. Locke's **Nobody's Claim** (9-3-83, Windsor) was an action-packed western that won a spot in touring bills for several seasons. Its hero is Ward Devereux (J[oseph] J. Dowling); its heroine, Madge (Sadie Hasson); and its chief mischiefmaker, Dell McWade (Richard French). Before Ward and Madge can tie the knot, he has to wrestle a bear and shoot out all the local telegraph wires to prevent a message from being sent. She in turn must rescue the tethered hero from a burning mill.

If giants such as Booth and Jefferson adhered to rigidly prescribed programs, so did many minor figures who toured incessantly and sometimes braved New York in the great actors' wake. One such player was George Edgar, an awkward, stolid actor who satisfied the road but found little except disfavor with the more brahmin critics in larger cities. His Booth-like agenda, during his week's stay

at the 14th Street Theatre beginning on the 10th, consisted of Othello and Richelieu. Edgar must have been embarrassed when his leading lady, Ellie Wilton, and his principal male support, Lewis Morrison (the Alexis of the late, unlamented *Vera*), garnered better notices than he did. His opening coincided with the return of Charles Wyndham and his company, who began their engagement at the Union Square with revivals of *Ruth's Romance* and *The Great Divorce Case.*

Another example of what the road had to put up with but Broadway would not tolerate was C. B. Lewis's **Yakie** (9-17-83, 23rd St.). Lewis was a popular writer with the *Detroit Free Press,* and his work was yet another comedy about a lovable German-American. Regrettably Lewis was not the best of craftsmen, and his star, Alf Wyman, was a poor substitute for J. K. Emmet. In keeping with the tradition of this sort of comedy, the evening was sprinkled with songs—or should have been until something went wrong in the orchestra pit and several songs had to be omitted. Onstage mishaps, among them a recalcitrant sled, also bedeviled the opening. The cast included a cow, but her performance could not compare with that of a trained dog, who earned some of the heartiest applause. There was not much applause for Lewis's unimaginative story or the jerry-built mounting. A woman and a young child flee from a villain, but their coach is upset in a snowstorm. Sensing her fate, the woman hands over the child to a kindly mountaineer, Yakie (Wyman). She has no sooner done this than she dies—and dies, according to the *Herald,* "on a sofa covered with a sheet which does duty for a snow clad mound." An intermission allows years to pass. The child has grown into the attractive Louisa (Lulu Wilson). Yakie is still shielding her from the villain but eventually is able to turn her over to the protection of the handsome, adoring Zouave Captain Custer (Harry D. Parker).

Vying for attention the same night was Clara Morris in *Camille* at the Third Avenue. Of course, outlying theatres such as this regularly played host to tried and true warhorses. At some time or other during the season, such stages offered Mrs. G. C. Howard, still as Topsy in *Uncle Tom's Cabin,* Chanfrau as Kit, Fanny Herring, the Bowery favorite of a quarter-century earlier, at fifty-two still romping as her hoydens or as *The French Spy,* Emmet as Fritz, and numerous other stars and plays long since relegated to second-class theatres but still beloved by a multitude of playgoers. As a rule, newspapers ignored these productions.

On the 22nd at the Union Square, Wyndham and

his troupe brought out a second double bill for the final fortnight of their visit. The main attraction was a revival of *Pink Dominos,* which was coupled with a new work as curtain raiser, **The Household Fairy,** in which Katharine (Kate Rorke), a country girl, persuades a citified aristocrat, Julian de Clifford (George Giddens), to accept both her and her country ways.

The continuing vogue for plays about Russians and nihilism was further exemplified by the fast-fading Charlotte Thompson's appearance in **The Romanoff** (9-24-83, 23rd St.). The drama was the work of Harry Marshall, who was actually Harry St. Maur, an actor in the play, and who claimed to have based his piece on Adolphe Belot's *La Drame de la Rue de la Paix.* Its story focused on the tragedy of a Hungarian princess, Etelka Zecksta (Thompson), whose nobleman lover is shot after he is falsely accused of being a nihilist. Later she becomes romantically involved with General Yopslokoff, unaware he is the same officer responsible for her former sweetheart's death. When she learns the truth she kills both the general and herself. Although filled with Russian characters, the play was set in Paris.

The *Times* suggested that one explanation for the fashion in matters Russian was Russian fashions, noting, "A Russian hero in top-boots and a fur-trimmed coat is unquestionably a more dashing and romantic person than any American hero in trousers." Two or three of the top-booted Russians—Count Derfenhoff, Etelka's lover; Col. Ivan Muscholaski, Derfenhoff's treacherous friend, who leads him into a nihilist conspiracy and later shoots him; and Yopslokoff, the name afterwards assumed by Muschollaski—all were played by the same actor, George Learock. Nothing in the story, such as a marked similarity of appearance, nor Learock's unexceptional talents called for such a showy but pointless tour de force. The play was a quick failure, prompting Miss Thompson to bring *Jane Eyre* out of storage for her second and final week. An unstated reason for its hasty withdrawal may well have been that a better and more famous play, one more sumptuously produced, was scheduled to open on Broadway during her final week.

That play was Sardou's **Fedora** (10-1-83, 14th St.), which the playwright had written expressly for his greatest star, Bernhardt, and in which she had scored a Paris triumph the preceding December. Its American star was Fanny Davenport (who also served as her own producer). As early as 1877, when she assumed the part of the old, haggard Posthumia in *Vesta,* she had taken on a role French theatregoers

identified with their "Divine Sarah." Now, and for the rest of her career, Davenport would appear in virtually no play not similarly identified with the illustrious French star. Naturally comparisons had to be drawn, and they were not altogether favorable to the beautiful American. Indeed, her ravishing, almost regal beauty was the one point on which Davenport won hands down; yet it never truly compensated for Bernhardt's incandescent stage presence. No one questioned Davenport's intelligence or her thoroughly schooled theatrical technique, but, again, they were hardly a match for Bernhardt's uncanny instincts and her superior utilization of every known stage trick. Perhaps in one respect the contest, if in fact it was a contest, was a draw. Both women were renowned for their gorgeous, expensive costumes. Yet significantly, many looked on Davenport's beautiful clothes as the most salient feature of her appearances, while Bernhardt's sumptuous wardrobe always was a mere ornament to her overpowering acting. Fanny Davenport never overpowered any playgoers. Nonetheless, she was good enough and popular enough to surmount any comparisons. And she was, after all, one of ours.

Like Etelka, her Fedora discovers that her lover has been slain through the machinations of another man. The seeming villain is a purported nihilist, Loris Ipanoff (Robert B. Mantell), and she sets out to destroy him. To this end she determines to make him fall in love with her and then to betray him to the secret police. But after her trap is set her plans go awry, for Ipanoff proves to her that he is no nihilist and that her lover had been an unfaithful scoundrel. Realizing that she has fallen in love herself and that there is no way of calling off the secret police, she poisons herself.

The death scene demonstrated the differences between the two actresses. Bernhardt luxuriated in writhing final moments. In this respect she might have found a better American competitor in the unfortunately uneven and undisciplined Clara Morris. By contrast, Davenport apparently thought being more reserved meant being more effective and more dignified. Certainly modern thinking would agree with her, although by modern standards even her emoting was probably overdone. To 1883 American tastes it was just fine, so *Fedora* held the boards in New York until late December, then toured. Its success also helped secure Mantell's fast-rising reputation as a matinee idol. His dashing good looks obscured the fact that his style was somewhat out of sync with newer, less fustian styles of acting, which smaller theatres and better lighting were encourag-

1883–1884

ing. Thus the *Evening Post* could only rejoice that he stood "in striking contrast to the mincing mannikins who had posed recently as stage heroes by the grace of tailors and hairdressers."

The Florences, too, scored a hit that would remain in their repertory for several seasons when they offered George Jessop and William Gill's **Facts; or, His Little Hatchet** (10-1-83, Grand Opera), although this time around they could play it only for the first week of their three-week stand. They starred as Governor Pinto Porterhouse Perkins, a man who simply cannot tell the truth and can always top someone else's experience with one of his own, and as Mrs. Matilda Starr, a London fashion magazine's elegantly dressed correspondent who has no trouble reading French so long as it is translated into clear English and who is proud of a friendship she has maintained for "yahs and chahs." When she comes to interview Perkins he recalls his experiences as a Mississippi riverboat captain and as a marshal in the French army. Before long the pair have fallen in love, and not even the absurd sight of Perkins absentmindedly donning half a dozen overcoats—none of which belongs to him—can cool the ardor. Forced to return the coats, he sheepishly asks the owners to leave him with his "liver-pad." For the remainder of their stand the stars offered *Eileen Oge* and *The Mighty Dollar,* and by the time they returned they had rechristened their new vehicle *Our Governor.*

The same busy night also saw Wallack's relit for the new season, with the conservative, English-oriented manager selecting a revival of Charles Reade and Tom Taylor's *Masks and Faces* to launch his season.

Only one play opened the next night, but it quickly joined the ranks of successes brightening the still young theatrical year. **Dollars and Sense** (10-2-83, Daly's) was the latest in the theatre's Americanization of German farce, in this case L'Arronge's *Die Sorglosen.* Saphira Lamb (Mrs. Gilbert) is a domineering, tightfisted Pennsylvania Dutch matron, and her husband, Eliphet (James Lewis), hankers for a couple of wild nights on the town. To engineer his escape he brandishes a "red hot" telegram from his friend Peabody, beseeching his urgent presence in Washington, only to have Saphira solemnly enter the room in mourning with news of Peabody's passing. Nothing daunted, Eliphet proceeds to attempt a fling with Sybilla Briggs (Virginia Dreher), the fiery Latin wife of an English colonel in the Egyptian army. Interfering for better or worse are an elegant but ridiculously moralizing young lawyer, Harry Latimer (John Drew), and a charming

girl, Phronie Tremont (Ada Rehan). As so often happened at Daly's, a previous booking forced the run to be cut short in early December when the play was still profitable, but it later enjoyed frequent revivals so long as the company survived.

Great stars in old plays were the order of the night on the following Monday, the 8th. Jefferson, perhaps taking to heart the critical digs a few weeks before, or possibly invigorated by the success of his mounting of *The Rivals,* set aside *Rip Van Winkle.* But classicist, or at least conservative, that he was, he eschewed anything truly new, instead opting to return to plays in which he had won acclaim in his younger years. His Caleb Plummer in *The Cricket on the Hearth* and his Mr. Golightly in *Lend Me Five Shillings,* in which the hero frantically tried to borrow enough money to escort a widow home in a carriage, were remembered with affection and received again with enthusiasm, so he prospered during his six-week stand at the Union Square.

Charles Coghlan was made far less welcome when he appeared at the Fifth Avenue, first in *Money,* then moving on to *A Celebrated Case* and *The Duke's Motto.* The *Times* called him "spasmodic in manner, forced in articulation," adding, "His action often amounts to swagger." These complaints were echoed by the *Herald,* which found he was "hard, utterly lacking in sympathetic quality, spasmodic in gesture and utterance, declamatory instead of intense, and annoyed everybody by hoisting or lowering one or both shoulders every time he had a line with any point to it." Scarcely noticed by the critics was the fading Rose Eytinge's opening at the inconvenient Mount Morris in Harlem, where her bills included *The Winter's Tale* and *Oliver Twist.*

The first new play of Wallack's season was **Moths** (10-18-83, Wallack's), derived by Henry Hamilton from Ouida's novel. The saintly Vere Herbert (Rose Coghlan) is forced by her frivolous, heartless mother, Lady Dolly Vanderdecken (Caroline Hill), to marry Lady Dolly's former, abusive lover, Prince Zuroff (Gerald Eyre). Vere would prefer to marry Raphael de Carreze (Osmond Tearle). Another suitor of Vere, Lord Jura (Charles Glenney), solves her problem when he challenges Zuroff to a duel, which proves fatal to both men. Critics pounced on the adaptation, observing that it reflected all too well Ouida's shallow cynicism and romanticism and that it gave the putative hero, de Carreze, nothing much to do but stand around and look handsome. They also questioned whether Caroline Hill, who was the wife of Herbert Kelcey, was right in making a comic figure out of an essentially cruel, thoughtless person. Yet Wallack's had a sufficiently large and loyal clientele to give the drama a reasonably prosperous run of six and a half weeks.

For nearly two weeks thereafter, first-class theatres presented no premieres, although lesser houses continued to bring in touring revivals. For example, Kate Claxton starred in the late Laura Keene's once popular vehicle, *The Sea of Ice,* at the Rankins' Third Avenue Theatre. Whether or not the lull at the major theatres was intentional, it served to build further, feverish interest in the next important opening, although that opening for months past had been the season's most eagerly awaited event. Tellingly, this was not the premiere of a new American play or even the first appearance of a leading American performer in an untried role. Rather, it was the New York debut of two of England's greatest players—Henry Irving and Ellen Terry—in their London repertory. It underscored again how, for all the intermittent cries for more emphasis on native plays and actors, foreign attractions still exercised a certain hegemony on the Rialto. Not since Bernhardt's visit had New York been so abuzz or had prices been so brazenly raised.

For many seasons Irving had craftily ballooned his own reputation until he was, almost unarguably, the most renowned actor in the English-speaking world. It did not follow that he was the most admired. His poor posture, his curious waddle, his often grating voice, and his puzzlingly regional accent (different critics descried different regions in his speech) were all held against him. Nor was he a handsome man. He was slender, tall, and flat-chested, but between his high forehead and long, slim jaw were large, deepset, dark eyes that could be wonderfully expressive. He was nearly forty-six. His reputation had been carefully built with comic and melodramatic roles, and not until he felt his place was secure did he seriously venture into the lofty realms of tragedy, where many of his detractors felt he was never fully at home. Yet even when he seemingly dared to overreach, he surrounded himself with some of the finest physical productions the English stage had ever seen, and these magnificent mountings, as much as or more than his sometimes questionable interpretations, established his right to his hard-earned fame.

His leading lady was the perfect foil. At thirty-six Ellen Terry was a fine-featured English beauty with a queenly stance, a deep and compelling voice, an ethereal manner of floating across a stage, and a charming simplicity ("as fresh as an English garden").

Although the pair worked magnificently in tandem, very few plays allowed them an equal opportu-nity to shine. So Irving arranged for what amounted to two successive opening nights at the Star, offering his Mathias in *The Bells* on the 29th, with no part for Miss Terry, and Miss Terry as Queen Henrietta Maria in Wills's **Charles I,** with Irving in the title role, on the 30th. The high point of this costume drama was the queen's plea to the unfeeling Cromwell, who has betrayed and seized the king. Later in their engagement the stars were seen together in *Louis XI, The Merchant of Venice* (considered by many their greatest achievement), *The Lyons Mail, The Belle's Stratagem,* and sections of *Richard III.* New York critics, although most duly noted Irving's flaws, were caught up in the excitement and ballyhoo, and so handed the stars and their excellent supporting cast highly flattering reviews. They also praised the richly designed, apparently historically correct settings and costumes and the fine staging. Among the dramatic effects singled out was the lighting of Mathias's vision with Mathias and the hands of the mesmerist followed across the room by a searing white light while most of the other figures in the drama stood deadly still on a dimmed stage. At $3 top, the four-week stand grossed nearly $76,000.

When the company returned for another month at the end of March, Irving and Terry added *Much Ado About Nothing* and *The Captain of the Watch* to their program. Perhaps by then critics had had time to mull over their first impressions and had decided they had reacted too acceptingly. Reviews harped more damningly on Irving's insistent mannerisms. His Benedick won little praise. Miss Terry's incomparable Beatrice stole the show. Irving's Hamlet, which had been bruited to be part of the spring season, was not offered, possibly because of the chilling reception it had received during the winter tour.

Not all English goods were unquestioningly received. Critics, if not playgoers, were growing angrily impatient with English melodrama, so most were unkind to Sims and Pettitt's **In the Ranks** (11-1-83, Standard), even though it was advertised as "the Grandest Melodramatic Production of Modern Times." Perhaps the rude reception was in good measure deserved, for their plot involved another young man, Ned Drayton (Frederic Bryton), who, thanks this time to the nefarious Richard Belton (F. F. Mackay), is framed and imprisoned for a crime he did not commit, escapes his jailers, distinguishes himself in the army, and returns home to vindicate himself and bring his persecutor to justice. The *Herald* snarled that Bryton was "not manly enough," a charge increasingly leveled at younger leading men. Whatever critics thought, enough playgoers relished theatrically effective clichés, set against Voegtlin's superb scenery, including a moon-lit woods, to give the play a month's run before it went on tour.

Of course, Americans could produce equally shoddy goods. A. C. Gunter's **Courage** (11-5-83, Third Ave.) served as a vehicle for Effie Ellsler, trying to cling to the stardom she had won as Hazel Kirke. She played Blanche Grey, whose swarthy, duplicitous suitor, Ignatio Ortiz (Frank Weston), a double agent in the Cuban-Spanish struggle, plants an incriminating letter on the man Blanche really loves, Howard Temple (H. A. Weaver, Jr.). Blanche and Howard are quickly caught up in the dangerous international intrigue surrounding Cuba's attempt to become independent. The play was a failure. For the next decade Miss Ellsler would try to find another role like Hazel Kirke. She would not succeed, although she enjoyed some minor hits, including one before the same month was out. Only late in her career would one last juicy part in a major hit come her way.

Matters hardly improved, if they improved at all, with **The Stranglers of Paris** (11-10-83, New Park), David Belasco's translation of Belot's play. Much like *In the Ranks* and *Courage,* it was what the *Tribune* called "a sensation piece, embellished with showy scenery." In later years Belasco himself called it simply "buncombe." The real stranglers are the mentally deranged hunchback, Jagon (Henry Lee), and his accomplice, Lorenz or Lo-renzo (Fred Huebner), who murder their victims for their money. Jagon has a daughter, Mathilde (Agnes Booth), who is innocent of his occupation. Jagon is caught and implicated not with his true accomplice but with Blanchard (Waldon Ramsay), whom Lorenz had disguised himself to resemble. Jagon and Blanchard are sentenced to be trans-ported. During the voyage they escape (or, in some versions, the ship is wrecked and they sail free on a raft). Meanwhile, Mathilde has learned the truth about her father and Lorenz. She confronts Lorenz, who strangles her. Just then Jagon returns. He denounces Lorenz to the police, and Lorenz is shot while attempting to flee. But all this proves too much for Jagon, who dies, exclaiming, "I am done with justice, done with prisons, done with crime, done with life." While the play was not a success, it managed to hold the boards for the next season or two.

Many years later, when films were the most popular entertainment, a distinct pattern emerged for distribution, with a new film moving predictably from a major first-run palace to a second-run house and then through a hierarchic chain of neighborhood theatres. Similarly, television developed a relatively clear pattern of fall and winter premieres with spring and summer reruns. Until the decade following the Civil War, theatrical bookings had also followed a simple plan, with every city having its principal stock company, most of which sometimes played host to a touring star. The rapid development of railroads and the population explosion played havoc with this comfortable simplicity, promoting the proliferation of touring shows, destroying the stock companies, and bringing about the rapid rise in the number of theatres. Perhaps contemporaries saw a certain logic and order in bookings during the 1880s. Perhaps, too, they recognized some meaningful nuances in what, a hundred years on, often seems haphazard and confusing.

Even in this still young season such a towering figure as Jefferson had first appeared at a neighbor-hood combination house and afterwards returned for an extended stay at a first-class auditorium. Now Fanny Janauschek looked to be treading in his wake. She opened a week's stand at the Grand Opera on the 19th, later appeared at other outlying houses, and then in the spring spent a fortnight at the prestigious Star Theatre. She carried much of her repertory with her, offering *Bleak House, Mary Stuart, Mother and Son, Marie Antoinette, Mari-anne, a Woman of the People,* and one new play. This was **Zillah, the Hebrew Mother** (11-23-83, Grand Opera), taken from Victor Séjour's *La Tireuse des cartes* and telling of an old Jewish fortune teller who spends agonizing years searching for her kidnapped daughter. Critics still held the actress in high esteem, but their comments on her often pitifully small audiences revealed how her public had dwindled.

Attendance was much larger at **Storm Beaten** (11-26-83, Union Square), a sensation-melodrama by the popular Scottish poet and novelist Robert Buchanan. Priscilla Sefton (Effie Ellsler) is courted by Christian Christianson (McKee Rankin) and by Richard Orchardson (Joseph E. Whiting), even though Orchardson has already promised to marry Christianson's sister, Kate (Maud Harrison). Pris-cilla and her suitors find themselves aboard a steamer, which Orchardson attempts to set afire. In the confusion that ensues no one notices an iceberg approaching. The berg hits the ship, which sinks. The three principals are stranded together on an ice floe; Christianson hurls his rival into the sea. But Orchardson is rescued. However, his close brush with death brings about a reformation. Christianson weds Priscilla, and the repentant Orchardson marries Kate. Although the men had the more dramatic roles, Miss Ellsler's "charm of manner and frank method" and Miss Harrison's "genuine pathos" elicited the heartiest applause. Once again playgoers were more welcoming than critics, and the play prospered for two months. On the same night, Robson and Crane bounced into the Star with *Our Boarding House*, and James O'Neill emoted at the Fifth Avenue in *Monte Cristo*.

At Wallack's on December 3, *The Road to Ruin* was revived. Not many years earlier such a revival would have been part of a repertory schedule, but the repertory system of nightly changes of bill, never the most profitable way of mounting plays, had all but disappeared in the face of growing audiences and rising costs. So Holcroft's old comedy stayed on the boards for several weeks, until the next new play was ready.

Yet while the repertory system had become obsolete, the idea of truly long runs, allowing a show to remain until its potential audience was completely exhausted, had not fully taken hold. Daly especially was given to blocking out in advance as much of his season as he could. As a result, he was forced to close his still profitable *Dollars and Sense* to offer Pinero's **Girls and Boys** (12-5-83, Daly's). A circus performer, Gillian West (Virginia Dreher), wants to marry Mark Avery (Yorke Stephens), the adopted son of the gouty, rural Squire Papworth (Charles Fisher). Yet when Papworth disowns Avery and insists the girl marry the local schoolteacher, Simon Prothero (James Lewis), she immediately agrees. Just as the church bells are chiming, however, she has a second change of heart, concluding poverty with Avery is preferable to the dull comforts Prothero could offer. Happily for Prothero, a sweet village maiden, Jenny Kibble (Ada Rehan), is delighted to take the wedding ring he is free to place on her hand. Critics were baffled by the lack of motivation and tension in the play, flaws not concealed even by lovely settings, such as "a blue and red twilight" against which the country lovers woo. After a single discouraging week Daly withdrew the play, but since he had sent *Dollars and Sense* on the road with a second company, he was forced to rush in a revival of *7-20-8* on the 12th.

Two nights before, on the 10th, Booth replaced Irving and Terry at the Star. Comparisons were inevitable, although Booth diplomatically saw to it that his selection of plays—*Richelieu, King Lear, Hamlet, The Fool's Revenge, Othello, Macbeth, The Merchant of Venice,* and *Katherine and Petruchio*—scarcely encroached on Irving's. While the *Times* lamented that Booth's voice had become "wire-like

and nasal," it concurred with others in deeming him far more poetic and elegant. What disturbed many observers was Booth's intransigent refusal to try something new. They pointed to Irving's less classic but more variegated programs. Even worse was Booth's indifference to the quality of his productions (though critics recalled how he had, once upon a time when his own theatre had been new, offered magnificent mountings), and he was also again assailed for his refusal to surround himself with superior supporting casts. The *Times* bemoaned, "It is astonishing that Mr. Booth should lag so far behind other actors in enterprise and courage. . . . The example set by Mr. Irving ought not to be lost upon him altogether. Public taste is, we are convinced, growing beyond Mr. Booth's dull and slow methods as a manager." On Saturday nights, when Booth continued to refuse to perform, W. E. Sheridan and D. H. Harkins took over, presenting *A New Way to Pay Old Debts, Ingomar, Louis XI,* and *Richard III*. Booth returned for a fortnight at the 14th Street Theatre in late March.

Two new plays vied with Booth for attention. Henry C. de Mille's **Delmer's Daughters; or, Duty** (12-10-83, Madison Square), which Belasco staged, dealt with a character that had been popular the previous season—the difficult mother-in-law. De Mille's Martha Delmer (Mrs. Thomas Whiffen) is married to the newly rich John Delmer (W. J. LeMoyne). Her attempt to force her daughters to climb socially nearly destroys their marriages, but since this was a comedy the curtain fell on a scene of domestic felicity. Until now the Madison Square had been the home of unusually long runs. *Delmer's Daughters* was its first failure, surviving only a single week and prompting one wag to suggest the daughters had gone to meet Pinero's girls and boys. *The Rajah* had to be brought back.

Princess Chuck (12-10-83, New Park) was a vehicle for Lizzie Harold, who played the daughter of a man sentenced to hang as a horse thief. He escapes, taking her with him. A relative dies, leaving her a million dollars, and she must spend most of the evening warding off sinister figures who would steal her inheritance. To this end she disguises herself for a time as a man. One critic noted that the play was "laid in California in order that certain slang words . . . may be introduced." The lively star stayed for just a fortnight before returning to the road, for which the play really had been contrived.

If all these openings were not enough, playgoers wanting to reassess Mansfield's Baron Chevrial could see him at the Third Avenue, on part of a tour that was to prove financially unrewarding to him.

Sims and Sydney Grundy's **The Glass of Fashion** (12-17-83, Fifth Ave.) made a comedy from material melodramatists often drew upon. A rich brewer, John Macadam (Frank Mordaunt), buys a fashion and gossip magazine, *The Glass of Fashion,* which has printed an article linking the happily married Mrs. Trevanion (Sara Jewett) with a Russian adventurer, Prince Borowski (Lewis Morrison). The article upsets Colonel Trevanion (Herbert Kelcey). Of course, tragedy is averted in the last act. At a crucial moment Mrs. Trevanion's sister, Peg O'Reilly (Stella Boniface), switches places, thus taking matters on her more rugged shoulders. The play failed to catch on, closing after three weeks.

While divorce may have been touched on lightly in *The Glass of Fashion,* it played a crucial role in a play that opened the same night and a second that premiered the following evening. Leander Richardson's **Expiation; or, The Old, Old Story** (12-17-83, Park Theatre, Brooklyn) took its plot from the cruel inflexibility of French divorce laws and used a telephone conversation, still a rarity onstage, to confound its villain and bring about a happy ending. The heroine is a Frenchwoman who believes herself legally free of her first husband and so takes on a second, an American. The first husband reappears, bent on making trouble. Fortunately, a neighbor who is a retired detective recognizes the man as a onetime convict. The play apparently never moved beyond its Brooklyn showing.

Judge G. C. Barrett's **An American Wife** (12-18-83, Wallack's) also dealt with French law. As a young girl Edna de Beaumar (Rose Coghlan), an American, had been pushed into a marriage with the barbarous Comte de Beaumar (Gerald Eyre), but his cruelty has led her to flee back home, taking her young son, Paul (a trouser role played by May Germon), with her. Here she is befriended by the kindly Colonel Gordon Linsay (Osmond Tearle), a rising attorney. He advises her ruefully that technicalities in the law prevent her getting a divorce, even in America. The comte appears, demanding Edna return to France and threatening to take Paul back with him if she refuses. At the last moment it is discovered that the comte is a bigamist. He is forced to return home alone, while Edna and her lawyer can consider their own marriage. One of the rare American plays produced at Wallack's, it received some favorable notices but failed to draw. Judge Barrett, you may recall, was the man who had ordered *The Passion* closed.

By contrast, **The Pavements of Paris** (12-18-83, Niblo's) seems to have drawn reasonably well during its month's run, although Niblo's was more and more out of the way and unmistakably déclassé. Belot's melodrama was yet another piling on of shopworn clichés. Despite this, or possibly precisely because of it, it lured a particular class of patron unconcerned with growing critical disdain. Years before the main action of the play begins, a count, disgruntled because his wife has given birth to a girl instead of a boy, gives the baby to an obscure peasant. Eighteen years later the dissolute nephew of the count learns he will be heir to his uncle's fortune if he can prove the missing daughter is dead. Unfortunately for him, she is not. Instead, she has grown into a charming teenager, who is known as Marie by the Parisian rabble among whom she lives. Her cousin pays a man to kill her, but her screams frighten him away, and in attempting to flee he is killed by a speeding locomotive. Marie comes into the inheritance and marries a young soldier who saved her life during the Franco-Prussian War. Besides the spectacular railroad scene (which malfunctioned on opening night), sets included a luxurious chateau and the ragpickers' quarters in Paris (complete with a lively can-can). Another production played the 14th Street Theatre for a fortnight in April.

John T. Raymond closed out the year with a revival of *In Paradise* at the 14th Street Theatre on New Year's Eve. Two nights later, on January 2, 1884, Wallack brought back *Old Heads and Young Hearts* to occupy his stage, left empty by the failure of *An American Wife.*

On the 7th Lillie Langtry came into the Fifth Avenue. Her vehicle was yet another version of Sardou's *Nos Intimes,* which Americans already knew under such titles as *Bosom Friends, Our Friends,* and *Friends and Foes.* At first she called her version *Peril.* For some reason, Bartley Campbell took umbrage and threatened her with a lawsuit based on the fact that his own decade-old play had the same title, albeit he long since had rewritten it and changed its name to *Matrimony.* To avoid any unpleasantness, Mrs. Langtry changed her title to **A Wife's Peril.** She was well remunerated during her three-week visit. Charles Coghlan was her leading man.

Raymond soon abandoned *In Paradise* to present David Lloyd's **For Congress** (1-10-84, 14th St.). In the *Evening Post,* J. Ranken Towse described Raymond's character of General Josiah Limber as "an Illinois carpet-bagger, well versed in all the minor arts of corruption, with a plentiful lack of modesty and an abundance of lung power." Limber has two schemes afoot. The first is to get doddering, compliant Peter Woolley (William Cullington) elected to Congress as representative for Woolleyville. Despite all his string-pulling, the election ends in a tie vote because Woolley has voted for his own opponent, so Limber consents, with only a token show of reluctance, to run. At the same time, he is courting not one but two ladies. The comedy's high point came in the third act, when one of the ladies writes him accepting his proposal only to have her letter fall into the hands of the other lady. Limber must retrieve it before she can read it. The play was slight, but Raymond's surefire winks and other antics made it one of his most popular achievements.

A slight, silly play, **Deception; or, Aunt Ann** (1-17-84, Wallack's), profited from skillful playing to chalk up a month's run. Its ridiculous plot turned on the marriage of Ann Daley (Rose Coghlan) to Patrick Merrion. Only the groom is Emily Merrion (Helen Russell) in disguise. Naturally, the real Patrick (Osmond Tearle) enters to complicate matters.

At their own theatre the Rankins starred in **Gabriel Conroy** (1-21-84, Third Ave.), a theatricalization of Bret Harte's novel relating the adventures of a group of travelers stranded in a snowstorm in the California Sierras. Mrs. Rankin played the leading role of Grace Conroy, Gabriel's sister, and Rankin himself was the real hero, Arthur Poinsett, who is traveling under the alias Philip Ashley. Frederic Bryton took the part of the professional gambler, Jack Hamlin. Designed for the road rather than New York, the play was so coldly received that the projected tour was cut short.

New York critics continued to look down their noses on any performer who was not New York–trained, so it was hardly unexpected that they joined in a chorus of sneers when Emma Latham, a popular western star, braved Manhattan to offer Knowles's creaky *The Love-Chase* at the Star on the 21st. One week and the chase was over.

The same critics sometimes showed more leniency, albeit often grudging, to plays and players from such eastern theatrical centers as Boston and Philadelphia. So they had to confess that Joseph Derrick's London hit **Confusion** (1-28-84, Fifth Ave.), which had scored heavily in both those cities, was indeed a funny farce. The expected misunderstandings arise when the secretly married servants of Mortimer (Harry St. Maur) and Rose Mumpleford (Florence Gerard) sneak their baby into the Mumpleford home. Rose has been hinting that she has a surprise for Mortimer—she has surreptitiously brought home a little pug dog—but Mortimer discovers the baby and thinks that is the surprise. Somehow a fluttery spinster, Lucretia Trickleby (Maria Davis), and her aging suitor, Christopher

Blizzard (Henry E. Dixey), are each led to believe that the baby belongs to the other. In a curtain raiser, **Distinguished Foreigners,** Dixey and Miss Gerard spoofed Irving and Terry in *The Merchant of Venice.* Clearly the management had not expected a hit, for Gilbert and Sullivan's *Princess Ida* had been booked to open on February 9. As a result, the farce was transferred to the Comedy Theatre, until recently the home of the long-lived San Francisco Minstrels, and then to two other houses, where it continued its surprising attraction. Dixey walked away with the best reviews, but they were nothing compared to the ones he would receive in September when he began his record-breaking run in the musical *Adonis.*

Sharply divergent opinions greeted Bartley Campbell's **Separation** (1-28-84, Union Square). The *Times* dismissed it as "conventional and shallow"; the *Tribune* thought Campbell "might have been more effective had he thought more of dramatic point and less of moral significance." On the other side of the fence, the *Herald* praised it as "the best play the public has seen from the pen of its author. Its literary quality is superior to anything he has ever done. The construction is closer." The *Dramatic News* proclaimed it "a triumph." All these critics were no doubt aware that manager after manager had rejected the work before Shook and Collier agreed to give it a hearing.

The action of Campbell's play spanned nearly two decades and two continents, moving from America to France and then to Italy. Its heroine, Dora Blair (Eleanor Carey), has a beautiful voice and delights in singing for charity, but her puritanical husband, Benton (Charles Coghlan), is so offended even by this that he takes their baby daughter and disappears. Left to her own resources Dora becomes an opera singer and soon is established as a leading prima donna under the name of Mlle. La Chaise. At intervals in her travels she meets her husband and daughter, Mabel (Effie Ellsler), but for many years a coolness remains. Only long afterwards does Benton relax and allow a reconciliation. Coghlan's somewhat formal style made his reproving husband the center of attention. The play had a moderately successful run of ten weeks, then toured for over a year with another cast, once again meeting with divided notices.

Olive Logan's less famous sister, Celia, was the adaptor from the French of **That Man** (1-28-84, New Park). Like *Separation*, it spotlighted a man who deserts his wife. But in this case the scoundrelly Marquis de Tanguay (Barton Hill) walks out on not only his wife, Muriel (Agnes Booth), but his child as well, in order to enter into a bigamous marriage with Mme Clemence (Margaret Lanner). Mme Clemence's chivalrous brother, Baron d'Emonde (Arthur H. Forrest), who has fallen in love with Muriel, unmasks the marquis's treachery and hounds him until he commits suicide. Although the play's run was brief, it was later rewritten, reset in America, and toured as *An American Marriage*.

Another "western" star, Thomas W. Keene, ran into another dismissive eastern reception when he offered his Richard III at Niblo's on the same night, using Cibber's version. Actually Keene, a huge, florid-faced man, was a native New Yorker who had learned his trade at the old Bowery and at Wood's. Moreover, he did not confine most of his activity to the "West" but toured the whole country incessantly and was one of the most popular of road stars. His touring repertory consisted more of warhorse melodramas such as *Across the Continent, The French Spy,* and *L'Assommoir* than of Shakespeare. But New York critics largely ignored his wide-ranging travels and continued to embrace the notion that performing in western theatres coarsened any actor's art. While he remained at Niblo's only a week as part of his transcontinental trekking, he was not, like Emma Latham, easily discouraged. New Yorkers would see him again and again.

Another actor New York would see repeatedly and usually await more eagerly was Richard Mansfield. To his dismay his post-Broadway tour as Baron Chevrial had not proven profitable, so he abandoned it to assume a principal role in Hjalmar Boyesen's **Alpine Roses** (1-31-84, Madison Square). Boyesen was a Norwegian-American whose play dealt neither with Norway nor America. Set in the Tyrol, it told a story needing only some suitably arioso music to make it an operetta. That Mansfield selected it for his return to New York is interesting, since several of his later vehicles were eventually turned into operettas. The two mountain roses are Ilka (Georgia Cayvan) and Irma (Marie Burroughs). When Count Gerhard von Dornfeld (Mansfield) meets them he falls in love with both. Irma is responsive, but Ilka prefers a rambunctious mountaineer, Hansel (George Clarke), who is forced into the army and finds himself serving under the count. The girls move to Berlin, where Irma becomes a popular singer but where the count's mother, Countess von Dornfeld (Liska von Stamwitz), makes difficulties. Eventually the lovers are properly paired. Critics lauded the play for its charm, never a strong inducement to most playgoers. Nor were reviewers pleased with Mansfield; the *Post* felt he was "too obvious" in a "colourless" part. The play had a

slightly forced run that kept it alive until early April, by which time Mansfield, who had a passable singing voice, had left to accept a role in a real operetta.

Maurice Barrymore's **Nadjezda** (2-11-84, Star) was the initial offering of a projected month-long visit by the graceful Modjeska. The leading man and author had to settle for a single role while the star played two, mother and daughter. His play opens in Warsaw. To save her husband, the beautiful Nadjezda (Modjeska) agrees to sleep with the lascivious Prince Zabarouff (Ian Robertson). However, the prince reneges on his side of the bargain, and over the dead body of her husband Nadjezda drinks poison, but only after turning over her baby daughter to the nihilist, Khorvitch (Frank Clements), and extracting a promise that Khorvitch will raise the child to avenge her parents' deaths. At Nice twenty years later, Nadine (Modjeska) has grown into a woman every bit as lovely as her mother had been. She falls in love with the handsome Paul Devereux (Barrymore), who turns out to be one of Zabarouff's many bastards. But Zabarouff is still very much alive and falls in love with Nadine. Khorvitch jumps at this chance to enflame a father-and-son rivalry. However, the outcome is not quite what he envisions, for Nadine kills the prince and then, mirroring her mother, kills herself.

The word "dark" permeated critical assessments. In the *Tribune* Winter pontificated that Barrymore had handled his "dark theme" with "thoughtful and careful labor [that] has shown the correctness of his judgement." The *Times* observed that while the basic themes were "mixed up darkly," Barrymore had managed to draw his "scenes and characters without darkness of any kind." Barrymore also was praised for his performance but inevitably played second fiddle to Modjeska, who brought to her interpretation "the finesse of a sympathetic, tender, flexible nature."

Most patrons were probably unaware of difficulties behind the scenes, fueled by the offstage romance of the star and her leading man. When they began to surface unpleasantly during the second week, Modjeska's husband and manager forced the new play to be dropped. Performances of *Camille, As You Like It,* and *Frou-Frou* were substituted on all but two nights. Then it was given out that Modjeska was tired and the final week would be canceled, although the star proved strong enough to give a special performance of *Adrienne Lecouvreur* at the Madison Square during that week. A few years later Barrymore brought suit against Sardou and Bernhardt, claiming the idea of *La Tosca* was stolen from his play.

Charges of plagiarism also dogged Buchanan's **Lady Clare** (2-13-84, Wallack's), which Georges Ohnet insisted was stolen from his *Le Maître de forges*. Buchanan disarmingly professed that he had borrowed the basic idea from Ohnet's effort, apparently unaware that it was not all that new. For example, *Pique* and *The Banker's Daughter* both had recounted the saga of a woman, rejected by the man she loves, who marries another man on the rebound and with time comes to love her husband. However, Ohnet and Buchanan added another element—class differences. When Lady Clare (Rose Coghlan) is spurned by Lord Ambermere (Charles Glenney), she consents to marry the self-made John Middleton (Osmond Tearle), although she has no real love for him. Lord Ambermere returns and attempts to have Lady Clare flee with him, but a near-fatal duel between the men brings the woman to her senses. A light, puppy-love affair between two teenagers, Cecil Brookfield (J. C. Buckstone) and Mary Middleton (Adela Measor), served as counterpoint to the somber main story. Whatever its source, *Lady Clare* gave Wallack his most successful offering of the season, running until mid-April.

Rumor had it that the manuscript of **On the Yellowstone** (2-13-84, Cosmopolitan) was found among the papers of Salmi Morse after his suicide. True or not, it was produced at a fitfully used auditorium at 41st and Broadway by a determined actress-manager "from the West." Her name was Mary Blackburn, and in the play she portrayed the equally determined Nancy Jane, a survivor of an Indian massacre of a wagon train. She encounters a man called Kelly (Randolph Murray), who has survived a similar attack during which his wife was kidnapped by the Indians. For Nancy Jane it proves love at first sight, even if Kelly proclaims that he is married and will not look at another woman. She pursues him so relentlessly that the poor man finally attempts to kill himself by jumping into the Yellowstone rapids. Nancy Jane jumps in after him and pulls him out. He again attempts to escape, this time by joining the army. So Nancy Jane becomes a camp follower. Meanwhile, back at the Indian encampment, Mrs. Kelly (Lida Talbot) engineers a revolt and in the confusion runs away. She seeks out and finds her husband, leaving Nancy Jane to kill herself. The rescue from the rapids, with waving sheets passing for the white water, and buckets of real water thrown by stagehands adding to the effect, was a highlight of the production. Another set depicted the famous geysers. The *Herald* added that the stage Indians "rejoiced in paint and feathers enough to gladden the heart of the most fastidious aboriginal."

Of course, that "from the West" hit a nerve and set New York critics' conditioned reflexes going. Snide reviews abounded, and the play closed quickly. But New Yorkers had not heard the last of it, for it preempted paragraphs in several newspapers when one T. J. McGivney, who apparently had bankrolled the affair, charged the star and the playwright had "tried to ruin me" by their extravagance. The stage manager supported McGivney, offering a hilarious description of behind-the-scenes problems, among them the many gaucheries in the original text that required rewriting. Two examples he cited were the original opening, which had the curtain rise to disclose a pair of dead bodies onstage, and the final curtain, which fell on a child being scalped.

Daly's policies must sometimes strike modern theatre lovers as peculiar. Many a time, as with *Dollars and Sense* earlier in the season, he would withdraw a play that was still attracting good attendance simply because he had previously announced another play and dutifully prepared it. Yet at other times he would not keep to his published schedule. His hurried revival of *7-20-8,* rushed in to replace the failed *Girls and Boys,* had prospered beyond anyone's expectation and may have even been allowed to run past the slot allocated *Girls and Boys.* His next offering had long since been announced as *Love on Crutches,* with Garrick's *The Country Girl* to follow. Without any ado, the producer shelved the new farce in favor of the classic comedy on the 16th. The years when Daly or Wallack might mount a repertory of such classics were gone, but Daly and many of his regular patrons still loved such pieces. Daly's ensemble was now probably better suited to bring them to life than even Wallack's players. Critical huzzas greeted both the production and the cast. Ada Rehan's "singular charm of manner, sprightly action, and spontaneity" made her Peggy Thrift one of the great comic creations of the era. The play ran a month (its successor was in rehearsal at the time of its premiere), but its reception prompted Daly to include at least one such revival in almost all his ensuing seasons.

E. G. Lankester's **Warranted** (2-25-84, 14th St.) wasn't. Even its star, Nat C. Goodwin, passed over it when he came to write his reminiscences. Goodwin played Ananias P. Bliss, a matchmaker and head of the Domestic Fidelity Insurance Company. Claims by unsatisfied ladies against Bliss and his underwriting are so high that he hires a poet, Orlando FitzKrank (Jacques Kreuger), to woo ladies as a test before he writes policies on them. By mistake FitzKrank courts Mrs. Bliss (Eliza Weathersby). Bliss's plans turn into a shambles at the studio of Jack Scumble (Robert Coote) a portrait painter, where each of the lady applicants had gone for a seemingly innocent sitting. Typical of other characters' names was Mike Angelo Finnegan. Far more to most reviewers' liking was the short **Those Bells,** in which Goodwin mimicked Irving's Mathias. It was the sort of intratheatrical skit that later revues would have such fun with. Goodwin took off the rejected farce after one week and coupled *Those Bells* with a revival of *The Member for Slocum.* Later he bought the touring rights to *Confusion* and enjoyed a welcome wherever that was mated with his Irving sendup on the road.

For many months rumors had been circulating regarding John McCullough's increasingly erratic behavior. He was suffering, as only an inner circle knew, from paresis, an advanced stage of syphilis, which often led to insanity. Physically it had also taken its toll. His stentorian voice sounded pitifully weak at times, and his once manly vigor seemed sapped. He looked thin and pale. Fear of disappointment or perhaps the period's decorous habit of turning away from unpleasantness kept many seats empty. Only one thing remained constant during his four-week visit to the Star beginning on March 3, and that was his repertory—*Virginius, The Gladiator, Brutus, Othello,* and *Richard III.* He gave his last public performance the following autumn in Chicago, then, after a time in an insane asylum, died a year later. Many of his standard plays were rarely performed in first-class playhouses again. Other prominent figures came to town the same evening as McCullough, offering themselves in popular works from their own more recent repertories. Thus the aging Boucicault, who was considerably older than McCullough and also was nearing the end of his much longer career, starred in *The Shaughraun* at the New Park, while Oliver Doud Byron, still so welcomed by the gallery gods and on the road, continued traipsing in the "well-worn" *Across the Continent* at the Third Avenue.

A new play destined for a generation or more of popularity, again with the gallery gods and on the road, first amused New Yorkers the following Monday. From the start **Peck's Bad Boy** (3-10-84, Comedy), taken from George Peck's series about an almost lovable little brat, was assigned an unfashionable house. The play was advertised as "without plot, but with a purpose—to make people laugh." Young Henry (or Hennery) Peck (William Carroll) is the bane of his neighborhood, leaving behind him a trail of devastation whether he is at home, at the

corner grocery and drug stores, on a picnic, or simply out on the street. His "chum" Jimmy (Mollie Fuller) and his little girlfriend (Florence Bates) accompany him on his rampages. Henry's mayhem reaches a peak in the third act when he provokes his mother into hysterics, flings a scuttle of coal at his "pa," all but destroys the grocery store while swinging on a lighting fixture, shoves a pursuing policeman into a washtub filled with soapy water, and pushes a serving girl out a window. The endemic, sadistic violence in the piece was not unlike that featured years later in film cartoons and clearly appealed to the same atavistic instincts. Critics agreed there was no real story line but also acknowledged that uncritical audiences loved every minute of it. Future stars such as George M. Cohan and Frank Daniels gained invaluable experience heading two of the comedy's many road companies, which toured unceasingly until just before World War I.

Although they had not served him well, Daly could not overcome his predilection for the prototypical musicals of the period. So when he presented Jacobson's *Ein gemachter Mann* as **Red Letter Nights; or, Catching a Croesus** (3-12-84, Daly's), which he called "an entirely new eccentric comedy, in four acts and a Kermess," he sprinkled it with songs and dances. The Kermess took place at Belmonico's, which contemporaries recognized as New York's finest eatery, Delmonico's. A thin, serviceable plot told of a young girl, Tony Pogswog (Ada Rehan), whose upstart parents want her to marry a titled Englishman, but who prefers Tom Crayon (John Drew). A highlight was the moment in which Tony, set on discouraging her importunate suitor, Lord Muddleford (Charles Fisher), dons a man's dressing gown and galoshes and, with her hair drenched and disheveled from a soaking rain, romps through a tomboyish rendition of the old nursery song "Miss Jenny Jones." They play proved a downbeat finale for Daly's season, but the "Miss Jenny Jones" number so stopped the show that Daly found a way to insert it in subsequent revivals of *Dollars and Sense.*

Conquest and Pettitt's eight-year-old **Queen's Evidence** (3-17-84, Mount Morris) had been tried out several seasons before in Boston and elsewhere under the title *A Free Pardon* and had failed. Most likely only the need to fill the stages of a rapidly growing number of combination houses prompted its revival. An undistinguished cast played out its story of a wife, wrongly accused of infidelity, who is deserted by her husband. When he later recognizes her innocence he returns to her, finding she has gone blind and is menaced by a man who attempts to drown her by throwing her in a canal. Just the melodramatic escapism sought by patrons of neighborhood houses, it played a week here and a week there, remaining on lesser circuits for several seasons.

A short-lived failure, **Her Sacrifice** (3-24-84, New Park), supposedly was drawn from an unidentified French play. The heroine, Gabrielle (Kate Forsyth), believes her father, Michael Gerard (F. F. Mackay), is a murderer, and she nearly destroys both her marriage and her life to keep the secret. She at last learns that Gerard is not her father after all. Two weeks and the work was gone.

When Irving and Terry returned on the 31st it meant that, with Booth at the 14th Street Theatre, the most prestigious English and American performers were playing a few blocks from each other.

Some critics felt Ettie Henderson's **Claire and the Forge Master** (4-5-84, Fifth Ave.) was a better dramatization of *Le Maître de forges* than was *Lady Clare*, just then concluding its run at Wallack's. Mrs. Henderson's transcription hewed closer to the original, although the dramatic duel now took place offstage. However, they felt its star, Maude Granger, was too mechanical and whiny as the heroine. It ran a single week. Some indication of how rapidly a nonunionized theatre could function was indicated by the fact that the previous booking at the theatre, the peripatetic *Confusion,* closed on Friday night, the 4th, and the new play opened the following day—at a matinee.

David Belasco's **May Blossom** (4-12-84, Madison Square) had a story that dimly echoed the main theme of *Le Maître de forges*. Belasco set his play against a background of the Civil War, a background that would suddenly spring into vogue now that the war was twenty years behind us. And like so many of the Civil War plays in the offing, Belasco's would place its sympathies with the defeated Confederacy, although in this case those sympathies were more implicit than stated. At the outbreak of the war both Richard Ashcroft (Walden Ramsey) and Steve Harland (Joseph Wheelock) propose to May Blossom (Georgia Cayvan), the daughter of a fisherman who lives on the Virginia coast of Chesapeake Bay. May accepts Richard's proposal, but immediately afterward Richard is arrested as a spy. Only Steve witnesses the arrest, and Richard extracts a promise from Steve to inform May of what has happened. Assuming Richard will be shot, Steve breaks his promise and instead leads May to believe that Richard is already dead. When a year passes without word from Richard, Steve again proposes and is

accepted. Two years later, just before a gala party, Richard suddenly reappears, having escaped from prison. May is horrified but concludes she must remain wedded to Steve for the sake of their young child. Richard returns to the war, and Steve, surmising that May can never again truly love him, also enlists. Richard is killed in battle, but after the war Steve does not return either. Only six years later does he come home. Unca Bartlett (W. J. LeMoyne), their village parson, helps effect a reconciliation.

The pious Mallory brothers, who owned the theatre, at first balked at mounting a play with so perfidious a leading man as Steve, and later they found the *Times* in agreement, when it condemned him and his rewards as "immoral." Indeed, most critics felt that many of Belasco's turns of plot defied logic. Some also questioned the need for such scenes of treacly sentimentality as that in which children bury a dead bird. On the whole, however, they were pleased, seeing it as one of the few recent American plays of palpable merit. The *Dramatic Mirror* praised it for its "backbone," while the *Tribune*'s Winter, brushing aside objections to its morals and logic, insisted its "dramatic fabric captivates entire sympathy." The play's success—it ran for 169 performances—pushed Miss Cayvan into stardom.

• • •

Georgia Cayvan (1858–1906) was a native of Bath, Me. A brunette with a round face, wide eyes, and a hint of a pug nose, she had performed in Boston before replacing Effie Ellsler in *Hazel Kirke.* Her acting in *The Professor, The White Slave,* and *Siberia* had helped secure her reputation. Although initially her training in a dying old school of melodramatics had been evident from her "reeling, staggering, and clutching at furniture" in moments of high emotion, with time she adopted more reserved, modern methods of expression.

• • •

A far less successful play opened the same night. George Jessop and William Gill's **Stolen Money** (4-12-84, New Park), itself stolen from Charles Reade's *Singleheart and Doubleface,* told a story of a good, devoted woman, Hester (Kate Forsyth), married to a drunken, unfaithful husband, Paul Vansittart (Loudon McCormack), and used most of the same players seen earlier at the house in *Her Sacrifice.* One addition to the cast was co-author Gill, who assumed the part of Woolf Arons, a maligned but honest Jew who helps bring about a happy denouement.

A. R. Cazauran, who had adapted successfully so many plays for Palmer during Palmer's management of the Union Square, returned to his old haunt with what he claimed was an original drama, **The Fatal**

Letter (4-14-84, Union Square), although several critics proffered various suggestions as to possible sources. His story centered on yet one more woman who discovers her husband is not what he seems and, like *May Blossom,* unfolded against a Civil War background. When the fatal letter of the title discloses Captain Trevor (Joseph Haworth) betrayed Confederate troops to Union forces during the war and thus caused the deaths of her father and brother, Rachel Trevor (Helen Barry) leaves her husband, taking with her their six-year-old son, Harry (Master Tommy Russell). The captain is resolved to retrieve Harry, regardless how cruel the means. Fortunately, Rachel finds a wise counselor in Dr. Bell (Charles Walcot). Years pass. Harry (now played by Edwin Clearly) has grown to manhood. He knows nothing about his father's real history, so when he hears his father's reputation besmirched he challenges the disparager to a duel. His opponent's well-aimed shot might have killed him had not Captain Trevor, who had heard about the duel, stepped in front of his son and been killed in his stead. Unfortunately for Cazauran, his own skills seemed limited to translating better craftsmen's work. Instead of the long run so many of his adaptations had enjoyed, his original drama survived a mere two weeks.

On the same night, Wallack's put on F. C. Burnand's **Betsy,** an English version of the same French play produced years before as *Baby.* Two farce-comedies, those prototypical musical comedies, were also presented that evening—**Skipped by the Light of the Moon** at the Fifth Avenue and Hoyt's **A Rag Baby** at the 14th Street.

Leonard Grover's **A Great Scheme; or, The Dime Museum** (4-16-84, Comedy) seems to have started out as a theatrical spoof, twitting the ineptitude of playwrights and performers trying to supply the requirements of a dizzily expanding road. In fact the term "road" was apparently so new in describing the theatrical hinterlands that it was written with quotation marks in discussions of the play. Regrettably Grover, who had written the hugely successful *Our Boarding House,* was unable to sustain his comedy, which by the second act deteriorated into another primitive musical. His story centered on the Stuyvesant Square Travelling Company's attempt, under the direction of General Bunn Barkadoo (Leonard Grover, Jr.), to rehearse a new play starring Eager Charles (James Russell), a young actor who had paid for his position. (Knowledgeable playgoers may have read between the lines a particular sendup of Colonel Henry Savage's Castle Square Opera Company in Boston.) When their play fails, the actors accept work as freaks in a dime museum. The real

play was as bad as the play in the plot, although there is no record of what its performers did when the show was withdrawn abruptly.

Milton Nobles, so long confined to second-class houses with his perennial *The Phoenix,* captured a brighter limelight briefly when he starred in a new vehicle, **Love and Law** (4-21-84, 14th St.). The star played Felix O'Paff, an Irish-American lawyer, who must protect Rita (Dollie Nobles) after her dissolute and disowned uncle, Jasper Craddock (O. H. Barr), attempts to have Giovanni Conti (G. W. Barnum) kidnap her. Craddock is furious that Rita has been made heiress to the estate he had hoped to inherit. O'Paff must disguise himself as Conti to help confound villains. The play was really not designed for more sophisticated audiences, but having garnered that sought-after New York imprimatur it joined Nobles's bills in his tireless touring.

Selina Dolaro, who was a star in several of the period's musicals, displayed her versatility by assuming the title role in **Justine** (4-21-84, New Park), which she claimed to have adapted from a work by Sardou, *Les Diables noirs.* A wife is led to believe her husband is guilty of all sorts of horrible actions after he sells one of her rings to pay a debt of honor. She goes mad and attempts to kill both her husband and herself by setting fire to their home. Neither Miss Dolaro's writing nor her acting pleased most critics, so the play ran only one week. But one critic's observation about Eben Plympton, who played the husband, suggests how performing styles were in flux. The reviewer urged the actor not to "talk as a tragedian" when he presented "a man in every-day life."

Now approaching the end of his career and a few months earlier reported near death, Lester Wallack made one of his increasingly rare appearances on his own stage, beginning on the 23rd, when he came out as Prosper Couramont in *A Scrap of Paper,* which had been pressed into service to replace the failed *Betsy.* For an aging, ailing man he showed marvelous vigor and seemed to have lost none of his elan. One concession to his age was an auburn wig. On May 3, he returned to his "youthful" Charles Marlow in *She Stoops to Conquer.* He was sixty-four. John Gilbert and Mme Ponisi, who played Mr. and Mrs. Hardcastle, were seventy-four and sixty-four respectively. And they were the last of the great performers who had graced Wallack's stages. For all their excellence, the renditions at Wallack's by this time must have had a certain geriatric quality to them.

Random Shot (5-5-84, Comedy) was an Americanization of a German farce. Its star, J. Newton

Gotthold, was also its adaptor. His Random Shot takes on an alias, not realizing that the name he has selected belongs to another man in his neighborhood. Confusions are quick to arise. The play was a touring piece, which remained at its new home for three weeks before again wandering on.

Probably no playgoers expected the Star to sustain its parade of distinguished performers. Irving and Terry, Booth, Modjeska, McCullough, and Janauschek had followed one another in thrilling sequence. Yet patrons may well have been startled by the next offering, even though Lester Wallack was announced as one of the producers. The Frohman brothers, Gustave and Charles, were co-producers, but they had yet to make a name for themselves, while the play's director, David Belasco, was also a relatively new name to be reckoned with.

Robert G. Morris's **The Pulse of New York** (5-10-84, Star) was a "localized" sensation-melodrama. Although the playwright was also a well-liked drama critic, who possibly should have known better, his plot was as flimsy as it was exhausted. A young man falsely accused of a crime he did not commit loves a girl raised by a man she believes to be her father, but who is not. It takes an honest, rosy-cheeked detective to straighten out matters. What really counted were the scenes of New York life, including the Central Police Station and the Tombs. And since this was a sensation-melodrama there had to be a sensation. In this case, it was a novel variation on the endless shipwrecks and train derailments of earlier examples, with the villain, aided by a "crazed negro," pulling a switch that will cause two elevated trains to collide.

The *Tribune*'s critic, probably from his sentiments and discursiveness William Winter, gave the opening exceptionally extended coverage. But most of the review dealt with denigrating the play's genre as a whole, especially the "excessive prominence given to the life in the 'slums.' " Most likely it was the fact that this particular play offered "no slums and no squalor" that prompted the lengthy notice, which nonetheless rued that "a thin story . . . contains nothing new" and saw the work as "made tributary to the scenery." The reviewer went on to expose the transparency of the playwright's outline, with an act-by-act breakdown of the work. The first act showed the murder on the steps of Trinity Church on Christmas Eve; the second found the wrong man being arrested; the third recounted his grilling by the police; the fourth saw him booked and tried; and the final act witnessed his ultimate acquittal, thanks in no small measure to the work of Inspector Barnes (George Clarke), who conveyed a "strong image of taciturn authority and patient vigilance" and who was made up to resemble New York's actual chief of police. Despite critical carpings the play toured for several seasons.

More decrepit clichés abounded in Frank Harvey's **The Wages of Sin** (5-12-84, 14th St.), which was advertised as a London hit. Ruth (Agnes Booth) is led to believe that the man she loves, George Brand (Eben Plympton) has been unfaithful, so she marries Harry Wentworth (Gilbert Elliott) on the rebound. To her distress, Harry proves a criminally inclined weakling who forces her into a life of degradation and, when she balks, attempts to kill her. In the end it is Harry who dies, leaving Ruth free to wed George. However trite the basic motifs may have been, reviewers found the play solidly constructed and filled with thoughtful characters and dialogue. They also admired the excellent acting. As a result, the play enjoyed a month's run (twice as long as *The Pulse of New York* had lasted) despite the hot weather and went on to an even longer afterlife on the road.

At the very lowest level of Manhattan's combination houses, a melodrama called **On Hand** (5-12-84, 8th St.) allowed its persecuted heroine to suffer through several acts before finding vindication and happiness just as the final curtain fell. Because the theatre catered heavily to what a later generation would term "ethnics," the cast of characters was filled with such figures as a "Chinaman," a Jewish clothes peddler, and a volatile Italian, as well as a Yankee farmer. The play ran three weeks. Although the theatre made a point of attempting to please its relatively hard-up and not totally acclimated audiences with this play and such older pieces as *Mose, a Dealer in Second-Hand Clothes* (note the slight title change), it also offered many of the standard melodramas, comedies, and spectacles of the time along with a few such "classics" as *Ingomar*.

How quickly fashions in playwriting can arise was demonstrated when the season's third play about the Civil War appeared. Elliott Barnes's **The Blue and the Gray** (5-19-84, Niblo's) took as its main theme a motif that was ignored by *May Blossom* and *The Fatal Letter* but would prove virtually the sine qua non of later Civil War plays—the romance of lovers on opposing sides. When news of Fort Sumter reaches his New England village, Mark Stanley (Joseph E. Whiting) grabs his musket and enlists. On her father's Louisiana plantation, Ruth White (Elizabeth Hudson) watches her friends and neighbors go off to battle. Somehow Ruth and Mark meet and fall in love. Ruth's father has become a guerrilla leader in Mississippi, where Mark has been posted.

The father's maneuvers place him in a position where he might be able to kill Mark. Instead Mark captures the colonel (Horace Vinton), who later succeeds in escaping. Shortly after, Mark is blinded in battle and is in turn taken prisoner by the colonel. The colonel releases him on the condition that he renounce Ruth. After the war the colonel dies and Ruth inherits his estate. She goes in search of Mark, finds him and his mother in poverty and about to be evicted, and tells him she still loves him. They agree to marry. For a while the play was later known as *Ruth's Devotion*. By the time better handlings of the subject were offered, *The Blue and the Gray* had long disappeared.

Nor would **Whose Are They?** (5-26-84, Star) be long remembered, although its author would be—as an actor. He was E. H. Sothern, son of the late comedian. His plot centered on a haplessly married man, Theophilus Pocklinton (Joseph Haworth), who is badgered by a harridan mother-in-law and a suspicious wife, especially after an unidentified lady's garter unleashes complications. However, Sothern slyly added another role, which he hoped would steal the show and which did; of course, he himself played it. That was the part of Melchisidec Flighty, a jabberwockying lunatic. The farce was not a success, but that did not prevent its being taken on the road again in the following season, when it was retitled *Crushed* (hinting at his father's *Crushed Tragedian?*) and failed once more. Because he eventually became one of our most admired Shakespearean actors, it is sometimes forgotten that Sothern rose to fame as a comedian.

As they so frequently did in this era, comedy and melodrama went hand in hand in **Captain Mishler** (5-26-84, Comedy), a sequel to *One of the Finest* and another chance for Gus Williams, the dialect comedian, to portray his bungling police officer. Mishler's antics were set against the background of the story of an adventurer who deserts his wife and child, bigamously marries a rich heiress, commits a brutal murder in a park, unjustly implicates his brother-in-law in the crime, and is eventually shot to death in a courtroom. This odd, somewhat ghastly juxtaposition of hilarity and horror apparently pleased Williams's followers, so he toured with it for a season or more.

The New Park Theatre closed out its season by reaching back to *The Dead Heart,* a play once identified with Edwin Adams, Edward Eddy, and a departed school of emoters. The revival ran two weeks, beginning on the 26th, to mediocre business.

Business would soon be much better at another, seemingly unlikely theatre—Tony Pastor's. Precisely how the numerous vaudeville houses of the time were run is something of a mystery. At intervals many of them briefly abandoned variety to turn their stages over to a farce or newfangled musical. Thus when the Grand Central Theatre offered its patrons a play on February 4, the opening went largely unnoticed. An opening at Pastor's prestigious little auditorium was a different matter, so when the same play returned to New York to take the boards at Pastor's, the critics did come and the next day reported their findings. The authorship of **The Corner Grocery; or, The Bad, Forgetful Boy** (6-9-84, Tony Pastor's) was universally attributed to its star, the vaudevillian Dan Sully. Beyond that the reviewers found themselves at loggerheads—though not very urgently so. There were disagreements over whether the farce was in fact a farce or whether it was one of the new-style slipshod musical entertainments, dotted with songs, dances, and other variety turns. A melodramatic thread tied together the comedy's more lighthearted moments. And whatever it was, was it also a lampoon of *Peck's Bad Boy* or a blatant steal of that play's main idea? Reviewers further disagreed on just how good the entertainment was.

Michael Nolan is made the guardian of a rich orphan, who falls in love with Nolan's older son. A treacherous rival resorts to dirty tricks to prevent the girl from inheriting her money or marrying her sweetheart, but he does not reckon with Nolan's mischievous young son, Jimmie, who has his own bag of sly tricks to put the malefactor in his place. Sully impersonated the grocer into August, despite the hot summer nights, and returned regularly thereafter to Pastor's or elsewhere in the role. Of course, each year his tiny nemesis, first played by a tyke listed variously as Master Malvey or Master Fulvey, was played by a new youngster, and over the seasons more and more vaudeville bits seemed to intrude. Tugging on his goatee, scratching his closely cropped hair, or biting off the tip of his pipe in a temper, Sully kept on performing in the play for more than a decade, although never in first-class "legitimate" houses.

Late in the season several of the lowest-rung combination houses played host to an unusual band of performers. The actors, who appeared at the 8th Street Theatre at the end of June and at the Cosmopolitan a month later, were members of the Astor Place [Shakespearean] Company of Colored Tragedians, so many playgoers came disposed to laugh and did just that. The *Times,* never sympathetic to black actors in this era, was especially cruel. It characterized Benjamin G. Ford's Othello as "dull," Alice Brooks's Desdemona as "feeble," and J. A. Arneaux's Iago as "a passable 'amateur' delineation," then went on to record the "roars of laughter" provoked by "J. S. Webster's Rodrigo, an amazing specimen of namby-pambyism and awkwardness, and by G. F. Chinn's Brabantio, whose facial and tonsorial 'make up' was strikingly suggestive of the head of a skye terrier."

Another new play that baffled some critics was Charles F. Dunbar and Fred Wren's **Distrust** (7-21-84, 14th St.), the last new play of the season. Many were uncertain whether it was a drama or a comedy. Part of the problem may have been that it was first successfully mounted in Buffalo, which some of the reviewers no doubt perceived as part of the theatrically degrading West. But then the play seems not to have been much help either, for it revolved around a husband's attempt to bring to light a dark secret in his wife's past. The secret turns out to be that years before, when she had not been wealthy, she had worked as a chambermaid. Most critics dutifully recorded the audience's laughter but were loath to guess how much of it the authors had hoped for.

1884–1885

Denied the gift of hindsight, contemporary playgoers could well have set down the new season as another passable theatrical year, illuminated occasionally by the acting of some veteran performers or by the restoration of an older play. Certainly this season, like the entire first half of the 1880s, was not generously forthcoming with exciting new plays. And even many of the better novelties trafficked unthinkingly in timeworn clichés. Seemingly nothing could loosen the grip of the false accusation on playwrights' fancies, while all season long the unequal marriage provided the frame for plot after plot. Just as the preceding season had resurrected the Civil War as a popular theme, so for a time at the season's beginning another motif threatened to dominate plays, one that matched the inevitable lack of hindsight in an oddball way: no sight at all. Not even Kate Claxton, groping her way across the stage in the enormously successful *The Two Orphans* ten years before (and she was still playing it in combination houses), had triggered such a rash of blind heroes and heroines.

Only time would reveal the significance and durability of many of the mechanical and technological changes introduced during the season, of some interesting modifications of play construction, and of the firm footholds theatrical giants of decades just ahead were establishing. The engineering wonders were associated almost entirely with Steele MacKaye's newest theatre, but several playhouses brought out new works, often well received, that were singularly advanced in their rejection of the spatial and temporal excesses of mid-19th-century melodrama. A unity of place and time, which actually harked back to the earliest Greek dramas, was perceived as imparting a reasonableness, a tautness, and most of all, an encouragingly embraced modernity. And whether plays were old-fashioned or newfangled, they frequently were written by young authors and cast with young players soon to find their names above the title.

For some reason, as inexplicable to contemporary commentators as to historians, ticket sales to nonmusicals nosedived both in New York and on the road. National economics could not explain the drop, nor could the quality of plays and productions justify it. *The Private Secretary* chalked up the longest straight-play run of the season, 200 performances, at a tiny playhouse, the Madison Square, noted for its long runs. Elsewhere, a few stars, such as the sensational Irving-Terry team and the aging, dyed-in-the-wool traditionalist Booth, pulled strong grosses. So did most of Daly's productions. Other stars and other companies, greeted with equal or more fervent enthusiasm, regularly had to curtail engagements or play to distressingly small audiences.

The very first attraction of the new season offered one of the most promising of upcoming stars. **Caprice** (8-11-84, New Park) was a comedy-drama written expressly for Minnie Maddern by Howard P. Taylor. Its simple story depicted the difficulties besetting the marriage of a naive country girl, Mercy Baxter (Miss Maddern), and a young sophisticate, Jack Henderson (A. H. Forrest). At one low point in their marriage Mercy walks out, determined to become a "lady" on her own. Some critics still spotted all too cute touches of Lotta in Maddern's acting, but they agreed that she had marvelous vocal projection "distinct to the furthest corner of the deep gallery" and that "her performance, from beginning to end, was one series of triumphs with her audience." An especially memorable moment came at the close of the first act, when Mercy has been particularly humiliated. Cuddling up by the fireplace at the rear of the stage, with the firelight playing mournfully on her sad, pale face and red hair, she consoles herself by softly singing "In the Gloaming" as the curtain falls. After two weeks, the young leading lady began a cross-country tour with Henry Miller as her leading man.

If plays with black performers were rare and treated with ridicule when they did appear, plays with blacks as principal characters were equally rare and, *Uncle Tom's Cabin* excepted, seemed always to be comedies or to ignore specifically black problems. Much in the manner of *Our Colored Brother* and *Smoke* of ten or a dozen years earlier, **Our Colored Friend** (8-11-84, Tony Pastor's) told of a black man—played, naturally, by a white in blackface, in this case H. J. Myers—who helps whites out of several scrapes. One concerned Laura Lambert (Annie Ward Tiffany), a newlywed whose self-serving husband finds a richer woman, demands that Laura hand over their marriage certificate and, when she refuses, attempts to murder her. A second problem involved a young man deprived of his rightful inheritance. But a black was not the only figure whose characterization was tinged with condescension, however affectionate, for a Jew named Morris Levy Solomon (E. Walton), "a misfit clothing merchant," also wandered in and out of the action. *Our Colored Friend*, like *Caprice*, stayed two weeks, then moved on to tour.

Both plays may have suffered from a later summer heat wave, which also served to dampen enthusiasm for J. K. Tillotson's **Queena** (8-18-84, Union Square), another mounting designed primarily for the road. Queena Montrose (Lillian Spenser) has married Lord Walter Huntington (Eben Plympton), but their marriage has been kept a secret because Walter's father would consider it beneath his son's station. For all their caution, Walter's father discovers the truth and has Walter kidnapped. He is committed to an asylum, where he suffers an attack of brain fever, which leaves him blind. Thinking she has been deserted, Queena selects the path of several earlier heroines, taking up singing and becoming a famous opera star, under the name Mme René. A few years later, Walter hears Mme René perform, recognizes her voice, and, following some initial coolness on her part, effects a reconciliation. The beautiful Sadie Martinot, even then celebrated as a clotheshorse, virtually stole the show as Florence Nightingale Fletcher, a fortune hunter who has the good humor to see the absurdity of her schemes and so eventually settles for a poor boy she long has loved. After three weeks and some cast changes, *Queena* embarked on its own tour.

No other late summer offering was awaited with such great expectations as **Called Back** (9-1-84, Fifth Ave.). Hugh Conway's feverishly sensational novel had been a best-seller on both sides of the Atlantic, and the dramatization of the book, done by the author and J. Comyns Carr, had been drawing crowded houses in London since the preceding May. Backed by the Madison Square Theatre, young Daniel Frohman took charge of producing the work and seeing to it that it received considerable advance publicity. Playgoers' appetites were whetted with news that, since the physical production was so large it could not be handled by the Madison Square's unique moving stages, a search for a larger stage was under way. Moreover, Frohman revealed that to play the lead he had hired the tall, blond, and dashingly handsome Robert Mantell, who had garnered marked attention opposite Fanny Davenport in *Fedora*, and would pay him the then newsworthy sum of $10,000 to remain with the production for the whole season.

Mantell portrayed Gilbert Vaughan, a blind young man who inadvertently stumbles upon a murder being committed under the aegis of a dangerous spy, Paolo Macari (W. J. Ferguson). The victim is the brother of Gilbert's friend Pauline (Jessie Millward), who also witnesses the killing and is driven out of her mind by its horror. Sightless as he is, Gilbert resolves to bring the murderers to justice and see that Pauline is "called back" to sanity. He does both. His task takes him across the map of Europe, including a Siberian prison camp (nihilists were never far away from playwrights' thoughts at this time). The desolate Russian landscape was crowded with impoverished peasants, bedraggled prisoners, and romantically dressed Cossacks. Wing-and-drop settings were still employed, and on opening night one of the wing flats, representing trees in Regent's Park, stuck in its tracks so that it inadvertently became part of the next setting—a garret. A number of favorable reviews implied that critics felt expectations had not been raised unduly high. Mantell and Ferguson were accorded flattering notices. But playgoers, possibly discouraged by the persistent, suffocating heat wave, failed to respond. The drama hung on for eight weeks before departing for a season-long tour, not all of it with Mantell.

Heat alone could not be blamed for the short runs of two other plays that opened the same night. Morgan Bates and Elwyn A. Barron's **A Mountain Pink** (9-1-84, Comedy) hinted at the folk plays that would come into vogue some decades later, centering as it did on life among North Carolina moonshiners. But its approach was traditional blood-and-thunder melodrama. Harold Wilmot (Charles F. Tangay) comes trudging through the backwoods seeking a long-lost heiress but is nearly shot by some irate, suspicious moonshiners. Only the timely intervention of Sincerity Weeks (Ada Gilman), a naive but shrewd young lady who has been raised by the moonshiners, saves him. Before many minutes passed, most knowledgeable playgoers had figured out that Sincerity and the heiress were one and the same. For no small number of these patrons T. M. Hunter's Felix Bonnory, a murderous but likable moonshiner, was the highlight of the evening. The play had already enjoyed success on the road, so when Broadway would not buy it, it hastily returned to the hinterlands.

Walter Standish's **Fickle Fortune** (9-1-84, 14th St.) also survived only a single week. It recorded the comic misadventures of a carpenter, Alonzo Mooney (Eugene O. Jepson), who unexpectedly comes into a huge fortune and must spend the evening learning to live with his newfound riches.

Three nights later the season's biggest hit opened, but it was a musical. *Adonis* made a star of Henry E. Dixey, who had won such raves in last season's *Confusion,* and became the first show in Broadway history to run over 500 performances. Its tale of a statue brought to life had been used successfully before in nonmusicals, and would be soon again.

The unyielding heat wave may have had no effect on a new musical burlesque, but comedies and dramas were not so lucky. The better of the two major premieres on the next Monday was the second play of the young season by J. K. Tillotson. Like his *Queena* it was designed for the road and came into New York early on, so that it could boast of a Rialto run in its touring advertisements. Actually, the road had already seen it briefly the preceding season, when it was called *Belmont's Bride* and the principal characters had different names. Now it was known as **Lynwood** (9-8-84, Union Square). Tillotson went to the newly stylish Civil War for his background and, as Barnes had done in *The Blue and the Gray,* made his lovers espouse opposing causes. Since the playwright had pitted a northern woman against a former Confederate in his *The Planter's Wife,* such friction was not new to him, but his earlier play had a postwar setting.

In both his plays the leading lady was Maude Granger, who may have commissioned the works to prop up her faltering career. This time she played a Kentucky belle, Lucile Carlysle, who has been courted by both Victor Blanchard (Eben Plympton) and Dudley Middleton (B. T. Ringgold). With the outbreak of hostilities Blanchard becomes a Union officer and Middleton is made a lieutenant colonel of the Kentucky Independents. Blanchard is captured and imprisoned in a camp run by Lucile's brother, Edwin (W. S. Harkins). When Blanchard attempts to

escape he is caught by Edwin. A scuffle ensues, and Middleton, who long has hated Edwin, uses the confusion to kill him. Blanchard himself believes he has killed his sweetheart's brother, and when Lucile learns this she confronts him accusingly. Of course, Middleton's treachery is finally exposed—with the crucial help of a line drawing made at the crime scene by a war correspondent, Epencetus Carter (Charles Morris)—and Lucile forgives her future husband. New Yorkers continued to see Miss Granger as a limited actress, nor did they much like her new vehicle. After a month's run, she took the play on tour, where she was accorded a warmer welcome and still considered an important star.

E. J. Swartz's **Dad's Girl** (9-8-84, 14th St.) ran only half as long. Tomboy heroines were usually featured in plays about the appropriately wild West, but Swartz made his Mulvina Hoskins (Lizzie May Ulmer) a New Englander. Actually, she has not spent all her years there. Possibly to have the best of both worlds, the playwright also made her the adopted daughter of an old western roustabout who has earned a mint and retired to the East. Mulvina does not have to roam far from home to help solve a series of thefts and murders, or to find the right young man. However, some playgoers felt the evening's scene stealer was G. C. Boniface in the role of Vasco de Gama Biles, a crusty gentleman who lives by his wits. One striking setting was a view of Nantasket Beach with "the light from a monster moon falling upon a placid sea."

The dramatic action moved from New England to Illinois in David K. and Milton Higgins's **Burr Oaks** (9-16-84, Grand Opera, Brooklyn), a drama that enjoyed long years of popularity on the road but apparently never played Manhattan, at least not in its original form and under its original title. In the late 1890s, when David had made a small name for himself as the author of touring plays, a revised, rechristened version was performed at some of Broadway's combination houses. But in 1884 the brothers were Chicago journalists and unfamiliar to most playgoers.

Their story called to mind *The Silver King,* for their titular hero (Walter Bentley) flees home and family in the mistaken belief that he has killed his grandfather. Years later, having fought in the Civil War, he returns to his Illinois village. In tattered clothes and using a false name, he takes a room at the local inn, where by chance his wife, Margie (May Brookyn), and his young son also are lodged. One night he decides to sneak into their room to have a look at the sleeping boy. He is seen leaving the room and is accused of attempted theft. "Yes, I am a thief," he acknowledges. "I have stolen a kiss from a little boy." But he has also learned who really killed his grandfather. The murderer is none other than Eben Hartstone (B. F. Horning), the very man who is courting the presumably widowed Margie. Oaks's plan to expose Hartstone nearly is frustrated when the killer falls into some raging rapids. Oaks jumps into the turbulent waters (shown by waving canvas) and pulls Hartstone out, exclaiming, "Saved for justice!" But Hartstone is a tough cookie, not one to confess, until Oaks has a friend appear dressed as his murdered grandfather's ghost to scare Hartstone into blurting out the truth.

Many observers had suggested that Lotta was inching toward full-fledged musical theatre, so they may not have been surprised when she appeared at Daly's on the 15th in Hervé's *Mam'zelle Nitouche,* which she had watched the great Judic perform in Paris. Ironically, much of Hervé's score had to be discarded, since Lotta's voice was not of a character to do it justice. A few tinnier songs were inserted, but the mounting that packed the theatre for three weeks was less of a real musical than it had been in Paris.

If many critics held Lotta in disdain or at best retained serious reservations about her limited talents, they virtually all conceded she knew how to pick a vehicle that would show off her abilities and delight her fans. By contrast, Fanny Janauschek, for all her superb histrionic gifts, often displayed an embarrassing lack of common theatrical sense in her choice of plays. She demonstrated this again when she appeared in Henry Meredith's **My Life** (9-17-84, 14th St.), a play so convoluted that most reviewers despaired of figuring out its plot. The star only aggravated matters by assuming three different roles. The *Herald* reported that the curtain rose on a "Parisian garret with a view of Notre Dame illuminated by a vermillion moon. Mrs. Janauschek [in the role of Mico] lies behind an overturned table while Mr. Frank Clements sticks knives into her body and sprinkles the floor with petroleum. Then the house burns, the vermillion moon grows black, Notre Dame is blotted out, and Mrs. Janauschek rushes, blinded, through the smoke." She also saves a baby girl from the fire. Twenty years later, as Leben, the blind lady of the Moorland (role two, possibly an offshoot of Mico), she fends off the trickery of a none too savory actress, Circe Encore (role three), so that her adopted daughter can wed a baronet.

The Hoop of Gold (9-22-84, Grand Opera) spotlighted a young married couple, Richard Wrench (George Morton) and his heiress wife, Ruth (Georgia Tyler). (You knew Ruth was an heiress since her maiden name was Bullion.) Their marriage seems headed for years of bliss until a false accusation of theft sends Richard to prison, and his imprisonment somehow impoverishes Ruth, who is driven to attempting suicide. (She is thoughtful enough to jump from a beautiful recreation of the Thames Embankment, where another humongus calcium moon conveniently lights her rescuer's way.) To no one's surprise, villainy is trounced, and the couple and their money are reunited just before the final curtain. The vociferous gallery gods, still a feature of all combination houses such as the Grand, had a field day (or field night) cheering the goodies and booing the baddies, so *The Hoop of Gold,* though its first New York visit lasted only a week, went on to many years of profitable touring.

Gustav von Moser's *Der Bibliothekar* reached the Rialto the next Monday evening, and a headline-grabbing brouhaha followed in its wake. The reason for the ruckus was that two versions opened at the same time. **The Private Secretary** (9-29-84, Madison Square), was Charles Hawtrey's successful London translation, and was the initial offering at the playhouse after A. M. Palmer took over its directorship. **Digby's Secretary** (9-29-84, Comedy) was adapted by William Gillette as a starring vehicle for himself. Hawtrey called his absurdly timid hero Rev. Robert Spaulding (Spalding in the published text); Gillette called his Rev. Job McCosh. The curate, inevitably wearing galoshes and forever lugging with him his "goods and chattels," is mistaken by a doddering old man for the man's nephew, who the uncle is resolved should be a carefree gadabout. In the farcical mayhem that ensues, the meekly protesting religious is rushed from room to room, thrown in a coal bin, locked in a box, and mistaken for a spiritualist.

Beginning in his old Union Square Theatre days, Palmer had established a policy of suing infringers. He immediately brought action against several pirated versions in other cities and against Gillette. However, to his amazement, he learned that Gillette had paid von Moser for the American rights while Hawtrey had never paid the German playwright a penny. A gentlemanly agreement was quickly struck whereby Gillette took his play on the road and Palmer's more expensive Madison Square production was allowed to continue. The farce ran well into April, chalking up 200 performances, but ever afterward, at least in America, it was Gillette who was identified with the play, which he was allowed to retitle *The Private Secretary.* (In fact, he was allowed to revamp Hawtrey's work, and all the character names remained Hawtrey's.)

At the New Park on the same night, Antonie

Janish, who had gained some fame in German-speaking theatres in such plays as Schiller's *Kabale und Liebe,* tried her hand at performing in English. Her vehicle was the same play, now called *Louisa.* Its plot was familiar to opera lovers, for it was the same that Verdi had employed in *Luisa Miller.*

Palmer's production at the Madison Square of *The Private Secretary* was the first at a major New York house during the season to feature a theatre's resident company. For many theatregoers the return of these local ensembles signaled the real beginning of a new season. Across the nation the rapid growth of touring troupes had sounded the death knell for most such bands elsewhere, and even in New York writers were bewailing that surviving ensembles were spending more and more time away from home. Daly was even taking his company on European jaunts. Yet dying as they were, they still were perceived as the solid rock upon which the best theatres established and maintained their reputations. With the Madison Square leading the way, the other stock houses followed.

Elliott Barnes's **The Artist's Daughter** (10-6-84, Union Square) got Shook and Collier's faltering theatre off to a shaky start. When André Fauversal (J. H. Barnes) weds Blanche (Sara Jewett), the daughter of a noble family, her parents disown her for making a marriage beneath her station. As if that is not enough, the slimy Gaspard Lazette (J. H. Stoddart) stabs André and dumps him in the Seine, leaving him for dead. He disguises himself to resemble André. Blanche, dying of consumption and the effects of childbirth, is too ill to recognize the imposture. After her death her family persuades Gaspard to renounce all claim to her baby in return for a handsome sum of money. Years pass. André has not died, but when he recovers from his wounds he can no longer find his wife and child. He establishes himself under another name as a prominent painter. Commissioned to paint Marie (also Miss Jewett), a duchess's daughter, he is startled by her resemblance to Blanche. She is, of course, his own child, but their reunion is marred by the sudden reappearance of Gaspard demanding hush money. Only after Gaspard is handed his comeuppance can the curtain fall on a happy picture. As they had so often in the past at this theatre, Marston's settings all but stole the show. His snowy view of the bridge at Notre Dame by night and of a chateau garden decorated for a gala festival both earned him curtain calls. The Louis XV costumes were also praised, along with one supporting actress's handling of "her fan with the grace of a *grande dame* of bygone days." But the production's decorativeness could not hide the play's weakness. It ran less than three weeks.

Daly had better luck with his brother's translation and Americanization of von Schönthan's *Roderich Heller* as **The Wooden Spoon** (10-7-84, Daly's). The farce could have been seen as a comic version of the theme of Daly's *Pique* and other similar plays. As a young woman, Perdita Grumbleigh (Mrs. Gilbert) had loved Leonidas Plantagenet (Charles Fisher) but, after a falling-out with him, had married a wealthy cotton manufacturer, Titus Grumbleigh (James Lewis). Over the years Plantagenet has become a famous poet and writer, and Perdita, soon setting aside her quarrel with him, has become one of his most vocal admirers, though they never again have met. She also supports him when he enters politics, and this does lead to a meeting. To her chagrin she discovers he is now a crotchety, self-centered man, with his good looks and several wives all far in his past. A subplot recounts the romance of the Grumbleighs' daughter, Aphra (Ada Rehan), with a popular young editor, Paul Impulse (John Drew). The play was light and charming, but Daly's company, then at its peak, was clearly the main attraction. One newspaper reported that "in receiving Miss Rehan, Mrs. Gilbert, Mr. Lewis and Mr. Drew the audience forgot the conventionalities and broke into cheers." The comedy ran until mid-November, when Daly's policy of prescheduling required its withdrawal.

Two novelties, both edging toward musical comedy, came in on the same evening. **Vacation; or, Harvard vs. Yale** (10-13-84, Tony Pastor's) included some songs, dances, and a scene of bathing at Cape May in its lighthearted saga of two students and their professor who visit the home of the teacher's widowed old flame. Since two pretty young girls are staying with the lady, there are three happy pairs by evening's end. The other attraction was advertised as **"A Play—A Plot"** (10-13-84, Third Ave.) and offered a prize of $1000 to the patron who could devise the best title for it. Its story of comic blackmail focused on a photographer who snaps a picture of a passing trolley just as the trolley is jolted to a halt, throwing some young girls into the laps of strange men. If the play was ever given a real title, or, more important, if a patron was ever actually handed the $1000, no newspaper seems to have taken notice of it. But many playgoers would eventually take notice of the unknown playwright—Joseph Arthur.

The oldest, most august of the ongoing ensembles was the last to return. T. G. Warren's popular London farce **Nita's First** (10-16-84, Wallack's) was the slimmest of affairs, telling of the search for a baby left in the charge of a young man who promptly misplaces the child. Almost certainly the greatness of Wallack's troupe was a thing of the past. Virtually all the illustrious names were gone, and most of those who remained were not in this production. But the company's reputation and no small amount of professional know-how still sustained it. They helped the farce achieve a modest stay of three and a half weeks.

By late October, when shows mounted for touring had made brief appearances and been given the desired New York stamp, and when the great stock companies had all been heard from, it was time for revivals to be hurried in to take over the stages left empty by failures or a gap in the bookings. Of course, neighboring combination houses had been offering them from the start. For example, when Oliver Doud Byron came into the Grand Opera on the 20th in *Across the Continent*, loyal patrons of the theatre had already attended Campbell's *Separation, The Silver King, The Pulse of New York, The Sea of Ice* (with Kate Claxton starring), *Hazel Kirke,* and *Her Atonement.* Later in the season they could see *Moths, Caprice,* John T. Raymond in several of his successes, *Called Back, Confusion, Forbidden Fruit,* Campbell's *My Partner,* and numerous other works. This was an era when the most popular of the older plays neither died nor faded away. The first major theatre forced by a failure to bring out a revival was the Union Square, which replaced *The Artist's Daughter* with *French Flats* on the 25th. Two nights later, after the closing of *Called Back,* the Fifth Avenue was offering *The Colonel.*

One new play did come in, very briefly, to a combination house. The play was Joaquin Miller's **John Logan, the Silent Man** (10-27-84, Third Ave.). Since General John A. Logan was then running for vice-president, the title may have been opportunistic. Logan evidently thought so, for he brought suit immediately. He need not have, however, since the play was so bad it died an almost instantaneous death. The *Herald* noted the "long rows of empty benches and dreary waits between acts" on opening night and branded the drama one of "the most dismal" ever stage. Not even a lynching and a graveyard murder could stimulate interest. At best, Frank Mordaunt's rum-soaked but chivalrous Virginian, Colonel Jackson, garnered a modicum of praise.

November began with the return of Henry Irving and Ellen Terry to the Star on the 10th. New Yorkers had seen them before in most of their repertory, which included *The Merchant of Venice, Much Ado About Nothing, The Lyons Mail, Louis XI, Charles I,* and *The Bells.* Only two mountings were new to America. Their *Twelfth Night,* which they had first presented to London between American visits and which they brought out on the 18th, met with a divided press. So did *Hamlet,* first presented in America during last season's tour to highly critical comments and now initially offered to New York on the 26th. Winter led the cheering section, acclaiming Irving's reading as "poetic," while the *Times* called his performance "great acting," noting, "His fine, thoughtful face is rarely in repose. . . . There is a constant play of expression in the actor's features, and his face is a fine study in itself." On the other side of the fence, the *Herald* condemned his work as "melodramatic, grim and weird." However, the many dissenters had little effect on the box office, and even though prices were raised once again, would-be playgoers were turned away at almost all performances of the month-long stand.

Fanny Davenport made the mistake of bringing *Fedora* back to the 14th Street Theatre on the night of Irving and Terry's return and was nearly lost in the excitement. But her revival quickly caught on and ran for five weeks.

Lester Wallack also made a mistake, courteously waiting for the next night to give the American premiere of Robert Buchanan's **Constance** (11-14-84, Wallack's). Newspapers were able to devote more attention to his opening, and for the most part they were kind but discouraging. At least they could rejoice that some better-known players had returned. Lady Constance (Rose Coghlan) has been tricked into marrying the austere, cruel, and lecherous Duc d'Azeglio (E. J. Henley), although she long has loved Frank Harlowe (Herbert Kelcey). The duke is unaware that his secretary, Feverel (Osmond Tearle), is the husband of a woman he cynically had seduced and is determined to be revenged. Feverel sees his chance by helping Constance and Frank, especially after Frank is made a peer for his bravery in battle. Feverel arranges for the lovers to meet. The duke learns of the reunion and storms into the room, but finds only his wife and his secretary in a seemingly innocent discussion. They have hidden Frank under the couch on which Feverel is sitting. In the end, however, Feverel identifies himself and kills the duke in a duel. For all the carefully built tensions in the closing scenes, critics saw the play as absurd and lamely written. They agreed the actors did their best, but somehow that was not enough.

Matters also went awry for Daly when he removed his still prosperous *The Wooden Spoon* to bring out Pinero's **Lords and Commons** (11-16-84, Daly's). Pinero was a playwright always interested in proclaiming his modernism, but much of his writing style was rooted firmly in the past. His new play, like many of Robertson's two decades earlier, was set against a background of the struggle between the old aristocracy and the new democrats. In this instance Pinero added an element that should have interested Americans, for his story pitted haughty English peers against open-minded Yankees and some Englishmen who had spent time in America. A rich American, Mrs. Devenish (Virginia Dreher), buys up the estate of the impoverished Earl of Caryl (Otis Skinner). The earl curiously fails to recognize her, even though she is the same girl he had married years before and had abandoned at the insistence of his aristocratic mother, the Countess of Caryl (Mrs. Gilbert). Slowly Mrs. Devenish inveigles the earl into falling in love with her, and when he is totally smitten she tells him of a friend whose husband has deserted her and makes him promise to do all he can to have the erring husband return to his wife. The promise extracted, she reveals who she is. In a subplot Mrs. Devenish's steward, Tom Jervoice (John Drew), an Englishman who has lived in California and adopted American ways, finally melts the cold heart of the arrogant Lady Nell (Ada Rehan), the earl's sister. Despite its flattering portrayal of Americans and American ideals, the play was one of Daly's worst failures, running a mere ten performances. Some observers blamed Daly's casting of his favorites, which gave Mrs. Gilbert a thankless, unpleasant role and assigned Drew and Miss Rehan relatively subordinate parts. Of course, Otis Skinner had yet to conquer playgoers' affections.

L. R. Shewell's **The Shadows of a Great City** (11-17-84, Grand Opera) was another melodrama in which an actress had to play both mother and daughter. George Benson (O. H. Barr) persuades his aged uncle to disinherit the old man's daughter, Annie (Julia Stewart), but just before he dies the repentant father changes his mind and reinstates his daughter and her child. Learning of this, the nephew and an unscrupulous pawnbroker buddy, Nathans (W. W. Allen), contrive to have the woman and her baby sent to the almshouse on Blackwell's Island. The men thwart the efforts of the police to find the mother and child. They also frame a young sailor, Tom Cooper (B. R. Graham), who attempts to save the woman. He is imprisoned, escapes, and, learning that Annie has died ("*to slow music*"), rescues the child. Fifteen years later the daughter, Helen, has grown to be an attractive girl. But the villains, having located her, have Tom arrested as an escapee and obtain guardianship of the girl. She sets about to

prove Tom's innocence and convict her treacherous relative. She does just that, then marries Tom. Although this was a traveling show that toured profitably for several seasons, its scenery was elaborate. At one point, Tom's prison was shown with the almshouse juxtaposed. Hell Gate and a boathouse in Harlem were also recreated. A revealing spotlight is cast on the workings of such touring shows by the fact that Annie Ward Tiffany was awarded star billing almost as soon as the play opened. She played none of the principal roles in the drama but was Biddy Roman, the hero and heroine's comically impulsive friend. In short order her role was fattened to justify her billing, even if it set the main plot atilt.

Duprez and Son, Bankers and Brokers (11-19-84, Union Square) was taken from d'Ennery's 1857 *L'Aveugle*. Old as its source was, the play seemed a mere reshuffling of several motifs that had been virtually exhausted during the season. Its hero, Albert Morel (J. H. Barnes), is the illegitimate son of the great Lyonese banker, Duprez (John Parselle). Albert is made a member of the bank until his baleful half-brother, Armand (J. E. Whiting), falsely accuses him of embezzlement and persuades Duprez to disown him. Albert tries his hand at painting and becomes successful until he is struck blind. Luckily he is attended by a kindly hunchback, Dr. Darcy (J. H. Stoddart), who eventually helps him prove that Armand is the embezzler and who reconciles the father to his bastard son. Although the play was rewarded with a number of favorable reviews, it failed to draw and survived only three weeks.

The abrupt failure of *Lords and Commons* prompted Daly to rush forward **Love on Crutches** (11-25-84, Daly's), Americanized from Stobitzer's *Ihre Ideale*. Daly had originally announced plans for mounting the comedy the preceding season, yet Otis Skinner, who played a supporting role in the piece, recalled in his autobiography that the translation still had not been completed when rehearsals began. Such exigencies would not faze Daly's skilled comedians any more than would the play's slim and obvious plot. The five-month-old marriage of Annis (Ada Rehan) and Sydney Austin (John Drew) is a loveless one. They married each other in order to secure the money left them in a relative's will, and nothing has altered their fundamental detachment. In fact, Annis has fallen in love with one Marius, the pseudonymous author of a best-selling novel, and he with her. Never mind that they have never met. They have been corresponding and thus unburdening their souls—he about his cold wife, she about her unloving husband. Annis has signed her letters

"Diana," and Marius has signed his "Pascal," the name of his novel's hero. Of course Marius is none other than Sydney. Annis "mails" each letter by giving it to her widowed friend, Margery Gwynn (Edith Kingdon), who in turn passes it on to Dr. Epenetus Quattles (James Lewis), who hands it secretly to Sydney. Sydney's responses take the reverse route back to Annis. When Sydney discovers his wife is having a furtive correspondence, he demands a separation. Rather than jeopardize their social position and their inheritance, Annis determines to retrieve her letters from Marius and show Sydney how essentially platonic they have been. Marius and Annis agree to meet at an evening charity bazaar, a "bubble party," at Margery's home. To identify themselves, Marius-Pascal agrees to wear a primrose in his buttonhole and Diana a rose in her belt. Annis's mysterious correspondence also raises the hackles of Margery's languorous suitor, Guy Roverly (Skinner), a bored world traveler, and of the perennially suspicious Mrs. Quattles (Mrs. Gilbert). Quattles's antidote for his wife's suspicions is to tell her to "take one of these every hour till you feel better" while handing her a wad of money. The final curtain turns husband and wife into lovers.

Daly's superb mounting culminated in the last act, with Margery's conservatory bathed in dimmish blue lights and the roseate glow of the fireplace and with servants handing out bowls of soapy water and pipes to allow Margery's guests to fill the room with prismatic bubbles. More than one critic could not resist comparing those bubbles with the fragile, transparent nature of the comedy. The public loved every minute of it. Daly kept it on the boards until early February and revived it in several later seasons.

Lester Wallack also had been saddled with a failure, so he resorted to his own favorite remedy, revivals. On the 26th he presented a double bill of *A Sheep in Wolf's Clothing* and *A Bachelor of Arts.* In the latter Wallack himself appeared as Harry Jasper, a very young, very world-weary man who finds love and pleasure after accepting a post as a tutor to an old man's daughter. His big scene, reminiscent of one in *David Garrick,* had him feigning drunkenness to cool the ardor of his enamored pupil. Critics long since had despaired of persuading the fast-aging actor not to play youthful lovers, and Wallack apparently knew that his reputation and gaslights allowed him considerable leeway. Moreover, as one critic pointed out, his art was "so delicate, so significant, so brilliant and so rare" that the seeming absurdity did not matter much. Nonetheless, that art

was increasingly of limited appeal to a new generation. The bill ran only one week. However, Wallack made a major concession to his age on December 2 when he brought out one of his house's standbys, *London Assurance,* and assumed the role of Dazzle instead of Charles. His supporting cast included the stalwart John Gilbert as Sir Harcourt and Rose Coghlan as Lady Gay Spanker. But by the 8th Wallack had once again sipped from the fountain of youth and appeared as Charles Marlow in *She Stoops to Conquer.*

Other openings competed with the revival. **Three Wives to One Husband** (12-8-84, Union Square) was a Colonel Milliken's adaptation of Ernest Grenet-Dancourt's Parisian hit. For one reason or another—or for no good reason at all—Andrew Dobbs (J. B. Mason) marries three young ladies: a French girl pressed on him by his relatives, the daughter of his landlady, and an artist's model. Problems follow. The *Herald* reported that many in the audience could find no cause for laughter in some very French jokes. Thus when a lady asked who her father was and was informed by her mother, "My child, I cannot tell you. I met him at a ball and he wore a mask," there were as many disapproving gasps as there were guffaws. Even so, the play caught on. After a two-month run, during part of which it was coupled with *One Touch of Nature* (beginning on December 13), it toured profitably, sometimes under the title *Nice and Warm.* At the same time, Charlotte Thompson began a two-week stand at the Star, first offering *Jane Eyre,* then, the next week, *East Lynne.* The Florences returned to the Fifth Avenue in *The Mighty Dollar.*

The Outcast (12-15-84, 14th St.), billed as an "emotional society drama," was a short-lived adaptation of an Edmond About novel. When Margaret Mason (Louise Pomeroy) learns that she has inadvertently committed bigamy by entering into a second marriage (believing her first husband dead), she agrees to a divorce and to her husband's remarriage, which will legitimize their son. The woman whom the husband is to marry is said to be dying, so Margaret hopes that by the time she obtains her divorce her husband will be free to wed her again. Instead the husband's new wife finds marriage a tonic and recovers her health. Despairing of her own happiness and not wanting to stand in her husband's way, Margaret kills herself.

Henry Pettitt and Paul Merritt's **Brought to Justice** 12-15-84, Third Ave.) was no more successful. It depicted the wickedness and downfall of Stephen Byway (Frank Mordaunt), who would wreak havoc on a decent farmer, John Byrnes (McKee Rankin), and on Nell Forrest (Mrs. Rankin), the wife of a weak husband. The *Tribune,* gorged with such written-by-rote pieces compounded of "the usual elements," listed those in *Brought to Justice* as "the usual villainous lawyer, the usual English farmer, the usual secret marriage, the usual important packet of papers, the usual heartbreaking collection of afflicting circumstance . . . [leading] to the usual settings to rights and discomfiture of the bad people."

If Lotta could water down a French musical into a suitable vehicle, why could not Marie Aimée, the celebrated opéra bouffe star, attempt an American-made farce studded with special songs for her? The answer was provided with the arrival of George Jessop and William Gill's **Mam'zelle** (12-15-84, Fifth Ave.). The plot foreshadowed the Cinderella yarns that would dominate American musical comedy forty-five years later. Aimée's Toinette Jacotot is a milliner who dreams of being a famous singer. Over the opposition of his shocked family, she wheedles T. Tarleton Tupper (J. O. Barrows) into wangling an audition for her at the American Café Chantant run by Col. Hiram Poster (Newton Chisnell). Before long she is the star, although her name has been changed to Fleur de Lys. Her songs ranged from excerpts from opéra bouffe to risqué Spanish and French ditties. One clever if antiquated device had her first numbers interrupted by objectors. Mrs. Tupper (Laura Wallace), for example, protests from a box, and Toinette's fiancé, Bob Pritchard (Frank E. Lamb), rises bellicosely from his seat in the orchestra. Both have to be removed by ushers and police. Aimée's heavily accented English and suggestive charms drew good audiences for a fortnight and proved a lure on the road.

For some time the noted elocutionist George Riddle had been offering readings of a tragedy called *Memnon* by a young New Mexican, Henry Guy Carleton. How the two men met is uncertain, but their association had an element of cruel irony. For while Riddle was a fine speaker, Carleton suffered from a marked stammer, which he was never to lose but which never stopped him from insisting on personally reading his plays at their first rehearsal. His impediment in no way lessened the perception that he was a playwright of great promise.

That promise was furthered by the production and success of his **Victor Durand** (12-18-84, Wallack's), even though the play's story rested on one of the most overused of dramatic clichés, the false accusation that leads to unjust imprisonment. The victim of this treachery, Durand, escapes from the galleys and returns to Paris, where he assumes the name Henri Favart (Osmond Tearle) and marries an American girl, Ruth Vaughan (Rose Coghlan). Ruth had been engaged to the very man Durand was wrongly accused of bludgeoning and has been courted by the real villain, Baron de Mersac (Lewis Morrison). When her husband's true identity is revealed, she is firmly convinced of his innocence and is staunchly supportive. Nevertheless, until the baron is tricked into admitting his own chicanery, the hero remains guilty in the eyes of the law. Departing from convention, which often spread the action over years and miles, Carleton confined his story to the evening and following morning in which all the matters are brought to a head, thereby imparting a dramatic tautness to the work. His deft construction was embellished by fine performances. Miss Coghlan was a warmly affectionate, understanding wife to Tearle's virile, determined husband, but the evening was all but stolen by the aged John Gilbert's sympathetic portrayal of Rose's father, John. On opening night Carleton was called for after each act and took bows from his box. The play ran until mid-February, but few could know how far short of his early promise the smiling playwright would fall.

Another aging veteran fared less well than the still beloved Gilbert. At sixty-three the great Italian tragedienne Adelaide Ristori had learned English, and she came into the Star on the 22nd in translations of some of her most famous vehicles: *Mary Stuart, Marie Antoinette, Macbeth,* and *Elizabeth, Queen of England.* Critics split sharply over just how effective and clear her English was, but they agreed she had forfeited none of her artistry. Unfortunately, her mountings were tacky and her supporting players no more than adequate. From the start attendance was disappointing, so the distinguished visitor, for all her efforts, concluded her last extended American visit on a sad note.

Barney McAuley, who had been touring successfully for several seasons in *The Messenger from Jarvis Section,* found a new if similar vehicle in E. A. Locke's **The Jerseyman** (12-29-84, 14th Street). He played Gilderoy Punk of Mackerelville, N.J., an old whaler whose slovenly dress and unlettered speech conceal a shrewd mind and a good heart. Punk (and critics pounced on that name) finds a baby afloat in an open boat, adopts her, and calls her Dot. She grows up to be an attractive girl. After fending off a phony claimant, Punk proves that Dot (Lillian Chantore) is an heiress. He also springs an innocent man from unfair imprisonment. Between times he invents an "air-tight muzzle" for cats. The play gave every indication of being a crowd-pleaser, but McAuley increasingly was displaying the instability that would shortly remove him permanently from the stage. He failed to show up for the initial matinee, whereupon the management announced the play would close at the end of its first week.

By the end of the year, newspapers were taking a glum notice of the box-office slump. Headlines such as "Depression in Business Makes Retrenchment Necessary" and "Actors Paid Too Much" lured readers into detailed discussions of the problem. Of course, not everyone subscribed to the pessimism, at least not publicly. Lester Wallack, for one, was at pains to deny numerous rumors that he was planning a drastic cut in the size of his ensemble.

Lawrence Barrett ushered in 1885 by opening a six-week stand at the Star on January 5. He began with his highly praised revival of *Francesca da Rimini*, then moved on to *Julius Caesar, Yorick's Love,* and *Richelieu.* In February he also offered a new bill.

Only a revival of *The Wages of Sin* at the 14th Street Theatre on the 12th, a revival rushed in following the shuttering of *The Jerseyman*, stood between Barrett's return and that of Booth at the Fifth Avenue on the 19th. Whereas Barrett was constantly refreshing his repertory, Booth long since had abandoned any attempt at novelty. On this occasion he offered *Othello, The Iron Chest, Macbeth, Ruy Blas* (coupled with *My Uncle's Will,* in which he did not appear), *Hamlet, The Apostate, Don Caesar de Bazan, Richelieu, Richard III,* and *The Fool's Revenge.* Perhaps responding to another persistent criticism—his weak supporting casts and indifferent mountings—he joined with the company of the famed Boston Museum in the presentations. Regrettably, like Wallack's, the Museum's heyday had passed, so, wittingly or no, Booth still was the only real attraction. Yet his attraction remained potent enough to result in a healthy $45,000 take for the month's engagement—all the more remarkable in light of the persisting cries of bad business.

Joseph Arthur—author of the season's only untitled play—appeared again as the playwright of **A Cold Day When We Get Left.** No critic disputed its claim to be a "comic musical conglomerate" when it opened at the 14th Street Theatre on January 26, but it remains worth noting as another early effort by a dramatist who would soon become important in popular theatres.

Conversely, Joaquin Miller's reputation as a promising dramatist was wearing thin. All that could be said for **Tally-Ho!** (2-2-85, Mount Morris) was that it may have been a mite better than *John Logan.* Its romantic triangle consisted of Hank Monk (R. L. Dowling), the fearless stagecoach driver and singer of western songs; Rosie (May Woolcott), his sweetheart, who is sometimes known as "Rose of the Sierras"; and Tom Crabtree (H. W. Herman), the mustache-twirling villain, who covets Rosie. After Hank and Rosie are wed, Tom manages to frame Hank for a murder. Hank has a noose around his neck and is minutes from being hanged when Tom is discovered in possession of a bloody, incriminating knife.

Morning-after reviews were the sort that should have meant prosperous box office for **A Prisoner for Life** (2-4-85, Union Square), Louis Nathal's translation of Auguste Anicet-Bourgeois's *Stella.* Praise was heaped on the story of a young girl, Mignonne (Maud Harrison), whose father, the Count de Valney (J. H. Barnes), has been sentenced to life imprisonment for a crime he did not commit, and whose weak mother, Louise (Sara Jewett), afraid to acknowledge her marriage, has been forced to marry the cruel General de Montrail (J. E. Whiting), the count's jailer. Mignonne disguises herself as a mute, sadistic boy and is made an attendant at the jail. She soon brings about her father's release and even effects a reconciliation between her parents.

The cast was universally applauded, and so was Marston's scenery. His first-act set showed a park and luxurious lodge in autumn, with burnished leaves falling one by one. Even more spectacular was his second-act view of a hut dug in against a snowy mountainside; just as the heroine leaves the hut, an avalanche engulfs it. Yet for all the production's merits and the good notices it earned, something went wrong. As if to signal the problems, the portly John Parselle, who long had been a fixture with the Union Square stock company and who had the important role of Louis XIV in the play, died suddenly during the run. Perhaps because the company had lost its former cachet, perhaps because the theatrical center was continually moving away from 14th Street, business was so disappointing that Shook and his associates cut ticket prices, reducing the best seat to $1. And when the play closed in early April the once great, nationally admired Union Square stock company was disbanded.

Conversely, Daly and his troupe were moving from triumph to triumph. The producer's standard fare, his Americanization of German farces, may not have won him any prizes for risk-taking, but most were quickly embraced. Now he returned to his policy of reviving old English comedy classics, and here he often demonstrated his learning and daring. On the 7th he raised his curtain on Farquhar's *The Recruiting Officer.* This brilliant comedy had been a staple on American stages in the 18th and early 19th centuries but had not been given a major New York mounting since 1843. On that occasion its Sylvia had been Mrs. Henry Hunt, who later became Mrs. John Drew and thus the mother of Daly's Captain Plume. If she saw this revival, she may have felt it did not do her son full justice, since Daly, as was his wont, had bowdlerized the work to soothe contemporary sensibilities. Much of Plume's roistering behavior was deleted, as was the brazen pandering of his lackey, Sergeant Kite (James Lewis). Instead Daly emphasized the sometimes comic, sometimes sentimental romance between Sylvia (Ada Rehan) and Plume. Performing honors went to Miss Rehan, especially for the scene in which, disguised as a man, Sylvia attempts to assess the relationship between Plume and a wench he appears to be courting. Many of the critics lauded the "refinement" achieved by Daly's editing and expunging, but a few more modern, protesting voices were heard—one writer insisting whatever shortcomings were evident stemmed from spectators being credited "with a prudery which they did not seem to possess."

Like Daly, Barrett regularly ventured into theatrically uncertain waters. Even when he came a cropper, as he did with the major half of his new double bill, critics were kind. After all, he was one of those rare contemporary tragedians to seek not merely novelty but "novelty, too, of a high order." Although neither of his two plays was new, both apparently were receiving their first professional New York hearings. In Robert Browning's 1843 **A Blot on the 'Scutcheon** (2-9-85, Star) Barrett portrayed Thorold, Earl Tresham, who learns that Henry, Earl Mertoun (F. C. Mosley), the man he has agreed can marry his sister, Mildred (Viola Allen), has already seduced her. Thorold kills Henry. Mildred dies of grief on hearing the news. Thorold then takes poison, content to die knowing his family's reputation is unblemished. Accompanying this tragedy was **The King's Pleasure,** Alfred Thompson's translation of Théodore de Banville's 1866 one-act comedy *Gringoire.* Barrett assumed the title role of the starving poet who is given the promise of love and a better life by Louis XI (Louis James). While the Browning work was quickly returned to the closet, Barrett's Gringoire won praise for its sentiment and pathos and retained a niche in the actor's repertory even after the great French actor Coquelin brought his totally different interpretation across the Atlantic and revealed to some shocked audiences how raffish and loutish the poet could be made to seem.

The art of another fine actor, Lester Wallack, provided the centerpiece of **Impulse** (2-16-85, Wallack's), a London success B. C. Stephenson had adapted from *La Maison du mari.* Because she has not heard from her officer husband, Major MacDonald (Osmond Tearle), for eighteen months, Mrs. MacDonald (Annie Robe) decides he no longer loves her, so she takes up with an old flame, Victor de Riel (Harry J. Lethcourt). Naturally the major picks this moment to reappear. Unpleasantness, including telling Mrs. MacDonald's aged, blind father, Sir Henry Aukland (John Gilbert), about his daughter's impulsive actions, is forestalled by the thoughtful intervention of Colonel Crichton (Wallack). "For many years," the *Times* observed, "this artist has enjoyed a monopoly of personages whom coolness, elegant impertinence, and tranquil bravery endear to the average spectator, and no one has yet sprung up that can rival him in scenes calling for a revelation of these fascinating qualities." Similarly the *Herald* recorded, "The quietude and grace of his manner are still as marked as of old. It is a manner seen no longer either here or in England." Wallack loyalists kept the play lit for a month, a shorter run than Wallack had hoped for.

M. B. Curtis, a far lesser actor, had been crisscrossing the country for four years in a single role, the title part of *Sam'l of Posen.* When he now returned to a first-class New York theatre he was still playing the Jewish peddler, but he had found himself a sequel to his durable vehicle, **Spot Cash; or, Sam'l of Posen on the Road** (2-16-85, Fifth Ave.). Sam has come to Chicago to attend the wedding of a rival drummer, Fred Jerome (William Morris), to Hortense Larivandier (Albina de Mer). During his stay he passes some bad checks, is blown out of a hotel safe in which he has been hiding, and is caught by his wife, Rebecca (Josie Wilmere), with three beauties coddling him. Critics had never been fond of Curtis but had agreed he had found an acceptable vehicle in his first Sam'l play. There was less agreement this time. However, the *Herald* applauded the production, especially two sets. The opening scene of a Chicago hotel lobby was "put on the stage with admirable realism, with a telephone and colored bell boys, a telegraph operator, and daily and weekly newspapers." The last act offered an elegant drawing room with a view of Niagara Falls in the distance. After three weeks Curtis and his drummer took the suggestion of the subtitle and hit the road.

The same busy night that saw the openings of *Impulse* and *Spot Cash* welcomed the return of the Florences to the Star. Last season their play had been known as *Facts,* but with the new season it was given a new and more permanent title, *Our Governor.* Florence had a field day as the prevaricating Pinto Perkins, and Mrs. Florence ably assisted him as the pretentious writer.

218

On the 23rd Daly continued his short season of classic revivals by bringing out *She Would and She Would Not*. Because his was a first-class house, the revival drew the better critics and received longer notices than did Robson and Crane's return in *Forbidden Fruit* at the Grand Opera. But critical eyes turned to the popular comic pair when in midweek they changed their bill and offered a new play, Joseph Bradford's **The Cherubs** (2-26-85, Grand Opera). Two elderly twins, Phidias (Robson) and Vandyke Cherub (Crane), are supposed to be artists. But the sculptor has never been known to sculpt and the painter never seen to paint. Instead they spend their time scampering in and out of trouble. They propose marriage on behalf of each other, sign each other's names to checks, and figure out all manner of additional ways to make mischief. A love interest joins their younger brother, Joseph (Charles S. Dickson), and their ward, Dina (Flora May Henry). Robson and Crane's manifold skills could do little to save such farcical hash. It was immediately withdrawn, to go down in the record books as one of their few out-and-out failures.

To conclude his spate of revivals Daly restored his hit of the preceding season, *The Country Girl*, on the 28th, this time coupling it with a curtain raiser that would remain a standby for the troupe until the producer's death. **A Woman's Won't; or, Thank Goodness the Table is Spread!** was taken from *Dieu merci! le couvert est mis* and elaborated on the farcical contretemps that ensue when a housemaid (May Irwin) refuses to repeat the words that constitute the subtitle. Before long, a fellow servant (William Gilbert), the owner of the house (Otis Skinner), his wife (May Fielding), his father-in-law (James Lewis), and his mother-in-law (Mrs. Gilbert) are all heatedly taking sides.

Charles Osborne's swashbuckler **A Midnight Marriage** (3-2-85, People's), recounting the perils of falling in love at first sight, was advertised as "a grand romantic play." Such puffing was modest compared to the advance press accorded its leading man, the Boston favorite William Redmund. He was extolled as "possessing the grace and magnetism of Fechter, the easy manner and delicate refinement of Montague, the heroism and princely bearing of Rignold with the manly physique of Salvini." Since the actors mentioned were not around to defend themselves—two were dead and two were overseas—critics took up the cudgels for them, hooting play and players quickly out of town.

Daly's string of successes continued with **A Night Off; or, a Page from Balzac** (3-4-85, Daly's), an Americanization of Franz and Paul von Schönthan's most famous comedy, *Der Raub der Sabinerinnen*. For the most part reviewers were highly enthusiastic, though not quite as much as Odell, who looked back from a vantage point of fifty-five years to recall Daly's mounting as "the most delightful comedy ever played at his theatre." Even today, a hundred years after the original production, with allowances made for the fading of topical references and the need to visualize much of the physical fun, the farce still makes for uproarious reading. No synopsis can do justice to the hilariously interlaced complications.

A sentence in that page from Balzac is said to read, "Every bride that lives—if she could but know the past and secret life of her husband—would renounce him even at the steps of the altar." Although such a renunciation is out of the question for Angelica Damask (Virginia Dreher), she openly wonders what secrets her husband Harry (Otis Skinner) is hiding. Harry insists he has none. But Angelica's henpecked father, Professor Justinian Babbitt (James Lewis), has a long-buried one, which he has revealed only to his housemaid, Susan (May Irwin): in his youth he wrote a blank-verse tragedy! A broken-down theatrical combination visits the professor's small town, and its head, Marcus Brutus Snap (Charles Leclercq), comes to the professor to solicit patronage. Learning of the professor's play, Snap agrees to mount it immediately, even though he lacks the requisite costumes and players. Their discussions are interrupted by a strange, haughty man, Lord Mulberry (Charles Fisher), who had once met Babbitt on a train and has now come to tell him the rest of his story about his worthless son. Babbitt gets rid of the Englishman, gives Snap his manuscript, and sits down to write his harridan wife, telling her to extend her vacation for another two weeks—just long enough so she won't learn about his play. The letter is no sooner written than Mrs. Babbitt (Mrs. Gilbert) appears. She has cut short her vacation. Since Mrs. Babbitt condemns all theatricals, everyone must find a way of sneaking off to the theatre without her knowing it. At the same time, an actor from the combination named Chumley calls on Harry Damask. Chumley, it turns out, is really Harry's old schoolmate, Jack Mulberry (John Drew). Jack has decided to reform—to give up not only his theatrical life but to make amends to a girl he once wronged. To this end he presents Harry with some incriminating evidence, such as a lock of the girl's hair and some unpaid bills he ran up in courting her. Harry puts them in his drawer and agrees to help Jack, but when Angelica persists in demanding what secret Harry is hiding, Harry in desperation pulls out the items Jack has left and pretends they belong to him. Misunderstandings and mistaken identities pile on thick and fast. The production of the play is a howling disaster, provoking a riot at the theatre. But other than that everything ends happily. The professor has gotten his secret out of his system. Mrs. Babbitt is forgiving. Angelica accepts the fact that Harry actually has no dark past. And Jack is not only reunited with his father but wins the hand of the Babbitts' other daughter, Sophonisba or Nisbe (Ada Rehan).

The writing contained a number of in-jokes that probably only the most knowing playgoers caught. Many probably grasped the pun when Snap, telling of always trying to mount locally written pieces and having detailed the problems he encountered with a notorious one written by the daughter of a banker, promises to produce Babbitt's play even "if it's worse than the Banker's Daughter's." Less obvious to most would have been the allusion in Snap's entrance after his mounting of Babbitt's play has been hooted off the stage. Staggering in, dressed in *"his long ulster, the collar turned up, and hat over his eyes,"* the pseudo-classicist moans, "Oh, Professor! Professor, oh!" (remember Sophonisba was a character in the farce!). Those ignorant of a once famous but even then justly forgotten 18th-century play and its most celebrated line (as well as Fielding's devastating putdown) could at least enjoy an immediate sight gag. The professor and Damask pull off Snap's long coat, discovering him *"in full Roman costume—white tunic, belt, fleshings, bare arms, but on his feet old street gaiters."* A photograph of this third-act curtain helped promote the play. From the start *A Night Off* had been slated to run only until Daly's season closed in mid-April, but like several earlier hits it returned to his stage in later seasons.

When Irving came back for a four-week spring season at the Star beginning March 9, he brought with him only one new production, W. G. Wills's **Eugene Aram** (3-9-85, Star). The famous tale of a murderer who is exposed on the eve of his wedding by his accomplice was dramatized by Wills especially for Irving. The actor turned the guilt-obsessed central figure into a tour de force much as he had the similar Mathias in *The Bells*. All of the action in the play took place during a single night, and, as always with Irving, the settings and costumes were superb. The play began with a scene showing the sun setting behind a rural parsonage with "roses clambering over its trellised porch, and its tiny garden full of flowers of many hues, the little church in the background and luxuriant verdure all about it," and ended at dawn, with Aram sitting in a graveyard

confessing his crime. Irving gave only a few performances of the play, satisfied to bring out the rest of his repertory for the remainder of his visit.

Diplomacy was revived at Wallack's on the 16th. Critics found themselves at odds when comparing Osmond Tearle's Julian, Annie Robe's Dora, and Herbert Kelcey's Orloff to the interpretations of the original players' performances, but they were pleased that Rose Coghlan, Mme Ponisi, and Wallack himself were again cast in the parts they had assumed in 1878. Wallack particularly was praised. Perhaps because he again took on a role as a character nearer his own age than one of the dashing young heroes he still sometimes attempted, and because such a role brought home how quickly he must be approaching retirement, reviews echoed the flattering sentiments expressed about his playing in *Impulse*. Thus one critic saw his helpful elder brother "distinguished by many fine bits of detail, at times by a hint of latent force, very cleverly manifested, and always by that elegant repose which is characteristic of the school of comedians of which Mr. Wallack appears to be the last representative."

J. H. Wallick, one of the most popular of touring stars, rode his horses Charger and Raider across the stage in **The Bandit King** (3-23-85, Niblo's). Wallick was clearly a far cry, or war whoop, from Wallack as he portrayed Joe Howard, who disguises himself as Tom Small, a Texas cattle baron, and Sam Thorndale, "a tramp detective," to break up a confederacy of bad men. Other characters, good or bad, included Kolemah (an Indian girl), Kansas Jake, Old Bob, and Breezy Eagle. The play toured for many seasons.

Having been cruelly shoved out of his Madison Square Theatre, Steele MacKaye was soon ready to unveil another bijou playhouse. Once more his auditorium prefigured future theatres, not only in its intimacy—it seated fewer than 800 people—but in its technological inventions. Besides the devices carried over from the Madison Square, MacKaye's novelties included an onstage platform upon which the musicians played overtures and music between the acts; it was lifted to the top of the proscenium to allow the musicians to continue to perform during the play. Another was a stage curtain that parted rather than rose. Neither of these conceptions took hold, but two others did. First was the earliest successful employment of folding seats, making it so much easier for theatregoers to pass by prior arrivals on the way to their own locations. The second involved MacKaye's even more inventive close friend Thomas Edison. Together the men saw to it that the Lyceum was the first major theatre to be lit almost entirely by electricity. The closeness of the audience to the action combined with bright lighting of the players would gradually bring about drastic changes in both acting and playwriting styles, banishing or modifying the most exaggerated gestures and such dramaturgy as encouraged them.

MacKaye's play, **Dakolar** (4-6-85, Lyceum), was not as totally new as his theatre. Rather, it was the third redaction in two seasons of Ohnet's *Le Maître de forges,* although MacKaye used only the central idea and played fast and loose with the rest of the story. In his version Madeleine de Volney (Viola Allen) marries Alain Dakolar (Robert Mantell), a blacksmith's son, after learning the man she loves, the Duc de Villeflor (John Mason), has been unfaithful. Immediately after her wedding the duke appears, protesting his innocence and begging for a reconciliation. He convinces Madeleine of his innocence, and she falls to her knees in tears. Just then Dakolar is heard approaching. The duke hides on a balcony, but when Dakolar spots his glove and runs to search the balcony, the duke jumps. Thinking he is dead, Madeleine goes mad. Only Dakolar's loving care returns her to sanity, by which time the fickle duke has found someone else to court.

Although all three principals would soon be topflight stars, only Mantell, at the time the most established of the trio and newly released from the *Called Back* tour, garnered generally favorable reviews. Miss Allen was judged "too mannered" or "too weak," while Mason received divided notices. As she had on earlier occasions, Sadie Martinot earned applause for her knowing clowning and her modeling of gorgeous gowns in a supporting role. The *Herald* reported her Sophie "combines the vivacity of Lotta . . . with the presence of Rose Coghlan [whom the critic would have to report on the very next night]. She is the most sparkling of coquettes. . . . The sweeping limb revealed by her satin dress in the fourth act would be envied by a Venus Callipynge." By contrast, most critics berated the overacting of Joseph Frankau in the minor role of a retainer. His old-school emoting could not stand the intimacy and bright lights of the new era. Goatcher's settings included a view of the Britanny seacoast, with a castle perched high on a cliff, while at the cliff's base fishing boats and nets were seen and the sea "scatters foam upon the rocks." Moonlit views were sure of a hearty round of applause, so one, showing the sea at night, was offered. Despite good if not enthusiastic reviews, *Dakolar* did poorly at the box office. Part of its problem was its similarity to other recent plays; part was the unusually high prices—$2.50 top—MacKaye was

demanding. Not even an eventual lowering of prices helped.

Still less successful was **Favette, the Story of a Waif** (4-6-85, Union Square), dramatized by its star, Estelle Clayton, from a Ouida novel. Her barefoot village waif is seduced or abused by all manner of noblemen and noblewomen until she finds romance in Paris with a bohemian artist, Bernardus (F. de Belleville), who turns out to be as noble as any of the meanies. How artificial and conventional the stage remained was evident in the portrayal of Picto, the little black groom—performed in blackface by a white girl.

J. C. Roach and John Amory Knox's **McFadden's Spirits** (4-6-85, Third Ave.), for which Denman Thompson was a co-producer, was another of the era's innumerable farces that regularly spilled over into musical comedy. David Conroy of the popular variety act the Four Shamrocks had the role of Timothy McFadden in a story that debunked spiritualism.

Herman Merivale and Cecil Dale's **Our Joan** (4-7-85, Wallack's) combined the always popular motif of the unequal marriage with the trappings of sensation-melodrama but failed to weave them into a surefire evening. The troubled couple are rich, sophisticated Arthur Meredith (Herbert Kelcey) and his wife, Joan (Rose Coghlan), who has grown up in a small fishing community. One approving critic described Coghlan's first entrance: "With a round Scotch cap on a profusion of ruddy locks, with a red handkerchief twisted around her sailor's collar, with a short red petticoat, she had the true air of a fishing girl, the beauty of the coast." Joan suspects Arthur of still harboring affection for his cousin, Lady Ruth Burney (Flora Livingston), whom he has enlisted to help polish his sometimes uncouth wife. In turn Arthur grows suspicious after seeing Joan embrace a man, not knowing that man is his wife's brother. When hostilities become too much for her, Joan leaves Arthur and returns home. She takes up residence in a lighthouse run by her grandfather. A repentant Arthur follows her, but at first Joan remains adamant. Arthur sets out in his boat to return to his yacht but is caught in a sudden storm. Now it is Joan's turn to repent. She jumps into a lifeboat, undaunted by "the thunder . . . pealing with terrific crashes," and rescues her husband. After their reconciliation Joan, like so many other contemporary heroes and heroines, is shown to be of suitably noble birth to explain her courageous behavior. *Our Joan* failed to run out the month at Wallack's but immediately reappeared at combination houses. When Miss Coghlan left Wallack's at the end of the season, she purchased touring rights to the play, despite its cool New York reception.

Palmer fared better with Mrs. Julia Campbell Verplanck's **Sealed Instructions** (4-13-85, Madison Square). Her story centered on the scapegrace son and daughter-in-law of Lord Dorchester (Frederic Robinson), the British ambassador to France. The son, Captain Haughton (H. M. Pitt), could wind up being tried for treason for selling secret documents. The coquettish Mrs. Haughton (Mathilde Madison) has attempted to deflect suspicion about her own infidelities by implicating Katharine Ray (Jessie Millward), the high-principled governess of the Haughtons' daughter, Ada (Annie Russell). In the end it remains for Katharine to help the Haughtons escape punishment and to bring about an understanding between father and son. Only then does Katharine reveal that she is actually Lord Dorchester's granddaughter, the child of another of his sons, now dead, whom he once disowned for marrying beneath his station. Good writing and fine acting were embellished by a superior physical production. Palmer once again had Marston back in his fold, but he had also hired the young, promising Homer Emens. Together these scene painters devised two handsome, homey interiors and, always an applause-getter, a moonlit garden.

Twins (4-2-85, Standard) attempted to have the best of several worlds. This Joseph Derrick farce had been a London success, though it hardly matched the popularity of his earlier *Confusion*. Nonetheless, early American announcements and advertisements proudly proclaimed its pedigree. However, since a number of songs and vaudeville turns were inserted, the play was also listed as a "farce-comedy," thus suggesting to playgoers of the time a night interlaced with musical entertainments. Yet later in the tour it was called, no doubt preposterously, a "comic opera." Perhaps more and more musical numbers were added, but if so they were scarcely the arioso songs of operetta. In any case, the original story told of the confusion generated when an austere bishop, Dr. Titus Spinach, is mistaken for his twin brother, Timothy, a drunken waiter at a seaside resort. John A. Mackay romped through several quick costume changes as the two disparate men. After a fortnight the attraction headed back out on tour.

With his regular season finished and his famed company embarked on tour, Daly brought to his stage one of his earliest stars, Clara Morris, with whom he had not worked in many seasons. Neither the contemporary German comedies nor the 18th-century classics around which the producer was building his reputation would have suited the ac-

tress's emotive style, so he selected one of the younger Dumas's social-melodramas, **Denise** (4-21-85, Daly's). Dumas's heroine is a charming young music teacher whose parents were caretaker and housekeeper for the rich André de Bardannes (Joseph Haworth). André falls in love with Denise, but when she learns that André's sister, Marthe (Hélène Stoepel), hopes to marry a young neighbor, Fernand de Thausette (A. S. Lipman), Denise is forced to reveal that Fernand had once seduced and abandoned her. At first the shocked André considers forcing Fernand to marry Denise or else sending Denise to a convent, but André's sober and judicious counselor, Thouvenin (Frank Losee), persuades him to overlook conventional morality, forgive her, and marry her. As everyone saunters out to the dining room it appears that André will heed the advice.

In its use of a comparatively small cast, a single setting (a room in a luxurious chateau), and a story that unfolds between breakfast and dinner, the play was forward looking, as it was in its well-written but restrained handling of its emotional scenes. Unfortunately, restraint was not one of Miss Morris's fortes, so Daly's choice of a vehicle for her was not as perspicacious as first appeared. There was no scene in which she could pull at her hair, tear her gown, or writhe on the floor, and without such a moment something went unfulfilled. Still, while some critics praised her performance as "fraught with a strange, unexplained feeling of suspense" or "rich in pathos," others attacked her with a surprising viciousness. Her persistent regional burr was brought up once more. Several critics, including the prestigious *Herald*'s, complained that at thirty-eight she was much too old for the part (was improved stage lighting beginning to tell?). Some griped about her stiff movements, possibly unaware that her long dresses hid a cast protecting a long broken ankle. Though all this critical carping told at the box office, the three-week run was still financially profitable thanks to the actress's many unswayable fans.

If Clara Morris's best years were behind her, another actress had every reason to hope that hers lay ahead. Only a few seasons back, dark-haired, dark-eyed Helen Dauvray had been a child prodigy, regaling audiences under the stage name of Little Nell and called "the California Diamond." More recently she had studied and performed in Paris. Now she returned home with her new stage name (her real name has been given variously as Helen Williams and Ida Louisa Gibson), ready to embark on a career as actress-manager. For her initial venture she elected to star in a dramatization of a then popular novel, *Mrs. Geoffrey,* which for stage purposes was rechristened **Mona** (4-27-85, Star). At heart it was yet another retelling of the unequal match motif, in this instance a young American girl running into difficulties when she meets and marries Sir Geoffrey Rodney (Clarence Handyside) in Switzerland. Sir Geoffrey's nasty cousin, Paul (Frederic Bryton), attempts to seize Geoffrey's estates and seduce Mona, but the seemingly naive Mona and not her worldly husband is the one to give Paul his desserts. Her effective actions win the respect of all the Rodneys. Despite kind words for the young star, the talky, conventional play was a two-week failure. As such it was an ominous hint of how badly most of the actress's hopes would eventually be dashed, although she soon was to have one major hit on which she could look back happily.

Following the failure of *Our Joan,* Wallack briefly pressed *Diplomacy* back into service on the 27th, then ended his season with three nights of *Old Heads and Young Hearts,* beginning on the 30th. Age could not wither one old head, seventy-five-year-old John Gilbert, who brought all his comic skills and infinite variety to the role of Jesse Rural.

Two special performances in early May were of great interest to the most dedicated playgoers, for they were announced as Ristori's proud farewell to America, following her bitterly disappointing tour. The first performance paired Ristori with none other than Edwin Booth in *Macbeth* at the jam-packed Academy of Music on the 7th. The second occurred, a little anticlimactically, at the Thalia five nights later when Ristori, playing in English and supported by the house's German-speaking company, offered Schiller's *Maria Stuart.* In both instances critics treated the star and her associates politely and respectfully but plainly failed to share the unbridled enthusiasm of the patrons—an enthusiasm most reviewers nevertheless dutifully reported.

Plays that Booth could have performed in his sleep were also the stock repertory of that inveterate trouper W. E. Sheridan. For his visit to the People's, beginning on the 18th, he brought with him *King Lear, Ingomar,* and *Louis XI.* Sheridan was not quite fifty; his slowly rising leading lady, Viola Allen, was not yet twenty.

Like Booth, Ristori, and Sheridan, Frank Mayo had long been locked into an unchanging repertory. In fact, Mayo could scarcely be said to have had a repertory of late, but rather a single vehicle, *Davy Crockett.* However much many observers and commentators admired the play, they agreed it gave only partial rein to Mayo's never fully realized talents. So there was general rejoicing when he appeared in a new play of indisputable merit, his and John G.

Wilson's dramatization of the German novel *Vineta* as **Nordeck** (5-18-85, Union Square). Waldemar Nordeck (Mayo), the illegitimate son of the cruel, unnatural Princess Zulieski (Henrietta Vaders), must constantly battle his own mother's stratagems against him and in favor of his half-brother, Prince Zulieski (Edwin Mayo). The Polish princess has come to hate all Germans—and Nordeck's father was a German. But Nordeck's courage and goodness win the day, even melting the seemingly icy heart of the haughty Wanda (Kathryn Kidder), who had first loved and been deserted by Nordeck's half-brother. The excellent notices helped the play run until the onset of warmer weather in mid-June. Thereafter it remained on Mayo's roster for several seasons, always being welcomed by discerning critics and audiences but never supplanting the wider popularity of *Davy Crockett.*

Crockett, of course, made an interesting native figure for American playgoers, as did Colonel Sellers, the role so long identified with John T. Raymond. Unlike Mayo, Raymond regularly essayed new parts. He had met with varying success as such relatively diverse, if mostly forward, American types as Pemberton Pembroke in *Risks,* Ichabod Crane in *Wolfert's Roost,* Ferdinand Fresh in *Fresh, the American,* Major Bob Belter in *In Paradise,* and General Josiah Limber in *For Congress.* Although he had also played Herr Weigel in *My Son* on tour, Broadway audiences had not seen him attempt to play a foreigner since he attained stardom. Now, in his continuing search for new vehicles, he followed in Mayo's footsteps and did just that, though his Englishman undoubtedly was far less exotic than Mayo's noble-blooded Eastern European. Indeed, at the beginning of Pinero's **In Chancery** (6-9-85, Madison Square) the Englishman is not only not exotic, he is nameless, or at least cannot remember his name, having barely escaped with his life from a horrendous train crash. His rescuers have swathed him in a stranger's overcoat. In its pockets he finds papers belonging to a Montague Joliffe, and since his own linens are initialed "M.J.," he assumes that is who he really is. The assumption lands him in hot water and almost pushes him into an unwanted marriage with the daughter of the temperamental, unreasoning Captain McCafferty (T. H. Glenney). Only the lucky accident of spotting some knick-knacks he had once owned and an amateurish landscape he had once painted initiates the process of restoring his memory. It is fully restored when he recognizes a forlorn lady in Victorian widow's weeds as his wife. If her name is Mrs. Marmaduke Jackson (Bessie Hunter), then he must be Mr. Jackson, a

British "bagman" or traveling salesman. The exceedingly meek, retiring Joliffe-Jackson was not the sort of figure playgoers expected of Raymond, and this, coupled with shortcomings in the farce, weakened the play's appeal. Still, Raymond once more had displayed his skill and versatility. After a month he set aside the farce and restored *For Congress* for the remainder of his stay.

When Raymond left the Madison Square Theatre, seventy-year-old C. W. Couldock took over its stage. The heavy-set, curly-haired performer had once been described as "the beau-ideal wealthy farmer," and while he had successfully interpreted a wide range of roles in his long career, his patently old-style methods were seen to best advantage when he played emotional rustics. The part of Luke Fielding, the farmer driven mad by what he perceives as his daughter's staining of the family honor, in Boucicault's 1849 London success *The Willow Copse* was his choice of vehicle on August 3. Whether August critics were first-stringers or, more likely, young upstarts champing at the bit, most were quick to dismiss both the star and the play as hopelessly outdated, although the more dispassionate or compassionate ones were broad-minded enough to report the warm audience response. And enough oldtime playgoers survived so that Couldock had a not unprofitable four-week stand, despite the often sizzling weather.

As if balancing the relatively new Madison Square's plunge into a musty past, the much older 14th Street Theatre offered what was billed as a "modern comedy-drama," although several reviews suggested it was simply yet another prototypical musical comedy, albeit one with a somewhat unpleasant story. The spunky heroine of Edward E. Kidder's *Sis* (8-3-85, 14th St.) rescues her mother from her abusive stepfather. Sis was played by pretty young Myra Goodwin, the latest in a long line of pretty young ladies determined to find stardom in Lotta-like assignments. Miss Goodwin could sing and dance pleasantly, as could many in her supporting cast, but the new play represented her sole, brief moment in the limelight.

1885–1886

The new season was openhanded with pleasant surprises. The box-office blues of the preceding year largely vanished, chased away in part by a reason-ably steady progression of plays, performers, and productions that garnered both critical praise and public approval. Time has not been equally openhanded. Of course, performers and productions have passed beyond recall ages ago, and only one of the straight plays—Pinero's *The Magistrate*—is revived with any regularity on commercial stages. Yet several other works might withstand modern reconsideration. In any case, a season that a hundred years on is seen to have given birth to a classic is not to be demeaned, and more and more subsequent seasons would proffer new works that still hold some place in the repertory.

The perceived change for the better in quality was not matched by a real change in another important matter. American stages remained firmly in thrall to European theatre, most especially London's playwriting and acting traditions. The recent vogue for French social-melodrama had waned to no small extent, not because of a decline in French playwriting but because a new wave of English playwrights had emerged with whom American critics (who regularly had sniped at the "immorality" of Parisian drama) and American playgoers could feel more comfortable. Naturally, bringing over West End plays provided no work for American dramatists. Yet all too many American playwrights, particularly those who aimed to be produced at first-class houses, continued either simply to translate or adapt European plays, or else to write "original" works teeming with European characters and settings.

This attachment to European and, most of all, to English artistry was nowhere better illustrated than in the reception accorded Mary Anderson when she returned early in the season from two years in London. For many critics London's magic theatrical spell had allowed the young actress to fulfill her incontestable promise—not the first or the last time that London would receive such credit. By implication, these anglophilic, xenophilic, or masochistically antinative writers and playgoers rejected the notion that a performer could attain full flower with only American experience; indeed, by way of confirmation and by contrast, these same observers often condemned American players who learned their art by traveling across their own country. (At the very outset of this same season Gilbert would show that such nonsense was not confined to America when he spoke in *The Mikado* of "the idiot who praises, with enthusiastic tone,/ All centuries but this, and every country but his own.")

The Mikado began its season-long run on Saturday night, August 15, getting the theatrical year off to a splendid and indicative start. The next Monday evening a rash of openings inaugurated the season in earnest and further indicated some of the directions the theatre was taking and some of the problems it was confronting.

Traditionalists continued to express alarm at the proliferation of musicals, often on stages they felt should have been reserved for the "legitimate." No less than Wallack's played host to *Chatter,* a melodic but silly thing from the German. Wallack's former home, now called the Star and living up to its name by welcoming a parade of leading players, also relit. Adelaide Moore, despite her English pedigree, met with a discouraging reception in a group of plays that included *Romeo and Juliet, The Hunchback,* and *As You Like It.* Not everything English was welcomed blindly.

Two American works were also among the foursome of openings. Bartley Campbell's **Clio** (8-17-85, Niblo's) had been a one-week failure when it had been played in Chicago in 1878. Critics had complained that the playwright seemed to want the best of too many worlds, and it was this very complaint that many reviewers echoed when Campbell's supposedly revamped version was brought out seven years later. To an even then old-fashioned plot (set in Europe), Campbell added elements of sensation-melodrama (including an onstage earthquake) and of spectacle (an elaborate ballet with 100 dancers).

Probably the story needed all the help it could get. In the days of the Medici, a sculptor named Fabian (Frank Losee) comes across a beautiful young lady, Lucia (Adele Belgarde), dressed like a ragamuffin and begging alms for herself and her demented father. Fabian sees in the girl the perfect model for the statue of Clio he is planning. He takes the girl and her father home, gives them decent clothes and rooms, and sets to work on the statue. Before long Fabian and Lucia have fallen in love. But the idyll is shattered by the selfish Countess Ellice (May Newman), who leads Fabian to believe Lucia is unfaithful and who prevails on him to move to the French court, where, in fact, he discovers Lucia in the arms of the French king. Well, not really "in fact," since the whole episode is shown to have been a dream. Lucia has not only been loyal but proves to be the devoted daughter of the deranged Duke of Montmaitre (Montmartre in many programs). A meeting with the Duchess of Montmaitre (Mrs. Charles Poole) brings about a happy ending for everyone.

The *Dramatic Mirror* spoke for most commentators when it branded *Clio* "positively the least meritorious thing which has emerged from this playwright's workshop. It has neither coherency nor

dramatic interests. Plotless, soulless and devoid of dramatic reason and common sense, the singular jumble of detached ideas and improbable incidents reasonably excited mirth when they did not create interest." By some forcing the play was kept at Niblo's for a month, then taken on the road, where its reception was no better. The financial losses Campbell incurred week after week were one step leading to his eventual mental breakdown.

Another step actually had been taken earlier, the preceding April, when he had leased the jinxed 14th Street Theatre. While one more of his plays was in active preparation, **Mixed Pickles** (8-17-85, 14th St.) was brought in for a fortnight's stopgap booking. The comedy, and the title, stemmed from the fact that cutup Joe Pickle and the goody-goody Rev. Arthur Pickle (both played by star J. B. Polk) love Cherry Brown (Julia A. Polk). At one point Joe pretends he is Arthur. Neither very original nor very good, it nonetheless satisfied undemanding combination-house audiences for several seasons.

There were no more openings until Campbell's second play of the season premiered. **Paquita** (8-31-85, 14th St.) was the third and probably fatal step in the author's plunge over the brink into madness. Most critics thought it a better play than *Clio,* although they could not agree just where its faults and virtues lay. The *Times* felt the last two acts failed to maintain the vigor of the first three; the *Herald* thought only one of the five acts displayed any strength; the *Dramatic Mirror* admired only the second and fourth acts. Eschewing an act-by-act reckoning, the *Tribune* concluded, "There is much that is wild, fantastic, and absurd in this latest production of Mr. Campbell's restless brain, but there are some genuinely effective situations—his power of melodramatic effect has not weakened."

Some small idea of how unbalanced Campbell's "restless brain" already had become might be seen in the fact that Paquita was a relatively minor figure in the story, which instead centered on a brief romance between Hortense (Kate Forsyth), a married woman, and José Borosco (H. M. Pitt). When they suddenly repent and confess to Hortense's husband, Dr. Manuel Del Rey (Frederic de Belleville), he proves surprisingly forgiving. Not so Hortense's brother, Victor (Ivan Shirley), who shoots José. For good measure, Paquita (Mary Mills), who loves Manuel, also pumps a bullet into José. The wounds might have been mortal but for a risky operation performed by the magnanimous Manuel. All this, however, proves too much for Hortense, who dies cradling her young daughter in her arms while, according to the *Tribune,* "significant glances are exchanged by Paquita and the bereaved husband." Like *Clio, Paquita* had a month-long forced run. Although the *Times* rather condescendingly predicted the play would "please second-rate provincial audiences," it had only the briefest, most fitful afterlife. When the play closed in New York, Campbell abandoned his managerial ambitions. He never wrote or produced anything again and in late 1886 was committed to an insane asylum, where he died two years later.

A second new play opening the same night was **A Brave Woman** (8-31-85, Union Square). Like *Mixed Pickles* at the 14th Street Theatre, it was obviously a stopgap booking (this time for a single week) by producers seeking a New York stamp for their touring show. The producers were assuredly unhappy with the stamp they received, which was more like a swift kick. Several chagrined reviewers saw this story of how a wife's courage saves a disintegrating marriage as patently "stolen" from *Our Joan.* Recognizing the shoddy nature of their goods, the actors "played to the gallery." The approach paid off, for *A Brave Woman* continued to trek across the country long seasons after *Our Joan* had called it quits.

On the same night as *Paquita* and *A Brave Woman* opened, Thomas W. Keene came in from entertaining those provincial audiences to begin a one-week stand at the People's Theatre in the Bowery. Like all combination houses, the People's offerings were treated capriciously in newspapers. Some were reviewed; some were merely mentioned in passing; some were totally ignored. No paper seemed to have a wholly consistent policy. But then there was little point in constantly returning to the same production of the same play as it shifted week by week from playhouse to playhouse up and down the map of Manhattan. However, Keene was not quite your ordinary combination-house attraction. He remained a stalwart knight of the road, a highly respected star in theatrical byways, and so merited at least the grudging attention some New York newspapers accorded him. Even here, though, there was disagreement, for some dailies sent second-stringers to review his opening night while others waited until later in the week when their leading critic could attend and comment.

Although Keene offered the road a wide range of contemporary melodrama and classics, he brought in only a single play for his Bowery visit—Cibber's version of *Richard III.* One critic, who took the occasion to lament that the gallery gods no longer found Shakespeare as meaningful or exciting as they once had and that they had transferred their loyalty

to modern sensation-melodrama, felt that "vigor, motion, and a show of earnestness" dominated Keene's intelligent but unsubtle performance. His reaction was typical.

After Keene departed, the People's roster for the rest of the season indicated the sort of entertainment available at combination houses both in New York and on tour. Its bills included *Storm Beaten, Michael Strogoff, Nobody's Claim, Her Atonement, Fogg's Ferry, The Silver King, Fedora* (still with Fanny Davenport), *The Sea of Ice, The Wages of Sin,* and *Prisoner for Life.* If by chance a regular's favorite did not happen to play the People's, it was only a trolley or elevated ride to other houses, where among the attractions were *The Private Secretary, The Hoop of Gold, The Rajah, Miss Multon* (with Clara Morris), and *Kit, the Arkansas Traveller* (with Henry Chanfrau in the role created by his late father).

Antonie Janish, who had been acting in German-speaking theatres (where her name had been spelled Janisch), had essayed a brief, disastrous English-speaking engagement last season. She nearly came a cropper again when she was announced to star in *Anselma* at the Madison Square on the 31st. Since *Anselma* was merely Leander Richardson's version of the same Sardou play Agnes Ethel had done as *Agnes* and to which she owned American rights, Miss Ethel brought suit to prevent the opening. Behind the scenes the suit was complicated by the fact that the actress had sold some of the rights to Kate Claxton, who sold them in turn to Minnie Maddern. Miss Maddern counseled compromise. Matters were settled in time for a September 7 premiere, when Mme Janish managed to snatch the most meager of victories from the jaws of a second defeat. She was seen as being an adequate performer, and her production held the stage for three weeks, but following a short tour she disappeared from the records.

The delayed opening meant that four major theatres vied for first-nighters. The only truly new play among the four was **A Moral Crime** (9-7-85, Union Square), a drama by Elwyn A. Barron and Morgan Bates, who had written *A Mountain Pink* the year before. Catchy advertisements stated, "No claims made—the selection of adjectives left to the public." Like so many contemporary American plays, the numerous twists of plot unwound in overseas settings. Mathilde Courtney (Marie Prescott) was rescued from poverty while still a child by a seemingly virtuous priest, Father Dablon (H. A. Weaver), who turns out to be a lecher and a blackmailer. Though Mathilde takes no action when he demands money not to disclose he has seduced her, she shoots him when he attempts to seduce a friend of hers. That friend's brother, Philippe, Count d'Albert (Joseph Haworth), was a friend of the priest and determines to discover the shooter. Mathilde confesses the whole story, and the two fall in love. But when the priest dies and Mathilde learns she is to be arrested, she stabs herself and falls dead in Philippe's arms. The production was enhanced by fine settings, including a richly furnished room in a chateau with light filtering through a magnificent stained-glass window. Some critics complained that too many twists of plot were talked about rather than acted out, and the *Herald* regretted that the play did not spring to life until the shooting, although applause at the end of that scene forced the curtain to "rise again, fall, and rise, rise and fall, till it seemed the audience could applaud no longer." Whatever reservations critics held, the public took to the play, and after five weeks the play took to the road.

Robson and Crane returned to the Star on the 7th in a revival of *The Comedy of Errors* that far outdid their 1878 mounting in lavishness and gusto. Critics extolled the elaborate settings, painted with Victorian meticulousness and detail. They compared them to some Irving had presented and those Charles Witham had designed in his early years at Booth's. The *Herald* summed up critical impressions by asserting, "Probably never before was a farcical play produced with such magnificence." A panoramic tableau of a shipwreck opened the evening, which then moved on to the duke's palace with its canopied courtyard. Pillars at the rear framed views of the city. Especially striking was the set depicting the city docks, with "the pier in front of the stage, while behind the water stretches and fades away into a dim and skillfully managed perspective of hazy blue." And, of course, as the two Dromios there were Robson, with his deadpan, boyish face and preposterous squeaks, and Crane, who used every theatrical trick to pass as Robson's twin. Like *A Moral Crime, The Comedy of Errors* played five weeks, then headed out on tour.

At Daly's the Florences stopped by for a month with a repertory consisting of *Our Governor, Dombey and Son,* and *The Mighty Dollar.*

For much of the summer, Tony Pastor's famous vaudeville house, rented out to Dan Sully, had been home to plays that often featured vaudeville stars and that some critics viewed as simply enlarged olio sketches—which, after all, was how Harrigan and Hart had begun. Typical was **Whose Can It Be?** (9-7-85, Tony Pastor's), in which a young couple, for the

usual absurd reasons, cannot acknowledge their baby is theirs. In no time a wife suspects her husband, a young girl her beau, and right on down the line, until the simple truth, emerging late in the evening, clears up matters.

Despite their reliance on packaged post-Broadway tours, combination houses still regularly raised their curtains on productions that might later have been termed tryouts. Some of these went on to first-class houses, but most proved less worthy, although the best of these often toured backwaters for many years. One such offering was Robert Buchanan and Harriet Jay's **Alone in London** (9-14-85, People's). Annie or Nan Meadows (Cora Tanner) is a country girl, as her surname suggests. She naively rejects the proposal of an honest country lad and, bedazzled by the enticements set before her by handsome Robert Redcliffe (Herbert Archer), accepts Redcliffe's offer of marriage and moves with him to London. Unfortunately, Redcliffe is soon seen to be a thoroughgoing scoundrel—a murderer, in fact. When his and Annie's child is of school age, he abuses Annie for attempting to teach the little boy some prayers (the gallery gods booed such impiety) and starts to turn him into a thief. Infuriated by Annie's objections, Redcliffe ties her to a sluice house along the Thames and opens the floodgates. She is spared drowning only by the arrival of her old and still loving country swain. Interesting if somewhat clichéd characters wove in and out of the action. Among them were a philosophy-spouting crook and a fetching street arab, the latter performed by a woman as a trouser role. But the hit of the evening was the floodgate scene, with a deluge of real water inundating the stage and the players, and the gallery gods' boos turning to cheers, stamping, and whistles.

One of the season's most interesting plays followed on the next night. It was hardly new. A few inveterate playgoers had even seen a version of it the preceding week, for Steele MacKaye's **In Spite of All** (9-15-85, Lyceum) was merely the latest rewriting of *Andrea,* the Sardou play most American audiences knew as *Agnes* and the one Agnes Ethel and Minnie Maddern had allowed Mme Janish to produce as *Anselma.* Even at nineteen, the future Mrs. Fiske had developed shrewd, telling theatrical instincts. She must have felt certain that comparisons between Mme Janish and her would all be decidedly in her favor, and she probably also recognized the brilliance and uniqueness of MacKaye's redaction. Although, as a rule, the experimental playwright was far more daring and advanced when it came to nonartistic technical or mechanical matters and moved more cautiously in his playwriting, with *In*

Spite of All he executed a remarkable, if inevitably unappreciated, leap into the next century, turning what Sardou and all his translators had crafted as a standard contemporary social-melodrama into what later generations would call a black comedy. Mac-Kaye himself called it variously a "high comedy" or a "high comedy-drama."

MacKaye retained the basic plot and the name of the heroine's rival but otherwise resorted to both major and minor changes to radically alter the whole tone of the evening. The original Agnes (or Andrea or Anselma or what you will) becomes Alice Clandenning, a New York socialite, in whose plush Fifth Avenue home all the action, except the famous dressing room scene, takes place. Alice's brother, a clumsy deus ex machina in the earliest versions, is now merely a comic, flirtatious young man-about-town, who often joins his brother-in-law on his nightly capers. Indicatively, Alice's rival, Stella, is no longer a ballerina at the opera or an opera star but a leading light in comic opera. One totally original, delightfully conceived figure is Stella's manager, the worldly, cynical, thickly accented Antonius Kraft. Almost equally interesting is the jeweler, Hartmann, who risks losing a good client to help that client's distressed wife. Gone are the ugly incidents with the police (although the husband, Carroll, is arrested and quickly released between the acts). In MacKaye's version Stella proves sympathetic to Alice's plight and joins with Kraft and Hartmann, and with Alice herself, to bring about a happy ending, with Alice forgiving Carroll "in spite of all."

Superb and often clever casting augmented a strong script. Stella was assigned to Selina Dolaro, who had made her name as the very sort of comic-opera star she was impersonating. Manly and handsome Eben Plympton made a believable Carroll (or Carol, as most programs spelled it). But the successes of the evening were Richard Mansfield's Kraft and Minnie Maddern's Alice. Mansfield had suffered a streak of bad luck since his acclaimed Baron Chevrial but now went a long way toward recouping his reputation. His meticulously molded characterization, with its many carefully calculated movements and half-earnest, half-mocking shadings, might have been regarded as too studied and contrived by playgoers fifty or a hundred years later, but contemporaries saw it as an insinuatingly amusing, virtually show-stealing turn. But then no one ever really stole a show from Minnie Maddern, and for all the attention given Mansfield, in the end it was "probably the most interesting young actress now on the American stage" who walked away with the largest critical bouquets. Her growing assured-

ness and deftness were evident in her effectively mixed moments of warmth, nervousness, fear, and determination.

Largely because of these capital performances, *In Spite of All* ran until early November. Yet it never made money. Nor was the subsequent road trip, spoiled in part by Mansfield's desertion, any more profitable. Although Minnie Maddern later returned to the play, the work apparently helped unravel all of the impractical MacKaye's plans and dreams. Before the season was out he had lost his second new theatre.

October was ushered in with Palmer's revival of *Sealed Instructions* at the Madison Square on the 5th. Fast on its heels came **The Magistrate** (10-7-85, Daly's), the most enduring—and endearing—play of the season. Pinero's hilarious depiction of the problems that pile swiftly on top of one another after a woman lies about her age was greeted with critical rejoicing. Extractable quotes—"a laugh in every line," "as funny a farce as we are likely to see"—filled morning-after notices, and the public responded accordingly. Acting plums fell to James Lewis as the embarrassed judge, Aeneas Posket, and to Ada Rehan as his prevaricating wife, Agatha, whose amorous nineteen-year-old son, Cis (E. Hamilton Bell), must pretend to be a boy of fourteen. The carrot-topped, pop-eyed Lewis was a wonder of befuddlement and indignation, while the regally gorgeous Miss Rehan was a comically mature ingenue. There was no suitable role in the play for Mrs. Gilbert. Drew and Skinner were assigned out-of-line parts as bewhiskered, aging military men, one of whom is in a position to disclose Cis's age and the other of whom has just broken off his engagement to Agatha's sister, but seventy-year-old Charles Fisher won special kudos as Bullamy, Posket's old associate. The play ran until the matinee of December 9 and most likely could have continued prosperously for several more weeks, but Daly, as was ever his wont, withdrew it in favor of a change of bill.

Two young ladies of great promise, both still in their twenties, vied for first-nighters' applause one evening apart. Mary Anderson came first, opening with *As You Like It* at the prestigious Star on the 12th. And she came back home after two years of polishing at Irving's Lyceum and at Stratford-upon-Avon. Her welcome was largely rapturous, although a few querulous critics, like the man on the *Times,* carefully modified their rapture. Most reviewers and playgoers found her classic beauty unchanged but her understanding of her roles deepened, her readings more beautiful than ever, her demeanor and her heretofore questioned costuming the last word in elegance. Her performance emphasized her heroine's aristocracy, even when she was masquerading as Ganymede in a russet doublet with slashed sleeves, genuine russet trunk hose (not a silk imitation), a leather jerkin, long boots, a squat velvet hat, and a dark red mantle. Her virtually all-English supporting cast was headed by the Orlando of Johnston Forbes-Robertson, then at the outset of his own distinguished career. Irving's designers had created the sumptuous settings.

An equally elaborate and cumbersome production, this time of *Romeo and Juliet,* was crammed onto the small stage of the Union Square the next night as a setting for the debut of Margaret Mather. The square-faced, tawny-haired actress was the protégé of the theatre's manager, J. M. Hill, who had spent a year attending to her much needed education before arranging her debut, and who had more recently spent small fortunes not only on the mounting but also on an unheard-of, for the time, publicity campaign. Spectators were uncertain how to react. Clearly this newcomer had intensity and forcefulness as well as an acrobatic ability that allowed her to wow more easily impressed patrons with her dramatic fall down a long flight of steps at the end of the potion scene. But for all of Hill's careful nurturing, there remained something a bit coarse and uneven about her acting. Still, Hill's astute ballyhoo and generally accepting reviews allowed the debutante to record a remarkable run of over eighty performances before the production was withdrawn at the beginning of the new year. The heretofore hapless Frederick Paulding was Romeo, but most critics felt he had little except his good looks to offer. No one could foresee how brief and opposite the careers of Anderson and Mather would be.

Another young actress, of a less classical bent, was Effie Ellsler, who continued her uphill battle to maintain the precarious foothold on stardom she had won in *Hazel Kirke.* Her latest vehicle was **Woman Against Woman** (10-12-85, People's), in which she played Bessie Barton, who marries John Terssider (Frank Weston) only to have John's old flame, Rachel Westwood (Mattie Earle), turn John against her and nearly destroy the marriage. The play was no *Hazel Kirke,* but it was a reasonably competent vehicle that provided the star with a regular paycheck for several seasons and even afforded her a brief chance to play a first-class house when she brought the work into the 14th Street Theatre for a short, late-season return.

Oliver Doud Byron followed in her wake with F. A. Scudmore's **The Inside Track** (10-19-85, People's), a piece he advertised as the "London sensation." The *Herald* assessed it as "a thrilling melodrama of the old-fashioned kind." Its hero, Harry Benbigh, was one more in a lengthening line of young men ensnared in a false accusation. Byron's audiences cared little how trite or trashy his vehicles were, so long as he provided them with an evening's escapist fun. He usually did, and *The Inside Track* remained a prominent part of his repertory for the rest of the decade—and then some.

It was to be a Gilbert year on Broadway. With *The Mikado* running along gaily, Mary Anderson added to the ad hoc festival by offering a double bill of Gilbert's plays. One was *Pygmalion and Galatea;* the other was a novelty Gilbert had written expressly for her during her London visit, **Comedy and Tragedy** (10-22-85, Star). In it she played Clarice, a virtuous actress who is lusted after by a contemptible nobleman. The play's great scene had her entertaining dinner guests with examples of her comic gifts all the while her husband is just outside, dueling to the death with the duke. When she breaks down, the guests can only think she is offering a gratuitous example of her skill at tragedy. Of course, it is the duke and not the husband who is killed.

The rapid growth of New York and its theatre life was attested to dramatically on the last Monday in October, the 26th, when five productions, all demanding critical attention, opened. So many simultaneous premieres were unquestionably a record, albeit one qualified by the recognition that most occurred at combination theatres and were works designed primarily for touring. Contemporaries probably saw only two as genuinely first-class occasions.

One of these occurred not at a regular legitimate theatre but at the then new Metropolitan Opera House, where Tommaso Salvini began a three-week stand. His bills consisted of *Othello, King Lear, Ingomar, The Gladiator,* and *Coriolanus.* Reviewers came down hard on his supporting players, who performed in English to his Italian and seemed, according to the *Herald,* "engaged to resist rather than support him." But it was almost impossible to resist the often larger-than-life tragedian. Even the barnlike vastness of the auditorium could not swallow up his gestures, expressions, and intonations. His essentially old-school methods saw to that.

The season's opener at Wallack's—also the home of many old-school traditions—was a one-week fiasco, continuing proof of Wallack's faltering grip on new trends and tastes. Mark Quinton's **In His Power** (10-26-85, Wallack's) told of a woman who remarries after learning that her husband is dead and then finds herself the victim of blackmail, when her first husband turns up alive and as a German spy in the Franco-Prussian War. With so many of his old regulars deserting him, Wallack gave leading parts to newcomers. Sophie Eyre was cast as the harried Marie Hastings. She was to have only a minor career, but her leading man, handsome if somewhat precious Kyrle Bellew, who played her husband, Hubert, in time would become a major star. The villain, called Eugene Lyon in most productions but Eugene Scara at Wallack's, was played by George Clarke. Despite its humiliating failure, *In His Power* later toured for several seasons.

By contrast, Fred Marsden's **Eily** (10-26-85, Grand Opera) quickly disappeared from the boards. Marsden had written it as a vehicle for Annie Pixley, hoping to give her an alternate attraction to her still popular *M'liss*, which she had played at the Grand the preceding week. His young Irish lass is nearly deprived of her rightful fortune by a cagey old troublemaker, who kills her father (in a glen as Eily prances gaily unaware on the brow of the hill beyond) and nearly kills her sweetheart before he himself is brought to justice. But not even Miss Pixley could breathe real life into the piece.

C. T. Dazey's **For a Brother's Life** (10-26-85, Third Ave.) fared no better. Dazey went to the recently resurrected Civil War for his background. Two brothers have had a falling-out over a girl, and when the war erupts they enlist on opposing sides. The Confederate is caught and condemned to death as a spy, at which point his brother agrees to undertake a dangerous mission within rebel lines in return for his brother's being spared. Dazey filled his tale with a variety of standard characters: a drunken Irishman, a quaint hillbilly, a philosophic old black. For additional comic relief he added the dialect role of a chicken-stealing German immigrant who has volunteered as a substitute in the war. A setting in an army camp was praised, as was a quartet of "real darkies" for their singing of war songs and spirituals. (The *Sun* called the vocalists a "chorus of negro jubilee singers.") Yet taken as a whole, the play did not seem to work.

The Crimes of Paris (10-26-85, People's) was a hopeless hash and one of the season's most dismal failures. Its principal story depicted the agonies of a young husband who is falsely accused of murder by a villain who covets the man's wife and fortune. In fact, the play was rife with villains—no fewer than four of them, including a "dumb hunchback" who

recounts his villainies in pantomime. So determined and vile were the villains that "death by every known means was depicted" before a stalwart Parisian detective, Pepin Cardel (played by the show's star, Edwin Thorne), saw justice done.

The abrupt closing of *In His Power* forced Wallack to rush in a revival on November 2. He chose *The Rivals*. which his company always seemed to have ready at their fingertips. The production allowed the house's two regulars, John Gilbert and Mme Ponisi, to return and ran for two weeks, until Wallack had a more unusual revival to offer.

Critics saw no need to trek up to an out-of-the-way fading playhouse, thereby missing an opportunity to sit in judgment on a play that would have a long life in theatrical backwaters without their imprimatur. **Eagle's Nest** (11-2-85, Mount Morris) was set in California, where it followed the adventures of Jack Trail. Jack loves Rose Milford, but Robert Bissedon also covets her and has come into the possession of papers that incriminate Rose's father in an attempt to swindle Jack's father. Bissedon forces Rose to marry him, but the stalwart Jack proves the wedding was illegal. He also gets hold of the troubling papers and sends the villain on his way. The star and, apparently, the author of the play was Edwin Arden, who would tour with the melodrama for ten years (occasionally spelled by performances in other touring shows) before making a respected name for himself on Broadway.

Brooklyn saw a dramatization that toured the eastern seaboard but never reached Manhattan. Actually, it saw two, both based on the same work. *Dark Days* was a novel by Hugh Conway. Charlotte Thompson tried out a version called **Phyllis Denohr** (11-2-85, Grand Opera, Brooklyn), which closed almost as soon as it opened. Conway and Comyn Carr's version, called **Dark Days** (11-9-85, Criterion, Brooklyn), had a slightly longer life. Both told of good country people oppressed by the family of a corrupt nobleman. Bigamy, betrayal, murder, and a host of other melodramatic clichés were employed in attempts to enliven the story. In the more official adaptation an effective setting of a crossroads in a snowstorm garnered applause.

An already interesting season received a further boost with Palmer's beautifully cast and mounted production of Henry Arthur Jones's London success **Saints and Sinners** (11-7-85, Madison Square). J. H. Stoddart gave one of his most memorable performances in the juicy role of Jacob Fletcher, a devoted, self-sacrificing clergyman who refuses to knuckle under to a blackmailing deacon and so destroys his own career by admitting to his flock that his daughter has gone astray. He suffers through years of poverty and aimless wandering before the tables are turned and justice belatedly meted out. Bending to the newer style of writing and the sort of acting best projected in a small auditorium, Stoddart gave a portrayal that was "quiet, natural, and artistic," emphasizing the "gentleness, simplicity, and pathos" inherent in the characterization. In one of his great moments, as Fletcher is putting the finishing touches on a table he has prepared for his daughter and the man he hopes she will marry, his joy and expectation are shattered by the news that his daughter has eloped with a rakish army officer. Palmer's excellent supporting players, many of whom, like Stoddart, had worked with him for long seasons at the Union Square Theatre, gave a brilliant ensemble performance. W. J. LeMoyne was the greedy, vicious Samuel Hoggard; E. M. Holland the loyal parishioner, Lot Burden; Herbert Kelcey the philandering Captain Fanshaw; L. F. Massen the loyal suitor, Ralph Kingsmill; and Marie Burroughs was Fletcher's daughter, Lettie. Marston, another recruit from Palmer's Union Square days, earned applause and curtain calls for his settings, which included the minister's comfortable house, the chapel, and the hovel Fletcher eventually calls home. As Palmer had shown when he produced *Daniel Rochat*, a well-written, well-staged play with a religious theme could find an audience even in devil-may-care New York. *Saints and Sinners* confronted playgoers with its moral dilemma for over 100 showings.

Bronson Howard's **One of Our Girls** (11-10-85, Lyceum) followed and proved the season's biggest nonmusical hit, chalking up 200 performances. It marked the single real triumph in Helen Dauvray's short-lived attempt to establish herself as an actress-manager. With her silent partner, John Rickaby, she had taken over the Lyceum from the impractical MacKaye. Her choice of play represented a typical period compromise—an American play, but one set in Europe and largely peopled with foreigners. The titular heroine, however, was unmistakably American. Kate Shipley (Dauvray) is the daughter of an American father and a French mother. Her mother had been ostracized by her haughty French relatives for marrying a man who was not only foreign but unmonied. The family's attitude changed abruptly after Kate's father had become a millionaire. When Kate sails to France and spends some time with her French aunt and uncle, she shocks them by her refusal to be accompanied by a chaperone or suffer any of the other restrictions French propriety places on unmarried girls. She in turn is shocked to learn that her cousin, Julie (Enid Leslie), has been pushed into an arranged marriage with the arrogant, impoverished Count Florian de Crebillon (F. F. Mackay), on whom Julie's social-climbing parents have bestowed a huge dowry. The reappearance of Julie's former heartthrob, Henri Saint-Hilaire (Vincent Sternroyd), drives the young bride into a tizzy. She learns that Henri, disappointed at finding her married, has decided to return to his overseas post, and she rushes thoughtlessly to his apartment. Kate follows, hoping to forestall any complications, but she has no sooner arrived than the count knocks on the door. Kate and Julie hide in another room. Unfortunately, the count discovers a woman's glove and demands to search the rooms. When Henri refuses, the two men seize rapiers and start to duel. Their fight is interrupted by the arrival of their friend, the Englishman Captain John Gregory (E. H. Sothern), who also is Kate's suitor. John realizes that Henri has been wounded, and the count starts for the next room to get water and bandages. Once more Henri attempts to prevent him, but this time the door opens and Kate stands there. To protect Julie's reputation, she willingly risks her own. The count sneeringly hands John the lady's glove: "I ought to envy Captain Gregory. The hand to which this glove belongs has been promised to him in marriage. He will be obliged to share its caresses with other men." John takes the glove and slaps the count with it, thus challenging him to a second duel. Although the count is reported to be seriously wounded, another report discloses that his first wife, whom he thought dead, is still alive. While the count's woes are compounded, Henri and Julie understand they will soon be able to marry, and Kate has all the proof a girl could want of her lover's affection for her.

Society long since has junked the proprieties, strictures, and niceties that helped give *One of Our Girls* its tension and bite. Yet Howard's comedy remains pleasant enough and had to be much more so to contemporaries. A few flaws were obvious even then. The European characters, while theatrically effective, were frayed cardboard cutouts. Some of the exposition, especially the long letter-writing scene at the beginning of the second act, with its extended asides, was clumsy. And attempts to contrast American and French mores became annoyingly repetitive after a time. The other side of the coin was Howard's droll, memorable depiction of his heroine. Kate can be knowingly and proudly American, as when she tells her astonished aunt, "I am my own governess. . . . If a girl doesn't learn how to govern herself before she's married, I don't see how she can govern her husband and the rest of her household afterwards." She can be objective, if not dispassionate, about European codes:

Julie: The count proposed to father for my hand, of course.
Kate: Why didn't you tell him to *marry* your father?
Julie: Ha, ha, ha, ha! It's quite immaterial to me which of us he marries.
Kate: You do not love him, Julie! You cannot, of course.
Julie: Love him? No; I'm only going to marry him!
Kate: Oh! That's all.

Howard also gave her a touching humanity by adding such small details as her awareness of the value of money, and her indifference to it. Thus, having cabled her father that she loves Captain Gregory "very, very, very much," she muses, "Three 'verys'—at forty cents a word; they're worth it." She then concludes her message, "Please send me your blessing and enough money for my trousseau."

Few if any blessings were showered on Howard P. Taylor's **Dimples** (11-16-85, Third Ave.), written expressly for the Lotta-like Ida Mülle. Miss Mülle was petite and cute, but she lacked all those endearing charms and talents that made Lotta so compelling. And most certainly she was not in a class with young Minnie Maddern, who had done so much to find an audience for Taylor's earlier *Caprice*. Dimples, described cryptically in the program as "a winsome but vicious little village duckling," is the daughter of a country blacksmith who has discovered a rich mine. Two scoundrels, one young and one old, try to kidnap Dimples and to obtain the deed to the mine. Naturally, wealth and true love are both hers by the final curtain.

More sophisticated first-nighters could delight in a superior offering that same evening, when Wallack's supplanted its staging of *The Rivals* with a production of Mrs. Centlivre's rarely seen *The Busybody*. Like the Sheridan comedy, it ran two weeks. At that point many of the same regulars undoubtedly returned to the theatre for what proved to be the final success in a month of hits. Henry Arthur Jones and Wilson Barrett's **Hoodman Blind** (11-30-85, Wallack's) depicted the dangerous ruptures jeopardizing the marriage of Jack (Kyrle Bellew) and Nance Yeulett (Annie Robe), a country couple, after Nance is blamed for misdeeds actually committed by her look-alike outcast half-sister, Jess (also Miss Robe). Despite the huge cast of characters, only cameo roles could be found for several of Wallack's best players. John Gilbert, for instance, appeared for only ten minutes in the first act as a

figure who is no sooner introduced than he is murdered.

If both play and players won handsome applause, the scenery was even more applauded. Not since Marston's heyday at the Union Square had critics devoted so much attention to describing sets and lauding a painter. Philip Goatcher had to take at least three curtain calls for pictures that included "a moonlit grove, with a rustic stile and winding pathway," and a view of the Thames Embankment "showing the Egyptian Column, the semicircle of lights, and the 'dark, flowing' river." Goatcher's equally acclaimed associate, Harley Merry, created the setting showing a street in Abbot's Creslow, "with its quaint shops and houses facing the village cross."

Unlike Daly, Wallack was willing to allow his more successful productions to run as long as the public wanted them, but success was a relative thing for Wallack. His large house, fading ensemble, and aging clientele meant plays would no longer run there as long as they might elsewhere. Still, *Hoodman Blind*'s seven-week run was as profitable as any Wallack's had enjoyed in recent seasons.

Probably few of Wallack's loyalists were fans of Lotta. Most highfalutin' critics never had taken to her. But now time was beginning to put its cruel, ineluctable stamp on her and her career as assuredly as on Wallack's. She faced a "small and apathetic" audience when she began a two-week engagement at the Standard on December 7. Her vehicles were *Little Nell and the Marchioness* in the first week and *Mam'zelle Nitouche* in the second. Some critics undiplomatically suggested that she was now too old for her parts in the Dickens dramatization, but the *Times,* no admirer from the start, at least found some virtue in her playing: "No one can wink like Lotta. . . . No one can wriggle more effectively. No one can kick higher nor oftener. No one can display hosiery with such ingenuous grace or poetic abandon. Lotta is nothing if not athletic."

Two days later Daly revived *A Night Off.*

The old year was rung out with another of those concoctions that may or may not be perceived as a prototypical musical—George Hoey's **Oh! What a Night!** (12-28-85, Grand Opera), a vehicle for dialect comedian Gus Williams. The play might have been seen as a comic version of *Woman Against Woman.* Celeste Vavasour (Topsy Venn), a hot-headed burlesque star, sees nothing funny in her former fiancé, Howard Laing (C. F. Tingay), announcing he will marry the daughter of retired Major Herman Pottgeiser (Williams). The balloonish Pottgeiser hides in closets, scampers under a table, and uses all his homey philosophy to becalm the troubles. At one moment his wife misconstrues his behavior and in a fit threatens to "wipe him up mit de floor." If the evening contained many musical numbers, they were not good enough for critical comment. But then neither was the farce, which remained for only a week and was something of a disappointment on the road.

Modjeska opened the new year with a month-long visit at the Star, beginning on January 4, 1886. Her first role was Camille. Although William Winter persisted in branding the play "openly offensive," he recognized Modjeska's artistry. He recorded in the *Tribune,* "This actress from the first of her career upon the American stage has been remarkable for her power to express the passionate rapture with which true love looks upon the object of its adoration. With this power her performance, last night, was vital and beautiful. The outburst of despair, in the agonizing scene of the third act—when the tortured *Camille,* driven from her last refuge, cries out 'Why do I live?'—remains, as it has ever been, one of the finest strokes of dramatic art that have been accomplished within the memory of the present generation. Mme. Modjeska, like Sarah Bernhardt, portrays the death of *Camille* without the taint of physical decay, and without the least association of the sick-room and the medicine-chest." Modjeska's schedule also included *Mary Stuart* (her first New York attempt at the part, and one that prompted the *Times* to suggest that "in grace and beauty Mme. Modjeska's embodiment of Mary Stuart surpasses that of any actress who has been seen in Schiller's noble drama in this city"), *As You Like It, Adrienne Lecouvreur, Twelfth Night,* and *Odette.* She also presented a rarity, John Westland Marston's *Donna Diana,* brought out on the 14th. Marston's play was based on a 17th-century Spanish classic, Augustín Moreto y Cabaña's *El desdén con el desdén.* Though it was still popular in translation in New York's German-speaking playhouses, New York's regular theatres had not played host to it for nearly twenty years. In that earlier life it was sometimes called *Love's Masquerade.* Its heroine is an icy noblewoman who has sworn never to love any man; her coldness is thawed when Don Caesar pretends to be even more unloving and frigid.

Modjeska's return coincided with the second offering of Margaret Mather's extended debut. Following the surprising success of *Romeo and Juliet,* Hill and his young aspirant selected a much newer drama, but one even then fading from the stage—Daly's *Leah, the Forsaken.* The poetic deliv-

ery, the polish, and the subtlety looked for in a stellar Juliet were not requisite to depicting a moving Leah, so many observers felt that the role of the deserted Jewess was more in Mather's line. She enjoyed a month's run in the piece.

J. E. Brown's **Felix McKusick** (1-11-86, Grand Opera) allowed lanky, smiling Sol Smith Russell to portray a failed country newspaper editor who becomes the proprietor of a dime museum and must resort to all manner of disguises to keep his customers (and audiences) interested. These disguises include a Rube Goldberg–like inventor, an idiot from Australia, and a young man given to boring people by reciting long poems. His problems evaporate when his wife turns out to be an heiress. Russell and his cohorts also resorted to a number of musical specialties. Unfortunately the play, whose plot had an uncomfortable resemblance to Grover's *A Great Scheme,* bored too many patrons, so Russell soon dropped it.

Daly continued his excellent season with a revival of *The Merry Wives of Windsor* on the 14th. As usual Daly had tampered aggressively with the text. The comedy was given in four acts, with numerous scenes cut or rearranged. Daly gave Ada Rehan's Mrs. Ford speeches written originally for other characters and boldly took material from *Henry IV* to provide an epilogue for Falstaff. The casting also came under questioning, with some reviewers wondering aloud if Mrs. Ford and Mrs. Page should have been played by such beautiful young women as Miss Rehan and Miss Dreher, and if Ford and Page were meant to be as cavalier and elegant as Drew and Skinner made them. But the casting that elicited the most comment was Charles Fisher's Falstaff, for Fisher eschewed the traditional besotted charlatan. Instead Fisher let his own majestic figure and gift for pathos act as counterpoint to the absurd situations in which the old knight finds himself.

Some critics, such as J. Ranken Towse of the *Evening Post,* felt Daly was wrong to have his actors play the comedy as if it were another German farce, but others admired the fast pacing. The almost Oriental opulence of the settings and costumes, more or less typical for the period, similarly divided critics, some of whom felt Daly went overboard. For example, the costumes of E. Hamilton Bell, which the producer imported from England, dressed Mrs. Ford and Mrs. Page in luxurious lace-bordered silks that at best hinted at genuine Elizabethan designs. Daly's use of electric lighting to create eerie effects in the Herne's Oak scene also puzzled some less venturesome reporters, who were happier with the painted realism that showed Windsor Castle looming beyond the Garter Inn and the Pages' walled garden, or the heavy, solid period furnishings in Ford's wainscoted room. Yet for all the critical carping, the play ran merrily indeed for a whole month.

Modjeska's presentation of *Donna Diana* vied with Daly's revival for first-nighters, and the following Wednesday, the 20th, Wallack's restored *The Guv'nor* to its program.

W. C. Cowper was one of the players in his own melodrama, **Blackmail** (1-25-86, People's). The *Herald* reported the kaleidoscope of stock motifs jumbled together in this typical touring piece with a singularly impressionistic summary: "a fête, a recognition, a betrayal, a mother's death, the Fortress of Toulon, a wolf in sheep's clothing, an escape, the harbor of Marseilles, an abduction, a sister's prayer, a baby's voice, a victory, a death, a voice from the grave and a scene of harrowing despair," all leading to the curtain line, "I will love you all my life." Cowper was luckier than many of his playwriting colleagues. His play was awarded a fortnight's booking (no doubt another stopgap) in mid-March at the Standard, a first-class Manhattan house generally given over to musicals. *Blackmail* enjoyed a reasonably long, healthy life in the backwaters for which it was probably written.

As they had four years before, Booth and Barrett opened competing engagements on the same evening. The first night of February saw Booth ensconced at the comparatively small Fifth Avenue and again supported by members of the faltering Boston Museum company, while Barrett brought his own specially selected company into the larger Star. By the simple expedient of beginning his visit with an imaginatively selected revival, Barrett won a lion's share of space in the morning-after theatrical columns. His selection was Hugo's *Hernani*, which had disappeared from New York's first-class, English-speaking stages by the early 1840s. Its story told the tragic love of a high-principled outlaw. When Don Leo (C. M. Collins), who has saved the hero's life although they are rivals for the hand of Donna Zanthe (Minna K. Gale), demands that Hernani keep his promise to kill himself on hearing Don Leo blow a silver trumpet, Hernani does just that. But Zanthe joins him in drinking the poison, thus depriving Don Leo of a final triumph.

Barrett was always careful about his mountings. Three settings—a street in Saragossa at midnight, the tall, gloomy vaults at Aix-la-Chapelle, and a gaudily lit Moorish garden—"excited the spectators to loud demonstrations of approval." But it was Barrett himself who walked off with the most praise.

A few weeks earlier, after seeing the first performance in Philadelphia, Winter wrote in the *Tribune* that the star portrayed the hero "with splendid dash and touching fervor. The sonorous elocution was almost wholly discarded in favor of a vehement, impulsive delivery. . . . He spoke and acted with the true eloquence of heart, and he evoked a tumult of sincere public applause." Barrett offered only this production for the first two weeks of his visit, then in his last fortnight included it in a fast-changing repertory that also included *Francesca da Rimini, Julius Caesar, The Wonder, The King's Pleasure, David Garrick,* and *Yorick's Love.*

By contrast, Booth offered nothing so fresh. His long-ossified repertory consisted of *Hamlet, King Lear, Brutus, Macbeth, A New Way to Pay Old Debts, Richelieu, The Fool's Revenge, Richard III,* and *Julius Caesar.* Reviews of his productions were generally damning, and those of his own interpretations ran an astonishing gamut from ecstatic to scathing. One young supporting player, however, received almost universal praise. He was J. B. Mason, who took such roles as Laertes, Edmund, Titus, and Antony. Years later, as John Mason, he would become one of the luminaries of the American stage, albeit in a type of drama alien to Booth. Booth's repertory may have been stale, but it was not unprofitable. Newspapers reported some remarkable grosses, including a house record of $1730 for one Saturday matinee. At this same period Frederick Warde stopped briefly at the People's in a Booth-like program of plays.

All of hopeful Margaret Mather's offerings during her four-month debut had appeared on evenings when more established stars were beckoning first-nighters, or immediately thereafter. She had opened hard on the heels of Mary Anderson, proffered *Leah* against Modjeska's return, and now bucked both Booth and Barrett to bring out her last production, another fading old favorite, *The Honeymoon.* It gave her the opportunity to show her skills at comedy. Critics were divided in their judgments, but even the kindest felt she still had much to master. Unlike the dramas in which she had played, the comedy remained before the footlights for only a week, at which time she concluded her stand.

George R. Sims and Clement Scott's **Jack-in-the-Box** (2-9-86, Union Square) was the sort of hodgepodge that made critics shudder while it delighted the gallery gods. Its basic plot was pure melodrama—a man framed for a crime by a treacherous cousin (who always keeps a chloroform-soaked handkerchief "handy" in his pocket). Minor characters were a grab-bag of stock melodramatic figures. There was the rich old father seeking his long-lost son (guess who the son was!), an abducted maiden (the hero's daughter), a sleazy Italian (the villain's accomplice and the real criminal), and a smart-talking street arab. Somewhat quirkily, the street arab was played by the show's star, Carrie Swain, another Lotta-like player whose talents ran to some light singing, dancing a jig, and doing somersaults. (In fact, in England the show had been considered a musical.) As a result the drama was preposterously watered down, the more carefree moments tinged with unnecessary tension or starkness. After a few weeks the show returned to the hinterlands from which it had come.

On the 13th Daly restored *She Would and She Would Not* for a handful of performances. Despite so very limited an engagement, Daly coupled the play with **A Wet Blanket,** a two-character, one-act comedy from the French. This trifle had Drew cast as an English baronet whose ardent advances to an American lady, played by Miss Rehan, are cooled by her statement that his own wife is at that moment being wooed by the lady's husband.

The aging Lester Wallack, sensing his career was drawing to a close, told David Belasco, "I think I have one more 'study' in me" and asked Belasco to write a play for him accordingly. No doubt deciding that Wallack was too old for an extended role, Belasco contrived a work in which Wallack's part would not be large but would be crucial. To this end he wrote **Valerie** (2-15-86, Wallack's), a drama derived loosely but effectively from Sardou's *Fernande.* Belasco reset the play in England (possibly to please the anglophilic Wallack) and slightly tilted the emphasis of the story, which he might now have called something on the order of *Helena's Revenge.* Helena Malcolm (Sophie Eyre), who is the equivalent of Clothilde in the original, tricks Sir Everard Challoner (Kyrle Bellew), the André of *Fernande,* into confessing that he no longer loves her and that he has given his heart to an unknown youngster whom he met briefly when she had a fainting spell in the street. By some means the malicious, bitter Helena discovers that the girl is Valerie de Brian (Annie Robe) and that Valerie's father was a gambler who had murdered Everard's father. She passes off Valerie, whom she assumes has been a courtesan (as Fernande had been), under the name Marie de Ligneries and engineers a marriage between the girl and Everard. As the newlyweds leave the church Helena approaches, bent on disclosing the bride's background and thus destroying Everard's happiness. But the strong arm of middle-aged lawyer Walter Trevillian (Wallack) restrains her. He

later shows her that Valerie has never stooped to the degradation Helena believed she had. He also confronts her with some other home truths, all of which combine to humble the vixen.

Winter wrote that Annie Robe's "performance evinced a fine woman-like intuition and . . . was suffused with touching sincerity" but added that she displayed "a certain muscular vigor incompatible with the ideal of a sweet, fragile girl." Sophie Eyre's Helena was seen as forceful if not quite finished. Many critics felt Bellew was not manly and tough enough to play Everard. Most of the real praise was lavished on Wallack's performance, although some critics saw it merely as one in a line of such roles, at which he long had excelled. The drama ran one month, about as good a run as Wallack could expect any more.

Daly did not even expect that sort of stay when he returned *The Country Girl* to his bills, but though the revival was slated for only a week's visit, the healthy theatrical economics of the era and Daly's own high-mindedness again saw to it that the superb remounting was coupled with a new one-act curtain raiser, **A Sudden Shower** (2-18-86, Daly's). If Ada Rehan and John Drew shone most brilliantly in the Garrick comedy (and in the previous curtain raiser), the two-character comedietta, taken from the French, was a tour de force for the older half of Daly's great foursome. A friend persuades Christopher Peechick (James Lewis), an old bachelor, that he ought to think about marriage, and to that end the friend suggests that his spinster cousin, Triphena Skrimp, would make a good prospect. Dressed like a young dude, Peechick sets out to call on Miss Skrimp, but a sudden shower forces him to knock on a strange door for shelter. His knock is answered by a hatchet-faced lady sporting long, stiff curls and wearing a bright green dress. She proves, despite her appearance, to be so pleasant that Peechick finds himself confiding in her his plans to meet and court the stranger he calls "old Limp and Gimp." Naturally the strange lady turns out to be Miss Skrimp (Mrs. Gilbert). When she has heard enough and the shower has passed, she politely shows Peechick the door.

Another of the plays that straddled the line between comedy and musical was William Gill's **A Toy Pistol** (2-20-86, Comedy). It was written to serve as Tony Hart's first solo vehicle since his feud with Harrigan and departure from their company. He received a tumultuous reception on his initial entrance, but the joy soon turned sour. The comedy's basic plot was not unlike the one J. E. Brown had written for Sol Smith Russell in *Felix McKusick,* centering as it did on another embattled newspaper editor who must resort to all manner of disguises to keep his enterprise afloat. Hart's name alone kept the play afloat for a little over a month before it embarked on tour.

At the Madison Square Theatre the long run of *Saints and Sinners* finally gave way on the 23rd to a highly praised revival of Gilbert's *Engaged,* with Agnes Booth heading the cast as Belinda.

Daly capped his splendid season with **Nancy and Company** (2-24-86, Daly's), his brother's Americanization of Julius Rosen's *Halbe Dichter.* Pivotal to the preposterous plot was the secret collaboration of Kiefe O'Kiefe (John Drew) and Nancy Brasher (Ada Rehan) on a play that is about to be given its first New York performance. O'Kiefe is living on probation at the home of Ebenezer Griffing (James Lewis), who is determined to prove that O'Kiefe is not fit to marry his niece, Oriana (Virginia Dreher). Griffing's own daughter, Daisy (Edith Kingdon), is in love with Captain Renseller (Otis Skinner), but Griffing is conspiring to marry her to Sikes Stockslow (George Parkes), a broker whom Daisy dismisses as "a ninny who values a wife according as she harmonizes with his bric-a-brac and his *Louis Quinze* rooms." Her disdain is confirmed by his every babyish utterance, such as "Awful nice little girlie! Make awful nice little wifey! She'll dress up my housey splendidly [*Titters*]." Nancy rushes off to New York to attend the opening of the play but refuses to tell Mr. Brasher (William Gilbert) her real reasons. Angry and suspicious, he follows her. She takes a room at a posh hotel. By a happy farcical coincidence, the room on her left is occupied by Oriana and her mother, Mrs. Dangery (Mrs. Gilbert), and the room on Nancy's right by none other than the simpering Stockslow. Before long, characters are rushing from one room to another, slamming doors behind them, and misconstruing everything. At one point Griffing spots Nancy's feet hidden under a lap rug and thinks to discover her to O'Kiefe's discomfiture, but by the time he rounds up witnesses and returns to pull off the rug it is Captain Renseller who is revealed. A few minutes later Griffing again sees Nancy's feet under a cloak. In this instance by the time he collects his witnesses and pulls off the cloak, he finds only Mr. Brasher. It goes without saying that everything ends happily.

A few nitpickers aside, critics were as happy as the paired lovers. Looking back some years later, Edward A. Dithmar would rate *Nancy and Company* "the very best of the lighter and more farcical pieces in the Daly repertory." Even more joyous huzzas greeted the players, who were seen to be the finest ensemble of comedians in America and at the peak of their form. And certainly that is how this troupe long was remembered. Yet at the time there were some who perceived some fallings away from near perfection, with no one more conscious of this than Daly himself. Less than a month into the run (which continued until season's end on May 1), Daly posted a backstage notice that read, in part: "The performances of Nancy & Co. are drifting away from the true spirit of the piece—& from the condition desirable in a perfect representation.

"Some have grown listless—some slothful—some so by rote as to get their words & sentences tangled—gigglings and suppressed laughter are frequent & ill disguised—some have become *so easy* as to give no *force* to their voice & their words do not carry half the distance of the house—others have grown to make unnecessary pauses & breaks—others hurry & talk through laughs, altogether there is a lack of that freshness & alertness which I want to see at every performance."

Of course, such faults may have been evident mostly to Daly's hypercritical eyes and ears. When Daly took the play and his actors to London during the summer, English critics, often highly contemptuous of American acting, were bowled over. In its notice of *Nancy and Company,* the *Saturday Review* proclaimed, "There is not now in London an English company as well chosen, as well trained, as brilliant in the abilities of its individual members, or as well harmonized as a whole, as the admirable company which Mr. Daly directs. They suggest the Comédie Française at its best."

Clay Greene's **Forgiven** (3-8-86, Windsor) was a touring show that some reviewers felt displayed more merit, or at least promise, than most such dramas. Frederic Bryton was the star of the piece, in which he played Jack Diamond, a volatile, dictatorial, but essentially good-hearted professional gambler. When a scheming rival uses a forgotten coat and an ambiguously worded letter to make it appear that Jack's wife, Annie (Sydney Armstrong), has been unfaithful, Jack's mercurial response is so frightening that Annie flees. For ten years Jack seeks her out. Eventually he kills the troublemaker and is reunited with his wife. What pleased the more responsive critics were not the obviously melodramatic moments of the story but the early scenes in which the hardnosed but loving husband and his unworldly wife try to make an accommodating marriage in the face of social ostracism. Many playgoers had other ideas about what made the show go. One reviewer noted that after the shootout near the end "the gallery boys (mad with the scent of gunpowder, bless 'em!) cheer till their throats ache." Whatever the reason, *Forgiven* went on to a long theatrical life in lesser theatres. By the end of 1888 Bryton could announce, with apparent honesty, that he had performed the play 1000 times.

The romantic Irish swashbuckler found a welcomed example in **The Ivy Leaf** (3-8-86, Niblo's), in which fearless, versatile Murty Kerrigan (J. P. Sullivan) must jump to freedom from a high tower, fend off two archvillains, Robert Nolan (producer W. H. Powers) and Dennis Donovan (Grattan Phillips), and warble a few misty ballads before he can claim the hand of long-suffering Colice O'Brien (May Woolcot). Every now and then one of these Irish plays came in without the character of a drunken priest or a dastardly Britisher in sight. *The Ivy Leaf* was one such play and was applauded accordingly. But not everyone applauded. Certainly not A. M. Palmer, who, as trustee for Bartley Campbell's estate, was outraged at the play's similarity to *Grana Uaile*. The author, and sometimes star, of the newer work was Con Murphy, who had been the original Ryman O'Reilly in Campbell's play. Always ready to go to court to defend his rights, Palmer sued Murphy for plagiarism. Despite the era's lax copyright laws, he won. Given earlier charges that Campbell had borrowed brazenly from still older shows, there was a certain additional irony in the decision.

The appropriately named Star Theatre had played host to many of the world's best performers since it had been rechristened after the uptown move by Wallack's ensemble. Now another star came onto its stage, but a star whose once shimmering brightness had paled sometime back—Dion Boucicault. His reappearance after a prolonged absence was accompanied by a whiff of scandal, for the sixty-five-year-old actor-playwright, who was rumored to have murdered his first wife and who cruelly threw off his second, brought with him a new spouse, twenty-one-year-old Louise Thorndyke, a girl obviously young enough to be his granddaughter. Boucicault may have attempted to deflect some of the expected notoriety by his old trick of ballyhooing his new play as a bold departure in modern dramaturgy. It was a ploy he had used too often, and one observer lamented, "With all his gifts, Mr. Boucicault has always been a humbug." Boucicault's new play, **The Jilt** (3-15-86, Star), was seen by some as a rewriting of his old *Flying Scud*. Its colorful racetrack scenes and racing lingo were framed in a story that recounted how the romance and eventual marriage of Myles O'Hara (Boucicault) and the flirtatious Kitty Woodstock (Miss Thorndyke) were jeopar-dized by Lord Marcus Wylie's attempt to make public love letters Kitty's sister-in-law, Lady Millicent (Helen Bancroft), had written years before. It turns out Sir Budleigh Woodstock (Henry Miller) had known about and ignored the correspondence. One effective scene had various onlookers in a grandstand describe a race. *The Jilt* ran three weeks and later returned for an additional week. It had also played to good business in a number of other cities from San Francisco to Boston. Yet its limited success was a far cry from the huge hits Boucicault had once enjoyed, and it was to prove his last offering to win any sort of critical or public acceptance.

On the same night, the newer Wallack's offered revivals of *Home* and *A Happy Pair*, followed a fortnight later by a revival of *Central Park*.

The night after this latter revival welcomed a double bill of plays, which included its own revival, Bronson Howard's *Old Love Letters*. This short piece was familiar to New Yorkers, especially with Agnes Booth recreating the role of Mrs. Brownlee. Herbert Kelcey was the suitor. The "new" play coupled with the old was not all that new, for it was Gilbert's **Broken Hearts** (3-30-86, Madison Square), first done in London nearly ten years earlier. It had also been seen in some American cities, but New Yorkers' only previous exposure to it had been in the preceding season when it was given at one of those "special matinees" that had begun to serve as tryouts.

On a beautiful island where "real water bubbled amid moss-grown rocks," a band of ladies lives, avowedly isolated from men. The only male presence allowed on the island is Mousta (W. J. LeMoyne), a deformed dwarf. But handsome Prince Florian (Louis Massen) suddenly appears. At first he courts Lady Vavir (Annie Russell), a beautiful but weak girl who dies of a broken heart when the prince changes the object of his affections. The prince's new heartthrob is Lady Hilda (Maud Harrison), and for a time he whispers sweet nothings in her ear from behind a magical cloak that makes him invisible. Mousta steals the cloak and seemingly woos and wins Hilda. But when he reveals himself, she rejects him in favor of the prince.

Despite laudatory reviews, Gilbert's bittersweet blank-verse fantasy appealed to only a small number of playgoers. Two and a half weeks sufficed to satisfy their demand for seats.

Wallack's parade of revivals continued with *She Stoops to Conquer* on April 5, the incorrigible Wallack still representing young Marlow.

Many a star, Wallack among them, might play

longer or shorter seasons at a first-class house and also pop up now and then at combination houses. Thus while Lotta had spent time at the Standard earlier in the season, she, too, often came to her admirers in their own neighborhood. On a spring stopover she included one new play, Mrs. Charles A. Doremus's **Larks** (4-8-86, Grand Opera). The story was slight. Laura has been named for her rich uncle, Lawrence Peterhill (P. A. Anderson). Laura's family hoped this would allow them to eventually inherit the uncle's estate. When it becomes clear that old Peterhill has assumed his namesake is a boy, Laura must dress up as one, in knickers and a polo cap. The uncle soon sees through the ploy but has no trouble forgiving his winsome niece. There had been a time when the story did not matter to Lotta's fans; they came solely to see their beloved star and her turns. But that time was fast disappearing. Even a medley of popular songs from Harrigan and Hart shows was little help. The quick removal of *Larks* from her schedule may have been an early signal to Lotta to start thinking about retirement.

Édouard Pailleron's *Le Monde où l'on s'ennuie*, a superb comedy about political and social string-pulling, was Americanized by Clinton Stuart and Mrs. J. C. Verplanck and produced by Palmer as **Our Society** (4-19-86, Madison Square). The deft satire (heavy-handed and coarsened in translation, according to some critics) was framed in the simple story of two young couples, whom a pushy social climber would mismate but who finally are left to their own devices thanks to the intervention of a warm and wise grande dame. Of late the ladies had walked away with the laurels at this theatre, and in the new mounting they did so again. Annie Russell won applause as Sylvia Spencer, a spunky young girl who finds both independence and a husband despite her bluestocking relatives' attempts to control her, while Maud Harrison took bows for her Mrs. Ferdinand Tupper, a wife resolved on obtaining a consulship for her passive husband. The lateness of the season and previous commitments to tour confined the play's run to two weeks, although it would return briefly the following year.

Wallack's was also bringing its season to an end. Its final offering was another double bill of revivals—*The Palace of Truth* and *The Captain of the Watch*, whose run precisely paralleled that of *Our Society.*

April closed with Booth and Salvini joining hands to give three performances of *Othello* and one of *Hamlet* at the Academy of Music, beginning on the 25th. Booth was Iago in the former and Salvini was the Ghost in the latter. In the second performance, on the 28th, after the Moor had warned "Villain, be sure thou prove my love a whore, / Be sure of it" and had given Iago a shove, Booth staggered backward, tripped over the footlights, and nearly fell into the orchestra pit. Later he began to mumble and sank into a chair. Booth insisted it was only a dizzy spell, but a number of newspapers ran articles the next day insisting he had been drunk—an old charge revived with a vengeance. The scandal deeply wounded Booth, and, like Lotta, he began to ponder the virtues of retirement.

If Booth represented a waning school of high theatrical art, Richard Mansfield would eventually come to represent a more modern but equally lofty-minded school. That was hardly evident when he appeared for the first time as a star, in A. C. Gunter's **Prince Karl** (5-3-86, Madison Square). Gunter had conceived the piece as a serious drama, but Mansfield recognized its possibilities as light farce and developed these possibilities during a month-long run at the Boston Museum. The impoverished prince, who has been serving as a guide to some American tourists, has promised to marry a rich old woman. He changes his mind when he meets a beautiful widow, Florence Lowell (Maida Craigin), who is in line for an even grander fortune. Karl fakes a suicide and then reappears as his own "foster brother." In this guise he becomes Mrs. Lowell's courier. Although he is unaware that she had been the daughter-in-law of the widow he has overthrown, she learns of his ploy but mischievously pretends to be ignorant of it. In time romance blossoms, and in time she confesses not only her knowledge of his ruse but that the money she is to inherit was left her by Karl's long-lost uncle and actually belongs to him. Whatever critics thought of the play—and they were sharply divided about it—they agreed on the merits of Mansfield's careful performance. At a time when German-dialect comedians were flooding vaudeville and musical stages, Mansfield played the prince with a light, polished German accent. He sang a romantic number charmingly. And his comic skills were more evident than ever. In one scene he imitated a pianist doggedly playing over the incessant conversation of his audience, then performed a cello solo without a cello, and finally assumed all the roles—from basso profundo to coloratura soprano—in a burlesque of a comic opera. On the strength of his performance the comedy ran until mid-August and remained in his repertory for the rest of the century.

George Clarke assumed a secondary role in his

1885–1886

own new play, **A Strange Disappearance** (5-24-86, People's), which was advertised as a "pictorial comedy drama." Actually, it was a very mediocre melodrama, awash in tired or unimaginative turns of plot. A desperate scoundrel, Alfred Blackpool (F. McCullogh Ross), has married Mrs. Blackpool (May Roberts) for her money. The play deals with Alfred's attempts to dispose of both Mrs. Blackpool and her daughter, Lucy (Henrietta Crosman), in order to inherit the fortune. At one point he ties Lucy across the tracks of the elevated as trains approach from both directions (one critic asked aloud how he could do this unobserved), and when the attempt fails he tries pushing Lucy in the path of a horse. Mother Blackpool was treated no better, being unceremoniously shoved off a balcony. Like so many touring shows, it managed to insert several songs. Not surprisingly, *A Strange Disappearance* itself disappeared quickly.

Another dud, more ironically titled, was Conquest and Pettitt's **Bound to Succeed** (6-7-86, Niblo's). Robert Randall (James E. Wilson), believing he has blown Edward Fitzgerald (Augustus Cook) to bits, proceeds to assume his place—but not for long. After all, Fitzgerald has made one fortune overseas and has come home to inherit an even larger pile, so a few sticks of dynamite and a smug miscreant are not going to stand in his way. Following a single dismal week the play was supplanted by a real oldtime success, *Uncle Tom's Cabin,* with Mrs. Howard still in the cast.

The ghost of Frank Chanfrau's Mose may well have haunted **One of the Bravest** (6-7-86, People's). Its hero, Larry Howard (Charles McCarthy), a strapping young fireman, performs heroic rescues at a fire and at a steamboat explosion, prevents a murder, and finally wins the hand of Rose Grogan (Georgie Parker). Settings included a dock scene, a garret, and the intersection of Broadway and Mott Street. Spectacle, besides the fire and explosion, included a fireman's parade by the Zoave Veteran Association—"a pretty sight." Although the *Herald* waved away the play as a tawdry example of the "penny dreadful style of drama," it acknowledged that the entertainment was not designed to please critics but rather to delight the vociferous gallery gods. The paper's reviewer had no doubts about how well the work had achieved its aim, noting it drew a "top heavy house" and that "the burning house burned amid wild enthusiasm." That enthusiasm persisted long after the fake flames of opening night had been doused, and *One of the Bravest* held on tenaciously at minor theatres for many years.

James Schönberg's **Not One Word** (6-14-86, Grand

Opera) offered an interesting twist on the stock motifs of the false accusation and the unjust punishment, since by the time the curtain rose an innocent man had been hanged for a murder. The play centered on the growing feelings of guilt and the ultimate repentance and confession of the real culprit, who meanwhile had adopted the innocent man's daughter. Unfortunately, the play was not well written and so was soon withdrawn.

William Carleton's **Zitka** (6-21-86, People's) was a shocker destined for long popularity. Three officers of the czar's special guard get drunk, kidnap Zitka Marzoff (Charlotte Behrens), and despoil her. She escapes, but the shock of her experience kills her mother. She then goes to the czar to complain. In a dramatic second-act curtain she points out her attackers to the czar, who promptly exiles them, confiscates their property on her behalf, and forces the richest to marry her. Luckily for Zitka, the richest is also the handsomest, and in time she and her husband fall in love. She arranges for a pardon from the czar. The production featured a sumptuous interior representing the Winter Palace.

Tony Pastor frequently offered his famed vaudeville house to light full-length plays that were generally given the shortest shrift by critics. Yet many of these plays subsequently enjoyed long lives, although they almost never were sheltered at first-class houses. **Daddy Nolan** (6-21-86, Tony Pastor's) was a sequel to *The Corner Grocery,* with Dan Sully again assuming the part of the kindly if mercurial grocer. This time his experiences at a birthday party and a Christmas Eve party served as the slim plot. As usual, excuses were found to interject a number of variety turns, but at least one reviewer was grateful that this loose-jointed comedy was not "overcrowded with 'song and dance' business."

The season ended on a merry note with Fred Marsden's **Humbug** (6-30-86, Bijou). Its star was Roland Reed, always a favorite on the road if not in New York, which looked askance at his broad, brash style. Reed assumed the role of Jack Luster, a cobbler's son determined to live a life of ease without working for it. His game is to pretend he is scion to a wealthy, respected southern family. His goal is a rich, attractive widow. Only the lady he lands turns out to be as much of a fraud as he. Every now and then, when the comedy threatened to lapse, Reed and his associates burst into song, at one point offering a medley of hits from *The Mikado.* The play enjoyed a long life traipsing back and forth across the country.

239

1886–1887

The happy theatrical turnabout ignited during the preceding season continued apace in the new term. If none of the season's novelties proved to have the staying power of *The Magistrate,* no fewer than three received often excited critical attention, enjoyed prosperous runs, and subsequently held prime stages for years on end. The biggest hit of all was an English play, *Jim, the Penman,* but the other two were incontestably American—*Held by the Enemy* and *The Old Homestead.* All three plays long since have disappeared from the boards, but in their day they were hailed as exemplars of modern dramatic art offering new approaches to playwriting, and all retain an honorable niche in theatrical history. Several other American plays, whether successes or failures, also had enough merit to elicit growing hopes for a more native theatre.

Just as *The Mikado* had gotten the preceding season off to an exhilarating, augurous start, so William Gillette's **Held by the Enemy** (8-16-86, Madison Square) launched the new season in a similarly happy fashion. Moreover, *Held by the Enemy* was an American play with an American setting. Yet boosters of native theatre, however elated by the excellences of the new play, still probably recognized that they had to qualify their enthusiasm at least to the extent that the play's arrival merely exemplified a quirk in contemporary theatre practices. In recent years the startling growth of the American theatre, both in New York and on the road, had led to some odd compartmentalizations. For example, on one level surviving stock companies occupied a different pigeonhole than combination troupes. As a rule stock ensembles retained ownership of their own playhouses, while touring productions rented stages in houses often owned by men more interested in real-estate profits than in drama.

The theatrical season itself likewise was carved into convenient sections, with the main season still coinciding with the opening of the leading stock houses and continuing until they ended their programs. Flanking the main season were shorter periods known as the "preliminary season" and the "after season" or "summer season." It was in these secondary seasons—the latter running from about early May to late July and the former occupying the remaining hot-weather weeks—that a disproportionate number of American plays reached better New York houses. Producers long had accepted the fact that homespun goods were received more warmly in the hinterlands and in the less elite Manhattan theatres than they were in New York's first-class houses, but they were equally aware of the cachet afforded by a New York run. So for a decade or more, plays designed primarily for the road regularly had premiered in New York in August and September, then had gone dutifully and hopefully on tour. The summer season did not have so singular a purpose. Some bookings were given to plays and stars who had achieved unexpected success during the principal season but whose prior bookings had not allowed them to stay for an extended run. They were rewarded with return engagements. Other stages were assigned to plays and players who were not deemed front-rank and thus had to await leftover bookings. A third category included plays that had been touring and either decided belatedly on earning a New York stamp or else, usually with little reason, assumed they were now of a caliber for a major hearing. In recent years this last group had fought a losing battle with a new genre, those burgeoning musicals that were perceived as ideal entertainment for the torrid months.

In a curious fashion *Held by the Enemy* answered the demands for entry into both subsidiary seasons. Certainly Gillette was a rising figure, but nowhere near the front rank yet as either a performer or playwright. At the same time there was every reason to hope that his new play would be as well received on the road as *The Private Secretary* had been. Hopes were more than realized when morning-after reviews appeared, for Gillette had turned to the increasingly popular theme of the Civil War for his story, and his work was seen instantly as the best drama to date on the subject.

A martial overture concluded, the curtain rose to disclose the drawing room and veranda of a home in a Southern city. Drum rolls are heard, growing ever louder and nearer. The home belongs to Mrs. McCreery (Mrs. M. A. Farren), "blessed with no end of hauteur and white hair and lace caps." The drum rolls come from a band of Union troops, who are occupying the city. Mrs. McCreery has a daughter, Rachel (Kathryn Kidder). Two Union officers, Brigade Surgeon Fielding (Melbourne McDowell) and Colonel Prescott (George R. Parks), fall in love with her, although she is betrothed to a Confederate officer, Lieutenant Gordon Hayne (John E. Kellerd). Hayne sneaks through the lines to spy, but he is caught and brought to trial. The trial takes place "in the rough casement of a fort, with the big black breeches of the guns looming up on either side and a pile of real cannon balls between them." Fielding is the judge advocate and attempts to dispose of both his rivals by implicating Prescott along with Hayne. Shocked by Fielding's chicanery, Rachel blurts out that Prescott had, in fact, known Hayne was a spy. To save an innocent man, Hayne confesses and insists he was working alone. He is convicted and imprisoned. Rachel offers to marry Prescott if he will help Hayne escape, but he refuses. Nonetheless, Hayne does attempt to escape when the prison is shelled, but he is shot for his pains. At a church converted into an army hospital, Rachel convinces Hayne to pretend to die and then arranges for his removal. As the supposed body is being taken away, Fielding appears. He suspects a ruse and demands that the body be reexamined. Rachel whispers to Fielding that she will consent to his wishes if he will go along with the ploy. He examines Hayne and announces that the lieutenant is dead. In the last act Prescott, determined that Rachel shall not be forced to marry the vicious Fielding, tells him that he will confess to the chicanery, thereby implicating both himself and Fielding and dooming both men to the firing squad for abetting a spy's escape. Fielding triumphantly retorts that it will be Prescott's word against his, since Hayne is apparently safe somewhere behind Confederate lines. At that moment Hayne walks through the door. Fielding stalks out, and Hayne, conceding that Prescott "behaved like a white-man," grants that the northerner is the right husband for Rachel. Interspersed as comic relief was the romance of Rachel's sister, Susan (Louise Dillon), and Thomas Henry Bean (Charles S. Dickson), an illustrator for *Leslie's*, who has made all his war drawings in advance and hopes that circumstances will make them valid.

For reasons now lost the names of some principals were changed shortly after the opening, with Prescott becoming Brant and Rachel, Eunice. Moreover, the spelling of "Bean" in many early programs is odd, for the character makes a point several times in the play that his name is Beene and has nothing to do with Boston.

Although billed as a "five act war drama" and subsequently hailed as the first great play about the Civil War, *Held by the Enemy* was really a romance set against a war background. The issues crucial to the war—slavery and secession—were dealt with only in passing. And, of course, the romance was essentially that of lovers on opposing sides, a motif basic to most 19th-century plays set during the struggle.

Even at the very first a few critics recognized the absurdity of the play's most dramatic and memora-

ble scene, the closing of the fourth act, when the characters are determined to prove or disprove that Hayne is dead. In actual life such a bluff would have been improbable if not downright impossible. But this quibble detracted not a jot from the theatrical efficacy of Gillette's play (any more than did one southern production that allowed Hayne to win the girl). Its initial run was less than three months, but the play made a number of return stands (with Gillette occasionally playing Beene) and toured profitably for years and years.

Frederick Warde, a fine and dedicated player whose "years of itinerancy" had been propelled by the warmer welcome he always received on the road, came in for one of his occasional visits on the same night *Held by the Enemy* opened. Although he was an excellent actor, he was dedicated to an obsolescent repertory—the same repertory that had served Forrest, McCullough, and Booth for so long—and he was simply not in their class. He began his stand at the Windsor with *Virginius* and moved on to *Ingomar, Damon and Pythias, Richard III* (Cibber's version), and *The Lady of Lyons*. Even critics who held reservations about his talent acknowledged that he clearly won the approval of large audiences at the house. Warde's peregrinations were to bring him back throughout the season to several neighborhood theatres, where plays such as *Julius Caesar* were added to his programs. A January visit brought forth a "new" play.

Two weeks later, on the 30th, a greater, far more venturesome, and far more admired actor began the annual procession of luminaries at the Star. But for this engagement Lawrence Barrett was content to range broadly through his repertory and not present any novelty. His list consisted of *Yorick's Love, Richelieu, Hamlet, Julius Caesar, Francesca da Rimini, The Merchant of Venice, David Garrick, The Man o' Airlie, Richard III,* and *The King's Pleasure.* Daring as he often was, Barrett could also be an unthinking, archtraditionalist. Thus his *Merchant of Venice* was not the complete Shakespearean comedy but the truncated version, ending with the trial scene and deleting numerous other bits in earlier acts, that was standard on 19th-century stages. Its relative brevity, coupled with contemporary playgoers' willingness to remain snug in their seats for three or more hours, led to this and other plays on the list occasionally being offered as double bills. However, Barrett tried not to disappoint his more progressive followers, so when he returned late in the season for a second engagement he did bring a new work with him.

The Minute Men of 1774–1775 (9-6-86, People's)

had initially been done the previous season at Philadelphia's venerable Chestnut Street Theatre and represented James A. Herne's first major solo effort at playwriting. Its principal figures are the patriotic Yankee, Reuben Foxglove (Herne), and his self-assured, flirtatious daughter, Dorothy (Mrs. Herne). Dorothy is courted by an English officer but also is fond of a handsome, noble Indian, Roanoke. A locket Dorothy carries proves her to be the long-lost daughter of her British suitor's commanding officer. Roanoke in turn is shown to be the long-lost brother of Dorothy's friend, Rachel Winslow. He had been sold to the Indians by Dyke Hampton, who then contrived to bankrupt Rachel's father, an old soldier, and demanded Rachel's hand in return for helping Captain Winslow stave off eviction. Rachel is betrothed to the captain of the Minute Men, Ned Farnsworth, who had fled Hampton's abusive cruelty when he was a young boy. Another interesting character was the tough, good-hearted, would-be camp follower, Ann Campbell.

Herne was fair to both sides, portraying the Englishman as a thoroughgoing gentleman. In truth, however, the plot took a back seat to the sensational dramatic events and to patriotic spectacle. The former included an Indian attack on a fort, which eventually is set on fire and explodes for a ripsnorting curtain. The latter included glimpses of the battles of Concord and Lexington, and of Bunker Hill (a tableau based on Trumbull's famous painting). In the final scene no less than General Washington rode in astride a white horse.

Herne's dialogue for his regular characters was excellent and believable, especially that given to his finely delineated Dorothy. But the speech of his more colorful figures was sometimes strange. Reuben's was homey, if not corny: "Roanoke—there's a good deal o' man in yeou—as Jonah said to the whale's belly." And Roanoke could exclaim, "Roanoke is never lighter of heart, fleeter of limb, stronger of arm or surer of aim, than when serving a friend." *The Minute Men* found only small favor. Herne soon learned to drop unnecessary flag-waving and to put homespun humor to better use.

Among rising young actresses probably only Minnie Maddern was looked upon with higher hopes than Georgia Cayvan, yet following *May Blossom* Miss Cayvan's luck had soured, and her new vehicle, David and Milton Higgins's **Our Rich Cousin** (9-6-86, 14th St.), did nothing to help matters. Indicatively, several reviewers spent more time commenting on the refurbishing of the old playhouse than on the new play, despite some flamboyant preopening ballyhoo for the production. As her name suggests, Cynthia Merrygold is wealthy. But she is also spoiled, volatile, and covetous. She attempts to deprive her epileptic cousin, Zed Menard, of money due him, and this forces him to steal a package he believes contains the money, so that he can pay for an operation for his ailing mother, Martha (Mrs. Sol Smith). Milton Higgins, besides collaborating on the work, undertook the part of Zed—a character some reviewers felt would have been better left unwritten. A fortnight's stand was followed by a brief, profitless tour.

If Miss Cayvan could reasonably expect to become a major star on the strength of her remarkable talent, the better-looking Lillian Olcott believed her family fortune and the support of her rich society friends could achieve the same end more quickly. She had purchased the American rights to Sardou's *Théodora*, which had been a huge Paris success with Bernhardt in the title role. No expense was spared to recreate the lavish Paris scenery and costumes, and more money was poured out in another preopening publicity blitz. So elaborate was the production that one of New York's larger stages was required, and when **Theodora** (9-13-86, Niblo's) finally opened, the spectacle most certainly did not disappoint.

The play and the star did. Dressed in richly brocaded, heavily bejeweled gowns and framed in gaudy, cluttered settings that brought to life the streets and palaces of 6th-century Byzantium, Miss Olcott portrayed the faithless wife of the emperor Justinian (Hudson Liston). Though she is not at first aware of it, her paramour, Andreas (J. H. Gilmour), is a leader in the movement to overthrow Justinian. When his plot fails he is captured and slain. Her own perfidy exposed, Theodora, with a noose about her neck, is led away to be garroted. As if the melodrama of the story and the exotic appeal of the locale were not enough, Sardou filled the evening with additional theatrical spices—gypsy fortune tellers, magic potions, and spear carriers representing Goths, satraps, and eunuchs. Such romantic spectacle kept the play at Niblo's until late October, after which Miss Olcott toured with it for two seasons, bringing it back to New York several times. For a while the publicity attending Bernhardt's American appearances in the play undoubtedly helped this translated version. But Miss Olcott apparently understood her own marked limitations and the small likelihood of finding many more such colorful vehicles, so when her tour ended she bid the theatre adieu.

Periodically Tony Pastor turned over his vaudeville theatre to full-length dramas that apparently were not deemed elevated enough for the regular legitimate stages. Precisely why these works were thus exiled can no longer be learned. They appear to have been different in degree, not kind, from many of the plays presented at standard dramatic houses, so probably the perceived quality of the writing and the intellectual demands made by the play had much to do with it. On the surface **Eli Wheatfield** (9-13-86, Tony Pastor's) would seem little different from *Joshua Whitcomb, A Messenger from Jarvis Section*, or the soon to be seen *The Old Homestead*. Eli (Aaron H. Woodhull) is an eighty-year-old Vermont farmer whose levelheadedness helps save an innocent cashier from being convicted of murdering a bank president. Eli sees that the real culprit, a counterfeiter, is convicted instead.

Whether or not Henry C. de Mille and Charles Barnard's **The Main Line; or, Rawson's Y** (9-18-86, Lyceum) was perceived as part of the "preliminary season" is uncertain, but it nonetheless gave a small leg up to native playwriting. Advertised as "An Idyl of the Railroad," it made the most effective use of telegraphy and trains since *Across the Continent*. At the same time, it served as a harbinger of numerous later plays contrasting the virtues of the open, freethinking West with the narrow-minded, selfish, and overcivilized East, though this contrast was understated in the new play.

Possy (Etta Hawkins) is the energetic and determined daughter of Sam Burroughs (de Mille), who is stationmaster at Rawson's Y. Possy helps out by serving as the telegraph operator. She is also right pretty, so it is not surprising that several men find her attractive. The one she likes best is Lawrence Hatton (John Mason), a sophisticated, high-minded New Yorker who has come west to get away from his family and to paint. Hatton finds a perfect model in Possy. But this arrangement angers Jim Blakely (Ralph Delmore), a brakeman who is resolved to marry Possy and does not hesitate to blackmail her father to accomplish this. Blakely threatens to reveal that he once saw Sam push a man over a dam. Some of Hatton's friends and relatives come to Rawson's Y to beg him to return east. They point out that his mother is dying and her dying wish is that Hatton marry Dora Van Tyne (Lillian Richardson), an orphan his mother had raised. A rivalry immediately springs up between Dora and Possy, in which Possy believes that she has bested Dora by winning enough money at a poker game to provide Hatton with a proper studio. She is stunned when Hatton decides to return home. Hatton hops the last car of a freight train that will take him to the nearest junction, but the car breaks loose and heads down the same track on which an express is speeding. Alone in the station Possy frantically pulls

switches, hoping to prevent a crash, but she is too late. The last act takes place more than two years later, when Rawson's Y has grown into Grand Junction. It turns out that Hatton and Blakely had changed places on the train and that it was the villainous Blakely who had been killed in the crash. It also has been learned Blakely knew that the man Sam pushed over the dam had not died. Furthermore, Dora has proved unfaithful to Hatton. She has gone off with one of his friends and begun a career as an actress. So when Hatton reappears, he and Possy can consider marrying.

Critics divided sharply over the play's worth. While the *Times* deemed it "something far above the average of new native plays in the matter of literary merit, reasonableness, humor, and dramatic force," the *Spirit of the Times* felt it possessed "no value as drama." Among the specific points disturbing reviewers were Sam's references to seeing ghostly figures and ghostly red warning signals, presaging a tragic close that the playwrights eventually shunned, and the comic character of Zerubbabel Puddychamp (F. F. Mackay), a passenger agent turned evangelist, whose behavior prompted one critic to warn the playwrights to "let the Bible alone on the stage."

By contrast, director David Belasco's wily use of the telegraph's clicks and singing wires as a sustained background won widespread commendation. So did the sensation scene of the train crash. The crash occurred offstage, but the sound effects and, perhaps more urgently, the lighting effects achieved with still new electric lights were greeted, according to the *Tribune*, "with tremendous applause." The *Telegram* later stated that the effect "had become the talk of the town." How long it remained the talk is moot, for *The Main Line* remained at the Lyceum for only a month, although it played several outlying combination houses as part of its long tour. The work stayed on the road, often with several companies going at once, for four or five seasons. In 1891, de Mille rewrote it drastically, changing the characters' names and changing the title to *The Danger Signal* as well as inserting additional sensation scenes, including a huge avalanche. In this altered guise the play continued to tour for several more seasons.

Henrietta Chanfrau, a fine actress long content to play in her husband's shadow, was forced by his death to go it alone. Not yet fifty and still attractive, with a special flair for showing off clothes, she had every reason to hope for success. She chose as her vehicle **The Scapegoat** (9-20-86, 14th St.), a play by Sir Charles Young, whose eagerly awaited *Jim, the Penman* had expectant New Yorkers abuzz. But great expectations for one fine play could not prop up a weaker one. Linda Colmore (Mrs. Chanfrau), an American actress, is married to Victor Broughton (Myron Leffingwell), an Englishman who is wrongly convicted and imprisoned. He escapes, but Linda is led to believe he has perished in the attempt. One night on leaving the theatre, her carriage strikes a man. It proves to be Victor. She sets about clearing his name and points the real finger of guilt at Victor's brother, Lord Parkhurst (Horace Vinton). Critics found kind words for Mrs. Chanfrau, although they could find few for the play. It survived a fortnight. After it closed, Mrs. Chanfrau—who had played Ophelia to Booth's Hamlet in his historical 1864 production—was seen no more on New York stages.

Georgia Cayvan, equally luckless, moved from disappointment to disappointment. Her second assignment in this still early season was A. C. Gunter's **A Wall Street Bandit** (9-25-86, Standard). Critics noted its marked similarity to Boucicault's *The Streets of New York*. Sometime before the Civil War, Weston Minton (Charles Wheatleigh), a banker, steals a client's life insurance money, thus reducing the dead man's family to poverty. To assuage his guilt he later adopts the dead man's daughter, Ethel (Miss Cayvan). Ethel in turn rescues a man who is being arrested as a safecracker, a crime she knows he did not commit. She soon discovers the man she has saved is her own long-lost brother, Johnny (Atkins Lawrence). The play was by no means a failure, unlike Miss Cayvan's earlier *Our Rich Cousin*, but it had no more than a mediocre three-week run, touring thereafter with only modest results for the rest of the season.

A few nights before Gunter's premiere, massive Josephine Cameron came in for a week's stand at the Third Avenue. She was reputedly popular in theatrical backwaters. One paper referred to her as "a 'star' of the Western wilds," so she should have known how New York's chauvinistic reviewers would treat her. Actually, in her case their derision may have been justified. She began by playing a grotesquely robust Camille, then switched to Parthenia in *Ingomar* and Isabel in *East Lynne*. With no requests for her to extend her stay or to return, she hastily retreated to her one-night stands.

By contrast, the critics seemed almost too eager to applaud the American-born, European-trained Genevieve Ward when she began a short visit. Her opening vehicle was **The Queen's Favorite** (9-27-86, Star), Sydney Grundy's adaptation of Scribe's *Un Verre d'eau*. The story traced the rise and fall of Sarah Churchill as the darling of Queen Anne. For all their importance—or self-importance—New York critics could not sway playgoers. Certainly Josephine Cameron's many admirers—if they ever even heard the names of the New York critics—were impervious to their pontifications. Conversely, the reviewers' laudatory paeans could not induce many New Yorkers to visit the Star. Miss Ward played the Grundy piece for a week and then reverted to her most popular play, *Forget-Me-Not*. She toured for the rest of the season, apparently always to critical praise and half-empty houses. In her autobiography she treats the tour cursorily and in a manner suggesting it was just a sight-seeing sojourn to her.

A would-be star actress, Bertha Welby, who toured combination houses in a repertory of such standards as *Oliver Twist*, earned herself some rare attention when she brought out **The Martyr Mother** (9-30-86, Third Ave.), Ettie Henderson's rendition of d'Ennery and Tarbé's *Le Martyre*. Its preposterous story describes the disastrous consequences of a wife's pretending her illegitimate brother is her lover in order to save her mother's reputation. The husband kills the brother at the same time he abandons the supposedly faithless wife, she loses her child, and all manner of terrible things happen before an equally preposterous happy ending. The play was immediately withdrawn, as much because of a lawsuit by Palmer as because of the sharp critical turndown. Next year Palmer presented a bigger if not better version. Miss Welby soon relinquished her tenuous hold on stardom and spent much of her later career in minor supporting roles.

Several great ladies marched in the forefront of October's parade of entries. Since Lillie Langtry was, for the moment, the most glamorous and most newsworthy, she received the lioness's share of attention, after her return at the Fifth Avenue on the 4th. During her month-long stand she offered only two plays, both revivals: *A Wife's Peril* and *The Lady of Lyons*. Critics found her beauty still dazzling and her art more knowing than ever. The *Times*, grumbling that "the sources of her art do not lie very deep in her nature," continued, "She has nevertheless acquired the ability to counterfeit by the use of approved symbols all the emotions, and varying shades of emotion." Clearly, obvious and formalized technique was not disdained. So heavy was the crush of business that the star returned for two additional visits during the season.

The same night saw Clara Morris reappear at the Union Square, her first engagement at a major New York house in some years. She, too, came in with a pair of revivals, two of her old successes: *Miss*

Multon and *Article 47*. By now critical sentiment about her had hardened—and so had her performances. Her former flaws, such as her annoying accent and her unevenness, and her former virtues, such as her unquestioned emotive flair and her deftness at moving her audience, all remained, but her youth and the promise it held for even greater things to come long had gone. As temperamental and hypochondriac as ever, she refused to perform twice a day, leaving her company to mount *Engaged* on Saturday evenings. She stayed only a week, then moved to neighboring combination houses with these and other plays.

Mrs. D. P. Bowers, who was an important actress when Clara Morris was still a toddler, and who continued to uphold an older, more stately and artificial tradition of grand acting, competed for patronage at the 14th Street. For her four-week stand she selected a large, diverse repertory: *Mary Stuart* (Edmund Falconer's version of Schiller), *Elizabeth* (translated from Giacometti), *Lucretia Borgia, The Jealous Wife, Macbeth, Camille,* and *Lady Audley's Secret* (an adaptation by John Brougham of Mary Elizabeth Braddon's novel about a bigamous wife who thinks she has murdered her first husband, which the star had first presented to New York twenty-three years earlier).

Mary Stuart was also the attraction on the 4th at the Windsor, where Janauschek began a week's stand that included *Bleak House, Mother and Son, Marie Antoinette, Henry VIII,* and *Macbeth*.

Daly graciously waited until the ladies had enjoyed their evening before opening his new season with **After Business Hours** (10-5-86, Daly's), his brother's Americanization of Oskar Blumenthal's *Sammt und Seide*. The producer's courtesy assured him a house filled with the cream of New York first-nighters, who gave his players warm, prolonged greetings and seemed almost as receptive to the new comedy. Its slight story told of a young couple, Richard and Doris Brandagee (John Drew and Ada Rehan). Each gambles without the other's knowledge on the stock market, and a wily but good-natured broker, Tommy Chipper (James Lewis), plays one off against the other in order to forestall their going broke. According to Winter in the *Tribune*, "The new play proved congenial alike with the mood of the actors, the temper of the house, and the spirit of the occasion." Reading between the lines of this and similar notices, potential playgoers probably surmised the new comedy lacked the crescendoing mirth and vitality of Daly's better hits. Nonetheless, the play had a satisfactory six-week run. Lewis's penchant for making up to look like

famous, or infamous, New Yorkers, in this instance someone named John Bloodgood, probably attracted a few additional playgoers out for a topical laugh.

Wilson Barrett, a short but heavily built and rather handsome actor who had won fame in the West End in such plays as *The Lights o' London* and *The Silver King*, made an auspicious New York debut in a sumptuously mounted, sometimes archly poetic sensation-melodrama, W. G. Wills and Henry Herman's **Claudian** (10-11-86, Star). He played a profligate Byzantine noble who kills a hermit who is protecting a girl the noble lusts after. He immediately falls victim to the dying hermit's curse, which leaves him to roam the world unloved eternally unless an unpremeditated act of contrition releases him. He moves from place to place, much like the Wandering Jew, until the hermit appears to him in the aftermath of a terrible earthquake (depicted onstage) and confronts him with the choice of saving a blind girl or saving himself. He makes the right choice, so at last is allowed to die. Critics admired Barrett's rich, deep voice and clear, precise enunciation, but some questioned how well he could convey that aura of mystery or the supernatural implicit in the story. His delivery was often monotonous and his poses too studiously statuesque. There were also complaints that too many supposedly behind-the-scenes mechanisms—wires, ropes, stagehands—were visible during the earthquake. But these critical reservations apparently could not deter the public. Apart from a special matinee of one-acters, the Englishman gave over his entire three-week stand to *Claudian*.

One critic had likened Barrett to the late E. L. Davenport, a comparison possibly provoked subconsciously by the critic's knowledge that he would be sitting in judgment on Fanny Davenport the following night. Her vehicle was *Much Ado About Nothing*, which she was prepared to offer at the Union Square for a fortnight beginning on the 12th. Everything about the evening—her Beatrice, her lovely costumes, J. H. Barnes's Benedick, the supporting players, the scenery—left the critic satisfied but in no way excited. Still, for all her lack of the extra something that makes for greatness, the beautiful actress had enough of a following to ensure a respectable box office before she again took to the road.

Ominously, Philip Goatcher's scenery all but stole the show at the opening of what was to prove Wallack's last season. The play, torn to shreds by most critics, was Henry Hamilton's **Harvest** (10-13-86, Wallack's). For a crucial turning point in his work, the young playwright resorted to a motif that had been worked to death some years back—the differences in English and Scottish marriage laws. The highborn but impoverished Noel Musgrave (Kyrle Bellew), tiring of his wife, Brenda (Annie Robe), uses the technicality to callously desert her and his little son (played in the prologue as a trouser role by May Germon). Years pass. Musgrave has cynically married a very rich woman, who has helped him get a title and who then has died, leaving him a widower with a teenage stepdaughter, Lettice (Carrie Coote). Before long, his grown son (now played by Booth's nephew, Creston Clarke) and his stepdaughter fall in love. Brenda, horrified, refuses her consent. Musgrave belatedly offers to marry Brenda in a binding ceremony, but she scornfully refuses. It takes four acts of "aphorisms and epigrams, soliloquies and dialogues" before Brenda is persuaded to reconsider and two marriages can take place. Goatcher's outdoor settings, especially the rustic picture of Act I and the view of the ruins of an old castle in Act III, earned him as many curtain calls as the playwright or the actors got. But his "pretty" pictures were not enough to keep *Harvest* going beyond the first few days of November.

Two fictional ladies vied for attention the following Monday. One was called **Gretchen** (10-18-86, Lyceum); the other, **A Daughter of Ireland** (10-18-86, Standard). Gretchen was portrayed by May Fortescue, an attractive young Englishwoman who had garnered front-page columns some months before by her breach-of-promise suit against an English lord. Although she was able to rely on W. S. Gilbert's sardonic version of the Faust legend (admittedly not one of his best efforts), she could do little to bring it alive. After three weeks she switched to *Frou-Frou,* and three weeks later she offered a double bill of *King René's Daughter* and *Sweethearts.* She seems to have done reasonably good business, albeit largely on the strength of her notoriety and her often outlandish interviews with newspaper reporters, who found her delicious copy. But she must have realized wisely how fleeting such fame was, for after her post-Broadway road tour she never again came in front of American footlights.

At the Standard the translation of Henri de Rochfort's *L'Irlandaise* told of the ungrateful little Irish ward of the governor general of Canada. She becomes a Fenian spy, steals away the man betrothed to her guardian's daughter, and even tries to kill her guardian. The play was filled with brutal stabbings, wrestling matches between women, and other such roughhouse bits that should have been

expected to appeal to the gallery gods, particularly the working-class Irish who constituted such a large and faithful portion of these patrons. But something patently went awry, for *A Daughter of Ireland* seems to have run just a single week and not to have toured anywhere else.

The month-long procession of ladies ended with a very real and very great one—Modjeska. She began an extended visit at the Union Square on the 25th with *As You Like It.* Remembering her performance through the mist of nearly sixty years, Odell recalled, "What her Rosalind may have lacked in raillery and youthful buoyancy it made up in gentle humor, grace, poetry or even at times pensive charm. . . . Modjeska easily transcended all phases of technical efficiency, of which, indeed, she was past mistress, and arrived into a realm of poetic and spiritual beauty that few have reached. And this in spite of her foreign accent which one must admit detracted from utter enjoyment of her Shakespearian interpretations."

Seeming almost an afterthought was Boucicault's brief return at the Standard on the 30th in *The Jilt.*

November belonged to the men much as October had to the ladies. Its very first night brought in two of the most renowned. The more venerable of the two was unquestionably Edwin Booth. But once again his eloquent artistry was confined to his tried and true warhorses and shabbily framed with hand-me-down scenery and mediocre supporting players. He opened with *Hamlet,* then proceeded to *The Fool's Revenge, Othello, Richelieu,* and a double bill of *The Merchant of Venice* and *Katherine and Petruchio.* Business was excellent, but the projected four-week stand was interrupted for a week when Booth was put to bed with stomach troubles, which he ascribed to an actress's breaking a mirror in the theatre.

The other man was a reprobate named James Ralston, better known as **Jim, the Penman** (11-1-86, Madison Square). In Sir Charles Young's telling of his tale, Ralston (Frederic Robinson) employs his penmanship to perpetrate a number of mean forgeries. In fact, he long ago won his wife, Nina (Agnes Booth), by forging letters that broke up the engagement between her and Louis Percival (H. M. Pitt). Afterwards he used his pen to bankrupt Percival. Percival has now determined to track down the forger, and he enlists the help of Captain Redwood (E. M. Holland), a sly, seemingly blasé, but effective detective. Without knowing all this, Ralston has grown weary of his way of life and decided to reform. His cronies, led by heartless Baron Hartfeld (W. J. LeMoyne), press

246

him into one final escapade—which would bankrupt his own daughter's fiancé. At the same time, Redwood slowly but unyieldingly closes in. Just as he is about to be exposed, Ralston suffers a fatal heart attack.

The *Times*'s critic spoke for many of his colleagues when he hailed the new work as "a thoroughly good acting play." And good acting is what it got. Ironically, the weakest performance seems to have been that of the stiff, somewhat paunchy Robinson, although it was only his stiffness and not his paunch that well-padded contemporaries objected to. By common consent the stars of the evening were Agnes Booth and E. M. Holland. Miss Booth's greatest moment came when a casual comparison of some handwriting leads Nina to pull out the last letters Percival supposedly wrote her. As she silently reexamines them she gradually awakens to the horrible truth of their origin, and her love for Ralston turns to hatred. Coincidentally, her long-dormant affection for Percival, of which she herself was not fully aware, but which was evident to the audience from the beginning, is rekindled and allows for the possibility that the old lovers may finally wed. Holland's cool Redwood, soaking up incriminating bits of conversation all the while he pretends to nap, set a pattern for succeeding generations of stage sleuths. In fact, although *The Ticket-of-Leave Man* is usually credited with introducing the figure of the detective to the footlights, *Jim, the Penman* and its tremendous success may have provided the real spark for making the detective and the detective-play so popular. The Broadway company enthralled playgoers for a full six months—the longest run of any nonmusical offering during the season—and road companies soon abounded. The play held the boards regularly for a decade or so and was still revived occasionally, especially in stock, until World War I.

A third opening was W. J. Shaw's **Caught in a Corner** (11-1-86, 14th St.), a comedy designed to allow M. B. Curtis some relief from his incessant touring as Sam'l of Posen. His relief came in the form of new lines, for his Isaac Greenwald was simply a variation on the lovable Jew that served as his specialty. One paper described him as "not young as Sam'l, with a fringe of red hair around a bald head, a watch chain like a log trace, very big diamonds and a big collar." In a story with echoes of Daly's *After Business Hours,* Isaac is involved with a young lady who attempts to corner the wheat market. She does not succeed, but Isaac is there with his consoling philosophy to cushion her fall. The comedy was insubstantial but likable, and business

was no doubt augmented by the growing cadre of Americanized Jews who enjoyed seeing themselves depicted onstage—and depicted favorably at that. The play ran two months, then toured.

Robert Buchanan's theatricalization of *Tom Jones* was known as **Sophia** (11-4-86, Wallack's) and had been a huge hit at London's Vaudeville Theatre. At Wallack's, with Annie Robe in the title role and Kyrle Bellew as Tom, it struggled vainly for a month, probably supplying another nail for the company's coffin.

The Chouans (11-10-86, Union Square), Paul Potter's dramatization of Balzac's *Les Chouans,* provided Modjeska with a respite from Shakespearean heroines. Marie de Verneuil (Modjeska), daughter of a beheaded duke, is enlisted to entrap the Marquis de Montauran (Maurice Barrymore), a royalist insurgent. Instead she falls in love with him and helps him to escape. Later she is tricked into believing he has betrayed her, but she eventually understands that she too readily condemned him, and she sacrifices her own life to spare him. Critics sang their customary paeans to both Modjeska and Barrymore (whose billing was now virtually as prominent as his co-star's), but most thought little of the play, which continued for several weeks to dwindling attendance.

While Wallack's foundered, Daly moved from one success to another. His latest was **Love in Harness** (11-16-86, Daly's), taken from Albin Valabrègue's *Bonheur conjugal.* Just as the Joblotses (Charles Fisher and Mrs. Gilbert) are about to marry off their third-youngest daughter, Jenny (Lillian Hadley), their two married daughters, Rhoda Naggitt (Virginia Dreher) and Una Urquhart (Ada Rehan), appear. Una, all her belongings in hand, has left her husband, Frederick (John Drew), because he so objects to having to accompany her to balls four or five nights a week and to staying up until dawn that he has thrown her best ball gown out the window. Rhoda is brought back by her husband, Julius (James Lewis), who is furious at being served cold veal every morning for breakfast. Jenny announces that if this is what marriage comes to, she wants none of it. Mr. Joblots recognizes the problem at once—his wife has spoiled the girls and turned them into "social queens instead of women, wives and mothers." This astounds Mrs. Joblots, since from the day she was first courted, she has governed her behavior by the rules set down in *The Matrimonial Manual, or Hints to Hymen,* the same book she has presented to each of her daughters. Frederick, given to paroxysms of rage and jealousy, is not of much assistance, but the wilier Julius, by means of a few thoughtfully forged invitations, finally finds a way to reconcile the couples and to allow the third wedding to proceed.

Much of the laughter was provoked by humor no different from that on modern television situation-comedies. In one scene Jenny unintentionally frustrates every advance of her fiancé, the young doctor Charley Hoffman (Otis Skinner), by constantly having to thumb through her manual to find the proper response. Later a totally flustered Charley, having wiped his brow with his handkerchief and grabbed his hat, plunks the handkerchief on his head and tries to stuff the hat in his pocket. One obsolescent tradition that appears to have delighted both Daly and his audiences was his closing each play with a poetic tag. Thus Una ends the play by reading from the notorious manual:

For the men—
To go in "double harness" is your pet
Phrase for wedlock. Pray, don't forget
That means side by side, or better yet,
A tandem! One may lead, but both must strive,
And neither, mark me! *neither* one must drive.

Happily received all around, *Love in Harness* compiled a run of seventy-three performances and might have gone on to more had not Daly had his major offering of the season ready in mid-January.

November concluded with the arrival of Joseph Jefferson at the Star on the 29th. Once again, the greatest of 19th-century American comedians, like its greatest tragedian, whom he had followed, relied on a long-locked-in repertory. In Jefferson's case this meant several weeks of *Rip Van Winkle*, followed by a week of *The Cricket on the Hearth* coupled with *Lend Me Five Shillings*. Of course, Jefferson's polished, irresistible playing allowed most theatregoers to overlook the sameness in his bills.

Lillie Langtry returned to New York to star in Charles Coghlan's **Enemies** (12-6-86, Niblo's). The playwright was also the English beauty's co-star, and together they performed the parts of young lovers who triumph over the opposition of their feuding parents. The play had not pleased London and now failed to please New York. It was withdrawn after a fortnight, and *The Lady of Lyons* was rushed in to fill the remainder of the contracted stay.

The evening of Langtry's return also saw Modjeska present *Twelfth Night* at the Union Square. Her Viola was among her greatest achievements and was made to seem even richer when set against the handsome, manly Barrymore's Orsino.

The popular Rosina Vokes's bills generally consisted of short comedies and pasted-together little musicals, but occasionally she ventured a traditional, full-length farce. Such was the case with Pinero's **The Schoolmistress** (12-7-86, Standard), which the playwright had written for Mrs. John Wood and which had scored a long-run success in London with Mrs. Wood in the title role. The plot focused on a prim, proper, but ambitious schoolmistress who secretly marries a playboy aristocrat and takes herself to London to earn enough money to pay off his debts. While she is away, singing in comic opera under an assumed name, her hedonistic spouse piles up new debts by throwing a lavish party with several of his wife's pupils in attendance. Inevitably, the schoolmistress and several other people barge in unexpectedly, after which misunderstanding follows hard on misunderstanding.

Perhaps surprisingly, Miss Vokes did not assume the title role. Instead she played the greatly enlarged role of Peggy Hesslerigge, the schoolmistress's apprentice, throwing in several of her musical turns for good measure. Miss Dyott, the schoolmistress, was played by stately Helena Dacre, whose dignity was in shambles by evening's end, while the Hon. Vere Queckett, the partying husband, was performed with a superb blend of lordliness and idiocy by Weedon Grossmith, a member of a famous English acting family. Most critics seem to have liked the play better than their readers did, and the farce, which stayed one month in its initial appearance, never became as popular in America as it remained for many years in England.

That same evening saw a revival of *One of Our Girls* at the Lyceum, and the following night, the 8th, brought back *Moths* at Wallack's. The first revival featured many of the original players; the second virtually none. Wallack's company was as much in flux as in decline.

A noted New York newspaperman, John W. Keller, was the author of **Tangled Lives** (12-13-86, Fifth Ave.), which served as Robert Mantell's first starring vehicle.

. . .

Robert B[ruce] Mantell (1854–1928) was born in Scotland and began acting in England under the name Robert Hudson. He resumed his real name when he first came to America to play in support of Helena Modjeska in 1878. Following a brief return home, he established himself permanently in America. For a time he was Fanny Davenport's leading man, most notably as Loris Ipanoff in *Fedora* (1883). His blond good looks made him a matinee idol, although even from the start his detractors complained he subscribed to an outmoded, bombastic school of acting.

. . .

Keller's central figures are Raymond Garth (Mantell) and Helen (Eleanor Carey), the woman who has been Raymond's common-law wife and whom he has been beseeching to marry him. She has persistently refused but has never summoned up enough nerve to tell him her real reason for refusing—the fact that she has not been divorced from her first husband. In time Raymond falls in love with another young woman, Edith Ainsley (Effie Shannon). He decides to ask Helen one last time to marry him, and if she will not he will leave her and marry Edith. Again Helen refuses. But when he goes to seek out Edith, she has disappeared. A year or so later he finds her again, and since in the interval he has discovered Helen's secret, nothing stands between him and Edith, and the altar.

Critics recognized that the play was written "to suit Mr. Mantell's kind of acting" and thus described it with such expressions as "flamboyant" and "full of feverish emotions," qualities apparently reflected in Mantell's performance. Indeed, many of the reviewers were far kinder to a young actress making her New York debut. The *Times* praised Effie Shannon as "sweet," the *Herald* as "sweetly pretty." However readers might interpret criticism of the play and its star, *Tangled Lives* and Mantell pleased audiences for seven profitable weeks and on tour.

Modjeska did herself and her admirers a disservice when she closed her visit with a second new play, **Daniela** (12-13-86, Union Square), William von Sachs and E. Hamilton Bell's translation of Felix Philippi's German original. She portrayed a woman married to a man who is obsessed with unrealistically roseate memories of his first wife. It takes that dead wife's former lover to bring the husband to his senses and make him appreciate how loving and loyal his second wife is. Barrymore was the neurotic husband and Charles Vandenhoff the lover. Several critics thought the men's roles were more interestingly written and allowed Barrymore and Vandenhoff to appear to more advantage than Modjeska. (Such comments probably hastened the play's removal from Modjeska's repertory.) But all in all, the reviewers felt the whole effort was a waste of time. Even the scenery seemed tacky to them, the *Times* snidely concluding its notice, "The picture made to serve as that of the dead wife should be presented to some patent medicine firm to be labeled 'Before taking.' "

At the Lyceum, Helen Dauvray continued her season with a revival on the 20th of *A Scrap of Paper*. She won plaudits for the excellence of the mounting and for surrounding herself with a first-rate supporting cast. In fact, in many reviews her leading man, E. H. Sothern, walked away with the most appreciative comments. But to the more perspicacious observers it was becoming evident that for all her admirable purposefulness and intelligence, she, like Fanny Davenport, lacked that extra spark that meant the difference between good and great. She was, essentially, a well-meaning, accomplished technician, without Davenport's luck or flair.

Robert Downing may have been a sad anomaly. Extremely handsome and rugged, if given to corpulence, he seems to have been born a generation or two after his time. On the 20th he came into no less a theatre than the prestigious Star in a play that Forrest had made famous and the late McCullough had tried valiantly to keep alive—Bird's *The Gladiator*. Even critics who felt the drama was hopelessly dated acknowledged that Downing's performance had roused a blasé audience. Yet Downing was to struggle on for many seasons, ignoring the passing years and the changes in taste they brought with them.

When Modjeska closed her stand at the Union Square, its stage was taken over by Margaret Mather. She provided a vivid contrast. She had none of the poetry, the grace, or the delicacy that Modjeska brought to all her parts. For these she substituted determination and a theatrical dynamism. With Frederick Paulding and Milnes Levick in support, she offered the same three plays she had in the previous season: *Romeo and Juliet* (with her much publicized tumble down the stairs), *The Honeymoon*, and *Leah, the Foresaken*. But her novelty had worn off, and the demand for seats was hardly as pressing as it had been earlier. A month sufficed to attract her loyalists.

The decline of Wallack's was pathetically evident in its revival on the 27th of the house's traditional standby, *The School for Scandal*. Of course, John Gilbert presented his incomparable Sir Peter, the role with which he had made his debut with the company in 1862. One critic wrote, "He is thoroughly old-fashioned yet as fresh and buoyant as could be desired. He makes you forget that the play is old. . . . You think only of Sir Peter, his pardonable uxoriousness, his wounded pride, his genial egotism, and his harmless irascibility." Reviewers made it clear that only Harry Edwards's Sir Oliver and, possibly, Mme Ponisi's Mrs. Candour approached Gilbert's finish. Bellew's "effeminate"

Act Two : 1879–1892

Charles and Annie Robe's "watery" Lady Teazle were especially disappointing. Wallack kept the comedy before the footlights for a month, while he rehearsed a new play.

Two apple-pie-American comedians helped ring in the new year with laughter. Ever since September, John T. Raymond had been "dogging it" (the contemporary term for trying out a play) in a new vehicle. Apparently still not convinced it was ready for the big time, he decided to test New York's reaction gingerly by offering it for a week at a Harlem theatre. In David D. Lloyd's **The Woman Hater** (1-3-87, Theatre Comique), Raymond took on the role of an old bachelor, Samuel Bundy, whose years of happy bachelorhood end abruptly after he proposes to and is accepted by three different widows. Before his troubles are resolved, Bundy finds himself mistaken for another man and dragged off to an insane asylum. Raymond was a capital farceur, a master of deadpan withdrawals, double takes, and quizzical vocal inflections, and from all accounts might well have turned *The Woman Hater* into another success for himself. But laughter turned to tears for many when three months later the star died suddenly while continuing his tour. Over the years, however, several other players would keep *The Woman Hater* alive.

A week later, tears mingled with laughter for a different reason. Denman Thompson belonged to another order of comedian—one who tugged at the heart almost as often as he tickled the funnybone. His new vehicle was really not all that new, furthering as it did the adventures of his Yankee farmer, Joshua Whitcomb. In fact, Josh's latest adventures were hardly more than a rehashing of his old ones. Yet somehow, this time, everything fell wonderfully into place, and **The Old Homestead** (1-10-87, 14th St.), which Thompson wrote with George W. Ryer, quickly became one of the most popular of all 19th-century American plays, a veritable classic in its genre. Even while the warmhearted, steadfast New Hampshire farmer is welcoming all manner of visitors to his place, his mind is preoccupied. Months have gone by without Josh receiving any word from his son, Reuben (T. D. Frawley). The boy has gone to New York, and Josh, suspicious of city wiles, decides to seek him there. His childhood friend, Henry "Redhead Hank" Hopkins (Walter Lennox), is now a millionaire with an imposing New York mansion (complete with a statue of "Venus of Milo" in the vestibule), so Josh stays with his old schoolmate—even if Hopkins's wife, whom Josh once knew as Betsy, now haughtily insists he call her Elizabeth. Josh and Henry

discover Reuben has become a derelict. Josh sets about helping him reform and makes him promise that he will return home for the holidays. When a reformed Reuben and his friends keep that promise, Josh welcomes them and urges, "Now don't let this be your last visit to the Old Homestead. Come up in June when all natur' is at her best—come on, all of you, and let the scarlet runners chase you back to childhood."

The play was beautifully mounted. Homer Emens was praised for his first-act farm setting, showing the house with flowers on the front porch, outbuildings, and summery fields, and for the spacious but rustic kitchen of the last act—spacious enough for the cast to dance in to the music of a small rural band. A larger band, a Salvation Army ensemble, paraded in the moonlight through Hughson Hawley's third-act setting depicting Broadway and 10th Street, with an exterior of Grace Church at the rear. Surefire if clichéd turns and bits included the character of the comic slavey, Rickety Ann (Annie Thompson), and a third-act curtain-call tableau—after Josh has discovered Reuben—for which directions read "*Policeman with head bowed. Reuben stands with his head on Josh's shoulder.*" If photographs are to be relied on, a subtle but telling change also had taken place. The pictures of Thompson as Josh show him dressed essentially the same way he did for *Joshua Whitcomb*—the baggy pants, the glasses, the straw hat—but the clothes are no longer exaggerated for effect. The pants are no longer too baggy, the hat no longer a bit too large. Josh is no longer pictured as something approaching a traditional grotesque clown of the period but merely as a colorful, slightly unsophisticated rustic. In fact, the unsophisticated farmer has become a bit sophisticated, no doubt mellowing to reflect the growing sophistication of audiences. In its first New York engagement *The Old Homestead* ran out the season, compiling 160 performances. On tour and on repeat visits it continued to delight playgoers right up to Thompson's death in 1911.

When his unceasing wanderings brought Warde back for a brief stand at a combination house, he offered a seminew play, Leonard G. Outram's **Galba, the Gladiator** (1-10-87, Windsor), taken from Saumet's famous *Le Gladiateur,* which Salvini and others had made familiar to American patrons. Warde won praise for his portrayal of the gladiator-slave who discovers the young Christian he is ordered to kill is his own daughter.

Helen Dauvray had banked heavily on Bronson Howard's **Met by Chance** (1-11-87, Lyceum) to bolster her bid for a secure and select niche in the

250

theatre world. It proved otherwise. Edward Dudley Talford (Frank Rodney), an English earl traveling in America incognito with his friend, Dr. Harrington Lee (E. H. Sothern), meets Stella Van Dyke at an Adirondacks lodge, falls in love with her, and is disconcerted to discover she is engaged to a man posing as him. That man is Dudley Bretton (J. G. Saville). Stella and her friend, Hope Rutherford (Ellie Wilton), later get lost in the woods and wind up at Talford and Lee's camp. Bretton soon follows and shoots Talford, but the real earl recovers and wins Stella, just as the good young doctor and Hope begin to look longingly at each other.

The actress-manager spared no expense. The spectacular scene in the Adirondacks was so craftily contrived that some critics insisted even the rocks and trees had to be real. Certainly the rainstorm, with thunder and lightning, was as effectively recreated as such a tempest could be, and some patrons in the front rows were splashed in the downpour. But such carefulness backfired, at least on opening night. One of the solidly constructed rocks, lifted into the flies after it was no longer needed, broke loose and ripped a gaping hole in the ceiling of a drawing room, which could not be totally mended without canceling the rest of the play. There were also complaints that while some front-row patrons had been splashed, the stage waterfall "dried up under the influence of the presence of ladies." But the effects, when they worked, were not enough to overcome weaknesses in Howard's script, so the play was withdrawn after three weeks and at a frightful loss.

One of the era's countless aspirants, Helen Hastings, attempted to achieve instant stardom in **Pen and Ink** (1-17-87, Union Square). She portrayed Phyllis, "a child of nature," who meets Aristarchus Brent (Eugene Jepson) at a party at Irvington-on-the-Hudson. The pair join forces to establish a newspaper in the big city—and they succeed. The play did not. Its paltry claim to fame is that it marked the New York debut of a future star, William Faversham.

The hit of Daly's season and one of the most remarkable productions of his long tenure was his mounting on the 18th of *The Taming of the Shrew*. There were two salient reasons for its success. First of all, after decades of having to be content with the eviscerated and bowdlerized *Katherine and Petruchio*, playgoers could at long last enjoy something approximating Shakespeare's original text. One Daly student, Marvin Felheim, who wrote, "This revival was unquestionably his most successful venture into the field of Shakespearean drama and . . .

must be reckoned one of the truly great presentations of the play," details the changes made by the producer, beginning with the restoration of the Induction—and with it Christopher Sly (William Gilbert)—and of the subplot of Hortensio (Joseph Holland) and Bianca (Virginia Dreher). The remaining changes would not have pleased modern purists. By telescoping Acts III and IV into one heavily rearranged act, he cut an intermission and shortened the running time. As a proper 19th-century moralist, Daly deleted many lines for the sake of "refinement," and in so doing destroyed the bite of *Katherine and Petruchio*'s second-act verbal duel. (Bowdlerization was still the order of the night.) To spotlight Ada Rehan's shrew he teased audiences by delaying her entrance, then padded her part with lines from other characters and even other plays. Drew's Petruchio was similarly pampered, though to a markedly lesser degree.

Yet for all these infidelities, this was probably as true a *Taming of the Shrew* as American audiences ever had seen. And as beautiful. Daly's scene painters worked up stage pictures that resembled Veronese masterpieces come to life in all their color, richness, and fullness, from the gilded furniture, upholstered in red damask, of Baptista's house to the long, sumptuously laden dining tables of the final scenes, with the ornately columned buildings rising behind the pilastered terrace in the background. By consensus the cast was superb. And by a similar consensus Rehan's Katherine was the high point of her career. To modern eyes her picture, in a richly brocaded, drapey dress and a huge, befeathered hat rakishly atilt seems almost 18th-century. But that may be an unfair quibble. Winter wrote of her shrew, "She has no rival in it, and probably she never had an equal. The image of her Katherine will live in memory, and in stage-history, as that of an imperial blonde, tall, lithe, supple, with queenly demeanor, flashing eyes, a proud, scornful countenance, spontaneous posture of command, an impetuosity that seemed invincible, and a voice that now could cut like a knife, with its accents of sarcasm, and now could ring out like a clarion, in rage and defiance. But into her ideal of Katherine, Miss Rehan, by something in her voice, and by something in her manner, conveyed the suggestion of a loving and lovable woman, latent beneath the shrew—and that was the true charm of the embodiment, for the spectator felt that this glorious creature, with all her violence of temper, could love, and that her love would far excel that of all her silken sisterhood." The revival's amazing run of 121 performances established an American record for the play. Naturally, Daly brought it back in later seasons.

Conversely, the precipitous and lamentable decline at Wallack's again was made manifest when the house brought out another English melodrama and found that its scenery again was the most highly praised aspect of the evening. The play was George R. Sims and Henry Pettitt's **Harbor Lights** (1-27-87, Wallack's). It recounted the rocky path to the altar trodden by a young naval officer, Lt. David Kingsley (Kyrle Bellew), and his devoted sweetheart, Dora Vane (Annie Robe). Obstacles in that path include a wicked country squire, Frank Morland (Creston Clarke), and his cohort, Mark Helstone (Herbert Kelcey). Among Goatcher's applause-grabbing sets were a pier at a shipping port, an old country inn with the rolling hills beyond, and a "trick scene" that allowed the action to move from the top of a cliff to its base with the sea pounding against it, while the audience watched. A forced run kept the play on the boards until mid-March.

The failure of *Met by Chance* forced Helen Dauvray to rush in a substitute attraction. She chose *Masks and Faces,* mounting it on the 31st with the same artistic care and carelessness of expense that had exemplified her earlier productions. The problem was, she was all wrong for the leading role. The petite, reserved actress lacked the openheartedness, the zest, and even the animal presence required of anyone taking on the part of Peg Woffington.

To make matters worse for her, a more established star, Rose Coghlan, came in on the same evening—at the Union Square, virtually down the street—in a repertory that included the same play and for which she was much better suited. Miss Coghlan opened with *London Assurance,* and besides *Masks and Faces* offered *As You Like It* (in which her Rosalind was compared unfavorably to Modjeska's) and *The Lady of Lyons.* Because her productions were designed for traveling, they were not especially luxurious, but some reviewers rued they were not even imaginative or interesting. Nor, except for Charles M. Walcot, did her supporting players strike critics as noteworthy. But Miss Coghlan's reputation, her beauty, her vitality, and her intelligently acquired skills saw to it she played to good houses.

That final night of January also saw Mantell replace *Tangled Lives* with *The Marble Heart,* an old play neatly suited to his somewhat retrograde style. It ran for two weeks, until his engagement ended. The play was never again given a major mounting until Mantell himself did so years later.

For several seasons, although the modern notion of tryouts had grown rapidly, producers had re-course to another method of testing new works—the special matinee. Brander Matthews's *Margery's Lovers* had been given just such a chance a few weeks earlier and, like most similar experiments, got no further. But a few months before, another such matinee was so well received that a run seemed worth the gamble. **Jack** (2-14-87, Fifth Ave.) was a comedy taken from Augier's *La Pierre de touche* by Mrs. Harry Beckett, the widow of the late comedian. Jack Beamish (Eben Plympton), a mediocre painter, Noel Blake (Charles Kent), an effete composer, Madge Heskett (Georgiana Drew Barrymore), and their dog, Junior, live in a typically bohemian garret and support themselves on the money Jack earns by turning out trash, which the public wants. Then Noel comes into an unexpected inheritance. He sneers at his old friends, meanly kicks a fellow composer who had once pawned a coat to buy Noel some medicine (shades of another bohemian world), and, to show fully how worthless and villainous he is, shoots the dog. This all proves too much for Jack and Madge, who long have loved each other. The prospective bride and groom sit down to dinner, having just learned that the rich heiress Noel had hoped to wed has run off with a low-level bureaucrat. What had looked so promising at its special matinee apparently did not hold up on second hearing. The play quickly went on tour but seems not to have done well there.

Another of those borderline affairs—farces laced with a few songs and dances—was Cal Wallace's **Pa** (2-14-87, Standard), created as a vehicle for bean-pole Sol Smith Russell. The comedian played Perkimen Guinney, who must marry off his three daughters and who tries desperately to find suitors for the two older ones. Russell was always more welcome on the road than in New York, and this time around was no exception.

February's only other major entry was the return of Richard Mansfield. The actor was rapidly making a reputation and developing a following, so he recorded good business during his three-week stand in *Prince Karl* at the Union Square, beginning on the 21st.

On the other hand, Helen Dauvray's dreams of establishing herself as an important actress-manager fell almost completely to pieces with her production of Henry Wertheimer's **Walda Lamar** (3-7-87, Lyceum). The ineptly written play seemed at once a pastiche and a parody of some of the more torrid French melodramas, especially *Article 47.* Walda is represented as a celebrated Parisian actress, born the child of a Russian nobleman and a peasant woman. But something in her past has embittered her, and she applauds the behavior of a woman who threw acid in the face of her faithless lover. She has hardly said this when she discovers her own lover, the Duc de St. Germain (Alexander Salvini), is deserting her to wed someone else. She goes to him, dramatically throws all her love letters to her at his feet, and then stabs herself. The wound is not mortal, and when help arrives she accuses the duke of the stabbing. He is brought to trial, but in the courtroom the sight of the duke's aged mother, the Duchesse (Ida Vernon), bowing her head and wiping away tears, softens Walda's feelings and prompts her to retract her charges. At that point the old duchess raises her head, stares for a long minute at the actress, and then shrieks, "Walda, my daughter." Walda in turn recognizes the lady to be the mother she had not seen in many years.

As badly written and clichéd as the play was, a young Clara Morris might have been able to put it across a decade or so before. But Helen Dauvray was the wrong actress at the wrong time. The best notices were handed to Alexander Salvini, son of the great Tommaso, who made the duke seem sympathetic and believable. The Lyceum's small capacity and much forcing kept the play going until mid-April, when the star had one final offering to bring forth.

Then, after a long absence, Bernhardt came back, opening a three-week stand at the Star on the 14th. Her bills consisted of *Fédora, Le Maître de forges, Frou-Frou, Adrienne Lecouvreur, La Dame aux camélias,* and *Théodora.* The better, more probing critics again took time to expound on her limitations—her inability to convey true tragic feeling or plumb a character's depths. But to a man they conceded she had bowled over her audiences. Most confessed she had bowled them over, too, by her incomparable theatrical presence (from her first appearance in *Fédora* in a white lace dress), her magnificent voice (though here critics disputed whether "golden" or "silvery" was the more descriptive word), and her electrifying emotional pyrotechnics ("Who," the impressionable young Odell later asked, "could ever forget the wail that swept through the theatre when Bernhardt's Fedora realized that her lover had died, behind those closed doors?").

Frederick Hale and H. S. Hewitt's **The Commercial Tourist's Bride** (3-14-87, Union Square) tried unavailingly to make an evening's fun out of the comic obstacles thrown in the way of the courtship of Violet Granville Smith (Agnes Herndon) and a traveling salesman with the ridiculous name of O. N. Time (Frank Lane). Other musical comedy monikers included B. B. Catcher and Rose E. Flour. The characterizations were as preposterous as the characters' names, prompting the *Herald* to describe Time as "a 'drummer' such as the funny papers crack standard jokes about, but sensible merchants never employ."

David D. Lloyd's **The Dominie's Daughter** (3-24-87, Wallack's), probably not much more fetching a title than *The Commercial Tourist's Bride,* was a case of too little, too late. Raymond's death was to temporarily halt the tour of Lloyd's *The Woman Hater,* and now he was handed the dubious distinction of writing the last new play—and one of the precious few American plays—to be mounted by Lester Wallack for his historic ensemble. In Revolutionary New York City the Reverend John Van Derveer (Harry Edwards), his pretty young daughter, Molly (Annie Robe), and his gallant young son, Robert (Creston Clarke), are all staunch advocates of American freedom. This doesn't prevent Molly from falling in love with a redcoat, Captain Dyke (Kyrle Bellew). Naturally Dyke falls in love with her—but so does his arrogant superior, Major Barton (Herbert Kelcey). When the two men come calling on the Van Derveers, they discover that Molly has hidden a man in her room. They conclude it is her lover, and Barton attempts to use the incident to his own advantage. Of course, the man is only Robert, who is acting as a spy. With Dyke's help he escapes.

Superficially the plot outline suggests that of many period plays dealing with the Civil War, but for some reason American playwrights almost never chose to treat the Revolutionary War as seriously. So whereas lovers of opposing persuasions and trapped spies would be the cue for harrowing introspections and tense moments in a Civil War drama, they simply provided colorful pivots for a romantic Revolutionary War comedy. The distinction would apply, with the inevitable few exceptions, for all the ensuing decades. Though the play arrived too late to save Wallack's—and given Lester Wallack's age and lack of a willing heir, probably nothing could have forestalled its closing—most observers felt it was one of the most attractive new pieces offered at the house in many a season.

Once again, though, no small measure of its charm came from Goatcher's skilled brush. The *Times* praised "an old parsonage standing amid rolling meadows where the vilest part of the Bowery is now; a quaint churchyard that contains the simple memorials of early Dutch settlers, with a farmhouse here and there nearby, and the sun-lit East River in the distance; [and] the parlor of a fine old mansion on Wall-street where Dutch solidity is contrasted with the luxury tolerated by the British." But also once again, Wallack's could not lure playgoers in any significant number. Molly and her friends bid adieu after three and a half weeks.

Two English stars who had brought with them a certain excitement earlier in the season returned in April—one at the start, the other at the close—to frame a somewhat lackluster month. Wilson Barrett reappeared first, coming back to the Star on the 4th. He opened with his controversial Hamlet. Most controversial of all in many critics' minds was his insistence that Hamlet was scarcely out of his teens and that almost all the figures surrounding him, especially his mother, Ophelia, and his male friends, were accordingly much younger than normally perceived—even if the performers playing the parts did not always succeed in making them look so youthful. Barrett also tinkered cavalierly with the division of the acts and the order of the scenes. And he added such original if essentially quirky and unimportant bits as having the play-within-the-play take place outside, in a moonlit orchard. Three nights later Barrett brought out **Clito** (4-7-87, Star), his collaboration with Sydney Grundy. The story tells of a brilliant young man, at once a sculptor, poet, and rising politician, whose downfall is cleverly engineered by Helle (Miss Eastlake), a courtesan Clito had denounced. In London and on its American tour the play had been received rapturously, some writers hailing it as a modern masterpiece. New Yorkers thought differently. Barrett's repertory also included *Claudian* and *The Lady of Lyons*.

The McKee Rankins—she was Kitty Blanchard—were the stars of Clay Greene's **The Golden Giant** (4-11-87, Fifth Ave.). Mrs. Rankin played Bessie, a widow whose husband had been hounded to death by smirking Duncan LeMoyne (Nester Lennon), who is resolved upon stealing the deeds to a mine—deeds he knows Bessie is equally resolved he shall not have. A chase ensues. At one point Bessie's coach is overturned and thrown into a stream, and only Alexander Fairfax's daring rescue saves her from drowning. But Duncan still has another trick up his sleeve—the dead husband's twin brother, Max (J. Winston Murray), whom he hopes to pass off as the dead man. However, by 11:30 Duncan and all his cronies have received their comeuppance, and Bessie and Alexander (Rankin) can embrace, oblivious to all the eyes watching them from the other side of the footlights. Westerns still featured the comic "chinee," but in the case of *The Golden Giant* he was the real McCoy or, perhaps, McSoy. Ah Wing

Sing was advertised as "the first real English-speaking Chinaman on any stage." His role was small, but he apparently milked it for all it was worth and earned himself several solo bows. The play remained at the Fifth Avenue for a mere two weeks, then headed back to the road, where it already had done well and would continue to do so for several seasons. It played several return engagements.

Helen Dauvray was not so lucky, and she rang down the curtain on her largely unsuccessful attempt to become an actress-manager with a revival of Knowles's *The Love-Chase*. Its production at the Lyceum on the 11th was another egregious miscalculation on her part. Not only had the comedy long since fallen out of favor, but if she had any dreams of bringing it back into vogue, she and her co-star, E. H. Sothern, lacked both the flair and the experience required by older-style comic writing.

Fanny Janauschek had enjoyed more moments of glory, but her career, too, was patently in the descendant, as was made evident by the reception accorded her Meg Merrilies. Whatever kind words critics had—and many of them were generous in their appraisal—no one equaled Charlotte Cushman in their eyes. On this point playgoers and reviewers were in agreement. The actress's two-week engagement was disappointing at the box office.

Boucicault's career had been even longer and filled with greater triumphs—all far in the past. Yet his name was still glamorous and potent enough for him to be added to the distinguished roster moving in and out of the Star throughout the season. Unpacking his bags on the 18th, he presented playgoers with a double bill consisting of *Kerry* and a supposedly new play, *Fin McCool*, but the latter was quickly unmasked as a reworking of *Belle Lamar*. The play had been produced in Boston several months before, as *Fin MacCoul of Skibereen*, and had been rejected there as well. Boucicault had retained the basic story of a heroine and her husband who find themselves on opposing sides in the Civil War, but he had added the character of an Irish immigrant who joins the Union army. Naturally, the star himself played the young man. Unfortunately, the playwright failed the star, for the new title figure was not woven skillfully into the main plot and only provided a distraction in a script that had too many distractions to begin with. The play was quickly hustled away, and revivals of *The Jilt* and *The Shaugraun* followed. Old and ill as he was, Boucicault still cavorted as the boyish Conn, seemingly to the satisfaction of many observers. That illness, however, forced the canceling of several performances in what had been booked as a full month's stand.

At Wallack's, Boucicault's *Old Heads and Young Hearts,* first done in this country forty-two years earlier, was brought forth as what proved to be the penultimate offering of that once august company. So many careers were hurtling to a close. For the occasion, John Gilbert once again was Jesse Rural.

Plump but gamin Annie Pixley had reason to be grateful to A. C. Gunter, whose **The Deacon's Daughter** (4-25-87, Union Square) gave her a much welcomed respite from incessant touring in *M'liss.* It also allowed her to use her singing and dancing skills as Ruth Homewebb, who disobeys her deeply religious, puritanical New England parents and runs off to New York to seek stardom on the stage. Although Deacon Isaiah Homewebb (M. C. Daly) despairs, "I've heard of reformed murderers and reformed housebreakers, but never of a reformed actor," he and his wife hurry to the big city to save their child. Instead, they are transformed into theatre buffs. In a sense, *The Deacon's Daughter* was the reverse side of the coin of *The Old Homestead.* In the one a New England rustic goes to New York to rescue his child from degradation and bring him back to the wholesome countryside; in the other a young girl succeeds in New York and manages to make her New England parents see the virtues of some aspects of city life. Gunter's comedy was never as successful as Thompson's mellow melodrama. No doubt most playgoers preferred to think of parents as knowing more about life than their offspring. No doubt, too, especially on the road, many American playgoers still equated small town and farming communities with a certain innocence or virtue. And, probably, *The Old Homestead* was simply a better play. But for all that, *The Deacon's Daughter* was a hit, doing good business for six weeks and remaining a much demanded touring attraction for many years.

Tom Taylor's thirteen-year-old play known variously as *Lady Clancarty,* or as *Clancarty,* and subtitled *Wedded and Wooed,* had been produced in several American cities and at a special matinee in New York, but it remained for Lillie Langtry to give Manhattan's theatregoers their first chance to see a regular production of the work. Not unexpectedly, she chose the title **Lady Clancarty** (4-25-87, Fifth Ave.). She played a woman who was married as a young child to a small boy, has not seen her husband since, and now suddenly discovers him to be a leading agitator for the return of the Stuarts. She manages to save his life when he is condemned to death. She and Charles Coghlan made a pair of handsome, forceful lovers and were well received. Only the lateness of the season and the

limited advance booking probably confined the run, which was cut short to allow the company to close with a few performances of *The Lady of Lyons.*

With the long run of *Jim, the Penman* concluding at the end of April, the Madison Square revived its hit of the preceding season, *Our Society,* on May 2. But more dedicated playgoers certainly trekked downtown that night to an increasingly out-of-the-way, outmoded theatre to watch Lawrence Barrett essay yet another new play. Actually, like so many new plays of the time, **Rienzi** (5-2-87, Niblo's) was simply an old play reworked. At Barrett's behest Steele MacKaye had rewritten Mary Russell Mitford's tragedy, initially presented in America nearly sixty years before. Whether the original or MacKaye's revisions were at fault, many commentators suggested the story of the high-minded tribune's attempt to restore republican sentiments to a decadent Rome now lacked dramatic punch. Pageantry sustained the evening. It could not sustain it for long, so after three weeks Barrett bowed out with a final week that moved swiftly from *Yorick's Love* to *Francesca da Rimini, Hamlet,* a double bill of *The Merchant of Venice* and *David Garrick,* and *Richelieu.*

The night next saw the arrival of another new-old play, but this one became a landmark in American theatricals. The old play was Maddison Morton and Robert Reece's *Trade,* which the playwrights had created many years before as a vehicle for E. A. Sothern and which the actor had stored away without producing. The new play was **The Highest Bidder** (5-3-87, Lyceum), David Belasco's rehashing of *Trade* as a vehicle for E. A.'s son, E. H. With Helen Dauvray's bowing out, Daniel Frohman had taken over the running of the theatre, and his mounting of the comedy signaled his emergence as a major American producer.

. . .

Daniel Frohman (1851–1940), a wiry, balding man with a closely cut beard and mustache, was the eldest of three brothers who would figure importantly in American stage annals. He was born in Sandusky, Ohio, and came to New York as a young man to work in newspapers. However, by the mid-1870s he was advance man for a minstrel company. With his brothers, Gustave and Charles, he helped run MacKaye's Madison Square Theatre, and the men are generally credited with establishing the practice of sending out road companies, first of the Madison Square's long-run hits and then of other plays. (Some credit for first sending out road companies must go to Palmer.) Frohman then moved to the Lyceum but did not fully assert himself until he produced *The Highest Bidder*.

. . .

The leading figure in the play is Jack Hammerton (Sothern), a well-to-do young auctioneer, who can remain cool in the face of the most audacious villain yet grows perplexed and flustered when gazed at by a pretty, dewy-eyed blonde in a chaste white dress. Complications arise—and Jack is launched on a comic emotional roller coaster—when the pretty, dewy-eyed blonde, Rose Thornhill (Belle Archer), is threatened with having her family estate, the Larches, put on the block and with losing it to none other than the audacious villain, the unscrupulous Sir Evelyn Graine (Herbert Archer). Although Jack is helped at times by a fire-breathing curmudgeon with the proverbial gold heart, Bonham Cheviot (W. J. LeMoyne), he is nearly murdered by the villain and unjustly mistreated by Rose. The climax comes at the auction. Fortified by frequent swigs of champagne, Jack conducts a hectic bidding, with Sir Evelyn glowering and raising his bid on one side of the room and Rose watching desperately across the way. Other, less identifiable bids are called out from everywhere. The frantic pace, the excited murmurs, and the bidding continue until the exhausted Jack pounds the gavel three times, exclaiming, "Going! Going! Gone!" He then seems to crumple. In a sudden stillness Rose asks aloud, almost afraid to learn the answer, "Who has bought The Larches?" Jack identifies the successful bidder with a single word: "I!" He offers the deed back to Rose, who, after the initial shock, fully understands how deeply Jack loves her.

Although the accomplished and admired character actor LeMoyne garnered some of the most flattering notices, Sothern's playing of Jack marked him as an upcoming star. *The Highest Bidder* was greeted by critics as breezy, warm-weather entertainment, and the play continued to good business until hotter nights forced it to take a hiatus. It remained popular for several seasons.

The dichotomy of old and new that ran through this season may nowhere have been more graphically or poignantly illustrated than on the night *The Highest Bidder* opened—propelling a rising young producer and a rising young actor into the limelight and further turning up the brightest spots on the play's young adaptor. For on the same night, Wallack returned *The School for Scandal* to his stage. The rest of the week saw the Sheridan comedy alternate with Boucicault's play until, on Saturday, May 7, 1887, Wallack led his ensemble in their final bows. Sticklers may argue about the date. As if to inject a bit of comic confusion into theatrical history the company moved briefly to Daly's, where, for a fortnight beginning May 16, they offered another of Wallack's old favorites, *The Romance of a Poor Young Man,* and the oncoming season saw Henry Abbey's high-minded but futile attempt to keep both the company and its traditions alive.

Whichever date is accepted, the end of Wallack's unmistakably if not singlehandedly underscored the end of an era—the era of an American stage dominated by traditional English plays, traditional English acting methods, and to no small extent by the Anglo-American attitudes of largely Anglo-American audiences, producers, players, and dramatists. Immigration had been changing the very nature and face of American theatre for some time, and now the changes were to come into the open. The day when much of the best American theatre was unified in its ideals and its day-to-day working was soon to totally disappear. The old theatre had seen actors often become playwrights and playwrights become producers. In a sense the theatre and even its audience had been a tightly knit fraternity. From here on, men with little knowledge of old plays or players, men whose first interest was entrepreneurial or monetary, or who were merely "bricks-and-mortar men," were increasingly taking over theatre ownership and play production, and these men, like the changing audience whose patronage they sought, were not always of the old stock. The change was to have dismaying drawbacks and marvelous advantages.

The earliest wave of non-English immigrants— the Irish—had figured importantly on both sides of the footlights for many decades and would continue to do so for many more. At a certain level, this led to plays catering to special Irish tastes. Such a play was George Fawcett Rowe's **The Donagh** (5-18-87, Grand Opera), in which Lantry Killaly (Joseph Murphy) foils Dorsey McMurragh (O. J. Loring) in his attempts to take over Castle McBride and its heiress, Kate (Belle Melville). A panorama of Lake Killarney with a moving boat was featured. The play and the production pleased predominantly Irish audiences for several seasons.

On the 30th Mansfield came into the Madison Square to open an engagement that would defy the summer heat and run for five months. He began with a revival of *Prince Karl*, which held the stage until mid-July.

A number of fine players wasted their talents in Lawrence Marston and John A. Stevens's **The Hypocrite** (6-6-87, 14th St.). Set in Louisiana before the Civil War, it centered on an octoroon slave,

George (Newton Gotthold). His hatred for his master, Edward Walton (Osmond Tearle), has festered ever since Walton sold George's wife and sent her away. He sees a chance for revenge when Walton brings home a bride, Edith (Annie Robe). George knows that Edith has been the mistress of Walton's close friend, Richard Singleton (Herbert Kelcey), and he sets about planting suspicions in Walton's mind. This latter-day *Othello,* with colors reversed and with a happy ending, was filled indiscriminately with shootings, poisonings, suicides, mad scenes, and bits of driveling comedy. Another up-and-coming young figure, Charles S. Dickson, earned praise for his deft handling of the clumsy comedy with his portrayal of a dramatist whose plays were obviously as bad as *The Hypocrite.* Coming suddenly out of nowhere, the play ran but two weeks and apparently never attempted to tour.

Having pocketed $300,000 for her American tour, Bernhardt came into New York to await the sailing of her steamship. She did not let her few nights in Manhattan go for naught, bringing out *Fédora, Théodora,* and *Hernani* at the Star in three successive evenings beginning on the 15th. For good measure she offered a Friday matinee of *Théodora.* The *Hernani* was offered as a "benefit" to her, meaning, of course, that she received the entire gate. Papers reported that at the special prices she was asking Bernhardt was about to add $2800 to her bank account from that one night alone.

Travers House (6-20-87, Niblo's) was another inept melodrama given a better cast than it deserved. Its author, no doubt fearful of its reception, had refused to disclose his or her identity, and when the play's reception realized those fears, the playwright remained silent. The prologue tells how Reginald Travers (J. T. Sullivan), consumed by guilt, marries Stella (Adele Belgarde), a girl he has violated. The young wife thereupon dies. Many years pass. Travers has become a baronet, and so his second wife is known as Lady Travers (Adeline Stanhope). She is not a nice woman. She is particularly unhappy that Sir Reginald has left the bulk of his estate to his daughter by his brief first marriage, a sweet girl named Valerie (again, Miss Belgarde). One night Lady Travers confronts a burglar in the house and recognizes him as John Bland (Nelson Wheatcroft), her old partner in crime. Bland kills Sir Reginald, and then he and Lady Travers put their heads together to attempt to deprive Valerie of her inheritance. They fail.

Perhaps the most interesting thing about the play was the comment it elicited from the *Times,* suggesting how tastes continued to change. The paper's critic

remarked, "Audiences are prone to smile nowadays when the old-fashioned expedients of melodrama are brought too frequently into use, and there were moments last night when the smiles were quite audible." Of course, the critic could only have been speaking for the better cosmopolitan patrons, and then only when matters were handled ineptly onstage, for old-fashioned melodrama was more than tolerated, it was warmly embraced in backwaters all across America and would continue to be until the coming of films. And there were still sophisticated playgoers, even in New York, who relished the twists, turns, and sensations of melodrama when they were accomplished with panache. However, panache was in short supply at *Travers House,* which stood on Broadway for just two weeks.

All season long, old favorites popped in and out of combination houses. For example, on the same night *Travers House* premiered, *Hazel Kirke* began a brief stand at the Grand Opera. By now C. W. Couldock, who had remained with the play since its New York opening, had come to be perceived as the star and his old-school, emotive Dunstan as the play's main attraction. May Wheeler, who played the title role, had to be content with second billing and a back seat in most notices. But the waning season prompted some first-class theatres to accept touring shows. Thus the Bijou, a leading house devoted mostly to musicals, played host to Minnie Maddern in *Caprice* for three weeks beginning on the 21st. Once more most of her notices were glowing, hailing her as a young player of exceptional promise.

Colonel Joseph Nunez of Louisville was the author of the all too appropriately named comedy **False Steps** (6-27-87, Windsor), in which old moneybags Mr. Fielding (Harry Rich) marries Theresa D'Arnay (Hattie Russell) and thereby sets off fireworks. His family claims she is a notorious adventuress and even produces a man claiming to be her husband.

Another of the minor dramas briefly to usurp a vaudeville stage was **Bijah Frisby** (6-27-87, Tony Pastor's). Like the earlier *Eli Wheatfield,* its hero (J. W. Jennings) is an old New England farmer. It becomes Bijah's task to prevent his young friend, Marion (Queenie Vassar), from being bilked by her unscrupulous uncle and his sidekick, a French maid. Part of the action took place in Coney Island. After a single week the play disappeared forever from New York stages. Unfortunately, the trade sheets of the era, notably the *Clipper,* did not report completely on touring attractions, so what further career *Bijah* enjoyed, if any, is open to conjecture.

Henry Chanfrau, looking for a breather from touring in his late father's famous vehicle, *Kit, the Arkansas Traveller*, gave over the matinees of his stand at the Grand Opera House to a new play, George Hoey's **American Grit** (6-29-87, Grand Opera), in which a young American goes to Wales to seek his fortune. He finds a rich, abandoned mine and an even richer heiress, winning both after surmounting expected obstacles. One unexpected obstacle may have been the hero himself, who was depicted as a curious amalgam of bravery and boastfulness. He has no qualms about recounting his daring rescue of a young girl, and if it will further his macho image, he is even willing to accept the paternity of a child who is not his. The *Sun*, baffled by such a puzzling character, also berated the play for requiring too many scene changes and for "much needless profanity." Such comments and a few performances were enough to persuade Chanfrau to drop the work.

Mansfield's first new play of his engagement brought the season to a pleasant close. **Monsieur** (7-11-87, Madison Square) was doubly Mansfield's, for not only was he its star, he was its author. His André Rossini Mario de Jadot, an impoverished aristocrat, has come to New York to scratch out a living as a musician. He has fallen in love with Alice Golden (Beatrice Cameron) and she with him, but Alice's snobbish, nouveaux riches parents are outraged. However, they consent to allow André to perform at one of their musicales, where, weak from hunger, he faints during his performance. This further infuriates the Goldens. Defying them, Alice and André marry and set up housekeeping in a garret. After a time Alice's father, Ezra (D. H. Harkins), would relent and accept the pair, but Mrs. Golden (Josephine Laurens) adamantly refuses. Just as the Goldens are threatened with major financial reverses and even bankruptcy, André learns he has inherited the huge estate of his uncle, a French count. So all ends happily.

As in *Prince Karl*, Mansfield put his singing gifts and skills as a mimic to good use in *Monsieur*. He also won laughs and some tears in a scene in which André prepares his hungry wife a paper-thin "sandwich of cheeken" and serves it to her with the majestic flourishes of a grand maître d'. The play proved popular—doing surprisingly strong business through two months of hot weather—but not doing as well as the greedy, maniacally ambitious Mansfield wanted. Ever afterwards he blamed himself for this, saying his choice of title defeated the play since Americans were embarrassed by their inability to pronounce the word easily or correctly and thus

deprived the work of word of mouth. One result was that the play was sometimes offered later as either *Monsieur Jadot* or as *Jadot*, neither choice really more helpful if Mansfield were right in the first place. Another result would be seen when Mansfield came to mount Booth Tarkington's *Monsieur Beaucaire*.

1887–1888

Quite probably a majority of playgoers sat through the 1887–88 season reasonably satisfied with what they saw and heard. Gallery gods could still hiss ebony-black, snarling villains and still cheer heroes rescuing heroines from a blaze of illuminated tinsel and stage smoke. At the same time, thanks to new, smaller theatres and to stages brightened by electricity, the exaggerated writing and acting so dear to excitable newsboys and their fellow ragamuffin noisemakers was disappearing rapidly from smarter houses. In those, a better-dressed and better-mannered clientele, who could afford the better-located seats, applauded a handful of aging, traditionalist stars returning year after year in their aged, traditional repertory. They also enjoyed surviving stock ensembles (which now made only token bows to the classics) and a rising type of specially cast and mounted production. For the most part the plays both audiences saw were relatively new. Almost totally gone were the comedies and dramas of a bygone century, plays that for decades had been sprinkled liberally throughout the seasons. More and more, Broadway was given over, as it would be from here on in, to a diet of new, sometimes not fully ripened offerings. And for seasons to come these works would continue to be largely foreign. Even most American plays—though, significantly, often not the better ones—would be clothed in European garments.

Such was the case with Nelson Wheatcroft's **Gwynne's Oath** (8-15-87, Windsor), which was clearly earmarked for theatrical backwaters and was brought in as part of the so-called preliminary season to give it a New York imprimatur. Its heroine is Gwynne Archer (Adeline Stanhope), whose father is murdered in an argument over gambling debts and who vows to avenge the crime. The murderer is Harry Vesey (Herbert Archer), a nephew of the very man who shelters the orphaned girl. Gwynne is a sleepwalker, and when one night

Harry startles her and wakes her, she is jolted into recalling a tidbit that identifies and convicts him. The play's first New York stay was only a single week, albeit it toured for several seasons during which it made some equally brief returns. Did Americans look at this play as American? Why didn't Wheatcroft set his play on this side of the Atlantic and fill it with Yankee figures? After all, there is nothing inherently European about his story. But it must be remembered that Wheatcroft himself was British-born and British-trained. For a certain kind of playgoer, including many who bought the higher-priced seats, a play not only needed a New York sanction but also an English or Continental setting. No doubt a second, possibly larger group, less vocal or less able to find a public press for its sentiments, still awaited thoroughly American works.

The preliminary season also saw the hasty reemergence of more recent successes in various stopovers on their way out to the hinterlands, as well as revivals of older pieces. *The Duke's Motto* came into Niblo's on the 17th as *Lagardère*, a lavish production so replete with ballets and other spectacular paraphernalia that many critics treated it as a musical. In short order *Lost in London*, *The Highest Bidder*, *Held by the Enemy*, and *The White Slave* appeared before the footlights, and from the beginning until the season's close, other works delighted loyalists, especially at combination houses. Even such arthritic warhorses as *Uncle Tom's Cabin*, *East Lynne*, and *Ten Nights in a Barroom* found stages here and there.

Like the first, the season's second American work, A. C. Gunter's **One Against Many** (8-29-87, Union Square), unfolded in a European setting. Its heroine, Olga (Katie Gilbert), is a susceptible young countess conned by nihilists into doing dirty work for them. She is rescued from trouble by Pierre de Montelambert (John L. Burleigh). Burleigh was seen as rather burly for a leading man, and few of the cast seemed particularly good as performers. The play survived for a month, but its record, if any, on the road is obscure.

A far longer career was in store for Joseph Arthur's **The Still Alarm** (8-30-87, 14th St.), a play sure to thrill the gallery gods. And here was an American play with an American setting—even if the plot, trite as trite could be, might have been set anywhere. John Bird (Nelson Wheatcroft), spurned by Elinore Fordham (Blanche Thorne), tries to frame her father, Franklin Fordham (E. A. Eberle), for a murder he himself has committed. He tells Fordham he will forget the matter if Fordham forces

Elinore to marry him instead of the man she prefers, Jack Manley (Harry Lacy). Elinore reluctantly agrees.

Elinore: Jack Manley, the hour for you and me to part has come—Our dream of love is over—Go—go—go! (*She swoons in Jack's arms*)
Jack: My God! What does this mean? Whose work is this?

Curtain

When it looks as if his plans still will go awry, Bird decides to burn down Fordham's house. He also cuts the wires for the alarm boxes. This forces Jack to rush to the firehouse.

([Jack] seizes hammer and strikes alarm bell—Lights up—two horses run out and take their places under collars and before Engine—the bed clothes are taken off the beds by wires—the firemen slide down the poles—the horses are hitched—Jack mounts the Engine seat—he pulls reins, which releases crabs, harness drops on to horses' backs . . . The Engine is driven off amidst shouts of firemen, showing off red fire—Engine smoking.

In the end Bird is revealed as the kidnapper of a second Fordham daughter, who was abducted in infancy many years before. A secondary comic romance between Willie Manley (Charles S. Dickson) and Cad Wilbur (Blanche Vaughan) provides a subplot, with boozy Doc Wilbur (Jacques Kruger) helping both Manley boys get their girls.

What counted for the cheering idealists hanging intently over the gallery railings were scenes such as Jack's breaking a window to descend heroically down a fire escape, and, most memorably, the firehouse scene with Jack leaping on the engine and goading the "beautiful twin [white] Arabian horses" that pulled it into action. The *Herald* reported that "the audience howled with delight." The play's initial New York run was only two weeks, but it returned in late March to chalk up 104 more performances, and it gave Lacy a meal ticket for many years ahead. In an opening-night speech Arthur credited the famous critic A. C. Wheeler with a hand in the play's composition.

David Dixon Porter was a distinguished admiral, a superintendent of the naval academy of Annapolis, and a sometime historian and novelist. He sat in a box alongside his friend General Sherman on opening night when one of his novels was dramatized as **Allan Dare** (9-5-87, Fifth Ave.). His story seemed to want the best of both worlds, for while his characters were Europeans, the action moved them to the quaintly costumed New York of 1820. Sets included a thieves' den, a garden on the Hudson "where short-waisted girls danced in the minuet," and a prison. The play's principal characters are Dare (Frank Carlyle), a detective, and Robert le Diable (Wilton Lackaye), a notorious thief. They do not know that they are brothers. In the background of their battle for dominance are a treacherous uncle who is a banker, a long-lost father who reappears as a crazed man convinced he is a famous African explorer, and a long-lost mother. McKee Rankin and George Densmore had originally made the theatricalization for San Francisco. Despite an expensive mounting it was poorly if kindly received and folded after two weeks in New York.

Infinitely more memorable was a second translation from the printed page to the stage. This time the work was Robert Louis Stevenson's not yet two-year-old *The Strange Case of Dr. Jekyll and Mr. Hyde,* which Thomas Russell Sullivan had dramatized at the behest of Richard Mansfield. With **Dr. Jekyll and Mr. Hyde** (9-12-87, Madison Square), Mansfield triumphantly concluded the engagement he had begun the previous season. Sullivan's adaptation was not slavish. Among his additions was a love interest for the good doctor, a sweet girl named Agnes Carew (Isabelle Evesson), whose father is strangled by the evil Hyde at the beginning of the play. Neither Sullivan nor, more important, Mansfield attempted to contrast the two personalities as black versus white. Mansfield's Jekyll was a young man haunted by the secret of his increasingly uncontrollable demon. Moreover, the actor was careful not to overuse the obviously theatrical device of metamorphosing from one figure to the other in front of the audience. In the third act Hyde was transmuted into Jekyll; in the fourth act, Jekyll into Hyde. The change was accomplished not by any tricks of makeup but largely by a change of stance, facial expression, and voice. Jekyll's appearance and mannerisms were normal in every way. By contrast, the crouching, swaying Hyde walked on tiptoes and had an eerie shriek in his voice. Green lighting and shadows assisted in the effect. William Winter called the play "a tragic drama, alert with incident, cumulative with action, various with character, fluent in style and significant in picture and meaning," adding that it was wrapped "as well with an atmosphere of domestic life and love as with the otherwise unrelieved investiture of horror." Other critics also praised Mansfield's interpretation, seeing it as not merely theatrically knowing and effective but psychologically probing and true. Prior bookings limited this first New York stand to less than a month, but the star kept returning to the role until shortly before his death.

Stars of lesser magnitude had to be content with bookings at the Grand Opera. Thus the week before Mansfield unveiled his latest vehicle the dogged Robert L. Downing, one of many troupers more acceptable to the road than to New York, came for a week in *The Gladiator,* while the night of Mansfield's premiere the admired if not truly stellar Louis James, with his wife, Marie Wainwright, as his leading lady, began a week of hangdog repertory that included *Virginius, Ingomar, Hamlet,* and, of more recent vintage, Gilbert's *Gretchen.* In the spring he played the Fifth Avenue, at which time *Othello* and *Much Ado About Nothing* were part of the bills.

A star who far outshone even the rising Mansfield in the eyes of many playgoers was Lillie Langtry. For her autumn engagement she offered a new play, **As in a Looking Glass** (9-19-87, Fifth Ave.), taken by Frank Rogers from F. C. Phillips's best-seller. Its story recounted how an adventuress, Lena Despard, falls in love with the man she has married for his wealth and position and finally commits suicide to spare him public disgrace. It was a tricky and odd choice for a woman whose own reputation was none too savory, but with her beauty, her magnificent clothing, and her not unskilled acting she carried it off. Maurice Barrymore was her leading man. The attraction proved popular in its six-week stand.

A Dark Secret (9-19-87, Academy of Music) and **Two Roads** (9-19-87, Windsor) opened the same night as Mrs. Langtry. The former was a minor English play by J. Douglass and J. Willing, Jr., and was based on yet another novel, *Uncle Silas.* In the play Uncle Silas became Uncle Jonas and was rescued from some murderous friends by his nephew. What packed the huge house for nearly three months was not the plot but the spectacular production featuring a huge tank ("5,000 cubic feet of real water") serving as the Thames, down which floated real swans, canoes, and a steam launch. A recreation of the Henley Regatta featured George Hosmer, a leading sculler of the day. *Two Roads* was an ineptly written, ineptly acted piece about a man confronted with a choice between good and wicked ways. One week and it was gone for good.

In one of his volumes of reminiscences Daniel Frohman suggested that **The Great Pink Pearl** (9-20-87, Lyceum), a comedy by R. C. Carton and Cecil Raleigh, marked the beginning of his career as an independent producer. He passed over the other half of the bill, **Editha's Burglar,** which Augustus Thomas had derived from a story by Frances Hodgson Burnett. The British play told of a Russian prince's determination to retrieve both the jewel and his family honor, even if it means blowing up himself and his friends with an explosive concealed in a trick music box. The piece had enjoyed a modest success in London but failed to appeal to Americans. *Editha's Burglar* was another matter. Editha is a very young girl whose home is invaded by an intruder. Fearing for her father's life, she keeps the burglar engaged in conversation until he has finished his task. In the end it develops the burglar is her real father, who had long ago broken his wife's heart by his behavior. Although the up-and-coming E. H. Sothern portrayed the intruder, the show was stolen from him (and he neglects to mention it in his autobiography) by tiny, long-haired Elsie Leslie. For several seasons, in this and other plays, she became Broadway's darling, the Shirley Temple of her day. The success of the play marked a small win for the struggling American drama.

That little victory was nearly erased a few days later at one of the special matinees that stood in the stead of tryouts. The play was Mark Twain and W. D. Howells's **The American Claimant; or, Mulberry Sellers Ten Years Later** (9-23-87, Lyceum), a continuation of the beloved colonel's misadventures. It told of Sellers's belief that he was the heir to a large English estate and of his persistent attempts to market his harebrained inventions. Justifying the late John Raymond's rejection of it, *The Theatre* typified critical reaction by dismissing it as "a miserable lot of twaddle with neither dramatic construction nor reason."

Happily, American dramaturgy quickly bounced back with one of the biggest dramatic hits of the season, Bronson Howard's **The Henrietta** (9-26-87, Union Square). Nicholas Van Alstyne (W. H. Crane) is a successful stockbroker, rapacious yet not unfeeling. Concluding his younger son, Bertie "the Lamb" (Stuart Robson), is a ne'er-do-well, he has lavished all his affection and most of his wealth on his other son, Nicholas Junior (Charles Kent). Bertie is content to enjoy a leisurely life as a clubman and happy in the love of Agnes Lockwood (Jessie Storey), sister of the younger Nicholas's wife, Rose (Sibyl Johnstone). Unfortunately for everyone, Nicholas is an unprincipled cad. He has been unfaithful to Rose and ruined another woman in the process. He also steals his father's securities and attempts to destroy him by creating a run on the market. When a blackmailer proposes to expose Nicholas to Rose, Bertie takes the incriminating letters, casually burns them, and suggests he was the man to blame. He also uses his own monies to foil his brother and rescue his father from bankruptcy, buying stocks, since he knows nothing about them,

by the flip of a coin. He succeeds, but the shock kills his brother, who dies of a heart attack in his father's office as the ticker tape impersonally clicks out the dashing of all the troublemaker's hopes. At first, Rose refuses to believe anything bad about her husband and resigns herself to a long widowhood. But Mrs. Cornelia Updyke (Selena Fetter), a widow the elder Nicholas is courting, opens Rose's eyes, leaving her free to marry the self-sacrificing Dr. Parke Wainwright (H. J. Lethcourt), who long has loved her in a silence. Old Nicholas looks at Bertie with new respect.

The *Times* hailed the play as "a real comedy of American life . . . a keen satire of the foibles and failings of the men and women we see every day, a trenchant exposition in dramatic form of one of the greatest evils of our time." Similar bouquets were awarded the players, especially the stars. Crane abandoned his usual pompous buffoonery to create a character of genuine strength and pathos. Even Robson's famous deadpan and squeak were held in check to develop the most lovable central figure. The play was advertising "last weeks" when a fire destroyed the theatre and cut short its run at 155 performances.

To speak of a constant parade of revivals, as we did a bit earlier, may be a slight misnomer. Actually, many were more strictly speaking return engagements, since the plays and productions often had been touring nonstop season upon season, with at best short respites at the height of the summer's heat. Among the more important returns in October were *Jim, the Penman* at the Madison Square on the 1st, Minnie Palmer in her almost inevitable *My Sweetheart* at the 14th Street Theatre a week later, Jefferson and Mrs. Drew in *The Rivals* at the Star on the 17th (along with a handful of performances of *Cricket on the Hearth* and *Lend Me Five Shillings*), and *Baron Rudolf* at the 14th Street on the 24th.

The month's first new play was major indeed, although New York did not take to it as wholeheartedly as perhaps it should have. That new play also served for the most glittering first night of the still young season. But then Augustin Daly's ensemble always brought out an elite theatrical crowd. Pinero's **Dandy Dick** (10-5-87, Daly's) told of the farcical problems an unworldly minister and his sporting sister encounter when they become involved with the racehorse that gives the play its title. Except for Mrs. Gilbert, Daly's entire company was on hand, and each was given a tumultuous welcome on his or her initial appearance. Charles Fisher scored a hit as the quizzical Reverend Jedd, as did Ada Rehan as his down-to-earth sister, Georgiana

Tidman. In an unusual bit of casting, John Drew portrayed the aging, bald, wobbly-kneed Major Tarvor and was required to simulate playing a flute. For all the enthusiasm at the premiere and in the morning-after notices, business was so sluggish that Daly withdrew the comedy after one month.

The next important opening was something of a surprise, for in the preceding spring Wallack had announced his retirement and the disbanding of his prestigious troupe. Yet here was Wallack's reopening with no little hoopla. What had befallen in the interim was that Henry E. Abbey and Maurice Grau had taken over the house and announced they were maintaining the old policy and many of the old players. The season began inauspiciously with Sidney Grundy's **The Mouse Trap** (10-11-87, Wallack's), a drama in which a selfish wife attempts to poison her husband but is unmasked by a kindly physician. Whatever the faults of the play, Abbey did one thing to the theatre that had a lasting influence. At the time most stages featured vestiges of outsized, curving aprons, which cantilevered partially or entirely over the orchestra pit. Abbey removed the surviving apron, opening the entire orchestra to view and aligning the front of the stage and the footlights with the proscenium—essentially the way all theatres were thereafter constructed. The picture-frame stage was complete.

Clara Morris's glory years were gone forever. She had lost the allegiance of more demanding playgoers, long since dismayed by her inability or refusal to develop her great native talents. Nonetheless, she clung to a faithful following that was still eager to pack theatres for her appearances. These faithful no doubt were satisfied when she began a week's stand at the Grand Opera. Her program consisted of several old favorites—*Article 47, The New Magdalen,* and *Alixe*—and one new play, **Renée de Moray** (10-20-87, Grand Opera). Technically the play was not all that new. It had been seen the preceding season in a version called *The Martyr Mother* and would soon be seen again in a more significant production under its original French title.

On the 24th *Caste* was revived at Wallack's to take the place of *The Mouse Trap.* That same night Frederick Warde came into the Windsor for a week. His repertory offered *Galba, Virginius,* and *Damon and Pythias,* plus one novelty, **Gaston Cadol** (10-26-87, Windsor). This was Celia Logan's redaction of *Jean Dacier,* a tragedy in which a commoner attempts to rise through love and bravery. Because Americans were reputed to prefer "tragedy with a happy ending," Miss Logan altered the denoue-

ment, but the change could not give the play any vast appeal.

The month's finale offered excitement of a special sort—the professional debut in America of a lady known variously as Mrs. Potter, Mrs. Brown-Potter, or Mrs. Potter-Brown. This merry-go-round of names apparently stemmed from a celebrated lawsuit in which the lady's pesky brother-in-law, a minister, sued to prevent her from besmirching the family name when she went on the stage. Before her marriage she had been Cora Urquhart, daughter of a wealthy New Orleans man. Her marriage vastly increased her wealth but in no way diminished her striking beauty or her reputation as a superb dresser. She had appeared in numerous amateur productions before braving London the previous spring. Her vehicle now was Alfred Delpit's **Mademoiselle de Bressier** (10-31-87, Fifth Ave.), a saga of lovers who triumph over family hatreds and pledges of vengeance, which she had performed in London under the title *Civil War.* Kyrle Bellew was her leading man. Reviewers condemned the complicated plot but were divided on the star's abilities. Even the most critical allowed that she was no longer a "windmill . . . sawing the air," as she had been in her amateur days. Whatever her shortcomings, high society of the era packed the house to encourage her, despite her unhappy brother-in-law's misgivings.

All in all, October had been a barren month for American dramaturgy. November would be a little better, bringing one new American work and one quasi-American play.

David Belasco and Henry C. de Mille's **The Wife** (11-1-87, Lyceum) officially inaugurated the season for the stock company at the theatre, although many of the players had appeared in the earlier double bill there. Though these players were not yet as well known as those at Daly's, they, too, were greeted effusively as they made their first entrances. The story the authors had provided for them was not new. Critics pointed to similar motifs in *The Banker's Daughter, Pique,* and other plays. Helen Truman (Georgia Cayvan) rejects Robert Gray (Henry Miller) when she discovers he has jilted another girl. Instead she agrees to marry Senator John Rutherford (Herbert Kelcey), although in her heart she knows she still loves Gray. Later the senator arranges a political appointment for Gray, only to get wind of a rumor that his wife had inveigled the appointment because of her continuing warm feelings for her former suitor. Rutherford confronts Helen in his library, which is lit only by the moonlight pouring through the window and the glow from a dying fire in the fireplace. She confesses, but his reaction is one of tenderness and understanding: "Don't hang your head. What you did, you thought was for the best." As she leaves to go to bed he adds, "God—bless—you and give—you—rest." When she has gone, the moon passes behind a cloud and the fire goes out. Rutherford sinks abstractedly into his armchair. The confession has served as a catharsis. Afterwards, when he is planning to go on a trip, she begs to accompany him, insisting, "There is no life for me except when you are near." He is glad to acquiesce. The *Herald* called *The Wife* "a good play of American life, serious in its purpose, yet with its emotional scenes relieved by pleasant comedy . . . well written and quick in action, the interest never being allowed to flag." A careful production and fine ensemble acting furthered the play's attraction, and it ran out the season, compiling 239 performances.

The Railroad of Love (11-1-87, Daly's) ran less than half as long, only 108 performances, but clearly was no less appealing as an evening in the theatre. Only Daly's insistent policy of turning over productions curtailed its stand. As was his wont, Daly's brother Americanized the work from a German original, von Schönthan and Kadelburg's *Goldfische*. Phenix Scuttleby (James Lewis), an aging man-about-town, bewails, "Man alive! it's railroad time with women nowadays. If you are loaded with millions, you may court on way-freight time, or a particularly fascinating fellow may jog along on accommodation schedule. But the daredevil in love will flash across the switches, through the tunnels, and around curves with a strong heart and no flinching." In this mile-a-minute world Lieutenant Howell Everett (John Drew) pursues Viva Van Riker (Phoebe Russell) until he recognizes that she prefers the struggling artist Benny Demaresq (Otis Skinner). He then turns his attentions to Mrs. Valentine Osprey (Ada Rehan), a rich, beautiful widow. His only obstacle is a clause in her husband's will that disinherits her if she remarries and gives his estate to Scuttleby, unless Scuttleby marries first. That seems highly unlikely until events and friends conspire to foist Scuttleby on Eutycia Laburnam (Mrs. Gilbert), a country dowager who craves "a change from the eternal birds and crickets" and air with "not a trace of ozone."

Odell remembered the entertainment as "the most exquisite comedy I ever saw at Daly's." One scene he recalled with particular affection had the lieutenant waiting for Valentine while she dressed in an adjoining room. "Bidden to examine the photograph album on the table, he casually turns the pages till she calls from the adjoining room, asking

him what he thinks of her photograph in the book. Taking the cue, he finds the picture, slips it into his pocket, and replies there is no likeness of her in the album. She protests, comes to the door, sees what he had done, and in the silvery Rehan voice and with the inimitable Rehan smile, says in an aside (asides were permitted in those happy pre-Ibsen days), 'The wretch!' " Another charming bit had the lieutenant dutifully learning how to embroider, bending over the frame and counting "one, two, three, four, cross" as he bungled the assignment. The production included a pavane danced by the entire company dressed in costumes half-Elizabethan, half-modern. Daly would revive the play several times.

Another major opening followed apace—the return of Henry Irving, Ellen Terry, and their renowned company on the Star on the 7th. The schedule included W. G. Wills's version of *Faust*, a double bill of *The Bells* and *Jingle* (a sketch derived from *Pickwick Papers*), *Louis XI*, and *The Merchant of Venice*. Once again American critics performed somersaults in praise of the exceptional mountings, of Miss Terry's incomparable charm and talent, and of the excellent supporting cast. And once again they greeted with modified rapture Irving's obvious assets and his equally obvious eccentricities.

Some intrepid playgoers may have experienced a sense of déjà vu watching **The Martyr** (11-10-87, Madison Square), for it had already been seen in other translations as *The Martyr Mother* and *Renée de Moray*. Just as it had in d'Ennery's French original, the story recounted the attempts of a lady of position to keep secret the fact that her mother also has had a son—out of wedlock. Even a fine cast that included J. H. Stoddart, Alexander Salvini, E. M. Holland, William Davidge, Agnes Booth, and Annie Russell could not whet American appetites, so the production was soon withdrawn.

Mrs. Brown-Potter had a second exhibition ready with Ross Neil's **Loyal Love** (11-14-87, Fifth Ave.), an English play written in archaic blank verse and telling of a lady who risks death rather than be unfaithful to her fiancé. One week was all it was accorded.

Wallack's, evidently in trouble, resurrected Robertson's once popular *School* with John Gilbert welcomed back to the footlights as Dr. Sutcliffe. More welcome still was the return at the 14th Street Theatre on the 21st of Denman Thompson in *The Old Homestead* for a month's engagement. On the same night, Jefferson came into Niblo's in *Rip Van Winkle*, a limited one-week stand.

An elaborately mounted dramatization of Rider Haggard's **She** (11-26-87, Niblo's) straddled the

Act Two : 1879–1892

fence between drama and musical. It competed for critical attention with another hurried revival at Wallack's, this time *Forget-Me-Not*. And so November straggled to a close.

As recently as the 1980s Broadway revisited a musical Camelot, but not even with numerous playhouses sitting idle for whole seasons would it probably have considered a lavish mounting based on Tennyson's Arthurian poetry. Yet the sometimes adventurous Palmer did just that with **Elaine** (12-6-87, Madison Square), which George Parsons Lathrop and Harry Edwards had adapted for the stage and which had been tried out a season earlier at a special matinee with encouraging results. Annie Russell made an exquisite, believable heroine, and many of the applauded stage pictures were based on then famous paintings of the story. While such a presentation may have seemed theatrical caviar, Palmer was able to keep it on the boards for over a month.

Back in October, at another of those trial matinees then so popular, an aspiring young actress had made her New York debut. Now, on the same stage just vacated by Irving and Terry, she began her first starring engagement. Thus New York was given its first real exposure to the beauty and artistry of Julia Marlowe.

. . .

Julia Marlowe (1866–1950) was born in England but raised in America, to which her father had fled after injuring a neighbor in an altercation. Her real name was Sarah Frances Frost, but the family changed its name on coming to the New World, and she made her first theatrical appearance under the name Fanny Brough when she played in one of the many children's companies of *H.M.S. Pinafore* in 1879. Subsequently she acted with the touring company run by Colonel R. E. J. Miles. She has been described as "of medium height, slender and frail of aspect, with a pale and rather sallow face, great, dark, and wistful eyes, a head that seemed too big for her body, beautiful dark-brown hair."

. . .

Her program at the Star beginning on the 12th was brave, opening with *Romeo and Juliet* and, within its single week, moving on to *Ingomar* and *Twelfth Night*. Critics were unanimous in extolling her beauty and charm, but most felt she was a highly promising newcomer whose promise had yet to be fulfilled.

Outlying theatres remained home to much native drama. Some of these plays attempted to wrap themselves in an ersatz cachet of sophistication by relating the adventures of highborn Europeans.

However, most were content to deal with Americans not unlike those sitting on the other side of the footlights. Many were farce-comedies, but those with more dramatic pretensions usually fell into one of three categories: homespun regional comedy-dramas, prototypical westerns, or melodramatic, almost Dickensian looks at the horrors of city life. Walter S. Sanford's **Under the Lash** (12-12-87, Third Ave.) belonged to the last of these. It was set in the Italian area of New York's slums, where the villain persecutes a little blind girl, Marie, until she is rescued by the hero and his two cunning, intrepid dogs, Hector and Hero. The human hero was portrayed by the author. While the best stages may have been forever locked to him, Sanford, his drama, and his mutts trekked from lesser house to lesser house for several seasons.

On the 19th Mansfield came into the Fifth Avenue for the second of three visits he would make during the season. Most of his month-long stand was given over to *Dr. Jekyll and Mr. Hyde*, but *Monsieur* and *A Parisian Romance* were also on the roster briefly.

At the Star on the same night, Miss Marlowe gave way to Mr. and Mrs. Florence. Preseason announcements had suggested that they would offer a new play, *Uncle Bob*, in which Florence would portray an uncouth westerner courting an eastern widow. Its reception on the road prompted the couple to discard it, so their two-week stay offered only three old standbys—*Our Governor, Dombey and Son,* and *The Mighty Dollar*—all of which were sufficient to please mightily their many admirers.

By far the month's most interesting premiere was Steele MacKaye's **Paul Kauvar; or, Anarchy** (12-24-87, Standard). Inspired in part by MacKaye's anger over what he perceived to be the unfair trial and execution of the Chicago anarchists some months before, it first had been tried out under the title *Anarchy*. That was dropped to a subtitle in order to avert charges of trading on headlines. MacKaye's exceedingly complicated plot centered on Paul Kauvar (Joseph Haworth), a commoner who had risen to high rank in the French Revolution. But Kauvar is repelled by the upheaval's swift plunge into terror, so he attempts to harbor, under aliases, the Duc de Beaumont (Edwin Varrey) and his daughter, Diane (Annie Robe), whom he secretly marries. The treacherous former Marquis de Vaux, who now passes under the name Gouroc (Wilton Lackaye), betrays the duke and arranges to have it appear that Kauvar signed the death warrant. To prove his innocence Kauvar is willing to take his father-in-law's place at the guillotine. However, both men escape, although Kauvar is captured by royalists. He switches places with a royalist general, whom he allows to flee, and is united with Diane just as word arrives of Robespierre's death and the end of the reign of terror.

MacKaye's brilliantly staged mob scenes were a highlight of the production. Years later Belasco would recall, "It was the first genuine, thrilling mob we ever had. . . . It was a surging, thrilling, hideous mob, where every one had to act like a great artist to the minutest detail. There were women, men, children, old people—sprawling, starving—and wild, frenzied leaders—tremendous!" Critical judgments of the play were equally enthusiastic. Nym Crinkle (A. C. Wheeler) of the *Sun* called it "ruddy at times with the tongues of promethean fire . . . a work of great propulsive power, of genuine creative ingenuity, of massive dramatic effectiveness." Yet for all his mechanical inventiveness and for all his forward-looking ideas as a dramatist, MacKaye could not untangle himself from obsolescent theatrical encumbrances. Like so much of his work, *Paul Kauvar* is as resolutely retrograde as it is advanced. Thus it has little appeal to modern tastes. But contemporaries rarely took such a view. As a result the play ran profitably for over three months, a long run then for so serious a work.

Two nights later—on the 26th—two of the greatest luminaries of the contemporary stage, Booth and Barrett, joined forces in an elaborate mounting of *Julius Caesar* at the Academy of Music. Both men were long familiar with their roles, Brutus and Cassius, and by now brought to them a special ease and grace as well as force. During their two-week stand they were supported by E. J. Buckley as Marc Antony and John A. Lane as Caesar. While critics and audiences exulted, not everyone was happy.

The actor Milton Nobles saw another side to the pair's triumphant tour around the country. In an article for the *Dramatic Mirror* at season's end he bewailed, "This is an era of 'trusts' and 'combines,' and the Booth-Barrett tour was a mammoth 'trust,' and the local managers and more humble attractions have been the victims. . . . The clerk, bookkeeper, artist, artisan and small tradesman, with incomes ranging from nine hundred to two or three thousand a year, are the main support of the drama. They allow themselves a certain amount of money during the season for amusement. To see the Booth-Barrett 'combine' cost them just five times what it would cost to see Louis James, Annie Pixley, Fred Warde, Maggie Mitchell, or Milton Nobles. . . . So great an event demands unusual preparation in the matter of toilets, gloves, carriages etc., for wife or sweetheart. All of these extra expenses must be met by rigid economy before the coming, and total abstinence after the departure of the great 'combine.' In point of fact, the one attraction has absorbed the amusement fund for the season."

Nobles's curious complaint, no doubt partially self-serving, betrays his somewhat narrow theatrical view. The stars he names, including Maggie Mitchell at this late moment in her career, were hardly considered prime New York attractions. They were road stars. And his audience seems to contain none of the more affluent playgoers who regularly patronized first-class houses both in New York and in other large cities and whose budgets would scarcely have been cramped by a visit to the Booth-Barrett production. Yet this cannot negate some small truth in Nobles's perspective. Those who look back on a bygone theatre they see as more high-minded and less greedy might pause and ponder.

Because of the Booth-Barrett premiere, Henry Pettitt and Augustus Harris's **A Run of Luck** (12-26-87, Niblo's) was forced to accept second-string critics. But the flux of fashion also hurt the production. Not many seasons earlier, Drury Lane melodramas were such a rage that even the prestigious Wallack's succumbed to the vogue. But elite audiences had had their surfeit. Still, the gallery gods could and did rejoice. In this saga of racing chicanery, with real horses (six of them) again onstage, Harry Copsley (Forrest Robinson) must outmaneuver the devious, perfidious Captain Trevor (Frank Losee). To heighten interest celebrated jockeys, most notably "Snapper" Garrison ("the American Archer"), were brought in for guest appearances. The play ran for more than a month.

Selina Dolaro, the singing actress, turned playwright again with **In the Fashion** (12-26-87, Wallack's). Like so many contemporary American plays, the story unfolded for no good reason in Europe, where wives recklessly spend their husbands' money on expensive gowns and baubles. Those expensive gowns were a prime attraction, especially at matinees. The play's forced run was another nail in the faltering Wallack's coffin.

England and France were the sources of most of the major offerings seen at the beginning of the new year, 1888. In **Heart of Hearts** (1-16-88, Madison Square), Henry Arthur Jones's drama, the romance of poor Lucy Robins (Marie Burroughs) and rich Harold Fitzralph (Louis Massen) is nearly derailed when she is accused of stealing a ruby, which actually was heisted by her convict father, Daniel (C. P. Flockton). The play ran two and a half months.

The same night offered Frank Daniels in A. C.

Gunter's **Little Puck** (1-16-88, 14th St.). Daniels portrayed a father who must take his young son's place at school. The show was sprinkled with songs and dances and, like an increasing number of attractions, thus straddled the fence between straight play and musical. Many such pieces came in and out of lesser theatres. For example, about the same time, Jennie Yeamans was making the rounds of combination houses as the hoydenish heroine of Clay M. Greene's **Our Jennie.** For all their musical interludes these productions generally still were treated as farces or dramas by those critics who deigned to review them. Comic opera aside, it was hard for these tradition-bound critics to realize a new genre had sprung up.

L'Abbé Constantin (1-20-88, Wallack's) was Clinton Stuart's translation of Hector Crémieux and Pierre Decourcelle's dramatization of Halévy's novel. The glue that held its frail plot together was the shy love affair between a rich American heiress (whose even richer sister has purchased an old chateau) and the impecunious godson of the abbé. But the center of attention was most often the lovable old abbé, and the character gave John Gilbert, then approaching his seventy-eighth birthday, his last new role. Yet his fine performance was not enough to give the play more than a middling run.

Kate Claxton hoped to find a successor to her perpetual *Two Orphans* in Frank Harvey's **The World Against Her** (1-26-88, People's). "Her" is Madge Carlton, whose husband deserts her, whose child is stolen, and who is reduced to living off the charity of some kindly strolling players. The play was clearly no *Two Orphans,* but it did play Niblo's later in the season, and Miss Claxton was able to tour with it for several seasons.

Modjeska, like other performers before and since, had developed a bad habit of regularly announcing her retirement. Time would show these farewell performances were not farewells, but audiences attending her two-week engagement at the 14th Street Theatre beginning on January 30 could not be sure. What they could be sure of was most of her repertory: *Camille, As You Like It, Donna Diana, Much Ado About Nothing, Romeo and Juliet,* and her first New York appearances in two plays, *Cymbeline* and *Measure for Measure.* In each of these Shakespearean rarities Modjeska retained virtually the full text, although she reined in *Measure for Measure*'s most outlandish comedy. One critic called her Isabella, so beautiful dressed in the white robes of a novitiate, virtually "perfect." Her Imogen was lauded for her precise blending of dignity and pathos with

an almost girlish warmth and curiosity. Praise was also handed to the handsome Robert Taber (Julia Marlowe's first husband) for his Pisanio and Claudio, but critics were less in accord about the merits of other supporting players. At least one man complained about the scenery, apparently made to do service in more than one production and therefore not always right for the circumstances.

More Shakespeare was in store to close out the month when Daly presented his long-heralded version of *A Midsummer Night's Dream* on the 31st. For years afterwards it was recalled as one of the masterpieces of Daly's era and one of the great 19th-century American Shakespearean revivals. Against Henry Hoyt's exquisitely detailed, carefully painted scenic realism (romantic realism, to be sure) Ada Rehan was a "graceful," "sweet," "fruity" Helena; Virginia Dreher a "loving and lovable" Hermia; John Drew a "gallant" Demetrius; and Otis Skinner a "manly" Lysander. Both men were singled out time and again for their impeccable diction. James Lewis's Bottom was lauded as "one of the richest bits of low comedy our stage has ever known . . . nimble and quaint." Alice Wood was Oberon, Bijou Fernandez was Puck, and Effie Shannon was Titania. Reminiscing, Odell could recall that "Daly followed the custom of giving a moving panorama, this time on the return from the enchanted woods to Athens. The actors did not look particularly comfortable sitting or standing in the stationary boat while the scenery slid by."

Yet even contemporary critics were beginning to balk at such heavy-handed scenery, although the real rebellion was still decades away. Thus the *Times* observed, "The poetry of Shakespeare, intelligently spoken, conveys more than the use of painted pictures, ingenious grouping, rich dresses, and clever mechanism can possibly convey." But these were quibbles about a production that, for its own time, was as fine as one could ask. The revival played to crowded houses until Daly closed his season at the end of April.

Three weeks passed before another major opening, and then playgoers were treated to the return of Irving and Terry. Whether such returns reflected the theory that ticket buyers preferred to space out their visits or merely gave evidence of the often curious, geographically illogical theatrical circuities of the day is hard to say. Since lesser stars frequently appeared at widely spaced intervals in a single city's neighborhood houses, there is reason to suspect the latter. All that would change within a decade. Meanwhile, the English idols reopened at the Star on February 20, adding *Olivia* and *The Lyons Mail* to their schedule during their month-long stay. That same evening Wallack's, despairing of finding real success with new plays, resorted to revivals of traditional favorites. *London Assurance* was presented on the 20th, followed by *Old Heads and Young Hearts* on the 29th. Neither did well.

Between these resurrections New York saw its only premiere of the month. **Deacon Brodie; or, The Double Life** (2-27-88, Fifth Ave.), a play by Robert Louis Stevenson and W. E. Henley, had first been done in England nine years earlier. It recounted the last fifty hours of a man who is a respected citizen by day and a burglar by night. The title role was assumed by E. J. Henley, who was a brother of Stevenson's collaborator and who had created the part at the English premiere. Just what prompted the production, which had been given a trial matinee the year before, is moot. Possibly the example of *Dr. Jekyll and Mr. Hyde,* another Stevenson saga of a split personality, may have figured in the thinking. But this work was so filled with regional idioms as to be at times inaccessible to American audiences; nor was Henley in any way the bravura actor that Mansfield was. Business was so disappointing that for the final weekend of the two-week stay another play, **Fortune Hunters** (3-9-88), was substituted. It told of a rich man who leaves his estate to one of his three nieces, with the stipulation that the details of the will not be disclosed until after all three girls have married. Henley played a spendthrift with a heart of gold who lands the newly monied young lady.

The Union Square Theatre burned on February 28. Four nights later a new theatre opened, and its opening attraction announced that France would not allow the English to dominate American theatricals as they had in the preceding month. Americans are still familiar with the French play, if only as an Italian opera. Sardou's **La Tosca** (3-3-88, Broadway) starred the glamorous Fanny Davenport as the doomed prima donna. Once again she undertook a role created in Paris by the even then almost legendary Bernhardt, a practice she would continue for the rest of her career. So once again comparisons were inevitable. As usual she came out on the short end. But she was not without her virtues. One critic observed, "In the earlier scenes, even in the fit of jealousy at the castle, her acting does not count for much. The superlative wit and fascinating personality of Bernhardt are needed to make these scenes go with spirit. Miss Davenport looks well. The short waists and long straight gowns become her; she is handsome, graceful and imperious. Not until the beginning of the agony in the suburban villa,

however, did she thoroughly command the sympathy of her audience." Such reservations apparently did not deter audiences, any more than did some other critics' lamentations of immorality, although some of the dialogue between Tosca and Scarpia was toned down after the reviews appeared. Miss Davenport was rewarded with two months of very good business.

Poor waifs sequestered in derelict slums continued to be a staple of touring melodramas. Edwin A. Locke's **Never Say Die** (3-5-88, Third Ave.) was no exception, although his heroine was allowed some breath of city air, since much of the action took place on or under the Brooklyn Bridge. Innocent little Drift has put her trust in the wrong man. She should have had faith in Jack Wallingford, and she finally does after Jack rescues her from the river, into which the wrong man had just thrown her.

Before the next attractions could come in, the snow came—the Great Blizzard of '88. The openings were postponed for a night, and only two theatres, Daly's and the Star, remained lit. Both houses had sold out in advance, albeit in the event they were less than half-filled.

One of the delayed plays was another French work, Louis Nathal's translation of d'Ennery's *La Dame de St. Tropez.* Because it had been reworked as a vehicle for Robert Mantell, it was also rechristened. The titular hero of **Monbars** (3-13-88, Fifth Ave.) is a man who learns his wife married him out of gratitude (he had saved her from a rabid dog) and not for love. As it had in several recent American plays, the curtain fell with the wife professing she had, indeed, come to love her husband.

In glaring contrast to these sophisticated Gallic works was the lone American entry for the month. Fred Williams's **Maggie the Midget** (3-13-88, 14th St.) was Maggie Mitchell's newest starring piece, like her perennial *Fanchon* recounting the rise of a hoyden to a position of wealth and elegance. Even her fans felt it was inferior stuff, so matinees were given over to *Fanchon* (she had been portraying this youngster for twenty-five years) and *Jane Eyre.* David Braham wrote a few songs that helped turn the piece into another of those borderline works so plentiful at the time. But even the songs were no lure, so the show played out its two-week engagement, toured briefly, and was dropped by its star.

The night of the 13th also saw Daniel Bandmann unsuccessfully attempt his version of *Dr. Jekyll and Mr. Hyde* at Niblo's, while the desperately sinking Wallack's reached back for Thomas Morton's *Town and Country,* which had not been revived for more than a quarter of a century. In the mounting, John

Gilbert played Kit Cosey, the great city-lover who, like Eutycia Laburnam in *The Railroad of Love*, cannot stand unpolluted country air. Several critics felt that his brilliant acting sadly underscored changing styles of playing and stood in marked contrast with the less stylized playing of younger members of the company. On the 23rd *Money* reentered Wallack's bills.

The star-crossed Margaret Mather brought her repertory to Niblo's for a week, beginning on the 26th. She opened with *Romeo and Juliet*, then proceeded to *Leah, the Forsaken, The Lady of Lyons, The Honeymoon,* and *Macbeth*. Critics were cordial, if not excited; her public was reported to be enthusiastic, if not large. Nonetheless, the following week she moved to the Standard, where she added *As You Like It* to her list.

France was the source of April's openers, even if both French dramas had been reworked flagrantly. Robert Buchanan's **Partners** (4-2-88, Madison Square) was based on Daudet's *Fromont jeune et Risler aîné*, which once had served as basis for *Sidonie*. For this occasion, the wife was no longer the vicious manipulator. Instead, renamed Claire (Marie Burroughs), she was downgraded to an innocuous, almost innocent role in the story. The center of attention became her husband, whose younger partner bankrupts the company and is made to seem to be having an affair with Claire. The star of the evening was Alexander Salvini, son of the famous Tommaso, as the distraught Henry Borgfeldt. Only prior bookings forced the play's closing at month's end. The same night saw Sardou's *La Patrie* mounted under the title of *Dolores* as a spectacular musical. Clara Morris also made a brief return to the Madison Square in *Renée de Moray*.

Although Sydney Rosenfeld was better known as a lyricist, a librettist, a wit, and a gadfly, he already had made several stabs at nonmusical theatre pieces. His latest was **A Possible Case** (4-9-88, Standard), a farce about multiple marriages (without benefit of divorce) and the conflicting marriage laws in several states and territories. Violet Archer Mendoza's husband was kidnapped several years ago, and she assumes he is dead. Violet (Genevieve Lytton) currently is being courted by Otto Brinckerhoff (M. A. Kennedy), whose wife, Ethel, deserted him three years ago, which means he must wait two more years before he is considered free by New York law. Violet is also sought after by Allan Weeks (Robert Hilliard) and by Lawrence Gould (F. M. Burbeck). Allan's friend, Dick Hertel (E. D. Tannehill), courts Gladys Winston (Lelia Wolstan), daughter of Otto's lawyer. Ethel (Dorothy Dorr) suddenly reappears,

sporting a new surname, as does Violet's husband. A confused Otto can only say, "Just a word of advice Dick, and I give it in the presence of a lawyer. When you get married to Gladys, marry her in every State of the Union or you won't know where you stand before you are at the end of your journey." However, Allan points out, "That will make it all the harder for you when you want a divorce." Otto promises to think about that. Most of the dialogue was more succinct and crisp than usual for the period.

Several critics complained that Rosenfeld began with an interesting idea, then adopted the easy road by inserting all manner of Joe Miller jokes instead of letting the humor arise fresh from the characters and situations. It was a charge critics would level with increasing vexation at the playwright in coming seasons. Playgoers apparently decided a laugh was a laugh. The comedy had originally been scheduled to follow *The Henrietta* into the Union Square, but when that house burned it was given this interim booking. It did so well that it later was transferred to the Madison Square. It then toured for most of the succeeding season.

"Drums, guns, red fire, whooping Indians, soldiers, scouts and lots of excitement" were the attractions the *Herald* assured its readers they would find in **On the Frontier** (4-9-88, Windsor), another western destined for long popularity but always denied access to better stages. Its valiant hero was one of the scouts, Jack Osborn, and his devotion to an Indian princess, Blue Flower, was the source of its adventures. Not all the Indians whooped. At intervals a Sioux Indian brass band trooped on stage to blare away. Note how Jack is becoming the name of choice for a touring melodrama's hero.

The Star next played host to a self-proclaimed tragedian, James Owen O'Conor (or O'Connor). Reviewers and playgoers dissented, seeing him rather as an unfortunate reincarnation of the late Count Joannes. All during his valiant if absurd two-week stand, which began on the 9th and offered his interpretations of *Hamlet, Othello, The Merchant of Venice, Richelieu,* and *The Marble Heart,* he was hissed, hooted, and pelted with rotten fruit and vegetables. His Hamlet seemed to jig and prance rather than walk, and when he was sitting he kicked his legs wildly for no apparent reason. To score a point with Horatio, he chucked him under the chin in the ghost scene. He stopped the play at times to lecture audiences. Then, in his death scene, he wriggled all over the stage and finally announced that since he was supposed to be dead he would not give an encore. The rest was not silence, but pandemonium. Although he never again played a major New York engagement, he did take to the road, where he performed behind a protective wire screen, thus, like Dr. Landis, presaging vaudeville's famed Cherry Sisters.

A saner, if for other reasons equally sad, spectacle was *She Stoops to Conquer* at Wallack's, also on the 9th. By now it was generally known that the company would not survive. It switched on the 18th to a favorite of the house, *The School for Scandal*, and gave its final performance on May 5th. While Daly's and other stock companies (the ensemble at the Madison Square, for example) survived, they were devoted primarily to the presentation of modern plays, Daly's occasional magnificent revival notwithstanding. The day of the older-style stock company, which regularly maintained a backlog of "classic" plays and at times offered them in true repertory fashion, was gone forever. Admittedly Wallack's, even at its height, rarely attempted the great tragedies. That was left to the celebrated touring tragedians, who themselves were a dying breed. Nonetheless, an era was ending, taking with it the chance for playgoers to become familiar not merely with delightful bygone pieces but with the special style of playing they required.

Of course, if there had been a genuine demand for the older comedies and dramas, a group undoubtedly would have emerged to present them. Increasingly, however, American playgoers wanted only contemporary plays—a dismaying truism that remains dismayingly true a century later. Yet the jeremiads of the time, which bemoaned the proliferation of slapdash musicals and other fluff, could not be taken too seriously, given the continuing attraction of the aging Booth and his competitors. But fluff continued to attract as well and was beautifully exemplified by the era's most popular female impersonator, Neil Burgess, who romped into the Standard on the 23rd with two popular vehicles, *Vim* and *The Widow Bedott*. Burgess, unlike the grand tragedians, was not a member of a dying breed, but his successors would find a steadier paycheck in musicals, not straight plays.

The predictable, if not always warranted, vogue for English plays and the condescension accorded serious native efforts were made manifest again at the beginning of May, albeit with a twist. Some respected performers could not camouflage the weaknesses of Arthur Law and Fergus Hume's London melodrama **The Mystery of a Hansom Cab** (5-7-88, Academy of Music), which allowed two serio-comic detectives to absolve two innocents and pin a murder on the real villain, and which was trashed by critics, who branded it "dramatic rubbish" and "dull and stupid." Yet the *Dramatic Mirror* reported it enjoyed good business for its single week.

Not so James A. Herne's **Drifting Apart** (5-7-88, People's). Most critics did not deign to review it, and it struggled along for two weeks to empty houses. Herne's wife is reported to have pawned her jewelry to keep the play going on tour. Admittedly, People's was not a first-class house and so not likely to attract reviewers. At the same time, however, it and similar auditoriums regularly offered American plays that, like Herne's work, were refused better stages. Whether these plays were tryouts or simply touring attractions, they merited some attention and consideration if American dramaturgy were to grow in stature. Herne himself portrayed his hero, Jack Hepburne, a man so ashamed of his slavery to drink that he leaves his wife, Mary (Katharine Corcoran Herne), and child and runs off to sea. There he is first shipwrecked and then captured by Chinese pirates. When he returns home years later, he finds Mary is about to remarry. He takes her away, but she and their daughter die of starvation, and their death drives Jack mad. Picking up Mary's body, he says, "Let's go home, back to the old home in Gloucester—(*Kisses her*). Poor child—I have so loved—so wronged you. But I'll make amends—I'll drink no more, come. Mother, be sure to put plenty of onions in the stuffin'—Mother—see—here's Mary—she's not well, poor girl—quick, food. She's starvin', I tell you—come Mary, we'll go home—home—home." Happily for Jack, the deaths of Mary and his child are only a dream. The curtain falls as the family stands around a warm Christmas fire, singing the temperance song "Turn Your Glasses Upside Down."

Because Herne's play was preachy and riddled with all the obsolescent dramatic clichés of the time, he was not yet perceived as a purposeful playwright attempting to break away from outmoded traditions. Herne's biographer also suggests that audiences felt cheated, having been tricked into expending emotions on a tear-jerking dream sequence. Yet Herne persisted in touring with the play whenever he could obtain a booking and enough money to assemble a production. However, major acclaim was not far in the future.

Ned Buntline and Ed Chapman's **Queen of the Plains** (5-14-88, Windsor) was another western stubbornly relegated to neighborhood and small-town theatres. Its star was six-foot-tall Kate Purssell. She played a pistol-packing Calamity Jane bent on avenging her mother's killing. This was no small task, since five badmen had to be accounted for. Horses and dogs provided a certain theatrical verisimilitude. But audiences apparently never questioned the verisimilitude of the dialogue, such as one villain's warning, "Breathe a word of my disguise and in a second the leaden messenger of death will sink into your heart and stop its throbbing forever."

Far less to the liking of the backwaters was Robert Johnston's **Inez: or, a Wife's Secret** (5-14-88, Theatre Comique, Harlem). Julia Anderson starred as a woman who, thinking her first husband is dead, remarries. The play was set in Europe.

One more American play rounded out the month. Charles Gayler's **Lights and Shadows** (5-21-88, Standard) recounted the tribulations of Mark Milburn (J. H. Gilmour), who is falsely accused of a crime he did not commit, nearly loses his sweetheart as a result, and must recover his long-lost sister. Threadworn drivel perhaps, but Gayler was a knowledgeable hack, and so his play held the boards for several seasons—primarily in road houses.

At the end of May the *Times* published an equally age-old threnody, keening over the decline of great playwriting. Although most of the long article, headlined "Where is the Dramatist?" focused on the dearth of good English drama, it noted that Booth had never acted in a new American play (at least not since he became a star), that Barrett had despaired of finding acceptable new American works, and that even Daly, "our foremost American manager," had to resort to translating German plays. But no real remedy was suggested and no real hope held out. Indeed, for all the references to American playwriting, the now established Bronson Howard and his struggling compatriots went unmentioned, and the implication of the article was actually that when and if more good plays were forthcoming they would probably come from England.

An instance of why the *Times* held out so little hope for American drama could have been witnessed in Leonard Grover's **Lost in New York** (6-4-88, Bijou). In fact, the newspaper singled it out as an example of the sort of third-rate piece that first-class houses (such as the Bijou, usually given over to musicals) booked only late in the season to avoid dark weeks. Everything about the attraction seemed derivative. Its title must have reminded some playgoers of *Lost in London,* an older touring show. And its highly touted lure, a huge tank of water, once again did duty as a stretch of river. Of course, this time the river was the East River. And once again the hero must rescue a waif from the cold water, where another copycat villain has tossed her. The rescued girl is reunited with her long-lost, blind

mother. However unoriginal, the play appealed to a certain public, so toured for several years.

Charles Foster's **Under Cover** (6-4-88, Windsor) was not much better, if any. But it was designed primarily as a vehicle for George C. Boniface, whose fans were pleased and unquestioning. Boniface played Jerry Jummel, another serio-comic detective, whose aliases and disguises help right a multitude of wrongs. The play toured all of the next season.

An example of a touring American comedy was S. M. Monroe's **Parvenus** (6-4-88, Amphion Academy, Brooklyn). It offered one more example of Americans abroad. A family weighted down with money from a Colorado mine arrive in Paris and are nearly stripped of all their wealth by Parisian sharpers. The timely appearance of the sheriff of Slippery Gulch sets matters straight.

For seekers of more elevated fare, Mansfield came back to the Madison Square on the same evening and during his month's visit revived *Dr. Jekyll and Mr. Hyde, Prince Karl,* and *A Parisian Romance.*

Despite its title, Edwin Atwell's **His Lordship** (6-11-88, Standard) was an American play, even if it sought an instant cachet by making its hero a visiting English nobleman. Lord Blushington (H. M. Pitt) falls in love with an American girl, Kitty Saginaw (Lillian Chantore), but his duplicitous valet, Carrick (Mark Price), resorts to dirty tricks to try to scuttle the courtship and almost weds Kitty himself by pretending to have saved her life. Many critics thought Philip Goatcher's settings were the evening's best feature. These included an elegant boudoir and a recreation of the exterior of an actual New Rochelle church and its neighboring street. All this and the added inducement of a theatre "cooled by iced air" were not enough to secure the play's success.

William R. Wilson, a newspaperman, and his brother James were the authors of **Among the Pines** (6-11-88, People's). Captain Allen Hearty (Eben Plympton), a young seaman, loves Marion Dalton (Helen Windsor), the daughter of his employer, but Luke Lergott (P. Augustus Anderson), a sailor Hearty has discharged, convinces Marion that Hearty is untrue to his vows. She sends him away. Years pass, and after her father's failure she takes work as a schoolmarm. She is courted by a handsome lumberman who goes by the name Jim Blanchard and who she fails to recognize is really her old lover. This time he wins her. Although the critic for the *Sun* complained that the performers' accents were not Down East but a "cross between

Mississippi and Kansas," he and most other reviewers liked the play. Yet its career was short.

Henry A. Du Souchet, a newspaperman turned actor turned playwright, who would eventually find some success writing comedies, tried his skills with a melodrama called **Dollars and Hearts** (6-25-88, Windsor). His story dealt with efforts to retrieve a stolen lottery ticket. Critics and theatregoers alike gave it short shrift.

Several actresses of the period, rocketed to fame by a single early role, were to spend the remainder of their careers looking for a similar such piece. One was Kate Claxton. Another was Effie Ellsler. It was Miss Ellsler's misfortune to strike out twice in July. She first appeared in **The Keepsake** (7-2-88, Madison Square), Clinton Stuart's reworking of Raymond Deslandes's *Antoinette Rigaud,* a Parisian hit that subsequently had failed in London and at the Boston Museum. One reason for its failure may have been the underlying absurdity of its main scene. It was the sort of situation that might still appeal to some Victorians but that modern writers would have to rework as farce. Stuart's heroine, now called Christine Leroy, is married to a prosperous businessman. However, she once had written love letters to a young artist. He gallantly attempts to give them back to her when her husband is away—by climbing through her bedroom window at night. Naturally the husband returns at that moment from a trip, and the artist must hide under her bed and then in a closet. Stuart's dialogue was no help, running to such lines as "Miserable woman that I am! What shall I do?" With the play's quick failure the star turned to Frank Harvey's **Judge Not** (7-30-88, Madison Square). In this English play she portrayed Katherine Clare, an actress who abandons the stage for a man who at first proves unloving. Although she returns to the stage and becomes famous, her loyalty and goodness ultimately win her husband's respect and affection. Once more, however, Miss Ellsler's public was unreceptive.

"Serio-comic" had become a buzzword for critics during the season, which ended on an upbeat note for playgoers and, to a lesser extent, for American dramaturgy with William Gillette's serio-comic **The Legal Wreck** (8-14-88, Madison Square). In the New England village of Gap Harbor, old Cap'n Edward Smith (Alfred Hudson) lives in a parlor painted to resemble the bottom of the sea. His reading consists of outdated shipping journals. His adopted daughter, Olive (Nina Boucicault), is pursued by two men, the captain's loutish, brutal son, Ed (George Fawcett), and a handsome Boston brahmin, Henry B. Leverett (Boyd Putnam). At one point Ed tries to

have Olive kidnapped. At another, Ed and Henry have a knockdown-dragout struggle at the edge of a cliff. Henry throws Ed over the cliff and is led by a young lawyer, Richard Merriam (Sidney Drew), to believe he has killed Ed. When, at Richard's urging, Henry goes off to inform the police, Richard pulls the stunned but otherwise unhurt Ed up from below and leads him, in turn, to think he has killed his rival. A happy ending includes Olive's being reunited with her long-lost mother and sister. Originally booked as a summer filler, the play ran well into the autumn.

1888–1889

If summer dog days cramped theatricals, they could not totally discourage them. Established stars and stock players might desert the sweltering city for cooler haunts at the seashore or in the mountains, but managers continued to keep theatres open and more or less profitable, attempting to lure determined entertainment seekers with promises of ice-cooled air (barely perceptible), with mountings of plays deemed too uncertain for the height of the season, and with up-and-coming players anxious for a better chance in the limelight. As often as not, this was the time when newer American plays were given an opportunity. Actually, though many contemporary commentators failed to grasp the fact, important young American playwrights were coming increasingly to the fore. By now Steele MacKaye and Bronson Howard were well established, but James A. Herne, Augustus Thomas, William Gillette, Henry C. de Mille, and David Belasco also were carving out enduring niches for themselves. Gillette again had shown his mettle at the close of the previous season. De Mille and Belasco had a new play ready to launch the coming one.

Their offering might more precisely be termed a vehicle, since it was composed expressly to display the comic talents of a rising young performer with a famous name—E. H. Sothern.

. . .

E[dward] H[ugh] **Sothern** (1859–1933) was the son of E. A. Sothern. Although born in New Orleans, he was educated in England, where he planned a career as a painter. When he changed his mind, he made his debut in New York in 1879 as a cabman in his father's *Brother Sam.* He was apparently slightly smaller than his father but was considered handsomer and so was often assigned romantic leading-man roles. He toured with John McCullough and others before joining the Lyceum Theatre ensemble. Coincidentally, his leap into stardom came just months after that of Julia Marlowe, whom he would eventually marry and with whom he would share much of his theatrical glory.

. . .

To capitalize on the celebrity of the elder Sothern's Lord Dundreary, de Mille and Belasco centered the new vehicle on another English lord, thereby also allowing for another voguish English setting. They called their play **Lord Chumley** (8-20-88, Lyceum). Young Lord Cholmondeley (Sothern) is a seeming ne'er-do-well. His best friend is Lieutenant Gerald Hugh Butterworth (Frank Carlyle), who is known simply as Hugh, and his great love is Hugh's sister, Eleanor (Belle Archer), who haughtily disdains his love. What Chumley and Hugh's family do not know is that Hugh is an inveterate gambler and, to pay his debts, has stolen money his regiment collected for a fellow officer's widow. The evidence of the crime has fallen into the hands of Gasper Le Sage (Herbert Archer), who holds it over Hugh so that Hugh will promote Gasper's courtship of Eleanor. When Hugh goes off to fight the Zulu insurgency, Chumley discovers the situation. He contrives to reimburse the widow, even though it means he must live in relatively spartan rooms, and he eventually manages to cow a burglar who discloses that Gasper is an escaped convict. With this information he sets matters aright and wins Eleanor's affections.

Dialogue in the play ran to such give and take as:

Lord C: I have been crossed in love.
Lady A: Never mind, there are more fish in the sea.
Lord C: I don't want to marry a fish.

This choice tidbit comes while Lady Adeline (Fanny Addison), Eleanor's fat, middle-aged aunt, mistakenly thinks Chumley loves her. It clearly struck an 1888 funnybone, for the *Herald* commended the play as "clever and ingenious." But for all the knowing professionalism of the writing, the *Post* summed up the consensus by noting, "Sothern's triumph was the chief feature." Many of Sothern's most applauded moments were little more than "business" in the authors' text. He held the burglar at bay with a pipe he pretended was a gun; he filled a coal scuttle by doing a backward somersault through a trapdoor; and he cavorted with a tickling feather duster. The play ran three months before embarking on tour, and Southern was able to return to it as late as 1897.

Another American hit was Mary Fiske's **Philip Herne** (8-27-88, Fifth Ave.). Its hero (Joseph Haworth), despite the knowledge that he is illegitimate, accepts blame for a murder he believes his mother's husband has committed. He is sentenced to prison, finally escapes, and, after years of destitution and wandering, becomes a successful businessman. The long arm of coincidence allows him to discover that one of his employees was the actual killer. Through all this only the devoted Evelyn Armitage (Helen Russell) remains loyal. But even now his troubles are not at an end. A treacherous cousin who loves Evelyn threatens to expose him and have him returned to prison. He too, however, is put in his place in time for a happy ending (underscored by soft music, as one reviewer reported). Critics found the play disjointed and episodic but filled with good and intelligent dialogue and excellent characterizations. They were especially pleased by the delineation of the practical, independent, yet steadfast Evelyn. The show was such a surprise hit that it had to be moved to another playhouse to finish a ten-week run, but the road apparently was not as welcoming.

Three nights later *The Old Homestead* was brought into the huge Academy of Music. Its return attested to the gradually increasing, if not yet fully appreciated, assertion of American rights to American stages. The revival was lavish: real cattle and real bales of hay were used in the farm scenes; Hopkins's mansion seemed "something like the private palace of a modern Nero" to one critic, who speculated there was "probably nothing so luxurious in real life east of Chicago"; and Goatcher's recreation of Grace Church was thunderously applauded. Reviews were more than raves, they were downright loving, hailing the work as "noble" and "poetic." And of course there were paeans aplenty for Denman Thompson's time-tested Josh Whitcomb. Not even the long intermissions required to change the cumbersome sets daunted playgoers. The superb production, the play's fame, and the ecstatic reviews all combined to give the show a startling season-long run of 277 performances. (It would return after a summer respite in 1889 to an almost equally extended stand.)

But *The Old Homestead* was a relatively new play. All through the season, as was the practice of the time, still older plays reappeared with some regularity, albeit usually at second-class houses. The hit today, forgotten tomorrow mentality that prevails in modern theatre had only begun to take hold. And, surprisingly perhaps, many of the works that showed the most remarkable durability were American works from a day when American works were rarely held in high esteem. Thus, along with returns of more recent foreign and domestic plays, at least two separate productions of *Uncle Tom's Cabin* came in for respectable business and often uncondescending notices. Several of Bartley Campbell's plays traversed the outer circles. Frank Mayo returned in his still highly regarded *Davy Crockett*. Late in the season *The Octoroon* was lavishly revived. And, at the Star on September 3rd, Robert Downing once again emoted as Bird's *The Gladiator*.

The promise of cooler weather meant the onset of fashionable importations. In Robert Buchanan's **Fascination** (9-10-88, 14th St.) Lady Madge Slashton (Cora Tanner) learns that the apple of her eye, Lord Islay (pronounced eye-lee, don't you know?) (Edward Bell), is falling for the snares of adventuress Rose Delemere (Eleanor Carey). So Madge stoops to conquer by disguising herself as a derbied, dapper young man and calling herself Charles Marlowe, and then showing up her rival's real stripes. In the face of divided reviews the play chalked up a fair seven-week run.

Merritt and Conquest's London melodrama *The King of the Diamonds* was revised by Belasco and Edward J. Swartz and offered to Americans as **The Kaffir Diamond** (9-11-88, Broadway), with Louis Aldrich as star. The burly, blustering actor portrayed Shoulders, a man who has sought refuge in the African wilds after believing himself wronged and his marriage destroyed by the supposed treachery of a British army officer, Richard Gauntley (Fraser Coulter). In attempting revenge, Shoulders almost wrecks the reputation and life of a lady who turns out to be the daughter he has not seen since she was a child. Only when he has trapped and doomed his imagined enemy is he made to understand that Gauntley actually has been a devoted friend. However much the gallery gods rejoiced in Shoulders's plottings, misfortunes, and final rehabilitation, critics found little to praise except for Henry Hoyt's striking scenery, which included some sober South African interiors and a mist-laden swamp eerily illuminated by ignis fatuus. Yet as one aisle-sitter observed, even Hoyt's technical know-how could not prevent the shadows of players from being cast on the canvas sky. After a short New York run, Aldrich took the play on the road, where it was immensely popular.

The Paymaster (9-17-88, Star) may well have been a vanity production. Its producer, its director, its author, and its star were one and the same—Duncan Bradley Harrison. The handsome if monotoned young actor portrayed Lieutenant Robert Emmett O'Connor, a paymaster in the British army, who finds he has a rival for his fiancée's hand in his own scowling colonel. The play's main attraction seems to have been another of those water-filled tanks that passed for a river. O'Connor was required to jump in twice, once to pull out his drenched sweetheart. Each soppy reappearance brought a storm of applause from the upper reaches of the theatre. Whether vanity or a certain popularity kept the work on the boards is uncertain, but the show played around the country steadily for several years and was revived by Harrison as late as 1899. However, its stay at the Star was a mere two weeks.

Herminie; or, The Cross of Gold (9-17-88, Windsor) was no better, but it, too, toured subsidiary circuits for several seasons. It told of a husband and wife who are separated after the wife is imprisoned for a crime she did not commit. The husband is a soldier who rises from sergeant to general before he can be reunited with his wife and the play can be over. This engagement was for a single week and was followed by Alice Lewis Johnson's **Her Husband** (9-24-88, Windsor), which recounted a similarly weepy story, with the wife once more separated from her husband (this time by another woman's lies) in the first act and not reunited until the final curtain. In both plays the wife at first returns in disguise and passes unrecognized. Like its predecessor, *Her Husband* played just one week; but unlike *Herminie,* it soon was withdrawn.

Another short-lived failure followed. **The Quick or the Dead?** (10-1-88, Fifth Ave.) was a dramatization of Amélie Rives's then recent and popular novelette. But some sort of Victorian double standard still obviously applied, for drama critics resented this story's being transferred to the stage and condemned it as "unpleasant" and "malodorous." What was the story that so disturbed these critics? It told simply the plight of Barbara Pomfret (Estelle Clayton), who is torn between her love for her dead husband and her love for his look-alike cousin.

Charles Fawcett's **Katti, the Family Help** (10-1-88, Bijou) was derived from Meilhac's *Gotte* and told of a household drudge who inherits a fortune. Larded with songs and dances, it was yet another of the era's many offerings that teetered equivocally between farce and musical comedy.

The spate of lackluster openings came to an abrupt end with a pair of premieres on two succeeding evenings. Both were more or less French, the first purely Gallic, the second adulterated. At Palmer's Theatre, which until some months before had been Wallack's, New York's playgoing cognoscenti gathered on the 8th to welcome the great Parisian comedian Constant Coquelin and the noted actress Jane Hading. Their bills included *Les Précieuses ridicules, La Joie fait peur, Le Maître de forges, L'Aventurière, Gringoire, Le Député de Bombignac, Les Surprises du divorce, Don César de Bazan, Frou-Frou, Tartuffe, Mlle. de la Seiglière, L'Etourdi, Jean Marie,* and *La Dame aux camélias.* All this, and more, in just three weeks. Some audiences were disappointed by Miss Hading, who was no Bernhardt. But others admired her sparer, more restrained interpretations. About the short, stubby Coquelin there was no dissent. He was magnificent—droll, deep, subtle, and blessed with an astonishing range. The Frenchman returned twice more later in the season, introducing still other novelties.

Theatregoers who could not understand *Les Surprises du divorce* in the original French could enjoy it in Daly's Americanized version, **The Lottery of Love** (10-9-88, Daly's). It marked another major success for Broadway's leading ensemble, by now generally acknowledged as the finest such group in the English-speaking world. Zenobia Sherramy (Mrs. Gilbert) is a "strong-minded, woman's rights, female suffrage platform apostle" who once was jailed in her youth for parading in bloomers. The years cannot mellow her. She makes life so miserable for her new son-in-law, Adolphus Doubledot (John Drew), and his bride, Diana (Sara Chalmers), that on the same day they are married they agree to a divorce. Two years later Adolphus has married Josephine (Ada Rehan), the daughter of a widower, Benjamin Buttercorn (James Lewis). Imagine Adolphus's horror when Buttercorn brings home Diana as a bride, with her bellicose mama in tow. The dear old girl again makes life so unbearable that they foist Diana on the doting Tom Dangerous (Frederick Bond), who promises to take the ladies far off—to Brazil.

Daly filled the play with bits of business that delighted his regulars. In the original, the mother-in-law had been a ballet dancer and put on her moth-eaten tutu to do some ballet steps. The producer changed that, dressing Mrs. Gilbert in faded bloomers and a little round hat and having her do an absurd hornpipe until her appalled son-in-law grabs her and hustles her offstage. Unexpectedly, Drew's Doubledot seemed to many a more polished, restrained performance than Coquelin's Doubledot (Duval in the French)—"lighter, daintier" than the Frenchman's "broad, rather violent manner." For example, when Mrs. Sherramy made her sudden, unforeseen reappearance, Drew's face told his whole reaction. Coquelin, on the other hand, grimaced vigorously and jumped up and down.

Some critics had reservations about making light of divorce and about showing a woman who marries men simply for the purpose of obtaining an alimony (although Joseph Daly's adaptation had minimized this aspect), but virtually everyone agreed audiences had a wonderful time. The comedy was still doing excellent business when Daly, as was his wont, removed it for a change of fare. But it was revived regularly for more than a decade. Because by standards of the time *The Lottery of Love* was a short play and because Ada Rehan's part was so small, the producer added a curtain raiser, Justin Huntley McCarthy's **The Wife of Socrates** (10-30-88, Daly's), derived from Théodore de Banville's play. In this Miss Rehan romped as a noisy, belligerent Xantippe until she was brought to her knees by the unyieldingly philosophic Socrates of Charles Wheatleigh. **Popping the Question** and a shortened version of *The Critic* called **Rehearsing a Tragedy** later supplanted it in turn, both as afterpieces.

A. C. Gunter was a novelist as well as a playwright, and an 1887 novel of his had become a best-seller, reputedly surpassing the million mark in sales. Given his shunting between hardcovers and footlights, it was not improbable that he should dramatize the work. But his **Mr. Barnes of New York** (10-15-88, Broadway), at least on the stage, had precious little to do with Mr. Barnes and even less with New York. Instead the spotlight usually focused on Marina Paoli (Emily Rigl), a hot-blooded Corsican. She has sworn to avenge her brother's murder and through a misunderstanding comes to believe her own suitor is the killer. A bloody mistake is narrowly averted. The emphasis on these incidents prompted Nym Crinkle of the *World* to suggest they were a more fitting subject for tragedy than for so essentially comic a play. He was further disturbed by J. H. Gilmour treating Barnes as something of a ladykiller instead of the more reserved, levelheaded American Gunter had drawn in print. But he was pleased with the colorful costumes of the Corsicans and of the French and English army officers, as well as with the sunny Mediterranean settings. For all the book's fame, it was the tiny, German-accented ex-ballerina who proved the main draw; ironically, her casting was said to have been a last-minute inspiration. Miss Rigl toured in the play for several seasons, but like Kate Claxton, Effie Ellsler, and a number of other well-liked actresses, she was to spend most of her career trying to recapture or merely retain an earlier promise or glory.

American dramaturgy was also represented the

same night by Charles Hoyt's **A Brass Monkey** (10-15-88, Bijou), another of the playwright-producer's many efforts to transform farce into musical comedy. This spoof of superstition and fetishism, by the by, had a character named "Mr. Barnes of New York."

A third offering on that busy night brought forth one more example of popular English theatricals. Tom Craven's London melodrama **The Stowaway** (10-15-88, Niblo's) moves from slum to yacht to mansion and lawn while Tom Ingliss (Walter L. Dennis), its singularly uncomprehending, self-pitying hero, tries to recoup the inheritance he wrongfully has been deprived of. His vicious cousin, Charles Ethering (Mark Lynch), plots to kill him, but his father's trusty old servant, Dickey Dials (H. Hawk), finds ways of helping him. Following two weeks at Niblo's, the show toured second-class theatres.

The public's rejection of *The Quick or the Dead?* prompted its star, Estelle Clayton, to hastily mount a substitute. **A Sad Coquette** (10-17-88, Fifth Ave.) was a dramatization of Rhoda Broughton's novel *Good-bye, Sweetheart.* Its heroine, Leonore Merritt, is cast aside by her fiancé when he discovers her dancing and flirting with another man. In despair she marries the other man but never comes to love him. He in turn proves equally unloving. On her deathbed she asks to see her old flame, but her husband hastens her end by telling her that her former lover is to be married at that very hour. For the second time in a month Miss Clayton found herself and her play thrashed by the critics, so she departed quickly.

Revivals and returns wound up the month, with four of note on the 29th. *Held by the Enemy* was at Palmer's, and Frank Mayo starred in *The Royal Guard* (*The Three Musketeers*) at the Grand Opera. Jefferson and Mrs. Drew reappeared in *The Rivals* at the Fifth Avenue, with the interesting addition of Wallack's old favorite, John Gilbert, as Sir Anthony Absolute. And the Star played host to a lavish touring revival of *A Midsummer Night's Dream,* one of several mountings of that play apparently prompted by the success of Daly's the previous season. (One with an "all-star" cast had been offered to Chicago.)

November's more interesting and prestigious openings were bunched together. First and foremost in many playgoers' eyes was the Booth-Barrett "combine," which came into the Fifth Avenue on the 12th, this time with *Othello*. There was little critics could add to their many earlier judgments of Booth's Iago and Barrett's Moor. They did call attention to the excellent crowd scenes, with real crowds, not merely, as the *Times* noted, "two unwashed Irish-Americans in baggy tights to represent the masses." Even the street pictures were carefully executed, including one with a "covered bridge across the road and the luxuriant garden to which the bridge led." Many critics, however, felt the physical production fell short of Irving's high standards. In short order *The Merchant of Venice* was added to the bills, and before the engagement was terminated in early January, *Julius Caesar* and *The Fool's Revenge* were brought out, the latter coupled variously with *The King's Pleasure, David Garrick,* or *Yorick's Love.*

Such was the power of Booth and Barrett that all other major openings for the week, which normally would have been consigned to Monday night, were postponed until Tuesday. Tradition's tug was just as strong, so most leading critics elected to review not one of the new plays on display, but yet another theatrical classicist—the young, ravishingly beautiful Mary Anderson. For her premiere on the 13th at Palmer's she bravely chose a rarely done Shakespearean comedy, *The Winter's Tale*. Still more courageously, she opted to play two parts, Hermione and Perdita. She had first essayed the roles in London at Irving's Lyceum, where she had employed Irving's set designers and costumers to brilliant effect. It was this beautiful production she brought to New York, thus in at least one respect instantly outshining Booth and Barrett's mounting. Some critics carped at her doing two roles, but since the characters meet only once and then briefly, no more than a few minor alterations of the text were required. William Winter's gushing that her interpretations were "like windows to a sacred temple" is hardly revealing, except in the most general way, but he suggests something more of her artistry when he concludes that her Hermione was "majestic, tender, pitiable, transcendent, but its color was the sombre color of pensive melancholy and sad experience" and that her Perdita "became the glittering image and incarnation of glorious, youthful womanhood and fascinating joy." Her sublime figure and face seemed all the more perfect in the simple white dress she wore in the trial scene, and, as she had in *Pygmalion and Galatea,* she made a perfect statue. Her coming to life after Paulina draws away the red curtain was a high point of the evening. She also gave a few performances of *The Lady of Lyons* and Gilbert's play. But these were her final New York appearances, for during the subsequent tour she announced her retirement to marry. Unlike so many other stage figures who regularly announced their retirements, she never returned to the footlights.

Two new plays opened the same night as *The Winter's Tale.* One was Pinero's **Sweet Lavender** (11-13-88, Lyceum), in which a young law student (Henry Miller) and the daughter of his housekeeper (Louise Dillon) find their romance nearly destroyed after the girl's mother recognizes the boy's foster parent as the girl's real father. The Lyceum cast, chosen from members of the ensemble, included Mrs. Whiffen, Georgia Cayvan, Herbert Kelcey, W. J. LeMoyne, and the Charles Walcots. The play's long run lasted until mid-March, a far more protracted stand than better and less treacly Pinero plays had been accorded in this country.

The other new play was Augustin Daly's **The Undercurrent [of Human Life and Human Passion]** (11-13-88, Niblo's). Some mystery attaches to the work. First of all, it may not have been all that new (though it never before had been produced). And it may not have been primarily by Daly. In interviews Daly implied he had written it a decade earlier, hoping to have it mounted when he was working in London. But Daly's private correspondence suggests that Daly had actually conceived only the basic outline and that, as usual, his brother had written most of the dialogue. A greedy physician's attempt to deprive two sisters of their inheritance provided a pivot for the action; a long-lost father reappeared to help resolve the problem. The clichéd story allowed for the sort of spectacular effects with which Daly had made his name early on. Thus there was once again, as in *Under the Gaslight,* a character tied to a railroad track and the theatrically stunning sight of the train approaching at full speed. There was also a grim thieves' den with a trick circular staircase that collapsed whenever anyone (in this case the heroine) tried to escape. Although such melodramas had become passé as far as more sophisticated playgoers were concerned, it should have appealed to a larger audience still eager for its black-and-white, blood-and-thunder excitement. Somehow, it didn't. Two weeks and it was gone, without benefit of any further tour.

It was followed by Denman Thompson and George Ryer's **The Two Sisters** (11-26-88, Niblo's), suggested by Paul Giroux's original. In a sense the story was merely a variation on a theme the authors had employed so successfully in their gold mine, *The Old Homestead.* Mary (Lavinia White) and Martha Howard (May Merrick) are siblings who have left behind their bucolic country home and come to the city to make their way in the world. Martha is soon seduced by shiny baubles and a good-looking scoundrel. Before long, polite doors are closed to her. Mary, helped by the sly, sympathetic Hiram Pepper

(Eugene Jepson), sticks to the straight and narrow and is suitably rewarded. The new play never won the acclaim *The Old Homestead* had received, but it did four weeks of excellent business at Niblo's, then continued on its tour. It remained a staple on secondary circuits for many years.

Popular novels continued to be a source for stage plays, and few recent novels had been as popular as Frances Hodgson Burnett's **Little Lord Fauntleroy** (12-3-88, Broadway). Virtually everyone who entered the theatre knew the story beforehand. Because the aristocratic Earl of Dorincourt (J. H. Gilmour) would not accept an American for a daughter-in-law, Mrs. Errol (Kathryn Kidder) has raised her precocious, garrulous young son, Cedric, in her homeland, democratically allowing the boy to befriend shopkeepers and bootblacks. (The boy's father has died before the story opens.) But when Cedric becomes heir apparent his mother takes him to England. There the gouty, crotchety earl refuses to allow Mrs. Errol to live in his mansion and tries to discourage Cedric's democratic ways. Then a false claimant appears, and only with the help of the bootblack and Cedric's other American friends are the claims discredited. This leads the earl to recognize the errors of his foolish snobberies.

London had seen a version by E. V. Seebohm months earlier, but this New York version had the special cachet of being the author's own. It also had the era's brightest meteor, little Elsie Leslie, in the title role. She was dressed and curlishly coifed to replicate the portraits Reginald Birch had drawn for the book, which initiated a velvety, lacy fashion that soon became the bane of real little boys. The role was seen to be so taxing that the original schedule called for young Tommy Russell to alternate with her. Such was her fame, however, that she quickly was called on to give more than her share of performances. Of course, she eventually outgrew the part. For years other bright youngsters honed their talents on the juicy assignment, and the play continued to tour profitably until silent films appropriated it a quarter of a century later.

Second-stringers sent to review **The Fugitive** (12-3-88, Windsor) saw an opportunity to unsheathe daggers. "Mr. Tom Craven wrote the play," the *Herald's* man observed, "and that's not the worst of it. There was the cast." The story those demeaned players enacted told of a clerk who loves his boss's daughter only to learn that his employer has been blackmailed into consenting to the girl's marriage to a loutish squire. The clerk challenges the squire to fight and, believing he has killed his opponent, flees. He runs off to sea, where, naturally in this sort of play, he is promptly shipwrecked. Later he returns, intending to confess. But he learns that someone else had killed the squire and that the boss's daughter is still waiting for him. The *Herald*'s man concluded his review, "I prithee 'Fugitive' chase yourself away and get lost or something of the sort. At any rate, forget to come back soon." Oblivious to its critical drubbing, *The Fugitive* toured backwaters for several seasons.

Maurice Barrymore was the star of Haddon Chambers's London hit **Captain Swift** (12-4-88, Madison Square), which told of another "child of shame" who is raised in the slums and becomes first a criminal in Australia and then a well-received figure in London society until his past catches up with him. At A. M. Palmer's behest Dion Boucicault reworked the piece, giving it, among other things, an equivocally happy ending. Some strenuous critical objections prompted the quick restoration of the hero's offstage suicide. The supporting cast was showered with praise, especially Agnes Booth as the hero's long-suffering-in-secret mother. But Barrymore inevitably came in for the most extended, laudatory comments. *The Theatre*'s reviewer recorded that he acted with "a dash, nonchalant and devil-take-you air that was simply superb. He is altogether a splendid specimen of manly grace." The play ran out the season.

Mrs. Brown-Potter came into Palmer's for an eight-week stand on December 25. The engagement began with Tom Taylor's *'Twixt Axe and Crown*, but most of the run was given over to the rarely revived *Antony and Cleopatra*. Critics were unkind, finding both Kyrle Bellew's soldier and the star's queen much too ladylike. Some idea of the mounting can be gleaned from the fact that a ballet was inserted. When she returned in April at Niblo's, the star offered *Romeo and Juliet*, *Camille*, *The Lady of Lyons*, and *She Stoops to Conquer*.

One of the most popular of touring stars, Oliver Doud Byron, found some success with **The Upper Hand** (12-31-88, Windsor). He played Happy Jack. Only Jack isn't happy very long, for at the end of the first act he is framed and imprisoned. His cruel mother-in-law has no small hand in his framing. An explosion at the prison allows Jack to escape. He soon clears his name and is reunited with his faithful wife (played by Byron's real wife, Kate).

That same night Margaret Mather opened a brief six-night stand at Niblo's, changing bills nightly. Her schedule listed *The Honeymoon*, *Romeo and Juliet*, *Masks and Faces*, *The Lady of Lyons*, *Leah, the Forsaken*, and *Macbeth*.

January 7, the first Monday of 1889, saw two more

stars return. Lillie Langtry's repertory at the Fifth Avenue was even larger than Margaret Mather's, but then she lingered for two months. Her programs moved from *A Wife's Peril* through *As in a Looking Glass*, *Macbeth*, *As You Like it*, *Lady Clancarty*, *The Lady of Lyons*, and *Pygmalion and Galatea*. For most of the time Charles Coghlan was her leading man. Odell recalled he played Macbeth "in a slow, intelligent, ruminative way," and his Jaques won the highest praise. The star drew qualified approvals, though to a man critics admired her beauty and gorgeous gowns.

Louis James, supported by Marie Wainwright, came into the fading Star for a week with another *As You Like It* as well as *Virginius* and *Much Ado About Nothing*. When they moved on to neighborhood theatres other plays were added to their agenda.

The repertories of these touring stars rarely contained anything unexpected. Perhaps they had to play it safe, especially on the road. But Daly did not, so on the 8th he supplanted *The Lottery of Love* with Farquhar's relatively obscure *The Inconstant*. It became one of the surprise hits of the season. Of course, it was bowdlerized a bit, so as not to offend narrow contemporary sensibilities. But lavishly mounted with sumptuous period costumes and acted with the company's singular elan, it delighted audiences who watched the Oriana of Ada Rehan rewin the wayward affections of John Drew's Mirabel. Daly's reward was a month's run. (The opening, it should be noted, was part of a Tuesday night subscription series, which Daly used to revive favorite old productions and test new ones.)

McKee Rankin once had been a first-class leading man on Broadway but more recently had found a warmer embrace on the road. He now was the co-author, with Fred G. Maeder, and star of **The Runaway Wife** (1-14-89, Niblo's). The wife is a formerly rich English girl married to an artist who goes blind and is reduced to poverty. Unable to stand the degrading conditions in which they must live, she runs away. Later she hears that the artist has died, which means she is free to marry a rich man and reenter the best society. She does not know that her new husband has lied to her. He knows her first husband is still alive. At a soirée some years later her first husband and their now grown son appear. The son is a famous artist, so they are well-to-do again. The woman faints when she recognizes them. But the son—clever lad—inveigles her to pose for a portrait, and, guilt-ridden, she agrees. The young man uses the sittings to expose the current husband's villainy and effect a reconciliation. The reunited family all sail for America, where the blind man's sight is restored and everyone is happy. As with so many plays of this sort, the better critics sneered and a large, less sophisticated public accorded it many seasons of good business on tour.

William Yardley's **A Royal Revenge** (1-21-89, Grand Opera) was merely another version of *Gringoire,* which Coquelin was offering that same season and Barrett had done as *The King's Pleasure.* Yardley's version was written to order for Nat Goodwin. Most critics liked Goodwin as usual, but not his vehicle, which was dismissed as commonplace. No matter. Coupled with *Confusion,* the bill was designed for the road and, according to Goodwin, was highly successful there.

John G. Wilson's **The Silver Age** (1-28-89, Thalia) was set in 1862 in Idaho. An old man and his lovely young daughter are hounded by an implacable villain until the scoundrel is run off by Cool Jack (Edwin F. Mayo). (For what it's worth, note how many heroes or recent touring melodramas were named Jack.) Mayo was the son of Frank Mayo of *Davy Crockett* fame, and the Thalia once had been the glorious Bowery Theatre.

George H. Jessop's **22, Second Floor** (2-4-89, 14th St.), a vehicle created for dark-haired, plump Annie Pixley, was one of the myriad entertainments of the time that wavered between pure farce and prototypical musical comedy. Besides giving its star chances to sing and dance, it allowed her to portray identical twins—one the rigidly proper Mrs. John Ellis, the other the carefree, bohemian chorus girl, Flora Featherstone. The requisite farcical arrangements bring them to the same hotel, where the requisite farcical misunderstandings follow apace. At one point poor Flora must even claim she is the mother of her sister's child. Miss Pixley was another of the numerous players more popular on the road than in the better New York houses, so she stayed only a single week.

Beacon Lights (2-4-89, Thalia) revolved around a miscreant's attempt to lure a ship onto dangerous rocks and an intrepid heroine's battle to alert and save the ship.

With such a long string of hits to his credit, it was inevitable that Daly would finally make a misstep. That little slipup was **An International Match** (2-5-89, Daly's), taken from Franz von Schönthan's *Cornelius Voss.* Although set in a richly appointed New York mansion, it recounted how Lord Ravenstoke (John Drew) hoodwinks his uncle's emissary, who has been sent to bring him back to England to marry an English girl, and marries his real love, Doris Smith (Ada Rehan). The duenna of the house, Mrs. Merriday (Mrs. Gilbert), lends the lovers a helping hand or two and in the process snares for herself an aging bachelor, Quincy Caramel (James Lewis). Theatregoers failed to line up at the box office, so Daly rushed another production into rehearsal.

The peripatetic Maggie Mitchell followed Annie Pixley onto the same stage when she opened in C. Wallace Clifton's **Ray** (2-11-89, 14th St.). For the umpteenth time she played a tempest-tossed waif who finally finds wealth and happiness. Ray's father has been falsely imprisoned and her mother harassed by the very malefactor who framed her father. A labor agitator becomes her foster father. What was unusual about the play was its background of labor strife, a topic then usually still kept at arm's length in the theatre. The strife included a strike, a factory burned by strikers, and killings by the strikers. Like her predecessor, Miss Mitchell stayed one week, then moved on.

Ramsay Morris's **The Tigress** (2-11-89, People's) was set in France and centered on Lise Troubert (Selena Fetter), an adventuress and gambler's decoy whose murder of a man is witnessed by the man's sweetheart, Sara (Blanche Weaver). Lise flees after Sara warns, "I will remember you." Years later Sara is employed as a governess for a rich family. She comes across Lise and her brother, who are posing as Count (Morris) and Countess Barrotti, exposes them for theft, and has the satisfaction of learning that Lise has taken poison. The drama was sourly received and quickly folded.

Brander Matthews and George H. Jessop had written **A Gold Mine** (3-4-89, Fifth Ave.) for John Raymond, and the actor had tried it out on the road little more than a week before his sudden death. (That fact was later to win a law case for the authors when they were sued for plagiarism.) Now it suddenly reappeared, and its reappearance testified further to the often curious peregrinations of the contemporary stage, for its star was Nat Goodwin, who just a short time earlier had been relegated to a second-class theatre with a second-rate show. Most commentators considered this new vehicle first-rate, albeit they realized it had no claim to immortality. Silas K. Woolcott (Goodwin) is a rough-hewn but good-natured American who has known numerous financial ups and downs. He gave up one fortune to pay off his ne'er-do-well brother's debts. Since then he has discovered a gold mine and has come to London to sell it. The crafty Everard Foxwood (R. G. Wilson) is interested in buying the mine, but only if the purchase price is a mere steal. However, Silas is smitten by Sir Everard's sister, Mrs. Meredith

(Kate Forsyth), even if Mrs. Meredith turns up her nose at the uncouth American. The Foxwood household (its expensive main room is the play's lone setting) is also home to young George Foxwood, Sir Everard's gambling son. To pay his debts the boy speculates in a stock in which he knows his father has invested heavily. What he doesn't know is that his father is privy to bad news and is hastily disposing of his holdings. When the stock goes bad George is in serious trouble. Silas decides to use the money from the sale of the mine to help out the boy. Wily old Foxwood senses how anxious Silas is to sell and, unwittingly, offers precisely what his son requires to honor his obligations. Although Silas had hoped to sell for much more, he agrees to Foxwood's price. Realizing that Silas is broke, the snobbish knight callously cancels a dinner invitation he had proffered. But when Mrs. Meredith learns of Silas's sacrifice, she changes her feelings about him.

Some extraneous bits of comedy irritated the critics. For example, an excuse was drummed up to allow Silas to play the balcony scene from *Romeo and Juliet* with a dowager actress (portrayed by Ida Vernon). But they also found much of the dialogue superior and several scenes very touching. Among these was Silas's reaction to Foxwood's final snub. Left alone in the dusky room, he picks up a rose Mrs. Meredith had worn and, contemplating it, finds all the consolation he needs. For Goodwin, who had heretofore confined himself largely to vaudeville, the piece offered an opportunity to display a new range and depth and marked an early move away from his former fripperies.

Jessop, co-author of *A Gold Mine,* was also a collaborator, with Henry Lee, on **The Cavalier** (3-4-89, Palmer's), a play based on a d'Ennery drama. The play was one of a pair of entries vying with *A Gold Mine* for first-nighters. Lee was the swashbuckler's star, too, and portrayed the brave hero who must adopt a variety of disguises before dueling his way to victory. The entertainment was an interim booking (one week only) and a quick failure as well.

Maude Granger, still a star only in the eyes of outlying audiences, was allotted a single week on the fringes of the big time with J. K. Tillotson's **Two Lives** (3-4-89, Niblo's). She played a woman falsely accused by her treacherous brother-in-law of murdering his father. One interesting setting was a sordid, smoky gambler's den run by immigrants on Hester Street.

Two hits opened the next night. The era's leading female impersonator, Neil Burgess, was given the honor of unveiling a new theatre in Charles Bar-

nard's **The County Fair** (3-5-89, 23rd St.). Bernard's story was as simple and homey as the crispy-crusted pies baked by his spinster heroine, Abigail Prue. Her good heart prompts her to take in a waif, Taggs (Clara Thropp), and eventually she locates Taggs's long-lost parents. That good heart also induces the painfully shy Otis Tucker (Archie Boyd) to court her. Unfortunately, Solon Hammerhead (Julius Scott) also courts her, and he holds the mortgage on her family farm. She will lose the farm if she spurns Hammerhead or cannot come up with sufficient money to make her mortgage payments. Luckily, Abigail has a horse named Cold Molasses, and when, despite his name, she runs him in a race at the county fair, he wins, thus providing his mistress with the $3000 she needs to buy back the mortgage. His reward is a hug and kiss from his overjoyed owner. The race was run with real horses on a treadmill. A second setting depicted a barn with real cows in the stalls. Burgess, who played his ladies straight, without any of the campiness of later transvestites, found himself another durable vehicle. His original stand scored 105 performances, and he returned the following two seasons for even longer runs. An additional note of respectability was offered by Barnard, long associated with the distinguished *Scribner's Monthly.*

Yankees were clearly staging a theatrical comeback. John Whitcomb was welcoming folks to the old homestead in record numbers, Silas Woolcott was winning his expensive victory, and Miss Prue was ridding herself of her debts. Now Charles Hoyt added a passel of old-line Americans to the list. Hoyt had gained his fame with farces that were in reality primitive musical comedies, but his **A Midnight Bell** (3-5-89, Bijou) was an unalloyed rural comedy. To frame his action he recorded how Ned Olcott (Hart Conway) takes the blame for stealing securities from his uncle's bank when he learns that Squire Olcott (T. J. Herndon) is to be arrested for the crime. Ned is convinced (and so is the audience) that his uncle's cashier, shifty-eyed Stephen Labaree (W. J. Humphries), is the culprit and that Labaree hopes to win away Ned's girl, Annie Grey (Beth Bedford). A number of other uncertain romances were threaded through the story. Would John Bradbury (Richard J. Dillon), the minister, recognize how much he loves the pretty young schoolma'am, Nora Fairchild (Isabelle Coe)? And would the youthful lawyer, Napier Keene (W. H. Currie), propose to the minister's winsome little sister, Dot (Maude Adams)?

The only uncertainty, of course, was on the part of the characters. Savvy playgoers knew from the start how everyone would be paired. Much of the delight of the play came in waiting for, and finally watching, expectations realized—not just lovers happily united and Labaree exposed, but the village's spiteful, gossipy biddies given their comeuppance. These comfortable, reassuring feelings were enhanced by the settings. Act I showed the squire's dining room, with food on the table and a mutt scampering about for scraps. Act II showed the interior and exterior of a one-room schoolhouse, and children sledding and throwing snowballs. The parlor of the village old maid was the background for the next act, while the last took place in the meetinghouse, with pews, organ, and hymnals, and with the bell ropes visible at the bottom of the belfry. Some of the humor was more clownish than comic.

Deacon: You know I never lose my dignity. [*Falls on icy step*] Land o'gosh! [*Rises and falls again*]

Some was obvious, as when the deacon (Thomas Q. Seabrooke) makes way for one of the gossips with "Age before beauty." And some resorted to homespun aphorisms, such as "True consistency is a jewel, but jewelry is vulgar." However, much was on the order of Keene's probing Dot's sentiments.

Dot: I expect to marry a man I can love, honor, and obey.
Keene: Obey? Would you promise to obey?
Dot: Why, of course!
Keene: And would you obey?
Dot: Yes, but I guess I'd have something to say about what the commands would be.

Good, clean fun, *A Midnight Bell* ran out the season and afterwards toured for many years.

The failure of *An International Match* caused Daly to restore *The Taming of the Shrew* to his stage on the 7th. It filled out the month there.

Nor did Daniel Frohman have a new play on view when he offered his regulars **The Marquise** (3-18-89, Lyceum), for this was merely Louis Nathal's reworking of *Ferreol*, which had played the old Union Square a dozen years earlier. Georgia Cayvan and Henry Miller undertook the leads once performed by Kate Claxton and Charles R. Thorne, Jr.

Coincidentally, when a new playhouse opened on the site of the burnt-out old Union Square, it, too, opened with an old play wearing a new title. **A Woman's Stratagem** (3-27-89, Union Square) was another version of Scribe and Legouvé's *Bataille des dames*, a comedy New Yorkers had seen long years before as *The Ladies' Battle*. The English actress Helen Barry was starred.

The month ended jovially enough with **Samson and Delilah** (3-28-89, Daly's), taken from Bisson and Moinaux's *Un Conseil judicaire*. Daly billed the play as "an eccentric comedy," and one eccentricity must have surprised his regulars. If they had assumed that John Drew and Ada Rehan would impersonate the title figures, they were only half right. The Delilah of the piece is Audrey Ollyphant (Miss Rehan), an outrageous spendthrift. Her husband, Julius (Frederick Bond), is so exasperated by her extravagance that he sues to have a trustee look after her monies. The judge, impressed by the arguments of Goliah Puttybank (James Lewis), an attorney famed for husbanding other estates, appoints him as trustee. But poor Puttybank is no match for the determined, seductive beauty, and he ends up giving her all she asks for and then some. He also ends up with a lot of explaining to do to Mrs. Puttybank (Mrs. Gilbert). And Audrey is left to go her merry way, buying a new dress each week and a new hat whenever the fancy strikes her (last year it struck sixty-eight times). Drew was relegated to a minor role, the opposing counsel. Perhaps because of this, and certainly in the face of mostly enthusiastic notices, *Samson and Delilah* ended Daly's season on something of a down note as far as attendance was concerned.

Rose Coghlan had been touring all season in a heady, romantic drama by her brother Charles and now brought **Jocelyn** (4-1-89, Star) into a prime New York theatre for a fortnight as part of that tour. The story, set against the religious turmoil of Louis XIII's day, was simple. The notorious Prince Saviani (Wilton Lackaye) is determined to marry Jocelyn de Boissac. She is equally determined that he will not. Hoping to leave her defenseless, he slays her brother and her lover. But he has not bargained on Jocelyn's strength. She dons a man's clothing, challenges him to duel to the death, and wins.

No play of the season received more scathing reviews than Charles Stow's **An Iron Creed** (4-8-89, 14th St.), although most critics had tolerant words for the author's attempt to portray American Jews in a realistic, sympathetic light. However, the results were so banal that one critic concluded the play would make Jews "squirm." David Delmont (did the name purposely hint at Augustus Belmont?) (J. F. O'Brien), a rich Jew who has spent his life on good works, dies of grief when his daughter, Ruth (Marie Cross), runs off with a swindler. Ruth in turn commits suicide after finding her lover attempting to rob the room in which her dead father lies. Critics also bewailed the introduction of such an absurdly farcical character as Lord de Pettypate and found fault with outlandish gowns such as one "gray and terra cotta dress, cut kangaroo-wise."

Another quick failure was **Reuben Glue; or, Life among the Bushrangers** (4-8-89, Windsor), which Fred Marsden derived from W. H. Thomas's novel. What once had been a melodramatic story of a man transported from England to Australia seems to have become in its transfer something of a farce, possibly unintentionally. The *Herald* felt someone should have taken a lesson in basic English, pointing to such curious juxtapositions as a "sneering eye" and a "gloating heart."

Frank I. Frayne, one more touring stalwart, was the star of his own **Kentucky Bill** (4-22-89, Third Ave.). The "crack of the pistol and the gleam of the Bowie knife" were important features of the play, as were trained dogs, a horse ("Kentucky Boy") trained to perform special tricks, a bear, a lion, and two hyenas. The dynamite-toting villains of the piece were an odd couple, to say the least, Rev. and Mrs. DeWitt Graball (George Weller and Mrs. S. K. Chester) of the Salvation Army. Along with serving them their just desserts, Bill also helped an Indian, Kiola (T. A. Clinton), get a civilized job—carrying a sandwich sign advertising a dry-goods store.

The perpetual comet Thomas W. Keene, still a name to be reckoned with in the theatre's far-flung outer reaches, came into the People's Theatre on the 29th with a repertory that included *Richelieu, Brutus,* and Shakespearean standards—a repertory as redolent of Forrest as of Booth.

That same night William Gillette came a cropper when he dramatized Mrs. Humphrey Ward's controversial novel **Robert Elsmere** (4-29-89, Union Square). The drift of the work was that Christianity would do better to struggle for social improvement and not worry about metaphysics, but such a philosophic discussion seemed best left to the printed page. The production survived for two weeks, doing little business.

Leonard Grover and Nathaniel Childs's **My Brother's Sister** (4-29-89, Fifth Ave.) was another of the countless offerings of the time that came perilously close to being musical comedy. It was poorly received, so its star, Minnie Palmer, quickly switched to her older if not dissimilar favorites.

A far greater Minnie followed when Minnie Maddern came in for a two-month run in **Featherbrain** (5-6-89, Madison Square), James Albery's translation of *Tête de linotte*. Her empty-headed Mrs. Coney misplaces some old love letters, and the search for them leads to no end of complications and misunderstandings. A hot-tempered Portuguese, Don Stephano (Wilton Lackaye), who would like to have an affair with the pretty wife, only adds fuel to the fire. In the end Mrs. Coney discovers she has

been carrying the letters about on her person the whole while. Even in this early stage of her career the actress had little time for clichés. She refused to play the heroine as a chirpy, wide-eyed innocent. Her deep voice and her carefully considered style made the heroine a believable woman rather than a caricature, although some critics felt this detracted from the farcical possibilities. This was the last time New Yorkers would see the name Minnie Maddern on programs. When the actress returned after a brief retirement she would be billed as Mrs. Fiske, a name that would become a theatrical legend.

William Gill and Richard Golden's **Old Jed Prouty** (5-13-89, Union Square) was a blatant attempt to capitalize on *The Old Homestead.* Golden impersonated Prouty, who, like Josh Whitcomb, leaves his New England (Maine) farm to see his child in the big city (Boston), stays with a rich friend, and, thanks to his own naiveté, suffers a number of comic indignities. These include pulling a rope to summon a servant and drenching himself in the process, since the cord is for the shower. But the theatre was so vast and healthy in the 1880s that it could support such a cynical ripoff. The play toured the hinterlands and lesser metropolitan theatres well into the 1890s.

Grover was as prolific at this time as Jessop, but hardly as successful. His **A Noble Son** (5-13-89, Niblo's), a play about theatrical life, was spared the season's most vicious pans only because *An Iron Creed* had preceded it. The *Times* gave some idea of its demerits when it described a crucial scene: "The hero's wife is persuaded to run away from him while he is in the next room playing the banjo. The wife has scarcely gone beyond the door when the hero enters and discovers her flight. Instead of going after her and fishing out what it all means he goes crazy and after raving around awhile falls flat on the floor, evidently for no other purpose than to bring down the curtain." One week and the play fled, too.

Matters failed to improve with Wilton Payne's London melodrama **The Mystery of Fernley Abbey** (5-27-89, Windsor), in which the hero is accused of a murder, which he did not commit, but apparently is never accused of being a bigamist, which he is. Some fine actors, probably in search of a summer income, were involved, but their paychecks terminated after the first week.

Before the next major opening occurred theatrical columns in leading newspapers were abuzz with news from London. The critics were not merely divided, they were at war with one another, about a new play presented there. That war would soon reach American shores, for the play was Henrik

Ibsen's *A Doll's House.* For better or worse, it would enduringly change playgoers' perceptions of drama.

No hint of Ibsen tinged **Jeanne Fortier, the Bread Carrier** (6-10-89, Niblo's), which Emily Soldene, formerly a star of opéra bouffe and more lately popular in variety, had adapted from *La Porteuse de pain.* Its plot was propelled by the season's umpteenth false accusation, which sends the heroine to prison, reduces her to a street vendor, and forces her to watch the real murderer attempt to destroy the romance that develops between her daughter and the son of the murdered man. Mrs. D. P. Bowers, the Emilia in the 1886 Booth-Salvini *Othello,* played the lead.

The Dear Irish Boy (6-10-89, Windsor) belonged to the school of romantic melodrama that for decades had a special appeal to Irish-Americans. Set in the old country, it told of a villainous lord who loves a girl who loves a simple Irish lad. Other components included a stolen letter, a haughty father, a visit to a mysterious cave by moonlight, bagpipes, jigs, and Irish airs.

Another Irish lass, this time an Irish-American, was the title figure in **An American Princess** (6-17-89, Third Ave.). If her name seemed to be Juniatto Trattori (Jennie Calef), that was because she was attempting to pass herself off as a Mexican, a rich lady's long-lost daughter. The name itself, which sounds as much Italian as it does Spanish, should have awakened suspicions. Nevertheless, it took a wily pet bear (played by W. H. Benney in costume) to expose her. A few songs dotted the nonsense, ranging from "There Was an Old Nigger" to "Nearer, My God, to Thee." The *Herald*'s critic, back at his desk after sitting through the play, reported, "Criticism is paralyzed into silence born of amazement."

French performers, such as Bernhardt or Coquelin, regularly performed to sold-out houses in which many of the spectators probably understood no French at all. And French plays could still often attract good business, despite their waning vogue and the ongoing assault on their immorality. Snobbery no doubt contributed to their success. Things French were chic. Not so things Chinese. So when the Royal Company of Hong Kong visited New York for two weeks, beginning June 24, it was assigned a second-class theatre, the Windsor, and had to rely almost entirely on the city's small Chinese community for its trade. There was little attempt among the critical fraternity or even the theatrical intelligentsia to appreciate either the plays or the productions, both of which were so far

removed from the Western mainstream. The offerings were dismissed with condescension as boring, unintelligible, and overlong.

Overlong was also a charge leveled against **The Burglar** (7-1-89, Madison Square). In a way the play was too much of a good thing and nothing at all of a possibly better one, for it represented Augustus Thomas's attempt to turn his one-act *Editha's Burglar* into a full-length drama. The old play served, with modification, as the middle section. The first act showed the burglar's earlier, happier married life, and the final act struggled to tie up all the loose strings of the original. Perhaps more important, no comparable replacement could be found for Elsie Leslie. But these changes really mattered little, except to a handful of sophisticated regulars, for the entertainment was designed for the road, which was loathe to accept one-acters. And there an especially dramatic scene ensured its popularity. When the burglar (played in this month-long engagement by Maurice Barrymore) realizes that the little girl is his own daughter, his paternal feelings overwhelm him and he determines to hug and kiss her. Her stepfather's entrance would seem to frustrate his plans, so he pulls his gun and threatens to shoot. Then, in a change of heart, he hands Benton, the stepfather, the gun as a sign of his good intentions. Now it becomes Benton's turn to grasp the situation and show compassion. He returns the burglar's gun and tells Editha to give the man a kiss. The proof that Thomas's changes were professionally knowing is that *The Burglar* held the boards for more than a decade.

Before a few latecomers closed the season, the *Times* published another season's-end overview, again ruing the lack of fine dramas. But this time the paper's critic, E. A. Dithmar, dwelt solely on American drama. He used *The Burglar*'s big scene for a springboard, suggesting that it might be theatrically effective but was dramatically dishonest. He rested his hopes for a turnabout on an odd postulate—that a series of dire failures was necessary to force producers to look around for better, more progressive, and more artful material. Time would show that was not the answer. Commercial success and the militant prodding of some enlightened critics would do far more for American drama than failure.

Two lightweight pieces brought down the curtain on the theatrical year. Will R. Wilson and Julius A. Lewis's **The Lion and The Lamb** (8-5-89, Bijou) was a quick flop. It centered on Lyon Lamb (Charles Coote), a middle-aged, Walter Mitty–ish hero who desperately wants to be thought of as a roué and is willing to bribe his way into ill repute. One scene hinted that the authors had attended the recent revival of *The Rivals,* for the hero embroils himself in a preposterous duel and is saved only by a deluge (with real water inundating the stage).

The British offered a more acceptable piece and gave Kate Claxton the biggest hit she had enjoyed in some while. **Bootles' Baby** (8-5-89, Madison Square) was Hugh Mose's dramatization of John Strange Winter's (Mrs. Arthur Stannard's) novel. The hero (C. A. Stevenson), an officer in the Lancers, discovers an abandoned little girl in his barracks and decides to raise her. He also loves Helen Grace (Miss Claxton), not knowing she is secretly married to the villain and is the child's mother. The villain's convenient death allows for a happy ending. The play ran through the summer and well into the fall.

1889–1890

Odell labeled the new theatrical year "a very brilliant season." Of course, he was writing about it more than half a century afterwards, and he was writing about the stage of his youth, which almost always seems better when looked back on with age's tinted memory. Odell was an affectionate chronicler of the era, and he earlier had called the late 1870s Broadway's palmiest days. Such assessments were tinged with absurdity even in the 1930s and early 1940s, when he made them. Now, another half-century later, despite myriad reevaluations of the Victorian period and its arts, they still seem questionable. Unfortunately, the performances and productions have vanished beyond recall, and in any case we would be inclined to judge them, if we could watch them, by standards that were not the standards of their contemporaries. Moreover, few if any of the season's new plays would be anything but quaint period pieces, for all our attempts to be open-minded. Nonetheless, the season was very important. For one, it introduced three men who soon would loom gigantically over the American theatre. And, however gingerly, it gave New Yorkers their first chance to see a play by Ibsen, whose influence would be even more pervasive.

The season opened unpromisingly with **La Belle Marie; or, A Woman's Revenge** (8-12-89, Windsor). Notwithstanding her sobriquet, the heroine (Agnes Herndon) is a Fall River lass who, after being led down a primrose path, runs away to New York.

There she rehabilitates a handsome young flophouse denizen who has been driven to drink by the machinations of his wicked half-brother. Much of the play's humor stemmed from jokes about the derelicts' use, or lack or use, of soap. For all its coarseness and clumsiness, the drama found a welcome in minor theatres.

Not so **Myrtle Ferns** (8-17-89, People's). Most papers did not even bother to review it, and the *Herald,* which did, simply acknowledged it to be another compilation of the period's stock characters and motifs: "The plot introduced us to the deep, designing villain, a heroine with a profusion of taffy colored hair, an old man who spoke with a young man's voice, and who died a tragic death in three breaths and a strangle, and an Irish servant who did any number of things which would not be tolerated in any decent household." It disappeared quickly.

So did Pierre Leclercq's **The Love Story** (8-19-89, Fifth Ave.), which was a one-week flop. The play starred a throaty, monotoned, wooden English actress, Adelaide Moore, as Madeleine Booth, whose love for poet Paul Falshawe (Otis Skinner) is nearly undermined by the dirty tricks of a duplicitous banker, Charles Marchcastle (Frazer Coulter).

The same week also saw *Lord Chumley* lead the seasonal parade of revivals and returns. *Mankind, Captain Swift,* and others followed.

E. E. Kidder's **A Poor Relation** (8-26-89, Daly's) was a play destined for long years of popularity. It was written as a vehicle for Sol Smith Russell, a lanky, slightly stooped comedian with huge dark eyes and a winning, sad smile. Russell portrayed Noah Vale (the name set the tone for the play), an unworldly, eccentric inventor who is clad in black tatters and goes around accompanied by waifs he has befriended. When he tries to sell his latest invention to Roderick Faye (Alfred Hudson), Faye's devious partner, Jasper Sterrett (Charles Kent), steals the plans and sets about patenting them. Faye's equally devious wife, Eunice (Maud Hosford), catches Sterrett in the act and blackmails him. She also attempts to pin the theft on her stepdaughter, Dolly (Grace Filkins). For all his unworldliness Noah has a certain instinctive cunning. Jasper discovers that the invention he has patented does not work, since Noah had carefully omitted some crucial information. Jasper comes to Noah's shabby garret to see if he can unearth the missing pieces, but the appearance of a strange woman wrecks his plans. That woman, Rachel Warriner (Lillian Owen), turns out to be the wife Jasper had deserted, a desertion that drove her mad for a time. Russell beguiled his waifs and his audiences by telling them odd tales and by singing little nursery ditties. This first visit lasted one month. Russell would return with some regularity, but he was always more popular in the West than in the East.

What would our late 19th-century drama have done without waifs? Some, like those in *A Poor Relation,* were mere children, but probably as many were young girls just entering a marriageable age. The heroine of **The Buckeye** 8-26-89, Windsor) was one of the latter, a pretty orphan who weds a good-natured but weak gambler. He loses everything betting on horses, but just as matters seem darkest the orphan learns she is a millionaire's heir. Lizzie Evans was the star, and she belonged to the Lotta school of performing, offering songs and dances to enliven even the most somber dramas. Her admirers preferred to see her happy, so in midweek she switched to *Fine Feathers,* a comedy that gave her vaudeville arts freer rein.

George H. Jessop and Ben Teal's trite if solid melodrama **The Great Metropolis** (8-31-89, 23rd St.) was a huge hit on the road. The story spotlighted Will Webster (Harry Meredith), a prodigal son who returns home just in time to be accused of murdering his father and who must then spend the rest of the evening tracking down the villain and proving his own innocence. As usual with this type of play, spectacular scenic effects glossed over some of the weak points. These effects included a sunset and moonrise off Sandy Hook, followed by a storm during which local people attempt to rescue victims of a shipwreck, aided only by the intermittent illumination from a lighthouse, and then a New York elevated station complete with all the latest advertisements and with crowds buying tickets and rushing through the collection booths. Critics singled out for praise a young actress, Annie Mayor, who portrayed a wronged girl. The *Herald* predicted she "has won a place beside the two or three foremost actresses on the New York stage. She has the strength, truth and charm of Agnes Booth." The *Times* opined, "There is nothing stupid or conventional about her work, and she has, evidently, sufficient artistic intelligence and personal force to secure an important place." Inexplicably, she quickly faded from the scene. But two other figures associated with the production did not. The first was its producer, Abe Erlanger, in his maiden New York producing venture.

· · ·

Abraham [Lincoln] **Erlanger** (1860–1930) rose to important theatrical positions in his native Cleveland under the tutelage of his notorious mentor, Mark Hanna. A blocky, balding, bull-faced man,

who openly admired Napoleon and became famous for his collection of Napoleonana, he joined forces with a lawyer, Marc Klaw. The pair came east, bought out a thriving actors' agency, and set to work producing. Within a few years Erlanger, clearly the dominant partner, became the most powerful and most reviled man in the American theatre.

· · ·

The second man, whose connection with *The Great Metropolis* was simply that he had taken over the running of the theatre where it played, was Charles Frohman. But Frohman was also the producer of the very next major arrival.

· · ·

Charles Frohman (1860–1915) was the youngest of three brothers who went on to achieve some measure of theatrical fame. The more important of the other two was Daniel, by then established at the Lyceum. The least of the trio was Gustave. Charles was born in Sandusky, Ohio, the son of a itinerant peddler. He came to New York at the age of twelve to work in newspapers but soon found himself selling tickets at a Brooklyn theatre. After serving as advance man for minstrel shows, he joined his brothers at Steele MacKaye's Madison Square Theatre, where the boys were credited with establishing the policy of sending out duplicate road companies of Broadway hits. He also became an actors' and authors' agent. He has been described as a "little, round, slant-eyed Buddha."

· · ·

One of the men Frohman represented was Bronson Howard, and he was dismayed when a Howard play he admired was tried out at the Boston Museum but was rejected by all the supposedly knowing New York managers. He borrowed money to bring the play into New York himself. **Shenandoah** (9-9-89, Star) used the Civil War to give a little bite and background to several interwoven love stories, much as *Held by the Enemy* had. Because happy endings were contrived for all the love stories, more than one critic viewed the play as a comedy rather than a drama. The play begins in Charleston as the citizens congregate excitedly in expectation of Beauregard's opening fire on Fort Sumter. The first shots mean that two West Point friends, the New Yorker, Kerchival West (Henry Miller), and the Virginian, Robert Ellingham (Lucius Henderson) find themselves on opposing sides. Their chagrin is all the more heartfelt because the men love each other's sisters, Madeline West (Nanette Comstock) and Gertrude Ellingham (Viola Allen). In time the war touches the Ellingham homestead in the Shenandoah Valley. The home is occupied by Union troops under General Haverill

(Wilton Lackaye). Haverill's colonel is none other than West. Gertrude is captured attempting to carry a message to Confederate forces, and her examination by West is chilly indeed. But West is stabbed by another prisoner, Captain Thornton (John E. Kellerd). This same vicious spy had attempted to enter Mrs. Haverill's bedroom in Charleston. At the time Mrs. Haverill had fainted, and West had used his handkerchief to help her. Haverill had discovered the handkerchief but had accepted the explanation given him. Now West has taken a locket from Thornton. The locket contains Mrs. Haverill's picture. She had presented it to their erring son, who had gone off to fight under an assumed name, Lieutenant Bedloe (G. W. Bailey), and Thornton had obtained it after the boy was wounded. But Haverill's suspicions are aroused again, and he is certain his wife is having an affair with West. The dying boy is returned in a prisoner exchange, but he dies before he can straighten matters out. Luckily, just before his death he dictated a letter. The note is read only after the war is over, just as several of the lovers, who have been reported dead or missing, all reappear within minutes of each other at a Washington gathering. There are hugs, kisses, and reaffirmations of affection all around.

As this synopsis suggests, the war itself played the smallest part in the story. The slavery question and arguments about secession or union are totally absent. At best the soldiers' uniforms, offstage cannon and rifle shots, distant torch signals, a series of cavalry bugle calls (all carefully specified in accordance with army manuals by Howard in his directions and appropriately trumpeted by Frohman in his advertisements), and the thundering, upstage ride of General Phil Sheridan and his men served as constant reminders of the wartime setting. The changing audience (and with it the changing theatre) was noted somewhat archly by the *Times* when it observed that the play's sentiments were applauded by "immigrants and the sons of immigrants who have settled in this country since 1861." New stock or old, playgoers delighted in Howard's professional know-how. *Shenandoah,* which moved to Frohman's own 23rd Street Theatre after a few weeks, chalked up a run of 250 performances.

The Civil War also served as little more than background for a short-lived failure, William Haworth's **Ferncliff** (9-9-89, Union Square), which added a touch of rural Americana and a touch of old-fashioned melodrama for good measure. Tom (E. H. Vanderfelt) and Annie Howins (Belle Flohr) are happily married on their small New England farm. Annie cooks a wonderful Irish stew filled with

onions, their children are careful to say their prayers every night before going to bed, and dear old Dad Howins (T. J. Herndon) is always around for some kindly philosophy. Into this happy picture comes clenched-teeth, sneering Willard Hilton (Harry Pierson), who attempts to seize the farm and Annie by arranging for Tom to be drafted into the army. Tom circumvents this by having his brother, Jim (Haworth), go as his legal substitute. But when Jim is reported missing, the guilt-ridden Tom enlists. Before long he, too, is among the missing. Time passes, and the farm begins to fall apart. To save it and ensure a good home for her children and father-in-law, Annie finally consents to marry Hilton. Then, just as the wedding is about to take place, two figures are spotted coming down the road arm in arm. Guess who! Hilton commits suicide. The second-stringers who reviewed the play were kind but unenthusiastic. Still, after a fortnight *Ferncliff* moved on to houses reserved primarily for touring shows.

Those touring houses always welcomed the "juvenile" star N. S. Wood. His latest vehicle was **Out in the Streets** (9-9-89, Third Ave.). Wood played Harry Farley, a fearless young bank clerk who triumphs over his treacherous boss and other malefactors to save the deposits of many innocents, including a little blind girl. Advertisements promised "realistic views" of St. Patrick's Cathedral, the Washington Market, Wall Street, City Hall Park, and the Brooklyn docks, along with "A River of Fire" proclaimed "the acme of scenic realism."

Another "open-and-shut" case as far as Broadway's first-class theatres were concerned was Pettitt's London melodrama **Hands Across the Sea** (9-16-89, Standard), although it, too, toured month after month elsewhere. Gustavus Levick, grown absurdly fat, played the hero, Jack Dudley, who joined a seemingly interminable line of victims of false accusations. He is imprisoned, escapes, sails overseas, is shipwrecked and rescued, and eventually returns home to right all wrongs and claim his heroine. Neither the star's obesity nor Pettitt's shopworn clichés bothered lovers of such hokum. Reviewers recorded that the galleryites hooted, cheered, hissed, and stomped with abandon. Were they still caught up in legitimately overwhelming emotions, or were they, by this time, simply having a good time at the expense of a bad play? No real hint of the latter seems to lurk between the lines of the critics' reports.

The critical dismissal of *Hands Across the Sea* was nothing compared to the critical brickbats that greeted **Love and Liberty** (9-23-89, Union Square),

T. Malcolm Watson's dramatization of Charles Gibbons's *For the King*. Reviewers were at odds only over which was more inept, the play or its incorrigible English star, the somewhat mannish Helen Barry. She portrayed a German girl who, during the Franco-Prussian conflict, is forced to choose between her French soldier-husband and her father. When she elects to remain with her husband, her father steals important papers and attempts to incriminate his son-in-law. There was apparently no subsequent tour.

By contrast, John A. Stevens's **Wife for Wife** (9-23-89, People's) enjoyed a long, prosperous career on the road, even though those better critics who deigned to review it saw it as a barely competent twisting of the *Othello* story. None of these reviewers mentioned *The Hypocrite* (6-6-87), an earlier play by Stevens with a similar theme. George (Davenport Bebus), a black man, learns his wife has been seduced. Embittered, he viciously sets about persuading Edward Walton (Stevens) that his wife, Edith (Florence Elmore), is faithless, too. Walton shoots and wounds the supposed seducer before the truth comes to light. After it does, George takes poison. At a time when popular playhouses reveled in a quirky attempt at realism, audiences saw nothing amiss in a white man's playing a major black role in blackface. Realism was a relative thing.

That curious idea of realism was evident again in the horses, cows, and pigs that moved about the farm that was the setting for **Diogenes Tramp** (9-30-89, Third Ave.). Diogenes (Frank I. Frayne), a self-educated hobo, rescues a farm family (the father has taken to drink) just as the mortgage is about to be foreclosed.

Among the fall revivals and returns *The Old Homestead* was relit at the Academy of Music on the 26th and once again ran out the season. That same night, around the corner on Irving Place at Amberg's Theatre, an auditorium devoted to presentations in German, *Nora; oder, Ein Puppenheim* was mounted (for three performances only). Playgoers who wanted to see it in English so as to understand what all the fuss was about would not have to wait long.

Before the next New York opening Chicago welcomed a novelty, Steele MacKaye's **An Arrant Knave** (9-30-89, Chicago Opera House). Its star, Stuart Robson, played Chiqui (pronounced Cheeky), a blustering, cowardly soldier who nonetheless manages to right a number of wrongs. Among his good deeds he restores a duke's long-lost son to his rightful place and helps the young man win the girl of his dreams. The play was apparently written in a labored, archaic blank verse, although the lone surviving manuscript has the dialogue in prose form. But antiquated dialogue did not stop the performance from eliciting largely favorable notices. It toured for six months, only to close before reaching New York after MacKaye refused to make changes that Robson requested.

The preceding winter Paris correspondents for major American newspapers had reported in no uncertain terms about Sardou's latest hit, *La Marquise*. They railed at the immorality of a story describing how a scarlet lady, in order to win acceptance and position, marries a seedy marquis, who agrees to disappear soon after the wedding, and sues him for divorce when he fails to keep his end of the bargain. This was the plot Daly had his brother use as the basis for **The Golden Widow** (10-2-89, Daly's). Of course, the material was scrubbed clean and trivialized to make it palatable for American audiences. The lady of ill repute was transformed into Tryphena Magillicuddy (Ada Rehan), a rich, flighty American widow determined to add a title to her name. To this end she selects a decrepit insurance adjuster, one Campanilla (James Lewis), whom she discovers to be an impoverished marquis. She is spared the need to divorce him when she learns he long since has misplaced another wife, who turns out to be Coralie Coraline (Mrs. Gilbert), the same irritable harridan who has provided the widow with slippers and lingerie. The discovery leaves Tryphena free to wed Tom De Camp (John Drew), "a protecting angel from New York." All the scrubbing apparently was not thorough enough, and possibly the mention of certain unmentionables by Mrs. Gilbert also offended the pretentious sensibilities of some playgoers. In any case, Daly's season got off to a false start.

Several big guns vied for attention on the 7th. All were English. To many the foremost attraction was the Kendals—William and his matronly wife, Madge, sister of the famous playwright T. W. Robertson. They were the Lunts of their day. Both were in their forties, but audiences continued to allow older players to portray younger characters. They opened at the Fifth Avenue with Sardou's *A Scrap of Paper*. Notices were laudatory, even if some were tactless in expressing surprise at how good the underrated Mr. Kendal was. Many reviewers seemed to miss the more romantic approach that Lester Wallack and Rose Coghlan had brought to the parts. The Kendals were advocates of a newer, more soberly realistic school of playing. Before ending their month's visit they also brought out *The Ironmaster*, Ohnet's *Le Maître de forges*, which

Americans already had seen under several titles. When they returned in February they had some novelties to offer.

Two players of lesser repute, the handsome, debonair William Terriss and his attractive vis-à-vis, Jessie Millward, both stars in London's Adelphi melodramas, came into Niblo's, where their initial offering was **Roger La Honte.** The play was adapted from the French by Augustin Daly and Robert Buchanan. Daly also managed to find time in his busy schedule to help stage the production. Its plot centered on two men, the good Roger La Roque and his evil look-alike, Luversan, who sees to it that Roger is blamed for his wicked deeds. Later the company switched to *The Lady of Lyons,* and on their trouble-plagued, foreshortened tour they added such standbys as *Frou-Frou* and *Othello.* The Kendals had brought their own company; the Adelphi stars had settled for American support. This may partially explain their disappointing reception.

Louis Nathal's **The Suspect** (10-7-89, People's) starred Henry Lee as a French duke sympathetic to the cause of the downtrodden during the French Revolution. His fiancée's brother accuses him of treason. All ends happily, with the future brother-in-law repentant.

More bad American support undermined another foreign visitor. An aging Salvini came into Palmer's on the 10th, with a repertory that provided no surprises (*Samson, Othello,* and Saumet's *Gladiator*) and with a roster of American players (performing in English to his Italian) that provoked howls from the critics. When he returned in March to the Broadway he also presented *La Morte Civile* (billed as *The Outlaw*) and *Don Caesar de Bazan.* This proved to be the final American tour for the sixty-year-old star, though he survived another quarter of a century.

Time was also running out for Edwin Booth—far more swiftly, in fact. Illness had forced Barrett to withdraw from his co-starring assignments, but he continued as manager, seeing to it that a touch of quality was imparted to Booth's mountings and to his support. For this season that support included one of America's greatest actresses, Modjeska. It included as well the rising young Otis Skinner. But Skinner was shocked when he started to work with Booth. He later recalled that "years had dug devitalizing claws into his strength, his spirit, and his ambition. It was more the shell of the great actor; symmetrical still, but the echo of youthful inspiration growing fainter." Of course, when they opened at the Broadway on the 14th Booth was nearing fifty-six and Modjeska was less than three weeks

away from her forty-ninth birthday. Their schedule for their two-month engagement was a busy one, bringing out *Richelieu, Much Ado About Nothing, The Merchant of Venice, Hamlet, Macbeth,* and two double bills, *The Fool's Revenge* and *Donna Diana,* and *Don Caesar de Bazan* and *Mary Stuart.* As had become their custom with these venerable stars, most critics emphasized the virtues and discreetly minimized the flaws, even when the stars had an off night. Yet there were high points. Odell long remembered Booth's final moments in *Macbeth:* "Realizing defeat, wounded, dying, he threw, like a madman, his sword and shield at Macduff, and sank, a crumpled heap, at the feet of his conqueror."

More great, elderly players competed with Booth and Modjeska when *The Rivals* reappeared at the Star the same night. A sixty-nine-year-old Mrs. Drew impersonating Mrs. Malaprop may not have been extreme, but Joseph Jefferson, at sixty, was again Bob Acres. W. J. Florence, a mere fifty-eight, was a believable Sir Lucius O'Trigger. Perhaps we can see why the fortyish Kendals, portraying figures in their twenties and thirties, were not all that disconcerting to contemporaries.

The perennially touring Frederick Warde braved this awesome competition when he opened in **The Mountebank** (10-14-89, Grand Opera), a play he had assembled himself from several older works. In late 18th-century France, William Belphegor (Warde), a strolling player, marries Madelaine (Stella Rees), the daughter of the exiled Duke of Montbazon (L. F. Rand). When the duke returns to power he snobbishly tries to dissolve the marriage. New Yorkers wouldn't buy, but according to Warde it became one of his most requested vehicles on the road.

Our Flat (10-21-89, Lyceum), an English comedy about a young couple living beyond their means, won no admirers. Even a scene in which the pair entertain in a room filled with crates, barrels, and a discarded bathtub, their furniture having been repossessed, garnered only a modicum of laughs.

Daly, who had suffered his own disappointment with his season opener, fared only a mite better with **The Great Unknown** (10-22-89, Daly's), derived from Gustav Kadelburg and Franz von Schönthan's *Die berühmte Frau.* The great unknown is Arabella Jarraway (Annie Yeamans), a famous authoress who is unknown to her family because she prefers to spend her time across the ocean in Paris. This leaves the flirtatious Mr. Jarraway (James Lewis), his hoydenish elder daughter, Etna (Ada Rehan), her sister, Pansy (Isabel Irving), and the girls' censorious Aunt Penelope (Mrs. Gilbert) to fend for themselves until Etna's admirer, Ned Dreemer (John

Drew), tricks mama into returning and reembracing her family. Playgoers knew Annie Yeamans as the beloved leading comedienne of Harrigan and Hart's heyday. Another new face this season was the ubiquitous Wilton Lackaye, who played "the O'Donnell Don," a preposterously chivalrous Irishman. But neither of these fine players truly fit into Daly's carefully honed organization. Both soon left. Critics could not agree on the play's merits. The *Tribune*'s long-winded William Winter proclaimed, "It is a good comedy, good because copiously fraught with action, interesting in story, abundant in diversified characters, cheerful with humorous traits and amusing dialogue, pungent with playful satire." By contrast, Winter's friend on the *World*, Nym Crinkle, dismissed the piece succinctly as "loose in structure and verbose in treatment." Nor could critics settle on which player shone most brightly, some opting for Miss Rehan, some for Drew, and some for Lewis. The play ran until mid-December, but it was never considered one of Daly's real triumphs.

Clara Morris returned to the site of her old glories in a performance of *Camille* on the 28th and then, the next night, switched to a new play, Martha Morton's **Hélène** (10-29-89, Union Square). She played a woman who, unjustly, has gotten a bad reputation. To overcome this she rejects the proposals of Dr. Clermont (Frederic de Belleville), a man she loves, and marries instead an old invalid. When the invalid dies, another rejected suitor spreads the rumor that Hélène and Clermont arranged his death. Hélène determines to confront the liar, but when she does he grabs her and kisses her, just as Clermont appears. Clermont challenges his accuser to a duel. Another, quicker solution is found. The men agree to write their names on scraps of paper. These and similar scraps will be placed on the table, and Hélène will draw from them until a name appears. The man whose name appears will be exonerated. The other will shoot himself. After several false starts Hélène picks a piece with writing on it. It bears Clermont's name. The loser shoots himself, but before he dies he confesses his guilt.

Even at her peak Miss Morris was an undisciplined, controversial actress. Now the *Times,* never one of her supporters, described her playing in unflattering terms before launching into a brutal pan: "She speaks many lines of inflated sentiment in the strange tone of a person talking in a dream. Her face assumes a great variety of startling expressions. Her body and limbs frequently tremble as if she were in danger of spasms. She indulges in frantic outbursts of emotion, and often paces the stage in a strange, wild, restless way of an untamed animal in captivity." The play itself was waved away as "preposterous rubbish." It played a mere two weeks, but Miss Morris's name kept it alive on the road for the rest of the season, sometimes rechristened for no good reason *The Refugee's Daughter.* And Miss Morton decided to make playwriting her profession.

Palmer enjoyed a season-long success with a double bill consisting of Augustus Thomas's **A Man of the World** and Ralph R. Lumley's English hit **Aunt Jack** (10-30-89, Madison Square). Thomas's brief curtain raiser had the worldly-wise Captain Bradley (Maurice Barrymore) lecture his ward and her husband to prevent their marriage from falling apart through the husband's inattention and the bored wife's flirting. Most critics relished this trifle, but the moralistic Winter could not resist chiding Barrymore for preaching concern and fidelity on the stage while philandering off it. However, the real success of the evening was the English comedy. Agnes Booth stole the show as Joan Bryson, who sues Colonel Taverner (Frederic Robinson) for breach of promise after he breaks off their engagement because she has sung a music hall ditty. Matters are complicated when she falls in love with the bachelor S. Berkeley Brue (E. M. Holland) and he with her—only to discover that he is to be Taverner's lawyer in court. The comic climax comes in the courtroom with Joan in a huge hat, topped by ridiculously undulating feathers, giving her rendition of the trouble-making ditty—"If You Want to Know the Time, Ask a Policeman." J. H. Stoddart won special applause for his Gilbertian Judge Mundle.

More visiting Englishmen ushered in November, both on the 4th. Charles Wyndham led his Criterion Theatre Company of comedians into Palmer's; Wilson Barrett and his more serious-minded entourage came into the Fifth Avenue. Wyndham began with *David Garrick* but soon switched (on the 11th) to **The Candidate,** Justin Huntley McCarthy's translation of *Le Député de Bombignac,* which had fun with a politician who prefers making whoopee to campaigning. The work was coupled with *Cut Off with a Shilling.* He then reached back for *Wild Oats* and *Trying It On.* Next, on December 9, came a mixture of old and new, *Delicate Ground* and F. C. Burnand's **The Headless Man,** whose hero was a scatterbrained young lawyer desperately and disastrously trying to improve his memory. Barrett opened with his and Hall Caine's dramatization of Caine's *The Deemster,* now called **Ben-My-Chree** and relating a sort of provincial Romeo-and-Juliet tragedy set on the Isle of Man. Moving on, he revived *Claudian* and *The Silver King* before embarking on a busy week that included *Clito,* his own rural melodrama **Nowadays** (on December 11), *Hamlet,* and a triple bill of shorter plays.

On November 11, Neil Burgess brought back *The County Fair* and settled down at the Union Square for a run that would preclude the house's having to book another attraction until June.

Another smash hit was Belasco and De Mille's **The Charity Ball** (11-19-89, Lyceum), a play that seems to exist for the sake of one startling scene—in which a minister forces his brother to marry a girl whom the brother has violated but whom the minister loves. The minister is John Van Buren (Herbert Kelcey), who has invited Phyllis Lee (Grace Henderson) to visit him in New York. He is unaware that Phyllis has been seduced by his stockbroker brother, Dick (Nelson Wheatcroft), who promised to marry her. But Dick is ruthlessly engaged in a Wall Street power battle and, forgetting his promises, is determined to marry Ann Cruger (Georgia Cayvan), the daughter of his archrival, thus further securing his place at the top. To complicate matters still more, Ann is secretly in love with brother John. But John learns the truth about Phyllis and Dick when the heartbroken, conscience-stricken girl sees a light in John's window, knows it means he is at home to anyone seeking help, and pours out her heart. He summons Dick and shames him into marrying Phyllis. Soon after the wedding, however, Dick dies of a heart attack. (Grasping stockbrokers always died of heart attacks as *The Henrietta* also attested.) By that time John has begun to fall in love with Ann. Despite his earlier confession to her of his love for Phyllis, she is happy to accept his proposal. Phyllis must be content with a rich widowhood. Few pieces of the period found a single story line sufficient, so *The Charity Ball* introduced two contrasting romances for comic relief. They embodied May and December. The first was the sometimes tempestuous courtship of John and Dick's young sister, Bess (Effie Shannon), by an eager-beaver photographer, Alec Robinson (Fritz Williams). The other had old Judge Knox (W. J. LeMoyne) courting the widowed Mrs. De Peyster (Mrs. Charles Walcot). This courtship is nearly derailed when the judge naively believes Alec's mischievous remarks that Mrs. De Peyster has a cork leg. Many of the evening's laughs came from Knox's inept attempts to check the leg for himself.

By modern standards, of course, the more serious dialogue is dissuadingly stilted and sententious. It often deprives the characters of a helpful subtlety and pushes them dangerously close to caricature. Thus the resolute, power-mad Dick announces to his rival, "You are the only man that blocks my way. And do you think I'll stop? I have no religion, no God, but one ambition—to be master of the street!" But after he is browbeaten and humiliated by his brother, he is almost cringing and whiny when he speaks to Phyllis: "Phyllis, is there love enough left in your heart for me, forgive me all the misery I have caused you? . . . False to myself, false to those at home, false to you, I come with my eyes open at last." Virtually the sole hint that Dick is ever torn between his lust for money and inherently decent feelings comes from an early aside to the audience, "If I could only tear this love out of my heart! I will!" One fascinating character is the men's blind mother (Mrs. Whiffen), whose heart tells her what her eyes cannot show her. Whatever the flaws in the writing, superb acting and magnificent settings turned the play into compelling theatre. The settings—"beautiful stage pictures," according to the *Star*—included a reproduction of the lobby of the Metropolitan Opera House (where the ball that gives the play its title occurs) and the rectory's homey sitting room, with a fire sending out a glow and the reassuring light in the window (the minister's "watches of the night") illuminating the snow falling outside. The play ran 200 performances and continued to be revived with some frequency until about the time of World War I.

While new plays—and, more significant, new American plays—were increasingly taking over the ever growing number of stages and earning longer and longer runs, Shakespeare could hardly be counted out, although hindsight would show his grip on theatricals was loosening ineluctably. But he returned with a flourish in mid-December when three of his works were mounted on two successive nights. The least eagerly awaited of the productions presented Marie Wainwright, a good but not great actress, as Viola in *Twelfth Night* at the Fifth Avenue on the 16th.

That same evening tiaraed and white-tied first-nighters gathered at Palmer's to assess Richard Mansfield's interpretation of *Richard III*. Alerted by reports from London, where Mansfield initially had tried out his ideas, and from the first American stops on his tour, playgoers could be sure in advance that this interpretation was idiosyncratic, to say the least. Flying in the face of an unmistakable drift toward restoring Shakespeare's original texts as purely as possible, Mansfield leaned heavily on Cibber—liberally adding his own alterations. Thus the play opened with a prologue lifted largely from *Henry VI* and proceeded to a scene of lavish pageantry in the tower before allowing Gloucester to make his dramatically belated entry and launch into a truncated "Now is the winter of our discontent" soliloquy. As in Cibber, richly drawn figures such as Clarence and Queen Margaret, who might have stolen the limelight, were deleted. More singular, Mansfield was determined to convey something of the historic passage of years and avoid Shakespeare's effect of having the action seem almost continuous. Gloucester, therefore, first was seen as a man of nineteen or twenty who aged perceptibly in subsequent scenes. Ostensibly, Mansfield also rejected the unmitigated malevolence of Shakespeare's portrait and attempted to show Richard battling between his conscience and his conception of political expediency.

Many of the leading critics were disturbed by the production and thought Mansfield failed to convey his own published notions. J. Ranken Towse of the *Evening Post* placed himself squarely among the naysayers. Even recalling the performance years later he blanched at Mansfield's delivering a soliloquy "squatting like a toad upon a stone." To Towse, the actor presented the king "as a hangdog looking, beetle-browed fellow, whose face suggested nothing but a dull malignity. . . . His entrance into King Henry's chamber in the tower, his studied pause upon the threshold, his warming his hands at the fire, the careful drawing of his sword, and the testing of the tip exhibited a calculated mechanism in which there was no quiver of life or emotion. He passed his sword through the body of his victim with the nonchalance of a poulterer skewering a fowl, and wiped his sword upon the curtain with the same passionless indifference. . . . All was mere action without informing soul." Mansfield kept the mounting on the boards for a month, despite poor attendance, and gave a bitter curtain speech on the play's final evening in New York.

Meanwhile, back at the ranch, or at least at one of the cheaper, outlying theatres, playgoers would thrill to more contemporary, native adventures. **The Indian Mail Carrier** (12-16-89, Third Ave.) starred Go-Won-Go Mohawk, who was supposed to be an authentic Indian. Newspapers and programs could never agree on how to spell or hyphenate her name, and some commentators questioned whether she was truly an Indian. But they all agreed she could ride a horse and fling a knife. The star was also billed as author of the play, although the manuscript credits one Charlie Charles as collaborator. Colonel Stockton loves his eastern-educated daughter, Nellie, and his "red brothers," especially Wep-Ton-No-Mah, a mail carrier. The Indian rides on for his first entrance to the strains of "Oh, My Gallant Steed." What the colonel does not know is that his debt-ridden nephew, Captain Franklin, and a Spaniard, Joe Lopez, are conspiring against him. A big birthday party for the colonel provides an excuse for the specialty turns required of every touring show. The party ends when a violent thunder-and-lightning storm breaks loose. Wep-Ton-No-Mah gallops onstage to rescue Nellie first from the stampede that follows, and then from Joe.

Wep.: The White Fawn need have no fear for Wep-Ton-No-Mah will shield her with his life.
Nellie: (*aside*) My hero.

A furious Joe kills the Indian's father and sets out to get his nemesis.

Joe: (*coming on looking about*) Wep-Ton-No-Mah is very cunning, he is concealed somewhere, and if he don't show up soon I'll burn him out of his concealment. Now to see who is the most cunning. (*Exit R.2.E. Red fire. Everybody rushes about yelling and screaming and off at different entrances*) . . . (*rushing on knife in hand*) . . . [*he fires on man loyal to colonel*] You are unarmed, wounded and alone. All I have to do is cut your heart out. (*turns savagely, sees Wep-Ton-No-Mah, is horrified*)
Wep.: Then you'll have to cut through me.
Joe: Wep-Ton-No-Mah!
Wep.: Yes, Wep-Ton-No-Mah. (*Terrific knife combat. Joe is conquered.*)
Curtain

Playgoers accepted this picture of "rugged frontier life" as reasonably accurate and unquestionably exciting, so the lady rode dauntlessly on for many seasons, sometimes using the title *Wep-To[n]-No-Mah, The Indian Mail Carrier*. There seems to be a hint of burlesque in these Indian names.

The third Shakespearean production of the week was *As You Like It* at Daly's on the 17th. While the producer-director offered virtually all of Shakespeare's comedy, he radically rearranged the order of scenes; for example, Daly's second act began with the third scene of Shakespeare's second act, then progressed through scenes five, one, and four—all three combined into one—before concluding with scenes six and seven). He also softened expressions that might offend, changing "God" to "Heaven," "bastard" to "child," and "spit" to "cough." He enlisted such leading scene painters as Hoyt, Goatcher, and J. H. Young to create a bright, cheerful Forest of Arden. The cheerfulness spilled over to the performance, which emphasized the comedy and happier aspects of the romances. Ada Rehan was Rosalind, Drew was Orlando, and Lewis was Touchstone. No place could be found for the fourth member of Daly's famous quartet, Mrs. Gilbert, but young Henrietta Crosman, later herself a famous Rosalind, was Celia. Again, not all the critics were pleased. The *Herald*'s man thought the production gave Shakespeare's poetry short shrift and was too "modern" in its approach. He similarly rejected Miss Rehan's "arch" heroine and Drew's "trooperlike" hero. But unlike Mansfield, Daly long since had established a reputation and won a steadfast clientele. His revival ran for sixty-two showings and remained in his repertory until his death.

If some of Mansfield's notions were retrogressive, in other ways he was enlightenedly and courageously forward-looking. So on the afternoon of December 21, he gave New York its first English version of **A Doll's House;** a repeat performance was offered on January 9. Several other cities on Mansfield's tour had seen it earlier (always at a single, special matinee), and, of course, amateur Scandinavian-speaking theatrical societies had presented it. (We have already noted the professional mounting in New York in German.) But for all practical purposes (since Modjeska's *Thora* was an unfaithful redaction and had only been given one performance in Louisville in 1883), this represented America's real introduction to Ibsen. Mansfield himself did not appear in the production, but critics and notably small audiences applauded Beatrice Cameron's warm if rather ingenuous Nora. The *Times,* which in earlier notices had condemned much of the play while admiring its craftsmanship, softened its stance. Its anonymous critic, probably Dithmar, conceded Nora was "not a pretty character" but concluded the play "deserves to hold its own on our stage." Winter disagreed, but his disapproval was nowhere as virulent as his fulminations against Ibsen would become shortly thereafter when he appointed himself leader of the anti-Ibsenite Americans. (Several nights later *The Pillars of Society* was given at the Amberg in German.)

Benjamin Landeck's **My Jack** (12-23-89, Grand Opera) was the latest English melodrama imported for the touring circuits. Its heroine, Dorothy Prescott (Isabelle Evesson), loves a simple fisherman, Jack Meredith (J. H. Gilmour), but Sir Howard Vanberg (Wilton Lackaye, who seemed to be everywhere in the last few months) is determined to get rid of Jack and marry Dorothy himself. In the end Vanberg is shown to be no nobleman. The real nobleman, as everyone might expect, was Jack. The play included an explosion in a lighthouse, a shipwreck, and other creaky melodramatic clichés. Its single week at the Grand Opera was part of a cross-country tour.

Some knowledgeable playgoers had been puzzled by the failure of Terriss and Millward to bring with them one of their major and most recent Adelphi successes, a melodrama set primarily in America. The hero of Sydney Grundy and Henry Pettitt's **The Bells of Haslemere** (12-23-89, Windsor) is forced by a perfidious rival to flee to Louisiana. The villain follows him there and accuses him of being a counterfeiter. He is nearly lynched and flees into the bayou, dogged by bloodhounds, before all is set right. Another touring production stopping only briefly in New York, it was revived in America as late as 1902.

Fanny Davenport rang out the old year when she returned on the 30th to the Star for a fortnight's visit in *La Tosca.*

James H. Wallick, one of the most popular stars of cheap western melodramas, assumed the title role of **Sam Houston, the Hero of Texas** (1-6-90, Third Ave.). The action harked back to 1836 when Sam, aided by his buddies Col. Davy Crockett and Col. Jim Bowie, bested Santa Ana on the banks of the San Jacinto and won independence for Texas. Santa Ana was shown as a gentleman who gallantly hands over his sword to the victors. A horse was not so gentlemanly on opening night, knocking down the scenery as it galloped across the stage. In 1986, nearly a hundred years on, when such stage melodramas and neighborhood playhouses had bitten the dust decades before, CBS noisily publicized its special, three-hour-long made-for-television movie *Houston: The Legend of Texas,* which covered much the same ground.

Dan Sully was another popular touring star, whose vehicles usually contained enough songs and dances to nudge them into the musical category. **Con Conroy and Co.** (also called *Conroy, the Tailor*) (1-6-90, Theatre Comique, Harlem) was probably no exception, but its plot touched on potentially serious problems such as Con's having to save his prospective son-in-law from the snares of a sharp banker. It was not a success.

The popular team of Robson and Crane had announced its dissolution late in the 1888–89 season. Most playgoers probably had preferred the lovable, deadpanned, squeaky-voiced Robson and would have predicted he was better able to survive the breakup. But discerning observers had noted a certain sameness in everything Robson did and, on the other hand, a willingness to range and explore on Crane's part. As a result they were not surprised when Crane fared better than his erstwhile partner, though Robson remained an attraction for many seasons.

In the autumn Crane had tried out several plays on the road, apparently determined to bring in only the best for his reemergence as a solo comedian. He dropped several foreign vehicles and put one American piece on hold, selecting instead another domestic work. He thereby scored the first hit of the new year when he appeared in **The Senator** (1-13-90, Star), a comedy written by David D. Lloyd and polished after Lloyd's death by Sydney Rosenfeld. Crane played the kindly, knowing Senator Hannibal Rivers, who agrees to help Silas Denman (J. G. Padgett) and his attractive daughter, Mabel (Lizzie Hudson Collier), to press a claim dating back to the War of 1812. Mabel hopes the money will speed her marriage to a suave Austrian diplomat, Count Ernst von Strahl (Henry Bergman). But Rivers soon gets wind of rumors that Strahl is a fortune hunter and a faithless philanderer, so the senator enlists a rich, notoriously coquettish widow, Mrs. Hilary (Georgiana Drew Barrymore), to abet him in exposing the count. Mrs. Hilary also lures away another senator, who plans to vote against the claim and whose vote could be crucial. The excitement of winning proves too much for old Denman, who dies of a stroke. Left alone and with her former suitor out of the picture, Mabel is receptive to Rivers's proposal of marriage. However, she does have one question.

Mabel: (*to Senator in low tone*) And why should you marry me, you a Senator and a millionaire?
Senator: I'll tell you why; you've got $75,000 in your pocket this minute. I'm marrying you for money.

Mrs. Hilary wins the hand of an officer she has had her eye on. Although the *Spirit of the Times* exclaimed, "Think of an original American comedy with quotable lines! Such a phenomenon has not been known before in this generation," the play in this instance was not the thing. Contemporaries instantly enrolled Crane's Rivers in the pantheon of memorable theatrical portraits, alongside Jefferson's Rip, Sothern's Dundreary, Raymond's Sellers, and Florence's Slote. Mrs. Barrymore also won kudos for her hilarious widow. The play compiled 119 performances before reembarking on its tour.

Uptown at the Fifth Avenue on the same night, Julia Marlowe returned in what was hoped would be an eight-week stand. Her repertory offered *Ingomar*, a pensive, autumn-hued *As You Like It* (in marked contrast to Daly's festive, springlike mounting), *The Hunchback*, and *Pygmalion and Galatea*.

Critics were cordial, seeing a distinct maturing of her artistry. But apparently she was not yet a big enough name to attract playgoers to an often obsolescent schedule in sufficient numbers. After a month, during which she lost $29,000 because of poor houses, she headed out again to a more conservative road that had proved receptive and profitable.

A third opening, this time at the 14th Street Theatre, saw Robert Mantell delight audiences in the sort of romantic swashbuckler he did so well, *The Corsican Brothers*.

Broadway's darling, Elsie Leslie, starred in the dual roles of **The Prince and the Pauper** (1-20-90, Broadway), which Abby Sage Richardson adapted from Mark Twain's story. Most audiences knew in advance the saga of young Prince Edward and ragged Tom Canty, who exchange garments and are promptly mistaken for one another. The prince runs off with Sir Miles Hendon (E. H. Vanderfelt), a disinherited knight, who treats him kindly and is amused at his pretensions to royalty. Meanwhile, the courtiers are baffled by the unprincely behavior of Tom. Annie Mayor won praise for her Mrs. Canty. On opening night Twain made a long curtain speech as he held Miss Leslie's hand, while she stared smilingly but uncomprehendingly at the audience. She probably had no notion that this would be her last important New York opening. After two seasons of touring in the play she would outgrow the sort of roles that had made her famous. She retired, and when she returned nearly a decade later, she confirmed what many critics had said about her—that while she was cute and blessed with winning childish ways, she was no actress.

A theatre on 8th Street, which had tried its luck with Jewish offerings and vaudeville, took on a new name and converted to straight plays. Its first offering was **A Chase for a Duck** (1-20-90, Comedy), not the most encouraging of titles. The plot told of a hypochondriac's search for absurd cures. Critics thought neither the duck, the doctors' advice, nor the play itself was all they were quacked up to be. The following Monday another play (Arizona Joe in something called **Black Hawk**) opened and closed on the same night, after which the playhouse went dark for several months.

At the more prestigious Palmer's, Mansfield, having been forced by disappointing business to set aside *Richard III*, restored *Dr. Jekyll and Mr. Hyde* on the 20th and brought back *Prince Karl* the following Monday. Mansfield's failure with his offering of theatrical caviar prompted him to leap to the other end of the theatrical spectrum and present what Winter, in his biography of the actor, called "a drama that exhales the fragrance of boiled cabbage." The critic meant a melodrama that pandered to the lower classes by depicting a poor hero hounded by a rich villain. The untiring Pettitt and George R. Sims were the authors of the London piece Mansfield selected, **Master and Man** (2-5-90, Palmer's). In this instance the poor hero was not all that poor but was a young engineer, and the rich villain, an ironmaster, was not the real villain but was under the baleful influence of his vile, hunchbacked foreman, Humphrey "Humpy" Logan. Naturally Mansfield played Logan. But this was not the season for hunchbacks. *Master and Man* lasted less than two weeks.

Mansfield was not the only celebrated figure having an off season. The far more experienced Daly was not faring well either. Even his generally praised *As You Like It* had a shorter run than his earlier Shakespearean revivals. He suffered his second real flop of the season with **A Priceless Paragon** (2-12-90, Daly's), taken from Sardou's *Belle-Maman* and recounting the downfall of a meddling, self-important mother-in-law. Audiences might have expected Mrs. Gilbert to be assigned the title role, but Daly, somewhat oddly, awarded it to his favorite, Ada Rehan, who only recently had been portraying an eighteen-year-old. Neither the play nor the casting satisfied playgoers' expectations. Furthermore, *A Priceless Paragon* was one of the very rare instances in which Daly's brother Joseph had no hand in the adaptation. The play struggled on for three weeks. During its last week it was accompanied by a short piece, **The Prayer** (2-25-90, Daly's), which Maurice F. Egan had translated from François Coppée's *Le Pater* and in which a young girl named Rose (Ada Rehan) is taught to forgive the Communards who murdered her beloved brother, a priest.

A hundred years on, Thurman Noyes, the central figure in Sydney Rosenfeld's **The Stepping Stone** (2-17-90, Standard), might have been a smirking, palms-up television preacher, soliciting an audience of foolish millions to send him their dollars. But Noyes (Gustavus Levick) has no such access to masses of people or money. This phony seer, spouting his faddish theosophy, can only prey on small groups of susceptible housewives. His chief victim is Mrs. Arden (Rose Eytinge), whom he prevails upon to hand over to him monies entrusted to her. He is finally exposed through a photographer's ruse in a dark room with a then newfangled flashbulb. The play's life was brief, but in that short time it underwent such amazing changes of cast that Odell devotes several paragraphs to them in his *Annals*.

When the Kendals returned in February to the Fifth Avenue they presented two plays already familiar to American playgoers, *Impulse* and *The Queen's Shilling*. The novelties were Pinero's **The Weaker Sex** (2-17-90, Fifth Ave.), in which a man falls in love with the daughter of a woman he once had courted, and Grundy's **A White Lie** (2-24-90, Fifth Ave.), telling how a woman's attempts to help an erring friend involve her in difficulties.

The indefatigable Thomas W. Keene came in on the 17th to the 14th Street Theatre with his hidebound repertory that for this visit displayed *Louis XI, The Merchant of Venice, Julius Caesar, Richelieu,* and *Richard III.*

For the most part March was given over to revivals and return engagements. These included Salvini, *A Midnight Bell, The Rivals* (followed by *The Heir at Law*), and Daly's productions of *A Midsummer Night's Dream* and *The Taming of the Shrew.*

Mlle. Rhéa, the French actress who reputedly had been popular on Russian stages before coming to America in the early 1880s, had never won acceptance in Manhattan. Somehow, despite her inability to master English pronunciation and her equally distressing inability to project her voice to the farthest reaches of a theatre, she had found steady employment and loyalty as a touring star. She met with failure once again when she braved New York in Albert Roland Haven's **Josephine, Empress of the French** (3-17-90, Broadway), which narrated the rise and fall of the empress. The elegantly costumed star danced at a sumptuous ball at the Tuilleries, gave pieces of her mind to the important figures of her day, was bid a tender farewell by Napoleon in a setting drenched in romantic moonlight, and finally was given a protracted death scene. But the play was heavy-handed, and Rhéa's "sing-song, loudly-pitched delivery" disaffected many critics and playgoers. After two weeks she looked for solace on the road.

Daly's unlucky season stumbled to a close with a double bill of **Miss Hoyden's Husband** and **Haroun Al Raschid and His Mother-in-Law** (3-26-90, Daly's). Neither play was totally new. The preceding season the producer had offered a condensed version of one play by Sheridan, *The Critic. Miss Hoyden's Husband* was a short curtain raiser made out of another of his plays, *A Trip to Scarborough,* which in turn had been based on Vanbrugh's *The Relapse. Haroun* was Sydney Grundy's English redaction of the same German play Daly had mounted in 1879 as *An Arabian Night.* Since Daly had announced in advance that his season would end on April 12, the plays' relatively short stand did not wholly reflect their poor reception.

Blind mothers seemed to be a theatrical fashion during the season. They had appeared as subsidiary characters in *The Charity Ball* and *My Jack,* among others. Now one played a small role in Sedley Brown's **A Long Lane; or, Pine Meadow(s)** (3-31-90, 14th St.), which had been tried out the previous season at a special matinee under its subtitle. In fact, both the play and its mounting thrived on period clichés. Thus the farm setting, with a long lane painted appropriately on the backdrop, featured real sheep patiently munching real grass in a small enclosure down by the footlights. The farm, not unexpectedly, was a New England farm, as were most of the era's stage farms. And the story centered on two farm sisters. One goes on to fame and fortune in the big city as an actress, while the other suffers at the hands of a caddish, rich neighbor. Matters go from bad to worse—at one point the actress must represent the seduced sister's baby as her own—before the actress finds means to pay off the mortgage on the family farm, set her erring sister on the right track, and win a proposal from the man she loves. Poorly received, the play was withdrawn after three weeks.

Not even a disastrous opening night could dampen the late-season success of Steele MacKaye's **Money Mad** (4-7-90, Standard). What one reviewer referred to as "a chapter of accidents" stretched a planned two and a half or three hours of entertainment into five grueling hours. It also gave critics time to think up all manner of reason for condemning the show despite the audience's obviously happy opening-night clamor. MacKaye's story was hardly new. He had used it before in his *Through the Dark* (3-19-79). But this reworking was reset in America, and more particularly in Chicago. Names, too, were changed. The villain was now called Cary Haskins (E. J. Henley) and the hero Jack Adams. (Note, again, how many of the period's American heroes were named Jack—clearly the all-American boy.) Adams was played by the seemingly omnipresent Wilton Lackaye.

The major critical complaint was that MacKaye had cheapened his work, sacrificing drama for the sake of theatre. The *Evening Sun* went into detail about the revision's melodramatic high point: "The great scene came when a drawbridge was revealed, stretched diagonally across the stage against the background of old rookeries—a most striking illusion!—and the crossing of a steamboat, when the bridge swung out over the orchestra to let it pass, brought forth the mightiest cheers and applause of the evening. This act closes with an attempted murder on the street-end of the bridge, while Wilton Lackaye . . . is trying to get to the rescue from the open draw. . . . The cries of Lackaye to the bridge-keeper, who refuses to close the draw, the oaths and shouts for help of four figures fighting in the dark, were almost too real to be pleasant." All the reviewer neglected to mention was that a huge water tank sat beneath the bridge to represent the river and that the hero jumped into it to swim to the rescue. Another spectacular setting, representing a thieves' den sunk in the bowels of the earth, was built on three levels, running from the height of the rear of the stage to a lowest level partially below the stage close to the footlights. No wonder set changes took so long! New roles included a comic cameo for Annie Yeamans and a street urchin, which the popular vaudeville star Queenie Vassar played in boy's clothing and in which she found occasion to sing "Little Annie Rooney." The play ran until summer and was given productions around the country. MacKaye's son, Percy, claims his father coined the expression "money mad."

Another thieves' den and another jump into a river were to be seen that same evening in **The Knights of Tyburn** (4-7-90, Niblo's). However, as spectacular effects they fell flat. The *Times* complained that in the dreary den "the oceans of ale drunk by the mellow roysterers are symbolized in the old-fashioned way by a few empty pitchers and tin cups." More embarrassing, "when wicked Sir Rowland meets his death under London Bridge he steps carefully into the dark Thames, lifts up one end of the water, as if it were a blanket, and crawls under it." The play, supposedly translated from a d'Ennery drama, retold the story of Jack Sheppard, with the picaresque hero played as a trouser part by Clara Louise Thompson. It lasted two weeks, then toured briefly.

An unusual return was *The Henrietta* at the 23rd Street Theatre on the 21st, unusual in that it starred Robson without Crane. Frank Mordaunt, so often saddled with villain roles, played the elder Van Alstyne. The consensus was that the play and Robson were as good as ever and were all that was needed to make a satisfactory evening. The stand was for four weeks.

Guilty Without Crime (4-21-90, People's) was a new, melodramatic title for a dramatization of M. E. Braddon's older, sensational novel *Aurora Floyd.* In the 1860s Matilda Heron and other emotive stars of the epoch had appeared in other theatricalizations of the book. Now only second-rate touring players were featured, but whether because of the title or a lingering awareness of the novel's bygone fame, playgoers thronged to outlying theatres to see it.

One week sufficed for **The Blue Officer** (4-28-90, Madison Square), a French play touted, and duly reported by some critics, as having been banned in Paris. The vicious Mme Delcroff (Rose Eytinge) and Prince Doblansky (Henry Holland), each for reasons of his or her own, attempt to destroy the Count (Henry Lee) and Countess Jassy (Selena Fetter). The prince's position as a blue officer, a member of the czar's secret police, makes it easy for him to plant incriminating papers. When the innocence of the Jassys is finally established, the prince commits suicide.

Louis Aldrich found himself a successful vehicle in **The Editor** (5-5-90, Palmer's), which he co-authored with Charles T. Vincent. Heretofore he had been known largely for his "heavies," downright villains or sombre, tormented men such as his recent Shoulders. His Colonel Joseph Hawkins marked a refreshing departure, for the editor and publisher of Tucson's *American Eagle* is a smiling, homey, good-natured, pat-on-the-back sort of fellow. So what if the editor's grammar and pronunciation leave something to be desired. Perhaps the play missed an opportunity to depict life in the still primitive Far West when it resorted to a device that was old when the Far West was still virgin, plunking down its small-town hero amid big-city sophisticates and slickers. Hawkins's visit to New York and his loosely tied together adventures there served for a plot. Probably the most memorable of these adventures concerned his encounters with the scoundrelly Stephen Morton (John E. Kellerd), whom he holds at bay with a pistol that is really a banana (shades of Lord Chumley) until the police can arrive. Later, when Morton has escaped from his captors, the men again confront each other. This time, however, Hawkins comes to the realization that Morton is not all that bad and ought to be given another chance. The colonel lends him his own slouch hat, his overcoat, and one of his ever present cigars and gives him not only a $10 gold piece but his own ticket back to Tucson. As the grateful, disguised Morton is about to leave, the colonel reminds him not to forget these kindnesses after he, Morton, talks his way into Congress. Another comic situation dealt with Josephine Jeffries (Dora Goldthwaite), a widow who has decked out not only herself but her home and even her little dog in black, in memory of her "sainted Simon." But a jeweler's bill reveals hubby had spent more on a mistress than he had on his wife. Into the trash goes all the mourning, right down to the dog's black

ribbon. The play ran out the month and toured the following season, but injuries sustained in a Syracuse hotel fire during the tour put an end to Aldrich's acting career for all practical purposes, although he later served as president of the Actors' Fund.

On the same evening, Mansfield began a summer stand at the Madison Square Theatre. His first two weeks were devoted to *A Parisian Romance*.

Less critical playgoers, looking for thrills rather than laughs or tragedy, could watch two popular touring stars, J. J. Dowling and Sadie Hasson, struggle to foil chicanery in a western mine in **The Red Spider** (5-5-90, Third Ave.). To them the West was home to romantic adventure.

Another type of romance provided the plot for **The Shatchen** (5-12-90, Star), written as a vehicle for M. B. Curtis by Henry Doblin and Charles S. Dickson. For years Curtis had been touring in one play or another as the benevolent Sam'l of Posen. Now he turned to another Jewish figure, the professional Jewish marriage maker. His name in the play is Meyer Petowsky, and he has been asked by the rich merchant, Joseph Lewis (Lewis Morrison), to find a bride for his son, Leo (Russ Whytal). But before Meyer can arrange matters, Leo arranges them for himself. To his family's horror, he weds a Christian. His father promptly disowns him. While Meyer has lost a commission, he has not lost an iota of his essential warmth and goodness. He determines to reconcile the elder Lewis to his son and new daughter-in-law. However, Meyer's best intentions are nothing compared to the arrival of a grandchild to bring about a happy ending. *Abie's Irish Rose* could not be far off. The play ran a month, then toured during the 1890–91 season.

Jacquine; or, Paste and Diamonds (5-12-90, People's) told of a poor girl's struggle to become an actress. Since it was sprinkled with musical numbers, the play inched noticeably toward musical comedy.

Mansfield provided the waning theatrical year with some special excitement when he came forth as **Beau Brummell** (at first spelled *Beau Brummel*) (5-19-90, Madison Square). Beau is vain, effete, and supercilious, interested only in savoring life's pleasures. He is so hopelessly irresponsible that he tells his valet, Mortimer (W. J. Ferguson), to hide his bills where he "would not see them," so that he might "think that they are paid." Only his gambling debts are honored promptly. His empty purse prompts him to offer his hand to Mariana Vincent (Agnes Miller), daughter of a rich, vulgar London merchant. Brummell is unaware that his own nephew, Reginald (F. W. Lander), and Mariana are in love.

For some time he has amused the Prince of Wales (D. H. Harkins), but he alienates him when, on leaving a ball, he snaps, "I shall have to order my carriage. Wales, will you ring the bell?" His attempts to gloss over the gaffe are rebuffed, and his creditors pounce. To his further dismay, Brummell overhears Reginald and Mariana exchange endearments. Head high, he determines to leave London. Years pass— unkind years. Aging and impoverished, and kept company only by his devoted valet, he sits in his shabby French rooms, where, by the light of a single candle, he provides a regal if imaginary supper for his old companions, who themselves are now but figments of his fantasy.

For many playgoers and critics Mansfield's Brummell was his quintessential performance—a brilliant tour de force that was showy and wide-ranging, yet ultimately deeply moving. A few carpers claimed that his "invincible stiffness and angularity" detracted from his impersonation of the exquisite dandy in his younger years, but Mansfield's playing of the defeated old man won universal admiration. In the first scene of the final act Beau is "discovered sitting in front of the fireplace with his back to the audience. He is dressed in a yellow brocaded dressing-gown, apparently the same one worn in Act I, but with its glory gone,—faded and worn, torn in places." His final entrance, at the beginning of the next and last scene is more dramatic. As Winter described it, "The place is dimly lighted. The slow, heavy, uncertain steps of *Brummell* were heard, as he came toiling up the bare, hollow-sounding stairs, outside. Then came a momentary pause and silence, as though the broken man had stopped to recover himself. When he appeared he was the image of abject misery,—still, however, striving bravely to endure. His lips moved, as though whispering to himself, but no sound came from them. His strength was almost exhausted. He moved weakly a few steps into the room, and sank into the chair that was brought forward by *Mortimer*. After a moment he recovered a little and tried to straighten his body—then sat, crouched and still. His old hat was pulled low on his forehead; his threadbare coat, buttoned close to his chin, wrinkled over his shrunken body; his fingers aimlessly plucked at the frayed tips of his gloves; his eyes vacantly stared, as though he saw the light of other days around him; his mind was far away: presently, at first in a quavering whisper and then in a low, weak voice, thin and tremulous, but wonderfully sweet,—the voice of a broken, dying man,—he sang, without appearing to know that he was doing so." *Beau Brummell* spanned the summer, compil-

ing 150 performances before heading back out on tour. Mansfield kept the play in his repertory until his death. He also kept up a long, acrimonious debate over how much of the writing of *Beau Brummell* was his and how much was contributed by Clyde Fitch, who was credited with the authorship on programs. Whatever the truth, the production introduced to the public the dramatist who would become the leading American playwright of his time.

. . .

Clyde [William] **Fitch** (1865–1909) was born in Elmira, N.Y., the son of a Union army officer and a Maryland belle. His sissified ways isolated him at school but earned him ladies' parts in plays while a student at Amherst College. Coming to New York, he tried his hand at architecture and interior decorating. He also wrote short stories and plays. One of his plays, *Betty's Finish*, had been tried out earlier in the year at the Boston Museum. At the same time, he made a number of theatrical friends, among them Dithmar and Winter, and it was these men who suggested to Mansfield that he work with Fitch.

. . .

At the Lyceum a revival of *The Private Secretary* wound up the season.

Several times during the year stars or supporting players had appeared in plays of which they were co-authors. Except in the case of the cantankerous Mansfield, there was rarely any argument over whether they genuinely had contributed a share of the writing. Nor was there any unpleasantness about authorship when Edwin Arden, for years a popular leading man on tour, opened in **Raglan's Way** (5-9-90, Union Square), which programs credit him with writing in partnership with Arden Smith. The only unpleasantness was onstage, where critics found a story condemned by some critics as too continuously nasty and by others as too continuously absurd. Its incidents did border on the ridiculous. But then its hero, Guy Raglan, sometimes had to be crossed and kicked and spat upon before he could become truly angry. At other times he was quick to anger and just as quick to cool down. Guy (Arden) stumbles across his best friend, Ivan Robeloff (Nelson Wheatcroft), forcing his attentions on a woman in the ruins of an old abbey. The woman is able to flee, but Guy picks up a bracelet she has dropped (it looks a lot like one he has given his girlfriend). Ivan attempts to seize the bracelet, which is torn in half. And when he gives Guy a good smack, Guy suggests they fight a duel—not an ordinary duel, but a very odd one (echoes of *Hélène*). The men will shoot at each other in pitch darkness. However, each will be smoking a cigar, and that will indicate his whereabouts. No longer annoyed, Guy decides to shoot to miss. Unfortunately, Ivan holds his cigar at arm's length, so Guy's bullet pierces him. He appears to be dead. From out of nowhere, Guy's sweetheart, Vivian (Minnie Seligman), arrives, sees what has happened, and shrieks. Guy does not seem to notice her bracelet is missing. Many years elapse. Suddenly Ivan returns. It seems he was not killed and has been roaming the world these many years. For some reason Guy has kept the half-bracelet and never wondered why Vivian has not worn hers since the night of the duel. But Vivian, though she once had a certain affection for Ivan, does not want him to reenter her life. She writes a letter to him, which she leaves unfinished on her desk. Since she had left it blank side up, Guy appropriates it when he needs a paper on which to draw pictures for his child. Later, however, he turns it over, reads it, and finally understands why Vivian has not worn the bracelet. He invites Ivan to see him and sets upon him, hoping to strangle him. Just at this moment the child calls. Guy relents, but soon after Ivan commits suicide. The play ran three weeks, then toured for a time in the fall before Arden returned to the security of his *Eagle's Nest*.

Actor-playwright Mark Price put both his skills to work in another melodrama, **Branded** (6-16-90, Third Ave.). It centered on two brothers, Clarence and Warren Stanton (E. J. Buckley and M. J. Jordan). One is a forger who has served his time and is now down and out. The other is rich and self-righteous but not all that decent. He would have his hungry brother forge again, this time to destroy an innocent man, Tom O'Hare (Price). O'Hare and the ex-forger combine to teach the rich brother a lesson.

A cast filled with favorites probably explains why Fred Maeder and McKee Rankin's **The Canuck** (7-28-90, Bijou) did good business despite the heat during its six-week run. These favorites included Annie Yeamans and her daughter, Jennie, and Wilton Lackaye. But Rankin was the star, assuming the role of a French-Canadian farmer, Jean Baptiste Cadeaux. Cadeaux's daughter, Archange (Mabel Bert), loves Tom (S. Miller Kent), the son of a Vermont farmer. Tom, however, has gone off to Wall Street, where he sees a chance to make a killing in mine stocks and persuades his father to mortgage the farm in order to buy the stocks. Also, he has married another girl. But the girl turns out to be a bigamist, and the mine stocks soar in time to save the farm. Lackaye was assigned the role of a serio-comic villain "who wears good clothes and calls a

lady a 'lala,'" and Annie Yeamans provided more comic relief. A number of songs and dances, mostly for Jennie Yeamans, probably added to the play's hot-weather appeal.

A double bill wrote *finis* to the season: Augustus Thomas's **A Woman of the World** and George Manville Fenn and J. H. Darnley's English comedy **The Balloon** (8-4-90, Star). Thomas's one-act afterpiece was bruited to have been written especially for Georgiana Drew Barrymore in hopes that it might serve as a companion for her husband's *Man of the World*. Its reception was cool enough to counter the summer heat, and it quickly disappeared. Crane had tried out the English comedy earlier in the season and found it, too, wanting. New York saw it with a totally different cast. In *The Balloon* a young doctor is pursued by a ridiculous widow and led to believe he has poisoned his sweetheart's aunt, so he attempts to flee by sailing away in a friend's balloon. Not even an excellent cast that included Robert Hilliard, Sidney Drew, and Mrs. Barrymore could make it acceptable to Americans.

1890–1891

"Times are a-changin'," a character in one of the season's lesser plays observed. The observation was unoriginal even then. At varying tempi times always are changing. But during the 1890–91 theatrical year two matters sharpened this sense of change in an appropriately dramatic way. The more apparent was the electrification of auditoriums. For several seasons theatres had been converting from gas lighting, but the transformation had been slow and very often tentative. Many a playhouse owner, wary of the new invention, had either converted only a small area or else timidly opted to employ the old and the new side by side. However, during the summer hiatus of 1890, a number of major playhouses—such as the Fifth Avenue—plunged headlong into the brave new world. As a result, when playgoers returned en masse with the cooler weather they time and again entered brightly lit lobbies, sat beneath glittering chandeliers, and saw stages illuminated to a remarkable degree. Inevitably, stage electricians felt they had to show off their wondrous facilities. So before long a critic could write, tongue in cheek, about a new mounting, "There are no light effects. We are not permitted to look upon the sunset when it is red or the moonlight when it is an impossible but attractive shade of green.

A servant does not once come upon a darkened stage with a single lamp that causes an instantaneous and dazzling general illumination."

Concurrently, the expression "fin de siècle" began to crop up in reviews, acknowledging that a tired old century was coming to an end and a new century was in the offing. As used in notices the expression also implied a certain wearied decadence, a perception that the high moral fiber the century had boasted in its vigorous heyday had become distressingly flabby. Yet interestingly, these sighs for a passing age contained an undertone of acceptance, as if writers grudgingly were recognizing that the Victorian moral fiber was sometimes absurdly muscle-bound. For the moment at least, protestations of immorality—though they most certainly did not disappear and would swell anew with the anti-Ibsen movement—seemed muted. It was the beginning of a stance that eventually allowed some real fresh air to waft across our stages.

More than one critic insisted that James Schönberg's **The Banker** (8-11-90, Windsor), which was advertised as a "new and powerful emotional drama," was neither, seeing it instead merely as a lame rehash of Tom Taylor's *Henry Dunbar,* a play Broadway had applauded in the late sixties and early seventies. After one week this version disappeared from the records.

Many of the same reviewers detected something hand-me-down about **The Tale of a Coat** (8-14-90, Daly's). Its star was Sol Smith Russell, and as he had in the preceding season's *A Poor Relation,* he played an impoverished, eccentric inventor, Jeremy Watt. A tailor by trade, Jeremy is secretly in love with Mrs. Cora Welby (Linda Dietz). Unfortunately for him, Cora believes she is a widow and is faithful to the memory of her husband. Then the handsome Richard Doubleday (John E. Kellerd) orders a new coat from Jeremy, and while making the coat Jeremy discovers that Richard is not only Cora's husband but is a bigamist as well. When one of Jeremy's inventions suddenly brings him a fortune he attempts to bribe Richard, whose first wife had died, into returning to Cora. Cora learns of this and rejects Richard's proposal. Instead she consents to marry the loyal, honorable Jeremy. The play's author was a name out of the gaslit past—aging, ailing Dion Boucicault. Boucicault had suffered a heart attack during rehearsals in Philadelphia, and he died just days after Russell was forced by "four weeks of disastrous business" to replace the vehicle with *A Poor Relation.*

Matters went from bad to worse with Webster

Edgerly's **Christopher Columbus; or, The Discovery of America** (8-18-90, Windsor). Edgerly, who ran an acting school in Washington, not only wrote the play—"in execrable blank verse"—but produced it and enlisted his own services as star, using the moniker Edmund Shaftesbury. He was not a good actor, cursed with "a whistling voice that justified the inference that Columbus must have worn false teeth." Nor was he too brainy when it came to mounting his play. At one point he argued his case that the world was round by producing a Rand-McNally globe on which playgoers in the front rows could see the undiscovered new world clearly outlined. If Edgerly hoped his masterpiece would still be touring during the Columbian celebrations two years hence, he was quickly disabused. The play lasted a single week.

Despite its title, Edward E. Kidder's **One Error** (8-26-90, Fifth Ave.) did a bit better. The play was a vehicle written expressly for Cora Tanner, whose husband, Col. W. E. Sinn, an important figure in Brooklyn theatricals, produced the piece. Miss Tanner played Judith Orme, a rich young girl who passes as a poor one so that no man will want her for her money. She is led to believe that the man she loves is a fortune hunter and aware of her ruse, so she marries another man, who *is* a fortune hunter and aware of her ruse. This man's mistress attempts to poison Judith's coffee, but Judith's husband drinks it by mistake and dies, so Judith is able to remarry more wisely. The play ran four weeks and toured briefly before a lesser cast was allowed to take it out to the hinterlands.

The first real success of the season was the first incontestably English play, Jerome K. Jerome's **The Maister of Woodbarrow** (8-26-90, Lyceum), which gave a further boost to E. H. Sothern's escalating renown. Sothern portrayed Allen Rollitt, a country lad who goes astray in the big city, then returns home to find peace and happiness.

The next "star," a big, strapping fellow, won a noisy round of applause when he first appeared, wearing a loose white shirt bordered with ruffles, knee-smalls, black silk stockings, and pumps. Exactly why a man impersonating a village blacksmith should dress so luxuriously remains a mystery. But obviously the audience approved. They were even more vociferous when he donned a pair of boxing gloves, for the "star" was John L. Sullivan, America's most admired boxer. (A year earlier Sullivan had beaten Jake Kilrain in the last bare-knuckle championship fight—in seventy-five rounds.) His vehicle was Duncan B. Harrison's comedy-drama **Honest Hearts and Willing Hands** (9-1-90, Niblo's), and Sullivan played Jim, whose brother, John (Harrison), has been falsely accused by Arthur Dare (Basil West) of murdering Arthur's uncle, General Dare. Actually Arthur himself was the killer, but since it was known that the general was reluctant to allow his niece and ward, Emily Poignsford (Virginia Nelson), to wed Jim, Arthur felt he could provide a plausible motive. The brief, wildly cheered boxing match at the end was fought not with Arthur but with Arthur's hired cohort, the hooligan Tug O'Brien (Joe Lannon). Before that Jim twice had to rescue his sweetheart from Arthur's clutches. Spectators cared not a whit that Sullivan seemed unaware of modern punctuation, turning two sentences into one, such as "What not gone yet get out or by heavens I'll choke you," or that whenever he was interrupted in midsentence by applause he invariably had to retreat to the beginning of the sentence again. After two weeks downtown, Sullivan moved on.

Another Irishman, one who was often to employ Sullivan's rival, Corbett, and was to move on to greater theatrical fame, was William A. Brady.

• • •

William A[loysius] Brady (1863–1950) was born in San Francisco and began his career there in 1882 as an actor. He turned to producing in 1888 and soon found himself in legal hot water after mounting an unauthorized production of Boucicault's *After Dark*. Ten years passed before he hit the big time. In 1899 he married Grace George.

• • •

In 1890 Brady was still struggling as an actor, as a playwright, and as a fledgling producer. He served in the last two capacities for **The Bottom of the Sea** (9-1-90, People's), which he supposedly derived from a French sensation-melodrama. The play featured a collision at sea and a ship's sinking. The hero is helping to lay cable in the Atlantic, but he must dive to retrieve the heroine's jewel box, lost in the sinking, before the villain can reach it. The play toured for many years.

Rose Osborne was the star of **Satan** (9-1-90, Windsor), in which, as Madeline de Sevigne, she assumed the guise of the devil to save an innocent young girl. Oldtimers recognized the play as a reworking of *Satan in Paris*, which Laura Keene and other bygone actresses had popularized in the 1850s and 1860s.

The season's initial American hit, **All the Comforts of Home** (9-8-90, 23rd St.), was American only in that its author was the fast-rising William Gillette. In keeping with an all too common practice of the time, it was simply a redaction of a foreign play, Carl Laufs's *Ein toller Einfall*, and was reset not in New York or some other American city but in London.

There Egbert (Robert in some programs) Pettibone (T. M. Hunter), suspecting his wife is falling in love with another man, removes his family to the Continent and hands his mansion over to his nephew, Alfred Hastings (Henry Miller). Alfred decides to turn his situation into a financial windfall by renting out rooms. He generously promises to split his take fifty-fifty with his friend, Tom McDow (J. C. Buckstone), whose principal thought thereafter is "And I gits half!" The renters are an odd lot. Christopher Dabney (Ian Robertson) is a difficult, eccentric composer, who boasts, "I quarrelled with the conductor, the soloists, orchestra, chorus singers, was insulted by the stage-manager, and finally hissed by the audience." Fifi Oritanski (Maud Haslam) is a singer of comic operas. Judson Langhorne (Lewis Baker) is a gaudily dressed man-about-town. Another renter—never seen—keeps calling down to find out the time. There is also a persistent visitor, Victor Smythe (J. B. Hollis), who has been courting Pettibone's daughter and whom Pettibone mistakenly has believed to be his wife's heartthrob. Complications begin to come fast and furious after Theodore Bender (M. A. Kennedy), a retired produce dealer, takes rooms for himself, his harridan wife (Ida Vernon), and his daughter (Maude Adams), and when Fifi contrives to have Mr. Bender underwrite her career. Flirtations, mistaken identities, and wild accusations pile one atop another, reaching a frenetic peak just as Pettibone returns home unexpectedly. Rapid-fire pacing (not always evident on opening night) helped gloss over the gaps in plausibility. The farce ran until mid-October and returned later in the season to another theatre to chalk up an additional three-month stand. At that time the cast included W. A. Faversham as Alfred and Rose Eytinge as Mrs. Bender. The play remained a favorite for many years and in 1919 served as the source for the musical *Fifty-Fifty, Ltd.*

John A. Stevens's **The Mask of Life** (9-8-90, Grand Opera) used the once voguish problems of Russian nihilism for background. In the foreground Countess Vera (Annie Mayor) marries Leon (J. H. Gilmour), to the chagrin of Prince Oscar (Frazer Coulter). The prince thereupon insinuates that Vera is not faithful. The play was as stale as the setting and soon disappeared.

The longer second run of *All the Comforts of Home* was not unusual at a time when many new plays first were given a limited New York booking as part of an extended prearranged tour. The active 8th saw the return of both *The Senator* and *The County Fair*, now a pair of established hits, whose return runs surpassed their original stands. *The Senator* ran at the Star until the end of January. The even more popular Neil Burgess vehicle stayed on at the Union Square until late March. Clay M. Greene's 1882 play, *Chispa,* also made an appearance. But it remained for just a lone week at the Park before heading out to the road.

So busy, largely successful, and largely American a Monday night was followed a week later by an evening that saw only two important premieres, neither of which was American and neither of which succeeded. The Parisian hit Dumas fils and Achille Artois's *L'Affaire Clemenceau* was offered as **The Clemenceau Case** (9-15-90, Standard). It starred Wilton Lackaye as an artist who devotes himself to his wife until he discovers she is under the thumb of her greedy but impoverished mother, a countess, and is unfaithful. Wilson Barrett and Hall Caine's London melodrama **Good Old Times** (9-15-90, 14th St.) centered on a husband transported to Australia after publicly assuming guilt for shooting a molester whom his wife actually attempted to kill. The injured villain pursues both the man and his wife until he is finally given his comeuppance. An episodic piece, it relied heavily on scenic effects, such as a boat cruising a Tasmanian river, for much of its appeal. But that appeal proved stronger on the road than in New York.

Fred Darcy's **The Devil's Mine** (9-15-90, Third Ave.) was to enjoy a long life on the touring circuits. Set in Bear Gulch, it recounted the tribulations of a drunken miner who is framed for a robbery and nearly lynched. The hero, a young, high-principled gambler, arrives in time to shoot down the rope with which the miner is about to be hanged. His reward is the miner's daughter. Apaches and an overland coach added some theatrical realism to the settings.

A tempest in a theatrical teapot was stirred up by C. A. Byrne's **Goggles** (9-22-90, Fifth Ave.), taken from Labiche's *Les Petits Oiseaux.* Palmer long since had announced he would have a version ready in October. One look at the morning-after reviews, and playgoers decided to wait for Palmer's mounting.

A beautiful new pink and white playhouse, the Garden, part of the Madison Square Garden complex, opened its doors with an English version of a French farce. In this adaptation by Hamilton Aide, *Dr. Jo-Jo* became the more prosaic **Dr. Bill** (9-27-90, Garden). Wilton Lackaye, so recently the unhappy artist Clemenceau, took on the part of the perplexed physician. In his younger days he had been quite a rake, so a neighbor, Mrs. Horton (Sadie Martinot), persuades his wife to test his fidelity. He gets wind of the plot and sends a substitute. But though Lackaye

got laughs when he was accidentally drenched, the show was stolen from him by two ladies. Edith Kenward was imported from England to recreate her popular "Kangaroo dance." It made such a hit that her small role was quickly enlarged; unfortunately, a fall forced her to leave the show immediately afterwards. Sadie Martinot, playing a retired ballerina and wearing gowns just this side of shocking, had fun trying to retrieve a key that had fallen down her back. To bolster attendance the producers soon added a curtain raiser, Jerome K. Jerome's **Sunset** (10-6-90, Garden), which told of two sisters in love with the same man. For all its faults, and despite numerous cast changes, the double bill ran into the new year.

Helen Dauvray came a cropper when she attempted to reactivate her career as an actress-manager by producing and starring in Sydney Rosenfeld's **The Whirlwind** (9-30-90, Standard). Rosenfeld looked to recent headlines about the run on the Sixth National Bank for his inspiration. He could feel certain that many in his audience would remember the major details. A young man had speculated illegally and disastrously in funds belonging to the bank where he worked. His socially prominent father, a stockholder in the bank, had proclaimed, "I'll save the bank if it costs me a million a day!" Unfortunately, Rosenfeld could not decide whether he wanted to be a melodramatist or a satirist. His Pine Street Bank is nearly ruined by the wheelings and dealings of Robert Brent (J. G. Saville), who couldn't care less if some of the bonds he has stolen belonged to his betrothed, Polly Fargus (Miss Dauvray). But Polly, a determined and skilled young lady, sets about saving the bank and wins the hand of a decent young lawyer in the process. The scene at the Clearing House, with desperate depositors shouting outside, was a high point. Polly, vaguely echoing the real father's statement, tells the bank president, "I love your wife. For her sake I will help you. I must have half a million dollars at once. . . . The bank will be saved!" Some attempts at localization and topicalization went wide of the mark. Thus a character called Mr. Prime was made up to resemble the contemporary superintendent of the New York Clearing House, even though, as one critic observed, not one person in five thousand had any idea of what he looked like. More telling was Rosenfeld's sketching of a moneyless go-getter, Press Fenwick (Sidney Drew), who can publish his *Weekly Financial Budget* if he can only scrounge up $100. Fenwick never does find the money. Nor could the play find a large audience. It lingered one month. In its Sunday afterview the *Herald* observed that the play typified a failing of American playwrights—they could not write well about love. Just why this play should prompt such a remark is unfathomable, but the *Herald*'s man returned to it several times later in the season.

October brought in a rash of hits, beginning with its very first premiere. Joseph Arthur's **Blue Jeans** (10-6-90, 14th St.) quickly secured a niche in the pantheon of American stage classics, largely because of one sensational scene that soon became a cliché in period melodrama. Its hero, Perry Bascom (Robert Hilliard), has returned to his Indiana home to run for Congress and to marry Sue Eudaly (Judith Berolde), a beautiful girl who had once been a "snake-charmer" in a traveling circus. The marriage angers Sue's old suitor, Ben Boone (George Fawcett). He is therefore easily persuaded to oppose Perry, and with the help of some cagey, corrupt politicians, he wins. But Perry has discovered that Sue is an adventuress and a bigamist. He divorces her and marries June (Jeannie Yeamans), a waif from the county poorhouse. Believing that Perry cannot prove her first marriage, Sue turns the tables and threatens to bring him to trial for bigamy. At the same time, she tells Boone that Perry is the only obstacle to their marrying. Boone lures Perry and June to the Bascoms' sawmill. He locks June in a small office and, after knocking out Perry, places him on a belt that is moving toward the gigantic, whirring buzz saw. June breaks down the door in time to save Perry, who later succeeds in identifying Sue's other husband. Naturally there were plenty of those homey touches, which audiences of the time so craved, in the staging. Perry climbed an apple tree to shake down blossoms on the beguiled June, and June fed real leaves to a lovable black calf, which curled its long red tongue to receive them. And there were also audience-rousing lines, such as when Sue appears with a constable, bent on making trouble, and June tells Perry, "I can lick her if you can do him." But the scene that gave the play its instant and long-lived fame was, of course, the sawmill scene. The initial engagement lasted until early March. For decades thereafter *Blue Jeans* was an incessant touring and stock favorite.

Marie Corelli's novel *The Vendetta* was the source of Arden Benedict's **Fabio Romani** (10-6-90, Third Ave.). Romani (Walter Lawrence) is supposedly slain by his wife, Nina (Frances Field), and her lover, Guido Ferrari (John Jay Palmer), but rises from his tomb to wreak vengeance. Spectacle included a reproduction of the 1620 eruption of Vesuvius. Only it wasn't all that spectacular. One

paper found it no more alarming than a small, contained bonfire.

A beloved rural comedy, *The Old Homestead,* returned the same night to the Academy of Music. Embellished for this visit with a boys' choir of twenty-four voices, it remained, with one brief respite, into the spring. A second return was *The Editor,* but this was a single-week stopgap booking at the Fifth Avenue.

Daly began his season by presenting the third Jerome K. Jerome work to be staged in New York in the still young theatrical year, **New Lamps for Old** (10-7-90, Daly's), a singularly appropriate title considering that over the summer Daly's had joined the rush to electric stage lighting. The play dealt with two married couples who fail to realize how well off they are and who decide to run away with each other's spouses (this in the day before car keys could be openly exchanged). Farcical coincidence demands that both new pairs run away to the same hotel. John Drew and Ada Rehan played one of the couples, Burr McIntosh and Anna Franosch the other. Mrs. Gilbert was the landlady of the hotel, which was really a rather rundown country inn. To James Lewis fell the juiciest part of the evening, the old solicitor, Mr. Buster, who finds himself trapped in an unstoppable elevator. Lewis played his brief scenes through the lift's open grillwork whenever the elevator passed by on its way up or down. He was seen sometimes taking evidence for a divorce case, sometimes munching on a makeshift dinner. But the play, for all the enthusiastic welcome accorded the players, was not a hit, so Daly hurriedly put another work in rehearsal.

On the 13th Joseph Jefferson, W. J. Florence, and Mme Ponisi brought in their old favorite *The Heir at Law* to Palmer's for a month's stand. Young Viola Allen was Cicely Homespun. At the Fifth Avenue the Kendals settled in for a two-month visit, bringing out such standbys as *The Squire, The Queen's Shilling, All for Her, A Scrap of Paper, The Ironmaster,* and, for their final week, a bill of one-acters. Both theatres were displaying old-line stars who often assumed roles much too young for their years, but there were still enough traditionalists around to ensure them good box office.

Just how quickly a new sensation began to slide into a cliché was made evident by **The Limited Mail** (10-20-90, Windsor). This thriller starred Florence Bindley, another well-liked road star, whose costume regularly included a pistol and a holster. Her new vehicle allowed her to portray a beautiful, heroic telegraph operator. One sensation was rather old hat, a train wreck. But a second found Miss

Bindley tied to a belt moving slowly toward a whirring buzz saw. *Blue Jeans,* famous for introducing such a scene, was only two weeks old. Audiences were not deterred by the imitation. *The Limited Mail* toured for four or five years.

The same bank scandal that had prompted Rosenfeld to write *The Whirlwind* inspired de Mille and Belasco's **Men and Women** (10-21-90, 23rd St.), which gave Broadway and young Charles Frohman another success. During a run on the Jefferson National Bank, its officers discover that bonds kept in the vault are missing. Suspicion falls on the youthful assistant cashier, Edward Seabury (Orrin Johnson), who has just announced his engagement to Dora Prescott (Maude Adams). Dora is the sister of Edward's fellow cashier, William Prescott (William Morris). Will also has just become engaged, to Agnes Rodman (Sydney Armstrong), daughter of Arizona's governor, Stephen Rodman (Frank Mordaunt). Calvin Stedman (R. A. Roberts), who had hoped to marry Dora himself, determines to pin the theft on Edward, and when Governor Rodman comes to Edward's defense, Stedman reveals that the governor has a criminal record—a bank theft at that. This attack on his future father-in-law, coupled with the realization that Agnes has stumbled on the truth, prompts Will to disclose that he is the real culprit. He is dismissed and cannot find work, but he is not prosecuted. The kindhearted bank president, Israel Cohen (Frederic de Belleville), quietly obtains another job for him, leaving all the lovers free to marry.

The midnight meeting at Cohen's luxurious home was the high point of the play. As Will bewails, "Does the mercy of God reach down as far as the depths of my sin?" the green moonlight, shining in through the window, illuminates a stained glass painting above the mantel, which depicts Jesus pardoning a repentant Magdalen at his feet. (Leave it to William Winter to ask why a Jew would have such a picture in his home.) Will takes the handcuffs, which are resting on the table and obviously awaiting Edward, and places them on his own wrists. Cohen enters, sees what has transpired, and exclaims, "My God! William! William!" At this point the stage directions read, "*Agnes staggers toward William, and looking at Stedman, places her hands upon the irons, and half fainting, falls across the table.*" End of act.

Except for the *Herald,* the next-day reviews were largely favorable, the *Star* considering it de Mille and Belasco's best work. With time to remove himself from the skillful production's witchery, the critic for the *Dramatic Mirror* was less enamored but

objective, writing, "Its sentiment is cheap enough, its characters are false enough, its comedy vulgar enough, and its construction mechanical enough to meet the requirements of a class that does not know good art from bad art and habitually praises that which deserves condemnation. From which the readers of THE MIRROR will infer that this play is a box office success." And a success it was, chalking up 204 performances as well as playing to crowded houses on tour. It was revived with some regularity for about fifteen years. However, it was the last of the de Mille–Belasco collaborations, with the men parting amicably, de Mille to write one more hit before his early death and Belasco to move on to decades of fame.

The indefatigable Wilton Lackaye was the leading figure in **Nero** (10-21-90, Niblo's), which Max Freeman theatricalized from Ernest Eckstein's novel. Real lions stalked the stage, and a Spanish dancer, Señorita Rosita, found an excuse to perform an anachronistic fandango in ancient Rome. Critics felt that the supposedly lavish spectacle cut corners on scenery and costumes. It certainly cut the traditionally long running time of such overscale pieces. The curtain fell on opening night at 10:30. The axe fell two months later in a welter of charges, countercharges, and lawsuits over nonpayment. In that time, however Lackaye portrayed an artistic, loving emperor who only turns against the world (and finally commits suicide) after his mother, Agrippina (Alice Fischer), sells his beloved Acte (Carrie Turner) into slavery.

Maurice Barrymore found himself a full-fledged star—with his name alone above the title—for the first time when J. M. Hill presented Augustus Thomas's **Reckless Temple** (10-27-90, Standard).

. . .

Maurice Barrymore (1849–1905), whose real name was Herbert Blythe, was born in India. He later studied law in London and won some small renown as an amateur boxer before turning to the stage. He migrated to America, making his debut in New York in 1875 as a replacement for John Drew in *The Big Bonanza.* Subsequently he married Drew's niece, Georgiana. He performed increasingly important roles with Edwin Booth and at Wallack's before becoming Helena Modjeska's leading man. He then joined Palmer's company. A fellow player described him as "a tall man, dark and pale, with cool Northern grey eyes. . . . He was lightly built, but of a round-muscled, strong-shouldered powerful lightness."

. . .

Barrymore and Thomas's Edgar Temple came close to being an antihero in contemporary eyes, a handsome, hard-drinking gambler with one foot in bohemia. But he determines to reform when he falls in love with Dana Hamlin (Dallas McLean). He is also a lawyer and has defended Jean Clautice (Joseph Holland), a man accused of murder. Clautice's sister has been seduced by George Hamlin (Frank Lander), the brother of Temple's fiancée. Temple takes the blame in Hamlin's stead, and Clautice demands a duel. They elect to draw lots, with the loser to shoot himself. Temple loses, but his shot is not fatal, and the play ends on an upbeat note. Like Rosenfeld earlier in the season, Thomas found himself torn between the essential melodramatics of the basic story and the satiric possibilities of its background of St. Louis society. Several critics found his stabs at satire too angrily cutting. Nor, some of these critics suggested, was Barrymore altogether helpful. He had, it seems, developed a very quirky, annoying delivery. The *Dramatic Mirror* recorded, "His method is to explode the first word or two of a speech like a bomb, and then glide to the end of a sentence with a *diminuendo* that shrouds the final words in the mystery of inaudibility."

Barrymore's fame was not yet so solid that he could override bad notices for himself and his play. After two weeks the show was taken on the road, where its tour had to be cut short because of poor business. One puzzling sidelight remains. In his autobiography Thomas wrote, "Somewhere from the South there was a newspaper item of two men who had fought a duel by drawing lots from a hat with the understanding that the man who got the marked card was to suicide," and he stated that this item provided him the germ of his ideas. Did he really read such an article, or had he seen or read last season's *Hélène*? Perhaps he and Martha Morton drew from the same source.

Down in the Bowery yet another distressed heroine had to be rescued from the path of a train (this time a New York el) by the hero. The play was **The Plunger** (10-27-90, People's), and its stars were Oliver Doud Byron and his wife, Kate. The work remained in the Byrons' repertory for several seasons.

One rationalization for *Reckless Temple*'s brief run was that it came in just before election time, when theatres of the era generally suffered a box-office slump. That feeble excuse was given the lie when Daly presented his brother's version of von Schönthan's *Das letzte Wort* as **The Last Word** (10-28-90, Daly's). It was an immediate hit, although no one could foresee the irony hidden in the title, for, as Odell ruefully noted, this was to prove "almost his last success with modern comedy." Times were,

indeed, a-changin'. After Faith Rutherwell (Isabel Irving) announces that she will not obey her father and marry Baron Stuyve (Sidney Bowkett), but instead will wed Boris Bagoleff (Sidney Herbert), she is ordered out of the house. However, she is immediately taken under the wing of the beautiful and rich "Witch from the Neva," Baroness Vera Boraneff (Ada Rehan), whose laughter is "a full yard of velvet sunshine," and who is Boris's sister. Faith's bookish brother, Harry (John Drew), is under their father's thumb, too. He visits Vera to chide her for helping his sister, but Vera not only shows Harry what a scoundrel the baron is, she wraps him around her finger and, when he has fallen in love, kids him that he cannot kiss her without his father's approval. They agree to confront the old man and make him accept the lovers. Daly gave the play a splendid mounting. The *Times* noted, "The first scene is an exact representation of a large social gathering in the house of a man of wealth and position. It is a charming picture and a true one. The bustling gayety, the constant movement, the hum of conversation, are perfectly imitated." For many the evening's triumph belonged to Miss Rehan, with her gorgeous, gasp-provoking gowns (furred red velvet for her first appearance; black and silver, and black and yellow for later scenes) and her impeccably honed sense of high comedy. The play ran until mid-January and easily could have run longer had Daly allowed.

The month's final offering was Palmer's presentation of **A Pair of Spectacles** (10-30-90, Madison Square), which Sydney Grundy had adapted from the same *Les Petits Oiseaux* that had been the source of *Goggles*. The simple story recounted how a benevolent man's rosy outlook on life is soured when he loses his glasses and must wear those of his misanthropic brother, and how his sunny view is restored when his glasses are retrieved. In a striking instance of casting against type, J. H. Stoddart was assigned the role of the good brother and E. M. Holland that of the mean one. The cast was widely applauded, the play deemed slight. To make a fuller, more satisfying evening Palmer revived *Old Love Letters* (with Agnes Booth again in one of the two leading roles), then replaced it with Augustus Thomas's **Afterthoughts** (11-24-90, Madison Square), in which a young widow, Mrs. Fairfield (Agnes Booth), reunites a younger suitor, Donald Barclay (Louis Massen), with the girl she knows he should marry. The double bill was by no means a failure, but business fell short of expectations in its nine-week run.

Annie Ward Tiffany, one more inveterate tourer, was the star of L. R. Shewell's **The Stepdaughter**

(11-3-90, Windsor). Ruby (Tiffany) falls in love with her stepmother's secret lover, a man the woman has persuaded her husband to take on as a secretary. Her stepmother imprisons Ruby in a tower before the wicked woman and her paramour are sent packing.

A self-sacrificing woman was at the center of Paul Potter and David Belasco's **The Ugly Duckling** (11-10-90, Broadway). Kate Graydon learns that her sister, Hester (Helen Bancroft), is to marry Viscount Huntington (Ian Robertson), a man who once had courted her. She holds her peace. After the wedding Count Malatesta (E. J. Henley), believing Huntington has had an affair with the countess, lures Hester to his apartment and lets Huntington know she is there. Kate learns of this treachery and contrives to take her sister's place, thus blackening her own reputation.

However claptrap the play was, it proved a historic occasion. Not every critic recognized this. In fact, William Winter snobbishly elected to attend the opening of an English performer and apparently had no interest in seeing to it that a second-stringer was assigned. It sufficed, he felt, to append a short notice to his own extended review: "Among the minor theatrical events of last night in this city was the production of a farce called 'A Texas Steer' by Mr. Hoyt at the Bijou, and the first performance of a piece called 'The Ugly Duckling' at the Broadway Theatre, in which a debutante named Mrs. Carter played one of the parts." Mrs. Carter's debut as Kate was no minor theatrical event. She was, in fact, the first in a long line of Belasco protégés.

. . .

Mrs. Leslie Carter (1862–1937) was born in Lexington, Ky., where she was christened Caroline Louise Dudley. She grew up in a comfortable but not exceptionally wealthy home. That great wealth came to her when she married and found herself in Chicago society. However, her world came crashing down after an acrimonious, highly publicized divorce. Although she had had no acting experience, she turned to acting in order to support herself and her mother. A tiny, willowy woman with piercing green eyes and flaming red hair, she subjected herself to long coaching by Belasco before making her first appearance.

. . .

For a novice, she acquitted herself handsomely in her first outing. Nevertheless, the play was not a success, except in Chicago, where her notoriety stimulated sales.

Nor could the premiere of **A Texas Steer** (11-10-90, Bijou) be branded a minor theatrical event by

anyone except a snooty brahmin such as Winter. Hoyt again eschewed, at least initially, bedecking his farce with musical numbers. Maverick Brander (Tim Murphy) is a rich Texan who is goaded by his wife (Alice Walsh) and his daughter (Flora Walsh), affectionately known as Bossy, to run for Congress. Winning costs him a trifling $30,000—that's $5 a head for the community's 6000, bribable voters. Life in Washington amazes the Branders. Bossy, for example, wonders aloud why the ladies, who all ride sidesaddle, can't afford stirrups. But Brander's own path to political wisdom is not obstacle free. He is tricked by a blackmailer, whose mother "had been kissed by Daniel Webster," into letting her kiss him in front of a concealed camera. The chagrined Brander can only inquire if it also cost Daniel Webster $100. Before he learns Washington's wily, wicked ways, Brander is buncoed and fleeced by other resident sharpers. Minor characters had such typical farcical monikers as Brassy Gall (he's a lobbyist), Christopher Columbus Fishback, Othello Moore, and Knott Initt. A typical bit of dialogue ran:

— Red Dog, Texas has a great future. All it needs is a little better society and more rain.
— That's all hell needs.

Playgoers voted to keep the play going until the end of January, and it remained popular wherever it played for many seasons.

However history might mock Winter for cavalierly waving away two not unimportant first nights on the New York stage, his selection of a premiere to attend was certainly the correct one from a contemporary vantage point—and even history might not disdain it. On that busy night of the 10th Winter found his aisle seat at Palmer's and sat back to watch the American debut of one of the finest English actors of the period in a new play by one of England's leading young playwrights. The star was E. S. (for Edward Smith) Willard, a "compact," dark-complexioned, blue-eyed man with a "rich and resonant" voice, whose acting Winter was to praise for its "simplicity and sincerity." His vehicle was Henry Arthur Jones's **The Middleman,** a tale of a potter who believes his employer's son has violated his daughter and who, in revenge, destroys his own invention rather than allow his employer to profit from it. Both the play and the star were hailed almost universally. For Willard the opening marked not merely the beginning of a five-month Manhattan stand but the start of years of transatlantic popularity.

Haddon Chambers crossed the Atlantic to personally direct the American production of his West End hit **The Idler** (11-11-90, Lyceum). Although it was set entirely in London, one of its leading characters, the highly respected Sir John Harding (Nelson Wheatcroft), had spent some of his early years in the American West, where he had been a gambler known as Gentleman Jack and had killed a man. The dead man's brother, Simeon Strong (Eugene Ormonde), vowing vengeance, has finally tracked him down and has persuaded a notorious, handsome wastrel, Mark Cross (Herbert Kelcey), to bring about Harding's ruin. Cross needs little persuasion, since he long has coveted Harding's wife (Georgia Cayvan). In a foolish attempt to save her husband she goes to Cross's apartment to confront him, but in the midst of the visit Harding himself is announced. Lady Harding attempts to hide but forgets to take with her an incriminating fan. Harding challenges Cross to a duel but quickly is convinced of his wife's innocence. A shamed Cross orders his servant to pack his bags. The scene between the men, with the wife's fan in full view of the audience, was the culmination of the evening. (Wilde would use the device in *Lady's Windermere's Fan* a few seasons later, and years afterwards a similar trick would thrill audiences in *Angel Street.*) But despite critically lauded playing, the drama was only a middling success. It ran until mid-January.

William R. Wilson's **The Inspector** (11-13-90, Park) had its opening delayed several nights, apparently because police felt the leading character was a caricature of the inspector of police. With some quick rewriting and a new actor in the title role, the play was finally allowed to open. The Inspector (Frazer Coulter) is all over town, nabbing millionaire Simon Vendervere (Edwin Varrey) for murder, Ben La Bree (John E. Kellerd) for impersonating an English lord, and all other manner of wrongdoers. Scenes moved from a police boat in the river to the Battery and uptown. An organ grinder and other immigrants helped people the stage. But only for a month.

The emotionally troubled, seemingly foredoomed Margaret Mather appeared never able to grasp the theatrical brass ring. She suffered another costly failure when she starred in **Joan of Arc** (12-8-90, Fifth Ave.), which the admired William Young had translated into stodgy blank verse from Jules Barbier's *Jeanne d'Arc*. Something of the star's personal difficulties came through in the most emotionally charged scenes, such as when Joan is hounded by her jailers in her cramped cell. The *Times,* calling her acting "hard, labored, ultra-theatrical," nonetheless granted she was "effective." The real problem, as the same critic smugly suggested, was that "the heroine of Orleans is not a fit personage for dramatic treatment." He insisted her inspiration and character must "elude the dramatist's touch." Even backed by music Gounod had written for the original production, the play could not excite theatregoers. It lingered for only two weeks, but the star included it in her post-Broadway tour along with several standards (*The Lady of Lyons, Romeo and Juliet, Leah, the Forsaken*) and the rarely done *Cymbeline.*

Annie Pixley briefly had offered New Yorkers a revival of *The Deacon's Daughter* before essaying a new play, James C. Roach's **Kate** (12-8-90, Grand Opera). The heroine follows her lover into battle during the Civil War and even takes his place when he is wounded. She must also help unmask the treachery of her fiancé's cousin, a Confederate spy posing as a war correspondent. Miss Pixley's many fans always rejoiced as much in her singing and dancing as in her acting, so she not unnaturally offered a number of turns, including "I Dreamt that I Dwelt in Marble Halls," which she sang in the thick of the battle. After a single week she headed back out on tour.

There was no train wreck in Lincoln J. Carter's **The Fast Mail** (12-8-90, Windsor), merely a frustrated attempt at derailing. But patrons were hardly deprived of thrills. Walter West loves Mary Martin, a banker's adopted daughter, but the banker's adopted son, Philip, who has forged his father's name to important papers, assures his crony, James Reed: "Trust to me, these forgeries have astounded the old man, he will never suspect me! Can't you see that we must place these forgeries against your rival West, and that will be the end of his matrimonial chances." At the same time, Philip is plotting to kill not only West but Reed, too. Instead Reed is murdered by the father of a girl he has violated. Philip implicates West in the killing. West and Mary, who have wed secretly, flee westward. A cross-country chase ensues and includes a knifing, an axing, a drowning by being thrown into Niagara Falls, and a steamboat explosion. Philip learns that Mary and West are on separate trains and wires the police to pick up West. Mary attempts to warn West by telegraph but is stopped by Philip. She manages to pin a warning to a mailbag. The act ends with a train speeding through the station and grabbing the bag with a hook. It turns out that West is actually the banker's son, kidnapped years before, and that Philip's real father is a notorious Italian crook. The villain is nabbed by a detective (whose name was spelled variously as Sleuth, Sluthe, or Sluth) with the help of his comic wife, who earlier had disguised herself as West to aid in his escape. With so many attractions the melodrama was guaranteed a long life in the hinterlands.

Not so E. J. Swartz's **The Clipper** (12-15-90, People's), a comedy-drama that told how a murderer's daughter was able to rise above her seemingly doomed fate thanks to a mysterious inheritance. It sped into oblivion at a high clip.

Émile Moreau and Victorien Sardou's **Cleopatra** (12-23-90, Fifth Ave.), following in the wake of *Fédora* and *La Tosca,* confirmed that Fanny Davenport had set herself up as Sarah Bernhardt's English-speaking standby on American stages. In this instance spectacle helped save the day—or evening—although perhaps too little was left to the imagination. Miss Davenport made her first entrance at the quay in Tarsus stepping from a barge slavishly copied from Shakespeare's description. Huge, mammoth-pillared palaces and temples imparted an exotic flavor. What Hollywood would later call "special effects" was offered in a simoom, with lightning and thunder, windblown dust, and palm trees bending in the gale. The critics were less thrilled with the star. The *Sun*'s man, while acknowledging she was accepted "with respect and esteem," regretted "she had no electrical effect upon the assemblage." Moreover, he and other reviewers were dismayed by her growing girth. He called her "a cumbersome and unwieldy temptress." Another reported there were snickers when she was lugged in at one point concealed in an all too bulging rug. How long the drama might have run in the face of disappointing notices will never be known. Just over a week after the premiere the theatre burned to the ground. No torrid Mediterranean passions ignited the blaze; the culprit was a carelessly discarded cigarette. But when new costumes and scenery were ready three weeks later, Miss Davenport had a good reason for reopening on tour instead of in New York.

The year ended with E. S. Willard introducing a second Jones play, **Judah** (12-29-90, Palmer's), in which a minister falls in love with a quack faith healer and, on discovering her true nature, perjures himself to save her good name. Most critics felt both the play and the star's performance outshone his highly lauded earlier vehicle and acting.

Two great American actors accompanied the new year in. In a way, one represented the fast-receding past, the other an equally onrushing future. The older man was Barrett. Venturesome to the last, he began his stand in the title role of a new play, William Young's blank-verse **Ganelon** (1-5-91, Broadway). Ganelon is the son and namesake of the notorious warrior who had betrayed Roland at Roncesvalles.

He has vowed to expunge the infamy attached to his name and has spent his years fighting the Saracens. But after he breaks the siege of Aleria in Corsica, he discovers that the Corsican prince, Count Colonna (Ben G. Rogers), has reneged on a promise to allow Ganelon to wed his daughter, Bianca (Minna K. Gale). Ganelon unsuccessfully attempts suicide and then is persuaded by the Saracen leader, Malec (John A. Lane), to disclose a secret passage into the town. Bianca learns of his treachery and denounces him. Shamed by her outburst, he dies fighting to save the city. As he dies Bianca arrives and forgives him. All the action supposedly occurs in a single day. The beauty of the mounting and the fervor of Barrett's acting impressed most critics, but theatregoers seemed indifferent. After a fortnight (which included a matinee of *Much Ado About Nothing*) Barrett withdrew it in favor of *Francesca da Rimini*.

The younger, notoriously money-mad Richard Mansfield always had his eye on box office, so he rarely was as daring as Barrett. For the first of two engagements during the season he offered only a single work—his recent money-maker *Beau Brummell.* He played it for three weeks at the Garden, along with a single matinee of *Prince Karl*. His wife, Beatrice Cameron, was more willing to take a risk than he was, so, with his help but without his presence, she again gave a special matinee of *A Doll's House* during the stand. Attendance was meager and critical comment largely as dismissive as it had been earlier.

Rosina Vokes, the Englishwoman so beloved for her vaudevilles, dropped her songs and dances to appear as a coquette turned actress, after a misunderstanding has caused her to be separated from her husband, in Grundy's **The Silver Shield** (1-6-91, Madison Square). Even though Odell records that the play's most memorable scene found her attempting to learn a part while being distracted by an organ grinder churning out a popular tune, she refused to bow to hints from the gallery and never burst into song. Still, her loyal coterie supported her happily for a month.

Apparently wearying of his long run in *The Old Homestead* but not of its central character, Denman Thompson interrupted the favorite's engagement for two weeks beginning January 12 to restore the play that he had used for so many years before, *Joshua Whitcomb*. So similar were the plays that much of *The Old Homestead*'s scenery sufficed for the brief revival.

Daniel Frohman and his Lyceum stock company, again relying on importations, provided New Yorkers with an attractive double bill in Haddon Chambers's curtain raiser, **The Open Gate,** and J. Comyns Carr's adaptation of *Les Femmes nerveuses,* **Nerves** (1-19-91, Lyceum). The shorter work centered on a spinster who keeps her gate opened for fifteen years in hopes her old lover will return. He does. Georgia Cayvan and Nelson Wheatcroft played the leads, while Fritz Williams and Effie Shannon played two younger lovers in danger of repeating the quarrel that had separated the old maid and her beau. Carr's work dealt with ways modern men might treat restless young women. Some critics felt not all the players were adept at this sort of comedy. But there was praise for Mrs. Whiffen's nervous mother-in-law and, most of all, for May Robson as a fluttery, often hysterical, and totally unreliable serving girl. The scenery, too, as was so often the case during the season, garnered encomiums. The old maid's little cottage with a view of its garden and its open gate and a busy confectionary shop in the longer play were singled out most often. The bill ran until early April.

Beautiful scenery, some of it made in London, was also an attraction in Daly's revival of *The School for Scandal* on the 20th. There was interest as well—and no little displeasure—in the fact that Daly, as was his wont, had rearranged the order of scenes. But in this instance, the cast was the thing. Two great favorites, James Lewis and Mrs. Gilbert, succeeded as best they could in the relatively unrewarding roles of Moses and Mrs. Candour. Charles Wheatleigh won reserved praise for his Sir Peter (after all, who could replace the late John Gilbert?), and Harry Edwards (late of Wallack's) was applauded for his Sir Oliver. George Clarke made an acceptable Joseph. Drew was better as a brittle, dashing, yet at heart compassionate and carefully tactful Charles. But the star of the evening was unquestionably Ada Rehan. Her ravishingly handsome Lady Teazle looked like a Gainsborough or Reynolds come to life. And for her interpretation she went back to that of the famous Dora Jordan. Hers was an honest, warmhearted country girl aching to break loose from her own other self, that conniving, affected city sophisticate. Winter called it "womanlike, true, vivacious, fascinating with a buoyant ripple of enticing levity in the lighter scenes, treated throughout with a suitable perception of the author's meaning, and made symmetrical and distinctive with the unerring skill of trained dramatic art." Albeit no film or recording exists to attest to her excellence, she is generally considered the finest interpreter of the part in American annals. The mounting ran six weeks.

Barrett continued his engagement by bringing out a second new play, Oscar's Wilde's tragedy *The Duchess of Padua.* Since he was the star, he offered the play not with Wilde's title but as **Guido Ferranti** (1-26-91, Broadway). Guido is determined to murder the Duke of Padua (Frederic Vroom), not only because the duke had murdered Guido's father but because Guido loves the duke's much abused wife, Beatrice (Minna K. Gale). When he enters the sleeping duke's bedroom intent on carrying out his plan, he discovers Beatrice has done the job for him. He shrinks back appalled, and Beatrice screams bloody murder. Guido is arrested, tried, and condemned to die. A sorrowful Beatrice visits him in his dungeon, where the pair commit suicide. Brave as Barrett was, he was also in some need of funds, so the play was produced using scenery from older works in his repertory. The gloom of the tragedy and the shopworn settings told against the production. Barrett could keep it going only for three weeks. After inserting a few performance of *Yorick's Love, David Garrick,* and *The King's Pleasure,* he brought back *The Man o' Airlie* on February 23.

Two other actors vied with Barrett for first-nighters. The established Nat Goodwin came out in Leander Richardson and William Yardley's **The Nominee** (1-26-91, Bijou), another version of the same play seen by New Yorkers with Coquelin as *Le Député de Bombignac* and with Wyndham as *The Candidate.* For a curtain raiser he initially offered **The Viper on the Hearth,** an English piece depicting a lovers' quarrel. When it failed to please he substituted Jerome K. Jerome's **Barbara** (2-23-91), in which a long-lost heiress, who all unknowingly loves her brother, is rediscovered and restored to her fortune. The play featured a newfangled phonograph blaring away onstage. Goodwin's legion of followers kept the box office busy until the beginning of May. At the Park the rising, not yet established James T. Powers cavorted in J. J. McNally's **A Straight Tip,** a farce-comedy perhaps closer to musical comedy than to pure farce. Powers's best years were spent in musicals.

Three years earlier A. C. Gunter had turned his best-selling novel *Mr. Barnes of New York* into a theatre piece. Now he did the same for his almost equally successful **Mr. Potter of Texas** (2-2-91, Star). Sammy Potts, as a young man, fled to America to escape being wrongfully implicated in an English bank scandal. Years later he is able to return to London as the Hon. Samson Potter (Frank Mordaunt). He comes wearing expensive boots, a huge sombrero, and gilt pistols in his holster. And he sets about vindicating himself and convicting the real culprits. He also rescues innocent Charlie Errol

(Louis Massen) from the designs of the tricky Lady Amersley (Minnie Seligman). Comedy often touched lightly on matters that later historians would look upon differently.

Potter: Is that 'ere lunch ready? I'm like an Indian on a reservation—starving.
Lubbins [*a waiter*]: (*admiringly*) And to think if hi 'ad hemigrated I might 'ave been like 'e.

Palmer, chided for having pulled out his Madison Square Theatre stock company to give its stage over to Rosina Vokes, restored the players to their home in early February. What many of his denouncers may not have known was that the once powerful producer was sinking into a financial mire. His double bill featured an English play, R. C. Carton's **Sunlight and Shadow** (2-2-91, Madison Square). In its soap opera–like story, just before the marriage of Helen Latimer (Maud Harrison) and Mark Denzil (Maurice Barrymore), the pair learn that Denzil's first wife, believed dead, is still alive. Helen eventually agrees to marry the crippled George Addis (Edward Bell), who soon learns that Mrs. Denzil now has actually died. Should he reveal this and lose Helen, or marry her and let her learn the truth later? Bell's performance as an essentially good man caught in a frightful dilemma was the evening's best. Barrymore was still criticized for his "spasmodic delivery." The play at first was paired with Augustus Thomas's **A New Year's Call,** in which a young man pretends to be drunk in order to test his fiancée's devotion. One critic suggested the Mr. Wilton listed as playing the black servant might well have been the author performing under a stage name. Whether or not he was correct was probably a matter of small interest, but it could have reminded some readers that most American stages still usually were closed to blacks and that black roles were generally taken by white actors in black makeup. Poorly received, the one-acter soon made way for Thomas's *Afterthoughts.* This double bill ran just over a month.

Willard continued his extended visit with Joseph Hatton's **John Needham's Double** (2-4-91, Palmer's), in which a criminally minded man murders his look-alike to claim the dead man's inheritance. Part of the play was set in America, and Palmer found some of the American characters had been given such preposterous English bents that he had Augustus Thomas rewrite much of the play. The skillful reworking and another fine performance by Willard (or performances, since he portrayed both look-alikes) gave the star another triumph.

The reason Fanny Davenport had been loathe to reopen her rebuilt *Cleopatra* became clear when the great Bernhardt swept onto the stage of the Garden Theatre on February 5. Her initial offering was *La Tosca,* but she quickly moved on to *Cléopatre, Fédora,* and *La Dame aux camélias.* All the fire, depth, and restraint wanting in Davenport's sometimes superficial emoting were evinced by this sinuously slim, spellbindingly attractive woman. Davenport was certainly serviceable enough for the multitudes of American playgoers never so fortunate as to witness Bernhardt in action, but for those who saw the immortal Sarah there was no comparison. Her Cleopatra seemed endowed with magical powers that bewitched her audiences as much as they bewitched her Antony. Savagely stamping on the messenger who brought her the news of Antony's marriage might not seemed restrained to modern theatregoers, but by the standards of the day her own conception appeared strengthened by a reining in of excessive melodramatics.

Melodrama combined with musical comedy touches sometimes found acceptance at a time when ideas of what musicals should be were not firmly established. Charles Klein and Charles Coote's **A Mile a Minute** (2-9-91, People's) was a case in point. Its story centered on the abduction of Agnes Dale (Beverly Sitgreaves) by her husband's cousin, Richard Blackstone (Myron Calice). He sequesters her in a thieves' den, but not before she tells him, "Base varlet, even though it were possible to become your wife—I am already married—I would die rather than yield to the indignity of accepting your hand." Her husband hunts the pair down, and the play ends with a chase on a train—at a mile a minute. Yet the star of the show was Minnie Palmer as Nelly Sparkle, a role tied to the main plot by the slenderest thread. And, of course, her fans came to see Miss Palmer sing and dance as much as act. Her reputation alone gave the work its success on tour.

There were some songs and dances, too, in **Grimes' Cellar Door** (2-9-91, Windsor), which seems like a mismating of *The Old Homestead* and *Pygmalion and Galatea* (or, perhaps, *Adonis*). Josiah Grimes (Charles Burke), a Yankee farmer, buys a statue of Pandora, and troubles are set loose after his nephew, Bill (James B. Mackie), kisses it and it comes to life.

Uptown, Oscar Hammerstein was having problems booking and filling his theatre on 125th Street. To rectify the situation he attempted to form his own stock company. He introduced the group in B. F. Roeder's **Husbands and Wives** (2-16-91, Harlem Opera House), a farce taken from the German comedy *Fifi.* Fifi is a dog, and she is used by a duplicitous valet to cause problems between a young husband and his bride. Comic scenes included a theatrical snowstorm (at a rehearsal) gone amok. The company enlisted some excellent performers—Robert Hilliard, Charles Dickson, Louise Thorndyke Boucicault—but their ensemble playing in a weak piece left much to be desired.

George L. Stout's **Noah's Ark** (2-16-91, Niblo's) was billed as a melodrama and was filled with generic clichés. Thus the villain sets fire to a Five Points tenement, which is soon totally involved. While the firemen, with a real engine onstage, futilely attempt to extinguish the blaze, the hero rushes up to the sixth floor to effect a daring rescue on a makeshift fire escape. But the play also offered two brass bands with "150 men (count them)" and a plenitude of songs and dances performed in spectacular settings such as Printing House Square with a view of City Hall and local dignitaries waving to the crowds. But Niblo's was increasingly out of the way, and this sort of entertainment could no longer lure suburbanites from their patronage of neighborhood houses. The production lasted for two weeks.

On March 2, Booth joined Barrett at the Broadway. Because Booth was so doggedly traditional, the repertory now had to reflect his conservative tastes. The announced schedule promised *The Merchant of Venice, Julius Caesar, Hamlet,* and *Macbeth.* Everything that could go wrong did. Critics were aghast at how exhausted and indifferent Booth's playing had become. He dragged down with him his ailing co-star. A. C. Wheeler, writing in the *World* as Nym Crinkle, condemned the men as "mummified actors . . . who are enduring by reason of packed spice and frankincense, that keep them in an unchangeable and antiseptic condition." After watching *Julius Caesar,* Wheeler condemned a "tottering Mr. Booth . . . whose work was marked and marred by careless feebleness." On the 18th, during a performance of *Richelieu,* Barrett's physical problems overcame him, and he collapsed. Two days later he was dead. Booth finished the forlorn engagement alone. He gave a single performance in Brooklyn the following week, then retired forever from the stage he had once dominated. Times were more than changing; a whole era was swiftly approaching its close.

Daly, too, was on the receiving end of some unhelpful if respectful notices, when he produced a truly oddball thing, a full-length, entirely wordless pantomime, **The Prodigal Son** (3-3-91, Daly's). The entertainment was his version of an unexpected Parisian hit that had also delighted London, *L'Enfant prodigue,* with a story line by Michel Carré, Jr., and music by André Wormser. The pantomime's

Pierrot rejects the flowers offered by sweet, virtuous Virginie (a Daly addition) (Isabel Irving) and instead runs off with the voluptuous Phrynette (Adelaide Prince), who eventually discards him for a more promising suitor. Sadder but wiser, Pierrot joins the army to prove himself worthy of the waiting Virginie. Pierrot was played by Ada Rehan in a white Pierrot costume, her whitened face capped by a white skullcap. More than one critic suggested her makeup reminded him of George L. Fox's Humpty Dumpty, the most famous role of America's most famous exponent of pantomime. Even those critics who found kind words for the production predicted it would not please contemporary audiences. Daly's customarily loyal subscribers stayed away in such sickening numbers that the producer withdrew the piece at the end of its first week—one of his worst failures. He rushed in a revival of *A Night Off* on the 9th to keep his stage lit and his actors employed.

Just before that revival appeared, graduates of the American Academy of Dramatic Arts took over the Lyceum for a single matinee performance on March 6. Their choice of play was Ibsen's **The Pillars of Society.** Three days later, on the evening of the 9th, Hammerstein's Harlem company brought out the same play with J. B. Studley as Consul Bernick and Hilliard as Johan. Reviewers who bothered to attend gave the play short shrift but did report that the orchestra seats were packed albeit the upstairs was largely empty. The week's run at the Opera House was the first extended stay, if it can be called that, for any Ibsen work in New York.

First-string critics neglected Ibsen to sit in judgment on Willard in his third Jones play of the season, **Wealth** (3-9-91, Palmer's), in which his self-made man, still haunted by memories of his early poverty, pretends to lose his money when his daughter refuses to marry the nephew he has chosen for her. In the end the nephew proves treacherous and the daughter's good sense prevails. This time the star was deemed far superior to the play. Nonetheless, the play served the star until the last week of his engagement when he repeated his earlier offerings, then bowed out with a double bill of lesser plays on his final day. The engagement had been too long, so business had been disappointing, but Willard had established himself in the eyes of American playgoers and critics.

The evening's third opening presented the work of another busy English (if Australian-born) playwright, Haddon Chambers's **Love and War** (3-3-91, Garden), derived from *Devant l'Ennemi.* The love of two men, one good and one evil, for the same girl propelled the plot. But the welcome was chilly, and the play soon departed.

American drama could only find a berth at a fast-sinking house. Milton Nobles, one of the most dogged of the perennially circulating players, and his wife, Dolly, were the stars of **From Sire to Son** (3-9-91, Niblo's). Alfred Armitage, a California gambler, and his wife are shot by a robber seeking Armitage's gold. The wife dies, but Armitage survives, although he is stricken dumb. The killer abducts their daughter, whom he takes to Europe, where he assumes Armitage's name. The mute Armitage traces them first to Venice, then, when they flee, to a castle on the Rhine. There he regains both his speech and his daughter. In the first act trained broncos and a Rocky Mountain stagecoach added to the excitement. Dolly played both mother and daughter. The title puzzled at least one reviewer, but the Nobleses, who had been touring with the play for several seasons, chalked up another commercial success.

Before the next play could open, newspapers' foreign correspondents were reporting that Ibsen's *Ghosts* had been played in London, where critics were violently divided on its worth. Several weeks later reports told of a similar London reception for *Hedda Gabler*. The *Times* rushed to reassure possibly nervous readers, "There is no demand for Ibsen here."

Palmer, his fortunes ebbing fast, next offered another double bill. Mrs. Lancaster Wallis and Malcolm Watson's English drama **The Pharisee** (3-16-91, Madison Square) centered on a dying man attempting to make amends to a woman he once had wronged. The play afforded Barrymore a chance to redeem his own recently shaky reputation, and the *Spirit of the Times* advised his readers that "Mr. Barrymore did some of the best acting of his career," but many other critics could not overcome their unyielding distaste for his mannerisms. The curtain raiser was **Dinner at Eight** by J. A. Ritchie, best known at the time as an actor's agent. In its tissue-thin plot a man appears for a dinner party on the wrong night and must hide himself until the dinner is finished. Odell recalled a minor bit of the play ignored by critics. The character of Dorothy Dimple (Maud Harrison) lives in terror of the sound of popping corks, and when a champagne bottle is opened soundlessly, she faints from the shock. Unfortunately, the players' celebrity was not able to counteract discouraging notices, and Palmer found himself saddled with a two-week failure to add to his growing woes.

Some critics felt American drama took a step forward with Augustus Pitou and George H. Jessop's **The Power of the Press** (3-16-91, Star). The play's pivotal figure is a basically good but hard-drinking ship carpenter, Stephan Carson (Wilton Lackaye), who in a drunken moment is led to abet a burglary and attempted murder. Afterwards he is framed for the crime by the real culprit, Turner Morgan (Myron Calice), who plants an incriminating pistol in his pocket. By having Steve sent to prison Turner hopes to be free to court Steve's wife, Annie (Minnie Seligman). In Sing Sing, Steve is converted to the straight and narrow, vowing never again to touch liquor. His behavior leads to a surprise parole, and Steve is able to appear on the doorstep just as his harassed but stubbornly loyal wife has finished cooking the Christmas goose. He would return to work, but Turner prevents his rehiring. Luckily, Steve has learned that Turner expects to flee to Brazil, so he calls the newspapers to advise them of this, and the news prompts the police to remove Turner from a ship that has just sailed.

The *Times*'s man, admittedly a second-stringer, rejoiced in a play in which "real people came out on the stage and did things such as real human people do is real life." The critic who wrote the Sunday followup hailed the work as an "uncommon play." Of course, both men had reservations. The first-night reviewer felt that the authors tugged too much at the heartstrings and cited as an example Annie's teary and unsuspectingly wrong "He will eat his Ch-Christmas dinner in Sing Sing." The scenery was also excellent, including a recreation of the exterior of the Manhattan Athletic Club, a shipyard setting (with a ship weighing anchor), and two views of the Battery. Pitou was to make a career of writing and producing such plays for a hinterland that clung to them long after first-class playhouses had dismissed them as superannuated and was to earn himself the sobriquet "King of the One Night Stands." But in 1891 this sort of melodrama continued to have wide appeal. It ran for over fifty performances and was still touring actively six years later.

Kate Claxton, looking vainly for a new hit, was the star of Frank Harvey's **Cruel London** (3-16-91, People's). She played Helen Clyde, who finds herself in trouble with disbelieving police after some fleeing burglars dump their loot on her doorstep. Critics were cruel, too, so Miss Claxton quickly retreated to her main meal ticket, *The Two Orphans*.

On March 28, Daly brought out his closing offering of the season, a revival of *Love's Labour's Lost*. Once again, as he did with virtually all old pieces he revived, he drastically cut and reordered the play, mounting it in four acts. He occasionally sacrificed sense for scenic effect, so that much of what had been Shakespeare's Act IV, scene iii, in the woods, was played in moonlight and the lovers required to pretend to read by its meager glow. In Daly's last act, a bleak winter scene changed into a verdant spring setting while the audience watched. The performances were hailed as good, but none excited special praise, not even Drew's King of Navarre or Miss Rehan's Princess of France. Nor was the public excited. The play went on before only modestly filled houses until the matinee of April 11, then Daly wrote *finis* with a single evening showing of *The Railroad of Love,* ostensibly to allow Mrs. Gilbert (who had no role in Shakespeare's comedy) to participate in the closing festivities.

A magnificent, moving performance by Agnes Booth could not save **Betrothed** (3-30-91, Garden), an uncredited adaptation of Alphonse Daudet's *L'Obstacle,* which Paris had first seen just over two months earlier. The modern cry that Broadway will not accept unpleasant plays (even one, like this, with a happy ending) is nothing new. When Madeleine's guardian learns that the father of her fiancé, Henri, Marquis d'Alein (J. H. Gilmour), died insane, he forces Madeleine (Isabelle Evesson) to break off her engagement. The rupture drives Henri himself to the brink of madness. To save him his mother (Miss Booth) tells him that he was illegitimate—a lie that will ruin her own reputation. Fortunately, the loving Madeleine prevails over the guardian. The play lingered for a mere month.

Scathing reviews and police threats to shut the theatre for presenting an immoral play closed **Thou Shalt Not** (3-30-91, Union Square) after its first week. The play was adapted from Albert Ross's novel. Hector Greyburn (Gustavus Levick), a man who has reveled in every conceivable sin, falls in love with a sweet village maiden, Clara Campbell (Maida Craigin), and is reformed by her. In the book Greyburn's past catches up with him, and he is made to pay for it. Not so in the play. This failure to punish a sinner seems to have been what disturbed the authorities. What also disturbed the critics, besides the weak dramatization, were Levick's stiffness and old-style declamation and Miss Craigin's cloying coyness.

The happiest opening of that busy night was **Mr. Wilkinson's Widows** (3-30-91, 23rd St.), William Gillette's redaction of Alexandre Bisson's *Feu Toupinel.* Mrs. Dickerson (Henrietta Crosman) and Mrs. Perrin (Louise Thorndyke Boucicault), two newly remarried widows who live in the same apartment house, meet after one hears the other

playing a song written by the musician husband of the first. The meeting leads to a friendly, gossipy chat in which the women exchange their histories. Mrs. Dickerson, it seems, was formerly married to a Mr. Wilkinson, a wine merchant. Now isn't that interesting, for Mrs. Perrin's first husband was also a Mr. Wilkinson, a wine merchant. Their amusement turns a bit sober when they discover that their Mr. Wilkinsons both had the same given name, looked exactly alike, and married them on the very same day. It soon dawns on them that Mr. Wilkinson was a bigamist. Enter Major P. Ferguson Mallory (Thomas Burns), who promises to clear up matters and does nothing of the sort. By the time the curtain falls, all remain as confused as they were early in Act I. For many the show was stolen by Joseph Holland as the ridiculously jealous Percival Perrin. Is the flirtation the major describes with a former Mrs. Wilkinson a description of a flirtation with his new wife? Acted deftly and with suitably distracting breakneck speed, the farce regaled audiences, except for a summer respite, until October.

Far away from the glitter of first-class theatres a bit of Americana was being played out in **On the Trail; or, Daniel Boone** (3-30-81, Windsor). Pioneers fought Indians and Indians fought back in what the *Herald* described as "blood curdling border scenes." A minor actor, W. J. Lanigan, surely no member of the Players, portrayed the dauntless hero. Sophisticates might sneer, and most New York newspapers sent no reviewers, but the play eked out a couple of seasons on the road.

Alabama (4-1-91, Madison Square) probably was the season's best new American play. It provided major proof of Augustus Thomas's coming of age as an important native dramatist.

· · ·

Augustus Thomas (1857–1934) was born in St. Louis, where he initially contemplated becoming a lawyer but turned instead to journalism and also worked for a time on the railroad. He wrote several plays for local amateur groups. One of these plays was *Editha's Burglar,* which, with some reworking by Edgar Smith, was brought to New York. Shortly thereafter he replaced Boucicault as play doctor and adaptor for the Madison Square Theatre.

· · ·

Residents of the isolated bayou community of Talladega have mixed feelings about the arrival of the railroad. Most adamantly opposed is an unregenerate Confederate veteran, Colonel Preston (J. H. Stoddart). He has never forgiven the destruction of his property, nor forgotten that his son left to serve with the Union troops. He has not answered his

Act Two : 1879–1892

son's letters nor seen him in twenty years. The coming of the railroad interests the corrupt Raymond Page (Walden Ramsey) in another way. Realizing that his sister-in-law's lands will appreciate in value, he claims that she was never legally married to his brother. He believes that since two of the witnesses to the wedding, the minister and the colonel's daughter-in-law, are long dead, and the third witness, the colonel's son, is forever out of the picture, his case is ironclad. He has hired another old Confederate, Colonel Moberly (E. M. Holland), to take his case, but when Page is openly rude to his sister-in-law, Mrs. Page (May Brookyn), the chivalrous Moberly refuses to continue as attorney. An advance agent for the railroad, Mr. Armstrong (Edward Bell), has arrived and, somewhat surprisingly, is housed by Preston out of courtesy. Armstrong falls in love with Preston's granddaughter, Carey (Agnes Miller). Of course, the colonel will not hear of a southern belle marrying a northerner. When the malevolent Page also insults Preston, Preston throws a glass of water at him, thus challenging him to a duel. Moberly, citing the colonel's age, agrees to take his place on the field of honor. The chief engineer for the railroad, Captain Davenport (Maurice Barrymore), appears. Preston does not recognize him, but the faithful old retainer, Decatur (Reuben Fax), and Mrs. Page do. He is, of course, Preston's son, who assumed another name during the war. Davenport once had been engaged to marry Mrs. Page, but the marriage was prohibited on the grounds of consanguinity. The two are cousins. Davenport stops Armstrong and Carey from eloping but has them stage a fake elopement instead. He also confronts Page, forcing him to apologize to his father and Mrs. Page. Then he reveals himself to his father. Not only are father and son reunited, but Armstrong and Carey, Mrs. Page's son, Lathrop (Henry Woodruff), and Colonel Moberly's daughter, Atlanta (Nannie Craddock), and the now middle-aged cousins all can plan happily for their weddings.

Thomas's characters were carefully delineated, even such relatively minor figures as Squire Tucker (Charles L. Harris), "a large baby of fifty . . . tied for life to the apron strings of his mother," who made his first entrance wearing a tattered straw hat, a rumpled shirt, and pants falling down on one side since he has only one suspender. He comes with a pail full of frogs and the gig he used to catch them. It was a choice example of the sort of theatrical eccentricity beloved by the era. The sentiments expressed by the characters might offend some modern sensibilities but were certainly not con-

ceived that way. Thus the gentlemanly Moberly tells Davenport he heads "the Talladega Light Artillery . . . recruited only six years ago, when the county felt the need of some military organization for its moral salutary influence upon the blacks." The squire also expresses what must have been the sentiments of many southerners when, talking of Decatur, he notes, "Ef they is any white folks, Colonel, that despise a niggah, it's because they neveh own one, I say. . . . Who could be more intelligent or discriminatin' than that old man? I really believe he would have voted the Democratic ticket, if permitted to exercise his ballot." Of course, much of the dialogue was formal and melodramatic by later standards. Mrs. Page asks Davenport if his return grieves him. He replies, "Grieve me—grieve me—It is the sight of land to a starving shipwreck." At that point the stage directions call for incidental music, with "The Vacant Chair" to be played softly. The singing offstage, supposedly by blacks, of plantation songs similarly reinforced the mood in other scenes. The settings were excellent: Mrs. Page's lovingly tended garden with a glimpse of her vined cottage; Colonel Preston's rundown mansion; and a ruined gateway in the moonlight. For this romantic night setting, the odor of magnolias was wafted through the auditorium.

In an interesting observation the *Dramatic Mirror* noted that the play "would seem to point to the speedy realization of Mr. [William Dean] Howells' prediction that the future American drama will be 'a prolongation of character sketches.'" Almost all important reviews looked favorably on both the play and the players. For a pleasant change, some of Barrymore's most persistent critics acknowledged that he gave a sterling performance—apparently free of his bothersome mannerisms. The play remains an affectionately written, moving, late 19th-century idyll. But its place in theatrical history is not so happy. Palmer, losing confidence in it during rehearsals, had allowed other managers to book his theatre for the spring and summer and also had scheduled a Chicago engagement. Refusing to go back on his promise, he was forced to hustle the original company off and also to supplant it briefly with another company (and new sets and costumes) until the other managers came in. All these costs meant Palmer missed the opportunity to make some desperately needed profits. His stubbornness or integrity caused him to lose the Madison Square (although he still retained Palmer's) and signaled the beginning of the last phase of his downhill plunge.

Daniel Frohman revived Boucicault's *Old Heads and Young Hearts* at the Lyceum on April 6. In his memoirs he states he was "giving way to a general demand" and praises his stock company's performances. He never specifies where the general demand arose, but apparently it did not come from the public at large. Nor did a majority of critics agree with his appraisal of the acting. Most reviewers felt that such otherwise fine players as Georgia Cayvan and Nelson Wheatcroft were not up to the specialized demands of this sort of period comedy. W. J. LeMoyne's Jesse Rural was deemed the most satisfactory interpretation. Preopening ballyhoo made much of the fact that the play was to be performed in correct period costumes, but here, too, some reviewers were not so certain about the results. Frohman had to force the month's run to carry him to the end of his season. At the 14th Street Theatre Rose Coghlan cavorted as Peg Woffington in *Masks and Faces,* while Julia Marlowe starred at the Harlem Opera House in a week that saw her do *As You Like It, Ingomar,* and *The Hunchback.*

Playgoers seeking a new play's premiere had to be content with **A Lucky Man** (4-6-91, Niblo's). Supposedly based on a French play, it unfolded the adventures of a man beset by troubles through mistaken identity. The *Times*'s man, short and sarcastic, had praise only for the title and wondered aloud about a hero "who as each misfortune is heaped upon his head remarks, 'Now I am having my good time.' " The masochist hung on for just a single week.

On the 11th Kate Claxton and Kitty Blanchard came in from the road to the Union Square for a week of their old fallback vehicle, *The Two Orphans.*

Similarly settling in after a cross-country tour, the Kendals unpacked at Palmer's on the 13th, beginning their second stand of the season with Pinero's *The Weaker Sex* before moving on to *A Scrap of Paper, The Ladies' Battle, A Happy Pair, Impulse, The Queen's Shilling, The Ironmaster,* and *The Money Spinner.* Their two-week return played to crowded houses.

The characters in Thomas Woods's **Two of a Kind** (4-18-91, Union Square) included two rich old maids dead set against marriage, two old, poor bachelors, two pretty young girls eager to wed, and two young men. Since the play was a comedy, audiences had a good idea of how the pairings would turn out.

Rose Coghlan had a new role for critics to judge when she appeared in her brother Charles's **Lady Barter** (4-27-91, Palmer's). His story was simple. Lady Barter is a woman with a past who is determined to put that unfortunate past behind her by means of a new marriage. The man she loves, Lord Brent (Hugo Tolland), hears rumors about

letters she has hidden. He demands to see them. She refuses. He stalks out. She faints and the curtain falls. In the final act she comes into an inheritance left her by a former lover, so walks away, head high, to seek a better life elsewhere. To the critic for the *Herald* the production appeared shamefully cheap, with Lady Barter's gaudy salon reminding him more of 23rd Street than of a Mayfair drawing room, where the action supposedly occurred. The vivacious star with the beguiling deep voice won applause when she appeared in an olive satin gown, yet she could not whet interest in the play. Three curtain raisers or afterpieces offered on different nights during the two-week run— **Dream Faces, The Lost Thread** (4-29-91), and Charles Reade's **Nance Oldfield** (5-15-91), in which an aging actress must disillusion a lovesick young playwright—were no help.

One American play that was to enjoy many years on the road was Philip G. Hubert, Jr., and Marie Madison's **The Witch** (5-4-91, People's). Its hero, Walter Endicott (Charles Jehlinger), is a New Englander who strays into Indian territory and at a Catholic mission there meets Leontine (Marie Hubert). He falls in love with her and marries her, but he subsequently is waylaid and attacked by an Indian who also loves the girl. The attack causes Walter to lose his memory. He returns to Salem and becomes engaged to Elizabeth Leyden (Flora Redding). Leontine comes to Salem seeking her husband. Her religious garb, her constant crossing herself, and the dove (a gift from Walter) she insists on carrying all strike the villagers as odd. Before long, rumors that she is a witch have spread throughout the town. At first Elizabeth is sympathetic, but when Leontine refuses to renounce Walter, she turns against her. Elizabeth scratches her own face and claims Leontine has bewitched her. Leontine is convicted and sentenced to death, only to be pardoned at the last moment. In one scene Leontine releases the dove, hoping it will carry a message back to her priestly mentors. In another, her fetters break asunder just as the judge taunts her by asking for a miracle. The judge does not know that the chains have been weakened by a compassionate jailer. The settings, of simple Salem homes, a drab jail, and the woodlands, lacked the richness and elegance playgoers were said to prefer but were appropriate to the story.

The "Play of American Life in Three Acts" that ousted *Alabama* was Martha Morton's **The Merchant** (5-4-91, Madison Square). It had won a $1000 prize given by the *World* for the best American play submitted to it. But this sort of contest was suspect, designed largely for publicity, and few of the better reviewers agreed with the award. The majority felt that beautiful settings and superb, restrained acting saved the evening from bathos. In Miss Morton's saga Carroll Vanderstyle (Henry Miller) has speculated unwisely and is on the verge of bankruptcy. Fred Dupré (E. J. Henley) offers to lend him the money he needs to attempt to retrieve his fortune. What Vanderstyle does not know is that Dupré is in love with Mrs. Vanderstyle (Viola Allen) and hopes to enjoy her favors as a result. She sharply rebuffs him, and a contrite Dupré apologizes. However, Vanderstyle overhears him and returns his check. The couple are left to face a possibly dismal future together. Despite critical harrumphs, the public was taken by the entertainment, and it ran until the summer heat forced its closing.

Miller and Miss Allen represented the newer school of reserved acting. James O'Neill and Louis James stood for an older school when they co-starred in E. J. Swartz's **The Envoy** (5-4-91, Star). The piece was claptrap, patently designed as a vehicle for its stars. James was seen as the better actor, though some felt that at just short of fifty he looked absurd in a blond wig, trying to play a young man. O'Neill was lambasted for his incessant posturing and his failure to learn his lines. After two weeks the play left.

If *The Witch* had faint echoes of *From Sire to Son,* William Bourne's **Work and Wages** (5-4-91, Grand Opera) brought to mind *The Middleman* and several other recent plays. Its hero, Tom Wentworth (John E. Kellerd), is a working man and an inventor, whose invention is stolen from him by an industrialist. A strike and a trial follow. The strike provided much of the vivid action, with striking ruffians invading and breaking up an elegant ball and also blowing up a blast furnace. *Work and Wages* did not please New Yorkers.

Nor did a lighter work, **Home Sweet Home** (5-4-91, Academy of Music), which was proffered as a worthy successor to *The Old Homestead.* It wasn't. After Richard Lambert (Mason Mitchell) steals money and fastens the guilt on Fred Pringle (John B. Maher), one of the robbery victims, Jeremiah Makepeace (Robert Fisher), takes it on himself to prove Fred's innocence. Uncle Jerry likes Fred, and so does his daughter, Kate (Hattie Harvey). Settings showed a grist mill and a working cider press, although the *Herald* noted that neither had anything to do with the plot.

In the face of all these new plays, Richard Mansfield began a summer-long visit to the Garden. He started with recent favorites—*Beau Brummell,*

A Parisian Romance, and *Prince Karl*—but did bring out one novelty early on, his own **Don Juan; or, The Sad Adventures of a Youth** (5-18-91, Garden). His approach was fresh and perhaps singularly American. This Don Juan is not a jaded, sometimes cruel cynic but a happy, overeager young man newly released from the shackles of a rigid upbringing. And all his wild, amorous escapades notwithstanding, he genuinely loves his devoted Julia (Beatrice Cameron). The hero's death comes after he is wounded defending his sweetheart and is thrown into jail. Don Alonso, Duke de Navarro (D. H. Harkins), his implacable enemy, has vowed to torment him to the end, but though Don Juan is beset by moments of delirium, he forces the duke at swordpoint to sign an order of release. For Don Juan the victory is short-lived. Still, he dies content, knowing he and Julia, who has sacrificed her own life, have been united in death. Looking back, Winter summed up the star's interpretation as "gay, gallant, heroic, impetuous, a creature all sunshine, and his hero, by a pathetic death, in prison, dignified the character, dispelling the remembrance of its volatility and endearing it to the heart." But at the time of the opening, critical opinion was divided and warm weather no help. Mansfield doggedly kept the play on the boards until late June, at one point inserting a happy ending that allowed the don and Julia to leave prison alive and filled with hope. Before long, however, Mansfield dropped the work from his repertory.

D. K. Higgins was both the star and author of **Kidnapped** (5-18-91, People's). As Louis Rhinegold, "the Dutch Dude," he vanquished murdering abductors. Sensations included a fire in a slum wine shop, and a police wagon and its horses rushing across the stage.

Delirium, besides giving actors a chance to chew the scenery, was a useful device for contemporary playwrights. The hero of Albert Roland Haven's **The Veiled Picture** (5-25-91, Lyceum), while delirious, had killed his best friend and fellow art student. All that was years ago in Rome and was hushed up. The death was made to seem a suicide. When he returned home, George Felton (Robert Mantell) married a pretty girl. But the rest of his life, and his art as well, have been haunted by the killing. Only now, so many years afterwards, does he discover that his wife, Alice (Charlotte Behrens), is the dead man's sister. The discovery drags him to the brink of madness, but with Alice's careful nurturing his raging furies are exorcised. Neither the play nor the performers were well received. Mantell, though relatively young, was an actor of an older school given to declaiming. The best one critic could say was that he looked handsome in his plum-colored velvet frock coat. During the play's second week a companion piece was added, John Ernest McCann and Nugent Robinson's **A Lesson in Acting** (6-2-91, Lyceum). It gave the somewhat hammy Mantell a tour de force. He portrayed Maurice Lasarge, an actor who brings home an aspiring tyro and asks the young man to improvise a scene in which he learns that his wife has just left him. The improvisation is not very convincing, and Lasarge decides to show how he would play the scene. In doing so he picks up a letter, which informs him that his own wife has, in fact, left him. The young man watches first in awe and then in horror as Lasarge becomes delirious. All the emoting was in vain. Theatregoers would not buy, so that second week was also the final week.

The *Herald* castigated J. B. Runnion's **Miss Manning** (6-1-91, 14th St.) as "a ghastly piece of work," quite possibly the season's worst. Trapped as its star was Effie Ellsler, who played a woman required by a will to marry at once or lose her inheritance. A collection of seeming loonies materializes out of nowhere to court her. Since the play was peppered with songs and dances, it straddled the fence between straight play and musical. Miss Ellsler was trapped for only one week.

Those critics who reviewed **Apple Orchard** [or **Blossom**] **Farm** (6-8-91, Windsor) were at a loss to explain it. It appeared to be a comedy-melodrama, with the villain kidnapping a child and harassing its mother until everything is reset in apple-pie order by Aunt Ollie. Aunt Ollie was played by a female impersonator.

Apart from some special matinees and evening performances, which served during those years in lieu of tryouts, *Miss Manning* and *Apple Orchard Farm* rang down the curtain on the season. However, one of these tryouts deserves brief mention, since it came from the pen of Augustus Thomas. **A Night's Frolic** (6-10-91, Union Square) was his version of von Moser's *Eine Frau die in Paris war*. A woman learns that her brother's prospective father-in-law will not allow his daughter to marry anyone except a soldier. She disguises herself as an officer and, to disgust the father, purposely misbehaves. Ordered to sleep outside in a gazebo, she meets there the soldier whom the father had expected. The two fall in love, leaving the father little choice but to accept the girl's brother as his daughter's husband. The all too masculine Helen Barry, never welcomed in New York, had enjoyed some success with the play on the road, but reviews of the one-night stand warned that neither she nor the play could expect much from Broadway.

All in all, it was a season marked by an uncommon number of failures (which could not be rescued even by tacking on curtain raisers or afterpieces) and by tragic losses (most notably Barrett's death and Booth's retirement). Of course, away from first-class houses old stalwarts continued to provide a lure. Touring stars, many of whom rarely or never played Broadway, brought neighborhood and regional playgoers everything from Shakespeare to Boucicault to *Uncle Tom's Cabin* to more recent successes such as *The Henrietta* and *Paul Kauvar*. The theatre remained a leading outlet for escape for virtually every station of society. Still, as the old codger in *Home, Sweet Home* said, times were changing.

1891–1892

To call the 1891–92 season unimportant would be to condemn it with a gratuitous severity. On its musical stages it saw, first, in *Robin Hood* the appearance of the earliest American work to enjoy a long, respected afterlife and, almost immediately following, in *A Trip to Chinatown* the American work that more than any other moved farce-comedy into the realm of modern musical comedy. It also witnessed, if only for a single matinee, the breakaway drama that introduced Ibsenite influences into native dramaturgy. For dedicated playgoers it brought forth any number of evenings of more than passing interest. Yet on the whole, it can fairly be termed lackluster. Truly exciting nights seemed fewer and farther between than in many superior seasons, both before and since. Nonetheless, even with these caveats in mind, the season secured itself a minor place in American theatrical history, for it served as a small, rickety bridge between eras, the one ending with the death of Barrett and the retirement of Booth, and the other beginning with the opening of a major new theatre.

The season began with the sort of "audience show" that often defies the sadistic bludgeons of nose-in-the-air critics. **Jane** (8-3-91, Madison Square) was a London farce by Harry Nicholls and William Lestocq, taken from Maurice Desvallières's *Prête-moi ta femme*. Its heroine, played by the "mannish" Johnstone Bennett, is a wily servant who helps her master outwit a persistent nuisance by posing as her master's wife. Late in the run an American curtain raiser, Edward S. Belknap and Mason Carnes's **The Better Part** (10-16-91, Madison Square) was added to the bill. In its spotlight was a struggling young actor who relinquishes a part he badly needs so that the husband of a girl who jilted him can take it and support her. Alone or with its accompanier, *Jane* delighted audiences for more than 100 showings. By the time it left, the theatre had been taken over by Charles Hoyt, who lodged his *Trip to Chinatown* there, thus removing the playhouse for some time as a home to straight plays.

Harry P. Mawson's Civil War drama, **A Fair Rebel** (8-3-91, 14th St.), was less successful, though by no means a failure. Like so many Civil War plays (possibly a majority of them), it centered on a romance that transcends sectional rivalries. Clairette Monteith (Fanny Gillette), a Virginia girl, loves Col. Ezra Mason (Edward E. Mawson), a Union officer. He is captured and imprisoned, and the girl's vile cousin, who himself hopes to marry her, arranges to have the man put to death. But the girl persuades her fiancé to tunnel to freedom. She will be waiting at the tunnel's end. The digging succeeds but the girl is shot. The *Herald*'s critic deemed the play more interesting than *Shenandoah* or *Held by the Enemy*, although he allowed that much of the dialogue seemed pretentious "nonsense." He cited two examples: "I am proud to say that his manhood is my admiration" and "I would rather die of starvation with my face to the enemy than turn my back to the foe to live in selfish luxury." Striking scenes included a Union soldier being shot while attempting to telegraph a message from the top of a telegraph pole. Comic relief included a scene taken from the recent disclosures of life in Libby Prison (where much of the action was set), in which a man is brought before a court-martial for trying to take a bath. After filling out the month on 14th Street, the play took to the road.

John J. Kennedy's **She Couldn't Marry Three** (8-17-91, Windsor) teetered precariously toward musical comedy in telling the story of a young lady loved by a haughty nobleman, a villain, and a nice seaman.

The same German farce that had served Augustus Thomas for *A Night's Frolic* the previous season now served as a vehicle for Rose Coghlan under the title **Dorothy's Dilemma** (8-20-91, Park). Unfortunately, Leopold Jordan's adaptation did not serve her well. The star's entrance as a mustachioed dragoon in a red coat and gold-striped dark pants, with her saber rattling comically, won a round of applause, as did an exit that had her jumping on a handsome black stallion and riding offstage. But all her charm and skill could not work wonders on a weak piece. Still, helped by publicity from Helen Barry's attempt to get an injunction, the play ran nearly a month and toured all season.

Frederick R. Giles, a newspaperman, was the author of a "romantic carnival drama," **The Black Mask** (8-24-91, Union Square). His young hero, Leon (E. J. Henley), is loved by Queen Forzunette (Julia Arthur), who elevates him to the peerage and sends him, with a piece of the true cross, to counteract a plague raging nearby. While he is away jealous noblemen poison the queen's mind against him, but he returns in the midst of a grand masquerade ball. Dressed all in black, he is at first assumed to be the dreaded plague incarnate. However, he soon drops his mask, announces his success, and reinstates himself in the queen's good opinion. Not satisfied with an evening of exciting swordplay, Giles also found excuses for introducing dancers, wrestlers, weightlifters, and "living statues." While the acting was praised along with the scenery, the play was brutally dismissed by most reviewers. It was a quick flop.

Two English hits and an American one shouldered each other for attention on the same night. The American play was Sydney Rosenfeld's comedy **The Club Friend** (8-31-91, Star). In his story a middle-aged doctor who had sowed many a wild oat in his earlier days lends $10,000 to an imprudent young married woman, hoping to become her lover. But her husband's friend and fellow club member, Stuyvesant Filbert (Roland Reed), knows that the physician is actually the wife's father and quietly acts to prevent a scandal. At one point the husband has received an anonymous letter warning him of his wife's behavior. He suspects Filbert and shows him the letter. Filbert tears it up. Just then the doctor comes in. "Your patient is there," Filbert says, pointing to the thunderstruck husband. "I'll attend to Mrs. Oaks!" End of act. Filbert's self-portrait is a simple one: "I am constantly reminding myself of Puchinello . . . the maddest, merriest fellow, even when his heart was breaking." After more than a month at the Star, the comedy embarked on a season-long tour.

The first of the English plays, albeit it had toured the provinces, had not been seen in London. Harry and Edward Paulton's **Niobe** (8-31-91, Bijou) was a bit of light fluff about a classical statue brought to life by an electrical shock. To contemporaries the picture of wiring wrapped around ancient marble and left there overnight by workmen who were in the process of electrifying a home must have heightened the contrast between the old and the modern, and possibly imbued a touch of pride in those affluent and progressive enough to welcome the innovation in their own homes. The American edition of the text, published as *Niobe, All Smiles* several years later by Samuel French, poses a small but interesting question. Although the play, both in the 1891 production and in the 1896 printing, was reset in America, the text contains phrases such as "our English law" and mentions characters moving to and fro with amusing unconcern between American and a few obviously English localities. Did American players follow the patently careless resetting faithfully, or were the errors rectified by the actors? The answer almost certainly must be the latter. Yet either way, playgoers unquestionably enjoyed themselves. The farce chalked up just over 100 performances before setting out on tour.

The second British work was more serious-minded, and in it E. H. Sothern continued on his climb to the very heights of theatrical fame. Henry Arthur Jones's **The Dancing Girl** (8-31-91, Lyceum) told of a dissipated duke who has lost his chance to marry the girl he loved and who has made a loose dancing girl his mistress. Her devout Quaker father discovers what his daughter is doing, creates a scene at the duke's party, and leaves the now virtually broke duke to contemplate drinking a vial of poison. His hand is stayed by a crippled girl who has served as his conscience and whom he agrees to wed. Virginia Harned and Jenny Dunbar were the naughty and good girls respectively. Some notions of a changing climate can be gleaned from the *Times*'s man, who scoffed at the thought that "to be virtuous is to be happy" and branded it "buncombe." Moral or not, the evening was superb theatre, which Sothern took on tour as soon as his New York engagement ended on November 14.

Far from the main stem, up on 125th Street, a fourth play was offered for public assessment. Lawrence Marston's **Credit Lorraine** (8-31-91, Columbus) looked like a rehashing of Rosenfeld's *The Whirlwind,* reset in Europe. Leonora de Castiglione (Lillian Lewis) wins a husband after she saves a failing bank during the Franco-Prussian War. The play was no failure, either, touring for at least a couple of seasons.

Paul Merritt and Augustus Harris's six-year-old *Human Nature* had been brought to America in 1890 and enjoyed a long run in Boston. Now, using its Boston title, **The Soudan** (9-3-91, Academy of Music), it was offered to New York. Its saga of an attempt to relieve the siege of Khartoum was really an excuse for spectacular scenes—a wild thunderstorm, a noisy, bloody assault, and a triumphant march in Trafalgar Square. The hero, Captain Temple (Lewis James), is also reunited with his long-separated family. Although not as well received as it had been in Boston, the melodrama ran till late November.

American melodrama was represented by William Irving Paulding's **The Struggle of Life** (9-7-91, Standard). The play starred the ambitious but rarely successful Frederick Paulding. The young Paulding was the nephew of the author and revised the play, which had not been performed previously, for production. The hero, another victim of false accusations, has been forced to adopt an alias, Hamilton Spread, in his search for vindication. His search takes him to a thieves' den, where the man who can exculpate him dies in his arms. Just then the thieves return, and Hamilton elects to hide in a sewer. The thieves realize this and seal the hatch at the same time a flood rushes into the sewer. Hamilton struggles to save himself. His attempts are aided by a ragged woman he has befriended, who frantically brushes the snow from a manhole cover. Hamilton escapes, clears his good name, and rewards the bedraggled lady. If the sewer filled with water and a dead body floating by showed life's seamier side, other, more pleasant settings depicted Battery Park at night, with the Statue of Liberty in the distance, and St. Patrick's Cathedral (again at night) decorated for Christmas, with glimpses of neighboring homes. Such scenery failed to thrill jaded first-nighters at a house such as the Standard, but Paulding had found a vehicle that provided him with a meal ticket for several seasons.

The same night, Marie Wainwright (with Henry Miller as her leading man) found a meal ticket in a revival of *Amy Robsart,* which held the stage at Palmer's through October.

While a statue-come-to-life cavorted at the Bijou, Henry E. Dixey, who had won long-lasting fame in another such role, tried out a new play for size—one more English farce, J. H. Darnley's **The Solicitor** (9-8-91, Herrmann's). Darnley's story featured a solicitor, Gilbert Brandon (Dixey), who, on a dare at a party, agrees to take over an unattended cab waiting outside and see what happens. Among his fares are his own wife, whom he takes to an unknown address and witnesses kissing a handsome soldier, and a burglar, who leaves part of his loot in the cab. Complications, then explanations, follow. Years later Dixey would star in an even more successful piece with a similar story, *The Man on the Box.* But for the nonce *The Solicitor* provided him with a modest hit.

Lucy H. Hooper was a Paris correspondent for an

American newspaper and Richard Davey a promising poet. Together they had written a play that had been tried out in late 1889 as *Helen's Inheritance* at one of the era's many special matinees. It was handed vicious notices. Nonetheless, an intrepid or foolhardy producer opted to chance the road with it, and it was revised as **Inheritance** (9-14-91, Windsor). Its heroine learns that her mother died insane and refuses to heed warnings of a family history of insanity. She marries and goes mad. When her husband, having obtained a divorce, attempts to remarry, she appears at the wedding and tries to kill him and his bride. The play itself died a swift death.

Richard Mansfield, nearing the end of the lengthy engagement that had begun the preceding season, brought out a new work, **Nero** (9-21-91, Garden). His reward was ecstatic critical notices and chilling public indifference. The play was not the same presented the previous October at Niblo's. Mansfield had sketched the outline for Thomas Russell Sullivan, who had also worked with him on *Dr. Jekyll and Mr. Hyde* and who actually wrote the drama. Their Nero was an unmitigated villain, abusive to women, cruel to anyone he no longer needs, selfish, hedonistic, and cowardly. In the end, the doting Acte (Beatrice Cameron), whom he has savagely discarded, shows him how to accept his fate by killing herself in his presence. Recognizing what must be, the terrified, craven emperor wails at the mute corpse, "Is there no pain? Is there no pain?" So unrelievedly stark a portrait probably was foredoomed, but Mansfield, himself not a nice man, apparently felt a certain kinship with it, so he attempted to retain it in his repertory—something he did only briefly for his more humane *Don Juan*.

Clara Morris, two decades before one of the brightest luminaries of the American theatre and still blessed with a vast following on the road, made one of her increasingly infrequent appearances in a first-class New York house when she starred in *Odette* at the 14th Street Theatre for a week, beginning on the 21st.

If the title of John Douglass's English comedy **Darlington's Widow** (9-21-91, Columbus) smacked suspiciously of *Mr. Wilkinson's Widows*, its plot seemed a steal from Pinero's *The Magistrate*. Mrs. Darlington (Grace Huntington), a widow in love with Adonis Featherfield (Al Roberts), is careful to hide the fact that she has a stepchild older than she. Adonis also has a secret—a stepchild older than he. The play was purportedly taken from *Les Suites d'un premier,* but it had only small appeal for American audiences.

A cast recruited largely from August's mishap,

The Black Mask, was featured in a play about another unrelenting villain, **The Marquis' Wife** (9-28-91, Columbus). Hélène Barriche (Julia Arthur), the marquise, a poor girl who has married a rich man, is ungrateful, unloving, and a political plotter. When the marquis (Mark Price) discovers the truth he warns her she will live out her life, for all practical purposes, as his prisoner. She feigns remorse, puts opium in his brandy, and when he is unconscious tries to persuade George Cecil (E. J. Henley), an acquaintance, to kill him. The shocked man refuses, so she does the killing herself, then pins the blame on the man who has demurred. He is sent to prison but escapes, hunts down the marquise, and strangles her. The play was by Sidney Bowkett, a young actor. Despite some good acting, the play had an even shorter life than *The Black Mask.*

Clinton Stuart's **Will She Divorce Him?** (9-28-91, Harlem Opera House) survived for only a few months, entirely in neighborhood theatres, no doubt out of a certain courtesy. After all, its star, Cora Tanner, was the wife of a popular Brooklyn theatre owner. The play's preposterous premise was probably no more preposterous than that of many, more successful plays. Lawrence Senlyer (John Glendinning) sends a love letter to Julia de Sardonna (Esther Williams), a married woman. When her husband discovers the letter the embarrassed writer says oops, it was meant for someone else. That someone else is Isobel, a woman he has never loved but who has pursued him, as the husband knows. A wedding ensues. In time, of course, Isobel learns the truth, which confronts her with the dilemma of the title. But that same passing of time has allowed the young husband to find he does love his bride, so all ends well.

The excesses of the French Revolution were pitted against the ultimately suicidal stubbornness of a religious fanatic in Sardou's **Thermidor** (10-5-91, 23rd St.). A woman brings about her own death (and that of her faithful lover to boot) by refusing to renounce a vow, despite the unceasing efforts of a kindly friend. In a startling move, Elsie de Wolfe (later better known in other fields) was cast as the girl; the fine English actor, Johnston Forbes-Robertson, was the lover; and Frederick Bond was the helper. The play, despite numerous dissuasive notices, ran until mid-November.

Financial difficulties and scathing reviews turned George I. Ulmar's **The Volunteer** (10-5-91, Harlem Opera House) into a one-performance fiasco. By 1891 its story was dreadfully clichéd. During the Civil War a girl loves a soldier who fights for the opposing side. Their romance nearly is derailed by a second, treacherous suitor, whose black marks include fratricide and bigamy. Paunchy Gustavus Levick was the hero, Col. Jack Chadburn. One scene offered an elopement in a balloon. The play was advertised as being in "four acts and a vista." That vista was a battle scene in which, on the only night, the blues and grays were intermixed in befuddlement. The following morning the scenery was seized for nonpayment of debt.

Scott Marble's **The Patrol** (10-5-91, People's), slammed as a ripoff of *The Still Alarm,* had a slightly longer existence but also soon disappeared.

On the 12th at the Garden a distinguished first-night audience assembled for the latest return of Jefferson, Florence, and Mrs. Drew in their version of *The Rivals.* During the second week of the fortnight stand *The Heir at Law* also was dusted off for a few performances.

Other loyal playgoers foregathered the same night at the Star to welcome back similarly familiar visitors, the Kendals. The couple's repertory offered no novelties, relying instead on *Still Waters Run Deep, Home, The Ironmaster,* and *A Scrap of Paper.*

Leonard Grover's **Wolves of New York** (10-26-91, Windsor), filled with scenes of city life, opened attractively in a music hall with patrons drinking and dining, and a show being performed on its tiny stage. But the play soon proved to be another ripoff, this time of *The Two Orphans.* A pair of innocent sisters, one of them blind, come to the big town and are entrapped by a false friend. In one scene a sister is strapped to a wheel above a vat of oil, and a fuse leading to the vat is set afire. One more buzz saw figured in the action as well. Other scenes depicted the Jefferson Market Prison and a Salvation Army barracks. However, like all of Grover's later plays, this one failed to find a responsive audience.

November was ushered in by a return of *Alabama* (at Palmer's) and Henry E. Dixey's second starring vehicle of the season, **The Man with One Hundred Faces** (11-2-91, Herrmann's). Carl and Hugo Rosenfeld adapted the farce from a German work. Dixey played a vaudeville mimic who so cleverly makes himself resemble a well-known lawyer that the lawyer hires him to take his place at home while he goes out for a night on the town. In the course of the action Dixey also devised pretexts for making himself up to resemble the president and other notable figures as well as the star of *Adonis* (who, as everyone knew, had been none other than Dixey). The play ran a month. Neither vehicle apparently satisfied Dixey or his audiences as much as had been hoped. Before long he was romping again in *Adonis.*

Another play that opened the same evening was

Charlie Reed and William Collier's **Hoss and Hoss** (11-2-91, Park). The young comedians played a pair of judges, Charlie and Willis Hoss, whose tour of the town leads to all sorts of complications. Most critics treated the play as a farce, although it followed the practice of the time by inserting a few songs and dances. Before long, however, more musical numbers were added, making the entertainment a full-fledged musical.

The next night Bernhardt was back. Her opening selection at the Standard was Barbier's *Jeanne d'Arc,* which afforded comparisons with Margaret Mather's earlier interpretation. Once again an American artist recieved the short end. But then who could compete with Bernhardt? No wonder she packed the house at a whopping $3 top. Her utterly unique theatrical magic was also displayed in *Théodora, La Tosca, Cléopatre, La Dame aux camélias, Adrienne Lecouvreur,* and *Frou-Frou.* New to Americans were the murderous heroines she portrayed in **Pauline Blanchard** (on November 28) and **La Dame de Challant** (on December 3).

Henry C. de Mille enjoyed one final success when Charles Frohman produced his version of Ludwig Fulda's *Das verlorene Paradies* as **The Lost Paradise** (11-16-91, 23rd St.). Reset in America, it recounted how Andrew Knowlton (Frank Mordaunt), a rich Boston industrialist, hands over his factory's day-to-day operations to his trusted, warmhearted manager, Reuben Warner (William Morris), in order to devote his time to his daughter, Margaret (Sydney Armstrong). His hope is that she will wed Ralph Standish (Orrin Johnson), an arrogant young man whom Knowlton has taken in as a partner. When a strike explodes at the factory, Knowlton is shocked to discover that first Warner, then Margaret side with the strikers. She announces, "Amid all the selfish arguments, there comes to my soul the voice of God, crying for mercy upon His poor. I heard it in the grinding of the machinery over at the factory. I recognized it in the cries of these people for bread. And to-day I heard it again by the bedside of sickness, in the homes of wretchedness." She consents to marry Warner, who had learned in the first act that he had invented the device that had helped Knowlton become so wealthy but who has kept quiet to spare Margaret's feelings.

Growing sympathy with the plight of many laborers earned this speechy yet gripping play favorable notices. While all the performances were praised, several critics singled out the acting of little Maude Adams in the small role of Nell, the hungry, hope-denied child worker, who has been crippled in a factory accident ("I can't do much hard work since that steel bar came down on my foot") and who knows that Warner will never reciprocate her love for him ("I saw the look in his eyes. He loves her. She's beautiful, and her frocks ain't all patched up like mine."). Special commendation also was given the factory set, with its huge, cumbersome machinery noisily grinding away and shrill steam whistles adding to the din. The production recorded 138 performances. Seekers of trivia may delight in the play's use of a one-sided telephone conversation at the start of the first act for expository purposes. This may be the earliest such employment of what soon became a cliché.

Pinero's **Lady Bountiful** (11-16-91, Lyceum) signaled the return of the Lyceum stock company. When Donald Heron (Herbert Kelcey) learns that the lady of the title, Camilla Brent (Georgia Cayvan), has lost a substantial amount of money by quietly supporting his scoundrelly father (W. J. LeMoyne), he breaks off his engagement to Camilla and marries another girl (Effie Shannon). Only after his first wife dies and Camilla is about to marry someone else does he realize how absurd his actions have been. He persuades the heroine to marry him, however belatedly. The settings, including a riding academy, won applause, while May Robson gathered laughs simply by attempting to wheel a baby carriage around the stage. For some reason, Pinero was never as popular in America as he should have been or as he was in England. *Lady Bountiful* was no exception. It enjoyed a good run, until mid-January, but created no real excitement.

Daly's troupe returned from a successful European tour and relit his theatre on the 25th with a revival of *The Taming of the Shrew*. As usual, Miss Rehan, Mrs. Gilbert, Drew, and Lewis were welcomed thunderously. But audiences probably awaited them more eagerly in something new. The obstinate Daly, however, had other plans. He embarked on a series of resurrections, bringing *The School for Scandal* in on December 2.

Jack Royal of the 92nd (12-7-91, Grand Opera) may have sounded vaguely English to some potential ticket buyers. It wasn't. Andrew C. Wheeler, the author, was better known in theatrical circles as Nym Crinkle, the critic. His play returned to the popular theme of the Civil War, but with a difference. No lovers were torn asunder after finding themselves on opposing sides. In fact, if his fellow critics' summaries can be trusted, no love interest found a place in the drama. Jack Royal (Harry Lacy) is an Irish-American and an engineer who is assigned by the War Department to run the Manhattan Iron Works. His lot is made difficult by strikers,

draft rioters, and saboteurs. Naturally Jack triumphs over the odds. Although the play offered, as had *The Lost Paradise,* another factory setting, with sweating workers and clanging machinery, its interest was not class difference or social justice but patriotism. At least one reviewer noted the irony of making the hero Irish when so many of the draft rioters were Irish. Roaring good theatre, the play lingered for a fortnight before heading out on the road, where it allowed Lacy some relief from his always popular *A Still Alarm.*

The Junior Partner (12-7-91, Herrmann's) was taken from the French of Alexandre Bisson and Albert Carré but was listed as a world premiere by producer Charles Frohman, who announced that he had commissioned it. Its plot told of two dentists who work together and how one is tricked into marrying the other's sweetheart. A carefully recreated dentist's office, with the dentist drilling away on a yowling patient, set the comic tone at the opening. Other people's pains can sometimes be fun, so the play ran for more than two months.

One of the era's many special matinees brought in the season's most interesting American work, James A. Herne's **Margaret Fleming** (12-7-91, Palmer's).

. . .

James A. Herne (1839–1901), whose real name was James Aherne or Ahearn, was the son of a poor Irish immigrant who embraced the rigorous teachings of the Dutch Reformed Church. At the age of thirteen he was removed from school in his native Cohoes, N.Y., and sent to work in a brush factory. A secret trip to watch Edwin Forrest perform determined his future plans, although he waited until he was twenty before running off to join a traveling company performing then popular dog dramas. Years of touring with various troupes followed and eventually led him to California. There he met and married Katharine Corcoran, who would often be his leading lady, and worked in collaboration with David Belasco. Their *Hearts of Oak* was Broadway's introduction to Herne. His penchant for the newer, more naturalistic drama was evident in *Drifting Apart,* which called him to the attention of Hamlin Garland and William Dean Howells, both of whom thereafter promoted his work. Because his plays were considered so avant-garde, they were rarely major commercial successes, so he was forced to supplement his income by continued acting and by directing other men's works.

. . .

Margaret Fleming (Katharine C. Herne), the wife of a successful businessman, Philip Fleming (E. M. Bell), is going blind as a result of an illness contracted during a recent pregnancy. She does not know that her husband has also fathered a child by one of his mill girls, and Fleming is fearful that knowledge of this will aggravate her condition. Margaret is asked by her maid, Maria (Mattie Earle), to visit the maid's sister, who is dying after a troubled childbirth. The sister is Fleming's mill girl, and when Margaret discovers the truth the shock leaves her totally blind. After the girl's baby dies despite Margaret's efforts to save it, Margaret flees. Her desertion marks the beginnings of hard times for her husband. Years later they meet accidentally when Margaret comes upon her own child, whom Maria has reared. A squabble follows, and they are hauled into the police station. Margaret determines to keep and raise her child but never again to see Fleming.

Herne was confessedly attempting to bring Ibsenite reforms into American drama. He discarded soliloquies and asides, omitted unnecessarily stagey scenes, especially at the end of acts, and concentrated on truthful characterization. The play had been seen earlier in Boston, where notices had been for the most part uncomprehending and unaccepting. New York's reviewers were, perhaps, even more savage. The *Herald* waved it away as "monotonous and talky." The *Critic* blasted Herne's views of human nature as "abnormal" and insisted, "His 'realism' when it is not unreal is often ridiculously trivial." The *Times* found the work "commonplace," adding, "The life it portrays is sordid and mean, and its effect upon a sensitive mind is depressing." In the *Tribune* William Winter, who by now had begun to establish himself as the archanti-Ibsenite, bewailed that it offered nothing but long conversations "interrupted from time to time by the falling of the curtain." He dug his knife in to continue, "Several babies are introduced, and at one time the stage is replete with bathtub and sponges, baby pins and diapers, scented soap and powder puff, towels and carminative; and this paraphernalia of the nursery is exploited with abundance of that soft nonsense of prattle which always sounds well beside the cradle and always make people sick in public." That public seemed to agree. There was no call to transfer the play somewhere for a regular run. Subsequent revivals were intermittent and never particularly well received. To this day the play, whatever its importance, holds the allegiance of academia in a way it never has the working stage.

That evening Daly continued his parade of revivals with *The Last Word*.

Frank Mayo, of *Davy Crockett* fame, had long been relegated to second-class theatres. He ap-

peared briefly at a fading first-class theatre (if, indeed, it was still looked upon as such) when he offered **The Athlete** (12-14-91, Niblo's). The piece proved to be a reworking of Wilkie Collins's *Man and Wife* and was poorly received, so Mayo hurriedly returned to the safety of *Nordeck* and *Crockett* before heading out again to the road.

The muscular R. D. MacLean, another road star with serious albeit antiquated pretensions, came into the Union Square on the 21st and harked (and barked) back to the days of Forrest with a mounting of *The Gladiator*. The production's scenery was shabby and travel-weary. One supporting player who received some good notices as Phasarius was the youthful William S. Hart.

On the following evening, the 22nd, Daly introduced the last of his revivals, *As You Like It*.

A plot about a girl who runs away from home, joins a circus, and later is found there by her father after she has become a famous and happily married bareback rider sufficed for Charles Barnard's **The Country Circus** (12-29-91, Academy of Music). Spectacle was the thing. Besides an elaborate circus parade through a small New England city in the third act, the circus of the fourth provided any number of thrills. Along with bareback riders there were acrobats, trained baboons, monkeys, mules, and dogs. Grotesque clowns cavorted around the ring and in the stands. At one point, for no understandable reason, a huge mirror was lowered onstage so the audience could see its own reactions. The production enriched the coffers of the rising young partnership of Klaw and Erlanger, who mounted it in conjunction with Joseph Jefferson's son. The author of *Margaret Fleming*, Herne, staged the piece. Even miserable weather could not keep the public away from the huge auditorium, where the entertainment compiled more than 100 performances.

The new year, 1892, began with the return of another audience pleaser, *Blue Jeans*. Its saw buzzed along merrily and terrifyingly at the 14th Street Theatre from January 4 to April 9.

One minor play also tried its wings the same evening, Herbert Hall Winslow's **Birds of a Feather** (1-4-92, Third Ave.). This hodgepodge was offered as a "melodramatic comedy" with, according to the *Herald*, "songs and dances, gory tragedy and flame, deep-voiced villains and helpless maidens all jumbled together." The hero was Dr. Bob Pellet, and one of the rescued ladies promised to become his wife. Whatever its faults, it toured for the rest of the season.

Modjeska came into the Union Square on the 11th. Her repertory was heavy with standbys: *As*

You Like It, Measure for Measure, Mary Stuart, Much Ado About Nothing, and *Camille.* However, she was not without something new: Paul Kester and Minnie Maddern Fiske's **Countess Roudine** (1-13-92, Union Square). The countess's name is Liana, and she is engaged to marry Count Sagenoff (John A. Lane), a man who has come under suspicion by Russia's nervous authorities. To remove doubts the count agrees to expose another nobleman the government has doubts about, Prince Moronoff (T. B. Thalberg), and he enlists Liana to help entrap the prince. She agrees, but before long she has fallen in love with the prince. Risking all, she tricks Sagenoff into destroying the evidence against the prince and escapes. Even though she was past fifty-one, Modjeska was so radiant, so warm, and so persuasive a performer she had little trouble portraying a susceptible girl of twenty or so. But her performance was not enough to justify a mediocre play, and the new work soon disappeared from her bills.

The night before Modjeska presented her new play, two other new works premiered. Pinero's **The Cabinet Minister** (1-12-92, Daly's) was Daly's first new offering of the season. It told of a spendthrift English lady who falls into the snares of a black-mailer and is saved only because her husband has overheard the blackmailer's demands. Strangely, although there were two good roles for her in the play, Ada Rehan was absent. Apparently even good notices could not compensate many loyalists for her absence. Daly was forced to make another precipitous withdrawal.

The second play was American and had some fun with the same labor strife that earlier dramas had viewed with concern. **For Money** (1-12-92, Star) was a vehicle written expressly for W. H. Crane. He portrayed Colonel W. Farragut Gurney, a wealthy man who has become convinced some of his friends like him only for his money and who decides to separate the frauds from the true believers. He has been impelled to his doubts by the discovery of his dead wife's locket, which contains not his picture but that of another man. A young lady, boasting of her parentage, shows him a picture of her father and—lo and behold!—there, as Gurney exclaims, is "the man whose picture I found on my dead wife's bosom." He knows the man. To achieve his purpose, Gurney engineers a strike among employees of his streetcar company, a strike he announces could bankrupt him. The strike quickly gets out of hand, and mob rule is threatened. Gurney is a colonel in the local militia, and he is called upon to restore order. But this presents a problem, for although he is afraid of water, Gurney is also the commodore of

the Larchmont Yacht Club. When the call comes he is busy delaying a yacht race, because he has grown seasick looking at the sound. He eventually solves matters by bribing the strike leaders. At the same time, he also wins the hand of a rich widow (or, more accurately, she wins his) and encourages several others moonstruck or dumbstruck lovers to clasp hands in the bargain.

Crane had a field day. He had asked the authors, Clay M. Greene and Augustus Thomas, to provide him with a comedy-drama that would allow him to display the range of his abilities. Yet somehow he made what the playwrights had conceived as touching or dramatic moments irresistibly funny. At one point, for whatever minor value it had, he became the second unlikely star of the season to prance across the stage on a black stallion. He also, wisely, surrounded himself with good players in amusing roles. There were, for example, Mrs. Rittenhouse Webb (Hattie Russell), the rich, practical, persistent widow; Norman Stewart (T. D. Frawley), an embarrassingly deaf suitor; Violet Bell (Gladys Wallis), a gushingly sentimental young girl; and Winona (Anna O'Neill), Gurney's daughter with a roving eye. Settings, too, were superb, including a magnificent green and gold interior and a scene on the Larchmont landing with a view of the windswept sound. Yet for all its excellences, Crane seemingly was dissatisfied, so after a profitable run that lasted until the beginning of April, he dropped the work.

Squire Kate (1-18-92, Lyceum) was Robert Buchanan's adaptation of Armand d'Artois and Henri Pagat's *La Fermière.* An elder sister makes sacrifices to bring up her younger sister, only to have the younger girl steal the older one's fiancé. The big scene gave Georgia Cayvan a real chance to show her mettle, and most critics felt she rose to the occasion. But the play itself was weak, and even the added attraction of a one-acter, **Catching a Fairy,** could not stimulate the box office. The two-month run was forced.

On the 19th, to replace the failed *Cabinet Minister,* Daly breathed new life into *Nancy and Co.* Naturally, Ada Rehan was back in the cast. The next night Palmer brought back *Jim, the Penman* with Maurice Barrymore heading the cast. It was a stopgap booking that kept Palmer's lit for only a week and a half.

Both Daly and Palmer had new presentations ready early in February. Both offered plays taken from the French. Sydney Grundy's **The Broken Seal** (2-3-92, Palmer's) was derived loosely from Busnach and Cauvin's *Le Secret de la terreuse.* A young man learns that his late, respected father was actually guilty of a crime for which another man has been imprisoned, so the man endeavors to absolve the wronged man even at the price of his own family's good name. He does so with the help of a priest willing to break his vow of silence (thus the title). The prisoner, his life ruined, refuses to allow the young man's family to have its reputation besmirched. Palmer culled from his roster of players as fine an ensemble as could be gathered for this sort of drama. Edward Bell was the hero, J. H. Stoddart the wronged man, Frederick Bond the priest, Agnes Booth the dead man's erring, recalcitrant wife, and Mrs. D. P. Bowers the hero's distressed mother. However, the play offended many clergymen and religious theatregoers and proved too uncompromising for others.

That was not the case with **Love in Tandem** (2-9-92, Daly's), which Daly's brother reworked from Henri Bocage and Charles de Courcy's *La Vie à deux*. The basic plot was simple. A young married couple, Aprilla and Richard Dymond (Ada Rehan and John Drew), begin to get on each other's nerves and so agree to a divorce, whereupon Aprilla sets out to find Richard a suitable second wife. She brings in several candidates, and they bring with them a host of farcical complications. As everyone on the other side of the footlights knew from the beginning, the comedy concludes with the Dymonds cheerfully reconciled. Most critics enjoyed the play, all the while conceding it required its remarkable comedians to put it over. There was some lamenting that no part could be found for Mrs. Gilbert, but Lewis won plaudits for his droll delineation of a selfish father-in-law (with the typical period farce moniker of Mr. Skinnastone), whose bungling efforts to improve matters merely make them worse.

The absence of Mrs. Gilbert in this production, the absence of Ada Rehan in an earlier one, and the fact that neither Lewis nor Mrs. Gilbert would be in the next production may have been intentional on Daly's part. He already knew and was bitter that Drew had signed on with Charles Frohman and would leave the company at season's end. His casting may therefore have been to prepare his regulars for the permanent breakup of his famous foursome. Bit by bit another piece of the theatrical scene was being unraveled, another small era drawing to a close. *Love in Tandem* was successful, but Daly long since had announced his final offering of the season would be unveiled in mid-March. The comedy drew good houses as long as Daly allowed it to continue.

Gloriana (2-15-92, Herrmann's), taken from the French by James Mortimer, had fun with switched identities, not unlike *Quits* and *Vice Versa*. They begin when Leopold Fitz-Jocelyn (Charles B. Welles), about to be married, receives a call from Gloriana Lovering (Henrietta Crosman), a widow he once had met briefly. To discourage her he pretends that he is his own valet. She invites him to become her servant, but when this gains her nothing, she pretends to have been a serving girl who had been out on the town in her mistress's fancy clothes. By chance Mrs. Lovering lives in a house owned by Fitz-Jocelyn's prospective father-in-law, and Fitz-Jocelyn's real valet, Spinks (Joseph Humphreys), at times has courted the serving girl there, Kitty (May Robson). A further complication arrives in the person of the mercurial Count Vladimir Evitoff (E. J. Henley), the widow's would-be second husband. Believing Spinks is Fitz-Jocelyn, the count demands a duel. By the final curtain Fitz-Jocelyn and Mrs. Lovering have ironed out the problems. The play ran two months, but not always alone. Because the evening was perceived as too short, Clyde Fitch's **Frédéric Lemaître** (2-29-92, Herrmann's) was added to the bill. The short piece told how the great actor impersonates a brokenhearted lover so touchingly that he persuades a stagestruck young milliner to return to her suitor. Quinn has called the play "a charming character study," but in 1892 Fitch's reputation had not been established and critics gave far more attention to the rising Henry Miller's performance. The *Herald* extolled it for its "poetry of interpretation and carefulness of portrayal." Curiously, Miller had not been slated to play the part and was given it only after another player rejected it.

A dramatized novel, **The Wide, Wide World** (2-15-92, Niblo's) found its heroine, Marie (Helen Blythe), in the clutches of a villain who is not only a kidnapper but a forger. He hides her in a Hester Street den presided over by the haggish Mother Mouton. Of course, Marie is eventually restored to her friends and fortune. Mother Mouton's shaggy hair covered her face, and on opening night a raspy-voiced wag in the gallery got a laugh by yelling, "Say, Mag, get your hair cut." He and other spectators were treated to a tour that took them to, among other places, the Little Church Around the Corner and a Parisian foundling hospital.

Mansfield returned to his New York home, the Garden, on the 15th. *Beau Brummell, Prince Karl, A Parisian Romance,* and *Dr. Jekyll and Mr. Hyde* were all on his bills, as was *Don Juan,* disguised under a new title, *The Weathervane.* He also had one new play ready, but before that appeared another theatrical event occurred.

The Amberg Theatre, on Irving Place, was given over to performances in German. On the 17th the management gave New Yorkers their first chance to see *Hedda Gabler*. Several of the more responsible papers sent critics. Many found the mounting execrable, and this may have tinged their judgment of the play. Except for the *Times*, which found the play a "finely written prose drama" and liked the cast, reviews ranged from indifferent to outraged. The play usurped the *Herald*'s Sunday theatre page, but the report was low-keyed. Ibsen still was having an uphill battle.

Edward M. Alfriend's **The Louisianian** (2-18-92, People's) was another of the many plays tried out at special matinees. Now Robert Mantell added it to his repertory, only to discover the validity of the original unfavorable judgments. He played Louis St. Armand, a French Creole who loves the daughter of the American governor. Both fathers oppose the marriage, and an adventuress claims St. Armand is already married to her. A duel ensues. St. Armand is wounded. When he recovers he hires a detective to entrap the adventuress. Then he is free to wed. Mantell had given a few performances of the piece earlier as part of his touring repertory and gave a few after this single-week stand, but he soon dropped the work.

Mrs. Romualdo Pacheco's **Incog** (2-22-92, Bijou) has for its hero the resourceful Tom Stanhope (Charles Dickson). Unfortunately for Tom, his resourcefulness lands him in a whirlpool of hot water. Tom's father, General Rufus Stanhope (Harry Davenport), demands Tom marry the general's ward, Isabelle Howard (Nellie Buckley), and when Tom insists he will marry Kate Armitage (Ellen Burg) he is ordered out of the house. Walking along the seashore (the play is set in San Francisco), he comes across a man's photograph, opts to disguise himself as the likeness in the picture, and returns home to pursue his courtship under an assumed name. The photograph turns out to be one of Dick Winters (Louis Mann), a happily married man who has a twin brother, Harry (Robert Edeson), who is engaged to Mollie Somers (Clara Lipman). Mollie and Mrs. Winters (Alice Shepard) are friends of Kate and Isabelle, but their friendships and their sanity are strained when the look-alikes, Tom, Dick, and Harry, are constantly being confused for one another. Not surprisingly, they all converge on an insane asylum before matters are straightened out. The farce was performed with zest by a troupe of rising young players (Fanny's brother, Harry, was only twenty-six when he played the old general), many of whom later moved on to stardom.

The play itself became the source of the very popular musical *Three Twins*. Coupled with the longer farce was a one-acter, **The Saltcellar,** which Henry Doblin took from a German play by C. A. Görner and which dealt with a domestic quarrel and its happy resolution. This short piece subsequently gave way to another, **Book III, Chapter I** (4-11-92, Bijou), in which a wife attempts to scare away her husband's pesky friend by flirting with him and finds that he is game for flirtation. With one curtain raiser or another, the play ran a month and toured profitably for many years.

Mansfield's new vehicle was **Ten Thousand a Year** (2-23-92, Garden), dramatized by Emma Sheridan from Samuel Warren's old novel. Tittlebat Titmouse is a cockney shopkeeper who, through an error, is pronounced the heir to a large estate. He is quick to revel in gaudy new clothes and everything else he believes to be the perks of his high position. He long has loved Tessy Tagrag (Beatrice Cameron) but knew her higher social standing precluded any serious thought of marriage. Now, as the Squire of Yatton, he must look down on her. Although he would appear to be a rascal, at heart he is decent and loving. So he hands over his inheritance to the rightful heir, knowing he himself has won Tessy. Mansfield played the piece as low comedy with sentimental overtones. Low comedy, however, was not his forte and not what his admirers expected from him. The play soon disappeared from his repertory.

Augustus Pitou, slowly making a name for himself as a producer of shows designed for the road, brought in his itinerant players for New Yorkers to assess. His opening double bill started with Lorimer Stoddard's **Her First Love** (3-7-92, Union Square), in which a caddish suitor discards an ingenuous girl when he finds out she has lost her fortune, and then moved on to Fred Horner's adaptation of Paul Ferrier's farcical *L'Article 231*, **The Last Straw.** The last straw comes when a husband (William Faversham) forgets his wife's birthday. Wife (Minnie Seligman) and husband agree to a divorce but eventually are reunited through the efforts of her father (W. H. Thompson) and her worldly admirer (Nelson Wheatcroft), both of whom become anxious to get the volatile young lady off their hands. The players, all excellent, were well received, but the farce, in a season top-heavy with them, was not. Since Pitou had already scheduled a successor for the next week, reviews did not matter.

That same night the Kendals began a fortnight's stand at Palmer's. Their program included many of their expected favorites: *A White Lie, Impulse, A*

Scrap of Paper, The Ironmaster, Still Waters Run Deep, The Squire, The Queen's Shilling, and *My Uncle's Will.* They also, very briefly, had a novelty to present.

Edward E. Rose would soon gain renown as an adaptor of novels for the stage, but he also wrote numerous original works, although most of these were consigned to combination houses. An early example was **The Westerner** (3-7-92, Windsor). Its title may have deceived playgoers into expecting gunplay and settings with mountains painted on the backdrop, but the drama was played out entirely in New York. Jim Errol has come east from Nevada, in part to court Mary Lawton. Her father has been speculating in mine stocks, something about which he knows little but with which Jim is very conversant. A troublemaker spreads rumors that Lawton's stocks are worthless and attempts to create a run on the shares. He has not bargained on Jim's acumen. Jim saves the day and wins Mary. The drama sometimes toured as *Jim, the Westerner.*

George R. Sims and Robert Buchanan's **The English Rose** (3-7-92, 23rd St.) was essentially the sort of romantic melodrama that catered to Irish audiences at neighborhood theatres. Its English heroine remains faithful to her Irish sweetheart even when he is falsely accused of murdering her uncle. The play featured a steeplechase and a beautiful setting of a bridge by a waterfall (with real water), seen, of course, in moonlight. It survived a month and a half.

Pitou's second mounting was the first Clyde Fitch play to suggest the road he would take in his more mature writings, **A Modern Match** (3-14-92, Union Square). Robert Hunt (Nelson Wheatcroft) and George Synott (W. H. Thompson) are partners in a failing business. To his horror Hunt finds himself caught in a room with his associate bent on suicide and his callous wife, Violet (Minnie Seligman), prepared to run off with Gerald Rankin (George Backus), a wealthy clubman who can provide for her better than Hunt now can. He is helpless to prevent either from carrying out the threats. Indeed, at least in Fitch's subsequent revision, he orders Violet to leave. As the years pass, Hunt sets about recovering his wealth and position. He also finds himself falling in love with his partner's widow, Eleanora (Adelaide Stanhope). Eventually, when he is once again secure, he proposes to Eleanora and she accepts. He also makes preparations for his daughter's wedding. But his contentment is shattered by Violet's return. She professes to be contrite, but Hunt has his doubts. He shuts the door on her, telling her she will not even be admitted to their child's wedding.

Critics agreed that Fitch showed tremendous promise and hailed the acting, but Pitou's commitments would only allow the work a two-week run.

Fine scenery and stylish gowns may partly account for the longer run of **Merry Gotham** (3-14-92, Lyceum), which was derived from Ernest Blum and Raoul Toché's *Paris, fin de siècle* by Elisabeth Marbury (later more celebrated as an agent, producer, political string-puller, and friend of Elsie de Wolfe). The scenery included several posh drawing rooms and a rather faithful recreation of a real, luxurious New York restaurant. The play, with its large cast, had no primary plot—unless a loosely organized attempt by New York society to put down some California mining upstarts could be called one—but offered a number of interwoven themes to present a potpourri of that New York society. Romances include one in which a man discovers another man has paid his fiancée's extravagant bills, and a second in which a man agrees to marry a girl he has never met, then unwittingly falls in love with her at a cotillion. Daniel Frohman's fine ensemble combined to present a feather-light, pleasant evening, which held the boards for six weeks.

The Kendals' novelty was **Katherine Kavanagh** (3-14-92, Palmer's), in which a respectable matron's past as a gambling house decoy catches up with her. Its reception was anything but kind.

While touring with *The Nominee* Nat Goodwin added a curtain raiser to the bill, **Art and Nature** (3-14-92, Grand Opera), which William Yardley adapted from a French play. It was a piece on the order of *Nance Oldfield* or *Frédéric Lemaître.* An actress who had promised to disillusion a young lawyer finds herself falling in love with him in the process.

Fine scenery and gorgeous costumes contributed to the next entry's success. Much ballyhoo had preceded the opening of Daly's final play for the season—the world premiere of Alfred Lord Tennyson's **The Foresters** (3-17-92, Daly's), with special songs and much of the incidental music by Arthur Sullivan. The play was a retelling of the Robin Hood story, a story many American playgoers had recently become reacquainted with in DeKoven's operetta. Indeed, the popularity of the musical had forced Daly to change Tennyson's original title, which also had been simply *Robin Hood.* Applause commenced with the rising of the first curtain to reveal the terrace of a medieval castle and a sunlit landscape in the background. The cheering was more boisterous still when Maid Marian (Ada Rehan) made her first appearance in a brocaded satin gown of old rose and salmon pink. Later the exigencies of the plot forced her to dress as a Norman knight and carry a huge, triangular shield painted with a large cross, a shield whose rounded small end could rest on the ground while its larger end touched Marian's chin. Not all the story paralleled Harry B. Smith's operetta libretto. Tennyson introduced a fairy scene in a glen beside a river bank. There Titania (Percy Haswell) emerged in the moonlight from a tree trunk, and her fairy coterie, starlike lights twinkling on their foreheads, danced and waved flowers that glowed in the dark. Drew, of course, was Robin Hood. The spectacle was undoubtedly necessary for the work, which, for all its literary merit, was often adramatic. Still, the publicity, the rave notices, and Daly's policy of limited runs saw to it that the play was performed to packed houses until the Saturday matinee of April 23. That evening's performance saw a double bill of *As You Like It* and *A Woman's Won't*, brought out so that Mrs. Gilbert, as she had last season, and James Lewis could participate in the closing celebrations.

Three American plays finished out the month. Frank G. Campbell's **Gettysburg** (3-21-92, Harlem) was simply one more in the long catalogue of plays providing variations on the theme of lovers caught on opposing sides of the Civil War. Tom Markham, whose sympathies are with the North, and John Fairfax, who supports secession, both love Florence Pryor, daughter of a Richmond gun-factory owner. Both work for her father. Fairfax maneuvers to have Markham fired because of his views. Many of the workers, who like Markham despite his leanings, go on strike to support him. A melee follows, and Markham is shot and wounded. When the war breaks out Markham enlists in the Union army. At Pickett's charge (depicted onstage) he is taken prisoner. An explosion in the prison permits him to escape. By the final curtain the war has ended and he and Florence are reunited. Campbell and his wife, Camille, played the leads during much of the tour, at theatres whose lobbies were often decorated with flags and bunting to set the mood for the play. Tours continued for the remainder of the decade.

The next entry was seen by many as a blatant attempt to capitalize on the success of *Alabama* and, like that play, to help rehabilitate southern sentiments in northern eyes. With the generous assistance of Augustus Thomas (who did most of the writing), F. Hopkinson Smith dramatized his best-selling novel **Colonel Carter of Cartersville** (3-22-92, Palmer's). There was a touch of Colonel Sellers (as well as Colonel Moberly) in the central figure, albeit the play has a partially happy ending. Colonel Fairfax Carter (E. M. Holland), a displaced Virgin-

ian, lives in genteel poverty in New York, served by his loyal former slave, Chad (Charles L. Harris). He survives largely on "loans" from a distant aunt and the goodwill of friends such as T. B. Fitzpatrick (Maurice Barrymore). The colonel's dream is to develop a railroad back home. That dream comes to naught, as does a December-May romance of his, but coal is discovered under his lands, thereby reviving his fortunes. Holland played the role with "a whimsical drollery, thinly veiled by a sweet, grave, demure composure," in much the same makeup he had employed for Colonel Moberly in *Alabama*—white, receding wig, full white mustache, and large white goatee. The makeup was fast becoming a cliché for depicting southern colonels. Like *The Foresters*, the story was too adramatic for contemporary tastes (Winter called it "frail"), and although the characters were warm and picturesque there apparently were limits to how many pleas for rehabilitation, however carefully couched, northerners would sit through. The puritanical Winter took a different slant, writing in *The Wallet of Time*, "Coming, as it did, at a time when the Stage was being freely used for the dissection of turpitude and disease, that play came like a breeze from the pine woods in a morning of spring." His was a minority view, or at least one not designed to beckon playgoers. The play ran little more than a month.

Augustus Pitou and his traveling band had one final play ready with Martha Morton's **Geoffrey Middleton, Gentleman** (3-31-92, Union Square). Middleton (Nelson Wheatcroft) is a gentleman who marries Margaret Merritt (Minnie Seligman) for her money, money her father Thomas (W. H. Thompson) amassed in railroads. But Middleton is a fortune hunter with a difference. He doesn't want the money for himself. Rather, he needs it to help his own father avoid a humiliating bankruptcy. What's more, he is led to believe that Margaret is a social climber, willing to buy or marry her way to the top. Bitter recriminations ensue before husband and wife both perceive each other's fundamental decency and agree to head off for a new life in South America. The playwright's idea of comedy was seen in the character of Harry Middleton (Jane Stuart). Harry had once been Harriet, but, forced to assume a man's responsibilities, she assumes a man's name and dress, too. As scheduled, the play ran only a week and a half.

The preceding season had witnessed two dramas based upon a recent bank scandal. Now an international dispute that had made headlines found echo on a Broadway stage. In late 1890 a New Orleans policeman had been murdered, and rumor blamed the Mafia. When no one was convicted, angry citizens stormed the local jail, seized all prisoners with Italian names and lynched eleven. Three of these proved to be not Italo-Americans but subjects of Italy. Despite nudgings from Washington, no action was taken against the lynch mob. The Italian king withdrew his minister, and Washington recalled its representative in Rome. Matters were not resolved until early 1892.

A bank failure was one thing—a good subject for a sturdy drama. An international squabble somehow seemed less menacing, so Paul Potter turned it into a comedy-drama for W. H. Crane, **The American Minister** (4-4-92, Star). When Benjamin Franklin Lawton arrives to take over his post, he finds the American legation awash in intrigue. Most alarming of all, an important document is missing, and his son, Thomas Jefferson Lawton (James Neill), a secretary at the legation, is the prime suspect. The foreigners (at least that's what Lawton calls them) are crafty, but Lawton is craftier. He gulls a wicked Italian princess (Hattie Russell) into unwittingly assisting him, exposes the Italian foreign minister (Joseph Shannon) as a Mafia leader, and exculpates his son. He finds time, too, to court a sweet American lady, Delphine Carondelet (Annie O'Neill). Some of the humor was almost slapstick, such as Lawton's shoving a troublesome woman into a safe and locking her in. Some of it reflected accepted American attitudes, such as Lawton's complaint that Rome had too many statues and too little soap. And some of it was simply oddball, such as Lawton's proposal to Delphine, for which he employed the language of the diplomatic treaties. The Roman settings and the costumes of the worldly diplomats and exotic courtiers gave the action a colorful frame. *The American Minister* was more successful than *For Money* had been earlier in the season. It ran nearly two months, and later Crane took it on tour. But it did not give him the durable successor to *The Senator* that he had been seeking.

Our troubled relations with Chile also had been in the news lately (we had taken the wrong—the losing—side in the Chilean civil war), so when Wilson Barrett and George R. Sims's **The Golden Ladder** (4-4-92, Park), which originally had been set in England and Australia, was presented for American consideration it was reset in New York and Chile. The change was gratuitous and had little to do with the story, which told of a man's struggle to clear his banker father-in-law of a false accusation. Edwin Thorne was starred, and when he took ill in midweek the play was forced to close abruptly.

A. Y. Pearson's recipe for a successful melodrama included such tried and true ingredients as a waif, a Yankee farmer, a kidnapper, and fire engines. He called his play **A Midnight Alarm** (4-4-92, People's) and christened his waif Sparkle (Edith Julian). (Remember Nelly Sparkle in *A Mile a Minute*?) The good farmer, Gideon Tillwell (George B. Berrill), comes to town to find Sparkle and let her know she is an heiress, but he falls into the hands of a bogus lawyer, E. Chippenton Chaser (George F. Hall). Chaser kidnaps Sparkle, but when the building in which he hides her catches fire, a handsome fireman, Harry Westmore (Robert Neil), dashes to the rescue.

The Holly Tree Inn and **Spooks** (4-11-92, Union Square) comprised a short-lived double bill. The curtain raiser, taken from a Dickens story by Mrs. Oscar Derringer, recounted the "elopement" of two children. Charles Barnard had originally written *Spooks* as a vehicle for the great female impersonator Neil Burgess and had called it *Cynthia's Lovers*. Now Sarah McVicker took over the role of Cynthia Burdock, an old maid faithful to the memory of a long-dead suitor, Clarence Dullwitte. Even at this late date she is courted by Deacon Wishy (J. J. Coleman) and Continue-in-Well-Doing Jones (David B. Steele). The deacon loses after he reveals that Dullwitte was not as faithful to her as she has been to him. Some of the action takes place in a haunted house where all manner of odd things, such as a door opening unaided, occur. At another point a battle rages with dough and flour as the lethal weapons.

O'Flynn in Mexico (4-11-92, Park) was so ineptly written and performed that the *Herald* wondered aloud whether the whole affair was meant to be a joke. Its author and star was Alfred Kelcey. As Piper O'Flynn he foiled every effort—and they apparently were numbered in the dozens—of a greedy uncle to murder his rich niece.

The month's second double bill fared better than the first. Its curtain raiser was William Echard Golden's **Hearts** (4-16-92, Garden). The play had grabbed one of several prizes being awarded by local newspapers (in this instance, the *Herald*) to spur American playwrights. A canny, sometimes sharp-tongued, yet endearing young widow, Mrs. Cavendish (Cora Tanner) discovers that Cuthbert Devlin (Harold Russell), the man she once had loved—and still loves—is about to marry her younger friend, Marion Carew (Tessie Butler). In a pique Marion had broken off her engagement to Jerome Rutledge (Cuyler Hastings), who had gone off to lick his wounds. Now he has returned. So, using soft lights and irrefutable logic, Mrs. Cavendish wheedles to reunite the youngsters and to win a proposal from

Devlin in the bargain. Golden's dialogue was smart and clever.

Mrs. C.: Mr. Rutledge will complete our party, and can entertain me while you are pouring "dulcet nihilities" into Marion's ears.

Devlin: Rubbish.

Mrs. C.: I didn't think you would be frank enough to admit that.

Devlin: I remember a time when you didn't call it rubbish.

Mrs. C.: I beg your pardon. You called it that.

In the glow of the firelight and flickering lamps, the play had an air of romantic fantasy about it. Although it took only about half an hour to perform, and no curtain was lowered or no lights dimmed to indicate any passage of time, the action supposedly transpired over six hours. F. C. Phillips and Percy Fendall's **Husband and Wife** saw its husbands and wives aligned in separate clubs, each dedicated to subjugating the opposite sex. The clubs are in the same building, and only a door with a convenient keyhole divides them. But the door is no protection when the police raid both rooms on the mistaken impression that they are gambling dens. Cora Tanner starred in the second play, too.

It often seemed that American playwrights dealing with the Civil War could not resist the temptation to have their lovers set squarely in opposing camps. In writing **Across the Potomac** (4-18-92, 23rd St.) Edward M. Alfriend and Augustus Pitou made no effort to resist. In fact, they went one better, having two pairs of lovers caught in the conflict. The Garlands of Virginia and the Bakers of Massachusetts have gathered in Northampton to celebrate the wedding of John Garland (Mason Mitchell) and Helen Baker (Charlotte Tittell) and the engagement of Capt. Ralph Baker (Robert Hilliard) and Edith Garland (Henrietta Lander). Joy turns to gloom when news of secession reaches the party. Helen agrees to follow John to Virginia, but Edith and her captain are separated. Four years pass. Ralph is now a colonel. He is captured along with the beautiful Madge Hanford (Alice Fischer). Edith is left to wonder if Ralph has been unfaithful. But his position becomes clear when the trial reveals that Madge is a northern spy. Realizing that Ralph still loves her, Edith decides to ride forty miles to appeal personally to General Lee for a pardon. A Confederate officer who had once courted her and still admires her agrees to ride in her place. He is shot for his pains, but before he dies he delivers the pardon. A vivid battle scene, with horses charging across the stage, enlivened the drama. The *Herald*'s man didn't

like the show, complaining it was written in a "toploftical wrap-me-in-the-American-flag kind of style." Designed primarily as a touring show, the play ran for a month before moving on to spend several profitable years on the road.

Bernhardt returned briefly on the 19th to give a few performances of *Leah, the Forsaken* (in a French adaptation) and one of *Fédora* in the vastness of the Metropolitan Opera House. Daniel Frohman's players ended their season with George R. Sims and Cecil Raleigh's **The Grey Mare** (4-25-92, Lyceum), in which a young doctor's improvised tale of an imaginary ride lands him in trouble when his tale happens to parallel that of a real abduction. Accompanying the farce was Lottie Blair Parker's study of a selfish girl, **White Roses.** This latter piece did not please, so it was replaced by Henry Arthur Jones's **The Organist** (5-9-92, Lyceum), in which a young organist finds himself in the awkward position of having to ask the consent of the man he replaced to marry the older man's daughter.

Rosina Vokes's bills of one-acters were generally sprinkled with songs and dances and were generally of foreign origin. Many belonged as much in the realm of farce-comedy, the era's name for its prototypical musical comedies, as in that of straight theatre. But one play she offered on her spring visit is of special interest, for its author was Minnie Maddern Fiske. **The Rose** (5-2-92, Daly's) told of a chivalrous old New Orleans doctor who comes to learn that his young wife secretly loves a much younger man and who hastens his own death so that the young man will not leave town without a proper bride. A simple, tender piece, well written, its obvious quality was attested by the fact that Miss Vokes staged it although it contained no part for her. It enjoyed a long afterlife.

Young men in supposedly bohemian worlds were principal figures in two May entries. **Friends** (5-9-92, Standard) was by Edwin Milton Royle, who was forced to take over one of the leading roles on opening night when an actor called in sick. He played John Paden, Jr., a struggling poet who shares a spartan apartment and one dress suit with an aspiring musician, Adrian Karjé (Lucius Henderson). Both men fall in love with the same girl, Marguerite Otto (Selena Fetter), but when it becomes clear she is fond of Adrian, John gallantly steps aside. The boys also take swift, effective action when a rascally manager, Harold Hunting (John Glendinning), attempts to bamboozle Marguerite's father, Hans (Edmund Lyons). In doing so, they discover that Marguerite is an heiress.

On the 16th at the Grand Opera, the eccentric,

problem-haunted Margaret Mather appeared as Esmeralda in **The Egyptian,** her oddly titled version of *The Hunchback of Notre Dame.*

Edelweiss (5-16-92, People's), advertised as "a Swiss play," depicted the sometimes rocky road to the altar for its yellow-braided Edelweiss and Jack Dutton. Some songs and dances alleviated the tension.

Sydney Rosenfeld's **Imagination** (5-23-92, 14th St.) was more lighthearted than *Friends.* Mrs. Jelleman (Georgia Dickson) has locked her husband, Harry (Harry Hotto), in their apartment while she attends a woman's rights meeting. Using the building's dumbwaiter, he escapes with the aid of his nephew and his nephew's buddy. He pays the boys, Dick Brennan (Wilton Lackaye) and Tom Dawson (W. W. Wilson), to take him for a wild night on the town in the bohemian underworld. Instead they take him to a boisterous masked ball given by the socially prominent Mrs. Solomon Ricketts (Helen Kinnaird). During the ball Mrs. Ricketts's daughter elopes and by mistake leaves a note saying "Bearer will explain" in the pocket of Jelleman's coat. He and the boys have more explaining to do after the police arrive, for a janitor has reported seeing "burglars" use the apartment's dumbwaiter to escape. Rosenfeld's idea of humor ran to the order of having one man, asked whether he is connected to another man (of the same last name), reply, "By telephone." Electricity continued to have its effect on casting. A critic observed wryly that the thirty-year-old Lackaye looked more like an out-of-training prizefighter than the Princeton athlete he was supposed to represent. The comedy survived for just two weeks.

A longer history lay in store for Howard P. Taylor's **Irish Inspiration** (5-23-92, People's), but then these professionally crafted romantic melodramas set in the old country usually were assured a prolonged welcome by the vast Irish-American audiences around the nation. Squire Fox (Daniel Jarrett) and his malicious sidekick, Michael Rooney (John F. Ward), labor to prevent the widowed Lady Margaret (Belle Melville) from marrying Alan Fitzgerald (Nestor Lennon). Rooney even threatens to drown Margaret's baby in the river to discourage her. The arrival of two-fisted Con Reilly (R. A. Roberts) sends the troublemakers scurrying. A horse race with real horses on a treadmill was a popular feature, however hackneyed, of the piece. And, of course, as in almost all of this genre, Irish jigs and airs provided a special embellishment. The play ran only a week on its first New York outing but toured for several seasons, including at least one return visit to New York.

A similar, less successful effort got no closer to Manhattan than Brooklyn. In Edmund E. Price's **Wicklow** (5-30-92, Lee Ave. Academy), decent Terrence Duffield (Mason Mitchell) is rescued from his murderous uncle, Darby McShane (Ben Horning) by Lanty McGuire (Andrew Mack). Unlike R. A. Roberts, who was a skilled character actor, Mack possessed a fine Irish tenor. Within a very short time Mack would be starring in song-filled Irish romances that let him sing to his audiences' content and that were really musicals.

Back across the river playgoers could savor **The House on the Marsh** (5-30-92, People's), which Mervyn Dallas dramatized from Florence Warden's novel. Dallas played the hero, Jim Woodfall, who assumes a disguise to expose a villain who has falsely accused Jim's friend, Violet Chrystie (Minnie Dupree), a governess, of burglary. The *Herald* felt Dallas had "warped" the original story and intent of the novel to achieve a hoped-for dramatic effect. According to the critic, all Dallas actually achieved was "a marsh of wearying talk and rubbish called dialogue." Such thrashings did not deter the play from touring the following season.

Robert Hilliard, so recently of *Across the Potomac,* was the star of the season's last major opening, a double bill that included one of his own plays. The curtain rose on his one-acter, **Adrift** (6-6-92, Union Square), to disclose a memorable stage picture. The setting showed the dreary, back-alley stage door of a playhouse, an equally shabby dressing room, and, on the right half, a stage, ready for a production to begin. Richard Grey, an old, clearly unwell, white-haired, hollow-eyed actor, enters the theatre, exchanges a few courtesies with the doorman, and moves on to his dressing room, where, with the aid of costuming and makeup, he transforms himself into a youthful, blond, and red-cheeked steeple-chase jockey. In the process he muses aloud, and the audience learns that he is dying of tuberculosis and that for many years he has been separated from his wife and daughter. Dashing onstage, all smiles, he begins to perform a scene in which he reads of his fame in a newspaper, but the paper he is handed as a prop carries the story of his wife and daughter's deaths. He collapses and is carried back to his dressing room, where he dies reaching for a letter his little child sent him years ago and he has always carried with him.

The play, a tour de force, was reminiscent of *A Lesson in Acting,* which Robert Mantell had brought out a year earlier. Hilliard was not the colorful emoter Mantell was. He relied more on his good looks (no doubt here well concealed by makeup), clear diction, and simple honesty and intelligence to put the play over. Of course, even the makeup represented a sort of minor tour de force, with the thirty-eight-year-old actor made up to look like an old, ailing man who must make up to look like a young one. Most critics felt his acting was believable but not moving. Still, in one way he succeeded handsomely. The main play of the evening received far less attention than his curtain raiser. W. Stokes Craven's **The Fabricator** was a farce in which a man's stolen coat is found in a train wreck, whereupon (shades of *In Chancery*) all manner of absurd misunderstandings arise. By the time Sunday followups on the bill were released, the bill was gone.

ACT THREE
1892–1899

The Rise
of an Empire

1892–1893

Although victories over the Spaniards at Manila Bay and in Cuba at the decade's close confirmed our emergence as a world power, throughout the not-totally-gay nineties the nation was flexing its muscles, growing apace, and reconsidering its perceptions. Even the grim panic that began in the spring of 1893 with the failure of the Reading Railroad and the National Cordage Company, while hurtling the economy into temporary disarray, ultimately led to reorganizations that served to strengthen that same economy and promote a more vigorous enterprise. Inevitably the theatre partook of the expansion.

During the 1892–93 season no fewer than three new first-class theatres opened their doors in Manhattan alone. At the same time, around the country, city after city, small town after small town boasted the erection of additional playhouses. It would have been well-nigh impossible for contemporaries to recognize that in retrospect one of these new auditoriums might be seen to signal the start of an era in American theatricals. That theatre was the Empire, and only time would reveal how appropriately it was named, for within a very few years its builders, aligned with several other aggressive entrepreneurs, would meet to establish a syndicate that would put playhouses, plays, and players on a modern commercial footing. To the delight of many and to the indignation of many more, they would succeed in bringing a new order and stability to the American theatre, albeit often at the price of a cynical, brutal monopolization. Of course, monopolization was a feature of much of the period's enterprise. The hegemony the theatrical syndicate so quickly established marked the end of a certain localization and intimacy in American theatres. The likes of a Wallack or Daly, who owned a playhouse, kept an established company there, and often wrote, directed, or acted in the productions himself, was to pass away forever. The new breed, whatever their affection for drama, were primarily "bricks and mortar" men, more interested in profits than in art or entertainment. They were businessmen first, men of the theatre only secondarily.

There were other reasons for suggesting a fresh theatrical era had arrived. Booth's retirement some months earlier clearly suggested the end of a period,

a suggestion his own contemporaries picked up on. His death at this season's end underscored the transition. At the other theatrical extreme, Lotta Crabtree, probably the nation's most popular entertainer, also had waved good-bye to the stage after sustaining an injury in a fall late in the 1890–91 season. Death or retirement claimed numerous other figures as well.

Whatever the initial resistance to Ibsen and his plays, critics plainly were tiring of time-honored but increasingly threadbare genres, notably sensation-melodramas. The problem play and similar newer forms of dramaturgy were ready and waiting to supplant more jaded ones.

Charles Frohman's Comedians inaugurated the season. Their offering was **Settled Out of Court** (8-8-92, Fifth Ave.), William Gillette's adaptation of Alexandre Bisson's *La Famille Pont-Biquet*. Newly-wed Mark Harriman (Joseph Holland) creates the farce's complications with his blind belief in phrenology. He insists a person's "bumps" tell all, and when the bumps and reality fail to coincide, he points an accusing finger at reality. His young, attractive mother-in-law, Lucretia Plunkett (Georgiana Drew Barrymore), the third wife of the eccentric Judge Plunkett (M. A. Kennedy), becomes his chief victim. Refusing to accept her as a queenly matron, he forges a series of impassioned love letters to her. They promptly fall into the wrong hands, and pandemonium ensues. Matters are ensnarled further after Mark attempts to help his future brother-in-law shake off an old flame. Both Holland and Miss Barrymore received enthusiastic notices, but many felt Kennedy stole the show. He was forever losing his glasses whenever he had to read something and went stone deaf on approaching a beautiful lady (a telltale giveaway to his watchful wife). Enthusiasm for the play was markedly less, but the farce ran a month before setting out on tour.

A far shorter run (one week) and a not very profitable post-Broadway tour was the lot of **Jerry** (8-13-92, Windsor), which supposedly had been performed in England first although it was an American play. Nana Leigh (Kate Troncay) was saved from a steamboat explosion in which her mother had been killed and was adopted by a couple who had been aboard at the time of the accident. They are well-to-do and have arranged an excellent marriage for Nana. Their nasty nephew covets Nana for himself and hires a tramp, Jerry (J. W. Summers), to claim he is Nana's long-lost father. In fact, Jerry turns out to be her real father. He also turns out to be a petty thief and jailbird. However, he has enough innate nobility to expose the nephew and to walk away without disclosing his true identity, so as not to blast his daughter's expectations. Summers was co-starred with Grace Emmett, who took the part of a comic domestic. The *Herald* dismissed the play as "a stilted melodrama of the vintage of 1860."

Rising American jingoism was exemplified by James W. Harkins, Jr.'s **The White Squadron** (8-15-92, 14th St.). Advertised as a "Big $28,000 Patriotic, Romantic and Spectacular Production," it was laid in Brazil, where an international naval conference has been assembled and where the foreigners join to protest the murder of tourists by Brazilian bandits. More murderous treachery follows before a heroic American, Victor Staunton (Robert Hilliard), trounces the devious Latin, Demetrio de Romacio (Henry Lee). De Romacio is not only a leading Brazilian general but also the head of a band of brigands robbing trains carrying silver from the mines. He is mean and tricky enough to send his prospective son-in-law, Paulo (William Harcourt), to attack the brigands, hoping Paulo, whom he dislikes, will be killed. Further complicating the plot is the fact that Paulo's sister, Onesta (Alice Fischer), loves Staunton, who commands the White Squadron. Staunton is captured and brought to a secluded monastery, where he is confronted by the general's gloating nephew, Francisco (Bryan Douglas).

Francisco: Staunton, you have played a desperate game, and lost. 'Tis the fortune of war, my friend. Have you any last request to make?
Staunton: None, but the consolation of prayer.
Francisco: You shall have it. The monks are at service inside. Would you like their attendance?
Staunton: I would die happier.

Francisco does not know that the monks are disguised American sailors.

Critics applauded the patriotic intent, but not the play. Those who could spare a few kind words found them for the scenery, including a square in Rio, a ruined monastery, and a final tableau representing the sailing of the White Squadron. Unable to extract much quotable praise, subsequent ads excerpted the comments on the audience's cheering response to the flag-waving and promised future playgoers "the Congress of Navies, the Moorish Slaves Yoked to the Ox, the Silver Train, the South American Llamas, the Ruined Monastery, the Funeral March of the Monks, the Departure of the White Squadron, U.S.S. Chicago." Within a few days theatrical columns were announcing that demand for seats was so great that the producer was trying to buy out the contracts for the theatre's future bookings. Either this was sheer puffery or the producer failed, for the play lingered only three weeks. However, it did find a welcome on the road for the rest of the decade.

Marguerite Merington's **Captain Lettarblair** (8-16-92, Lyceum) proved more pleasing to Broadway's sophisticated, demanding critics. Perhaps a modicum of their pleasure came from being able to acknowledge that a schoolmarm, one who taught Greek at a normal school, could supply so cheerful and competent an entertainment. Whatever faults the comedy possessed were glossed over by Daniel Frohman's skilled players, headed by E. H. Sothern as Captain Lettarblair Litton. He may look like a million in the uniform of the Royal Irish Fusiliers, but in truth he is on his uppers. Indeed, while his valet and a friend keep a creditor at bay Lettarblair hastily sells his horse to a fellow officer to scrounge up some quick cash. His empty purse, however, is only half his problem, for his well-heeled fiancée, Fanny Hadden (Virginia Harned), is all too anxious to aid him financially, even if the idea of accepting money from a lady goes against his grain. She inadvertently makes matters worse by demanding her solicitor collect a huge debt long owed her family, not realizing that this is part of the debt left behind by Lettarblair's father, which her fiancé is attempting to pay off in dribs and drabs. The contretemps that develop are fueled by malicious gossip circulated by another of Fanny's suitors, the scheming Francis Merivale (Morton Selden). The dialogue between the two men is indicative of the play's humor.

Merivale: I hope you're not put out by my arrival.
Litton: Your arrival? Whose rival are ye, Merivale?

In the scene that follows, Litton mimics Merivale's posturings. More puns, so popular at the time, peppered the scene in which Lettarblair reviews his tries at mollifying his creditors with some of his goods.

Jorkins [Lettarblair's valet]: Haberdasher sent back the Venus, Captain! He was mad as the hatter! Said he wouldn't take her in payment because she was broke!
Litton: Well, now, haberdash it all, I sent her in payment because I was broke! He needn't have

been annoyed with her, poor dear! Seeing she's quite *armless!*

The comedy's most celebrated scene occurs when Fanny attempts to storm out of Lettarblair's room. She catches the train of her dress in the door and, since the doorknob has come loose and fallen out of reach, she is helpless to do anything but stand there and listen to Lettarblair's pleas. (In their autobiographies the producer and the star offer conflicting accounts of how the scene came to be inserted.) At the close of the play Lettarblair wangles a proposal from Fanny. Minor characters included Dean Ambrose (C. P. Flockton), who condemns popular novels in his sermons but reads them on the sly. One interesting critical quibble was the complaint of the *Dramatic Mirror* that Sothern's Irish accent was both wrong and inconsistent. After a two-month run, the play embarked on a cross-country tour.

By contrast, critics savaged Lawrence Marston's **Lady Lil** (8-16-92, Standard). The *Dramatic Mirror* dismissed it as "gruesome and lurid," while the *Times* took up the cudgels against the actors' mispronunciations, observing, " 'Clambering' came as 'ca-lamb-er-ing,' and there were enough 'rs' in 'revenge' to stock a spelling book." Lady Columba Lil (Lillian Lewis), an Austrian bareback rider, tells Severin de Rohan (Gustavus Levick) that she would marry him but that she was once betrayed. Vaclay Hassan (W. A. Whitecar) decides to prevent the marriage by besmirching her. She learns of his plan and lures him to a room where a tiger is waiting. He is fatally mauled, but before he dies he implicates Lil. She commits suicide. One act was set on a smoky battlefield during the 1866 Austro-Prussian War; another in the wings of an amphitheatre, where Miss Lewis was able to demonstrate her ability on a not very threatening old white steed. The tiger was even less formidable—it was stuffed. Despite critical sneers Lady Lil pranced about the hinterlands for a couple of seasons.

A Kentucky Colonel (8-22-92, Union Square) was taken by Opie Read from his own novel. He called it "a character comedy," but by any label it apparently wasn't worth the effort. His central character is Col. Osbury (McKee Rankin), who must mediate a feud between the Savelys and the Britsides. Among the lesser figures is an oddball flutist who will play only after someone feeds him. Osbury and his neighbors lingered for only a week and found a cold shoulder on the road.

To confuse matters, Oscar P. Sisson's **The Colonel** (8-22-92, Windsor) arrived the same evening. In this instance the old officer is Alfred Hummer (Harry St. Maur), who brings a slew of troubles down on himself by introducing a buxom vaudevillian, Diana Dimple (Mabel Huntington), to his wife, Rose (Florence Wolcott), as his niece. The arrival of Alfred's mother-in-law, Mrs. Griswold (Kate Vandenhoff), only worsens his difficulties. Like his Kentucky brother, this Colonel moved out after a single week.

An equally short life was in store for **Nora Machree** (8-22-92, People's), although she fared a little better on the road. In Charles T. Vincent's play Nora became the latest in a long line of heroes and heroines falsely accused of murder. When her brother rushes to her defense he finds himself in hot water, too. Since the hefty star, Sadie Scanlan, was popular on variety stages, her grim plight failed to prevent her singing several songs.

Another Irish lass, Kitty Burke, was the pivotal figure in Con T. Murphy's **Killarney** (8-22-92, Star). Kitty (Katie Emmett) is deprived of her inheritance by two scheming rascals, Felix Driscoll (Frazer Coulter) and Martin Cavanagh (George C. Boniface). No slouch, she dons a man's clothing, assumes the name Terry Doyle, and accepts work as a bouchal (serving boy) to the villains. Before long she not only has won back her estate but has won the hand of Allan Tracy (Harry Leighton), a rugged Irish-American, as well. *Killarney*'s initial stand was two weeks, but it afterwards supplied its star, Miss Emmett, with a sturdy vehicle well into 1895.

Robert Mantell found a similarly acceptable piece in Charles Obsorne's **The Face in the Moonlight** (8-29-92, 23rd St.), which sent chills up and down New Yorkers' spines for six weeks before embarking on a long tour. It offered the hammy Mantell the sort of juicy double role he relished. He first appeared as the lumbering, scowling Rabat (Jacques Ferrand in some programs), who viciously murders an innocent man. The murder is witnesssed by Lucille Munier (Charlotte Behrens). Because it is dark, she mistakes him for her own fiancé, the trim, erect Captain Victor Ambrose, to whom he bears a remarkable resemblance. Her error nearly costs Victor both his life and Lucille before justice is served. Some critics noted the applause Mantell received for his startlingly quick costume changes and for his careful delineation of the men's differences. They also granted the entertainment was a crowd-pleaser, however much many of them disdained it.

The same reaction greeted D. K. Higgins' **The Vendetta** (8-29-92, People's), the story of a husband who is estranged from his wife by a villain's lies, then finally sees through the treachery and hands the cur his just desserts. Sensations lured in patrons. These included a crash of two steamships, with the heroine being found and rescued after a "modern" searchlight scoured the sea for her, the burning of Paris, and an explosion, which allows the hero to escape from a prison where he is being held on a false charge of murder (this last scene was accomplished with the aid of a revolving stage). The play had toured profitably during the preceding season and continued to circulate for several more seasons.

Like *Killarney*, Edwin Hanford's **The Shamrock** (8-29-92, Windsor) was designed for the vast contingent of loyal Irish-American playgoers, but this tale of a grasping nobleman hounding a good peasant had small appeal and was soon withdrawn.

Many of the same Irish-Americans were dedicated to the growing labor movement, so they must have numbered among the potential audience sought by Frank Norcross's **Monongahela; or, Homestead in '92** (9-5-92, Columbus). As the subtitle suggested, the play dealt with the Homestead strike, in which steel company guards fired on workers. The story hewed closely to the facts, embellishing only to have an anarchist attempt to foment additional trouble and an Irish laborer rout him. A comic Irishman provided comic relief. Unfortunately, the play was not nearly as gripping as recent newspaper accounts had been, and it died aborning.

Roland Reed's vehicle **Lend Me Your Wife** (9-5-92, Star) was a version of the same French farce that had been seen the previous season as *Jane*. This version originally had been written by Boucicault shortly before his death and had been done at the Boston Museum in 1890. By the time New Yorkers saw it, Sydney Rosenfeld had tried his hand at revising it. The results were more than satisfactory. The production garnered laughs for three weeks, then embarked on a slated tour. By chance, *Jane* returned the same night to another theatre.

Richard Mansfield was on the receiving end of flattering notices when he appeared as Arthur Dimmesdale in Joseph Hatton's dramatization of Hawthorne's **The Scarlet Letter** (9-12-92, Daly's). Especially lauded was his death scene, in which the quiet, guilt-ridden minister discovered the passionate strength to expiate his sins. He dragged himself to the pillory and tore away the minister's band to reveal a scarlet letter on his own chest. His bitter expression turned into an ecstatic smile, his eyes glowed, and his arms and hands reached upward as he died in Hester's embrace. Critics were less happy with Mansfield's supporting players. Moreover, virtually to a man they questioned the feasibility of transferring the novel to the stage and certainly saw this dramatization as largely unsatisfactory. Since

Mansfield had rewritten much of Hatton's text, he himself had to share the blame. The production ran three weeks and completed its planned tour, but Mansfield rarely returned to it.

In Charles Klein's **By Proxy** (9-12-92, Harlem Opera House) a scapegrace English lord is ordered to marry the daughter of an American millionaire. Since he already is married, he prevails on his friend, Redfield Winters (A. S. Lipman), to sail to America and take his place. Winters, an American, is something of a scapegrace himself, so he is happy to assume the disguise.

The Rambler from Clare (9-19-92, Third Ave.) starred Dan McCarthy as Tony Sullivan, a young lad who thwarts every attempt of Squire Malone and the squire's no-good son to rob him. Like most Irish plays, it found a number of occasions for Irish airs and jigs.

There were apparently a number of songs and dances introduced into another play opening that evening. In a way, the play was an oddity, for it was the late Bartley Campbell's **Bulls and Bears** (9-19-92, Columbus), which Campbell had taken from von Moser's *Ultimo* and which had been offered successfully to San Francisco in 1875. New Yorkers knew the play better as Daly's *The Big Bonanza*. Of course, throughout the season revivals and returns of recent hits served as fillers in first-class theatres and as standard bookings in combination houses. A few of the visitors early in the year were *Fabio Romani*, *The Private Secretary*, *The Still Alarm*, and *The Lost Paradise*. Even *East Lynne* was resurrected. Classics of an older vintage also reappeared, although not with the frequency with which they had been presented in preceding decades.

Larry, the Lord (9-26-92, People's) also had its quota of musical turns, since it was one of those farce-comedies still straddling the fence between straight play and musical. In it Larry (R. E. Graham) goes to work to find a wife for his master. Rowers in sculls "raced" before a moving panorama.

John Drew was the star of **The Masked Ball** (10-3-92, Palmer's), Clyde Fitch's adaptation of Alexandre Bisson and Albert Carré's *Le Véglione*. Broadway wags gleefully noted that it was housed at a theatre directly across from Daly's, where Drew had been a fixture for so long. But Drew was reputed to have been annoyed that Daly chose his plays more with Ada Rehan than with him in mind, and the producer, Charles Frohman, had his own score to settle with Daly, who once had slighted him. The play made light of a man who wins a girl through deception. Louis Martinot (Harold Russell), learning that he is called away, asks his buddy, Dr. Paul

Blondet (Drew), to woo Martinot's sweetheart, Suzanne (Maude Adams), for him. Blondet agrees, only to fall in love with Suzanne himself. So he writes Martinot warning him that Suzanne's family is disreputable and that Suzanne is something of a tippler. By the time Martinot returns (disguised in a false mustache), Blondet has married Suzanne. His return coincides with a masked ball. When Blondet discovers that Martinot will attend the party, he ships Suzanne off to mama's, but Suzanne makes her escape and goes to the ball. There the truth comes out. Although she loves Blondet, she is outraged—not so much by his betrayal of his friend as by his depiction of her as a secret boozer. She stages a drunk scene to put hubby in his place. Drew's feather-light, throwaway style was perfect for a comedy with somewhat unpleasant undertones, and accordingly he was awarded the lion's share of encomiums in the morning-after notices. But Maude Adams was also singled out for her skillful rendition of the drunk scene—knowing and comic enough to be telling and amusing, all the while never offending late 19th-century strictures. The play ran until late January. The tour that followed set a pattern for years to come, with Frohman offering Drew to New York in a new vehicle, usually in the fall, then heading out across the country with New York's praises (they hoped) serving as advance insurance. It was a policy that Sothern and others also had adopted.

Using a forged IOU, two men attempt to get a young player to throw the Harvard-Yale football game. When he refuses the young man is drugged. But his friend, Captain Harcourt, take his place on the field. The gallery went wild when Harcourt made his first entrance in Edmund E. Price's **The Man from Boston** (10-3-92, Columbus), for he was played by John L. Sullivan. Later the young man's father wagers $10,000 on a bout between Sullivan (who apparently had dropped his characterization) and another man. A third-round knockout assures the old man he will collect. By coincidence, James J. Corbett, the man who recently had wrested the heavyweight crown from Sullivan, opened the same night in a vehicle of his own in Elizabeth, N.J. Most newspapers sent reviewers to both plays and printed their notices side by side. But New Yorkers would have to wait a few weeks to see the Corbett show.

The Drewless Daly braved critics and a questioning public with **Little Miss Million** (10-6-92, Daly's), taken from Oskar Blumenthal's *Das zweite Gesicht*. It was an unwise choice that the producer pulled off the boards after a mere two weeks. Its best-drawn figure was Beverly Primrose (James Lewis), a debt-ridden social butterfly who has spent what little money he has trying to break his older brother's will, which left everything to Beverly's sister-in-law. Primrose is convinced the woman, Venetia (Adelaide Prince), is a money-grubbing adventuress. In the end she selflessly agrees to help him maintain his expensive ways and plays a hand in uniting his daughter, Rena (Ada Rehan), and Ned Candid (Arthur Bourchier). The big question was whether Bourchier could fill Drew's shoes; the answer seemed to be that they were the wrong size. Moreover, Ada Rehan, still lovely but no longer very young, was absurdly miscast as a schoolgirl. Nor was there a role for the beloved Mrs. Gilbert.

Henry Guy Carleton's **Ye Earlie Trouble** (10-10-92, 23rd St.) was set in Revolutionary War times and recounted the romances of two American officers with the daughters of a known Tory. The more earnest couple are Ralph Izzard (Joseph Haworth) and Joan Van Twillet (Mary Shaw), while Anthony Buck (Henry Woodruff) and Charity Van Twillet (Jane Stuart) take their romance more lightly. But earnest or carefree, the men barely escape hanging as spies. General Howe (R. F. McClannin), who also loves Joan, gallantly defers to Ralph and helps the men out of their predicament. The romances are set aside for a scene in which a statue of the hated King George is pulled down and for one depicting the surprise attack on the British at Trenton. But all was not that good in love or war, so the play closed after three weeks.

Two theatrical giants also opened on the 10th. Modjeska began her visit with a mounting of *King Henry VIII* at the Garden; Jefferson presented his *Rip Van Winkle* at the Star. Modjeska's version omitted Shakespeare's final act, ending instead with Katharine's death. The warmth and poetic beauty of her interpretation were extolled, but little else was. Her scenery seemed skimpy and hand-me-down, albeit at least one critic praised the panorama of Anne Bullen's passage through London. Nor was her supporting cast much admired. Young Otis Skinner's Henry, for example, was dismissed by the *Dramatic Mirror* as "immature." Critics spent little or no time on Jefferson's scenery or fellow players, devoting themselves instead to paeans for the star. The *Times* hailed his Rip as "flawless." Jefferson kept to the one play for his fortnight's engagement, but for the last two weeks of her month-long stand Modjeska brought out, in addition to *Henry VIII*, *As You Like It*, *Mary Stuart*, *Much Ado About Nothing*, and *Cymbeline*.

Walter C. Bellows and Benjamin F. Roeder's **The Old, Old Story** (10-17-92, Windsor) was a case of like father, like son. Without his father's knowledge the son has speculated in family stocks and lost. Years before, the father had defrauded and bankrupted the father of his son's fiancée. When the son commits suicide, the shamed father makes restitution to the fiancée for the crimes of long ago.

On the 18th Daly gave over his stage to a hurriedly mounted revival of *Dollars and Sense* to replace his failed opening. A more carefully prepared revival came in on the 24th at the Star, earning some of the season's happiest reviews. The play was the fourteen-year-old *Diplomacy;* its stars, Rose Coghlan and her brother Charles. They played Countess Zicka and Henry Beauclerc to the Julian of John T. Sullivan and the Count Orloff of Frederic Robinson. Sadie Martinot was somewhat surprisingly cast as the slandered Dora. The fact that the crucial dispatch box would not open on the first night was laughed away and quickly forgotten, but fifty-five years later Odell still could call back to mind "the scene in which Dora's innocence and Zicka's guilt dawns upon [Henry] by the finally recognized scent on the papers. . . . In this scene Coghlan did but little talking, but his face, the intensity of his listening, betokened a great artist in perfect control of his medium." Equally vivid to Odell were Rose Coghlan's initial haughtiness and vengefulness and her "complete collapse" in the face of incriminating proofs. Prior bookings confined the revival to a month's stay, but it returned for a run later in the season. At that time Miss Coghlan also brought out *Masks and Faces,* which she retitled *Peg Woffington.*

Far downtown and far down in the artistic pecking order, **Current Cash** (10-24-92, Niblo's) shunted between a familiar England and an exotic Afghanistan to unfold its saga of a young officer wrongly branded as a coward. Henry Lee, so often a villain, was the hero, Captain Milton, while Charles E. Verner answered numerous curtain calls in the sort of eccentric part that so delighted contemporary playgoers, a picaresque tramp.

Frances Hodgson Burnett's **Love's Young Dream,** yet another version of Dickens's *Boots at the Holly Tree Inn,* served as curtain raiser to **The Family Circle** (10-31-92, Standard). The play was derived by Sydney Rosenfeld from the French of Bisson, and its plot seemed a variation of that of *The Masked Ball,* which also had been taken from the French playwright's pen. Old Jasper Quigley (W. H. Thompson) falls in love with his own son's fiancée, so he attempts to marry his son to a business partner's daughter. Since that girl is engaged, Quigley claims his partner's intended son-in-law is a murderer. All

is set right only minutes before the final curtain. The double bill was a touring production and was brought in for a fortnight as a stopgap booking.

J. J. McCloskey's **The Black Detective; or, The South as It Was** (10-31-92, People's) starred Wash T. Melville, playing in blackface, as Jeff, who defends a brother and sister from the sinister machinations of Capt. Jack Howard. The Southern Quarter provided musical interludes.

If McCloskey's subtitle suggested that many Americans saw the Civil War as a major dividing line in the country's history, a play that opened across the river on that same night tried and failed to use the war for some flag-waving. A. T. Treloar's **U. S. Grant** (10-31-92, Bedford Ave.) was a historical pageant with chintzy costumes and cheap scenery that recapitulated Grant's most celebrated exploits. The separate scenes were poorly tied together. And the scrimping producers apparently created another problem. The *Herald* rued, "Alas for human expectations Stonewall Jackson was killed in the second act . . . to allow the same player to depict General Lee in the third and fourth." The critic goes on to note similar doublings, although the cast printed in the review lists different actors for every role. Did the critic spy something behind the makeup?

A Gilded Fool (11-7-92, Fifth Ave.), Henry Guy Carleton's second play of the season, fared better than his first and gave Nat Goodwin a vehicle he could return to in later years. Chauncey Short, although newly rich, is deemed a fool by all who think they know him. A scoundrelly stock broker, Bannister Strange (Clarence Holt), certainly thinks so and sets about misadvising him. But Chauncey has his suspicions and gets his detective friend, Jacob Howell (Theodore Babcock), to dig out the truth about Strange. Posing as a minister soliciting for missionaries in the Congo, Howell snoops around and confirms Chauncey's doubts. As a result, Chauncey buys stock whenever Strange tells him to sell and sells whenever Strange tells him to buy. Each move makes him all the richer. So when a company headed by Matthew Ruthven (Henry Lee) teeters on the edge of bankruptcy, Chauncey is there to save the day and also to win the hand of Matthew's daughter, Margaret (Lizzie Hudson Collier). The play ran out the year on its initial visit. Some idea of contemporary players' hasty transpositions can be gauged from the fact that an important role was assumed by Henry Lee, who two weeks earlier had opened in another play at Niblo's.

W. F. Carver, billed for some unknown reason as "the Evil Spirit of the Plain," was the star of **The Scout** (11-7-92, Niblo's). None of the major newspaper critics recorded any plot, with one or two suggesting the entertainment was merely loosely tied together scenes from the more rough-and-tumble sections of western life. The program listed every character as played "By Himself." These included not only Carver and another cowboy named Whispering Willie, but Indians flouting such monikers as Red Hatchet and Man-Afraid-of-His-Horse. The scene in which the scout and his horse plunge twenty feet down a ravine and into a creek after a bridge has been destroyed assured the play of wide popularity. (Niblo's ad boasted of "the biggest tank ever used on any stage.") Even if the tank could not accompany the production on its tour, hordes of cowboys, Mexicans, and horses did. And the tour continued in the backwaters for many seasons, although this initial New York stand was only for a month.

With much ballyhoo the new heavyweight champ finally reached town in Charles T. Vincent and William A. Brady's **Gentleman Jack** (11-7-92, Grand Opera). Corbett played Jack Royden, whose rival for the hand of Alice Saunders (Lee Lamar) is George Halliday (Edward Wade). Ever the gambler, Halliday arranges for Jack to fight with Charles Twitchell (John Donaldson) at the New Orleans Olympic Club. Corbett may not have been the great fighter that Sullivan was, for Sullivan had knocked out his opponent in *The Man from Boston* in three rounds. Corbett took four. Of course, he may have been tired since the previous act included a sparring match at the training camp. The scene at the Olympic Club was praised for its verisimilitude, with a large, noisy crowd milling around the roped-in ring, the loud gong, and fighters' assistants at the ready with bottles and towels. The play stayed at the Grand for only a week before moving on to other neighborhood theatres.

A Test Case; or, Grass Versus Granite (11-10-92, Daly's), based on Blumenthal and Kadelburg's *Grossstadtluft*, was the second major disappointment in Daly's still young season. Jonathan Pognip (James Lewis), a confirmed rustic from East Lemons, is so disturbed by the high life he sees when he visits his niece, Juno Jessamine (Ada Rehan), and her husband, Ned (George Clarke), in New York that he invites them to come back with him, his daughter Salvina (Isabel Irving), and her big-city suitor, Rob Fleming (Arthur Bourchier), to savor small-town life. Their visit is made miserable by the narrowness and hypocrisy of Pognip's snooping neighbors, chief of whom is Mrs. Dr. Tinkey (Mrs. Gilbert). Her henpecked husband (William Gilbert) only highlights the problem by incessantly reminiscing about his carefree undergraduate days.

He is cheered when the youngsters teach him the latest "college" song, "Ta-Ra-Ra-Boom-Dee-Ay." Mrs. Gilbert, got up in long, yellow corkscrew curls, was made rapturously welcome on her first entrance, but even she could not win an audience for the farce.

Bisson was represented for the third time this season when his *Les Joies de la paternité* was offered as **Little Tippett** (11-12-92, Herrmann's). Both Oliver Newton (Edward Bell) and Austin Tippett (Charles Bowser) have wed and divorced the same adventuress. Both have remarried. When Newton receives a letter from his former wife saying she has had his baby, he readdresses the letter and forwards it to Tippett. Complications erupt as the baby is passed back and forth. Finally the affair is cleared up and the adventuress exposed as a would-be blackmailer. A curtain raiser, William D. F. Verdenal's **A Victim of Science,** was added midway into the month's stand.

Gorgeous gowns and sumptuous settings could not mask the weaknesses in Bronson Howard's **Aristocracy** (11-14-92, Palmer's). His story centered on the socially ambitious Stocktons. Jefferson Stockton (Wilton Lackaye) is a self-made San Franciscan whose wife, Diana (Blanche Walsh), is determined to marry their daughter, Virginia (Viola Allen), into New York society. Virginia loves Stuyvesant Laurence (S. Miller Kent), but his family resolutely opposes any marriage. Stockton suggests the best way of entering New York society is by way of London, so he moves his family there. When Virginia is led to believe that Stuyvesant has been unfaithful, she rushes into marriage with Prince Emil von Haldenwald (William Faversham), a "polished sensualist." The marriage proves unhappy, and the prince is finally killed in a duel. The more discerning critics generally belittled the play, seeing its figures as cardboard and attitudinalist. The effects of Ibsen already were being felt, and the *Times* cried out against the overuse of soliloquies and asides in the work. This was a stance it would reiterate later in the season. Yet the play was not all that displeasing to contemporary theatregoers, chalking up a fine run of nearly three months.

Mrs. [Sara] Bernard-Beere became the latest English performer to try her luck across the Atlantic. She was by no means a negligible artist, but her choice of plays, her productions, and having to act in a barn of an auditorium failed to show her off to advantage in the huge new Manhattan Opera House, where she debuted on the 14th. Moreover, she invited comparison with an established favorite when she opened with *Lena Despard,* the same play

Lillie Langtry had presented under the title *As in a Looking Glass.*

The next Monday, the 21st, another English player, E. S. Willard, returned to consolidate the name he had begun to make for himself since his American debut two seasons earlier. His initial bills at the Star offered familiar pieces—*The Middleman, Judah, John Needham's Double, My Wife's Dentist,* and *A Fool's Paradise.* This last was a reworked and retitled verson of *The Mouse Trap,* one of the final plays mounted at Wallack's. Only at the end of his stand did Willard bring out a novelty.

The following night Mrs. Bernard-Beere offered her lone new work, **Ariane** (11-22-92, Manhattan Opera), taken from Mrs. Campbell Praed's novel by an uncredited adaptor. The heroine of this "trashy" drama is goaded into leaving her drunken, loutish husband despite the heartrending pleas of their child ("a stage brat in a crimson 'mother hubbard' "). After her divorce she agrees to marry a baronet, but her first husband appears at the wedding and kills her. (To make matters worse, on opening night the pistol would not fire.) The *Dramatic Mirror* described the star as a deep-voiced, exceedingly large-framed actress possessing "a breadth of gesture that would be decidedly useful to her in a scene with the American actor named John L. Sullivan." Even with Maurice Barrymore portraying the besotted spouse, the evening was waved away as hopeless. After some performances of *Adrienne Lecouvreur* the star resigned herself to the verdict and called it quits.

William Sanford's drama of the London slums, **The Power of Gold** (11-28-92, People's), began a career that would keep it on the stages of secondary (or tertiary) theatres for the next several seasons. It did so despite a horrendously mishap-filled New York opening. When the villain went to light a "poisoned candle" his matches wouldn't work, forcing him to grab a knife and stab his victim. When horses started to pull a canal boat the boat fell apart. These and other absurd disasters temporarily forced into the shadows a plot in which the villain, in order to inherit a fortune, kidnaps a baby and has its mother committed to a mental institution.

Desperate for a choice role for Ada Rehan, Daly reached back sixty years to revive Sheridan Knowles's fading if still popular *The Hunchback* on the 29th. It proved a felicitous selection. The *Times* hailed Miss Rehan's Julia as an "unequivocal triumph" and, unwittingly reflecting the gradual but ineluctable alteration in ideals of fine acting, continued, "She is not formal, sepulchral or statuesque. She does not attitudinize, nor does she seem to wait for her catch phrases and then overemphasize them.

Her portrayal is remarkable for variety of tone. . . . It is all sincere, moving and satisfying." The production ran a month, until Daly had another major revival ready. By way of a historical footnote, the original Julia, Fanny Kemble, died in London just a few weeks after the mounting was withdrawn.

No such long life was in store for William Haworth's **The Ensign** (12-5-92, 14th St.), although it was well received on touring circuits for the rest of the century. Set in the Civil War against a background of the Mason-Sidell incident (two Confederate loyalists removed from a British ship by the U.S. Navy), its hero is the quick-tempered Bill Baird (James Neill). When a deserter not only maligns his girl but tramples on the American flag, Bill shoots him. A court-martial and exoneration follow. Charles T. Parsloe won applause as another Bill, comic old salt Bill Bolin. The scenery also was applauded, especially a set depicting the U.S.S. *San Jacinto.* But some critics had reservations about the makeup employed by actors who impersonated such figures as Gideon Welles, Admiral Farragut, and President Lincoln. (The curtain had to be lowered and raised five times on opening night to quell the patriotic applause greeting Lincoln's entry.)

More nattily dressed first-nighters elected to attend a premiere farther uptown. Reports suggested that Sardou's **Americans Abroad** (12-5-92, Lyceum) had been written to order for Daniel Frohman, and these items in turn prompted some heated correspondence and threats of lawsuits, since Augustin Daly claimed he had signed a prior contract with the French playwright to provide a vehicle for Ada Rehan. Such claims and counterclaims held small interest for most playgoers, who asked simply to be entertained. And entertained they were. Sardou ostensibly had written a comedy about rich Americans seeking entry into European society (his original title had been *Les Riches*), but to American audiences his work seemed yet another version of *She Stoops to Conquer.* A "society broker," Baroness de Beaumont (Mrs. Walcot), has selected a seedy nobleman for Florence Winthrop (Georgia Cayvan). However, Florence is suspicious of the nobleman's motives. With her uncle, Richard Fairbanks (W. J. LeMoyne), and her cousin, Jessie (Effie Shannon), she takes humble rooms in a Parisian attic (with a balcony overlooking romantic Paris rooftops) and sets herself up as a struggling artist. Jessie sets about becoming an actress. The girls are helped in their struggle by a neighbor, another American, Gilbert Raymond (Herbert Kelcey). Before long Florence and Gilbert are in love. Just as the wedding is about to take place,

Florence is led to believe that Gilbert is a duplicitous conniver. By the time matters are cleared up, Jessie has found a suitor in the carefree Landolphe (E. J. Ratcliffe). The players were as nattily dressed as their audience. The *Herald,* extolling the costumes, wrote that Miss Cayvan's last-act gown, "a clinging skirt of sage green brocade and pale blue corded silk Directoire body[,] was daring, to say the least." This light yet knowing fluff enjoyed a profitable four-month run.

John G. Wilson's **A Society Fad** (12-5-92, Bijou) took a tongue-in-cheek look at the same phenomenon—newly rich Americans wedding European title-holders. In this case an Englishman, Lord Farandole (Tyrone Power), sails over to find an heiress. He also finds he must watch any number of vaudeville turns. The comedy offered yet another instance of how thoroughly the period's theatre fudged the distinctions between musicals and straight plays.

Mrs. Brown-Potter, by now generally called merely Mrs. Potter, and her handsome, epicene leading man, Kyrle Bellew, braved New York in Zola's **Thérèse Raquin** (12-12-92, Union Square). The story told how a young married couple who have murdered the wife's first husband are driven to suicide by guilt and by the dead man's invalid mother (who is also the wife's aunt). Although critics again reminded their readers of the star's good looks and her gift for wearing beautiful clothes beautifully, they accorded the play and the production a generally frigid reception.

Repeated return engagements were a theatrical commonplace during these years, yet not all were successful. The *Dramatic Mirror* reported that attendance at the Broadway Theatre during the return of *The Country Circus* had been "dismal," so the play's producers—Klaw, Erlanger, and C. B. Jefferson—rushed in another mounting, Glen MacDonough's **The Prodigal Father** (12-12-92, Broadway). The two plays were markedly different, the first a combination of spectacle and drama, the second a simple farce. Stanley Dodge (G. W. Denham), noting a slight similarity in name to African explorer Sir Henry Morton Stanley, presumes he can win some renown on the dark continent as well. Unfortunately, in New York he misses his boat. To compensate for his failure he encounters Dollie Bonde [or Doude] (Blanche Chapman), an attractive vaudevillian. After a reasonable amount of time he returns home, filled with farfetched accounts of his adventures. His prospective son-in-law, Tom Breeze (G. C. Boniface, Jr.), is forced to disguise himself as an African prince to continue his courtship (shades of

Le Bourgeois Gentilhomme). And, of course, who should come to town in a vaudeville bill but Dollie. Inevitably, some vaudeville turns were sprinkled through the entertainment. One of these was performed by a character called Birdikins and played by a tot listed on programs as Little Irene Franklin. Carmencita, a then more celebrated dancer, was also enlisted for part of the run, which lasted only till New Year's Eve.

The Midnight Special (12-12-92, Niblo's) was a hodgepodge of rickety clichés and had no more than a brief life on lesser stages. One trade sheet summed up these clichés as "the murder of a rich broker, a hero wrongfully accused, a daughter's oath of vengeance, the escape of the villain pursued by the heroine and like incidents." Only its setting of a railway station was singled out for commendation.

Even in the healthiest theatre keen observers can detect a tug-of-war between established traditions and experimental innovations. Every now and then, however, the war erupts noisily and more bitterly. The increasingly open rebellion against once exciting motifs and against once useful dramatic devices such as the soliloquy testified to the dissatisfaction and ferment among many playgoers and critics. Newspaper columns and sometimes full pages debating the merits of Ibsen (and shortly of other emerging European dramatists) cast a telling spotlight on the turmoil. The trial matinees of recent seasons may have been a gentlemanly precursor of the eruption. So may the play contests held by several newspapers, albeit these, besides promoting circulation, somewhat narrowed the focus of discontent by attempting to evoke a totally native, American response. Now the turmoil was institutionalized. A group of ivory-towerish devotees joined forces with a few solid professionals to found the Theatre of Arts and Letters, one of America's earliest examples of a concerted endeavor to elevate the standards of commercial stages. Throughout the season, sometimes at special matinees, sometimes for slightly more extended stands, the group offered subscribers in New York, Boston, Baltimore, and Washington bills calculated to unite belles lettres and show business.

The organization's introductory offerings were **Drifting** and **Mary Maberly** (12-15-92, 23rd St.). *Drifting* was a one-acter by Emma Sheridan, an actress, and Evelyn Sutherland, later a well-known playwright. It chronicled the breakup of the summer romance of a naive girl and a young, handsome drifter. *Mary Maberly,* by the novelist J. S. Stimson, told of an old lover's attempt to rescue his former sweetheart from an unfortunate marriage. Major players such as Mrs. Whiffen, Charles Walcot, John Kellerd, and Eben Plympton were among the cast, whom playgoers paid the then outlandish price of $5 a ticket to see. The critical reaction, as it would be to all the group's productions, was "well-intentioned, but . . ." (For what it's worth, within days the theatre, by then known as Proctor's 23rd Street, switched to vaudeville.) Subsequent bills presented Clyde Fitch's **The Harvest,** which he would rework as *The Moth and the Flame,* and Frank Stockton and Eugene Presbrey's **The Squirrel Inn** (1-26-93, Fifth Ave.), which would return for a run in April. A month later a triple bill was offered. Brander Matthew's **The Decision of the Court** (3-23-93, Herrmann's) presented Agnes Booth as a wife whose repentant husband persuades her to call off divorce proceedings. Richard Harding Davis's **The Other Woman** had a bishop confront his daughter's suitor who, the bishop knows, is having an affair with a married lady. John Harrison's **Hal o' the Hall** was a blank-verse idyll set in rural England in the days of Charles II. The group's final presentation was Presbrey's dramatization of Mary Wilkins's **Giles Corey, Yeoman** 4-17-93, Palmer's), a tale of the Salem witchcraft trials. Corey's whole family is accused of complicity with the devil. His daughter is pardoned, but his wife is hanged and he is crushed to death. Following this opening several of the prior mountings were restored in repertory for two weeks, after which the Theatre of Arts and Letters disappeared into history. High prices and poor selections undoubtedly doomed it, but with rare exceptions the future would suggest that well-meaning idealists had better let the commercial theatre alone.

Just how good and how sensible that commercial theatre could be was evinced at the very next premiere, the play Willard selected to close his engagement. **The Professor's Love Story** (12-19-92, Star) introduced playgoers who were not readers of novellas and short stories to a new name—James M. Barrie. His Professor Goodwillie, for all the learned doctor's knowledge and experience, cannot recognize a curiously debilitating illness as love sickness. But even his frustrated old-maid sister is unable to prevent eventual enlightenment and the professor's engagement to his attractive secretary. Commitments allowed the comedy to remain only for a week, but Broadway would enjoy several revivals, and the play remained a favorite in stock for decades.

John Crittenden Webbs's **After Twenty Years** (12-19-92, Niblo's) told of a villainous brother who attempts to seize his sibling's inheritance. He eventually flees England and comes to America, where he

is killed fighting for the Confederacy. The star, Edwin F. Mayo, assumed several roles, including that stock figure, the devious Jewish money-lender, in this instance with the obvious name Aaron Abraham. The *Herald* suggested that "a fair idea of the disregard for the incongruities" displayed in the work was evidenced when a duel scene was followed promptly by a bevy of young women dancing in Turkish costumes.

Daly's revival on the 20th of *As You Like It* gave Ada Rehan's admirers another chance to witness her Rosalind. More adventurous theatregoers could attend the premiere of **If I Were You** (12-20-92, Herrmann's), which William Young had written as a vehicle for the popular comic opera favorite Marion Manola. The play, set in a place called Fernymead, had a bucolic charm about it and an appropriately simple story. Doris Carew (Miss Manola) and Jack Charteris (John Mason) fall in love, quarrel, drift apart, and finally are reconciled. Although the star naturally inserted a song or two, she was hailed as a promising straight comedienne. Even more promising to many was Mason, who indeed went on to become one of our finest actors. Stanislaus Stange, who would be remembered primarily as a lyricist and librettist, was the author (and leading man) of the curtain raiser, **The Army Surgeon,** in which a lovely widow hides a Union doctor from a vindictive Confederate colonel.

Broadway was not overwhelmed by its Christmas presents. **The Crust of Society** (12-26-92, Union Square) was the first of several versions of the younger Dumas's *Le Demi-monde* to be displayed during the season. A young soldier's narrow escape from a probably disastrous marriage to a notorious woman was its theme. This version by William Seymour survived for a fortnight, then toured.

In James E. Sullivan's **Manhood** (12-26-92, Niblo's) the hero, George Ashford (Edwin F. Thorne), is a signalman who is hounded by a typical snarling villain. No doubt for scenic purposes, the villain's lair was deep in an abandoned mine. And to provide moments of comic relief the author wrote himself the part of Blue Peter, a drunk who lives in constant fear of seeing a snake.

At the Star that same evening Minna Gale-Haynes, supported by Eben Plympton, Milnes Levick, Mary Shaw, and other competent players, began unfolding a repertory of old standbys, several of which had been better done recently at Daly's: *The Hunchback, As You Like It, Romeo and Juliet, The Lady of Lyons,* and *Ingomar.* Although critics were sharply divided over the merits of the star, her supporting cast, and her mountings, she enjoyed five weeks of good business. Clearly there was still life in these time-tested or time-tattered showpieces.

By contrast with Christmas's disappointments, the new year began with one of the season's most interesting plays, Clay M. Greene and Joseph Grismer's **The New South** (1-2-93, Broadway). Its story combined a vicious indictment of black corruption under carpetbagger influence with a traditional romance. Jefferson D. Gwynne (Charles Mackay), a member of an old, distinguished Georgia family, has run for Congress and seems certain of election until the blacks, goaded by their leader, the arrogant, unprincipled Sampson (James A. Herne), steal the ballot boxes. Sampson offers to return them for a personal bribe and assurances that a black will be appointed postmaster. Gwynne's answer is simple and direct. He horsewhips Sampson. But the appearance of Capt. Harry Ford (Grismer) worries him, for he assumes that the officer is another carpetbagger bent on humiliating white southerners. A fight ensues, and Gwynne is hurt. When Ford rushes off to obtain aid for his opponent, Sampson slinks in, finds Gwynne defenseless, and kills him. Ford is convicted of murder, but he is finally exonerated and freed. The irony of all this is that Ford was not about to badger Gwynne. Rather, he merely wanted to pay court to Gwynne's sister, Georgia (Phoebe Davis). With the ugliness in the past the two are finally free to marry.

The evening did not completely please the critics. The *Times* wrote, "Here is a good subject for a better play," while the *Herald* concluded, "It is all wrong, but it is all interesting." Nym Crinkle, William Winter, and several others were harsher. Particularly displeasing to many reviewers were the southern accents, which some felt were laid on too thick and others heard as inaccurate and often unintelligible. The acting palm was handed to Herne, who naturally performed in blackface. But he eschewed burnt cork for the more realistic greasepaint and wore a carefully made wig, not one smacking of minstrel caricature. His scene depicting Sampson's growing fear and panic as retribution nears all but stole the show. The producer, William A. Brady, tried a novel stunt, publishing advertisements featuring the most adverse reviews and offering money-back guarantees. His ploy failed. Many nights the box office took in no more than $100. At the end of the month he threw in the towel.

Competing for first-nighters was **Deception** (1-2-93, Fifth Ave.), the season's second version of *Le Demi-monde*. This one was by Mattie Sheridan, and aisle-sitters were uncertain just how to take it. Reviews were snide when they were not downright ridiculing. The producer and star was Baroness Blanc (in reality the much married Libby Nicholson of Philadelphia), and most of the rest of her cast were unknowns. She tried to emulate Margaret Mather's Juliet by tumbling down a flight of stairs to underscore her undoing. It was all to no avail. Another forced run kept the production on the boards for three weeks.

Daly's third revival in a row was Hannah Cowley's *The Belle's Stratagem* on the 3rd. The mounting allowed Ada Rehan as a resourceful Letitia Hardy to subdue the absurdly demanding Doricourt of Arthur Bourchier. Coupled with the old comedy was a new curtain raiser, Clothilde Graves's **The Knave.** The scene is a medieval German village where the illiterate citizenry are at a loss to read a proclamation that has been tacked onto the door of their town hall. Along comes Mockworld (Ada Rehan in a trouser role), a notorious knave. Since he can read he is ordered to explain the notice. It turns out to be his death warrant, so, of course, he does not read it correctly. Before he wanders off he sees to it that a young girl who loves him finds a more suitable sweetheart.

The continued popularity of the Civil War as a setting for native drama was demonstrated again in Margaret Barrett Smith's **Captain Herne, U.S.A.** (1-9-93, Union Square). Howard Herne (E. J. Henley) has defied his southern family and joined the fight for the Union. His half-brother, Jeoffrey Colchester (Lawrence Hanley), who covets Howard's wife, and a spurned octoroon, Inez (Dorothy Dene), conspire against him. But Howard thwarts their intrigues. Critics slammed the play and its cardboard figures. The good Captain was simply too good, expostulating nobly at length and acting with unbelievably selfless heroism. Even the insistent use of asides and soliloquies was blasted, although at one point Inez was recorded as interrupting one of Colchester's to complain, "Your habit of speaking your thoughts aloud will get you into trouble." Another device fast becoming a cliché was the use of a quartet to provide mood-enhancing songs. They sang such songs as "Annie Laurie," "Tenting Tonight," and "Nearer My God to Thee" while Herne strutted manfully on the battlefield. The New York engagement lasted only two weeks, but despite its critical rejection the play lingered on the road for several seasons.

Leaves of Shamrock (1-9-93, Windsor), a failure designed with Irish audiences in mind, saw Carroll Daly, a gossoon (serving boy), and his girl rescue an orphan, Moya O'Connor, from the wiles of some villains.

Two Detroit newspapermen, Edward Weitzel and

Fred S. Isham, had no better luck with **At the Carnival** (1-9-93, People's). A Rome street singer, Lucia, is persuaded through deception to marry Count Morini instead of a young American, Neal Russell. Years pass, and Lucia has become a famous prima donna. She meets Russell, falls in love with him again, learns of the deception, so kills the count and herself. Comedy relief was provided by a flirtatious widow, Mrs. Harmon, and a superpatriot, Charlie Wells.

That same night Marion Manola and John Mason switched from *If I Were You* to a revival of *Caste* at Herrmann's.

Sutton Vane, father of the author of *Outward Bound*, was himself a successful London melodramatist. In America his shows were generally relegated to cheaper touring circuits. One of his most popular plays on this side of the Atlantic was **The Span of Life** (1-16-93, People's). His hero, Richard Blunt, and heroine, Kate Heathcote, are hounded by the implacable Dunstan Leech even after they are wed. At one point Leech tries to prevent Blunt from reaching the top of a lighthouse to signal a ship of danger. The scene had canvas "waves washing round" the lighthouse and the "illuminated ship" in the distance. Later, in Africa, three men (acrobats Luke, James, and Lawrence Wilson) must form a human bridge over a chasm to allow Kate and her baby to make an escape.

Another big scene helped accord William Haworth's **The Flag of Truce** (1-16-93, Columbus) a long life span on the touring routes. In this instance the villain, who at one point was loudly booed for proclaiming "I always hated the Irish," traps the hero in a New England quarry and attempts to crush him under a huge rock suspended by a derrick. The villain gets his chance because the hero, Tom (Gustavus Levick), is too trusting. Tom, a stable married man, has allowed his wilder single brother, Jim (Haworth), to take his place in the Civil War (a legal practice at the time). But then the villain, who naturally covets Tom's wife, leads Tom to believe that Jim has deserted.

Daly's rapid turnover of revivals continued on the 17th with *The School for Scandal*.

Although critics in an era of robust acting often had professed to admire actors capable of a studied "repose" on stage, many theatrical historians credit one great actress with initiating the tradition of modern underplaying. To contemporaries, and in retrospect, her American debut was a high point of the season, and alone ample justification for suggesting the 1892–93 season opened a fresh theatrical epoch. Eleonora Duse was a small, slender woman,

by no means beautiful but with a simple, dark face dominated by lustrous, expressive eyes. When she opened her slightly pouty mouth to speak she disclosed a rich, deep, mellow voice. Whenever possible, she performed with little or no makeup.

For all her modernity, she subscribed in several ways to an older school. For one, she refused to perform nightly. Initially, too, her selection of plays was anything but advanced. And unfortunately, like so many great stars, she surrounded herself with mediocre supporting players. Also like so many stars, she made financial demands that forced producers to hike admission prices. The top ticket at the Fifth Avenue Theatre, where she debuted on the 23rd, was pegged at $3, double the going rate.

She opened in *Camille* (using the American title of the play) and moved on to such standards as *Fernande*, *Fédora*, and *Divorçons*. Less well known to American audiences were Giovanni Verga's **Cavalleria Rusticana** (source of the opera); Carlo Goldoni's **La Locandiera**, in which she played Mirandolina, who humbles a nobleman before marrying her waiter-lover; the younger Dumas's **La Femme de Claude**, with Duse as Caesarina, a scheming, unfaithful wife who attempts to steal her husband's invention and is shot for her treachery; and the same Dumas's **Francillon**, with the star in the title role of a woman determined to get even with her boulevardier husband by pretending to have an affair of her own.

Some snobbish critics complained about the crass dress and rude manners of Italian-Americans in the audience, but as a rule they were beguiled by the star. The *Sun* extolled her "personal magnetism" and her ability to convey the flux of emotions without saying a word. The *Herald,* smarting from her refusal to grant an interview, nevertheless conceded she was "indubitably one of the subtlest and most interesting actresses of the modern school" and had achieved "an unqualified triumph."

The contrast between Duse and Bernhardt was exemplified by simple, telling differences in their Camilles. With her consummate bravura, Bernhardt was unmatchable as the hard, knowing, successful demimondaine of the first act. Duse was softer, more ladylike. When symptoms of incipient tuberculosis tired the courtesan during the dance in the first act, Bernhardt broke away, leaned on a table, then clutched herself in patent alarm. Duse merely stopped the dance and stood still with a look of quiet fear. A memorable moment came as Duse's Marguerite met Armand's father and her initial hope turned to shock and despair. She held a flower in her hand. It was fresh and erect, but as her dismay mounted she bent the stem, seemingly without meaning to, letting the flower droop and its petals finally fall. Duse was silent, but the dying flower spoke her speeches. As yet Duse's fame was far overshadowed by Bernhardt's. This, along with many playgoers' inability to comprehend her new style and the fact that things Italian were not as voguish as things French, left many seats empty during the stand. The New York engagement at an end, Duse toured major cities, sometimes meeting with a surprisingly mixed reception, especially in Chicago and Boston.

Those who couldn't or wouldn't attend Duse's debut could sit through **My Official Wife** (1-23-93, Standard), A. C. Gunter's dramatization of Capt. Richard Savage's novel. That "wife" is actually Helene Marie (Minnie Seligman), who meets Arthur Bainbridge Lenox (William F. Owen), an ex-army man going to visit relatives, on the Russian border and bamboozles him into taking her across as his spouse. She is, in fact, a nihilist, determined to kill the czar. Realizing her game, Lenox feeds her opium powders to make her too drugged to commit murder. But the vindictive Russian police come to her apartment and stab her. Before she dies she tells her story to Lenox's wife, so that the woman will not misconstrue matters. As she staggers across the room, she hears a street band playing the very music played at the ball: "It's the masked ball music—that with death in it—That which came to me at the ball when I was to kill the czar! When I dreamed as I danced—when I was fighting—fighting with sleep! That's all we Poles can do—fight! Fight! and Die! (*falls dead as Lenox catches her*)." At least one reviewer labeled the show a "musical," but neither he nor any of his colleagues gave any suggestion to justify the label. Curiously, a similar story, albeit with a happy ending, was used in the 1911 musical *The Red Widow*.

Shiloh (1-23-93, Niblo's) appeared and disappeared almost as quickly, telling in its short tenure another tale of the Civil War. The two brothers who are the central figures naturally, for theatrical purposes, join opposing sides. But when the Union officer is condemned as a spy, fraternal feelings replace sectional differences. The Confederate brother, with the help of a freed slave, wangles the prisoner's release.

Whether it was an indication that he could not find suitable new plays, or whether he felt the new plays he liked would not suit changing public tastes, Daly proceeded with his parade of revivals, bringing out *The Foresters* on the 24th.

Hard on the heels of Duse's entry came another of the season's major occasions, the opening of the Empire Theatre on the 25th. The playhouse was located just below 40th and Broadway, across from the new Metropolitan Opera House, and this helped propel the northward surge of the theatrical heartland—now almost within reach of Longacre (afterwards Times) Square. It was an attractive theatre, with a long lobby, eventually hung with marvelous theatrical portraits. Its seating capacity of about 1100 reaffirmed that the barnlike auditoriums of old were, for the time, passé and that a certain intimacy would affect the nature not only of acting and writing but of playgoing itself. Of course, in time, before its demolition slightly more than sixty years on, it became Broadway's most venerable, venerated theatre. Among the men behind its construction were Charles Frohman, Al Hayman, and William Harris—all of whom very soon would loom large and possibly ominously over the theatrical scene.

Frohman was in charge of running the theatre, and he hired David Belasco and Franklin Fyles, then a drama critic for the *Sun,* to write a play with an American setting for the premiere attraction. The result was **The Girl I Left Behind Me.** (The title was suggested by Charles's brother Daniel, and coincidentally the old song had been featured prominently in Daniel's production of *Captain Lettarblair* a few months earlier.) Belasco and Fyles eschewed the overworked Civil War background, opting instead for a setting that largely had been ignored on first-class stages in recent years, the battles between white men and Indians. The Indian insurrections of 1876 and the Custer debacle of that same year were still fresh in memory. Fresher still—indeed no more than three years old—were the incidents at Wounded Knee, Pine Ridge, and Rosebud. The Indians, led by the American-educated Jack Ladru or Scar Brow (Theodore Roberts), are angered at their mistreatment. Scar Brow informs an American officer that "since last winter's cold and hunger, the rations have grown smaller and poorer, and last month there was no food at all." That officer is General Kennion (Frank Mordaunt), the very man whose sword years before had inflicted the scar on Ladru's brow and who now commands Post Kennion. Anger turns to outrage after Kennion insists the Indians not hold their traditional sun dance. Kennion's daughter, Kate (Sydney Armstrong), is one of the many women at the post. She has accepted a marriage proposal from Lt. Morton Parlow (Nelson Wheatcroft), although she since has had second thoughts about it and recognizes she really loves Lt. Edgar Hawkesworth (William Morris). When the Indians defy Kennion's prohibition, the general sends out a company to stop the gathering. Several of its members are ambushed but might have been saved except for Parlow's cowardice. Parlow pleads with Hawkesworth not to disclose his cravenness. Hawkesworth reluctantly agrees, only to have Parlow accuse him of being responsible for the deaths. The Indians attack. With the post surrounded Hawkesworth agrees to ride for assistance. Meanwhile, Scar Brow's beloved daughter, Fawn Afraid (Katherine Florence), comes to the post to help the Americans. She is shot by mistake. Kennion hopes to stall for time by showing Scar Brow that his daughter is in the encampment, but she dies of her wounds. Since Kennion cannot show him a dead body, Scar Brow concludes Kennion is lying and presses the assault. Luckily, Hawkesworth and the rescuers arrive in time. Seeing Kate and Hawkesworth embrace, the general remarks, "This looks like—union forever."

Raves filled the morning-after notices. The *Herald* acclaimed it as one of the best American plays yet produced, while the *Tribune*'s William Winter called it an "excellent piece of romantic melodrama." Writing on it again in 1916, he still felt it marked a high point in American dramatic literature. "Its superiority . . . is very great. The story is clear, direct, animated, sympathetic and thrilling. The persons introduced are various, natural, interesting, discriminated, and finely drawn." He also recorded a vivid description of Belasco's stage picture at the opening of the third act: "The place is within the stockade of logs surrounding the Post. There has been an all-night vigil, with fierce intermittent fighting. The time is just before daybreak. The first faint gray of light is beginning to steal into the sky; there is a reflected glow of distant fires, and, far off, yet clear and indescribably horrible, are heard the 'blip-blip' of the Indian war-drums, and the shrill, hideous cries of the savage warriors, working themselves to frenzy for the last murderous rush to storm and overwhelm the defenders of the Post." By modern standards some of the authors' dialogue and devices appear hackneyed. Thus Fawn Afraid speaks stage-Indian: "It is six moons since Scar Brow gladdened his Fawn's eyes by looking into them." And, of course, there were still occasional asides. When Parlow learns that a woman he violated has died without apparently revealing her seducer, he gloats to the audience, "That dead woman kept my secret well." After two months the original company was packed off to Chicago to entertain visitors to the Columbian Exposition, and a second, unexpectedly inferior company replaced it. In all, with one cast or another, the play ran five

months. In touring versions and in stock it remained popular for the rest of the century.

The next night Marion Manola and John Mason gave New York Erckmann-Chatrian's **Friend Fritz** (1-26-93, Herrmann's) and enjoyed the biggest success of their stand. This story of young lovers helped in their romance by an understanding rabbi had a month's run. Like *Cavalleria Rusticana*, it was later better known as an opera (*L'Amico Fritz*), but even in this version it came perilously close to being a musical, for lyricist Stanislaus Stange and composer Julian Edwards created several songs for Miss Manola to warble.

W. H. Crane had first tried out Brander Matthews and George H. Jessop's **On Probation** (1-30-93, Star) in the fall of 1889 but had withdrawn it for revisions. The new version was less serious and more comical than the original, a fact that distressed some critics but delighted Crane's following. The irrepressibly flirtatious Jonathan Silsbee (Crane) is put on probation by Mary Marlowe (Amy Busby), who promises to marry him if he can restrain his running after other women for a whole year. The year will be spent traveling in Europe with Jonathan's sister and niece, with Mary serving the sister as a paid secretary. Of course, Jonathan fails time and again and is caught every time. Still, after he discovers that Mary is entitled to a large piece of European real estate, buys off the large mortgage, and hands her the deed, Mary reconsiders. (In the earlier version they went their separate ways.) Some critics felt that Crane's exclamations of surprise on being discovered wore a bit thin in the course of the evening. But the comedy was enjoyable enough to run till mid-March and tour for a season or two.

The effort of a rich landowner, Lord Montgomery, to win Kathleen O'Connor from Terrence O'Toole (J. K. Murray) was the subject of Edward S. Gurney's **Glen-da-Lough** (1-30-93, 14th St.). No Irish romance was complete without some Irish airs, and since Murray had played minor roles in operettas he was more than capable of handling them.

Some songs and vaudeville turns were also featured in Forbes Dawson's **The Outsider** (1-30-93, Park). They were worked into a story in which a rascally English nobleman, a cockney Jew, and a stableboy drug a horse to ruin Squire Henry Fellows (Edwin Thorne). But the race was the big thing, with "4 colored jockeys" on four thoroughbreds competing on another treadmill.

There were no songs, but there were a buzz saw, a speeding express train, and a moonshiner's still in Fred S. Gibb's **A Kentucky Girl** (1-30-93, Third Ave.). The girl was Charity Jarvis, and it required

Harry Condon's persistent heroism to save her from the murderous plans of Virginia Vale and Harold Rudley.

William Gillette's **Ninety Days** (2-6-93, Broadway) featured a typical theatrical will, which decrees that Matilda Watkins (Kate Denin Wilson) must marry a certain young man within three months or forfeit her inheritance. Simple, except that the man is a missionary in Egypt. Matilda is undaunted and goes to Egypt, where she is pursued by the other possible heirs, all determined to sabotage her trip, and where she must stop off to watch a baseball game. The *Times* described her harrowing return voyage: "An Atlantic liner strikes an iceberg, and as the bow of the ship slides upon the berg the rear of the stage rises in the air and the whole structure trembles and heaves in a very realistic manner. Lifeboats are launched, the berg goes careening by, and the scene is full of thrilling action. Again a party on the berg is besieged by a polar bear, but part of the berg is made to split off and float away, carrying bear and villain." The hokum ran for six weeks.

The evening's other opening ran longer, ten weeks, and remains the only play of the season to hold the stage actively to this day. But it was not an American work. Palmer's production ("by arrangement with Charles Frohman") of Oscar Wilde's **Lady Windermere's Fan** (2-6-93, Palmer's) was superbly set and superbly cast, at least on paper. The principals included Edward Bell as Lord Windermere, Maurice Barrymore as Lord Darlington, Julia Arthur as Lady Windermere, May Brookyn as Mrs. Erlynne, and Mrs. D. P. Bowers as the Duchess of Berwick. In his *Annals* Odell says audiences were not prepared for Wilde's departures from tradition, that the "topsy-turvy wit" went over their heads, and that they were baffled by the play's construction. Certainly the better critics did not agree. The *Times*'s first-stringer (Dithmar?) understood and welcomed the work. But he disagreed sharply with Odell—who, looking back, felt "chief honours of the performance" went to Mrs. Bowers and Barrymore—when he complained that Mrs. Bowers was "too vociferous" and that Barrymore "makes love to another gentleman's wife in the manner of a foreman of a fire-engine company calling for another line of hose." The *Herald* was among the naysayers, asserting, "Unfortunately, epigram and neatly pointed moral may adorn a tale and yet fall far short of making a play."

At Daly's, where the producer obviously was not having one of his better seasons, the 7th saw the return of another revival, *The Taming of the Shrew.*

Mrs. Potter and Kyle Bellew were the stars of **The Marriage Spectre** (2-13-93, 14th St.), a version of the same *Francillon* Duse would bring out the very next week. Perhaps because they had been relegated to a lesser house (a sign of fading esteem?), or perhaps because they were wearing out their welcome, the stars were roundly criticized. Mrs. Potter's monotonous, sometimes shrill delivery was condemned, and her interpretation of the leading role as well as her dressing for it were assailed as shocking, without specific details being offered. The translation was heard as dull. And the *Times* even found an opportunity to continue its season-long attack on asides.

Scott Marble's **The Diamond Breaker** (2-13-93, Windsor) was the latest backwater thriller this prolific hack had churned out. His heroine, Rexina Alden, is an Allegheny Mountain girl who first must escape from an insane asylum to which she has been wrongly committed and then must rescue her man after he is thrown into a machine designed to crush coal. (Advertisements claimed ten tons of machinery were on stage.) The *Herald* complained that the scene in which the asylum inmates were abused by the wardens was "almost lunatic in [its] unreality," but the paper had no objection to the commonplace practice of inserting some lighthearted songs and dances into the harrowing tale.

Uncle Tom's Cabin had been touring assiduously for forty years and would continue to do so for decades more. But its appeal was obviously waning. When it returned to Niblo's on the 13th, the theatre announced not only gifts for all patrons but a special "novelty": lady ushers to assist patrons to their seats.

Charles Frohman's Comedians were featured in **The Sportsman** (2-14-93, Standard), which William Lestocq drew from a Feydeau farce, *Monsieur chasse!* Harry Briscoe (Joseph Holland) is an inveterate gambler, but whenever he goes out to gamble he dresses in hunting clothes and tells Mrs. Briscoe (Georgiana Drew Barrymore) that he is going shooting with his friend, Perkins (T. C. Valentine). The appearance of Perkins, who is looking for a daughter who has eloped, exposes the scheme, so Mrs. Briscoe runs off to her old friend, Dr. Holroyd (M. A. Kennedy), for consolation and advice. By farcical coincidence Holroyd's flat is directly above the gambling den. This leads to a curious interview between the Briscoes, with Mrs. Briscoe hiding under a blanket and pretending to be a little French girl. Then a police raid occurs—but by mistake it is Holroyd's flat that is invaded. The doctor and the lady are carted off to jail. After they are released she returns home, to be greeted by her husband, who

Act Three : 1892–1899

had escaped the raid in the doctor's clothes. He smilingly offers her his bag of game, all actually purchased at a poulterer's. During the short run various curtain raisers were offered.

All during the Union Square Theatre's glory years, when Palmer was introducing New Yorkers to the latest in French drama, Milton Nobles was circling the outer theatrical reaches with crude, alluring, homemade melodrama. Although he had trained under notable old stars such as John Mc-Cullough, few considered him a great performer. Nonetheless his name on the marquee was sufficient to draw hordes of blue-collar playgoers. Now he was booked to tread the famous boards, even if the playhouse had fallen on hard times and, at season's end, would leave the legitimate fold. Nobles's vehicle was his own play, **For Revenue Only** (2-20-93, Union Square), and it marked another unusual change for the star, since it was a comedy. And it was a rather odd, picaresque comedy at that, for as the *Herald* noted, the hero was a "quickwitted rascal," and "all the male characters were seen to be utterly devoid of high minded principles." Tom Knowall (Nobles), a tramp printer who has set himself up as editor and reporter for a shoestring newspaper, climbs through a window to interview Jefferson Potter (Luke J. Loring), a millionaire candidate for Congress on a fly-by-night ticket. He soon has wangled the position of Potter's manager. Potter loses the election, but not before Knowall helps an heiress (Mrs. Nobles) find true love or before he discovers that Potter is his own long-lost father. Reviews ranged from condescending to condemning to no review at all. Noble stayed a fortnight, then pushed back out to the road, but apparently not with this play. Instead he was soon offering his loyalists his inevitable *The Phoenix*.

The next night Daly brought out another revival. This time, however, it was a freshly rethought, freshly (and elaborately) mounted production—one that many observers were to consider Daly's finest triumph. With Ada Rehan as Viola, Sidney Herbert as Sebastian, George Clarke as Malvolio, James Lewis as Sir Toby Belch, and Catherine Lewis, a Daly alumna who had gone on to achieve fleeting stardom in comic opera in America, as a scene-stealing Maria, *Twelfth Night* garnered critical kudos left and right. Henry Hoyt's ornate scenery and Graham Robertson's rich damask and satin costumes were eye-filling, if cumbersome. Songs and dances used music by Purcell, Arne, and Schubert and, most successfully, Sir Henry Bishop's rendering of verses from *Venus and Adonis*. Odell presents a detailed, dissenting account of the

mounting, which ran until the close of Daly's season in early April.

Only a few weeks had passed since the villain in William Haworth's *The Flag of Truce* had threatened to zonk the hero by dropping a huge stone on him from a derrick. The villain in Haworth's latest opus, **A Nutmeg Match** (2-26-93, 14th St.), must have seen the play, for he was quick to employ a dastardly variation on it. Wiliam Hartley (Earle Browne) goes to Connecticut to build a dock and while there falls in love with Cinders (Annie Lewis), the adopted daughter of Farmer Lucas (E. A. Eberle). Shortly after they are married, Tom Stoddard (Henry Herman) arrives and spoils their bliss by disclosing that Hartley's sister is a woman with a past. This leads to a fight between Hartley and Stoddard. Stoddard knocks out Hartley, who falls with his head resting on a partially driven pile. Stoddard starts the engine of the pile driver. Its hammer slowly rises. But Cinders rushes in just in time to save her husband. Before the final curtain another truth comes to light: Cinders is the daughter whom the mustachioed Stoddard long ago abandoned. Many critics insisted the minor characters were the most interesting, at least in the original production. One was Nervy Kate, played in drag by the humongous Oscar Shoening. Better yet was George Washington Littlehales, otherwise known as Brick, "a country lout with a gaping mouth and a generous instinct." The part was assumed by a young man who would become one of the American theatre's giants, David Warfield.

Italian-Americans rarely figured as characters in native plays, not even as the villainous gangsters who would be prominent in casts of the future. A hint of things to come could be seen in Richard F. Carroll's **The Dago** (2-27-93, Third Ave.), in which Carmencelli Vidette (R. M. Carroll, the author's father) plots to kidnap a banker's daughter. The heavy is abetted by "a very withering and wicked adventuress [who] wander[s] about the stage flourishing a dagger." With the help of C. E. Morse (the author), the babe is restored to her family. The action took the players to Five Points (the city's most notorious slum), a Fifth Avenue mansion, and the Brooklyn Bridge and also offered a rescue from a burning building. As usual, some songs and dances broke the tension.

Stanislaus Stange's **Yesterday** (2-28-93, Herrmann's) was the curtain raiser to a revival of *Our Club*. The one-acter told of an old man who recalls the day he killed his brother in a quarrel over a girl. The excitement of the reminiscence proves fatal.

At the Union Square Theatre, the perpetually

touring Nobles was supplanted by Thomas W. Keene, another actor more at home on the road than in even a fading first-class playhouse. His repertory was strictly old-school "legitimate": *Richard III, Othello, The Merchant of Venice,* and such non-Shakespearean "classics" as *Richelieu* and *Louis XI.* Less kind critics reported some horse-laughs and hisses, but by and large he was dismissed as a good, if minor actor whose talent had been cheapened by catering to non–New Yorkers.

W. H. Crane replaced *On Probation* with Martha Morton's **Brother John** (3-20-93, Star), a comedy in which John Hackett, a successful, self-made hat manufacturer, underwrites the attempts of his brother and sisters to enter Long Branch society, rescues them fron newfound, false friends, and convinces them that the simple life is best. The play was deemed trite, but Crane's avuncular humor glossed over any number of weaknesses. After a month's run it was added to his touring slate.

Joseph (3-20-93, Union Square) was George Giddens's heavily bowdlerized version of Léon Gandillot's enormously popular French farce. Giddens, an English actor who some critics felt resembled Stuart Robson in appearance and in his deadpan delivery, took the title role of an absurdly foolish young man who is pressed by a widowed roué into marriage with his daughter.

Isaac Henderson, an expatriate litterateur, was the author of **The Silent Battle** (3-27-93, Standard), which he took from his own novel *Agatha Page.* Mercede da Vigno (Grace Henderson), a married woman, falls in love with Filippo, Marchese Loreno (Frank Gillmore), who is also married. His wife is a quiet, faithful American girl, the former Agatha Page (Evelyn Campbell). Mercede is not really an adventuress but a freewheeling soul who resents being tied down to an unimaginative husband and feels that Filippo would do better with a more colorful wife. They prepare to elope, but Agatha's cousin, John Dow (Joseph Holland), appears on the scene and talks sense to Filippo. This and Agatha's careful tending of their sick child reunite the pair. Mercede is forced to return to her husband. Literary dialogue, a lifeless heroine, and a dissuasive title all told against the work.

Sidetracked (3-27-93, Third Ave.) was also fated for a short life. It starred Jule Walters as a tramp who prevents a homicidal railroad superintendent from fastening blame for one of his killings on his rival in love. A few songs and dances were woven into the action.

A more successful touring show was **The Operator** (3-27-93, People's), which spent no fewer than three full seasons on the road. Part of its attraction came from such standard sensation scenes as a locomotive crashing into a bridge, a steamship sinking, and "a horseback ride for life." But it also offered an interesting departure. Its stars were Willard and William Newall, identical twins ("alike as two peas," the *World* assured its readers), who played the hero and villain. Look-alike characters were nothing new in drama, but having identical twins to play them was a rarity.

April's first entry was an English farce, George R. Sims and Cecil Raleigh's **The Guardsman; or, The American Girl in London** (4-3-93, Lyceum). Lady Jones (Mrs. Whiffen) agrees to pay of all the debts of her nephew, Captain Eustace Bramston (Herbert Kelcey), if he agrees to marry her American protégé, Daphne Lovell (Maud Harrison). Since Bramston has fallen in love with a girl whose name he doesn't know, he decides to misbehave and alienate Daphne. His plan works, but then he realizes that Daphne is the unknown he has fallen in love with. Explanations take up the last act. A pleasant bon-bon, the farce ran until mid-May.

Alexander Salvini, son of the great Tommaso, began a stand at the Manhattan Opera on the 3rd. His vehicles mixed the old and the new, starting with *Don Caesar de Bazan* and *The Three Guardsmen* before switching to a double bill of *L'Ami Fritz* and *Cavalleria Rusticana.* The son, a fine, good-looking actor, had none of his father's intensity, but what he lacked there he made up in romantic dash. With a good supporting cast and excellent scenery to back him up, he enjoyed both encouraging notices and profitable business. The scenery, however, was so mammoth that intermissions of half an hour frequently were required to permit changes.

While brother Daniel was reaping rewards from *The Guardsman,* Charles Frohman's Comedians presented a double bill of Henry Arthur Jones's **Sweet Will** (4-10-93, Standard) and a revival of Grundy's *The Arabian Nights. Sweet Will* turned on the generosity of a poor young man who is willing to release his betrothed so that she may accept an offer of marriage from a rich, older man. As he helps her to write her letter of acceptance she comes to the realization that money is not everything. Special interest was elicited by the casting of Mrs. John Drew in the Grundy play as the comic mother-in-law, which presented New Yorkers with a rare opportunity to see her in a modern role. But the bill lingered only three weeks. For all practical purposes, the 1892–93 season came to an early end in New York, at least as far as most major companies were concerned. Daly rushed his ensemble eastward, to London; most of the other players and troupes hurried west, to cash in on the Chicago fair.

A young exponent of the Booth-Forrest school, Walker Whiteside, came into the Union Square Theatre on the same night. He failed to cause much of a stir during his two-week engagement with either his Hamlet or his Richelieu. Significantly, his arrival coincided with a change in the playhouse's masthead. Programs now listed B. F. Keith as owner and E. F. Albee as manager. Playgoers knew what that meant for the theatre's future.

Neither of the major openings two Monday nights later was exactly new. *Squirrel Inn*, at Palmer's, had been presented earlier by the Theatre of Arts and Letters. It hoped to charm its audiences into titters, not guffaws, with a story centering on Ida Marberry (Grace Kimball), a philosophy teacher who spends her summers acting as a baby's nurse. She lulls her charge to sleep by reciting Greek poetry, in Greek. Another guest at the Catskill inn is Professor Tippengray (F. F. Mackay), who is busy translating Dickens into ancient Greek. The two meet, and a courtship ensues. Lanigan Beam (John E. Kellerd) attempts to divert the professor's interest away from Ida to a neighborhood spinster, Calthea Rose (May Tyrell), who has been pursuing Lanigan. But a marriage of like minds cannot be deflected, and Lanigan must fend for himself where Calthea is concerned. The hoped-for charm was evident to many critics but not to many playgoers, so *Squirrel Inn* shut its doors for good after a single week.

The Froth of Society (4-24-93, Union Square) was the season's third version of *Le Demi-monde*. Even Emily Rigl as the adventuress could not infuse life into Mrs. Frank Leslie's translation. It, too, survived only a single week.

Thomas Bailey Aldrich's short tragedy **Mercedes** (5-1-93, Palmer's) was, according to one reviewer, "justly considered the most important of the unusually large number of more or less noteworthy theatrical incidents of the night." Its tale was a simple, unpleasant one. A soldier named Louvois (E. J. Henley) was forced to abandon his pregnant sweetheart, Mercedes (Julia Arthur), and now finds himself assaulting her Spanish village. After the village is seized, his fellow soldiers learn the wine Mercedes has served them is poisoned. They force her to drink some, and she gives still more to her baby. Too late, Louvois appears on the scene and, realizing what has happened, drinks the last of the wine. In a rare move for the time, the play's two acts (really little more than scenes) were performed without intermission, the transition from the forest bivouac, lit by campfires, to a sunny Iberian village

being effected quickly. Two lighter works completed the bill. **Twilight,** which A. E. Lancaster and Arthur Hornblow derived from Octave Feuillet's *Le Village*, depicted the efforts of a restless old bachelor to have his married buddy go a-wandering with him. The third piece was James Mortimer's farce **Two Old Boys.** The plays ran for a fortnight.

Two weeks was also all the run accorded Fitzgerald Murphy's **The Irish Stateman** (5-1-93, 14th St.), a vehicle for yet another Irish tenor, Carroll Johnson. Johnson portrayed the slightly roguish yet likable Osmonde O'Sullivan, who graduates from teaching school in Killarney to being elected to Congress and marrying a millionairess. Settings included a view of Killarney, the deck of a transatlantic steamship, Castle Garden, City Hall Park, a luxurious drawing room, and the Capitol rotunda in Washington.

High expectations were brought down to earth when critics got a look at Stuart Robson's version of *She Stoops to Conquer* on the 1st at the Fifth Avenue. The comedy was heavily rewritten, with Robson's role of Tony Lumpkin much inflated, and with the introduction of a whole bevy of cornball characters (Landlord Stingo, Farmer Bouncer, Jack Slang, etc.) totally unknown to or barely suggested by Goldsmith. Settings and costumes were praised for their 18th-century authenticity. But on opening night Lumpkin's final entrance astride a horse was spoiled when the horse misbehaved. Robson hurriedly brought back *The Henrietta*.

To all intents and purposes the Union Square Theatre ended its career as a legitimate playhouse with Wilson Barrett's three-week engagement, beginning May 1. Barrett opened with *Ben-My-Chree* and proceeded through *Othello, Claudian, The Lady of Lyons,* and *Hamlet* before bringing out, on the 15h, a triple bill consisting of *Chatterton, A Clerical Error,* and a dramatization of S. Weir Mitchell's treatment of the Faust legend, **The Miser.**

With the Union Square Theatre winding up its legitimate career down on 23rd Street and the magnificent new Empire greeting well-heeled patrons on Broadway at 40th Street, changes in the theatrical world were progressing apace. Those changes were underscored again when the American Theatre opened and became the first playhouse on 42nd Street. Little more than a decade later 42nd Street would become the nation's principal theatrical thoroughfare, but the American would contribute little to its celebrity. Its history would be relatively short and constantly troubled. To be right too soon is to be wrong. Indeed, the theatre was not totally right to begin with, although it took a while for that to become evident. For one, it was huge at a time when most of the better new playhouses were increasingly intimate. However, that vastness proved just right for its opening attraction, Henry Pettitt and Augustus Harris's London hit **The Prodigal Daughter** (5-22-93, American). The daughter in question is Rose Woodmere (Julia Arthur), who is disowned by her truculent father after he is led to believe she had eloped with a man he detests. Actually, she has eloped with the very man he hoped she would marry, Capt. Harry Vernon (Leonard Boyne). The good captain prevents the villains from throwing a race by riding his own horse to victory. As was so often the case in this type of melodrama, the plot was not the thing. Spectacle was. Applause-grabbing settings included a grand hotel with cabs driving up and discharging their passengers and their luggage, the start of a fox hunt with horses and hounds onstage, and, most of all, the steeplechase itself, complete with hurdles and water jumps. Six horses competed. The melodrama spanned the summer, then ran on with a new cast till mid-December.

Walter C. Bellows's **No. 3A** (5-22-93, Standard) had no such luck. A slipper (size 3A) is found and passed from hand to hand with supposedly farcical results. But the *Dramatic Mirror* condemned the shenanigans as "funereal." In desperation Bellows added **The Missis** two nights later. The play had won one of the many prizes contemporary newspapers offered to encourage American playwriting. Ralph Kendrick (George W. Leslie) has married a crippled girl, Alice (Grace Kimball), for her money. Alice learns the truth and pretends she has lost her fortune. In time Ralph grows to love his wife. He takes her to a mountain camp, where they encounter a guide known as Profanity Joe (E. J. Henley). In the course of conversation Joe recognizes Alice is his long-lost daughter, but he leaves without telling her for fear of spoiling her life (echoes of *Jerry* at the season's start). Although this play received welcoming notices, it could not save the farce. The bill closed at the end of the first week.

At Daly's, Kellar the Magician came in with his sleight-of-hand. His entertainment was joined with a revival of *The Loan of a Lover,* in which Catherine Lewis's Gertrude walked away with the best notices.

Held in Slavery (6-5-93, Columbus) was a nautical drama that reminded the *World*'s critic of Mme Celeste's vehicle of sixty years before, *The Cabin Boy.* Some musical turns helped the impressed (by force) crew to forget their hard lot and their cruel captain. Ignored or slighted by most critics, it soon disappeared.

This play was followed by a double bill that brought the season to a close. **Tangled Up** (6-12-93, Columbus) exhibited the perplexity of Walter Sedgely (Louis de Lange), who has mixed his stockbroking business with his love life, and Burr McIntosh's **Why?** dealt with the plight of a young man who must not use the word "why" for a whole day.

1893–1894

The new season was one of the finest Broadway had ever seen, although Broadway was not prepared to acknowledge that at the time.

Of course, contemporary viewpoints and hindsight frequently provide disparate perspectives. Certainly there was no reason for late nineteenth-century American playgoers to conclude that the preceding season had initiated a new era on American stages. A few did, not many. In any case, breaking up theatrical history into eras is usually a matter of arbitrary convenience and not irrefutable. But the quality of so many of the plays to reach Broadway in this new theatrical year was striking. First of all, American playwrights did themselves proud. Second, England gave us two plays that are still occasionally revived. And from the Continent came several plays that remain accepted as classics, even if they are rarely presented any more on this side of the Atlantic. In some instances the failure of the Continental plays here may be attributed to faulty initial mountings. But the utter neglect now of the season's best American work is sadly indicative of our modern theatre's smug refusal to reexamine its past with the same dedication that Europe brings to exploring its own.

The first major theatre to relight was the Lyceum, when E. H. Sothern came in on August 7 with his hit of the previous season, *Captain Lettarblair*. All the while he was playing it, he was rehearsing a new work.

When the curtain rose on Blanche Marsden's **The Player** (8-14-93, Star), a few excitable patrons may have lit matches and rushed to reread their programs, for what they saw was a performance of *Hamlet* in progress. Behind the actors were footlights, and behind the footlights was another audience watching the tragedy. Except for some supers in supposed stage boxes, this second audience and the theatre it was in were all painted on a backdrop. The actor playing Hamlet was purported to be

Gustavus V. Brooke. Seasoned theatregoers knew that Brooke had been a stentorian-voiced performer who had dissipated away a promising career before his death in 1866. Now Brooke was a sort of stand-in for Garrick, for once the scene from *Hamlet* had been played out the rest of the drama proved to be a reworking of T. W. Robertson's *David Garrick*, which New York first had seen twenty-four years earlier. Lawrence Hanley, another fine player who never really reached the top, took the leading role. But his efforts went for naught.

If one audience briefly had been baffled, another was so rowdy that an interesting European play never got through its first performance. Part of the problem was that the evening consisted of a mixed bill of vaudeville, light comedy, and drama, and that all too many patrons clearly were interested only in the vaudeville, which featured the popular skirt dancer Loie Fuller. The lighter play, Charles Dance's old duologue *A Morning Call*, came first and presented no difficulties. But then Edvard Brandes's **A Visit** (8-16-93, Garden) raised its curtain. The visit of a newlywed husband's old friend reveals that the husband's supposedly pure-as-snow bride has a soiled past. Olga Brandon, who had performed the role in London, was the wife and was said to have been excellent. But the catcalls became so loud that John Kellerd, who played the husband, tried to reason with the audience. Then, after the frightened, teary pleas of Miss Brandon were fruitless, the curtain was lowered. The play was not done again.

By contrast, R. C. Carton's comedy-drama **Liberty Hall** (8-21-93, Empire) was an immediate hit. Blanche Chilworth (Viola Allen) loses her family estate and rejects the offer of her cousin to maintain the old homestead and to marry her. She moves to far more spartan quarters, where she is wooed and won by a poor salesman named Mr. Owen (Henry Miller). Everyone on the other side of the footlights knew what Miss Chilworth could not discern, that Owen was her cousin in disguise. Miller was praised for bringing warmth to the role of a rather unsympathetically drawn hero. However, the most laudatory notices went to W. H. Crompton in the part of William Todman, a Dickensian eccentric who runs a circulating library where nothing circulates. Before heading out on tour with a different cast (the original principals were tied by contract to the theatre), the play chalked up a two-month run.

Since Daly and his company were in London, his theatre reopened on the 21st with a curiosity, French actors in the same *L'Enfant prodigue* that had been such a heartbreaking failure when Daly's own players had offered it. As Odell pointed out, that first production had run seven performances, while this ran seven weeks. However, reports in trade sheets suggest that part of the run may have been forced to keep the house lit. Nonetheless, the French players reappeared briefly in late winter.

Augustus Thomas's **In Mizzoura** (9-4-93, Fifth Ave.) was the season's best American play—a superb work long since unjustly ignored. It was written as a vehicle for Nat Goodwin and clinched his hold on stardom.

. . .

Nat[haniel Carl] Goodwin (1857–1919) was described by Thomas as being at the time "under average height [5′7″], and then, was slight, graceful, and with a face capable of conveying the subtlest shades of feeling. The forehead was ample; the eyes were large and blue, clear and steady. The nose was mildly Roman; the fair was the colour of new hay. His voice was rich and modulated." Born in Boston, he was given his start by Stuart Robson. He made his name in vaudeville, musicals, and farce-comedies before turning to more serious work.

. . .

Goodwin played Sheriff Jim Radburn, a middle-aged man who is so thoughtful that he never shoots to kill (though he has been shot at many times) and will even stop to make a cast for an injured dog. His thoughtfulness has not been unappreciated, and his neighbors repeatedly have reelected him. Now he stands a good chance of being sent to the Missouri legislature as Bowling Green's representative. His friends are unaware that he has paid for the education of Kate Vernon (Mabel Amber), his neighbors' daughter. In this case his motives have not been entirely unselfish, for he loves Kate and hopes to marry her. He tells her father, Jo Vernon (Burr McIntosh), how warm he feels "whenever I hear her purty voice—soft an' low like verses out of a book—whenever I look at her face—purtier than them pictures they put in cigar boxes." But Kate has returned home with newfound airs. She rejects him, favoring instead a dashing young man, Robert Travers (Emmett Corrigan). However, Travers turns out to be a train robber, and after he shoots a man, Radburn gives him a pony on which to escape rather than see Kate's feelings hurt. He also withdraws as a candidate so that Kate's father can run unopposed. The villagers would turn against the sheriff, until they are shown the good-heartedness behind his actions. Kate learns of his help and sacrifices and begins to love him, but Radburn realizes her love would now stem from gratitude and not from the more fundamental affections he had longed for.

When Mrs. Vernon (Jean Clara Walters) suggests that Kate is "comin' to her senses" and that he need only talk to her to win her hand, Radburn replies laconically, "Some other time."

The *Times* praised the play, saying among other things that it was "as full of details as a Dutch painting." Harking back, Odell fondly remembered several of these vignettes, such as Kate's sister, 'Lisbeth (Minnie Dupree), constantly having to give up her comfortable rocking chair to visitors and Jo's complaint that all the songs they sing are about home and mother, never about father, except that he's drunk. In his opening-night curtain speech, Goodwin spoke of "the thin line between laughter and tears," and it was both his and Thomas's adroit balancing of the two that most critics gave lengthy attention to. Perhaps the play's bittersweet qualities and touch of rustic idyll militated against it, for it had no more than a modestly successful run of less than two months. Goodwin blamed the disappointment on the fact that some loyalists still demanded he be a clown. But he claimed that outside of New York and San Francisco the play did excellent business. It remained popular for more than a decade.

The two plays competing with *In Mizzoura* for first-nighters didn't fare nearly as well. **The Other Man** (9-4-93, Garden) was taken by Fred Horner from Georges Feydeau and Maurice Desvallières's *Champignol malgré lui.* Its hero is a young officer, St. Fontaine (Joseph Holland), who takes an old flame, Agnes (Henrietta Crosman), on a picnic, even though she is married to his fellow officer, Champignol (Thomas Burns). St. Fontaine is immediately mistaken for the husband and required to pretend he is Champignol until shortly before the final curtain. Two highlights were a thoroughly unmilitary military drill and St. Fontaine's attempt to draw a sketch of his captain (since the real Champignol is reputed to be a fine limner). Charles Frohman's comedians performed to mediocre business for a month before the play was shunted out to a more accepting road.

If Loie Fuller's admirers could be blamed for hooting *A Visit* off the stage, they probably did little to seal the doom of George Sims and Cecil Raleigh's **Fanny** (9-4-93, Standard), although Miss Fuller and her dances were an added attraction. The play was its own worst enemy, detailing without wit or snap how Florence Barnes pretends to be her dead sister, Fanny, to obtain money for her crooked husband. Its star, that virile lady Johnstone Bennett, dropped it in midweek and substituted her popular *Jane*.

A much finer performer had better luck. E. H. Sothern's new offering for the season was Paul Potter's **Sheridan; or, The Maid of Bath** (9-5-93, Lyceum). In a way its story, based very loosely on fact, was a variant of that John Drew had played in *The Masked Ball.* The action centered upon *The Rivals*'s disastrous first night but was really another boy-meets-girl romance. The boy in question was the playwright, and the girl was the Bath beauty Elizabeth Linley (Grace Kimball). Sheridan falls in love, but his rival, Captain Matthews (Morton Selden), tells him that he has secretly married Elizabeth and, when he is called away for a tour of duty, puts her in Sheridan's charge. Sheridan is torn between his increasing passions and his sense of obligation to a supposed friend until a lady in black appears and reveals that she is Matthews's abandoned wife. A duel follows, but since it is fought in the dark, no one is wounded. Afterwards Sheridan is free to marry Elizabeth (which he did, in fact). Costumes and settings were lavish and lavishly praised. Little details such as food served on glass dishes and a live parrot added to the color. One scene in a moonlit tavern room and another backstage at Covent Garden were heavily applauded when they were revealed. An example of Potter's wit had a character telling Dr. Linley (C. P. Flockton), Elizabeth's father and an aspiring composer, "Your music will be played after Handel's is forgotten—and not till then." Critics had reservations about the play, but none was serious. Although the play ran until mid-November and recorded good business on a season-long tour, Sothern apparently was uncomfortable with it. (He makes no mention of it in his autobiography, and neither does Daniel Frohman, the producer.) Audiences apparently thought once was enough, too. No major revival followed the tour, albeit it popped up now and then in stock for a decade or more.

About this time a play started to tour the Midwest. In Henry Dobbins and Charles Klein's **Admitted to the Bar** a young lawyer, Jefferson Ward (Charles Dickson), is presented with a touchy problem. His client, Helen Yarnelle (Margaret Fitzpatrick), is determined to see that her illegitimate son receives an inheritance to which he is entitled. But she insists her name not be mentioned, even though the law demands proof of parentage. The matter is doubly difficult because Helen is the mother of the lawyer's fiancée, Jessie (Dolly Nobles). Jessie, too, must be kept in the dark about her mother's secret. Despite good reviews, the play was soon withdrawn, although contemporary trade sheets are silent as to why. Yet the era's theatre was so alive that within months Dickson would reach Broadway in a new Klein play.

An older order of theatre was evident when Frederick Warde and Louis James's touring company came in for a month's engagement. Their bills included *Julius Caesar, Othello,* and *Virginius,* but their initial attraction was a new play, Henry Guy Carleton's **The Lion's Mouth** (9-11-93, Star). The story, which several reviewers likened to *Romeo and Juliet,* was set in Venice during the inquisition and centered on young Paul di Novara (Warde) and Linora (Edythe Chapman). The lovers marry, unaware that Linora's father, the usurping doge, had arranged the murder of Paul's father, who was the rightful doge. Paul is committed to avenging that murder. Francesco (James), the usurper's crony, who has entered the church and become head of the Venetian Inquisition, fans the interfamily feud, although, as opposed to Shakespeare's tale, potential tragedy is averted at the end. Warde had been touring in the work for two years. He described it as "an Italian romance of the sixteenth century, written in fine English blank verse, admirable in construction and redolent with poetic imagination." Critics dissented. Besides finding the plot old hat, they lambasted the blank verse as artificial and labored. The *Herald* brushed the plot away as "brimful of bombast" and as "one of the sins of Mr. Carleton's youth." Another paper's critic was amused at Warde's habit of holding his hands like a baseball player about to catch a ball.

Two farces romped in to enliven the season. Many critics had been complaining about a surfeit of farces (and musicals) in recent years, but there were few complaints about the new arrivals. One was American, one was English—and they indicated clear distinctions between transatlantic styles. Charles H. Hoyt's **A Temperance Town** (9-18-93, Madison Square) was the American entry. Fred Oakhurst (E. F. Nagle), who lost an arm rescuing another soldier during the Civil War, runs a saloon in a small Vermont village. The local do-gooders have voted to shut down the bar. Of course, the do-gooders aren't all that good themselves. The druggist, Deacon Kneeland Pray (Joseph Frankau), derives much of his income from selling booze in the guise of prescription medicine, and the town physician, Dr. Caldwell Sawyer (Frank A. Lyon), supplements his own income by writing those prescriptions. They are supported by the stern minister, Ernest Hardman (Richard J. Dillon). One character asks of him, "Did you ever hear him utter a cheering word to his wife? Did he ever offer to buy her a new dress or tell her that her dinner was good? Did he ever return from a walk and bring her even a bunch of wildflowers?" No wonder his son ran off and never returned.

Hardman blamed whiskey, not his own coldness, for the boy's flight. Using the ruse of a sick person needing immediate stimulant, they get Oakhurst to sell them some whiskey, then close his saloon and bring him to trial. The jurors keep asking for more of "Exhibit A," the whiskey, but they eventually bring in a guilty verdict. A huge fine is slapped on the impoverished Oakhurst. Just then a young man appears. He is very wealthy. He is also the soldier Oakhurst had saved at the price of his own arm. What's more, he is Hardman's long-lost son, Frank (Frank Russell). He pays the fine, converts his father, and routs the hypocrites. Colorful local types—the town drunk, a wild old man—augmented the character list, and several romances were laced into the plot. Much of Hoyt's humor ran on the order of:

—If I had a wife like that, I'd lick her.
—Oh, would you? Boys, Uncle Joe's going to treat!
—No, I ain't! I said, "lick her"!
—Well, that's what we want, "liquor"!

Some of it was old vaudeville repartee:

—Mink, is it true that married men live longer than single men?
—No. Married men don't live any longer. It just seems longer.

And no small part of the fun was roustabout and visual. Thus a towel with varnish on it sticks to one character after another. And when, at the close of Act II, the drys try to dispose of Oakhurst's beer keg, it explodes, sending them flying in suds and tatters. The farce ran for 125 performances, toured for years, and later inspired a failed musical.

While the democratic American play looked for laughs at the expense of yokels and their small town, the English farce took aim at much richer, more worldly figures and was set in the lordly environs of Oxford University. It was an even bigger hit, running twice as long, enjoying revivals to this day, and providing the inspiration for a smash hit musical in 1947. Brandon Thomas's **Charley's Aunt** (10-2-93, Standard) unfolded the misadventures that befall some undergraduates after one of them, Lord Fancourt Babberley (Etienne Giradot), in order to provide a chaperone for his classmate, Charley Wykeham (Henry Woodruff), dons a wig and black satin dress and poses as Charley's aunt from Brazil ("where the nuts come from"). The appearance of the real aunt, Donna Lucia (Ellie Wilton), provides the embarrassing complications. Much of the humor came from Fancourt's—and Giradot's—absolute refusal to be at all feminine. The absurdity of so many knowledgeable characters blithely accepting the gruff, rebellious man as a woman added to the hilarity. Giradot won overnight renown—and spent the rest of his long American career trying to find a similar success. Some idea of the freewheeling nature of contemporary theatre can be gauged by the fact that in midrun advertisements claimed a "new" version of the play was being offered.

That same freewheeling could be seen in W. J. Thompson's **Signal Lights** (10-2-93, People's, Brooklyn), which never played Manhattan but enjoyed a long, successful tour. Ostensibly the piece was a melodrama based on a famous Peekskill murder and reset in New York. Its story told of a mysterious killing, a hounded heroine, and an ambitious lawyer. Among its scenes were a view of the East River and one of the elevated trains. But critics passed over the plot quickly and slightingly. What appealed to them and the audience were the vaudeville acts so regularly inserted into touring melodramas. They were especially taken with trained St. Bernards, "Sam" the talking goat, "Pete" the educated donkey, and some Russian ponies. Most of all they had high praise for "John L. Sullivan," billed as "the world's only fighting lamb." The dogs helped rescue the heroine, but just what the other animals did, or if they even had the most meager relationship to the story, no critic revealed.

Another great new English play opened a week after *Charley's Aunt* when the Kendals returned to New York and promptly created a scandal. Pinero's **The Second Mrs. Tanqueray** (10-9-93, Star) told of a woman with a past who hopes for a better life after she makes a fine marriage but who is driven to suicide by society's unwillingness to forgive or forget. The very idea of pleading for such charity struck many reviewers and playgoers, led by the *Tribune*'s sanctimonious William Winter, as reprehensible. Even the relatively liberal *Herald* allowed that "the audience seemed intensely interested in a story that for audacity is nearly without parallel in dramatic literature." To compound the problem, Mrs. Kendal's Paula was a shocker. It totally lacked the sympathetic delicacy and pathos that Mrs. Campbell had brought to the part in London. The *Dramatic Mirror* denounced her interpretation as "crude, noisy and vulgar," as if she were bent on undermining the playwright's premise and justifying Paula's fate. The scandal helped sell tickets for three weeks, but it also sullied Mrs. Kendal's reputation in many eyes.

Sol Smith Russell came in for a stand on the same night, and his first vehicle, E. E. Kidder's **Peaceful Valley** (10-9-93, Daly's), also ran three weeks. But it

made no waves. Indeed, its central figure, Hosea Howe, is an exemplar of good behavior. He doesn't smoke, drink, swear, or wager on the ponies. To pay his way through college he accepts a job as a writer at a White Mountain summer hotel. There he falls in love with rich Virgie Rand (Minnie Radcliffe) and eventually wins her. Before that, however, he must set his erring sister on the right path again without alerting their mother that the girl has strayed too far. He does so. Kidder's humor often had a homey bite to it, such as when he described a razor as having "an edge like the feelings of an old maid at another woman's wedding." Critics deemed the evening harmless entertainment. Their reception of Russell suggests that he was beginning to wear a bit thin. He was a performer, a personality, and not truly an actor. Whomever he played, he was always Russell, with the wondering eyes, the sad smile, and total likability, but no more. For many, that was enough.

Richard Mansfield began a month-long visit on the same night, housed, somewhat surprisingly, at the déclassé Herrmann's. For most of the stand he was content to present his more successful old standbys. Not until late did he venture a new role.

Joseph Arthur's **The Corncracker** (10-10-93, 14th St.) received sharply divided notices. It lingered a month, then failed on tour, even though it was filled with the sort of roughhouse action and sensation scenes Arthur's followers expected and loved. It contained a tarring and feathering, a fistfight between two women, a second fistfight between the hero and his prospective father-in-law, and an elevator supposedly crashing eight floors and starting a fire. Besides being so dramatically evident in the elevator scene, the carpenter's and scene painter's arts were displayed in the sight of a steamboat, its stacks spewing smoke, cruising down a river, and in autumn leaves and hickory nuts falling from the trees. Most of the action took place at a fair and temperance meeting in Patriot, Ind., but the elevator effect was seen during an act unfolding in a plush Cincinnati apartment house. And what was the story that called for these settings and incidents? Critics shied away from their customary painstaking synopses of the plot, virtually to a man insisting that it was so complicated or so ineptly jerry-built as to defy a totally rational explanation. The *World* viewed it as "a remarkable combination of horse play, farce-comedy and melodrama." It focused on David Buckhardt (William Ingersoll), a Kentuckian or Corncracker, who falls in love with Helen Strange (Judith Berolde) and, in order to win her, must overcome the often violent objections of her father, John (Walter Edward), a fiery temperance advocate.

David also comes across his long-lost mother and sister (when the mother applies for a job as David's housekeeper) and brings about a happy ending when he discovers a long-lost will (hidden in the handle of an old cane). The weaknesses in the plot were exacerbated by the stiltedness of Arthur's dialogue: "It was that metaphysical marvel, love, that brought me back to you."

More fights, an explosion, and a horse race (again with real horses on a treadmill) provided excitement, while a "pickaninny brass band" offered a touch of humorous verisimilitude, in a play that became an American classic of sorts, Charles T. Dazey's **In Old Kentucky** (10-23-93, Academy of Music). The audience "shouted itself hoarse in approval," the *Times* reported. Set against a background of mountaineer feuds and of class rivalries between the mountain folk and the "blue grass" people, Dazey's story spotlighted Madge Brierly (Bettina Gerard), "the flower of the mountain." She has a touch of the tomboy in her, happily confessing, "Why[,] my pony and I take to racing like a pig to carrots." And she can admonish a haughty, lorgnetted young lady, "Gracious! That's why you couldn't see—spectacles at your age—and only one at that." But she is not against rich people. In fact, she loves the patrician Frank Layson (William Courtleigh). He loves her in turn, and so do his friends, such as Colonel Sandusky Doolittle (Burt G. Clark), who calls her "a thoroughbred even if she hasn't a pedigree." On the other hand, Horace Holton (William McVay), "a trader in niggers," is determined to destroy Frank and to seize Madge's land. Horace, years earlier when he was known as Lem, had killed Madge's father and another man, then fled the area. No one recognizes him on his return. As a result he can safely approach Joe Lorey (George W. Deyo), the son of his other victim, to assist him. Joe loves Madge and therefore hates Frank. In fact, he has threateningly warned Madge, "If that town bred dandy comes between you and me, I'll spoil his handsome face for ever." Horace adds fuel to Joe's burning anger by telling him that Frank has reported Joe's still to federal authorities. Horace has also attempted to enlist the colonel in his schemes, and when the colonel refuses, Horace snarls to the audience, "I'll teach him what it is to stir the hate of Hell in a man's heart." Joe and Frank meet at a chasm and fight. Joe knocks out Frank, destroys the bridge, and lights a fuse to some dynamite. Touched by compassion, he then extinguishes the flame and leaves. Horace appears and relights the fuse. He is no sooner gone than Madge arrives and recognizes the danger. She grabs a rope, swings across the chasm, and hurls the bomb into it, where it explodes harmlessly.

But Frank is short of cash. He has debts and also needs $25,000 to buy land he has learned the railroad wants. He decides to enter his horse, Queen Bess—"the prettiest, fastest mare in old Kentucky"—in the Ashland Oaks, hoping her winnings will provide him with enough money. Horace sets fire to the stables, only to have Madge rush in and rescue the horse. He then attempts to drug the jockey. Madge dons the jockey's uniform and wins the race. Although some of the Kentucky aristocrats might be shocked, Madge confesses what she has done. Horace is exposed, and a sadder, wiser Joe acknowledges, "I see now you were never meant for me. I see where your heart is and I put your hand in his and say good-bye. God bless you both." The original production ran at the huge playhouse for nearly six months, and thereafter the play remained a staple on all theatrical circuits until the 1920s.

There is an interesting sidelight. Dazey slapped his fellow playwright, J. J. McCloskey, with a suit charging plagiarism. McCloskey's play was called *Kentuck* (sometimes *Old Kentuck* or *Kentucky*) and was also a racing drama, with a "real" race onstage. McCloskey countered that his drama predated Dazey's. It did. It had been circulating through the backwaters since at least 1881 and had played at Hyde and Behman's in 1885. Either newspapers failed to disclose the outcome of the case or it was settled quietly out of court. So under one or another title McCloskey's play continued to tour, probably to many playgoers' annoyed confusion.

A more elite crowd assembled that night at Herrmann's to see Mansfield essay a new part. His Shylock, with a long, scraggly white beard, unkempt white sidelocks, and cumbersome, heavy garments, was a study in unmitigated hatred and malignity. To Mansfield, Shylock was a wholly irredeemable villain without a trace of compassion. If such a totally black villain denied the production some dramatic values, matters were made worse by the pale, ineffectual, and girlish Portia of his wife, Beatrice Cameron. Some commentators and many in the growing Jewish contingent of playgoers were offended, but Mansfield kept both the play and the interpretation in his repertory until shortly before his death.

The plot of **The Younger Son** (10-24-93, Empire), which David Belasco adapted from the German play *Schlimme Saat*, was so involved that the *Dramatic Mirror* required two full columns to give a synopsis. Several dailies needed almost as much space. It dealt with two brothers, the older a corrupt wastrel, the younger, a struggling artist. Their widowed mother favors the elder and connives to have the younger shipped off to Italy, where he can paint to his heart's content and be out of her way. The maneuver nearly costs him his sweetheart. But understanding and reconciliation are finally achieved. Despite an excellent cast that included Henry Miller as the younger brother, Viola Allen as the sweetheart, and Mrs. Bowers as the mother, the play failed abysmally. Charles Frohman, its producer, removed it after only four showings and rushed *Liberty Hall* back in.

By contrast, Belasco's former collaborator, Herne, scored a resounding success and made himself no small fortune with a play that ran over 200 performances (in a slightly broken run at two theatres). Curiously, the play had suffered some rocky going under several different titles before racking up a long run the preceding season at the Boston Museum. There it figured as a profitable but dubious milestone in the history of that old house, for it was the last play offered by the theatre's stock company. By the time **Shore Acres** (10-30-93, Fifth Ave.) was repeating its Boston success in New York, the nationally famous Museum was trying a short-lived stint hosting touring companies, after which it was demolished. Herne added to his coffers by assuming the leading role of Nathan'l Berry. Uncle Nat is a kindly old soul who has been content to let life pass him by. The property he inherited with his brother, Martin (Charles G. Craig), now is wholly in Martin's hands. Indeed, the greedy, narrow-minded, unsentimental Martin even married the girl Nat loved. Martin is so callous that he would sell to developers the plot their mother is buried on. Martin's daughter, Helen (Katherine Grey), loves Dr. Sam Warren (David M. Murray). Although Martin implacably opposes the match, Nat encourages the youngsters to elope on the *Liddy Ann.* A storm arises, and the ship is in danger of being wrecked on the rocks nearby. Martin is keeper of the Berry Light, but in his fury he refuses to light the beacon. After a tussle Nat manages to light the beacon, thus saving the ship. When the newlyweds return home Nat offers his pension money to keep the property in the family. A shamed Martin finally acknowledges how mean he has been. With the others gone, Nat slowly turns out all the lights at Shore Acres and puts the house to bed.

Except for William Winter, who detected a strong, displeasing odor of Ibsen about the play, critics fell solidly into its corner. The *Mercury* felt the play "marks an epoch in the drama of the American stage," while the *Journal,* going a bit further, called it "one of those pieces of theatrical

work that comes but a few times in a century . . . the best American play that we have had." After an ominously slow start the play caught the attention of playgoers, who especially liked a scene in which a turkey dinner was cooked and served onstage, with the food's aromas wafting through the auditorium, and the then unusual, subdued ending, with Herne's quiet, five-minute pantomime of making the house safe for the night. Herne toured with the play for five seasons. It remained a stock favorite at least until World War I.

A czarist infiltrator holding up a bomb and threatening to detonate it at a nihilist meeting provided much of the excitement and the title for the Kendals' next vehicle, Henry J. W. Dam's **The Silver Shell** (10-30-93, Star). Mrs. Kendal played a Russian prince's naive widow tricked by the nihilists into joining them. The play lasted only a week. When the Kendals returned in the spring they offered nothing new.

On the 31st Sol Smith Russell restored *A Poor Relation* to his programs at Daly's.

Charles Frohman had a modest success with Eden Phillpots and Jerome K. Jerome's **The Councillor's Wife** (11-6-93, Empire). Although it was a comedy, some critics detected an "Ibsenite" touch in its ending, which allowed the councillor, bigamist and manipulator that he is, to walk merrily away, rich and scot free.

In Leander Richardson's **Under the City Lamps** (11-6-93, Park), stalwart Arthur Burton (Harry Mainhall) assumes all manner of risks to free Mary Jasper (Helen Lowell) from the snares of a gang led by Bill Rochester (Mark Lynch). His task is made all the more difficult since Mary is not only a trusting innocent, unaware she is an heiress, but also blind. Settings included the Casino Roof Garden at night (with a show being performed), the safe deposit vaults at the Marine Bank, the Fulton Ferry slip, a Five Points thieves' den presided over by a notorious hag, Mother Bergman (Marion P. Clifton), and the Little Church Around the Corner. The *Herald* acknowledged that the audience was receptive and responsive, with the villains "vociferously hissed." No doubt similar audiences hissed just as vociferously on the play's seasons-long tours.

Olaf (11-6-93, Niblo's), a play taken from the German, enjoyed a month's stand far downtown. Olaf (T. B. Thalberg) is a handsome woodsman who courts trouble by courting Thora (Minnie Seligman), the niece and heir presumptive to King Marbed (C. B. Hanford). All ends happily when Olaf is discovered to be Marbed's long-lost son. Romantic medieval settings, thrilling swordplay, and a moonlit climb up a rope to enter Thora's chambers added to the appeal.

That same night Jefferson began a three-week stay at the Star in his almost inevitable *Rip Van Winkle*. He and the play returned in April for an additional fortnight.

When Irving and Terry came in for a two-month visit, their baggage contained such expected favorites as *Louis XI, The Bells, The Merchant of Venice, Henry VIII, The Lyons Mail,* and *Nance Oldfield.* However, they wisely opened with their lone novelty, Tennyson's **Becket** (11-8-93, Abbey's). Gorgeously set in Fair Rosamund's bluebell woods and in magnificent Gothic cathedrals, and sumptuously costumed, the production somehow made Tennyson's closet drama seem gripping theatre. The ascetic, determined Becket was one of Irving's greatest interpretations. But Fair Rosamund became virtually poor Rosamund; despite her ravishing gowns and glittering jewels, she was left in the shadows by Irving's tour de force. The new playhouse was filled to standing room so long as Irving elected to continue the piece.

The *Herald* sneered at the "goody-goody sentiment" that colored Clyde Fitch's **April Weather** (11-13-93, Daly's) noting that the play was loaded with surefire theatrical tricks designed to please less demanding audiences, such as "dear children, who are undressed and put to bed and made to say their prayers in full view of the audience." Fitch had thrown off the play as a vehicle for Sol Smith Russell. The hero, Raphael Reed, was another of the impoverished, tattered, yet sunnily disposed figures who were Russell's stock in trade. Reed is a struggling artist about to wed a lady who believes she is the widow of a forger. Her husband returns and proves not only that he is very much alive but that the charges against him were false. Reed can do nothing but smile and walk away. The bittersweet play failed to catch on with New Yorkers but remained popular on the road.

Cloying sentiment gave way to pompous pontification in Howard P. Taylor and Henry Meredith's **Maine and Georgia** (11-17-93, 14th St.), the latest theatrical look at the Civil War. As usual in these affairs, a Union soldier, Carroll Snow (Harry Mainhall), loves a southern belle, Olive Golden (Marie Burress). He is captured, imprisoned at Andersonville, and falsely accused of murder, so she helps him escape, clears his name, and sets the date. The theatre resounded with such noble statements as "A general's place is at the head of his army," but most of all with cannonades and volleys of rifle shots. The *Times* dismissed the play as "beneath

contempt" but hailed as the best ever staged the battle scene, witnessed from a rebel fortification along a riverbank and augmented by "well-disciplined steeds" and "the deft use of electric wires and incandescent lamps." However, the *Dramatic Mirror* complained the scene had nothing to do with the rest of the play and merely filled the playhouse with smoke. The opening had been delayed several nights, ostensibly because the scenery had not arrived. However, there was little delay in hurrying the play back onto the more receptive road.

The play served as a breather between two Fitch openings. The second was **An American Duchess** (11-20-93, Lyceum), which the youthful dramatist had derived from Henri Lavedan's *Le Prince d'Aurec.* The widowed Duchess of Holderness (Mrs. Whiffen) once had been simply Sally Rhodenbush, daughter of a prosperous Illinois canner. She is tremendously proud of the family she has married into, but she also is aware that she is heir to American gumption and wiliness. So when her son, the young duke (Herbert Kelcey), lets his irresponsible, spendthrift ways push him and his wife (Georgia Cayvan) to the brink of bankruptcy, she knows just when to let him extricate himself and just when to quietly help. A major problem is an upstart Jew, Baron Phillips (Eugene Ormonde), who is determined to seduce the duchess and to force the duke to assist in his gaining entry into society (shades of Pinero's *The Cabinet Minister*). One colorful albeit extraneous scene was a masked ball in which the duke was dressed in an ancestor's medieval armor and the duchess appeared as Nell Gwynn, and in which Lord Danby's (Fritz Williams) two left feet wreaked havoc on an elegant pavanne. For all the fine acting and excellent mounting, producer Daniel Frohman felt compelled to withdraw the play after a month, blaming its failure on the nation's financial crunch.

A fascinating sideshow was a special matinee at Palmer's on the 21st by the Professional Women's League. It turned Elizabethan tradition topsy-turvy by presenting *As You Like It* with an all-female cast. The most notable name on the program was Fanny Janauschek, who played Jaques. Later in the season it played a full week at the Garden Theatre.

Two foreigners vied for attention on the 27th. At the Garden, E. S. Willard opened a nine-week stand. His offering included *The Professor's Love Story, The Middleman, Judah, John Needham's Double,* and beginning on January 22, his eagerly awaited, distressingly lackluster *Hamlet.* At the Star, Alexander Salvini's repertory consisted of *The Three Guardsmen, Ruy Blas,* and *Don Caesar de Bazan,* three swashbucklers all a little long in the tooth, as well as one premiere. Paul Kester's **Zamar** (12-11-93, Star) was a melodrama of the same ilk but not as well made or as durable. Nonetheless it adequately served the dashing, athletic scion of the great tragedian. The scene is laid in 16th-century Portugal, where King Manuel (John A. Lane) has persecuted the gypsies. On his deathbed the king confesses to Prince Joam (William Redmond) that he once had another son, by a gypsy mother. That son is now Zamar (Salvini), and he is a king in his own right—king of the gypsies. He is willing to marry his beloved Hinde (Maude Dixon) and live the only life he has known, until Isabel de Braganza (Eleanor Moretti) foments trouble between the half-brothers. Lines such as "Take my life, if you will, but her [Hinde's] honor is safe" set the tone.

A better, more durable play raised its curtain the same night. Rose Coghlan was the star and producer of Oscar Wilde's **A Woman of No Importance** (12-11-93, Fifth Ave.). In a stellar cast she played the wronged Mrs. Arbuthnot to Robert Taber's Gerald Arbuthnot, Effie Shannon's Hester Worsley, Ada Dyas's Lady Hunstanton, and Mrs. Bowers's Lady Caroline Pontefract. The only player to receive damaging notices was Maurice Barrymore, who, as the callous Lord Illingworth, "jumbled and fumbled line after line." (In fairness, he was a late replacement for the star's brother, Charles.) Miss Shannon's pastel dresses and Miss Coghlan's black velvet gown won ahs and oohs, while E. G. Unitt's lovely, elegant settings, particularly the spacious terrace scene, earned him his own curtain call. Still, the comedy ran only a month, with the poor economic picture again receiving some of the blame. Later, when Miss Coghlan decided to tour in the play, the scandal of Wilde's London conviction forced her to drop her plans.

At the Lyceum *An American Duchess* was replaced on the 21st by a revival of *Sweet Lavender*.

The year ended with Mrs. Drew's arrival on the 25th at the increasingly out-of-the-way 14th Street Theatre. She began with *The Road to Ruin*. At a time when many older players were still impersonating much younger people it was interesting to see her as the aged Widow Warren, who pretends to a comically false youthfulness in order to steal Mr. Dornton (George Osbourne) from her own daughter. After a week she switched to *The Rivals*, then, following a short hiatus, she reappeared at the Star in these plays and in *The Jealous Wife*.

A less discriminating audience may have relished Elmer E. Vance's **Patent Applied For** (12-25-93, People's). Luckily for Vance, who was also the

author of *The Limited Mail,* clichés could not be copyrighted. His hero, Robert Lansing, is an inventor, whose invention is stolen by Grafton Chase. Lansing chases Chase onto a ship, which is promptly shipwrecked. Coming ashore, Lansing is rescued and carried to safety on a horse by his sweetheart, Helen Millburn. Somehow, although plot synopses in reviews do not make it clear just how, a stereopticon acts as a "silent witness" to prove Lansing's claim and entrap Chase.

If a great American performer helped close out 1893, two great French players raised the curtain on 1894. The inimitable Coquelin and Jane Hading were the attractions at Abbey's for six weeks starting on January 1. Their first week was devoted to *Thermidor,* but thereafter they changed bills almost nightly to present a repertory of more than a dozen plays ranging from Molière to the moderns.

England's turn came next. Sydney Grundy's **Sowing the Wind** (1-2-94, Empire) told of a rich man, Brabazon (Henry Miller), who tries to prevent his ward from marrying a young actress, Rosamund (Viola Allen), only to discover that she is the illegitimate daughter he long ago had abandoned. The play's great scene was the confrontation of the two principals. The scene soon became known as "Sex Against Sex," from the phrase used at its opening. So famous did both the play and the scene become that when the first American revue, *The Passing Show,* appeared a few months later a spoof of the plot tied its skits together and one of its big songs was "Sex Against Sex." In a departure striking enough to elicit comment from several critics, no incidental music accompanied the performance. (Instead the house's full-sized orchestra offered such pieces as Beethoven's "Prometheus" overture during the intermissions.) Despite late 19th-century pruderies and the atrocious slump in business everywhere, *Sowing the Wind* ran until mid-May and reaped huge profits.

Another look at sexual problems was received with howls of outrage when some lesser players rented the Berkeley Lyceum for the matinee on January 5 to give a performance of Ibsen's **Ghosts.** "Unclean," "fetid," and "vile" were some of the adjectives with which critics pelted the drama, even those who were willing to admit the performance was fine. Yet the tragedy managed to receive a few more scattered playings during the season.

Hardly a year passed without some comedy turning on the provisions of a preposterous will. Last season it had been *Ninety Days;* now it was **Our Country Cousins** (1-8-94, Lyceum), which Paul M. Potter took from Augier and Foussier's *Les Lionnes* *pauvres.* This will demands that a man prove he is happily married or forfeit an inheritance. Since his country cousins know he is in love with another woman, they do all they can to make his life miserable. As usual, the Lyceum ensemble, led by Herbert Kelcey, E. J. Ratcliffe, W. J. LeMoyne, Georgia Cayvan (resplendent in a yellow silk gown), and Mrs. Whiffen, was showered with praise. The play was not, so had to be content with a six-week run.

Another period cliché assured playgoers that virtually any drama set in Russia dealt with nihilists. H. Grattan Donnelley's **Darkest Russia** (1-8-94, 14th St.) was no exception. The rebels, Ida and Ivan Barosky (Selma Herman and Sheridan Block), enlist Alexis Nazimoff (E. L. Davenport), son of Count Nazimoff (M. H. Jordan), in their cause. At a party Ida, a violinist, refuses to play the national anthem and smashes her violin. The count has them arrested and threatens to send them to Siberia, but a happy ending follows. Critics bewailed that the dialogue and overblown acting were as old hat as the story, but trade sheets reported that the play was the theatre's biggest hit since *Blue Jeans.* Unfortunately, the era's trade sheets were not always dependable, and the fact that the play ran only six weeks leaves their comments suspect.

Theatregoers who elected not to visit darkest Russia could journey to **The Heart of Africa** (1-8-94, People's), where Lionel Roy (Oliver Doud Byron) must retrieve a magnificent diamond discovered by his father and taken from him under hypnosis. Lionel and his wife (Kate Byron) "suffer untold miseries," all vividly told, until the jewel is restored. The play was a quick failure.

It was supplanted at the same house by Robert Drouet's **Doris** (1-15-94, People's). With Effie Ellsler as star, the play depicted English prejudices against a divorced woman who remarries while her first husband is still alive. No matter that the rejected spouse was a criminal whose inconvenient reappearances keep cruelly troubling his former wife. Like its predecessor, the drama was a short-lived dud.

Another stock figure in contemporary theatre was the "ruined" woman. The season already had seen plays dealing with the effects of the misstep on the woman herself (*The Second Mrs. Tanqueray*), on her husband (*A Visit*), on her son (*A Woman of No Importance*), and on her daughter (*Sowing the Wind*). **Poor Girls** (1-22-94, American), which was taken from a de Maupassant story by an uncredited adaptor, told of the effect on a sister. Ada Taylor (Kitty Cheatham) discovers that Herbert Blair (Frank Mills), who has proposed to her, has despoiled her sister, Deborah (Odette Tyler). Ada's other suitor, Tom Osborne (Joseph Holland), steps in quickly to prevent the marriage, nearly shooting Blair in the process. At first he is also hard on Deborah: "With all your silks and perfumes, what are you? I repeat it, what are you?" But Blair is made to see the error of his ways, and the figures are properly paired at the end. A touch of theatrical realism, as in *Shore Acres,* meant another meal was cooked onstage—this time fried ham. All for naught, since *Poor Girls* closed after two weeks.

Drama of a higher order became available to discriminating playgoers when Modjeska returned to New York. Her vehicle was one of the great European plays of the 19th century and a beacon in the new wave of dramaturgy, Hermann Sudermann's *Heimat.* The play was known in America by its heroine's name, **Magda** (1-29-94, Fifth Ave.). Magda has left her provincial German home in disgrace and has gone on to become a famous opera prima donna. She returns to give a concert and possibly effect a reconciliation with her estranged father, the dour, crippled Major Schubert (Otis Skinner). She is even willing to consider marriage with the man who apparently betrayed her, Privy Councillor von Keller (R. Peyton Carter). He is willing to marry her, too, but refuses to accept her illegitimate child lest his political career be destroyed. She is outraged. Her father demands the marriage take place. She turns and asks him why. After all, how can he be sure that von Keller was her only lover? The shock of the revelation kills the old man. Artificialities of the casting—a fifty-three-year-old actress portraying the daughter of a thirty-six-year-old actor—bothered no one. In fact, Modjeska's performance was hailed as beautiful, compelling, and persuasive. The *Times* praised her "force, grace and sympathy," while Skinner remembered her Magda as "temperamental and buoyant." Winter was a dissenter, decrying her interpretation as too lofty, a view strangely in line, if not in agreement, with Modjeska's own. The star insisted Magda was one of her favorite roles because of the heroine's "consciousness of the high mission of an artist." Knowing she had a drama that might be too advanced for many playgoers, and aware of the generally dismal business at box offices, Modjeska limited her stand to a fortnight.

W. H. Crane stayed for six weeks after arriving at the Star on the same night, but then he had a schedule of better-known, more widely acceptable plays (*The Senator, Brother John,* and *On Probation*). Among the other revivals or returns on first-class stages during January were *A Texas Steer, Lady Barter, Playmates,* and *Forget-Me-Not.*

John Drew, still new to stardom, found himself in a ticklish situation when a supporting player all but stole the show from him in Henry Guy Carleton's **The Butterflies** (2-5-94, Palmer's). Carleton's story told how love forces Frederick Ossian to give up the life of an irresponsible man-about-town and settle down to earning his way in the world. Maude Adams was the heroine. But critic after critic stopped his review in its tracks to hurl garlands at Olive May for her portrayal of Suzanne Elise, a happily chortling, scatterbrained ingenue. She bounced about in bright, flower-bedecked gowns, and when she bounced, a bun that sat atop her head like a cupola bounced in quick response. Yet although she also received excited notices in some later shows, Miss May's career was shaky, while Drew and Miss Adams remained major stars for decades. Carleton's humor was also enjoyed. In one instance a snobbish woman, determined that everyone should be aware that she and her family are the Stuart-Dodges of Philadelphia, has her vanity punctured when someone asks in response, "Where is Philadelphia?" Winning further applause was a setting of a San Augustine drawing room, with a moonlit lighthouse seen through its windows. Pleasant fluff, the play drew patrons determined to forget the nation's economic woes and so prospered for three months.

Some blocks northward an English melodrama of a style slipping from vogue was not as welcomed. In Pettitt's **A Woman's Revenge** (2-5-94, American) a former, rejected suitor leads a married woman to believe her husband is unfaithful. After the wife leaves her home and has been falsely accused of murdering the old suitor, her husband brings about a reconciliation by successfully heading her courtroom defense. Following a three-week struggle, the play folded, and the still very new American Theatre sank to a combination house. Forty-second Street remained a bit too far north to be part of the theatrical mainstream, while the auditorium's huge size stamped it as belonging to a passing era.

A similar piece was Edwin Barbour's **The District Fair** (2-8-94, People's), and it, too, found no acceptance. It was another of the era's many racing melodramas (with real horses running on treadmills). This time an erring son reforms and rides on to victory. Even the sticks wouldn't buy it, at least not for long.

For many months newspaper readers had been besieged with ballyhoo about an actress named Kathrine Clemmons. Press releases extolled her beauty, confessed that lovers had nearly fought duels over her, and leaked any snippet of information, true or not, that would implant her name in playgoers' minds. What was unprintable by the standards of the time was that she apparently was Buffalo Bill's mistress and that his money was behind the press agentry. When the blonde beauty began her one-month visit with **A Lady of Venice** (2-12-94, Fifth Ave.), supposedly a fifty-year-old English drama revamped for the occasion, reviewers agreed she was not unattractive. But her skills as an actress were clearly minimal. Wisely, she surrounded herself with superior players and a physically magnificent production. Nina Sforza has married Raphael Doria, Prince of Genoa (Francis Carlyle), but his enemy, Ugone Spinola (Maurice Barrymore), who covets Nina, lures him away and then surrounds the town. A single combat follows with Nina in the guise of her husband. To her horror, she trounces Spinola only to learn that Raphael has been seduced by Spinola's bedmate, Laurana (Jennie Goldthwaite). Nina takes poison. Happily, Raphael appears in time and repentant. He provides an antidote for her.

On the 15th at a special matinee at the Empire for the benefit of the Maternity and Training School departments of Hahnemann Hospital, Mrs. Fiske performed as Nora Helmer in *A Doll's House.* Some of the scenes most likely to give offense were cut—the bits with Nora's stockings, and Dr. Rank's description of his ailments—but even this could not assuage many critics. The *Times* again assured its readers that "there is no hope for a 'dramatic revival' under the influence of Ibsen." Yet the star was praised, with the *Dramatic Mirror* singling out "the pathos of the kisses upon the door of the nursery when [Nora] realizes that she is no longer fit to be with her children." Largely drawn by Mrs. Fiske's growing reputation, the audience was reported to have been the largest Ibsen yet had enjoyed in New York.

One of the year's biggest hits was Pinero's **The Amazons** (2-19-94, Lyceum). A fanatic mother gives her three daughters mannish names and raises them, with the help of a determined female gym instructor, to be like boys (she even encourages them to smoke cigarettes) but then must watch as some nice young suitors undo all her plans. This tale struck a note in an era when agitators for women's rights were going through one of their periods of noisemaking. The last act was set in a gymnasium the mother had built on her estate and in which the girls could exercise in special gym clothes that showed off their legs. Georgia Cayvan, as one of the daughters, won a round of applause for a routine with Indian clubs during the act. Two other players proved particularly popular: Mrs. Whiffen as the martinet instructor, "Sergeant" Shuter; and Ferdinand Gottschalk as a suitor, Lord Tweenways, scion of an old family where curses come home to roost and bad genes become dominant with the odd-number generations—and he is very odd indeed. Like *Charley's Aunt* and *The Butterflies, The Amazons* was the very sort of escapist frippery hard times called for. It ran out the season and remained popular for years. Tom Taylor's *A Sheep in Wolf's Clothing* accompanied the Pinero piece.

In short order Edwin Barbour, author of *The District Fair,* had a second melodrama ready with his dramatization of Hall Caine's *The Bondman,* which he called **The Land of the Midnight Sun** (2-19-94, 14th St.). To the *Dramatic Mirror* this saga of two half-brothers—one charitable and loving, the second bent on avenging his wronged mother, even at the expense of his innocent sibling—exemplified all that was meretricious in such touring shows: "The whole gamut of melodramatic interest is sounded; its cheap humor, direful catastrophes [a volcanic eruption, a bloody impaling], 'sacred secrets,' exaggerated sentiments, conventional love scenes, and well-known types of characters; while above all hovers ever and anon the inevitable soul-stirring pulsations of the tremulo fiend of the orchestra." Recalling the attention *Sowing the Wind* received for omitting incidental music, the last comment is especially interesting.

On February 26, Irving and Terry came back into Abbey's for a fortnight, offering nothing but revivals. Two new plays premiered the same night. One was veddy British, the other distinctly American. Barrie's **Walker, London** (2-26-94, Park) starred the great rubber-faced comedian James T. Powers as a barber who, the night before his wedding to a notorious battle-axe, has one last fling on the town by disguising himself as an African explorer and joining a party on a houseboat.

No other American play of the season was so heavily advertised in trade sheets as was **Blue Grass** (2-26-94, People's). It was a touring melodrama, and its lone, brief Manhattan booking was part of a cross-country trek. Although the play was set in Kentucky it had nothing to do with horses, racing, or any other matter normally associated with the state. In fact, the story was so general—and so trite—it could have been set anywhere. John and Mary Brand (R. A. Roberts and Mrs. Cyril Norman, the producer's wife) are happily married, but Louis Berthelot (Emmett C. King), long covetous of Mary, persuades John's hardboiled old flame, Mrs.

Violet Raymond (Florence Ashbrooke), to come between the Brands. Furious at her when she fails, Berthelot strangles her and implicates John. He is rescued in the nick of time from a lynching and kills Berthelot. Disdainfully received, the play was hustled back to the hinterlands.

Lloyd S. Bryce and Stanislaus Stange's **Mrs. Dascot** (3-5-94, Fifth Ave.) filled out the final week of Kathrine Clemmons's month-long grab for stardom. The play, set in England and Egypt, recounted how a widow makes a doctor who once had betrayed and jilted her marry her, even though it means he must abandon plans to marry a rich nobleman's daughter. She does this by locking herself in his office with him while his fiancée is outside, and then screaming that he made a pass at her. Solely for theatrical effect, one act unfolded in Alexandria during a bombardment, with a cannonade (supplied by a bass drum), the sound of breaking glass (from the prop men's crash box), and theatrical flame (made with lycopodium powder) for verisimilitude. Miss Clemmons looked lovely in a rose-pink dress, but her acting was as hopeless as the play. Even Maurice Barrymore, as her leading man, could do nothing. Some critics expressed surprise that Bryce, editor of the prestigious *North American Review,* would be associated with such drivel.

Coincidentally, several critics pounced on the same line in William C. Hudson's **A Man Among Men** (3-5-94, 14th St.) as establishing the tone and nature of the play, although they were at variance in recording the line's precise wording. One reviewer heard it as "A daughter's duty is always to her father," while a second wrote it down as "A daughter's place is with her father." (Remember a similar line in *Maine and Georgia*). The daughter is Edith Olyphant (Amelia Bingham). Her father is a professor (Erroll Dunbar) who has invested all his savings in the Round Top Mining and Smelting Company after discovering a valuable deposit on its property. John Morrow (William Harcourt), the mine's superintendent, plans to foreclose on the mine's mortgage, which he holds, and Edith entrains from Saranac to New York City in hopes of changing his mind. Some unsavory trustees goad Morrow on and even kidnap Edith. At one point rebellious miners burn buildings attached to the mine. But after Edith and John fall in love a happy ending ensues, albeit it turns out one of the lowly miners and not Olyphant is really Edith's father. Olyphant proves to be her uncle. The mine settings won applause, as did the play, from many critics. But the many good notices somehow failed to ensure a success.

Lincoln J. Carter's **The Tornado** (3-5-94, Niblo's) pulled out all the melodramatic stops and enjoyed a long life on the touring circuits. Its basic story recounted the plight of a young married couple separated by an especially "energetic villain." But the story assumed second place to the stunning effects, which included a violent storm and a collision of ships at sea. Of course, playgoers knew the husband and wife would be reunited at the end, but they almost certainly could not guess that the reunion would occur when the husband discovers his long-lost spouse on a hospital operating table.

Return engagements (such as *The Girl I Left Behind Me*), revivals, and premieres made the night of the 12th busy. For many the revivals held more interest than the novelties. Critics were divided over how noticeably age had withered Wallack's old standby *Rosedale*, which was given an affectionate mounting (and exceptionally extensive newspaper coverage) at the Star. At Abbey's Stuart Robson, so beloved for his deadpan and squeak, brought back *The Comedy of Errors*. Of course, his erstwhile partner, Crane, had gone his own way. In his place Robson enlisted a minor comedian, Giles Shine, apparently because Shine's resemblance to Robson gave added credence to the twin Dromios.

A maid with a feather duster opened the next play, thereby setting its tone. **Love's Extract** (3-12-94, Fifth Ave.) was taken from a French farce, *Les Petites Voisines*, and reset in New York. It followed the comically complicated lives of two French chanteuses who have somewhat loose morals. They also have adjoining apartments. Problems pop up when one of their flats is sublet to a rural family. No one does more to add to the mayhem than Don Pedro de Mancha (Max Figman), the hot-tempered suitor of one of the ladies. He soon is discovering suspicious men hidden in closets, in chests, and even in a clock. The piece survived for less than a month.

The Pride of Mayo (3-12-94, Third Ave.) was supposedly from the pen of its star, Dan McCarthy, who played Dick Fitzgerald, a lad always available to lend a helping hand. That help is needed by Michael Clancy after Frank Driscoll foists the blame for a murder on him. Michael flees to America but eventually returns to Ireland to be exonerated. When this touring show reappeared the following season, Con T. Murphy was credited with authorship.

The respected French tragedian Mounet-Sully came a cropper during his four-week visit to Abbey's, beginning on the 26th. His repertory ranged from Corneille and Racine through Victor Hugo, with an obligatory attempt at Hamlet. Held

at a polite distance by most reviewers, his New York stand and the ensuing tour were a financial fiasco.

Nor did Clara Morris fare much better during a one-week stand, which began on April 2. She presented *Camille, Article 47, The New Magdalen*, and *Renée* along with one new work. **Claire** (4-4-94, 14th St.) was based on Richard Voss's German drama *Eva*. Its heroine, after jilting her first husband, killing her second, and learning, on her release from prison, that her first husband has forgiven her, dies in an ecstasy of joy. Long past her heyday and perceived by numerous critics as burnt out, the star soon resumed her travels.

On the same evening, the Kendals opened their second, much shorter visit of the season at the Star, but they offered nothing new.

Since C. T. Dazey was one of the authors of **The Rival Candidates** (4-9-94, Madison Square), playgoers might suspect rightly that horse racing would furnish part of the plot. But Dazey and his collaborator, I. N. Morris, hoped to add an extra punch to the story by closely reflecting a recent New York political scandal. John Douglas (Joseph Wheelock) is a candidate for office and a stable owner. What his friends are unaware of is that he is bogged down in debt. He orders his jockey, Tim Tipton (Louis Haines), to throw a race. Douglas's rival, Richard Bashforth (Francis Carlyle), has bet heavily on Douglas's horse. After the incorruptible Tim wins the race, Bashforth wins his bet, the election, and Janet Kendran (Victory Bateman) in the bargain. This time there were no horses onstage. The race was merely described. Nor did reflections on New York's perennially sordid politics grip audiences. The play was soon withdrawn.

So was a rewritten *Margaret Fleming*, which opened the same night at the Fifth Avenue and eked out a month of mediocre business in the face of discouraging notices.

Like *Love's Extract,* the action of **The Sleepwalker** (4-9-94, Bijou), which C. H. Abbott based on W. S. Gilbert's story *Wide Awake*, transpired in a pair of conveniently adjoining apartments. Robert Hilliard played the hero, who pretends to be a sleepwalker in order to court one woman all the while he is engaged to another. Paul Arthur stole the show as a nearsighted minister. The piece failed.

The Sleepwalker was replaced by another instant failure, Charles Klein's **Willie** (4-23-94, Bijou). This was the piece Klein offered to Charles Dickson when *Admitted to the Bar* proved disappointing on the road. If connecting flats played no part in the story, the fact that the main female characters lived in the same boardinghouse did. Dickson assumed the role of Willie Furbelow, who concludes that Florence Bignold (Lillian Burkhart) has thrown him over, and so decides to marry just to spite her. A matrimonial agency gives him the name of an old spinster, Sarah Tugstock (Gertrude Whitty). On visiting the house in which she lives, Willie discovers not only that Florence lives there, too, but that Florence actually has not rejected him. So Willie gives his name as Willie Selwyn, whereupon a real Willie Selwyn (John H. Bunny) enters the scene.

The *Dramatic Mirror* called **Rory of the Hills** (4-23-94, 14th St.) an "out-and-out, plain, unvarnished Irish play" and listed its components as "the iron-hearted landlord, the tender-hearted colleen [Grace Darley (A. Cushman)], the young man with an evil disposition, and an accomplice in his power because the young man knows he is a ticket-of-leave man, the missing document[,] . . . the shooting in the back." Fortunately, Rory O'Malley (James C. Roach), "nimble in gait, genial in expression, and facetious in speech," comes to the rescue. As always in this sort of play, jigs and Irish airs were laced through the action. Roach was also the playwright, thus providing his own meal ticket for several seasons.

In Mark Price's **The Wicklow Postman** (4-30-94, Third Ave.), the titular hero reunited a long-lost heiress and her legitimate fortune despite the dark workings of a villain. Critics saw the play as refreshingly free from the clichés of Irish romantic drama despite its hackneyed story, and some compared it favorably with *The Shaughraun,* although that play told quite a different tale. Naturally, Irish songs and dances interrupted the action.

Even before the next play opened it received some unusual publicity. E. T. Gerry, that self-appointed protector of children, took action to prevent the show from being staged. This prompted the *Dramatic Mirror* to note that the noisy do-gooder "has long been offensively active against the children of the theatre, who never have needed his solicitous interference[,] . . . while he has been studiously inactive with reference to the miserable children of the street." Not everyone agreed. Some theatrical writers suspected that the show's producers had never really intended using a fifteen-year-old child but simply had announced her casting to bring on the public brouhaha and had a small, youngish-looking but older actress ready to assume the part. However, since that part was the leading role, it was a matter of no small moment. The play itself was of no small moment, either. It was another of the important examples of new Continental drama, Gerhart Hauptmann's *Hanneles Himmelfahrt,* ever after known in America simply as **Hannele** (5-1-94, Fifth Ave.). Hauptmann himself came over from Germany to help with the staging (and promptly found himself hauled into court by Gerry). The "dream poem" recounted the visions of a dying little girl (Anna Blancke), little more than a street waif, who has been institutionalized after being abused. By standards of the time the play was almost free form, moving back and forth between the illuminating visions and squalid reality. This alone was enough to upset many hidebound reviewers. Less imaginative critics also could do little more than compare Hannele's final assumption into heaven with the famous, not dissimilar scene from *Uncle Tom's Cabin.* Their comparisons were not very favorable, since the production was shabby and the acting little better than inept. Then, too, the holier-than-thou among the reviewers found the play, with its representation of Christ and other "shocking" scenes, utterly blasphemous. The hypocritical *Times* pointed out that the American theatre was given over largely to musicals and vaudeville and that a serious work should be accorded every consideration—then went on to savage the play. The result of all the hand wringing and wailing was that *Hannele* ran less than two weeks.

Ellie Norwood's English comedy *The Noble Art* made the mistake of encouraging more unfavorable comparison by coming into New York with the title **Charley's Uncle** (5-7-94, Bijou). Uncle Andrew (George Woodward) hires Professor Tranz (Albert Bruning), a hypnotist, to rid his nephew, Charley (Charles B. Welles), of his gadabout habits. Charley learns of the plot and bribes Tranz to pose as a prizefighter, engage his uncle in a sparring match, and hypnotize him between jabs. When the actors walked out, complaining they had not been paid for the first two weeks, the show closed. But the producers promised to take the show on the road, using its original title and a different cast.

Arthur Hornblow was the adaptor of **Musotte** (5-7-94, Star), which folded the same week it opened. Its story told of a husband who must persuade his young bride to accept his baby by his dead mistress.

Equally short-lived was Charles Coghlan's **The Check Book** (5-9-94, Madison Square), in which the poor husband of a rich wife and the poor wife of a rich husband form a partnership to help out each other. When a gown the poor husband purchases for the poor wife is mistakenly delivered to the rich wife, the arrangement is exposed. An excellent cast included Rose Coghlan, Effie Shannon, and Joseph Holland. Some critics admired the playwright's clever if untheatrical wordplay, but such compliments could not save the piece.

A double bill ended the seaon for another house. Bret Harte's **The Luck of Roaring Camp** (reputedly dramatized by the late Dion Boucicault) was coupled with Thornton Clark and Louis N. Parker's **Gudgeons** (5-14-95, Empire). In the former, May Robson walked away with most of the laurels as Baby, the undiscourageable miner's wife, who refuses to be kept away from the camp where women are not welcome and who disguises herself as a Chinese boy to nurse a foundling. In the second work, a nouveau riche American, Howard R. Harrison (W. H. Crompton), and his daughter, Persis (Kitty Cheatham), determine to enter London society. With the aid of the Anglo-American and Universal Agency they are introduced to James Ffolliott Treherne (Henry Miller), who is willing to oblige if the price is right. Romance and good fortune follow after Treherne's nephew, Reginald (William Faversham), meets Persis. The bill ran for two weeks.

One hard-luck theatre came back briefly into the limelight when Wilson Barrett and Clement Scott's **Sister Mary** (5-15-94, American), a play written ten years earlier, was mounted there. The saintly Mary Lisle (Julia Arthur) assists a betrayed woman in getting back on her feet and also turns a young army officer away from the bottle. She later agrees to marry the officer, then discovers he is the woman's betrayer. The *Times* described one scene. The officer settles down "in a rocky glen near an abundant and soul-inspiring waterfall [and] paints a portrait from memory of Sister Mary. Meanwhile, the band plays softly, and Mary, in a fine house dress, with lace-trimmed petticoats and dainty shoes, trips blithely down the rockly path from the fly gallery, carrying a hatful of hothouse flowers which she has plucked by the way. So it happens that when the noble officer, having finished his portrait, proceeds, as British officers handy with brush invariably will, to address it in endearing terms, calling it 'Mary,' Mary herself answers 'Here I am.'" Since Mary and her officer finally do wed, audiences could leave the theatre satisfied. But not for long, for the play closed after two weeks.

Robert Buchanan's **Lady Gladys** (5-28-94, Madison Square) was also an importation from London. Minnie Seligman played the title role of a woman who avenges herself on the mean man who has foreclosed on her family estate by marrying his son, getting the deed for the property, then ordering father and son out in the driving rain (this to "a plaintive wail" from the orchestra pit). She comes to learn, just before the final curtain, that to forgive is divine. One critic, while admiring Miss Seligman's

interpretation, evoked an ages-old cry, complaining that though the theatre was small she spoke "so low in unemotional passages that she can scarcely be heard at the back of the house." The play was yet another two-week dud.

An American play, Scott Marble's **Tennessee's Pardner** (6-5-94, 14th Street), wrote *finis* to the season. It also gave Cora Van Tassell, a popular touring star, a chance to show her stuff to more sophisticated New Yorkers. After old Tennessee dies, his fellow prospectors keep writing letters in his name to his daughter back east. She is not deceived and hurries west. To the miners' consternation, she is soon running the camp, with an iron fist in a velvet glove. She reforms a cynical adventuress, saves a miner's life, and puts everything in four-square order. By contrast to comments on the well-liked, New York–trained Minnie Seligman, Miss Van Tassell was seen as a bit coarse, given to all too short skirts and a broad style of acting. But there was no doubting that she got her points across—and then sometimes waited tellingly for applause or laughter.

Of course, all through the season old favorites returned to combination houses and, occasionally, to fill in booking gaps at better theatres. From the unavoidable *Uncle Tom's Cabin* through such more recent plays as *Sam'l of Posen*, *The Crust of Society*, or *The Stowaway*, they were accorded their two or three hours onstage and then moved on.

That all was not well in this year of generally bad business could be seen in the advertisements even relatively prominent players took out during the season. In May, for example, one trade sheet ad ran: "Wanted: Authors are requested to submit Modern Comedies and Costume Plays suitable for Miss SADIE MARTINOT." A month later another advised, "Robert Hilliard at Liberty Invites Offers for This Summer and 1894–95."

1894–1895

Except possibly for the succession of marvelous seasons that so rightly excited theatregoers beginning about the time of World War I, great theatrical years rarely follow one another. Coming after the brilliant showing made by the previous season, 1894–95 was no exception. True, two of the best 19th-century English comedies had their New York debuts, and England also sent over some other good plays and noteworthy players, one of whom gave

New Yorkers their first glimpse of yet another Ibsen tragedy. But these instances aside, the new theatrical year was mediocre at best and often downright bad. Most discouraging of all, American playwrights presented little they could acknowledge with genuine pride. They seemed to be on a self-awarded sabbatical. (From here on, we will follow the division of seasons found in the *Best Plays* series.)

When William Niblo first began providing entertainments at Broadway and Prince Street in the late 1820s, his site was in Manhattan's northern suburbs. For many years, as the town moved northward, the theatres built there, and promptly replaced after they burned down, were elegant and prosperous. But by the mid-1890s time and the theatrical center had passed by. To begin what proved to be its final season—and not a full one at that—the house relit with George C. Jenks's **In the Name of the Czar** (8-11-94, Niblo's). As far as the house's loyalists were concerned, it was a rousing beginning. At least, according to the *Herald,* the audience "shouted itself hoarse with delight." But the gallery's clamorous joy did not prevent the paper's reviewers from assailing the drama as a mere "concatenation of scenes . . . not a logical, serious or well constructed play." Within the confines of those scenes Hector Delmont prevents Norman Daryell from embarrassing the American government by acting as a mercenary instigator of an anticzarist uprising. Stock characters such as a boozy Irishman and a French maid provided comic relief. An elaborate ballroom scene was sprinkled with vaudeville turns. After a single week the players were looking for other jobs.

Vaudeville turns also found a place in Charles Taylor's melodrama **The Derby Mascot** (8-20-94, People's). Set in Texas, it pitted Jack Marston against Andrew Knight for the affections of Nellie Cheneworth, daughter of a miner. Jack has a horse running in the big race, and Andrew drugs Jack's jockey, forcing Jack's niece, Little Tex, to ride the horse to victory. But Andrew isn't finished with his dirty work. He kills Nellie's father and implicates Jack. Little Tex turns detective to get the goods on Andrew. Before he can be brought to trial he is crushed to death by a huge snake. As there had been with some plays in the previous season, there were complaints about the poor quality of the incidental music. However, the play apparently was a crowd-pleaser, so after a week it moved on to a season-long tour.

That was the case, as well, with Edwin A. Locke's **The Life Guard** (8-20-94, Niblo's), which also utilized vaudevillians to gloss over dull moments and also had a hero named Jack. This Jack is surnamed Wallingford, and he is a proud member of the United States Life Saving Station in New York. He finds true love after he organizes a "living ladder" to save a pretty waif named Drift.

The season got under way in earnest the next Monday, the 27th, even if Augustin Daly, who lured out the most glittering first-nighters, insisted his offering was part of a preliminary season. His attraction was a revival of *A Night Off* and allowed patrons to welcome back James Lewis, Mrs. Gilbert, and almost all the other regulars, fresh from their London triumph. Only Ada Rehan was missing, and she was promised for later bills in the "regular" season. One added inducement to go to Daly's was that Henry E. Dixey had joined the company. His broadly farcical Marcus B. Snap, the old producer, usurped many of the morning-after notices.

Daniel Frohman's loyalists were of the same high order as Daly's, so another crowd of swank first-nighters was on hand for Paul M. Potter's **The Victoria Cross** (8-27-94, Lyceum). The play was a vehicle for E. H. Sothern, and since its story unfolded in India it was indeed a color-splashed vehicle, filled with exotic settings to frame the regal uniforms and elegant gowns of the English and the more unusual garb of the nabobs, khitmatgars, and wallahs. Using the excuse that Joan (Grace Kimball), daughter of General Allan Strathallan (C. P. Flockton), has entered a "sacred" horse in a race, the treacherous Ahmedoollah (Arthur R. Lawrence) precipitates a mutiny. The English are trapped in a fort. But Joan's fiancé, Ralph Seton (Sothern), who has been accused of cowardice, leaves the fort, rides through the enemy, and brings rescuers. He comes none too soon, for the natives have dug tunnels under the fort (the audience could hear the digging) and filled them with explosives. Though the mutineers do blow up the building, the English survive and win. In many ways the story was that of *The Girl I Left Behind Me* reset in India. One odd scene had Seton attempt to dance with a broken arm and disrupt the dancers by fainting. Disaster was narrowly averted on opening night. As the walls caved in after the explosion, some of the "stone" fell on Flockton. He was able to continue although he was hurt. The play ran a month, then embarked on a national tour.

Lesser houses presented two other shows that enjoyed much longer successes on the road, touring for years even if their initial Manhattan outings were very brief. A dam bursting and spewing water ("à la the Johnstown disaster"), a steamboat race, and a working cotton compressor were among the added inducements to see Charles E. Callahan's **Coon**

Hollow (8-27-94, 14th St.). A few songs and dances also enlivened the work. Its heroine, Georgia, has run away from a North Carolina home where she had been left by a kidnapper and has come to live in Sulphur Springs, Tenn. There she is courted by Jared Fuller, whose mutterings to the audience reveal that he is really Tom Eastman, the man who had abducted her. Georgia is also pursued by Ralph Markham, who in turn is hounded by the jealous suitor of his former girl. In the end Jared is killed and Ralph weds Georgia. The more brahmin critics condemned the writing as trashy and had little use for the players' fist-on-the-forehead, broad school of acting, but less demanding playgoers ate it up.

Similarly, Frank Bixby's Shaft No. 2 (8-27-94, Columbus) and its performers were on the receiving end of disdainful notices, which did not prevent ticket buyers from lining up at box offices on the road. They wanted to see if Hiram Ely could prevent Jim Rathburn from making improvements to a mine. When Jim takes his girl, Maggie Daly, down the shaft to show her his plans, Hiram sets loose a mine car to run over them. They escape by cramming into an air shaft. Foiled once, Hiram has his cohort, Alfred Nelson, attempt to chloroform Jim. A storm arises, Alfred is struck and killed by lightning, and Jim is indicted for his murder. He is strapped to the electric chair as Maggie rushes in with a pardon from the governor. Critics did agree with patrons that the lightning and thunder effects were, well, electrifying.

The Cross Roads of Life (8-27-94, Star) was yet another melodrama designed for the road, even if it was allowed to open at a still prestigious albeit fading theatre. It was written as a vehicle for Edmund Collier by the star himself in collaboration with Thomas Garrick. Dick Hawthorne (Collier) doesn't know that his fiancée, Ethel Stratton (Carrie Francis), is an heiress. Ethel doesn't know it either. But Julian Ashwood (J. H. Hutchinson) does, and he plots to gain the inheritance for himself although that means he must kill Dick and marry Ethel. He attempts to blow up a train on which Dick is riding as it speeds through the Harlem Tunnel. The attempt fizzles, and the lovers leave for a European honeymoon. Julian is waiting for them when they return. This time he plans to scuttle their ship off Sandy Hook. He is foiled again, caught, and carted off to jail. Advertisements for the play promised a "Carload of Scenery." Those settings showing Park Avenue, the railroad tunnel, and Sandy Hook elicited the most praise. Other characters included a comic tramp and another manly crew from the United States Life Saving Station.

The Academy of Music played host on the 30th to a return of Shenandoah. Although the play itself was not tampered with, the vastness of the stage allowed for some spectacle, most notably when a whole "troop" of cavalry rode across the stage. Since there was always an audience that relished this sort of showiness, the play added 108 performances to its record.

John D. Newman, the hero of Edmund E. Price's A True American (9-3-94, Third Ave.), comes incognito, as a Mr. Desmond, from Ireland to oversee his uncle's estate. He prevents a dissipated cousin from abducting their uncle's daughter and heir. Furious, the cousin hires a professional boxer to beat up John. John happily takes on the boxer and the cousin and beats them both. The men should have known better, for John was played by John L. Sullivan. As usual, critics complained about Sullivan's very meagre acting ability, but his fans paid no attention to their cavils.

Elmer Grandin's Slaves of Gold (9-3-94, Columbus) followed the unsavory exploits of a man sent away for robbing a safe. When he is released from prison he kidnaps the safe owner and the owner's daughter and barricades them in a mine, which he threatens to blow up.

Another Irish-American celebrity was the star of R. N. Stephens's On the Bowery (9-10-94, 14th St.). How big an attraction he was remains moot. The Dramatic Mirror observed that the playhouse was "by no means crowded"; the Times reported that the theatre "was packed." The play told of a betrayed young woman, Blanche Livingstone (Valerie Bergere), who hunts down her betrayer, Thurlow Bleekman (Mark Lynch), determined to give him his due. He in turn hires two thugs to drown her by throwing her from the Brooklyn Bridge. A heroic young saloon keeper comes along just in time. He jumps from the bridge to rescue the girl. Later Bleekman locks Blanche in a building on an East River pier and sets fire to the building. The saloon keeper again has to come to the rescue. The actor who played the saloon keeper was actually a saloon keeper, and he had some experience in jumping from the Brooklyn Bridge. In fact, he used his real name in the play, and that, of course, was Steve Brodie. For the next several years, whenever he became bored with his bar he returned to the play, performing primarily in the New York area. A line of his in the play summed it all up: "This ain't art. It's on the Bowery." In the original production Frank Bush, a famous vaudeville dialect comedian, played several parts, including an Irish tough and a "sheeney [Jewish] huckster." Other variety acts garnished the entertainment (especially in Act II, which was set in a replica of Brodie's saloon), with Brodie himself essaying a song and dance or two.

At the other end of the theatrical spectrum Thomas W. Keene came into the Grand Opera on the same night for one of his brief, infrequent New York stands to give Manhattanites an increasingly rare chance to enjoy a full week of Shakespearean repertory. The days when Forrest, Booth, and others constantly afforded New Yorkers prolonged engagements of Shakespearean drama were irretrievably gone. Keene's programs—*Richard III*, *The Merchant of Venice*, *Othello*, and *Hamlet*, along with *Richelieu* and *Louis XI*—were respectfully received but only moderately well attended.

The first new hit of the season was Charles Frohman's production of Henry Arthur Jones's sentimental comedy **The Bauble Shop** (9-11-94, Empire), which told how a middle-aged English lord is saved from despair and disgrace by the affectionate attention of a young daughter of a poor, besotted toymaker. For John Drew, his part marked a refreshing departure from the light-as-air farces of recent years. For his leading lady, Maude Adams, her glowingly warm portrayal gave her a further boost toward stardom. Beautifully mounted and filled with excellent supporting players, the piece had to be held over for an additional month beyond its two-month booking before setting out on a cross-country tour.

In the topsy-turvy world of theatre there was nothing illogical about the sad fact that a far better play—a bright gem, in fact—came in next and failed. Its short run could be ascribed to Richard Mansfield's bringing it in as part of his repertory. Yet when he read the largely delighted notices Mansfield was prepared to keep it running. A poor response at the box office removed any incentive. The comedy was George Bernard Shaw's **Arms and the Man** (9-17-94, Herald Square), an antiwar spoof about a soldier who prefers nibbling chocolates and making love to fighting. The simple sets were charming, and Mansfield's Bluntschli was crisp, nonchalant, and whimsical. Rather than incur losses, Mansfield filled out most of the month of October, until he had another novelty ready, with old favorites: *Beau Brummell*, *A Parisian Romance*, *Dr. Jekyll and Mr. Hyde*, and *The Scarlet Letter*.

Egregious miscasting seemingly made a hash of Arthur Law's hit London farce **The New Boy** (9-17-94, Standard), in which a baby-faced groom must pretend to be his wife's son by an earlier marriage in order to retain an inheritance. After James T. Powers was hurried in to assume the leading role,

business picked up. The play ran ten weeks and toured.

Horse racing, an erring son, and a lady detective—three popular motifs of the era—were welded together in **The Great Brooklyn Handicap** (9-17-94, Grand Opera). The erring son is Howard Clews, and since he is known to have misappropriated funds at his father's bank he is saddled with the blame when some diamonds are stolen. His cousin, Fredericka Van Aucken, believes he is innocent. To help him, she bets on a long shot at the Brooklyn race and wins. She also unmasks the real culprit behind the theft, "a woman with a black dress and a past." The race was not shown onstage. That was left for Fredericka to describe. Instead, the big sensation scene had a trolley car hurtling down on the hero while he fought an accuser in the middle of the street.

Attempts to wreck the American consulate in Chile and to scuttle the U.S.S. *Baltimore*, the ship's escape to sea, and an ensuing naval battle provided the thrills in **Old Glory** (9-17-94, Columbus). William A. Brady and Charles T. Vincent adapted the work from an English melodrama by Henry Pettitt and Paul Merritt. It was set in the South American republic at a time when American interests were interfering in a civil war there in real life.

Edward Weitzel's **Tide of Life** (9-17-94, Niblo's) was also bolstered by some spectacular scenery and effects. The first act was set on a South Street dock, with a ship alongside the pier. The third act showed a house by some railroad tracks, with trains speeding by. And the villain's death occurred when he fell from a five-story building, became entangled in wires, and was electrocuted. That villain is Dan Gillette, a river pilot who kidnaps Jill Worthey and then spends the next three acts trying to kill her father, Judge Worthey. Jill and her fiancé, Captain Stoddard, manage to undermine all Gillette's efforts and pursue him until he jumps to his destruction. For better or worse, the play remained popular on the road for half a dozen years.

When A. M. Palmer relit his theatre he announced that Augustus Thomas's **New Blood** (9-19-94, Palmer's) would be the initial offering in a season-long program devoted solely to American plays. That was not to be, and the new play's failure was one reason why. Thomas's drama centered on a confrontation between Courtland Crandall (E. M. Holland), a dying magnate who has vowed to form a huge industrial trust before his death, and his liberal son, Van Buren (Wilton Lackaye), who is just as determined to oppose him and to better the conditions in which his employees live and work. When Van Buren is shouldered out by his father and the old man's associates, he forms a new company with the help of his rich friend, Barstow Adams (Maurice Barrymore). The trust gives battle, but by the final curtain Van Buren appears to be winning.

Many of the reviews were nasty, not because they condemned the quality of the play so much as because they abhorred its stance. One reviewer derided the hero as "a sappy sentimentalist posing as a leader of practical reform." The drama had opened initially in Chicago at a time when strikers were burning trains and when soldiers guarded the streets. Its topicality helped sell tickets. But Thomas felt that New Yorkers were surfeited with news about such distant happenings, so rejected the work. Charles Frohman gave him a different reason, suggesting that patrons who paid top price for tickets were not sympathetic to a play in which a laborer tells a rich man that workers would be content with the scraps the rich leave on their plates.

Henry Guy Carleton's **Lem Kettle** (9-24-94, Bijou) was in no way controversial but was no more successful, folding after two weeks. Its protagonist, played by Tim Murphy, is a farmer who neglects his fields to tinker in his workshop. He devises a beer-bottle stopper that is sure to make him rich, only to have it stolen by a pack of rascals led by the oily Matthew Holliwood (George Macomber). Lem spends the three remaining acts reasserting his rights, taking time out from this effort to court and win a pretty girl named Barbara (Dorothy Sherrod). Stock figures such as a stage Yankee and a latter-day Mrs. Malaprop comprised the supporting characters.

Most critics felt that W. H. Crane had overleapt himself and stumbled badly when he unveiled his Falstaff in *The Merry Wives of Windsor* at the Star on the same evening. He was best at modern, homespun parts and lacked the depth and richness to convey fully all the old knight's absurdities. There was, the *Herald* rued, "no merry twinkle in his eye, no mirth in his voice, no exuberance in his spirits." Alluding to a more successful role of the star's, the critic branded his portrayal "a senatorial Falstaff." As usual with Crane's productions, the mounting was physically attractive (if much overweighted by modern standards). For example, the exteriors of the Pages' house and the Garter Inn, both ornately Victorian-Elizabethan, occupied opposite sides of the stage while between them a street led to a painted view of Windsor Castle in the distance. The Herne's Oak scene made clever use of blinking electric lights to simulate fireflies. A good businessman, Crane accepted the inevitable and soon withdrew the comedy.

Clyde Fitch would have no new play on Broadway this season, but he did have one that opened in Chicago after a single-night tryout in Rockford, Ill., then toured until summer. The play was offered to Brooklyn in June but never crossed over to Manhattan. It's producer and director also took the leading role and elevated himself to stardom, although New York would not acknowledge that elevation until later. In **His Grace de Grammont** (9-24-94, Grand Opera, Chicago), Charles II (Frederick Mosley), in exile in France, asks the Count de Grammont (Otis Skinner) to court the lovely, ingenuous Mistress Hamilton (Maude Durbin) for him. The count agrees, only to fall in love with the girl and pursue her for himself. The infuriated king orders Grammont's arrest for treason. But in time he comes to accept that the young couple are genuinely in love, and he allows them to wed. (Before the tour finished, Miss Durbin had become Mrs. Skinner in real life.)

When *The Victoria Cross* set out on tour, its New York cast remained behind to appear in Jerome K. Jerome's **A Way to Win a Woman** (9-26-94, Lyceum). The story recounted how a man commits some despicable acts in order to become rich enough to satisfy his mercenary sweetheart and how both eventually see the errors of their ways. The play received divided notices, but E. H. Sothern's reputation had grown sufficiently to permit the comedy a modest run.

Florence Bindley, a popular touring star, put away her revolvers to appear in **The Captain's Mate** (10-1-94, People's), a play by a New York journalist, John Ernest McCann. For this occasion she was Margie, a waif who comes to New York to unearth some villains she believes are depriving her of an inheritance. For a time she disguises herself as a bootblack named Crullers. But later she and the villains find themselves together aboard a ship (she as stowaway). The villains throw her and the captain's wife overboard, but heroic little Margie saves herself and the floundering woman. It soon turns out that the inheritance wasn't Margie's after all. Still, her bravery does not go unrewarded. She is made the ship's first mate.

Echoes of Lotta Crabtree, now retired, reverberated through the auditorium when Belasco and Clay M. Greene's **Pawn Ticket 210** (10-1-94, Niblo's) finally reached Manhattan. It had been written in 1887, and Lotta had toured with it, getting no closer to Broadway than Brooklyn. Now a minor actress, Amy Lee, attempted to fill her shoes in the role of the little girl left with a Jewish pawnbroker as security for a $30 loan. Years pass, the girl grows up, and the pawnbroker decides to marry her. But her mother and a handsome young man redeem the ticket just in the nick of time. Miss Lee was no Lotta, and the production disappeared after a single week.

Charles Hoyt's **A Milk White Flag** (10-8-94, Hoyt's) was a big hit, tallying 153 performances in its first New York stay. But was it a play or was it a musical? Hoyt, who had taken over the Madison Square Theatre and rechristened it after himself, had been instrumental in moving farce-comedy into full-fledged musical comedy. However, he had not been consistent in his advances, sometimes loading a work with song and dance, sometimes merely spiking a play with a handful of musical turns. *A Milk White Flag* seems to fall smack in the middle, with four song lyrics included in the published text and indications elsewhere for other musical bits. Its plot interwove two stories. In one, the Ransome Guards, a ludicrous, small-town paramilitary group, strives doggedly to outclass a rival organization. In the other, an unprincipled contractor hides and arranges to be declared dead so that he can collect on an insurance policy. His funeral is supposed to afford the Ransome Guards a chance to surpass a funeral staged by their opposition. Hoyt reached deep into his bag of hoary tricks. There were his customarily preposterous names: Phil Graves (an undertaker), Mark Tombs (a doctor), Steele Ayres (a composer). There was the free-for-all between the rival bands, which ends Act I. And there was the homey, unsubtle humor:

—They say he [General Hurley Burleigh] is wonderfully brave.
—He is. He's come to town to visit his mother-in-law.

The show toured for several seasons. In 1916 a totally musicalized version, *Go to It,* failed.

A Ride for Life (10-8-94, Grand Opera) starred its playwright, Walter Fessler, as yet another touring hero named Jack. Jack Woodruff is poor. Edwin Marston is rich. They both love Annie Powers. Edwin frames Jack for murder, then attempts to run away. Jack follows him, and the pair fight it out to the death on a speeding locomotive engine. To play the part of the engineer, the producers hired James Root, who was not an actor but an engineer-hero who had driven his train through raging forest fires in Minnesota. The play toured lesser theatres for two seasons.

The play was definitely not the thing when A. W. Gattie's **The Transgressor** (10-15-94, Palmer's) premiered. Gattie's story reminded more than one

critic of *Jane Eyre.* A woman agrees to marry the man she loves despite his odd demand that the marriage be kept secret. She soon learns that her husband has another wife, who is in an asylum and is hopelessly insane. A blackmailer and legal problems beset the couple before the first wife's death puts an end to their troubles. Few critics had kind words for the play, but then the drama was of only secondary interest. The primary attraction was the debut of a well-publicized English actress, Olga Nethersole. Miss Nethersole was a slim, dark, almost Latinate woman with beautiful eyes and long, flowing hair. She exuded "sex." Her passionate playing evoked memories of Clara Morris in her heyday. Wilton Lackaye was her leading man, but when after a fortnight she switched to *Camille,* Maurice Barrymore became her vis-à-vis. Lackaye, Barrymore, and all her supporting players were members of Palmer's company, attesting how quickly Palmer had surrendered his ambitious plans for a season of American drama. On her later tour, *Romeo and Juliet* and *Frou-Frou* were added to the star's programs.

Crane, too, had seen his ambitious plans come to naught when his Falstaff was coolly received, so he returned to the kind of contemporary comedy he excelled at. Perhaps in his own mind he slyly compromised, for Paul Potter's **The Pacific Mail** (10-22-94, Star) was a modern rewriting of Tom Taylor's *The Overland Route.* To allow Crane to shine all the more brightly, Potter combined two of the best characters from the older play, the hero and the runaway husband, into a new part for the star. Thus as Sylvanus Urban, the coward turned savior, Crane could not only demonstrate his gift for low comedy but display his gifts with more sophisticated humor. He elicited gales of laughter as a manacled man trying to drink a cognac and light a cigar at the same time, and later, after the shipwrecked characters are stranded on an island, he performed the admirable Crichton with a delightfully insouciant hauteur. It was all good fun, but somehow the public did not want to be entertained by it.

Julian Magnus and A. E. Lancaster's **Daughters of Eve** (10-22-94, Harlem Opera) called to mind older plays such as *The Two Sisters.* Like them it centered on siblings, in this case twins, who leave their rural home and come to the big city (London) to try their luck. One is virtuous; the other is not. But when they find themselves in love with the same man, the fallen girl selflessly discloses her past so that her sister can find happiness. Recognizing that her erring sister is genuinely regretful, the good sister sees to it that the penitent wins the man. Marie Wainwright played both girls.

An "obstreperous" gallery enthusiastically greeted James W. Harkins, Jr.'s **The Man Without a Country** (10-22-94, American) even if critics could find little to commend. For some reason the play was set during the Civil War. Yet its story had nothing to do with the conflict. The only real conflict in the play was between Robert Hampton (William Harcourt) and Victor Saville (E. J. Henley), who falsely accuses Robert of a crime. Robert hides in the Louisiana swamps and in New Orleans before he is able to prove Saville is the actual criminal. One big scene had Saville attempting to kill a blind child by throwing her into a sugar crusher.

Mansfield closed his fall season with his second novelty, Lorimer Stoddard's **Napoleon Bonaparte** (10-27-94, Herald Square). The play was a loosely connected chronicle moving from Tilsit, to the emperor's return from Moscow, to Elba, then to Waterloo, and finally to St. Helena. For all practical purposes Mansfield treated it as a pageant, which allowed him a tour de force. As the scenes of the action moved, Mansfield moved from comedy to melodrama to tragedy. The highlight of the evening came in his encounter with the defeated but hardly cowed Queen Louisa of Prussia (Beatrice Cameron). However much critics disdained the play, they extolled Mansfield's bravura playing. The mounting attracted capacity houses on tour, while *Arms and the Man* drew poorly.

Glen MacDonough's **Miss Dynamite** (11-5-94, Bijou) was a farce written for the comic opera favorite Marie Jansen. As such it had its share of interpolated songs (including one about John and Jane, who had never tasted champagne). The Miss Dynamite of the title does not appear in the show. Instead Georgia Day, on learning that the lady owes her hubby money, dons bright red tights and poses as the music-hall singer. Complications follow, a cake explodes, and a cuckoo clock tells more than the time before matters are resolved. The entertainment was a two-week dud.

George Hoey's **A Tale of Corsica** (11-5-94, Niblo's) was supposedly taken from an old play by d'Ennery, although the play was not identified. Its story centered on the dilemma of Father Angelo (Harry Mainhall), a priest who hears Toraldi (Hoey) confess to a murder for which the priest's brother, Mateo (Frank Lander), is about to be hanged. The priest knows he cannot violate the confessional. His agony is ended when Toraldi is killed in a duel. This allows the priest to come forward just as Mateo is being led to the scaffold. Some clergymen also came forward to point out that the priest's vow still applied, but the argument was moot, since the show folded after a single week.

Two plays with similar titles, both hinting that the latest upsurge in women's rights agitation would not soon go away, opened on the same night. One was an English play—the second in less than a month to open at a theatre that had promised a season-long slate of American dramas. Sydney Grundy's **The New Woman** (11-12-94, Palmer's) spotlights a young girl who marries above her station and discovers that her husband is pursued by an emancipated, freethinking "new" woman (a married lady, at that), but whose quiet loyalty ultimately is rewarded. The centerpiece of the evening was Annie Russell's radiant performance, which discreetly underscored both the humor and the pathos in the role. Virginia Harned was perceived as being too coquettish and insufficiently intellectual as the troublemaker, while reviews implied the ubiquitous Wilton Lackaye was playing the husband by rote and wearing out his welcome (a sentiment that would change dramatically later in the season). The play ran five weeks.

The Coming Woman (11-12-94, Fifth Ave.) packed her bags after eight performances. As a girl she ran away from home to join a circus and later established a stable of horses and suitors. The suitor she loves is an English lord, but she is blackmailed into an engagement with another man. So that he may ride to town for a license she lends him her most recalcitrant horse, and as she suspected he would be, he is thrown. The accident is not fatal, but it lets him see how determined a young lady she is. He relinquishes his claim on her. Carrie Turner, who played the lead, Kate Melton, was a good actress but not in Annie Russell's league. Moreover, there was general agreement that the play was feeble. Where there was no agreement was over who wrote the play. Despite its failure, three writers came forward to take credit for it.

Daniel Frohman suffered a major disappointment when he staged Abby Sage Richardson's translation of Sardou's **A Woman's Silence** (11-20-94, Lyceum). Its silent woman, Dorothea March (Georgia Cayvan), an American in Paris, risks social ostracism and even contemplates suicide rather than testify against her worthless brother, whom she believes guilty of the murder he has been accused of. The play was sumptuously mounted, with highly applauded Paris interiors. Miss Cayvan received almost universal praise for her sensitive, restrained performance, but whether she felt she had been saddled with too many failures or simply wanted to try her luck on her own, she left her longtime home at the Lyceum after the play finished a month's forced run.

Wilson Barrett began his latest American visit with his dramatization of Hall Caine's **The Manxman** (11-26-94, American). When Pete Quillian (Barrett) goes off to seek his fortune he leaves his sweetheart, Kate (Maud Jeffries), in the care of his friend, Philip Christian (T. W. Percyval). On his return Pete marries Kate, unaware that she is carrying Philip's child. After the child is born, Kate flees. She leaves the baby behind, feeling Pete will give it a better home. But after a time she regrets her decision. She returns to steal the child but unexpectedly encounters Pete. His goodness is brought home to her by his willingness to sacrifice his happiness for hers. William Winter called *The Manxman* "a powerful play, [made] out of a trite, though touching story" and hailed Barrett for the patent, simple humanity of his interpretation. Other critics were less receptive, noting that the Manx dialect was often unintelligible to American players and that for one reason or another playgoers snickered at odd times throughout the performance. Barrett kept the play on the boards for three weeks, then filled out the rest of his booking with *Hamlet, Claudian, Ben-My-Chree, Othello, Virginius,* and *The Silver King.*

William Gillette provided the season with its biggest hit when he turned Maurice Ordonneau's *La Plantation Thomassin* into **Too Much Johnson** (11-26-94, Standard). For those occasions when the philandering Augustus Billings (Gillette) leaves his home to entertain his French mistress in New York he has a glib story ready to foist on his wife (Maud Haslam)—he has to go to Cuba to visit his sugar plantation. His problems begin when his wife and mother-in-law (Kate Meek) decide to take a vacation and accompany him. The problems balloon after the women find an incriminating letter in his pocket. Luckily for Billings, the letter is addressed to Mr. Johnson, the name he uses when he is having an affair. He tells the ladies that Johnson is his overseer. On board is a father (Samuel Reed) who is taking his daughter (Marie Greenwald) to marry a man sight unseen. The man is named Johnson. Billings hopes to use the plantation of an old college buddy, unaware that the buddy had sold out to a cantankerous man named Johnson (Ralph Delmore), the very one who is to marry the reluctant girl. Leon Dathis (Henry Bell), the French mistress's irate husband, is also on the ship, brandishing the top half of a photograph (forehead and scalp) with which he hopes to identify his wife's lover. The action moves from the ship to the Cuban plantation before Billings's sangfroid and ingenuity get everyone out of the scrape. Since Gillette was writing for himself he incorporated his airy, staccato style into Billings's dialogue: "Suddenly remember—pocket knife! Snatched it out—cut myself loose—and fell exhausted into the ash-pan!" The *Herald* noted that the star's "assumed imperturbability was almost marvelous" and lauded both the farce and the production, finding "no horseplay in it, no exaggerated situations, no strained effects." Performed at breakneck speed against settings that had a slightly unworldly look, the production gave playgoers no time to worry about any implausibilities. The result was a run of 216 performances. The play remained a stock favorite for many years.

In the eyes of many of his followers Daly's season began late and was a major disappointment from beginning to end. Daly may have felt differently, for the season marked a major change in his thinking. Years earlier Daly had mounted some of the period's prototypical musicals, albeit with little profit. During his season-long visit to England he had recognized the advances made in musical comedy by George Edwardes and decided not only to become a major importer of the British bon-bons but to offer them as part of his program—thus allowing his stock company more time on the highly lucrative road. In September Daly had introduced American playgoers to *A Gaiety Girl*, often considered the font of much modern musical theatre. The show kept his playhouse lit until the producer brought back his regular players for a revival of *Twelfth Night* on the 26th. Ada Rehan was Viola; Sybil Carlisle, Olivia; Francis Carlyle, Orsino; Sidney Herbert, Sebastian; and James Lewis, Sir Toby Belch. As usual Miss Rehan received paragraphs of high praise, but several reviewers gave the lion's share of their notices to Henry E. Dixey's Malvolio. A few thought it was a solid, traditional interpretation, happily eschewing the broader clowning Dixey employed in musicals. Some others said precisely the opposite. The production lasted a month. Revivals and new offerings were to come and go with ominous rapidity during Daly's season.

A single scene in Henry Arthur Jones's **The Masqueraders** (12-3-94, Empire) sent shock waves through the audience and assured the play a long run. The bankrupt, ne'er-do-well Sir Brice Skene (William Faversham), a compulsive gambler and husband of Dulcie (Viola Allen), consents to cut cards ("best two out of three") with Dulcie's rich admirer, David Remon (Henry Miller). If Sir Brice wins David will hand over his fortune to the Skenes;

if David wins Sir Brice will relinquish all claims to his wife and child. As Dulcie watches, David wins; then, sensing Sir Brice may attempt to renege, he throttles him to ensure compliance. At a time when so much theatre remained presentational as well as representational, bow after bow was demanded before the players could wind up the evening. Dissenters objected to the play and especially to the big scene on moral grounds, but in a changing society and theatre their jeremiads were brushed away. *The Masqueraders* compiled 120 performances, then toured.

Rose Coghlan fared less happily when she starred in Mrs. Romualdo Pacheco's **To Nemesis: or, Love and Hate** (12-2-94, Star). She portrayed Mlle. Walanoff, née Madelon Flaubert, a rich widow who has vowed to be revenged on the Marquis d'Aumale (Henry Jewett), who years earlier had seduced and abandoned her. She contrives to involve him in a duel, in which he is seriously wounded. Only then does she discover that he is not her betrayer but rather his twin brother. Unlike many stars Miss Coghlan was willing to surround herself with skilled and attractive players. She and they walked away with whatever laurels the critics could bestow. There was praise for Cecil M. York's comically stuttering Englishman, but most of all for the ladies. The *Times* professed, "Seven handsome women, better dressed, never took part in a play in this city." The "dark brilliancy of Miss Maxine Elliott's marvelous beauty" especially delighted the reviewer. But the public proved so indifferent that after less than three weeks Miss Coghlan replaced the work with a repertory that consisted of *London Assurance, Diplomacy,* and *Forget-Me-Not.*

A melodrama designed primarily for the road, Sutton Vane's **The Cotton King** (12-3-94, Academy of Music) packed the huge house for eight weeks and subsequently spent several seasons touring profitably. Once again the hero was named Jack. Jack Osborne (Eben Plympton), the American cotton king, comes to England to buy some mills. Richard Stockley (Cuyler Hastings) tries to ruin his business and to foist the blame for a seduction on him. He manages to have him committed to an insane asylum in America. Jack escapes and returns to England in time to prevent Stockley from crushing Hetty Dawson (May Wheeler) under an elevator. A full, operating cotton mill with, naturally, a functioning freight elevator elicited applause when it was disclosed.

When Americans moved into a haunted English mansion in Oscar Wilde's *The Canterville Ghost,* their dinner small talk, "the ordinary conversation of cultured Americans of the better class," touched on such urgent matters as "the immense superiority of Miss Fanny Davenport over Sara Bernhardt as an actress." New Yorkers had another chance to debate the point when the American star appeared in Bernhardt's latest Parisian hit, Sardou's **Gismonda** (12-11-94, Fifth Ave.). Truly discerning playgoers and commentators of course held a different view than the Otises. But for many, in the case of *Gismonda,* the matter was secondary—the scenery stole the show. The play was set in Athens during Florentine rule. No fewer than five of the era's most distinguished scene painters (Joseph Clare, D. Frank Dodge, Homer Emens, Richard Marston, and Ernest Albert) combined their talents to design settings that intermingled Renaissance richness with bits of classical ruins and touches of Oriental splendor, moving the action from a luxurious palace to a forest hut. The play ended with a Palm Sunday pageant. A woman's absurd snobbery and fickleness fueled the plot. When the widowed Duchess of Athens's son is menaced by a tiger she vows to marry any man who will save him. Almerio (Melbourne MacDowell) rushes in and rescues the boy. But Gismonda, learning that he is merely a falconer and illegitimate to boot, goes back on her word. Even after he gives himself over as a hostage to prevent a revolution against her and later takes the blame for a murder she committed, she still will not have him. Only when he releases her from her vow does she decide that she loves him and that he is worthy of her. Sardou's surefire theatrics, the eye-filling production, and solid if not great acting led to an eleven-week run.

On the 15th Daly revived *Love on Crutches,* performing it for a time in repertory with *Twelfth Night.*

Another Daly's, a famed gambling establishment, was, along with the Hoffman House, a celebrated hotel and watering hole, and the 30th Street Police Station, among the settings for the kidnapping, murder, arson, and conning (called bunco steering at the time) that gripped audiences at Edmund E. Price's **In the Tenderloin** (12-17-94, People's). For a change, the villain was called Jack.

The hero in Daniel H. Scully's **Special Delivery** (12-17-94, Columbus) is a postman. His rival for the hand of the heroine murders the heroine's father and implicates the mailman, in part by planting an incriminating letter in his coat pocket. The hero escapes from jail and jumps into the Harlem River to rescue a man who can tell him and the police all about his rival's unsavory history.

Twins were one of the season's stock gimmicks. In

E. E. Kidder's **A Back Number** (12-17-94, Harlem Opera) the twins were a rural schoolmaster, Benjamin Bennett, and his brother, Shiftless Ike. Although they often seem to work at cross-purposes, their combined efforts prevent a city slicker from depriving a local lass of her inheritance. The rising William Collier played the twins. A pair of spectacles and a studied reserve marked Benjamin off from his more broadly comic sibling. When both men had to appear together, a double, who showed the audience only his back, was employed.

The Kendals came into Abbey's for a stand beginning on the 24th. They offered nothing new, content to display *Lady Clancarty, The Second Mrs. Tanqueray, A White Lie,* and *The Ironmaster.* When they returned for a short stay in April they also offered *Impulse, The Queen's Shilling,* and *A Scrap of Paper.*

On the 27th Daly brought out *The Taming of the Shrew* again. His quick turnovers were a sign Daly was not enjoying a satisfactory season.

Henry Arthur Jones's third play of the season, **The Case of the Rebellious Susan** (12-29-94, Lyceum), was his least successful in American eyes, perhaps because playgoers were tiring of stories of "modern" women. Lady Susan Harabin (Isabel Irving) discovers her husband has been unfaithful and decides that what is sauce for the gander can be sauce for the goose. She runs off to Egypt, where she has a brief affair. After she learns that her lover has wed another woman, she reaches a compromise with her husband, letting bygones be bygones. The comedy was enhanced by the fine ensemble playing of the Lyceum's stock company, with the black-haired beauty, Miss Irving, now its leading lady. It stayed at the house for ten weeks.

Playgoers could preface their New Year's Eve revels with a visit to Haddon Chambers and B. C. Stephenson's London hit **The Fatal Card** (12-31-94, Palmer's). A set depicting two offices separated by a corridor and a staircase allowed audiences to see Harry Burgess (R. A. Roberts) commit a murder and escape. He next contrives to have Gerald Austen (E. J. Ratcliffe) accused of the crime. When the accusation fails to stick, Harry ties up Gerald and places a time bomb in the room. Remembering that Gerald once did him a good turn, he loosens the bonds, lets in Gerald's fiancée, Margaret Marrable (Amy Busby), and leaves, locking the door behind him. Gerald throws the bomb out the window. It explodes, shattering glass, bringing down plaster, and killing Harry. May Robson won laughs as a pretentious spinster who returns from a canoe trip soaking wet and minus her false teeth. Like *The*

Case of the Rebellious Susan, The Fatal Card ran ten weeks.

Scott Marble's touring melodrama **Down in Dixie** (12-31-94, Columbus) made the first of several brief visits to New York to recite how the unscrupulous Abe Lampton hounds Georgia Hale, an orphaned "cracker" (backwoods) girl, who is loved by Jack Calhoun. Lampton's cohort, Alvin Curtis, blackmails his relations in a subplot. Both men are taught a lesson by the seemingly lackadaisical Squire Loundes. A "pickaninny" brass band and drill team provided diversion from the tension. The author won plaudits for his performance as Loundes, but he missed another opportunity to throw the hero or heroine into a menacing machine. In this case a huge cotton compressor was onstage. All it did was bale cotton harmlessly. Note how the heroine, like so many others, was named for her home state.

More traditional or sentimental playgoers could see the old year out with a return of *The Old Homestead,* which settled down snugly at the Star until late April.

Other touring standbys were 1895's earliest arrivals. The new year's first novelty was Émile Moreau and Sardou's **Madame Sans-Gêne** (1-14-95, Broadway). This amusing saga of a laundress-become-duchess, who prevents Napoleon from destroying her marriage by reminding him of his unpaid laundry bill, featured Kathryn Kidder and Augustus Cook in the leading roles. Possibly too Gallic for American tastes, the play was only a moderate success.

Far less lofty, but perfectly suited to the taste of theatrical backwaters, Charles E. Blaney's **A Run on the Bank** (1-14-95, Bijou) never played for more than a week in any of its New York visits. In order to court a rich man's daughter, a pair of tramps adopt the names of two noblemen lost at sea. As Lord Percy Soakup ("Happy" Ward) and Baron Harold DeCanter (Harry Vokes) they open a combination bank and bar. When a run ensues the men hire a counterfeiter to print money for them, and when this is about to be exposed they flee to San Francisco. A grand marriage ball concluded the evening. The bar portion of the bank and the ballroom both permitted the insertion of vaudeville turns.

If Daly hadn't enough problems in his rocky season, an utterly disastrous public response to his first new play of the year forced him to withdraw it after a single week. The play was **The Heart of Ruby** (1-15-95, Daly's), Justin Huntley McCarthy's adaptation of Judith Gautier's *La Marchande de sourires,* in which a Japanese courtesan's attempt to reform and lead a respectable life comes to a tragic end. Daly's canvas-and-paint Japan was highly admired, especially a scene showing a moonlit garden with a pond filled with lotus flowers. (Critics gave varying lists of the garden's other blossoms.) But Daly unwisely kept most of his popular performers offstage. Only Ada Rehan was present, and she was confined to acting as an intermittent commentator. One addition to the producer's roster was Maxine Elliott (this time, one reviewer called her "surely the most beautiful woman on the stage"). The following week Daly rushed in a revival of *The Railroad of Love.*

"Muckraking" was not yet part of the American idiom, yet Charles Klein and Harrison Gray Fiske's **The District Attorney** (1-21-95, American) certainly foreshadowed it. The *Dramatic Mirror* (owned by Fiske) required three long paragraphs to detail the plot. More briefly stated, it tells how the corrupt political boss, Matthew Brainerd (Frank Mordaunt), pushes his daughter, Grace (Annie Irish), to marry the young, idealistic district attorney, John Stratton (Wilton Lackaye), in hopes of bringing him under his thumb. His ploy fails. Instead, encouraged by Grace and aided by a crusading journalist who has been elected to the state legislature, Stratton interrogates a young man who has been framed and imprisoned by the machine and uncovers the evidence he needs to prosecute the politicians. Since well-written interrogation scenes, strongly worded confrontations between good and evil, and touching encounters between family members on the opposite sides of an issue are usually surefire onstage, *The District Attorney* was rattling good theatre. The *Times,* turning jingoist, added, "Such plays appeal more strongly to this community than foreign pieces full of allusions to Trafalgar Square, 'Ounsditch, and ' 'arf-and-'arf.' " The appeal lasted for only five weeks at the huge auditorium. (The *Dramatic Mirror* said the uncredited staging was reputedly by Mrs. Fiske.)

Herbert Beerbohm Tree was to many Englishmen Irving's logical successor. In London he had taken over the Haymarket Theatre, where it soon became evident that he was following in the "sumptuously illustrative Lyceum tradition" of mounting. (His long career at His Majesty's Theatre was still in the future.) In many ways his playing was like Irving's. Weak at truly tragic figures, he throve when portraying all manner of eccentrics. He was over six feet tall and slim, with red hair and blue eyes. For his American debut at Abbey's Theatre on January 28 he presented a double bill. W. Outram Tristam's **The Red Lamp** was the latest in a long line of contemporary dramas or melodramas dealing with Russia and her nihilists; Walter Besant and Walter Pollock's **The**

Ballad Monger was a new version of *Gringoire,* which Americans had seen in several other translations. His only other novelty was not all that novel either, since Sydney Grundy's **A Bunch of Violets,** offered two nights later, was an English redaction of *Montjoye,* which had entertained Americans in 1877 as *The Man of Success. Captain Swift, The Merry Wives of Windsor,* and *Hamlet* rounded out his bills. Critics saw him as a polished, intelligent actor, but he was never to enjoy the adulation accorded Irving in this country by the theatregoing public.

Nothing was working for Daly in this ill-starred season. His double bill of **The Orient Express** (1-31-95, Daly's), F. C. Burnand's translation of Blumenthal and Kadelburg's *Orientreise,* and his revival of *A Tragedy Rehearsed* drew flattering notices and sparse attendance. In the former Hettie Featherston (Ada Rehan) reads that her traveling husband, Robert (Frank Worthing), and "his wife" are being held by bandits who stopped and robbed a train in Greece. Of course, everything is explained away in the last act (hubby had sold the spare ticket, which had been issued in his wife's name). James Lewis and Mrs. Gilbert drew curtain calls for their portrayal of the sort of couple they had portrayed time and again, a henpecked husband and his sharp-beaked hen. The restaging of the Sheridan comedy permitted Henry E. Dixey as Mr. Puff and Lewis as Don Whiskerandos to have fun departing from the text to twit each other's acting styles playfully.

In Sutton Vane's **Humanity** (2-4-95, 14th St.), set in South Africa, Major Fordyce Dangerfield (Frazer Coulter), a corrupt and eventually demented war correspondent, tries to bribe a Jewish money-lender, Manasses Marks (Dore Davidson) to ruin Lt. Bevis Cranbourne (Joseph R. Grismer). The Major then hopes to be able to marry the lieutenant's betrothed, Alma Dunbar (Phoebe Davies). Marks refuses, so Dangerfield lures the hero to an old house, stuns him, ties him to a post, places a bomb beside him, lights the fuse, and exits. The heroine, who happens to be on the roof, hears her lover's cries for help and uses a rifle to batter down the door. As in *The Fatal Card,* the hero throws the bomb out the window. It explodes, collapsing the wall but leaving Cranbourne and his girl unharmed. Not until they all return to London is the villain finally routed. More excitement was provided by a duel on horseback, while sentiment and humor were found in the person of the Jew's smiling little boy, Ikey—who was played by a winningly smiling little girl, Sadie Price. If *Humanity*'s first New York stand lasted only a month, it came back periodically during its years of touring.

William Haworth's **On the Mississippi** (2-4-95,

People's) also toured for many seasons. Despite its title, its action began in Tennessee's Walden Mountains and ended on Lookout Mountain. Only the middle three acts occurred on or near the river. The *Dramatic Mirror* summed up the most exciting scenes in this saga of Virginia Tyson's misguided marriage and her eventual rescue by Ned Raymond as a "Ku Klux Klan outrage, a mob's attack on a jail, a shooting in a gambling house and other harrowing details of lawless life along the Mississippi." Haworth apparently had run out of derricks and pile drivers. During the second act, which took place on a river levee, a group of black youngsters entertained with songs and dances.

Alfred H. Spink, the author of **The Derby Winner** (2-4-95, Columbus), was described by one newspaper as a "well-known Western racing man," which no doubt accounts for the subject of his play and may explain why it was more popular beyond the Alleghenies than it was in the East. It opened with an unusual setting, Grant's log cabin near St. Louis. There Alice Noble stalks off when she hears that Milt West loves one Missouri Girl. She is unaware that Missouri Girl is a race horse. If the horse doesn't win at the St. Louis Fair Grounds Race Course, Milt will be bankrupt. Jack Wright, a slippery, "darkbrowed" bookie, tries to bribe the jockey to throw the race. However, by this time Alice has learned the truth. At gunpoint Alice locks away the jockey and mounts the horse herself. She outrides a field of six other horses (on treadmills, naturally). The celebration in the last act was filled with songs and dances. Scenes at the racetrack were said to duplicate faithfully the real St. Louis course.

Although Oliver Doud Byron and his wife, Kate, were the stars of F. A. Scudmore's **Ups and Downs of Life** (2-11-95, People's), a drama about a marriage in jeopardy, they did not play the married couple. The difficulties arise in the marriage of Vivian (Byron) and Constance Ransome (Florence Stone) when Constance attempts to shield her dissolute brother. To Kate fell the role of June Judkins, an Irish serving girl who advertises for a mate in *Cupid's Dart*. The play was not one of the Byrons' bigger hits, but it toured for about a year.

Two weeks later Charles Frohman began counting his profits from the fourteen-week run of E. M. Robson and William Lestocq's **The Foundling** (2-25-95, Hoyt's). It wangled laughs from the slimmest of plots. Dick Pennell (S. Miller Kent) is a foundling who decides to seek out his parents. He finds plenty of mothers but no fathers. Songs and dances covered up the slow spots. No fewer than four different curtain raisers were tried out during the run, the

most successful of which was Augustus Thomas's **The Man Upstairs** (4-9-95, Hoyt's). Even less of a plot—no more than a mistaken identity—served this shorter piece. A newly hired cook thinks a man who enters the apartment is her new employer. Actually, the man is the upstairs neighbor, who, for farcical purposes, can't recognize that the furniture isn't his.

His Wife's Father (2-25-95, Fifth Ave.), advertised as being taken from an unidentified L'Arronge play by Martha Morton, opened on the same night and ran precisely as long. The play had been adapted as a vehicle for W. H. Crane and gave him his biggest hit in years. Buchanan Billings (Crane) is a rich widower who turns over his home to his recently married daughter and his butchering business to his new son-in-law. Billings's well-meaning but incessant unsolicited advice and interference finally drive the newlyweds to a home of their own. (And this, of course, provides a splendid third-act curtain with Billings sitting dismayed and alone in a room emptied of everything except his own portrait.) However, there were four acts. So when the incorrigible Billings follows the pair to their new home, the son-in-law hits upon the only solution to get the old man out of their hair. That solution comes in the form of an attractive middle-aged widow. The part of Billings suited Crane's homespun, avuncular style to a tee, and he kept it in his repertory for several seasons.

The Two Gentlemen of Verona had not been given a major mounting in New York for forty-nine years. At any time it was a risky proposition, and for Daly to bring it out, on the 25th, near the end of a singularly bad season seems foolhardy. His reward was one more costly disappointment. As usual with Daly, the mounting was gorgeous. Minstrels in pleasure boats crossed a moonlit lake as they sang "Who Is Sylvia?" A brilliant electrical storm lit up the final scene. But Daly's distortions of the text in order to amplify Julia's role for Ada Rehan merely led to obfuscation of a story that is not always easy to follow as it stands. Nor could the actors get proper handles on often thankless parts. The audience on opening night was encouraging, but when attendance quickly fell Daly began to alternate the Shakespearean comedy with a revival of *Nancy and Company*.

If, at least in America, Herbert Beerbohm Tree was forever consigned to linger in Irving's shadow, so Réjane was overshadowed by Sarah Bernhardt. Tree and Irving were not all that dissimilar, but whereas Bernhardt excelled at drama (perhaps more accurately, melodrama and pseudo-tragedy), Réjane was at her best in comedy. Réjane, whose real name was Gabrielle-Charlotte Réju, was a small, lithe, ordinary-looking woman given to quick speech and quick movement. She and her company from Paris's Vaudeville Theatre wisely began with *Madame Sans-Gêne,* and the response was such that most of her season was devoted to it. Also in the schedule were Henri Meilhac's *Ma Cousine,* Alphonse Daudet and Adolphe Belot's *Sapho,* Meilhac's *Lolotte* (a one-acter written for Réjane), and two older plays, *Divorçons* and *Maison de poupée.* More than one partisan critic gloated publicly that this last work drew pathetically small attendance in contrast to the generally good box office for the other plays. But then to such men *A Doll's House* by any name was despicable.

A divorced woman's brave struggle to prevent an impetuous friend from leaving a happy home and running off with a lover provided the tensions in Clyde Fitch and Leo Ditrichstein's **Gossip** (3-11-95, Palmer's), which the authors acknowledged had been suggested by Jules Clarétie's *Monsieur le ministre.* The play had been created as a vehicle for Lillie Langtry, so while reviewers took time out in their notices to mention that it was well crafted, the piece took second place to their observations about the star. The consensus was that her acting had improved, her beauty was as compelling as ever, and her gowns and jewels (including a coronet of diamonds and a diamond and ruby brooch) would be the envy of all the ladies in the audience. The actress was careful to see that the play was given an attractive mounting. A scene set on the beach at Trouville earned a particularly fervent round of applause. Her fine supporting cast included Effie Shannon as the erring wife and Eben Plympton as the wife's lover. But for all the thoughful work that went into the play and all its encouraging notices, it ran a mere three weeks.

Like Daly and Palmer, albeit to a somewhat lesser extent, Daniel Frohman was going through a disappointing season. His latest setback came when he introduced New Yorkers to Oscar Wilde's **An Ideal Husband** (3-12-95, Lyceum). The tale of a gentleman whose one early lapse from grace comes back to haunt his marriage received mixed reviews. It was, after all, second-drawer Wilde. But reading between the lines of polite, perfunctory commendation for the cast raises the suspicion that Frohman's players could not quite catch the tone the playwright required.

Daniel's brother Charles fared no better with Haddon Chambers's **John-a-Dreams** (3-18-95, Empire), which dealt with the understandably trouble-plagued romances of a drug addict (an "opium-eater") and a woman with a past but a heart of gold. Commentators not upset by the moral implications of the play were upset by its unremitting dullness. Most kind words were reserved for the players, led by Henry Miller and Viola Allen, and for E. G. Unitt's fine settings, especially "a schooner yacht in motion under mainsail and forestaysail, with a moving panorama of Southampton harbor, with its lights and a moonlit sea in the background."

The Saturday night after the Empire Theatre's latest premiere, the 23rd, Niblo's closed its doors. At the time it was New York's oldest playhouse still devoted to plays in English. The slightly older Bowery Theatre still stood, although it long since had been renamed and given over to foreign-language entertainments.

Mrs. Potter and her leading man, Kyrle Bellew, paid a month-long visit to the Herald Square, beginning on the 25th. They opened with **Charlotte Corday,** which was written by Bellew under the pen name of J. C. Montesquison. Bellew surprised many by abandoning his prettified strutting to portray a pale, emaciated, filthy, pimply, and hacking Marat. His drama, conceded by critics to be a crowd-pleaser, had Charlotte Corday see herself as a biblical Judith, with Marat as Holofernes. The pair also brought out *Francillon* and, when they returned later in the season to the American, *Thérèse Raquin.*

Daly suffered another distressing failure when he was forced to pull **A Bundle of Lies** (3-28-95, Daly's) after a single week. The farce, taken from the German, detailed the misfiring attempts of Washington Brownie (James Lewis) to stop his harridan wife from lording it over him about a bad debt. He has two old friends pretend to repay the money. His ruse fails because (1) the friends happen to be married to his wife's nieces, who pick that moment to pay a visit, and (2) the debt has already been paid back quietly to Mrs. Brownie (Mrs. Gilbert). Daly felt the failure could be ascribed to the play's stock characters and stock situations, although both had served him so well and so long. Tastes were changing.

Murder and merriment were combined in Murphy O'Hea's **Garry Owen** (4-1-95, Grand Opera). Spurned by Nora (or Mona) Conway, Stephen Purcell murders a Protestant minister and fastens the blame on Nora's brother, a priest. To save the priest, Nora's suitor, Garry Owen, professes to have been the killer. He is exonerated in time for a happy ending. But before that romantic finish, Maggie Cline, a well-known vaudeville singer, offered songs, and other variety artists presented jigs and a bagpipe specialty.

The central figures in William Richard Goodall's **The Two Colonels** (4-2-95, Palmer's) had been enemies during the Civil War but eventually had become close friends. When Colonel Sloane (Frank Mordaunt), a Virginian, comes to Vermont to visit Colonel Whittaker (George C. Staley), he learns that Whittaker's son, Ralph (Charles S. Abbe), has been accused of stealing bonds from the bank in which he works and that the elder Whittaker believes that the accusations probably are justified. Sloane helps prove Ralph's innocence, and then they all set out for Virginia, where Ralph marries Charlotte Sloane (Georgia Welles) on her father's plantation. An old minstrel favorite, Willis P. Sweatnam, stole several scenes as a faithful "darky" retainer, not above shuffling to an old minstrel tune. But the play itself was mediocre and departed after two weeks.

On the opening night of George Hoey's **The Pace That Kills** (4-2-95, 14th St.), the newest in the growing list of racing melodramas, a near panic was averted after several horses knocked down "bushes" in a steeplechase and tumbled one over the other. The story leading up to the incident begins when worthless Richard Fielding kidnaps Blossom Herrick, daughter of the trainer, Stephen Herrick, and then persuades a Jewish money-lender, Sim Sylvester, to foreclose on Herrick's properties. Edward Herrick, who is supposed to be Stephen's adopted son, attends the auction and buys Blossom, who has been named after Stephen's daughter. He races the horse in the Grand National, and, of course, it wins. Edward then is revealed as the real heir to the Fielding estate and Richard shown to be an imposter.

At Daly's the producer revived John Tobin's old *The Honeymoon* on the 4th, with no more luck than any of his other nonmusicals had enjoyed during the season.

When Beerbohm Tree returned on the 8th to Abbey's he braved some possible brickbats by opening with Ibsen's **An Enemy of the People.** By this time sides had been drawn sharply between those who favored Ibsen and the anti-Ibsenites. Yet the actor-producer must have been gratified not only when he and his production were lauded, but when the play itself was not subject to the vituperation so many other Ibsen works had been (and would continue to be) subjected to. (Winter possibly did not write the *Tribune* notice, since he later claimed not to have seen the play until 1905.) Even so, the star was cautious enough to offer only one performance. The rest of his week he spent on remountings of the plays he had performed earlier in the year.

Daly closed his season with his remounting of *A Midsummer Night's Dream* on the 13th. It corralled enthusiastic notices and did some of the best business Daly had seen in months. Unfortunately, Daly already had announced his season would end in late April, so there was little chance for him to reap much profit for his belated success.

John C. Dixon, who a few weeks earlier had played a major role in *The Pace That Kills,* was a featured player in and author of **The Queen of Night** (4-13-95, 14th St.). Dixon's preposterous plot focused on a wife who, in order to prevent a duel between her husband and a man who has attacked her, attempts to shoot her attacker. When it seems she has shot and killed her husband by mistake, she runs away and is adopted by a band of gypsies. Both her husband, who was not actually killed, and the villain seek her out and find her. She pushes the villain off a cliff, but he clings to a bush just long enough to assure her husband of his wife's total innocence. Apparently such absurdity was too much for playgoers, and the play is said to have been removed from the stage in midweek.

The season's most memorable success was **Trilby** (4-15-95, Garden), taken by Paul M. Potter from George Du Maurier's novel. It was, in fact, one of those shows that was virtually an assured hit before it opened. Word from Boston had been so exciting that crowds jammed the lobby hoping for cancellations, and scalpers were having a field day. Trilby O'Ferrall (Virginia Harned), a Scotch-Irish waif, has grown up in Paris, where her boozy parents drank themselves to death. She darts about in a striped dress and a threadbare, oversized army coat, and whenever possible she darts about barefoot. The girl is the pet of three more expatriates, who share bohemian digs. Talbot Wynne is better known as Taffy (Burr McIntosh); Alexander McAlister is called the Laird (John Glendenning); and William Bagot goes by the nickname Little Billee (Alfred Hickman). When Trilby is not eking out a few sous by serving as an artist's model, she runs the boys' errands, cooks their dinners, and mends their clothes. Naturally, all three young men have fallen in love with her, and all three intend to propose. But when they learn that Trilby prefers Little Billee the other two defer to him. Just then Little Billee's illusions are shattered by the discovery that Trilby has posed in the "altogether." He plans to run away. At the last minute his heart won't let him, so he returns, prepared to accept Trilby as she is.

His return might have led to a quick, happy ending were it not for a shabby, malevolent Jewish mesmerist. The mesmerist has found out that Trilby has a breathtakingly beautiful voice, although for some reason she cannot or will not sing. He hypnotizes Trilby, puts in a few viciously destructive words about her when he meets Billee's mother and uncle, forces Trilby, again under hypnosis, to write Billee a farewell note, and takes her away. Five years later they return to Paris. Trilby now carries his name and is a famous singer. And the mesmerist is rich, and decked out accordingly. But the strain of keeping the girl under his evil spell takes its toll, and he suddenly dies. Freed from the mesmerist's sinister influence, Trilby is once again simply Trilby. Billee remains anxious to marry her. However, when a mysterious figure delivers a portrait of the mesmerist, Trilby sees it, falls in a faint, and dies. There were hosannas for all the cast. Miss Harned was hailed for her unaffected, beguiling depiction of the innocent girl. The three bohemians were made up to resemble Du Maurier's descriptions and published drawings of them and were carefully differentiated by the performers. But the sensation of the evening was the villainous hypnotist, Svengali. Wilton Lackaye's performance in the role made him a star overnight.

. . .

Wilton Lackaye (1862–1932) was born in Loudon County, Va., and educated at Georgetown University. He no sooner left the school than he obtained a part in Lawrence Barrett's revival of *Francesca da Rimini*. Among his early assignments was the treacherous revolutionary Gouroc in *Paul Kauvar*. He remained a busy, prominent player, but one who always narrowly missed grabbing the brass ring until Svengali came his way. From then on he was a prominent light, appearing in important new plays and major revivals until shortly before his death. He returned on many occasions to Svengali, the role with which he was hereafter identified.

. . .

Several critics thought that Lackaye came on too strong, painting the hypnotist's coarse yet unctuous villainy with overly bold strokes, but they confessed that by evening's end they, too, had been hypnotized by his portrayal. His death scene, in which he fell back on a table with his head hanging down and his open eyes staring out at the audience, evoked thunderous applause. Pictures of him with his unkempt long hair, scraggly beard, low thick brows, and penetrating glare imprinted themselves on a generation of playgoers. Critics also praised the deft adaptation by Potter.

. . .

Paul M[eredith] Potter (1853–1921) was born in England. His real name was said to have been either

Walter McEwen or McLean. He worked as a journalist before a scandal forced him to leave England and settle in America under a new name. Although he tried his hand at a variety of plays, the success of *Trilby* prompted him to devote the rest of his career largely to dramatizing novels.

. . .

Trilby ran for over six months and sent out numerous road companies. It was revived regularly and long remained a standard in stock. In the 1920s a musical version folded during its tryout.

The dramatization of another famous novel had less luck, although Frank Mayo's version of **Pudd'nhead Wilson** (4-15-95, Herald Square) was by no means a failure. Mark Twain's story of an eccentric lawyer whose fascination with fingerprinting leads him to unravel an old case of baby-switching and send a worthless "white nigger" down the river at the same time the real heir is restored to his rightful place, was excellently mounted and cast. The scene of the Driscolls' yard, with its view of the Mississippi, and the exterior of a ruined mill earned special praise. Mayo himself assumed the title role, while E. L. Davenport was the murderous Chambers (although in the play the judge is wounded, not killed), E. J. Henley was Tom, and Mary Shaw was Roxy. Such future celebrities as Harry Davenport, Lucille LaVerne, and Adolf Klauber had supporting roles. The play's problem was that it was episodic, never achieving the incessant, crescendoing tension of *Trilby*. Yet it proved pleasing enough to run six weeks and provide a popular touring attraction for many years.

Meanwhile, houses catering to other touring attractions also had novelties to offer. Will R. Wilson's **The Police Inspector** (4-15-95, People's) took patrons to the Battery, the 13th Street Police Station, and Billy McGlory's dive.

In Leonard Grover and Clay M. Greene's **The Vale of Avoca** (4-15-95, Columbus) a worthy Irish lad's sweetheart is lured by a caddish adventurer from her homeland to Colorado, where she is soon deserted. The lad follows and, after saving her from lecherous miners and treacherous Indians, finally weds her. Saving the heroine did not take all that long, so the hero also restores a mine to its real owner and reunites a long-separated father and son.

That arthritic theatrical device, an absurd will, precipitated the complications in **Fortune** (4-16-95, Lyceum), which Frederick Horner took from Adolphe Belot's *Le Testament de César Giradot*. In this instance the will stipulates that the presumptive heirs must vote to give the inheritance to just one of their group. When chicanery mars the balloting, a clause in the will allows the money to go to a pair of young lovers, for whom the audience was rooting from the start. The piece was a two-week failure.

Edward E. Rose and Alfred M. de Lisser's **Captain Paul** (4-22-95, 14th St.), taken from a Dumas story, was a swashbuckler that seemed to fit its star, Robert Hilliard, like the proverbial glove. As skipper of the American ship *Ranger,* he had to fight foreign malefactors (dueling with two at once), show how much he could drink without getting drunk, and save a beleaguered American heroine. The ship was shown under full sail, with the wind in the sails coming from offstage electric fans "capable of delivering 100,000 cubic feet of air per minute." At one point a cannonade blasted the mainsail to smithereens. Another effect, more standard, was a cliff seen by moonlight. The New York run was short, and Hilliard let another actor take the play on tour.

In Frank Harvey's **Fallen Among Thieves** (4-22-95, People's) Hester Hawthorne is lured from a happy farmstead and the prospect of a good marriage by the deceptive Roderick Maxwell. She is saved from further degradation when she stumbles on her long-lost mother. However chilly its New York welcome, the play was embraced by the touring circuits for several seasons.

On that same night the younger Salvini began a short stay at the Grand Opera with a repertory that offered only *The Three Guardsmen* and *Hamlet.*

But the most important opening of the evening, at least by later lights, was unquestionably Oscar Wilde's **The Importance of Being Earnest** (4-22-95, Empire). Yet modern playgoers would be aghast at its initial reception. The *World*'s banner read "WILDE'S NEW PLAY NO GO," and its review allowed for only a single bright act. The *Evening Post* condemned it as "laborious." The *Times* dismissed it as "a burlesque comedy in the manner of W. S. Gilbert's 'Engaged' and 'Tom Cobb' and 'Fogarty's Fairy,' or Sydney Rosenfeld's 'A Possible Case.' And it does not compare favorably with any one of those plays." The critic then filled out his review by citing nearly two dozen of Wilde's epigrams and commenting, "They do not seem very smart in print, do they?" The *Herald,* echoing the sentiment, noted, "A whimsical story is . . . the string on which are threaded a series of sham brilliants in the way of epigrams." But then the paper may have put its finger on the reason for such all but universal disdain when it observed, "A fairly appreciative audience . . . greeted it, but not a very large one. The present unpopularity of Mr. Wilde's personality has evidently stigmatized the play."

Unfortunately for everyone concerned, the play opened just as Wilde's infamous London trial was making sensational headlines.

Charles Frohman's fine cast included Henry Miller as Jack, William Faversham as Algernon, Viola Allen as Gwendolen, Ida Vernon as Lady Bracknell, and May Robson as Miss Prism. Because of the scandal or for whatever reason, this so-good-on-paper cast may not have had its heart in it. The *Evening Post* spoke for several papers when it deemed the acting competent but not brilliant. The public reacted to such icy greetings by staying away, so this farce about snobberies and pretensions—and about the importance of having a name your sweetheart prefers—ended the Empire Theatre company's regular season (apart from some hastily returned mountings) on a distinctly down note. The play closed after two weeks—ever to be revived again.

The next night Richard Mansfield brought back *Arms and the Man* to initiate a spring season of repertory. But in doing so he earned the enmity of many Broadway regulars, since he opened the play at his "new" theatre. The theatre had been built by the beloved Harrigan and called Harrigan's. Mansfield had promised to retain the name and immediately broke his promise by renaming it the Garrick. Within a year or so he was to commit an ever baser perfidy.

Typical of a circus atmosphere that often prevailed in the contemporary theatre, where prizefighters and bridge jumpers were billed as stars, was the arrival of the elder Salvini's famous vehicle, *Samson,* at the People's Theatre on the 29th. Its "star" was no actor but a famous, muscle-bound strong man of the day, Walter Kennedy.

When Mansfield brought out his only novelty of the spring season, Louis N. Parker's **The King of Peru** (5-7-95, Garrick), he further raised some hackles by calling the premiere a "public dress rehearsal," all the while charging full prices. The play dealt with a mother-dominated, financially irresponsible pretender to the Peruvian throne, who lives in London, marries a rich merchant's daughter, squanders her fortune, and finally accepts reality by taking on a paying job (as fencing master) and renouncing his claim to the nonexistent throne. Mansfield quickly dropped the drama from his bills.

Another quick closing was B. C. Stephenson and William Yardley's **The Passport** (5-13-95, Bijou). It was based on Savage's *My Official Wife,* and New Yorkers had seen an earlier version under that title in 1893. The play shut down in midweek, when its producer-star, Sadie Martinot, told the cast she could not pay their salaries.

Russ Whythal's **For Fair Virginia** (6-3-95, Fifth Ave.) introduced a modest twist in Civil War dramas. No soon to be married lovers or old friends find themselves on opposing sides. Instead a husband and wife are torn apart. The play's title, as a synopsis of the drama shows, was something of a pun. To please his southern wife, Virginia (Marie Knowles Whythal), Edward Esmond (Edward J. Morgan) has bought and overseen a Virginia plantation. However, when the war breaks out he feels he must fight for the Union. She is left to look after the property. The Confederates, commanded by John Laughlin (Whythal), occupy the house. Laughlin once had courted Virginia and now threatens to destroy the plantation unless she will become his mistress. Union troops, with Edward at their head, come to the rescue minutes before the final curtain. Critics noted that the war provided hardly any background for the production, serving merely as an excuse to get the husband out of the house. The rest of the play was simply not-so-good old-fashioned melodrama. Although the play lingered only a week, it held the boards in road houses for several seasons.

So did Hal Reid's **Logan's Luck** (6-3-95, People's), which soon changed its title to *Human Hearts*. Tim (or Tom) Logan (Reid) has married a cynical adventuress, Jeanette. She goads Frederic Armsdale into killing Logan's father and pinning the blame on Logan. The action moves from an Arkansas blacksmith shop to Chicago before Logan can exculpate himself.

Probably the most interesting of the season's last nonmusical entries was the American debut of Janet Achurch, a beautiful English actress whom Shaw had hailed as England's finest tragedian and an "untamed genius." Unfortunately for her subsequent career, she was also an alcoholic and a drug addict. She arrived on the 3rd at Hoyt's with little fanfare, and in her lone week (her only American appearance) she gave a double bill—of *Forget-Me-Not* coupled with Langdon Mitchell's **In a Season**—and *A Doll's House*. Her rich, deep voice and elegance appealed to critics in the opening bill, but their assessment of her Nora clearly depended on their feelings about Ibsen. Anti-Ibsenites were not able to separate the two.

As usual, all though the season revivals and returns kept houses lit. They ranged from recent hits to such older works as *Rosedale, The Shaughraun, Paul Kauvar,* and the seemingly indestructible *Uncle Tom's Cabin.*

1895–1896

Recovery from the panic of 1893 had been remarkably swift. By late summer of 1895 business was rosy almost everywhere, and theatrical columns, offering their predictions for the new season, were universally optimistic. The *Dramatic Mirror* echoed a prevailing sentiment when it prophesied that the new theatrical year would be one of the best ever, though it quickly added "from a pecuniary point of view." One sign of resurgence did not sit well with all crystal-ball readers. Four major theatres announced, virtually in unison, that they intended to raise the top ticket price from $1.50, where it had been since the Civil War, to $2.00. Their reasoning was that higher prices would make theatregoing "higher toned." Dissenters dismissed such rationalization as self-serving. But their cries were lost in a swelling of production records and the building of new playhouses. What even the gloomiest dissenters could not see was that four managements simultaneously announcing higher prices was a small harbinger of another development, for during this new season the organization that came to be known as the Theatrical Syndicate (or Trust) was formed. Of course, it was merely one more contemporary instance of an attempt at monopolization in business, and both contemporaries and historians would argue its merits and demerits ever after. But its motivations were entirely commercial. The men who formed the syndicate professed to be interested in making money by rectifying ills stemming from a largely chaotic system of booking. In all the talk of monopoly and pecuniary points of view, precious little was mentioned about the quality of the writing and staging. And in fact, as far as quality was concerned, the theatre was distinctly bearish.

The season began in the middle of a hot spell, so advertisements for Eugene Bertram and Bassett Willard's **The Engineer** (8-18-95, People's) promised patrons would be "cooled by electric fans." They also promised an "exciting engine room scene," the "Plumbville cornet band," a "great July 4th celebration," and the "Village Church Choir." What they failed to mention was yet another plot in which the hero is falsely accused by his rival for the heroine's affections. The soubrette role was played by an as yet unknown Eva Tanguay. Since these touring melodramas regularly featured some songs and dances, the future queen of vaudeville probably did a turn or two, but critics took no more notice of her than they did of the play.

A switch from melodrama to farce brought no improvement. Edward Owings Towne's **Other People's Money** (8-19-95, Hoyt's) was set in Chicago, where it was first produced. Its story of an obdurate father duped by a prospective son-in-law was old hat. Naive construction and disappointing performances did nothing to help matters. The rich, blindered father is Hutchinson Hopper (Charles Dickson), who has vowed that his daughter, Marjory (Georgia Welles), will make a suitable society marriage. When his clerk, Oliver Starbird (Aubrey Boucicault), tells him the sad tale of a poor young man in love with a wealthy girl, Hopper agrees to advise the poor young man on how to steal the girl away from her home—in return for 5 percent of her dowry. He counsels tricking the girl into an elopement. Oliver gets Marjory to elope with him and, in the end, gives back to the flabbergasted Hopper 5 percent of the dowry he had promised his daughter. Dickson was a jack of many theatrical trades (actor, author, director, producer) and master of none. Several critics pounced on Hopper as a natural part for the likes of W. H. Crane. Unfortunately, Dickson was no Crane, so the play was withdrawn after two weeks.

The season's first hit came, as did a disproportionate number of the era's successes, from London. There it had been called *The Derby Winner,* but since an American play with a similar story had usurped the title, the Drury Lane melodrama was rechristened for American audiences **The Sporting Duchess** (8-29-95, Academy of Music). The duchess saves a fellow nobleman from bankruptcy and disgrace by outbidding the villain when the nobleman's prize stud is put up for auction. However, she does so only on the condition that the earl's handsome friend will marry her. The play was deemed "mouldy with age" and its star, Agnes Booth, wasted. But Charles Frohman's fine production, which offered a splashy military ball, a horse auction, and, of course, another treadmilled race, saved the day. The play packed its huge auditorium until late winter and toured for several seasons.

Frohman was less lucky with another importation. **The City of Pleasure** (9-2-95, Empire) was George R. Sims's adaptation of *Gigolette* by Adrien and Pierre Decourcelle and Edmund Tarbé. It dealt with the plight of several half-sisters, and it was gone after three weeks.

Harry and Edward Paulton's **A Man With a Past** (9-2-95, Garrick) fared no better. E. M. Holland and his brother, Joseph, were starred as totally disparate cousins. To please his wife, whose mother has filled her with absurd notions of a bachelor's life, the staid cousin appropriates his rakish cousin's history, and the complications set in.

The only new American play to open that same busy night, W. A. Tremayne and Logan Fuller's **Lost—24 Hours** (9-2-95, Hoyt's), also ran three weeks, but it enjoyed an afterlife of several seasons on the road. It, too, resorted to an old farcical cliché. After a night on the town, Dick Swift (Robert Hilliard) sleeps for a whole day without realizing it. So when his wife, Mildred (Maud White), returns on what seems to him a day ahead of schedule, she finds him in the arms of a beautiful lady in a red and black dress. That lady is Mrs. Bertha Dacre (Madeleine Bouton). She was an old flame of his, and the hug is really very innocent. However, the flustered Dick introduces her as his sister. Naturally, one lie leads to others, and when Dick's strait-laced brother, David (Grant Stewart), attempts to sidestep Dick's prevarications, his truthfulness only pours more hot water on the situation. Hilliard was a handsome and technically competent actor, but his comic skills were second to Stewart's and Miss Bouton's. They stole most of the laughs. Harry Rogers, in another role fast becoming a cliché, the Jewish pawnbroker, also garnered a fair share of the guffaws.

Initially, the play was coupled with a curtain raiser, **The Littlest Girl,** which Hilliard took from a Richard Harding Davis short story, *Her First Appearance.* In it a man-about-town persuades the father of a tot, whose dead mother had been an unfaithful wife to him, to take back and rear the child. Critics stated that the piece was extremely true to the original, even to employing much of Davis's dialogue, but they neglected to comment on the story's strong stand against theatre people. On its subsequent tour the longer farce was renamed, unimaginatively, *A New Yorker.*

The string of credits for **The Queen's Necklace** (9-3-95, Daly's) read like one of the credit catalogues that Hollywood became so prone to in its heyday. Decourcelle's drama, which had been taken from the novel of Dumas père, had been translated by the English critic and playwright Clement Scott, then adapted by Charles Henry Meltzer, and finally "freely revised" by Kyrle Bellew. Its story of how Cardinal de Rohan was duped, by the use of a double, to trick Marie Antoinette into authorizing the purchase of a bejewelled pendant was well known, so the necklace was not of prime importance to playgoers and critics. What counted most was seeing Mrs. Brown Potter model one beautiful gown after another as she portrayed both the willful, whimsical queen and her kittenish look-alike. For all his revisions Bellew failed to provide an interesting role for himself as the cardinal. However, the production remained in the stars' repertory all season. After its month-long run, its tour included a brief return stand in March.

The third night (Wednesday) of this busy week saw the premieres of two more plays destined for long years of popularity. One was Edward M. Alfriend and A. C. Wheeler's **The Great Diamond Robbery** (9-4-95, American). When Mrs. Bulford (Blanche Walsh) learns that her husband has gained possession of the fabulous and missing Garbiadoff jewels, she poisons him to gain ownership of them. Years before, she had helped a notorious thief steal them, only to be cheated out of her share. Frank Kennett (Orrin Johnson), a young clerk who has been falsely accused of embezzlement, comes to plead with Mr. Bulford (George Boniface) not to press charges, and the murderess manages to make it seem that Frank is the poisoner. He flees, is shanghaied on a ship bound for South America, but escapes and arrives at the house of his fiancée, Mary Lavelot (Katherine Grey). There he meets Dick Brummage (W. H. Thompson), a detective assigned to the murder case. To Frank's relief, Dick is certain that Mrs. Bulford is the killer. However, he is under pressure from corrupt police officials to bring in Frank. He tells the young lovers, "We've got a big fight, but if you'll be steered by Dick Brummage, we will run the real culprit to earth." Dick's plan is to place Mary in Mrs. Bulford's household as a maid. He himself will take on the guise of a local delivery boy, and Mary can slip messages to him whenever he appears at the door. The crafty villainess becomes suspicious of Mary and arranges for the notorious Mother Rosenbaum (Fanny Janauschek) to kidnap her. At the busy, boisterous Hoffman House Café, Dick tells Count Garbiadoff (George Middleton) to go to the home of Mrs. Bulford's lover, the venal Senator McSorker (Odell Williams), and identify the jewels. He assures the count that everything will be cleared up by midnight. Sheeny Ike (B. R. Graham), Mother Rosenbaum's cohort, overhears Dick tell Frank that the two of them will have to rescue Mary first, and he rushes off to alert the old crone. Frank is drugged, but Dick manages to effect his and Mary's escape. Confronted at the senator's home with the evidence, Mrs. Bulford swallows poison and falls dead. McSorker threatens Dick, whose curtain line is, "Stand back! The lady belongs to the law—her diamonds to the Count Garbiadoff! . . . Senator, it is twelve o'clock!"

Thompson had a field day as Dick. Besides his Irish delivery boy's disguise, he appeared as a loquacious old tar, an escapee from a mental institution, and a drunk. Critics felt he and almost all his associates were very much up to the parts. But the sad cynosure of the evening was Fanny Janauschek, in what proved to be her last Broadway assignment. Denied star billing, she still received a huge, show-stopping welcome on her first appearance. As a criminal mastermind, she brought remarkable shadings to her interpretation, suggesting the cruel injustices of her early years as much as any naturally evil bent had determined her chilling course. Contemporaries knew that the part reflected an infamous New York criminal, Mother Mandelbaum, but Janauschek accorded it a richness and humanity the original most probably lacked.

Not only were living figures mirrored in the story. The settings took audiences to two rich Lexington and Madison Avenue homes, to a poorer home on Houston Street, to a sordid thieves' den (at Rivington and Canal streets), and to a careful reproduction of the popular Hoffman House (where, in preunion days, a vast horde of supers could depict all manner of New York high life, from the truly wealthy, to showy gamblers, to young football fans out for a night on the town). So excellent was the production that critics readily overlooked the improbabilities and shopworn motifs of the story and instead hailed it as a gripping slice of life. The play ran nine weeks and for over a decade remained one of the best-patronized touring plays.

An even bigger hit, albeit not so totally American, was **The Prisoner of Zenda** (9-4-95, Lyceum). Edward E. Rose adapted it from Anthony Hope's best-selling novel, and Daniel Frohman served as producer. This tale of Rudolf Rassendyll, who takes the place of his look-alike, the abducted Ruritanian king, falls in love with Princess Flavia, but secures the king's release and relinquishes his beloved to the monarch, remains a classic. The show initially starred E. H. Sothern in the dual roles of king and substitute. Sporting a "hideous red wig," he cast aside many of the artificial mannerisms some believed had marred previous interpretations and played the more or less swashbuckling parts in an "easy and natural" yet "strong and convincing" style. Grace Kimball was the princess. A full, robust score accompanied the romantic developments, and the offstage sounds of horses' hoofs and clattering carriage wheels won special commendation. The *Times* reported that the play "charms the fancy, stirs the blood, and touches the heart." The *Dramatic Mirror* went a step further, calling it, "unquestionably, the best dramatic fare that has been presented so far this year." The press for tickets forced Frohman to add a third weekly matinee in October, and when the demand failed to subside and prior road bookings required him to send the original company on tour, a second troupe, headed by James K. Hackett, took its place. Together the companies chalked up more than 200 performances.

Recalling the rationale for higher prices aired just a week earlier, it is interesting to note one newspaper's report of galleryites condemning Augustus Thomas's **The Capitol** (9-9-95, Standard) as "too high-toned." Conceivably it was meant as an intentional dig at the pronouncement. Critics themselves had other complaints, ranging from the lack of "sincerity" and the puppetlike quality of Thomas's character drawing to indifferent performances. The complicated ins-and-outs of the playwright's tale may also have militated against the drama. Reduced to essentials, an ambitious politician, Will Dare (or Dale) (Andrew Robson), succumbs to the blandishments of a cynical lobbyist, Mr. Carroll (Frazer Coulter). Years before, Dare's mother-in-law, Margaret Doane (Mary Shaw), had married one man, then eloped with Carroll. She long since has left the hateful Carroll and has believed her first husband dead. Actually, he has become a priest. They are reunited, though naturally not in marriage, and work hand in hand to thwart Carroll. The play struggled for several weeks before folding.

Paul Burgenhoff, the villain in R. N. Stephens's **The White Rat** (9-16-95, People's), has murdered a Danish sailor in order to steal a diamond crescent, which the sailor had hidden in a stuffed white rat. He keeps the crescent but gives the rat to Albert Lindley, who is promptly imprisoned for the sailor's murder. Lindley just as promptly escapes. Meanwhile, Burgenhoff has learned that Lindley has an incriminating note written by the dead man. He kidnaps Lindley's girl, Edith Kenwell. A chase through a Chinese opium den, over rooftops, and into a Salvation Army meeting room follows before Burgenhoff is brought to heel. John H. Young's fine settings garnered the best notices.

On the same night, Clara Morris began a fortnight's engagement at the 14th Street Theatre, relying on four old favorites: *Camille, Raymonde, Miss Multon,* and *Article 47.* Since her loyalists were still loyal, reviewers reported crowded, receptive houses, and some even detected a few sparks in the embers of her former fire. But a two-week stay was little compared to the months of packed houses the star once enjoyed. Across the river, in Brooklyn, Frederick Warde offered William Greer Harrison's

retelling of the Robin Hood story, **Runnymede** (9-16-95, Columbia). It was poorly received, so Warde also took refuge in his old standbys as he resumed his ceaseless trekking. (By his own account, the previous season he had played 246 performances in eighty-six cities in thirty-four weeks.)

In contrast to these fading players, the young producer Charles Frohman was staking his claim to theatrical prominence with noteworthy rapidity. He opened two more productions on a single evening. The more publicized and eagerly awaited of the pair proved a disappointment. John Drew was the star of Henry Guy Carleton's **That Imprudent Young Couple** (9-23-95, Empire), with Maude Adams again as Drew's leading lady and his niece, Ethel Barrymore, in a minor role. Carleton's story centered on John Annesley and Marion Dunbar, both of whom have been promised in marriage to others, but who after a whirlwind courtship marry secretly. Marion gives John some letters to mail to the folks back home, telling them the news, but John forgets to post the letters. As a result, the newlyweds return to Tuxedo and instantly cause consternation. When John's quick-tempered uncle discovers that Marion is the daughter of a woman who years before had divorced him, he cuts John's allowance from $15,000 per annum to $1000. This would be bad enough in itself; however, Marion compounds their problems by blithely arriving home at the same moment to announce that she has just been on a shopping spree and that her bills total $1000. The couple attempts to live valiantly, if comically, on the installment plan before the playwright balances the books for a happy ending. Critics felt the comedy fell to pieces after a promising first act. Skilled playing, E. G. Unitt's excellent settings, and William Furst's attractive incidental music could not repair the damage, so the comedy was taken off after two weeks.

The Gay Parisians (9-23-95, Hoyt's) was derived from Georges Feydeau and Maurice Desvallières's French hit *L'Hôtel du Libre-Échange.* The farce recorded a wife's misfiring stabs at making her neglectful husband jealous and included a door-filled set that depicted several apartments and an intervening hallway. The doors received a workout during the fast-paced developments. An excellent tonic for tired playgoers, it ran for four months.

Frank Harvey's **The Land of the Living** (9-23-95, People's) moved from London to a South African gold mine as it unfolded a tale of business partners, one of whom covets the other's wife and attempts to kill his associate in order to marry her. Although it was disdained by the few critics who condescended to review it and ran only one week in its initial New York playing, it toured steadily into the new century.

On the other hand, **A Social Highwayman** (9-24-95, Garrick), dramatized by Mary T. Stone from a story by Elizabeth Phipps Train, collected highly favorable notices, only to attract such meager box office that its producer, Richard Mansfield, took it out on the road after a red-ink fortnight. Its hero, Courtice Jeffrey (Joseph Holland), is a good-looking, raffish roué, who lives in style by stealing and selling the jewels of the women he entertains. He is threatened with exposure by one of his victims, Señora Caprices (Olive Oliver), until his valet, the equally crooked Jenkins Hanby (E. M. Holland), reveals that the lady once was known to him as Julia Goldsborough and is a bigamist. Jeffrey would seem to be home free, but his life of crime is ended abruptly when he is accidentally killed. The play had several high points, including a scene in which Jeffrey tests his society friends' reaction by telling them the story of an acquaintance who steals ladies' jewels (their reaction leads him to contemplate suicide) and a seance in which the blackmailer attempts to reveal the truth without seeming to do it herself. Since the Holland brothers and many of their associates were known primarily as comedians, audiences may have been taken aback by the uglier aspects of the story. Whatever the problem at its first hearing, the play's popularity built slowly, and Mansfield was able to recoup some of his losses eventually by road tours and leasing the rights to stock companies.

Tall, slim, weak-mouthed, weak-jawed Walker Whiteside continued his pursuit of Booth's mantle when he began a short stopover at the Herald Square on the 20th. He offered *Hamlet* and *Richelieu* but was rejected by New York's demanding critics as "provincial."

Frohman's response to *That Imprudent Young Couple*'s debacle was to offer a hasty mounting of Madeleine Lucette Ryley's **Christopher, Jr.** (10-7-95, Empire). Actually, the mounting was not all that hurried, for Drew and his fellow players had been offering it on the road. Since Christopher Colt, Jr. (Drew), has mistakenly entered a young lady's stateroom, fallen asleep, and remained there overnight, he has been forced to marry the girl. Once ashore, however, he conveniently forgets her—an easy thing to do since he never really got a good look at her. Although he lives a costly man-about-town life, he takes a room in an attic and pretends to poverty when his father comes to visit him. But his father's mission is to insist that his son marry, and, for farcical purposes, the old man will not listen to his son's explanation of why he cannot. The father (Harry Harwood) introduces the bride-elect, Dora (Maude Adams), and Christopher proceeds to make himself as undesirable as possible. Of course, it turns out that Dora was the girl on the ship, and all ends happily. Mrs. Ryley's dialogue ran to the order of:

—Take care, Sir. You'll 'urt your 'and.
—Don't drop your "H's," Job.
—Don't you drop the 'ammer, Sir.

Drew had several juicy scenes, at one point turning a headache on and off to suit his purposes. Miss Adams also had an applause-getting scene, which required her to run a gamut of confused, often conflicting emotions in response to Drew's remarks. The *Times* praised both players, suggesting that Drew's role was "measured to fit him." But other critics were wearying of Drew's tried and true mannerisms, which, the *Dramatic Mirror* complained, often consisted of little else than "rolling his eyes at the heroine and making grimaces at the audience." But his audiences clearly loved it, and the farce ran out the rest of his season, eight weeks.

Two other luminaries also came to town the same night. Nat Goodwin, at the Fifth Avenue, garnered divided notices for his double bill of *David Garrick* and *Lend Me Five Shillings*. Modjeska fared better at the Garrick. She may have loaded the dice in her own favor by resorting to that favorite trick of 19th-century performers—announcing her stand as her "farewell" appearances. (Happily, she would reappear for several more farewells.) Her engagement began with *Measure for Measure, Mary Stuart,* and *Camille.* For the second week she brought out a new piece, Clyde Fitch's **Mistress Betty** (10-15-95, Garrick). Set in the 18th century, the play begins in the green room of a London theatre, where Betty Singleton is also making a farewell appearance. She is about to marry the Duke of Malmsbury (W. S. Hart). She is almost hysterical with happiness, and as her play ends she goes onstage to give her admirers her farewell speech—a speech delivered directly to the real audience. Unfortunately for her, the duke proves callous and hard-drinking. Rumors reach her of his affairs with grander ladies. Heartsick, but determined to provide the duke with justification for leaving her and leading his own libertine life, she pretends to an affair with another man. Years pass, and she lives ignored, impoverished, and ailing in a wretched garret. Half crazed, she recites the same farewell speech she had given under more promising circumstances so long before. The repentant, sober duke arrives in time for her to die in his arms.

The play allowed Modjeska to evolve from a

bubbly, beautiful woman of thirty-five to a dejected, prematurely aged relic, and she brought all her grace, delicacy, and poetry to the part. Reviewers were not kind to Hart (twenty years on, a cowboy star in silent films), whom they condemned as wooden and declamatory. The engagement ended after a week of Fitch's play, which soon was dropped from Modjeska's repertory. (It would reappear a decade later with a new star, a new title, and a happy ending.)

The night of Fitch's premiere saw Joseph Jefferson return, at the Garden, in a double bill of *The Cricket on the Hearth* and, in competition with Goodwin, *Lend Me Five Shillings*. Whatever fresh approaches Goodwin brought to his Golightly, a largely tradition-bound press preferred Jefferson's time-honored interpretation. The reaction of playgoers, a group then in flux, was not recorded firsthand.

In any case, Goodwin quickly moved on to a novelty by the productive Henry Guy Carleton, **Ambition** (10-22-95, Fifth Avenue). Like September's *The Capitol*, it took a disdainful look at some of Washington's unsavory, behind-the-scenes intrigue. Yet for all its telltale period references it has, a hundred years later, a more modern feel to it. Obediah Beck is chairman of the Senate's foreign affairs committee. He is a man of singular integrity, decency, and warmth, devoid of pomposity and well aware of the humor in life's supposedly serious side. His name is constantly bandied about as presidential timber, but he is not interested. He recalls all too well the vicious, unfair vilification he endured when running prior campaigns. "An editor," he tells a listener, "in a political campaign is like a boy in a frog pond with a bean shooter. He may have no ill feeling for any particular frog—but he has a bean shooter." Over the incumbent president's opposition, Beck sponsors a bill giving Cuban sugar favorable tariff treatment, hoping that such treatment will smooth the way for Cuban independence. When he leads the successful fight to override a veto, American sugar interests conspire against him. He is offered and rejects a nomination as secretary of state. His enemies then plan to put his name in nomination at the presidential convention, intending to defeat him so crushingly that the embarrassment will mortally wound his career. Beck learns of the plot, derails it, and decides he will be happiest living simply with a lovely, loyal young lady named Ruth (Annie Russell).

Critics divided sharply in their assessments of the play. Even those in favor sensed a falling away in the last act, which Carleton had not handed over to Goodwin until a few days before the opening. But

Goodwin, who played the part in a black wig, and his supporting cast were applauded for their excellent performances. As he almost always did, Goodwin improvised bits nightly, not always to the play's advantage. At first business was, as Goodwin noted in his autobiography, "simply ghastly." The play was quickly withdrawn but later proved popular on the road.

Goodwin might have done better had his opening not conflicted with one of the most memorable first nights of the decade, Belasco's **The Heart of Maryland** (10-22-95, Herald Square). The play could not pretend to any of the literary qualities many reviewers detected in *Ambition*. Still, it featured the increasingly self-assured Belasco's brilliant staging, culminating in the sort of scene that becomes an instant theatrical legend. The production securely established Belasco's reputation. As in most dramas of the Civil War, the conflict split asunder families and lovers. Col. Alan Kendrick (Maurice Barrymore) fights for the North at the same time that his father, Hugh (Frank Mordaunt), serves as a Confederate general. Alan's sweetheart, Maryland Calvert (Mrs. Leslie Carter), has also remained loyal to the South and so has broken off their engagement. When Alan sneaks through the lines to see Maryland, he is captured by Col. Fulton Thorpe (John E. Kellerd), a former northern officer whom Alan once court-martialed and who now fights for the rebels. The vengeful Thorpe arranges to have Alan shot as a spy. When Maryland comes to plead for Alan's life, Thorpe attempts to seduce her. She grabs a bayonet, which Thorpe has stuck into a table to use as a candlestick, and stabs him with it. This gives Alan time to escape. The wounded Thorpe orders the local church bell rung to announce the escape, but Maryland climbs into the belfry and, shouting "The bell shall not ring!" grabs the clapper and swings with it to prevent the bell's sounding. Later Alan returns with Federal troops and besieges Thorpe. He also intercepts letters from General Lee, which reveal that Lee has discovered Thorpe to be an untrustworthy double agent. Thorpe is imprisoned; Alan and Maryland are married.

The production was magnificent. For example, the first act showed "an old Colonial mansion, deep-bowered among ancient, blooming lilac bushes and bathed in the fading glow of late afternoon and sunset light." The redheaded star and her supporting players, particularly Barrymore and Kellerd, were enthusiastically received, although, as always, enthusiasm for the mustachioed Barrymore was somewhat tempered. Thus the *Spirit of the Times* reported, "Maurice Barrymore never appeared to better advantage and never had less to say and do." Since a majority of leading critics elected to attend *Ambition,* the aisle-sitters at Belasco's opening were mostly second-stringers. Very few found much to praise in the play itself, although they conceded that it was a crowd-pleaser. What most pleased the crowd was the close of the third act when, "lantern in hand, the indomitable heroine speeds up the rickety staircase to the belfry. We see her going up, up, up. She reaches the bell just as it begins to move, and seizing the clapper swings to and fro with it in midair." Within a few weeks critics were allowing that the public had second-guessed them. No less than the cantankerous William Winter discovered good things to say about a work his subordinate had clobbered as "wild . . . shrieking melodrama." The drama played to packed houses until the onset of hot weather in mid-May and toured first-class theatres for several years before being handed over to lesser companies.

By now the vast majority of imported English sensation-melodramas were relegated to lower-class and touring houses. **Sins of the Night** (10-28-95, People's), Frank Harvey's second play of the season, was no exception. It transported audiences from a Mexican silver mine to London (his first had moved from London to a South African gold mine) in recounting the saga of a man's determination to prevent his disinherited cousin from reclaiming his estate. One scene found the hero trapped in a cellar being inundated by floodwaters from the Thames.

But English dramas with loftier ambitions, especially if mounted by Henry Irving, were a different matter. His bills, when he opened at Abbey's on the 29th with Ellen Terry as his leading lady, promised such old favorites as *Macbeth, The Lyons Mail, Louis XI, Becket, Faust, Much Ado About Nothing, The Bells, The Merchant of Venice,* and *Nance Oldfield.* New to New Yorkers were Laurence Irving's **A Christmas Story,** W. G. Willis's dramatization of **Don Quixote,** John Oliver Hobbes's **Journeys End in Lovers' Meeting,** A. Conan Doyle's **A Story of Waterloo,** and J. Comyns Carr's **King Arthur.** Of these only *King Arthur* was given more than two or three performances, holding the boards for three full weeks. First offered on November 4, it was a breathtakingly beautiful spectacle. Scenes included a moonlit fen, a forest in spring, and a flag-draped Camelot with a host setting out to seek the Grail. In them costumes "of tourmaline and topaz, pale amethyst, jasper and jacinth" were "blended with mystic colors from the dreamland of Burne-Jones [who designed the sets]." Miss Terry's glowing,

restless Guinevere stole the show. Commentators were less pleased with Irving's gaunt, graying, "Mephistophelian" king and Ben Webster's Lancelot. Indeed, critics were more and more intolerant of Irving's clumsy waddle and his curious, often mumbled delivery, although there was no gainsaying his ultimate magnetism. When the company returned briefly in May, Laurence Irving's one-acter **Godefroi and Yolande** was also offered.

The great female impersonator Neil Burgess proved fallible when he came a cropper in Charles Barnard's **The Year One** (11-2-95, Star). To attract customers the house had been freshly redecorated, matinees were to begin at 1:30 (to avoid the 5:00 crush), and a lavish mounting was advertised. The story centered on a vestal virgin named Gabbylaria, who loves a dashing charioteer but whose curious, manly resemblance to Caesar Augustus prompts her being pressed into service as his double. On opening night mishap followed mishap. At one point the curtain came down in the middle of a scene. Later the orchestra and a chorus of vestal virgins each had their own ideas about tempo. Most disastrous, the chariot race in the Circus Maximus turned into an unexpected farce. Two chariots were to race on treadmills. The four black horses propelling one chariot acquitted themselves handsomely. But three of the four white horses pulling the opposing chariot had their own ideas, too, and refused to trot. Nor was all of the costuming up to snuff. The supers appeared in tights that "hung upon their legs in the loosest way imaginable." But allowances regularly were made for such opening-night flubs. What seemed to bother many people was the air of what would now be called "camp" about the whole affair. Burgess always had imbued his ladies with an inherent dignity. However, his first entrance, descending from a sedan chair in an outlandish white vestal gown and an absurd red wig, set a tone that apparently was maintained throughout. The result was at best a modest run (followed by a return of *The Country Fair*) and tour.

Charles T. Vincent's **In a Big City** (11-4-95, People's) was set in *the* big city and retailed the difficulties encountered by an immigrant who arrives with a will that can make him wealthy. His efforts to receive his inheritance are stymied for a time by greedy troublemakers. One scene took place on the Battery with a view of Castle Garden and, in the distance, scurrying little ships and ferries, their proportions, according to the *Sun,* "harmonizing exactly with the demands of the perspective." Chatham Park and City Hall by night also were shown. Minor characters, so typical of this sort of play, included a comic Irishman, a fat German, a dudish black gambler, and a street waif.

The best that most English sensation-melodramas could hope for was a hearing at the huge, relatively new American Theatre on 42nd Street, and this is what Sutton Vane's **In Sight of St. Paul's** got on the 5th. It was set entirely in London, and each setting, if only on the backdrop, dutifully accorded audiences a glimpse of the cathedral. One scene took place on the dome, with a panoramic view of London. In the end the company assembled in the church to celebrate the release of Tom Chichester (John T. Sullivan) after he had been held on a trumped-up murder charge and exonerated. The play stayed a month, then moved out for a season-long tour.

A much finer play was accorded much shorter shrift, possibly because it was mistranslated and misstaged, or, just as likely, because it was misunderstood by the critics who condemned it. The play was Sudermann's *Die Ehre,* offered to Americans as **Honour** (11-11-95, Standard). In this version Sudermann's Robert became Gunther Hartmann (George F. Nash). He returns to Berlin (which he had left in the original after being snubbed by his sister's seducer, whom he had challenged to a duel) following years overseas. The experience is disillusioning, since he finds his impoverished family crude and uncaring. He finally is able to marry his old sweetheart, Renata Muhling (Lenore Mühlingk in the original) (May Wheeler), thanks to money from his rich, cynical friend, Count Trast (Frederic de Belleville). The cast also included F. F. Mackay, a fine, old-school actor who long had been a mainstay at the Union Square. The major complaint was that the work often was played for laughs. In many critical eyes this destroyed its much vaunted new-style naturalism, but modern exegeses have discovered an underlying satirical bent, which this production may have explored. Whatever its rationale, it was gone after a single week.

Jane May, a Parisian actress admired there for her performances in pantomime, recruited a supporting cast of American players to help her present a wordless entertainment listed variously as **Miss Pygmalion** or **Mademoiselle Pygmalion** (11-18-95, Daly's). Either title hinted at the plot, but neither secured her an audience.

With his designed-for-touring production of *The Prisoner of Zenda* having crated its sets and begun its cross-country trek, Daniel Frohman belatedly reintroduced his stock company. Their initial presentation was yet another London success, R. C. Carton's **The Home Secretary** (11-25-95, Lyceum),

in which a self-involved wife nearly destroys her devoted husband's political career by flirting with an anarchist. Perhaps because American audiences were finding American-written drama ever more acceptable, the play was only a modest hit.

Opening in competition with Frohman was Charles Klein's **A Happy Little Home** (11-25-95, 14th St.). The play had plump George W. Monroe, in the role of Owen Moore, masquerade as a housekeeper to be near his sweetheart. What with songs sprinkled through the first two acts and the last act given over to a lengthy vaudeville, many critics treated the entertainment as a musical.

The day of the oldtime stock ensemble was fast approaching its end. Their shortened seasons were irrefutable testimony to that. Thus the greatest surviving ensemble, Daly's, did not open its own season until the night after Frohman's group returned. Their offering was their old standby, *The School for Scandal.* Once again Ada Rehan cavorted in her incomparable Lady Teazle, with James Lewis as Sir Oliver, Mrs. Gilbert as Mrs. Candour, and Frank Worthing as Joseph. In Worthing, Daly may well have found a truly capable successor to John Drew, but the shadowed, limited future of ensembles and Worthing's premature death a few years later prevented his achieving the fame he was entitled to.

A rash of premieres occurred on the first Monday in December. The Frohman brothers joined forces to bring Olga Nethersole into the Empire. Her programs revived *Denise, Frou-Frou,* and *Camille* and introduced one novelty, **Carmen** (12-24-95, Empire), as taken from the French by Henry Hamilton. Bizet's opera was well known and popular, but many staid playgoers were shocked by the same story told without Bizet's romantic, distracting music, and especially by the star's portrayal of the cigarette girl as wanton and sluttish. Yet her Carmen held the boards for as long as all her revivals combined.

Charles Hoyt's **A Runaway Colt** (12-2-95, Hoyt's) starred one more stage-struck athlete, Adrian C. ("Cap") Anson of the Chicago White Stockings. The play, while still called a farce, had more serious undertones than earlier Hoyt pieces. A gambler persuades the weakling brother of the athlete's sweetheart to bet trust money on a game. When Anson hits a winning home run the gambler must pay up, and Anson also wins the respect of the heroine's ministerial father, who had thought all athletes "low down." Initially the sounds of the game came from behind the scenes, the grandstand and the bustling crowd blocking the view, but then the set swung around to allow the audience to see the star his hit four-bagger. Like most athletes, Anson was no great shakes as an actor. The *Dramatic Mirror* suggested he spoke his lines like an "artillery officer," and the *Sun* complained about his restlessly shifting stance. Audiences seemingly missed the rambunctious horseplay they had come to associate with the "Aristophanes of the modern stage," so the New York run was brief.

Although its first New York showing was even briefer (sixteen performances), Scott Marble's **The Sidewalks of New York** (12-2-95, 14th St.) remained a road favorite for many years. Marble's characters were a representative list of stock melodramatic figures: a dissolute, wicked son, his victimized banker-father, an affectionate but unsophisticated sister, a treacherous Italian villain, and a long-suffering hero, falsely accused of the banker's murder. One sensation scene had the hero jump into the river from a shot tower on the Brooklyn waterfront to rescue the heroine. In this instance the actor who played the hero was not all that heroic. A double, a famous athlete, was employed for the dive. Another well-received setting showed a view of Herald Square with the newspaper building featured prominently.

A second Italian (no doubt reflecting the onset of sizable Italian immigration) was the villain in Ada Lee Bascom's **A Bowery Girl** (12-2-95, Grand Opera). Cesca Bertolina attempts to force Agnes Delorine to marry Nicholas Franklin, even though he knows Franklin is married. Nora Hallihan, the wholesome daughter of a very unwholesome ward heeler, rights matters. The settings were supposed to take audiences not only to the Bowery but to the Palisades. However, much of the play's scenery had been destroyed in a train wreck on the way to Manhattan. By the time the scenery was replaced, Agnes and her cohorts were back trouping across the nation.

Russians and Englishmen replaced Italians as the villains of J. W. Harkins's **Man-O-War's Man** (12-2-95, People's). The Russians arrest Capt. Jack Conway of the U.S.S. *New Orleans* on charges trumped up by Capt. Basil Haviland of the H.M.S. *Scorpion* and attempt to hold him incommunicado. Jack helps engineer his own escape and gives the malefactors the back of his hand. Once restored to his post on the American warship, he sinks the *Scorpion* "amid the boom of real cannons, the belching forth of real fire and the rising of real smoke," if one critic can be trusted. He also persuades a Russian Mata Hari to cross over to the American side. (For what it's worth, note how persistent was the use of Jack as the name for the all-American hero.) Like *The Sidewalks of New York* and *A Bowery Girl, Man-O-War's Man* found a long welcome in the hinterlands.

However, the longest run chalked up by any of the evening's openings went to an English play, Robert Buchanan and Charles Marlowe's **The Strange Adventures of Miss Brown** (12-2-95, Standard). (Charles Marlowe was a nom de plume for Harriet Jay.) It was a farce on the order of *Charley's Aunt,* with the hero donning a blue dress and a curly red wig to pass as a girl in a seminary. The red wig was the third red wig of the season to garner critical comment. Curiously, the red-haired Goodwin had been required to don a black wig for his role in *Ambition.* Following a ten-week stay, the farce headed out to the road, where it failed to find the large audiences that American melodramas enjoyed.

Mansfield also began an engagement on the 2nd, but he offered only a single performance of *Beau Brummell* before turning to Charles Henry Meltzer's dramatization of *Crime and Punishment* under the unattractive title **The Story of Rodion, the Student** (12-3-95, Garrick). The evening hinged on an overused device of the period, a hero's delirium. As the guilt-ridden murderer reenacts the killing, one commentator wrote, "The face of the wild, tortured, hopeless fanatic is alabaster, his eyes blaze deep, black and purposeful. He waits for the unspoken horror which his eyes and twisting hands announce. He reaches out and seizes this ghastly intangible nothing. He wrestles with it. . . . It oozes out of his grasp. It presses with unearthly force against him. With brutal bravery he brings the awful phantom to the ground and slinks away with stealthy terror." Many reviews agreed with the man from the *Times,* who called the performance "the greatest artistic triumph" of Mansfield's career. (Most descriptions of the scene, however, say the murder was committed with an axe or pick.) The descriptions proved too ghoulish for potential patrons, and Mansfield, embittered, was forced to close the show. Its closing, coming on top of other losses he had suffered in producing ventures, meant he had to give up the Garrick. He told audiences he would hereafter confine himself to the road. Luckily, this was another promise that the great but duplicitous artist was not to keep.

But Mansfield was not alone in his problems. For his first new play of the season Daly went to his accustomed German well and came up dry. **The Transit of Leo** (12-10-95, Daly's), taken from *Das Schösskind,* began with the elegantly dressed guests and members of a wedding party entering two by two through a doorway and then performing a polonaise. From there the story unfolded a modern taming of the shrew. Ada Rehan was the spoiled bride, Worthing her distressed husband, and Lewis and Mrs. Gilbert the bride's eccentric uncle and aunt. The reviews were favorable, if qualified. The critic for the *Dramatic Mirror* probably earned the ire of Daly's principals when he reserved one glowing sentence for Maxine Elliott, who had only a small part. He reported, "The eyes of the audience were glued to her all the time she was on the stage." But even that probably prompted no more than a handful of men-about-town to buy seats. Daly blamed "vile" business on a pre-Christmas slump but ruefully acknowledged that the slump could not account for all the empty seats. After a mere ten playings the comedy was gone.

Sidney R. Ellis's **Bonnie Scotland** (12-16-95, 14th St.), a touring play, was larded with Scottish airs as it recounted how love triumphs over an ages-old feud after Walter McFarlane saves the life of Mary Colquhoun.

A fine English actor, John Hare, made his American debut in Pinero's **The Notorious Mrs. Ebbsmith** (12-23-95, Abbey's). Also making their American debuts were his leading lady, Julia Neilson, and C. Aubrey Smith, for so long Hollywood's stereotypical Englishman. Pinero's saga of a widow who makes a home for an unhappily married man but takes umbrage when, on deciding to return to his wife, he asks her to be his mistress, rubbed against American sensibilities. So did the play's most famous scene, when the heroine throws a Bible into the fire and then, as a sign of her probable redemption, risks burning herself to retrieve it. Hare did not play the husband—that role fell to Fred Terry—but the calculating *raisonneur*, the Duke of St. Olpherts. The play was quickly pulled, and the company proceeded to *A Pair of Spectacles*, coupled at different times with *Comedy and Tragedy*, **Two Old Cronies** (1-6-96), in which a pair of bachelors, trying to compose a love letter, conclude bachelorhood is best, and **A Quiet Rubber** (1-13-96), Charles Coghlan's adaptation of *La Partie de piquet*, in which an old man is talked out of a duel by being persuaded he dreamt the affront.

An unusual and potentially fascinating figure was the central character in Edwin Barbour and James W. Harkins, Jr.'s **Northern Lights** (12-23-95, American). John Swiftwind (William Courtleigh) is a Sioux Indian who has been educated at Yale and is now an assistant surgeon at Fort Terry, Mont. He is a man alone, for his white associates are condescending and his tribesmen resent his leaving the reservation to enlist in the ranks of their persecutors. Yet Swiftwind is instrumental in rectifying two dangerous situations. In the first, his superior, Dr. Sidney Sherwood (Clarence Handyside), anxious to marry another woman, attempts to murder his drug-addicted wife by injecting her with a cholera virus. Swiftwind rescues the woman in time. In the second, Wallace Grey (George A. Wright), son of the fort's commander, is convicted of cowardice, but Swiftwind, relying on the latest medical theories, shows that the cowardice is hereditary, stemming from his mother's having been frightened by seeing his father wounded in action.

The realistic scenes in Montana, with their pictures of army and Indian life, and the references to contemporary medical thinking all prompted the *Dramatic Mirror* to see the play as an "attempt at American photography" and hail it as "the best melodrama written by an American in ten years." Other papers, while acknowledging the play's theatrical effectiveness, were more moderate in their praise. For example, the *Times* judged it "an excellent olla podrida" of "old things from many widely-separated styles of playwrighting." In truth the drama, for all its potency on stage, missed an opportunity. Its authors were too much creatures and creators of their own time. Swiftwind's real dilemma is touched upon only in incidental speeches. Instead he is utilized as that stock dramatic fallback the deus ex machina, who rectifies essentially clichéd wrongs. Contemporaries were indifferent to such artistic failings, so the drama lingered for five weeks at the huge auditorium and then spent several years touring.

Hard on the rejection of *The Notorious Mrs. Ebbsmith*, Pinero suffered another if lesser disappointment when Daniel Frohman brought out his **The Benefit of the Doubt** (1-6-96, Lyceum). Curiously, this story of the conflict that arises between two families when the wife of one is thought to have been compromised by the husband of the other garnered largely laudatory reviews. Isabel Irving and Herbert Kelcey especially were praised in the principal parts. Yet Frohman pulled it after thirty performances. The following season his brother Charles took it on the road with his own players.

R. N. Stephens's **A Girl Wanted** (1-6-96, 14th St.) starred Frank Bush, a protean vaudeville clown, who disguised himself as a stranded variety actor, a farmer, a waiter, a girl, an Italian, and a Jew in order to court a restaurant owner's daughter. It was one of many touring plays of the day to straddle the fence between straight farce and musical. This visit was for a single week.

One week was also all that was allowed Arthur Shirley and Benjamin Landeck's **Saved from the Sea**

(1-6-96, Columbus). Its hero, Dan Ellington, is lashed to the mast of a sinking ship and must cross safely over a collapsing suspension bridge and risk the gallows (which, happily, won't work) in order to free his wife, Nancy, an heiress, from the snares of "Surly Jim" Weaver.

Stuart Robson had not been as successful as his erstwhile partner, Crane, in carving out a career for himself after the partnership was dissolved. Earlier in this season he had toyed with Daniel L. Hart's *Government Acceptance,* a comedy about an oddball inventor who eventually strikes it rich, but the play had gotten no nearer Manhattan than Brooklyn. Now his squeaky voice and deadpan were more profitably employed in the role of the henpecked hero of **Mrs. Ponderbury's Past** (1-7-96, Garrick), which F. C. Burnand drew from Blum and Toché's *Mme. Mongodin.* The harridan Mrs. P. (Henrietta Vaders) keeps her husband under her thumb by prominently displaying a large knife, which, according to her, she once used to put an all too persistent suitor in his place. Only when the truth about the knife comes to light does the husband gain the upper hand. Slight as the play was, Robson's appealing comic skills—his ability to punctuate a seemingly innocent sentence hilariously, his ludicrous gestures of surrender—helped secure the farce a passable run. Twelve years later Richard Carle would star in a musical version called *Mary's Lamb.*

The abrupt shuttering of Daly's first novelty for the season prompted him to revive *Twelfth Night* as a stopgap until his next new offering was ready. That play was **The Two Escutcheons** (1-7-96, Daly's), which Sydney Rosenfeld translated from Oskar Blumenthal and Gustav Kadelburg's *Zwei Wappen.* It detailed how the social prejudices of an old German aristocrat and an upstart American pork packer nearly wreck their children's plans to marry. Somehow the humor proved untranslatable. Daly's first novelty had run a week and a half. This did slightly better. It ran three weeks. Once again Daly was not having the sort of brilliant, well-attended season he had had so regularly in the past.

Edward W. Townsend's **Chimmie Fadden** (1-13-96, Garden) was described by the *Herald* as "a sensation melodrama in slang." Much of the action took place on or near Division Street. The "quarter fairly swarms with foreigners. There are 'Dago' organ grinders and 'Dago' fruit peddlers, German grocers and Hibernian gin mill keepers." When the Van Courtlands go slumming there they are pestered by the mean-mouthed Moxie (Will Cowper), looking tough and menacing in his yellow coat and red scarf. Chimmie (Charles H. Hopper) comes to the socialites' aid. Furious, Moxie steals some of Chimmie's tools and leaves them at the site of a burglary at the Van Courtlands'. When Chimmie is finally exonerated his reward is the Van Courtlands' "French" maid, who comes, it would seem, from Paris, Ky. For many, Mrs. Murphy (Marie Bates), the "rum-soaked bum" who comments wryly on the events while leaning out of her window, was the star of the evening. "Really," the *Herald* began its notice, "they should have called it 'Mrs. Murphy.' " But as *Chimmie Fadden* the play remained popular for many years.

A much more pretentious, ballyhooed drama opened two nights later. The ballyhoo spotlighted the fact that the New York premiere of Henry Arthur Jones's **Michael and His Lost Angel** (1-15-96, Empire) was to occur simultaneously with its London premiere. Of course, given the time difference the London opening would be over before the Empire's curtain went up. The producer, Charles Frohman, was talking with Henry Miller in the latter's dressing room prior to the start of the play and was handed a telegram, which he read and pocketed witout comment. Miller later learned that the message informed Frohman of the play's unfavorable West End reception. Its fate was no different on Broadway, and this tale of a devout, unyielding Anglican minister who is nearly brought to perdition by a rich, beautiful temptress survived for only thirteen showings. Frohman wrote off his $17,000 investment. However, Miller and his vis-à-vis, Viola Allen, were both able to clip paragraphs of praise to paste in their scrapbooks.

The story of another temptress followed apace. This time, however, the Buddhist hermit she would seduce seemingly does not fall for her wiles but instead converts the courtesan. When she kills a rajah who would force her into marriage, she is stoned to death. The hermit arrives to comfort the dying woman and confesses that, in fact, he did love her. The settings for Armand Sylvestre and Eugène Morand's **Izeyl** (1-20-96, Abbey's) provided lavish and exotic pictures of Himalayan India in the 5th century B.C. But the play's real attraction for American audiences was its star, Sarah Bernhardt. Even playgoers unschooled in French understood that the actress's electrifying histrionics would make all but the most subtle nuances of the play comprehensible. She devoted a full week to the play, then offered *Camille, Adrienne Lecouvreur, Fédora, Magda, Gismonda,* and *Phèdre.* When she made a brief return in May she also offered *La Tosca* and *La Femme de Claude.*

The death of Dumas fils in November had sparked

a resurgence of interest in his work. The two Dumas plays in Bernhardt's repertory reflected that interest to some extent, although both had been announced earlier.

Similarly, R. C. Carton's adaptation of his *L'Ami des femmes* as **The Squire of Dames** (1-20-96, Palmer's) had been offered to London shortly before the playwright died. But the lack of announcements in American papers suggest that the producer, Charles Frohman, only became interested in importing it after columns of eulogies had filled theatrical sections. Having decided to do it, though, he gave it his best shot. John Drew was starred—his third starring role of the season—and many of the players regularly associated with him were reenlisted in support: Maude Adams, Arthur Byron, Ferdinand Gottschalk, and Annie Irish. The slightly watered-down story told of a capricious, rebellious wife who leaves an erring husband for a doltish lover. It takes the sometimes subtle, always sensible counsels of a blasé, no-longer-young man of the world to bring about a curtain-time reconciliation. Drew and the increasingly admired Miss Adams won the most laurels, and the play ran, with a slight interruption, for three months.

Robson's ex-partner, W. H. Crane did not fare quite as well in a "serviceable" vehicle, Franklyn Fyles's **The Governor of Kentucky** (1-21-96, Fifth Ave.). Fyles's tale, like *The Capitol* and *Ambition*, played up to the political fever building in this election year. Governor Lee hopes to be named senator (this was the era before direct election of senators), but he refuses to bow to the will of a corrupt commercial syndicate, which has the pull to prevent his nomination. One of the syndicate's cronies, Mason Hix (Edwin Arden), with the reluctant compliance of Lee's good but weak-willed old secretary, forges Lee's signature on a document meeting the syndicate's stipulations. Rather than inculpate his secretary, Lee is prepared to abandon all political ambitions. Just in the nick of time, Daniel Boone Bingley (Burr McIntosh), a former moonshiner who has turned detective, uncovers the facts. The settings by Walter Burridge earned critical encomiums, notably a recreation of the governor's office with huge portraits on the wall, and a veranda offering a view of the Cumberland Mountains in the distance. If Drew had become the consummate avuncular, citified man of the world, Crane had no peer as a similarly avuncular and knowing man, but one with unconcealed countrified roots. His performance, with McIntosh's droll support, sustained the play, which ran five weeks and then toured. Whether for publicity purposes or because Crane

had a genuine fear of a cast with thirteen characters, an additional minor role was added two days after the play opened.

Three weeks after he was first seen as a devout Anglican minister, Henry Miller was featured as an almost saintly Jew in Charles Brookfield and F. C. Phillips's **A Woman's Reason** (1-27-96, Empire). His leading lady, Viola Allen, played a woman whose impoverished but highborn family presses her into a marriage with the rich Jew who holds the mortgages on their properties. She eventually runs off with another man, but his brutality and the Jew's obvious goodness soon bring her to her senses. The new play, again from London, was no more welcomed than its predecessor had been and left after three weeks.

Daly's shortened season ended with his brother Joseph's adaptation of Franz von Schönthan's **The Countess Gucki** (1-28-96, Daly's), which the producer announced had been written by the German playwright expressly for Ada Rehan. She portrayed a merry widow whose fussy brother-in-law, Court Counsellor von Mittersteig (James Lewis), and his sharp-tongued wife, Clementina (Mrs. Gilbert), find their daughter, Cilli (Helma Nelson), is being courted by a dashing young officer, Horst von Neuhoff (Charles Richman), a man not to their liking. But with some modifications, which she sets about putting in order, he is very much to the liking of the countess. As she says at the end,

Let wise old heads instruct us as they may,
Young hearts will rule and *Love* will have its *way*.
So if our friend approve this oft-told theme,
Join hands once more—applaud *our* Little Scheme.

William Winter was happy to report that the "fine feeling and buoyant beauty" Miss Rehan brought to the part resulted in "an illuminative study of woman's nature." The entire action took place in an 1819 Carlsbad drawing room, with one highly praised effect of the wind blowing through an opened window and disturbing curtains and pictures on the wall. The play's month-long run to good business brought Daly's otherwise disappointing season to a happy conclusion.

A heroine being evicted from her home by a rejected suitor was the first piece of business in Henry Pettit and Augustus Harris's Drury Lane hit **Burmah** (1-28-96, American). But that was only prelude to the big scenes in the Far East, where the English must battle the natives before setting to rights more domestic wrongs. The spectacular battle scene had an officer jump a huge chasm to ride for reinforcements when the troops are about to exhaust their ammunition. The play ran into March, but one critic made the interesting observation that "the few New Yorkers who want to see everything 'made in England' can't support a playhouse." Such a remark would have been absurd even a decade earlier. But then a few days before, one trade sheet, remarking not on the source but on the nature of current plays, bewailed "this dark hour of morbid problem exposition." Some critics are rarely happy.

Having provided himself with a lifelong meal ticket by writing *In Old Kentucky,* C. T. Dazey tried again—and almost succeeded—with **The War of Wealth** (2-10-96, Star). The play had been reaping a fortune since it opened the previous February in Philadelphia. Dazey abandoned horse country and set his play in a banker's mansion overlooking the Hudson and in the bank's offices. Speculations by a junior partner, Sanford Farley (A. S. Lipman), have threatened the bank headed by John Warfield (Lawrence Hanley), a onetime Montana rancher, with a run that could destroy the enterprise. Farley had attempted to enlist a cashier, Philip Norwood (Malcolm Williams), in his scheme, but Norwood, along with Marcia Dudley (Madeline Bouton), an heiress who is the girl of his dreams, and Major Pinckney Poindexter (Thomas A. Wise), a big-hearted southerner, join forces to save the bank.

Typically for plays of this kind, the plot was an excuse to introduce sensation-scenes. Most sensational of all was the rescue of the heroine, who has fallen from a platform on the edge of a precipice and is clinging for dear life. Norwood swings from an American flag on a flagpole bent nearly double to prevent her falling any farther. Lesser sensations included an explosion, which releases the hero from a bank vault in which the villain has locked him, and the arrival of an express wagon, "driven pell mell on stage," with the monies to stop the run. The melodrama ran into the spring and returned regularly on its tours, which lasted for several more seasons. It remained a favorite of regional stock companies for more than a decade thereafter.

Quick oblivion was Edward Vroom's merciful lot. Vroom was a socialite with acting ambitions. He secured the rights to Charles Renauld's translation of François Coppée's **For the Crown** (2-11-96, Palmer's) and, abetted by some of his rich friends, mounted it with himself as star. He at least had the wisdom to surround himself with fine artists. Rose Coghlan was his leading lady; Richard Marston and Homer Emens designed the sets; costumes were said to be copies of the Paris originals. The tragedy centered on a son who kills his traitorous father and

then, rather than besmirch his father's name, accepts blame for his own seemingly unwarranted act and is condemned to death.

Some interesting announcements appeared in New York newspapers during the week. Foreshadowing the "package deals" of a hundred years later, several New York trolley lines announced that special cars would take playgoers to and from their theatres and provide them with meals on board. Details were not spelled out, but even horse-drawn trolleys were probably swift enough so that the meals must have consisted of a 19th-century equivalent of fast food. The plan seems to have flopped.

An excellent cast, which included William Faversham, Robert Edeson, Viola Allen, Elsie de Wolfe, and Joseph Humphreys, could do nothing with Brandon Thomas (of *Charley's Aunt* fame) and Henry Keeling's **Marriage** (2-17-96, Empire). A couple in the throes of a divorce—and the husband about to marry another woman—are reconciled in time for a happy curtain. Coupled with the comedy was Emma Sheridan Frye and Mrs. E. G. Sutherland's one-acter **Marse Van,** in which a southern belle scorns her lover for joining the Union army, then relents and accepts him.

On the 22nd the *Dramatic Mirror* contained a small squib alerting readers that there was a "plan afoot for a combination of theatrical interests." In oncoming weeks the trade sheet ran further notices and briefly interviewed several of the participants. These men assured the paper that nothing sinister was in the works, that they were merely trying to introduce some order and logic into the traditionally disorganized business. For the time being, the trade sheet accepted their word.

Duse began a stand at the Fifth Avenue on the 24th. Besides her double bill of *Cavalleria Rusticana* and *La Locandiera,* she offered little but *Camille, Magda,* and a single performance of **Pamela Nubile** (3-19-96), Goldoni's dramatization of scenes from Richardson's novel *Pamela.* Thus both in her person and her schedule she invited renewed comparison with Bernhardt. And again critics divided ranks according to their predispositions. But even the *Times,* which was not in her corner, granted she was the "idol of the hour."

In the prologue of Clifford Dempsey's **Arm of the Law** (2-24-96, People's), Indians attack a lone "prairie schooner," killing the adults and kidnapping a baby. The baby grows up to be a beautiful girl who, the villain knows, is also an heiress. Among her harrowing experiences before she can claim her riches, she is bound in a hut, which the villain sets afire. A friendly Indian attempts to break down the door, and when that fails he mounts his horse, which rears up and pounds in the door.

For a number of seemingly petty reasons, Augustin Daly had developed an implacable hatred for Julia Marlowe. Early in the season he had announced plans for a *Henry IV* revival (subsequently dropped), only to learn that Miss Marlowe would be presenting it during her visit with herself as Prince Hal—the same role Daly had reserved for Ada Rehan. When he discovered that *Romeo and Juliet* was also on her programs, the incensed producer settled on a mean trick. A week before Miss Marlowe's opening, and with his own ensemble on tour, Daly mounted a lavish *Romeo and Juliet* at his theatre on March 3, with Mrs. Brown Potter and Kyrle Bellew. His stars were beautiful to look at, but so were Miss Marlowe and her husband of the moment, Robert Taber. However, her still youthful appearance, her "graceful low-toned voice," and her exquisite readings gave Marlowe a distinct edge, while Taber, so virile and high-spirited, left Bellew in the shade. Having won her point, the star moved on to *Henry IV, As You Like It, The Hunchback,* and *She Stoops to Conquer* during her stay at Palmer's. Later in the season, at some of New York's neighborhood houses, she added performances of *Twelfth Night* and *The Lady of Lyons*.

In competition with Miss Marlowe's opening, Charles Frohman brought out **Bohemia** (3-9-96, Empire), Clyde Fitch's dramatization of the Henri Murger story that remains so popular as Puccini's *La Bohème*. Henry Miller was Rudolph, and Viola Allen, Mimi.

A lesser tragedian, George Miln, came in on the same night to the Broadway. His week-long stand, coolly received, offered *Julius Caesar, Hamlet,* and *Othello.* Miln had won a loyal audience in the Midwest, but New York would have none of him.

On the other hand, New Yorkers would always welcome Mrs. Fiske, so her coming out of her premature retirement was good news. Her play, according to many critics, wasn't. **Marie Deloche** (3-16-96, Garden) proved to be an American dramatization of Daudet's *La Menteuse.* The heroine, an illegitimate daughter of worthless parents, schemes and commits bigamy to rise to the top, only to resort to suicide when her methods are exposed. Several reviewers compared the character to Becky Sharp (whom the star would portray so memorably a few years later). Also in her repertory were *Cesarine* (*La Femme de Claude*) and *A Doll's House,* the latter mated with Mrs. Fiske's own one-acter **A Light from St. Agnes** (3-19-96). In this playlet the heroine, Toinette, attempts to prevent her vicious lover from

stealing a diamond cross, which admiring villagers of her bayou community have placed on the body of a saintly neighbor. As she dies, the sunlight streams through the chapel's colored glass windows, illuminating her figure. The star also gave a single performance of Brander Matthews's one-acter **This Picture and That,** which related the wooing of a widow, who at first persists in mourning an unworthy husband, by a former suitor. The response to virtually all Mrs. Fiske's mountings was the same—she was a superb actress, but why could she not choose less offensive plays? Writing in the *American,* Alan Dale theorized that if Mrs. Fiske had come to New York as Bernhardt or Duse had, with a ready-made European reputation, there would have been no such carping, and he predicted that given time and experience she would rival these great ladies.

· · ·

Minnie Maddern Fiske (Mrs. Fiske) [née Mary or Marie Augusta Davey] (1865–1932) Born in New Orleans into a theatrical family, she employed her mother's maiden name when she was first carried onstage at the age of three. Her New York debut came in 1870. She soon was recognized as a preeminent child actress, and with time the short, redheaded girl won equal acclaim in ingenue roles. In 1890, after marrying Harrison Grey Fiske, the publisher of the *Dramatic Mirror,* she retired briefly. Although some critics and playgoers disliked her nervous, erratic manner of speaking, there was general agreement that her performances had depth, subtlety, and finesse. She could even convey an impression of great beauty, despite her unexceptional appearance.

· · ·

Another fine actress, Rose Coghlan, tried her luck in one of her brother Charles's plays, **Madame** (3-23-96, Palmer's). She was cast as Mme Morensky, the widow of a rich, unloved money-lender. Pining for her long-lost lover, she brazenly places an advertisement seeking him. The ad is answered not by the lover—who had died—but, on a whim, by his brother, Gerald (Harrington Reynolds). In short order the pair fall in love. Only the wiles of the deceptive Priscilla Bellamy (Amy Busby) serve to delay their eventual alliance. *Madame* was the sort of play that offers critics little to disparage and just as little to delight in. Miss Coghlan was something of a beauty and a clotheshorse, and a good, robust actress. She never found wide appeal but remained popular with a small, knowing coterie. Her problem was that without a compelling play her coterie was too small to ensure more than a meager, profitless run.

But Miss Coghlan could boast she kept *Madame* on the boards for a longer time than a competing comany was able to stay afloat. And that play not only offered a younger, more beautiful leading lady but, in this election year, dabbled in politics to boot. The glamorous leading lady was the fast-rising Maxine Elliott. The play was Sydney Rosenfeld's **A House of Cards** (3-23-96, Fifth Ave.). His plot begins its twisting when Eleanor Cuthbert is pressed into announcing her engagement to a suave millionaire, Gerald Pryor (Campbell Gollan), unaware that Pryor is having an affair with her married sister, Gwynne (Henrietta Crosman). Gwynne's husband, Peter Burlap (Frazer Coulter), is also unaware of the liaison, for he is too preoccupied calling the political shots behind the scenes. At the moment he is promoting the senatorial candidacy of Ned Garland (Frank Worthing). From the moment Ned and Eleanor met, audiences could guess the outcome. However, they had only two weeks in which to guess.

The evening's biggest moneymaker proved to be I. N. Morris's **The Last Stroke** (3-23-96, Star). It, too, reflected current headlines—not political infighting, but Cuba's attempts to free itself from Spain. Richard Vance (Joseph T. Kilgour), an American with Cuban sympathies, is falsely accused by Don Julio Valdez (Frederic de Belleville) of being a spy. Vance is shot by Valdez, who once had courted Vance's wife, Lucile (Helen Lowell), and who now kidnaps her. The wounded Vance is tied to a post in a wooden building, which is then set on fire. The ship on which Valdez has taken Lucile sinks, and the two are separated. Of course, all three figures escape—Lucile to take the veil (believing Richard to be dead), Richard to hunt for his wife, and Valdez to set up a few more sensation scenes, before villainy is punished and the lovers reunited. On opening night, when the Cuban flag was brought onstage, the whole house responded in unison to one playgoer's appeal for three cheers. The melodrama toured successfully until after the Spanish-American war. Its success further fattened the coffers of Jacob Litt, a young producer who was also gleaning huge profits from *In Old Kentucky* and *The War of Wealth*. When he died a few years later, still in his mid-forties, his estate was valued at over $1,000,000.

On April 1, at the Irving Place Theatre, a house given over to performances in German, Hauptmann's *Die Weber* was accorded its first professional playing in America. For the most part, those critics writing in English-language dailies who attended the premiere decided that the play would be of little or no interest to American playgoers. Americans would have to wait nearly twenty years to decide for themselves.

Der Raubenvater was the sort of German farce that Daly at his peak might have turned into a smash hit. A. M. Palmer's presentation of it, as **His Absent Boy** (4-6-96, Garden), did little for Palmer's fading fame or pocketbook. The story concerned a playboy husband who collects money from his wife under the pretext that it is being forwarded to his unfortunate son from an earlier marriage. The fact that no such boy exists presents farcical problems for the husband when the wife demands to meet and adopt the lad. Sydney Rosenfeld was credited on programs with "colloquial embellishments." Reviewers regularly had spanked Rosenfeld for his heavy reliance on slang, so his name in the playbill merely served as one strike against the play in their books.

Although the hero was a lion tamer and one scene was set at a circus, no lions stalked the stage in Arthur Shirley and Benjamin Landeck's sensation-melodrama **A Lion's Heart** (4-6-96, People's). In settings that moved from France to New Caledonia, the hero had to escape from unjust imprisonment to be avenged on one villain who stole his wife and on another who tried to seduce his daughter. Despite a resounding critical rejection, the play held the stage in backwaters for several seasons.

George Hoey's **The Law of the Land** (4-7-96, American) apparently was less of a crowd-pleaser, for its life on the road was measured in months rather than seasons. Set in the pre–Civil War South, it dealt with the consequences of a treacherous Jew's foreclosing on the mortgage of a troubled plantation. To compound problems, an octoroon named Huldah (Jeffreys Lewis) purposely lies about the parentage of the two foundlings the kindly plantation owner had raised. She insists the all-white Blossom (Amy Busby) is her own daughter, thereby allowing the other foundling, who actually is her daughter, to pass as white. A determined, resourceful Richard Payton (Frank Losee) must rescue Blossom when she is put on the block for sale. At the same time, a red-sealed envelope is delivered. Its contents prove which woman is which. The opening of the play elicited favorable comment. The curtain rose on a view of a southern mansion. Negroes were heard singing from the wings. The *Sun* noted, "Fully two minutes [pass] before a character appears." But such a subdued beginning held only academic interest.

Bygone Americana of another variety supplied much of the appeal in Jerome H. Eddy and Alice E. Ives's **The Village Postmaster** (4-13-96, 14th St.). Their scene was laid in 1852 New Hampshire, when its favorite son, Franklin Pierce, was running for president. Seth Huggins (M. A. Kennedy), the village postmaster, wants his daughter, Miranda (Bertha Creighton), to marry the politically ambitious Ben Deane (Edward J. Morgan), but Miranda has eyes only for a struggling young inventor, John Harper (Forrest Robinson). John goes to New York to try to sell his inventions, and Ben, helping out at the post office, intercepts and destroys his letters, leaving a tearful Miranda to conclude that John really does not love her. She agrees to marry Ben, and the church is bedecked with flowers for the wedding when John returns to unmask Ben's perfidy. Homer Emens's superb settings helped bring to life a country general store (with the post office in one corner), a village green (where the local militia marches, since it is "Training Day"), the Baptist minister's parlor (with his choir singing to enliven a donation party), Seth's farmyard (with live chickens pecking on corn), and the interior of the church. The bucolic piece played until hot weather crimped business, then returned for an even longer stay in the fall. It also found a protracted welcome on the road.

A more contemporary American picture was revealed in **The Speculator** (4-18-96, Fifth Ave.), whose young playwright, George Broadhurst, would soon loom large in American theatricals. Many critics pointed out the obvious: Broadhurst's plot was a comic version of Romeo and Juliet. Its opposing houses were headed by tough businessmen, the implacable Henry Duncan (Atkins Lawrence) and the more compassionate John Fullerton (Thomas Q. Seabrooke). They are cutthroat rivals, so neither is very happy when Robert Fullerton (Sydney Smith) falls in love with Kate Duncan (Lorraine Dreux). To mollify old man Duncan, Robert, dressed in a sombrero and silver-lined trousers, and sporting two revolvers (which he hasn't the faintest idea how to shoot), agrees to try his hand out west. Meanwhile, Duncan hopes to destroy Fullerton by causing a run on wheat futures. Just as things seem to be going Duncan's way, news arrives that war may break out in Europe. Wheat futures soar. Duncan is wiped out. Fullerton comes to his enemy's rescue, so the play ends with the fathers agreeing to their children's marriage. Added color was provided by an English duke, a French count, a society duenna, and a young American anglophile. One striking set showed both fathers' offices, with ticker tapes rattling away and lackeys coming and going, as the two men fight out the futures battle. Seabrooke, better known for his slapstick clowning in musicals, walked away with the best notices. But they were not enough to ensure the show a long run.

On the other hand, an English importation chalked up nearly 100 performances (in two slightly separated engagements). Ralph Lumley's **Thoroughbred** (4-20-96, Garrick) starred another player better known for his clowning in musicals, Henry E. Dixey. The star portrayed a stiff-necked mayor who becomes hopelessly flustered when he is saddled with a horse that is entered in the Derby. While Seabrooke had eschewed any song or dance in his production, Dixey was allowed a number or two in the racetrack scene. Curiously, Dixey soon withdrew from the show—to be replaced by none other than Seabrooke.

The season's final novelty had sufficient songs and dances to allow some commentators to pass it by as just another summer musical. Furthermore, its very title was stolen from a popular song of the day. Surprisingly, **The Sunshine of Paradise Alley** (5-11-96, 14th St.) was the work of Denman Thompson and George W. Ryer—the same two men responsible for the solidly constructed, wildly popular *The Old Homestead*. This time around, the *Dramatic Mirror* rued, the result was as "formless and invertebrate as a jelly-fish." The trade sheet dismissed it as a not wholly successful "attempt at local photography." Its "photographs" included an East River dock with a view of the Brooklyn Bridge and the Bronx Park in autumn. Against these backgrounds were played out the trials, tribulations, and ultimate triumph of Widow McNally's (Mrs. Charles Peters) pure-of-heart daughter, Nellie "Sunshine" (Julie Ring).

As usual, both first-class and combination houses played host during the season to touring versions of old warhorses: Knowles's *The Love-Chase*, Boucicault's *After Dark* and *The Colleen Bawn*, Herne's *Shore Acres* (for a surprisingly long stand), *Fabio Romani, A Celebrated Case, The Struggle of Life, The Witch,* and many others. Apparently missing from the scene—at least in the houses regularly chronicled by Manhattan newspapers—was *Uncle Tom's Cabin.* But Topsy, Eva, and the gang would be back in force during the coming season.

1896–1897

America continued to expand and prosper. At least most Americans thought so. William Jennings Bryan was not so sure, and when he was nominated to run for the presidency he warned the opposition that they could not crucify underdogs on "a cross of gold." The issue was debated all summer and fall. But when ballots had been counted, Americans had opted for gold and McKinley.

Both class divisions and shared pride in America's newfound muscle and importance were evident when the season's first drama premiered. "Those who sat in the orchestra seats in evening dress, and gallery gods who roosted aloft in their shirt sleeves," joined forces to cheer a native work, which, the *Dramatic Mirror* informed its readers, displayed "a hundred times more vigor and coherence than any recent importation." The play was David Belasco's reworking of Clay M. Greene's **Under the Polar Star** (8-20-96, Academy of Music), which, the trade sheet added, initially had been offered to San Francisco several seasons earlier. William A. Brady, increasingly making his mark, was the producer. A scientist named Silas Rodman (Charles Kent) organizes an Arctic expedition to be led by his two nephews, Harry Carleton (Francis Carlyle) and William Brandon (Cuyler Hastings), both naval officers. (The exploits of Fridtjof Nansen and his associates on the *Fram* were just then front-page news.) Shortly before the expedition sails, Rodman is murdered. His ward, Helen Blaine (Grace Henderson), who is engaged to Brandon, believes Carleton is the killer. To gain proof she takes passage on the men's ship, disguising herself as a cabin boy. She soon discovers that her fiancé is the real culprit. The ship is crushed by icebergs and explodes in flames, with the crew taking refuge on ice floes. A blow from Brandon, who is determined that the truth will not come to light, causes Helen to lose her memory. However, it returns in time for her to help convict Brandon. She also realizes that she loves Carleton. The destruction of the ship and the scene on the floes, with the midnight sun glowing on the horizon and northern lights playing in the sky were major applause-getters. Brady, Belasco, and Greene reaped the rewards of their efforts for ten weeks at the huge house and then on tour for several years.

By contrast, the galleryites sat on their hands at Scott Marble's **The Cotton Spinner** (8-29-96, Grand Opera), and its career was very short. Marble set his play in North Carolina, where a good-natured gambler, "a legitimate k'yard dealer," Heath Honlore (P. Aug. Anderson), sees to it that all manner of villainy is thwarted. The villain of the piece is a treacherous mill superintendent, who tries to provoke a strike and attempts to blow up the secretly married hero in the cotton mill and thus win the hand of the heroine.

Nor did Herbert Hall Winslow and Will R. Wilson's **In the Heart of the Storm** (8-29-96, Columbus) fare much better. It continued the movement southward, set, as it was, in the Everglades. There Paul Hudson (Williard Lee) has vowed to be avenged on a murderer who had framed Hudson's father for the killing. That man is Farnum (Sheridan Block). Hudson's determination melts when he falls in love with pretty young Florida (Jessie Bonstelle), who turns out to be Farnum's daughter. Fate takes a hand, killing Farnum in a building's collapse. Before that, audiences could watch a duel in a storm, the heroine saved from drowning by the hero on horseback, and several figures nearly engulfed by quicksand. Not all the action was out in the open; one act took place in a luxurious hotel room. Jessie Bonstelle, of course, went on to fame years later as the great "star-making" duenna of several notable stock troupes. By that time even she probably had forgotten the play.

The same authors were also responsible for the next wide swing on the season's dramatic travels, **The Great Northwest** (8-31-96, American). Amid the tall old trees, the open prairie, and an effective stage blizzard, Robert "Cap" Sheaf (William S. Hart) is hoodwinked into marriage with Stella Cross (Maud Hosford), a conniving adventuress. She plots with Bart Foxwell (John E. Kellerd) to ruin Sheaf. Their first ploy is to steal some horses and implicate him. After Sheaf is acquitted, Foxwell tries to have him lynched. Not even Sheaf's rescue of Stella from a prairie fire earns him any gratitude. By this time Sheaf has fallen in love with Grace Harding (Frances Drake). She offers to play poker with Foxwell—the loser to leave the country. Foxwell proves a bad loser and attempts to kill Sheaf. Grace climbs a windmill to signal for help, but Foxwell starts the mechanism and sees to it Grace is caught on one of the sails (during the blizzard). She is rescued; Stella is shown to be a bigamist; and all ends happily. But the play itself proved little more appealing than the playwrights' earlier effort.

For many playgoers the theatre season started only when the first importation appeared. Two appeared the same night as *The Great Northwest*. The lesser of the two was Charles Darrell's **When London Sleeps** (8-31-96, 14th St.). While the great city slumbers, Capt. Rodney Haynes (Edwin Walter) kidnaps Queenie Carruthers (Perdita Hudspeth), a slack-wire performer who he believes is an heiress. He hopes to force her to marry him and not her sweetheart, David Englehart (Leander Blanden). Critics savaged the work, but audiences clearly enjoyed it, so it toured for many years. What audiences relished were circus scenes, with live animals and real circus acts, a scene in which the heroine is tied to a fake Hindu altar in an amusement park (from which she is released by a convenient explosion), and a scene in which the heroine escapes from a burning building in which she has been locked by breaking a window and recreating her tightrope act on telephone wires. Another scene, which elicited gasps by its prurient display, showed a hustler picking up a customer, then taking him inside a brothel.

The season's first big success at a prime playhouse was Murray Carson and Louis N. Parker's **Rosemary** (8-31-96, Empire), which Charles Frohman mounted for his star, John Drew, supported by an excellent cast that included Maude Adams, Arthur Byron, and Ethel Barrymore. Drew played middle-aged Sir Jasper Thorndyke, who takes a pair of eloping lovers under his wing only to be smitten by the bride-to-be. He resists temptation and sees to it that the pair are married. Years later, after the youngsters have lived out their lives and died and he is a doddering old man, he revisits the inn where he took the girl to watch the coronation procession and there briefly remembers the idyll. Drew was "delightfully light and airy in the gay passages. . . . Always essentially the man of the world, he composed with admirable skill the picture of senility in the last act or epilogue." Many reviewers felt Miss Adams gave her most beguiling performance yet, and they found promise in Miss Barrymore's portrayal of a rustic maid. The play ran into the winter, then toured.

One night later, Charles Frohman's brother Daniel presented his own most popular leading man, E. H. Sothern, in Robert N. Stephens's **An Enemy to the King** (9-1-96, Lyceum) and was rewarded with an almost equally long Broadway run and a prosperous tour. In a way the play represented a daring gamble, since heretofore Stephens had been known only for cheap touring dramas such as *On the Bowery* and *The White Rat*. For faithful opening-nighters it marked a distinct change of pace, following a bit of frothy sentimentality with swashbuckling folderol. Ernanton de Launay is a brave, dashing, white-plumed Huguenot leader whom the authorities have been unable to capture. In desperation they promise Julie de Varion (Virginia Harned) to release her imprisoned father if she can ensnare de Launay. She agrees, but then falls so deeply in love with him that she offers her life in return for his. Naturally de Launay reciprocates her feelings, and he rescues her father before the lovers go off to promised marital bliss. Gorgeous period settings (an inn on the edge of a forest, a ruined chateau, and a sumptuous hall in a castle) and colorful period costumes embellished the evening.

Clyde Fitch's **The Liar** (9-2-96, Hoyt's) was taken from a Bisson farce. Gustave Bravot (Fritz Williams) invents a heroic history for himself in order to impress his fiancée and her mother. Although his rivals follow suit with similar tall tales, he finally wins his girl even though his lies are exposed. For some odd reason the farce was preceded by scenes from Boucicault's old play *The Long Strike*. The bill was coolly received and quickly withdrawn.

One week was all Frank Harvey's **A House of Mystery** (9-14-96, 14th St.) could manage. Its story told how a woman takes poison meant for a mysterious stranger when she discovers that the stranger is her husband's first wife, whom the husband had believed dead.

One of the era's loveliest, most soulful, and most natural of actresses, Annie Russell, found a mite of success in Bret Harte and T. Edgar Pemberton's **Sue** (9-15-96, Hoyt's), taken from Harte's story "The Judgment of Bolinas Plain." In the title part the star played an innocent young girl who is married off by her worthless, drunken father to a dull, loutish farmer, Ira Beasley (Joseph Haworth). Her cows and her colts provide her only happy moments until a handsome young man in spangles and brightly colored tights appears at Lone Farm. He is Jim Wynd (Guy Standing), a circus acrobat who is fleeing from a posse. For the briefest time Sue knows the ecstasy of passion, but when she discovers that Jim would plant the blame for the crime he committed on her husband, her illusions are destroyed. At the saloon that has been converted into a makeshift courtroom, she helps exonerate her husband and prepares to return with him to their farm and their dreary existence. Harte's stories usually did not transfer well onto the stage, and *Sue* was no exception. Only the perceptible glow of Miss Russell's personality saw to it that the drama had a modest run and similarly modest post-Broadway tour.

Another admired actress, Georgia Cayvan, on her own since leaving the Lyceum Theatre company, was not so fortunate. Her vehicle was an English play, W. R. Walkes's **Mary Pennington, Spinster** (10-5-96, Palmer's). The star was cast as a rich, highly educated Englishwoman who takes in a young man as partner to help her run the business she has inherited. A manipulative woman comes between them just as the plant is hit by a strike. Mary loses the business but retrieves and weds the man. The play was a quick failure.

So far during the still young season, American

plays outnumbered importations (counting Fitch's adaptation among the foreigners) by six to five. Any such imbalance was not noteworthy, since what was still called the "preliminary season" regularly saw a rush of native mountings designed primarily for the road and brought to New York early and briefly merely for its stamp. But when the next play opened, was a resounding hit, and was followed by a string of other American plays, several dailies and trade sheets mused publicly on the possibility that within a few years a Broadway season could be sustained almost wholly with native writings. That sort of season was still far off, but the drift was unmistakable.

The play that elicited this prophesying was William Gillette's **Secret Service** (10-5-96, Garrick), still one of the best of all American melodramas. Its action is virtually continuous, beginning at eight in the evening and ending about eleven—the very hours its audiences spent in the theatre. Most of the action occurs at the Richmond home of General Varney, where Confederate women are busy making bandages and otherwise ministering to the needs of the wounded in their besieged city. Varney's daughter, Edith (Amy Busby), is in love with a man she knows as Captain Thorne (Gillette), and to keep him from being sent to the front has persuaded Jefferson Davis to give him a special commission to the telegraph service. She is dismayed when he refuses, insisting he must go back to battle. Benton Arrelsford (Campbell Gollan), Edith's rejected suitor, works for the Confederate Secret Service and is convinced that Thorne is actually a Union spy. Arrelsford has caught one of the Varney's Negro house servants, Jonas (H. D. James), receiving a message from a Union prisoner, Henry Dumont (M. L. Alsop). Jonas refuses to reveal for whom the message is intended, so Arrelsford decides to bring Dumont to the Varney home and let him, supposedly unobserved, confront Thorne. Of course, Thorne is actually Dumont's brother, Lewis. At the meeting Henry recognizes the trap, seizes his brother's gun, and shoots himself in such a way that it seems Thorne shot him. For the time being, Thorne appears to be in the clear. Thorne, now knowing what message he must send, one that will lead to a suicidal Confederate retreat, rushes off to the War Department's telegraph office. He contrives to clear the room and begins to send the message, when Arrelsford arrives with soldiers and attempts to arrest him.

The entrance of General Randolph (Joseph Brennan), the commander at Richmond, affords Thorne the opportunity to twist matters and engineer Arrelsford's arrest, especially after Edith comes and shows Randolph Davis's commission. By now she has realized that Thorne is a spy and whispers to him to use the commission to escape through the lines. He continues to send the message until a sense of guilt and shame overcome him. He tells the operator, "Revoke the order! it was a mistake! I refuse to act under this Commission!" Back in the Varney home, Thorne is arrested and ordered shot. Jonas removes the musket balls from the rifles, but when Thorne learns of this from Edith he alerts the soldiers to the trickery. His life is saved by the second arrival of General Randolph, who points out that since the damaging message was never sent there is no capital case against Thorne. As he is escorted to prison he asks Edith, "What is it—love and good-bye?" She responds, "No no—only the first—and that one every day—every hour—every minute—until we meet again!"

Writing in the *Times,* Edward A. Dithmar noted, "Not a word is spoken in 'Secret Service' except in conversations that might be overheard by an eavesdropper properly placed. Every person in the audience is made to feel himself in each scene an intensely interested occupant of a room in which something stirring is always going on. This is a good play, a fine play, a welcome play." Discussing the drama some years later, Walter Pritchard Eaton made another critical observation: "You will note that in the telegraph office scene especially, the stage directions often occupy double or triple the space of the dialogue. . . . What the actors *did* was of more importance in creating the illusion and excitement than what they *said.*" Thus the click of bayonets and the glint of their metal protruding from the Varneys' curtains was a crucial, thrilling adjunct to the brothers' second-act interview; and Gillette, alone in a dimly lit telegraph office, coolly playing with his cigar and his revolver, turning abruptly to assess each untoward noise and seeing a possible menace in every shadow, made for gripping theatre. The drama ran until early March, toured for many years, and long was a favorite in stock. Its New York stand gave Charles Frohman his second smash hit of the season. Before the theatrical year ended he would be on record as producer of the season's three biggest nonmusical successes.

H. A. du Souchet's **My Friend from India** (10-6-96, Bijou) ran less than a month on Broadway but remained a road and stock favorite for many years. Given the importance of telegraphy in *Secret Service,* it is a curious coincidence that du Souchet worked in the telegraph office of a New York daily. But his farce had nothing to do with telegraphy.

Instead it recounted how Charles Underholt (Edward A. Abeles), after a boozy night on the town, brings home a Five Points barber he met on his barhopping. The barber is clad in a yellow bedspread and introduced into the household as a Buddhist wise man, even though his real name is a typical farce moniker, A. Keene Shaver (Walter E. Perkins). Charlie's father, Erastus Underholt (Frederic Bond), is anxious to move into New York society and tries to use the Buddhist to open doors. A high point of the evening centered on a broken full-length mirror, which a repairman is continually trying to fix. Hoping to escape the seemingly loony Underholts, Shaver puts on a lady's dress. At that moment a silly spinster, garbed in an identical gown, enters. Shaver, on one side of the empty mirror frame, is forced to mimic her gestures to make her think she is seeing herself in the mirror.

Old-fashioned sensation-melodrama was Joseph Arthur's forte, and he enjoyed his final success with **The Cherry Pickers** (10-12-96, 14th St.). The drama was set in Afghanistan during the British-Afghan War. John Nazare (William Harcourt), a half-caste, serves as an officer with the Eleventh Hussars, who are known as "the Cherry Pickers." Col. Brough (Ralph Delmore), although a married man, is Nazare's rival for the affections of another half-caste, Nourmallee (Roselle Knott). Brough accuses Nazare of trying to kill him. Nazare is convicted but escapes. Brough also tortures and kills Nourmallee's father. When Nazare is recaptured, Brough ties him to the fort's walls within range of Afghan bullets, but Nourmallee rescues him. The villain also chains Nazare to a cannon and incites a native to fire it. Again, Nourmallee saves his life. The furious native kills Brough, so Nazare and Nourmallee at last are free to wed. Augustus Pitou's production ran for four months before heading out for a long life on the road. The *Dramatic Mirror* hailed the clearly obsolescent work as "good, wholesome melodrama," adding much the same praise it had accorded *Under the Polar Star* some weeks before by suggesting the work "surpasses any imported melodrama" of recent vintage.

Critics were not so pleased with A. C. Gunter's **A Florida Enchantment** (10-12-96, Hoyt's), to some extent because public moral posturing was not changing as openly as fashions in playwriting, and also because the playing left some doubt as to whether the work was meant to be a comedy or a drama. In Gunter's story Lillian Cruger Travers (Marie Jansen) and her black maid, Jane (Dan Collyer), using a magic pill, turn themselves into men in order to be avenged on faithless lovers. As a man, Lillian successfully courts the pretty widow her fickle suitor is now chasing. Just why a woman saying "damn," smoking a cigarette, or making love (disguised as a man) to another woman should have so offended reviewers is hard to fathom. Gunter also pointed out that it was all clearly meant as good fun and had been labeled accordingly "a comedy frolic." Critical cries, rather than killing the play, helped give it a modest run, although it seems not to have prospered in the hinterlands.

Three touring melodramas similarly evinced a lack of consistent tone, though clearly such tonal hodgepodges were what their public wanted. Since Clay M. Greene and Ben Teal's **On Broadway** (10-12-96, Grand Opera) starred the popular vaudevillian Maggie Cline, the hodgepodge was inevitable. She played Mary Brady, "a womanly woman with a man's nerve." She is a subcontractor, taking over her father's failing company and helping to erect a building the villain causes to collapse. Her friend Dan McCloskey bloodies the nose of the mean-spirited Harlem Hyena to teach him his place. But in the end Mary does not marry Dan. Instead she settles for a nice young detective. One scene was set on a cable car, with City Hall and other structures passing by on the panorama behind; another, also set before a moving panorama, took place on a ferry. Of course, Miss Cline sang her most famous song, "Throw 'em Down, McCloskey," as "supers chucked loose lumber" in the wings.

Barney Gilmore and John F. Leonard's **Hogan's Alley** (10-12-96, People's) was taken from the popular comic strip. Programs warned that "the Yellow Kid [a popular comic strip figure] has swiped the plot." What little story there was depicted the rough-and-tumble life on the East Side. The *Herald* concluded, "The play no doubt would fall flat at a Broadway house, but on the Bowery it is a howling success."

According to the *Sun*, Scott Marble's **The Great Train Robbery** (10-19-96, People's) was so atypical a melodrama that it 'left the identity of villain and hero in doubt for fully fifteen minutes." Of course, the critic was being sarcastic, since the basic plot once again pitted a good guy and a bad man, both of whom seek to win the same girl, against each other. To eavesdrop, the villain runs a wire from a telephone pole into a room, hiding the wire's end under a hat. When he learns on which train a large amount of money is to be sent, he goads his Indian friends into attacking the train. The baggage car is blown up, with its roof and sides flying off in different directions. The heroine, dressed as a man, with "real saucy boots," helps the hero settle the score. A second-act barroom setting allowed for the expected specialties. In 1903, when Edwin S. Porter made his famous one-reeler, he appropriated Marble's title but not his story.

The parade of American plays ended for the time being with George Day and Allen Reed's farce **The Mummy** (11-2-96, Garden). A mischievous young lady, Hattie Van Tassell Smythe (Amelia Bingham), on a visit to a famed Egyptologist, sends an electric current through a mummy of Ramses II, bringing the mummy to life. Hattie and her friends dress the revivified mummy (Robert Hilliard) in modern clothes, while she pretends to be the ancient Egyptian. Her adventures were secondary, since Hilliard was the star, but he finds himself pursued by an old maid while he in turn courts a black serving girl, Cleopatra (Vivian Bernard), who reminds him of Isis. Finally tiring of running around, he returns to the sarcophagus. Yet when its lid is raised again for a final peek, nothing is found in the coffin except a hat, an overcoat, and an empty whiskey bottle. Trite and excessively complicated, the farce found few takers.

The Dutch-born English actor and cellist Auguste Van Biene had played **The Broken Melody** (11-5-96, American) more than 1000 times on English provincial circuits before bringing it to America. He portrayed a composer who cannot remember a melody until his wife, alienated from him by a malicious duchess, returns. Neither he nor the play proved popular.

However, another British drama did win favor, if not a long first New York run. Wilson Barrett had premiered the work, with himself as star, in St. Louis some months earlier, but by the time **The Sign of the Cross** (11-9-96, Knickerbocker) reached Broadway, Barrett had returned to England and relinquished the lead to Charles Dalton. Dalton was cast as a Roman prefect, ordered by Nero to kill Christians, who becomes enamored of a Christian girl and accompanies her to face the lions in the arena.

Theodore Kremer, a hack probably best known for his version of *Bertha, the Sewing Machine Girl*, was the author of **The Nihilists; or, the Assassination of the Czar** (11-9-96, People's). His was a theme long since worked to death by better writers. Rafaelle Alexis (Kremer), a Moscow University student, is engaged to the Baroness Olga. His rival, Ivan Arkoff, makes it seem that Rafaelle is plotting to kill the czar, until Ivan's discarded mistress, Doris, spoils the scheme.

An example of a drama that folded on the road was Ernest Lacy's unappealingly titled **Crom-a-Boo** (11-9-96, Park, Philadelphia). The Earl of Kildare (Charles Maclaine) wants his daughter, Moya (Miss Santje), to marry Sir Henry Hardcastle (Prince Lloyd) although she loves a young surgeon, Edward Doyle (James Skelly). Edward's foster brother, Gerald O'Brien (John Skelly), who is the earl's steward, exposes Sir Henry as a miscreant, helps unite the lovers, and turns out to be the real earl. Although the play was called a "romantic Irish drama," it was rather sedate. There were no fisticuffs, no roistering drunkards, no warbling laborers. The critics, if not the public, found these changes all in the play's favor. What they objected to were the indifferent and inept performances. But for whatever reason, the primarily Irish audience for which it was intended would not accept the piece.

Back in New York, a more famous figure than Kremer was starred in his own work when Maurice Barrymore opened in **Roaring Dick & Co.** (11-16-96, Palmer's). Barrymore played a scapegrace, disowned son who returns home, saves his miserly father from being murdered, inherits the estate, wins his girl, and reforms. One scene, in which Dick sets out to demonstrate how generous he can be with his newfound wealth, had dozens of children ravenously wolfing down food at long tables under a large marquee. Rumor had it that Barrymore—and his producer, William A. Brady—recruited the youngsters from local orphanages to ensure their hunger would drive them to eat wildly. Not all critics were as harsh as the *Tribune*'s William Winter, who branded the entertainment "rubbish," but the four-week stay was not particularly profitable, and the subsequent tour ended abruptly. When the show closed in New York, the failing Palmer gave up his lease on the playhouse, having moved to try his luck in Chicago. Barrymore's career, crippled by syphilis, was also nearing its end. Only Brady represented the wave of the future.

The success of *Trilby* may well have served as the inspiration for **An Innocent Sinner** (11-16-96, Star). Lawrence Marston and Lillian Lewis set their drama in the Kentucky mountains, where Hinda Beckman is accused of murdering her abusive husband, a crime committed while under the mesmeric influence of the baleful Dr. Jacob. Tom Bridges, a young mountaineer, loves Lillian and helps clear her name. One week and the play was gone.

Few things better exemplified the inevitable change in theatrical fashions than the situation at Daly's. By now Daly more or less had resigned himself to the loss of John Drew from his famous quartet. Then in September the other male stalwart from the group, James Lewis, died suddenly. Nor, apparently, could Daly find a suitable new vehicle. The early months of the season had been given over to an imported English musical. His entire "regular" season was devoted to old plays. He began on the 23rd with *As You Like It* and moved on, at varying intervals, to *London Assurance, The School for Scandal, Much Ado About Nothing, The Magistrate, Meg Merrilies, The Wonder,* and *The Tempest.* Of these only *Meg Merrilies* and *The Tempest* were new to his repertory. In a way, that repertory now looked more like Wallack's in its heyday, but even Wallack's had found room for new works. Ada Rehan and Mrs. Gilbert were back, and some excellent players such as Tyrone Power joined the ensemble. Yet the simple truth was that Daly's time, and the time for a company and repertory like his, had passed. (The English musical was even played on occasional evenings during the early weeks of the "regular" season, and no sooner had his shortened season ended than another London musical took over his house.)

In his own way Richard Mansfield was battling against the current as much as Daly. When he opened a six-week stand on the 23rd at the Garden, he brought with him nine productions. Eight were revivals of his standbys: *Richard III, The Merchant of Venice, Beau Brummell, A Parisian Romance, The Scarlet Letter, Prince Karl, Dr. Jekyll and Mr. Hyde,* and *Arms and the Man.* He saved his novelty for midway in his visit.

Two insignificant plays opened on the same night, although one was rewarded a modicum of popularity. Charles Klein was the adaptor of Decourcelle's *Les Deux Gosses.* As **Two Little Vagrants** (11-23-96, Academy of Music) it centered on a girl waif, actually well-born, and a gamin (played as a trouser role by Minnie Dupree). They are raised together by thieves and try to restore the girl to her proper station when they learn her history. The play had been a hit in Paris and London and on its pre-Broadway tour before compiling seventy-two Manhattan showings.

David K. Higgins's **Turn of the Tide** (11-23-96, People's) was the latest touring melodrama to employ an Italian immigrant as a villain. He is Luigi Sinabaldia (P. Aug. Anderson), but true-blue-American Hal Vandeleur (Oliver Doud Byron) confounds his attempt to blackmail a gentlemanly widower who once had been kind to Hal. Not all Italians were depicted as evil. Byron's wife, Kate, was cast in the sympathetic, comic role of Peggy Tarrabocia, an "Irish-Italian-American."

Daniel Frohman's stock ensemble, more forward-looking than Daly's, began its season with a new English play and promptly laid an egg. Henry V. Esmond's **The Courtship of Leonie** (11-24-96, Lyceum) unfolded the tribulations of a young widow after circumstances make it seem years before had murdered her bigamist husband. Mary Mannering made her American debut playing opposite her own husband-to-be, James K. Hackett.

Herbert Beerbohm Tree opened his second American visit with Gilbert Parker's **The Seats of the Mighty** (11-30-96, Knickerbocker), a romantic melodrama set in rebellious Quebec during the reign of Louis XV. The star took the role of the king's speechifying illegitimate son. When the play failed to draw, it was replaced by *The Dancing Girl, Trilby, A Bunch of Violets,* and *Hamlet.*

Another short-lived disappointment was Arthur Bourchier and Alfred Sutro's version of Bisson and Carré's *Monsieur le directeur* under the title **The Chili Widow** (11-30-96, Bijou). During its lone week it described the ploys of an aggressive sister-in-law to win a promotion for her timid, punctilious brother-in-law and marry his boss, a political bigwig, at the same time. The English company included Bourchier, and Violet and Irene Vanbrugh.

The single American novelty of the night had still less intrinsic merit, but since it starred James J. Corbett it packed the gallery with cheering supporters. Charles T. Vincent's **The Naval Cadet** (11-30-96, Grand Opera) cast the fighter as Ned Correll of the USNA at Annapolis. He invents a new machine gun, the designs for which are promptly stolen by a scoundrelly Frenchman. A chase, with suitable intervals for fisticuffs, ensues, taking the characters from the gymnasium at Annapolis to the deck of the luxury liner *St. Louis* and finally to a thieves' den in the slums of Paris hard by the Jardin de Paris. The one-week stopover was part of a cross-country tour that lasted for two seasons and, producer William A. Brady recorded, netted a small fortune. McKee Rankin directed.

W. H. Crane, who had returned to New York a week earlier with a revival of *His Wife's Father,* now switched to a new play, Martha Morton's **The Fool of Fortune** (12-1-96, Fifth Ave.). Elisha Cunningham (Crane) comes back from Europe with his wife (Kate Lester), his daughters, Marjorie (Effie Shannon) and Jennie (Dallas Tyler), and Count de Cluny (Edwin Arden) in tow. The count hopes to wed Marjorie, but she prefers a young stockbroker, Karl Worresdorf (Boyd Putnam), so de Cluny settles for Jennie. When Ezekiel Powers (F. F. Mackay) ruins Elisha financially, Karl turns the tables by bankrupting Ezekiel and restoring Elisha's wealth. All this proves too much for the old man, who dies as the ticker tape taps out his victory. Some critics complained the death beside the ticker tape smacked of an earlier Crane hit, *The Henrietta*. There were also quibbles about whether or not Elisha needed to die in the play. On the pre–New York tour Crane had experimented with several endings, finally deciding this, Miss Morton's original conclusion, was best. His disintegration from a robust, buoyant man to a shattered wreck allowed for a tour de force that helped pack the theatre for five weeks and on the continuing tour.

E. S. Willard joined the long list of London players peddling their talents on Broadway during the season when he opened in Henry Arthur Jones's **The Rogue's Comedy** (12-7-96, Wallack's). The play recounted the undoing of a likable swindler by a young man who does not know he is the swindler's son. During the three-week stand Willard also gave a few performances of *The Middleman* and *The Professor's Love Story*. Competing for attention with Willard's first night were two new-old plays. At the Bijou, Arthur Bourchier's troupe brought out **The Queen's Proctor,** Herman Merivale's reworking of *Divorçons*, while at the new Murray Hill Theatre, Roland Reed, a popular touring comedian, starred in **The Politician,** which Sydney Rosenfeld adapted from David Lloyd's *For Congress*.

Ticket sales picked up for Daniel Frohman when he replaced *The Courtship of Leonie* with a double bill consisting of Sydney Grundy's **The Late Mr. Costello** and Theodore Burt Sayre and Helen Bogart's one-acter **The Wife of Willoughby** (12-14-96, Lyceum). In the former a young widow exploits her widowhood to tantalize her sister's suitors. In the short American piece an aging painter discovers his youthful wife's infidelity when, simply to have her give him a hurt expression to paint, he accuses her of having an affair. This curtain raiser was replaced on the 31st by Mrs. Fiske's **The White Flower,** which once had been *The Rose* and in which an aging husband takes poison so his young wife can marry her lover.

Frank Harvey's **Brother for Brother** (12-14-96, Star) was a touring melodrama that made several brief stops in Manhattan during the season. Its action begins as the dissolute, spendthrift Eric Redford decides to rob his father's safe and cast suspicion on his decent half-brother, Allan Foster.

Mansfield's new play provided him with one of his strangest and most memorable opening nights. H. Greenhough Smith dramatized his own novel **Castle Sombras** (12-16-96, Garden). The story begins somberly enough, with Sir John Sombras, the inheritor of an ages-old tradition of cruelty and baseness, brooding over the refusal of Thyrza (Beatrice Cameron) to marry him. She loves Hilary Dare (Henry Jewett), who is besieging the castle at the behest of King Charles. When Sir John, disguised as a minstrel, enters the enemy camp, he is recognized and captured. But Hilary finds a portrait of Thyrza on Sir John, and, learning that she is a relative of Sir John and lives in the castle, he releases him. Hilary in turn is permitted to enter the castle alone. There Sir John spies on the pair, realizes how deeply they love each other, and accepts the inevitable. Because of its "happy" ending the play was billed as "a romantic comedy." The billing backfired. As Mansfield recorded, "We rehearsed the play as a melodrama. I played the part of a deep, dark villain. My first remark, as I came on the stage, intended to be taken seriously, was greeted with a laugh. . . . I knew it would be fatal to attempt to act that play seriously." And so the rest of the piece was played for laughs. But even this sudden change could not win much approval, and *Castle Sombras* never entered the list of Mansfield's favorites.

The Gay Mr. Lightfoot (12-16-96, Bijou) had initially been tried out as *When the Cat's Away,* a title that gave more of a hint of its plot. Its authors, Louis De Lange and Lee Arthur, almost certainly were familiar with older farces such as *Forbidden Fruit*, which employed the same basic situation to precipitate the comic confusion: a married man sends his wife on vacation so that he and a young assistant can have a night on the town. In this instance Mr. Lightfoot (W. H. Thompson) shaves off his whiskers and dons a wig (in front of the audience) to help compound the misunderstandings. These begin when a rich widow, Mrs. Beaumont (Mabel Amber), mistakes the assistant, Mr. Jerome (Wright Huntington), for Lightfoot. Moreover, Jerome had once saved the life of a pretty young girl, Helen (Bijou Fernandez), and begun a correspondence with her. Unfortunately, the letters fall into the hands of her maiden aunt, Ellen Opie (Agnes Findlay), who assumes that Jerome's proposal of marriage is meant for her. As if these confusions were not enough, Te Jim (Charles Bradshaw) appears on the scene. He is an Indian being pursued by Lieutenant Farsely (Frederic Conger), an army officer who has orders to arrest the Indian for bigamy. Te Jim is also given to long, boring pronouncements, ergo his name. By the final curtain Lightfoot has squared matters with his wife (who naturally returned prematurely); Jerome elects to marry Mrs. Beaumont; Helen and Lieutenant Farsely exchange troths; and Te Jim has added the old maid to his list of conquests. Much of the action took place in the new Manhattan Hotel, and one newspaper suggested the hotel may have defrayed some of the production costs to have its rooms duplicated onstage. The expense was wasted, for *The Gay Mr. Lightfoot* died an early death.

Our changing vocabulary has added a certain unintentional humor to one critic's description of the situation at the start of McKee Rankin's **True to Life** (12-21-96, Murray Hill), although the critic himself obviously was poking fun at some absurd theatrical clichés: "A young woman, abandoned by her mother, grows up to be a typewriter, and the forgetful mother, abandoned by her husband, who languishes in Sing Sing, becomes a great operatic singer." The husband is Philip Garth (Rankin), who had been imprisoned for a crime he did not commit. When he is released he sets out to find his wife, who has finally decided she ought to find her daughter. At first the girl spurns her mother, but after Garth rediscovers his wife and restores his good name there are hugs and kisses all around. The daughter was played by a debutante, Nance O'Neil, who for years was known euphemistically as Rankin's "protégée." Some songs and dances larded through the drama "jarred harshly," but after a single week the play moved on to a long circuit of combination houses.

Mark Price's ironically titled **A Man of Honor** (12-21-96, American) played two weeks, then also toured at length. Its titular hero-villain deserts his wife, flees with his daughter to America, later returns to England under an assumed name, remarries, and commits his first wife to a mental institution when she reappears seeking a job as a housekeeper. She is rescued from there by the daughter's suitor.

From a late 20th-century point of view, the most interesting of the evening's openings may have been **Darkest America** (12-21-96, People's), for it suggested that even some late 19th-century audiences could be racially mixed. The *Dramatic Mirror* noted that "the upper ten of Thompson Street and Minetta Lane joined last night with whitefaced East Siders in according rapturous greeting" to the play. A Mississippi steamboat race was the evening's high point, and minstrel songs enlivened the entertainment, which was able to tour for more than a year.

The season's biggest dramatic success was Charles Frohman's importation of a London hit, Edward Rose's dramatization of Stanley Weyman's novel **Under the Red Robe** (12-28-96, Empire). Its story was much like that of *An Enemy of the King,* with sexes reversed. Gil de Berault (William Faversham), a bankrupt, is hauled before Cardinal Richelieu (J. E. Dodson) for an unauthorized duel. To avoid punishment he agrees to spy on Henri de Cocheforêt (Lewis Baker), until he falls in love with de Cocheforêt's sister, Renée (Viola Allen). Critics came down hard on the performance. The *Times,* more tactful than many, reported it was "marred by nervousness." The *Dramatic Mirror* saw little hope in Faversham, complaining that he was "the last man in the world one can swallow as a hero of romance. He squints from the corners of his eyes, he stands with arms akimbo, and he speaks his lines stupidly. . . . Oh for a Fechter, or a young Salvini, or a James O'Neill to give life, and fire, and grace, and impetuosity to such roles." Yet the swashbuckler, bedecked with colorful period costumes and settings (among them a gambling house, a chateau, a mountain crossroads, and the cardinal's sumptuous palace) had huge audience appeal and ran into the summer. It survived as a touring and stock favorite well into the early years of the new century.

Not so **Society Shadows** (12-28-96, Savoy), which was advertised as "an American play by an American author." The hero, Rodney Gray, is a poor Yankee inventor with a dying mother. He is offered a fortune to marry a wealthy man's daughter, pregnant by another man. Does Rodney accept? You bet he does. But audiences could not have cared less.

Yet one more London star, John Hare, drew the most elite first-nighters on the first Monday of the new year, 1897. He opened with Arthur Wing Pinero's **The Hobby Horse** (1-4-97, Knickerbocker), in which an old racing fanatic is taught by his youthful wife that there are more charitable pleasures. Besides revivals of *Caste, A Pair of Spectacles,* and *A Quiet Rubber* he also offered two short plays in which he did not appear: Frances Moore's **When George IV Was King** (2-8-97), in which two old men realize their ward is mature enough to fend for herself; and Israel Zangwill's **Six Persons** (2-15-97), telling of a young couple who come to recognize they are an ill-suited match.

A Superfluous Husband (1-4-97, Fifth Ave.), reworked from the German of Ludwig Fulda by Clyde Fitch and Leo Ditrichstein, recounted how a famous woman enlists her ex-lover to help give her bookish, retiring husband a moment in the public spotlight. Although the wife was played by Olive Oliver, the Holland brothers, E. M. and Joseph, were starred. The consensus was that everybody's efforts were wasted. Nor was there much praise for Augustus Thomas's one-act condensation of *Col.*

Carter of Cartersville, which served as a curtain raiser.

The best-received of the wholly American plays to open on that hectic evening was Charles H. Hoyt's **A Contented Woman** (1-4-97, Hoyt's). But his story of a wife who runs against her husband in a mayoral contest was so larded with songs and musical turns that it straddled the fence between genres.

Edwin Milton Royle's **Captain Impudence** (1-4-97, American) employed the rarely used Mexican War, just before the Battle of Buena Vista, as background. The author played the happy-go-lucky Capt. Willard Shields. A hot-tempered Mexican, Jovita Talamanca (Selena Fetter Royle), loves him, but when she hears that he has "spoken slightingly" of her and that his heart is set on Lucretia Bugg (Ellen Burg Edeson), she plots revenge. She becomes a Mexican spy, is captured, and is brought before the captain, who laughingly dismisses her. For this Shields is ordered court-martialed. Jovita rushes to his defense and wins his freedom. The American flag waving over Chapultepec in the last act elicited a barrage of applause. A subplot featured the comic romance of Lucretia's father, Major Hannibal Bugg (McKee Rankin), and a feisty widow, Mrs. Trigg (Amelia Bingham). Airily played, the comedy lingered in Manhattan for three weeks before embarking on a seasons-long trek.

James R. Garey's **Fatal City** (1-4-97, People's) was an unsuccessful touring melodrama that frittered away a fresh theme by trafficking in stock characters and motifs. Eureka is a utopian community founded by Robert Nelson. His superintendent, Paul Coudert, and a dedicated anarchist, Madelaine Warden, connive to hand over the city to "the trust king," an opportunistic capitalist named Alexander Wilson. His methods bring about a strike, and when this leads to a falling-out with Madelaine, Coudert kills him and foists the blame on Nelson. A young reporter, William Locke, uncovers the truth. Madelaine kills Coudert, then kills herself.

Henry Miller tasted stardom for the first time when Charles Frohman placed his name above the title in advertisements for Charles Klein and Joseph I. C. Clarke's **Heartsease** (1-11-97, Garden).
. . .
[John] **Henry Miller** (1860–1926) was born in England and raised in Canada, where he decided upon an acting career after seeing Oliver Doud Byron in *Across the Continent.* He first played New York in 1880, then rose to leading assignments under Daniel and later Charles Frohman. A round-faced, slightly stocky man, he was an advocate, despite his early admiration for Byron, of thoughtful, natural acting. He also became famous for his explosive temper.
. . .
Miller portrayed Eric Temple, a well-born but impoverished Englishman who in 1785 writes an opera on King Lear. The opera is stolen and performed under another name at Covent Garden. Before Eric kills the rich, titled thief in a duel and rights all other wrongs, he is accused of tricking his mother-in-law-to-be into supporting him, forced to break off his engagement, and stricken with a case of brain fever. While first-night jitters spoiled the duel scene, Miller was praised for his restrained, intelligent action. The production was not so well received. Apparently it skimped on costs; several players were observed wearing but one costume, although the action supposedly took place over several months. Even more absurd were careless anachronisms. When the play had been tried out its setting was contemporary, but when its action was moved back to the 18th century the message apparently failed to get through to everyone. Some of the furnishings were distinctly modern, and, more comical, the newspapers characters read were contemporary New York dailies. The slips reportedly were hastily rectified. This initial mounting ran ten weeks. Subsequently, it toured and was produced in stock for many years. Miller himself returned to it on and off for nearly a decade.

London and Brighton at the other end of the 18th century were the settings for George Fleming (Constance Fletcher) and Frances Hodgson Burnett's **The First Gentleman of Europe** (1-25-97, Lyceum). As the title indicates, the central figure is George IV (James K. Hackett), then merely heir apparent. Under an assumed name he courts Daphne (Mary Mannering), a goldsmith's daughter. Daphne's humble suitor, George Carteret (Edward Morgan), attacks the supposed Mr. Ffolliott and is jailed. The efforts of worldly Lady Sark (Marie Shotwell) and Daphne's concern for Carteret soften the prince's resolve. This time there were no complaints about Daniel Frohman's thoughtful costuming and settings. Coupled with the piece was **When a Man's Married** (of uncertain authorship), in which a young couple, trying to remedy another pair's falling-out, have their own quarrel. The double bill ran until spring.

During the preceding season, as election fever was building, Jacob Litt had toured H. Grattan Donnelly's **The Woman in Black** (1-25-97, Columbus) with considerable success. It had even gotten as close as Brooklyn, where it was rechristened briefly

Tammany Tiger. Now it arrived belatedly in Manhattan, betraying the influence of at least two recent Broadway hits. John Crane, a cynical, corrupt millionaire hoping to gain a seat in Congress, aligns himself with an equally cynical, corrupt political boss, Simon Krantzer. They are opposed by the forthright Frank Mansfield, who hopes to marry Crane's ward. But Crane is determined the girl shall marry his son, John junior, who prefers a music hall singer, Mlle. Ruby. Krantzer hires a notorious mesmerist, Mme (or Mother) Zenda, to hypnotize the girl and force her to marry Crane's son. Naturally, goodness prevails, the lovers are properly paired, and Krantzer's power is broken. John H. Young's settings evoked the biggest applause. These included Krantzer's headquarters, the thieves' den where Zenda reigns, and, most of all, Madison Square, with the Hoffman House and the Fifth Avenue Hotel in the background and a huge calcium-lit sign projecting election returns. McKee Rankin directed. By now audiences were sated with politics. The play ran a single week but reappeared briefly during the season at several other combination houses.

The next night the ill-fated, emotionally troubled Margaret Mather came out of retirement to present *Cymbeline* at Wallack's. Her production was sumptuous, with John H. Young, Homer Emens, Richard Marston, Harley Merry, and Walter Burridge all combining to create much lauded sets. Critics also admired the fervor and clarity of the star's performance, although there were complaints that some of her supporting players had not yet learned their lines. Unfortunately, the play was too esoteric for most playgoers. It did two weeks of indifferent business. In the following year Miss Mather died, still in her thirties.

The opening of Sutton Vane and Arthur Shirley's **Straight from the Heart** (1-26-97, Academy of Music) had to be delayed for one night when its scenery became lost in transit from Philadelphia. Even then much of it would not work properly, including a supposed fire aboard an ocean liner. As in *Fatal City,* anarchists, led this time by Ventry Fox (E. L. Walton), are the villains. They persecute Clara Nugent (Blanche Walsh), her brother, Harold (also played by Miss Walsh, as a trouser role), and her lover, Dr. David Walters (George Paxton). In fact, their treachery brings Walters right to the guillotine, and he is saved only when Clara rides up on horseback, waving a pardon from the French president. The action moved from a stately English conservatory, to a rocky pass in the Algerian desert, to the ship, and to Paris. The ubiquitous McKee Rankin staged the play, while the comparatively new

firm of Gates and Morange was responsible for the settings.

The seemingly luckless Holland brothers suffered another quick failure when they starred together in F. Marion Crawford and Harry St. Maur's dramatization of Crawford's novel **Dr. Claudius** (2-1-97, Fifth Ave.). Joseph impersonated the young Swedish doctor who must prove he is a legitimate heir, while E. M. Holland played his adversary, Silas Barker.

Equally luckless were A. C. Wheeler and Edward M. Alfriend, who had scored so heavily with *The Great Diamond Robbery.* Advertisements proclaimed their new opus, **New York** (2-1-97, American) was "A Drama of Local Interest—Not a Melodrama." Critics rejected both the distinction and the play. Kate Haviland (Mabel Amber) kills a married man who had violated her. She later marries the politically powerful Dr. Follin Sanger (Herbert Carr). At the time of his death the murdered man was carrying papers that bequeathed a fortune to Colin Carteret (Charles Mackay). The papers have disappeared. Carteret is the illegitimate, unacknowledged son of a detective, John Wilder (Burr McIntosh), and it falls upon Wilder to uncover the papers. His problem is that he must do this without involving Mrs. Sanger, with whom he sympathizes. His search takes him to yet one more theatrically contrived thieves' den before he brings the affair to a satisfactory conclusion. There he grabs the papers and makes good his escape by smashing an oil lamp on the table. The *Sun* disparaged this and other settings, including a "longshoreman's tower," a boudoir, and an office, as seeming "about as much like New York as . . . ancient Babylon." At one point the action was interrupted to allow an octet of black singers and dancers ("the real thing," one critic rejoiced) to show their stuff.

The next entry made no attempt to hide its nature. Programs called J. J. McCloskey's **Cuba's Vow** (2-8-97, Star) a "realistic melodrama." Cuba Varona was the latest in a line of heroines whose given name was the same as her birthplace (witness Georgia, Maryland, and, this season, Florida). Cuba returns home to find her family has been murdered on orders of Donna Dolores Vasquez, the sadistic wife of a Spanish general. She vows revenge, and she succeeds with the help of a handsome American naval officer, Lt. Percival Grant. She also discovers her father had escaped the massacre. Donna Dolores's end comes when Cuba dumps her down a well. Slangy, roistering American sailors provided comic relief and some musical moments.

The Star, where *Cuba's Vow* played out its brief run, once had been Wallack's, until Wallack built a newer theatre uptown. That now more prestigious Wallack's served as host on the same night to Julia Marlowe and her husband, Robert Taber, when they opened in *Romeo and Juliet.* Review after review used the same word to describe the star: "charming." But the Tabers quickly switched to a novelty, **For Bonnie Prince Charlie** (2-15-97, Wallack's), Joseph I. C. Clarke's translation of François Coppée's *Les Jacobites.* Miss Marlowe portrayed Mary, an urchin who sacrifices her reputation and life for the Stuart cause. Taber was seen as her uncle, a blind beggar. The warmth of the star's acting, the picturesque settings and costumes, and the skirling bagpipes combined to give the play a six-week run.

Three weeks sufficed for Sardou's **Spiritisme** (2-22-97, Knickerbocker), which told of a faithless wife who allows her husband to believe she has died in a railroad station fire, then discovers her lover no longer wants her. Nelson Wheatcroft and Virginia Harned were the husband and wife, Maurice Barrymore the suave, caddish lover.

Many critics were happier with an American play that opened the same evening at a less classy playhouse, David K. Higgins's **At Piney Ridge** (2-22-97, American). The critic for the *Times* commented, "The American drama is growing and will grow in just the direction indicated by Mr. Higgins in this play. We have no blasé and degenerate 'society' to analyze, and what romance there is among us must be found in those communities in which men are not wholly given up to the weary grind of making money, or trying to make it, and in which 'modern civilization' has not yet nearly annihilated nature." Yet *At Piney Ridge* was little more than a skillful compiling of stock situations found in many older American plays. Years before the curtain rises, Dagmar (Mrs. McKee Rankin), an octoroon, secretly has exchanged her own child, Mark (Charles Canfield), for Jack Rose (Burr McIntosh). Mark is given all the benefits of a rich upbringing and becomes a respected banker. But Jack, too, has grown rich. Both men love Azelle (Mabel Amber), a bank president's daughter. To advance his own suit, Mark denounces Jack as part Negro. Naturally, he says nothing about his own seduction and abandonment of Cindy (Georgia Waldron), a mountain girl. Moreover, Mark's defalcations have brought his bank to the verge of ruin. Dagmar, pursued by a lynch mob, reveals the truth, but Mark escapes through a window. Just then a shot is heard, and Zeb (B. J. Murphy), Cindy's father, appears at the window with a smoking gun. Jack uses his own monies to save the bank and weds Azelle. There was little mountain atmosphere in the settings, which included the exterior and reception room of the banker's home and Jack's home—all of which might have served for any "society" drama. Only the one act set outside Cindy and Zeb's humbler home suggested a country background. The play ran for five weeks and immediately was added to the lengthening list of touring favorites.

One of the most glowing of theatrical evenings followed, when Mrs. Fiske appeared in Lorimer Stoddard's dramatization of **Tess of the D'Urbervilles** (3-2-97, Fifth Ave.). Virtually all the critics were ecstatic, although the cranky William Winter complained her Tess had more intellect than feeling. Many unhesitatingly compared her—and compared her favorably—with Bernhardt and Duse. The critic for the *Dramatic Mirror* proclaimed she possessed the "divine essentials" and called her murder of the vicious Alec "one of the most marvelously natural and thrillingly effective things ever seen on stage." Dithmar said she combined "great sympathy and clearness of expression with so rare a gift of poetry." The rising James Huneker described in the *Advertiser* the ending (at Stonehenge): "The Wessex Pagan, Tess, [is] saluting the god of day as the law closes in about her. The scene is Wagnerian, it is superb, and is a final stroke of genius, for it sums up Tess's character, her love of nature, of light, of love. It gives us in a breathless moment . . . the atmosphere of the half wild, unsullied sweet creature." When *Harper's Weekly* appeared a short time later, William Dean Howells concluded that "this fine actress" made audiences believe in the inevitability of Tess's fate "by her almost invariable truth." Charles Coghlan as Alec, Edward Bell, a once promising actor beset by alcoholism who now temporarily licked his demon, as Angel, and Annie Irish as Marian all won praise. The Fiskes had been forced to book the not very desirable Fifth Avenue Theatre because of their battle with the rapidly expanding Trust. But the reviews brought them eleven weeks of good business and a prosperous road tour, despite the efforts of the Trust to deprive her of theatres everywhere.

In Louis N. Parker's second play of the season, **The Mayflower** (3-8-97, Lyceum), the daughter (Mary Mannering) of a confirmed Puritan is hounded by the scapegrace son (James K. Hackett) of the Puritans' persecutor. Daniel Frohman's Lyceum ensemble did capable work against settings that depicted Holland at tulip time, an old quay at Plymouth, and sunrise over Massachusetts Bay, with the partly cleared forest in the foreground. But the play ran less than a month.

On the other hand, a French farce gave Charles

Act Three : 1892–1899

Frohman the season's last (or last but one) nonmusical hit. **Never Again; or, The Tricks of Seraphin** (3-8-97, Garrick) was T. R. Birmingham's adaptation of Anthony Mars and Maurice Desvallières's *Le Truc de Seraphin*. It offered nothing new, only lots of laughs. Its story was much the same that had been told in *The Gay Mr. Lightfoot* in December and in countless farces before that: two men (both married) out for a lark. Expectations that the artist and his father-in-law would somehow bump into their wives as well as the cellist (the second cellist of the season) who is the husband of the woman with whom they have the flirtation were not disappointed. Fritz Williams and E. M. Holland (performing, for a change, without his brother) were the fun seekers. Elsie de Wolfe, handsomely costumed, and May Robson played the wives. The cellist, Mr. Katzenjammer, and his wife were played by Ferdinand Gottschalk and Agnes Miller, with Gottschalk made up to resemble a celebrated orchestra conductor. The play ran until the hot weather wilted it, then toured for years.

Townsend Walsh's **The Boys of Kilkenny** (3-15-97, Star) ran a single week and did poorly on the road. It offered so many songs and dances that some reviewers called it a musical. But virtually all these musical numbers occurred in the second act (there were five) in a hayfield, where farmhands were entertaining themselves. Walsh's heroine is Mona O'Hara, daughter of the richest and most miserly man in the region, Darby O'Hara (Walsh). Darby is tossed in a blanket and robbed by the Dugans, who throw blame for the robbery on Mona's suitor, Matt Annesley. Matt is imprisoned, flees to America, makes a pile of money, and comes back to claim Mona. Walsh, besides writing and acting in the play, was credited with designing the scenery.

Some of the most distinguished names on the American art scene were associated with the mounting of *L'Arlesienne* (3-22-97, Broadway), a translation of Alphonse Daudet's story of a young man driven to suicide by his love for an unattainable girl. John E. Kellerd was the doomed hero, and Agnes Booth his tragically obsessed mother. David Belasco joined Eugene Presbrey in staging the show. Ernest Gros and John H. Young designed the settings. And Anton Seidl conducted Bizet's score. But all their efforts were to small avail, for the play did two weeks of lackluster business.

By coincidence, Olga Nethersole opened on the same night at the Garden, and her first attraction was *Carmen*, without Bizet's music. For what she announced as her "farewell tour," she also brought out *Denise*, *Frou-Frou*, and *Camille*, plus one novelty.

The mixture of English and French theatre seen in Nethersole's Gallic repertory was evident again when a double bill was presented for a single week. The principal offering was Harry St. Maur's **A Divorce Cure** (3-29-97, Murray Hill), which was the season's second rewriting of *Divorçons*. It was coupled with Gilbert's *Comedy and Tragedy*.

French and English plays usually were assured at least a modicum of respectful attention. California plays were a different matter. So it was not surprising that one critic, reviewing Clay Clement's **The New Dominion** (3-29-97, American), began his notice by observing snidely, "The ushers and the 'paper' applauded vigorously from the beginning." Another reviewer suggested the play was merely a character study with "only a mere thread of a plot." Clement, assuming a thick German accent, also assumed the leading role of the Baron von Hohenstauffen, who falls in love with a girl and pays off a villain threatening to foreclose on her mortgage if she refuses to marry him. After eight performances Clement was heading back to California.

Nethersole's only novelty was Giuseppe Giacosa's **The Wife of Scarli** (4-5-97, Garden), in which an unfaithful wife and her lawyer-husband are reconciled by the pleadings of their youngster. A draggy play, it was given short shrift by most critics.

If November's *An Innocent Sinner* and January's *A Woman in Black* may have sought to capitalize on *Trilby*, Charles Klein's **Dr. Belgraff** (4-19-97, Garden) most certainly did. Triply so, for not only was it housed in the same theatre in which *Trilby* had played, but its titular hero-villain was something of a hypnotist, and he was portrayed by none other than Wilton Lackaye. Even Lackaye's makeup—long, unkempt hair, scraggly beard, shabby clothes—reinforced the resemblance. Belgraff is a patent madman, neglecting his apothecary shop to work in his laboratory on a chemical so murderous that it will put an end to all wars. When he learns that a nobleman has betrayed his sister, he kills the seducer. The baronet's own sister, Agnes (Marie Wainwright), has witnessed the crime, so Belgraff hypnotizes her and induces her to blame her sweetheart, Gerald Fenton (Forrest Robinson). Belgraff's fears of discovery drive him to drink and ultimately kill him before the lovers can be reunited. There was little subtlety in Lackaye's characterization. He portrayed Belgraff as a "blood-curdling demon . . . with a droll German accent." Nor was the play more satisfactory. It departed after a few disappointing weeks.

Two other plays that opened the same evening fared better. Madeleine Lucette Ryley's **The Mysterious Mr. Bugle** (4-19-97, Lyceum) served as Annie Russell's second starring vehicle of the season. Obviously the star was not the mystery man. In fact, he didn't exist. Rather he was the invention of Tom Pollinger (Joseph Holland), who is waiting for his rich aunt to die or to change her mind and allow him to wed. In the meanwhile, he uses his imaginary friend to keep other suitors away from his fiancée, Betty Fondacre (Miss Russell). Several characters are mistaken for the nonexistent man, and one character, a man, must even dress up as an equally imaginary Mrs. Bugle until the fiction is exposed concurrently with a happy ending. Although Miss Russell never aimed as high as Julia Marlowe, she, also, was admired for warmth and charm, and many critics felt that she probed deeper than Miss Marlowe ever did in seeking to understand figures she was impersonating. The farce chalked up seven weeks, then toured.

Du Souchet's second play of the season, **The Man from Mexico** (4-19-97, Lyceum), also ran seven weeks but enjoyed a longer afterlife both on tour and as a 1912 musical, *Over the River*. It, too, was a farce in which a single lie precipitates the comic difficulties. In this instance Benjamin Fitzhugh (William Collier) is sentenced to time in prison for contempt of court but tells his family that he will be away on business in Mexico. Collier's cool, bone-dry style of playing added to the merriment. Much laughter came from the disclosure of an art-bedecked prison. It seems the warden, William "Foppy" Loveall (Theodore Babcock), is a lover of painting and sculpture. The play was adapted from Gondinet and Bisson's *Un Voyage d'agrément*.

Lillian Lewis and Lawrence Marston, like du Souchet, had a second offering for the season, **The Widow Goldstein** (5-17-97, 14th St.). Its villain is the vicious skinflint speculator, Cyrus Russell (R. F. Cotton), who warns Judith Simpkins (Sarah McVicker) that he will bankrupt her father if she refuses to marry him. Russell had once driven Mr. Goldstein to suicide, so his widow, Hettie (Jennie Reiffarth), who is fond of Judith, takes it upon herself to give Russell his comeuppance. The farce, filled as it was with magicians, singing college boys, and a street band, was seen by some as a musical. The *Times* tried to balance its assessment, noting, "The thing is rather more like contemporary 'musical comedy,' with fewer songs than usual." Whatever it was, it lasted only one week.

The season's final play was William Gill's **The Alderman** (5-24-97, 14th St.), written as a vehicle for

Odell Williams to follow up on his success in *The Great Diamond Robbery*. He portrayed Andrew McSlathers, an alderman running for senator, opposed by the snooty reformer, Blanchard Maxwell (Mark Price). His life is complicated by the fact that his daughter, Fanny (Zenaide Williams), loves Maxwell's son, Jack (Paul Menifee), and by the fact that he himself is courting a rich widow, a determined "new woman," Mrs. Tremont Fordham (Marion Abbott). When he finally despairs of taming her, McSlathers dictates a marriage proposal to his "typewriter," Dora Wellesley (May Wheeler). It takes her a while to realize the letter is meant for her and not for Mrs. Fordham, but she finally accepts. The *Dramatic Mirror* saluted Gill's delineation of Mrs. Fordham as a "breezy and captivating sketch of the species of the new woman who makes politics her special study," and most critics had kind words about the rest of the play and the performance. But like its predecessor at the same house, it survived for only a week before disappearing into theatrical history.

As was still the custom, older plays made repeat stops in New York during their incessant touring. This year even *Uncle Tom's Cabin* returned. On one visit (to the Star for three weeks beginning May 3) it was offered in a new version, with each of its five acts containing only one setting. The rewriting was by J. W. Harkins, Jr., and Edwin Barbour.

1897–1898

Theatre business had become spotty the preceding spring and plummeted alarmingly during the summer. Looking for a reason or a scapegoat, pontificators pointed an accusing finger at "the bicycle craze," which found many potential playgoers pedaling merrily in the balmy weather instead of crowding into cramped, often sizzling theatres. In March of 1898 the *Maine* was blown up. A month later we were at war with Spain. After a brief spell during which Americans were preoccupied with the new war, box offices again were confronted with the old, accustomed lines. Yet the rage for bicycling persisted, leaving the commentators baffled but happily counting their profits. Another reason—an ineluctable change of tastes—may have accounted for some of the falling off. The season's very first show hinted at the problem. The season itself was often interesting without being as constantly rewarding as the last one. So the real cause of the downfall and rise of ticket sales may never be fully understood.

The prolific Frank Harvey was the author of **A Fight for Honor** (8-21-97, Grand Opera). His villain, James Rockley (George C. Robinson), commits forgery and foists the blame on George Clive (Myron Leffingwell). Clive is convicted and imprisoned, escapes, and is shipwrecked with a fellow passenger, Isabelle Damer (Annie Mortland). They fall in love, and after they are rescued Clive, disguised in a false beard, lives with her family. Rockley reappears and attempts to force Isabelle to marry him, until he is exposed not merely as a forger but as a bigamist as well. The *Dramatic Mirror* saw "the regulation Harveyized pattern" in the work, and similar remarks popped up in other reviews. Throughout the season many critics, but especially those on the trade sheet, sniped continually at the threadworn clichés of popular melodrama. The playgoing public frequently ignored them, yet it could not help heed, if only subconsciously, the ongoing attack. In this instance the critics and public were in accord, and *A Fight for Honor* flopped.

Opening-night mishaps hurt chances for Harrison Grey Fiske's **The Privateer** (8-21-97, Star), but the playwright, who was also the publisher of the *Dramatic Mirror* and the husband of the great actress, hadn't helped matters beforehand by noisily applying for an injunction to prevent the mounting, which he insisted was unauthorized and incompetently reworked by other hands. Critics heard echoes of *Black-Eyed Susan* and, more important, of *Damon and Pythias* in Fiske's tale. A decent man, given too much to drink, befriends the man who rescues him from a burning windmill. Later the villain, who pretends to be a long-lost heir, contrives to have the reformed drunkard (the real heir) convicted of a crime. His rescuer agrees to stand in as hostage aboard the villain's ship while his newfound buddy says farewell to his family ashore. In the midst of his good-byes the reborn co-hero learns that his hostage-friend's life is in danger, so he swims out to the ship to save his life and give the villain his comeuppance. Among the first-night foulups was the failure of the canvas "water" to move properly, so that the actor, instead of appearing to swim, seemed to be floating on a raft. The play survived for three weeks.

Coyne Fletcher's **A Bachelor's Baby** (8-28-97, Murray Hill) had an even shorter life—a single week. It was the first of several plays to open in fairly quick succession with "Bachelor" in the title. Mrs. Ponsonby (Annie Leonard), long ago jilted by Col. Roderick D'Arcy (McKee Rankin), hopes her nasty son, Robert (William Friend), will marry the colonel's ward, Geraldine (Nance O'Neil). To this end she attempts to make Mrs. D'Arcy (Lucille Flavin) believe a telegram addressed to "Roderick D'Arcy" and reading "Baby is on the way" applies to her husband. Roderick junior (Franklin Ritchie) nobly suggests the telegram is meant for him. It turns out it is, for "Baby" is the nickname Geraldine has given herself, and her message is to alert the younger Roderick that she is coming home to marry him. Nance O'Neil's warm, discreet performance won numerous compliments but couldn't save the show.

The season began in earnest when three plays opened on the last Monday in August. Leading the parade was George Broadhurst's **What Happened to Jones** (8-30-97, Manhattan). Jones (George C. Boniface, Jr.) is a traveling salesman who peddles Bibles to backwater yokels and playing cards to city sophisticates. While in New York he has attended an illegal prizefight, which has turned into a free-for-all and is raided by the police. He escapes in tatters, following his ringside neighbor, Ebenezer Goodly (George Ober), to Goodly's home. Goodly is a professor who is expecting a visit from his brother, Anthony (R. F. Cotton), a bishop in Australia. Ostensibly the bishop is coming to see Ebenezer, but actually he wants to court Alvina Starlight (Mrs. E. A. Eberle), Ebenezer's spinster sister-in-law, with whom he has been corresponding. He has asked Ebenezer to order him a new clerical suit, and it is this suit the bedraggled Jones dons. Alvina straightaway assumes Jones is the bishop and becomes eager to help him pursue the courtship. But Jones is smitten by Ebenezer's ward, Cissy (Anna Belmont). After innumerable complications Jones's real love for Cissy allows him to tell a fib that gets everyone off the hook and brings down the curtain. All the action took place within a few hours.

Some idea of the comic mayhem can be gauged by the program's descriptions of minor figures, such as William Bigbee, "who thinks he is an Indian," and Henry Fuller, "superintendent of a sanatorium." Bigbee had escaped from the asylum, and when Fuller arrives in search of him he finds the bishop dressed in a blanket and wearing what looks suspiciously like war paint. The humor was a grab bag. Occasionally it played a game of brinkmanship with the era's perceptions of naughtiness. Thus Jones, attempting to explain why he looks much younger than the bishop's age would suggest, remarks, "It's the climate. Australia has the dam—the dampest climate!" Sometimes it was simply silly or banal:

Jones: The sweetest sight in the world is to see a dear, old mother-kangaroo hopping around with her baby on her back.

Mrs. G: On her back! Why, I thought they carry their young in pouches.

Jones: Not now. They used to carry them in that way,—but not now.

Mrs. G: How can that be?

Jones: Didn't you hear? The style in baby carriages changed last summer.

Occasionally Broadhurst came up with a wonderful one-liner, such as Cissy's complaint, "The boys here are so slow that they make New Year's calls on the Fourth of July." (The line is interesting in that it, along with several other comments in the play, implies a small-town setting, although the action purportedly occurs in New York.) The unsteady quality of the play's humor seemingly bothered no playgoers, any more than similar situation comedies on television fail to entertain viewers a century later. So successful was the farce that when its booking at the Manhattan expired it was moved to the Bijou. There another farcical contretemps developed. The producers announced they would give away "cold tea," which proved to be small bottles of whiskey. Government authorities clamped down, so the producers settled for handing out chits good at a neighboring bar. The play returned for another run in late winter, in all chalking up over 130 performances in its first year. It was revived frequently for a quarter of a century.

Frank Harvey's second offering of the fledgling season, **Shall We Forgive Her?** (8-30-97, 14th St.), profited from the skillful handling of its resourceful producer, Jacob Litt. It may also have been a slightly better play than his earlier one. Its protagonist, Grace (Hannah May Ingham), is lured to Australia by a false promise of marriage from Neil Garth (E. T. Stetson). She returns to England and marries another man, only to have Garth enter and accuse her of having been his mistress. The shock drives her husband blind. Grace becomes a famous and rich writer and pays for an operation to restore his sight. A month-long stand was followed by a two-season tour.

A play designed strictly for touring was **New York Day by Day** (8-30-97, People's), from the pen of W. J. Thompson, who had composed such similar pieces as *Under the Lash* and *Signal Lights*—the latter with "the fighting lamb." Its opening occasioned another attack on the genre by the *Dramatic Mirror,* whose critic complained, "The plot is like a thousand others and deals with the triumph of virtue over vice, with a thrill every three minutes and a laugh sandwiched in between every two thrills." The real hero was a street waif, a bootblack named Rags (a trouser role), who helps free Polly Horn from the grip of the sinister Mother Cantwell and her nefarious crew of miscreants. The trade sheet allowed that the villainess "earned plenty of hisses" but insisted the star of the show was Calson, a huge, trained St. Bernard. (St. Bernards had also been featured in *Signal Lights*.)

The month ended sadly for theatre aficionados with the death of Mrs. Drew. One by one the giants of the American 19th-century stage were stepping into history.

Not all critics were so down on cheap melodrama. Writing in a Sunday followup in the *Times*, Edward A. Dithmar confessed, "I retain and cherish a liking for the old tricks and manners." Yet he was glad to learn that some of the most melodramatic moments had been cut after opening night from **A Southern Romance** (9-4-97, Fifth Ave.), which B. B. Valentine and Leo Ditrichstein drew from Dolly Higbee's novel *In God's Country*. God's country was Kentucky. There Lydia Ransom (Katherine Grey) agrees to marry Beverly Johnstone (Emmett Corrigan) to save the plantation of her father, Col. Wyckoff Ransom (Frank C. Bangs). However, she soon has second thoughts, for her heart long since has been given to the colonel's kind but untidy gardener, André (Ditrichstein). The pair grab a horse and ride off to the railroad station. Furious that a "white nigger" would even look at his fiancée, Johnstone dashes out in pursuit. At the station a battle ensues. Lydia, her clothes torn, is seized, and André is shot jumping from the train as it starts to move. Back at the plantation the lovers confront the colonel. André is revealed to be a count. Johnstone stalks away, damning everyone. The performances underscored distinct schools of acting. Bangs had often played in support of Booth and offered "a spell of old-fashioned emotion in the 'grand style.'" Miss Grey, whose bedraggled entrance astride her horse in the last act presented a memorable picture, was all "naturalness, spontaneity, and sympathy." Taking a middle ground but leaning toward the modern, Ditrichstein charmed with his quaint broken English and his fervor. The play ran a month.

As had become his custom, Daniel Frohman, before bringing in his Lyceum stock company, relit his house with a vehicle for his touring star, E. H. Sothern. This year's vehicle was Murray Carson and Louis N. Parker's **Change Alley** (9-6-97, Lyceum). The star played a young sailor with the telling name Kit Heartright, who suddenly is discovered to be an heir, loses his fortune in the South Sea Bubble, and struggles through to renewed riches, not to mention romance. Magnificent period settings (a decrepit Portsmouth canteen, a wainscoted manorial hall with blackened oak rafters, the statue-filled garden at Sadler's Wells, and Change Alley itself) and equally colorful period costumes ("noble lords in bag wigs and fine ladies in farthingales") enhanced the mounting. But the play proved less inviting. Sothern acted it for five weeks, then returned to such old reliables as *The Lady of Lyons, Lord Chumley,* and *An Enemy to the King* before heading out on the road.

George Broadhurst's second hit of the season, **The Wrong Mr. Wright** (9-6-97, Bijou), was not new to some New Yorkers, since it had tried out the previous spring in Harlem. Indeed, it had been circulating around the country for more than a year. The play itself was in a way transcontinental. Its leading figure, Seymour Sites (Roland Reed), is a San Francisco businessman who is on the verge of bankruptcy because a clerk has forged a check for $50,000 and disappeared with the money. Sites puts a detective on the clerk's trail but then learns the thief has gone to Old Point Comfort, Va. He heads there himself, hoping to nab the criminal and thus forestall having to pay the detective a reward. When he arrives at the hotel he signs in as Mr. Wright, unaware the clerk is hiding under the same name. The detective appears in the person of pretty Henrietta Oliver (Isadore Rush). Sites immediately falls in love with her and starts courting her. But his spendthrift ways lead her to suspect he is the forger.

Broadhurst's style was neither consistent nor readily identifiable. He plugged for laughs opportunistically. Some humor entailed merely mock brashness, as when Sites attempts to evade an erstwhile crony whom the years have made stuffy.

Clingstone: I'm so glad to see you.
Sites: Excuse me! You are making a slight mistake. The man you are looking for has just gone into the office, so pass right along—pass right along—(*turns . . . and shakes coat tails*).
Clingstone: The man I am looking for?
Sites: Yes, Mr. Hayseed Wayback from Cassopolis, Kansas, who came here with a carpet-sack in one hand and an itch for experience in the other. He may want a gold brick, I don't.

Some of the humor reflected a slightly soured, urbanized cynicism, such as Sites's remark on seeing his onetime sweetheart, a beauty now grown painfully buxom: "And to think she drove me into the wholesale liquor business." And some seemed a Wilde stab at epigram: "The lucky man is the one who doesn't get what he is sure he wants." Settings included the hotel lobby and the parade grounds at Fort Monroe, with the navy's "White Squadron" at anchor in the background. Reed's brash, "explosive" style, "with his manner always suggesting 'What are you pleased to bid, gentlemen?' " apparently was more acceptable to the road than to New Yorkers. Still, the farce compiled a month's run and retained its popularity for many years.

The season's second "bachelor" play was John Stapleton's **A Bachelor's Honeymoon** (9-6-97, Hoyt's). It, too, trafficked in the stock farcical tricks of the day, among them a comic detective, a misdirected letter, and transposed garments. His father's will stipulates that if Benjamin Bachelor (M. A. Kennedy), a widower, remarries without the consent of his spinster sister, Minerva (Isabel Waldron), he will lose his inheritance. Bachelor's problem is that he has remarried, secretly. His wife is a young actress, Miss Arbuckle (Berenice Wheeler). A letter Bachelor has sent from New York to be posted from Quisset is delivered stamped "Received from New York to be re-mailed," and the cat is out of the bag. But Bachelor's problems are complicated when his daughters' suitors turn out to be old friends of his new wife. Typical of the evening's shenanigans was the plight of one of the suitors, Stephen Howston (W. J. Ferguson). Howston is a teetotaling dude, but after his suit is mauled by a dog, the skinny caller is forced to traipse around in a suit belonging to the outsized Bachelor and is tricked into getting drunk. The antics were lamebrained, but Kennedy and Ferguson added to the appeal. The farce enjoyed a month of profitable business before embarking on its predestined itinerary.

Lorimer Johnstone's **The Indian** (9-6-97, People's) may have been inspired by the commercial success of *Northern Lights*. Like that 1895 work, which still was touring, it attempted to deal with the red man's efforts to adjust in a white civilization, and also like the earlier drama, it squandered an interesting idea by wallowing in stock motifs. Actually, despite the title, there were two Indians—brothers, and both were portrayed by A. S. Lipman. One brother goes by the name of Red Feather; the other, seeking a more active role in the white world as an army officer, has assumed the name Rex Sterling. When Allan Leech (Frank Sheridan) tries to goad the Ogallalas into rebellion and force Rex to stand against his own people, Red Feather must come to his brother's rescue. Romance was provided by a subplot featuring Capt. Robert Dudley (Francis

Byrne) and Dolly Sutton (Olive Berkeley). A poor house greeted players on opening night. This and another one-week engagement at a second combination house comprised the drama's New York history. Its road tour was equally unimpressive.

Charles Hoyt's **A Stranger in New York** (9-13-97, Garrick) ran sixty-four performances, a far cry from the long runs some of Hoyt's earlier plays had enjoyed. But it was Hoyt's last taste of success. His stranger (Harry Conor) finds a letter introducing a man to a club, only to discover that no one will listen to his explanation, instead taking him for the man mentioned in the letter. Like so many of Hoyt's works, it was liberally larded with songs and dances, thus again straddling the fence between straight play and musical.

So confused was Madeleine Lucette Ryley's story for **A Coat of Many Colors** (9-13-97, Wallack's) that several critics threw up their hands in despair. This confusion might have been acceptable in farce, but not in a purportedly serious drama. At heart the play described the efforts of a lady lawyer to seek out on behalf of a client a woman he had once loved and now wishes belatedly to marry. What the lawyer does not know is that the client is her real father and the woman she seeks is her mother. The lawyer's seemingly cynical associate is a man who loves her. Effie Shannon and Herbert Kelcey starred, but not for long.

The Captain of the Nonsuch (9-13-97, Star) was a designed-for-touring farce taken by J. F. Milliken and J. M. Morton from *La Flamboyante*. It centered on a man who hides his extramarital escapades by telling his wife and domineering mother-in-law that he is a sea captain who must spend long stretches away on duty. The story would seem to have served as the basis for Jerome Kern's 1920 hit *The Night Boat*, although another show was listed as the source.

The season's third "bachelor" play, Martha Morton's **A Bachelor's Romance** (9-20-97, Garden) proved the most popular of the trio, thanks in large measure to its star, Sol Smith Russell, and the fine playing of Annie Russell (no relation). Its story was simple. David Holmes is an unworldly literary critic who loves his ward, Sylvia Somers, but fears she will never love him and so sets out to find her a suitable husband. His widowed, knowing sister, Helen (Blanche Walsh), and Aunt Clementine (Fanny Addison Pitt), "a maiden lady, with a sharp tongue," recognize that Sylvia does care for David and that they would make an ideal match. They bring about a happy curtain. Aunt Clementine also convinces David's pleasure-loving brother, Gerald (Orrin John-

son), that fresh milk can have almost as many charms as wine, women, and song. The action shuttled between David's book-cluttered study in Washington Square and Helen's fashionable home in Murray Hill before taking all the characters out to Aunt Clementine's farm. The lanky Russell's gangly legs, sheepish grin, and dry humor were the star's stock in trade, all he had and all he really needed for the part. Miss Russell again displayed "her artistic sympathy and sensibility, her nice sense of proportion, her good taste, personal humor and delicate prettiness." Russell had been touring with the show for a year; Miss Russell joined the company only for its Broadway run, which lasted for six weeks.

If *A Bachelor's Romance* typified some of the standard theatre of its day, the bill at another house that same night exemplified the strange combinations playgoers tolerated. The bill began with *The Gay Deceiver,* which was not a play but simply a succession of vaudeville acts, including a sharpshooter, acrobats, a buck-and-wing dance, and a baritone singing Bizet and Fauré. As the lights dimmed after intermission, Oriental figures moved about the aisles hawking joss sticks and incense. With music of the "Lady picking mulberries kind" by the often admired Edgar Stillman Kelley setting the tone, the curtain rose on San Franciscan Chester Bailey Fernald's **The Cat and the Cherub** (9-20-97, Olympia Music Hall) to reveal One Eye Alley in the Celestial Quarter of San Francisco's Chinatown. Two men are conversing as a policeman strolls by. When he is out of sight, one of the men takes a hatchet to the other's head and spews out curses as his victim dies. Hearing the policeman returning, he props up the dead man and seems to engage him in conversation until the unapprehending policeman again disappears. The murdered man is Chim Fang (Richard Ganthony), proprietor of an opium den. He has kidnapped the baby of the uncle of the girl he loves, Ah Yoi (Ruth Benson), holding it until the uncle agrees to a marriage. His rival for Ah Yoi's hand, the widower Wing Sun Luey (Edward Morrison), threatens to expose him and is killed for his pains. Wing Sun Luey's son, Wing Shee (Holbrook Blinn), resolves to avenge his father's death and, of course, does. The play, the first nonmusical to be presented at a first-class theatre on Times (then Longacre) Square proper, ran four weeks and quickly became involved in a cause célèbre. But before that happened several more shows came in, among them the season's biggest hit.

That runaway success was James M. Barrie's **The Little Minister** (9-27-97, Empire). Barrie supposedly dramatized his story specifically with Maude Adams in mind, and whether or not that is true (the play was performed first in America), the play launched the radiant young actress on a career as one of America's most enchanting, beloved stars.

. . .

Maude Adams [née Kiskadden] (1872–1953) was born in Salt Lake City and was carried onstage by her actress mother, Annie Adams. She was still a youngster when she played her first speaking roles in small California towns before moving to San Francisco. She came east in 1888, where she performed in such plays as *Lord Chumley, A Midnight Bell,* and *All the Comforts of Home.* After a time she was John Drew's leading lady until Charles Frohman elevated her to stardom. At this time stage historian Lewis Strang wrote, "In figure almost painfully slight and girlish; her face elfishly bewitching in its very plainness; her eyes large, blue and roguish; her hair ashen brown and delicately rippling; unusually gifted intellectually, and with a personality of the most persuasive magnetism, Maude Adams is to-day the most popular woman on the American stage."

. . .

Two of the most unusual figures in the town of Thrums, a town torn by labor strife, are its austere young cleric, the Rev. Gavin Dishart (Robert Edeson), and the daughter of Lord Rintoul, Lady Barbara (Adams), a girl who sympathizes with the discontented weavers and sometimes disguises herself as a gypsy to help them. She is known affectionately as Lady Babbie or "the Egyptian." When troops are called in to arrest rebellious workers, the seeming gypsy girl tricks the minister into sounding the alarm. Later, after she has changed her garments, the soldiers question her and the minister. She leads them to believe she is Dishart's wife, and in his confusion he does nothing to deny this. By the time Dishart learns the truth and an accommodation has been reached between the authorities and weavers, Dishart has totally succumbed to Babbie's charms. That old Scottish law (used in so many plays a decade or more back) to the effect that if a couple declare themselves man and wife before witnesses they are considered married brings about a happy curtain. Strang observed of Miss Adams's playing, "She was dashing, careless and free as the tantalising gypsy girl; as the daughter of Lord Rintoul, graceful and spirited, serious and sympathetic." Other critics and audiences agreed. The play was soon moved to the Garrick, returning to the Empire for its 300th and final performance in mid-June, when Frohman presented an American Beauty rose to each lady in the audience.

Another play by an English author but with ties to America was the next major opening. In this instance the connection was the comedy's American setting, for the work was Shaw's **The Devil's Disciple** (10-4-97, Fifth Ave.), which spoofed both Yankee and British behavior during the Revolution. Critics were coming around to accepting, even delighting in, Shaw, and Dithmar called the play "a boon to the jaded mind." Winter was never to care much for Shaw, but he allowed that Richard Mansfield's Dick Dudgeon was "made brilliant and touching by his impetuosity, incipient kindness, and winning serio-comic humor." The scene-stealing role of General Burgoyne, the gentlemanly, discomfited soldier, was awarded to Arthur Forrest, who carried it off handsomely. Settings were praised, although photographs suggest they were encumbered by Victorian clutter and heaviness and would not seem colonial to a modern eye. But contemporaries welcomed the comedy, and its eight-week run was the longest Mansfield had enjoyed since *Beau Brummell.* When the run was finished, Mansfield offered a hectic week of repertory, bringing out seven of his standbys.

E. S. Willard returned the same evening as Mansfield and for the first fortnight of his stand offered Henry Arthur Jones's **The Physician** (10-4-97, Wallack's), in which a young country-bred lady has her blind infatuation with a worldly scoundrel brought up short by a compassionate doctor. The final two weeks of Willard's visit were devoted to some of his prior hits.

The Proper Caper (10-4-97, Hoyt's) was a heavily bowdlerized version of Maurice Hennequin, Paul Bilhaud, and Fabrice Carré's *Le Paradis.* Its comic confusions arose from a portrait of a woman, mistakenly thought to be a portrait of the woman's daughter. The painter's son, himself an artist, must not only set matters straight but must convince his father-in-law-to-be that he is a bit of a rake. The farce ran five weeks.

Charles E. Blaney's **The Electrician** (10-4-97, Third Ave.) had been a huge success in second-class theatres across the country, but its New York visits were confined to several one-week stands at combination houses. Tom Edson and his father, who have a contract to electrify Denver's streets, are nearly bankrupt. Edith Sessions, who loves Tom, lends him her money after her own banker-father denies the men help. Kenneth Sauvage, rebuffed by Edith, attempts to destroy the generating plant and electrocutes Tom's father in the process. However, he manages to place the blame on Tom. It takes two years and two more acts before Sauvage is brought to confess and commit suicide.

The story and setting of Francis Powers's **The First**

Born (10-5-97, Manhattan) must have seemed familiar to many regular playgoers. Man Low Yek (Charles Bryant) kidnaps Chan Lee (Carrie E. Powers), wife of Chan Wang (Powers), and later returns to abduct Chan Lee's son—the first born. In the process the child accidentally is killed. Chan Wang vows vengeance, and he is supported by all his friends in San Francisco's Chinatown. Here is Winter's description of the final scene: "An alley-end in the same district is shown, with a glimpse of contiguous gambling halls and opium dens, under the darkening shadows of evening. There the inexorable avenger lounges, leaning against a door post,—apparently an idler smoking his evening pipe and talking with a Chinese girl, who leans from a window; in fact, vigilantly observant of *Man Low Yek,* visible within a shop, and intent on slaying him. The alley grows dark and becomes deserted. The neighboring houses are illumined. The chink of money and the bickering chatter of unseen gamblers are heard. A police officer saunters by and disappears. *Man Low Yek* comes forth from his shop, closing it after him. Then, suddenly, as he passes, *Wang,* with fearful celerity, leaps upon him wielding a hatchet, strikes him down, drags his dead body into convenient concealment, and is back again at his former loitering place, outwardly placid, before the fire in his pipe has had time to become extinguished."

Director David Belasco produced the play with Charles Frohman. After two weeks the original company was replaced and rushed to London, but William A. Brady's production of *The Cat and the Cherub* beat it to the punch. West Enders thought two similar shows were one too many, and *The First Born* failed. The original troupe was returned to New York at the Garden Theatre. Between the two companies a run of seven weeks was compiled in New York. *The First Born* resembled *The Cat and the Cherub* in another way. Since both plays were short, both were presented as part of a double bill. No vaudeville this time. At the Manhattan, Georges Feydeau's **A Night Session** told of a man planning a night on the town who sends a letter of excuse to his wife and a letter of invitation to a friend. The letters are switched. E. M. Holland played the lead. At the Garden the farce was Meilhac and Halévy's *L'Été de St. Martin,* offered as **Indian Summer** (11-29-97). In it a rich uncle who disapproves of his nephew's fiancée comes to want her himself. The staging emphasized the pathetic rather than the comic aspects of the story.

Madeleine Lucette Ryley's romantic drama **An American Citizen** (10-11-97, Knickerbocker) found most critics in one corner and the public in another. Beresford Cruger (Nat Goodwin) at first refuses to accept an inheritance, which requires him to become a British subject and marry a British girl. He changes his mind and his name when his law partner absconds with their firm's cash and when his English cousin, Beatrice Carew (Maxine Elliott), advises him that she, too, could lose her fortune if he does not. Egerton Brown (William Ingersoll), who had been engaged to Beatrice but had faked a suicide when he believed she had been disinherited, comes back to make trouble. Beresford persists, winning back Beatrice and retrieving his American citizenship.

The action moved from a New York law firm to Nice at Carnival time and finally to London. The *Dramatic Mirror,* one of the harshest commentators, condemned the play for "the sort of dialogue usually heard from variety sketch teams." Miss Elliott, it concluded, was "no more an actress than before, although her undoubted beauty is quite sufficient again to make one overlook other shortcomings." Of Goodwin, the trade sheet observed that he won audiences with "the same tricks of speech, the same grimaces, the same impetuous stride, the same everything." Even less unhappy critics called him to task for staring out at and playing to his audience instead of to his collaborators onstage. But audiences clearly loved it. The play was rewarded with three months of excellent business and a long, prosperous tour.

In Lillian Lewis, Lawrence Marston, and Albert B. Paine's **For Liberty and Love** (10-11-97, Grand Opera), a Cuban girl, Carlotta Cassanova (Lewis), daughter of an insurgent officer, loves the Spanish Captain Mario Navarro. Navarro's rival, Captain Mora, accuses her of betraying the Cuban cause, and she does, in fact, hide Navarro when the insurgents come looking for him. Optimistically but prophetically, the Cubans win the war for independence, and Carlotta gets to keep her beloved soldier. Some critics bewailed the "stagy, unnatural and ineffective" acting, but they laid the blame on the need to please less discriminating audiences in the hinterlands for which the show was created. Like those of so many other touring pieces, its New York stands were confined to one-week visits at various combination houses.

But another touring show fared much better. **Cumberland '61** (10-18-97, 14th St.) was from the pen of Franklyn Fyles, drama critic for the *Sun.* Perhaps because of this the play, which one of his colleagues characterized as belonging to "a series of American plays for the multitude which Augustus

Pitou has been producing," was treated at greater length and with considerable respect by most of his fellow reviewers. As a result it had a profitable six-week stand and crisscrossed the country for many years.

Fyles's story mingled two popular motifs—taking sides in the Civil War, and mountaineers' family feuds. Col. Leslie Murdoch (Frank Losee) of West Point has helped educate Alice Ainsley (Florence Rockwell) on the understanding with her father that the colonel would marry her eventually. Alice's father, Benner (C. G. Craig), is a Cumberland mountaineer whose family long has fought its neighbors, the Graynes. What Benner does not realize is that, despite this age-old feud, Alice loves George Grayne (Edgar L. Davenport). When war breaks out Murdoch returns to serve the Confederacy; George becomes a Union guerrilla. Murdoch insists the time has come for the wedding, but as the wedding is about to take place at a war-ravaged mountain church George and a friend appear. The colonel has them seized, shouting, "Don't honor him with a bullet—I'll hang him as a spy." The men escape. Ainsley is still not aware of his daughter's real feelings, and he and George meet on a wooden bridge over a ravine separating the Ainsley and Grayne properties. During the fight Murdoch contrives to have the bridge set on fire. He does this by telling George's friend, Dick Kansett (John E. Kellerd), who is actually Murdoch's half-breed, illegitimate son, that he will acknowledge his paternity and spare George. A red glow in the sky from the burning pines shows Dick has done his job well. Then the flames break through. Alice's pleas prompt George to save her father as the bridge collapses. When Dick realizes his father has no intention of keeping his promises, he kills him. Benner consents to George's marrying Alice. Besides the colonel's home at West Point, the church, and the bridge, settings showed the exterior of Ainsley's home, complete with smokehouse, and its interior.

Not all American plays were set in America. The appeal of an English setting remained irresistible. Of course, **A Lady of Quality** (11-1-97, Wallack's) was taken up by Frances Hodgson Burnett and Stephen Townsend from Mrs. Burnett's novel, and Mrs. Burnett was English-born, albeit by this time long an American citizen. The lady in question was Clorinda Wildairs (Julia Arthur). In the novel much had been made of her tomboyish youth, when she had dressed in breeches and shared a bumper of hard liquor with rough or roguish colleagues in a tavern. Only one scene at the beginning of the play put her in trousers. The rest of the dramatization, unfolding in the early 18th century, recounted Clorinda's problems when, adult, wealthy, and recently widowed, she would marry the Duke of Osmonde (Scott Inglis). The rotten, disgraced Sir John Oxon (Edwin Arden) uses an old lock of her hair to frustrate her, and he attempts to seduce her. She grabs a horsewhip and, striking him, kills him. Since guests are waiting to be received, she hides the body under a sofa and coolly greets her visitors. When the duke learns the truth he is forgiving. Several critics registered the same complaint, that Miss Arthur, while manifesting "lightning flashes of temperament," was essentially too dignified and restrained a performer to sustain such a role or such a weak theatre piece. Yet her acting and her play satisfied the public. *A Lady of Quality* ran six weeks in New York, found some measure of success on the road, and made Miss Arthur a star.

• • •

Julia Arthur (1869–1950) was a Canadian whose real name was Ida Lewis. She rose from amateur theatricals to a place in Daniel E. Bandmann's Shakespearean company. Assignments in New York and with Henry Irving's London company followed. She was a small brunette beauty, with large, dark eyes and a "Madonna-like" face.

• • •

The 18th century, with its elegantly gilded and painted rooms and gorgeous costumes, also served as the setting for Sydney Grundy's London success **A Marriage of Convenience** (11-8-97, Empire), which the playwright based on Dumas père's *Un Mariage sous Louis XV*. The story told of a French count and a young convent girl who do not care for each other but are forced to marry, then come to love each other. Slight as the plot was, it was capably acted by John Drew, Isabel Irving, and an excellent supporting cast. The comedy ran for two months.

Scott Marble's touring melodramas never played theatres like the Empire, but he achieved one of his longest New York stands when his latest work was housed at a once prestigious, now fast-fading playhouse. Reports suggested that **The Heart of the Klondike** (11-8-97, Star) was based on an actual 1878 incident in which a miner adopted a Russian baby he had found still alive beside her dead father. Mortimer Drew (Ernest Hastings), a miner who is being treated for snow blindness, loves Olga (Laura Burt). However, he believes his good friend, Joseph McCutcheon (E. L. Snader), who had discovered and raised the girl, hopes to marry her, so he is loathe to express his own feelings. Olga loves Drew, but she thinks he is cool to her because he prefers

Beatrice Wall (Jessie Bonstelle), a woman of some question. Naturally, all ends happily. Settings included a mine with water running down a sluice. Some of the play's most theatrical moments, such as a murderer being forced by a gathering mob to jump off a cliff, came from its subplot. Critics' growing annoyance with overused devices was evident in one's dismissal of Beatrice as "a conventional adventuress." But lovers of this sort of theatre packed the old playhouse for a month and continued to support the piece on tour for several seasons.

By contrast, Michael Morton's **Miss Francis of Yale** (11-8-97, Manhattan), a farce designed for a better level of theatre and audience, came and went quickly. The play clearly was a vehicle for bantam Etienne Giradot, written to capitalize on his success in *Charley's Aunt.* When the troublemaking Miss Mann (Sarah McVicker) discovers a lady in the rooms of Frederick Anderson (Raymond Capp), she sees a way to sabotage his romance with Vesta Fitz Allen (May Monte Donico). What she does not know is that the lady was actually Frank Staynor (Giradot), got up for a part in a play. Misunderstandings and complications abound until matters are cleared up in the last act. Giradot had a field day in his disguise, smoking his cigar and using very unladylike slang, but these were the same ploys he had milked in *Charley's Aunt,* a much superior farce.

An even shorter life, at least in New York, awaited Robert Fulgora's **Old Money Bags** (11-8-97, People's). It lasted one week, a typical run at this combination house. But trade sheets reported it had been a success in parts west, a point not likely to endear it to Manhattan's chauvinistic critics. Its central figure, Moses Levi, makes a pile in Nevada City, then finds adventures in Cape May and New York. For the second time in the season, according to one trade sheet, a dog stole the show. Only "Nip" was not a St. Bernard but a mongrel.

It was followed promptly by **Always on Time** (11-15-97, People's), which no author came forward to claim. Nell is the mascot of Poker Flat. When her father loses his money and his holdings to a card sharp, Nell takes on the gambler and wins everything back. She really did not have to work so hard, for she turns out to be an heiress. The *Dramatic Mirror,* continuing its onslaught on such plays, condemned it as "regulation Western melodrama," also noting that it was interspersed with "specialties at short intervals." One week and it, too, was gone.

The season's shortest run (apart from special matinees) was the fate of Edward M. Alfriend's two-performance fiasco, **The Magdalene** (11-15-97, Mur-

ray Hill). The theatre's manager, Frank Murtha, had established there something resembling an old-fashioned stock company, headed by McKee Rankin, and had offered revivals of such favorites as *Led Astray, Camille,* and *East Lynne.* He now ventured this new work. Kate (Nance O'Neil) is forced to beg in the streets of Baltimore by her father, John Morrison (Rankin), a bankrupt gambler and drunkard. She is seduced by Melville Scott (Thomas J. Powers). When Edward Day (Thomas Tuther), a rich man, falls in love with her and proposes, she tells him the truth about her past. Her father, who would have forced a marriage, is furious and kicks her out of his home. She goes to New York, where she becomes Scott's mistress. When she returns to Baltimore for her mother's funeral, her father is abusive. But the Rev. John Hinson (Andrew Robson) defends her and takes her in. A romance blossoms. Deciding to marry her, the minister battles his outraged congregation and finally wins them over. Sentimentality played as important a part in the work as did creaky melodrama. On the minister's birthday, seven little girls, all dressed in white, offer him flowers but shrink back as Kate enters the room. He convinces them to shake hands with her, one by one. Those critics who reviewed the play savaged it. Just over a month later, Murtha gave up his lease.

One special matinee that same week deserves to be noted. On the 18th at Hoyt's Theatre an ambitious group called the Criterion Independent Theatre presented the American premiere of Ibsen's **John Gabriel Borkman,** with E. J. Henley in the title role. The *Times,* which saw much of the play as "uncommonly tedious" and "preposterous," assured its readers "it is not likely to be acted here again."

In telling contrast to the lone performance accorded Ibsen, Cecil Raleigh and Henry Hamilton's Drury Lane sensation-melodrama **The White Heather** (11-22-97, Academy of Music) ran 184 times as long at a huge auditorium. Another "Scottish marriage" provided the basis for the story. In its climactic scene two divers, one paid by the treacherous husband, the other by the disowned wife, struggle to retrieve evidence from a sunken yacht. The "dive" was shown with the divers remaining in place while the boat from which they jumped and the "waters" disappeared up into the flies. As the two men dueled, shadows of swimming fish, projected onto a backdrop, heightened the illusion. No fewer than six well-known scene painters helped prepare the settings for Charles Frohman's latest money-maker.

Another double bill opened the same night, but

unlike some earlier double bills it did not offer contrasting pieces. George Day's **A Close Shave** was a one-act musical farce that burlesqued comic opera, while the main attraction was **His Little Dodge** (11-22-97, Manhattan), Justin Huntley McCarthy's adaptation of a farce by Georges Feydeau and Maurice Hennequin, *Le Système Ribadier*. Its plot centered on a man who mesmerizes his wife so that he can have a fling. The bill ran two weeks.

Daniel Frohman was rewarded with a ten-week run when he carefully mounted Arthur Wing Pinero's roseate, languorous pavane **The Princess and the Butterfly** (11-23-97, Lyceum), in which a widowed princess and her old admirer contemplate marriage together but finally decide on younger mates. James Hackett and Mary Mannering played the leads.

Youthfulness seemed the order of the day. While the Frohman brothers were moving from success to success, Augustin Daly, once among the brightest lights on Broadway, was slowly flickering out. He now relied on musical importations for his real profit. His once brilliant, vital company was decimated by desertion and death and depended almost solely on revivals. With Ada Rehan and Mrs. Gilbert as its staunchest props, the ensemble returned on the 29th to offer *The Taming of the Shrew*. Only one novelty was sandwiched in between subsequent remountings of *Twelfth Night, The Country Girl, The Merry Wives of Windsor,* and *As You Like It.* Nor was there much excitement on the other side of the footlights. Loyalists were drifting away—or passing away—so business all during the season was disappointing at Daly's.

Disappointment was also voiced at the debut of Alexandra Viarda, a Polish beauty with magnificent eyes and a mobile face but without any special magnetism. She had made a name for herself in Germany and had learned little or no English. She therefore performed in German while the rest of the cast played in English. This only aggravated difficulties, since her opening vehicle, Richard Voss's oddly titled (given the star's name) **Alexandra** (11-29-97, Fifth Ave.), was an inept, unpleasant drama. The heroine has been seduced and jailed for infanticide. When she is released she determines to be avenged on her seducer. Instead she falls in love with him, and when he once again spurns her she commits suicide. Poor reviews and meager audiences prompted her to switch to *Deborah,* but when this, too, failed she made her final exit from the American theatrical scene.

Arthur D. Hall's **A Guilty Mother** (11-29-97, People's), a touring melodrama, goaded the *Dra-matic Mirror* into yet another jeremiad. Its critic bewailed such plays could appeal only to "audiences enamored of the class of melodrama that reeks of villainy of every type . . . [and] from which virtue rises phoenix-like at the fall of the curtain." The guilty mother is Madeline Verrill, who leaves her husband after his partner whispers lies about him into her ear, has a child by the partner, then deserts him when she learns the truth. The father kidnaps the child, and Madeline hires a detective to rescue her. Years pass. By the time the dogged detective locates the child, she is a grown woman who has attempted suicide after a nobleman seduced and abandoned her. Meanwhile, the despicable partner has taken to burglary. He attempts to rob Madeline, and she kills him for his pains. Somehow Madeline and her long-neglected husband are reunited, as are her daughter and the repentant nobleman. Trash, acted in an antiquated fist-on-the-forehead manner, it failed to find a public, but its failure did little to assuage the trade sheet's reviewer's misgivings about many American playgoers.

Madeline clearly was a popular name of the hour, for the very next entry centered on **Madeline of Fort Reno** (12-6-97, People's). This Madeline is Madeline Hartman, daughter of a well-born English lady and a reformed bandit. She lives in a stockade filled with real horses and keeps a real lion as a pet. She is loved by handsome Jack Curley and plagued by the inevitable mustachioed villain. At one point she runs into the lion's cage to escape the villain. At other points she and her friends relieve the tension by breaking out into song and dance.

Daly's lone novelty of the season was **Number 9; or, The Lady of Ostend** (12-7-97, Daly's), which F. C. Burnand took from Blumenthal and Kadelburg's *Hans Huckebein*. It was doubly novel, for it featured a scene in which its characters (and the audience) watched a motion picture. This was not the first instance in which a film sequence had been used. Two seasons earlier a musical called *The Bicycle Girl* had employed a "Kinetoscope" to depict the crucial race. Edison's "Vitascope" had been featured as part of vaudeville bills since April 1896. But this was its first use in a straight play. The hero, a young married man, is persuaded to smooch on film with a pretty girl. It's all very innocent, but the prizefighter who is the girl's fiancé doesn't see it that way. His comic attempts to redress matters provide the rest of the story line. For some reason, probably her age, Ada Rehan was not cast for the piece. The decision may well have hurt Daly's already hurting attendance, and the play was taken off after three weeks.

Franklyn Fyles and Eugene W. Presbrey's **A Ward**

of France (12-13-97, Wallack's) also ran three weeks, a run that became the subject of bitter controversy. Its story was simple enough. A French lady, Flower Moyne (Una Abell), is exiled to Louisiana for her royalist sympathies. There she is courted by two men, both of whom, it turns out, are sons of the very revolutionary who deported her. One is a young soldier, Victor Laussat (Stephen Gratten); the other is the notorious pirate, Jean Lafitte. A happy ending comes when she is reunited with her father, whom she had believed guillotined, and when she accepts Victor's proposal. Lafitte was played in grand swashbuckling style by Maurice Barrymore, who garnered some excellent notices. Elita Proctor Otis as his mother, the witch Zabet, also won high praise. So did settings, which included a nighttime fête in the governor's garden. Crowds outside the garden walls consisted largely of Spaniards and Frenchmen, each noisily clamoring about their nation's superiority. But the gallery broke out in spontaneous cheers when one actor, portraying a native American, began tooting "Yankee Doodle" on a fife. In his Sunday followup, Dithmar took occasion to lament the sorry state of most American dramaturgy, writing, "We have no body of plays we can point to with pride. 'Alabama,' and 'The Heart of Maryland,' 'Young Mrs. Winthrop,' 'The Henrietta,' and 'Secret Service' are all very well, but they are exceptions, and they tell a story of many years of unproductiveness."

Such a discussion nearly deflected the burning issue, which, inexplicably, the mounting brought explosively to the surface—the growing domination of the Theatrical Trust. Papers favorable to the Trust praised the show; papers opposed to the Trust sneered at it. Anti-Trust critics suggested openly that those who lauded the production were in the Trust's pay; Trust supporters claimed those who panned it did so simply because Klaw and Erlanger had produced it. Proponents announced that although the play had been slated to remain only a fortnight, it was held over an extra week to accommodate demand. Would-be Trust-busters claimed the show was brought in for the run and had to be withdrawn after three disappointing weeks. For the next several years, much theatrical reporting would be unreliable, time and again tinged with feelings about the Syndicate.

Elmer Grandin and Eva Mountford, a popular touring husband-and-wife team, were both the stars and authors of **The Secret Enemy** (12-20-97, Grand Opera), which stopped over briefly on its extended sojourns. Their story revolved around disputed wills, one genuine, one bogus. Miss Mountford portrayed the heroine, Marcelle Beauchard; Grandin played both her father, Pierre, and her husband, Louis Romains. A duel in a darkened cellar provided the evening's thrilling high point.

Another player-dramatist, Charles Coghlan, whose career had been faltering, scored a personal triumph in his redaction of Dumas's *Kean* as **The Royal Box** (12-21-97, Fifth Ave.). He rechristened his troubled, emotion-prone actor James Clarence. Tensions have been rising since Clarence discovered his friend and benefactor, the Prince of Wales (Harold Russell), quietly courting Clarence's own difficult inamorata, Countess Helen (Elizabeth Garth), wife of the Swedish ambassador (Albert Bruning). During his performance of *Romeo and Juliet,* Clarence watches with growing fury the prince's attentions to the countess, who is sitting with her husband and the prince in a box (an actual box at the theatre). Finally he can stand it no longer and, forgetting his Juliet up on her balcony, stops the play to berate the prince. His performance brought Coghlan the sort of encomiums he had not savored in many seasons. Winter wrote, "In the attitude of reverential devotion to woman, allegiance and deference to royalty, protection to innocence, fiery scorn for meanness, craft, and villainy . . . Coghlan's acting showed a consummate mastery of his art. He bore himself with impressive sincerity and acted with passionate vigor that created the illusion of truth." Some illusion was necessary since Coghlan was fifty-five. His play ran eight weeks, toured, and returned the following season for another month.

The new year began disappointingly. Joseph Arthur never may have been the critics' darling, but his sensation-melodramas had attracted enormous patronage and made him rich. With **The Salt of the Earth** (1-3-98, Wallack's) he turned his hand to what programs called "a country comedy." It was a highly melodramatic comedy, set, as were so many of his plays, in his native Indiana. In hopes of providing an additional incentive to playgoers, Annie Russell was given a leading role. She played the part of Ann May, daughter of a prosperous farmer. Her affections are claimed by her father's attractive young ward, Tom (Theodore Babcock), who all the neighbors agree is the salt of the earth. Into this idyllic scene strides a painted Louisiana beauty, Cynthia May (Alice Fischer), claiming to be a distant relative, and her nattily dressed sidekick, Jean A'Lairable (Frank Landers). They smear Tom's good name and attempt to seize the property held in trust for him. Matters look dark indeed for Ann and Tom until sweet Kate Boudinot (Maude Odell) appears to throw a happy light on the situation. Some critics enjoyed Arthur's homey dialogue, such as "She folded her hopes and laid 'em away, like the pants of a dead friend," while others complained that such "slang" as "Just tell them that you saw me" and "Don't blow out the gas" sounded harsh coming from Miss Russell. Verisimilitude was provided by glimpses of rural Indiana folk at work and play. The piece was a quick failure in New York but was reported to have been popular in the Midwest.

An echo of Arthur's *The Cherry Pickers* could be found the same night at Edward E. Kidder's **Shannon of the Sixth** (1-3-98, People's), when its hero, Lt. Laurence Shannon, a young Irish officer during the 1857 Sepoy rebellion, must rescue Dora Kimber, who has been tied to the mouth of a cannon by blackguard Captain Arlington. There were echoes, too, of *Trilby*, since Arlington is also something of a mesmerist. A group called the Boston City Quartette found an excuse for songs in the last act.

Nor was Paul M. Potter's **The Conquerors** (1-4-98, Empire) all that original. The virulently anti-Trust *Dramatic Mirror* devoted an entire page to detailing similarities between Potter's story and two French works, de Maupassant's "Mlle. Fifi" and Sardou's *La Haine*. Potter's play unfolds one evening in 1870 when some crude, destructive German officers are occupying a French chateau. Among the most brutish would seem to be Eric von Rodeck (William Faversham). He breaks family heirlooms and defaces old portraits. Later he attempts to rape the elder daughter of the house, Yvonne de Grandpré (Viola Allen), but her hysterical despair shames him, and he slinks off. Yvonne faints, and while she is unconscious another lout enters her room and tries to assault her. Eric returns in time to save her and kill him. When Yvonne regains consciousness she sees the dead body and believes the man was murdered trying to defend her. Her hatred turns to love after she finally learns the truth. Since Eric, too, has fallen in love, he is not above allowing her brother, who is wanted as a French spy, to escape. For this, he is condemned to be shot. His sentence is commuted, and he is instead assigned a very dangerous mission. As he goes off, Yvonne can only pray that the war will end and Eric will return safely. There was nothing in Charles Frohman's production that the *Dramatic Mirror* saw fit to spare. It noted sneeringly, "Electric lights [in supposed oil lamps], American upright pianos and American champagne hardly existed in remote Brittany in 1870." But less committed papers praised the play, the mounting, and the players. Faversham was admired for his dashing good looks and the warmth that ultimately

made Eric likable; Miss Allen for her charm, sincerity, and ardor. The play ran into spring and long remained a staple on tour and in stock.

One scene merits a footnote. For insulting French womanhood, Eric has a glass of wine thrown in his face. When Weber and Fields satirized the show, the hero received a pie in his face, thus initiating a time-honored slapstick tradition.

During the week of January 3, two productions of *As You Like It* vied for attention. Most critics preferred Daly's sumptuous revival, with Ada Rehan's buoyant Rosalind. At the Knickerbocker, Julia Marlowe's lush heroine was seen against backdrops more suitable for touring. After one week she dropped the comedy and offered **The Countess Valeska** (1-10-98, Knickerbocker), based on *Der lange Preusse*, a German play by Rudolph Stratz. Its heroine is torn between the man she loves, who is determined to kill Napoleon, and a guest in her house, Napoleon himself. Her sweetness and wiles allow her to be at one and the same time the perfect mistress and the perfect hostess. Those favorite critical kudos "charm and sincerity" were brought out again to welcome the star, and she continued with the play for the remaining three weeks of her engagement.

Five companies reportedly were playing Lincoln J. Carter's **Heart of Chicago** (1-10-98, People's) around the country and in England, but its New York stands were few and brief. A shady lawyer, who has stolen from his own firm and loves his partner's wife, is caught by his partner, whom he murders. Just then the great Chicago fire breaks out. The sound of panicky horses is heard offstage. Soon the building is aflame (thanks to "transparent scenic curtains, electrical appliances, calcium light effects and magnesium combustion"). The building collapses. Twenty years elapse. The lawyer has come to believe he will never be caught, and he has grown rich. But a clerk and a maid know his secret and blackmail him. He is driven to suicide. The innocent parties celebrate at Court of Honor at the Chicago World's Fair. One other highly praised setting showed a busy railroad station.

Another railroad station, this time Grand Central, along with a New York mansion, a Juneau saloon, and the S.S. *Golden Hope* (which catches fire to permit the requisite sensation scene) were locales for the action of **The Ladder of Life** (1-10-98, Third Ave.), a circulating melodrama whose authorship went uncredited. Its plot centered on yet one more heroic Jack, Jack Ellsworth, falsely accused of murder. The leading man accepted his fate when tiny Fanny Gonzales all but stole the show from him as Bats, a newsgirl who is "the darling of the alley." He probably was more disconcerted on opening night when his gun refused to fire yet the villain fell dead. He could only think to mutter, "I thought I heard a shot," a comment greeted by snickers and guffaws from the audience.

The beautiful Fanny Davenport made what proved to be her final major New York appearances when she returned for a fortnight beginning on the 24th. Most of her visit was given over to standbys *La Tosca, Cleopatra,* and *Fédora,* but she also offered a few performances of **Joan** (1-29-98, Fifth Ave.), Frances Aymar Matthews's retelling of the Jeanne d'Arc legend in uninspired blank verse. Her buxom maid lacked fire. The star died the following September. She was forty-eight years old.

The night of Miss Davenport's reentry also witnessed the premiere of R. C. Carton's sharply written saga of a selfish, money-grubbing woman who wrecks the lives of her husband and her old lover, **The Tree of Knowledge** (1-24-98, Lyceum). Daniel Frohman's fine troupe and tasteful production brought in playgoers for six weeks.

Eugene Presbrey's **A Virginia Courtship** (1-31-98, Knickerbocker) may not have been as literate, but it was skillfully contrived (in avowed imitation of classic 18th-century English comedies) and had the added attraction of W. H. Crane as star. So it ran longer—ten weeks. When war breaks out in 1815 between England and France, the pro-English Major Richard Fairfax (Crane) falls out with his pro-French neighbor, the widowed Madame Constance Robert (Annie Irish). This puts a crimp in the romance of his son, Tom (Walter Hale), and Madame Robert's daughter, Prudence (Percy Haswell). It also leads to a preposterously comic duel, not unlike that fought by Bob Acres in *The Rivals.* Of course, everything ends happily, with Fairfax and Madame Robert agreeing to wed along with Tom and Prudence. Crane cavorted in "his Anthony Absolute manner." The mounting included correct period costumes and two settings, one "decorated and furnished in a sort of combination of Louis XV and Empire modes, while the other is in the heavy old English style." Late in the run A. E. Lancaster's **His Last Appearance** (4-4-98) was added to the bill. Crane played an old actor who tricks a shy young man into proposing to an equally shy young girl.

When Daly restored *The Country Girl* he accompanied it with **The Subtleties of Jealousy** (2-1-98, Daly's), Sydney Rosenfeld's adaptation of a short Feydeau farce. Ada Rehan assumed the principal part of an absurdly suspicious wife. The piece failed to please and soon was replaced by a one-act operetta.

Way Down East (2-7-98, Manhattan) was a hackneyed melodrama that became for a time an American theatrical classic. Written by Lottie Blair Parker, an actress with playwriting ambitions, it was substantially reworked by a more experienced, deft actor-playwright, Joseph Grismer, and presented by two rising producers, William A. Brady and Florenz Ziegfeld. Grismer's wife, who used the stage name Phoebe Davies, was given the leading role of Annie Moore. Annie, having been seduced and having lost the child of that liaison, drifts aimlessly until she is taken on as a servant at the New England farm of Squire Bartlett (Odell Williams). Not knowing her history, the Bartletts treat her with kindness, but when her past is discovered the squire drives her out in the midst of a blinding snowstorm. She loses her way and nearly dies before the squire's son, David (Howard Kyle), finds her and brings her back. He finally convinces his parents that Annie is a decent girl, worthy to be his wife. The story was reminiscent of so many old warhorses. Critics quickly called to mind *Hazel Kirke* and *The Old Homestead.* The *Sun,* one of the harshest naysayers, complained that the play had "not a throb of life in it" and that its humor came solely from "exaggerated twangs." The critic, suspicious of the audience's "uncomfortably enthusiastic" response, hinted the house had been papered (which Brady later admitted) and reported, "The applause was deafening at every juncture of the play and it was admirably distributed throughout the theatre." The *Journal,* though tiring of the clichés, was a bit more accepting, noting that "at the end of the third act, when the heroine with the usual melodramatic past is thrust out into the usual melodramatic snow storm, while the hero puts on his melodramatic fur cap and worsted muffler to follow her, the gallery howled its approval."

For other reviewers, there was a restraint and honesty in the writing that they found appealing. And there was a homespun humor they knew audiences of the day would find irresistible. At one point a rube (in fact, his name was Reuben Whipple) enters to announce excitedly, "Big doin's in town— pust-office bruk into and robbed last night—gret loss fer th' gov'mint—three dollars wuth o' stamps stole!" And the requisite production values were also there: honest-to-goodness barnyard animals mosied across the stage, and the paper blizzard, using newly patented tricks, was somethin' awful. According to Brady, the 152-performance run was forced, without a single profitable week. But the producers didn't care. The long New York run was a potent advertisement on the road, and the play soon was greeted by packed houses everywhere. Over the next dozen or so years Miss Davies performed her part more than 4000 times, and after her death other actresses replaced her. The play eventually became one of the most famous silent films.

Oh, Susannah! (2-7-98, Hoyt's) was a farce by three Englishmen. A drudge who works in a boardinghouse falls wildly in love with a young doctor living there. Her comic efforts to convince him to marry her come to naught when she discovers he has a wife. Business began to falter after a month, so a second farce was added to the bill. Mildred Dowling's **Dangerfield '95** (2-28-98) recounted the reaction of a young lady (Annie Russell) whose beau mistakenly sends her a package that contains a letter describing her as "Miss Goody-goody." She takes it upon herself to show him how wickedly she can behave. She smokes in public, gambles, and even, heaven forfend, sits on the floor.

Modjeska also came into town on the 7th, at the Fifth Avenue. She brought nothing new, contenting herself and her faithful followers with *Mary Stuart, Magda, Macbeth,* and *Measure for Measure.*

Charles Frohman, on the other hand, had plenty of new plays on the fire. He brought two of them in on two successive evenings the following week. Both were English. Each was headed by an important star. John Drew was the center of attraction in Henry V. Esmond's **One Summer's Day** (2-14-98, Wallack's). He portrayed a self-sacrificing, put-upon officer blackmailed by a gypsy (Elsie de Wolfe) and misunderstood by his fiancée (Isabel Irving) until the air cleared minutes before an eleven o'clock curtain.

Henry Miller provided a striking contrast to Drew, who rarely ranged beyond the safe boundaries of light comedy or sentimental drama. In his easy, throwaway style, Drew had impersonated a figure about his own age—in his middle forties. Miller, still in his thirties, assumed the more testing part of an older man, implacable and cruel, who drives his son, daughter, and wife away, and who only learns to bend and love when his family returns to him after he has precipitated his own ruin. The play was Stuart Ogilvie's **The Master** (2-15-98, Garden). Franklyn Fyles, in his capacity as critic for the *Sun,* observed, "Mr. Miller acts throughout with sincerity and fervour. Nothing has ever done more to justify his claim to a high position among the artists of our stage." By the time the father, seeing his son marching in the ranks, waves his handkerchief and cheers on his boy, Miller had skillfully turned his audiences' feelings about him 180 de-

grees. Miller was awarded a ten-week run; Drew lingered only seven weeks.

W. R. Waldron and Lionel Ellis's **A Midnight Trust** (2-28-98, People's) was set in England and found the villain and hero dueling over an inheritance. A huge, ugly stone-crushing machine added menace to a sensation scene. Continuing its season-long attack on this school of touring melodrama, the *Dramatic Mirror* dismissed the piece for belonging to an all too "familiar order," telling a "regulation story."

On March 30, *Hedda Gabler* was given a special matinee at the Fifth Avenue. Elizabeth Robins was Hedda, and Leo Ditrichstein was George Tesman. A lesser actor, Ernest Hastings, was Lovborg. Once again the audience was small. But several reviewers, including Dithmar in the *Times,* gave the play extended, flattering notices. Slowly but surely, Ibsen and his new theatre were making headway.

At the same time, an older theatre was giving way just as slowly and surely. Players in the old tradition were dying off or retiring. But some diehards remained. Louis James, who had performed with Mrs. Drew and Barrett and at Daly's in its early years, continued to travel doggedly in a Shakespearean repertory. He long since had become a major star on the road, if not in New York. When he returned briefly for a stand at the lowly Metropolis Theatre on March 28, he presented *Hamlet, Julius Caesar, Othello,* and *Romeo and Juliet* along with Bird's *The Gladiator,* here called *Spartacus.* However, he also essayed one new play, Espy Williams's **A Cavalier of France** (4-3-98, Metropolis), a drama written in outdated blank verse and telling how René de Froisace (James) is allowed to marry Gabriella (Alma Kruger) after aiding his erstwhile enemy, Henry III (Barry Johnstone), to escape some dangerous conspirators.

Most critics continued to ignore such traveling productions, consigned to out-of-the-way houses and the shortest visits. As a rule, when they did deign to attend, they were condescending, seeing such mountings and plays as of little interest to sophisticated playgoers. So Creston Clarke's **The Last of His Race** (4-4-98, People's) met with the same indifference that greeted James. Clarke, who was Booth's nephew, was the star of his own play. He impersonated Louis Cardel, a man discovered to be a long-lost prince, who marries his beloved Marie de Neuville despite the efforts of Nicolai Karacheff to besmirch him with the taint of illegitimacy.

But then a weak farce at a first-class house received little better treatment. W. H. Allerdice, who wrote **The Old Coat** (4-4-98, Bijou), was a navy officer who dabbled in belles lettres. His play concerned two law partners who wear look-alike coats. One accidentally places his wedding money in his partner's coat; the other mistakenly places legal papers and an invitation to a party in his associate's jacket. The expected complications followed, albeit not for long. Arthur Voegtlin's recreations of a typical law office and of a smoking room received more commendation than the play did.

Broadway's brightening lights glowed even more brightly the next Monday, when two of the season's most interesting bills premiered. In the first instance the play (or, more accurately, the plays) was not the thing, since the star was America's finest young actress, Mrs. Fiske. Her offerings were Mrs. Oscar Beringer's one-act **A Bit of Old Chelsea** and Marguerite Merington's **Love Finds the Way** (4-11-98, Fifth Ave.), taken from an unidentified German play. In the curtain raiser she played Saucers, a bedraggled cockney flower girl. Sitting on a doorstep, shivering with cold, she is taken in by a compassionate young sculptor, who offers her warmth and food. Naturally, she falls in love with him, only to discover that he is engaged to another girl, and so she ruefully goes on her way. To an extent the story resembled *Oh, Susannah!*'s, but without that play's coarseness and farcical turn. The star's performing counted for everything. She eschewed heart-tugging sentimentality or elaborate, theatricalized characterization. The essence and wonder of her performance was its simplicity and truthfulness, its fundamental happiness in the face of poverty and rejection.

By contrast, a gnawing bitterness was the keynote of her Madeline Winfield, a rich girl who should have enjoyed all the blessings of her station but has been soured since childhood because she is crippled. An understanding doctor is her best friend, and he believes her lameness may be psychosomatic (although that expression had not yet gained currency). Madeline is goaded into a self-forgetful act and suddenly discovers her handicap has vanished. While this was a pre-Freudian era, it was the epoch of Mary Baker Eddy and her preachments, and many of her followers saw in the play a dramatic confirmation of her Christian Science. According to reports, numerous handicapped people were taken to the play in hopes of encouraging cures. As usual, Mrs. Fiske underplayed, never unduly emphasizing either Madeline's lameness or morbidity and thus making both more telling. The play did eight weeks of excellent business. Before that, she had revived *Tess of the D'Urbervilles* for two weeks, and subsequently she brought out *Divorçons*. In all she defied the Trust, at the only first-class theatre besides Daly's that it did not control, for more than three months in New York.

The other major opening was Clyde Fitch's **The Moth and the Flame** (4-11-98, Lyceum), a full-length "society drama" the young author developed out of his one-act *Harvest*. Ostensibly the play was presented by the Kelcey-Shannon Company, which consisted of Herbert Kelcey, his wife, Effie Shannon, W. J. LeMoyne, and his wife, Sarah Cowell LeMoyne. Actually the company was one of several subsidiary organizations financed and guided by Daniel Frohman. Forming companies within companies was a common practice of the day, and such Byzantine pyramids permitted special players a second opportunity for billing. Fitch's plot was reasonably straightforward. The curtain rises to disclose a reception room and ballroom at the Woltons' elegant home. A fancy ball is in progress, with the guests all dressed as children. Several of the guests take turns performing songs and dances. Conversations reveal that Marion Wolton (Shannon) has rejected a proposal of marriage from forthright Douglas Rhodes (Bruce McRae). Further dialogue, demonstrating Fitch's surehanded dramatic technique, offers more revelations at the same time it delineates some characterizations, suggests the theme of the play, and even sneaks in the title.

Mrs. Lorrimer [Mrs. LeMoyne]: Who's here?

Johnstone [Edward See]: Everybody.

Mrs. Lorrimer: Anyone I can marry?

Kitty [Edna Phillips]: Oh, Mrs. Lorrimer, do be decent. You haven't been divorced a year yet.

Mrs. Lorrimer: My dear, divorce isn't like death—you don't have to go into mourning! Besides, that's what I want to get married for! I find I've a perfect passion for divorce! Just like men have it for drink. I've only had two divorces, and I want another!

Johnstone: You must be damned careful—I beg your pardon.

Mrs. Lorrimer: Oh, don't apologize, I say it myself!—careful about what?

Johnstone: What sort of *husband you choose.*

Mrs. Lorrimer: Exactly! None of your ideal men for me! I want a man with a bad record! Plenty of proof concealed about his person, or not buried too deep in his past for me and my lawyer to ferret out. I've a perfect duck of a lawyer! He made up every bit of evidence about my last husband; that won me my case, and, my dears, it just *happened* to turn out to be true!

Ethel [Leila Ellis]: Speaking of records, who do you think is here to-night?

Mrs. Lorrimer: Ned Fletcher—!!
Kitty: Yes.
Mrs. Lorrimer: Girls—I'll tell you a secret—
Johnstone: I don't want to hear it.
Mrs. Lorrimer: I'm crazy about him! Where is he?
Kitty: You've no chance; he's going to marry Marion, if she'll have him.
Mrs. Lorrimer: What a shame! And will she?
Ethel: She's mad about him.
Mrs. Lorrimer: The moth and the flame!

Rhodes also warns Marion that even if she will not have him, she would be well advised to keep away from Fletcher (Kelcey). Another visitor to the Wolton home is Mr. Dawson (LeMoyne), Mrs. Wolton's brother. He has come to warn Wolton (E. W. Thomas) that Wolton is bankrupt and no further aid will be forthcoming. Wolton goes upstairs and commits suicide while the guests cavort below. Fletcher advises Dawson that he will assume all of Wolton's debts, so that Mrs. Wolton (Isabel Waldron) and Marion will not be embarrassed. But a year later, at the wedding service, when the minister asks if any man can show just cause why the marriage should not take place, a woman appears with a child to announce that Fletcher is her husband, or at least the father of her child. Fletcher strikes the woman, Jeanette (Eleanor Gross), knocking her to the floor. Calling Fletcher a coward, Marion rushes to help her. Afterwards, at Marion's home, Fletcher tells Marion that if she will not marry him, he will disclose the truth about her father's debts. Luckily, Rhodes appears on the scene and lovingly agrees to assume the debts himself and to marry Marion, if she will have him. She will.

Beautifully mounted and acted, the play made for compelling theatre. One much voiced complaint, however, was that none of the characters truly enlisted sympathy. The most interesting figure was Fletcher, who seems genuinely willing to put his ugly past behind him and reverts to his baser self only when the woman whom he sees as his sole chance for salvation spurns him. The drama ran ten weeks, until the onset of summer stifled business. It toured all of the following season and long remained a favorite in stock.

But New York did not follow the lead of the road in embracing Augustus Thomas's **The Hoosier Doctor** (4-18-98, 14th St.), even though it starred Digby Bell, so popular a comic in musicals. Perhaps the problem was that the work was too adramatic, a character study that minimized all its story's dramatic opportunities. The character was Dr. Willow, who had taken up medicine in middle age after a life

of failures. A widower, he is beset by three demanding daughters, a loutish son-in-law, and a virago of a mother-in-law. He also has a run-in with the White Caps, a Ku Klux Klan–like group. But his fundamental goodness is rewarded: Little Rosie (Ethel Vance), a waif he has taken in, proves to be another long-lost heiress, and he wins the hand of a sweet widow, Mrs. Bunce (Emma Butler). Comic bits included Willow's dictating his proposal of marriage to a typist; among the sentimental scenes was Little Rosie's undressing for bed and then saying her prayers sitting on Willow's lap. The dictation scene had been used in *The Alderman,* but since both plays had begun touring about the same time the preceding season, which borrowed from which is moot. Putting a child to bed was an old trick to win appeal. Although many critics admired Thomas's writing, poor attendance forced the show to be pulled after its first week.

Critics also felt that **The First Violin** (4-25-98, Garden) missed some dramatic potential and wallowed in talk and patent sentimentality. The play starred Richard Mansfield, who, under the pen name Merridan Phelps, collaborated with J. I. C. Clarke in bringing Jessie Fothergill's novel to the stage. The role of Eugen Courvoisier marked a change of pace from the darker figures the actor had been portraying. Eugen has been forced into exile and poverty after publicly accepting blame for forging a check, a forgery actually committed by his irresponsible wife. As a struggling musician, he helps a beleaguered young English girl, May Wedderhorn (Lettice Fairfax). Learning that his wife had died, he proposes to her. Anna Sartorius (Olive Oliver), a vicious minx who knows Eugen's history, attempts to come between them. For a time she succeeds, but eventually she is discomfited. Despite critical complaints, this sort of soppy romance appealed to a sizable audience. Although wartime excitement was keeping many playgoers away from the theatre and hurting ticket sales, *The First Violin* did good business during its prebooked, month-long visit, so Mansfield kept it in his repertory for a while.

A slighter piece ran longer, thanks no doubt to the capering of the ever popular W. H. Crane, who had set aside *A Virginia Courtship.* **His Honor the Mayor** (4-26-98, Empire) was a farce by Charles Henry Meltzer and A. E. Lancaster, derived "partly" from Meilhac and Halévy's *Le Mari de la débutante.* Its action moved from a prima donna's apartment to City Hall to a theatre's green room. The journey is not surprising if you realize that Bartholomew "Jonesy" Jones, a politician suddenly elevated to mayor pro tem, is also a would-be theatrical producer. The comedy came from his constantly mixing up the duties of his disparate offices.

The title of Mark Swan's **Princess of Patches** (5-2-98, People's) undoubtedly gave the plot away to knowing playgoers, for its heroine, Selma, is an ill-treated foundling who turns out to be an heiress. Her first entrance was an eye-opener. A barrel rolls onto the stage, and when it comes to a standstill, Selma peeks out and announces, "I went swimmin' an' somebody stole my clothes."

C. T. Dazey, who was still coining a mint with *In Old Kentucky*, tried his hand at farce and stumbled badly. **The Tarrytown Widow** (5-9-98, Bijou) is Mrs. Constance Raymond (Madeline Bouton), a pretty young lady given to boasting, "It isn't everybody who is lucky enough to be a widow two years at nineteen." She is courted by a monkeylike, dagger-brandishing French count (George W. Barnum) and by Benjamin Bascom (W. J. Ferguson), whose wife is away. But Madeline prefers Benjamin's son, Augustus (Charles Lothian), even if, although he is over twenty-one, he is kept in knickers by his termagant mother. Before long Benjamin has some explaining to do, and Augustus is wearing long pants. A much applauded set showed the 42nd Street railroad terminal's waiting room, a natural place for all manner of folk to pop in and out.

The ongoing Spanish-American War provided the basis for Willis Arden's **A Spy of Spain** (5-16-98, People's). Its heroine is a Spanish girl with Cuban sympathies. She is courted by an American officer and a Spanish officer, and in one scene she dons an American uniform to help the Cuban cause. Its action took place in a U.S. Army camp in Cuba, a Havana prison, the captain-general's palace, and a Spanish blockhouse, the capture of which ends the play.

The drama of the new war was followed by a play about an older one, but David K. Higgins's **A Union Soldier** (5-23-98, People's) proved to be nothing more than a rewriting of his former *Burr Oaks*. Indeed, Higgins must have been very busy revamping previous hits, for the next offering at this popular combination house was **The Cuban's Vendetta** (5-30-98, People's), which was a reworking of his 1892 *The Vendetta*, reset in contemporary Spain and Cuba.

The same playhouse offered the season's last play, and this, too, was not totally new, since **Shadows of the Past** (6-6-98, People's) was merely a quirkily and misleadingly titled dramatization of Mark Twain's *Tom Sawyer*. It was also a singularly inept translation.

Of course, from *Sidetracked*, which appeared at People's in August, through *The Banker's Daughter,* which was seen at the Columbus in late May, older plays made brief visits all season long, mostly at houses devoted to such touring attractions, but occasionally as stopgaps at first-class theatres.

1898–1899

Prosperity, in no small measure war-bred, kept box offices humming. By spring one trade sheet was cheering on "the most successful season the American theatre has ever known." Of course, the paper was speaking largely of the financial situation. In the excitement of roping in huge profits, even badgering of the hated Trust became muted for a time. And more American plays were coming to the fore. Yet such was still the quality of most native works that the only two plays still revived a century later were both importations—and both took a highly romanticized view of bygone days.

The ongoing war provided material for R. N. Stephens's **The Ragged Regiment** (6-20-98, Herald Square). Dick Morris (Aubrey Boucicault) and Billy Gibbings (Frank Doane) land secretly in Cuba to rescue their friend, Hartley West (Donald P. Bowles), who is being held in a Spanish prison. Dick falls in love with Felicia de Lautana (Blanche Walsh), daughter of the prison commander, and persuades both of them to switch allegiances. The Spaniards get wind of this and besiege the prison. To scare off the besiegers Dick tries to get some Cubans to pretend they are an American group known as "the Ragged Regiment," a band of Bowery boys recruited by Tom Crosby (Edgar L. Davenport). The boys are known for singing "Marching Through Georgia" as they go into battle. But the Cubans' singing of the song is so pathetic that the Spaniards can only sneer. Just as they are about to begin their assault, however, the song is heard again—this time sung lustily by the real Americans. The Spaniards retreat. A printer's error left out the word "Regiment" from the placards plastered all about New York, but before new posters could be readied Boucicault was injured in an accident, and the show closed at the start of its second week.

No more major openings occurred for two months, until the arrival of Louis Eagan's **The Midnight Flood** (8-15-98, People's). Eagan's story reached back nine years to the Johnstown disaster. According to the playwright, the flood was the purposeful work of one murderous man, Dr. Sheldon. Before the rise of the curtain, Sheldon has killed the wife of his friend, Tim Westleaf (Eagan), dumped Tim's baby in the ocean, and had Tim committed to an insane asylum. Sheldon does not know that the baby has been rescued and grown to womanhood. She is now called Alice Sedley. A beautiful woman, she is courted by Archibald Lacy, Walter Wilkins, and none other than Sheldon himself. To clear his way, Sheldon kills Lacy and frames Wilkins for the murder. Now he demands that Alice's kindhearted guardian, Squire Morse, who owes Sheldon money, approve the match. But Westleaf has escaped from the asylum and comes to town disguised as a tramp. He uncovers proofs of Sheldon's villainy, whereupon Sheldon opens the gates of the dam. But his plans go awry when "the doctor's intended victims save themselves miraculously, and come floating across the stage on house roofs and other old things." The play had toured the preceding season and after a week at the combination house continued on its travels.

The four-year-old Dreyfus affair was also grist for America's theatrical mills, albeit once again real issues were shoved aside in the name of cheap melodrama. The hero of Vera De Noie and Arthur D. Hall's **Devil's Island** (8-29-98, 14th St.) was rechristened Maurice de la Tour (William Harcourt). When he spurns the advances of Countess Nina Petrovsky (Emily Rigl), she frames him for treason. He is convicted and sent to Devil's Island. Then Nina repents. She sails to French Guiana, seduces and drugs the prison warden, gives de la Tour the warden's uniform, and, with the help of some comic American "yellow journalists," assists in de la Tour's escape. Among the elaborate effects was one of a fully rigged ship approaching head on from the horizon. The drama played three weeks, then sailed out on a season-long tour.

Back to the war. Hamilton Harris's **The Maine Avenged** (8-29-98, People's) begins with two Spaniards about to press the button that will blow up the battleship. José Cordovas (Harris), a Cuban, enters the room and accuses the Spaniards of treachery. A fight ensues, and both Spaniards are killed, but before one of them dies he manages to crawl to the detonator. The ship, seen through a window, explodes. Unfortunately, José's problems are not over. He must rescue his sister from imprisonment, gingerly sidestep the wiles of a Spanish officer's tricky wife, and participate in the grand finale, the taking of Santiago.

Stuart Robson scored a small success in Augustus Thomas's **The Meddler** (9-1-98, Wallack's), keeping "the Robson falsetto and the Robson stare and other Robson methods of eliciting laughter within reasonable bounds." As the cowardly but interfering Francis Eli, who discovers his sister is engaged to a man notorious for affairs with married women, he brings all manner of trouble upon himself and his friends. To begin with, since his sister's fiancé has a reputation as a duelist, he attempts to appeal not to him but to the married woman the man is seeing. Naturally, the woman's husband appears and misinterprets the situation. Later Eli must hide the same lady behind some portieres and, when she is discovered, pretend she is a foreign maid who understands no English. Critics felt the best thing about the play was its bright dialogue. Booked in advance for a cross-country tour, the play ran only four weeks.

Having failed to find a truly popular vehicle in the preceding season, late in his tour E. H. Sothern had finally turned to Anthony Hope's picture of 1720 England, **The Adventure of Lady Ursula** (9-1-98, Lyceum). Sothern portrayed Sir George Sylvester, a professed woman-hater, who falls in love with Lady Ursula (Virginia Harned) only after he realizes she is willing to fight a duel with him while she is disguised as a man. The comedy was set aside after a profitable two-month stand.

A second importation was William A. Brady and Florenz Ziegfeld's production of **The Turtle** (9-3-98, Manhattan), Léon Gandillot's Paris hit, adapted by Joseph W. Herbert. Its story told of a long-suffering French grocer who wins back his butterfly ex-wife by marrying the very same young girl whom the ex-wife's new heartthrob actually loves. W. J. Ferguson and Sadie Martinot were the divorced couple, and beautiful, youthful Grace George was the girl. The farce was the season's first smash, running until spring.

An equally good press but a far less enthusiastic public response greeted another importation, Robert Ganthony's **A Brace of Partridges** (9-7-98, Madison Square), in which two cousins, one virtuous and one scoundrelly—and both named Partridge—pursue the same innkeeper's daughter. H. Reeves-Smith assumed the dual roles. To perk up business A. C. Fraserwood's **Goodbye** was added on October 6th. It recounted a bride-to-be's last visit to the man she truly loves, but whom her parents will not let her marry. Shortly afterward the Ganthony play headed out to try its luck on the road.

Despite its title, the central figure in Joseph Le Brandt's **A Factory Waif** (9-12-98, People's) is a foreman whose sympathies rest with the workers and not with the mill owner. As a result the owner frames him for murder. The owner also brings in a barrel of gasoline to set fire to the mill. The *Sun* reported the boisterous response of the gallery when the gasoline was ignited with a "fine bang and spatter," followed by "bursts of flame and showers of sparks."

Sutton Vane's latest London melodrama, **John Martin's Secret** (9-19-98, Star), had such a ridiculously convoluted plot that it required half a column of small print to summarize it. Suffice it that the titular villain owns a safe whose combination is D-E-A-T-H and that to protect his secret he has murdered the man who built the safe. His assistant is a Jew who is searching for his long-lost daughter, Zillah, unaware she is Martin's mistress. But Martin is determined to get rid of her so he can marry Madge—after he also has disposed of Madge's husband. In the play's famous sensation scene he lures Zillah to a hilltop above his mine. "He contrives to start the sloping ground so that a landslide occurs. . . . Zillah is left standing in front of a hut, which is about to fall. At this moment Madge, who has been in the mine, comes up in a small car, suspended on a cable, that runs to the works on a hill on the other side of the stage. The car is in midair. Madge calls to Zillah to jump. She does so, and is caught by Madge's outstretched hands and borne to safety." Although the play enjoyed some popularity on the road, it had to be content with one-week bookings in Manhattan's combination houses.

Two American melodramas, both dealing with the war in Cuba, opened the same evening. Jean Mawson's **A Daughter of Cuba** (9-19-98, People's) was a quick failure. The "daughter" is actually an American named Adele (Miss Mawson). She learns her sweetheart, Jack Price, has enlisted and berates him, "You care more for glory than you do for me." Then, ladylike, she changes her mind, confiding to the audience, "I, too, can be brave. I, too, shall go to war." So when Jack is seriously wounded in the battle for Siboney (which occupied the whole of Act III), she is there, in the hospital tent, ready to minister to him.

The heroes of Myron Leffingwell's **The Dawn of Freedom** (9-19-98, 14th St.) are Antonio Lopez (Paul Gilmore), whose sister, Paquita (Laura Alberta), has been seduced by a Spanish officer, and Ruy Ximenes (Edwin Holland), a Cuban-American who loves Paquita. At one point an American newspaperwoman, Jane Fortune (Ida Glenn), covers Ximenes with an American flag to hide him from the Spaniards. For a time the principal figures languish in prison, but they are on the ramparts at Santiago to watch the American navy sink the enemy ships and to welcome the marines and "jackies" pouring ashore. After an initial fortnight, the play toured all season.

James O'Neill, enjoying one of his rare respites from *Monte Cristo,* appeared for a single week at a combination house in Joseph Hatton's dramatization of his own novel **When Greek Meets Greek** (9-26-98, Columbus). There were no Greeks in the play, which was set against the background of the French Revolution. O'Neill played Henri Lavelle, a dashing aristocrat who vies with his rebel half-brother, the Deputy Grebauval (Edmund Breese), for the hand of Mathilde (Minnie Radcliffe), a duke's daughter. Grebauval attempts to have both imprisoned for treason, but Henri duels him to the death and flees with his beloved. The *Dramatic Mirror,* calling O'Neill "the representative romantic actor," reported he "reveled in splendid opportunities for the display of his fine talents, giving a performance at once picturesque, powerful and sympathetic, while compelling the audience to frequent outbursts of enthusiasm."

However, newspapers gave far more attention and a more prominent position to their reviews of two importations that competed with O'Neill's opening. **The Liars** (9-26-98, Empire), Henry Arthur Jones's cynical look at conniving, unloving, untruthful English society, starred John Drew as the one man sensible enough to save the tottering marriage of his friends after the wife has strayed. It was what had become a typical Drew role, and this time the *Dramatic Mirror* observed that the star "implied more by the nod of his head, the elevation of his eyebrows, the shrugging of his shoulders than was dreamed of in Henry Arthur Jones' philosophy." The play ran a little over three months.

Cecil Raleigh and Seymour Hicks's London melodrama **Sporting Life** (9-26-98, Academy of Music) ran a month longer. The hero, an English duke (Robert Hilliard), finds his engagement to a nice girl threatened by a schemer with whom he once had had a liaison. A prizefight (with the hero bravely substituting for a drugged pugilist) and a race with horses on the usual treadmills provided special thrills. Lavish settings included a stable, a mansion, the national Sporting Club, and Epsom Downs on Derby Day.

Edwin Jerome must have bet that he could lure in two huge groups of devoted playgoers—the Irish and the Germans—with his **Killarney and Rhine** (9-26-98, People's). He won his bet, for the play remained a touring favorite for several seasons. Its simple story recounted the adventures of Conrad

Rosenvonvurkelenops on a visit to Ireland. Songs and dances helped the entertainment.

Scott Marble's name was synonymous with touring American melodrama, but devotees were in for a surprise at his **Have You Seen Smith?** (10-3-98, Star), since his comic saga of A. Bleeker Knight and I. Work Days, divorced men who have married each other's ex-wives, was so filled with musical numbers that most reviewers considered it a musical.

The same evening welcomed the touring company headed by Frederick Warde, Louis James, and Kathryn Kidder at the Grand Opera. Their repertory offered *Hamlet, Julius Caesar, Othello,* and *Macbeth,* along with *The School for Scandal.* At Manhattan's leading second-string stock house, Hannah May Ingham's **The Young Wife** (10-3-98, Murray Hill) proved to be a reworking of *East Lynne.*

But it fell to Richard Mansfield to present the season's most awaited opening night and its most enduring play, Edmond Rostand's **Cyrano de Bergerac** (10-3-98, Garden). The story of a homely man who, sight unseen, courts the woman he loves for another, handsomer man was hailed immediately as a classic. Not everyone was totally pleased with Mansfield's interpretation. The *Times* complained about his lack of facial expression (which it suggested might be attributed to heavy makeup) and his sometimes careless enunciation. But all in all, the evening was seen as a triumph. Settings were sumptuous and crowd scenes, with more than 100 costumed people on stage, awesome. Augustin Daly presented another version that same night in Philadelphia, with Charles Richman as the Gascon and Ada Rehan as Roxane, but Mansfield's success dissuaded him from bringing it into New York. That success kept the Garden packed for the entire six-week engagement. Mansfield returned to the play in later years and was contemplating a revival at the time of his death.

Another major hit followed on the next Monday evening. Hall Caine's dramatization of his own novel **The Christian** (10-10-98, Knickerbocker) had been rejected by West End and Broadway producers until that astute agent Elisabeth Marbury gave it to Viola Allen, who immediately sailed for London to help rework the piece. Her production made her a star of the first rank.

. . .

Viola Allen (1867–1948) was born in Huntsville, Ala., the daughter of players. She first appeared in New York as Annie Russell's replacement in *Esmeralda* in 1882. Subsequently she performed with John McCullough and Tommaso Salvini, before winning attention in *Shenandoah* (1889). She toured

as Lydia Languish in Joseph Jefferson's company, then joined Charles Frohman's stock ensemble at the Empire. Lewis C. Strang wrote of the wide-eyed, round-faced, sad-miened beauty, "Miss Allen acts mentally rather than emotionally. Her conception of a part is always intelligent, comprehensive, and logical."

. . .

Miss Allen's Glory Quayle rejects a proposal of marriage from John Storm (Edward J. Morgan), who becomes a clergyman ministering to the poor. Glory starts out to be a nurse but soon finds a more glittering success as a music-hall singer. Storm pursues her, determined to save her soul, and, when his own world falls apart, threatens to kill her rather than see her doomed to perdition. She agrees to help him in his slum work. Few critics thought much of the play, but audiences quickly spread the word that it was rattling good theatre. It did solid business for twenty weeks.

The same evening saw Joseph Jefferson return for one final revival of *The Rivals.* A minor but able actress, Ffolliott Paget, acquitted herself admirably when she took on the difficult task of replacing the late Mrs. Drew as Mrs. Malaprop. Wilton Lackaye played Sir Lucius, and the up-and-coming Otis Skinner won good notices for his Captain Absolute. The mounting was enjoyed for a month at the Fifth Avenue.

No author was given for **The Wheel of Fortune** (10-10-98, Metropolis), and it was accorded the skimpiest notices when it was noticed at all. One report alerted readers that "murder, robbery, dynamite explosions and the collapse of a house follow in swift succession." Musical specialties were also part and parcel of the entertainment. By way of novelty, one character in the play was a gypsy fortune teller, and during intermissions she roamed the auditorium offering to read patrons' palms.

A touring play patently designed to capture the appeal of *The Old Homestead* had to be content with a one-week booking. Charles Manley doubled in brass, serving as both playwright and star of **Down on the Farm** (10-17-98, People's). His hayseed, Seth Huckins, comes to New York, visits the Bowery and has an adventure at a tenement roof-garden, then hurries back to the safety of the countryside. The roof-garden scene allowed for some song and dances.

A more knowing, successful piece was **On and Off** (10-17-98, Hoyt's), which was taken from Alexandre Bisson's *Le Contrôleur des wagons-lits.* Its story was reminiscent of *The Captain of the Nonsuch.* In this case the harried husband pretends to be a railroad inspector to cover up his flings. E. M. Holland was featured. A prosperous run was followed by a long tour. This show was credited as the source for Jerome Kern's 1920 musical *The Night Boat,* although the musical's plot is closer to that of *The Captain of the Nonsuch.*

On and Off was one of the season's many productions by Charles Frohman, as was the next hit. **Catherine** (10-24-98, Garrick), too, was from the French. Its author, Henri Lavedan, was much admired at the time for his social comedies. But Frohman offered playgoers an added incentive, raising the equally admired Annie Russell to stardom in the title part.

. . .

Annie Russell (1864–1936) was born in Liverpool and grew up in Canada, where she made her stage debut in 1872. Her first memorable New York assignment was in *Esmeralda* (1881). Illness kept this frail, darkish woman from the stage for many years and probably prevented her from fully realizing her possibilities. But Odell gratefully recalled "her charm, her grace, her exquisite voice, her genuine dramatic power."

. . .

As Catherine she portrayed a sensitive young woman torn between her love for a poor mechanic and the proposal of a rich, handsome duke. Her support was outstanding, with Frank Worthing as the duke, Joseph Holland as the mechanic, Elsie de Wolfe and Ethel Barrymore in lesser roles, and Mrs. W. J. LeMoyne all but stealing the show as a wise, regal dowager. Frohman announced that the sets were replicas of those employed at the Comédie Française. His care was rewarded with an eleven-week run.

The rut into which touring melodrama had dug itself was nicely exemplified by two openings the same night. Both were what one trade sheet called "olla podridas," utilizing many of the same stale clichés in virtually a codified order (a spectator, if miraculously fast enough, could have jumped from one theatre to the other without missing a beat in the story), and both were sprinkled with "specialties, without which no modern melodrama is complete." Both even resorted to the same first name for their hero—that most popular of all melodramatic heroes' names, Jack. (Authors and producers of these works could not foresee that within a decade films would all but wipe out the market for the genre.)

In Scott Marble's **On Land and Sea** (10-24-98, Star), Jack Farrell and James Durham are rivals for the hand of Lucy Massey, the daughter of a skipper for whom Durham works. Believing he is the skipper's heir, Durham murders him and makes it seem that Jack is the killer. His expectations are dashed when an octoroon named Zada appears with a later will, which leaves everything to Lucy. So Durham plots to scuttle a ship on which Lucy is sailing. When this, too, fails he lures her to an abandoned sugar factory and tries to have her sign over her estate to him. Once again Zada enters to obstruct injustice. Durham grabs Zada's baby and throws it into a wheat crusher, but Zada is able to save her child because her own lover rushes in and shoots Durham. Jack, who really hasn't done that much, is free to clasp Lucy.

The rivals in Octavius Cohen's **The Sleeping City** (10-24-98, People's) are Jack Morton and Charles Creston, and the object of their affection is Ethel Baintree. Charles's false accusation lands Jack in Sing Sing. With Ethel's help, he escapes from there by plunging from the prison wall onto a speeding freight train. Meanwhile, Charles has had Jack's brother, Lou, confined to an insane asylum. Lou also escapes, if not so sensationally. The brothers then rescue Ethel, whom Charles has kidnapped and locked in an East Side thieves' den. Charles is shot. Among the differences between the two offerings were the whistling act that won applause in Cohen's play and the "coon shouter" whose songs stopped the show in Marble's play.

While Charles Frohman seemingly had a hand in production after production, his brother Daniel remained satisfied largely to mount offerings at the Lyceum. Since *The Adventures of Lady Ursula* had been brought to town after an extensive tour, he now needed a new vehicle for E. H. Sothern and Sothern's wife, Virginia Harned. His selection of yet another costume drama for them was not particularly fortunate. Grace Livingston Furniss and Abby Sage Richardson's **A Colonial Girl** (10-31-98, Lyceum) was billed as "a play of Old New York." On the rebound from losing Judith (Eleanor Moretti) to an English officer, Godfrey Remsen (Sothern) marries Mollie Heddin (Miss Harned). The guileful Judith gets the innocent Mollie to deliver a letter proving that Godfrey is a spy for the Continental army. At first Godfrey believes Mollie to be duplicitous, but when he learns the truth he forces a silly fop to exchange clothing and a powdered wig with him, entertains the British officers at dinner, then throws off his disguise and avenges himself. He and Mollie flee. In one excellent, early scene Mollie describes her lot under a harsh stepmother by putting it in rhyme and singing her ditty as she accompanies herself on a spinet. Most critics preferred the late 18th-century costumes and settings to the writing. After three weeks the play set out on tour, where it found a warmer welcome than New York had offered it.

A less elite audience "howled approvingly" and "vociferously applauded" Walter Sanford's **Tempest Tossed** (10-31-98, Grand Opera). Richard Wentworth marries Nellie Preston, then arranges to have her kidnapped so that he can marry a richer girl. Once he has the rich girl's money he tries to kill her by blowing up a lighthouse so that the ship she is on will be wrecked. His perfidy is exposed, and he is forced to flee into lonely exile. His wives find better mates.

On the same evening Julia Arthur opened at Wallack's with a repertory that offered *A Lady of Quality, Ingomar, As You Like It, Pygmalion and Galatea,* and *Mercedes.*

As was his wont in recent years, Daly had given over his theatre during the season's early months to an imported English musical comedy. What was left of his once great ensemble returned to the fold in mid-November. Even with the loss of Drew and Lewis it was still an illustrious group. But when it reappeared on the 19th no one could foresee that this would be its final season or that Daly would die at season's end. Happily, the great producer and his band went out with a flourish, enjoying their best year in a long while. The opening attraction was *The Merchant of Venice,* cut and reordered by Daly to spotlight Ada Rehan's Portia. Cuts included anything that could be construed as lewd, such as Portia's line "I am much afeared my lady his mother play'd false with a smith." Rehan was featured prominently in the final scenes of Acts II and III and was given the closing lines of the final three acts. Dithmar, lauding the variety of her readings, concluded that "she filled every one of Portia's scenes with distinction and sympathy." Sidney Herbert, among the company's lesser lights, was Shylock. Mounted with Daly's expected largesse, the production delighted critics and playgoers alike, so ran to good business into early January.

No fewer than three critics used the term "made-to-order" to characterize Eugene Presbrey's **Worth a Million** (11-21-98, Knickerbocker). The man whose measure it was cut to was William H. Crane, he of the avuncular, hearty-pat-on-the-back brand of acting. Indeed, one reviewer noted that so many similar plays had been written especially for him in the past few years that the expression "Crane plays" had become common parlance and needed no explanation. In his latest outing Crane took the guise of Colonel Amory West, "a retired millionaire." He is entrusted with finding Phyllis Gregg (Gladys Wallis), the heiress to a stolen fortune. He finds her, sees that she receives her rightful monies, helps her marry the young artist she loves, rectifies a number of other wrongs, and lands for himself a much divorced grass widow. But though the play fit Crane, its "childish simplicity" was not attractive, so he immediately put another vehicle into rehearsal.

One of the season's biggest hits—and, with *Cyrano,* the only play of the season still revived with any regularity—was Arthur Wing Pinero's **Trelawny of the Wells** (11-22-98, Lyceum), which told of a young actress who marries into a snobbish Victorian family, finally resents their restrictive way of life, and returns to the stage. Mary Mannering gave one of her finest performances depicting "the pathos, humor and weakness of the truly good girl who could not live . . . in a conventional atmosphere." Indeed, the entire cast was so fine that Pinero told producer Daniel Frohman it was better than the original London cast. Rising young players included William Courtleigh as the swaggering Gadd, Henry Woodruff as Rose Trelawny's husband, Grant Stewart as a boisterous stage manager, and Hilda Spong, in her American debut, recreating her London role of Imogene. Period flavor was enhanced by the old-school artistry of Mrs. Thomas Whiffen, Charles Walcot, and George C. Boniface. Play, cast, and mounting came together to give the Lyceum a long run—132 performances.

A lesser English play, with its original but minor London star, came and went swiftly. Arthur Shirley and Benjamin Landeck's **A Grip of Steel** (11-28-98, Star) was set in France and told of a farmer, imprisoned unjustly, who becomes the head of a robber band after his release. Henry Bedford played the hero-villain.

The just-ended war (the Treaty of Paris was signed two weeks later) was the subject of James Schönberg's **The Red, White and Blue** (11-28-98, Grand Opera). In it the American owner of a Cuban plantation is killed by a wicked Spaniard, who then attempts to court his widow. Cubans coming to her rescue are nearly routed before a troop of American marines save the day. The play was feeble stuff, and not even advertisements promising the appearance of heroic sailors from the *Maine* and the *Oregon* could inject much vitality. Nonetheless the drama did circulate for a while among neighborhood touring houses.

The indefatigable Scott Marble was the author of **Lost in Siberia** (12-5-98, Columbus). The father of its heroine, Sophie Kuton, is framed and shot by the treacherous Governor Meckelvitch after Sophie spurns Meckelvitch's proposal of marriage. Sophie tries to kill the governor but merely wounds him. She is sentenced to be whipped. Her lover, Basil Nordeff (Richard Ganthony), rushes in to rescue her, and the pair are exiled to Siberia. More adventures await them there. With the help of some of the governor's bodyguards, who secretly are nihilists, they finally wreak revenge and escape.

Having stumbled badly with *Worth a Million*, Crane endeavored to place himself on a proper footing again with **The Head of the Family** (12-6-98, Knickerbocker), which Clyde Fitch and Leo Ditrichstein "freely adapted" from Adolf L'Arronge's *Hasemanns Töchter*. That its story centered on a father with three troubled daughters, spoiled by their mother, recalled *Our Daughters* and *The Way We Live*, both of which had been taken from another L'Arronge play and presented during the 1879–80 season. However, in this case the plot turns principally on the father's exertions to rescue one daughter's marriage after her husband unjustly believes she is seeing another man. The play proved hardly more satisfactory than Crane's earlier vehicle, so he threw in the towel after a month's struggle.

Like Scott Marble, Lincoln J. Carter relentlessly churned out touring melodramas. His latest was **Under the Dome** (12-12-98, People's), which had traveled the country for much of the preceding season. Based on fact, the story depicted the German navy's failed attempt to seize Samoa from American forces. Carter's biggest sensation scene showed both fleets suffering from a typhoon's violent pounding at Apia. Another setting allowed a wood and canvas reproduction of a North River ferry to cross the stage. When the melodrama left after a single week, the playhouse presented **Chain of Destiny** (12-19-98, People's), which turned out to be a revised version of *The Courier of Lyons*.

On that same evening a second old play was given a new life and a new name. Russ Whytal's **Vagabondia** (12-19-98, Harlem Opera House) was simply a rehash of Watts Phillips's forty-year-old *Camilla's Husband*, in which a girl flees from an unwanted, forced marriage and finds happiness with an itinerant painter.

Even Creagh Henry's **The Sorrows of Satan** (12-24-98, Broadway) was not all that original, taken as it was from Marie Corelli's novel of the same name. This semimystical, semiallegorical work planted the devil, in the guise of prince Lucio Rimanes (John E. Kellerd), in modern London, where he strives nobly but ineffectually to have people reject him so that he may return to heaven.

Another dramatization of an English novel opened two nights later. If H. V. Esmond and

Edward Rose were hoping for another *Prisoner of Zenda* with their adaptation of Anthony Hope's **Phroso** (12-26-98, Empire), they no doubt were disappointed, although their work was by no means a failure. There were marked similarities. Once more a brave Englishman finds himself in a colorful, imaginary country, falls in love with a beautiful noblewoman, and fights off adversaries. However, this time there was no bittersweet ending, for Lord Wheatley (William Faversham) wins the hand of the voluptuous Phroso (Jessie Millward).

Lincoln J. Carter's second play of the month was **Remember the Maine** (12-26-98, People's). The war's end could not douse passions. All Americans and Cubans were lily white; all Spaniards pitch black. The *Dramatic Mirror* recorded, "Not one of Mr. Carter's American Americans, from General Fitzhugh Lee to a comedy sailor, failed to devote a good portion of his remarks to references to 'Uncle Sam,' 'the land of the free,' 'the Stars and Stripes,' *et al.*, which never failed to draw a round of applause." The sleazy Spaniards included General Weyler (who slinks around in disguise), Rufina Romora (who presses the button that blows up the ship), and the man who loves her, Count Fernando Rujaero (who is arrested, to more audience cheers, when he tries to stab a sweet Cuban girl on board the *City of Washington*). The sinking of the *Maine* and Dewey's bombardment of Cavite were the evening's scenic high points.

Playgoers welcomed in the new year by applauding a fine new American play, Clyde Fitch's **Nathan Hale** (1-2-99, Knickerbocker). "One of the brightest and best of this Winter's . . . theatrical programme" and "one of the best plays ever written by an American author" typified the response of elated critics. Fitch wrapped Hale's real if quiet heroics with a fictitious, emotionally charged love story. Young Hale (Nat Goodwin), fresh from Yale, teaches in a Connecticut one-room schoolhouse, where he has fallen in love with his brightest pupil, Alice Adams (Maxine Elliott), and she with him. The Revolution has just broken out. Guy Fitzroy (William Ingersoll), a loutish young Tory who also loves Alice and has threatened to have her no matter what, commandeers the schoolhouse for a loyalist rally. Hale and his young pupils head off to enlist in the patriots' cause. In the following year Hale, who has made a name for himself as a valiant soldier, and Alice meet again at her uncle's New York home. She makes him promise he will not risk his life again. But a spy is needed to secure British plans. When Hale volunteers, Alice wails, "If you go on this mission, it is the end of our love!" At an inn Hale secures the plans, but Fitzroy bars his leaving. Having no proof that Hale is a spy, he decides to trick Alice into identifying Hale by writing her that he is dangerously wounded. Despite her disclaimer, she rushes to meet him. Luckily, Hale succeeds in warning her, and she pretends not to recognize him. Then her uncle's black servant appears and unwittingly betrays Hale. The lovers are permitted a silent, tearful farewell by a moonlit tent. As dawn breaks, Hale is led off to an orchard. Reciting his famous last words, he climbs the scaffold. By modern standards much of the writing was naively formal and declarative:

Col. Knowlton: Hale's done a hundred brave things since then! The eyes of the whole Army are upon him.
Alice: I know something very few are aware of. Not long ago the men of his company, whose term of service had expired, determined to leave the ranks, and he offered to give them his pay if they would only remain a certain time longer.

And there was the sentimentality the era loved, mixed with period humor in scenes such as that where the black servant, unobserved, watches the young lovers:

Jasper: Dat's right, kiss on, ma honeys. Smack each other straight from the heart. It does ole Jasper good to see you. Thah's a little yaller gal lying out in the graveyard, younder, dat knows ole Jasper was fond of kissing, too! Don't stop, ma honeys, don't stop!

The last few minutes of the play—the lovers' parting and Hale's being led to his death—were beautifully contrived pantomime, all but wordless except for Hale's pronouncement. One critic hailed the orchard setting as "a stage picture that has rarely been equaled." Fitch worked assiduously with the electricians and their still primitive equipment to realize his directions: "It is the moment before dawn, and slowly, at the back through the trees, is seen a purple streak, which changes to crimson as the sun creeps up. A dim gray haze next fills the stage, and through this gradually breaks the rising sun. The birds begin to wake, and suddenly there is heard the loud, deep-toned, single toll of a bell, followed by a roll of muffled drums in the distance. Slowly the orchard fills with murmuring, whispering people; men and woman coming up through the trees make a semicircle amongst them, about the gallows tree, but at a good distance." Goodwin, although still thought of primarily as a comedian, once again showed he could handle more serious material, while his wife, Maxine Elliott, furthered

her own reputation as an exceptionally lovely and not unskilled player. The drama's eight-week New York stand capped a profitable year-long tour for the play.

The next evening, the 3rd, Daly offered *Madame Sans-Gêne* with Ada Rehan in the lead. It was followed in quick succession by *The School for Scandal* and *The Taming of the Shrew* before the producer brought out his final novelty.

In Paris the great Réjane had starred not only in *Madame Sans-Gêne* but also in the next play to reach Broadway. **Zaza** (1-9-99, Garrick) was Belasco's version of Pierre Berton and Charles Simon's drama and starred the redheaded Mrs. Leslie Carter. Its heroine was a music hall singer who becomes the mistress of a rich man, Bernard DuFrène (Charles A. Stevenson). She learns he is married, visits his home, and is so touched by his little child that she renounces him. His attempts to win her back are indignantly repulsed. The censorious William Winter stood for many critics when he wrote in the *Tribune*, "It is the story of a wanton, coarsely and offensively told." But some critics, among them the *Times*'s Dithmar, who warned that Mrs. Carter's own little son should not be allowed to see the play, still granted it was moving, even electrifying. Mrs. Carter's fiery renunciation scene achieved something rare in the theatre of its day, a spontaneous standing ovation. Critics were also divided on Belasco's production. Some praised his fine eye for detail, while others noted such jarring slips as American photographs in a French home and a clock that (at least on opening night) would not work. But such quibbles could not deter playgoers, so *Zaza* ran out the season.

The sultry Olga Nethersole tried her luck with Louis N. Parker and Murray Carson's "poetic" drama **The Termagant** (1-9-99, Wallack's). She portrayed a 16th-century Spanish lady, Beatriz, who, until the final curtain, always can find some snappish reason for fending off her dashing suitor, the explorer Rodrigo (Hamilton Revelle). Theatregoers would not accept the play, so she padded out her limited engagement with revivals of *The Second Mrs. Tanqueray* and *Camille*.

A touring comedy, **Looking for Trouble** (1-9-99, Metropolis), spent a single week in Manhattan. Its central figure, O. Bliss, goes out for a night on the town while his wife is away on vacation and brings home a pretty vaudeville singer. Of course, his wife returns unexpectedly. The singer and her friends provided excuses for songs and dances.

A far longer run—sixteen weeks—was enjoyed by **Because She Loved Him So** (1-16-99, Madison

Square), which William Gillette took from Bisson and Leclercq's *Jalouse* and which gave Charles Frohman his umpteenth hit of the season. An unduly suspicious wife provided the crux of the story, but Kate Meek and J. E. Dodson won the lion's share of critical acclaim as the wife's parents, who propose to banish their daughter's concern by pretending to similar ones—only to have a falling-out of their own when the old lady proves as suspicious as her daughter.

Jealousy and a music hall singer were featured in Anita Vivanti Chartres's **That Man** (1-16-99, Herald Square). Three husbands, claiming business in Philadelphia, make too frequent trips there, thus arousing their wives' ire. They select a "country cousin," Theophilus Montjoy (Reuben Fax), to trail the men, and, sure enough, the men's business turns out to be with a pretty young singer.

Ernest Lacy and Joseph Humphreys's **The Ragged Earl** (1-16-99, Academy of Music) starred Andrew Mack as a down-at-the-heels Irishman who rescues a boy from cruel guardians and discovers the boy is actually a very lovable girl. As in any Mack show, the star worked in some Irish ballads to sing.

More products from the Scott Marble and Lincoln J. Carter factories were put on sale at combination houses the same busy evening. Marble's **Daughters of the Poor** (1-16-99, Star) told of rich John Lindsay, a kindhearted man who owns some tenements with his flint-hearted brother, Robert. One of their tenants is sweet, lovely, blind Hester Dean. John loves her, but Robert, seeing a chance to get higher rents from others, evicts her and kidnaps her, hiding her in a South Street attic. John comes to the rescue, and even Richard, disguised as John, cannot prevent a happy denouement.

Sparkling lines such as "Beware, my proud beauty!" and "Curse her coolness" excited the galleryites at Carter's **Chattanooga** (1-16-99, People's), yet another Civil War saga in which lovers' affections cross political boundaries. However, the climactic scene was novel. The principal figures find themselves hanging on for dear life to a speeding locomotive. Practiced stage carpenters took a back seat on this one, since the scene was projected on a screen, having been filmed in advance. Still, one reviewer called it "as thrilling as anything of the sort that Mr. Carter has ever devised."

Between *Chattanooga* and a second Civil War drama, one other work tested the waters at a combination house. The play was **Through the Breakers** (1-30-99, Metropolis) and its author was Owen Davis, who years later would go on to better pieces. But Davis served his apprenticeship in the

school of touring melodramas. Finding the woman he loves, Maud Radford, is married to another man, Peter Turner abducts her and the minister who performed the wedding. He immures them in a smuggler's cave. A fight on an overhanging cliff, Maud's escape through the breakers on a lifeline, and a passing ship under full sail provided the most cheered and applauded moments.

A far superior Civil War drama fared hardly any better than Carter's claptrap, although many critics were respectful and a few ecstatic. James A. Herne's **The Reverend Griffith Davenport** (1-31-99, Herald Square) was freely adapted from Helen H. Gardener's novel *An Unofficial Patriot*. Davenport (Herne) is a Methodist circuit rider whose beliefs cause him to detest slavery. His feelings are not shared by his aristocrat wife (Mrs. Herne) or his son, Beverly (Sydney Booth). He is ostracized by his neighbors. Only his second son, Roy (Bert Young), sympathizes. Davenport frees his slaves, albeit he is aware that their lot as "free niggers" will be difficult. Reluctantly he accepts a commission from Lincoln to spy on the Confederates. He is caught by his own son and sentenced to prison, but before he is sent away he is allowed one idyllic meeting with his wife. The play was often philosophic but just as often replete with tense, dramatic scenes. As Davenport manumits his slaves, a runaway dashes into the room, his vicious master hot on his heels. Davenport offers to buy the man and free him but is rebuffed. When the owner approaches to seize the black, the slave cuts his own throat and falls dead. His owner snarls, "There's $1,500 gone!" William Dean Howells called the drama "the only new thing of importance" and said it was better than *Cyrano* or *Trelawny*. The *Dramatic Mirror* praised it as "a thing of beauty." Of Herne's performance the reviewer wrote, "Quiet always, there is strength in every moment and superb reserve." But such commendation was to no avail, and the play closed after three poorly attended weeks.

William A. Brady and Florenz Ziegfeld continued their producing partnership with **Mlle. Fifi** (2-1-99, Manhattan), Leo Ditrichstein's translation of Dumanoir and Carré's farce. Echoes of *Because She Loved Him So* were heard in its story of a faked falling-out turning comically serious. In this case a spendthrift vicomte (Aubrey Boucicault) and his American bride (Grace George) are kept on such a tight financial leash by the bride's mother (Rose Coghlan) that they decide to go through the motions of a hot-tempered divorce in hopes she will become more generous. The husband's supposed attachment to yet another of the season's innumerable music hall singers, one Mlle. Fifi (Louise Beaudet), is the putative cause. The real Mlle. Fifi's unexpected arrival sets the plot spinning. Some critics thought Miss Coghlan was less the Boston brahmin she was meant to represent and more the nouveau riche Chicago matron, but virtually all the men praised Grace George's charmingly ingenuous wife. Miss Coghlan, from an older school of playing, had come almost to the end of her career as a major star; Miss George's stardom was just ahead. Although *Mlle. Fifi* was far from the season's best farce, it played for two profitable months.

A German farce, one day to provide the source for a classic operetta, also fared well. Sydney Rosenfeld made the adaptation of Blumenthal and Kadelburg's **At the White Horse Inn** (2-6-99, Wallack's). Its kaleidoscopic incidents pivoted around the plans of the attractive innkeeper (Amelia Bingham) to hook one of her guests (Joseph Holland). Her jealous headwaiter (Frederic Bond) sees to it another guest (Miriam Nesbitt) steals his boss's intended. An important role was assigned to Ditrichstein, translator of the competing *Mlle. Fifi.*

Hal Reid's **The Knobs o' Tennessee** (2-6-99, People's) was set in moonshine country. When Joe Preston (Reid), one of the moonshiners, and his brother, Henry, kill a revenue officer, Henry is captured and sentenced to death. He escapes, but just as he faces recapture his mother shoots him rather than see him hanged. Joe is imprisoned but also escapes. He goes to Washington to visit President McKinley. Reminding the president of a time he and Joe's father worked together in the Civil War, Joe persuades the president to grant him a pardon.

Daly's production of Cecil Raleigh and Henry Hamilton's **The Great Ruby** (2-9-99, Daly's) recalled for many that Daly had first made his mark with sensation-melodrama. Its story was as absurd as it was complicated. The high point, in more ways than one, was reached when two men fight over the jewel, which is stolen at the beginning of the play, as they go flying in a hot-air balloon. Ada Rehan played a titled sleepwalker on whom the thieves plant the ruby for a time. Daly had imported the original Drury Lane scenery for the production. His efforts were rewarded with the biggest hit he had known in years.

Unfortunately, Daly died in Paris on June 7, and the play was immediately closed, after its 135th performance. With its closing an era ended. Although nominally a few first-class stock companies remained, such as Daniel Frohman's at the Lyceum, none had the durability, the reputation, or the clearly identifiable signature that Daly's had possessed in its heyday. From here on plays would be cast largely from open calls, and once a play closed its players might never again work together. The ensemble feeling that the old stock companies developed would be a thing of the past, as were the clean, homey German farces on which Daly once had relied so successfully. A catch-as-catch-can attitude became the accepted one on Broadway. The mercenary masters of the Trust had won, although Broadway would probably have changed in similar directions even if they had not appeared.

A raging blizzard could not prevent Charles Frohman from chalking up one more hit with R. C. Carton's London comedy **Lord and Lady Algy** (2-14-99, Empire). William Faversham and Jessie Millward were featured as the separated young couple who are brought together again after Algernon clumsily serves as go-between in his brother's amours and Lady Algy reconciles the aggrieved participants. (On the same night, Frohman also offered a revival of *Her Atonement* at the Academy of Music.)

Mark E. Swan's **Brown's in Town** (2-20-99, Bijou), a two-week flop, described the plight of a young couple who must keep their marriage a secret from the groom's father or lose an inheritance. When the father suddenly turns up at the couple's hideaway, another, unmarried couple are introduced as the Browns, the name the married couple have adopted in their love nest. A "coon" song and several other musical turns punctuated the action.

Joseph Arthur's star had faded, although his *Blue Jeans* continued to tour prosperously. One week at a combination house was all his **On the Wabash** (2-20-99, People's) was offered in New York. His hero, Abe Early, is an orphaned "plow boy" taken under the wing of Ephraim Early. Actually, Abe owns the land that Ephraim farms, but Ephraim does not plan to tell him that until the young man matures a bit. Ephraim's second wife, Sincerity, plots with a gambler named Warman to put Ephraim in an asylum and seize Abe's lands. When young Abe is made a sheriff, Sincerity and Warman spread the word that he secretly married a schoolteacher who immediately disappeared. The reappearance of the schoolmarm gives the lie to their slander. Abe does promise to marry Ephraim's daughter, Esther. One out-of-town critic asked, "Can a popular song make a play popular?" The song he referred to was Paul Dresser's "On the Banks of the Wabash," which was performed as an overture and sung behind the scenes throughout the play. Apparently the answer was no.

All season long, adaptations of *The Three Musketeers* had popped up in various road towns and at New York's neighborhood theatres. Now "the long impending Musketeers epidemic" began at Manhattan's first-class theatres with Henry Hamilton's version, **The King's Musketeer** (2-27-99, Knickerbocker) which Daniel Frohman mounted for E. H. Sothern. Critics admired the eye-filling costumes and interiors along with a moonlit mere, but they were divided on the merits of the adaptation and the acting. The dropping of such beloved lines as "One for all and all for one" was rued, while Sothern was slapped for not being sufficiently swashbuckling by one man and for not enunciating clearly by another.

Sothern vied with Mrs. Fiske for first-nighters. Her engagement at the Fifth Avenue offered *Magda, Love Finds the Way, A Bit of Old Chelsea, Frou-Frou, Divorçons, Tess of the D'Urbervilles,* and one new, short play.

George Broadhurst's **The Last Chapter** (3-6-99, Garden) was bruited to be his first "serious" play. His hero was Richard Stanley (Edgar L. Davenport), a California mine superintendent, who is working to repay debts his father incurred after a cashier absconded with his money. Into town comes Katherine Blake (Grace Filkins), the cashier's innocent daughter. She hopes to be the village school-marm. The villagers turn against her, but Richard, falling in love, helps her by buying some seemingly worthless mine stocks she owns. A lode is discovered in the mine, and the couple can go to the altar knowing they will have no financial problems. At this stage of his career, Broadhurst was more adept at farce, so the public soon wrote *finis* to *The Last Chapter.*

James O'Neill, suffering from a cold and not up on his lines, was the season's second D'Artagnan. His vehicle was called **The Musketeers** (3-13-99, Broadway) and was the work of Sydney Grundy. Critics once again were sharply divided over the acting but united in praising the beautiful mounting. As far as playgoers were concerned, it was a tossup. Both versions ran forty performances.

There was too much hand-me-down in Grace Livingston Furniss and Abby Sage Richardson's **Americans at Home** (3-13-99, Lyceum) to satisfy either critics or theatregoers. The story reminded many of the ladies' effort earlier in the season, *A Colonial Girl,* and even the odd name of Gerald Fitzgerald had been used by a leading character in *The Ragged Earl.* The latest romance found Elliot Tremaine (E. J. Morgan) marrying Mildred Grey (Mary Mannering) after Loraine Grandin (Hilda Spong) had rejected him in favor of Gerald (William Courtleigh). A suspicion arises that Elliot and Loraine may be having a furtive affair, but that is dispelled in time for a happy ending.

High-minded critics and a less demanding public went their separate ways when it came to Charles E. Blaney and Charles A. Taylor's **The King of the Opium Ring** (3-13-99, Columbus). George Macy, the mastermind of San Francisco's opium traffic, lures Georgette (Madeleine Merli) into his den and sells her to Wah Sing. Just before the wedding can take place three decent Chinese men, forming a "human tower," help her climb down from a balcony and flee. She eventually finds her long-lost father, a sea captain. Settings, "realistic in the extreme," included a San Francisco dock with smugglers at work, the ring's underground den, and glimpses of a theatre and joss house in Chinatown. Although all Chinese characters who spoke were played by white men, "real Chinamen" were employed as supers for verisimilitude. The play ran only one week at the Columbus (a typical run at a typical combination house), but its success was such that it was brought back in May to the Academy of Music and did a month of good business.

London Life (3-20-99, Columbus) was Martyn Field and Arthur Shirley's version of Paul Audry, Max Maurey, and George Jubin's *Le Camelot.* A nephew and daughter of Sir George Ferrers (Richard Ganthony), who has disowned them, are framed for his murder by the actual killer and must spend the evening exonerating themselves. Their exertions take them to Piccadilly and Fleet Street, both of which were depicted in settings singled out for notice.

Outcasts of a Great City (3-27-99, People's), for which no author was given, had been touring the country since 1893, yet it was accorded only a belated, single week's hearing in New York. It was standard sensation-melodrama. The villain kidnaps one of the heroine's twin sons and tells her husband that she not only has been unfaithful but has drowned. She takes work as a typist (then still called a typewriter) and is rescued from the path of an oncoming train before the requisite happy ending. The train was advertised as "120 feet long and 8 feet high."

J. K. Tillotson, who had not been heard from for many years, returned with a new play on a favorite subject of his, the Civil War. **Report for Duty** (3-28-99, 14th St.) proved to be a compilation of clichés. Despite his southern heritage, Earl Gordon (A. S. Lipman) enlists in the Federal army. His defection does not keep his sweetheart, Virginia Dowling (Selma Herman), from promising to remain true.

But when he is not heard from for a long time, her father forces her to wed Claire Randolph (Stephen Wright), a Confederate officer. The wedding is no sooner over than Earl appears and is arrested by Claire. Claire finds that Earl is carrying plans for an attack, and he goes to signal Union troops false details of the plans. Virginia climbs a tower and signals the real plans. As she finishes, Claire blows the tower to bits. Luckily, Virginia is not seriously hurt and, after Claire is killed, reaffirms her love for Earl. Critics had high praise for the special effects, the blowing up of the tower, "and in the battle which follows, the bursting of shells in the treetops, and the roar of the artillery coming closer and closer, are as realistically produced as even a veteran could wish." There were fewer kind words for the drama.

The second-class stock company, which brought out a different revival each week, was best represented in 1899 Manhattan by Henry V. Donnelly's Murray Hill group. Earlier in the season they had presented one seminovelty with their rewritten version of *East Lynne*. As a curtain raiser to their mounting of *Our Boys,* they offered a more genuinely original farce—although its basic plot was scarcely new. Emmett C. King's **The Father of His Country** (3-27-99, Murray Hill) had nothing to do with George Washington. In fact, its hero, Archibald Scorcher (King) could tell a lie. The lie is meant to keep his wife from learning that he is going to a fancy dress ball without her. Since his wife will have nothing better to do for the evening, she advises him that she will go out—to the very ball he plans to attend.

Following one failure with another, Daniel Frohman's company found few takers for Jerome K. Jerome's **John Ingerfield** (3-29-99, Lyceum), in which a penny-pinching, scheming chandler marries a rich girl and is brought to understand the rewards of love and generosity. The last act, set forty years after the rest of the action, allowed the actors to paint wrinkles on their faces, don gray wigs, and luxuriate in a tear-jerking death scene.

Along with her revival of *Divorçons,* Mrs. Fiske offered her only novelty, Horace Fry's one-act **Little Italy** (3-30-99, Fifth Ave.). Giulia (Mrs. Fiske) has immigrated to America with Fabio Ronaldi (Frederic de Belleville), the vulgar, hostile husband her family forced her to marry. But she has never stopped loving Michele (Tyrone Power), and when he crosses the sea and appears at her doorstep, he has little trouble persuading her to elope. They are intercepted by Fabio, and Giulia is killed attempting to escape in a dumbwaiter. The men stand arguing over the dead body as the curtain falls. In his morning-after appraisal William Winter noted, "The essential charm of Mr. Fry's work—a charm so delicate that it might pass unnoticed—is its suggestiveness of vague, tearful, desolate emotion." Of the star's "shining" performance he wrote, "Her identity was absolutely merged in that of the passionate, sorrow-stricken, common Italian woman," and he singled out as an example "the poor creature's ecstasy at sight of her lover." Both men were also lavished with praise. But, possibly goaded by agents of the Trust, Italians, themselves not regular playgoers, protested, so Mrs. Fiske reluctantly withdrew the play after a few performances.

Another vulgar husband (Thomas Wise), whose wife (Amelia Bingham) takes a lover (Joseph Holland), was the central figure in **The Cuckoo** (4-3-99, Wallack's), which Charles Brookfield took from Henri Meilhac's *Décoré.* The farce had caused a sensation in London, so Charles Frohman optioned it and brought it into Manhattan just a month after its West End premiere. The husband is startled to learn he is to be decorated for bravery. Actually the brave man is the wife's lover, who had registered at a hotel under the husband's name and there performed not one but two outstandingly courageous acts. When the truth comes out, so does another sad truth—for hubby was cheating on his wife, too. So all ends forgivingly. Some critics professed to share London's outrage, but others just had a good time, and Frohman put one more venture down in the black-ink side of his ledgers.

Infidelity of sorts was also the crux of **The Purple Lady** (4-3-99, Bijou), derived by Sydney Rosenfeld from an unidentified German farce. A painter (Sydney Booth) who gained fame with his portrait of a model with purple hair is about to be married when the model (Maude Harrison) shows up and threatens a breach-of-promise suit. In desperation he palms her off as the wife of a wedding guest, a timid professor (Etienne Giradot). The professor's wife, when she arrives, is then forced to act as if she were a lady's maid. More complications follow before the model finds a suitable suitor and the wedding can proceed. Giradot, of *Charley's Aunt* fame, walked off with acting honors: "He was delightfully droll in a lamblike way, and delivered his lines with a naivete of manner that was excruciatingly funny." The play survived for six weeks, one week less than did *The Cuckoo.*

There were no acting honors handed out when a band of traveling players, led by Odette Tyler, R. D. MacLean, and Charles B. Hanford, arrived the same night at the Herald Square. This was especially sad to the *Times,* which rued that under the new theatrical order (led, of course, by the Trust with both its eyes on the box office) "Shakespeare's tragedies are not often seen on our stage in these days." Their repertory of *Othello, Romeo and Juliet, The Merchant of Venice,* and *Julius Caesar* was hurt by playing that, according to the *Dramatic Mirror,* "did not rise above the dead level of conventionality." Despite poor business and poorer notices, the players struggled on for three weeks.

Daniel Frohman, who, unlike his brother, had not enjoyed the best of seasons (except for *Trelawny*), suffered disappointment when he essayed that risky venture, a sequel. No matter that the original had been *The Prisoner of Zenda* and that the sequel had not been unpopular as a novel. Anthony Hope's **Rupert of Hentzau** (4-10-99, Lyceum) failed to duplicate its predecessor's success. On its tryout (and tryouts, then known as "dogging it," were becoming increasingly commonplace), Edward E. Rose, the director, worked feverishly rewriting. The story was rather straightforward. Rudolf Rassendyll (James K. Hackett) learns that an incriminating letter written to him by Queen Flavia (Jobyna Howland) has fallen into the hands of the treacherous Rupert (Arthur Hoops). Rupert hopes to ingratiate himself back into the favor of King Rudolf (also Hackett) by showing him the letter. Instead the men have a further falling-out, and Rupert slays the king. Rassendyll hunts down Rupert. He finds him in Rupert's cellar and there, in the play's most exciting and highly praised scene, duels him to the death. The duel begins with swords but temporarily turns into a wrestling match before Rupert is slain. Rassendyll's triumph is short-lived, for an assassin, mistaking him for the king, kills him. Hackett's handsome, virile Rassendyll won critical applause, but his doddering king was deemed less acceptable. One interesting bit of casting was Jobyna Howland as the queen. The statuesque redhead was a celebrated Gibson Girl who had not acted professionally before. Although she acquitted herself nobly, much of her subsequent career was spent decorating Broadway's gaudiest musicals. Such were the vigorous theatrical economics of the day that *Rupert* was hardly a total loss. It closed for the summer after a month, then returned briefly in the fall prior to an extended tour. At least one other company circulated among smaller towns.

Julia Marlowe's presence as star accounted for whatever popularity was enjoyed by Henry Guy Carleton's translation of G. Lenôtre and Gabriel Martin's **Colinette** (4-10-99, Knickerbocker). Colinette's husband has been imprisoned for his Bonapartist sympathies. The venal d'Albarede (John Blair) offers to secure his release if Colinette will sleep with him. He gives her a candle to place in her window as a signal of her submission. She blows out the candle, then faints. When she recovers she hurries to Louis XVIII (William Beach) to beg for her husband's freedom. She learns her husband is in the next room and, taking a hint from a story the king has told her, she exchanges clothes with him so that he may escape. The king, secretly amused, orders them to be painted in the exchanged costumes. The leniency so excites Colinette that she ignores protocol and kisses the king. He in turn is so delighted by this breach of etiquette that he pardons the pair. The two adjectives most often brought out to describe Miss Marlowe at this stage of her career—"charming" and "sweet"—ran like a thread through her notices. Her public did not have to be told, so *Colinette*'s seven-week Manhattan stand ended a season-long tour on a happy note.

The curtain raiser of a double bill, W. P. Kitts's **The Hen-pecked Husband** (4-10-99, Third Ave.), featured the author as a much harried husband who turns the tables on his wife. The main attraction was supposedly George Conquest and Henry Pettitt's **In the Trenches,** adapted by H. Percy Meldon. Most newspapers ignored the productions; reading between the lines of the small notices that did appear, the longer play would seem to have been a revision of the sixteen-year-old *In the Ranks*. (Pettitt himself had been dead for six years.) But a play called *In the Trenches* had toured briefly in 1887, when it was suggested that its author had borrowed much from the older play. However, that *In the Trenches* eschewed sensation scenes. Although it was set against the backdrop of the Civil War, the action took place in sumptuous drawing rooms (with troops seen through windows marching to and from battle). The hero, like the hero of *In the Ranks,* enlists after being falsely accused of a crime. But in the 1887 American work there were no battle scenes, and the main interest seemed to be a confusion of parentage, with the mother of the hero's sweetheart proving to be his mother and her daughter proving to be merely adopted. Even the villain, despite the Civil War setting, was not a wartime rival but a Frenchman. Critics at the time implied it was a society drama rather than a war play. If there was any connection among the three mountings, it is probably not even of academic interest any more. In any case, the new double bill lingered for only a week.

While his sister Rose was struggling vainly to retain her stardom, Charles Coghlan was still keeping his name above the title, even though it meant he had to write his own vehicles. He made his last New

York appearance before his mysterious death (by drowning) in his **Citizen Pierre** (4-11-99, Fifth Avenue). At its simplest, his wildly convoluted plot centered on Pierre's attempt to help Marie Antoinette, who does not appear in the play, evade the guillotine. His plans are thwarted by Madame Tison (Rose Eytinge), the rabidly revolutionary mother of Pierre's sweetheart, Heloise (Margaret Anglin). When his efforts come to naught he gives his passport to a friend and, singing the "Marseillaise," takes his friend's place at the guillotine. Coghlan's striking stage presence and clear diction won commendation, but his carefully chosen supporting cast often received more enthusiastic reviews. Rose Eytinge, another actress whose stardom was behind her, created a vivid portrait of a "coarse, vengeful and repulsive woman," while Miss Anglin, soon to be a star, was lauded for her "sensibility and dramatic aptitude." But the play was dismissed as hopelessly talky and confused. When the audience assembled at the beginning of its second week, they were informed that their money would be refunded.

Brady and Ziegfeld, in their third production of the season, slipped badly with **The Manicure** (4-24-99, Manhattan), a French farce by Sylvane and Artus, adapted by Joseph Grismer. A married man's attempt to pursue a coquettish manicurist brings problems on himself, her jealous Greek lover, and others. Typical of the play's humor was the drenching several characters received when they inadvertently pulled a shower cord.

An American Hero (5-1-99, People's), for whom no author stepped forward to claim credit, was the last new touring melodrama to play the combination house in the Bowery. Its story was old hat. A fine young man is wrongly blamed for a murder he did not commit. He goes into exile, with the actual murderer on the same ship. The ship is wrecked, and the men confront each other on a lonely island. Only then can the vindicated young man return home with his head held high. A week after the play closed, the theatre ended its policy of offering touring shows and announced that in the coming year it would join its neighbors, the Thalia (the historic old Bowery) and the Windsor, in catering to Yiddish audiences.

The charge that Shakespeare's tragedies were neglected by the young, Trust-affiliated producers because they could not make money on them was silenced for the moment when Charles Frohman spared no expense on a revival of *Romeo and Juliet* that was booked to run for only a fortnight. Even the most virulently anti-Trust reviewers conceded the production was ravishingly beautiful (though they

gave no details). Frohman's principals represented some fascinating, daring casting. Maude Adams was Juliet; Faversham, Romeo; and Hackett, Mercutio. Critics agreed that Miss Adams was no tragedian, but her youthfulness, beauty, charm, and sincerity carried the evening. (Winter was a rare, dour exception to the judgment.) Faversham, boyishly handsome, was physically an ideal choice for Romeo, but in his case the reviewers divided into two sharply disparate camps. The commentators drew together again to belittle Hackett's rough, boisterous Mercutio. Most playgoers, asking only to be entertained, seemed to feel that Shakespeare had been reasonably well served.

American dramaturgy was not well served by Lee Arthur's **We'Uns of Tennessee** (5-9-99, American). Set during the recent Spanish-American War, it focused on a group of volunteers in Chickamauga. Jack Gray (Robert Drouet) and Seth Thomas (Stephen Wright) both love Lucille Courtney (Victory Bateman). As Gray's superior, the shifty Thomas sets about making life as difficult as possible for his rival. His lies provoke a fight between Lige Monroe (Theodore Roberts) and Gray, in which Monroe is mortally wounded. The fight is held in the dark, and no one can be sure who the stabber was (although the audience knows it was Seth). Before he dies Monroe dictates a letter exonerating Gray, but the letter falls into Thomas's hands. Just then Uncle Ned (Charles K. French), Gray's faithful family retainer, a black, comes forward to claim he is the guilty one, and with true southern chivalry Gray allows him to be arrested. Critics lambasted the play as "overwrought" and Arthur's oddly delineated hero as a "cad" and "an inconceivable ass." The best performance was Roberts's "impersonation of the rough, simple-minded, strong-hearted mountaineer." But it was not enough to give the play a profitable run.

Charles Frohman combined some of his own contract players with performers from his brother's Lyceum Company to give the season its last hit, Robert Marshall's **His Excellency the Governor** (5-9-99, Lyceum). Guy Standing took on the title role of the ruler of an island where a yellow aloe blooms once every hundred years, and its wind-blown pollen induces everyone to fall in love. Troublesome visitors arrive from England, including an investigating M.P. and the season's staple character, a music hall singer. Romances blossom left and right, but not always logically, and there is even a supposed native rebellion, before everything ends the way it should. Commentators had given up counting the number of Frohman's hits. His latest succumbed only to a July heat wave.

Two flops closed the season. **Ma Cousine** (5-22-99, Wallack's) was Frank Tannehill, Jr.'s version of Meilhac's farce. It recorded how a knowing wife scuttles her husband's attempt to court a married woman by foisting a sexy music hall singer on him.

Uptown, Olga Nethersole portrayed a meddlesome woman who is quick to condemn men as profligates, only to discover her idolized husband is no better. The play was Arthur Wing Pinero's suitably titled **The Profligate** (5-22-99, Harlem Opera). Its London success counted for not a whit with Harlemites.

Thus another season ended, and with it another American theatrical era. Had Daly survived two more years the era might have closed with the century (considering 1901 the proper beginning for the 20th century), but that was not to be. Real history rarely obliges with convenient dates.

The last era had witnessed the retirement of Booth. His death at the start of this epoch was almost an afterthought. With Booth died the classical stage, the old "legitimate" that leaned so heavily, perhaps too heavily, on Shakespeare and a handful of other great plays along with some late 18th-century and Victorian imitations of them. The *Times*'s lament in April about the paucity of Shakespearean productions spotlighted how abruptly the old repertory had disappeared from our stages. Not only did poetic drama vanish, but so did Booth's school of poetic acting.

The last major vestige of Booth's theatre had been the first-class stock company. The growth of the railroads had done more than anything else to kill this sort of ensemble. Although ongoing companies were maintained by the Frohman brothers at the Lyceum and the Empire in these years, they served really as training and testing grounds for players, who were quickly raised to stardom and given their own vehicles when they proved they had the artistic wherewithal and an equally important allure. Daly's company was actually the last in the old tradition, where actors remained for decades, where a distinct style of playing was brought, as often as not, to a distinct type of play. Daly's hard luck in his final years came as much from his failure to find plays of the sort on which his company had built its name as from the defection of Drew and the death of Lewis.

To many the new theatre seemed less wholesome, less comfortably secure. It was more opportunistic, more uncertain—at least artistically—and blatantly more mercenary (although the theatre had always been all three to no small extent). Yet in a way, by so systematically organizing schedules the Trust allowed the theatre to become less uncertain, thus offering some comfortable security of its own. If this benefited theatre owners and producers more than it benefited players and playwrights, that was unfortunate. Still, by expanding the number of theatres and endeavoring to keep them lit, the Trust also helped provide work for actors and authors.

Of course, the Trust could not have succeeded so well and so rapidly if it had not presented playgoers with the sort of entertainment they wanted. The remarkable lightning rise of Charles Frohman, who by 1899 virtually dominated theatrical production, attested to this. What the public wanted and what, indeed, the best authors seemed to want to write were romantically realistic dramas and giddy farces. And this is what Frohman and his colleagues offered. However some diehards might rue the change, the public did not want the old-style, poetic drama. Yet to say that the Trust trafficked in cheap goods is unfair. Some cheap goods have always provided a mainstay for a healthy theatre and always will. (Modern Broadway's refusal to welcome them may explain in part why so many playhouses remain closed year after year.) In truth, while presenting the public with what it wanted, it also served it much that was best. True, a handful of great European plays received no real hearing in America. But the plays of this era that have proved durable were generally offered in conjunction with the Trust. Mansfield had joined them, and he offered *Cyrano;* Charles's brother Daniel, while not an active member, was never openly or strongly opposed, and he presented *Trelawny.* The Trust generally found a place for worthwhile ventures along with all the froth. In fact, the real junk, the material that has not endured and could not be revived, except to sneer at, was the mainstay of second-rate touring houses, in which the Trust took little interest.

One final point. Although Frohman and others still relied heavily on London and, to a lesser extent, Paris for plays, the theatre was becoming more and more American. The anglophilic Wallacks and the translation-prone Dalys would find few advocates in the ranks of rising producers. Frohman's alleged anglophilia stemmed from his need to find ready-made importations to keep his production factories and the Trust's theatres busy. But he was always amenable to looking at native writers and their works. Younger, aspiring producers were even more willing to gamble with American dramatists. From here on, the American theatre would be identifiably American.

ACT FOUR
1899–1906

The Growing Americanization
of the American Theatre

1899–1900

The seasons from 1899–1900 through 1913–14 witnessed an open, incessant struggle by native playwrights to take over American stages they felt rightly belonged to them. They battled relentlessly against producers who were not unsympathetic to their claims but who regularly, and perhaps understandably, sought safety in proven importations. Their battle was an unwritten drama in itself. Initially, to get a foot in the stage door, they may have seemed to compromise by crafting, more often than not, American vehicles for American stars. But this was still a common practice in many of the world's theatre capitals. The era of the star vehicle continued, albeit it was soon to come crashing down. Of course, there would be exceptions. Fitch's *The Climbers* and several of his other dramas were notable instances. Compromise also took the form of setting a seemingly inordinate number of their plays overseas, especially in England. Then, too, they could be reasonably assured of obtaining a mounting if they adapted for the stage a best-selling book, a famous short story or poem, or an established, beloved legend. But the truly "American play" was being granted a hearing only slowly—slowly, but certainly.

Just short of midway in these sixteen seasons a change occurred. It may not have been a drastic change, rather something like the lowering of a curtain during an act to denote the elapse of time. But the change did signal that American plays on American themes, plays not written for stars, were emerging front and center.

For many playgoers the new season served a dual purpose, helping to bid adieu to the old century and welcome in the new. If sticklers carped that the new century did not begin technically until 1901, that was of small concern to the multitude of pleasure-seekers. Historians might take a different view, seeing the theatrical year as a shaky bridge between two theatrical eras and arguably closing one rather than opening another. For all that, and for all the frustrations American dramatists encountered, native playwrights, working hand in hand with conscientious producers and fine performers, offered theatregoers a season filled with marvelous evenings.

A combination house, not many years earlier the prestigious Wallack's, reopened the dramatic mills. Apart from two continuing summer musicals and some vaudeville bills, most at open-air roof gardens, the playhouse had no competition. As a result, the *Dramatic Mirror* reported, "Humid and hot though the night was, the audience was so large as to tax the capacity of the theatre. Every seat was occupied and 'standers,' tightly wedged, filled the aisles and the rear of the orchestra. As for the gallery, every street gamin in New York, it seemed, was there." Neither playgoers nor critics could guess that within the coming decade those uncertain flickers that were now a part of so many vaudeville bills would put an end to most lower-class combination houses and the made-for-touring plays they offered.

But the "heat did not affect the enthusiasm of the audience" for Joseph Jarrow's **The Queen of Chinatown** (8-19-99, Star), a play that wedded traditional ten-twent'-thirt' melodrama to the new interest in Orientalia of sorts and to a bit of New York history. The titular heroine, Beezie, was based on a real figure, Bessie McGarity, and was played by Jeffreys Lewis, who once had been a promising young actress at Daly's and other first-rank theatres. Although Beezie is white, she is highly respected in "the Mongolian quarter." She loves Lieut. Harry Hildreth, U.S.N., even if he is engaged to Frances Parker. When Harry's sister, Mary, is kidnapped by Chinese highbinders, Beezie follows Harry through gambling and opium dens, a music hall, and the streets of Chinatown to help rescue her. At one point Harry is arrested on trumped-up charges; at another he engages in hand-to-hand combat. Beezie's reward is to be shot, as was the historical Bessie, by her jealous lover, Danny Driscoll. While the play was "devoid of literary merit, its action . . . not plausible or logical," yet "thrills and laughs, in about equal quantities" delighted patrons, as did the gorgeous gowns Miss Lewis wore, gowns far lovelier, according to the critic, than any the real Bessie ever owned. In keeping with another tradition of touring melodramas, variety turns larded the evening. These include a "coon shouter" and "Mlle. Elsieta, in abbreviated skirts, giving a pleasing dance in the centre of Doyers Street."

Along with interest in things Oriental came a resurgence of interest in revolutionary and Napoleonic France. A harbinger of this was the very next play to arrive at the same combination house, Howard Hall's **A Soldier of the Empire** (8-28-99, Star). Set in the Hundred Days following Napoleon's return from Elba, the play centered on Gilbert de Montville (Hall) and Louise de Vere (Rose Stahl). Gilbert, a member of Bonaparte's host, rescues Louise after soldiers scare her horse and she is almost thrown. Later Louise tends Gilbert when he is wounded in a skirmish. Louise's brother, Count Eugene, is virulently opposed to Napoleon, while the governess at the de Vere home, Hortense, has jilted Gilbert but still expects him to love her. The pair make trouble for Gilbert and Louise following the latter's wedding, but all ends happily. Hall eventually would have plays produced on Broadway, without much success, and would spend much of his career in supporting roles, but Miss Stahl became a major Broadway star for a time.

Two other plays opened the same night, one at a combination house and one at a better theatre. The touring play was **Dear Hearts of Ireland** (8-28-99, Third Ave.), a typical Irish romantic drama, which allowed the hero to raise his tenor voice in song. Myles McCarthy starred.

Brahmin critics bewailed that the American stage was dominated by slapdash farce and even more slapdash musicals. But in days before satisfactory air-conditioning such attractions were just right for hot-weather entertainments. A London hit, Mark Ambient and William Heriot's farce **A Little Ray of Sunshine** (8-28-99, Wallack's), led off the season at first-class houses. An old lord who has made a fortune in Australia returns to England to help his debt-ridden family but is mistaken for all manner of tradesmen and other unwanted souls until minutes before the final curtain. A short New York stand was followed by a longer tour.

The season's second farce was Georges Feydeau's **The Girl from Maxim's** (8-29-99, Criterion), now recognized as a classic of its kind. Its story depicted the comic plight of a henpecked husband who discovers after a night on the town that he has brought home a grisette. W. J. Ferguson was the forlorn, desperate spouse, and Josephine Hall, equally adept in musicals and farce, was the girl of the title. Charles Frohman kept his production in town for two months before hitting the road.

August's lone drama, J. K. Tillotson's **A Young Wife** (8-31-99, 14th St.), was not really new. In 1889, when it was first known as *Two Lives* and later as *Dens and Palaces,* Maude Granger had employed it

in a futile attempt to save her sinking stardom. This time around no star was billed above the title, but the rehashing ran longer than the original, chalking up fifty-four performances.

What very small acclaim **Mr. Smooth** (9-2-99, Manhattan) garnered it owed to its star, not to its author, although both were the same young man, William Collier. Collier's dry, detached humor wrung laughs from his feeble comedy about an unprincipled scamp who lies about his age, his name, and practically everything else, but whose striking imperturbability wins him the lady of his choice. The character's real name is Joe Patten. He comes from Chicago to New York, where he introduces himself to a banker, Arthur Chilleigh, as Cornelius Smooth, son of Chilleigh's late partner and a young man whom Patten knows to be gallivanting around Europe. Chilleigh accepts the impostor and even plans to marry him off to his shrewish, old-maid sister, Angelica. But Smooth falls in love with the banker's beautiful daughter, Rose (Helena Collier). When the real Smooth appears inconveniently, the impostor convinces everyone that the newcomer is a madman. And when the phony Smooth convinces Chilleigh's lackadaisical son, Frank, to role up his sleeves and show some industry, the banker consents to the charlatan's marrying Rose.

George Broadhurst fared better with **Why Smith Left Home** (9-22-99, Madison Square). Smith left home for a simple reason. He wanted to enjoy his honeymoon away from his pestering relatives, friends, and servants. Hefty, double-chinned Maclyn Arbuckle, with his heavy features and high-foreheaded, balding pate, was the romantic lead, a role he made more than acceptable by his skilled clowning. He needed his skills, for his competition was stiff. It included Annie Yeamans, once so popular as the harridan in the Harrigan and Hart series, who portrayed Smith's tyrannical cook, Lavinia, militantly proud of her position as president of the Lady Cooks' Union. She cooks a purposely horrendous meal to try to get rid of a particularly pestiferous aunt, but she is not above attempting a little blackmail of Smith. Miss Yeamans's broad, rambunctious humor won many a laugh. Reviewers admired the "up-to-dateness" of the farce, which one hailed as "funny as a new hand at the steering gear of an automobile." What more "up-to-date" allusion could you have? They also praised the absence of the "salaciousness" that soiled French farce in their eyes. Good notices and Broadhurst's growing reputation earned the play a three-month run (in two separate stands).

That very salaciousness was all too apparent to some critics in Louis Harrison and B. B. Valentine's **In Paradise** (9-4-99, Bijou), a translation of Maurice Hennequin, Paul Bilhaud, and Fabrice Carré's *Le Paradis*. The basic plot was preposterous. In order to satisfy his prospective father-in-law, a young artist must break off an imaginary relationship with a wicked woman. Since the artist knows no wicked women, he hires his buddy's foster child to impersonate one and gives her a copy of *Camille* so that she can have some idea of how to behave. In one scene all the principal men were found in the girl's bedroom, dressed in their pajamas. Playgoers, who may have recalled a more bowdlerized version, *The Proper Caper* (10-4-97), were not as finicky as some critics, so *In Paradise* ran for two months.

The incessant turnover of popular melodrama continued with the arrival of Walter Fessler's **The City of New York** (9-7-99, Star), which told three loosely interwoven stories and took place only partially in New York. The main plot detailed the rivalry of decent Tom Saunders and an unprincipled member of the Four Hundred, Gerald Leighton, for the hand of Nellie Montrose. Leighton had robbed Saunders of his fortune through trickery. The two fight at Grant's Tomb, and Saunders, believing he has killed Leighton, flees to Montana. There he becomes a railroad engineer. There, too, comes Leighton, to hold up a small station. Saunders prevents the heist from succeeding, so Leighton vows vengeance. He wrecks Tom's engine. (One critic noted, "The locomotive that came thundering across the stage was more realistic than any situation in the piece.") In the end Saunders slides down a flume that leads from a mountain to an old mill to rescue the kidnapped Nellie and kill Leighton. The other stories related the romance of a newsboy-turned-telegraph-operator who weds the soubrette (who sang and danced nicely), and the good deeds of a high-minded gambler, Jack Morgan (Fessler). Additional settings showed an elegant hotel at night and the Bowery.

Three of the season's longer-running hits arrived in quick succession. The Frohman brothers produced the first two, both comedies and both English. However, Jerome K. Jerome's **Miss Hobbs** (9-7-99, Lyceum) was said to have been written for Annie Russell and was, in fact, offered to Broadway before it was presented in the West End. Miss Russell was seen as Henrietta Hobbs, a feminist so determined to put men in their places that she breaks up marriages and romances, until a strong man comes along and shows her hers. The women were the strength of the cast. Besides Miss Russell, there was

old Mrs. Gilbert, who had remained loyal to Daly until the very end. Just as her crustiness had served as foil to the sugary lovers of Daly's farces, so her sensible spinster, Susan Abbey, was a telling counterpoint to the sharp-tongued heroine. Clara Bloodgood called attention to herself as a troubled wife. The play was judged thin, but it was unmistakably a woman's play (despite its antifeminist stance). Women swarmed to the matinees and dragged their husbands to evening performances, allowing the comedy a twenty-week run. The play was the last to be done at the Lyceum by Daniel Frohman's ensemble.

A woman also got a resounding putdown in Haddon Chambers's delightful "comedy of emotions" **The Tyranny of Tears** (9-11-99, Empire). The play recounted the plight of a popular novelist forever being cowed by his officious, meddling, saccharinely bitchy wife, a lady not above resorting to a timely crying jag as her ultimate weapon. However, in this instance the husband, not the wife, was the leading figure, and he was deliciously brought to life by John Drew, who rolled his eyes, grimaced, and meandered with practiced casualness through his speeches and business. The play prospered for sixteen weeks before embarking on its slated tour.

The next opening provided New Yorkers with one of the most memorable theatrical experiences of the epoch. A journeyman adaptation, sumptuous settings and costumes, and luminous performances combined to make **Becky Sharp** (9-12-99, Fifth Ave.), Langdon Mitchell's transcription of *Vanity Fair*, a rare, thrilling evening. Circumstances conspired to keep the production from fully realizing its possibilities. Mitchell was the son of novelist S. Weir Mitchell and would go on to write several other adaptations and one great original comedy. Wisely, in his first outing, he did not attempt to encompass the whole of Thackeray's masterpiece onstage, concentrating instead on Becky's marriage. The first act depicted the trickery the ambitious, unscrupulous Becky resorts to, initially to hide and then to reveal her elopement with Rawdon Crawley (and her unexpressible dismay when she learns that she might have wed Rawdon's rich father, Sir Pitt, newly widowed). The second act unfolded at a lavish ball, with beribboned officers and bejeweled women seen dancing through a large arch. Here Becky meets the malevolent Marquis of Steyne just as the soldiers are summoned to Waterloo. Eight years pass. Becky and Rawdon are reveling in high life. "We're socially successful!" she gloats. "The women who cut me last year would give their eyes to be where I am this.

Next week I'm to be presented to the first gentleman of Europe, his Christian and debauched majesty, George the Fat, and then who will say us nay?" But their life is paid for at a price. Although Rawdon thinks his gambling winnings are paying their debts and keeping their creditors at bay, in truth most of their coin comes from the marquis, who is now Becky's lover. Rawdon's unexpected return one evening unmasks the tryst and shatters the marriage. In the last act Becky is living in a quaint, somewhat rundown German inn, tutoring for pennies. But the appearance of her old admirer, the corpulent, fatuous Joseph Sedley, promises a modicum of hope.

The marquis was played by Tyrone Power (grandson of the earlier Irish comedian), an actor who many felt never achieved the renown he deserved. While Thackeray's marquis was short and homely, Power was tall (6'1") and handsome. His Steyne, according to William Winter, was "a carelessly-elegant person, grim in aspect, nonchalant in customary demeanor[,] . . . cynical in temperament and speech, evil in personality. . . . He uttered sarcasms in a bland yet icy manner which enhanced their venom." Of course, Rawdon was meant to be tall and handsome, and he found the perfect embodiment in Maurice Barrymore. "As *Rawdon Crawley*," the *Evening Sun* observed, "he was superb. In looks, speech and manner he might have stepped directly out of Thackeray's pages. His performance was a blending of sterling manliness and the gentlest pathos. Who that heard it will forget his reading of that letter from his little boy? . . . His *Rawdon Crawley* must rank as the finest performance of his career." Other critics assented, not realizing it would be his final appearance in a play in New York before his paresis-induced insanity removed him from the stage. Indeed, some critics implied he almost stole the show—almost but not quite. After all, his leading lady was America's greatest young actress, Mrs. Fiske. Lewis C. Strang wrote, "Never knew I insincerity to be shown with such convincing sincerity,," and he continued, "Mrs. Fiske never glossed Becky's failings—Becky's heartlessness, her selfishness, her flattering cajolery of her easy victims, her falseness to everyone and everything except herself—yet she never sacrificed Becky's charm." Strang concluded, "For the future, the Mrs. Fiske Becky Sharp and the Thackeray Becky Sharp will be inseparable."

About the play itself critics were more reserved. Few were as harsh as the lofty J. Ranklin Towse of the elitist *Evening Post,* who waved away Mitchell's work as "a theatrical monstrosity," "a rather poor joke," and "a feeble travesty." (It is hard to realize at this far remove how susceptible many newspapers were at the time to the fear of displeasing advertisers. A number of important papers were said to be in the pocket of the Theatrical Trust and to judge plays accordingly.) Yet the good notices the play did receive, and excited word-of-mouth, immediately made *Becky Sharp* the ticket of choice. Houses were packed, and the original engagement was extended twice. A previous, ironclad booking at the Fifth Avenue forced the show to take to the road after 116 performances, since the Fifth Avenue was the only adequate auditorium not controlled by the Trust, and in no way would either the Fiskes or the Trust compromise.

Before the Broadway season had opened, several major critics had traveled down to the Lower East Side to attend and report on Jacob Adler and his fellow Yiddish players when they offered Jacob Gordin's *The Jewish King Lear.* The play was not new. Its premiere had occurred seven years earlier. But regular playgoers and venturesome reviewers and commentators were taking a growing cognizance of the art of these recent immigrants. Of course, uptown the Jews had largely taken over ownership of playhouses and rapidly had become Broadway's leading producers. And Jews increasingly represented a sizable share of Broadway's audiences. Yet plays about Jews were still rare. That prejudice began to crumble noticeably in the new season. One instance of change was a Dutch play, Hermann Heijermans's **The Ghetto** (9-15-99, Broadway), which had been translated by Chester Bailey Fernald. In a way *The Ghetto* was as backward-looking as it was advanced, for while it examined Jews and Jewish life in uncommon detail it was not very sympathetic. In fact the *Times* saw the thrust of the play as embodying "the spirit of revolt in the Jewish nature against the meanness and sordidness with which the race had been afflicted." Its story smacked of *The Merchant of Venice* or *Leah, the Forsaken,* but with the religion of the principals reversed. In this case the son of an old, blind Jewish businessman falls in love with a Christian girl and must battle the fervent opposition of his father and his co-religionists. Reports condemned the play as more declamatory than dramatic. All the Jews were played by Christians—there were still few Jewish actors on the Broadway stage—but the critics suggested they imbued their parts with more warmth and tolerance than did the playwright.

Henry Miller is said to have felt in afteryears that the role of Sydney Carton secured beyond doubt his hold on stardom, and the part was bruited to have been his favorite. **The Only Way** (9-16-99, Herald

Square), Freeman Wills's adaptation of Dickens's *A Tale of Two Cities,* had been a London hit with Martin Harvey in the lead. Harvey had expected to use it for his American debut as star (he had been seen before as a member of Irving's troupe), but Charles Frohman reputedly told Harvey that if he did not release the rights to him he would have another adaptation made for Miller. Harvey capitulated. Miller's performance was a tour de force, his determination, restlessness, and resignation all swathed in the silken elegance that was becoming his trademark. He elicited tears and applause standing at the guillotine and exclaiming, "It is a far, far better thing I do . . ." Margaret Anglin brought all her "rare sensibility" to the part of the pathetic Mimi (a character not in the novel). So successful was the mounting that after its originally planned one-month booking it was moved to another theatre for six more weeks. Miller revived it several times in later seasons.

A major oddity followed. Even before its opening, controversy enveloped **The Gadfly** (9-18-99, Wallack's), purportedly adapted from Mrs. E. L. Voynich's novel by Edward E. Rose. Word from the tryout had said the leading lady wanted to quit, unhappy with Mrs. Voynich's lines, and this led to the question of who actually made the dramatization. Some commentators implied the controversy was designed for publicity. Oddest of all was that this serious drama, with an admittedly off-putting theme, starred a fine comedian. Stuart Robson abandoned his deadpan and squeak to portray the deeply religious Arthur Burton. Learning his real father is a cardinal, he turns violently against the church. He becomes a notorious cynic. He also takes upon himself the blame for his sweetheart's belonging to a secret revolutionary society. He is arrested and condemned to death. In prison the cardinal visits him, and Arthur demands his father choose between the church and his own flesh and blood. All the cardinal can do is pray for divine forbearance. Arthur is left alone and desolate. More than one critic used the adjective "crude" to describe the dramatization, and most agreed that Robson was more convincing as the cynic than as the devout young man. Hopes clearly were small for the production. When it opened, playgoers already knew that Wallack's was booked to house another play two weeks later, one starring Robson's erstwhile partner, W. H. Crane.

There was more than one stranger in Sidney Wilmer and Walter Vincent's **A Stranger in a Strange Land** (9-25-99, Manhattan). A scapegrace young Englishman, John Thorndyke (Cyril Scott),

is sent to America in hopes he will reform. He is supposed to go to the Wild West, where fresh air and hard work will do the trick. Instead he settles for Buffalo and writes home about his imaginary adventures with cowboys and Indians. His kindly Uncle Charles (M. A. Kennedy) suggests he bring a redskin back with him. The letter is lost in the mail, so on his return Thorndyke enlists his friend, Arthur Lowe, to pose as an Indian who supposedly saved his life. At the same time a self-proclaimed medicine man, Dr. Boiler, arrives in the village with a real Indian, Ta-Mo-Nee, and Thorndyke's family mistakes the genuine for the fake. Before long a third Indian appears on the scene. He eventually turns out to be a Scotland Yard detective, seeking the missing Lowe. The American figures were played as caricatures of dime-novel denizens, but it was Kennedy's bubbly, infectious humor as the uncle that won the most laughs. Wilmer and Vincent were vaudevillians, and some critics saw their comedy as a bloated two-a-day sketch. Yet it managed a passable run.

On the other hand, Leonard Merrick and George R. Sims's **My Innocent Boy** (10-2-99, Garrick) was a two-week failure, although it had appealed to West End playgoers. Otis Harlan was elevated to stardom to portray a man named Valentine, whose seafaring father refuses to believe he has grown up. Actually, Valentine has been married secretly, become a father, been widowed, and now is about to enter into a second secret marriage. Farcical complications were inevitable.

Two distinguished writers, Bronson Howard and Brander Matthews, tripped over themselves when they wrote **Peter Stuyvesant** (10-2-99, Wallack's) as a vehicle for William H. Crane. Their story, set against a background of English attempts to capture New Amsterdam, had the cantankerous but basically warmhearted Dutchman interfering in two love affairs. One involves Stuyvesant's niece and a titled Englishman. The Englishman is revealed as a spy and is condemned to death, but his manly courage melts the old Dutchman's heart. The sentence is withdrawn and the lovers allowed to wed. Edward A. Dithmar of the *Times* insisted that Crane was still performing in his Anthony Absolute style, a style plainly palling on audiences. Despite good reviews, the comedy ran only a month. On opening night Howard addressed playgoers, saying, rather startlingly, that the time had arrived for American playwrights to look to American history for subject matter. Native dramatists had been doing just that throughout the century. But this was the last opening-night speech Howard would give. Although he was to live for nine more years, this was his last play to be produced. For nearly three decades he had provided his theatre with some of its finest plays, tautly written dramas and comedies. Now a new generation of dramatists was waiting in the wings, and within a few years his works would come to seem little more than interesting period pieces to that generation.

A further echo of the past was heard the following Monday, the 7th, when two young, up-and-coming producers from Ohio, Lincoln A. Wagenhals and Collin Kemper, presented a troupe headed by Louis James, Kathryn Kidder, and Charles B. Hanford in a repertory of the old "legitimate": *The Winter's Tale, Macbeth, The School for Scandal,* and *The Rivals.* The performances at the Grand Opera were adequate, but attendance, except for *Macbeth,* was sluggish. After a single week the company resumed its peregrinations.

One interesting hit was **The Dairy Farm** (10-16-99, 14th St.) by Eleanor Merron (Mrs. Archie Cowper). It blended the "humanity and purity" of *The Old Homestead* school of rural drama with traditional melodrama and added a touch of rarely used history to boot. The scene is upstate New York in the mid-1850s. The beloved if stubborn Squire Hurley disowns his nephew, Nathan Newkirk, after Nathan weds Lucy, niece to Hurley's blackguard enemy, Simon Krum. When Simon is murdered and suspicion falls on Nathan, Hurley is torn but adamant. Then the truth comes out. Hurley and his nephew—and most of the town—have been ardent abolitionists. Indeed, the village is a stop on the underground railroad. But Krum, a secret Confederate sympathizer, pretending to help the runaways, actually has returned them to their owners. Krum has grown wealthy on his treachery, while Hurley is almost bankrupt from expending money on the blacks. The killer is shown to be a vengeful ex-slave. Hurley and his nephew are reconciled, and Nathan, who has become rich working in Albany, assists in restoring his uncle's fortune. Believable acting and realistic sets, with the inevitable livestock onstage, gave additional richness to the play. It ran ten weeks and had a long, profitable tour.

Just as *The Ghetto* was winding down its stand, **Children of the Ghetto** (10-16-99, Herald Square) arrived. This was not a sequel but rather was a dramatization of his own novel by Israel Zangwill, then a well-known English-Jewish writer. Two more fast-rising producers, Theodore Liebler and George Tyler, operating as Liebler and Company, brought in the highly heralded work. Like most adaptors, Zangwill was forced to jettison much of his novel,

and like Mitchell in the case of *Becky Sharp,* he opted to focus on a story of doomed love. In a moment of levity Hannah Jacobs (Blanche Bates) allows Sam Levine to place a ring on her finger and recite the wedding vows. She then discovers that under Jewish law she is legally wed. But since she is betrothed to David Brandon (Frank Worthing), a divorce is obtained. However, since David is a "Cohen," a member of an aristocratic Jewish priesthood, Hannah's father, the Reb Shemuel (Wilton Lackaye), refuses to allow the marriage. A "Cohen" cannot marry a divorced woman. Torn between her father's edict and David's ardent pleadings, Hannah reluctantly bars the door to her suitor. The play was convincingly acted and superbly staged. The slum scenes, filled with ragged crowds, were highly praised. But the play's success was limited. *The Ghetto* ran forty-three performances; *Children of the Ghetto,* forty-nine. However, the latter did enjoy a moderately profitable tour of major cities, where sizable Jewish communities provided a large portion of the audience.

If Christian actors could portray Jews, two Jewish players were to be seen across Herald Square playing non-Jews. Clara Lipman and Louis Mann were husband and wife offstage. Their vehicle was a German farce, **The Girl in the Barracks** (10-16-99, Garrick). Miss Lipman was cast as a French café singer who disguises herself as a man in order to win a bet that she can spend a whole day in an army barracks without being found out. Mann played the part of the father of the soldier whose identity she assumes.

Bronson Howard's reaction to the next opening has not been recorded, but it certainly responded to his hope that American playwrights would have recourse to American history, or in this case American history and legend. Of course, the Civil War long had provided a rich lode for our dramatists, even if, as in this new work, the war was romanticized. The new play also fell back on that hackneyed motif of so many Civil War plays—lovers from opposing sides. But with Clyde Fitch's **Barbara Frietchie** (10-23-99, Criterion) this particular genre of Civil War romance reached its apotheosis. Fitch played fast and loose with the story most Americans knew well, making Barbara a beautiful young girl and adding a tragic ending.

The curtain rose to disclose three homes, two brick and one of wood, side by side in the evening light in Frederick, Maryland. One house belongs to the Frietchies, and from inside it Barbara (Julia Marlowe) can be heard accompanying herself on the piano. Two young neighborhood girls are sitting on the Frietchie porch, and their conversation reveals that "the whole town is angry about Barbara." The townsfolk are chagrined because Barbara is openly in love with Captain Trumbull (J. H. Gilmour), one of the Union officers occupying the town. Everyone had hoped she would marry her next-door neighbor, Jack Negly (Arnold Daly). But Barbara, not without a certain irony, rejects him, calling him a "coward" to his face for refusing to enlist. Barbara's brother, Arthur, wounded fighting for the Confederacy, is hurried into the house under cover of darkness, just as Trumbull saunters down the street. He pretends not to notice. However, Union soldiers appear, on a house-to-house search for spies and rebel soldiers. Mammy Lu, a servant of the neighboring Royces, who own the third house, tries to shoo them away. (Mammy Lu was played by a white actress in blackface, and Fitch's characterization of her typifies the ongoing attempt to portray southern blacks of the era as happy with their lot.) She scolds, "Is you froo? Bress the Lawd! Is you done giv' up fin'in' any pore Southern sojers hyah? Ain't you gwine to look inside the roses agrowing on de bushes, you devils? And don't yer forget to look under the stah carpet."

Before the soldiers can enter the Frietchie home, Trumbull assures them no one is there, and they move on. In the love scene that follows, Barbara refuses to glance at the star Trumbull points to, saying it is only a trick to steal a kiss from her. Seconds later Barbara reverses the ploy and kisses Trumbull. Their idyll is interrupted when Trumbull is ordered to attack Hagerstown in the morning. Barbara agrees to go to Hagerstown and marry him there before the battle. At the minister's the wedding has to be put off when Trumbull is called to the front. As he leaves, a turncoat Yankee attempts to shoot him, but Barbara shoots the turncoat in the arm to prevent his firing. Back home, Barbara is confronted by her father (George Woodward), who tugs at her heartstrings to have her change her mind: "The night before she died, [your mother] called you mine, and said: 'Find her a husband, Southern, like her father; don't let her go away into the cold North! Keep her near you—to take—my place—.' " Trumbull is brought into the house, shot in the chest by Arthur, who did not know at whom he was aiming. Negly storms in and would rush upstairs to finish off his rival. When Barbara bars his way he wails, "Oh, Barbara! Barbara! You have broken my heart!" She replies, "Forgive me—by not breaking mine."

But Trumbull is beyond help and dies. Before they were supposed to be married, Barbara had given Trumbull the Frietchies' old American flag.

Trumbull had carried it under his coat. Now Barbara takes the bloodstained flag and appears on her balcony with it. The townsfolk greet her with catcalls. The soldiers order her to take it down. "Shoot, and I'll *thank* you!" she answers. "But *spare* your flag." Stonewall Jackson enters on horseback and, seeing the soldiers about to shoot, commands, "Halt! Who touches a hair of that woman, dies like a dog!" One newly recruited soldier, Jack Negly, refuses to listen. He shoots Barbara, who falls dead. Jack's father, Colonel Negly (W. J. LeMoyne), looks on in horror. The other soldiers seize Jack and ask the colonel what is to be done with him. After a moment's hesitation, he responds, "Carry out your orders!"

The *Times*'s Dithmar was one of the drama's enthusiastic boosters. He called it "a noteworthy and memorable play," which told, "simply and tenderly, yet with much dramatic ingenuity, a love story with a tragic ending, which does not depress the spectator's mind, but leaves him elated by its exhibition of heroism and devotion." In his Sunday followup he termed it "a work of art." William Winter of the *Tribune* was less elated, seeing the play as too simple and its ending forced. But he added that Julia Marlowe's performance, "by turns arch, capricious, tender, passionate and almost tragically strong," raised the evening to high drama. The *Dramatic Mirror,* which praised the play and the acting, expressed one amused reservation about the staging and blamed it on the star's vanity. "According to her usual custom, the limelight pursued her with unrelenting fidelity. In the moonlit scene of Act I, when she came out, the house door remained open and a great light was shed upon her, not, however, from within but from up over the first entrance on the prompt side, and one wondered whence such stunning illumination should come in a country town on a Summer night." The play ran eighty-three performances, toured and was revived for many years, and eventually was turned into the successful 1927 operetta *My Maryland.*

Miss Marlowe's biographer has provided one fascinating footnote. Apparently both Fitch and his star were anxious to retain Whittier's famous line, "Shoot, if you must, this old gray head." To that end they proposed to have Barbara's hair turn white from the trauma of Trumbull's death and her other troubles. Only practical considerations ruled out the quick change.

A more historical and ultimately unhappy romance was the subject of Émile Bergerat's **More Than Queen** (10-24-99, Broadway), which was translated by Frederic Nirdlinger and Charles Henry

Meltzer. Beginning with the love-at-first-sight meeting of Josephine (Julia Arthur) and Napoleon (William Humphrey), when Josephine tells the soldier that a Martinique sorceress once predicted she would be "more than a queen," it recounted with reasonable fidelity Josephine's rise and final lonely years. In Paris the play had been a tour de force for Jane Hading and Coquelin, but despite Miss Arthur's lovely Empire gowns, neither she nor her associates could make it seem other than a tensionless string of incidents.

Many critics who had begun to complain of the rash of farces and musicals, which they saw as demeaning the theatre, were no more happy with the growing fashion for romantic swashbucklers, which *The Prisoner of Zenda* and similar pieces had ignited. *Zenda*'s original star, E. H. Sothern, tried his hand at another when he appeared in Leo Ditrichstein's **The Song of the Sword** (10-24-99, Daly's). The play's setting also might have been deemed voguish since—along with *The Only Way*, its own first-night competition, *More Than Queen*, and even, indirectly, with *Becky Sharp*—it mirrored the turmoil of revolutionary France and the Napoleonic reaction. Its hero was Captain Egalite, the erstwhile Marquis de la Tour, now fighting the Austrians as a Republican officer. He encounters some rough soldiers attempting to molest a beautiful girl (Virginia Harned), rescues her, learns she is a former countesss, lords it over her, falls in love, and then finds he has a rival in the treacherous Napoleon, who arranges to have Egalite hurried before a trumped-up court martial in a lantern-lit tent. Some battle scenes, allowing for dashing swordplay, follow. Naturally, all ends happily. In the final act, after Egalite has won his Francesca, Napoleon is caught fleeing in some of the Marquis's discarded clothing. And when asked who he is, he identifies himself as de la Tour. By theatrical coincidence Egalite himself must confirm the identity. After a dramatic pause, he does. Napoleon snarls, "Now you and I are quits," and stalks out. One critic noted the large number of "youngsters" in the opening-night audience and suggested the fashion for swashbucklers was designed to lure them to the theatre. True or not, the play was only a moderate success, as was its tour.

However, France of a century ago continued to intrigue playwrights and playgoers. When Henry Irving and Ellen Terry opened their American tour, the premiere attraction on October 30 at the Knickerbocker was Sardou's **Robespierre**. By now judgments about both players had ossified. If Irving was condemned, it was for his curious diction, his strange gait and bearing, and his need to occupy the limelight. Even his detractors granted that all his faults could not override his unique, compelling charisma. Miss Terry, beautiful, regal, affectionate, and shallow, was as beguiling as ever, although once again Irving saw to it she played a distinct second fiddle on opening night. As always, the mountings were magnificent. Miss Terry had a better chance to show her stuff in *The Merchant of Venice* and in a matinee double bill that included *Nance Oldfield* and Alfred C. Calmour's **The Amber Heart** (11-4-99). In the latter Miss Terry portrayed a maiden given an amber amulet to prevent her suffering the pangs of love. Her curiosity prompts her to throw the charm into a lake, but it is retrieved in time to forestall her dying of a broken heart. The evening of Miss Terry's double bill Irving brought out one of his own, coupling *The Bells* with Arthur Conan Doyle's *(A Story of) Waterloo*, in which a senescent veteran recalls the great events of his early years. The pair returned briefly in March with the same plays, but while speculators cleaned up on the fall engagement, the spring return inexplicably proved a financial disaster for everyone.

To replace the disappointing *Peter Stuyvesant*, Crane brought out **A Rich Man's Son** (10-31-99, Wallack's), which Michael Morton took from H. Karlweiss's *Das Grosse Hemd*. This time Crane played another Peter, Peter Dibdin, a wealthy but unlettered man (he pronounces "Wagner" with a *W* and thinks his operas are done at Bay Ridge). Dibdin sends his son, Arthur (William Courtleigh), to Europe to be educated. When the boy returns he is haughty, ungrateful, and spouting socialistic tenets, so his father brings him down to earth by feigning bankruptcy. The play was hardly more satisfactory than Crane's previous vehicle, and the star found himself looking around for another one.

There was little question that Arthur Conan Doyle, as dramatist, owed the success of *Waterloo* to Irving's acting. Doyle was listed as co-author of the next play to arrive, but it was generally acknowledged that the work had been written mainly by his collaborator. That collaborator was William Gillette, who was also the play's star, and their effort was the season's runaway hit, **Sherlock Holmes** (11-6-99, Garrick). The vile, unprincipled Larrabees (Ralph Delmore and Judith Berolde) are holding Alice Faulkner (Katherine Florence) captive. Alice has hidden letters and photographs that bear on a breach-of-promise suit and can bring a small fortune, since they implicate a European prince. But Holmes has been put on the case. He comes to the Larrabees' home and, with the help of some servants he has planted in the house, starts a smoky fire. In her alarm Alice betrays the packet's whereabouts. Holmes returns it to her and warns the Larrabees not to take it. However, the Larrabees enlist Professor Moriarty (George Wessels) on their side. Moriarty long has been determined to do away with Holmes and sees his chance. With the coolness of an archcriminal, and keeping 19th-century proprieties in mind, he wangles his way into Holmes's apartment to suggest the detective desist. Holmes demurs, so Moriarty lures him to an old gas works. Just as he is about to be seized by Moriarty's men, Holmes hurls a chair at the single lamp lighting the room, throwing the room into darkness. Only the glow of Holmes's cigar can be seen. The men rush toward it. Just then the safety light reilluminates the room, and the men discover that Holmes has left his cigar on a window sill and is making his escape on the other side of the room. At the consulting office of Dr. Watson (Bruce McRae), the victim of a cab accident is brought in. He is really Holmes, disguised to evade the men Moriarty has had surround Watson's house. He has with him a set of fake letters and photographs, which Moriarty has sold him. These he offers to the men who have employed him. However, they instantly recognize them as frauds. Alice, who has been in the next room, enters and gives the men the real ones. She understands that if Holmes had taken them at the time of his ruse they could have been considered stolen documents. She confesses she has fallen in love with Holmes, and he in turn embraces her—which, given Holmes, may mean something or nothing at all.

Gillette played Holmes to the hilt. His tall, slim figure, his clean-cut features, his hauteur, his clipped speech, and "his manner of suggesting that underneath that quiet, casual mask there were tremendous things afoot" made him a natural for the part. When the play allowed, he donned the cape, the deerstalker cap, and all the other accoutrements Doyle's readers expected to see. Nor was Holmes's uncannily quick, observant mind ignored. On Watson's entrance Holmes remarks that the good doctor has been getting wet and has a careless servant. How does he know? "Too simple to talk about," he answers. "Scratches and clumsy cuts, my dear fellow—on the inner side of your shoe there—just where the firelight strikes it. Scratches! Cuts! Somebody scraped away crusted mud—and did it badly—badly! Scraped the shoe along with it. There's your wet feet and your careless servant all on one shoe!" To Watson's exclamation of amazement, he retorts, "Elementary, my dear fellow! Elementary!" Moriarty's headquarters in an underground vault, with its

electrical gadgets and telephones, must have seemed almost like science fiction to 1899 audiences. Moriarty's authority and precision were quickly established: "Bassick—notify the Lascar that I may require the Gas Chamber at Stepney tomorrow night—and have Craigin there at a quarter before twelve with his crew. Mr. Larrabee, I shall want you to write a letter to Mr. Sherlock Holmes, which I shall dictate—and tomorrow night I may require a little assistance from you both. Meet me here at eleven." Surprisingly, there were no loud complaints about the scene in which Holmes injects himself with cocaine and admits he regularly uses both it and morphine. Charles Frohman's production ran out the season, compiling 256 performances. Gillette returned to the play regularly for the rest of his career, including his farewell tour in 1931.

Make Way for the Ladies (11-13-99, Madison Square), the latest play to have fun at the expense of women's rights, was taken from Maurice Hennequin and Albin Valabrègue's *Place aux femmes* by an uncredited adaptor. A militant mother raises her daughters to wear trousers and snub romantic men. Two of her three daughters follow her teachings, but the third makes such a happy marriage that the other two soon succumb. So does mama, albeit only after her own misbehavior in court (where she has brought suit against her husband) brings her more humiliation. Although such fine comedians as E. M. Holland, Fritz Williams, and May Robson were in the cast, the center of attention was Eric Hope, who in real life was the Earl of Yarmouth. But even the publicity surrounding him could not give this Charles Frohman mounting a long run.

The Carnegie Lyceum was not a regular legitimate theatre. A small house, seating 650, it was given over to lectures, concerts, and amateur productions as well as occasional professional dramatic fare. It was run by Franklin H. Sargent, who had founded what became the American Academy of Dramatic Arts. For the 1899–1900 season an ambitious, high-minded actor, John Blair, offered a series there of subscription performances of avante-garde European theatre. The initial presentation, on November 15, was José Echegaray's eighteen-year-old **El Gran Galeoto**, done in English although the Spanish title was retained. Echegaray was never to become popular in this country, despite his winning the Nobel Prize in 1904. His story was not new. Slander leads a husband to suspect his wife is having an affair with his nephew, and the suspicion leads in turn to the husband's death and the innocent wife and nephew's exile. Ostensibly the play was an example of new drama, freed from old and tired conversations. Echegaray professed to be showing how a society and its unreasoning mores govern lives. Only a few principals appear onstage, while the forces that really are supposed to propel the drama remain unseen. American critics were not impressed.

Five nights later, on the 20th, Richard Mansfield began an engagement at the Garden with a repertory of past favorites: *Arms and the Man, Beau Brummell, Cyrano de Bergerac, The Devil's Disciple, Dr. Jekyll and Mr. Hyde, The First Violin, A Parisian Romance,* and *Prince Karl.* In short, the star was presenting a virtual recapitulation of his career. The engagement marked the last time his wife, Beatrice Cameron, performed, and also his own final appearances as Bluntschli and Karl.

When Irving and Terry moved out to tour, the stage they had occupied was given over to two other notable English players, Mr. and Mrs. Kendal. The Kendals' vehicle was Ernest Hendrie and Metcalfe Wood's **The Elder Miss Blossom** (11-20-99, Knickerbocker), in which a middle-aged spinster mistakenly believes that a letter, sent by a noted anthropologist-explorer and containing a proposal of marriage, is meant for her. This was the only play they offered New Yorkers, but on tour they also presented Sydney Grundy's **The Greatest of These** (2-12-00, Power's, Chicago), which told how an uncharitable husband learns that his wife, who once had strayed in the early years of their marriage, has not been unfaithful a second time but merely has tried to protect their son's forgery from being exposed.

Henry Arthur Jones's light comedy **The Manoeuvres of Jane** (11-27-99, Daly's) gave Daniel Frohman's players a handsome measure of success, a success doubly welcomed since the production marked Frohman's moving his contract players from the Lyceum to Daly's. Jones's story centered on rich, self-assured Jane Nangle (Mary Mannering), who defies her parents and marries a poor but worthy young man (William Courtenay). The light-headed lord (Ferdinand Gottschalk) her family wanted her to wed is snared by a designing poor girl (Elizabeth Tyree). Although Gottschalk's almost slapstick caricature of a veddy British nobleman regaled audiences, Miss Mannering's subtle, sophisticated acting was more pleasing to the critics.

A petite actress named Rose Melville had scored a huge success in a touring play called *Zeb,* in which she had played an Indiana hayseed, Sis Hopkins. The play was not long-lived, but the actress quickly adapted her character into a vaudeville sketch. The character proved so popular that she performed little else until she retired in the 1920s. Inevitably, a play was built around the freckled "jay girl."

Although her awkward country bumpkin was fundamentally comic, the *World* saw **Sis Hopkins** (11-28-99, Metropolis) as a "melodrama on the good old lines." And it was. In between laughs, Sis outmaneuvers the bounder who would steal her family's farm and then marries a local boy who becomes a great lawyer and walks arm in arm with her into society. For the next decade, when she was not a headliner on some vaudeville stage, Miss Melville returned regularly to the play.

No play of the season was more successful than **Ben Hur** (11-29-99, Broadway). It offered a thrilling tale and what, for the time, was mind-boggling spectacle. Those masters of 19th-century spectacle the Kiralfy brothers had offered General Lew Wallace a small fortune for the stage rights to his novel and had been rejected. Wallace also had turned down two great actors, Lawrence Barrett and Tommaso Salvini, who had seen theatrical possibilities in the book. Just why he eventually relented and allowed Klaw and Erlanger to produce it is moot. But he did, and the producers selected the once promising William Young to make the dramatization. (Since Young had worked closely with Barrett, the probability remains that his redaction already was stashed away in his drawer.) A prologue relating the tale of the three wise men (each holding the reins of a real camel) gave way to the main story. Judah Ben Hur (Edward Morgan), a warmhearted Roman Jew who has been betrayed by his supposed friend Messala (William S. Hart), serves as a galley slave to Arrius. Arrius frees him when he recognizes his selfless heroism in a sea battle. Judah goes to Antioch, where his father's old servant, Simonides, has carefully husbanded the Hur fortune. At first Simonides contemplates deceiving the young man, but his daughter, Esther, dissuades him. Advised that Messala has entered a chariot race, Hur enters his name, too. By carefully placing bets, Ben Hur and Simonides goad Messala into staking his own fortune on the race. Messala tries to panic the hero's horses, but Ben Hur interlocks his wheels with Messala's. Messala is thrown and crippled. Ben Hur wins the race. Messala is later killed, and when Judah learns that the man who once gave him water when he was thirsty and who has cured his mother and sister of leprosy is the Nazarene, he becomes a Christian.

Among the spectacular scenes was one showing Ben Hur and Arrius on a raft, "with all the stage, excepting a few feet of space beneath the flies, where the horizon is pictured, given up to a waste of tumbling canvas water." Of course, the climax was the chariot race, horses and chariots laboring on treadmills and a shaky, "quickly rolling panorama" reinforcing the sense of movement. One critic regretted that the braces used to restrain the horses and chariots "were painfully obvious." In fact, several commentators suggested the chariot race in the failed *Year One* had been better staged. Among other well-painted settings were the first-act panorama of Jerusalem, the interior of the galley, the grove at Antioch, and moonlit views of the sea and a lake. Apart from Mary Shaw, whose portrayal of the loyal old nurse was singled out for praise, most of the players were deemed little more than competent.

Critics accepted that the play would find an enthusiastic public, but they nonetheless expressed reservations both about the play as drama and about the nature of theatrical spectacle. Dithmar, commenting on the latter, observed, "So far from being dramatic, such stage pictures are essentially the reverse. They destroy the very illusion they are intended to create in the minds of the sincere dramatic student." Even at this early date the possibilities of still primitive motion pictures must have begun to condition reviewers' and some playgoers' responses. Writing nearly a decade later, Walter Prichard Eaton wondered aloud how such "a thing of bombastic rhetoric, inflated scenery, pasteboard piety, and mechanical excitement" could be "so enormously patronized." But patronized it was. The original production ran 194 performances, closed for the summer, and reopened in September to add an additional 40 showings to its records. Road companies abounded, and so did major Broadway revivals until 1916, when films finally pushed this sort of mounting from the stage. *Sherlock Holmes* ran longer and endured longer, to no small extent because of Gillette. But a 1974 revival, both in London and New York, showed the drama was sturdy enough to survive without Gillette or any star (albeit John Wood was certainly a rising player). No first-class stars ever appeared in *Ben Hur,* even if some performers subsequently went on to theatrical and cinematic fame. While no figures survive, *Ben Hur* was unquestionably seen by more playgoers than *Sherlock Holmes,* but they were an order of patrons who went primarily for visual and emotional thrills, and there is small if any place for them in modern theatre. *Ben Hur* almost certainly could not be revived onstage. However, it has been filmed successfully several times.

For years some of New York's Catholic clergy and many more of its Protestant religious leaders had railed heatedly against the theatre. Now a leading Jewish figure joined the noisy chorus. He was Rabbi Joseph Silverman of the prestigious Temple Eman-

uel, and his timing was awkward, coming as it did immediately after a play appeared showing a good Jew convert to Christianity. But Silverman was ecumenical, including *The Christian* and *The Children of the Ghetto* alongside *Ben Hur*. He presented numerous arguments, none new, but his tirade boiled down to a single sentence: "The presentation of religion on the stage tends to bring religion into contempt."

Howard Hall's second melodrama of the season, **Kidnapped in New York** (12-4-99, Star), was a fictionalized retelling of a story that had been headlined by the city's yellow journals a few months earlier, the abduction of Marion Clark. In Hall's version the mastermind is "the King of the Kidnappers," Mazzeotti. This robber-turned-abductor convinces the Clarks that their nurse is not to be trusted. She is fired and replaced by Mazzeotti's cohort, Birdie Bolen. After Baby Clark (Baby Bessie Burt) is stolen, Mr. Dooley, a yachtsman-newspaperman-detective, tracks her down, rescues her, and sees that the culprits are imprisoned. He also helps release Henry Brandon, who has been framed for some of Mazzeotti's dirty work, and marries Brandon's daughter. One of the few critics who reviewed the play suggested that hewing to the true story would have made a better play, but, like his colleagues, he accepted without comment the insertion of numerous vaudeville turns throughout the play.

R. C. Carton's **Wheels Within Wheels** (12-11-99, Madison Square) presented a variation of a story told in other society dramas, notably *Lady Windermere's Fan*. An older woman risks ostracism in order to prevent trouble for a rash, younger relative. Hilda Spong and Grace Elliston were the female leads; John B. Mason, Robert Hilliard, and Grant Stewart did honors for the men.

Another English play was not so well received, Frank Harvey's touring melodrama **Wicked London** (12-18-99, Third Ave.). A poor boy who marries a rich girl is framed not once but twice for crimes he did not commit. He corners and exposes the villain, his rich rival for the girl, only after escaping from prison. Settings included a hospital and a grog shop that serves as an after-hours gambling den.

John Blair's attempt to introduce New Yorkers to avant-garde foreign drama continued with **Ties** (12-20-99, Carnegie Lyceum), a translation of Paul Hervieu's *Les Tenailles*. This study of a small-minded domestic despot ends when his wife reveals he is not the father of their son.

By the time Clyde Fitch's **The Cowboy and the Lady** (12-25-99, Knickerbocker) reached Broadway it had behind it a long, successful American tour and a short, failed London run. New Yorkers seemed more inclined to agree with Londoners than with their own compatriots, even if two popular stars, Nat Goodwin and Maxine Elliott, headed the cast. (The play had been written for them.) Goodwin played Teddy North, a Harvard-educated rancher in Silverville, Colo. The Westons come from the East on a visit. North quickly falls in love with Mrs. Weston (Miss Elliott) but says and does nothing to reveal his feeling, although he does save her life when she and her horse are caught in a landslide. By contrast, Weston is a scalawag who openly courts Molly, the proprietress of the local dance hall. For this Weston gains the enmity of Molly's half-breed lover, Quick-Foot Jim. When Mrs. Weston throws a ball at the dance hall, Jim uses the occasion to kill Weston with a gun belonging to Mrs. Weston, which she has entrusted to North. North is brought to trial. Hoping to prove that there was no collusion between him and Mrs. Weston, he asks her if she loves him. She hesitates, but when the judge orders her to answer she says yes. North is convicted. Molly rushes in, claiming she can name the real killer. Jim shoots her. She is removed to another room, and moments later Mrs. Weston appears, to announce Molly is dead. Overcome, Jim confesses to murdering Weston. Then Mrs. Weston reveals Molly is alive and her announcement was a trick. As the courtroom empties, North asks the new widow if she meant what she said and would "stick to it." Her reply is, "I'm game."

Aspects of the mounting amused the critic for the *Dramatic Mirror.* He noted, as he had earlier in *The Conquerors,* the use of electric lights in supposed oil lamps and concluded, "Some boulders . . . couldn't have been very bold, for they yielded comfortably when stepped upon." The players were more welcome. Goodwin again demonstrated, as he had in *In Mizzoura,* that he could deftly intermingle drama and a touch of pathos with his comic skills. Miss Elliott was saluted for her beauty and for her "gowns of bewildering splendor, somewhat uncommon on the frontier." Many observers felt that a minor figure, Midge (Minnie Dupree), a waif adopted by North, was the most interestingly drawn. In Miss Dupree's hands, her scene on the witness stand won special plaudits. But *The Cowboy and the Lady* ran for only forty-four performances.

H. V. Esmond's London comedy **My Lady's Lord** (12-25-99, Empire) ran half as long. It was set in Esmond's answer to Ruritania, Vasungia, where everyone dresses in medieval-style clothing. An Englishman who has seen a beautiful girl on a London street follows her, discovers she is a noblewoman, and rescues her from an undesirable marriage to a boozy, lecherous prince.

Theodore Kremer's designed-for-touring melodrama **The Bowery After Dark** (12-25-99, Star) opened the same evening. Although it lacked spectacular settings—a burning building, an onrushing locomotive—it otherwise typified the genre. At first audiences saw, according to Kremer's script: "Interior of typical Bowery dive. L[eft], up stage, Oblique is the stage on which several specialties are performed at rise of curtain. R[ight] Oblique is the bar—bartender behind it." Many of the subsidiary characters are onstage. Kremer offered no detailed descriptions but supplied capsule characterizations, which found their way to programs.

Michael Quirk ["who wants to reform the Bowery"]: Look here, you little shrimp. This lady here will do me the honor of becoming Mrs. Quirk as soon as I get a steady job on the police force, and don't you forgit it.
Pete ["a Bowery ornament"]: I wouldn't dream of insulting so estimable a lady as Mrs. Guggles.
Michael: Her name isn't Guggles, it's Guggenheimer.
Pete: Mrs. Goo-o-gen (*gasps*) I'll have to oil my pipe before I can spring that jawbreaker. (*calls*) Waiter, give us a lager.

And, at another table:

Bertie ["a jolly good fellow"]: Say Nellie, won't you join me in a drink?
Nellie ["a Bowery waif"]: No thanks, I don't drink.
Bertie: Why?
Nellie: Because I promised mother I'd never touch liquor. I've never broken that promise and I never will.

But the principal figure is Flora, who has married the gambling Robert Morris after he treacherously employed forged letters to lure her away from Joe Howe. She has been subjected to numerous indignities, and now Morris has tossed with Lee Twang, owner of an opium den, for possession of her. Flora naturally is outraged. When she tries to leave, Twang starts to chloroform her. Nellie and Fing, Twang's mistress, rush in to her rescue. Nellie has mentioned a cross, and Fing, raised in ignorance of Western religions, asks her what it is.

Nellie: Look, here is one. My darling mother had it carved out of wood as she lay in agony on her death bed, and when she felt that her hour had come, she called me, put her arms around me neck, and whispered, "Nell, me little girl, me time has come. I'm going to leave you all alone in this cruel world, without care or protection. Don't cry, me little one. Whenever you are tempted to sin, look upon this cross and think of your dead mother." (*Nellie's head sinks down, she sobs.*)

Fing: (*wiping tears from her eyes*) Will you teach me to pray to your God?

Nellie: Indeed I will

Flora: And I will help you.

Fing: You! (*enter Morris and Twang*)

Morris: Look Lee, here they are, and praying.

Flora: (*whispers*) We are alone—we're lost.

Fing: No, no, courage. (*clings to her, holding cross to Flora's breast*)

Twang: You Fing, you praying with a cross? Throw it away.

Fing: No, never (*stage grows darker*)

Twang: Give it to me that I may break it to pieces. (*tries to get it*)

Fing: Don't you dare.

Morris: Yes, trample it to atoms.

Twang: Help me tear your wife out of that devil's arms.

Fing: No, you'll have to break them first.

Twang: Kill the tigress. (*draws knife*)

Morris: Yes, brain her with the cross.

Fing: Back, you blasphemers. You have outraged every human feeling. You have tried to disgrace the wife and dishonor the mother. You gambled for the possession of souls, and now you want to outrage the highest symbol of God. (*tragically*) You have gone too far. (*shrieks*) Down, down on your knees, tremble at the power of the cross. (*Men drop to their knees in horror. Women in praise.*)

Morris kills Twang and then himself. Michael and Joe have hurried in.

Michael: Mrs. Morris, your husband's committed suicide. He's dead.

Flora: Dead! (*falls on Joe's breast*)

Joe: My darling, you're free at last.

Nellie wins Pete, and the curtain falls. Harley Merry's scenery offered various views of the Bowery, especially less savory dens in the Chinese quarters. Once again a dismayed reviewer admitted that the galleryites were "wildly enthusiastic."

No one was wildly enthusiastic about David Belasco's **Naughty Anthony** (1-8-00, Herald Square). Although the play was by no means a failure, both the critics' and the public's reaction fell short of the producer-director-playwright's expectations. (Years later he would rationalize his disappointment by suggesting the public could not accept him as a writer of farce.) Belasco's Anthony Depew (Frank Worthing) is a self-anointed professor of morality. Most of his pupils are attractive ladies, so it is not surprising that the professor flunks his own test when he kisses a pretty hosiery salesgirl, Cora (Blanche Bates). The kiss is witnessed by a newly appointed policeman, who reports it. Depew's attempts to keep from being identified, mistaken identities, and misinterpretations lead to the usual farcical mixups before Depew reluctantly concludes, "I don't think I'll try any more to teach people how to be good." When Cora asks him what he will do hereafter, he replies, "I will ask some nice girl to teach me. Will you?" Worthing played Depew with an unflagging earnestness that made his farcical antics especially comic, but Miss Bates stole the show. Her "strip tease," taking off one set of brightly colored stockings after another, provoked more laughs than gasps. Immediately after the opening, Belasco decided he would need an afterpiece to bolster *Naughty Anthony*'s uncertain fortunes. He set about preparing it.

Galleryites and critics again found themselves at odds over W. J. McKiernan and E. J. Gallagher's **The Gunner's Mate** (1-9-00, Grand Opera). Its hero is Clement Carroll. Besides being a fine seaman on the U.S.S. *New York,* he is the guardian of Arthur "Blizzard" Gladden (a trouser role), who is the son of a buddy killed in the recent war. The ship's doctor is Herbert Quayley. He covets not only the estate that little Blizzard is heir to but Clem's girl, Mildred Emerson. He determines to get both by hook or crook. First Quayley attempts to inject the boy with tuberculosis germs. Clem stops him. Then he attempts to set Blizzard adrift in a rotten hulk. Clem, with the help of Plum Duff, a waif, stops him again. When the warship develops boiler trouble, Clem volunteers to fix it. The bad doctor locks him in the boiling-over boiler room, and Clem is saved in the nick of time by his shipmates. Clem has also helped a foreign sailor who is in love with an American girl by penning a love letter for him. Quayley gets hold of this, shows it to Mildred, and persuades her that Clem is unfaithful. Just as Quayley and Mildred are about to be united in a swank wedding, Clem and his friends appear. Quayley is thrown off a balcony, and Clem takes his place at the altar. Along with the cheer-grabbing boiler-room scene were settings showing other views of the ship, with sailors singing, dancing, gambling, and even staging a prizefight.

Lillie Langtry was the sole attraction in Sydney Grundy's **The Degenerates** (1-15-00, Garden)— "Mrs. Langtry in flesh-colored satin with sapphires,

Mrs. Langtry in pale-blue satin with diamonds in dazzling array, Mrs. Langtry in white with pearls." Reviewers were less happy with her acting in the part of a woman with a past who rescues another lady from disgrace by claiming (echoes of *Lady Windermere's Fan* again) a glove the careless lady has left behind is actually hers. However, her Mrs. Trevelyan is rewarded for her gallantry by a forgiving husband. Thanks largely to Mrs. Langtry's admirers, the play did good business during its month-long stand.

A rural drama that had been touring for many months came in the same night to a combination house. **Hi Hubbard** (1-15-00, Third Ave.) was the work of its star, Hi Horton, who undoubtedly didn't mind if playgoers confused him and his rustic philosopher. Hi's philosophy is put to the test when his daughter, Helen, supposedly is about to wed a young artist, Ralph Benedict. For just before the nuptials a lady named Celia Dupress appears and announces she is Ralph's wife. Ralph confesses but claims he thought his wife had died. Then comes another revelation. Ralph and Helen already have married, secretly. Is Ralph a bigamist? Not really, for Hi slyly wangles the truth. Celia is the twin sister of Ralph's dead spouse, and she long had hoped to marry Ralph herself.

Leo Trevor's **Brother Officers** (1-16-00, Empire) had been a hit in London and was a success all over again when Charles Frohman produced it with William Faversham in the lead. Faversham portrayed an officer who has risen from the ranks. He is a good, often self-sacrificing man, but none of his sacrifices is greater than when he gives up the woman he loves to another officer. The play ran eleven weeks and was brought back the following season for a brief engagement.

A play given the following evening for a single performance has held the stage to this day. The play was Ibsen's **The Master Builder** (1-17-00, Carnegie Lyceum), in its American premiere, and it was greeted by such observations as "Its meaning is known only to Henrik Ibsen himself" and "The symbolism in this drama . . . is particularly occult and mystifying." Players below the first rank could do little to elucidate matters.

Paul Bilhaud and Michel Carré's **The Surprises of Love** (1-22-00, Lyceum) was hardly obscure. Its comedy centered on a young widow (Elsie de Wolfe) who has become engaged to a tiring academician. He presents her with a lottery ticket, and when she wins she discovers the prize is a handsome young man (H. Reeves-Smith). From there the audience could guess the ending. Miss de Wolfe, Olive May,

and the other ladies in the cast wore "gowns that were poems." Poetry and farce combined to give the piece a modest run.

Less demanding audiences flocked to two openings at houses catering to touring shows. The villains in James H. Wallick's **The King of Rogues** (1-22-00, Star) were two Jews, Manuel Levigne and his crony, Solomon Isaac Silver. Their protean disguises turn them into everything from priests to porters as they hustle from Johannesburg to Paris, at one point locking the hero and heroine in a speeding mail-and-baggage car and unleashing a huge, venomous snake. But the snake is not their most effective weapon, for they also carry with them in a silver box an equally venomous spider "trained to jump out, kill a man, and then return to captivity." The *Journal* gleefully reported that the spider "never missed a cue." The pair are eventually brought to justice, but the fate of the spider is unrecorded.

There were more snakes (they were voguish this season) in the latest representative of what one reviewer branded "the 'Frisco-Chinese school of dramatic literature." If **A Night in Chinatown** (1-22-00, Third Ave.) found its authorship in dispute, no one cared. Its clichés sufficed. John O'Hara loves Clara Martin, but she is abducted by Duke Desta, "the King of the Highbinders." O'Hara's search for her takes him through the streets of Chinatown, an opium den, and a snake pit and finally to Duke's lavish apartment. But O'Hara does not prove Duke's nemesis. Instead a vengeful woman of the streets called Crazy Jane does in the villain, allowing the lovers to flee. Carrie Ezier as Mag, a tough girl, won loud applause for her songs and dances.

The next week the same combination houses again competed for first-nighters. Mark E. Swan's **A Man of Mystery** (1-29-00, Third Ave.) pitted a forthright detective, Ned Keene, against an unusually adroit thief, Richard Glenwood. No one can remember seeing Glenwood near the scene of any of his crimes. The reason soon becomes clear. The crook had apparently attended a performance of *Trilby* and trained himself to become a mesmerist. Keen's task is further complicated when he falls in love with Glenwood's sister, Flossie. Charles H. Langdon and Eric Hudson's **Man's Enemy** (1-29-00, Star) was a disguised prohibitionist tract imported from England. The hero comes from a distinguished family, which disowns him when he marries the mistress of a notorious gambler. The villain and his mistress turn the young man into a drunkard. The action—and there was plenty of it, including a scene in which the drunkard throws the gambler out of a window—moved from London to Monte Carlo. Of course, sobriety triumphs.

The first Monday in February was chock full of openings on first-class stages, but only one of the plays was American—and that was based on a French story. However, while the importations—all moderately successful—came and went quietly, the native work precipitated the season's more blazing pyrotechnics. Clyde Fitch's **Sapho** (2-5-00, Wallack's) was derived from a play by Alphonse Daudet and Adolphe Belot, which in turn had been taken from Daudet's novel. Only after Fannie Legrand (Olga Nethersole) seduces Jean Gaussin (Hamilton Revelle) into falling ardently in love with her does he learn she is the notorious courtesan Sapho. Twice others convince him to break off the affair, and twice he returns, hat and heart in hand. But Sapho herself has begun to fall in love with him, something beyond her own ability to deal with. So on his last return she persuades him to take a nap, and when he does, she writes a loving farewell note and leaves.

Nethersole's Sapho was, according to one admiring critic, "a languorous, insinuating siren with a musical, coaxing voice and wistful eyes." A conflicting opinion was voiced by the outraged William Winter, who railed in the *Tribune* that "her acting, always plainly artificial, prevails by force and not by tenderness" and proceeded to damn her as "hard, dry, monotonous and frequently tame." Even those who approved of the star agreed the play did nothing to improve the moral climate. Particularly offensive to many was the scene in which Jean seizes Sapho and carries her up a circular stair to the bedroom. Moralists yowled so loudly that police ordered the play closed, and the star was hauled into court. After she was acquitted, the play was allowed to reopen. In all the play recorded more than eighty performances and was brought back for a month during the next season.

Between its closing and reopening, Miss Nethersole mounted *The Second Mrs. Tanqueray* and *The Profligate*. Other companies, playing other versions of the play, also encountered trouble. A troupe in Connecticut hurriedly entrained across the border to New York, a step ahead of the police. Ripples touched even nontheatrical enterprises when a Philadelphia bookseller was arrested for offering the original novel. After the court decision, the companies returned to the footlights, where some presented the play with the spelling *Sappho*. One of these ensembles played Manhattan late in the season.

With their own Clyde Fitch vehicle having run its course, Nat Goodwin and Maxine Elliott turned to Henry V. Esmond's second play of the season, **When We Were Twenty-one** (2-5-00, Knickerbocker). In this September-May romance, a forty-year-old bachelor finds the orphan he has raised prefers a music hall singer to the young lady the bachelor has chosen for him, so the bachelor marries the lady himself. Goodwin's skill at mingling comedy and pathos and his wife's beauty again were sufficient to give the piece limited popularity.

Another orphan was the central figure in **The Ambassador** (2-5-00, Daly's), a society comedy by John Oliver Hobbes (Mrs. Craigie). She is Juliet Gainsborough (Mary Mannering), who becomes engaged to her guardian's stepson, only to realize she does not love him. She diplomatically breaks the engagement. Her diplomacy is also evident when she learns that her guardian's son has forged a letter and she risks her reputation to retrieve it.

Almost anything French was viewed by some Americans as salacious, and Albin Valabrègue and Maurice Hennequin's farce **Coralie & Co., Dressmakers** (2-5-00, Madison Square) was no exception. Its comic contretemps unfolded in a boutique where trick sliding panels give entrance to concealed, tiny bedrooms. One major figure is a wife who has bought an expensive rose-colored dress, which, with the flip of a knowing wrist, can be prim or provocative and which she tells her husband she bought elsewhere at a sale. The husband, learning of the boutique's reputation and of the dress's source, comes to check out matters. The panels start sliding furiously. While the *Dramatic Mirror* had been reasonably tolerant about *Sapho,* it warned this play contained "some exhibitions that might possibly provoke police interference." They didn't. The reviewer was especially aghast when, "as a climax to this carnival of adultery, one of the male characters was discovered in the same bed with a negress!" Perhaps significantly, of the evening's four major openings only *Sapho* enjoyed more performances.

Another French comedy, adapted by Henry St. Maur as **The Countess Chiffon** (2-6-00, Fifth Ave.), was a one-week failure. Its story told of a neglected wife who decides to have a fling.

By contrast, Charles Frohman scored a major success when he imported Cecil Raleigh's Drury Lane melodrama **Hearts Are Trumps** (2-21-00, Garden). A titled Englishwoman gambles herself deep into debt. She enlists her daughter to bring her luck, but the daughter is falsely accused of cheating. Later the daughter poses in the nude, and when mama sees the painting at an exhibition she takes a knife to it. Then the daughter goes onstage as a music hall performer, and mama creates a scene from her box. (The setting showing both the stage and the audience was one of the evening's highlights.) Finally a vicious Jewish money-lender lures the daughter to the Alps and threatens to kill her in a landslide if mama does not pay her debts. The Jew accidentally triggers the avalanche and is killed. (However much the American theatre had begun to evince a newer, more balanced view of Jews, unsavory Jews were another popular cliché of the season. In *The Degenerates* one had talked about how he hated his own co-religionists; in *When We Were Twenty-one* a rich Jew steals the ward's music hall entertainer from him.) Amelia Bingham, who would briefly go on to better things, was the mother. Well-produced sensation-melodrama still occasionally could find an audience at first-class houses, so *Hearts Are Trumps* ran into May.

Fabrice Carré and Paul Bilhaud's *Ma Bru* was offered to Americans as **My Daughter-in-Law** (2-26-00, Lyceum). A troublemaking mother-in-law attempts to break up her son's marriage, but her daughter-in-law turns the tables on her by showing her that her own husband is having an affair. Much of the cast was English, with Seymour Hicks and his wife, Ellaline Terriss, as the young marrieds.

That a century and its theatre were passing was signaled by the arrival of one of the last active 19th-century greats, Helena Modjeska. Although she had previously announced farewell tours, no one could know that this was, in fact, her last. She opened at the Fifth Avenue on the 26th. By now her repertory long had been set, and from it she offered *Mary Stuart, The Ladies' Battle, Macbeth, Twelfth Night,* and *Much Ado About Nothing.* Her only novelty was Clinton Stuart's **Marie Antoinette** (3-1-00), which critics dismissed as weak and old-fashioned. Reviewers agreed that the star's fire, poetry, and grace had not deserted her, but her old loyalists had. Apparently, only *Macbeth* was well attended, as was the case earlier with the James-Kidder-Hanford combine. The company stayed for three weeks.

If interest in an older school of theatre was waning, the "new" drama was made even less welcome. The band of pioneers who were trying to bring it to Broadway tried again with a performance of Alexander Ostrovsky's **The Storm** (3-2-00, Carnegie Lyceum). This "new" drama was forty years old, and Ostrovsky himself had been dead for more than a decade. His story told of a girl who, to escape from a humdrum, oppressive family, takes on a lover and commits suicide when he later rejects her. Once again critics dutifully attended the single performance and informed their readers that they had not missed much.

The first Monday in March was as busy as the first Monday in February had been, although only two of its openings were at first-class houses. Belasco finally had readied an afterpiece to accompany *Naughty Anthony.* He found his inspiration in a short story that John Luther Long had published two years earlier in *Century Magazine.* In Long's story a Japanese girl weds an American naval officer, but when she realizes that he has left and will never return, she resigns herself to a lonely life, raising their child in a society that will no longer accept her. Belasco made two crucial changes. He allowed Pinkerton (Frank Worthing) to return in time to discover that Cho-Cho-San (Blanche Bates), despairing of his coming back, has killed herself. (No one seems to have noticed that this was the very story used in Messager's 1893 operetta *Madame Chrysanthème.* Of course, the musical appears not to have made it across the Atlantic.)

Working with scene painter Ernest Gros, Belasco gave **Madame Butterfly** (3-5-00, Herald Square) a stunning production. Before the action began, three drop curtains set the scene and mood by depicting in turn a rice paddy, a harbor with fishing boats in the setting sun, and a tea garden by moonlight, with a snowcapped volcano in the distance. The lights then dimmed and went up again to disclose a Japanese house, with yet another view of a distant harbor seen through a vista of cherry blossoms. The dialogue audiences heard was not always inspired. Cho-Cho-San speaks of her two years of expectation as "jus' waitin'—sometimes cryin'—sometimes watchin'—but always waitin'!" It sounds more like something written to suggest a black dialect than what we would now expect for an Oriental. At least it avoided much of the "chop-chopee" of contemporary Chinese characters. Butterfly's suicide took place offstage. Dying, she staggers forward to clasp her child and to confront Pinkerton, who has entered the room. Her last words are "Too bad—those robin'—never nes'—again." But the scene that was most discussed, and that showed how Belasco had mastered almost every aspect of stage art, had no dialogue and lasted, according to William Winter, for fourteen minutes. It served as a link between the play's two principal scenes. Cho-Cho-San dresses herself and her child, decks the house with flowers, lights the lanterns, and then waits at the window with her maid and baby for the morning to come. The evening turns to night; the stars appear, first dimly and finally brightly; the maid and the baby fall asleep. In time the stars start to fade, and dawn, gray to begin with, then rosy, leads to a bright, sunny morning. Birds are heard in the trees.

Critics divided over the merits of the play, but to a

man they applauded the magnificent mounting. Most also applauded Blanche Bates, who was dainty, humorous, and poignant as the situation demanded. The play made her a star.

· · ·

Blanche Bates (1873–1941) was born in Portland, Ore., to a theatrical family. She grew into a dark-haired, handsome woman, whose acting was often described in terms such as "animated" and "vivid." Her debut came in San Francisco in 1894. Three years later she joined Daly's company, first appearing as Bianca in *The Taming of the Shrew*. Her playing of Hannah in *The Children of the Ghetto* brought her widespread acclaim earlier in the season.

· · ·

For all its good reception and its story's later fame (in Puccini's opera, first done just four years later); this original production ran a mere three weeks.

Opie Read and Frank Pixley's **The Carpetbagger** (3-5-00, 14th St.) ran only two weeks in its first New York outing, but it had been playing on the road since September 1898. (Some idea of how ubiquitous legitimate theatres were at the time can be gauged by the fact that the play had its world premiere in Warren, Pa., pop. 10,000.) The carpet-bagger is Melville Crance, the corrupt, detested governor of Mississippi. After his daughter, Nellie, graduates from school in the North, he brings her to Jackson, where she is ostracized by the locals. Her only friend is Roy Fairburn, son of a widow who lives near the governor's mansion. Nellie and Roy fall in love, and after they introduce the governor and the widow, so do the oldsters. Before long Nellie, Roy, and the widow have gotten Crance to change his outlook and his ways. Settings showed the governor's office, his home, and a magnolia grove in the inevitable moonlight.

No author came forward to take credit (or blame) for **The Missouri Girl** (3-5-00, Third Ave.), a rural drama awash in stock situations. Once Phil Sweatnam learns a vein of priceless ore lies under the farm of Silas Grubb, he employs every dirty trick to seize the farm, but Silas's daughter, Daisy, and her fiancé, Zeke Dobson, finally ride him out of town.

Edith Ellis Baker's **Mrs. B. O'Shaughnessey, Wash Lady** (3-5-00, Metropolis) was a vehicle for the buxom female impersonator George W. Monroe. Monroe had won acclaim as Bridget McVeigh in a series of musicals in the 1890s. His latest Bridget was a widowed washerwoman working to support her three daughters. She inherits a legacy of $100,000, which is promptly stolen by a scheming lawyer, Hold M. Upp. He hides it under a pillow in his home, and Bridget and her friends spend the rest of the evening trying to retrieve it. They do.

Charles Frohman added one more title to his growing list of money-makers when he offered New Yorkers **The Pride of Jennico** (3-6-00, Criterion), which Abby Sage Richardson and Grace Livingston Furniss drew from Agnes and Egerton Castle's novel. For some reason, the work's billing as a "romantic play" led several critics to muse on the difference between these swashbucklers and everyday melodrama. After all, both had their ardent lovers, their crafty, resolute villains, their hair-breadth escapes. Of course, romantic plays were usually set in some real but exotic land, or in some equally exotic if imaginary Ruritania, and romances often substituted dashing swordplay for fisticuffs and gunshots. *The Pride of Jennico* unfolded in Middle Europe, where Basil Jennico (James K. Hackett) has promised his dying uncle he will marry only a girl of noble birth. After he is tricked into wedding Marie Ottilie (Bertha Galland), a supposed commoner, he is torn between his love and his vow. His plight is made all the harder by the schemes of the perfidious Eugen Von Rothenburg (Brigham Royce) and Eugen's gypsy cohort, Michel (Grace Reals). When Basil decides that love is more important than a promise, he dons a monk's disguise, comes to where Eugen and his men are, grabs a sword, and battles the whole group until help arrives. Only then does Marie Ottilie tell him what the audience learned in the first act, that she is really a princess who, on a lark, had changed places with her maid. The play ran until the hot weather, took a summer hiatus, and reopened in the fall. Hackett's acting confirmed his claim to stardom.

· · ·

James K[eteltas] Hackett (1869–1926) was the son of the famous 19th-century comedian J. H. Hackett. Born in Canada, he studied law before turning to acting. He made his debut in 1894, played briefly with Daly's ensemble, then worked for Daniel Frohman in comedies and drama. The tall, virile, handsome actor's gifts for romantic drama became evident when he replaced Sothern in *The Prisoner of Zenda*.

· · ·

The garden variety of popular melodrama was represented by Hugh Gibson's **Just Before Dawn** (3-13-00, Third Ave.). Richard Demming, the foreman of the Big Six coal mine, loves Olga Carriston, whose father owns the mine. But Carriston's debts drive him to suicide. Edwin Brandon, who covets both Olga and the mine, makes it seem that Demming killed Carriston, and it takes the hero two more acts to exonerate himself and prove Brandon a scoundrel.

Things Oriental remained trendy (one of the season's musicals was *Broadway to Tokio*), so it was not surprising that when a troupe of Japanese players gave a few performances at the Berkeley Lyceum their success was such that they were invited to occupy the Bijou for several weeks, beginning on March 12. Reviews give little idea of the productions other than to imply that they were very "primitive," but it seems clear that they were not Kabuki or Noh plays. Actresses performed alongside men. Most of the plays appeared to be contemporary Japanese attempts to write of their history and legend in a Western mode. However, two of the mountings were particularly interesting. One was *Sairoku*, which was as close as the Japanese could come to Shylock, for the play was a version of *The Merchant of Venice*. Shylock's greed was minimized, because, as one of the cast informed the audience, no such character existed in Japan. The other play was *Sahoko*, which proved a quick Japanese stab at adapting *Sapho*.

Oliver Goldsmith (3-19-00, Fifth Ave.) was purportedly inspired by playwright August Thomas's perception that Stuart Robson resembled the 18th-century author. When Goldsmith mistakes a private home for an inn, it gives him the idea for a comedy. The finished work appears to be in trouble until David Garrick (Henry E. Dixey) attends a rehearsal and shows how to bring it off. Goldsmith has fallen in love with Mary Horneck, but she agrees to wed the vitriolic critic, Mr. Kenrick, who has threatened to expose secrets in her dead father's past and who also is determined to prevent *She Stoops to Conquer* from being performed. In the last, act, Goldsmith is discovered hounded by bailiffs in his seedy attic. Garrick enters in disguise, pays the writer's debts, and routs Kenrick. Goldsmith learns that Mary reciprocates his own feelings. The play was pleasant but episodic; the acting, despite the presence of two accomplished comedians, apparently was no more than capable. For many critics a minor actor, H. A. Weaver, Sr., walked off with honors as the gruff Samuel Johnson.

The title of Charles E. Blaney and J. J. McCloskey's **Across the Pacific** (3-19-00, Star) suggests they were trying to capitalize on McCloskey's long-lived hit of thirty years before, *Across the Continent*. Reduced to not-quite-bare essentials, their convoluted plot told of the love of Joe Lanier (Howard Hall), a Montana miner, for his ward, Elsie Escott. Two bad men, Bud Stanton and Sam Drysdale, also have their eyes on Elsie. Luckily, in the first act Elsie overhears a conversation that alerts her to the miscreants' real nature, but this in no way discourages the men. In a Chinatown opium den (the story has moved to San Francisco), Bud sees to it that Sam is drugged, steals his wallet, and plants it on Joe. But when he accuses Joe of theft a witness reveals the truth. Joe then enlists in the Montana regiment heading for the Philippines. Aboard the ship about to sail, Bud and Sam reappear, and again Joe must give the lie to false accusations. They also disclose that Elsie, who has disguised herself as a soldier, is on the ship. Elsie performs a military drill so snappily that the men's word is doubted, and they slink away, to be arrested. In the Philippines they crop up again, this time posing as a captain and a Red Cross surgeon. They hope to sell Joe to cannibals. But a battle at a blockhouse, complete with a working gatling gun, writes *finis* to their perfidy. Joe and Elsie can marry. The scenes in the opium den, aboard ship, and at the fort were praised as "elaborate and handsome." Songs, dances, and other vaudeville accoutrements, so necessary to touring melodramas, enlivened the entertainment. The play succeeded on the road but never matched the popularity of McCloskey's earlier play.

Kinsey Peile's London comedy, **The Interrupted Honeymoon** (3-20-00, Daly's) found few takers. A spoiled girl invites her father to accompany her on her honeymoon. When another, unwed couple is mistaken for the pair, complications arise. Mary Mannering and William Courtenay as the newlyweds, John Mason as the father, and Hilda Spong and Grant Stewart as the second couple could do little with the weak material.

Other excellent players had somewhat better luck with a play theatregoers might more readily have expected to see at the "new" drama series at the Carnegie Lyceum, Gerhart Hauptmann's **The Sunken Bell** (3-26-00, Knickerbocker). Charles Henry Meltzer was the translator. Forest gnomes overturn a cart carrying a bell molded by Heinrich (E. H. Sothern). The bell sinks into a lake, and the injured bell-founder is nursed back to health by a benevolent forest sprite, Rautendelein (Virginia Harned). He goes to live with her and starts work on another bell, which will ring with the sound of her magical voice. But a vision of his children, carrying an urn containing the tears of his dead wife, appears to him. He deserts Rautendelein. When he reconsiders and wants her back, she will not come. But she does allow him to hear his sunken bell pealing at the bottom of the lake before he dies. The play was beautifully mounted, with E.

G. Unitt's poetic settings and novel, effective electric lighting winning special praise. Many critics complained that the actors' mundane enunciation sometimes worked against the play's fantastic atmosphere. However, Sothern won universal admiration for "his poetic grace in speech and action," hinting at his Shakespearean career to come. He himself would return to the play in later years.

Two quick failures may have given playgoers a sense of déjà vu. **Little Nell and the Marchioness** (3-26-00, Herald Square) was Harry P. Mawson's reworking of many of the same incidents from *The Old Curiosity Shop* that Brougham long ago had dramatized for Lotta. But Mawson was no Brougham, and Mary Saunders certainly no Lotta. The play ran two weeks, or twice as long as the stand of **Twelve Months Later** (3-26-00, Madison Square), taken from the German of Oscar Blumenthal and Gustav Kadelburg. This loosely structured farce showed what happened a year later to the characters from *At the White Horse Inn*. Like all too many sequels, it was not nearly as interesting as the original.

Combination houses were also busy that same night. Jack Rutledge, an all-American boy, is the central figure in Joseph Le Brandt's **On the Stroke of Twelve** (3-26-00, Star), which programs called "the plausible American comedy-drama." Jack, an athlete, is persuaded by James Horton and his Jewish buddy, Moses Levi, to bet on a race. Jack loses, so Horton gives him a check to pay off his debt. But the check is a forgery, and Horton convinces Jack's father that Jack is the forger. He also tricks the elder Rutledge into a marriage with Marie Bergere, who is actually Horton's wife. Horton hopes to have Rutledge disown his children and leave everything to Marie. But when his plans go awry he kills the old man and implicates Jack. Jack escapes from prison and traces Horton to a counterfeiter's den, where all wrongs are righted.

The Ten-Ton Door (3-26-00, Third Ave.), another of the season's touring melodramas for which no author came forth, told of two half-brothers serving in the British army in Egypt. One brother plots to have the other killed, but a fight at the foot of the Sphinx settles matters in favor of the hero.

Charles Frohman's lucky streak ran out when he presented a double bill headed by **A Man and His Wife** (4-2-00, Empire), which Constance Fletcher wrote under her pen name, George Fleming. William Faversham played a husband who discovers his irresponsible wife (Jessie Millward) is having an affair with his best friend (Guy Standing). The friend eventually is killed in an accident, and the husband forgives his wife. Louis N. Parker and Addison Bright's **The Bugle Call** told simply of a girl (Margaret Anglin) who rejects the rich Jew (Edwin Stevens) her mother (Mrs. Whiffen) wants her to marry in favor of a young officer (Joseph Wheelock, Jr.). Rose Eytinge, once a star, had a bit role.

For less fashionable playgoers the evening's novelty was William H. Rightmire's **The California Detective** (4-2-00, Third Ave.). Harry Saunders (Rightmire), the titular hero, assumes at least three disguises to bring Jasper Blackburn to heel. It seems Blackburn has an irrational hatred of Mr. Thorton. He has killed Thorton's wife, and he slanders Carrie Thorton so that Thorton will disown her. Lest Thorton change his mind, Blackburn attempts to burn Carrie alive in an old mill. Other settings included a boathouse and the Brooklyn Bridge.

The following Monday night intrepid first-nighters had a choice of two theatres but, in a sense, of only one play: **Quo Vadis** (4-9-00, Herald Square and New York). The version at the Herald Square, by Jeannette L. Gilder, had the dubious merit of being authorized; the version by Stanislaus Stange at the New York, a theatre usually given over to burlesque and extravaganza, had the advantage of months of playing on the road. Of course, many playgoers were already familiar with Henry Sienkiewicz's novel, to which both retellings remained as faithful as possible. Once again the Christian girl, Lygia (Bijou Fernandez or Roselle Knott), pursued the often dangerous path to the altar with the Roman tribune, Vinicius (John Blair or Joseph Haworth), in the corrupt days of Nero (Robert Fischer or Edmund D. Lyons). Most critics concurred that the writing was more literate if not more effective at the Herald Square, while the mounting at the New York was eminently more theatrical. Certainly the latter won hands down in the realm of spectacle. Both versions showed Nero playing his lyre as Rome burned all around him, but at the New York Lygia was brought into the arena on a bull, while at the Herald Square the scene was merely described by spectators. The public opted for the New York, whose version ran into the hot weather. John Blair's presence in one cast was interesting, for he had initiated the series of "new" drama at the Carnegie Lyceum. He had dropped out as producer, in favor of the surer income of the commercial theatre.

The popular Henry V. Donnelly stock troupe (top ticket twenty-five cents) rarely ventured a new play but, along with its revival of *Turned Up*, brought out Ralph Stuart and D. A. Bragdon's **The Peacemaker** (4-9-00, Murray Hill). A young couple decide they are mismated and elect to go their separate ways

Act Four : 1899–1906

until an old friend professes to show how foolish anyone is to marry in the first place, thereby uniting them against him and saving the marriage.

Critics implied that Arthur Shirley and Benjamin Landeck's London melodrama **Woman and Wine** (4-11-00, Manhattan) seemed sometimes to be played for laughs, or should have been even if it wasn't. Its story centered on a young law student who is lured to Paris by a wicked woman, loses his inheritance gambling at the races, is drugged at a Japanese ball at the Café d'Afrique, and immediately thereafter is falsely accused of murder. In one unusual twist, his accuser is none other than he himself. Elita Proctor Otis walked away with the best notices for her "florid, effulgent, baleful picture" of the wicked woman. Apart from her, only the scenery fared well at the hands of the critics.

A second gambling Englishman was the hero of F. A. Scudmore's London melodrama **Dangerous Women** (4-16-00, Star). After he kills a man in a gambling argument, a priest persuades him to take a vow of poverty for a year and help the poor. The poor he aids is a "poor," beautiful girl who is being hounded by the proprietress of the gambling den. This wicked woman is determined to be revenged on the girl's father for having jilted her years before when he discerned her true nature. At one point the heroine is drugged and left for dead in a coffin. A quack doctor from a nearby insane asylum administers a "life-restoring" potion he has concocted and takes credit for her resuscitation, not recognizing she was not really dead. After more harrowing experiences, and the lapse of the avowed year, hero and heroine plight their troth, and the evil adventuress is removed in shackles.

Like Modjeska, Joseph Jefferson—the most beloved comedian of his century—also was winding down a great career. His engagement, which began at the Fifth Avenue on the 16th, offered a review of all the most popular vehicles of his later years: *Rip Van Winkle, The Rivals,* and *Lend Me Five Shillings* coupled with *The Cricket on the Hearth* (*Dot*). Reviews were affectionate but surprisingly brief. Perhaps it was a warning to him. Although he appeared two years later in Harlem, he never again performed on a first-class stage in the heart of Manhattan. Coincidentally, when his month-long visit ended, the Fifth Avenue left the legitimate fold, joining the ranks of vaudeville houses.

The organization dedicated to producing "new" drama—it changed its name in midseason to the dissuasive "Course of Modern Plays"—ended its series with Edward Martyn's **The Heather Field** (4-19-00, Carnegie Lyceum). John E. Kellerd was cast

as an idealist who attempts to make a wasteland productive. His family is hostile, his attempts drive him hopelessly into debt, and in the end he stands, uncomprehendingly insane, looking at his failed venture. Paired with the novelty was a new translation of Coppée's *Le Passant,* **A Troubadour.** But the Course of Modern Plays had not wholly failed. Not only had it provided venturesome theatregoers with fresh, challenging dramas and ideas, it had goaded at least one commercial producer to follow its lead. A week earlier William A. Brady had presented a special matinee of Berte Thomas and Granville Barker's **The Weather Hen** (4-13-00, Manhattan) with no expectation of transferring it for a run. A weather hen is a fickle woman. In this instance she is a married lady, an ex-actress, who contemplates leaving her husband, first for a spoiled, silly rich man, and then for an actor. To be rid of her, her husband gets her a job at a provincial theatre. The weather hen has swung full circle.

Joseph Le Brandt's second touring melodrama of the season, **Caught in the Web** (4-23-00, Star), mixed hints of *Men and Women* with stock melodramatic motifs but also offered something original for the time. His hero was not all white. Tom Stanley, like several other recent melodrama heroes, gambles himself into debt. Since he is a banker, he "borrows" some of his bank's funds to pay off the debt. When his rival in love, Robert Blackwell, who is a cashier at the bank, gets a whiff of Tom's peculations, he goes public with his discovery and also accuses Tom of being the leader of a counterfeiting ring. A run on the bank ensues. It takes a saucy, young, handsome, skirt-chasing detective, Dick Leonard, to unearth Blackwell's own stealing and set Tom back on the road to redemption and romance. James Carew stole the show with his new-style sleuth.

The season's last offering at a mainstem playhouse was Eva Foster Riggs's **Borderside** (4-30-00, Lyceum). The work originated in Baltimore and "starred" Virginia Calhoun, a newcomer. Scuttlebutt proffered that her own money or that of an admirer had bankrolled the mounting. Miss Calhoun, who was pretty enough, played a young girl who has never seen her father. An attractive young man arrives at her home, and, knowing that her father is about to return from a long exile, she takes him for her father. The new arrival is happy to go along with her error. When her father finally does appear, he tells her the young man is his adopted son. Sister and adopted brother announce they are in love. One reviewer opined that such an absurd case of mistaken identity was grist for farce, not drama. The play survived only two weeks. Miss

Calhoun disappeared from the theatrical scene, but her leading man, Robert Haines, carved out an excellent career for himself.

If first-class theatres had had their say for the season, combination houses sputtered more slowly to a close. There was **A Day of Reckoning** (5-14-00, Star), which was said to have been "by Moore and Osborne, revised by Frederick Henderson." None of the three seems to have been heard from again. For no good reason the play was set in Paris. When a dying man is asked who killed him, he blurts out his wife's name. He was only calling her to come to his side, but she is convicted of his murder. After she escapes from prison, she disguises herself as a naval officer and tracks down the real murderer.

Frank Harvey's **The Wages of Shame** (5-21-00, Third Ave.) brought up the rear. Billed as a "romantic Irish melodrama," it told of Kathleen Malone, "a motherless school mistress" loved by both Sir Terence O'Moore and Larry Beamish. When Larry Beamish learns that Kathleen prefers Sir Terence, he helps them to confound Terence's mother and her unprincipled lawyer, who employ a lot of mean tricks to try to stop the wedding. Irish songs and dances were interspersed.

As usual, throughout the season both first-class theatres and combination houses offered returns of recent hits and revivals of older favorites. Even *Uncle Tom's Cabin* made an appearance.

1900–1901

The coming of the new century was accompanied by a wave of national optimism that was echoed up and down the length of Broadway. Indeed, 1901 was the year in which Broadway was christened "the Great White Way." Nighttime strollers from Madison Square to Longacre Square (later Times Square) delightedly lifted their eyes skyward to feast on glittering, beckoning electric signs, which invited them to an evening's entertainment. At the season's outset the *Dramatic Mirror* listed nearly sixty auditoriums in Manhattan, approximately two dozen of them offering first-class or major touring productions. Except briefly at election time (when Americans opted for McKinley's reassuring silences over Bryan's fiery jeremiads), business boomed. True, no play chalked up the long run Gillette's *Sherlock Holmes* had the previous season nor sent out as many companies as *Ben Hur*. Yet by season's end *Theatre*,

just then embarking on a thirty-year path as America's most popular theatrical magazine, could speak without exaggeration of "phenomenal runs" and conclude that "the substantial success that has attended many of the metropolitan productions has been a remarkable feature of the past season." Curiously, *Variety*'s retrospective count of productions (*Variety* was not founded until 1905) recorded a noteworthy plunge in the number of new plays. Its figure is fifty, down from sixty-three in 1899–1900, plus a doubling of the number of revivals and musicals, for a total of ninety-six mountings. (Our count, including novelties at combination houses, is seventy-plus.) More important than mere figures was the perception that the American theatre was increasingly American. If some of the home-baked goods were stale or poorly made, no matter. Others were definitely occasion for hope.

Home-baked goods were in evidence when a combination house launched the season. The *Dramatic Mirror* gave a rare, detailed description of the scene audiences saw when the curtain rose on Edward Weitzel's *The Tide of Life* (8-4-00, Third Ave.). That scene depicted "a South Street dock, with a junk shop L[eft], of which both the exterior and interior are seen. The stern of a ship is visible, U[pstage] C[enter], and there is a shanty labeled 'Office,' R[ight]." The junkman is Dan Gillette, "a husky fellow with a guttural voice." Gillette is also a river pirate and a villain. He plots to kill Judge Morley, a rich shipowner, and marry the judge's adopted daughter, Helen. But his plans are foiled by Richard Stoddard, a handsome young sea captain, and by an honest waif, Jill.

More villainy and female heroism were on tap two weeks later in Theodore Kremer's **The Angel of the Alley** (8-2-00, Star). Walter Bennett, a cavalry officer, is lured into a Bowery dive by an adventuress, Ethel Sheridan. A fight ensues, a man is killed, and the killing is pinned on Bennett. He is strapped to the electric chair when the angel of the alley "comes through a hole in the wall that the lighting courteously punches for her at precisely the right moment." She reveals the actual killer. The angel is none other than Ethel, who has had a convenient change of heart. Whatever critics thought of the play, "the noisiest audience that has assembled in [the] playhouse in years" clearly relished it.

Any play with Andrew Mack straddled the fence between romantic melodrama and musical. James B. Fagan's **The Rebel** (8-20-00, Academy of Music) was no exception. The star played a loyal Irishman who must kill his sweetheart's brother when the brother proves to be a British spy. Whatever the play was, it delighted audiences for nine weeks, then toured.

At a time when Turkish atrocities were making headlines, **Slaves of the Orient** (8-27-00, Star) was set against a background of an earlier Turkish massacre of Armenians, but a young American girl was front and center. She is kidnapped and taken to the sultan's harem in Constantinople, where she must languish until her rescue in the final act. Colorful, exotic settings provided much of the appeal.

Although Daniel L. Hart's **The Parish Priest** (8-30-00, 14th St.) had enjoyed enormous success on the road during the preceding season, its New York reception reversed the common order of things. Most reviewers admired its simplicity and honesty, its careful avoidance of "smart" talk. Playgoers wouldn't buy it. Hart was a Wilkes-Barre newspaperman who set his scene in his native Lucerne County, Pa. His story was hardly new, but his treatment of it was direct and unadorned. James Welsh, a miner, has scrimped for years to put his brother, Edward, through medical school. James also hoped that Edward would marry Helen Durkin, niece of the parish priest, Father John Whalen (Daniel Sully). To the dismay of James and the priest, Edward spurns Helen when an older physician offers him both a partnership in his practice and the hand of his daughter. But Father Whalen's wise, quiet diplomacy reunites Edward and Helen, without alienating the other doctor. The doctor's daughter settles happily for her former sweetheart. Much of the evening's appeal came from Sully, a tiny man with a distinct brogue, who heretofore had specialized in roustabout touring farces. He was credited with what little trade the play received in New York.

While the Academy of Music and the 14th Street Theatre were technically first-class houses, they were located far downtown at the bottom of the theatrical district. They were no longer the most desirable auditoriums. The prime theatres waited until September to relight. Their initial offerings did not bode well for the season. In Leo Ditrichstein's **All on Account of Eliza** (9-3-00, Garrick), a pretty village schoolmarm (Clara Lipman) confronts the petty jealousies and sniping of some mean local ladies. One of her few defenders is an immigrant member of the school board (Louis Mann). Several reviewers compared the work unfavorably to *A Midnight Bell,* a comparison no doubt called to mind by the very recent death of Charles Hoyt. Moreover, some felt that Mann's clowning, with his heavy dependence on a thick dialect, destroyed whatever serious implications the subtext offered and belonged more to musical comedy.

Prince Otto (9-3-00, Wallack's) was taken from Robert Louis Stevenson's novel. A prince, wandering incognito, learns of a planned revolution. The uprising is engineered by the prime minister (George Nash), who, for a time, even manages to recruit the unhappy, seemingly neglected princess (Percy Haswell) into his ranks. But when he attempts advances, the princess stabs him. The prince assumes blame and is hurried off to prison by a rebellious mob. Of course, his throne is finally restored. A number of dramatizations of the story had sprung up and were touring. Critics complained that this one retained the plot but none of the charm of the original. The star's costumes, sometimes displaying his knees, were dismissed as ugly and ridiculous. Still, the actor, who was both star and adaptor, was such a fine performer that the five-week stand did good business. The new star was Otis Skinner.

. . .

Otis Skinner (1858–1942) was born in Cambridge, Mass., the son of a minister. He made his debut in Philadelphia in 1877, then joined the ensemble of that city's Walnut Street Theatre. He followed this with stints in support of Edwin Booth and Lawrence Barrett before becoming a member of Daly's celebrated troupe. His first starring assignment was actually in *His Grace de Grammont* in 1894, but the mounting came no closer to Manhattan than Brooklyn. Skinner's luxuriant style of acting caused George Middleton to describe him as "flamboyant and scene-filling, like a rich claret running over everything."

. . .

Way down on 13th Street, at a playhouse once known as Wallack's, less discriminating playgoers attended the premiere of Charles W. Chase's **Uncle Sam in China** (9-3-00, Star). Uncle Sam's representative was Jack Harkins, a sailor. He responds heatedly to the pleas of Yu Sien's wife and children when Yu Sien, a Christianized coolie, is pressed into the Boxer army by the evil men on Gee Wo's tea plantation. All the Chinese were played by Occidentals. The American flag was referred to and waved a lot, always to cheers from the gallery. At one point "a tin locomotive was dragged across the stage by a rope, plainly visible." Songs and dances larded the action.

Charles Frohman and his star, Annie Russell, braved oppressive heat in a theatre one critic described as a furnace to provide New Yorkers with the season's first smash hit. Unfortunately for boosters of American drama, Robert Marshall's **A Royal Family** (9-5-00, Lyceum) originated in London. A "dainty and attractive" comedy set in Ruritanian Arcacia cast the star as a princess who refuses to marry the prince of a neighboring country even though the alliance could prevent a war. A tactful prelate induces the prince to court her incognito. The denouement was brought about in the same manner as that in *The Parish Priest*, except that on our democratic stage an ordinary clergyman sufficed in dealing with miners, doctors, and other commoners, while the English play trafficked in kings, queens, and cardinals. Unlike Hart, Marshall had frequent recourse to showy epigrams. But Annie Russell's sweet warmth, always coupled with an unstated or understated vulnerability, plus gorgeous gowns and regal throne rooms lured in playgoers for five months.

A weirdly matched pair of plays pleased few reviewers or theatregoers. The main item was Alfred Capus's **The Husbands of Leontine** (9-8-00, Madison Square), a French comedy greeted with the tongue-clucking that greeted most French comedies. A hopelessly flirtatious, irresponsible wife (Isabel Irving) has been twice divorced from the same exasperated spouse (Fritz Williams). Her latest husband (E. M. Holland) catches her in a compromising position with another man and summons the police. The new chief of police turns out to be husbands one and two. He uses all his powers of persuasion to convince the new husband not to abandon his wife—lest, of course, he himself might become saddled with her a third time. Joined with this as a curtain raiser was **Ib and Little Christina,** Basil Hood's dramatization of a Hans Christian Andersen tale. Ib and Little Christina are childhood sweethearts, but when they grow up Christina marries someone else. Later the heartbroken Ib learns that her marriage was unhappy and that she has died. His mother, a fairy, restores Christina to life—not as a grown woman, but as the little girl who once reciprocated Ib's affections. Youngsters played Ib and his sweetheart in the first scene (and the little girl in the final scene). Good if unimportant actresses played the grown Christina and Ib's mother. However, the best notices went to Holbrook Blinn for his reserved yet touching depiction of the mature Ib. Still, all too many sentimentalists found the comedy naughty, while lovers of French comedy dismissed the curtain raiser as gooey. The pairing hurt both at the box office.

Nothing hurt Augustus Thomas's **Arizona** (9-10-00, Herald Square). A fine American play, superbly cast and beautifully mounted, it found a welcome from critics and public alike and ran for 140 performances. On its programs and in published form it was called a drama, but in his autobiography Thomas referred to it as a melodrama. It was both, for while it resorted to several stock melodramatic situations, it presented them with an artful subtlety missing in older melodramas and sometimes approached an elementary, unaffected poetry. Estrella Bonham (Jane Kennark) still resents that her rancher parents, the Canbys (Theodore Roberts and Mattie Earle), pressed her into marrying Colonel Bonham (Edwin Holt) of the 11th U.S. Cavalry, stationed nearby. One of the men she would have preferred to marry was Bonham's subordinate, Captain Hodgman (Walter Hale). She is unaware of his true nature, that he has fathered an illegitimate child with one of the girls on the ranch, Lena (Adora Andrews), and that, since he is really after the Canbys' money, he is now courting Estrella's young sister, Bonita (Eleanor Robson), on the sly. Even when she catches him bantering with Bonita he can throw her feelings into turmoil and make her uncertain of herself.

Hodgman: Now, don't say I stole your peace of mind. Lethargy isn't content. You were dreaming here in the hot sands like a torpid nestling. I talked of the ocean and the smell of the low tide, and you began to wake up—and you breathed deeper—as you are breathing now. (*Smiles and watches her*) The languor went out of your eyes, as it is going now, and your soul came into them—
Estrella: I have the love of the best man in the world.
Hodgman: Which should *fill* every empty hour, and yet—
Estrella: And I love *him.*
Hodgman: Almost like a father.

Lieutenant Denton (Vincent Serrano), Bonham's protégé, also loves Bonita. He learns that Estrella finally has succumbed to Hodgman's blandishments and is planning to elope, having first handed over her jewelry to the captain. At gunpoint, he forces Hodgman to give him the jewels and leave. Estrella locks the door of the room and attempts to explain her situation. But Bonham suddenly arrives and, angrily accepting appearances, demands that Denton resign. Denton takes work on the Canbys' ranch, and his proposal to Bonita is accepted. The cavalry stop by on their way to a new assignment. Lena's fiancé, Tony (Edgar Selwyn), has learned about Hodgman's perfidy and shoots him. Unfortunately, Denton is in the room at the time and his gun goes off. The dying man implicates him. The colonel has Denton arrested and sets up a trial. But the physician has removed the bullet from Hodgman's body, and it proves Denton's innocence. Estrella then reveals the whole story, which the gentlemanly Denton had refused to disclose, even at the risk of his career. She claims she has come to truly love Bonham and begs his forgiveness. At first he answers coldly, "When I come back," but, sensing how much his own rigid behavior has affected their marriage, he turns around and tellingly picks up a rose that Estrella had dropped on the floor and thrusts it into his shirt.

Critical paeans ran to "a perfect work of its kind" and "one of the best plays written by an American." Acting honors went to beautiful young Eleanor Robson, whose "captivating Bonita" was played with "charming vivacity and girlishness." Roberts's manly Canby was a close second. The settings and lighting were also praised, especially the adobe courtyard of the first and last acts, with the ranch on the right, the stables on the left, and the mountains that border the Aravipa Valley "in bold relief against the hot summer sky" and in the yellow light of an Arizona sunset.

Second-stringers had to suffer through one of the most inane, unpleasant farces in Broadway memory, Frederick Stanford's **Cupid Outwits Adam** (9-10-00, Bijou). A man named Adam, who had made money manufacturing yeast, leaves his money to a young girl on the condition she marry a man who, like him, is bald and harelipped. The girl prefers to run away with her fiancé, but they are involved in a train wreck, which leaves her new husband with a misshapen lip and hairless pate—and leaves her rich. The play gave up the struggle after Saturday night.

Two plays to premiere at combination houses the same evening were not much better, if at all. Charles E. Blaney and Charles A. Taylor, both usually so adept at catering to blue-collar audiences, came a cropper with **A Wife in Pawn** (9-10-00, Grand Opera), recounting how a debt-ridden young man will stop at nothing to scrounge up cash. He will even, as the title revealed, hock his wife. Critics felt the specialty acts were better than the comedy. J. E. Toole, "the singing comedian," was star and author of **The Gypsy German** (9-10-00, Third Ave.). As Rudolph, the gypsy, he woos the pretty Nadine away from rich Paul Volstein, but only after Volstein arranges to have Mercy Meldon, whom he once violated, kidnapped. Mercy escapes and spills the beans.

Switch parts if not partners became the byword briefly in midmonth. First to do so was John Drew, whose career lately had been given over to a succession of blasé *raisonneurs*. For the moment he joined the swelling ranks of swashbuckling heroes

in Charles Frohman's sumptuous production of **Richard Carvel** (9-11-00, Empire). Winston Churchill's novel was adapted by Edward E. Rose. Carvel loves Dorothy Manners (Ida Conquest), but the flirtatious girl has kept putting him off. Her father has prodded her to go to London to look over the mean, tricky Duke of Chartersea (Frank Losee). Having been kidnapped, then rescued at sea by John Paul Jones, Carvel also finds himself most conveniently in London. The duke provokes a sword fight with Carvel, first having planted one of his men in a position to stab Carvel in the back during the duel. Carvel catches on to the villain's intent and by his quick movements manages to have the duke's man stab the duke. Later Carvel serves nobly in the Revolution and thus wins Dorothy's hand. Some commentators carped that Drew was too old for the role (he turned forty-seven during the run), but almost all agreed that his knowing technique allowed him to belie his age most of the time. Edward G. Unitt's three interiors, including Carvel Hall in Maryland and a London tavern, garnered high praise. Frohman's ledger books remained comfortably in the black for the sixteen-week run and long tour.

Conversely, E. H. Sothern abandoned the type of modern romance he had played so profitably and turned to the dramatist who would supply him with roles for much of his remaining career—Shakespeare. His plunge into *Hamlet* at the Garden on the 17th was greeted enthusiastically, with more than one reviewer suggesting his "intelligent," "discreet," "poetic" interpretation established him as the logical heir to Booth. Even his appearance underscored the similarity. Dithmar observed, "His clustering dark hair, his handsome, mournful eyes, his broad, pale brow, his fine profile are all reminders of the greatest of our Hamlets." His wife, Virginia Harned, did not fare as well. Her Ophelia was dismissed as monotonous and saccharine. Sothern's text was traditional, although he did omit Hamlet's soliloquy on finding Claudius at his prayers. Unitt's massive, colorful settings were also admired, even if critics split on how well they were lit. One innovation was the illumination of ghost's face by a "ghastly light" hidden in his beaver. The production did two weeks of satisfactory business.

Caleb West (9-17-00, Manhattan) was Michael Morton's dramatization of F. Hopkinson Smith's novel. It was produced by one of the more responsible touring managers, Jacob Litt. Smith was purportedly himself a lighthouse builder, and his story centered on the building of one off Connecticut. Three men involved in the construction are the middle-aged West (Edwin Arden), a master diver; young Bill Lacey (Malcolm Williams), a rigger; and Captain Joe (George Fawcett), the superintendent. West has married a child bride, Betty (May Buckley), whom Lacey lusts after. When a storm swamps the construction site, Lacey is hurt attempting to rescue another workman. West carries him home and leaves Betty to nurse him. Lacey takes unfair advantage of the situation to lure Betty aboard a boat and head out to sea. The impression is that Betty has gone voluntarily. Captain Joe knows better and sails out to bring back the girl, but she is snubbed by the other women and by the heartbroken Caleb. It takes two years for the good captain to reconcile everyone. The first act, with the lighthouse not even half-finished and the storm hitting it, was hailed as a superb stage picture. In the last act the completed lighthouse was shown and its beacon lit in time to celebrate the happy finale. Fawcett's intuitive, kindly, and forceful captain was roundly applauded. The drama remained a month before heading back out on the road.

For the time Owen Davis continued to churn out cheap melodramas, which gave no hint he would one day win a Pulitzer Prize. (Of course, Pulitzer Prizes were also far in the future.) His latest to stop over for a week at a combination house was **Reaping the Whirlwind** (9-17-00, Star). Set during the Franco-Prussian War—no doubt for its colorful period settings and costumes—it told how Lisle Martel is tricked into marrying Max Von Loon, although the real love of her life is Lucien de Polonaise, heir to the estate on which her father is a steward. During the war Max captures Lucien, who is sentenced to be shot. Instead Lisle shoots Max, who with his dying breath orders his men to conduct the lovers safely across the frontier.

In **The Real Widow Brown** (9-17-00, Third Ave.), a man disguises himself as the widow only to have the lady herself appear inconveniently. Spiced with songs and dances, the farce-comedy, like so many earlier ones, teetered between straight play and musical comedy.

A beginning and an end were marked when **Sag Harbor** (9-27-00, Republic) opened. The beginning was the unveiling of Oscar Hammerstein's new theatre, which signaled the real beginning of 42nd Street as a major theatrical thoroughfare (since the American, near Eighth Avenue, never really caught on). But the premiere also marked the last time James A. Herne would offer a new play and his last New York appearance. His story, by his own admission, was not very fresh. In fact, he had used a similar one in *Hearts of Oak*. Two brothers, Ben (Forrest Robinson) and

Frank Turner (Lionel Barrymore), both court the orphaned Martha Reese (Julie A. Herne), whom Ben has helped raise. Although Martha prefers Frank, a sailor, she marries the older Ben out of a sense of obligation. Frank goes off to sea, but when he returns two years later he almost persuades Martha to elope with him. The kindly Captain Dan Marble (Herne) intervenes and, by telling a tale of a disastrous elopement, dissuades the couple. Frank settles for a schoolmarm who long has loved him.

The play had enjoyed a remarkable success on the road the previous season, including a "record-breaking" run in Boston. Contrary to legend, the New York press was not hostile, but it was sharply divided about the play. Among the naysayers, the *Commercial Advertiser* wrote, "It looks as if he had set about the construction of a popular drama with a certain local atmosphere, without having a story to tell, a character to present, or one strong mood to create; in short, without having anything to say." On the other hand, the *Herald* observed, "It is a charming reproduction of life and character. . . . Realism has been so often applied to problem plays of the Ibsen type that it has come to be associated with the gloomy and forbidding in drama. Mr. Herne is realistic in a wholly different way. His realism illumines the quaint and kindly side of life." Herne's performance was seen as "lovable," but not all the other actors were treated kindly. Lionel Barrymore was taken to task for not making anything of an "ungrateful" role, and he soon left the cast. To many, the best performance of the evening was given by William T. Hodge as a village gossip. Virtually all the critics agreed the mounting was excellent. A shipyard setting was littered with pine shavings (as two genuine boatbuilders worked away), sawhorses, ropes, and tools, and the stern of a large sloop was center stage. There was also another real dinner served, with clam pies brought in nightly from a nearby restaurant. The drama stayed two months, then continued on tour until shut by Herne's failing health. He died in June.

No pedant or phrasemaker ever spoke of "coastal dramas," but plays such as *Caleb West* and *Sag Harbor* were obviously near relations to rural dramas, in which outwardly unsophisticated figures demonstrated an understanding of human nature and a homey skill in handling it that put city slickers to shame. A classic of this genre was turned into an immensely popular theatre piece with the arrival of **David Harum** (10-1-00, Garrick). Edward Noyes Westcott's best-seller was dramatized by R. and M. W. Hitchcock, with an uncredited assist from Edward E. Rose.

Although Harum is the banker in the small upstate New York village of Homeville, his clerk tells a visitor, "He'd sooner make ten dollars on a hoss trade than a hundred right here in the office." One "hoss" trade Harum made some time back with wily Deacon Perkins left him stuck, and he is determined to get back at his neighbor. He sees his opportunity when he finds himself stuck a second time, on this occasion with a horse that he has been promised will "stand without hitchin'." It will, because it is a balker. Harum learns a trick that will make the horse move like lightning briefly, and he uses it to snooker the deacon, assuring him in turn that for all its apparent speed the horse will "stand without hitchin'." But Harum also has other concerns—notably two new arrivals in Homeville. One is John Lenox, Harum's prospective assistant, who was recommended to him by his friend, General Wolsey. The other is the new schoolmarm, who introduces herself as Cordelia Prendergast but soon turns out to be Wolsey's ward, Mary Blake. She has come to Homeville to be near John. Zeke Swinney, the town usurer, gains Mary's ear and turns her against Harum. Among other matters, he makes her believe that Harum is trying to swindle Widow Cullom out of her property—though it is really Swinney who is trying to do just that. Wolsey, concluding that Lenox may want Mary only for her money, comes to Homeville resolved to take her back to New York City with him. He is shocked to hear her opinion of Harum, and they agree that if Mary is correct she can remain in Homeville. Harum has overheard the conversation, and, deciding that Mary would be better staying close to Lenox, he rather showily offers her seeming proofs of his meanness. Mary storms furiously at him, but hers is nothing compared to the storm raging outside Harum's office window. A flash of lightning reveals the drenched deacon futilely attempting to goad his new mare, triumphantly confirming Mary's opinion as the second-act curtain falls.

In the last act, all the principals have assembled in Harum's home, where his widowed sister, Aunt Polly (Kate Meek), is preparing Christmas dinner. Harum tells them of how Widow Cullom's husband had given him his first chance to escape from an unhappy childhood. Now, in gratitude, he burns her mortgage. Mary realizes how unfair she has been, and her guardian consents to her marrying Lenox. Harum happily toasts the young couple, "the prettiest pair't I ever put in harness." Mary's disdain for Harum was not in the original novel but had been added by the adaptors to inject some theatrical tension into an essentially adramatic story. Several reviewers pounced on the change, condemning it as trite and unimaginative at the same time they acknowledged it was probably needed.

The play as a whole, while dismissed as literature, was welcomed as "pure and simple" and "hearteningly wholesome." Raising the evening to something approaching theatrical high art was William H. Crane's Harum, the best role he would ever have and, for many, the best performance he ever gave. Commentators ranked it alongside Jefferson's Rip and Raymond's Sellers. The *Sun* offered a detailed description, recording, "The clean-shaven red face with a wart near the large, firm-lipped mouth, the red and gray hair that left the crown of the head bare, the thick nose and the small blue eyes were all reproduced with fidelity. . . .Such divergence from the original as the actor permitted to himself was in urbanity. He was a genial old chap who grinned most of the time that he was not laughing right out loud. The crustiness and gruffness which the author had told of were moderated to almost the vanishing point." Charles Frohman's production became one of the era's biggest money-makers. Crane played Harum for three solid years (including this initial nineteen-week New York stand) and returned to it later. Without Crane, lesser road companies and stock troupes kept it alive for nearly twenty years, while Charles Coburn headed a major revival at the 1938 Mohawk Drama Festival.

Richard Mansfield also had a resounding, if less profitable, hit when he presented *Henry V* at the Garden on the 3rd. For sheer magnificence New York had rarely seen its like. Not only were Shakespeare's scenes lavishly mounted and his characters gorgeously bedecked, but eye-filling pageantry was added where Shakespeare probably never even imagined it. One long scene was a color-strewn pantomime representing the return of Henry's troops from Agincourt. In a large plaza at the end of London Bridge, townspeople and officials gathered to welcome the soldiers. Venders hawked their wares, watched from windows and housetops by citizens unable to crowd the street below. Flags and banners waved in the breeze as trumpets heralded the arrival of the army. Company after company of battleworn fighters paraded by. Wives and sweethearts broke through the mob to kiss loved ones. One young girl kept scanning the marchers, obviously looking for a familiar face. When the last of the marchers passed by she approached an officer. He whispered something, and she fainted. The excited crowds scarcely noticed. Mansfield's performance split the critics. The loyal William Winter called it "noble, authoritative, eloquent, and sympathetic." Dithmar, while generally impressed, regretted that some of the more fiery speeches lacked a "trumpet-toned magic." The *Dramatic Mirror,* displeased, called the actor physically and temperamentally "unfitted for the role." The entertainment ran four and a half hours, but that could not discourage playgoers. Only a previous booking (Bernhardt and Coquelin) forced Mansfield to take to the road after seven weeks, where he was equally successful all season.

Joseph Arthur's **Lost River** (10-3-00, 14th St.), representing a lower order of theatre, ran twelve weeks. It proved to be Arthur's swan song, but he still could provide his type of audience with the sort of sensation-melodrama they thrived on. Robert Blessing (William Courtleigh) is engaged to marry Gladys Middleton, daughter of his partner in a construction firm. The firm is building an aqueduct, and on his visits to the Indiana site Blessing has been smitten by Ora, a girl whose past is wrapped in secrecy. When the workers' pay is delayed en route from New York, they threaten to dynamite the aqueduct. Gladys and Ora's other suitor, Bill Loucks, conspire to come between Blessing and Ora by preventing the pay from being delivered. The results are a feverish bicycle race (with a picket fence speeding by on the panorama behind); an attempted holdup of Ora, who has taken it upon herself to deliver the money, when she arrives on horseback at a tollgate; and Blessing's rescue of Ora from the Lost River after Loucks has grabbed her and jumped in the water with her (the river was represented by the usual tank). It turns out that Ora is Gladys's illegitimate sister, the daughter of her father's youthful indiscretion.

There were touches of what a later generation would call "soap opera" in Harriet Ford and Beatrice de Mille's **The Greatest Thing in the World** (10-8-00, Wallack's). Mrs. de Mille was the widow of Henry C. de Mille and mother of William C. and Cecil B. de Mille. The ladies' plot spotlighted Virginia Bryant (Sarah Cowell LeMoyne), whose late husband had been loving (the greatest thing in the world) but a drunkard. One of her two sons presents little problem, but the other (Robert Edeson) seems to be following his father's dissolute path. He is also a forger. To save his impending marriage, she agrees to abandon the gentleman (Wilton Lackaye) who has been courting her and wed someone she does not love. The son discovers her willingness to sacrifice her own happiness and promises to mend his ways. Good acting was all that saved this treacly Liebler and Co. production from quick failure. To bolster sagging attendance, the

producers soon added Israel Zangwill's **The Moment of Death** (10-24-00), in which a duchess faints and during this state dreams she has caused a duel to the death between her elderly husband and her lover.

Blanche Walsh, often publicized as the quickest study in the theatre, was the star of Eugene W. Presbrey's **Marcelle** (10-8-00, Broadway). The heroine is a French Huguenot who loves an English soldier (Joseph Kilgour) but renounces him and agrees to marry a Catholic chevalier in hopes of sparing her co-religionists. The chevalier proves treacherous, so the girl and the soldier flee to Canada, followed by the Frenchman. There, as a lit fuse burns slowly toward a powder magazine below them, the girl watches the soldier and Frenchman duel. The chevalier is killed, and the lovers run out just as the magazine explodes. Critics felt the confused, dull play was not worth the study—quick or otherwise. Originally scheduled for a month's run, it was taken off after three weeks, and Miss Walsh substituted a revival of *More Than Queen* for her final week.

Pierre Decourcelle's *Le Petit Huit,* done as **Self and Lady,** (10-8-00, Madison Square) was an even shorter-lived failure. It told of a wife who arranges a liaison with an opera singer, not knowing the singer is actually her own despised husband.

Combination houses were busy, too. In Walter Fessler's *A Ride for Life* (10-8-00, Third Ave.), another heroic Jack is falsely accused of murder by the real murderer and must hustle between Chihuahua and New Orleans to clear his name. At least the settings were unusual. **A Wise Guy** (10-8-00, Star), which had toured prosperously during the previous season, found an English lord mistaking an actress for an heiress. She enlists a piano mover to impersonate her supposedly rich daddy. At the Grand, Louis James and Kathryn Kidder brought in their touring *Midsummer Night's Dream.*

If romantic swashbucklers were riding a crest at the moment, George C. Hazleton's **Mistress Nell** (10-9-00, Bijou) represented a novel twist: a lady wields the sword. The actress Nell Gwyn (so spelled in the programs) knows that her rival for the affections of Charles II (Aubrey Boucicault) is the Duchess of Portsmouth, who is in league with the Duke of Buckingham to trick the King into signing papers that will benefit the French. Nell comes to the duchess's ball dressed as a man, courts the duchess, gets hold of the papers, and briefly crosses swords with the king. During the duel she learns that she, not the duchess, is the king's favorite. Yet she must be content to know that though she is "Charles's queen" she can never be England's. Little was expected of the play. Rain and these low expectations kept opening night box office to a little over $60. Morning-after reviews changed all that. The *World* typified reaction when it called the entertainment "a complete surprise and a complete success." Her performance as the former orange vendor elevated Henrietta Crosman to stardom.

. . .

Henrietta Crosman (1861–1944) was born in Wheeling, W. Va., and made her debut in 1883. She had performed for Augustin Daly, A. M. Palmer, and the Frohman brothers before landing this role so relatively late in her career. An attractive if somewhat pouty-faced woman, she was admired particularly for what J. Rankin Towse called her "spontaneous vivacity."

. . .

A not too dissimilar piece, **Her Majesty** (10-15-00, Manhattan), which J. I. C. Clarke took from Elizabeth Knight Tomkins's novel, also featured a lady in the leading role. Honoria (Grace George) is Queen of Nordenmark, which lies "somewhere between Germany and Austria." Her government, headed by her self-serving prime minister, Baron Hausman (Fraser Coulter), is corrupt and her people on the edge of rebellion. Honoria has refused to wed any of the worthless nobles Hausman has chosen for her. As Prince Otto had earlier in the season, she goes out among her people incognito. There she meets a dashing, charming young man, who proves to be Count Waldeck (Frank Worthing). An uprising breaks out, and the pair are arrested. They are imprisoned together long enough for Honoria to fall in love. Waldeck is removed to a dungeon and sentenced to death. Honoria manages to escape. The next day Honoria holds court. (She is worried if her hair is properly coifed and if her crown is set straight.) When Waldeck is brought before her, she pardons and proposes to the startled count. Together they banish the wicked Hausman and his cronies.

Yet another lovely star appeared in short order. With Fanny Davenport dead, one question was who would perform Sarah Bernhardt's roles on American stages. For the moment the answer seemed to be Maude Adams. The play was Edmond Rostand's **L'Aiglon** (10-22-00, Knickerbocker), which Charles Frohman offered in Louis Parker's translation. The story of the brief life and pathetic death of Napoleon's son was well known and, in this drama, had been a huge success in Paris. Critical response to the work was largely favorable, but interest in the star overwhelmed it. Dithmar's reaction was representative: "She looks the scion . . . to the life. One never

thinks of her as a woman from the beginning of the play to its sad last scene. . . . Her portrayal is flawless. Not a gesture or a pose is out of place. . . . The young artist's integrity of purpose, her dramatic aptitude, and sympathy shine through all the performance." The production fattened Frohman's coffers for nine weeks and did even better on tour.

The fast-rising Liebler and Co. scored another success when it reached back to revive *Monte Cristo* at the capacious Academy of Music on the 23rd. Five of the nation's leading set designers—Ernest Albert, Homer Emens, Gates and Morange, Ernest M. Gros, and John Young—painted the stage pictures. Albert's fourth-act ballroom set won the loudest applause. And of course there was James O'Neill to play Dantes—a role he already had performed about 4,000 times. There was no hint that he could play the role in his sleep. According to one critic he gave "fullest value" to every word and gesture. The play did ten weeks of good business.

The last of October's premieres was at a combination house. Dan Darleigh's **Old Si Stebbins** (10-29-00, Third Ave.), with the playwright in the title role, was at heart a rehash of *The Old Homestead*. When Stebbins, a Maine farmer, objects to his daughter's marrying the man of her choice, the youngsters elope to Boston. Si follows and, after numerous encounters with city folk, some comic, some menacing, persuades the newlyweds to return to the farm.

The villain in Walter Fessler's **The Great White Diamond** (11-5-00, Star) was rather unusual. First of all, he is a "nyctalops," a man who can see well in the dark but is virtually blind in bright light. Moreover, he has a mania for chloroforming his victims. When the hero arrives in London from South Africa he has in his possession a large diamond. The villain chloroforms him and steals it, but the heroine steals it from the villain and flees to America. There the villain chloroforms her and places her in a mailbag suspended on a crane, to await a speeding train that will pick up the bag. The hero rescues her, so the villain chloroforms her again and leaves her in an old mill, which he sets afire. Thanks to a human bridge (shades of *The Span of Life*) formed by his friends, the hero rescues her again. The villain (played by Fessler) is finally brought to justice, and the lovers are allowed to wed.

Many of the original London company, including John Hare and Irene Vanbrugh, recreated their roles when Charles Frohman imported Pinero's **The Gay Lord Quex** (11-12-00, Criterion). Pinero's tale focused on a reprobate lord who promises to reform if a young lady will marry him. The girl's sister tries to stop the marriage, but the lord's determined good intentions win the day.

M. E. Henley's **Slaves of Opium** (11-12-00, Third Ave.) retraced well-trodden paths through the worst of Chinatown to tell of a young Irish-American hounded by a malevolent Italian baron. As Fessler had a week before, the author assumed the role of the villain.

Heavyweight champions of this era were sure to find a spot on its stages, so no one was surprised when Jim Jeffries, the latest title-holder, was offered as star of Clay M. Greene's **A Man from the West** (11-12-00, Grand Opera). Jeffries played a he-man Montana sheriff who is painfully girlshy. The usual false accusations and other typical melodramatic incidents test his mettle before he and his friends join a Wild West show and come to Coney Island, where the sheriff fights a three-round bout that settles some nasty old scores.

South Africa, during the Boer War, was the site of Madeline Merli and Charles E. Blaney's touring melodrama **An African King** (11-19-00, Star). Their heroine was an American girl, the niece of a Boer general. She loves an English officer but is coveted by her treacherous cousin. The cousin wangles the officer's arrest and, when the Englishman escapes, shoots and wounds him. At this point the heroine agrees to marry her cousin to spare her lover further harm. However, after the marriage the cousin discovers his wife is still seeing the Englishman. He locks them in a diamond mine and blows it up. The lovers escape across a chasm bridged by a fallen tree. The forced marriage is declared illegal. Critics sneered but admitted the audience thought the play "a go."

The theatre moved from the ridiculous to the almost sublime when the curtain rose on the troupe headed by Bernhardt and Coquelin at the Garden on the 26th. They opened with *L'Aiglon*, thus pitting the fifty-six-year-old French star against the twenty-eight-year-old American. If reviewers allowed that Bernhardt's performance was matchless, with her magnificent voice and regal bearing untouched by age, the production seems not to have hurt trade at the Knickerbocker and may indeed have helped it. Coquelin received short shrift in this outing but was compensated by the acclaim his Cyrano was accorded. The company offered *La Tosca*, *La Dame aux camélias*, and a controversial *Hamlet*, with Bernhardt raising eyebrows as the prince and Coquelin all but stealing the evening as the gravedigger.

Daniel Frohman found few takers for his production of Walter Frith's London hit **The Man of Forty** (11-26-00, Daly's). A widower (John Mason) would marry a woman (Hilda Spong) who may or may not be a widow. When her long-missing, rascally husband (Edward Morgan) suddenly reappears, the widower confronts him, and the confrontation leads to a fatal stroke. The widower and the lady are free to wed.

If November was a relatively slow month for midseason openings in New York, the theatre was bustling across the nation. The *Dramatic Mirror* listed over 400 dramatic companies (musicals were listed separately) crisscrossing the nation. Some plays were decades old. For example, *Fabio Romani* spent two weeks giving one-night stands in Custer and Edgemont, S.D.; New Castle and Sheridan, Wyo.; and Billings, Big Timber, Great Falls, Butte (two nights there), and Anaconda, Mont. A new play called *The Honest Blacksmith* was trekking through upstate New York.

The unappealingly titled **The Sprightly Romance of Marsac** (12-3-00, Republic) was derived by William Young and Molly Elliot Seawell from the latter's novel. It provided a starring vehicle for hefty Maclyn Arbuckle, who played Marsac, a young man living with a roommate in the Latin Quarter. They are so badly in debt that Marsac plants an item in the newspapers saying his roommate's uncle has died and left the roommate millions. Formerly glowering creditors bow and scrape until the landlady exposes the scheme. When things look blackest the uncle appears and pays their debts.

The busy Edward E. Rose, already responsible for *Richard Carvel* and, in good measure, for *David Harum*, worked with novelist Paul Leicester Ford to dramatize Ford's novel of Revolutionary days, **Janice Meredith** (12-10-00, Wallack's). Stardoms were being awarded left and right, and the play's premiere let round-faced, dark-haired Mary Mannering see her name above the title. Janice (Mannering) is the daughter of a Tory sympathizer, but she loves Charles Frownes (Robert Drouet), whose real name is John Brereton and who, though the son of Lord Howe, is pro-American. Frownes is arrested and led to believe that Janice has betrayed him, but after he escapes and requires a hiding place, Janice offers him the sanctuary of her bedroom, where she has time to make the proper explanations. At Yorktown the British attempt to abduct Janice. This time it becomes Frownes's turn to play rescuer. The surrender settles matters to the lovers' liking. Adjectives such as "conventional" and nouns such as "twaddle" summed up the critics' judgment of the comedy, but virtually to a man they found Miss Mannering charming. The play ran three months.

Premieres beckoned at two combination houses. H. Grattan Donnelly's **The American Girl** (12-17-00, Third Ave.) was a rather tame affair. A Virginia girl marries an Englishman, but he is called home to accept a large estate. While in England the villain leads him to believe that his wife has died, so he makes no attempt to return to America. After a time his wife crosses the Atlantic to find him. The villain manages to keep them apart until the wife is down to her last pennies. In desperation she puts up for sale a painting her husband had made during their honeymoon. One guess who comes in to look at the painting. Songs and dances relieved what few tensions the play had.

Songs and dances were also offered in Lincoln J. Carter's **The Flaming Arrow** (12-17-00, Star), but some of the dances were of a type rarely seen on the stage. They were Indian war dances. The melodrama starred Go-Won-Go Mohawk. By now commentators apparently had given up disputing whether or not she was a genuine redskin. More than half the players sported such Indian names as Chief Red Flash, Chief Kenjockety, and Corn Planter. The star, her first entrance on horseback, impersonated an Indian brave, White Eagle, who loves the daughter of an army colonel. An American lieutenant and a Mexican are White Eagle's rivals for Mary's affections. The lieutenant incites the Indians to revolt and kidnaps Mary. White Eagle quells the uprising and rescues his sweetheart. As one critic reported, "all ends happily," but whether this meant turn-of-the-century playgoers accepted a racially mixed marriage is unclear. Perhaps the fact that White Eagle was a trouser role allowed prejudices to be set aside for the night. One point audiences could not accept, at least not without snickers and more unconcealed laughter, was the orchestra's accompanying the war dances with "couchee-couchee music."

Daniel Frohman had a hit when he presented R. C. Carton's London comedy **Lady Huntworth's Experiment** (12-21-00, Daly's). A duchess, after being divorced on trumped-up grounds by her besotted husband, takes employment as a cook. She leaves the job when she comes into an inheritance and falls in love with an army man. Hilda Spong and John Mason were the leading players.

George Broadhurst's **The House That Jack Built** (12-24-00, Madison Square) had won acclaim and done excellent business on its long pre-Broadway road tour. New Yorkers, as so often, had other ideas about it, so after just over two weeks it headed back into the hinterlands. Still, it had its moments. Having built his house, Dr. Jack (John Findlay) hires Sir Edward Singleton (Charles Cherry) to decorate it. Sir Edward, smitten by Dr. Jack's daughter, Hester, and learning she dislikes titles, bribes a workman to lend him overalls and call him brother. That workman was Willie Slab (Thomas A. Wise), and he stole the show. Although hired as a paperhanger, he claims he is "at heart a plumber." Whatever his calling, he is not above adding Sir Edward's bribe to his "collection of souvenir ten-dollar bills." A high point was the end of the second act, when Willie and Sir Edward wager they can paper a whole room in three minutes. They do. Then the curtain rises again to show two scrub-women cleaning up the mess they have made. Second only to Wise as a laugh-getter was the irrepressible Annie Yeamans, who played Willie's Irish inamorata, "using all her old and desirable stock of nods and becks and wreathed smiles."

Special matinees, which often served in lieu of tryouts, remained commonplace. One curious instance was the production of Harrison J. Wolfe's **Cashel Byron** (12-27-00, Herald Square). Pirated from Shaw's novel, it prompted one critic to say, "Shaw's story might make a good play." Shaw made his own version a few months later.

New Year's Eve gave firstnighters a handsome choice of openings. Most successful was Lorimer Stoddard's dramatization of F. Marion Crawford's **In the Palace of the King** (12-31-00, Republic). It was mounted by Liebler and Co., which had begun to vie with Charles Frohman as Broadway's leading producer. Prince John (Robert T. Haines) has returned victorious from his battles against the Moors. He loves Dolores (Viola Allen) and she loves him, but the Princess of Eboli (Marcia Van Dresser), who wants John for herself and knows that King Philip II (Eben Plympton) is fond of Dolores, plots to break up the romance. Moreover, the king has attempted to murder Cardinal de Torres (Edgar L. Davenport) and turns on John as a scapegoat when news of the failed attempt becomes public. Dolores appeals for reason and justice. Her appeal, "first but a whispered one[,] . . . becomes persuasive then seductive, and, finally, in an outburst in which her love for her Prince is coupled deftly with an appeal to their admiration for his heroism" she wins over the courtiers and king.

No such good fortune greeted the season's second play about Nell Gwynne, Paul Kester's **Sweet Nell of Old Drury** (12-31-00, Knickerbocker). The occasion marked Ada Rehan's first appearance before the footlights since Daly's death. She was welcomed noisily; the play was not. Nell, who sells oranges outside the theatre, loves her savior, Sir Roger Fairfax, but when she discovers he is engaged to

Lady Olivia Vernon, she selflessly agrees to help them. They need help because the vindictive Lord Jeffreys (D. H. Harkins), chief justice of England, is out for Roger's head simply because Roger's father once had whipped Jeffreys. Charles II admires Nell's beauty and spunkiness and promotes her ambitions as an actress. The jealous courtiers side with Jeffreys. Nell uses her histrionic gifts to masquerade as Jeffreys and exculpate Roger. The king, who for a time thought she had become an ingrate and troublemaker, appreciates her all the more. The play mixed farce and melodrama deftly, but the writing was "puerile" and old-fashioned, even including frequent use of the obsolescent aside. Thus when the king first meets Nell (who does not recognize him) and proposes to buy her oranges he discovers he has no money.

Nell: (*Aside. As she draws out her purse*) Poor fellow! (*To Charles*) There! My week's profits! (*Counts out money; tosses some in her hand*) I'll keep a few halfpence.

The play's two-week run marked the last time Ada Rehan ventured a new work. Although she was only forty, her few remaining appearances before her premature retirement would be in roles Daly had trained her for.

Charles Frohman fared much better with his importation of Henry Arthur Jones's **Mrs. Dane's Defense** (12-31-00, Empire), which ran for three months. Margaret Anglin headed the cast as a woman with a past who, even after she is exposed, heads out to make a better world for herself.

From England, too, came E. S. Willard and his company. In their month-long engagement at the Garden they offered *David Garrick, The Professor's Love Story, The Middleman,* and one new play, **Tom Pinch** (1-8-01), taken from incidents in *Martin Chuzzlewit.*

Herbert Kelcey and his wife, Effie Shannon, were starred in Madeleine Lucette Ryley's **My Lady Dainty** (1-8-01, Madison Square). A young governess (Miss Shannon) must choose between an upright architect (Guy Bates Post) and a lord's ne'er-do-well son (Kelcey). The lord's son persuades her to elope secretly with him to America. There he falls in with bad company and goes broke. When his father writes that all is forgiven if he will return and marry an heiress, he deserts his wife. The architect comes to America and proposes that she forget her worthless spouse, but she returns to England and helps bring about her husband's reformation.

Paul Kester did better by Julia Marlowe than he had by Ada Rehan. His **When Knighthood Was in Flower** (1-14-01, Criterion), adapted from Charles Major's novel, was one of the season's biggest hits, chalking up 176 performances. It provided yet another gold mine for Charles Frohman. Henry VII wants his sister, Mary Tudor (Marlowe), to marry decrepit old Louis XII of France. Since she loves Charles Brandon (Bruce McRae), her response is: "Say to the King my brother that I will see him and his Kingdom sunk in hell before I'll marry Louis of France." When she discovers that Charles's letters to her have been intercepted, she disguises herself as a cavalier, flees the palace, and meets Charles at the Bow and String Tavern. There she persuades him to elope with her to New Spain. But the lovers are caught, and Mary is forced to wed the French king. The exertion of attempting to dance with her proves too much, and he drops dead. Louis's successor would keep her in France, but Brandon rescues her. Having done her duty, she is allowed to marry Charles, and he is made Duke of Suffolk. Scenery and costumes were attractive, but it was Miss Marlowe's "infinite grace" and "captivating show of spirit" that accounted in large measure for the romance's success.

The prolific Owen Davis had another thrill-packed melodrama ready, **Lost in the Desert** (1-14-01, Star). Davis's hero, one more in a long line named Jack, is falsely accused of robbing a bank. Jack, his sweetheart, and the real robber, who loves Jack's girl, all board a ship. There Jack attempts to uncover evidence in the villain's stateroom. He is caught and put in chains. Seeing his chance to be rid of Jack once and for all, the robber sets fire to the ship. The next act finds the principals on a desert island. The robber goads a band of Arabs to take the goodies captive. Jack is tied to a horse and the horse sent wandering over the waste. Luckily, one friendly Arab frees Jack. The villain has several other tricks up his sleeve, but he is finally confounded and the heroine secure in the hero's arms. The "Arabs" were more than the robber's accomplices. They were also acrobats whose turn was included among the specialties.

The feisty, busty Amelia Bingham, determined to become a leading actress-manager, gave New York one of the season's most memorable plays when she produced Clyde Fitch's **The Climbers** (1-15-01, Bijou). From the very moment the curtain rose, the audience knew this would be no run-of-the-mill social drama. Noticeably subdued servants are seen restoring chairs, obviously assembled for some sort of congregation, to their accustomed places. Four women, dressed all in black and veiled, enter. The ladies are Mrs. Hunter (Madge Carr Cook) and her daughters, the spoiled, selfish Clara (Minnie Dupree), the pleasant Jessica (Maud Monroe), and Blanche Sterling (Miss Bingham), the only married daughter and the only family member apparently genuinely grieved by her father's death. Clara is upset because her mourning means she cannot have her coming-out party and will not be able to wear the expensive gowns she has bought. The women receive a new shock when their family lawyer advises them that Mr. Hunter died broke. Paying their formal respects are several women and a social butterfly of a man, who, like Mrs. Hunter, have been determined social climbers.

Their visit provides one of the play's few bits of comic relief—savage comic relief at that. The guests' private remarks are brutal, one observing, "Mrs. Hunter went to the most expensive decorator in town and told him, no matter what it cost, to go ahead and do his *worst!*" Their behavior toward the mourners is cruelly thoughtless, especially when the sharp-tongued Miss Godesby (Clara Bloodgood) haggles with Mrs. Hunter over the price of gowns Clara will no longer need. Even Mr. Hunter's sister, Ruth (Annie Irish), is not kindly disposed to her sister-in-law, but she agrees to help the family and shows her confidence in Blanche's husband, Richard (Frank Worthing), by entrusting bonds to him. She does not know that Richard is a crook and is on the verge of bankruptcy. Blanche discovers the truth in a letter left by her father, but, hoping to change her husband's ways, she burns the letter. Blanche's hopes are shattered when Richard uses Ruth's bonds to speculate and fails. Richard is confronted by his oldest friend and Blanche's longtime admirer, Edward Warden (Robert Edeson). His actions to protect the family make Blanche realize she loves Edward. Richard, sensing the hopelessness of his situation, takes an overdose of sulphate of morphine. He writes a note asking Blanche to "forget all my sins, wipe out the memory of my name." Blanche and Edward enter the room, and Edward understands what has occurred.

Warden: (to Blanche) Give me your hand. (*Softly, with a man's tenderness in his voice.*) He is going away for good.
Blanche: Away?
Warden: For good.
Blanche: (slowly withdrawing her hand) For good? (*She looks from Sterling to Warden*) What does he mean?
Warden: We will know when he wakes.

According to the *Times*, the first-night curtain fell in silence because the audience, hitherto "friendly," was dismayed by the ending. Even some perceptive critics did not know what to make of the play. The *Dramatic Mirror* remarked that Fitch had "ventured daringly, for the sake of novelty, to the very edge of the possible in stage-craft." Some passages of infelicitous writing, such as Blanche's awkward soliloquy at the end of the first act, were pounced upon. On the other hand, Fitch, who staged most of his own plays, devised a startling bit of stage business by having Sterling's second-act confession spoken in total darkness, so that he would not confront the eyes of his accusers. All in all, most critics agreed with the trade sheet that the audience had been gripped by "a very human and very sympathetic play." Performances, too, were extolled. If Miss Bingham was not the strongest of emotional actresses, she was a very intelligent one. Worthing earned the highest praise for imbuing an outwardly evil man with a certain inner warmth. Surprisingly gratifying was the characterization offered by Clara Bloodgood, a relative newcomer, as the clawing, tactless Miss Godesby. The drama ran five months.

The most popular actress of the season had been long dead, but she was resurrected for a third time in Mrs. C. A. Doremus's **Nell Gwyn** (1-21-01, Murray Hill). The play was dismissed and quickly disappeared, but two players did not. In a bit of nepotism the Henry V. Donnelly Stock Company's Nell was Mr. Donnelly's sister, Dorothy, who went on to become a noted actress, librettist, and lyricist. In the small role of Frances Stuart was another Frances, Frances Starr, whom David Belasco would make famous.

The Honest Blacksmith (1-21-01, Star) came in from the backwaters for a one-week stopover. William Gill, best known as librettist of the 1884 musical *Adonis,* was the author. Starred was the season's second celebrated prizefighter to trod the boards, Bob Fitzsimmons. The play purportedly was based on incidents in Fitzsimmons's life. In the first act he made a horseshoe and shod a horse. Then he decided to become a fighter. Slocum Dunlap, "a very well-fed, oily villain," tries to throw monkey wrenches in his path, but in the last act Fitzsimmons punches his way to a $30,000 prize. Critics announced that Fitzsimmons was a better actor than Sullivan, Corbett, or Jeffries, but with that they ran out of encouraging words.

No prize was awarded to **Midnight in Chinatown** (1-21-01, Third Avenue), certainly no prize for originality. Perhaps his awareness of how unoriginal he was kept the play's author from coming forward. His hero was Joe Wallace, "an engineer who is falsely accused of most of the crimes common in sensational melodrama." To clear himself he travels from the Mountain Top House to the Bonanza mine, the Owl Saloon, San Francisco's Market Street, a prison, and, finally, Chinatown.

With so many hits creating a theatre shortage, producers were desperate. A newly built music hall had been hurriedly converted to a playhouse so that *Mistress Nell* could continue its unexpectedly successful run. Now it offered a new play, Leo Ditrichstein and Robert Grant's **Unleavened Bread** (1-26-01, Savoy), based on Grant's novel. A spotlight coldly picked out Selma White (Elizabeth Tyree), a selfish, social-climbing "new" woman. She walks out on her first husband at the merest hint of infidelity, drives her second husband to an early grave, and corrupts her third-husband-to-be, a governor (George Fawcett), into vetoing a bill so that he will be appointed senator. Despite its unpleasant story, the play was billed as a comedy. Its best comic performance was given by Eleanor Robson, whose "engaging personality, sweet, rich voice, and dramatic skill" shone in her portrayal of a lady from high society. It was a role she would one day play in real life.

Charles Frohman's newest star would also marry, albeit unhappily, a socially prominent figure, but she would spend most of her long, distinguished career on the stage. She was, of course, Ethel Barrymore.

. . .

Ethel Barrymore (1879–1959) was born in Philadelphia into an old, respected theatrical family. Her parents were Maurice and Georgiana Drew Barrymore. She made her debut in 1894 playing opposite her grandmother, Mrs. Drew, in *The Rivals*. She played several minor roles before sailing for London to perform with William Gillette in *Secret Service* and then act with Irving at the Lyceum. Her "fluttering eyes, the throaty voice, and the imperious beauty" gave her a "special alchemy."

. . .

For her first starring vehicle Frohman selected a Clyde Fitch play. (Fitch would have a third new play on Broadway two nights later, and all three would be unquestioned hits.) **Captain Jinks of the Horse Marines** (2-4-01, Garrick) was a change of pace for Fitch, a frothy romantic comedy. A Cunarder has docked in New York. On the pier is a crowd of reporters, obviously waiting for the appearance of a special celebrity. Most of the passengers have disembarked. Then a newsboy's shrill whistle alerts the reporters. There at the top of the gangplank stands a beautiful young woman. she is wearing an ermine fur tippet and carrying a muff and a tiny black-and-tan dog. Rushing down the gangplank she shouts, "Hip! hip! hurrah! Here we are at last on

American soil—planks—never mind, *soil—E Pluribus Unum!*" The young lady once had been Aurelia Johnson of Trenton, N.J. But now she is Mme Trentoni, an international prima donna. If she charms the reporters, she utterly beguiles Captain Robert Carrolton Jinks (H. Reeves-Smith), who makes a written wager for $1000 with his friends that he can win her love. He quickly does. Even the starchy disapproval of his nose-in-the-air mother (Mrs. Whiffen) cannot discourage the young couple. But on the eve of her major concert Aurelia is shown the note. At first she is too upset to sing. It remains for Jinks to convince her how genuine his love is, so all turns out for the best.

Time has imparted a rosy glow to this famous debut, but contemporary notices were hardly glowing. Many were downright hostile. "It is not a good play, not even a tolerable character picture" and "weak stuff" were among the assessments of Fitch's effort. Nor did Miss Barrymore send all the reviewers into rapture. "Not better than probably some score or more young actresses presently rated as ordinary," "The charm of Ethel Barrymore as yet is only the charm of high-spirited youth and infectious gayety," and "The triumph scored last night is a personal one for Miss Barrymore, who . . . acted with taste and spirit" illustrate the gamut of critical response. Yet Frohman clearly knew what his public wanted. *Captain Jinks* ran twenty-one weeks and returned for a fortnight in the fall prior to heading out for a long tour.

Henry Miller starred in an equally weak play, Madeleine Lucette Ryley's **Richard Savage** (2-4-01, Lyceum), but it was not the sort of drama the public would flock to. The dissolute poet loves Elizabeth Wilbur (Florence Rockwell). Savage discovers that her guardian, Mrs. Brett, is actually his own mother, who angrily refuses to acknowledge her maternity and becomes his enemy. He must also fight a duel with his rival, Mr. Sinclair, and when Sinclair is killed, Savage is imprisoned for murder. His friends arrange a pardon, but it comes too late. Savage dies embittered.

Over the Sea (2-4-01, Third Ave.) was an English melodrama consigned to touring houses. Its hero loves a village maiden. His rival makes a false accusation stick, and the hero is exiled to Australia. There he becomes rich. He returns to England in time to confound the villain, who is threatening to foreclose on the mortgage of the heroine's mother if the heroine will not marry him.

Another hit in a season of hits was **Under Two Flags** (2-5-01, Garden), which Paul Potter took from Ouida's novel. Other versions had been around for years, but this was the first to play a major Broadway house. Although the dramatization was condemned as errant claptrap, Frohman and David Belasco combined to mount a stunning production. When the Marquis of Chateauroy (Campbell Gollan) presents a forged will that deprives Bertie Cecil (Francis Carlyle) of his rightful inheritance, Bertie's fiancée, Lady Venetia, deserts him in favor of Chateauroy. In despair Bertie, under an assumed name, joins the French forces in Algiers. There he falls in love with Cigarette (Blanche Bates), a camp follower or *vivandière*. Chateauroy is appointed head of the regiment, and when Bertie learns that Lady Venetia has come with him, he attempts to arrange a meeting. Cigarette gets wind of the tryst and blurts it out to Chateauroy, not knowing he is the woman's husband. Chateauroy comes in on the meeting, a fight ensues, and Bertie is arrested and sentenced to death for striking an officer. Cigarette appeals to General Lamoriciere to spare Bertie. She gets her way after she saves the life of the general's son, who had fallen into the hands of a "witch-doctoress."

The scene now changes to the Chellah Gorge, "the finest setting of its kind ever exhibited in New York. In the foreground is a spring and drinking pool besides which stands a solitary palm tree. Beyond, and stretching up to the flies, is a series of rocky peaks, in splendid perspective. Up through the rocks winds a trail upon which, when the scene is first disclosed, stand groups of Bedouin, watching for the coming of Cigarette, whom they believe is a witch and whom they plan to murder." As the Bedouin seize her "the outposts give warning of an approaching simoon. The wind shrieks among the crags, the palm tree bends almost to the ground and the sand whirls in clouds over the prostrate Bedouin. In the midst of the storm Cigarette mounts her horse and . . . dashes this way and that, and escapes." Bertie is freed and learns of the marquis's chicanery. They fight a duel. Bertie's shot kills Chateauroy, but Chateauroy's bullet strikes Cigarette, and she dies in Bertie's arms. Blanche Bates, known in private as something of a tomboy, found the role of Cigarette even more than congenial than that of Cho-Cho-San. Coupled with Ernest Gros's magnificent settings—which also presented, among others, a curio shop, the winter garden of a French mansion, an Algerian wine shop, and the Casbah—and Belasco's brilliant stage effects, the play was an indisputable crowd-pleaser. It ran sixteen weeks, then toured.

The opening of William A. Brady's production of **Lovers' Lane** (2-6-01, Manhattan) meant that Clyde Fitch had not only given playgoers three successful works in short order but, with Effie Shannon starring in an upscale remounting of *Barbara Frietchie* at the Academy of Music, had a then record-breaking four works playing in Manhattan at the same time. Many critics who took note of the fact also used the occasion to snipe at the playwright for churning out pieces too quickly and thoughtlessly. The public disagreed. For the new play, whatever its demerits, worked capitally onstage. Furthermore, it offered yet another change of pace and style for Fitch. If nothing else, no one could accuse him of copying himself. In an interview at season's end he was asked what made his plays so popular. His reply was, "The power of amusing. . . . It will be a long time before the American theatregoer will give substantial encouragement to psychological and poetical plays such as Hauptmann, Sudermann and Ibsen are producing. As regards my plays, I always strive to convey a moral in each of them without making the lesson obtrusive. But preaching on the stage is unpopular; to amuse and interest is the thing."

The moral of his rustic idyll would seem to have been goodness and kindness pay. The Reverend Singleton (Ernest Hastings) is a good-hearted, open-minded man, who has no objection to billiards or cards. In this he is the opposite of Deacon Steele, who proclaims, "A hell that was good enough for our grandfathers is good enough for us." Most of the old biddies who cross the reverend's path seem in league with the Deacon. When they learn that Mrs. Woodbridge (Brandon Douglas) is divorced, they force her to resign from the church choir and ostracize her. Singleton takes her into his house, already crowded with village needy. By theatrical coincidence—and it was for points such as this that reviewers jumped on Fitch—Herbert Woodbridge (Edward J. Ratcliffe) appears and asks the minister to marry him to Mary Larkin (Nanette Comstock). The clergyman persuades the couple to wait a while and give the idea of marrying more thought. Through his good offices the Woodbridges are reconciled within a few months, and he himself weds Mary. The mounting touched a responsive chord in playgoers. The first act showed the minister's simple but appealing home. The second act took place in front of the schoolhouse, with children playing all the games theatregoers had played when they were young. The last two acts showed the orchard path—Lovers' Lane—behind the minister's house, first in autumn with apples on the trees, and then in spring with the apple blossoms in bloom. Playgoers ignored reviewers' cavils, so the work ran profitably for 127 showings.

Another playwright who could point to more than one success in the season was Augustus Thomas. And, like Fitch, he achieved it with a notable change of pace. His farce **On the Quiet** (2-11-01, Madison Square) starred William Collier as Robert Ridgeway, a young man who has dropped out of Yale to marry Agnes Colt (Louise Allen). While Agnes has inherited $4 million from her late father, his will gives her another $16 million if she marries with her brother's approval. But the brother (Brigham Royce) is a snob. Having married off one sister to an English duke, he is seeking another title for Agnes. However, he is finally talked into permitting the marriage—provided Robert first finishes his schooling. Too impatient to wait, Robert and Agnes wed secretly. At Yale, Robert is visited by the duke, who proposes to test his own wife's fidelity by inviting some chorus girls to join him and have his wife informed of the gathering. To further complicate Richard's life, Agnes has written that she has lost their wedding certificate and that it has fallen into the hands of a blackmailing bookmaker. Before long the chorus girls, the duchess, Agnes, the bookmaker, and a snooping reporter have all converged on Robert's rooms. Agnes and Robert flee to Robert's yacht, named—ironically, considering the introduction of the chorus girls—the *Coryphee*. The others soon follow. In hopes of getting rid of the reporter, Robert tells him the truth. The reporter allows that he cannot ethically print such confidential information but will publish a list of who was on the boat. Agnes's brother arrives and learns of the reporter's statement. Fearing scandal, he suggests that Agnes and Robert had better marry at once. Keeping straight faces, they agree. The bookmaker appears and promptly finds himself swimming ashore. As in any good farce, doors were slammed and characters pushed into hiding in closets and adjoining rooms, but it was Collier's hilarious, insistent deadpanning and nasal monotone that highlighted the evening. Arthur Voegtlin was praised for his settings, especially the yacht, with cabins and much of the deck revealed. The farce had been touring all season. It ran until late June. Collier returned to it for much of the next season and on several later occasions.

. . .

William Collier (1866–1944) was the New York–born son of performers who objected to his following in their footsteps. He had to run away from home to make his debut in a juvenile company of *H.M.S. Pinafore* in 1879. His parents forced him to return to school, but in 1883 he joined Daly's ensemble. He played minor roles there for five

seasons. He subsequently called attention to himself in *The City Directory* (1890), *Hoss and Hoss* (1891), and *The Man from Mexico* (1897). His dry voice and "inscrutable" face soon became his hallmarks.

. . .

Hal Reid's **Hearts of the Blue Ridge** (2-11-01, Third Ave.) used an old mountain family feud for background. The Carter and Reynolds families have been shooting at each other for years, but when a Reynolds boy marries a Carter girl and they have a baby, the feud is set to rest.

Maurice Hennequin and Georges Duval's **The Lash of the Whip** (2-25-01, Lyceum) was a farce despite its melodramatic title. It recounted the misadventures of a provincial stove manufacturer who leads a double life by pretending that he has a look-alike in Paris. Fritz Williams was the comic cheater, and E. M. Holland was his friend. When business needed propping up at the box office, Robert Marshall's one-acter, **The Shades of Night** (3-18-01) was added as an afterpiece. The story told of two lovers who encounter ghosts in a haunted house where they have gone to smooch. Holland and Elsie de Wolfe were the ghosts; Grace Elliston and Arnold Daly, the lovers.

Myron Leffingwell's **The Master-of-Arms** (2-25-01, American) gave new adventures to Don Caesar de Bazan. The don pursues Maritana, who he believes is only a peasant. In a fight he kills Malatesta. The dying man discloses the girl's true lineage. At the court, de Bazan and Maritana encounter a guard whipping Inez, who is Maritana's sister but is disguised as a boy. The don is sentenced to death for interfering, but Maritana persuades the king to pardon him. A wicked cousin prevents the pardon from being delivered, but Inez, still dressed as a boy, removes the shot from the executioners' guns. The don, learning that his cousin is conspiring against the king, kills him, and there are smiles all around as the curtain falls. The play was the first of several new dramas presented in late season by the city's second-class stock companies, dramas seemingly designed to cash in on the fame of older plays.

There was more swordplay in E. F. Buddington's adaptation of Mary Johnston's novel, **To Have and To Hold** (3-4-01, Knickerbocker). When the English king sends over some women as brides for the Jamestown colonists, Ralph Percy (Robert Loraine) selects a girl named Jocelyn. She remains distant and secretive. Only when Lord Carnal (Holbrook Blinn) arrives to find her does she confess she is Lady Jocelyn Leigh (Isabel Irving) and has fled England to avoid marrying the lord. The cruel peer arrests Ralph and has him exiled to a lonely island, where he is rescued by pirates, who make him their leader. He is captured and sentenced to death. Lady Jocelyn's intercession saves his life, and they sail for England to get the king's permission to marry. Only Blinn's "polished, sinister" villain found general praise. For Loraine, his American debut was singularly inauspicious. Despite only so-so business, Charles Frohman kept the play on the boards for its scheduled five weeks, not doubt encouraged by one reviewer's remark that it would be "a go" on the road.

Another play found an audience despite a disastrous first night. Drops would not drop (or rise), and when the house curtain did come down at one point it stranded an actor and a horse on the apron. But *Uncle Tom's Cabin,* which William A. Brady presented in a lavish revival at the Academy of Music on the 4th, was all but indestructible. The settings were superb, among them a snow-covered, rock-strewn mountain pass, St. Clair's New Orleans house and garden, and cotton fields with Legree's manse in the distance. Nor did Brady stint on casting. Wilton Lackaye's Tom was "a quiet, unpretending, honest rendering of a role commonly misplayed," and Theodore Roberts's Legree was "splendid" and carefully modulated. Annie Yeamans won a hand for Aunt Ophelia, even though she played it with a marked Irish brogue. Only Georgie Florence Olp was criticized—for something she could not help. She was patently too old to impersonate Little Eva. A band of blacks sang and danced, while "horses, carriages, pony carts, donkeys and dogs" added verisimilitude on the Academy's huge stage. The box office did land-office business for eleven weeks. Playgoers turned away the first week only had to walk a block further to see a touring version, which was berthed at the Star for a brief stand.

Russian nihilists once had threatened to run rampant on American stages, but by the turn of the century an anonymous touring melodrama seemed to be their last preserve. **The Voice of Nature** (3-11-01, Metropolis) told of a young student whose love of a beautiful duchess prompts a jealous nobleman to unjustly accuse him of joining the malcontents' ranks.

When a Kentucky gentleman in J. A. Fraser's **The Convict's Daughter** (3-18-01, Star) refuses to reveal the paternity of his adopted daughter, her vicious cousin sees an opportunity to prevent her marriage, which would deprive him of the money he hoped to have by marrying her himself. He helps a convict escape from Sing Sing (the escape was the play's main sensation scene) and attempts to pass him off as the girl's real father. The convict turns out to be the girl's father in fact, but he also discovers he was imprisoned on account of the cousin's perjured testimony. Without revealing his identity to the girl, he sees to it she marries the man she loves.

A dramatization of L'Abbé Prévost's **Manon Lescaut** (3-19-01, Wallack's), reworked by Theodore Burt Sayre, featured Herbert Kelcey and Effie Shannon. The new version offered considerable violence, with des Grieux killing a fellow gambler, Manon shooting an ex-lover, and des Grieux whipping "a la Uncle Tom's Cabin" another of Manon's lovers, who pursues them all the way to Louisiana. All to no avail, for Manon still dies in des Grieux's arms. The dramatization was booked for only two weeks, and that was as much as the traffic would bear.

An M.P. who has reneged on his promise to help a self-sacrificing friend's wife and child and who is prepared to sell out his own country was the chief villain in Cecil Raleigh's London melodrama **The Price of Peace** (3-21-01, Broadway). The prime minister is forced to shoot the villain's accomplice, a notorious spy, but he himself dies of a heart attack after heatedly denouncing the M.P. The spectacular scenery was the same used in the Drury Lane production, and critics bewailed that it showed distressing marks of long service. Most sensational was a transverse view of a sinking yacht, in which the M.P. is finally trapped and dies. Interestingly, the juiciest role, that of the prime minister, was assumed by Wilton Lackaye, who had left *Uncle Tom's Cabin* after only two weeks. (His part was assumed there by John E. Kellerd.) Little Mabel Taliaferro was the dead friend's orphaned child. The thriller chalked up sixty performances.

Are You a Mason? (4-1-01, Wallack's) had a shorter original run, only thirty-two showings. But Leo Ditrichstein's adaptation of Carl Laufs and Kurt Kraatz's German farce *Die Logenbrüder* returned in the fall for another month and subsequently was revived several times. Amos Bloodgood (Thomas A. Wise) and his son-in-law, Frank Perry (John C. Rice), both pretend to be Masons to please their wives. The men mimic each other in giving supposedly secret signs but, when they claim they are going to Masonic meetings, actually head out for an evening with the boys. However, for all these proclaimed allegiances Amos will not lend Perry money. Perry knows that Amos, before his marriage, had enjoyed an affair with a girl who was reputed to have died later. So Perry enlists George Fisher (Ditrichstein), a former actor who had once played Charley's aunt and now is a suitor of Perry's sister-in-law, to pose as the daughter of that bygone romance and blackmail Amos into giving Frank the money. A suitor (Cecil B. de Mille) for a second sister-in-law and the appearance of the old flame, who, of course, never had died, help solve matters. As he had been in *The House That Jack Built,* Wise was showered with rave notices for his easy, unctuous comedy.

The leading man in W. H. Collings's **Across the Trail** (4-1-01, Third Ave.) played the roles of two brothers whose surname was Faithful. When one is shot and killed by the "three terrors of the Yosemite," the surviving brother spends the rest of the play avenging the death.

A revival of *Diplomacy* at the Empire on the 15th, with what Charles Frohman billed as an "all star cast," was generally well received. William Faversham was Henry; Charles Richman, Julian; Jessie Millward, Zitka; and Margaret Anglin, Dora. Critics gave no hint that they perceived the old drama as "dated."

The tired theme of a southern girl and a northern boy in love during the Civil War was resurrected by Edward McWade's **Winchester** (4-22-01, American). McWade even resorted to the equally threadbare device of naming the heroine for her state. Virginia Randolph had been taught telegraphy by Frank Kearney, who is now a Federal cavalry officer. She uses her knowledge to spy on the northern forces. When she is caught by another officer, who just happens to be a rival for her hand, things look dark for her mentor. Virginia rushes in with a reprieve just as Frank is about to be shot. One critic wondered what cavalry regiment had taught Frank to dismount his horse "by lifting his right leg gracefully upward and over the animal's neck."

The same stock company had another novelty in Frank Lindon's **The Prisoner of Algiers** (5-13-01, American), which turned out to be a "sequel" to *Monte Cristo.* In a prologue Edmond Dantes discloses his undying hatred for Colonel Danglars (Lindon), but that does not prevent his son, Albert, from duelling and otherwise exerting himself to win Danglars's lovely daughter, Eugena.

The last new play to open at a first-class house was Frederick W. Sidney's farce **The Brixton Burglary** (5-20-01, Herald Square). When the wife goes on a visit, the husband slips off to Brixton for a night of fun, and that allows his servant to don one of his master's suits and also go to Brixton. Complications set in when the servant is forced to change clothes with a burglar. Joseph Holland as the husband and W. J. Ferguson as the servant walked away with the best reviews. Critics virtually ignored young Lionel

Barrymore, who was also in the cast. Nor could they imagine that the production inaugurated an era, being the first Broadway show to announce "Sam S. Shubert presents."

Although he had moved skillfully from farceur to dramatic actor, Nat Goodwin overreached himself when he assayed *The Merchant of Venice.* Reports from the road had been encouraging, and business even more so. When he came into the Knickerbocker on May 24 for three performances, most critics found little to like. Even his ornate scenery and patently expensive costuming were carped at. On paper his was an illustrious if not especially distinguished or promising cast. His wife, Maxine Elliott, naturally played Portia; Maclyn Arbuckle, Antonio; Vincent Serrano, Gratiano; Henry Woodruff, Lorenzo; Effie Ellsler, Jessica; Annie Irish, Nerissa; W. J. LeMoyne, Gobbo; and Aubrey Boucicault, Bassanio. At best Goodwin was judged intelligent and competent, but lacking that magic touch to make the Jew memorable. Miss Elliott's beauty was hailed, as it always was, but her reading was uneven, apparently best in flirtatious, comic moments. Yet playgoers were not to be discouraged, if the figures Klaw and Erlanger released were correct. According to the producers, the four-week tour grossed $61,000, a high total for the times. In his autobiography, written many years later, Goodwin excoriated one critic (seemingly Winter), who, he said, came late and drunk, left early, and wrote a vicious pan. Contrasting the critical response with the box office, Goodwin called the production one of his "successful failures."

Three nights later critics had to judge the work of one of their fellow reviewers when the curtain rose on Franklin Fyles's **Kit Carson** (5-27-01, American). They were not impressed. Set in New Mexico in 1846, just before the territory was annexed, the play found its hero prepared to lead a band of pioneers across Indian-infested wastes. Marian Kent is one of the band, but her own uncle, Manuel Alvarado, the Spanish governor of the area, is determined to marry her for her money and so asks Carson not to let her join the group. Carson loves her, although she scorns him, thanks to rumors she has heard. He disobeys Alvarado, who goads the Indians and other bad hombres into making trouble for the train. Of course, the train arrives safely at its destination, by which time Marian's feelings about the scout have changed. In the interval, "a hand-to-hand conflict, a race for life on real horses, a rescue of the heroine from death as a sacrificial offering, and divers other lurid and dime-novelish developments" provided excitement.

1901–1902

Coming after such a splendidly hit-filled season, the new theatrical year was perceived as a letdown. "Mediocrity has been the rule" was *Theatre*'s sad conclusion when June came around. To add to its discouraging assessment, the magazine rued that English playwrights had served the New York stage better than native authors had. Certainly offerings by such major American dramatists as Thomas and Fitch were not up to their best of the previous year, and the only novelty that probably could be revived today without too much trepidation was an English play. Yet the season's longest runs went almost exclusively to American pieces, suggesting American audiences were increasingly comfortable with native efforts. Even so, they must not have been too comfortable, for the number of long runs was down markedly.

Howard Hall and Madeline Merli's **The Mormon Wife** (8-19-01, 14th St.) reflected ongoing prejudice against the sect. Since Charles E. Blaney was the producer, it also reflected the continuing allure of highly wrought melodrama. The play was set in Salt Lake City, where John Turner informs his wife, Mary, that he has converted to Mormonism and married a second wife, Sally. Mary leaves her home to take up residence with an old friend, Dr. Mason. Her little son, Georgie, accompanies her. When Mary refuses to return home, John offers to renounce his new religion. "The Destroying Angels" hear of this, kidnap the boy, and kill him. As a choir (dressed in "vestments of the Episcopal Church") performs in the illuminated Tabernacle, detectives and Secret Service men arrive to arrest the killers. A repentant John dies after an operation, and Mary and the good doctor swear eternal love. As usual in this sort of fare, vaudeville turns popped up throughout the evening. One found a musical-comedienne playing a parlor organ with her nose. The play stayed a month before heading out on the road.

More sophisticated playgoers found much to like in Charles Frohman's importation of **A Royal Rival** (8-26-01, Criterion). The play was Gerald Du Maurier's reworking of that old warhorse *Don Caesar de Bazan*. Frohman gave it a sumptuous mounting and, to whet interest further, elevated its leading man, William Faversham, to star billing.

· · ·

William Faversham (1868–1940) was born and trained in London. His American debut was in 1887,

but the play was a quick failure. His boyish, curly-haired good looks and acting ability caught Daniel Frohman's attention. For the next eleven years he played ever more important roles under both Frohman brothers and with Mrs. Fiske. Edward Knoblauch, in his autobiography, further described him as "slim and straight-backed, with the rough voice of a Guardsman."

· · ·

The new don would regale audiences for three months in New York, during which time several other Don Caesars would compete for applause.

The casts of the three Don Caesar stories averaged nineteen players, not counting supers. That large a cast was not uncommon at the time. Even touring shows moved from city to city with sizable rosters. Thus Theodore Kremer's **An Actor's Romance** (8-26-01, Metropolis) listed seventeen performers. Four of them were pivotal. An actor and his new bride are rent apart by a scheming adventuress's trickery. This lady, in the adventuress's traditional red dress, makes an innocent encounter seem like an illicit love affair, and she is abetted in her designs by her own hopelessly infatuated, hot-headed suitor. In the evening's big scene, the actor interrupts a play within the play to denounce the schemer, who is sitting in a box. A shot rings out from the auditorium. The actor falls, wounded. Ushers seize the lover, who is running up the aisle.

Andrew Mack's career had been devoted largely to that peculiar breed of Irish romantic drama and comedy that mixed intrigue and song and appealed primarily to one ethnic group of playgoers. His latest vehicle, Theodore Burt Sayre's **Tom Moore** (8-31-01, Herald Square), was hardly much different, but critics treated it a bit more seriously, if not more enthusiastically. In Sayre's largely fictionalized account, Tom's singing of his songs, including "The Last Rose of Summer," wins over not only his recalcitrant landlady and the Prince of Wales, who had been led to believe that the poet had mocked him, but the apple of Tom's eye, Bessie Dyke. A month's stand was followed by a cross-country tour.

As he had often in the past, Charles Frohman launched the new season at his flagship with a vehicle for his reigning star, John Drew. Also in keeping with custom was his selection of a London hit as Drew's vehicle. Robert Marshall's **The Second in Command** (9-2-01, Empire) told of an army officer who is willing to lie to retain the affection of a young lady, but who later realizes the error of his ways. Continuing yet another pattern for these Frohman-Drew offerings, the comedy ran out the fall, then toured.

The patience of some steadfast first-nighters was probably tried the evening after Drew's premiere, when another leading star, James K. Hackett, began his season. Serving as his own producer, Hackett presented **Don Caesar's Return** (9-3-01, Wallack's), Victor Mapes's redaction of the Don Caesar de Bazan story. Since a third version opened a few nights later at the Murray Hill Theatre, where Henry V. Donnelly's popular stock company held forth, three dons were vying for acceptance. Hackett's cast included such fine players as Wilton Lackaye (King Carlos), Theodore Roberts (Don José), and Florence Kahn (Maritana), as well as the respected W. J. LeMoyne in support. Arthur Voegtlin designed and painted the sumptuous settings. Critics had split in their judgment of Faversham and were equally divided in their opinion of Hackett. Their main objections were his lack of comic flair and his stolidity ("rather a Saxon than a Latin adventurer"). However, on balance the verdict was that this was the superior presentation. Nevertheless, to no small extent because of advance bookings for his subsequent tour, Hackett remained in New York for only eleven weeks to Faversham's fourteen.

Before the next play could open, the nation suffered a jolt to its pride, self-confidence, and optimism. For the third time in less than forty years an American president was attacked by an assassin. McKinley was shot at close range while visiting the Buffalo Exposition. Although he failed to receive proper treatment, initial reports suggested he could survive. The shock stunned Americans and seriously affected theatrical attendance. Several shows arrived during what proved to be McKinley's hopeless struggle.

Richard Lovelace (9-9-01, Garden), like *Tom Moore* before it, played free with the life and love of a real poet, albeit in this instance its author, Sir Henry Irving's son, Laurence, gave the story a tragic bent. Lovelace (E. H. Sothern) is cheated out of marriage to the "Lucasta" of his poems, Lucy Sacheverell (Cecilia Loftus), by the treacherous Colonel Hawley, who marries her instead. Years later the crippled, impoverished poet and Lucy learn the truth, whereupon Lovelace challenges Hawley to a duel. Lovelace is mortally wounded but forgives his nemesis. Sothern received rave notices; the play was panned. (At the same time, at the Donnelly players' production of *Don Caesar*, Sothern's specially written prologue, "Never Trouble Trouble Till Trouble Troubles You," also was handed a drubbing.) The poor reception forced producer Daniel Frohman to put a new play into hurried rehearsal for the actors he had under contract. This, too, would be based on the life of a poet and would give all concerned one of their most memorable hits.

Frederick W. Bayley's **The Devil's Doings** (9-9-01, Third Avenue) was savaged by the few critics who bothered to review it. A wicked stepbrother attempts to murder virtually his whole family to get his hands on the family's wealth.

Daniel Frohman had a second show ready the next night, when he offered **The Forest Lovers** (9-10-01, Lyceum). This medieval romance was one playwright's revision of another dramatist's adaptation of a novel and centered on a girl named Isoult (Bertha Galland), brought up in ignorance of her high birth and eventually restored to her rightful place by a handsome knight. The play marked Miss Galland's debut as a star, a position she was never able to fully consolidate. Indifferently received in New York, it later enjoyed considerable popularity on tour.

McKinley died on September 14, a Saturday, and his death briefly stirred a ruckus in New York when many producers, who relied on Saturday grosses to compensate for emptier houses earlier in the week, refused to cancel performances. Perhaps feeling guilty that she had to perform that evening, Miss Galland published a poetic tribute to the dead president. As a poet she was no better than Sothern.

Coincidentally, Broadway saluted the feisty Teddy Roosevelt's assumption of the presidency by offering a batch of new American plays. **Up York State** (9-16-01, 14th St.) exemplified what some theatrical wags called "the 'B'gosh' school of drama," pictures of rural life that rarely appealed to citified New Yorkers. The Fourteenth Street Theatre had housed many such plays in recent years. In this case the stars, David Higgins and Georgia Waldron, were the authors. Higgins played Darius Green of Stony Creek. He loves his ward, Evelyn Blair, and when a Fourth of July accident nearly blinds her young brother, David mortgages his land to pay for the necessary operation. But David's avaricious Aunt Sarah poisons Evelyn's mind against David. Evelyn marries the aunt's choice, rich Allen Woodford. Woodford turns out to be a scoundrel, so Evelyn leaves him and, after giving Sarah a piece of her mind, is reconciled with David. As he had the year before in *Sag Harbor*, young William T. Hodge stole the show, this time as a backwater "sport." Manhattan was still home to enough "unsophisticated" playgoers to allow the comedy to run nine weeks in two slightly separated engagements, after which it circulated among other cities and small towns for several profitable years.

In the not too distant future Sam Harris and A. H. Woods would become prominent Broadway producers, but now, as two-thirds of the firm of Sullivan, Harris and Woods, they trafficked in touring melodramas. So their production of **The Road to Ruin** (9-16-01, Metropolis) was not a revival of Holcroft's famous old comedy but a new work by Theodore Kremer. It followed the journey of a weak young man under baleful influences and his stalwart rescuer to the Tombs, the Tenderloin, a tunnel, and finally a house (which was set on a revolving stage). The tunnel is a subway tunnel where the hero, one of countless heroes named Jack, and his sweetheart are tied to the tracks and rescued in the nick of time by his Jewish buddy, with the transparent moniker Izzy Cohen. Terry McGovern, one of the era's many pugilists who supplemented their incomes by acting, was starred. The most popular of these sensation-melodramas—and *The Road to Ruin* clearly was extremely popular—toured for years. When it returned a few seasons later, a critic addressed the very essence of these pieces. He noted that Jack "inside of 80 seconds holds in his arms a pretty little country girl, as his promised wife, and goes off to New York with a murderous adventuress, deserting the girl." This prompted the observation, "There is nothing gradual in Mr. Kremer's art. Things are done, not because human nature is what it is, but because movement is necessary, and change of scene, action, and 'Curtains.' " For what it's worth, the critic regretted that "whenever a policeman shows up, whether a roundsman or a sergeant, he is almost immediately bribed."

Some questions could be raised about how totally American the next opening was. **The Red Kloof** (9-21-01, Savoy) was written by Paul Potter, an American by adoption, and its stars were the husband-and-wife team of Louis Mann and Clara Lipman. Most of Mann's celebrity had been earned in "Dutch" dialect roles, the road to stardom taken by many Jewish actors of the time. "Dutch," of course, was often a contemporary euphemism for Yiddish. However, Potter allowed Mann the luxury of a real Dutch accent, since he set his tale in South Africa, where Piet Prinsloo is a Boer farmer. Prinsloo's hatred of the British is turned on his daughter, Mona, when she falls in love with an English spy and helps Jameson's raiders to escape. The comedy ends happily only after Mona's pleadings prompt the British to spare Piet's life following a death sentence.

Two nights later David Warfield, another performer heretofore known as a "Dutch" comedian, tried his hand at a dramatic role and scored one of the era's most memorable successes.

. . .

David Warfield (1866–1951), whose real name has been given variously as Wollfeld or Wohlfelt, was born in San Francisco. There he launched his career and met David Belasco. He moved to New York in the 1890s, soon becoming a favorite in Casino Theatre musicals for his comic portrayals of bearded, thickly accented Germans or Jews. He later played similar roles at Weber and Fields's. The stocky, square-faced actor was disbelieving when Belasco approached him to urge he abandon his comic parts and try a more serious role.

. . .

Three writers—Lee Arthur, Charles Klein, and Belasco himself—worked on **The Auctioneer** (9-23-01, Bijou). The curtain rose on a high-ceilinged, cluttered auction room, where Simon Levi (Warfield) presides, in the slums of Five Points. He is a bearded Jew with a sallow complexion, thin, wiry hair, a splayfooted, shambling gait, and voluble gestures. His manner is sometimes aggressive, sometimes fawning. To his delight, his adopted daughter, Helga (Maude Winter), announces that she will marry Richard Eagen (Brandon Tynan), the son of his friend, Mrs. Eagen (Marie Bates), an East Side "matron." Making the occasion happier still, Levi learns he has come into an inheritance. He uses some of the money to buy his prospective son-in-law a partnership in an investment firm and to purchase stocks in a trust company. He also announces he will move his family to a fine home on Lexington Avenue.

The play's most famous scene, reminiscent of the closing moments of the 1893 hit *Shore Acres*, in which James A. Herne went about putting out the lights in his home, occurred at the end of Act I, when Levi takes a last look at the surroundings he is leaving forever. As Alan Dale described it in the *Journal*, "The blinds are down, the final auction is over; one light burns in the old familiar shop; Mrs. Levi calls him to dinner. The old place is finished with; no more will he see the dinginess of the vicinity or the friendly racket of the poor old neighborhood. The old man stands aghast, a pitiful picture of dejection. His lank arms hang by his side. He gazes as though stunned at the irrevocable finality of the thing. Then, slowly, blindly, lumberingly, he goes up the wooden stair to the evening meal." But Levi's fortunes soon suffer another abrupt change. At a reception for the young couple, a detective appears and advises that Levi's stocks are worthless. The real malefactors are

Eagen's partner, Groode, and a venal politician, Callahan, but they have skillfully made it appear that Eagen is the culprit. Levi is reduced to peddling in the streets until the criminals get their comeuppance and the stocks prove valuable.

Few critics thought much of the play, although almost all of them lauded Warfield's portrayal. *Theatre* hailed it as "the best stage characterization of a local type since the heyday of Edward Harrigan's Mulligans. It is a study worthy of Dickens or Balzac." After a run of 105 performances, the play provided Warfield with work on the road for three years.

Following the play's opening, Warfield, in conjunction with a social worker, Margherita Arlina Hamm, published an interesting collection of short stories, *Ghetto Silhouettes,* which Warfield claimed grew out of his researching the role on the Lower East Side. Just how much he wrote and how much Miss Hamm contributed is moot. However, in 1905 two much publicized lawsuits, arising out of Belasco's attempt to break the stranglehold held over him by "Dishonest Abe" Erlanger and the Trust, led to interesting revelations about the play's authorship. It was generally conceded that Lee Arthur, whose real name was Arthur Lee Kahn, had written the first draft from an idea Belasco had given him. The draft was so bad that Belasco enlisted Klein's help and after the first tryout took over the revamping himself. It also showed that Belasco was forced to give the Trust half his profits to ensure decent bookings. By the time Belasco and Warfield revived the play in later years, the Trust's power had been broken.

On the same night that young Warfield was beginning his career as a major star, J. H. Stoddart, who had been a highly respected supporting player since 1854, was making what proved his farewell when he starred in **The Bonnie Brier Bush** (9-23-01, Republic), which Augustus Thomas and James MacArthur took from the novel *Beside the Bonnie Brier Bush.* The sort of drama in which yet another irate, unreasonable father casts out his daughter, crying, "Oh, the shame, the bitter shame o' it," it still found an audience for seven weeks, no doubt thanks in good measure to Stoddart's fame.

A third opening was Elmer E. Vance's dramatization of **Treasure Island** (9-23-01, Third Ave.). A young lady known only as Beatrice played Jim Hawkins.

If Belasco's battles with the Trust did not become public for several years, the next opening, **Miranda of the Balcony** (9-24-01, Manhattan), underscored the difficulties so many theatre folk encountered

with the monopoly. The producer was Harrison Grey Fiske; the star, his wife, Mrs. Fiske. Unwilling to bow to the Syndicate's greedy demands and unable to secure proper bookings as a result, the Fiskes took over the Manhattan as a New York base. (On the road Mrs. Fiske still occasionally was forced to play in tents.) The Manhattan had been built as an early vaudeville house, the Eagle, and opened in 1875. With its name changed to the Standard it later was home to many Gilbert and Sullivan American premieres. William A. Brady and Florenz Ziegfeld, then fighting their own battle with the Trust, took over the playhouse in 1898 and renamed it the Manhattan. The theatre went dark for a time after they made peace with Erlanger. When the Fiskes leased it, they converted it into one of the most elegant and comfortable theatres in New York. Their opening production was equally elaborate, with a cast of thirty-five and five gorgeous scenes, including a multitiered reception hall and a highly praised desert setting. Before the curtain rose on opening night, Ethelbert Nevin's "An African Love Song," a piece dedicated to Mrs. Fiske and with a lyric by the black poet Paul Lawrence Dunbar, was sung. The song was not entirely inappropriate since the play's story focused on Miranda Warriner, who, believing her cruel husband is dead, has fallen in love with a young, idealistic engineer, Luke Charnock (Robert T. Haines). However, just as a marriage is arranged, Miranda learns that her husband is alive and being held as a slave by the Moors. Charnock dutifully goes to rescue him. The three meet in Tangiers, where Warriner (J. E. Dodson) soon is murdered by a Moor he had mistreated. Miranda and Luke are now truly free to wed. Like so many plays of the time, especially the more romantic ones, this was a dramatization of a novel. Unfortunately, Anne Crawford Flexner's treatment of A. E. W. Mason's tale missed the requisite theatricality.

The play that forced *Up York State* to suspend its successful engagement temporarily was Charles Klein's **The Cipher Code** (9-30-01, 14th St.). Its story detailed an attempt by the villainous James Kelso (John E. Kellerd) to put the blame for a Wall Street swindle on his half-brother, an assistant secretary of state. Kellerd was the latest player to be pushed into stardom, a practice increasingly ridiculed by critics. Kellerd was a good, but probably not a great, player, and his hold on stardom proved fitful. His one dubious moment of theatrical immortality lay nearly a dozen years in the future.

No author was listed for **The Village Parson** (9-30-01, Third Ave.). A small-town minister orders his wife to leave him after he sees her in intimate conversation with another man. Actually, the man was attempting to blackmail her by revealing her father is a convict. She flees to New Orleans, where she becomes a concert singer. The minister also is forced to leave his home because the villain makes it appear he is a murderer. (Of course, the villain was the real killer.) Eight years of wandering, and several more thrill-packed acts, follow before the minister and his wife are reunited.

The season's biggest hit was Richard Ganthony's **A Message from Mars** (10-7-01, Garrick). Whether its message was Martian, English, or American was debatable, for Ganthony was an American playwright who, finding no takers for his show in his homeland, took it to London. Only after it ran for 544 performances in the West End did Charles Frohman bring it to New York. The premiere marked the New York debut of the original London star, Charles Hawtrey (who had bought all rights from the author). Hawtrey was a pudgy, moon-faced actor with a large, bristly, carefully twirled mustache. His very expression was innately comic, and his style seemed so effortless as not to be acting at all.

The play was a curious thing, progressing from a deliciously funny first act of social comedy, to a second act that was pure morality play, to an indifferent final act. Horace Parker is a hopelessly spoiled young man who dabbles in astronomy, especially questions about Mars. He pleads "a delicate throat and supersensitive lungs" to escape having to take his fiancée to a ball and even refuses to be bothered to call a cab for her and his aunt. The aunt berates him as "wrapped up in selfishness, and egotism, and conceit." When the ladies leave, in the car of the fiancée's admirer, a down-at-the-heels inventor appears, sent by a friend. But Horace is not interested in helping him. Left alone, Horace picks up his astronomy magazine and begins reading. The oil lamp flickers out. Suddenly a strange man is seen in the room. He announces he is a Martian (Henry Stephenson), whose punishment for vanity has been to come to Earth and teach Horace selflessness, or, as he calls it, "Otherdom." He forces Horace to go out in the snow to the steps in front of the house where the ball is being held. There, by allowing Horace to eavesdrop on his friends' unkind remarks about him, he shows Horace what they really think of him. News then arrives that Horace's bank has gone under and Horace is broke. Hot upon that comes word that his home has burned down. Horace is reduced to shoveling snow for pennies. In the last act Horace awakes from what has been a bad dream,

but he has learned a lesson. When a nearby tenement burns, Horace offers the victims shelter in his own home. Although an oil lamp figured in the plot, then novel electrical effects were employed strikingly. While Horace and the Martian stood in the evening snow, the scrim representing the house was lit from behind to allow the ballgoers their brief scenes; at the beginning of the third act, the setting was seemingly the same as Act II, with Horace (played here by a double) and the Martian onstage, but it immediately "dissolved" to disclose Horace asleep in his study. The comedy ran nearly six months and was frequently revived over the next several years.

In **A Royal Prisoner** (10-7-01, Third Ave.), another touring play that acknowledged no author, two prisoners, a pretender to the Russian throne and an army officer, exchange clothing so the pretender may escape. The empress comes to visit the supposed pretender, likes what she hears, and brings him to her court. Even when he is finally exposed, he is forgiven.

A pair of dramas mounted hastily to take the place of failures came in next. Sydney Grundy's **The Love Match** (10-12-01, Lyceum) was the vehicle Daniel Frohman offered Bertha Galland when New Yorkers would not accept *The Forest Lovers*. Like *Miranda of the Balcony*, its heroine has a supposedly dead husband return to prevent a better second marriage. Only his suicide leaves her free to wed. This English play had a slightly longer stay than Miss Galland's earlier vehicle but on the road proved less acceptable than *The Forest Lovers*.

Two nights later Frohman had his second replacement on the boards, this time for E. H. Sothern and Cecilia Loftus, and in this instance he found a work of long-lasting appeal. **If I Were King** (10-14-01, Garden) was written for Miss Loftus by her ex-husband, the Irish poet and novelist Justin Huntly McCarthy. For the third time in the still young season a real poet's imagined amours served as the basis for a play. The poet was the late medieval jongleur François Villon, of "Where are the snows of yesteryear?" fame. (A few seasons earlier Otis Skinner had toured in his own play based on the poet's life, *Villon, the Vagabond*.) Katherine de Vaucelles, a kinswoman of King Louis XI, has come to the Tavern of the Fir Cone to meet the poet, who has written to her, "If I were king what tributary nations I would bring to kneel before your scepter." Louis also is at the tavern, in disguise. He hears François sneeringly refer to him as "Louis Do-Nothing, Louis Dare-Nothing." Goaded by François's taunts, Louis makes François constable of

France, in which capacity the poet rids the king of his enemies. An ungrateful Louis still would hang him, until the suicide of Huguette (Suzanne Sheldon), who loyally loves François but recognizes that she stands in his way, and Katherine's willingness to marry the poet made the king relent. Sothern's lush, soaring, poetic style proved just right for the hero, giving the star what many afterwards considered his most memorable role. Even Miss Loftus, who had worked mainly in vaudeville, came across more than credibly. Prior bookings confined the run to seven weeks, but the show was revived regularly and in 1925 provided the basis for the operetta *The Vagabond King*.

Eugene Presbrey's **New England Folks** (10-21-01, 14th St.) marked the second time this season that rustic settings took over the theatre's stage. While glib phrasemakers may have classified all rural plays as "B'gosh" drama, some contemporaries apparently discerned a special distinction where plays relating to New England and especially Maine were concerned, for the *Times* noted, "A 'Down East' play that did not preach a sermon would not be the real thing." Much of the preaching came from a devout, hard-working farmer, Consider Morton (Frank Mordaunt), who is known popularly as Sid and who must mortgage the family holdings after conniving city slickers force his ne'er-do-well son into debt. Besides Consider, such character names as Weasel Clapp and Stuttering Sim added color to the piece, which ran for eight weeks, until *Up York State* was ready to return.

Snazzier playgoers rarely if ever trudged downtown to the Fourteenth Street Theatre any more. On the night *New England Folks* opened, they assembled at the Knickerbocker to welcome Irving and Ellen Terry in what proved to be the English players' last joint American appearances. Although the great pair hardly had worn out their welcome, short, rather perfunctory notices suggested they had come to be taken for granted. Moreover, they offered nothing fresh, falling back on such old dependables as *King Charles I, The Merchant of Venice, Louis XI, Madame Sans-Gêne, The Bells, The Lyons Mail, Nance Oldfield*, and *Waterloo*.

To shore up sagging attendance at *A Royal Rival*, Faversham added a one-act curtain raiser, Robert Marshall's **Prince Charlie** (10-22-01, Criterion). Faversham portrayed a playboy who, to return to his father's good graces, switches places with the hunted prince and loses his life in the process. The piece was not well received.

A barn with honest-to-goodness animals and a rustic kitchen were among the settings for Edward E. Rose's dramatization of Irving Bacheller's novel **Eben Holden** (10-28-01, Savoy). Holden (E. M. Holland) brings about a reunion of his niece, Hope, and her fiancé, William, after a misdirected letter threatens their romance and after William is mistakenly listed as killed in action. Holland's sputtering delivery annoyed some critics, but not as much as a supposedly comic character with a harelip (echoes of last season's *Cupid Outwits Adam*). For all its faults, Charles Frohman's production found an audience both in New York and on tour.

So, too, in its own way, did Sullivan, Harris and Woods's latest Theodore Kremer melodrama, **The Fatal Wedding** (10-28-01, Grand Opera). A malicious man and his lady friend spread lies about a married woman, leading her husband to divorce her. After the deceptions are unmasked, the wife and husband are reunited. Untrusting spouses were regularly forgiven in this sort of trumpery. The *Dramatic Mirror* could only lament that "despite the play's several crudities in the shape of impossible and overdrawn characters and situations, it suits the popular taste."

A Romance in Ireland (10-28-01, Third Ave.) was typical of its genre. A good-natured Irish hero is put upon by some sleazy gamblers and an unscrupulous jockey, but he wins the day and his girl with the help of some pleasing Irish songs.

Daniel L. Hart's **Australia** (10-28-01, Metropolis) originally had been produced the previous season under the title *Melbourne* and after a few weeks on the road had been withdrawn for revisions. Both versions were dramatizations of B. J. Farjeon's novel *The Sacred Nugget*. A convict transported to Australia strikes it rich there and sends for his wife and child. But the wife has run off with another man. An adventuress poses as his daughter but is soon unmasked, and the real daughter is discovered to be the woman's maid. Even this rewriting apparently could not help the work. Nonetheless, the production was historic in a small way, for Augustus Pitou, "King of the One-Night Stands," mounted it in conjunction with J. J. Shubert. This marks the earliest known instance of J. J.'s name appearing in producing credits.

Trend-spotters were offered grist for their mill with the next opening. First of all, like the much more declassé *Road to Ruin* before it, it appropriated the title of a famous old play. Happily this proved no trend at all. More dismaying to many, it came featuring yet another new "star." Theatrical astronomers were to be given little respite. The latest to be proclaimed with her name in lights above the title was Elsie de Wolfe. Her vehicle was Clyde

Fitch's **The Way of the World** (11-4-01, Victoria). That a theatrical logjam had prompted the conversion of yet another vaudeville house was also good for publicity purposes. In Fitch's story Mrs. Croydon's husband (Frank Mills), though loving and loyal, is absorbed at the moment in pursuing a nomination for governor. Her loneliness and boredom push Mrs. Croydon into a seemingly harmless flirtation with Mr. Nevill (Vincent Serrano), a cad who is also in league with Croydon's opponents. When Mrs. Croydon announces she is to have a baby, a rumor circulates that Nevill is the father. To antagonize his insipid wife, whom he hopes to divorce, Nevill tells her the rumor is true. Croydon overhears the remarks. In a scene reminiscent of Fitch's *The Moth and the Flame,* Croydon appears drunk at the baptism and shouts that he is not the father. He is led away. Mrs. Croydon and Mrs. Nevill (Allison Skipworth) put their heads together and manage to expose Nevill as a liar. With crowds outside shouting, and with fireworks exploding, the Croydons are reconciled as news arrives of Croydon's election.

The stage effects were superb. In the first act, the Croydons go for a drive through Central Park in their automobile, their chauffeur sitting in a seat behind and above them as he might have in an old hansom. A panorama gave the effect of movement, while on the sidewalk a girl on a tricycle (its rear wheels much larger than the front one), a nurse pushing a baby carriage, and other passersby passed by. (One critic, observing that Fitch often wrote to meet specific players' requirements, praised him for finding a clever way to slake Miss de Wolfe's penchant for waving at friends in the audience. She now waved at imagined strollers.) The fourth-act baptismal ceremony and the fifth-act fireworks garnered applause, too.

By now critical lines on Fitch were hardening. There was a feeling that the play offered further evidence of Fitch's surehanded theatricality and his ability to depict the world of high society, as well as his unwillingness to probe deeply. A reviewer regretted, "However well he may know his five o'clock tea, he really does not know human nature." Theatricality won the day, so the play enjoyed two successful stands in New York during the season and toured to good business. Whether from lack of interest, tenacity, or real ability, Miss de Wolfe's hold on stardom was brief, but she subsequently became a famous decorator and later a social lion as Lady Mendl. Ironically, Clara Bloodgood, the young supporting player who stole the show (much as she had in *The Climbers*) as a sharp-tongued divorcée,

quickly moved on to a more deserved stardom, equally short-lived and tragically concluded.

A forged will, a stolen deed, and a villain not above trying to blow up a tunnel with the heroine inside it were among the claptrap clichés of the anonymous **Sunset Mines** (11-4-01, Third Ave.). Besides being a forger, thief, and dynamiter, the blackguard kills a man for the man's property and deserts his own wife and child. It goes without saying that the heroine escapes all his traps. But how could anything truly baleful happen to a heroine named Sprightly Merriway? The curtain saw her holding the criminal at bay with a large pistol until the law arrived.

Winsome Maude Adams gained further laurels when Charles Frohman presented her as Phoebe in James Barrie's **Quality Street** (11-11-01, Knickerbocker). The play was set in Napoleonic times, and its impoverished, schoolmarm heroine must resort to disguise to ensnare her vacillating soldier-suitor.

Lottie Blair Parker's **Under Southern Skies** (11-12-01, Republic) was mounted by William A. Brady, who had co-produced her *Way Down East.* He brought in the new work with much ballyhoo, unwisely touting it as the successor to the earlier hit, although it was set in the South instead of New England and had no characters in common with the other play. What carried over was a sense of rattling good melodrama. (The week following the premiere, *Way Down East* returned to a second-class house for a six-week revival.) A disrupted church service, the same device employed in several recent Fitch plays, was the evening's high point. Lelia Crofton, a girl who has been told nothing about her mother except that she died long ago, is courted by two men, Burleigh Mavor and Steve Daubeny. She favors Burleigh, but Steve threatens to reveal that her mother had Negro blood if she will not marry him. To avert a scandal, she agrees. However, at the wedding, when she is asked to say "I do," she falters, then cries, "I cannot." At that moment a woman (Grace Henderson) rushes forward and reveals that she is Leila's mother. She has not died, and she has no Negro blood; rather she had run away with another man and now repents her action. Critics lavished praise on the beauty of the production (including an autumn-colored Hallowe'en party with "a pretty jack o' lantern dance") but, surprisingly in retrospect, had only perfunctorily kind words for another performer newly elevated to stardom, the play's Lelia, Grace George.

· · ·

Grace George (1879–1961) was born in New York and studied at the American Academy of Dramatic

Arts. She made her debut in *The New Boy* (1894) and played her first major role four years later in *The Turtle*. Fair-haired, dark-eyed, and strikingly beautiful, she developed an acting style that Brady, who was her husband, described as "the fast-building, vivacious, chin-up and tongue-sparkling sort of thing, with wit and tears mingled."

. . .

The *Times* observed that she was "an actress . . . who without any very evident show of sincerity, yet fills the requirements," and *Theatre,* employing almost identical language, concluded she was "a young woman of singularly attractive appearance who seems to be lacking in spontaneity and sincerity, but yet easily enlists the sympathies of her audience." Whatever the star's and the play's shortcomings, the piece did nine weeks of good business.

A second entry perceived by many as a sequel was Augustus Thomas's **Colorado** (11-18-01, Wallack's). The play most critics looked back to was *Alabama,* although others referred to *In Mizzoura* and *Arizona,* apparently latching on to Thomas's proclivity for simple titles with states' names and ignoring the fact that the playwright was consciously attempting to depict a broad spectrum of traditional American life. The central figures of the new work were young Frank Austin (John W. Albaugh, Jr.) and Tom Doyle (Wilton Lackaye), the father of Austin's fiancée, Kitty. Austin is a prospector who has developed the rich Happy Strike mine, which he has offered to share with Doyle. But the treacherous Colonel Kincaid, who spots Austin as a former army deserter, blackmails him into relinquishing the deed for the mine. Doyle comes to believe that Mrs. Doyle is having an affair with Kincaid, and he attempts to kill Kincaid, Mrs. Doyle, and Kitty when they go down into the mine. Austin forcibly dissuades him. The mine is flooded and ruined, but this proves to be a disguised blessing. With an unexpected source of water, the ranch above the mine can be irrigated easily. Kincaid and his crony, Ned Staples, their deed now worthless, meet the Doyles and Austin on the staircase of a swank hotel. Staples shoots at Doyle, but Kitty, at the top of the stairway, shoots Staples. In the end Kincaid is arrested, Doyle realizes he misjudged his wife, and Austin and Kitty prepare to wed. Hardly in a class with *Alabama, In Mizzoura,* or *Arizona,* this shoot-'em'-up western (one paper complained the stage often looked like an arsenal) nevertheless was a modest success.

Kate Mortimer's **The Power of Truth** (11-18-01, Third Ave.) told a not dissimilar story. In this case the villain attempts to force a girl to marry him by blackmailing her father about the father's unsavory younger days.

Moguls of the Trust may have been chagrined to learn that a white-tied, bejeweled audience made the premiere of **The Unwelcome Mrs. Hatch** (11-25-01, Manhattan) one of the most glittering social events of the season. Of course, the fact that Mrs. Fiske was the star was not the primary reason for all the swank. Rather, the play's author, Mrs. Burton Harrison, was counted among the Four Hundred. Belasco was angrier still, for he claimed that he had actually written the drama and had handed it over to Mrs. Harrison for her to add the proper social touches. He went to court to obtain an injunction, thus giving the Fiskes valuable publicity even though his suit was thrown out. Before the action of the play began, a Mrs. Lorimer had left her crass, selfish husband, who had flaunted his infidelities and even made Mrs. Lorimer invite his mistress to dinner. Unfortunately, Mrs. Lorimer left a note suggesting she herself was having an affair, and Mr. Lorimer (J. E. Dodson) used this note to obtain a divorce. Years speed by, and Mrs. Lorimer, who now calls herself Mrs. Hatch, has learned her daughter is about to be married. She comes to New York to see the girl (Emily Stevens), but her husband will do no more than allow her to glimpse Gladys, who is helping other society figures entertain poor East Side children in Central Park. Later Mrs. Hatch disguises herself as a dressmaker and, with the aid of a faithful old servant (Annie Ward Tiffany) still in Lorimer's employ, visits Gladys. But the new Mrs. Lorimer appears unexpectedly. She orders Mrs. Hatch from the house and fires the servant. Mrs. Hatch and the maid take cheap rooms, and Mrs. Hatch supports herself by sewing cotillion favors. Her daughter and new husband (Jefferson Winter) come to call, as does a man (Robert T. Haines) who has fallen in love with Mrs. Hatch. But their kindnesses come too late. Her heart strained beyond endurance, Mrs. Hatch dies in her would-be suitor's arms.

Mrs. Fiske's performance won raves from papers not under the thumb of the Trust. The *Dramatic Mirror,* owned by Fiske, may have been any more unbiased, but it offered a description of the star's big moment: "The pallor of death could be seen stealing over her face and her eyes seemed to grow glassy, while the physical weakness became ever greater. At the moment of Marian's death Mrs. Fiske's back was toward the audience, but the convulsive start and then the limpness of the body showed graphically that the end had come." The reviewer added, "Even the men had to choke back tears." Impartial critics could not be as complimen-

Act Four : 1899–1906

tary to the play itself, with its similarity to that old warhorse *East Lynne.* Even William Winter, whose son acted a prominent role in the play, pounced on the likeness with malicious glee. Nonetheless, the actress's following remained loyal, and after eight weeks she took both this play and *Miranda of the Balcony* on tour.

Most novelties at combination houses by this day were American-made. Martin J. Dixon's **Gypsy Jack** (11-25-01, Third Ave.) reportedly was an English play. But that was about the only difference critics could find in this run-of-the-mill melodrama. Its hero had been kidnapped by gypsies while he was still a tot. Now a young man, he undergoes all manner of vicissitudes (interrupted by vaudeville turns) to reclaim the vast estates that rightfully should have been his.

Virginia Harned, who for so long had performed in the shadow of her husband, E. H. Sothern, now came out as the season's umpteenth new star in **Alice of Old Vincennes** (12-1-01, Garden).

. . .

Virginia Harned (1868–1946), whose real name was Hickes, was born in Boston but raised in England. She made her debut after returning to America in the late 1880s. Her rise was swift, and for all practical purposes she had been a star for some time. After all, she was the original Trilby in 1895 and subsequently played numerous leading roles opposite her husband. An actress of singular maturity, she exuded, according to one writer, "sex, vitality, dignity and beauty."

. . .

Charles Frohman's in-house adaptor, Edward E. Rose, shaped the play from material in Maurice Thompson's novel. Alice is a young American girl caught up in the battles of the Revolutionary War. She sends her lover, John Fitzhugh Beverly (William Courtleigh), to call for reinforcements to save her beleaguered town. Although the British capture him, all turns out well.

But most first-string critics were not at Miss Harned's opening. Monday night was still the evening of choice for unveiling new productions, and this Monday was no exception. Two other first-class playhouses vied for first-nighters, and when it came to luring in major reviewers, Richard Mansfield won hands down. **Beaucaire** (12-2-01, Herald Square) was Booth Tarkington and Evelyn Greenleaf Sutherland's dramatization of Tarkington's novel *Monsieur Beaucaire.* However, Mansfield refused to utilize the full title, insisting that American playgoers could not pronounce "monsieur" correctly and might be too embarrassed to suggest

seeing the play as a result. The comedy remained faithful to Tarkington's story, in which a French nobleman flees his homeland and sets up as a barber at Bath. He persuades a friend to pass him off in society as a duke and in that guise is welcomed. When his plot is unmasked he is ostracized, so he reveals his true history, thus exposing in turn the hypocrisy and absurd snobbery of English high life.

Although Winter hailed Mansfield's performance as "an incarnation of chivalry and grace," other critics felt he was not at his best in comic parts. Even many who admired his performance reflected a snobbery of their own, not uncommon to the profession of the time, by ruing that he would waste his talents on such trivial material. Richard Marston painted the superb settings. Playgoers ignored critical reservations and gave *Beaucaire,* as they did *Alice of Old Vincennes,* a profitable two-month run, after which both plays headed for the hinterlands.

The least of the evening's three openings was **The Helmet of Navarre** (12-2-01, Criterion), a swashbuckler that Bertha Runkle and Lawrence Marston adapted from Miss Runkle's novel. Charles Frohman imported the English actor Charles Dalton to play Etienne de Mar, who wins his beloved Lorance de Montluc (Grace Elliston) only after foiling her uncle's attempts at treason and at marrying her off to his nephew. One reviewer described Dalton as "a somewhat picturesque melodramatic hero of the good old London Adelphi school." In the very minor role of Princess de Retz was Rose Eytinge, a star of decades earlier, now faded into relative obscurity. Her regular advertisements in trade sheets advising that she was available to coach theatrical aspirants was a poignant reminder of her decline.

One actress whose decades-old popularity never had declined, although she recently had turned eighty, was Mrs. Gilbert. The storm of applause that broke loose when she entered disconcerted her and all the other players. Yet she was not the star of Clyde Fitch's **The Girl and the Judge** (12-4-01, Lyceum). Annie Russell was. However, many critics felt that what should have been the play's most important role was assigned to neither of these favorites, and at least two commentators offered the suggestion that Fitch may have made a hasty rewrite to accommodate Miss Russell's star billing. When Judge Chartris (Orrin Johnson) mediates the Stantons' plans for separation, he allows their daughter, Winifred (Miss Russell), to select which parent she will live with. She chooses to live with her mother, for she knows the most cogent reason for the separation, a reason withheld from the judge: Mrs. Stanton (Mrs. McKee Rankin) is a kleptomaniac.

Chartris has fallen in love with Winifred and proposes. His mother (Mrs. Gilbert) visits Mrs. Stanton, who promptly steals the lady's jewels. For a time it is Winifred who is accused of the crime, because she has learned that her mother has pawned the jewels and she attempts to retrieve them. The judge prompts his mother to deny the pawned jewelry is hers lest Winifred be arrested. Finally Mr. Stanton (John Glendenning) agrees to look after his wife. In the play's big scene, mother and daughter are alone in the bedroom at night. Mrs. Stanton almost has convinced her daughter that she is not the thief when the doorbell rings. Assuming it is the police, Mrs. Stanton breaks down in hysterics and confesses. Charles Frohman's latest hit recorded 125 performances. When it closed, the historic, though not really very old, Lyceum was demolished.

Only one touring melodrama came between Fitch's second and third plays in little more than a month (a fourth had opened recently in London). That melodrama was one of a growing list circulating anonymously. Its title, **The Orphan Heiress** (12-9-01, Third Ave.), no doubt gave away most of the plot to the Third Avenue's regulars. The poor young girl is hounded by a dastardly couple bent on depriving her of her inheritance. They fail in Act V.

The Marriage Game (12-10-01, Victoria) was Fitch's version of Émile Augier's half-century-old masterpiece *Le Mariage d'Olympe*. Reset in England, it described how a lord is driven to kill the deceitful, gold-digging, title-chasing music hall singer he married. Sadie Martinot starred, but neither she nor the play was well received.

Nor did critics think highly of Louis Evan Shipman's **D'Arcy of the Guards** (12-16-01, Savoy), but they conceded it was entertaining. Donning a powdered wig and speaking with an Irish brogue, Henry Miller assumed the role of a British officer billeted in a Philadelphia mansion during the Revolutionary War. He is smitten by the daughter of the house, Pamela Townshend (Florence Rockwell), even though she steals plans for the English attack on Valley Forge and shoots him in the wrist when he tries to prevent her delivering them. Of course, for all her rebel sympathies, she falls in turn for the handsome major as she treats his wound. One applauded stage picture showed the redcoats gathered around a table, smoking long-stemmed pipes, drinking punch, and singing "Sally in Our Alley" as D'Arcy led the chorus using his pipe as a baton. The play did good business for six weeks and provided Miller with an acceptable vehicle for more than a year.

Charles Frohman added another production to his swelling roster of successes with H. V. Esmond's London hit **The Wilderness** (12-23-01, Empire). Margaret Anglin, Charles Richman, and William Courtenay were featured in this tale of a woman who marries a man for his wealth and social position but who comes to genuinely love him and so refuses her former lover when he returns and entreats her to elope.

Hal Reid's **At Cripple Creek** (12-23-01, Metropolis) provided surefire thrills for less demanding playgoers. Martin Mason kidnaps Belle Gordon, but she is rescued by Joe Mayfield and Ann Marbury, who also are harboring Mason's abused daughter, Maggie, and his grandchild, Tatto. Mason and his buddy, Alvares, know that a vein of gold lies hidden in Mayfield's mine. To persuade him to sign over the deed they throw little Tatto over a cliff, but the child is caught by Mayfield's Indian friend, Waketah, who swings out into the canyon to grab it. The villains next try to flood the mine, then, aiming at Mayfield, they shoot Ann Marbury. They are caught and lynched. Belle marries Joe and then discovers that Maggie is her long-lost sister. In short, both girls were Mason's daughters. For what little it may be worth, Tatto was played by the same Beatrice who earlier had portrayed Jim Hawkins.

Belasco's Christmas present to New Yorkers was his production of his own **Du Barry** (12-25-01, Criterion). As with so many plays to which he attached his name, his authorship was disputed. He was soon hauled into court again, where it was shown that he had lifted his "own" play from one by Jean Richepin. (The case was not settled until 1908, when Belasco paid Richepin a trifling $1000.) Set, of course, in 18th-century France, the story told how the Parisian milliner Jeanette Vaubernier, although she truly cares for a young soldier, Cosse-Brissac (Hamilton Revelle), marries Comte Guillaume Du Barry and becomes the plaything of royal society. Her secret meetings with Cosse-Brissac prove painful, and at the last nothing can save her from the guillotine. Screaming and "palsied with fear," she goes to her death with Cosse-Brissac vainly trying to console her. The fiery Mrs. Carter brought all her sizzling intensity and verve to the title role. She ran a gamut of wild emotions while hiding her lover under her bed as the king and his men search her room; she beat a would-be informer senseless with a candlestick; and, to some playgoers' consternation, she cavorted tauntingly in her bare feet. Like the real Du Barry, she refused to wear a wig, so her red hair added further coloring to her acting. Belasco surrounded her with a production of "unprecedented splendor," overflowing with gorgeous velvets and silks, which even the grouchiest critics acknowledged. But they did grouch. Winter complained in the *Tribune*, "The piece contains a plentitude of needless talk, and is overweighted with scenery, people [over fifty in the cast], and the accessories of spectacle. As a production 'Du Barry' is costly and ostentatious, but luxury counts for little unless it is used with judgment," only to conclude bitterly and correctly, " 'Du Barry' will undoubtedly have a prosperous career." In fact, the show's 165 performances made it the longest-running American play of the season, and after leaving New York it toured lucratively for three years.

Although no producer of the time could match Belasco's stagings, **A Gentleman of France** (12-30-01, Wallack's) was another lavish production that enjoyed a long run. Derived by Harriet Ford from Stanley Weyman's romantic novel, which was set in the same period and recruited some of the same historical figures as *The Helmet of Navarre,* it was presented by Liebler and Co. with the controversial Kyrle Bellew as star. He portrayed the dashing Gaston de Marsac, who can rout a bevy of villains to win the hand of Mlle. de la Vire (Eleanor Robson).

Detractors who insisted Charles Frohman cared little for American drama and imported London plays wholesale could point accusingly again when he brought over Basil Hood's **Sweet and Twenty** (12-30-01, Madison Square), which unfolded the love of two brothers for the same girl. Despite the presence in the cast of Mr. and Mrs. Sidney Drew and of young Richard Bennett, audiences did not take to the play, so two weeks later, in an unsuccessful bid to stimulate business, the producer added a one-act curtain raiser, Edmond Rostand's **Les Romanesques** (1-13-02), in which two fathers contrive to have their children wed by seemingly keeping them apart. Musical theatre buffs will recognize it as the source for the longest-running of all American musicals, *The Fantasticks.*

J. O. Stewart and Joseph J. Dowling's **Roxanna's Claim** (12-30-01, Third Ave.) depicted the bravery of an American army captain (Dowling) in lawless Colorado, where he thwarts schemers who would deprive the heroine of her lands. The audience "shouted, cheered and hissed itself hoarse at the almost continuous thrills."

The last offering of 1901 was perhaps its most daring and intriguing: Otis Skinner's revival of Boker's 1855 blank-verse tragedy *Francesca da Rimini* at the Victoria on the 31st. Lawrence Barrett had rescued it from apparent oblivion in the 1880s, but a Broadway absorbed mainly with preposterous

swashbucklers and society plays could only view the offering as a "perilous experiment." No one ever had thought much of Boker's blank verse, and Skinner's production did nothing to change that opinion. On the other hand, the playwright's compassionate characterizations and total theatrical effectiveness were still very much in evidence. Although some critics had reservations about the beautiful Marcia Van Dresser's Francesca, they generally agreed the other principal figures were exceptionally well served, with Aubrey Boucicault as a handsome, believable Paolo, William Norris as the malicious jester, Pepe, and, of course, Skinner, subtle and memorable, as the deformed, bedeviled Lanciotto. Winter, who was, if possible, growing increasingly cantankerous, laid aside his barbs long enough to suggest, "There could not, in the dramatic world, be a brighter augury for the New Year." The revival, which had opened in Chicago in August and toured for four months, ran seven weeks in New York, no mean achievement for so esoteric a mounting. But Skinner recorded in his autobiography that, for all the critical huzzas and reasonably good houses, the production had not begun to recover its costs—$20,000, including losses on the road—when it closed.

The new year began with the unveiling of a new theatre. The opening was hardly gala, since the playhouse was designed to be merely a combination house. But the theatre bore a not undistinguished name, the Star. The older Star, which had been built as Wallack's on 13th Street, had been demolished over the summer. The new auditorium was uptown on Lexington. Its opening attraction was **The Penitent** (1-6-02), which Lawrence Marston adapted from Hall Caine's novel *The Son of Hagar.* A duplicitous brother makes all manner of outrageous claims, including a charge of illegitimacy, to try to keep another brother from receiving his share of an estate. The play was poorly received, and that reception was a harbinger of things to come, for despite Weeping Willie Winter's optimistic prophecy, the last half of the 1901–02 season was a letdown.

The story, something about a young lady who sets up shop, pacifies warring social cliques, and wins her man, was not the thing in **Frocks and Frills** (1-7-02, Daly's), Sydney Grundy's version of Scribe and Legouvé's *Les Doigts de fée.* Daniel Frohman's production, set partly in the modiste's boutique, served as occasion for a display of new fashions designed by Mrs. Osborne, one of the era's leading costumers. It also served to demonstrate how regularly many of the theatre's more versatile craftsmen found employment, for the director, Edward E. Rose, was equally well known as a dramatizer of novels.

The high point of the waning season came at the Republic Theatre on January 13 when London's Mrs. Patrick Campbell, who could model gorgeous gowns as voluptuously as any mannequin, made her American debut under the aegis of Liebler and Co. She opened in *Magda*. J. Rankin Towse, writing in *The Critic,* praised "her faculties and power of expression," continuing, "Her voice is a charming instrument, rich, soft and musical, with sufficient volume. . . . Her eyes, large and dark and deep, often partly veiled, as in Orientals, by drooping lids, lighten finely, in her moments of excitement, and become wonderfully expressive and attractive. Her great height, her graceful, sinuous figure, and her long arms make her poses singularly picturesque and her gestures uncommonly eloquent and striking." She also presented two Pinero works, which had made her famous in England but which others had first offered to America, *The Second Mrs. Tanqueray* and *The Notorious Mrs. Ebbsmith.* Her novelties were Bjørnstjerne Bjørnson's **Beyond Human Power,** in which she played a minister's wife who does not share her husband's faith, José Echegaray's **Mariana,** whose heroine is shot by the man she married but confessed she did not love, and a few performances of Max Beerbohm's **The Happy Hypocrite** and Maeterlinck's **Pelléas and Melisande.** Winning high praise in supporting roles was a young actor who would remain in America and become one of its most notable players, George Arliss.

A Jolly American Tramp (1-13-02, Third Ave.) turned the tired clichés of touring melodrama into a fairly unusual comedy. A man imprisons his wife and claims she is dead in order to inherit her money. He also is very mean to his daughter. But a sly, smiling hobo comes along to undo his dirty work.

Con T. Murphy's **The Gamekeeper** (1-20-02, Third Ave.) was a typical Irish romantic drama in which a warbling Irish lad confounds villainy (in this case by taking on an alias) and wins his sweetheart.

William Bonelli was the star of his own sensation-melodrama **An American Gentleman** (1-20-02, Star). His rich young hero encounters a gypsy girl who is about to be forced to marry the winner of a wrestling match. The fashionably dressed hero saunters onstage and grabs the piratical-looking victor. He tosses him about the stage, "lifts him high over his head, spins him around as a drum-major spins his baton, and at last, smiling and cool, he flings the gypsy champion off stage." So much for the first act. Later the gypsies shackle the hero in a hut containing a powder keg. They light the fuse. The heroine rushes in to help her man, who breaks loose and throws out the keg just as it explodes. "In the midst of the smoke and the red glare of the fire," he carries the heroine to safety. She turns out not to be a real gypsy but an heiress who was kidnapped when she was a baby.

For all its excitements Bonelli's play apparently did not run out the week. Instead it was replaced by Daniel Hart and C. E. Callahan's **Pennsylvania** (1-25-02, Star). Having lost his memory, Henry Stroh cannot find the deed to his coal mine, which Charles Broadhead is callously exploiting. A reporter locates the deed, but Broadhead's jilted girl steals the papers. "While she is flaunting them in Broadhead's face he takes them from her by force and in turn has them immediately wrested from him by the demented Stroh. The excitement . . . restores Stroh's reason." Stroh then helps the miners when they rise against Broadhead. The interior of the mine, with a working elevator and with the miners' hats lit by flares, won applause when it was revealed, as did an explosion in the mine later in the act.

Amelia Bingham, endeavoring to consolidate the reputation she had earned as an actress-manager with *The Climbers*, made the mistake of appearing in a second version (this time by Edward Rose) of the same play that had been the source of *Frocks and Frills.* The failure of her **Lady Margaret** (1-27-02, Bijou) marked the beginning of her meteoric career's rapid decline.

In Lionel Ellis and George Comer's **The Red Barn** (1-27-02, Third Ave.) one brother frames another brother, then enters into a bigamous marriage with the jailed brother's wife. It requires three more acts for justice to prevail.

Most critics admired Charles Klein's third play of the season, **The Hon. John Grigsby** (1-28-02, Manhattan), but the public did not, so its run was short. Klein had written the work several years earlier for Sol Smith Russell, who tried it out briefly before his last illness forced him to withdraw. (Russell lingered on until shortly after this version opened in New York.) Frank Keenan, who would spend most of his career as a highly praised supporting actor, now assumed the lead. Set in Illinois in the 1840s, it purportedly was suggested by Lincoln's struggles there. Grigsby is a widower and a lawyer, given to helping the poor and thus usually in debt. Cynical politicians, hoping he will prove pliable, nominate him to the court, where they expect his vote in favor of slavery will be decisive. They are alarmed when they discover he is defending Meg Ronalds, who is teaching young blacks to read. The leading manipulator, James Ogden, attempts to make it appear that a bribe from a widowed friend of Grigsby's, Mrs. Marston, secured the nomination. He also attempts to arouse a mob against Meg. But Grigsby turns the tables by threatening to reveal that Ogden is Meg's father, having deserted her and her mother long ago. Grigsby wins both the judgeship and Mrs. Marston. Unfortunately for the play it arrived at a time when sentiments against blacks were hardening.

Like Amelia Bingham, Henrietta Crosman was determined to recreate the splash she had caused the previous season, in her case in *Mistress Nell*, and, like Miss Bingham, she made a mistake. Her vehicle was Evelyn Greenleaf Sutherland's **Joan o' the Shoals** (2-3-02, Republic). Its action took place in 1682 New Hampshire. An untamed American fisherwoman, appropriately named Joan Seastrawn, not only helps her shy local minister court the young lady of his dreams (Nanette Comstock) but also lands for herself an exiled British peer (Henry Woodruff). The last act showed a rocky shore on a stormy night, with a "rolling sea and the flying spray." Joan saves a passing ship by lighting a beacon. So bad were the reviews that Miss Crosman removed the play after a single week and revived her Nell Gwyn until she had a new production ready.

Three combination houses offered novelties the following Monday. In keeping with a not uncommon practice at these lesser theatres, at least one of the plays premiered in the afternoon. Lottie Gilson, a popular vaudeville belter, and J. K. Emmet, Jr., son of a more famous father who had created the lead in *Fritz, Our Cousin German*, found their names above the title of Edwin Barbour and James W. Harkins, Jr.'s **The Outpost** (2-10-02, Third Ave.). Both Gilson and Emmet were attractions of an order rarely seen at the Third Avenue or its rivals, and the play was clearly written for them. Not accidentally, Emmet played a character called Fritz. He is a Boer who loves Nora Desmond, but Nora's rascally guardian has Fritz imprisoned and rewrites Nora's father's will so that she will marry him, the guardian, which will allow him to inherit her money. After numerous trials and even more numerous songs, the lovers win the upper hand.

In Howard Hall's **The Man Who Dared** (2-10-02, Star), the husband (Hall) of a faithless wife masquerades as his own twin brother to bring his spouse and her lover to justice.

Brothers also figured in William B. Gray's rural drama **The Volunteer Organist** (2-10-02, Metropolis). Narrow-minded parishioners bring false charges against the fiancée of their liberal minister. The minister's brother, who had left home and become a

besotted tramp, returns and is reformed by the minister's good example. When the village organist refuses to play at the minister's wedding, the brother takes over the organ. (The action, imitating the striking staging in *A Message from Mars*, showed the self-righteous villagers standing sneeringly outside the church while the wedding, lit from behind a scrim depicting the church, was also revealed.) In the end, the villagers reconsider.

Jesse James, the Missouri Outlaw (2-17-02, Third Ave.) told of the escapades, captures, and escapes of Jesse and his brother, Frank, and of Jesse's death, but apparently so poorly that the few notices it was awarded were as scant as they were dismissive.

Following a three-week hiatus of openings at first-class houses, Martha Morton's **Her Lord and Master** (2-24-02, Manhattan) gave opening-nighters a play they obviously relished. The story was simple. A spunky American mining heiress, Indiana Stillwater (Effie Shannon), is made to accept the more reserved ways of her English husband, Viscount Canning (Herbert Kelcey). Contemporary commentators saw the play as a modern *Taming of the Shrew*, scarcely noting its implicit snobbish acceptance of foreign proprieties over American openness, or, for that matter, its advocacy of what a later generation would brand "male chauvinism."

Grant Stewart's **Mistakes Will Happen** (2-24-02, 58th St.) began with a secretly married young couple being threatened with eviction when they are caught together. But that is not their only problem. The husband is an unproduced playwright. Hoping to snare a backer for his latest play, he latches on to a rich married woman, arranging to meet her at an out-of-the-way inn so that he can plead his case. By farcical coincidence his wife arranges to meet the lady's spouse at the same inn for the same reason. One scene had the writer in a hayloft coaching the stagestruck married woman on acting tricks. Critics liked comic lines such as "Realism is what goes now on the stage. We have real oceans, real Niagaras, real buzz-saws, and some day we shall have real actors." The last phrase was ironic, since Stewart eventually would become one of Broadway's leading comedians. When the Fifty-eighth Street Theatre's stock company was not performing the play, the house was given over to vaudeville—often on the same day.

On the 100th anniversary of Victor Hugo's birth, Daniel Frohman mounted **Notre Dame** (2-26-02, Daly's), which Paul Potter had taken from the Frenchman's great classic. Edward G. Unitt's elaborate settings stole the show, since films yet had to demonstrate that they could more easily and credibly present the breadth and magnificence such historic spectacle demanded. But even in 1902 scenery alone could not make a hit, and Potter's journeyman adaptation coupled with Hilda Spong's competent Esmeralda and George W. Barbier's adequate Quasimodo proved insufficient to encourage a long run.

Henrietta Crosman handsomely atoned for her failure in *Joan o' the Shoals* when she brought out *As You Like It* at the Republic on February 27. For many playgoers and critics, her Rosalind was the high-water mark of her career. Shakespeare's poetry was given short shrift in her mounting, but the vigor and sprightliness that so characterized this actress at her best served admirably to animate the whole evening. Her fine Orlando was Henry Woodruff. One interesting point about this hurriedly-got-up production, a point several commentators noted but saw nothing wrong about, was its scenery and costumes. Those commentators had seen both before, since in easygoing, pre-union-regulated days, Miss Crosman simply had borrowed them from Julia Arthur's 1898 production.

Charles Frohman's Empire Theatre Stock Company had another minor success with **The Twin Sisters** (3-3-02, Empire), which Louis N. Parker had adapted loosely from Ludwig Fulda's *Die Zwillingsschwester.* Her performance as a wife who poses as her twin sister in order to reclaim her own roving husband gave a major boost to Margaret Anglin's growing stature.

A miser named Caleb Croc was the villain in **On the Suwanee River** (3-3-02, Third Ave.). His targets were another hero named Jack and a heroine called Dora. But the hits of the evening were Stella Mayhew, who was starred as a colored mammy and who belted her "coon" songs across the footlights, and the Clover Leaf Colored Quartette.

New England rusticity reclaimed another Broadway stage when Frohman next brought out Edward E. Kidder's **Sky Farm** (3-17-02, Garrick). The play was not especially successful, but if, as a few critics implied, it had the virtue of not taking itself seriously and was content to spoof good-naturedly many of its genre's clichés, then it signaled such plays were near the end of their days. Its basic story told how greedy Benjamin Breese (Frank Losee) attempts to undo the marriage of his son, Warren, to Marigold Towers, a minister's daughter. He wants Warren to marry a rich girl. Eventually Marigold's warmth and the tiny hands of a grandchild melt the old man's heart. Typical of the incidents was one in which Marigold, attempting to flee from her father-in-law, falls asleep and is covered with falling leaves. Still, Breese spies

her and exclaims, "Ah! Here's the woman." At that point a protector, "Neighbor" Nixon, jumps from the tree and adds, "And here's the man!" Rising young William T. Hodge once again won laughs as a typical country bumpkin, this time attempting to escape the clutches of another of the genre's stock figures, an amorous widow. Staging included the heroine riding a real horse-drawn raking machine.

Mid-March was not too late for yer another new star to be proclaimed nor, with Teddy Roosevelt now firmly in control in Washington, too early for a new play to wave the flag in an expression of growing jingoism and expansion. The play was **Soldiers of Fortune** (3-17-02, Savoy), Augustus Thomas's dramatization of a Richard Harding Davis short story, and the new star was Robert Edeson, a sternly handsome actor given to portraying sternly heroic figures. (His career as a star would be short-lived, and he would become one of the first important leading men to desert the stage for films.) As Robert Clay, a mining engineer who supervises the vast holdings of the American tycoon, Langham, in the banana republic of Olancho, he calls in bluejackets from the U.S.S. *Detroit* to thwart corrupt local politicians and wins Langham's daughter as a reward. The play ran until hot weather forced a summer recess, then resumed its run the following season.

Lincoln J. Carter's **The Eleventh Hour** (3-17-02, Third Ave.) featured a hero named Joe Manly, who takes on the alias Doby Dick and serves as a supposed tool to two married villains, called the Fowlers, as they attempt to rob a rich man. Like Clay's, his reward for restoring order is the rich man's daughter. Before that order is restored, a knockdown-dragout fight occurs, a fight so rough that the room in which it takes place is left a shambles.

With the opening of **The Diplomat** (3-20-02, Madison Square), Martha Morton had two hits playing simultaneously. Her latest was a comedy, which more or less reversed the presumptions of *Her Lord and Master,* and it provided William Collier with another sterling opportunity to display "his peculiar dry humor, his alert manner, and his quick, executive habit of speech." As the superficially irresponsible Nick Shortwick, he rescued a charming American heiress, Daisy Darling (Louise Allen), from foreign fortune hunters. By coincidence several notices quoted the same examples of Miss Morton's idea of comic dialogue, including this one:

—If I were to raise your allowance $5,000 a year, what would you do, eh?
—I don't do much now, but in that case I wouldn't do anything.

Amelia Bingham temporarily retrieved her shaky reputation as an actress-manager, which *Lady Margaret* had tarnished, when she presented **A Modern Magdalen** (3-29-02, Bijou), Haddon Chambers's English version of a Danish play in which the heroine sacrifices her virtue and becomes the mistress of a rich man in order to provide for her ailing sister. Her sister recovers and turns against her, so the would-be saint goes off to treat soldiers wounded in a war. Critics had serious reservations about the play, both on moral and aesthetic grounds, but were lavish in their praise of the fine mounting and the exceptional ensemble acting of her troupe, acting many felt among the best of the season. Her superior cast included Madge Carr Cook, Arthur Byron, Henry E. Dixey, and Wilton Lackaye. Good acting allowed the work to run out the season.

By contrast, Anson Ford's **Life** (3-31-02, Garden) ran only one week. Probably the play was not very good to begin with, but 1902 Broadway was not quite ready for the tale of a girl who runs away from home after an unhappy love affair and finds comfort in the company of a Bowery streetwalker. The only other first-class offering of the season with settings on the Lower East Side had been *The Auctioneer,* and that had dealt essentially with poverty, not with degradation. Moreover, for all the realistic tricks Belasco had employed, his play was sentimental at heart. *Life* apparently attempted something harsher (despite an ending in which the streetwalker sees to it the girl goes home) and was, accordingly, rebuffed. Even such respected players as Minnie Dupree (the heroine), Annie Irish (the streetwalker), George Boniface, and Maude Granger could not save it.

Elmer Walter's **A Thoroughbred Tramp** (3-31-02, Third Ave.) also ran one week, but that was all that was expected of most touring melodramas. Like *A Jolly American Tramp,* which had visited the same house in January, it recounted how a seeming derelict, one sporting the moniker T. Rush Thompson, confounds villainy and brings happiness to two harassed lovers.

Jolly and thoroughbred tramps were not the only people wandering from town to town in America. So were actors in modestly successful touring shows that never reached New York. Some, such as one called **A Man from Arkansas,** confined their travels to circumscribed areas. Apparently they dealt with matters and figures of localized interest. Others circulated more widely. The *Dramatic Mirror* devoted a lengthy column to six such shows, which opened in various cities on April 7. Of the six, one reached New York the following season, a second in

the 1903–04 season. The other four ran the gamut of the era's theatrical genres. To cite just one example, Thornall Styne's **A Country Editor** was unveiled at Troy, N.Y. It was a comedy-drama that touched fleetingly on the stage. In Coffeyville, Kans., the widowed editor of the *Thomas Cat,* the town's paper, adopts a girl orphaned when her actress mother dies. He attempts to have some of the townsfolk take her in, but they refuse. She grows up to be a lovely lady and falls in love with a young lawyer. The snooty townsfolk wonder aloud why a widowed man and a young woman live in the same house. And when these busybodies oppose the lawyer's bid for a seat in Congress, the editor exposes their ringleader as a hypocrite. In short, such plays may have differed from those that reached New York not in kind, but in quality. And given the quality of some of the works displayed at the combination houses, one can only ask if that was the only difference. No doubt financial and other such matters also determined a play's fate.

With the coming of April the season began to wind down, or unwind, with remarkable rapidity. Only two more novelties would be seen at first-class houses, and even combination theatres presented fewer fresh attractions. Leo Ditrichstein's **The Last Appeal** (4-14-02, Wallack's) had been doing well at prime theatres across the country all season long, but, as was so often the case, that meant little to New York. More than one critic looked upon it as an adult fairy tale that would not entrance grownups. When Crown Prince Waldemar (Robert Drouet) weds Melitta Arendt, both the king (D. H. Harkins) and Melitta's papa refuse to accept the marriage. The couple live isolated, but in princely splendor, for a year. Once a year the king opens his palace to all comers to hear their grievances. The youngsters join the line to plead for forgiveness, and since Melitta holds the king's new grandchild in her arms, the king (like crotchety old Breese in *Sky Farm*) relents.

One sure sign that fewer good plays are on the way is a rash of revivals. Producers ransacked the 19th-century repertory to help bring the season to a close. First to arrive was Charles Frohman's revival of *The Importance of Being Ernest* at the Empire on the 14th. When Frohman had presented the Wilde comedy originally at the same theatre seven years earlier, the play had flopped. This time it was a hit, with Charles Richman as Jack, William Courtenay as Algernon, and Margaret Anglin as Gwendolen.

A callous suitor threatens to throw the heroine's financially shaky father into bankruptcy if she refuses to marry him. Her answer is to enter the stock market and beat the suitor at his own game. She also clears her sweetheart of the villain's charge of embezzlement. Such was the plot of Richard L. Crescy and Owen Davis's **A Gambler's Daughter** (4-14-02, Third Ave.).

In James W. Harkins's **The Pledge of Honor** (4-21-02, Star) the hero had to travel farther from home, moving from England to Italy to Siberia and back to England, along with fighting the villain on a cliffside and rescuing the heroine from a burning building, before the fifth-act curtain fell on a satisfactory conclusion.

On May 6, Mrs. Fiske began a series of revivals at her family's Manhattan Theatre. *Tess of the D'Urbervilles* and *Divorçons* were the principal offerings, the latter coupled with *Little Italy*. She also presented a single performance of *A Doll's House*.

At first, a single week's run appeared to be the fate of **Hearts Aflame** (5-12-02, Garrick), another of the day's many society dramas. Mrs. Harmony (Dorothy Dorr) prevents Paul Charteris (Robert T. Haines), a sympathetic bachelor who long has been fond of her, from helping her brutal, drunkard husband, Harry (Arnold Daly), when he loses his fortune. She eventually leaves her husband for the thoughtful Charteris. Genevieve G. Haines derived the play from Louise Winter's novelette. Despite its abrupt closing, Mrs. Haines did not lose faith in the work. Instead she spent several months rewriting it and saw it enjoy a modest success when it was brought back the following season.

Hal Reid's **At the Old Cross Roads** (5-12-02, Grand Opera) spotlighted a heroine who is supposedly an octoroon and who is persecuted by a cruel landowner. She turns out to be an heiress who was surreptitiously switched with the real octoroon while still a baby. A "positive hit" was made by Thomas H. Ince in the comic role of a tramp disguised as an exiled count. Ince did little in the theatre but soon moved on to become a major director of silent films before his early, mysterious death.

The parade of revivals continued with Kyrle Bellew and Mary Mannering in *The Lady of Lyons* at the Garrick on the 19th. Mrs. W. G. Jones, who played the Widow Melnotte, had performed the same role in New York fifty years before. The Garrick later played host to revivals of *The Hunchback* and *Frou-Frou* during the week of June 2. Viola Allen, Eben Plympton, and Aubrey Boucicault were featured in the former, Grace George in the latter.

Frank W. Harvey's **John Jasper's Wife** (6-2-02, Third Ave.) found its hero beset by a wanton, extravagant wife and an irresponsible son who

squander his newly inherited wealth. He walks out, hinting he will find solace with his childhood sweetheart.

The dying season expired with a groan. Lorraine Hollis's **Jeanne du Barri** (6-3-02, American) endeavored to mine the same lode Belasco had worked so skillfully months earlier. Critics ridiculed the eccentric spelling of Du Barry's name as much as they ridiculed the playwright's ineptitude.

1902–1903

Despite the disappointing season just passed, optimism ran rampant along the Great White Way. No better sign of this existed than the construction busily under way from the bottom to the top of the fast-expanding theatre district. From Fourteenth Street to Columbus Circle no fewer than eight new playhouses were rising. Some would have short, difficult lives, but others—such as the new Lyceum, the Hudson, and the New Amsterdam—would have long, distinguished careers. Producers were eagerly scanning rosters for young players they could proclaim as stars, and they were also avidly searching for star vehicles. The play was still not the thing in this era.

With Teddy Roosevelt energetically leading a chorus of flag-waving, the source of many plays was an issue. A bill was introduced in Congress to impose a tax on all plays not by American authors. The idea of encouraging native writers was noble enough, but the plan simply did not make good sense. Citing figures, producers showed that even with the tax bite a foreign hit would remain more profitable and therefore more attractive than an American flop. Good sense prevailed, and the bill died.

At the same time a hue and cry was raised for a "National Art Theatre" or "Endowed Theatre," one proponents insisted could remain a home to great drama (from any source) and great acting, with the help of government subsidies. The hue and cry came mainly from some theatrical publications, most notably the two-year-old *Theatre*. Important actors and playwrights such as William Gillette and Augustus Thomas lent their support. Many others remained tellingly silent. In an interview in the *Herald* Clyde Fitch came down firmly against the proposal, remarking, "The people now clamoring loudest for the Endowed Theatre are the magazine writers and the playwrights who have failed, and one can draw his own conclusion as to the value of their advice or their competence to direct such a movement."

In the midst of all this hubbub, the season began. With "carriages at the curb, ticket speculators swarming the steps, [and] a wild scramble for programmes in the lobby," intrepid first-nighters bucked the evening's heat to attend **Quincy Adams Sawyer** (8-1-02, Academy of Music), Justin Adams's "crude" dramatization of Charles Felton Pidgin's novel. In one way the play turned traditional rural drama topsy-turvy, for the city slickers were the goodies and some of the rustics the villains. Sawyer (Charles Dickson) and his buddy, Arthur Hastings, are rich young men vacationing in Mason's Corner, Mass., where they fall in love with blind Alice Pettengill and Lindy Putnam. Sawyer licks the town bully, wreaking havoc on a grocery store in the process. Then, by holding a blotter up to a mirror, he learns that Lindy is really the daughter of an English lord and thereby thwarts the efforts of Lindy's greedy foster mother to prevent Lindy and Arthur from marrying. He also brings to town an eye doctor who cures Alice's blindness. A serving girl flying in from the wings, supposedly kicked by a cow she had been milking, and landing center stage was the play's idea of humor. So was an elderly pair dancing with For Sale signs stuck on their backs by a village wag. A lively corn-husking contest and the square dance that followed earned eight curtain calls. After a month, the play headed out for the road.

Brandon Tynan was both author and star of **Robert Emmet** (8-18-02, 14th St.), which one critic welcomed as "an Irish play . . . without thatched huts, an obdurate landlord, a wickedly splenetic bailiff, evictions, acushlas, mavourneens, shillelaghs and the like." Its simplistic construction was another matter. In the first act the famed rebel narrowly escapes capture when he goes to meet his sweetheart in Dublin. In the second act he narrowly escapes capture after a skirmish with British troops in the Irish hills. In the third act he again meets his fiancée, this time in a picturesque churchyard, and once more barely eludes his enemies. The final act shows him caught and imprisoned. An attempt to free him before he is executed fails. A large, primarily Irish audience applauded the play "vociferously." The play ran ten weeks, then toured.

Charles Frohman's first offering of the season ran only half as long and did not fare well on the road. H. M. Paull's English farce **The New Clown** (8-25-02, Garrick) told of a man who disguises himself as a circus clown after he mistakenly believes he has killed a friend.

The antagonist in Nain Grute's **Man to Man** (8-25-02, Star) abducts the heroine, attempts to kill her mother (or rich guardian, in some accounts), and imprisons her lover in a cave. But evil never triumphed in these thrillers.

Siegel Cooper's, then a popular New York department store, was the scene of the opening act of James R. Garey's touring melodrama **The Price of Honor** (8-25-02, Metropolis). The setting showed the busy, goods-filled counters and a working elevator. When the heroine realizes that the sister of her suitor, who is the store's detective, is a shoplifter, she claims she herself is the guilty one, hoping thereby to spare her fiancé humiliation. She is fired and lives from hand to mouth in a garret. The villain tricks her into marriage, deserts her, and then attempts to marry the detective's sister. At the wedding, at Trinity Church, the heroine shoots the villain in self-defense. He dies, but she is acquitted and reunited with her lover, who acknowledges he was wrong to believe her earlier confession.

Another salesgirl, another department store, and another practical elevator (this one used with dramatic effect) figured in Marie Wellesley Sterling and Charles E. Blaney's **Only a Shop-Girl** (9-1-02, Star). The heroine is loved by a rich young man and by a vicious, mustachioed floorwalker. She spurns the latter, so he, with the help of an adventuress who is after the rich suitor, decides to kill her. When his threats cause her to faint, he opens the elevator door, places the heroine with her head hanging over the shaft, and rings the elevator bell. The hero comes along and rescues the girl. There were so many musical specialties that at least one critic thought the melodrama could have been billed as a musical. The *Times,* which rarely deigned to notice such touring melodramas, for some reason devoted a whole Sunday feature article to it—if only to sneer. But in doing so it offered some marvelous glimpses of this kind of show. The writer was amused that the sidewalk outside the department store sported a red carpet and that the snow that fell on it fell temperamentally, hardly coming down at all except when the heroine was in trouble. Thus "when she repulses the bold, bad villain with those noble words, 'I may die out here in the snow, but rather [that] than accept the offer of a wretch like you,' the paper flakes have a veritable orgy of their own." In one act the outcast heroine has taken refuge with a waif, nicknamed "Little Mother," who finds room among her tiny siblings for the girl. But a "deep, double-dyed villain of a lawyer" comes demanding the rent or eviction. "This is me castle," the waif answers him, picking up a poker. At that point the hero suddenly comes in and offers to pay the rent. And when the adventuress tries to make trouble, the heroine informs her, "An honest, industrious shopgirl is as far above an idle doll of fashion as heaven is above the earth." With that "the gallery, always ready to recognize truth, no matter how humble the lips that give it voice, raises the roof."

Wills would play important roles in two of September's entries. The first was featured in Grace Livingston Furniss's **Mrs. Jack** (9-2-02, Wallack's). Jack Banaster, a highly successful upstart, had married and divorced a western waitress (Alice Fischer). His will leaves his ex-wife his $10 million estate for one year, after which a codicil is to be read. Banaster's family have no use for the "pie-handler," nor for each other. They care only about getting their paws on Banaster's money. But Mrs. Jack is different, even taking under her wing Banaster's one nice relation, his old aunt. When the codicil is read, it stipulates that whoever has taken care of the aunt gets the millions. The fluff delighted audiences in New York and elsewhere.

John Drew's annual vehicle was Isaac Henderson's London hit **The Mummy and the Humming Bird** (9-4-02, Empire). (Henderson was an American who had to go to London to have his play produced.) His story told of an older man whose neglect of his wife (Margaret Dale) drives her into the arms of a scoundrelly Italian (Guy Standing) until the husband opens his wife's eyes. Drew, who flubbed many of his lines on opening night, did not walk off with the best notices. They were reserved for his nephew, Lionel Barrymore, in the small but crucial role of the organ grinder, Giuseppe. Giuseppe's wife had died of shame after the Italian lothario had seduced her, and he is bent on revenge. His scene in which he tells (largely by pantomime) his history to the husband was a high point of the evening. As usual, Drew proved an attraction for the play's eleven-week booking and subsequently on tour.

George C. Hazleton, having dabbled loosely with English history in *Mistress Nell,* turned his attention to the American past in **Captain Molly** (9-8-02, Manhattan). His Molly Pitcher (Elizabeth Tyree) is not married, like the real one was, but instead has two suitors. The one she prefers is Barry Kenyon (J. W. Albaugh, Jr.), who nevertheless feigns a mortal wound to test her fervor. She also wins over the stern officers in a court-martial trial by her vivacity and wit. Of course, there was a noisy, smoke-filled battle scene in which soldiers fall one by one, leaving Molly to man the cannon. A muddled affair, the play had a short life.

Just for starters in Theodore Kremer's **The King of Detectives** (9-8-02, Star), the villain murders the heroine's brother with the heroine's Japanese paper-knife, thereby implicating her. But James Pierce, the titular hero, is on the heroine's side. Later she is kidnapped in Central Park and taken up in a flying machine, from which she is dumped. She lands unhurt on a church steeple and is rescued by Pierce, who has followed in a balloon. Pierce must resort to all manner of disguises, including pretending to be his own corpse at a wake, to nab the villain. In the end his mutoscope (a primitive motion picture camera) provides evidence to convict the villain. Local characters, such as a Bowery tough and a Jewish pawnbroker, provided comic relief.

Robert Marshall's **There's Many a Slip** (9-15-02, Garrick) was merely a new translation of Scribe and Legouvé's classic *Bataille de dames.* Its cast included James Erskine (stage name for the Earl of Rosslyn), Jessie Millward, and Leo Ditrichstein. It failed to draw, and to bolster attendance producer Charles Frohman added André de Lorde's brief Parisian sensation **At the Telephone** (10-2-02), in which a man talking to his wife on the phone hears her murdered by a burglar.

American sensation-melodrama was given another airing in an uncredited work, **The Gates of Justice** (9-15-02, Third Ave.). Treacherous moonshiners attempt to seize the heroine's property. They falsely accuse her of indecent behavior, have her committed to an insane asylum (from which she is rescued by a black with the odd name Woeful Danger), and throw her down the chute of a coal breaker.

There was more of the same at busy Theodore Kremer's second melodrama of the season, **For Her Children's Sake** (9-15-02, Grand Opera), which also offered the season's second circus settings. A reception celebrating the engagement of the heroine, a minister's daughter, to the hero, a young doctor, is disrupted by a woman who has loved the hero to no avail and so claims he has seduced her. She dangles an incriminating locket as proof. The hero is ordered out of the house, to which the heroine responds by announcing her departure, too. Her father warns her to think again.

Kingsley: (*sternly*) Edna, if you step over that threshold to-night you shall never again enter this house.
Edna: Father, I must go. I must follow the dictates of my own heart and conscience, but here are the proofs of that woman's crime. Jonathan [a minor figure] will tell you. (*Exits hurriedly and passes by window; Kingsley gives a cry of grief, calling to her; Florence* [the other woman] *screams; John*

grins and shows her the scissors and locket. Church bells ring.)

The heroine is tricked into marrying a cruel circus owner. He forces her and their children to perform by threatening to horsewhip them. The second act ends with the young doctor rushing in, seizing the whip, and using it on the villain as the children dance for joy on their bed. After the heroine is badly injured in a circus accident, one of her children kills the proprietor. The villainess disguises herself as a nurse, hoping to poison her rival. But the doctor who is summoned turns out to be none other than the hero. He manages to right all wrongs. The remorseful schemer pleads, "Edna, live, for your children, for your father, for me!" Edna's coy curtain line is, "All you to live for. Well, I'll try."

On the same day these plays opened, the *Times*'s new critic, John Corbin, published an extended essay taking note that most of the season's new plays were American and lamenting that they were not very good. Excepting Thomas and Fitch, he bewailed "the vacuity of the American playwright" and concluded, "The American playwright keeps on in the beaten path of old and outworn endeavor, or if he looks about him for something new, deliberately ignores what is real and true for the easy and the obvious and the ineffectual falsehood."

That English dramatists often took a similarly easy road was evident when the flamboyant Mrs. Patrick Campbell returned to New York. Her vehicle, E. F. Benson's **Aunt Jeannie** (9-16-02, Garden), was a variant on what one disgruntled English commentator had called "the Mayfair drama of cuckoldry." Benson's story focused on a widow who risks both her reputation and her chances for another marriage in order to prevent her niece from marrying the man who had demeaned the niece's mother. Even the warmth and intelligence of the star's performance could not kindle interest.

Nor could two weak American touring melodramas. In Malcolm Douglas's **A Fight for Millions** (9-22-02, Metropolis), the hero—he couldn't be otherwise, since his name was Tom Manly (or Manley)—is an inventor. He loves the daughter of a man with the majestic moniker of Hudson Rivers, who is president of the Great Central Railroad. Manly's competitor for the heroine's affections kills a woman claiming to be his wife and frames Manly for the killing. Manly is sent to Sing Sing, but he escapes with the help of the heroine and his own miniature submarine. (The sight of the submarine gliding through canvas waters, and that of the intrepid hero preventing a train from being dyna-

mited as it passed through a tunnel earlier in the play, were the evening's major thrills.) The lovers find a secluded spot, and from there Manly employs another of his marvelous inventions, a cordless telephone, to obtain a confession from the villain's accomplice, who is dying aboard a Europe-bound steamer and who is a typically corrupt Jewish pawnbroker with the obvious name of Solomon Moses.

Critics could not make heads nor tails of the plot of **A Mother's Heart** (9-22-02, Third Ave.), for which no author was listed. It seemed to have something to do with a woman whose daughter by a first, unhappy marriage falls in love with the son of her second marriage.

The second theatrical will of the season was crucial to one of the year's best plays, Pinero's **Iris** (9-23-02, Criterion). Mrs. Bellamy (Virginia Harned) has been left a fortune by her late husband on the condition that she not remarry. She is courted by two men—a rich, coarse Jew (Oscar Asche) and a poor young man (William Courtenay). She runs off with the young man, but then learns that her lawyer has absconded after frittering away her husband's money. Her response is to leave her lover, who goes off to make his fortune, and return to London, where the Jew can keep her in style. When the lover, now well-to-do, returns, he is appalled and leaves Iris. The Jew, discovering that she has seen her lover, casts her out into the streets. The best acting of the evening was by Asche, who had created the role of Maldonado in London. The heavy-set actor imbued the role with "passion . . . cunning and brute force." Charles Frohman added another success to his ledgers.

One more bit of early Americana found its way to the stage when Beulah Marie Dix and Evelyn Greenleaf Sutherland's **A Rose o' Plymouth Town** (9-29-02, Manhattan) premiered. Although the play took place in and around the home of Miles Standish, the spotlight fell on Rose de la Noye (Minnie Dupree), a Huguenot living with the Standishes. She shelters Garrett Foster (Guy Bates Post) when he dashes into the house after stealing some corn. She quickly falls in love with him, then falls out of love after misconstruing an overhead conversation. In a pique she promises to wed weak, mean John Margeson. But after Garrett warns the villagers of an Indian attack and is wounded in the fighting, she changes her mind. Comedy was provided by the deliciously drawn character of Standish's aunt, Resolute Story (Mrs. Sol Smith), who misses the fun and vigor of London life, and by the romance of Rose's shy, dull brother, Philippe (Douglas Fairbanks), and the captain's niece, Miriam. Critics lauded the latest young actress raised to stardom and Mrs. Smith as well, but they expressed disappointment at both the play and its production. Only the second-act setting, showing the autumn corn fields, the harbor, and the headlands viewed from Standish's yard, won any praise. Coy humor and an incessant attempt to recreate 17th-century speech were no help.

Philippe: I—I respect Miriam. I like not to see her pining. Doth all her love still turn to Margeson? Say true, sister!
Rose: Truly, the soup is boiling over!

The comedy ran three weeks.

September's last offering was Charles Frohman's production of a French comedy, Alfred Capus's **The Two Schools** (9-30-02, Madison Square). A divorced husband and wife take on new lovers, but when the two pairs meet at a restaurant it is the husband and wife on the one hand and the lovers on the other who leave together.

Frohman also produced one of October's first entries, a double bill. Both plays were foreign—one French, one English—and both starred Ethel Barrymore. In **Carrots** (10-6-02, Savoy), Alfred Sutro's translation of Jules Renard's *Poil de carotte,* she donned a red wig and boy's clothing (a coarse blouse and jeans) to play a youngster who believes neither of his parents loves him. A boy-to-man talk with his father discloses the father also feels unloved. Arthur Law's light-as-a-feather **A Country Mouse** came next, with Miss Barrymore playing a wily, superficially artless girl from the backwaters who comes to London and wins for herself a rich old duke (Harry Davenport). The star's knowing style, with "its arch simplicity, its soundness in humor as in emotion," pleased critics, one of whom added, "The rich vibrations of her voice and the subtle sweetness of her smile were never more happily in evidence."

But Frohman and his leading lady had plenty of competition that Monday evening. Weedon Grossmith's **The Night of the Party** (10-6-02, Princess) found servants taking over the digs of their master, who they believe has left for a long trip. His unexpected return and his talk of elopement with a married woman lead to some comic role-switchings and blackmail. The author impersonated the principal servant. The farce pleased Broadway, but its real importance rested in another credit. For the first time a Broadway banner read "Messrs. Shubert present."

. . .

[Levi] **Lee** (1873?–1953), **Sam S.** (1876?–1905) and J[acob] **J. Shubert** (1878–1963) [nés Szemanski]

were natives of Lithuania, brought to this country by their failed, alcoholic father. They grew up in Syracuse, N.Y., where Lee and Sam had odd jobs at local theatres. Sam's success after he purchased touring rights to *A Texas Steer* gave them the wherewithal to come to New York and lease the Herald Square Theatre. At this early date J. J. apparently still worked independently. Despite the birth years listed above, Sam was believed to be the oldest of the three sons.

. . .

As she had in *Mistress Nell* and *As You Like It,* Henrietta Crosman put on doublet and hose as Philippa in Ronald MacDonald's **The Sword of the King** (10-6-02, Wallack's). Her heroism impresses William of Orange, who presents her with his sword as a reward. But she has her difficult moments, too. She must hide her lover, Edward Royston (Aubrey Boucicault), in her bed to prevent his seizure by James's troops. She incurs Edward's ire when she allows her priest-brother, Philip, an opponent of the Orange claims, to escape. Not recognizing Philippa in her male attire, Edward fights a duel with her and wounds her. But all ends happily. The play was not a huge success, but its six-week booking proved profitable.

Theodore Kremer's third play of the still young season, **A Sister's Love** (10-6-02, Third Ave.), was written expressly for two girls better known as sharpshooters than as actresses. The girls played sisters who must fend for themselves when an adventuress and her disguise-prone lover persuade their guardian to attempt to murder them. The principals also partook in the specialty acts that were part and parcel of such touring melodramas. Thus the villain-lover won encores for his banjo and "bones" turn, and the heroines performed a xylophone duet "by striking the bars with bullets from their rifles."

So far none of the season's nonmusical plays had managed to run 100 or more performances. That distinction fell to a play from which little had been expected, and it did so at the city's largest auditorium devoted to straight plays. Ramsey Morris's **The Ninety and Nine** (10-7-02, Academy of Music) was purportedly suggested by a hymn of the same title. Its hero's real name is Charles Bradbury, but, to save a woman's honor, he accepted blame for a crime he did not commit and fled to the small Indiana town of Marlow. There, calling himself Tom Silverton (Edwin Arden), he has taken to drink. Ruth Blake sees good in him and hopes to reform him. Her hopes would seem to be dashed when rich, wicked, craven Mark Beveridge contrives to implicate Tom in a theft. Tom moves to another town and begins to drink more heavily. Then a telegraph message arrives warning that Marlow is surrounded by a huge forest fire, which threatens the town's inhabitants. The only way to save them is to run a train through the fire to bring out the townsfolk. The lone train available belongs to Beveridge, who refuses to endanger it. He holds would-be rescuers at bay with a gun until Tom tricks him into giving it up. There is a quick blackout, dramatic music from the orchestra pit, "then the curtain rises again on an exciting scene. The stage is literally covered with fire. Flames lick the trunks of the trees. Telegraph poles blaze and the wires snap in the fierce heat. Sharp tongues of fire creep through the grass and sweep on, blazing fiercely. In the midst of all is the massive locomotive, full sized and . . . almost hidden from view in the steam and smoke. Its big wheels spin on the track, and it rocks and sways as if driven at topmost speed. In the cab is the engineer [Tom], smoke-grimed and scarred, while the fireman dashes pails of water on him to protect him from the flying embers." (Tissue paper streamers, blown by concealed electric fans and colored by bright red and yellow lights, simulated the flame, while the panorama moved speedily in the background.) When the train arrives in the town the citizens fall on their knees and sing the Doxology. Tom and Ruth clinch. The *Dramatic Mirror* hailed the play as better than any English melodrama, while *Theatre* called it more moral than most society dramas. A majority of playgoers, while not rejecting such chauvinism or morality, enjoyed the play for the excitement it offered.

Cries that Charles Frohman never took his eyes off the box office had to be muted when he imported his next English play. This was no Mayfair society drama. Instead he offered the famous 15th-century morality play **Everyman** (10-12-02, Mendelssohn Hall). Ben Greet's production had been done first in London and now was brought forward for a few performances. The concert hall was only half filled, but rave notices whetted interest, so the mounting was soon moved, first to one legitimate theatre for a series of matinees and, when they were crowded, to another house for a regular run. In all, the mounting chalked up eighty-one showings. With Edith Wynne Matthison in the title role, the beautifully costumed presentation was offered on a stage designed to look like part of a Gothic cathedral. Throughout the show two actors dressed as monks sat silently, one on each end of the stage.

Lawrence Marston's **The Little Mother** (10-16-02, American) recounted the struggles of an orphaned newsgirl to support her young brother. ("Little Mother" had been the nickname of a similar waif in *Only a Shop-Girl*.) A wicked stepfather and a thieving sailor plot to force her into marriage, but she bucks them and eventually finds happiness with a more honest bluejacket.

Henry V. Donnelly's popular stock company, with Elita Proctor Otis as visiting star, offered a novelty, H. Holbrook Curtis and Rupert Hughes's **In the Midst of Life** (10-16-02, Murray Hill). In a fifteen-year-long fit of brain fever, a titled Englishman becomes convinced he is a wanted criminal, and he is encouraged in this delusion by a scheming adventuress.

The ongoing rage for showing actors' names above plays' titles led to brief stardom for two capable players, J. E. Dodson and Annie Irish. Their vehicle also attested to a persistent undercurrent of bad feelings between America and England. Its author was Madeleine Lucette Ryley, who had spent many years in America but recently had returned to her native London. **An American Invasion** (10-20-02, Bijou) depicted the resentment felt by some Englishmen in India when an American engineer comes there with a new and better way for draining swamps. They set an English widow to stealing his plans. She succeeds, but then she falls in love with him and repents.

Two revivals also came into first-class theatres on the same evening. At the Garrick, Frohman brought back *His Excellency the Governor*. More important, at the Herald Square, Martin Harvey was finally allowed to offer his interpretation of *The Only Way*. Critics divided sharply on their appraisal of the actor.

Nor were lesser playhouses idle. Lee Arthur's **Private John Allen** (10-20-02, American) had for its hero an ex-Confederate soldier who is running for governor of Louisiana. His enemies threaten to bring up an old matter that would embarrass his fiancée, so he throws his support to a rival, a Creole who secretly has married his daughter. When another of the era's innumerable adventuresses appears and tries to blackmail the Creole, Allen is forced to jeopardize his party's chances to win in order to clear everyone's name. The show had been popular on the road but found no favor in New York.

In Bruce Van Sant's **Tracy, the Outlaw** (10-20-02, Third Ave.), Tracy is induced by his treacherous brother to rob a train carrying a warrant for his, Tracy's, arrest. The brother then alerts the police. Tracy is captured and imprisoned. He escapes, only to be shot and killed later. At least one reviewer complained that Tracy, then still famous for his actual exploits, was made to seem more hero than villain.

A sense of slight disappointment, though not of pronounced displeasure, greeted Mrs. Patrick Campbell's second new play (she had revived *The Second Mrs. Tanqueray* in the interim). **The Joy of Living** (10-23-02, Garden) was the ironic title given by Edith Wharton to her translation of Hermann Sudermann's *Es Lebe das Leben,* and it was the play's and the performance's pervasive gloom that upset many. The star played an unfaithful wife whose husband confronts her and her lover and demands the lover commit suicide. Before he can do that, the wife drinks poison.

Dore Davidson's **The Judgment of King Solomon** (10-27-02, American) depicted the decadent court of the Jewish king. Innocent girls are brought there and seduced. In a dream Solomon sees the destruction of the temple as punishment for his court's sins. (The tumbling down of the great building was the evening's scenic sensation.) Two of the girls who have been ravished are brought before the king with a baby each claims is hers. Solomon decides that the baby will be cut in two, which of course brings wails of protest from the real mother. Solomon offers to marry her and reform his court's ways, hoping to forestall the temple's destruction.

"Probably in no existing play has a heroine been rescued from dire perils so often as occurs to Rene Ruthendale," wrote one reviewer of Hal Reid's **Old Sleuth** (10-27-02, Star). He added that the audience certainly lost count by the end of the second of the sensation-melodrama's five acts. Among the more noteworthy, if not original, thrills were her rescue from a burning bridge at Niagara Falls and from the path of a locomotive speeding through a tunnel. The actor who played the title role did so on crutches, having hurt himself the previous week in Philadelphia. But this did not stop him from donning all his quick-change disguises.

In his assessment of Clyde Fitch's **The Stubbornness of Geraldine** (11-3-02, Garrick), the critic for the *Dramatic Mirror* summed up a common consensus of the writer's work: "Mr. Fitch relies less upon his plots than do the majority of playwrights. It is his character drawing, his ingenuity in devising incidents, his originality in the matter of stage settings, and his clever lines that count." The new play underlined the accuracy of the characterization. Its simple story line told how rich Geraldine Lang (Mary Mannering) is prepared to marry a Hungarian, Count Carlos Kinsey (Arthur Byron), until she is led to believe he is a fortune hunter. Actually he has sailed to America to earn enough money to support her properly. To this end he takes a job with a Hungarian orchestra. The orchestra is booked to play at a ball given by Geraldine's aunt, and there Kinsey overhears the slanders that have hurt his courtship. His stout, heated defense of himself clears the air.

Miss Mannering was criticized for overacting, so Byron's polished performance took the laurels. But it was the opening stage picture that most playgoers remembered. "The setting represents the deck of an ocean liner home-bound from Europe. Sallow-faced passengers are laid out in their steamer chairs like rows of mummies, the big ship rocks and groans as she rises to the sea, and overhead are two great funnels and the usual steamer rigging." The setting became so famous that when Weber and Fields satirized the show they copied it as precisely as possible. Only they called their spoof *The Stickiness of Gelatine.* The original play ran eight weeks, then toured. Its New York run might well have been much longer but for contractual commitments.

Martin Harvey received excellent notices when he changed his bills to offer a translation of Ernst Rosmer's **The Children of Kings** (11-3-02, Herald Square), in which a young ruler encounters romance and adventure when he goes incognito among his people.

In E. Laurence Lee's **A Ruined Life** (11-3-02, Third Ave.), the central figure is a young gypsy queen with hypnotic powers. When she hypnotizes her captor he reveals that she was kidnapped as a child and is really a long-lost heiress.

A performer blessed with hypnotic powers of a different sort was Eleonora Duse, who began a two-week stand at the Victoria on the 4th. Her first offering was Gabriele D'Annunzio's **La Gioconda,** in which the wife of a sculptor loses her hands defending his work against the woman who inspired it and later loses her husband to the same woman. D'Annunzio's **La Città Morta** followed on the 7th, with the actress as a blind woman who finds her husband weeping over the body of a girl killed by an incestuous brother. The author's version of **Francesca da Rimini,** brought out on the 11th, concluded the engagement. Later in the season Duse returned for a brief stay at the Metropolitan Opera House. Despite generally ecstatic notices—for the actress, if not for the overwrought plays—this was Duse's last American visit for some years.

A fine American actress, Mrs. LeMoyne, could not save from quick failure **Among Those Present** (11-10-02, Garden), Glen MacDonough's weak drama about an avaricious grande dame whose dabblings in Wall Street lead her into trouble.

501

W. Howell Poole's English melodrama **The Blind Girl** (11-10-02, Third Ave.) centered on a sightless heroine who must expose her lover as her brother's killer after another brother is wrongly accused of the crime.

Martin Harvey concluded his first and last but one starring engagement in America with a double bill. In Freeman Wills and Fitz-Maurice King's **Rouget de Lisle** (11-12-02, Herald Square), he portrayed an impoverished, hounded musician who lives just long enough to hear his "Marseillaise" sung by an impassioned French mob. Harvey impersonated a similar figure in **A Cigarette Maker's Romance,** which Charles Hannan adapted from the work of his fellow novelist F. Marion Crawford. This time he was a dispossessed, penniless nobleman living in the futile hope his old friends would call on him.

Five new plays opened the following Monday. Of the three to appear at first-class houses, only one was American—and that had the shortest run of the three. Winston Churchill's adaptation of his popular novel **The Crisis** (11-17-02, Wallack's) resurrected the old saga of lovers torn apart by the Civil War. The northerner is Stephen Brice (James K. Hackett); the southerner, Virginia Carvel (Charlotte Walker). At the war's outbreak she opts in favor of another suitor, Clarence Colfax (Brigham Royce). During the struggles Brice saves Colfax from pursuing Federal troops, and when the war is over, although her father has been ruined by carpetbaggers, Virginia finally consents to marry Brice. The dramatization was episodic but beautifully mounted. One setting especially admired was an exterior view of the Colfax mansion, with folks doing a reel in the moonlight as banjos and guitars sing out the melody. Hackett, too, won praise for his "chivalrous warmth."

Hall Caine also dramatized one of his own novels, **The Eternal City** (11-17-02, Victoria). A revolutionary (Edward Morgan) denounces a woman (Viola Allen) for her alleged promiscuity, and she vows revenge. But in seeking to entrap her accuser she falls in love with him. After numerous vicissitudes and startling revelations (he is the illegitimate son of the pope), they end up arm in arm, and he is made prime minister. A sumptuous production increased the melodrama's appeal.

The fiancé (William Faversham) of a girl (Fay Davis) carelessly accused of having an affair with a married man (Richard Bennett) must help clear her of the charge. And he does in H. V. Esmond's London comedy **Imprudence** (11-17-02, Empire). The always dapper Faversham gave a graceful performance as star of the evening, but morning-after notices devoted more, glowing attention to Miss Davis. She was a Boston girl who had won her wings in London (she was the original Iris there). She would spend only a few seasons in her homeland before returning to finish her long career in the West End.

Joseph Le Brandt's **Not Guilty** (11-17-02, Star) begins with a rich mine owner disinheriting his daughter after she weds his superintendent. He writes a new will leaving all his wealth to his nephew, who promptly murders him and pins the guilt on the dead man's son-in-law. A Secret Service man helps send the real culprit to the chair.

Colonial settings and costumes added color to Sidney R. Ellis's **A Prince of Tatters** (11-17-02, Metropolis). An Austrian prince was married as a child to another youngster, but they were immediately separated and lost sight of each other. Years pass. Learning she is in New York, he joins a band of mercenaries who are sailing for America. In the New World he inadvertently becomes involved in a plot to assassinate the governor, his bride's guardian. He is jailed for a time before the inevitable happy ending.

During the season several stars had seen supporting players walk away with the best reviews. Even Mrs. Fiske found she was not immune when she opened in Paul Heyse's German play **Mary of Magdala** (11-19-02, Manhattan). (The uncredited adaptor was William Winter, who praised the translation in his review.) Mary has led a dissolute life after leaving her cruel husband. She had been seduced and deserted by Judas of Kerioth. Only when she hears Jesus (who was never shown onstage) preach and when he saves her from an angry crowd does she begin to repent. She appears in a sun-drenched, bustling Jerusalem square. "She stands humbly motionless near the wings, while a long and violent scene is enacted in the center of the stage, holding in her hands the alabaster box of ointment. Motionless, mind you, and without change of expression, and with no friendly calcium shaft to single her out—and yet that silent, obscure figure holds a steady heart-to-heart talk with you and brings you to the verge of tears." But her trials have only begun. Judas, for one, would have her back. He is not truly evil but torn between conflicting emotions, both about her and about Jesus. Jesus he loves, but condemns for his pacifism, believing it will ultimately lead to the destruction of the Jews. Flavius (Henry Woodruff), a nephew of Pontius Pilate, also courts her and promises to prevent the crucifixion if she will have him. Alone on a darkened stage, she prays for guidance. A single beam of light touches her face, signaling her vision of Jesus. She witnesses Christ's death, and Judas is seen ranting insanely in a storm.

The play was lauded for its sincerity and tact, but most critics felt it was not truly superior drama. Mrs. Fiske garnered excellent notices, but it was clear that Judas was the most compelling figure of the evening. Corbin wrote that Tyrone Power's Judas "was a creation of extraordinary simplicity and psychological grasp, sinister, yet dignified; of evil passions, yet strangely sensitive, even in his hatred." And he described the scene in which Judas decides to betray Christ: "The light fades from the full radiance of day, by degrees that are actually imperceptible, to the blue-black of starlight, in which Judas, now alone on the stage, is the merest blue of a shadow. Then Judas knocks on the temple door. The high priest comes out with a torch, and holding it toward Judas reveals to the audience the evil, agonized face of the betrayer." The play ran fourteen weeks, after which it toured as best it could given the opposition of the Trust to the Fiskes.

Beautiful Eleanor Robson was probably the only reason for seeing **Audrey** (11-24-02, Madison Square), which Harriet Ford and E. F. Bodington took from Mary Johnston's novel. Set in 1727, it told of a foundling who has grown up happy to wander barefoot in the woods. She is loved by Jean Hugon, a half-breed Indian she has befriended, and by wealthy Marmaduke Haward. For her carefree ways she is snubbed by society and denounced as a wanton by a fire-breathing preacher. When she must decide between Jean and Marmaduke, who has been repulsed in seeking a more advantageous marriage for himself, she selects Marmaduke. Jean commits suicide.

Although W. Howell Poole's **The Game of Life** (11-24-02, Third Ave.) was set mostly in California, it was an English play. Two partners in a mine have a falling-out, resulting in a fistfight. During the melee a Mexican shoots and kills one of the partners. The other, goaded by the Mexican, flees to England, where he claims an inheritance due his dead associate. Twenty years elapse. The dead man's son sets out to find his father's killer and avenge the murder.

Thrills and sensations were laid on "with a lavish hand" in James R. Garey and William T. Keogh's **A Kentucky Feud** (11-24-02, Star), with "knives, pistols, shotguns, rifles and horsewhips" seeing constant action. The background for all this violence was an ages-old feud between two mountain families. The moonshining son of one family (its operating still was shown onstage) attempts to force the daughter of his enemies to live with him, but her

lover puts on all manner of disguises to give the fellow his comeuppance. A colored band and four buck dancers "did some extremely funny 'stunts' that provoked unlimited encores."

Madeleine Lucette Ryley's **The Altar of Friendship** (12-1-02, Knickerbocker) was written to order for Nat Goodwin and Maxine Elliott. Goodwin played Richard Arbuthnot, a successful author, who must pretend to fall in love with Sally Sartoris to please her father. Of course, pretense turns to reality. He must also pretend for a time to have been guilty of an affair with his ward and secretary in order to protect the reputation of his sister's husband. The play was accepted as pleasant fluff. As usual, Goodwin was saluted for his acting and his wife for her beauty.

Settings and costumes for the *Julius Caesar* Richard Mansfield presented the same night at the Herald Square were by Alma Tadema and had been used first by Beerbohm Tree for his revival in London. The stage of His Majesty's was considerably larger than that in New York, leaving some viewers to complain the settings seemed cramped. But there was no denying their color: "orange temples[,] . . . the deep, hard turquoise of the Italian sky, the prophetic crimson of a scarf trailing down from the feet of Caesar enthroned in golden light." Adding to the sense of congestion, albeit effectively employed, were dozens of supernumeraries. Mansfield's Brutus split the critics, who resorted to such adjectives as "flexible and powerful," "singularly colorless," and "Ibsenish." Arthur Forrest was Antony; Joseph Haworth, Cassius. Following a fifty-performance stand, the revival, which had been touring since early October, returned to the road for the rest of the season.

A short time earlier, New Yorkers had followed with intense interest the ordeal of a good-looking socialite, Richard Burnham Molineux. A general's son and a popular club man, he had been accused of sending a bottle of poisoned Bromo-Seltzer to Harry Cornish, the manager of the Knickerbocker Athletic Club, after an argument. The manager's cousin took some and died. After two mistrials, Molineux was found guilty. The verdict was appealed, and he was acquitted in a retrial. His father and sweetheart had stood by him loyally throughout. Now a touring play based loosely on the affair was presented. When it opened in Newark, reporters, if not critics, rushed over to cover it.

Robert Molando (or Milando) arrives at his club in Victor C. Calvert's **The Great Poison Mystery** (12-1-02, Blaney's, Newark) with Christmas gifts: a necklace for his fiancée, Blanche, a walking stick for his father, and, almost as a joke, a bottle of headache remedy for his widowed father's friend, rich old Mrs. Adamson. Mrs. Adamson's unscrupulous nephew and heir apparent, Harrison Cornwall, whose eye "glitters like a snake," asks Molando to introduce him to his father. Molando replies, "I do not consider you a fit associate for a soldier and a gentleman, especially my father," and Cornwall retorts, "I'll wager that with twenty-four hours I'll prove to the world that your father will be more pleased to shake hands with me than with you—his own son." When Molando laughs scornfully, Cornwall snarls to the audience, "Curse him! I'll do it!" The lights dim, leaving only a "red glow effect from the crimson glass coals of fire in the realistically painted open grate." Cornwall is seen pouring poison into the Bromo-Seltzer bottle, which Molando conveniently has left behind. Mrs. Adamson later drinks some and dies. Molando is sent to Sing Sing. There Molando (and the audience) witness an electrocution. Molando's attempted escape fails, but his retrial is ordered. Cornwall dies in a fire on the then new East River Bridge. The play never reached New York, possibly because of a lawsuit initiated by Harry Cornish. But in a few years Molineux would become the first American convicted of murder to have a play of his own given a major New York mounting.

E. S. Willard opened a four-week stand with Louis N. Parker's **The Cardinal** (12-2-02, Garden), which reused the old story of a cardinal torn between revealing the secrets of a confession or allowing his brother to hang for a crime he did not commit. *David Garrick, The Professor's Love Story,* and *All for Her* occupied the rest of the schedule.

The next evening brought in the season's biggest dramatic hit, David Belasco and John Luther Long's **The Darling of the Gods** (12-3-02, Belasco). Dusting off an old play of his about Italian brigands, Belasco worked with Long to reset the story in Madame Butterfly's Japan, but at a much earlier era. The outlawed Prince Kara (Robert T. Haines), having saved the life of Princess Yo-San (Blanche Bates) yet respecting her innocence, is invited to a feast by Prince Saigon of Tosan (Charles Walcot). Yo-San is betrothed to the weak Tonda-Tanji (Albert Bruning). She does not love him, so hopes to discourage him by insisting that before their wedding he must kill a dangerous outlaw. Her wish falls in with the plans of the sinister war minister, Zakkuri (George Arliss), who is resolved to kill Kara. He plants assassins around Saigon's house, but Kara eludes them. When Kara and Yo-San meet again they fall in love, and for forty days she hides him and lives with

him. However, when he decides to return to his outlaw band he is captured. Zakkuri has him tortured in a vain attempt to make him reveal the whereabouts of his followers. Then the minister makes Yo-San watch the torture and, since she has lost her reputation, tries to turn her into a courtesan. She refuses, but she does blurt out the outlaws' hiding place. Zakkuri releases Kara, who rejoins his men. They are set upon, and Kara is mortally wounded. Yo-San appears, and the lovers agree they will meet a thousand years hence in the First White Heaven. A thousand years pass. Arm in arm, the reunited lovers prepare to ascend to the next celestial level.

The story appealed to turn-of-the-century romantic notions. While the dialogue sometimes fell back on theatrical pseudo-Oriental argot ("I am augustly sorry. But your husband eats happily well—your most noble husband?"), most of it was less pretentious ("We shall be exquisitely happy when we are married. I shall wear dark clothes and always meet you at the gates with kisses."). Haines was a handsome but stiff, metallic-voiced Kara. Miss Bates, less mincing than as Cho-Cho-San, was beautiful to look at and effective. However, acting honors went to Arliss. His villainy was subtle and commanding, with just a hint of malevolent humor underscoring it. Yet, as with so many Belasco productions, the mounting walked away with the bulk of most notices. "The Brink of the River of Souls" showed a vast gorge: "The smoke-like water swirls and eddies and rushes downward toward the fires of Hades. Through the water shadowy forms of men and women pass [projected from behind on a white curtain], striving against the current, to reach the harbor of paradise." Similarly, for Zakkuri's sword room, "the walls and the floor are of lacquer, richly decorated. In the midst of the room stands a huge image of the War God, and below are the torture chambers. When the doors of these subterranean rooms are opened a flood of red light illumines the scene." Sets of such "surpassing beauty" helped the play run for 182 performances.

More superb acting aided **The Cavalier** (12-8-02, Criterion), dramatized by Paul Kester and George Middleton from George W. Cable's book, to chalk up a successful nine-week run. But then, dimple-chinned Julia Marlowe and dashing Frank Worthing were two of America's best young players. Coming home from their wedding, Charlotte Durand discovers that her husband, Captain Francis Oliver, is a Federal spy. He is forced to flee. But he keeps reappearing to make trouble for the Confederates and for Charlotte's old suitor, Lt. Edgar Perry

(William Lewers). At one point Charlotte is shot and wounded during a Confederate raid led by Perry. She confesses to Perry that she has always loved him, not Oliver. When news arrives that Oliver is dead, Charlotte is free to remarry. The evening's most applauded scene came when Charlotte, setting aside her southern sympathies, soothes a dying Federal officer by singing "The Star-Spangled Banner" to him, and is joined in the singing by Federal prisoners, over the objections of their captors.

In Fred S. Gibbs and Herbert Hall Winslow's **A Montana Outlaw** (12-8-02, Third Ave.), the villain produces a phony will in his attempt to deprive a cattleman of his ranch. A young cowboy who loves the cattleman's daughter exposes the would-be cheater.

The Slaves of Russia (12-8-02, American) centered on a prince facing exile after being falsely accused of plotting against the government. The leading role was taken by Bert Lytell, one of the few players in such lesser theatres to move on to better things.

Aubrey Boucicault was both adaptor and star of **Heidelberg; or, When All the World Was Young** (12-15-02, Princess), taken from Wilhelm Meyer-Förster's *Alt Heidelberg*. The producers were the Shubert brothers, who would achieve one of their greatest successes years later when they presented a musical version of the play as *The Student Prince*. The beer-garden waitress who loves and loses the prince was played by Minnie Dupree. This version ran just five weeks.

Hal Reid's **The Peddler** (12-15-02, 14th St.) was a patent ripoff of *The Auctioneer*. Its star was Joe Welch, who, like Warfield, had made a name for himself as a Jewish-dialect comedian. Reid's peddler has risen from the streets to own a small East Side clothing shop and has taken a blind waif into his home. His son comes under the influence of a baleful woman who nearly bankrupts him and who turns out to be the waif's mother. An inheritance allows the Jew to pay for an operation to restore the waif's sight, while a reconciliation of father and son ends the play. There seems to be no record of the litigious Belasco suing Reid, though he might have won this one.

Lawrence Marston's **A Remarkable Case** (12-15-02, American) borrowed shamelessly from *Trilby, The Charity Ball,* and other older plays. Indeed, the villain strutted around in "Svengali-like" makeup. When a man learns that his brother has violated his blind, orphaned sweetheart, he forces the brother to marry her, although he himself still loves the girl. His action saves his life, since a country doctor with

hypnotic powers also covets the girl and mesmerizes her into murdering her new husband. With the help of the good brother she is cleared at her trial.

W. L. Lockwood's **Alaska** (12-15-02, Third Ave.) begins with one miner goading a half-breed Indian into killing another miner, and then pinning the murder on a third miner, who is the villain's rival for the affections of the heroine. When this fails to win the girl, the miscreants blow up her father's store. The girl and her father are unhurt and are rescued by men from a coast guard cutter. Later the heroine is locked in a cabin on the slope of a volcano about to explode, but the hero comes to her rescue just before the eruption.

Some idea of how loyal playgoers were to yester-year's hits was attested to by the fact that the same or following week brought in *Uncle Tom's Cabin, Ten Nights in a Barroom,* and *Monte Cristo*.

For playgoers who kept count, **A Desperate Chance** (12-22-02, Grand Opera) was Theodore Kremer's fourth new play of the season to see New York footlights. This time he based his work on a recent tabloid sensation and used real names. The play told how two notorious criminals were able to escape from a Pittsburgh prison with the help of the warden's wife, and how all three were brought to justice. One exciting scene showed the escapees being hunted down in a raging snowstorm; a more sentimental moment showed the heartbreak of the warden's little girl on learning of her mother's behavior.

Although critics kept harping on Fitch's limitations as "a photographer of the wealthy and frivolous," they could not deny he created some very effective theatre. That was certainly the case with **The Girl with the Green Eyes** (12-25-02, Savoy). At its best it was a gripping study of jealousy. The Tillmans are cursed with a streak of pathological jealousy. Geoffrey Tillman (J. W. Albaugh, Jr.), who has married a housemaid while he was drunk, enters into a secret, bigamous marriage with Ruth Chester (Lucille Flaven), lest a rival wed her. The craven Geoffrey tells his brother-in-law, John Austin (Robert Drouet), of the first marriage, hoping he will arrange an annulment, but says nothing of the second. John learns the horrifying truth from Ruth, who is unaware she has wed a bigamist. But the most jealous of the Tillmans is Jinny (Clara Bloodgood), Geoffrey's sister and John's wife. When she comes across John and Ruth discussing Ruth's problems, her jealousy of Ruth, which has grown since Geoffrey first introduced her, becomes almost insane. Ruth is forced to reveal the truth about Geoffrey. Jinny is stunned and contrite, but John has suffered enough from her. He walks out. After he is gone Jinny locks the doors, closes the windows and curtains, and turns on the gas jets. Only John's fortuitous return (when he breaks down the door to reenter) allows him to save her life.

Although Fitch thought this was the best play he had written to date, reviewers were not that pleased. They complained, among other things, about the husband's reluctance to confide early on in his wife and about the tacked-on "happy" ending. Yet they also, as they usually did, conceded Fitch's worth. *Theatre,* among the yea-naysayers, added prophetically, "But even if his work will not endure . . . he has qualities and capacities that single him out as the forerunner of the great race of American playwrights that are to come." On Broadway, aided greatly by the fine, naturalistic performance of Miss Bloodgood, *The Girl with the Green Eyes* endured for 111 performances.

Fitch provided an interesting glimpse of the slow spread of contemporary technology at the same time he demonstrated his dramatic and theatrical craftsmanship. His first act took place at the Tillman home immediately after Jinny and John's wedding. The distraught serving girl (Lucile Watson) gives the first hint of trouble, then Jinny jokingly remarks how jealous she is when John kisses the bridesmaids. The second-act setting was an eye-popper, the semicircular room at the Vatican dominated by the Apollo Belvedere. Groups of stereotypical but effectively comic tourists pass in and out before John and Jinny, on their honeymoon, enter. John's meeting with Ruth provokes Jinny's blindly jealous outburst. When John has reassured her, Jinny mentions reading of a French girl who killed herself with charcoal fumes after her lover deserted her, and she remarks, "In America that girl would have simply turned on the gas." John laughingly replies, "I shall install *electric light* as soon as we get home!" Theatres had been lit electrically for over a decade, and plays had made use of electric lighting in buildings and homes for some while. The 1891 comedy *Niobe* had depended upon a loose electrical wire, in a home being converted from gas, to spark the plot. So Fitch's foreshadowing would have been pointless if his audiences did not know that many otherwise affluent homes had yet to convert.

Before coming to America in **The Cross-ways** (12-29-02, Garden), Lillie Langtry had given a command performance of the play for King Edward, who long had been openly bruited as one of her many lovers. Press agents naturally saw to it that the performance and Edward's favorable comments received widespread coverage in American newspapers. The

play's spotlight fell on a duchess whose lover steals some of her jewels to pay for entering his horse in a race and whose brother takes the blame for the theft to spare the duchess a scandal. More complications ensue before matters are resolved satisfactorily. Mrs. Langtry was credited with co-authoring the play. Her collaborator, who also played the part of her brother, was J. Hartley Manners. This was his American debut. On tour the star tried out **Mademoiselle Mars,** a play about the famous early 19th-century French actress.

Fitzgerald Murphy's **The Power of the Cross** (12-29-02, Third Ave.) dealt with more ordinary people, and Americans at that. But their trials and tribulations may have been even worse. The villain has reduced a husband and wife to poverty after the wife refused to become his mistress. In his shame at his poverty, the husband wanders off and becomes a tramp. Meanwhile, the villain has lured a minister's sister to New York and attempted to seduce her. The tramp stumbles upon the pair and alerts the minister. At this point the would-be seducer kills the tramp, but the minister arrives to hand over the scoundrel to the law. Then the minister and the new widow look lovingly at each other.

The year's last offering was a return of Sothern in *Hamlet,* which began a three-week visit at the Garden on the 30th. Cecilia Loftus, "who has now lived down the handicap of a brilliant reputation as a mimic," was Ophelia.

At year's end several papers gave extended accountings of theatrical affairs for the past twelve months. The *Journal* was typical. Unfortunately, it usually did not cite specific plays but dealt for the most part in generalities. Even so, they are interesting in suggesting perceptions of the time. The paper was especially proud that "forty-one of our native playwrights have written 64 of the 116 new plays produced." This startlingly large figure undoubtedly included many works offered at trial matinees, but it may also have included touring shows. The writer added that "only 18 Englishmen contributed 27 of the total." Equally heartening to the reporter was the fact that melodrama and adaptations from novels appeared to be on the wane. He called *Mary of Magdala* and *The Darling of the Gods* the year's best plays.

The new year, which was to end so disastrously, began hopefully enough. The arrival of Grace Livingston Furniss's **Gretna Green** (1-5-03, Madison Square) brought with it the latest young actress to be hailed as a star, Elizabeth Tyree. She played Dolly Erskine, a most eligible maid in the England of 1801. Her suitor is an earl (Max Figman), courting her in the guise of a riding master. Their prospects seem uncertain until Dolly's sister, Lady Chetwynde, elopes to Gretna Green with a young officer. Dolly and her swain give chase, anxious to avoid tragedy, since Sir William Chetwynde has learned of his wife's flight. When they all meet, Dolly and her beau see no way out but to claim it was they who were eloping and that Lady Chetwynde was coming to give the bride away. Miss Tyree's seasons in the sun were to be few. *Gretna Green*'s life was even shorter.

Not every Broadway season can boast a play based on poems by an incumbent secretary of state. But this, after all, was the era of Teddy Roosevelt, himself no mean writer, and a president whose diplomatic halls echoed to the footsteps of Jusserand and Bryce. Yet **Jim Bludso** (1-5-03, 14th St.), which I. N. Morris adapted from John Hay's *Pike County Ballads,* was consigned to the bottom rung of first-class houses in Manhattan, while on tour it occasionally had to book one of the better combination houses. And this though Robert Hilliard had top billing. Jim, who has worked on riverboats, has been deserted by his wife, leaving him to care for his son, Little Breeches. A budding romance between Jim and Kate Taggart is nipped when the wife returns. She proves a troublemaker, removing sandbags shoring up a levee and allowing the waters to rush in (real water began to fill the stage as the curtain fell). Jim and his black buddy, Banty Tim, are blamed and nearly lynched before their innocence is confirmed. In the machine shop of Jim's boat, the *Prairie Belle,* workers hold an impromptu minstrel show, with Little Breeches doing a "coon" dance on the table. When they leave, Jim starts to prepare for a big race down the Mississippi with another steamer. But Ben Murrel, who had earlier persuaded Jim's wife to run away with him, enters and picks a fight. During the battle sparks from the forge set the ship afire. Two tableaux follow: one showing the ship in flames and passengers being rescued from the water, the second showing a few stragglers swimming ashore and the burnt-out vessel sinking. News comes that Jim's wife has died, so he now can marry Kate. Jim was the sort of role Hilliard "reveled in," and "he stepped right back into the place he used to occupy in the hearts of the patrons of the house when Blue Jeans was on the top wave of popularity." Another reviewer gave a glimpse of how primitively effects were achieved when he recorded the methods used to show sunrise on the river: "The calcium light is thrown with a red piece of glass before it on the upper half of the scenery, while stage hands at the rear are making the lower half flutter so that you can feel the waters are passing by."

The plot was more farfetched and the effects possibly more spectacular in an out-and-out touring melodrama, Joseph Le Brandt's **Over Niagara Falls** (1-5-03, Third Ave.). Long before the action of the play begins, a noted Chautauqua preacher had seduced and left for dead a young girl. She was found and restored to health by an Indian warrior named Starlight. Years later the preacher's son attempts to seduce the daughter raised by the girl and Starlight, but the girl is now a famous circus performer, and she is prepared to denounce both father and son. The men seize her and force her into a barrel, which they throw into the river. The scene then switches to the falls themselves, "the effect of the moon-lit waters being managed in a way to compare favorably with . . . more ambitious Broadway productions." The hero jumps in a boat and, just before the barrel would tumble over the cataracts, pulls the girl from it. They "are seen clinging to a rock in the foreground as the curtain slowly falls, while the orchestra strikes up a paean of thanksgiving, [and] the house fairly shrieks itself hoarse." Learning of the rescue, the old preacher drops dead of a heart attack; his equally vicious son falls off a precipice.

A cruel, faithless husband, his put-upon wife, her devoted lover, and a half-wit who invariably appears in time to rescue the goodies were the central figures in **Her Marriage Vow** (1-5-03, Star). The play was billed as a comedy-drama, but its tense moments dominated. Since railroading served as background for the story, one climax found the heroine trapped between tracks as approaching trains came at her from both sides. The illusion, one critic stated, was "almost perfect."

The Bird in the Cage (1-12-03, Bijou), Clyde Fitch's translation of Ernst von Wildenbruch's *Die Haubenlerche,* found little favor. The heroine (Sandol Milliken), a girl of the lower classes, must choose among her rich, decent employer (Guy Bates Post), his rich, unethical brother (Arnold Daly), and a member of her own class. She selects each in turn before definitely settling on the last. Edward Harrigan played a bit role added by Fitch specifically for the old actor, so fondly remembered for the parts he wrote for himself in the long-gone Harrigan and Hart series. His character—that of a labor agitator, somewhat crude, greedy, and unethical, yet basically kind and honest—paralleled the figures he had been wont to portray. When scolded for spitting on the employer's lawn, he retorts, "The poor laboring man can't even have his comforts in the open air, but Beerpoint Morgan can expeculate on his marble floor." Fitch even interjected a song for Harrigan to sing.

John Reinhart's **The Scales of Justice** (1-12-03, American) recounted how a murdered man's dying call for his daughter is mistaken for an accusation of guilt. Luckily the daughter's fiancé is a district attorney, and he manages to trap the real killer, the murdered man's adopted son.

A husband's not unreasonable but erroneous suspicions of his wife's past provided the interest in Robert Marshall's **The Unforeseen** (1-13-03, Empire). Margaret Anglin and Charles Richman were featured in Charles Frohman's latest importation, which did good business for three and a half months.

Frances Hodgson Burnett's **The Little Princess** (1-14-03, Criterion) appears never to have seen Broadway's night lights, for it was given only at matinees. But its story of a little rich girl who is sent to a cruel charity home after her guardian loses his money but who eventually is restored to her fortune and family appealed sufficiently to "children and grown up children" to compile thirty-four showings, tour, and return the following season for several more weeks.

A vehicle, the *Dramatic Mirror* noted, might be anything from a sedan chair to a modern automobile brougham. **The Consul** (1-19-03, Princess), Charles F. Nirdlinger's vehicle for dialect comedian Louis Mann, was a sedan chair—slow, unwieldy, and with room for only one person. Set in the imaginary principality of Carinthia, it focused on Charlemagne Hoch. Charlie, the American consul, runs a bierstube to support his diplomatic post. His efforts to annex Carinthia to the United States irk the local prince, who cagily makes Charlie his prime minister, then forces him to resign. When Charlie wires Washington for his post back, the reply is that no one there ever heard of him or Carinthia. Matters look bleak until Charlie helps the prince land the girl of his dreams. Broadway put up with the nonsense for three weeks.

By contrast Madeleine Lucette Ryley's **Mice and Men** (1-19-03, Garrick) allowed Charles Frohman to keep one of the Trust's theatres lit for fifteen weeks. The best-laid plans gang agley in the late 18th century when an English scientist (John Mason) who has adopted a foundling (Annie Russell) in hopes of marrying her accepts that he must lose her to his dashing, youthful nephew (Orrin Johnson). The play had been a London hit and was the last of Mrs. Ryley's to be given a major American mounting.

Will C. Murphy's explanation of **Why Women Sin** (1-26-03, Star) was that they have husbands too busy making money to give them proper attention. One such wife takes up with a scoundrel-lover, but when she changes her mind the cad holds her prisoner. She remains a prisoner for six months (hubby is too busy making money to notice she has not been home recently). She finally escapes. The villain pursues and almost nabs her. However, just then another woman whom he had debauched spots him, pulls out her handy revolver, and brings the play to a close.

Of course, there were other reasons wives seemingly might sin, as Lem B. Parker's **For Home and Honor** (1-26-03, American) showed. A wife leaves a callous English husband when she learns he is a bigamist. She sails to America and marries a naval officer. Then the first husband shows up and announces he was not really a bigamist, since his other wife died before his second marriage. Whether it is this news or a raging thunderstorm outside, something causes the wife to snap, and she shoots her former spouse. A man who has been ambling across the stage all through the play turns out to be a detective hired by the second husband, and he helps exonerate the woman by showing that the shot man was, in fact, a bigamist since his second marriage was actually his third.

One intriguing series of mountings occurred at what had been the Berkeley Lyceum but more recently had been rechristened Mrs. Osborn's Playhouse. On January 27, the auditorium having been converted into a replica of an Elizabethan theatre, *Romeo and Juliet* was offered in true Elizabethan fashion—that is, with no scenery. *Much Ado About Nothing* followed a few nights later. The acting was often little more than adequate. Of the youthful players, only Edmund Breese, who essayed Romeo, moved on to theatrical celebrity. Shouldering aside performances, critics did not know what to make of the venture. The very idea of sweeping away the heavy, elaborate productions of the time caught them off base. The *Times* sniffed that Shakespeare "Should not Be Archeologized." Once again a bold ensemble learned that to be right too soon is to be wrong. But that did not stop some more established actors from trying simplified outdoor mountings of Shakespeare later in the season.

A poor flower girl and her crippled brother were central figures in **Hearts Adrift** (1-31-03, Star). They help clear a man falsely accused of murder and in the end are reunited with their long-lost father. A fight in an airship between the villains and the children's defender was the evening's high point.

The James Boys in Missouri (2-2-03, Third Ave.) was the second new touring play on the subject in as many seasons, and older ones were still dusted off now and then. The new play began with two outlaws attempting to cheat the boys at a card game. Later the Jameses' stepfather is nearly lynched, and their home is burned by unprincipled townsfolk. All this drives the two boys into a life of crime, which ends with Jesse's death and Frank's surrender.

Fred Darcy's **Nevada** (2-2-03, American) was a mass—or mess—of timeworn situations and characters. The sneering villain attempts to steal the deed to a mine, and when that fails, he tries to implicate the mine owner in a theft by slipping a stolen bag of gold into the man's pocket. The hero, a rich young man who rushes to the owner's aid, is "tied to a tree facing a loaded rifle to which is attached a string. A match is applied to the latter, and when it burns off sufficiently, the weight of a stone on one end will cause the pulling of the trigger." Happily the heroine, the mine owner's pretty daughter, hurries in just in time.

The longest run—191 performances—among the season's nonmusicals went to Augustus Thomas's comedy **The Earl of Pawtucket** (2-5-03, Madison Square), and its success demonstrated that Charles Frohman was fallible. He had rejected the play after Thomas insisted on Lawrence D'Orsay for the leading role. Thomas admired the actor's air of "distinguished, opaque, English toleration, alternated with bland astonishment, not unmixed with good-nature, but always self-confident, self-sufficient, and aristocratic." To evade a summons and to seek a lady whom he has met three times but whose name he never learned, Lord Cardington sails to America and takes the name of his American friend, Putnam, who now lives in London. Those three meetings had been unusual. First he put out a fire in the lady's hotel room. Next he smuggled her dog into England, and finally he was stranded with her for a whole night atop a jammed ferris wheel. Each time his "delicacy" prevented his asking the lady's name. He discovers the lady, Harriet Fordyce (Elizabeth Tyree), at the Waldorf, and courts her, unaware she was once Mrs. Putnam. His attempts to pass for an American are amusing. He tells one American acquaintance, "You *watch* me. I'd have said 'you ken't deceive them,' not cawn't. Aha. I've practiced it all the way ovah." In England his mysterious disappearance has led to the belief that he may have been murdered and that the real Putnam may have been the killer. The ersatz Putnam finds himself pursued by lawyers seeking alimony, by the police, and by others. Thomas's change of pace surprised and delighted most critics.

Many of the same reviewers came down heavily on Clyde Fitch's **The Frisky Mrs. Johnson** (2-9-03, Princess), his adaptation of Paul Gavault and Georges Berr's *Madame Flirt,* but Fitch's public ignored them—at least for the first five weeks. The remaining five weeks were played to small audiences, but actress-manager Amelia Bingham wanted to be able to advertise a sizable New York run. Although Fitch borrowed his story from a French play, the theme was old and in no way exclusively Gallic. Mrs. Morley (Minnie Dupree) has a lover, but when her husband intercepts a telegram from the man, her sister, Mrs. Johnson (Miss Bingham), steps forward to claim the cable was for her. However, none of these characters proved the scene stealer that Wilton Lackaye made of gruff Jim Morley, Mrs. Morley's brother-in-law and Mrs. Johnson's admirer. The elegant, lavish settings and props that Fitch demanded were capped by an eye-popping tea service, all, including a three-foot salver, "presumably of solid gold."

Andrew Mack found few takers when he offered **The Bold Soger Boy** (2-9-03, 14th St.), Theodore Burt Sayre's variant on the traditional Irish romantic play. What made the play different was that it took place entirely in America. The hero is a soldier who loves an Irish-American lass. The villain is a German agent, who is after both secret plans and the girl. Mack sang four or five songs before coming out on top.

Charles A. Taylor's **The Queen of the Highway** (2-9-03, Star) presented the final day in the life of a lady bandit. She has deserted her husband for a fellow desperado. With the help of Indians they attack a pony express rider, throwing him over a cliff and leaving him for the wolves. An Indian girl rescues him from the animals. But when the lady bandit attempts to hold up a mail train, a bullet with her name on it finds its mark. The man who fired it was none other than her deserted husband. Before she dies she manages to shoot her confederate.

Simultaneous premieres were accorded to **Resurrection** (2-17-03, Victoria) at Tree's theatre in London and in New York. Tolstoy's novel had been adapted successfully by Henri Bataille for Paris's Odéon, and Michael Morton had then made his English translation. The principal roles were that of a count who recognizes how his thoughtless love-making has led a serving girl into prostitution, and the girl, whose life and spirit the count determines to save after she is exiled to penal servitude in Siberia. Tree and Lena Ashwell played the roles in London; Joseph Haworth and Blanche Walsh in New York. Both American players were hailed for their impassioned yet not overwrought interpretations. Reviewers also praised the honest, ungarnished production, but many asked aloud if so relentlessly gloomy a drama could lure in playgoers. It did, running eleven weeks despite the lateness of the season.

The Night Before Christmas (2-23-03, Star) also arrived a little late. What's more, its calling itself a "pastoral drama" was a gross misnomer. Regulars at the combination house craved gripping melodrama, and that was what they got. A philanderer is murdered on Christmas Eve by a man whose wife he violated. The killer escapes undetected, and the murder is blamed on a young man whose fiancée the victim had tried to seduce. The young man is tried and convicted, even though his father is the presiding judge. A short time later, the judge becomes governor but, heedless of his wife's tearful pleas, refuses to reprieve his own son. Fortunately, the murderer's dying confession does. As if all this were not enough for patrons, a blind fiddler roamed through the play to add to its pathos.

Come March the season began to wind down early and swiftly—at least at first-class houses. James K. Hackett tried his hand at producing and missed the mark badly with John Oliver Hobbes (Mrs. P. M. T. Craigie) and Murray Carson's English play **The Bishop's Move** (3-2-03, Manhattan). The cleric's move was to take sides when a pushy duchess and a demure debutante both crave the hand of his nephew. Perhaps sensing failure, Hackett did not appear in the play.

In late January, George Fawcett had brought his celebrated Baltimore stock company to New York for a single matinee performance of Ibsen's still controversial *Ghosts*. "Matinee girls[,] . . . intellectual persons, and theatrical reporters, and tribunes of the mid-Victorian moralities" mingled in the audience to give the performance a varied reception, but some reviews were encouraging. As a result the production was brought back on March 3 to the tiny Mrs. Osborn's, where its two-week stand constituted the first "run" Ibsen enjoyed in New York. Mary Shaw was Mrs. Alving. She was a dedicated, intelligent actress who usually won the respect of the critics but was forever perceived as unpalatable caviar by most playgoers. Her Mrs. Alving was lauded for its warmth and understanding. Good if now forgotten players offered her strong support: Frederick Lewis as Oswald and Maurice Wilkinson as Pastor Manders.

Joseph Santley, who became a star in musical comedy and later was a famous Hollywood director, began his career as a "boy star" in touring melodramas. In Charles T. Vincent's **A Boy of the Streets** (3-9-03, Metropolis), he played a Horatio Alger–like waif who is thrown from a window by his drunken, loutish, adoptive father and kept in ignorance of his inheritance by a scheming lawyer. He is restored to his proper estate only after singing some songs and doing an imitation of the well-known dialect comedians the Rogers brothers.

E. Hill Mitchelson and Charles H. Longdon's **The Dangers of Paris** (3-9-03, American) came from London. A man who had been imprisoned on the perjured testimony of an army officer serves his time and vows revenge. He eventually is able to throw the villain into the Seine. Sadly, a flower girl who has stepped between them receives a bullet meant for the hero, and she, too, sinks into the waters.

Hubert Henry Davies set his comedy **Cynthia** (3-16-03, Madison Square) in his native London. Cynthia (Elsie de Wolfe) and her English husband (Charles Cherry) have lived beyond their means in a swank London home. When she confides to an American friend (Arnold Daly) that they are broke, he offers to lend her money. She refuses, going instead to a Jewish moneylender (Max Freeman). Even with his loan, the pair are finally forced to move to a garret. The moneylender comes to collect. Cynthia, knowing she cannot pay him, offers to dance in the music halls. To prove her ability she dons a gaudy gown and does a skirt dance. The moneylender is impressed. But her father-in-law is shocked. He offers to pay the couple's debts if they will live more prudently. Elsie de Wolfe was no great shakes as an actress, but her charm and growing renown helped the play run a month.

Hal Reid's **In Convict Stripes** (3-16-03, Third Ave.) told of yet another man imprisoned for a crime he did not commit. The hero goes to prison for murdering his stepfather, although his stepbrother and a second man really committed the killing. He spends three more acts clearing his name and bringing the actual criminals to justice. A note on a surviving manuscript says the play once had been called *The Little Red School House,* hardly a catchy title for this sort of melodrama. Indeed, the first-act setting showed a one-room schoolhouse on the audience's right and a play yard on the left. A fence ran across the rear of the stage, and a view of faraway mountains could be seen beyond the fence. The opening was a comic idyll, although such openings were not uncommon in melodramas. Directions noted, "*Before curtain rises, the hubbub of school children playing is heard. Cowbells in the distance and the occasional mooing of cows is heard. Birds singing and effect of wind blowing and stirring branches of apple tree. At rise, school children discovered. A boy with paper dunce-cap on high stool on platform inside school. Boys* [mostly barefoot] *playing marbles and leap frog. Girls 'Ring-around-a-rosy,' and tossing bean bag.*" A black woman (played, naturally, by a white in appropriate makeup) enters.

Martha: Howdy you all white chilluns.
Children: Hello, Aunt Martha.
Johnnie: "Nigger, nigger, never die, black face and shining eye." . . . How come you're so black, Aunt Martha?
Martha: Cause God-a-mighty made me that way. I see how en He made something else, too.
Johnnie: What's that?
Martha: Sassy white boys, I reckon dats what!

Of course, the main drama began to unfold relentlessly, ending in a mixture of bombast and sentimentality when the heroine's father announces to the hero, "John Walton by my authority as Governor of the State I pardon you! You are a free man." The hero embraces his sweetheart and tells her, "Mabel, we're going home." (At a time when even small towns had playhouses, the drama was first performed in Rising Sun, Ohio.)

Fine staging turned Frances Aymar Mathews's uninspired **Pretty Peggy** (3-23-03, Herald Square) into a success. Peg Woffington (Grace George) makes her entrance on a donkey into the midst of acrobats, strongmen, clowns, and other performers at Madame Volonte's circus in London. There she meets David Garrick (Robert Loraine) and quick as a wink becomes London's most popular actress. She is toasted at a lavish reception in Covent Garden's green room. But Garrick's friend, Eva Sorrell, is jealous of the attentions accorded the actress and provokes a riot during one of her performances. Some thirty rioters, dressed in colorful 18th-century costumes and brandishing sticks, ran down the aisles and even "seized" a box at the Herald Square. "The galleries, which had hitherto been obstreperous, sank into an awed silence, and the floor, which had hitherto been glum, rolled forth peals of hearty laughter." On the stage-within-a-stage, poor Peggy faints. Miss George had yet to satisfy most critics, but the clever hokum gave the play a passable run, and it returned in the fall for an additional month.

Horseracing, as it did so often in his plays, figured prominently in C. T. Dazey's **The Suburban** (3-23-03, Academy of Music), which had been doing excellent business for Jacob Litt on the road since the preceding May. Donald Gordon (Charles F. Gotthold) has been disinherited by his father, Robert (J. H. Gilmour), for marrying a girl of whom the father did not approve. To compound his problems, his scurvy English cousin, Sir Ralph (W. S. Hart), robs the elder Gordon's safe and makes it appear that Donald did it. Donald goes away for six years, making a fortune seal-hunting in the Bering Sea. Meanwhile, his father has lost his money in speculations and risks what little he has on a horse, Hurricane, in the great race at Sheepshead Bay. Sir Ralph has bet on a different horse, so attempts to drug Hurricane. James Hyde, the jockey, must battle to prevent this. He does and, donning his red sash, heads for the track. "The grand stand, in the back, seems to be peopled with an animated throng, and by the device of waving handkerchiefs and moving parasols and figures, produces an illusion which has never before been accomplished. Twelve horses are paraded before the race. . . . The judicial gravity of the judges is seen, while the betting proceeds." Then, they're off. A bribed jockey attempts to knock Hyde from his horse. He fails, and Hurricane wins.

Critic after critic commented on the excellence and beauty of the thoroughbreds used and noted such attractive byplay as two young black stable boys who have bet their last quarter on the race and who "kick and squirm in an ecstasy that threatens to precipitate them from the fence where they are standing." Naturally, Donald has returned. He helps in thwarting the drugging and is reunited with his wife and young daughter. Happy playgoers packed the vast auditorium for seven weeks.

Richard Harding Davis may have been the quintessential American war correspondent, but when it came to writing a comedy, he was, like many other American authors, not above setting his play in London. The hero of his **The Taming of Helen** (3-30-03, Savoy) was Philip Carroll (Henry Miller), an American playwright trying to have his first play produced in the West End. Philip loves an American debutante, Helen Cabot (Grace Elliston). She, however, prefers to flirt with an English bounder. Philip tells her that if she continues to flirt she can do it without having him around any more. A great English actress, Marion Cavendish (Jessie Millward), takes a liking to Philip and his play and talks a major London producer into mounting it. This convinces Helen that Philip and Marion are in love. On opening night she sends a letter to that effect to Marion. Although Marion is dressed for her role and must go onstage in fifteen minutes, she rushes out to talk to Helen, who is preparing to return to America. In the green room those minutes tick by as an irate producer and a baffled author wait. Marion returns in the nick of time, rushing onstage and leaving Philip and a contrite Helen to come to an understanding.

In 1900, shortly before his premature death, Roland Reed had begun touring in Sydney Rosenfeld's **A Modern Crusoe** (4-6-03, Fifth Ave.). He never lived to bring it to New York, and it remained for a local stock company to give it its Manhattan premiere. Drexel Ward, a know-it-all millionaire, decides to take his family, some rich friends, and his "typewriter," George Arnold, on a round-the-world trip, on which he hopes to establish a new speed record. Instead his ship breaks apart, and the passengers are stranded on a deserted island. The know-it-all and his friends turn out to know nothing about how to survive in such conditions, so George takes over and establishes his own little kingdom. After they are rescued by a U.S. warship and returned home, Ward wants things to return to the way they were. But George and the millionaire's pretty ward decide they prefer island life, so plan to sail back. The comedy found few takers, for knowledgeable theatregoers were aware that London was applauding a fine James M. Barrie play with a similar theme, which was promised for the new Lyceum in the fall.

Hal Reid, one of the busiest authors of touring melodramas, offered another in **A Little Outcast** (4-6-03, Third Ave.). A clerk has secretly married his boss's daughter and has just about convinced his new father-in-law to bless the union when it is revealed that the young man once served a prison term (for a crime he did not commit, naturally). Driven from his home, he takes to drink. He is approached by a band of thieves who try to enlist him in a planned robbery. The robbery will occur at the home of his father-in-law. Luckily, he is able to inform his wife and a friend of the plans, so when the would-be burglars meet again a primitive recording machine is put to work and makes a record of the robbers' plotting. The young husband is rehabilitated. Among the vaudeville turns spicing the evening was the singing of the Newsboys' Quintette.

A blind daughter (how many blind heroines had groped their way across stages this season?), her sister lured to the big city by the villain, a mortgage about to be foreclosed, an unjust imprisonment, a man trapped in a burning building, and a horse race that allows the girls to win needed money were a few of the clichés in **The Minister's Daughters** (4-6-03, Star), one more of the many touring plays for which no author took credit. Yet the play was billed as a comedy. Besides the opening farm setting, playgoers saw reproductions of the Jefferson Market Prison, Printing House Square, a real East Side refinery, and a Tenderloin music hall. This last allowed for a rash of variety acts. One young actor in the cast—he played the sweetheart of one of the girls—was Donald Meek.

The success of Mrs. Burnett's *The Little Princess* in January prompted a revival of *Little Lord Fauntleroy* at the Casino on the afternoon of the 13th. Again, only matinees were offered. But without Elsie Leslie some of the attraction had gone, so the revival lingered only two weeks.

Theodore Roberts, a fine actor who never quite made it to the top, was featured in Opie Read's "character drama" **The Starbucks** (4-13-03, Daly's). The character he played was Jasper Starbuck, a Civil War veteran who lives in the Tennessee hills and keeps his family in whiskey by running a small still. The Starbucks long have been engaged in a feud with the Peterses, so when Lije Peters is appointed a federal marshal he hauls Jasper into a Nashville court as a moonshiner. The good-hearted Jasper not only convinces the judge of his innocence, he induces the judge to arrest Lije as a blackmailer. A minor player, William Vischer, was singled out in notices for his portrayal (in blackface) of "a wheedling, lazy old Negro." The show had been a big hit in Chicago. New York's critics gave it accepting notices, but not the kind that are called "money" reviews. So *The Starbucks* closed after three weeks.

Edith Ellis Baker, a favorite in Brooklyn stock, was both the author and leading lady of **The Point of View** (4-14-03, Mrs. Osborn's). Her heroine, Marjory Thorncroft, is the scion of an old family, all of whom must live in reduced circumstances because of their inability to handle money. They are restored to wealth after Marjory marries a rich cattleman, James Stiles. He is decent and loving, but his crude ways—at least crude to eastern eyes—lead to a clash. Only when East and West reach an understanding are matters settled happily. Neither the play nor the actress was received enthusiastically. They left after a single week. A few years hence *The Great Divide* would treat the same theme more effectively and become a watershed in American drama.

On the other hand, some light farces did find late-season audiences. George Broadhurst's **A Fool and His Money** (4-14-03, Madison Square) started out like *All the Comforts of Home* but then went its own merry way. Percy Merrill, a rich young man whose stern father has gone to Europe, turns the family home into a gambling casino. Papa returns unexpectedly and kicks out the gamblers, the roulette wheels, and Percy. Living on his uppers, Percy is shunned by his fair-weather friends. Only a young painter and a sweet girl remain friendly. Percy's luck turns only after he sells an invention to his surprised, forgiving father. The second-act setting was novel, a Long Island golf course situated beside some railroad tracks. The golfers signal a train to stop so they can retrieve a ball. However, the comic high point of the evening fell to May Vokes as a servant girl (then called a "slavey"). She rode a dumbwaiter up and down to carry on a conversation with people on the floors above and below. The play ran six weeks and returned the following season.

The Messrs. Shubert were the producers of a double bill that began with a sentimental comedy and moved on to a farce. The curtain raiser, Tom Gallon and L. M. Lion's **The Man Who Stole the Castle** (4-20-03, Princess), was set on a Christmas Eve during the 16th century. A young man (Aubrey Boucicault) who has inherited a castle bought by his father from the family that built it is confronted by two young runaways, an eleven-year-old boy and a girl of five or six. Belonging to the family that sold the castle, they have come to reclaim it. The young man is touched and bequeaths it to them as a Christmas gift. The boy was played by one actress, the little girl by another. That second actress was Louise Allen, who was thirty at the time. Some notices stated the "two" authors were one and the same. The farce was George Arliss's **There and Back,** in which two husbands inform their wives they are sailing to America on business but actually go hunting in Scotland. They have some explaining to do when they return, since the ship they supposedly sailed on was lost at sea. In his autobiography Arliss noted that, although the New York engagement was not a smashing success, royalties from road companies and stock presentations kept him in pocket money for the next fifteen years.

Touring melodramas continued their love affair with give-away names when Charles A. Taylor's **The Child Bride** (4-20-03, Star) took the stage. Taylor's heroine was Nellie Golden; his villain, Herbert Small. To escape Small's clutches, Nellie, who is a mere sixteen, marries her childhood sweetheart, and she marries him in the schoolhouse she is attending. Small then alienates her from her father, and the young couple are forced to flee to a New York slum. In hot pursuit, the villain implicates the husband in a counterfeiting scheme, kills the heroine's girlfriend, and locks the heroine in a boathouse, which he warns he will set afire.

A Svengali-like hypnotist was the miscreant in Martin Somers's **In the Shadow of the Night** (4-27-03, Third Ave.). He murders a detective trying to capture him and kidnaps a rich man's wife and daughter. But the dead detective's son is no mean sleuth himself, and he tracks down the hypnotist.

A marvelous suit of incombustible paper promised to make George Washington Skipper (Maclyn Arbuckle) rich in H. J. W. Dam's **Skipper and Co., Wall Street** (5-4-03, Garrick). Complications arise

when the father-in-law of Skipper's partner claims he holds the patent. The comedy was a two-week flop. Other shows that opened the same evening fared little better.

Frances Aymar Mathews's **My Lady Peggy Goes to Town** (5-4-03, Daly's) went back to the colorful days of George III to recount its tale of a country girl (Cecil Spooner) who goes to London disguised as a boy and fences her way to fame and romance. The play had been touring profitably for months, as had the other offering at a first-class house.

That play was Herbert Hall Winslow's **The Vinegar Buyer** (5-4-03, Savoy). Its star was a popular vaudevillian, Ezra Kendall, who took on the role of Joe Miller, the ne'er-do-well "humorist" of Buscomb's Corners. He fails as a vinegar trader, but he does win the hand of a rich widow. Turns by some of Kendall's vaudeville colleagues enlivened the comedy.

Of course, different critical standards applied to the lesser touring shows, and, hit or fail, they usually played only one-week engagements. Five came in before any more novelties were offered at first-class houses. Arda La Croix's **Defending Her Honor** (5-11-03, Metropolis) had the usual falsely accused heroine hounded by the usual villain. But his heroine once had rescued a tramp and his young son, and they take it upon themselves to see that she is exonerated. The boy even drives off in a big sleigh during a blizzard to obtain evidence.

A husband who was stranded all night atop a ferris wheel (recall *The Earl of Pawtucket*) tells his wife that he has spent the evening with a friend, a man named John Brown, in Pickleton. He even gets a real friend to pretend that he is Brown and confirm his story. But before he can do that his wife has telegraphed to Pickleton, and in response a man whose name actually is John Brown appears on the doorstep. Such was the basic situation in Frank Wyatt's **Who is Brown?** (5-11-03, Fifth Ave.), an English farce "localized" for American consumption. (The ferris wheel incident actually had occurred in London some months before.)

Just when Hal Reid slept is moot. Reid, whose full name was James Halleck Reid, already had seen four of his plays produced during the season and had three more ready in May. Two arrived in tandem. One was **A Working Girl's Wrongs** (5-18-03, Third Ave.). A wicked boss stabs a girl who has demanded that he support her and the child she had by him, and then pins the blame for the stabbing on the fiancé of another of his employees who has spurned him. He almost succeeds in sending the hero to prison. A comic subplot followed a tough Bowery girl's pursuit of a Bowery boy, who she claims is guilty of breach of promise. But comedy and treacly sentimentality were interspersed randomly in the main plot, too. Thus when the boss, nattily decked out in evening clothes and an opera cloak, comes face to face with the tot he knows is his he gasps, "My God, I cannot kiss my child." The child shakes her tiny forefinger at him and shouts, "Fraidy cat! Fraidy cat!" to "the manifest gayety of the house." However, when the child finds her murdered mother, she assumes she is asleep and snuggles up next to her as the curtain falls. Some idea of the musical accompaniment to the play can be gauged by the song the orchestra crooned whenever the doomed mother, whose name was Annie, appeared. The song was "Annie Laurie."

There were similar problems in Reid's second play of the evening, **A Mother's Love** (5-18-03, American). In this case the villain, named Haycraft, tricks the heroine, named Grace, into marrying him. He is confronted by her mother and by another woman whom, it turns out, the villain had also tricked into marriage. This first wife disposes of him by shooting him from behind a tree. She reveals she is consumptive and has only a few days to live, thereby sparing herself the ordeal of a trial and leaving Haycraft's entire estate to Grace. (Note how frequently a secondary wronged woman or remorseful female cohort slays the villain in these sensation-melodramas.)

In Marion Russell's **The Little Church Around the Corner** (5-18-03, Star), a venal lawyer attempts to seduce his secretary. He has her decent if alcoholic husband committed to an insane asylum, reduces her mother to poverty, kidnaps the girl's child, and does lots of other nasty things before a meeting in the yard of the church leads to a happy ending.

Henry E. Dixey, never to find another success to match *Adonis,* enjoyed a modest hit with a double bill. The curtain raiser was Clay M. Greene's **Over a Welsh Rarebit** (5-21-03, Garrick), in which two old men, one of whom is a puritan, the other a rake, reconcile their differences over dinner at the Lambs. James Henry Darnley's **Facing the Music** centered on an American, John Smith (Dixey), living in London. The flat above his is newly occupied by a Rev. John Smith. The American recently has been robbed in a pea-soup fog by a notorious actress known as "the Duchess of Piccadilly," and when the minister's wife enters the American's apartment by mistake, he phones for the police. A vain, not very bright policeman arrives and promptly concludes the minister and his wife are professional thieves. Indeed, he has his suspicions about everyone who

calls on the American, much to the American's embarrassment.

With his doleful face, sinuous movements, and comic drawl, Dan Daly was another popular player in musicals. Unfortunately his move into straight farce met with failure. Edward E. Rose and George V. Hobart adapted **John Henry** (5-25-03, Herald Square) from Hobart's popular short stories. To oblige a friend, whose prospective father-in-law (R. C. Herz) has threatened to take the bride (Julie Herne) to Egypt, John Henry pretends he is the groom-to-be. Never mind that he is engaged to another girl (Florence Rockwell). Both fathers-in-law-to-be arrive on the scene with their entourages, and Henry must frantically keep them all apart. One highly praised scene showed rooms in Henry's home lit and darkened at varying times as the action moved up and down the stairs and from room to room. Only at the act's end were all rooms lit. A lone critic complained that a backdrop showed a snow scene, although the action supposedly took place in the summer. In the last act the players all were found at a railroad station, where Daly won laughs trying to read fortunes in punched train tickets. But those laughs were not enough to give the show a run.

The same evening saw *Romeo and Juliet* revived for a week at the Knickerbocker. Eleanor Robson and Kyrle Bellew were the doomed lovers; Eben Plympton, Mercutio. Miss Robson was admired for her beauty and youthfulness, but the consensus was she lacked tragic intensity.

Another, more unusual Shakespearean mounting, also on the same night, packed the capacious American Theatre. The legal limit of standees was exceeded, a phenomenon not unknown then on Broadway, but unusual in that many of the playgoers must have understood much of the play. The revival was *The Merchant of Venice,* and while most of the cast recited Shakespeare's lines, Shylock spoke in Yiddish. Of course, he was Jacob Adler, the great star of the Lower East Side. If his was not "the Jew that Shakespeare drew" it was a compellingly modern, realistic, and sympathetic one. His Yiddish translation offered subtleties of its own. For example, in speaking of Lancelot Gobbo's eating habits, instead of employing the word *essen,* which means to eat normally, he said *fressen,* which implies a certain gluttony. The reception was such that the production was moved to the even larger Academy of Music for additional performances.

J. J. McCloskey's **Across the Rockies** (also known as *Home, Sweet Home*) (5-25-03, Third Ave.) was another saga of blackguards attempting to gain control of a mine, which is seemingly worthless but which they know contains a rich lode. "Knives, revolvers, railroad trains, hanging-ropes and poison all had their share in the action, and gore and death were common. Indians aided in supporting the 'heavy' business." The melodrama's title was designed to echo earlier McCloskey hits—*Across the Pacific* and, most especially, *Across the Continent*.

And then there was Hal Reid, whose latest opus was **A Wife's Secret** (5-25-03, Star). Busy as he was, he took time from his writing to play the hero of the piece. He portrayed another all too readily mistrusting minister who forces his slandered wife from his house. She and her little daughter, helped by a loyal "colored mammy" (the third such to appear in a Reid play this season), struggle in the slums. Somehow she manages to return one night to her husband's church. In the belfry she encounters a vicious old suitor who attacks her. Rather than submit, she jumps from the tower. She is caught in the minister's arms. Her explanations restore his faith in her. The minister's mean-tongued sister, who caused many of the problems, is exiled to missionary work in Timbuktu.

Within a few years Reid would fade from the theatrical scene and from the memory of all but a few persistent theatrical historians. By contrast, the author of the next melodrama to make a one-week appearance in Manhattan was beginning a long career that would establish him as a Broadway figure of some note. In his autobiography Channing Pollock branded his **A Game of Hearts** (6-1-03, 58th St.) "one of the worst plays in history."

. . .

Channing Pollock (1880–1946) was born in Washington, D.C., but raised in Omaha and Salt Lake City. He returned to Washington to serve as dramatic critic on several local papers. He also worked for the *Dramatic Mirror*. He then became a publicist for Ziegfeld, Brady, and the Shuberts. While working with Brady he was responsible for an uncredited revision of *Pretty Peggy* shortly before its New York opening.

. . .

Critics were not unkind to the play, although they expressed a special delight in the manner in which Pollock listed his characters in the program. Taking his hint from his title, he called his cast "the deck," his villain "the knave," his hero "the ace," his heroine "the queen," her sister "the trump," and, perhaps a little cruelly, the supers "the discards." The queen and the trump are Anna and Tatters Martin. They operate a mine in Rocky Gulch, Utah. Their foreman, the knave, is Lawrence Alston, who

courts Anna all the while he is cheating the girls on his accounts. Enter the ace, a young metallurgist named James Manners. He is smitten by Anna and sets about exposing Alston. A fight ensues. Manners is knocked unconscious and placed on a belt moving toward the mouth of a rock crusher. Tatters, who has been locked in an adjoining room, breaks down the door, jumps on another, faster-moving belt, and rescues Manners not a moment too soon.

The season faded away with William Manning's English farce **Kindred Souls** (6-15-03, 125th St.), which Louis Harrison Americanized. At a seance a charlatan spiritualist tells an unhappily married woman to wait alone in her apartment that evening for the arrival of a kindred soul. Naturally the spiritualist plans to be that soul. However, before he can appear, the lady's friends come visiting and her wildly jealous husband returns unexpectedly early from a trip. Closets and cloth-covered tables hid characters in the confusion that followed, but only for a single week.

1903–1904

Optimism continued to help brighten Broadway's lights. Just after the season got under way, *Theatre* published its predictions for the ensuing months. One indisputably happy fact was that six theatres that had been rising were ready to open their doors. Their stages, and others, had been promised not only some eagerly awaited London and Continental hits but an "unprecedentedly large" number of Shakespearean revivals. On the down side, although the article made no judgments, was word that the "list of dramatized novels . . . is longer than ever"; more discouraging, "very few new plays by American authors" were on the slate.

But facile optimism was soon clouded over. A minor financial panic during the summer was no help. Far worse, in December the most horrible theatre fire in American history persuaded thousands of potential playgoers to stay at home. However, disasters and cyclical business slumps never have had enduring effects on theatres. Almost unnoticed, and waved away if it was, the Grand Opera House, a leading home to combinations, had spent the hot-weather months showing motion pictures. Before the decade ended, all such lower-class playhouses would be film theatres.

In the meantime, it fell to these very auditoriums

to initiate the new season. Daniel Hart and C. E. Callahan's **Slaves of the Mine** (8-8-03, 58th St.) led off the procession. Its subject was labor-management strife, and since it was designed for lower-class audiences, management was necessarily evil and labor good. The sensation scene came in the third act, when the mine owner believes he has trapped troublemakers in the mine and so blows it up. But the tough leader of the mine workers and his long-suffering wife emerge triumphant.

J. W. Harkins, Jr.'s **The Winning Hand** (8-15-03, Metropolis) was a stereotypical melodrama with a spectacular opening and an unusual ending. The curtain rose to show a great ocean liner arrive at its pier. A man has been robbed during the crossing, but, since a woman he has become attracted to is suspected, he claims the money has been recovered. A hardnosed detective refuses to believe him and jails the woman (who turns out to be the detective's former wife) as the thief. This allows the real thief, an adventuress, and her cohort to kidnap the lady's blind father and little girl. Knowing the girl is an heiress, the adventuress dresses up her own little boy in skirts to claim the money. The detective tracks her down but, in an expected twist, is shot dead for his pains. The villainess commits suicide, while the robbed man and the lady are free to wed.

The relighting of first-class houses began with Leo Ditrichstein's farce **Vivian's Papas** (8-17-03, Garrick), which featured Hattie Williams, better known on vaudeville and musical stages, and two capital comedians, John C. Rice and Thomas Wise. Vivian is a chorus girl courted by two rich old men, one of whom is married and the other a widower. When they arrive in close order at Vivian's surprisingly luxurious boudoir, she confides to each that the other is her father. The married man's wife and similar complications follow promptly. Given generally dismissive reviews, the farce nevertheless provided good enough hot-weather entertainment to compile a passable run.

The Factory Girl (8-17-03, 58th St.) was advertised as "Charles E. Blaney's Great Labor-Play. A Thousand Heart-Throbs and a Smile for Every Tear." So what if its poor time-clock puncher "seems a little above her position and is vastly more refined than the other factory girls." The mill owner's good son loves her; his bad son is jealous and tries vainly to implicate her for stealing. When that fails he sets about robbing a safe. The good brother catches him, but the bad brother knocks him out and places him on a belt moving toward a triphammer used to pound aluminum sheets. The heroine breaks down the door and saves him in the nick of time.

No spectacular sets enhanced **Down by the Sea** (8-17-03, Third Ave.), in which an unscrupulous father places his own daughter in all manner of jeopardy to achieve his nefarious ends.

Several reviewers found Edwin Milton Royle's **My Wife's Husbands** (8-24-03, Madison Square) more wholesome and therefore more "American" than *Vivian's Papas*. Considering the sanctimonious attitudes of the time, their conclusion is puzzling, since the farce dealt cavalierly with divorce. Its heroine, Gwendolin Winston (Selena Fetter Royle), has been divorced three times, so she has her hands full when she falls in love with Ralph Kirtley (Royle), who is leading a movement to outlaw divorce. Her problems are compounded when all three of her former husbands reappear and when Ralph's father, himself much married, arrives and begins to court her. Of course, she not only wins Ralph, but she also softens his hard stance. Some idea of the farce's tone can be gauged by Royle's setting the action in the Hotel Buncono ("bunco" was a contemporary term for scam) and by his calling an alcoholic Mr. Drinkwater (Edward Abeles). Most critics complained that the Royles' playing was too exaggerated, but once again pleasure seekers didn't seem to care.

The farmer's daughter in Fitzgerald Murphy's **Beware of Men** (8-24-03, Metropolis) thinks only of marriage, not divorce. But after she is despoiled by a city slicker, her outraged father orders her from her home. She heads for New York, still naively trusting her seducer. He leaves her with his "aunt," who is actually the proprietress of a bordello. The farm girl's minister, who loves her, comes seeking her. This irks the city slicker, who hires a gang of hoodlums to break up a mission meeting addressed by the minister. In the melee the seducer is shot and killed. A sadder, wiser girl returns home with her true love.

The leading lady in Walter Howard's English melodrama **Two Little Sailor Boys** (8-24-03, Third Ave.) was not its heroine but its archvillainess. To keep secret her past—she has abandoned one husband and turned their son over to her accomplice to be reared in a life of crime—she resorts to false accusations, murder, and all the other stock wicked tricks of the genre. At one point her son (played as a trouser role) is caught in the act by the woman's incorruptible stepson (another trouser role) and shown the error of his ways. But when he confronts the mother, she hurls him over a bridge "into a tankful of troubled, splashing and very wet river." His stepbrother swims to his rescue. The audience's reaction was such that "the curtain soars again and again amid ear-splitting whistles and yells." More of the same follows until the wicked lady is exposed at the close of the fourth act. On opening night, when the actress who played the part took her curtain call, she was pelted with potatoes. The play was brought into the marginally first-class Academy of Music for a month's stand at season's end.

Advertisements for Sullivan, Harris and Woods's mounting of Theodore Kremer's **The Evil That Men Do** (8-29-03, American) boasted of the "Largest Scenic Production on the American Stage . . . A COMPLETE MARVEL OF STAGECRAFT." Since, even before the production opened, the same advertisements noted "Thousands Turned Away Last Night," the claims were suspect. Any playgoers who had been turned away had been turned away because the house had been dark, and, given the name of the theatre, even the phrase "on the American Stage" may have been a sly double entendre. Nonetheless, one sensation scene did elicit deafening cheers from the gallery. The villain and his dark-haired mistress murder his twin brother, a minister who stands in the way of an inheritance. The pair also engineer the divorce of a young couple (the good wife was a blonde, albeit with the help of peroxide, as one paper cruelly noted) and kidnap their son, who is placed in a private school where another of their accomplices promises to poison the boy. The boy escapes, scaling a wall while the accomplice and the other pupils play a game with a huge medicine ball. The scheming brother, who has taken his dead brother's place, is preaching a sermon when his mistress arrives. She has learned he plans to desert her, so she stabs him to death. In the confusion a fire, set moments earlier by the mistress, is discovered in the church's belfry. The boy has been hiding there. Hearing his shouts, his mother climbs into the belfry to rescue him as the bells ring wildly. After the smoke has cleared, all the good folk embrace and the murderess is led off.

One of Kremer's most stalwart rivals was Charles A. Taylor, whose **From Rags to Riches** (8-31-03, Metropolis) provided a vehicle for the rising young Joseph Santley. Santley played a newsboy-waif who roams the streets with his little sister until a rich old man recognizes them as children of his ward, who disappeared after her husband was convicted of a crime he did not commit. The unrecognized ward now serves as the old man's nurse. She identifies herself, and happiness seems just around the corner. Unfortunately, the man's base nephew, who had been responsible for the husband's conviction, enters and makes more trouble. This causes the old man to die of a heart attack. The nephew drives out the ward and her son but imprisons the little girl in a

Chinese opium den. She puts up a fight, and just when her energies flag, her brother rushes in to her rescue. The wronged husband also returns, clears his name, and helps jail the nephew. A wide-eyed, "frisky," nineteen-year-old actress who played the little sister received some of the best notices. According to the *Dramatic Mirror,* she furnished "a most lifelike sketch of a girl of the streets and won much applause by the deftness and vivacity of her sketch." She was billed as Laurette Cooney but afterwards, as Taylor's wife, assumed his surname in her billings.

Owen Davis also would move on to greater fame, but for the moment he, too, scraped out a living with touring shows. His **The Lighthouse by the Sea** (8-31-03, 58th St.) told of a miscreant's attempts to expel an aging lighthouse keeper and marry the old man's granddaughter. In the play's sensation scene, the girl tightwalks a thin wire in order to relight the signal, which the villain has put out. She thus saves a ship with her sweetheart aboard.

Distorted echoes of *Beware of Men* resounded throughout Thomas Oakley's **The Charity Nurse** (8-31-03, Star). The daughter of a blind minister is about to marry a good-natured mill foreman when a cynical city slicker lures her to New York with promises of marriage and a better life. Once there he forces her to sing at an elegant club. The jilted suitor arrives at the club, and a shooting spree follows, but the villain escapes. When the ruckus ends, the girl, leaning limply against a table, realizes she has a smoking pistol in her hand. She runs away and takes work at Bellevue as a nurse. She is hounded by the villain, but her still loyal suitor comes on the scene and proves to the girl not only that her marriage was a sham but that her supposed husband already has a wife. The police enter to arrest the seducer for forgery. More shooting erupts, but this time it leads to a happy ending.

The hero of *On the Frontier* (8-31-03, Third Ave.) is a rugged mountaineer who loves a supposed Indian girl named Blue Flower, Queen of the Hossowas. His reward for saving her from assorted perils is not only the maiden's hand but the knowledge that she is not really an Indian. Rather, she is the long-lost daughter of an army colonel. Real Indians from the Seneca, Cayuga, and Tonawanda tribes added verisimilitude, "though the only thing they had to do was to look fierce and give an occasional war whoop."

The curious late-summer dichotomy of melodrama for the masses and comedy for more bejeweled playgoers continued when Weber and Fields presented William Collier in Eugene Presbrey's **Personal** (9-3-03, Bijou). By now Collier had developed a distinctive, almost Cohanesque style, "marked by a dapper assurance near akin to the impertinent, and that rapid fire, pat readiness of repartee which wins laugh after laugh in succession too quick for sober thought." However, his new vehicle was rejected scathingly as "a bore." A retired businessman, conscience-stricken over his failure to keep his promise to his long-dead partner to raise the man's son, puts an ad in the paper seeking the boy. A young reporter (Collier) appears to find out more about the story and in the interview discovers he is that missing heir. He helps dissuade the businessman's elder daughter (Jane Peyton) from marrying a fortune-seeking foreigner (Brigham Royce) and wins the hand of the family's younger daughter (Nanette Comstock). Only Collier's popularity, plus some forcing, kept the play on the boards until a replacement was rehearsed.

In the preceding season Lillie Langtry had met with failure despite the fact that her play had been accorded some much publicized royal approval. Now, without a royal imprimatur, she failed again in Percy Fendall's comedy **Mrs. Deering's Divorce** (9-7-03, Savoy). The star played a society woman who backs away from a possible second marriage in order to remarry her former husband. Mrs. Langtry's beauty and her lovely gowns received the few kind words critics could muster.

As usual in this era, revivals and return engagements served frequently as filler bookings. However, one such revival reached exceptionally far back and met with surprising success when Andrew Mack appeared in Dion Boucicault's forty-year-old *Arrah na Pogue* at the 14th Street on the 7th. It was warmly welcomed and ran two months.

Combination houses were also busy on the same night. In Charles E. Blaney and Howard Hall's **Child Slaves of New York** (9-7-03, 58th St.) a vicious broker attacks a mine owner, steals his deed, and leaves him for dead. But the miner is not dead, and he and his Eskimo rescuer head for New York to retrieve the deed. Meanwhile, the broker, knowing that the miner's wife must sign the deed to validate it, kidnaps her child and places the infant with a gang of thieves who raise children to become pickpockets. A "boy detective" named Homer Sherwood (note the similarity to Sherlock Holmes) is put on the broker's trail. The thieves' den is alongside the river, and when the boy and the police arrive, the kidnapped child is thrown in the water, where she is saved by men from a police boat. One critic, condemning the play as "thoroughly exaggerated and very much overdrawn," concluded, "It fairly howls."

So did William Bonelli's **A Great Game** (9-7-03, Third Ave.), which another critic observed "has dramatic worth to appeal to those below stairs." The very first scene contained a sensational mine explosion. As in *Child Slaves of New York*, the villain steals the deed to the mine, but this time the heroine and her sweetheart must pursue him from Arizona to a harem in Algiers and to China. There they are confronted by rebellious Boxers. The American army comes to their aid, killing the villain in the process.

Three first-class stages relit the next Monday, but only one offered an American play, and that play came perilously close to being a musical. Indeed, with six new songs, Edward Harrigan's **Under Cover** (9-14-03, Murray Hill) was essentially a resurrection of the genre plays with music that Harrigan had reveled in during his heyday. Once more German-Irish antipathies and even more violent white-black disputes were at its core. Some whites want to obtain the deed of a neighboring black cemetery so they may expand a racetrack. Owney Gilmartin (Harrigan), a wise if not totally grammatical Irishman, brings about a sensible resolution. Of Harrigan's old troupers only the beloved Annie Yeamans was on hand. But she and Harrigan were enough to ensure an eleven-week run.

Stephen Phillips, the Christopher Fry of his day, was the poet-author of the blank-verse **Ulysses** (9-14-03, Garden). The story closely followed tradition. Tyrone Power's Ulysses, although not up to his earlier Judas, was hailed, while Rose Coghlan's Penelope caused several reviewers to lament that this fine, beautiful actress had been neglected for too long. First-night gremlins wrecked the important scene in Hades. Lighting was miscued, and Ulysses's barge groaned, creaked, and broke down during its passage across the stage. For all its problems, the drama ran eight weeks.

Charles Warner, billed as "England's greatest melodramatic actor," was the star of a revival of *Drink* (*L'Assommoir*) at the Academy of Music. His performance, which he had offered in his homeland more than 3000 times, was so harrowing "the audience shrank back shuddering in their seats with their hands to their faces." Rave notices kept Zola's play at the mammoth house for five weeks.

What might Warner have done to elevate Theodore Kremer's second touring melodrama of the season, **No Wedding Bells for Her** (9-14-03, Grand Opera)? Audiences assuredly had lost count of how many mines had figured in such plays, and probably didn't care. The evil partner in a mine covets his partner's daughter, but she loves the mine's foreman. When the workers strike and the foreman sides with them, the villain sees his opportunity to blame his rival for some violence. He commits other dastardly deeds before he is killed. Despite the title, wedding bells do ring for the heroine.

Playgoers may have been slightly confused by the title of another of the evening's openings, Kremer's **Wedded and Parted** (9-14-03, American). Three women were the key players. One, obsessed with her love for another woman's husband, frames the innocent wife for a crime. The poor wife is cast out into the snow, with her baby in her arms. Her heartless foe even finds a way of tormenting her when the guiltless woman is sent to prison and must serve in the prison's laundry. But the good wife's loyal maid removes bullets from a gun with which the villainess attempts to shoot her rival.

Owen Davis's second work of the season, **A Great Temptation** (9-14-03, Metropolis), featured a warm-hearted professional gambler as its hero. On a riverboat, he falls in love with a girl whose gambling-addicted father has been bilked of all his money and property by crooked players. The hero wins back the money and property, but the crooks kill the father, kidnap the girl, and hide her in a cave. While rescuing the girl and confounding the kidnappers, the hero discovers a rich vein of lead in the cave.

John Drew was apparently the only reason to sit through Anthony Hope and Harrison Rhodes's **Captain Dieppe** (9-15-03, Herald Square). The role Drew played was the role he usually played, the suave *raisonneur*. In this case he reunited a count with his debt-ridden countess and won the affection of the countess's best friend.

Charles Hawtrey, an English actor not unlike Drew, brought over his London company to allow Americans to savor the delights of F. Anstey's **The Man from Blankley's** (9-16-03, Criterion). A couple discover they have invited eleven people to dinner, and rather than have thirteen at table they "hire" an additional guest. When a gentleman-scientist knocks at their door by mistake, he immediately is assumed to be the rented extra man. The long second act found most of the characters seated at the dinner table, with a few servants providing the only movement. It was risky as theatre, but skilled British comedians handled it with flair.

The prolific Theodore Kremer's **Rachel Goldstein** (9-21-03, Grand Opera) begins on a ship, "which rocks and tosses in a most marvelous manner, throwing everybody into all sorts of heaps." On board, in steerage, is a Russian immigrant, Rachel. She witnesses a murder, and the shock of it leaves her in a strange torpor. Later, at a New York hotel,

she spots the killer and her senses are restored. The killer realizes she can identify him. He goes to her rooms in Hester Street, sees her father, seemingly asleep, and moves to kill him. But the "father" pulls off his disguise and proves to be none other than Rachel, pistol at the ready. The villain escapes, and more frightening adventures befall Rachel before she hands the murderer over to the police and marries a rich man whom she met aboard ship. Specialties included a turn by the Hebrew Boys' Orphan Asylum Band.

James R. Garey's **New York Life** (9-21-03, Star) also touched on immigrants, albeit not so directly. A banker frames one of his messengers for theft after discovering that the messenger is his rival for the hand of a young girl. The banker fails to reckon with the mistress he abruptly discards. She is a denizen of Little Italy, and she persuades her brother to stab the banker to death. The action moved from Madison Square and the new Flatiron Building to a Bowery dive and to Little Italy.

The season's first "long run" went to Clyde Fitch's **Her Own Way** (9-28-03, Garrick). The title was not Fitch's. Despairing at Maxine Elliott's rejection of all his suggested titles, he said, "Let her have her own way"—so she and the play did. Some turns of plot were reminiscent of *The Climbers*. However, that play, which opened with a funeral, was basically a drama. Since *Her Own Way* was a comedy, it started with a children's birthday party, the tots' chitchat providing much of the exposition. It seems that their aunt, Georgiana Carley (Miss Elliott), has two suitors, the gentlemanly Lieutenant Coleman (Charles Cherry) and the pushy upstart, Sam Coast (Arthur Byron). She prefers Coleman, but her family, with whom she lives, admires Coast. Misunderstanding a remark of hers, Coleman leaves for duty in the Philippines, where he is later reported killed. Her brother, Steven (R. C. Herz), discloses his speculations have bankrupted him, so Georgiana hands over her own fortune on the condition that Steven not speculate with it. Goaded by Coast, he does just that and loses it. Coast now believes that Georgiana must marry him or see herself and her family reduced to poverty. She vehemently refuses. At that point Coleman returns. Reports of his death were erroneous. The misunderstanding is cleared up, and he is free to wed Georgiana. Both play and performers were extolled in morning-after reviews. Typically, the *Times* welcomed "the most perfectly acted play seen in Broadway in many a long year. Taken all in all, it is the most evenly excellent of Mr. Fitch's social comedy dramas."

The hero of **Checkers** (9-28-03, American), which

Act Four : 1899–1906

Henry M. Blossom, Jr., adapted from his own novel, was Edward "Checkers" Campbell, a young man given to wagering. When he falls in love with Pert Barlow, he promises to give up his betting if she will marry him. She accepts. But Pert's father has different ideas. He insists Checkers first must earn $5000. So Checkers, breaking his promise, bets on a horse and wins the money. Pert is forgiving and her father satisfied. The comedy was praised and the racetrack scene, with stands climbing up one side of the proscenium, applauded, too. In 1920 the show was made into the musical *Honey Girl*, but by that time Blossom, who had become famous as a librettist, was dead.

Charles A. Taylor's latest rearrangement of sensation-melodrama clichés was offered in **Through Fire and Water** (9-28-03, Star). His plot centered on a girl, the daughter of the president of a railroad, betrothed to the line's sinister superintendent but in love with a young engineer. Naturally the superintendent resents her attitude, so he connives with a half-breed Indian to put the engineer out of the way and, failing that, kill the girl. At one point the heroine, clinging to the branch of a tree, saves the bound hero's canoe from going over a waterfall. He reciprocates by driving a locomotive through a fire (shades of *The Ninety and Nine*) to rescue her. According to one reviewer, at times "it seemed as if Bedlam itself was let loose." He also complained that the parlor car looked like "an East Side horse car on a rainy day" and that the poor hero dressed like a dude.

Faithful playgoers at combination houses had a pretty good idea in advance of what happens **When Women Love** (9-28-03, 58th St.). The woman in this anonymous thriller is a factory girl whose uncle and mother are murdered when they refuse to hand over some valuable papers. The evil genius behind the killings is the New York district attorney. Luckily, the girl's lover produces a gramophone on which he has recorded the D.A.'s planning the murders. The D.A. attempts to jump from a window at the Jefferson Market Court, but "he strikes a network of live wires and the vivid flashes that appear indicate that he is being roasted to death."

Mines continued to provide an inexhaustible lode for touring melodramas, even for one called **New York Day by Day** (9-28-03, Third Ave.). The blind daughter of a South African miner who was murdered by his partner has come seeking refuge in New York, where she is offered shelter by a kind young sailor. The surviving partner learns she is still alive and thus has a legal claim to a share in the mine. He travels halfway around the world to make trouble for her but is finally given his comeuppance by the sailor.

Two dramatizations of novels opened the next Monday, and both proved disappointments. **Hearts Courageous** (10-5-03, Broadway) was adapted by Franklin Fyles and Ramsey Morris from Hallie Erminie Rives's story and served to display Broadway's newest "star," Orrin Johnson. Johnson portrayed Louis Armand, Marquis de la Rouerie, who comes to America with documents pledging French support for the colonists against the British. He meets numerous rebel patriots, among them Patrick Henry (W. S. Hart). Henry cannot resist telling the Frenchman that his philosophy is "Give me liberty or give me death." But Armand also encounters his share of troubles. He is wounded and imprisoned. With the aid of a beautiful American, Anne Tillotson (Maude Fealy), he accomplishes his tasks, then marries Anne. Johnson was a strikingly handsome, capable enough actor but certainly not star material. *Theatre* commented, "The play is either too big, or he too small, for at no time did he appear to dominate the situations." Even the presumptuous cockiness with which he took his curtain calls annoyed some critics. His stardom lasted as long as the play did, three weeks.

A more established star fared only a little better when W. H. Crane arrived in **The Spenders** (10-5-03, Savoy), which Edward E. Rose transcribed from Harry Leon Wilson's novel. Peter Bines (Crane), a rugged pioneer type, has made a fortune with his One Girl mine and hopes his grandson, also named Peter, will follow in his footsteps. But the younger Peter rushes off to New York to enjoy its high life until his Wall Street plunge plunges him into bankruptcy. The old man, who has come east to watch over his grandson, secretly had hedged his bets but pretends to be bankrupt, too. He brings the youngster to his senses. Crane's "customary sincerity, emphatic manner, dry humor and wholesomeness" were not sufficient to carry so weak a vehicle. Before long he was touring again in *David Harum*.

The most glowing notices in morning-after reviews were reserved for Mrs. Fiske's week-long revival of *Hedda Gabler*, which opened the same night at the Manhattan. The production marked an important turning point in American acceptance of Ibsen. For all Mrs. Fiske's understatement, her Hedda conveyed "a lowering malignity, a low-browed intensity of tragic passion that chilled one's heart and seemed to stop the pulse." Wisely, she chose an excellent supporting cast. Carlotta Nillson's Mrs. Elvsted and William B. Mack's Tesman won high praise. Only Hobart Bosworth as Lovberg was chastised for overacting.

Healthy economics and easygoing practices of preunion days allowed William Collier to perform his failed *Personal* until the night before its replacement was ready. The change was made in midweek when Collier came out in Ernest Lacy's **Are You My Father?** (10-8-03, Bijou), based loosely on incidents in Captain Marryat's *Japhet in Search of a Father*. Both titles hinted correctly that the story was the reverse of *Personal*'s, for now a son seeks his long-lost parent. He asks his embarrassing question to everyone he meets, eliciting some odd responses. Eventually he discovers his father to be an old general (made up, according to one account, to resemble Ibsen). The play was set in the 1840s, allowing Collier to sport "coats of cinnamon-buff, asparagus green, and wine red" with brass buttons and ruffled cuffs. All to no avail, for bad notices forced Collier to abandon his search after a week and a half.

The lights of Broadway's newest theatres began to shine when Richard Mansfield came to town in **Old Heidelberg** (10-12-03, Lyric). Although Mansfield was a star of the first magnitude, the play was not new. Theatregoers had seen another version of it the season before. But the forty-six-year-old Mansfield was hailed for making the young prince, called Karl Heinrich in this redaction, seem a believable nineteen.

Mansfield's vehicle created no waves, but E. H. Sothern's did. During its Detroit tryout the mayor threatened to close it as blasphemous. Justin Huntly McCarthy's "Morality Play" **The Proud Prince** (10-12-03, Herald Square) opens with Robert the Bad, King of Sicily (Sothern), determined to seduce Perpetua (Cecilia Loftus), daughter of his executioner. She repulses him, and he curses heaven. At that "the skies darken, lightning crashes, and the statue of an archangel, hitherto motionless at the entrance to an adjoining shrine, descends from his pedestal, and, drawn sword in hand, pronounces an awful sentence on the now cowed and trembling king." He is transformed into a grotesque, crippled jester. His courtiers scoff at him. Meanwhile, Perpetua has been taken to his harem (the scene that offended so many). She continually repels his advances, and he begins to recognize her goodness. When she is attacked by another man, the king kills him with a huge iron cross he grabs from an altar. But Perpetua is condemned as a witch. The repentant king takes her place on the pyre and is transformed back to his original shape. The fire is extinguished, allowing him once more to claim his

throne. Despite sumptuous settings, gorgeous costumes, and fine acting, the principal players could not repeat the success they had enjoyed with McCarthy's *If I Were King*. Even so, for its last few performances the drama was moved to enable it to have the honor of opening the new Lyceum.

A snow scene in which the hero's mother is cast out of her home by his wicked brother, and the hero at the throttle of a locomotive speeding to the heroine's rescue, were highlights of Neil Twomey's **The Wayward Son** (10-12-03, Grand Opera). The supposedly wayward hero's brother is a counterfeiter who tries to implicate the hero in his chicanery. The heroine is a Secret Service woman who helps catch the villain and lands the hero. Twomey played his own hero, exciting the gallery to raucous cheers when "he throws his head back with a manly toss and cries, 'Stand back! You shall not touch a hair of her head!' "

Hal Reid was credited with having Americanized Lingford Carson's **The Heart of a Hero** (10-12-03, Third Ave.), whose heroine joins forces with the brother of a wronged girl to best the villain now attempting to wrong the heroine.

The Fiskes had not expected *Hedda Gabler* to draw as well as it had. They could not cancel its cross-country tour nor find another home for Mr. Fiske's next production. Unfortunately, that mounting, Angel Guimera's Catalan drama **Marta of the Lowland** [*Terra Baixa*] (10-13-03, Manhattan) was not to New York's taste. Marta (Corona Riccardo) is a beggar's daughter who has been sheltered and seduced by a rich landowner (Hardee Kirkland). When he tires of her and decides to make a proper marriage, he orders one of his shepherds (Hobart Bosworth) to wed her. The girl and the shepherd at first are suspicious of each other, but they eventually fall in love and flee to the hills.

Charles Frohman had better luck when he imported Cecil Raleigh's Drury Lane melodrama **The Best of Friends** (10-19-03, Academy of Music). The friends are an Englishman (Joseph Wheelock, Jr.) and a South African Boer (Richard Bennett), both students at Oxford. They find themselves rivals for the same girl's hand and, after war breaks out, on opposing sides. The Englishman wins the girl (Katherine Grey). Spectacular settings included a great banquet hall with 100 uniformed men at three long tables. The huge hall was lit by hundreds of candles. In later scenes Lionel Barrymore won applause for his delineation of an old Boer general.

Frohman had a second hit that same evening when he helped open another new theatre with a vehicle for Ethel Barrymore. Hubert Henry Davies's **Cousin**

Kate (10-19-03, Hudson) was a feather-light English comedy. A cynical young novelist, convinced she will never fall in love, encounters an Irishman (Bruce McRae) on a train. They later meet at an empty house and realize they are fond of one another. Then the authoress learns the Irishman is engaged to her own cousin. The cousin's decision to marry another man leaves the road clear for the young lovers. Miss Barrymore's gift for whimsical comedy aided the play's popularity.

A whimsical tramp named Willie Wildflower was the central figure in a touring "comedy-melodrama," The Ragged Hero (10-21-03, Third Ave.). Between specialty acts, he time and again saved the heroine from the villain's snares and finally helped put him away.

Henry Irving, no longer supported by Ellen Terry, made what proved to be his final New York visit, opening with a new play. Dante (10-26-03, Broadway) was translated by Laurence Irving from Victorien Sardou and Émile Moreau's original. While the third of its four acts was devoted to an elaborate pageant recreating Dante's journey through Hell, the rest of the play dealt with the poet's prolonged attempt, ultimately successful, to save his illegitimate daughter from his vengeful, highly placed enemies. The play was an unmitigated bore, but Irving's Dante was hailed for its intensity and austere dignity. The last week of his three-week stand brought back Waterloo, The Bells, Louis XI, and The Merchant of Venice.

Irving had to compete with the opening of another new theatre, one of the grandest of all Manhattan's playhouses, the New Amsterdam. Although the theatre later became identified mainly with musicals, its opening attraction was , Klaw and Erlanger's production of A Midsummer Night's Dream, with Nat Goodwin starred as Bottom. The mounting was as elaborate as the auditorium. "Fairies soared through the air[,] . . . electric bulbs twinkled in endless profusion among the flowers, and the woodland glade and Titania's bower were symphonies of soft light and subdued color." The ass's head had eyes that rolled, ears that wiggled, and a mouth that seemed to speak. Underscoring this was Mendelssohn's music, rearranged by Victor Herbert, who also added songs of his own. Some reviewers carped that Goodwin played Bottom too broadly and that Oberon and Puck were both assigned to actresses (Margaret Crawford and Lillian Swain). Among the other players, Ida Conquest was Helena; Florence Rockwell, Hermia; Kathryn Hutchinson, Titania; Etienne Giradot, Flute; and William Farnum, Demetrius. If one review was headlined "SHAKE-SPEARE TREATED AS MUSICAL COMEDY," that may only have whetted playgoers' appetites. The three-week engagement did land-office business, with the final two Saturday performances reputedly taking in a then astounding $5000.

Si U. Collins's At Duty's Call (10-26-03, Star) was an odd play, starting out as a melodrama and ending as a character study. In a prologue set during the Civil War, one cousin arranges to have another cousin, who has been shell-shocked, committed to an insane asylum so that he may claim his inheritance. Thirty-five years pass. The surviving cousin has been released from the asylum for twenty-five years. He is seventy-five and can remember nothing of his early life. He has become a village eccentric, claiming to be a fire marshal. He walks around in a fireman's helmet and brandishes a fire axe. A blow on the head causes him to forget his later years and recall only those before he became shell-shocked. Seeking out his treacherous cousin, he learns the man is dead. But he finally effects a reconciliation of sorts with the dead man's cold, stiff son.

One of the season's most successful bits of escapism was Raffles, the Amateur Cracksman (10-27-03, Princess), which Eugene Presbrey and E. W. Hornung dramatized from Hornung's short stories. A. J. Raffles (Kyrle Bellew) is a gentleman and a thief, delighting in stealing jewels then quietly returning them to their owners after Scotland Yard has thrown up its hands. While attending a party given by Lord Amersteth, he witnesses a real burglary. Raffles knocks out the burglar, appropriates the jewels, then alerts the dinner guests, who assist in arresting the burglar. One of the guests is Captain Bedford (E. M. Holland), an apparently somnolent man with a droopy blond mustache, who is actually a detective. He is convinced Raffles is a thief and has vowed to catch him, even though he rather admires the man's pluck and charm. He eventually makes things so hot for Raffles that Raffles confesses his guilt and returns Lord Amersteth's jewels. He darts into the next room, and a shot is heard. The horrified guests open the door to the room. No one is there. Helped by his fiancée, Gwendolyn Conron, who has guessed the truth, he has escaped. Bedford can only mutter, "I'm glad of it."

The Dramatic Mirror mused for a bit on what Theodore Kremer might have done with the material, but then concluded that the authors were wise to turn it into "a polite melodrama. . . . It is nice and genteel and repressed, and withal interesting." The handsome if slightly epicene Bellew abandoned costume drama to find an almost perfect part for his faintly dated style. Another critic observed, "His voice is tinged with the color of spectacular lime-light, his breathing with the musk and patchouli of the atmosphere of the theatre." Holland's detective was welcomed as a resurrection of the similarly sleep-prone Captain Redwood he had created seventeen years before in *Jim, the Penman*. The play, whose title frequently was shortened to *Raffles,* ran nearly six months, then toured.

By the time the new century would draw to a close, most Americans would think of Frederic Remington as a painter and sculptor, forgetting that he also wrote stories about the shaping of the West. Those stories provided Louis Evan Shipman with the basis for his **John Ermine of the Yellowstone** (11-2-03, Manhattan). Of course, contemporaries were equally forgetful. The play's star was James K. Hackett, who heretofore usually had played swashbuckling heroes or polished drawing-room figures. Few if any commentators remarked on the fact that his father, James H. Hackett, besides being his era's great Falstaff, had made a name for himself depicting earlier pioneers. Ermine is a white scout who had been kidnapped as a child by Indians and raised by them in Wyoming. He is largely ignorant of civilized ways, but he has found a photograph of a white girl and lovingly pocketed it. He is called in to help the army put down an Indian uprising. After a wagon train encampment is encircled, he bravely rides out to summon assistance. One of the members of the train is Katherine Searles (Charlotte Walker). She is the daughter of an army major (Theodore Roberts) and is the girl whose picture Ermine found. When Lieutenant Butler (William Harcourt) learns that Ermine is fond of Katherine, he is furious, since Major Searles has promised the lieutenant that Katherine would marry him. He visits Ermine's cabin, a fight ensues, and Ermine kills Butler in self-defense. He is brought up on murder charges, but Katherine, who had been hidden in the cabin, clears him. The production was praised for its verisimilitude, particularly the wagon encampment with the barricaded wagons close together among the sagebrush. Hackett's commanding figure and lithe grace were additional assets, as was Roberts's amusingly gruff major, but the play's run was short.

The old 14th Street Theatre, at the very bottom of the theatrical district, while not a combination house, regularly was assigned the lowest order of plays, works that might easily have found a comfortable home in lesser touring houses. Although Lottie Blair Parker was the author of the continuingly successful *Way Down East,* her **Lights of Home** (11-2-03, 14th St.) filled the bill. It just as easily could

have opened at the Star or the Third Avenue. Wallace Winfield hopes to gain the inheritance due his half-brother, Jack Stanton, by manipulating their father's will and by framing Jack for forgery. At first he succeeds, prompting Jack to flee the country. Even though Wallace is married, he also covets Jack's wife, Grace. When she persistently repels him, he imprisons her in a tide-washed cave on Staten Island. He also attempts to chloroform and strangle her boy, Archie. The boy escapes by jumping into the North River and swims to a ship, which by chance is carrying his returning father. Grace is also rescued (by a pair of characters who had provided comic relief), and the brothers meet for the final reckoning. Far from the huge hit *Way Down East* remained, *Lights of Home* enjoyed a month's run and some popularity on the road. *Way Down East* itself was given a successful revival in mid-December at the Academy of Music.

The two English plays that followed were greeted warmly, albeit for different reasons. R. C. Carton's **A Clean Slate** (11-3-03, Madison Square) was delicious froth, acted effervescently. A man (J. H. Gilmour) and a woman (Jessie Millward), whose respective spouses have eloped together, meet at a solicitor's office, where they have come to institute divorce proceedings. They were childhood sweethearts and fall in love all over again. When their eloping mates find they were not made for each other, they attempt to wheedle their way back into their deserted spouses' affections. They are too late. The divorces have been granted, and the newlywed couple is quite content.

George Fleming's dramatization of Rudyard Kipling's **The Light That Failed** (11-9-03, Knickerbocker) was perceived as talky and tedious, redeemed primarily by the playing of its star, the slim, aquiline Forbes-Robertson. He portrayed an artist going blind from a war wound, whose hopelessness is dispelled by a beautiful girl. The girl was played by Robertson's wife, Gertrude Elliott (Maxine's sister); the artist's loyal friend by C. Aubrey Smith. Fleming was the pen name of Constance Fletcher.

A real, headline-grabbing scandal provided material for Lawrence Russell's **The Buffalo Mystery** (11-9-03, Third Ave.). In Buffalo a Mrs. Burdick had persuaded her lover to murder her husband. The pair was killed while fleeing the police. Russell kept close to the facts, changing only the names. The actual denouement provided the main sensation, with the *American* reporting, "While the spellbound audience held its breath a property automobile that looked like a goat wagon came careening along the edge of the precipice and finally swerved . . .

dashing to eternity." The paper's critic complained strenuously about the players' enunciation, noting, among other horrors, that the leading lady kept pronouncing "love" as "leeove."

The Sign of the Four (11-9-03, West End), based on Conan Doyle's Sherlock Holmes story, opened the same evening. On behalf of Doyle, Charles Frohman went to court and was granted an injunction, so the play never finished out the week. Either the injunction was lifted or the parties came to a quiet understanding, since the thriller reemerged at other combination houses in the spring. Its tale of Holmes's preventing a girl from being slowly poisoned to obtain rare Indian jewels which she possesses was familiar to Baker Street Irregulars if not to many of these theatres' blue-collar patrons.

An English melodrama, Walter Melville's **The Worst Woman in London** (11-9-03, American), told how a vengeful lady dredged up an old murder in order to prevent her former lover from making a good marriage. According to one reviewer, she dredged it up again and again through four long acts.

Having offered playgoers John Drew and Ethel Barrymore, among others, Charles Frohman now brought forth the actress who was judged his leading attraction at the time, Maude Adams. "Were the young actress a Bernhardt, a Duse and Calvé rolled into one," *Theatre* remarked, "the ovation she received . . . could not have been noisier or more genuinely spontaneous." The magazine went on to opine that her "fair face is her fortune, and dainty gestures, coy glances, mischievous playfulness . . . a source of unmixed delight." Her vehicle was another matter. The play was Frances Hodgson Burnett's **The Pretty Sister of José** (11-10-03, Empire), and its leading role, that of a girl wary of men and matrimony, was not unlike Ethel Barrymore's a few weeks earlier. Pepita is a country girl who comes to Madrid and almost against her will kindles the first sparks of real love in the dashing, womanizing bullfighter, Sebastiano (Henry Ainley). She rejects him so persistently that he finally stalks off, vowing enough is enough. Only then does Pepita's heart melt, and she attempts to rekindle his ardor by dancing for him in a café garden. The dance unnerves Sebastiano. He becomes careless when he enters the bullring and is gravely wounded. Pepita devotedly nurses him back to health. The part of Pepita's simple-minded brother was so insignificant that many reviewers took no notice of the actor who played it, young Edgar Selwyn.

But Arthur Byron received plenty of favorable notice when he made his debut as a star. Wisely, his debut was played out against some superior scenery,

and he was supported by a truly first-rate cast. The settings included a British officers' quarters in Revolutionary New York, the officers' red coats and white breeches imparting a Christmasy feeling before the antique green of the walls and drapery; a pale rose salon filled with belles in colorful brocades; an especially striking autumnal glade; and a dismal prison made attractive by portraits the hero has painted. Among Byron's supporting players were Arnold Daly as his trusty servant, Mrs. Sol Smith and Mrs. Whiffen as grande dames, and such rising players as Wallace Eddinger and Thomas Meighan in lesser roles.

All Byron lacked was a play that would please critics and playgoers. Yet his vehicle was Clyde Fitch's personal favorite among all his own works, **Major André** (11-11-03, Savoy). Fitch told the traditional story of André's mission to Benedict Arnold, his capture (in the glade), and his execution, while giving the major a fictional romance with a Philadelphia girl, Barbara Allen (Chrystal Herne), and a rival for her affections in an American soldier, Nathan Goodrich (Guy Bates Post). In the last act Barbara steps out of the portrait André had painted of her to speak with him before he goes to his death. Commercially speaking, the drama was one of Fitch's worst failures, succumbing after only thirteen performances. But Byron's career, though not always as a star, continued for thirty-five more years.

· · ·

Arthur [William] **Byron** (1872–1943) was the son of the famous touring star Oliver Doud Byron. He was born in Brooklyn and made his debut in 1889 with his father's company. After performing with Sol Smith Russell and in San Francisco stock, he spent several seasons in support of John Drew. He then assumed leading roles in plays such as *The Stubbornness of Geraldine*.

· · ·

Charles Frohman remained indisputably Broadway's most active producer. So far, no fewer than eight of the season's plays and musicals had been presented by him. Two more now came in on successive evenings. The first was a two-week dud; the second proved one of the season's biggest hits and one of its most enduring works. The failure was **Lady Rose's Daughter** (11-16-03, Garrick), which was derived from a novel by Mrs. Humphrey Ward and recounted how a woman spurned by society nevertheless makes a titled marriage. The success was James M. Barrie's **The Admirable Crichton** (11-17-03, Lyceum). One commentator suggested that Barrie had borrowed the theme of his play from the same Ludwig Fulda drama that supposedly had been the source of Rosenfeld's *A Modern Crusoe,* but Barrie's comic saga of some highborn yet helpless ladies and gentlemen who must rely on the resourcefulness of their butler when they are stranded on a deserted island proved the tastier for American palates. In the original American production, William Gillette's clipped phrasing and economy of movement brought Crichton to life most admirably. The "fantasy," as it was called, chalked up 144 performances.

William Young, whose history as a dramatist had begun so promisingly, more recently had contented himself with dramatizing other authors' books. He wrote *finis* to his disappointing career with another such hack job, **A Japanese Nightingale** (11-19-03, Daly's), taken from Onoto Wotanna's novel. Yuki (Margaret Illington) marries an American (Orrin Johnson), but the proofs of their marriage are stolen by a vengeful suitor (Frederick Perry), leaving her irate brother (Vincent Serrano) suspicious of her claims. Some of the husband's American friends track down the villain and restore the proofs. The play was filled with melodramatic moments more appropriate to lesser touring plays. The production's main assets were its beautiful settings and costumes, culminating in a *bon odori* (dance of death), with Yuki leading a long line of girls "in clinging robes of rich and changeful colors."

Undoubtedly more by accident than by design, the new stars being trumpeted this season had been mostly men. Even this early, Orrin Johnson's celebrity was fading. His performance in *A Japanese Nightingale* was either ignored or lambasted by reviewers. Charles Richman's fate would parallel more closely that of Arthur Byron. He would remain a well-liked leading man for many seasons, then serve out his final years as a respected supporting player. His leap to stardom came in Victor Mapes's **Captain Barrington** (11-23-03, Manhattan). The background of the play, an attempt by the British to kidnap George Washington during the Revolutionary War, purportedly was suggested by a real such attempt, but, of course, a fictional love interest provided much of the story's spin. Complications arose from the fact that twin brothers, both played by Richman, were on opposing sides. The American soldier, Lieutenant Fielding, is, as the printed text insisted, "tender and serious, emotional and a trifle sad," while his English twin, Captain Barrington, is "brilliant, witty, reckless and brave," not to mention a notorious ladies' man. Ruth Langdon (Suzanne Sheldon) loves Fielding, but when she sees his look-alike brother flirting with another girl, she is hard-pressed not to believe Fielding is a philanderer and a spy. By the same token, the men's similarity allows Fielding to receive a letter detailing plans for Washington's capture and meant for Barrington. After Fielding is wounded and taken, he sends the distraught Ruth to alert Washington. Barrington is killed in the final skirmish.

Colorful settings and costumes (remember the redcoats!) and lively acting turned a mediocre drama into a minor hit. Gasps, then excited applause, greeted the appearance of Washington (Joseph Kilgour), "probably the most imposing presentment of The Father of his Country ever seen in a play." Washington's entrances and exits were accompanied by "Hail to the Chief."

The action of Robert Neilson Stephens and E. Lyall Swete's **Miss Elizabeth's Prisoner** (11-23-03, Criterion) was played out against the turmoil of the same war. To flee pursuing redcoats, an American, Captain Harry Peyton (William Faversham), steals a horse belonging to a pretty Tory, Elizabeth Philipse (Hilda Spong). He is shot and wounded, so returns to her house. When she threatens to turn him over to the British, he tells her he has fallen in love with her, woos and wins her. The play's reception was so cool that Faversham and his producer, Charles Frohman, soon replaced it with a revival of *Lord and Lady Algy.*

The season's biggest hit was an American play, George Ade's **The County Chairman** (11-24-03, Wallack's). Some observers had felt the season so far to be lackluster, leaving one wag to brand the play "First Ade to the Injured." The humorist's story was hardly novel. Jim Hackler (Maclyn Arbuckle) is the county chairman and vehemently opposes a bid for the office of prosecuting attorney by the shady Judge Rigby. Hackler encourages his young partner, Tillford Wheeler, to run against the judge. This creates a dilemma for Wheeler, who is courting Rigby's daughter, Lucy. Hackler has gotten hold of evidence that could destroy Rigby if released to the local newspaper, but Lucy and her mother prevail on him to tear it up. Even without the evidence, Wheeler wins.

The hefty Arbuckle, with his homespun burr, was ideal for the leading role, and it kept him busy for nearly three years. But from the start critics recognized that the play made its strongest appeal with its pictures of "quaint local types." Thus the *Dramatic Mirror* reported, "The inimitable performance of Willis P. Sweatnam [long famous as a minstrel] as Sassafras was the histrionic hit of the occasion . . . a perfectly faithful delineation of the normally mercenary negro, rendered with a subtlety of humor." Sassafras Livingstone is not above telling each of the candidates as well as the chairman that the latest arrival at the Livingstone home will be named for him. He informs the judge, "L. R. Livingstone is the appellation—the cognomen—the name—L. R. 'Lias Rigby Livingstone is the name selected—chosen—I mean—yes, suh," and for his news receives the promise of some easy labor. He next earns a dollar simply by advising the chairman, "Jim Hackleh Livingstone is what we decided on." But he almost comes a cropper with Wheeler, who has learned the baby is a girl:

Wheeler: Well, how can a girl baby be named Tillford?
Sassafras: Who said anything about Tillford?
Wheeler: You did.
Sassafras: Tillford? I said 'at baby's name was Tilly—Tilly, suh. We sometimes call it Tillford for short. Tilly is she for Tillford.

When Wheeler gives him fifty cents to buy something for the baby, Sassafras assures him, "I'll buy some peppehmint candy." And then there was the jingoistic Jefferson Briscoe, who holds firm, belligerent opinions on the Bering Sea controversy but, when asked where the Bering Sea is, responds, "Don't make no difference where it is. The question is, air we, the greatest and most powerful nation on earth, goin' to set back and be bullyragged an' hornswoggled by some Jim Crow island that looks, by ginger, like a freckle on the ocean!" In New York the comedy ran out the season.

The plot of Cosmo Gordon Lennox's **The Marriage of Kitty** (11-30-03, Hudson), taken from a French comedy, Fred de Grésac and Francis de Croisset's *La Passerelle,* had sustained several musicals, so it was not inappropriate that its star, Marie Tempest, had made her name on the lyric stage. Having abandoned musicals she had embarked on a career in straight plays that would make her a decades-long London favorite, and she had offered the play there first. To skirt provisions of a will that prohibit a man from marrying a certain widow, the man agrees to marry a pretty young girl, divorce her, and then wed the widow. Naturally, the young couple fall in love and the widow is sent packing. Miss Tempest's legions of American admirers ensured the play a good run. Years later the French original supplied the source for Victor Herbert's *Orange Blossoms*.

After a long absence, Robert Mantell returned to New York in W. A. Tremayne and Irving L. Hall's **The Light of Other Days** (11-30-03, 14th St.). In a prologue Maurice Desmond rushes from Ireland to attempt to save his beloved Countess Helene from the French Revolution. She is captured and killed, but Desmond flees with her daughter. Years pass, and the girl has grown into the beautiful Cerise (played by the same actress who had played her mother). She is kidnapped and returned to France, where Desmond again comes. This time his rescue is successful. For one month Mantell offered "a fine pictorial impersonation, a series of faultlessly effective poses, and a retinue of splendidly read speeches written obviously for applause getting." He then revived *The Corsican Brothers*.

Denman Thompson and George W. Ryer, still looking for another *Old Homestead,* tried again with **Our New Minister** (11-30-03, American). Their play reminded some of Fitch's *Lovers' Lane,* though it purportedly had been written ten years earlier. The new minister is Thaddeus Strong, who comes to a small New England town, preaching forgiveness and charity. His arrival coincides with the return of Lem Ransom from prison, where he served time for a crime of which he was actually innocent. Strong falls in love with Lem's daughter, Nance. The villagers take sides, with the nonchurch-going freethinkers generally favoring the preacher's stance while the church members harden their hearts against him. In the end he wins over most of the village. Critics praised the play's construction (with its largely comic first act), its dialogue, and its nicely drawn subsidiary figures. Typical of the dialogue was this bit:

—Do you believe in prayer?
—Well, I believe in prayer and hustlin', but the one ain't much good without the other.

At least one critic prophesied correctly that the play would find wider appeal on the road than in New York.

The pretty young girl dead set against accepting a wedding band was becoming one of the season's pet stock figures. The latest was the central concern of **What's the Matter with Susan?** (12-1-03, Bijou), which Leo Ditrichstein made over from an unidentified German comedy. Susan (Alice Fischer) serves as her brother-in-law's stern housekeeper. When she catches his maid in the arms of a cadet (William Harcourt) from nearby West Point, she orders them both out of the house. Then she catches a second look at the cadet and exercises a woman's prerogative. Ethel Barrymore or Maude Adams might have turned the play into a hit; Miss Fischer could not.

Nor could Fay Davis do much for Henry Arthur Jones's **Whitewashing Julia** (12-2-03, Garrick), in which small-town gossips wonder if a young widow once had a morganatic marriage with a grand duke. Her trusting admirer (Guy Standing) couldn't care less. In London a brouhaha over refusal to admit a critic from the *Times* on opening night resulted in notorious publicity. No such contretemps helped business during the play's five-week New York run.

All this while sensation-melodramas kept up their steady traffic at their regular berths. Theodore Kremer, taking time off from his own writing, was in the audience watching the premiere of Arthur J. Lamb's **The Queen of the White Slaves** (12-7-03, Grand Opera). A rich, unscrupulous Chinese-American hires the notorious Terrible Nine to kidnap a beautiful San Francisco heiress and help him bring her to Hong Kong. He either does not know or does not care that her fiancé is a famous detective. The girl is kidnapped and rescued "again and again." The final rescue takes place in China, where the hero, a gun in each hand, at last kills the villain. Before that audiences were treated to the sight of a thieves' den, a torture chamber, a "living tomb," and the villain and heroine on a raft at sea, saved by the timely arrival of a passing ship.

The troublemaker in Frank Lindon's **To Be Buried Alive** (12-7-03, 58th St.) was another of the era's innumerable unprincipled mesmerists. But a girl he has "ruined" and the heroine's lover ultimately succeed in unmasking him and saving the heroine.

The season's surprise hit began quietly enough with what was supposed to be a trial matinee. Arnold Daly, a rising young actor, and Winchell Smith, soon to be famous as a playwright, pooled their meager resources and with a mere $350 in hand mounted a performance of George Bernard Shaw's **Candida** (12-9-03, Princess), in which a woman must choose between a visionary and a practical socialist. Daly was Marchbanks, and Dorothy Donnelly assumed the title role. The reception was such that additional matinees were offered, then the comedy was moved, first to one theatre and finally to a second. By the time its run ended it had been given 133 times. For part of the run Daly also appeared as Napoleon in Shaw's **The Man of Destiny** (2-11-04, Carnegie Lyceum).

Among straight plays, only *The County Chairman* outran Belasco's **Sweet Kitty Bellairs** (12-9-03, Belasco), which the author-producer took from Agnes and Egerton Castle's novel *The Bath Beauty*. On opening night backstage difficulties, which Belasco publicly blamed on a hoodlum bribed by Erlanger, resulted in intermissions so long that the final curtain did not come down until well after midnight. Critics made allowances, for Belasco offered them another magnificent spectacle. His story was not all that complicated. The saucy Kitty (Henrietta Crosman) hopes to rekindle the ardor of the bored

Lord Standish (John E. Kellerd) for his wife (Katherine Florence) by making him jealous. She also hopes to tie the knot herself with Lord Verney (Charles Hammond). However, when Standish arrives at Verney's chambers while both ladies are there, Kitty realizes the situation is too dangerous. The women have hidden themselves in the bed's draperies, and Kitty self-sacrificingly steps forward to reveal her own presence. She afterwards is cut by society, with even the ungrateful Lady Standish refusing to help her. She is finally vindicated and, in a pouring rain, watches the soldiers march off. Belasco's gorgeous stage pictures gobbled up much of the next day's notices. A ballroom scene had more than fifty supers, all in exquisite 18th-century costumes, while the final downpour, though the rain had no bearing on the plot, made a stunning impression. The play ran until June, closed for vacation, and reopened in September, running a total of 231 performances.

Another dramatized novel, **Dorothy Vernon of Haddon Hall** (12-14-03, New York), which Paul Kester derived from Charles Major's work, allowed the red-wigged Bertha Galland a field day, offering her "a passage at swords with an unwelcome lover," a chance to pretend to be Queen Mary, and a meeting with Queen Elizabeth. This Dorothy is determined not to marry the scheming cousin (Sheridan Block) her father (Frank Losee) has selected for her, instead preferring John Manners (William Lewers), although the Vernon and Manners families have been at odds for years. Even when her father imprisons her, she remains stubborn. And she gets her way. The play ran five weeks, toured profitably, then returned for a time the following season.

Incessant touring was the lot of two dramas that opened the same night. The villain in Joseph Le Brandt's **Her First False Step** (12-14-03, 58th St.) tricks the heroine into marrying him by making it seem her true love is unfaithful. When he eventually deserts her, she takes work in a circus. The cad reappears and attempts to push her into the lion's cage, but her true love has remained true, so he shows up in the nick of time to rescue her.

The title of James R. Garey's **Gentleman by Day, Burglar by Night** (12-14-03, Star) hinted that it might be a ripoff of *Raffles*. It really was not. The hero cracks a safe to prevent a scandal erupting about his brother and to rid him of a pesky adventuress. The hero's reward is the hand of a girl who thought she had loved the brother.

If *Raffles* was not being ripped off, it was, for a time, being coupled with a curtain raiser, Louis

Tiercelin's **The Sacrament of Judas** (12-15-03, Princess). A defrocked monk (Kyrle Bellew) with revolutionary sympathies helps a fugitive nobleman, who is also his rival in love, win the girl and escape. For his pains, his fellow revolutionaries shoot him. The play was a weird choice for such a coupling, nor was it apparently well acted. One critic complained that not only did Bellew, in his death scene, indulge "in a Niagara fall from the top to the bottom of the stairs in the cottage," but that he persistently pronounced sacrament as "saycrament."

Pierce Kingsley's sensation-melodrama **Deserted at the Altar** (12-21-03, 58th St.) presented thrill addicts with an automobile and bicycle race in one act and a burning ship (with the heroine aboard) in another while relating how the queen of counterfeiters strews obstacles in the path of two young lovers.

One of the period's loveliest actresses, Eleanor Robson, imbued Israel Zangwill's **Merely Mary Ann** (12-28-03, Garden) with her special brand of enchantment, playing a young drudge who comes to the city from the country, eventually learns she is an heiress and marries a handsome, aristocratic composer (Edwin Arden). Calling hers "a voice of liquid pathos," *Theatre* went on to observe, "She gave expression to emotion so truly at all times that no note of artificiality crept in anywhere." Most other critics concurred. Audiences did, too, for 148 performances.

The same evening saw the premiere of the first of three American plays, which closed out the year. Clyde Fitch mischievously appropriated *Raffles*'s curtain line not only for his title but for the curtain line in all four acts. As was his wont, he also devised some theatrically effective settings. The first act showed the cloak section of a department store, with a working elevator riding up and down. The second showed the theatre's real stage, with scenery propped up against its brick wall, while rehearsals for a musical comedy supposedly took place. The final act displayed a hotel, fronted by a piazza. A man could be seen shaving in one of the hotel's rooms, a woman swatted mosquitoes in her chair, and Princeton boys ran across the stage yelling college cheers and singing. The story of **Glad of It** (12-28-03, Savoy) begins when handsome, rich Reginald Norton (Hassard Short), who is the principal backer of a forthcoming musical, bumps into a salesgirl, Connie Bowles (Millie James), while seeking his temperamental star, Clarita Baxter (Lucile Watson). He promises Connie a small part, which infuriates Clarita. At rehearsals, Clarita walks out. Connie is given her role, but it proves more than she can handle. Despite her failure, Reginald continues to see her, though Clarita, who knows all about Reginald's big bank account, throws obstacles in the path, hoping to nab Reginald for herself. Connie wins. The critics ganged up on Fitch, insisting his cleverness had gotten out of hand. W. D. Howells wrote appreciatively of the play, but his praise was too little and too late. Making his New York debut in a minor role was the last of the Barrymores, John.

In Fred Gibbs's touring drama **Paul Revere** (12-28-03, Metropolis), Revere loves the daughter of a staunch Tory and has a rival in a British officer. His own political feelings are ambiguous until his brother is killed by the British. This prompts a change of attitude and leads to his famous ride, which takes up the second act. At first he rides in slowly, alerts the townsfolk, then saunters off, but the rest of the ride is on a treadmill with a fast-moving panorama in the rear. His fiancée remains loyal, and together they convert her father.

The night after his brother made his New York debut, Lionel Barrymore again proved a show-stealer, this time in Augustus Thomas's **The Other Girl** (12-29-03, Criterion). Kid Garvey (Barrymore), the world boxing champion, has been taken under the wing of an easygoing minister, Dr. Bradford (Frank Worthing). The minister has been subject to fits of laughter at awkward moments and hopes a regimen of boxing will cure him. Garvey, though he has made considerable money in the ring, has never before been a part of high society. He finds it so to his liking that he decides to marry into it. The girl he chooses is Catherine Fulton (Drina de Wolfe). Never mind that Catherine is engaged to Reginald Lumley (Joseph Wheelock, Jr.). Catherine proves so susceptible to the Kid's magnificent physique and rough charms that she agrees to elope. Recognizing that such a match would be a disaster, Catherine's brash friend, Estelle Kitteridge (Elsie de Wolfe), contrives to take her place. In their haste the young couple accidentally run over Reginald. Hauled into court, Estelle seems willing to ruin her own reputation to save Catherine's, but the Kid's ever-loving girl, Myrtle, discreetly takes Estelle's place. Catherine and Reginald, Estelle and a forgiving Dr. Bradford, and the Kid and Myrtle all set the date.

The play's excellent settings included the rear terrace of a brownstone, with neighborhood homes looming over the fence. But the performances made the evening, and Barrymore's performance most of all. The *Times*, noting Barrymore, "has got the trick of genius in character parts," continued, "His utterance is no less vernacular than the wonderful assortment of language with which Mr. Thomas has supplied the part, and every motion and every gesture are of the ring." Thus at one point, Bradford is forced to confess that his vestry would be unhappy if they knew he associated with and paid a professional fighter. The Kid responds, "I *like* you, Doctor. You're sure a hit with *me*, and I don't need anybody's money. My saloon's worth 500 a week and I can turn ten thousand clear with a dub 'knock out.' I took your money just to make you feel easy, that's all, and you tell your vestry gazabos that I did *this* with the last 20 you gave me. (*Lights the bill by the lamp and starts to light his cigarette.*)" The comedy delighted audiences for twenty weeks.

An American comedy hit might have been a splendid way to end the year, but that was not to be. The next afternoon in Chicago, during a matinee packed with children at the "absolutely fireproof" Iroquois Theatre, fire broke out. So did panic. When it was over, the worst theatre fire in American history had claimed 600 lives. The shock depressed attendance at playhouses throughout the country for the rest of the season. In New York rigid inspections were initiated. They found so many safety lapses that several theatres, among them the Weber and Field Music Hall, were shuttered permanently, while others were closed until suitable repairs could be made. Yet for all the unhappy effects, there were enough good plays in good theatres and enough devoted playgoers that most stages remained lit, and the very first week of 1904 brought in another memorable success.

One disappointment and some touring melodramas preceded that hit. To some sentimentalists Leo Ditrichstein's **Harriet's Honeymoon** (1-4-04, Garrick) evoked memories of Daly's heyday with its farcical plot. Elliot and Harriet Baird (Arthur Byron and Mary Mannering) have come to Germany on their honeymoon but soon discover that Elliot has misplaced his passport and wallet. They decide to pretend they are an Italian diva and her manager. Meanwhile, the local prince has run away rather than go through with an arranged marriage. He finds Elliot's passport and registers at the same inn, using Elliot's name. The police, searching for him, have been told he may be masquerading as an opera impresario. The inevitable mixups and their resolution occupy the rest of the evening. Byron and Miss Mannering were popular, accomplished performers and received good notices, but they lacked the practice-perfected art of Daly's farceurs.

Combination houses also had New Year's presents. Hal Reid's **A Midnight Marriage** (1-4-04, Grand Opera) starred one of the best-known touring players, Florence Bindley. She portrayed a girl who sings in music halls to support her aged mother. Her

romance with the hero is jeopardized by the ploys of his jealous cousin. Lincoln J. Carter's **Too Proud to Beg** (1-4-04, Third Ave.) centered on a detective whose marriage is nearly destroyed by a slanderous inspector. After the detective appears to be killed in an old refinery fire (the play's sensation scene), the inspector tries to have his wife marry him, but the detective appears in time to save her from a bigamous fate.

Just about everything fell neatly into place for **The Virginian** (1-5-04, Manhattan). Writing in collaboration with his producer, Kirke La Shelle, Owen Wister skillfully transferred to the stage the accurate observations of western life, the believable, variegated characters, and the basic drama of his novel. His Virginian is a tough but humane Wyoming ranch foreman. When his best friend, Steve (Guy Bates Post), is shown to be in league with the skulking Trampas and Trampas's gang of cattle thieves, he unhesitatingly agrees to head the posse, even if that means he must kill Steve. It also may mean he could lose his sweetheart, Molly Wood, a moralizing schoolmarm from Vermont, who sees the posse as a barbarous lynch mob. Trampas escapes and vows to "lay for" the foreman on a street in Medicine Bow. In true western fashion the Virginian bravely goes to meet Trampas, although Molly is still protesting that it is wrong for one man to kill another. But when the drink-crazed Trampas's bullet goes astray and the Virginian kills him in self-defense, Molly understands the necessity of western ways. The evening was "a personal triumph" for Dustin Farnum. His manly, spirited hero, "with the bearing, almost a slouch, that is characteristic of men who live in Mexican saddles," made him a star, a position he retained until he became one of the first major Broadway figures to desert to films. He played the role for three months in New York and for two and a half years on tour. There were two other reasons for the show's immediate success. One was the novel's and play's most famous, often repeated line, "When you call me that, smile." The second was that Harrison Fiske, owner of the Manhattan, insisted on keeping a $1.50 top ticket at a time when the Trust was attempting to raise orchestra seats to $2.00.

The Trust's new $2.00 top was mentioned over and over in unflattering reviews of James M. Barrie's **Little Mary** (1-5-04, Empire). One annoyed critic summed up the evening as "two hours and twenty minutes of boredom, at $2 a bore." Little Mary was not a girl but the cutesy name for a stomach cure handed down by an apothecary to his equally cutesy granddaughter.

Sure enough, Chauncey Olcott sang his usual

quota of new Irish songs in **Terence** (1-5-04, New York), but, perhaps because he was appearing at a more prestigious, centrally located house than was his custom, critics treated Mrs. Edward Nash Morgan's dramatization of Mrs. B. M. Croker's novel as a play rather than a musical. Actually, it was typical both of Olcott vehicles and other Irish touring plays of the same epoch. For this occasion Olcott played an Irish soldier who returns home in the guise of an ordinary coach-driver to win the hand of his beloved and to thwart the machinations of a tricky lawyer out to deprive him of his inheritance.

A half-crazed boy on the trail of his sister's betrayer provided the plot for Dore Davidson's **His Sister's Shame** (1-11-04, Third Ave.). An avalanche added to the excitement, while numerous specialty acts broke the tension.

Richard Harding Davis's **Ranson's Folly** (1-18-04, Hudson) told of a cocky army officer (Robert Edeson) who openly boasts he can commit a holdup as daring as any committed by a local desperado known as "the Red Rider." When Lieutenant Ranson absents himself from a dance and a holdup takes place at the same time, his boast lands him in hot water until the real culprit is caught. The play was a modest hit, but Davis had a better work in the offing.

Amelia Bingham's faltering career as an actress-manager suffered another blow when she mounted Pierre Decourcelle's **Olympe** (1-18-04, Knickerbocker), in which she played an 18th-century actress who lures a novice (Henry Woodruff) from his monastery to become her leading man and whose fickleness leads to his death.

The saddest opening of the evening occurred at the Lyric Theatre, where Liebler and Co. presented Ada Rehan and Otis Skinner in a repertory of *The Taming of the Shrew, The Merchant of Venice,* and *The School for Scandal.* If vague memories of Daly's had been called up earlier by *Harriet's Honeymoon,* they were evoked more forcefully by Miss Rehan's reappearance. But Miss Rehan seemed to be a ghost of her once radiant self. Her technique remained, but the fire was gone. Some notices passed over her performance with a pathetic, telling silence. The lion's share of praise was accorded to Skinner.

By Right of Sword (1-18-04, American) was a touring melodrama derived by Arthur Marchmont and his collaborators from Marchmont's novel. It centered on an American who is visiting Russia and there takes the place of a Russian officer in a duel. He later exposes an attempt to assassinate the czar and finally wins the affections of the officer's sister.

In **The Stain of Guilt** (1-18-04, 58th St.), a greedy

banker arranges to have his cousin kidnapped and murdered. Instead the kidnapper secretly brings up the girl. A cashier in the villain's bank falls in love with her. The banker learns the truth. He falsely accuses the cashier of theft and fires him. The young lovers flee, pursued by the banker, and they discover themselves "facing death fully a dozen times" before the banker is jailed.

Broadway was charmed by Pierre Wolff's Parisian hit **The Secret of Polichinelle** (1-19-04, Madison Square). An underage couple marry privily and have a child. In time the secret comes out. When the husband's father visits the couple, he is delighted but fears his wife will be too straitlaced to be accepting. Later, when she pays a visit, she, too, is delighted but fears her husband's weak heart would not stand the shock. Of course, everyone embraces joyously at the final curtain.

Virtually no one joyously embraced E. H. Sothern's **The Light That Lies in Woman's Eyes** (1-25-04, Criterion), which the actor wrote as a vehicle for his wife, Virginia Harned. Critics lambasted the play as illogical and improbable and even accused Sothern of resorting to the Fitchian trick of whetting interest with unnecessarily novel settings. The settings included Anne Hathaway's tourist-packed cottage, a rehearsal of *As You Like It* (which allowed Miss Harned to don men's clothing as the disguised Rosalind), and a church with a wedding rehearsal in progress. Sothern's story told of a girl (Mabel Snider) who has gone blind over the shock of her lover's disappearance. A young Arctic explorer (William Courtenay) pretends to be the lover to soothe her, but this provokes the ire of his fiancée, Lorna (Miss Harned). She reassures herself of his love when she plays opposite him in an amateur mounting of Shakespeare's comedy. Then the explorer pays gypsies to stage a fake kidnapping of Lorna. It goes astray, and both find themselves left bound side by side. After they are rescued, the blind girl's lover turns up, and the young couples are wed. An embarrassment to everyone, the play quickly was whisked away.

So was Frances Hodgson Burnett's **That Man and I** (1-25-04, Savoy). Dick Latimer's sister dies after giving birth to a daughter out of wedlock. Dick (Robert Hilliard) vows to find the lover who betrayed her, not realizing it is his best friend, John Baird (H. Reeves-Smith). Time passes. Dick's niece, Felicity (Maude Fealy), is about to marry when Dick is offered the chance to purchase some letters that will reveal her father's name. At the same time, Baird returns from years in Europe. He has never known that Dick's sister was pregnant.

Dick's purchase discloses the truth, but not wanting to mar Felicity's wedding and seeing that Baird is genuinely remorseful, Dick decides to let bygones be bygones. The story was the sort that appealed to turn-of-the-century playgoers, but Mrs. Burnett was assailed for the crudity of her writing. Critics said she filled the play with outdated soliloquies and hammered "her ingot of sentiment down to the gold-leaf of sentimentality." The settings, two interiors and an exterior with "fine stretches of distant fields and hills," were praised, as was the acting, especially Hilliard's unusually restrained performance. But they were not enough to save the play.

Annie Russell and Mrs. Gilbert, who had worked together so successfully in several recent productions, were the mainstays of **The Younger Mrs. Parling** (1-26-04, Garrick), which Haddon Chambers freely adapted from Henri Bernstein's *Le Detour.* The play related how a child of the demimonde escapes from her world by marrying into a puritanical but loving family, only to be eventually lured back into the world she professed to despise. Although the aging Mrs. Gilbert's part, as the heroine's mother-in-law, was small, she made the most of it. The *Times*'s John Corbin lauded Miss Russell for "the subtlest and most exquisite art of the English-speaking stage" and continued his paean, "Her sensitive and sympathetic masque, with its sadly beautiful mouth, and its heaven-wide, heaven-deep eyes, are no more illuminating than her gracious and flawless method."

For more than a year *Theatre* had been ballyhooing its contest to promote American dramaturgy. The winning author first had been identified as a Mrs. Conheim, but when her full name was disclosed—Martha Morton Conheim—readers grasped that she was already an established playwright under her maiden name. After her entry, **The Triumph of Love,** was awarded a special matinee performance on February 8 at the Criterion and pelted with highly unfavorable notices, the perennial keening over the state of native playwriting crescendoed for a time.

The wailing was stilled briefly to welcome Viola Allen in *Twelfth Night,* which began a fortnight's stand that evening at the Knickerbocker. Her portrait of her namesake was seen as "girlish, tender, winsome, wistful, pathetic," and when she donned white kilts and a red and gold Zouave jacket, her camouflage swagger struck just the right note. The elaborate, Victorian-like settings were also praised, but John Blair's Malvolio split the critics sharply, with naysayers condemning him for overacting. The *Dramatic Mirror,* possibly indulging in a little Trust-bashing, reported an intriguing

sidelight, complaining that programs could not be read comfortably during intermissions since the house lights were not raised and reporting that the practice had become prevalent recently.

The title of Will C. Murphy's **If Women Were Men** (2-8-04, Star) seemed designed to lure inquisitive playgoers, since it had little or nothing to do with his plot, which related how a newlywed couple's lives are made miserable by prospective mates they had spurned. William B. Hurst's **The Black Hand** (2-8-04, Third Ave.) presented Jews, gypsies, and blacks (played, of course, by whites) among its characters, but no Italians—possibly because the action unfolded not in New York but in the South. A Kentucky colonel, blinded in one of the region's interfamily feuds, goads his son to avenge him by killing his enemies' young heir apparent. Instead the son is found with the heir apparent's knife in his heart and an impression of a black hand beside his body. The supposed murderer is, in reality, a peaceable young man. He is also an eye doctor. He restores the colonel's sight and unearths the actual killer, a member of a gang of professional murderers.

Although **The Pit** (2-10-04, Lyric) was a success, and its producer, William A. Brady, reputedly made half a million dollars from it, it, too, elicited musings on the state of American playwriting. Most critics agreed that Frank Norris's novel had little enough plot and that its virtues came from the novelist's ability to paint vivid verbal pictures. Channing Pollock, who adapted it, relied heavily on startling scenic effects for interest and excitement. Before the curtain rose, the quartet from *Rigoletto,* accompanied by a full orchestra, was heard coming from backstage. The rising curtain disclosed the lobby of Chicago's Auditorium Theatre, where Curtis Jadwin (Wilton Lackaye) is discovered talking about his speculation and casting an eye toward the beautiful Laura Dearborn. (Throughout this act snippets of opera could be heard offstage.) The second act took place on a lakefront lawn, during a rehearsal of *Romeo and Juliet.* Here Jadwin pursues his courtship of Laura, unaware that the owner of the estate, his speculations gone awry, has committed suicide. (Critics pounced on the scene as a marriage of scenes from *The Light That Lies in Woman's Eyes* and Fitch's *The Moth and the Flame,* though, of course, it was derived from the book.) If Jadwin at first devotes all his time to his new bride, he soon neglects her for his love of speculation. At his office, with tickers noisily adding to the confusion of scurrying clerks and messengers, Jadwin attempts to corner the wheat market. When the market goes against him, he hurries to the pit floor. There, watched by a crowd in the visitors' gallery, "coats are torn, hats smashed, and the air filled with flying scraps of paper and ticker tapes" as a hundred or more buyers and sellers deal frantically. A bell rings suddenly, and in the ensuing silence the failure of Jadwin's firm is announced. The neglected Laura had been preparing to elope with an old sweetheart, but seeing Jadwin so broken in spirit, she elects to remain with him. Lackaye's strong, emotive performance helped unify and thus strengthen what was actually a somewhat disjointed aggregation of scenes, but the stage pictures, especially the realistically reproduced, bustling trading floor, which one commentator called "the kinematograph of the wheat pit," ensured public acceptance. Brady earned some unusual publicity for the show by placing ads offering stagestruck brokers and commodity traders jobs as extras in the pit scene.

If American drama was not all that some high-minded observers might hope it would be, traditionalists could rejoice that Shakespeare was having his best season in years. No sooner had Viola Allen left the Knickerbocker than Charles Frohman brought in a second mounting of *Twelfth Night* to the same house. The production that opened on the 22nd was Ben Greet's English revival. In marked contrast to its predecessor, the production was simplicity itself, purporting to recreate for its single setting the very Middle Temple Hall where the comedy first was acted. A Beefeater (like the monks in last season's *Everyman*) stood guard on each side of the stage, and musicians in Elizabethan garb performed in a loft. Edith Wynne Matthison was Viola; Greet, Malvolio; and C. Rann Kennedy, soon to be an important playwright, Orsino. As had Miss Allen's version, this one played two weeks. Come March, the company appeared at Daly's, offering *As You Like It* and *The School for Scandal*.

In Howard Hall and John T. McIntyre's **An Heiress to Millions** (2-22-04, Third Ave.), a rich girl and her fiancé are hounded by two miscreants until the predictable denouement puts the bounders in their places.

John P. Lockney's **A Hidden Crime** (2-29-04, Third Ave.) was set in San Francisco. A wealthy old miner has made a will leaving everything to his daughter, whom he has not seen for seventeen years. A rascally gambler tries to have him rewrite the will, but the daughter's suitor and his loyal Chinese pal save the day. In the sensation scene the gambler chops away at the foundations of a wooden bridge over which the hero must pass. The bridge tumbles down, but the hero grabs a tree limb.

"Imagine," *The Theatre* begged its readers, "a

decrepit, half-demented old man in the last stages of senile decay, his face wizened and hollow like a grinning skull, the flesh a greenish hue, beardless, but covered with large warts from which sprout long, straggling hairs, saliva dripping from his toothless gums, and his hands and legs shaking from palsy." Such was the image of Richard Mansfield in Tolstoy's **Ivan the Terrible** (3-1-04, New Amsterdam). Ivan professes his eagerness to abdicate and orders the Boyars to select a successor, but the wily Boris Godunoff (Arthur Forrest) persuades the Boyars to tell Ivan that Ivan himself is the only man fit to rule Russia. The czar divorces his wife and prepares to do battle with King Stephen. While Ivan's troubles mount, Godunoff consolidates his own power. As he lies dying, Ivan recognizes Godunoff's true nature and "with a look of hatred that transforms his features into a terrifying masque" falls lifeless. Mansfield's striking performance could not hide the play's inherent dullness, so after two weeks Mansfield dropped the piece and for his final fortnight ran through a repertory of his older favorites.

The Shakespeare season peaked when Forbes-Robertson offered his celebrated *Hamlet* at the Knickerbocker on the 7th. In his autobiography Robertson recounted that *The Light That Failed* had met a disappointing reception on the road, so he ordered his *Hamlet* scenery and costumes rushed over from England. That physical production was viewed as rather threadbare by many critics. Nor, with one exception, was the star's supporting cast greatly admired. But the actor's fast-paced Hamlet was another matter. "A Triumph of Flawless Art" one banner read, while another reviewer echoed the sentiments of many when he called the interpretation "the most poetic, imaginative and beautiful Prince of Denmark seen here since Edwin Booth at his greatest." His Hamlet was neither a madman nor a vacillating weakling but a man whose sense of honor impedes his quest for vengeance. Among his supporting players only C. Aubrey Smith, who played both the Ghost and Fortinbras, was singled out for commendation.

Langdon McCormick's rural drama **Out of the Fold** (3-7-04, American) was a variant on an old theme. The hero is the local schoolmaster, who has temporarily taken the place of the vacationing minister. A young woman comes to live in the village and immediately serves as grist for the village's gossip mills. The village blackguard, who just happens to know something about her unfortunate past, stirs up further trouble for her. Although the schoolmaster defends her, he abandons any idea of marrying her until a shepherd, who knows his Bible, preaches him a lesson in charity. The stage pictures were familiar but not unwelcome: a black-figured heroine standing in falling snow outside a church as sounds of a hymn come from within; a farmhouse and barn with chickens and other animals moving about; a sylvan scene featuring a wooden bridge over a running brook.

By contrast, the city was the locale for Frank Tannehill's **Hush-a-Bye, Baby** (3-7-04, Fifth Ave.). The Budds, a widowed father and his son, both ladies' men, learn that a Mrs. Budd is coming to town with her baby. Each man accuses the other of being the guilty party. It turns out neither is.

The heroine of John Reinhart's **Because She Loved** (3-7-04, Third Ave.) is torn between her affections for the hero and for the suave leader of a Five Points gang. The gangster's perfidy finally opens her eyes. An inebriated character named Mixed Ale Liz provided comedy relief in a scene in the Tombs prison.

Complaints about the Trust's $2 top ticket emerged again in reviews of Ernest Denny's **Man Proposes** (3-11-04, Hudson). Critics felt the pleasant but frail comedy was not worth the new, steeper price. Its slim story told of a scapegrace younger brother (Hassard Short) who pretends to be his older brother, an Irish-born earl, and for a time wins the hand of the girl his brother loves. Henry Miller, performing with a subtle Irish brogue, was the star, but even his personal popularity could not override questionable, or questioning, reviews.

Mesmerism again reared its ugly head in Elwyn A. Barron's **The Ruling Power** (3-14-04, Garrick). Barron had seen several of his plays produced in New York in the 1880s and since that time had served as a Chicago drama critic. His latest effort introduced a novice, Katherine Kennedy, prematurely raised to stardom. Mrs. Harwood scoffs at the claims of her former suitor, Dr. Edward Maxwell (Vincent Serrano), that he can save a dying man through hypnotism. But when Mr. Harwood (Orrin Johnson) is brought home on a stretcher, having fallen out of a speeding automobile, Maxwell does just that. However, once Harwood is under his spell, Maxwell resolves to destroy him and wed Mrs. Harwood. Maxwell turns Harwood into a hopelessly dissolute gambler. Harwood's loyal wife is even willing to pawn her jewelry when his gambling costs him his fortune. Maxwell, fearing his plans might fail, orders Harwood to commit suicide. As Mrs. Harwood rushes in, her husband falls down, seemingly dead, but she summons all her strength and by sheer will power resuscitates him. Maxwell has won, and lost. Neither the play nor its new star was liked,

and her name never again appeared in Broadway programs.

For some time Sydney Rosenfeld had been promising to give New York an enduring company devoted to classical mountings, an ensemble not unlike Wallack's or Daly's. He called his troupe the Century Players and opened on March 14 at the Princess with a revival of *Much Ado About Nothing*. Jessie Millward, William Morris, J. W. Albaugh, Jr., and Florence Rockwell were featured. The performances were creditable, and the $1.50 top should not have discouraged playgoers, but business was no more than fair for the two-week stand.

An Orphan's Prayer (3-14-04, Third Ave.) was an anonymous touring melodrama in which an adopted child avenges the death of her foster father at the hands of the foster father's own murderous daughter. It gave way after the customary week to David De Wolf's **Born in the Blood** (3-21-04, Third Ave.). Set in California, the new work told of a gypsy who kidnaps his little daughter. Her mother and a gardener set out to recover her.

Having met with disappointment in their first outing, the Century Players tried again with the American premiere of Ibsen's **Rosmersholm** (3-28-04, Princess). Regrettably Rosenfeld did not have the requisite faith in the play. He reputedly rewrote much of it and, to compound his own problems, underrehearsed his cast. Their performances were uncertain when they were not wooden. After a single week, Rosenfeld threw in the towel, at least as far as Manhattan was concerned. The troupe, minus some of its better players, surfaced again a few weeks later in Brooklyn, where they offered Hermann Sudermann's **The Battle of the Butterflies** (4-18-04, Amphion), in which three sisters struggle against one another in their quest for mates. After that, the company appears to have faded into oblivion.

A surprise snowstorm on the 28th could not deter New Yorkers headed for an unusual revival at the New Amsterdam. Many may have come to laugh at an old warhorse, but they remained to cheer. The old warhorse was *The Two Orphans,* the great hit of thirty years before. The cast was an amazing all-star gathering, with Grace George as Louise, Margaret Illington as Henriette, Kyrle Bellew as Chevalier de Vaudrey, E. M. Holland as Picard, Charles Warner as Jacques, James O'Neill as Pierre, Annie Irish as Countess de Linières, and Elita Proctor Otis as La Frochard. But the wildest reception was extended to Clara Morris when she made a brief appearance late in the play as Sister Geneviève. The settings were acknowledged to be magnificent, with the snowfall on stage outclassing the snowfall on 42nd Street. Nor did critics suggest the play had aged. It seemed to them as powerfully moving as ever. A. M. Palmer, who had produced the 1874 success, was called before the footlights to receive his own personal accolade. The accolade was his last; he died a few months later. Rapturous notices and the potent tug of tradition kept the box office humming for all seven weeks of the engagement.

All but lost in the excitement of the revival was the opening of Lillian Mortimer's newest touring melodrama, **In the Shadow of the Gallows** (3-28-04, Third Ave.). The dark-eyed, dark-haired playwright took the part of a vengeful gypsy, whose mother had run away with a rich man. She seeks out the man, murders him, and then plots the ruin of his son and the son's new bride. Stabbings, false accusations, and a chase atop a moving train provided additional thrills.

The season's final success was Richard Harding Davis's **The Dictator** (3-28-04, Criterion). It marked a departure for Davis, his first play not based on one of his stories, but written from scratch. As the passengers and crew watch the steamer *Bolivar* slowly come up to the dock at Porto Baños, the capital of the Central American banana republic of San Mañana, two passengers seem especially edgy. They are known as Steve and Jim, but we soon learn they are really Brook Travers (William Collier) and his valet, Simpson (Edward Abeles). Back in New York they had gotten into a fight with a cabman who had overcharged them, and, believing Travers's punch inadvertently had killed the man, they had grabbed the first ship leaving the city. Another passenger is the new American consul to San Mañana, Col. John T. Bowie (George Nash). He boasts that he has engineered a revolution in the country and for all practical purposes now owns the republic. Travers reveals himself to Bowie, who, for an exorbitant price, agrees to protect the men. They will need that protection, for a detective, Duffy, has just boarded the ship seeking them. A fourth passenger is Lucy Sheridan (Nanette Comstock), a prim but pretty girl sailing to Porto Baños to dutifully marry a missionary. Bowie is informed that while the ship was slowly steaming southward yet another revolution has taken place (they occur almost every other Tuesday), and that the new strongman, General Campos, has vowed to kill him. The quick-thinking colonel agrees to sell his identity, the consulship—in fact, the whole country—to Travers for still another exorbitant payment, $5000.

Once ashore Travers-Bowie is confronted by more problems. Campos arrives and warns him if he

leaves the consulate he will be shot. The knife-wielding Señora Juanita Arguilla (Louise Allen) demands that Bowie keep an old promise to marry her. And the Rev. Arthur Bostick comes seeking Lucy. Discovering that Campos pays his men eighteen cents a day, Travers-Bowie offers them twenty (reviews said the figures mentioned in performance were twenty-eight and thirty), and the men switch allegiance. But Campos is still menacing, prompting the consul to telegraph the navy for help. By the time it arrives, the missionary and the señora are a pair and Travers has won Lucy. An officer advises Travers that the cabby did not die and that Duffy had been sent on a faster ship to bring the men home safely.

The comedy was applauded, as were Collier and his supporting cast, especially John Barrymore, who played a booze-loving telegraph operator, Charley Hyne. Some of Hyne's lines could have haunted Barrymore in later years, considering the reputation he developed. Thus in the first act he announces, "It's never too early for a drink." In the next act a café owner tells Hyne that he hangs pictures of Washington and Jackson in his barroom since "it makes the Americans in Porto Baños feel just like home," to which Hyne responds, "I guess I'll go over and see if I can't feel at home." Of course, most of the comedy fell to Travers. Typically:

Travers: And I said, "Campos has insulted a distinguished diplomat"—that's me—"for which reason the Liberal Party will tolerate Campos no longer."
Hyne: The Liberal Party?
Travers: Yes, I'm the Liberal Party. I'll bet I'm the most liberal party this town ever saw. The Governor alone cost me two thousand dollars.

The comedy ran until the onset of hot weather, took a respite, then returned in late summer for another month before touring.

Three other first-class houses offered competing openings, none of which fared well. The best-received, largely because of Charles Hawtrey and Fanny Brough's delightful playing, was F. C. Burnand's English comedy **Saucy Sally** (4-4-04, Lyceum). To impress his mother-in-law, the hero describes his imaginary adventures circling the globe on the ship that gave the play its title. The appearance of the ship's real captain bursts his balloon.

Fred W. Sidney's **An African Millionaire** (4-4-04, Princess), taken from stories by Grant Allen, spotlighted a pair of likable scam artists, husband and wife (H. Reeves-Smith and Minnie Dupree), who employ all manner of disguises and names in their ploys. And they escape scot-free at the end. Poor writing, not the unexpected conclusion, doomed the comedy to a single week.

A week's run was also all given to Paul Armstrong's double bill **The Blue Grass Handicap** and **The Superstition of Sue** (4-4-04, Savoy). In the first, an old Negro describes how his mistress's horse won a race. In the second, a young man's attempts to commit suicide are frustrated at every comic turn. He has become suicidal because his sweetheart turned him down on account of his proposing to her on Friday the 13th. Among the farcical characters was an Indian fakir named Spoo Katcha (read "spook gotcha"), who hides a snake in a sideboard to discourage would-be drinkers.

At a combination house, Dodson Mitchell's **Paul Revere** (4-4-04, 125th St.), the second play of the season with that title, offered a relative novelty. As Paul rode off to sound the alarm, the stage darkened and his ride was shown on "Pauley's kalatechnoscope motion pictures." At the end of the film, the flesh-and-blood "Paul rides in aglow with excitement." Paul's girl, Mary Waine, was played by Jessie Bonstelle, who later became a stock manager known as "the Maker of Stars."

And at the Third Avenue the umpteenth return of *Uncle Tom's Cabin* was given an enthusiastic welcome.

Virtually the whole biblical history of David was repeated in Arnold Reeves and Wright Lorimer's **The Shepherd King** (4-5-05, Knickerbocker). His friendship with Jonathan, his slaying of Goliath (done offstage, but with the giant's head brought in), his rivalry with Saul, his visit to the Witch of Endor, his crowning as king—all were offered against settings that evoked high praise, although critics felt that the staging and many of the performances, notably Lorimer's David, were often inept. For all its faults the play proved popular, returning for several respectable runs in later years.

Hal Reid's **Driven from Home** (4-11-04, Star) related how a puritanical father wrongly accuses his daughter of shaming him and orders her out of the house. Her crippled brother accompanies her. They suffer innumerable vicissitudes until the brother's skill as an artist helps bring a happy denouement.

At the Lyric *The Pit*'s bulky scenery was set aside for a single matinee on the 15th to allow Wilton Lackaye to star in *Pillars of Society*. As they usually did, reviews reflected critics' prejudices for or against Ibsen.

Two revivals of *Camille* opened on the 18th. Uptown at the Harlem Opera House, Virginia

Harned and William Courtenay played the leads; at the more centrally located Hudson, Margaret Anglin and Henry Miller starred. Reviewers still admired the play but agreed that in both productions the principal players were singularly colorless. The mountings were short-lived. On the final night at the Hudson, Miller gave a stinging speech assailing the critics, invoking the old argument that they were more interested in showing how clever they were than in offering readers a fair assessment.

Elizabeth Tyree's fitful hold on stardom moved nowhere, neither forward nor back, when she enjoyed a month's run in **Tit for Tat** (4-25-04, Savoy), which Leo Ditrichstein translated from *Heureuse*, a French farce by Maurice Hennequin and Paul Bilhaud. She played a snobbish wife whose aristocratic husband (Ditrichstein) prefers rough country life to effete city ways. After she takes on a lover (Joseph Kilgour), the couple separate. But her lover proves a disappointment, and the wife begins to receive amorous letters from a stranger. Naturally, the stranger turns out to be the husband.

When George H. Broadhurst's **The Crown Prince** (4-30-04, Daly's) had tried out in February in Harlem, it had been billed as "satirical romantic fantasy" and embraced as a delightful spoof of the very sort of Graustarkian folderol its star, James K. Hackett, often had performed. In transit to Broadway something went wrong. Scuttlebutt suggested Hackett quietly had rewritten much of it and restaged it in a more serious vein. As a result, what Broadway saw was a discouraging hodgepodge of styles. Robert, Crown Prince of Morantia, comes incognito to Rhodoland, where he is to wed Queen Cecilia (Charlotte Walker). Uncovering a plot by the minister of war to foment revolution, Robert disguises himself as a highwayman in order to attack the minister's coach. But his plan is thrown into confusion when a real highwayman (Brigham Royce) robs the coach. Robert becomes a fugitive, although he is aided by the queen, who has been smitten by the stranger. The truth comes out in time for a happy ending. Two weeks sufficed to exhaust the play's appeal.

The rest of the waning season belonged to combination houses. Victor Brandon's **The Signal Lights of Port Arthur** (5-2-04, Third Ave.) centered on an American engineer who aids in bringing important papers out of Russia. The spectacular scenery included a street in Port Arthur, "the billowy deep, with a warship, and plenty of firing and gallant rescues," and, finally, a barren islet, where all concludes satisfactorily for the hero and his girl. This was followed by Cecil Frederick's **The**

Voice of the Mountain (5-9-04, Third Ave.). A corrupt bank cashier, whose sideline is leading a band of Martinique brigands, robs the bank and attempts to foist the blame on his rival for the hand of the leading lady. The cashier chases the lovers and the lovers chase the cashier, until he is overwhelmed in Mt. Pelee's eruption, which brings the play to its sensational finish.

Alice E. Ives's **Starr's Girl** (5-16-04, Murray Hill) was a western "of the old-fashioned type." Its hoydenish heroine nurses a sophisticated easterner through an illness, and the two fall in love, much to the chagrin of the easterner's haughty fiancée. The hero buys some land from the hoyden's father, and it proves a bonanza. A further sweetening comes when a lady in the hero's party turns out to be the heroine's long-lost mother.

The tug of tradition was demonstrated again the afternoon before *Starr's Girl* opened, when Julia Marlowe and Tyrone Power gave a special matinee of *Ingomar* at the Empire. Actually, old plays such as *Uncle Tom's Cabin* and *East Lynne* still were paying profitable visits to combination houses, season after season. And, as *The Two Orphans* had attested, first-class audiences were equally responsive, given the right production.

In F. Marriot Watson's **The Black Mask** (6-6-04, Grand Opera), the heroine is tricked by the last of the season's gentleman-crooks into marrying him instead of her physician sweetheart. The woman comes to realize that her husband is not only a thief, but her father's murderer. She resumes seeing her old flame, which infuriates her husband. He plots revenge with his mistress. The wife is drugged and the physician brought in to perform an operation, ostensibly to save her life, but actually to disfigure her by removing her lips. Her loyal servants discover the plot, drug the mistress, and put her in the wife's place, with her face covered. The physician performs the operation, after which the husband pulls off his false wig and beard and gloats over his triumph. But the servants then pull off the facial covering, to the villain's consternation.

The season's finale was Edward E. Rose's **Fighting Bob** (6-13-04, Fifth Ave.). Rose was known to be an amateur horticulturist, leading one critic to suggest he had grafted Richard Harding Davis's *The Dictator* onto Anthony Hope's *The Prisoner of Zenda*. Rose's hero has just left college and gone to another banana republic for adventure and fortune. This republic is unusual in that it is ruled by a princess. The hero heads a revolution and wins the princess at the same time. The last act, underscoring the play's debt to *The Dictator,* was set at a telegraph station.

Another stock troupe brought the season to a close with Hal Reid and Bertha Belle Westbrook's **The Prince of the World** (6-3-04, Murray Hill), a play obviously hoping to cash in on the popularity of religious dramas such as *Ben Hur* and *Quo Vadis.* A prologue depicted such New Testament scenes as Judas accepting his silver and Peter denying Christ. The main play told how Caesar (Reid) loves Judith (Miss Westbrook), a Christian girl. When she spurns him he throws her in a cage of lions (real lions, according to reviews) and, after the lions refuse to touch her, subjects her to other harrowing trials. She survives and marries her Christian boyfriend. *The Dramatic Mirror* gave a small picture of the acting at this stock house when it reported that Reid, who played Simeon in the prologue, "bent nearly double" whenever he wanted to show that he was suffering from leprosy but stood erect to offer his speeches.

1904–1905

The outlook at the start of the season was gloomy. Memories of 1903–04's troubles were gallingly fresh when Charles Frohman returned from his annual early summer European trip to lament the paucity of good new English and Continental plays. Since importations were still the backbone of any strong Broadway season, that was ominous. *Theatre,* noting that "things often go by contraries," endeavored to cast a rosy limelight on the coming months by predicting that despite low expectations smiles might be in order at season's end. American playwrights, the magazine argued, were being handed a golden opportunity. Happily, the rationalization was not too far-fetched. If new American offerings were not as enduring as those that would begin to appear a decade down the road, they could, without much exaggeration, be viewed not only as good theatre pieces but as legitimate beacons of better things to come.

The season's statistics were equally interesting. *Variety's* retrospective accounting listed 63 new plays, 29 new musicals, and 35 revivals for a total of 127. But the *Dramatic Mirror's* contemporary figures were startlingly different. Its total was 313 productions, of which 224 were new and 89 were revivals. The discrepancy came from *Variety's* considering only regular runs at first-class houses, while the *Dramatic Mirror* accepted a handful of special tryout matinees as well as the numerous touring plays at combination theatres and attractions at two auditoriums devoted to foreign-language productions. By either accounting it was the busiest season Broadway had yet seen.

As usual the combination theatres relit first. Howell Poole and Henry Belmer's **A Child of the Slums** (7-30-04, Third Ave.) signaled that the same cobwebby motifs that had served sensation-melodrama so long and so well would continue to suffice. The action moved from Nigger Alley to the railroad tracks along the Hudson River to the Waldorf-Astoria and finally to a counterfeiter's den in recounting the saga of a street urchin who undergoes myriad tribulations before discovering she is really a long-lost heiress. The second act ended with the tiny heroine escaping her malevolent pursuer by precariously grabbing hold of a freight train speeding across the rear of the stage. The next act concluded with a reformed adventuress wielding an axe to prevent more mayhem. "To prove the worth of a play at the Third Avenue," the *Dramatic Mirror* advised, "one should go there and listen to the demonstrations at the close of the acts. It would seem that at the end of a season the roof would have to be nailed on again."

Another young waif, this time a boy, was the central figure in Hal Reid's **Alone in the World** (8-13-04, Metropolis). Actually, Reid told two unconnected stories. In the first, the boy rescues a "fallen" woman from the river, where she has jumped to escape a man who had hounded her. Later the boy wrests a revolver from the man, but the shock of the incident leads to the lady's fatal heart attack. Then the youngster becomes a bank messenger and prevents a second troublemaker from blowing up the bank's safe. The bank owner's daughter recognizes the lad as her long-lost son.

Such claptrap remained so popular that over the summer one relatively new combination house was redone with narrower seats to add capacity, regardless of possible discomfort to patrons. It reopened with Charles E. Blaney's **More to be Pitied Than Scorned** (8-15-04, 58th St.). Blaney's hero is an actor who violates company policy by secretly marrying. To exacerbate matters he marries the daughter of a neighboring minister who has been railing against the theatre. The villain learns of the marriage and spreads a rumor that the hero is a bigamist, so the hero loses both his job and his wife and becomes an alcoholic. His wife later regrets the separation and helps him to stop drinking. He also regains his job, but the villain plans to kill him during the performance. An oldtime actor gets wind of the plot and

switches guns. The villain is shot. Theatrical settings were the cue for the expected specialties.

Some curious if trivial parallels connected the new season with the one just gone by. Once again, for starters, a Leo Ditrichstein farce initiated the season at first-class houses. **Military Mad** (8-22-04, Garrick) was derived from Franz von Schönthan's *Im Bunten Rock,* and derived with too great fidelity to please most critics. Set in a German spa where soldiers are on maneuvers, it told how a diplomat (Henry V. Donnelly) asks an officer (Ditrichstein) to pay attention to an American heiress (Ida Conquest) who is being courted by the diplomat's son. He hopes by this means to prevent the heiress from becoming too enamored of the other soldiers, but his plan backfires when the heiress and the officer fall in love. The European-bred Ditrichstein's spirited playing was admired, but the patently American attitudes and dialects of the other actors clashed with the farce's Germanic style, and Miss Conquest was called to task for "her usual saccharine intonations, caressings of last syllables, and conscious poses of naivete."

A Fight for Love (8-22-04, Metropolis), Hal Reid's second play of the still young season, was written expressly for its star, the celebrated boxer Bob Fitzsimmons. Fitzsimmons played himself in a story that rehashed stock situations common to plays that had starred John L. Sullivan, Fitzsimmons, and other fighters before. The villain attempts to wreck the heroine's carriage by loosening a horse's shoe, but Fitzsimmons prevents the carriage from spilling and immediately reshoes the horse. (He had displayed his blacksmithing skills in earlier vehicles, but his audiences clearly never tired of seeing them.) Afterwards he prevents a robbery at the home of his sweetheart's father, and when the father, to recoup his failing finances, bets $10,000 on a match, he takes the place of the drugged boxer and wins the fight. He also wins the girl. One bit of boxing was not enough for patrons, so earlier in the play Fitzsimmons had offered them a "great bag-punching act."

The villain in Martin Hurley's **Dealers in White Women** (8-22-04, Star) is a Hindu who works in conjunction with an exotic woman named Karina La Strange. Their trade is white slavery, and they operate out of Chinatown. But they make a fatal mistake when they kidnap the heroine and her crippled sister, for the hero penetrates beyond the opium den where the Hindu presides and rescues the girls from a cell filled with captive women. The hero, like Raffles, is an expert cracksman, but seeing how base villainy can become, he vows to reform.

August's second and last show at a first-class house was Louis Eagan's **Jack's Little Surprise** (8-25-04, Princess). Jack (Arthur Byron), his bride, his father-in-law, and the father-in-law's young second wife have just finished a honeymoon in Cairo, when an Egyptian houri fleeing a harem seeks refuge in Jack's hotel suite. Jack agrees to carry her safely to America by hiding her in a steamer trunk. Somehow the girl survives the passage, but Jack has some explaining to do when the trunk is opened. Byron's "easy, buoyant manner, his splendidly sharp, incisive delivery" were not enough to carry the day.

But August's onslaught of sensation-melodrama was far from over. These often hurriedly written works might display their lack of careful composition, yet hurried writing did have one advantage. It allowed the plays to cull material from recent headlines. Thus the first of two Charles A. Taylor thrillers to appear in quick succession used the ongoing Russo-Japanese War for background. **The White Tigress of Japan** (8-27-04, American) spotlighted an Occidental ("an American girl of Roman Catholic faith") who had married a Japanese prince (referred to in some notices simply as a "Jap"). She had been maltreated in a Russian prison, where she had been held as a spy, and after her escape vowed vengeance. The Russians pursue her. At one point she hides in a huge flower basket. A Russian is about to thrust his sword through the basket when, possibly in a diplomatic breach, "a company of American marines, suddenly springing from nowhere, rushed in shouting and firing their guns with true soldierlike abandon. . . . The curtain fell to the crackling of guns, the waving of the Stars and Stripes, and the roaring and whistling of the gallery gods." But the heroine's troubles are hardly over. She is recaptured and dragged before the czar. An oriental turncoat rips her gown, exposing a special mark. "See," he cries, "the band of shame!! She is the White Tigress of Japan!" The girl, whose name is now Kinume, "raises [a] stiletto which she takes from her breast high above her head" and shouts, "Yes, the Tigress at bay! Lay your hands on me, and my soul shall be free! Free as Japan will be from the yoke you would place upon her people!!" The turncoat orders, "Seize her! Tear out her venomous tongue," but the czar interrupts, "Stop! She shall have freedom of speech," only to add, "It shall be her last!!" (Clearly Taylor's dialogue was all but indistinguishable from his rivals'.) A general amnesty saves the girl. She survives to see her blonde daughter, who is known as "the lady of Immeasurable Light," betrothed to an American naval officer.

Taylor's next entry was a vehicle for the Russell brothers, popular in vaudeville as female impersonators. In **The Female Detectives** (8-29-04, Metropolis) they portrayed policemen who pose as serving girls to save an old man from the machinations of a cutthroat villain and who recognize the old man's long-missing granddaughter in a fetching street waif. Thanks to its stars, this melodrama was long on laughs.

That was not true of Frederick Schwartz's **Thou Shalt Not Kill** (8-39-04, Third Ave.), which purportedly had been inspired by Tolstoy's antiwar pamphlet. But high-mindedness stopped with that brief announcement. The play was the same old gallery-pleasing hokum. The heroine, who does proclaim her allegiance to Tolstoy's ideas, learns that her fiancé's father has been murdered by a greedy rival for her hand and that the killer has successfully framed her fiancé. Since she has taken time out from preaching peace to learn hypnotism, she mesmerizes the villain into a confession. He hallucinates and reenacts the killing. If this were not enough, the play also featured a horse race with the horses on a dependable treadmill. Of course, there were lighter moments, in the specialty acts. One saw a lady bicyclist doing loop-the-loops.

The season's first big hit was the memorably titled **Mrs. Wiggs of the Cabbage Patch** (9-3-04, Savoy), which Anne Crawford Flexner dramatized from Alice Hegan Rice's popular material. Mrs. Wiggs (Madge Carr Cook), her son, and her oddly named daughters (Asia, Australia, Europeana) live in a ramshackle house by the railroad tracks in Louisville. The house is such a mess, she often wastes time looking for mislaid items. "One place is just as good as another," she tells a dismayed visitor. Her life is a mess, too. Years earlier her husband had run off, leaving her to fend for herself. Yet she remains sunnily disposed. To help her neighbor, Miss Hazy (Helen Lowell), win the food-loving Mr. Stubbins (William T. Hodge), she secretly cooks the dinners Miss Hazy claims as her own. After the marriage Stubbins cannot understand why his wife's meals always seem inedible. He becomes so sullen and drunk that Mrs. Wiggs assists in dumping him into a freight car, which immediately pulls away to points unknown. (The moving train recalled the faster freight in *A Child of the Slums*.) No sooner is he gone than a letter arrives informing him he is entitled to a sizable pension. He returns in time for a reconciliation. With his newfound wealth he will hire a cook.

But Mrs. Wiggs has fingers in lots of other pies. She convinces Miss Lucy (Nora Shelby) to leave her beloved South and head north with her sweetheart,

Bob (Thurston Hall), who has been offered work there as a newspaper editor. She also takes Lovey Mary (Mabel Taliaferro) into her already over-crowded home, along with the baby Mary carries in her arms. The baby is not Mary's. She has abducted it from an orphange, where it was placed after its mother died and where it was neglected. The baby's father appears, accompanied by a sheriff, with orders to arrest Mary. But the father turns out to be none other than Mr. Wiggs (Oscar Eagle). His forgiving wife welcomes her contrite husband and agrees to adopt the child.

Except for the better-educated Lucy and Bob, the characters wallowed in colloquialisms and malapropisms. Thus Mrs. Wiggs refers to "Stubbins-Hazy, with a syphon between the names." There were also some almost too cute passages, though they were frequently cut down by acid remarks. Mrs. Wiggs belongs to no religious denomination and views her garden as ecumenical. For example, the geraniums: "They're Methodists. They fall from grace and have to be revived. Like lots of encouragement in the way of sun and water. These hardy phlox is Methodists, too—easy to grow and needin' new soil every few years. Ain't that Methody down to the ground?" Mrs. Wiggs's lengthy analysis over, one soured neighbor concludes she'll just raise onions. There were effective sight gags as well, such as Miss Hazy moping about in a widow's black weeds and long black veil until Stubbins's return. While critics recognized that the dramatization was commonplace when it was not downright inept, they granted its appealing warmth and acknowledged that a cast "so near perfection" glossed over many of the faults. Madge Carr Cook (she was Eleanor Robson's mother) was praised for her sincerity and intelligence, but lesser players regularly grabbed the spotlight, especially Hodge as yet another bumpkin. The play, which had been touring for a year, ran 150 performances. It remained popular on the road and in stock for decades. Miss Cook performed virtually nothing else until her retirement.

John Drew appealed to a more elitist audience, yet he enjoyed almost as long a run in Charles Frohman's importation of Robert Marshall's **The Duke of Killicrankie** (9-5-04, Empire). The duke is rejected four times by the same lady (Margaret Dale), and when he abducts her to his castle she gives him the silent treatment. Only after he tells her he is cured of his infatuation does he win her.

Herbert Hall Winslow and Charles Dickson's **The Spellbinder** (9-5-04, Herald Square) failed to live up to its title and folded after two weeks. Howard Colby (Dickson), a young, unsuccessful lawyer who

has been nominated for the Senate by a political boss (Ralph Delmore), finds he must handle a breach-of-promise suit against the boss. To add to his woes, the boss is very fond of Colby's girl (Charlotte Townsend). For a time, after the girl jumps away when Colby discloses his feelings, he concludes the girl doesn't love him. He fails to take into account the onions he has eaten to cure a sore throat.

Another Frohman importation, Pinero's long and tedious **Letty** (9-12-04, Hudson), had a more than passable run thanks in good measure to William Faversham and Carlotta Nillson. They showed the final day in the doomed affair of a rich man and a shopgirl. An epilogue disclosed their fates some years later.

That same evening *The Old Homestead*, still popular after so many seasons, settled in for a run at the New York, with Denman Thompson as usual playing Josh Whitcomb.

Daniel Frohman elevated Cecilia Loftus to stardom when he presented her in Israel Zangwill's **The Serio-Comic Governess** (9-13-04, Lyceum). The star was cast as a convent-trained Irish lass who serves as a governess and moonlights as a music hall singer. She loves a soldier-hero (H. Reeves-Smith), but when he proves a faithless cad, she settles for a former suitor.

The next night saw a revival of the five-year-old *Becky Sharp* at the Manhattan. Mrs. Fiske again assumed the title role, but George Arliss now was Steyne and John Mason, Rawdon Crawley. Critics split in their judgment of Mason, many seeing him as less robust and dashing but more humane than Maurice Barrymore (then institutionalized with paresis). However, virtually all hailed Arliss's sinister portrayal, one man calling it "a moment of perfected theatric art." The revival ran nine weeks.

German militarism, which had served as a background for the farcical *Military Mad,* was depicted less attractively, along with rigid Germanic social protocol, in **Taps** (9-17-04, Lyric). The play was Charles Swickard's translation of Franz Adam Beyerlein's *Zapfenstreich*. A young woman (Effie Shannon), daughter of an aging sergeant (Herbert Kelcey), has an affair with a lieutenant (Robert Loraine). When the affair is revealed the father would kill the officer, but ingrained respect for his superiors prevents his doing it, so he kills his daughter instead. The forty-nine-year-old Kelcey and the thirty-seven-year-old Miss Shannon were husband and wife. Kelcey had to paint wrinkles on his face and wear a gray beard and mustache, while Miss Shannon had to doff a number of years. Yet even though electric lighting was far more revealing than gaslight, old practices still prevailed in many conservative circles, and no one complained. However, the play failed.

A second foreign play, Octave Mirbeau's **Business Is Business** (9-19-04, Criterion), fared better. It did so in part because of an odd bit of casting. William H. Crane laid aside his comic tricks and smiling bluster to play a sideburned, stern-visaged man whose very family must take a back seat to his implacable greed. Crane loyalists may have been unprepared for the change, but they came in large enough numbers to give the drama a respectable run.

The season's two biggest hits, both American, followed in short order, with only one swift failure intervening. The previous season had seen George Ade win the long-run sweepstakes and a Belasco production come in second. This year positions were reversed. Ade's comedy, **The College Widow** (9-20-04, Garden), arrived first. Even its title broadcast something of its freshness. Critics often had lambasted playwrights for excessive use of slang. The idea that dialogue should be loftier than everyday speech died hard. However, Ade had won his reputation with his slangy short stories, so critics were glad to make an exception for him. Unwittingly, their exception signaled a change in attitude toward stage dialogue. Fresher still was the notion of centering an entire play upon American collegiate life and its fun-loving, largely unstudious students. *Charley's Aunt* had employed an English university for its background, but its plot, relying on the need for a chaperone and the humor of a man masquerading as a woman, could have been set elsewhere. No way could *The College Widow* have been replanted to another setting.

A college widow is a young lady, affiliated in some manner with a school, who loves or flirts with students, only to lose them on graduation day. At Atwater the resident widow is pretty Jane Witherspoon (Dorothy Tennant), daughter of Atwater's president. One of her loves—she still wears his fraternity pin—has been Jack Larrabee (Edgar L. Davenport), a recent graduate who has returned to the campus not only to coach the football team but to continue his courtship as well. The campus is so tree-shaded that the view when the curtain rises merely hints at some buildings in the distance, except for a glimpse of the entrance to the main building on stage right. But students and faculty at Atwater have little time to appreciate the school's architectural or sylvan amenities. Concern focuses on the football team. It appears hopelessly green and puny. The trainer, McCowan (Dan Collyer),

groans, "Not one of 'em knows enough to pick up the ball. If they fell out of a boat, they wouldn't hit the water." To make matters worse, President Witherspoon is insisting that players maintain decent academic records if they are to play.

Things look bad for the traditional game with Bingham. One unexpected visitor to Atwater is Hiram Bolton (Edwin Holt), a buddy of Atwater's president from far back. But Bolton is Bingham's biggest benefactor—"does Rockefeller stunts" there, one student explains. Bolton gratefully attributes his success to his having flunked out at the school, forcing him to go to work at the railroad he now owns: "Oh, colleges do some good—they keep a good many light-weights out of the railroad business. But there ain't any money in a college education. Look at Pete Witherspoon. He was a smart boy—workin' now for three thousand dollars a year." Accompanying Bolton is his son, Billy (Frederick Truesdell). Billy has been a freshman at three colleges out west and now will try a freshman year at Bingham. Just what Billy will study is uncertain, and his father has hired a special tutor to help him get passing grades. What Billy really can do is run with that football.

There is consternation among Atwater's students until one of them gets the bright idea to have Jane persuade Billy to play for Atwater instead. She does this by inviting him to the faculty-student reception, where she promises him the first dance, and any more dances he desires. The dance in the gaily decorated gymnasium serves its end. "That was the best dance I ever had in all my life—honestly it was," Billy tells Jane. She replaces Larrabee's pin with Billy's. It takes no more coaxing to have Billy switch allegiances. He advises his apprehensive tutor, "I'm over twenty-one. . . . You're merely a tutor. Go ahead and tute as much as you please, but don't try to give me orders." The elder Bolton, who has been away, returns on the day of the big game and attempts to prevent Billy's playing, until the students kidnap the old man. Atwater wins on the strength of Billy's last-minute run. Then Billy learns about Jane's ploy. He is prepared to leave until he also realizes that, however insincere Jane may have been at the start, her feelings for him now are heartfelt.

Walter Prichard Eaton, one of the era's best new critics, hailed the work as "a genre picture of triumphant skill, executed with exuberant yet loving humor." He felt obligated to qualify his praise by adding, "But Mr. Ade has no power of dramatic development. He cannot penetrate the surface." Superficial as it might have been, the play allowed for wonderful stage pictures: town girls welcoming returning students; the faculty get-together; a rah-rah football rally and victory celebration, pennant-waving rooters looking down from the top of the stadium as the roughed-up Billy is carried through an archway on his teammates' shoulders. Ade peopled his story with amusing supporting figures such as the haughty, frustrated Flora and the mannish Bessie. If photographs suggest the actors today would seem too mature to impersonate college students (Davenport, who played the newly graduated Larrabee, was a not very young-looking forty-two), audiences again accepted them uncomplainingly. The comedy ran out the season, compiling a run of 278 performances, and later provided the basis for the musical *Leave It to Jane.*

Reviews called **The Coronet of the Duchess** (9-21-04, Garrick) Clyde Fitch's "first play of the season," attesting to the certainty of the playwright's ongoing productivity. They also called it some other, unkind things. Its plot was unpleasant and most unflattering to the English upper class, telling as it did of an American girl (Clara Bloodgood) who marries a duke and, after discovering him to be a conscienceless philanderer, is forced to buy his family's consent to a divorce. The drama could muster only two and a half weeks.

Belasco's production, one of his most memorable, was Charles Klein's **The Music Master** (9-26-04, Belasco). The play was written as a vehicle for David Warfield. Anton von Barwig's wife had run off to America with another man, taking Barwig's and her daughter with her. Leaving behind a promising European career, Barwig eventually came to America, too, hoping to find the girl. He has not succeeded. Nor has he been able to do better than eke out a living giving music lessons and playing in a dime museum, a fact he withholds from his friends. He has taken a room in a house on Houston Street. Both the house and its mistress have enjoyed better days, but now the neighborhood is rundown. Faded squares on the wall, suggesting pictures have been pawned for immediate income, underscore Barwig's plight. Even his heavy, square piano is in danger of being repossessed. But that does not prevent Barwig from buying a spaghetti dinner for his friends. Those friends are other down-and-out musicians, and they make the best of the meager meal, one of them claiming pretentiously that spaghetti is "a dish for aristocrats." Barwig's lone hope is the offer to lead an orchestra in a new concert hall, but his hope is dashed when an official from the bricklayers' union tells him the hall was not built with union labor, so the union will get violent if necessary to prevent its opening. "Wagner should be glad that he is dead,"

Barwig moans, and when the ignorant official asks who Wagner is, Barwig sends him away with the answer, "He was a scab."

An attractive young charity worker, Helen Stanton (Minnie Dupree), brings Barwig a talented slum boy and tells Barwig she will pay for the boy's lessons. Barwig is struck by her resemblance to the daughter he remembers. Just then men come to reclaim the piano. Rather than embarrass Barwig by offering him the few dollars needed to save the piano, Helen asks him to come to her house and give her lessons. Helen's father, Henry A. Stanton (Campbell Gollan), learns that Barwig is visiting his home and orders the servants to turn him away. However, Barwig does manage to meet Helen there again, and during the meeting Helen shows him her doll collection. One is a German doll with a missing eye, the same damaged doll his daughter had played with. When Barwig and Stanton come face to face, Barwig recognizes him as the man with whom his wife, now dead, had eloped. In his fury Barwig would expose Stanton, but the banker points out that such an exposure would destroy Helen's chance for an excellent marriage. Her fiancé's family, he remarks, would never receive her again. In the play's most famous lines, Barwig retorts, "Then if they won't take her—I take her! If they don't want her, I want her!"

Stanton cagily allows Barwig to witness an exchange between Helen and her betrothed, Beverly Cruger. Moved by the couple's obvious love, the devastated musician leaves without revealing the truth to Helen. His fortunes fall further, and he moves to an attic room in the Houston Street home. Reluctantly, he buys a steerage passage to return to Leipzig. He is packed and saying good-byes when Helen shows up. Her father has told her the true story, and she insists that Barwig accompany her and her husband on their European honeymoon. They will travel first class. Telling his landlady and his friends, "I am going to help take care of the baby," he starts slowly down the stairs while the others lean over the railing, waving an affectionate farewell.

Although Belasco could cull favorable quotations from reviews, such as the *Sun*'s "a magnificent success—a charming play, which runs from laughter up to tragedy," most critics branded the play trite and sentimental, all the while allowing that Warfield's acting and Belasco's staging turned the evening into a consummate piece of theatre. Of the star *Theatre* observed, "His methods are simple. His expression of feeling is delicate. His voice utters kindness in tones that come from a heart habituated to kindliness and forbearance and suffering. The lines about his mouth respond to sentiment and attention is centered on a face lit up by eyes aglow with the soul."

The *Times* called Belasco's mise-en-scène, particularly the Houston Street settings, "marvels of atmospheric realism." Some idea of Belasco's meticulousness can be gauged from the printed text. The play itself occupies 103 pages. The next 19 pages contain an awesomely detailed property plot (including recipes for cooking spaghetti and for the sauce), a light plot, a music plot, and a list of special effects (mostly door-slammings). In the original production the attic's skylight had cracked panes stuffed with cloths, which fluttered in the wind until they fell out and snow drifted in. According to Belasco's reminiscences, Warfield felt this was going too far and was distracting, so the business was dropped.

Cracked panes or no, *The Music Master* was the biggest straight-play success up to its time. It ran, with a summer hiatus, for a year and a half or 627 performances. The record held until *Peg o' My Heart* surpassed it nearly a decade later. Warfield continued to tour with the play until mid-1907.

The same night, Arnold Daly offered another Shavian double bill, reviving *The Man of Destiny* and coupling it with the American premiere of **How He Lied to Her Husband** (9-26-04, Berkeley Lyceum), in which a young man's attempt to deny he has written poems to a married woman leads to some unexpected, rough-and-tumble consequences. Second-drawer Shaw, it ran only a week.

Jane Maudlin Feigl's **A Texas Ranger** (9-25-04, 14th St.) brought with it a short-lived new star, Sydney Ayres, who publicity releases claimed had been one of Teddy Roosevelt's Rough Riders. He played "Freshwater Jack" Dallam, a cowboy and later a Ranger who loves his boss's daughter, Texas West. His life is complicated by the arrival of an English lord and the lord's niece. The lord develops a crush on Texas, and the niece is smitten by Jack. As if that were not enough, a cow thief accuses Jack of stealing cows. A shootout follows. Jack is wounded and nursed back to health by Texas. Jack also learns some land he purchased is rich in oil. The English return home empty-handed. On tour the play's title was cut to *Texas*.

The villain in Fran Allen's **Her Mad Marriage** (9-26-04, American) was an actor. As such he should have known that villainy doesn't pay. But that fails to stop him from tricking an heiress into marriage, murdering her father, and robbing the father's bank. He is leaving a fake suicide note beside the father's body when an office boy snaps a photograph of the incident. Even that cannot deter him from pursuing

the girl's true love, knocking him unconscious, and placing him on a belt moving toward a whirling saw. The office boy climbs a telegraph pole to cut the wires providing electricity to the saw. The villain eventually dies after accidentally drinking poison meant for his wife. One scene took place on the Brooklyn Bridge, where traffic and the show were stopped for the expected specialties. "This is circus, not drama," a critic wailed.

More of the same was offered in Lawrence Marston's **After Midnight** (10-3-04, Star). With the help of some sleazy Italians, a treacherous uncle kidnaps his nephew and niece. The boy is consigned to a school for young crooks and the girl to the Geisha, "a notorious resort in the Tenderloin." A "Hebrew" detective organizes their rescue. (Jews were to be treated more sympathetically this season than of late.) The action traveled from the children's posh mansion to Grand Central Station, the crook school, an East Side rooftop (with a view of the city), and finally to the Tenderloin.

The following Monday was monopolized at first-class houses by foreign works. None was especially successful although Henry Arthur Jones's **Joseph Entangled** (10-0-04, Garrick) held the boards for eight weeks. Jones's hero (Henry Miller) must pay the social consequences for spending the night in a home where, unknown to him, a married lady (Hilda Spong) also is sleeping.

In Paris, Sarah Bernhardt had found success in Sardou's *La Sorcière*. Mrs. Patrick Campbell offered New Yorkers the same play, translated, naturally, as **The Sorceress** (10-10-04, New Amsterdam). A Moorish woman with curative and hypnotic powers puts the bride of her faithless lover (Guy Standing) into a trance, but when she is hauled before the Inquisition she confesses to witchcraft rather than see the man condemned. Both are killed by an angry mob. Mrs. Campbell belonged to a newer school of acting. She handled the more quiet, subtle scenes well. However, in later, highly emotional moments, she could not hold a candle to Bernhardt's blazing pyrotechnics.

Otis Skinner appeared in a more congenial vehicle, Jean Richepin's *Le Chemineau*, which Skinner's brother, Charles, translated as **The Harvester** (10-10-04, Lyric), The star had the sort of romantic role on which he thrived, a life-loving, picturesque vagabond. A farm laborer seduces a young neighbor (Lizzie Hudson Collier), but the wanderlust seizes him, and he leaves before he learns that the girl is pregnant. He returns years later for a reconciliation with the now married girl and his grown son, then, heeding the call of the road, heads off again. Critics praised the play's poetry and Skinner's careful production. He had switched the action from France to French Canada and bought the costumes and many props from French Canadians among whom he had summered. Yet Skinner still was not a top star, nor was the idyllic play to everyone's taste, so the drama remained only a month before returning to the road itself.

The only new American play of the evening was a sensation-melodrama, Theodore Kremer's **A Prisoner of War** (10-10-04, Star). As his rival, Taylor, had in August, he looked to the ongoing Russo-Japanese conflict for coloring. A Japanese officer loves his countrywoman, whose father is a spy for Russia, but he is alienated by the secrecy she adopts to protect her father. When the hero is captured by the Russians, a Russian officer tells the girl he will release him if he, the Russian, can sleep with her. She refuses. The hero is sentenced to death but reprieved by an agreement to exchange prisoners.

Two great performers who eventually would marry and become one of the theatre's classic husband-and-wife teams made their first joint appearance at the Knickerbocker on the 17th. E. H. Sothern and Julia Marlowe began their six-week stand with *Romeo and Juliet,* then proceeded to *Much Ado About Nothing* and *Hamlet.* Although dyed-in-the-wool reviewers longed for bygone players and mountings, most critics were elated. Their consensus was that the *Romeo and Juliet* was "one of the very best and most intelligent productions of a Shakespeare play that the local stage has known in recent seasons." Even crotchety William Winter melted enough to note, "With one long sigh for summers passed away, Miss Marlowe combines physical beauty, tender sensibility, imagination, deep feeling, capacity of passion, and some measure of tragic force." A few reviewers perceived Sothern's Romeo as too moody and melancholy. The pair was seen as more evenly matched in Shakespeare's comedy, albeit here, too, Miss Marlowe was favored slightly. The balance tilted in Sothern's favor with *Hamlet.* Of course, with time and experience working together, the stars would be seen as virtually a perfect pair.

Dear friends in front, the curtain must not fall
Until a grateful woman says goodby to all.
Goodby, old friends, new friends, my children
    every one of you!
Listen, for it's true, I love each mother's son of
    you!
For wealth, for fame, my goodness, I don't care a
    filbert!
If only in your hearts you'll keep old Mrs. Gilbert.

Thus did the beloved Mrs. Gilbert, just turned eighty-three, say a final farewell to her admirers. Clyde Fitch had written her vehicle, **Granny** (10-24-04, Lyceum), taking it from Georges Mitchell's *L'Aïeule.* Its story centered on aged Mrs. Tompson, who tries to prevent her widowed son-in-law from making a second marriage. When she fails, she takes away her grandson (William Lewers), creating a breach between him and his father and new stepmother. Later she sees the error of her ways, admits she has been a "wicked old woman," and brings about a reunion. This was one occasion when the play clearly was not the thing. The star received a tumultuous welcome on her first entrance, and after she had delivered her poem on her final curtain, the audience joined in singing "Auld Lang Syne." The play enjoyed three weeks of excellent business, then embarked on its prearranged tour. Sadly, Mrs. Gilbert died a month later, shortly after the play had opened in Chicago.

Mrs. Henry C. de Mille, whose husband had been such a promising playwright and who had established herself as an important play broker, was listed surprisingly as producer of a hackneyed sensation-melodrama, Nain Grute and Wade Mountfortt's **The Missourians** (10-24-04, Metropolis). The villain tries to pretend that a mine is worthless, but his partner's son knows otherwise, so the villain contrives to have him killed. He already has murdered another partner and holds the mortgage on the widow's home. He forecloses on the mortgage and frames the widow's prospective son-in-law for killing the other partner's son. But the widow and her daughter own a horse, which has been entered into a race. A cohort of the villain, a corrupt jockey, is caught attempting to throw the race, so implicates his venal partner. Comedy was provided by a teetotaling tavern owner who calls his bar "the Road to Hell." The young man who both played jockey and directed the production was Mrs. de Mille's son, Cecil.

The next play to arrive at the same theatre also brought with it an actor who would be more famous in the future. The hero of J. L. Greenbaum's **Woman's Struggle** (10-31-04, Metropolis) was portrayed by Charles D. Coburn. He works in a shipping office and loves the firm's secretary (still referred to in 1904 as a typewriter). But he must compete for her attention with the office manager, who is a counterfeiter on the side. The crook senses he is losing, so he kidnaps the girl and causes the hero to be fired. Having nothing better to do, the hero accepts a position as pitcher on a New York baseball team. After he pitches and wins a crucial game (the game took up the whole third act), he hurries off to the counterfeiter's lair and rescues the heroine. Coburn's performance was praised as "manly and direct."

There was more trouble down at the mine in W. B. Patton's **A Struggle for Gold** (10-31-04, Third Ave.), where the hero is falsely accused of murdering his wife's father and where the "double-dyed villain" blows up the mine at one point. The hero doubled in brass in the specialty numbers. The actor who played him was billed as "the Great Sanderson, Europe's Comedy Poet of the Piano," and his routines stopped the show. When he said he would play a piece for two cents, the stage was showered with pennies. Jugglers who tossed axes and a singer who skipped rope while he sang also enlivened the evening.

John T. McCutcheon's popular cartoons provided the inspiration, if that was the word, for Glen MacDonough's **Bird Center** (11-3-04, Majestic). Critics found it singularly uninspired. A banker tries to court a widow who prefers a retired sea captain. The captain's daughter works at the bank, and when the banker discovers a $500 shortage, he holds the girl accountable. In fact, the girl innocently had paid out a $500 bill to her father. The bill turns out to be counterfeit and passes from hand to hand until the banker is forced to accept it as repayment. Much of the humor was of the Katzenjammer variety. A mischievous boy sets off fireworks. Later, at a July 4th celebration, the townsfolk become tipsy drinking from the captain's newly tapped well. It seems the captain drilled right down into an old buried sunken ship, which was carrying casks of whiskey. It also contained long-forgotten treasure, so all concludes happily for the captain, his daughter, and the widow.

On the 7th at the Lyric the great French actress Gabrielle Réjane began her first New York visit in nearly a decade. Her month-long engagement ranged from *La Dame aux camélias* to modern French comedy. By coincidence, a band of lesser French players had just offered a not dissimilar repertory at the American, down the street.

But on the night of Réjane's return that theatre was given over to another touring melodrama, David Higgins and Baldwin G. Cooke's **His Last Dollar** (11-7-04, American). A Kentucky gentleman comes to New York, where he loses his fortune through the schemes of a Wall Street con man. His fiancée is also in financial trouble and, to raise a mortgage on her property, sells the hero her horse. The hero promptly rides the horse at the Sheepshead Bay Futurity Stakes, winning the race, the girl, and a wad of money. The *Dramatic Mirror,* which

gave more attention to this school of drama than did other papers, hailed the performance of the actor who portrayed the hero, observing, "He was not at all the sleek, light-haired, long-suffering hero of conventional melodrama. Instead he was wiry, alert, none too handsome, and a very human person, who took his whiskey straight."

Edward E. Rose's **The Way to Kenmare** (11-7-04, 14th St.) represented a different, equally popular genre—the romantic Irish comedy-drama in which the tenor-hero warbled a handful of Irish ballads. The tenor in this case was Andrew Mack, and he portrayed the impoverished heir apparent to an Irish earldom who comes to America to make his fortune in mining. When he returns to Ireland he discovers a fake English claimant to the earldom, who also is attempting to steal his girl. He disguises himself "as a 'broth of a boy' in the knee breeches and red wig that invariably go with this sort of character," digs up proof of his legitimacy, and routs the villain.

Both Charles A. Taylor and Theodore Kremer also had novelties ready the same evening. Taylor's was **Tracked Around the World** (11-7-04, Star), in which a detective rescues his sweetheart and her jewels stolen by the villain and villainess while they were on the trail of a dangerous new explosive the sweetheart's father had developed. The trail took all the characters on a whirlwind world tour, from a New York mansion to San Francisco, Paris, Barcelona, Naples, and finally back to New York, only this time to an opium den. One setting was a railway sleeping car, where the principal characters were assigned berths next to a bevy of female minstrels who provided a series of specialties.

Comedy was even more up front in Kremer's **Fast Life in New York** (11-7-04, Windsor), billed as "an album of pictures of the life that kills in the metropolis." Playgoers may have been startled to see John Drew, Guy Standing, and Elita Proctor listed in the program, but they were listed on the left side since they were the names of Kremer's hero, villain, and villainess. The last two murder the lady's husband in order to obtain his money and to deprive the hero of the wealth he would have fallen heir to had the husband time to rewrite his will. The action moves from the murdered man's sumptuous home to a poolroom, then to Herald Square at night, during a snowstorm in which the poor are lined up for bread at a free-lunch wagon. From there the principals scurry to an artist's studio, where the villainess and the heroine fight a duel with fencing swords, to a bar run by amiable Jews, and finally to a gambling den. The repentant villainess, dressed as a man, kills her erstwhile cohort and hands the money over to the hero. Once again this season, Jews were depicted favorably. The hero's buddy is a Jew named Sammy who, got up in his long underwear, poses as a statue in the studio scene and draws a gun at a crucial moment.

The next Monday, the 14th, Charles Wyndham began an engagement at the Lyceum with a revival of *David Garrick.*

Fred Summerfield's **Why Girls Leave Home** (11-14-04, Star) regurgitated another batch of sensation-melodrama clichés. A bored country girl is lured to the big city by a slickly veneered operator. The girl's pure-as-country-air boyfriend rescues her just as she is consigned to a house of ill repute.

Comedies were rarer on tried-and-true touring circuits, but William Gill's **Mrs. Mac, the Mayor** (11-14-04, Metropolis) provided a healthy quota of laughs. Even so it also offered a quota of melodramatic clichés. Its star was the stocky female impersonator George W. Monroe, who played a Wild West washerwoman elected to mayor of a mining town on a reform ticket. She foils a plot to blow up a mine and converts her boozy spouse into a teetotaler.

Thomas Raceward's **Sunday** (11-15-04, Hudson), a badly written English comedy about the American West, which had succeeded in London, Australia, and South Africa, earned a respectable run in New York solely because its star was Ethel Barrymore, "the ideal of ultra-modern, Burne-Jones refinement." After tripping on a carpet and exclaiming "Damn!" offstage, she made her entrance "in an ill-fitting gingham gown of angry red, and her hair was braided double and tied tight with the most uncoquettish of red bow knots." Sunday is the daughter of an Englishman who died while mining in the West. His buddies have raised her, and after one of them has killed an Englishman who tried to abuse her, they send her off to London. There she falls in love with an Englishman (Bruce McRae), who is revealed to be her abuser's brother. She hurries back to America, followed by her persistent and ultimately victorious lover.

If Charles Frohman turned a profit with *Sunday*'s ten-week run, he was certainly out of pocket after another importation, R. C. Carton's **The Rich Mrs. Repton** (11-16-04, Criterion), shuttered four nights following its premiere. The wealthy widow (Fay Davis) finds herself in hot water when a bankrupt gambler (Ernest Lawford) announces their betrothal under the impression her name will soften some money-lenders' obduracy.

Last season's surprise success of *Hedda Gabler* prompted Mrs. Fiske to bring it back to the Manhattan on the 17th. Its revival caused H. T. Parker, later the great critic on the *Boston Evening Transcript* but then with the *New York Globe,* to muse on its probable future. Noting the polemics once set off by the original production of *Camille,* he wrote, "Fifty years from now, if Hedda Gabler lasts so long—and Camille is fifty years old—it may be a similar case. There will be no Ibsenites then. They are disappearing before our eyes even now, just as the professional Wagnerites have vanished. Current discussion of Ibsen's plays is tepid beside the turbid polemics of ten or fifteen years ago. We know them for what they are, and most of us have slipped them into their appropriate pigeon hole in the crowded rack of modern plays."

Four nights later, when Nance O'Neil began an engagement at Daly's, she opened with *Magda,* then quickly switched to her version of *Hedda Gabler.* Although she was relatively young, she belonged to a dying school of histrionics, and her floridly melodramatic Hedda suffered in comparison to Mrs. Fiske's more understated one.

Louis Mann, "this energetic disburser of mushy Dutch dialect," was the star of Gordon Blake's **The Second Fiddle** (11-21-04, Criterion), rushed in from the road to fill the gap left by *The Rich Mrs. Repton.* The play was a sort of comic *Heartsease;* the hero discovers his opera has been stolen by a nobleman, so he impersonates him and discomfits him before exposing the theft. Mann's "comic eccentricities, funny falls and general horseplay mangle all life-likeness out of the character as effectively as his mushy dialect removes all resemblance of the human from his speech," one critic lamented. Yet many similar complaints did not prevent the play's running a month.

Naturally, Theodore Kremer could never hope for even that relatively short run. His type of play had to be content with the customary one-week booking at a combination house. His latest was **A Race for Life** (11-21-04, Star), which presented spectators with their third treadmilled horse race of recent weeks. At least the setting was novel, Los Angeles. A repugnant horse owner endeavors to cripple a rival's horse and, failing that, hopes to bribe a jockey. The right horse wins.

Americans in England continued to be a popular theme, and a play that wove that theme into some deft comedy-melodrama seemed likely to appeal to playgoers. Alas, I. N. Morris's **The Usurper** (11-28-04, Knickerbocker) was not all that deft, but Nat Goodwin did his best to gloss over its inadequacies. John Maddox has risen from cowpuncher to millionaire. He comes to England seeking an English girl with whom he fell in love in his poorer days. He's really a nice chap, anxious to assure the English that cowpunchers don't punch cows all that often. His plan is to rent the girl's ancestral manor on the condition the family remain there, thus affording him time and opportunity to court Beatrice Clive. A monkey wrench is thrown in the works with the discovery that Beatrice is about to wed Sir George Trenery. She does not know that Sir George is a cad who has seduced her maid. The maid's father had attempted to shoot Sir George, shot an innocent man by mistake, and was sentenced to prison, from which he has escaped. In desperation John decides to take Beatrice up into the manor's haunted tower, and they are no sooner there than the butler unwittingly locks them in for the night. Scary sounds come from out of the darkness. At first they are believed to be made by a poodle, which somehow has gotten in, but even after the heroine holds the poodle in her arms, the noises continue. Then the maid's father reveals himself, and his story alerts Beatrice to Sir George's true nature. The "fat-cheeked" Goodwin's gift for light comedy helped the piece run a month.

Having offered *Magda* and *Hedda Gabler,* Nance O'Neil essayed the first of two novelties, Hermann Sudermann's *Johannisfeuer,* done as **The Fires of St. John** (11-28-04, Daly's). A gypsy girl has been adopted by a prosperous, conservative farmer (McKee Rankin). Just before the farmer's daughter is about to be wed, the gypsy has a passionate affair with the daughter's husband-to-be (Charles Dalton), only to be deserted by him. Again, the star was criticized for her crude, obsolescent, and patently too studied effects. As one reviewer recorded, "If she says, 'It does not reach your heart,' she slaps her lover's heart. If she speaks of her mother's breast, she clutches her own."

The inexhaustible Kremer had a new play on the boards that same night, **The Vacant Chair** (11-28-04, Metropolis). A young architect, who finally has received a major commission and does not want to tell his wife about it until his drawings are accepted, gives her no excuse for his protracted absences, thus allowing some malicious friends to cast doubt on his whereabouts. The troublemakers are disposed of by a convenient earthquake. Kremer may have sensed that the end was nearing for sensation-melodrama. The few critics who bothered to review his play remarked on how he increasingly was injecting comic notes into his plays, sometimes almost offering threadbare situations tongue-in-cheek. Perhaps, but comic characters had always abounded in these plays, just as specialty turns had.

A spiffily dressed, cold-blooded villainess and a precocious newsboy meet head on in Jean Caldwell's **The Secret of the Subway** (11-29-04, Third Ave.). Inevitably, a pasteboard subway car was the scene of one would-be killing thwarted by the young man's timely bravery.

Nance O'Neil terminated her engagement with a second novelty, Thomas Bailey Aldrich's **Judith of Bethulia** (12-5-04, Daly's). Apart from the minor acclaim his *Mercedes* had enjoyed, Aldrich's dramatizations of his own works rarely were seen as effective. This retelling of the Judith and Holofernes legend was a case in point. Nor did the production help, presenting as it did "the poorest apology for dancing girls and the most wooden-image soldiers and crowds seen on Broadway for many years." Moreover, the star's high-voltage, unmodulated emoting palled long before the final curtain. On her subsequent tour she added *Macbeth* and Giacometti's *Elizabeth* to her schedules.

Annie Russell's far more variegated art gave a leg up to Henri Bernstein and Pierre Veber's French farce **Brother Jacques** (12-5-04, Garrick), in which a naive, pliant girl is almost persuaded to marry an addlepated ninny (Joseph Wheelock, Jr.) until it dawns on her she really loves her self-sacrificing adviser (Oswald Yorke). Wheelock's farcical skills spiced the fun.

For the second season in a row, Shakespeare was making one of his periodic comebacks. His latest exponent was Robert B. Mantell. Opening night at the Princess on the 5th was jinxed. A snowstorm discouraged playgoers, and the small audience had to wait nearly an hour beyond the listed curtain time before stage hands could fit the cumbersome scenery onto the cramped stage. Even during the performance, grips could be heard, and sometimes seen, attempting to move or keep settings in place. At times their efforts provoked a hilarity that all but destroyed the proper atmosphere. Mantell's two-week stand began with *Richard III* (Cibber's version), Mantell luxuriating in a "robustious . . . good, old-time traditional Gloucester." *Othello* and Bulwer-Lytton's *Richelieu* followed. Mantell's outmoded, roaring style always would appeal more to the road than to New York. A lesser road star, Thomas E. Shea, had presented the same Shakespearean tragedies some weeks earlier at the Grand Opera.

Lillian Mortimer was the star of her own **A Girl of the Streets** (12-5-04, Third Ave.), portraying a waif brought up to a life of crime in Baxter Street. When she begins to question her criminality, she contrives to rescue two tots from the thieves' den. To do so she must first kill the gang's leader. The killing is pinned on one of the tots, so the young, tattered heroine writes a confession and jumps from a bridge. The accused girl's older brother, who loves the heroine, jumps into the river to save her. As usual, critics assailed heavy reliance on vernacular speech, one noting that "every slang phrase in the mother tongue was used." Obviously, Miss Mortimer was not George Ade.

Mrs. Charles A. Doremus and Leonidas Westervelt gave Charles Stuart a fictitious romance in **The Fortunes of the King** (12-6-04, Lyric). Fleeing from defeat at the hands of the Puritans, Charles (James K. Hackett) crops his cavalier curls and disguises himself as a yeoman. The sister (Charlotte Walker) of one of the king's guards befriends him and hides him, but when a Puritan officer (William Courtleigh) insults her, he reveals himself and promises to deliver Charles to the Puritans. Not realizing that the yeoman and Charles are one and the same, the girl disgustedly rejects him. The misunderstanding is cleared up in time for Charles to escape and await a more propitious moment for return. The drama was hackwork, but Hackett gave it his special stamp. "He sweeps through his scenes of adventure with compelling force," *Theatre* reported, "and makes love with a romantic fervor that will make the matinee girl his still more devoted slave."

Charles Wyndham continued his season with Hubert Henry Davies's **Mrs. Gorringe's Necklace** (12-7-04, Lyceum). A young house guest (Charles Quartermaine) steals another guest's (Mary Moore) necklace and manages to make it seem that his rival (Wyndham) for the hand of their host's daughter (Daisy Markham) is the guilty party. But the rival wheedles a confession from the thief, who walks out into the garden and shoots himself.

Another, luckier thief was the central figure in the best American play of the season, C. M. S. McLellan's **Leah Kleschna** (12-12-04, Manhattan). Writing under the pen name Hugh Morton, McLellan had achieved great popularity as a librettist, but this was his first major serious work to reach New York footlights. Leah (Mrs. Fiske) has been raised by her father (Charles Cartwright) in a life of thievery, moving across the map of Europe whenever they fear the police are closing in. For the moment they are living in a seedy room in Paris, a room with a dismal view of Paris rooftops. With them is Kleschna's servile crony, Schram (William B. Mack), who loves Leah. Both Kleschna and Schram are worried, for recently Leah has been acting strangely. She seems to be turning against them and regretting her criminal behavior. The change occurred after Leah saw a photograph in a shop. The photograph showed a man who, Leah is convinced, had rescued them from a sinking ship. Kleschna brushes this aside, since they are about to send Leah to steal Paul Sylvaine's family jewels.

Two visitors come to the Kleschnas' seedy flat. One is the degenerate, smirking Raoul Berton (George Arliss), who happens to be Sylvaine's prospective brother-in-law and who desires Leah as a mistress. The other is Sylvaine (John Mason) himself. He has learned of Kleschna's connection with Berton and wants him to leave Paris before Berton is corrupted further. Sylvaine is an odd man, a member of the Chamber of Deputies, who has pleaded publicly for compassion toward criminals, insisting that careful reformation, not harsh imprisonment, is the best way to help them. Leah was out when Sylvaine called, but she spotted him on the staircase and recognized him as her savior in the sinking. Kleschna denies that he visited the apartment. With reluctance Leah agrees to go ahead with the robbery. She enters the darkened room and places a flashlight on a stool so that the light shines on the safe, which she jimmies open. She has just removed the jewel box when Sylvaine appears. She pulls out a gun and warns him she will claim he had invited her to spend the evening with her even though he is about to be married. But when he flicks on the light, Leah is aghast to realize that Sylvaine is the man who saved her life.

A long dialogue ensues in which Sylvaine insists he has no intention of calling the police and no wish to hurt or chastise her. He professes to see much good in her, if only she will give that good a chance to rule her actions. At first she is sceptical, but she soon comes to accept Sylvaine's sincerity. Their tête-à-tête is interrupted by Raoul's appearance. He is furious, believing that Leah must be Sylvaine's mistress, and he threatens to stop Sylvaine's marriage. Leah enlightens him, telling him her history and pointing out, "Here we are—three of us—a gentleman—a thief—and a blackguard. I'm the thief." Sylvaine escorts Leah to the door, extracting a promise that she will visit him tomorrow. In their absence Raoul grabs the jewels and leaves. When Sylvaine returns and misses the jewels, he first thinks Leah cleverly tricked him, but, hearing Raoul and his buddies walking away singing and laughing, he reserves judgment. When Leah reappears the next day, Sylvaine is entertaining his fiancée (Emily Stevens), her mother, and her soldier-father. The general cannot comprehend Sylvaine's reluctance to call the police, and both Sylvaine and Leah have reached a tacit understanding not to mention Raoul. However, the general's increasingly angry persistence coupled with Raoul's sudden arrival wordlessly brings out the truth. Back in the apartment, Leah tells her father she is leaving. She recalls her mother, a simple peasant girl working in the fields.

Leah: I tell you I'm going a new road, Dad, and I've got to take it alone. Why, you couldn't follow it if you tried your best. How I'd take you if I could!
Kleschna: It leads back to the fields.
Leah: Back to the silent fields.
Kleschna: Among the peasants that labor with their faces to the ground.
Leah: Even on their knees with their faces to the ground.

Raoul arrives and offers to work a deal with Kleschna to share his loot. But Leah advises Raoul that one of Europe's best detectives is on his trail, and he is downstairs. If Kleschna tries to prevent her going, she will call the detective. Kleschna unlocks the door. As she leaves she says, "Poor old Dad. You never saw the true light, did you? Will it ever shine out to you? If it does, believe it, follow it; it's your only hope of peace in this world." The final act takes place three years later. Leah works quietly on a farm, "an Austrian lettuce garden bathed in sunlight." Sylvaine comes, tells her his marriage was called off, and asks her to marry him.

Some critics, such as John Corbin of the *Times* and Alan Dale of the *Journal,* held reservations about the drama ("The story progresses only by fits and starts"; a "dime-novel play"), but most critics lauded it unhesitatingly, even comparing it to the best modern European dramas. It might have been still more powerful had the Fiskes produced it as McLellan had written it, allowing Leah to walk out to an uncertain fate. The short, soppy final act was added as a concession to contemporary playgoers. Mrs. Fiske's mannerisms irked a few reviewers, one complaining that "at times her rapid, jerky utterance made her quite unintelligible," but the consensus was that the ensemble acting was nearly perfect. Cartwright, famous in England for his villains, was a harsh, forceful Kleschna, Mack a volatile Schram, Arliss an insinuatingly evil Raoul, and Mason a restrained, intelligent, sympathetic Sylvaine. The play ran until spring.

Theodore Kremer's fifth play of the season, **The Great Automobile Mystery** (12-12-04, Star), suggested his oddball humor persisted. John Drew and Guy Standing had been characters in his *Fast Life in New York;* now his latest hero was named John Barrymore. John is alienated from his wife through the machinations of a mesmerist. He divorces her and is given custody of their child, whom the wife then proceeds to kidnap and take to live in the slums. When John regrets his actions and attempts to locate his wife, the villain and his female sidekick hunt him down and shoot him. He is rushed to the very hospital where his wife and child are awaiting treatment. The two miscreants kidnap the wife. They are speeding through Central Park in an automobile when the wife is rescued. The mesmerist and his girl then fall on each other, since he has refused to marry her, but their troubles are ended when the car explodes.

Evelyn Saxton's **Down Our Way** (12-12-04, Third Ave.) was called a "rural comedy drama," but one notice referred to it as a "college play." It was both. A farm boy comes from New Hampshire to Harvard and a room filled with "bright flags, pictures and other paraphernalia of the collegian," including rum flasks. He lives beyond his means and speculates, losing everything. So his friends take up a collection, which allows him and a sweetheart to return to the farm.

Critics and the public quickly wrote off Pinero's attempt at whimsical satire in **A Wife Without a Smile** (12-19-04, Criterion).

A rash of plays arrived the day after Christmas. For many, prime interest rested with the first American appearance of Edward Terry, a London favorite. He was a polished comedian and considered a master at makeup, but his choice of an opening vehicle was unfortunate. Louis N. Parker's **The House of Burnside** (12-26-04, Princess) was derived from Georges Mitchell's *La Maison* and told of a rich man who determines to discover which of his grandchildren is illegitimate. Critics were complimentary to the actor but patently wished to withhold final judgment until they could see him in something more congenial.

Viola Allen added to the season's busy Shakespearean roster with a revival of *The Winter's Tale* at the Knickerbocker. Miss Allen's gleeful and exuberant Perdita contrasted effectively with her more passive Hermione. Her supporting cast and the mounting's attractive settings, particularly a highly lauded forest glade, were also admired. Several matinees during the month-long stand were given over to *Twelfth Night.*

American playwrights also were busy, although their entries this evening were short-lived. C. T. Dazey's **Home Folks** (12-26-04, New York) was booked into a theatre newly converted to a "one-dollar house." That meant seats ranged from 25 cents to no more than $1. Dazey's play, at least as New York saw it, was more of a spectacle than a drama. One act was devoted to a picnic, which featured a brass band, a sack race, a greased-pig chase, and a contest to climb a greased pole. Settings included a steamboat, an old mill, and a bridge with youngsters whose clothes have been stolen moving across from one end all dressed in barrels and a lynch mob (after a horse thief) marching across from the other. Somewhere in all this the plot was lost. When it did emerge it touched on several romances. There was the hero, who loves a city boarder, who in turn is loved by the bad man. The hero's widowed mother is courted by three comic rustics, and her maid is indulging in some amorous flings herself.

There was more rusticity in Charles W. Doty's **Common Sense Bracket** (12-26-04, 14th St.), which was billed as "an illustrated narrative of Maine life" and starred Richard Golden, a comedian better known on musical comedy and vaudeville stages. Golden played Bruce Bracket, who is president of the Winthrop school board and the town's lone barkeeper. Although the townsfolk have no objection to a tavern owner running the school board, they raise all manner of Cain when they discover the teacher (Florence Rockwell) he has hired once had been an actress. He befriends and defends the girl, and later he learns she is his long-lost daughter. Bracket also reconciles his brother and the brother's runaway wife. The man with whom the wife had eloped dies spectacularly by falling down the stairs at a posh hotel.

Echoes of *The House of Burnside* were heard in Louis Eagan's **Shadows on the Hearth** (12-26-04, American). Probably for the sake of colorful costumes, the play was set during the Civil War, though the war hardly touched on the story. A young man loves a girl whose sister has been secretly married. The girls leave town for a while and on their return bring with them a baby. Their father demands to know whose child it is. When they refuse to tell him, he grabs a kettle of boiling water to pour on the child. The hero's girl throws herself across the cradle, leaving her father to believe that she is the mother. She and the child are ordered out of the house. She finds shelter with her lover's mother while he angrily goes to hunt the father. When the sister's husband returns from the war, the true story comes out. No reviewer makes clear just why the sister could not acknowledge her marriage, but then there would have been no play.

The growing number of English-speaking Jewish playgoers was attested to again by Lee Arthur's **Cohen's Luck** (12-26-04, Metropolis), which starred the popular dialect comedian Joe Welch. Abe Cohen, who owns an unsuccessful restaurant, shares a lottery ticket with his Irish neighbor, but her pocket is picked and her half of the ticket stolen. Naturally their combination wins, so the rest of the evening is spent searching for the missing half.

Among first-class dramatists only Clyde Fitch usually was as prolific as authors who churned out sensation-melodramas. He started the new year with his third play of the season, **Cousin Billy** (1-2-05, Criterion). The play was based on Eugène Labiche and Édouard Martin's *Le Voyage de Monsieur Perrichon*. Although the characters' itinerary remained largely the same, Fitch made his figures Americans and updated the incidents, for example changing the spill from a horse to an automobile accident. Francis Wilson, a roustabout clown from the comic opera stage, brought his frequently slapstick tricks to the role of Perrichon-cum-Billy Jenks.

No one seems to have suggested that Genevieve Greville Haines had *Les Romanesques* in the back of her mind when she wrote **Once Upon a Time** (1-2-05, Berkeley Lyceum), but it should have been obvious. What was obvious was that her comedy found some of its fun at the expense of the Catholic church, and the play's failure was attributed, in certain quarters, to Catholic displeasure. Dona Ana (Gertrude Coghlan) is slated to become a nun. Two ardent admirers hope to dissuade her from taking the veil. One is a bandit, the other a man whose son, Don Juan (Robert T. Haines), is studying for the priesthood. Ana's wily, meddling duenna, Concepcion (Mathilde Cottrelly), sees that Ana and Juan are better suited for each other than for the church. She arranges for Ana to be abducted and for Juan to rescue her. The bandit gets wind of the plot and decides to abduct Ana himself. Juan and Ana foil the bandit's scheme. Typical of the comedy that some found offensive was Concepcion's lighting her cigarette in church by using the flame from an altar candle.

Even the lone novelty at touring houses on this evening had French antecedents, since Edgar Rawiston's **Banished by the King** (1-2-05, Star) was based on an unidentified French drama. Its hero rescues a murdered nobleman's baby daughter, raises her, and marries her, despite the efforts of the murderer to kill the girl, too.

That same evening saw a revival at the Academy of Music of Bartley Campbell's *Siberia*. Its timing could scarcely have been better, for as playgoers approached the theatre newsboys were hawking accounts of the fall of Port Arthur.

Arnold Daly, who had replaced Mansfield as Shaw's leading American advocate, scored another success when he starred in **You Never Can Tell** (1-9-

05, Garrick), a Shavian twitting of modern women and their supposedly liberating education.

A pair of equally successful, totally disparate American plays premiered two nights later. David Belasco and John Luther Long again combined their talents—and there was no question whose was by far the greater talent—to create **Adrea** (1-11-05, Belasco). Adrea (Mrs. Carter) is a 5th-century princess on an Adriatic isle. Since she is blind, she must be passed over as a ruler. Her ambitious younger sister, Julia, induces Adrea's betrothed, Kaseo (Charles A. Stevenson), to abandon the princess and marry her instead. Just as he is supposed to lead Adrea into the wedding, Kaseo plants his helmet on Echo (J. Harry Benrimo), a deformed, red-and-white-clad court jester, and gives the freak's hand to the princess. At dawn the next day Adrea has sensed something is wrong. Her prayers to the gods are answered with deafening thunder and brilliant flashes of lightning. Somehow the storm restores her sight. In her initial joy she carefully counts and plays with her fingers, but the horror of the trick perpetrated on her soon is brought home. Furious and resolved, she insists on claiming the throne. She orders her own coronation. "The pomp and circumstance of a semi-barbaric court, the symbols and curious weapons of forgotten dynasties, the tramp of armed men in strange-fashioned garb and headpieces, the smiles of courtesans and the cringing of slaves—all this mingled in a splendid, glittering pageant of pleasing sound and color. Here come the ambassadors of the then world-powers to pay homage to the new queen—the cultured Greek with wreath of gold encircling his classic brow, the haughty Persian with imposing beard and head-dress, a prince from India ablaze with precious stones, the black Ethiopian, insolent and opulent." The queen enters arrayed in cloth of gold. Her first action is to kill the false Kaseo, but her vengeance satisfied, she is overwhelmed with grief. She places her nephew on the throne, abdicates, and blinds herself.

Mrs. Carter's Adrea marked the high point of her career. She sounded every conceivable note "as a great master makes the Stradivarius throb to the slightest mood of his soul." Magnificent spectacle and fine acting allowed the play to run until spring. It returned briefly in the fall before embarking for the road.

The same long run, return, and subsequent tour were in store for Augustus Thomas's comedy **Mrs. Leffingwell's Boots** (1-11-05, Savoy). Mrs. Bonner (Dorothy Hammond) is preparing for a lavish dinner party, but she is unhappy at the high cost of food. Her large filet, trimmed and larded, has set her back four dollars, while her quail have cost fifty cents apiece. Nor can she get the elaborate fountain at the center of her table to stop spraying the whole room. Most galling of all, "the worst storm since Roscoe Conklin died," as she and other characters keep branding it, has forced most of her guests to cancel. And the only three guests she is left with present another problem. Mabel Ainslie (Fay Davis) had broken off her engagement to Walter Corbin (William Courtenay) after boots owned by Mrs. Leffingwell (Margaret Illington) were discovered on his fire escape. A late arrival was Mabel's demented, somewhat criminal brother, Richard (Vincent Serrano). In the farcical confusions that ensue, it is discovered that Richard maliciously planted the boots to embarrass Mabel and Walter. Moreover, Richard's weird, unsavory behavior is seen to stem from a blow he received at a collegiate ball game. Mrs. Bonner's old father, an osteopath, cures Richard. Late in the run, after the play had moved to another house, a curtain raiser was added. A. C. F. Word's **In the Eyes of the World** (4-17-05, Lyceum) dealt with a young woman (Margaret Illington) talked out of eloping with another man on the eve of her marriage.

Ida Conquest was an excellent actress who many felt was long overdue for stardom. Regrettably her first appearance with her name above the title was inauspicious, and she was never lucky enough to find the right vehicles to maintain her position. Her first starring vehicle was an importation, George Rollitt's **The Money Makers** (1-16-05, Liberty), in which she portrayed a young lady who brings a variety of difficulties on herself and her sweetheart when she elects to go into the betting business.

The hero of Charles E. Blaney's **For His Brother's Crimes** (1-16-05, Star) was an athletic blacksmith with the telling name of Victor Sterling. His conspicuous biceps help him no end when he assumes blame for his straying brother's misdeeds so that he can incriminate his brother's seamy cohorts and restore him to a better life.

E. S. Willard came a cropper when he starred in the late Wilson Barrett's **Lucky Durham** (1-22-05, Knickerbocker), playing the vengeful, illegitimate son of an English peer. He uses the fortune he has made in America to get even with his father for never marrying his mother.

College settings were coming into vogue during the season, and there were more football-playing collegians in William C. de Mille's **Strongheart** (1-30-05, Hudson), but their lot was not all fun and games. Three of the athletes, Frank Nelson, Dick Livingston, and a boy known as Strongheart (Robert

Edeson), are so close that they are called "a Damon and Two Pythiases." When one of their chums pretentiously corrects that to "Pythiae," others settle for labeling them "the Siamese Triplets." Strongheart is an Indian whose real name is Soangataha, but that's too much of a tongue-twister for the whites. The boys are students at Columbia. At halftime during the big game, the opposing coach comes to their locker room with a letter, which had been sent to him, revealing the Columbia team's signals. Strongheart recognizes the writing as Dick's, and since he knows that Dick hopes to win a girl by making an impressive showing in the game, he grabs the letter, withholds it from the others, and accepts blame. What Strongheart it unaware of is that Dick had no hand in sending the letter (it was stolen by a gambling student) or that the girl Dick hopes to impress is the very girl he himself loves, Frank's sister, Dorothy.

When both truths come into the open, the reaction is a shocker. Frank and Dick are outraged that an Indian would dare propose to a white girl. "You show the treachery of your race," Dick barks at him. Strongheart can only lament, "The knife of prejudice has cut the ties of friendship." To everyone's surprise Dorothy remains loyal to Strongheart, but just as it seems that they will surmount ingrained prejudice Black Eagle, an old Indian (Edmund Breese), arrives to tell Strongheart his father has died and he is now chief of the tribe. Strongheart informs Black Eagle of his decision to marry Dorothy. As shocked as Frank and Dick, Black Eagle advises Strongheart that the tribe will never accept a white girl, especially as the wife of its new chief. "The white men have been false to me," Strongheart wails, "but I thought my own would be true." Wounded to the core, he raises his arms and face upward and exclaims, "Oh, great spirit of my fathers, I call to you for help, for I am in the midst of a great desert, alone."

Northern Lights and other plays had touched on the Indian in the white man's world, but none to date as skillfully as de Mille's, which moved from the comedy of the dormitory (with ladies' brightly colored stockings hanging as trophies) to the drama of the locker room and the white-tie-and-tails postgame reception. Once again, by modern standards, the college boys would seem unacceptably old. Edeson, who was nearly thirty-seven, had always looked exceptionally stern and mature. However, in his bronze makeup and with his quiet but forceful acting, he made Strongheart believable and sympathetic. In a stand interrupted by a summer break, the play ran nearly 100 performances.

Edward Terry's second bill, Louis N. Parker's **Love in Idleness** (1-30-05, Princess), failed to excite critics any more than his opener had. Its story centered on a lovable perennial procrastinator.

Thomas W. Broadhurst's **The Holy City** (1-30-05, Fifth Ave.) recounted the romance of Mary Magdalene and Barabbas before her conversion.

William L. Robert's **On the Bridge at Midnight** (1-30-05, Third Ave.) told the tired tale of a kidnapped heiress who is finally reunited with her lover and with her long-lost, blind mother. Its highly promoted sensation scene began with the heroine being thrown from a drawbridge on a snowy midnight just as the bridge is opened to allow a ship to pass through. Disregarding all danger, the hero jumps in the river to save her. Besides the dramatic effect of the passing ship, playgoers could watch miniature trolley cars moving back and forth on the far side of the river.

Just as a Fitch play had helped open January, so one of his plays helped to close the month. However, **The Woman in the Case** (1-31-05, Herald Square) was among his best and most successful efforts. Margaret and Julian Rolfe (Blanche Walsh and Robert Drouet) have hardly returned from their honeymoon when Julian is arrested for the murder of his best man, who he thought had committed suicide. Claire Forster (Dorothy Dorr), a loose, grasping woman, has come forth with letters that suggest that Julian is her lover and that he was furious that his best man had stolen her from him. Julian admits writing the letters but insists they were written years earlier. He also admits to persuading the dead man to abandon Claire on the very night of his death. Other circumstantial evidence further appears to implicate Julian. There seems to be no hope until Margaret decides to take an apartment across the hall from Claire's, befriend her, and wheedle the truth from her. She succeeds on the eve of the trial, though the effort exhausts her and she collapses. Bedridden, she is brought the news of Julian's acquittal. The play was a mélange of Fitch's best styles. The first act was set in the Rolfes' elegant apartment, where Margaret and two of her bridesmaids are chatting.

Dora: I never knew a young married couple with so few hideous things!
Elsie: Yes,—Where are all your wedding presents?
Margaret: In the *Chamber of Horrors!*
Elsie: How do you mean?
Margaret: That's what we call the library, where we've put all the impossible gifts.
Dora: Do take us there, and let's see them.

Elsie: If I find *mine!!*

Margaret: Oh, don't worry, yours is in *my* room. It's a rule that the gifts of guests are always brought out and put somewhere else, when we *know* they're coming!

The second act took place in prison, where Margaret and the family lawyer interview Julian. The third act was set in the Tenderloin flat Margaret had rented under an assumed name. Her attempt to befriend Claire has succeeded beyond anyone's hope, and the two sit at a table enjoying an after-theatre snack of cold chicken and champagne. Softly, relentlessly, she brings Claire around to the fatal night and the confession that Claire saw Julian's friend kill himself. She only wanted revenge on Julian for preventing her from making a lucrative marriage. Triumphant, Margaret screams, *"You fiend!"* and lunges for Claire's throat: "I've lived day and night with you; I've lied to you and cheated you! I've sat and wallowed in the gutter with you! But it was all for Julian!" The witnesses hidden in the next room rush in. The last act ran less than ten minutes (less than the intermission), but it offered a typical Fitchian touch. Margaret, seemingly asleep, lies in her bed as the others discuss the elation in the courtroom when the verdict was announced. One character recalls, "Everyone wanting to shake his hand, and one woman *kissed him.*" At that point Margaret pops up and in a clear voice asks, *"What* woman?" It was almost a vaudeville sketch, deftly appended. The play ran eleven weeks.

Competing unprofitably with Fitch's opening was "Gyp" and Pierre Berton's French hit **Friquet** (1-31-05, Savoy), which described the rise of a waif to stardom in a circus and her pathetic, lovelorn death. Marie Doro played the title role.

Frank Wyatt's **Mrs. Temple's Telegram,** which opened on February 1, was something of a rarity. It was a touring farce that had been rewritten (with the aid of William Morris), retitled, recast, and brought forward in a first-class theatre. When it had stopped over briefly in Manhattan in 1903, it had been known as *Who Is Brown?* Even its berth was newsworthy, for it was housed at the Madison Square Theatre, which had been condemned to closure after the Iroquois Theatre fire and had been saved from the wrecker's ball only at the last minute. The theatre had been gutted down to the four walls, and even they had been broken through for additional fire exits. The farce was a surprise hit, running two months and touring under its new guise all of the following season. As for the playhouse, its reincarnation was to be short-lived. It would be demolished in 1908.

A curious coincidence in *Mrs. Temple's Telegram* and *The Woman in the Case* sheds interesting light on contemporary society. In Fitch's drama the lawyer almost gives away Margaret's ploy by inadvertently leaving a cigarette butt, but Margaret's manservant, who has accompanied her to the Tenderloin, saves the day by sheepishly confessing he was smoking on the sly. (Claire also mentions keeping a servant.) The farce opens with the butler's long, expository aside, beginning with his haughty admission that he smokes in the drawing room when his employers are away.

E. S. Willard's disappointing engagement—houses "two-thirds empty"—continued with Alfred Capus's *La Châtelaine,* translated by Louis N. Parker as **The Brighter Side** (2-6-05, Knickerbocker). Willard impersonated an eternally optimistic, self-made man who puts a harridan matchmaker in her place and helps a misused wife escape from her philandering husband. When this novelty proved no more successful than his first, Willard reverted to old favorites and once again enjoyed crowded houses.

Since late December Maude Adams had been playing in a revival of *The Little Minister.* As business began to wane, Charles Frohman added a curtain raiser, a second English play, Frederick Fenn and Richard Bryce's **'Op o' Me Thumb** (2-6-05, Empire). Miss Adams, in a broken straw hat and tattered, ill-fitting clothes, was cast as a laundress who lives in her dream world but is poignantly made aware that no Prince Charming awaits her.

Miss Adams was the most popular actress of her day, a satisfying position once held by Ada Rehan. Now at the end of her career, Miss Rehan appeared on a New York stage for the last time in an engagement that began at the Liberty on the 6th with *The Taming of the Shrew* and then turned to *The School for Scandal.* Charles Richman, who had been her leading man in Daly's final years, played opposite her again. Perhaps sensing these were her farewell appearances, she played with the zest and sparkle that once had been her wont. At least critics thought so. She retired quietly after her tour. Thus, in the same season, playgoers said goodbye to Daly's two most popular ladies.

Edward Terry finally found the right vehicle to please New Yorkers when he revived B. C. Stephenson and W. Yardley's English farce *The Passport* at the Princess on the 10th. For most New Yorkers the play was new, since the original 1895 production had shuttered abruptly after only ten performances when its unpaid actors refused to go on. They would have little chance to see it now, since Terry's booking had just one week to run.

Owen Davis's **The Confessions of a Wife** (2-13-05, 14th St.) spotlighted a country girl who had been lured into a bigamous marriage in the city and, after discovering the situation and having her husband imprisoned, returned to her country home in hopes of making a happier second marriage. She is hounded by her first husband, who has been released, and by a malevolent woman in a telltale red dress. At one point the girl is forced to push the villain out of a window and down a ravine—but he survives. Later the adventuress throws the girl's baby into the river, and the girl is forced to jump into a rowboat to rescue it. (The encore curtain—still a common practice—showed a ferry picking up mother and child.)

We generally have ignored special matinees—a regular form of tryout at the time—but one holds some zany interest. Aldora Shem, allegedly a popular actor in the West, offered his *Hamlet* to critics, who responded by gleefully unsheathing their stilettos. *Theatre,* assessing his Dane as "the most stupid performance ever seen in New York within memory," noted, "He was absolutely without emotion, and incapable of any surprise at anything that happened. When he takes the lamp to look behind the arras, he does express a very slight surprise, but the meaning of it seems to be that he was surprised that he had not really killed a rat." The *Times,* evoking the ghosts of Count Johannes and James O'Conor, concluded, "It has long been a tradition that no actor can fail in *Hamlet.* Aldora Shem's performance goes to prove one of two propositions. Either tradition lies or he is no actor."

The season's last success—at least the last play to run more than two months—was **The Education of Mr. Pipp** (2-20-05, Liberty), taken by Augustus Thomas from Charles Dana Gibson's cartoons. Its star, Digby Bell, like Francis Wilson in the previous month, had temporarily cast aside his comic opera clowning for a stab at the nonmusical stage. The henpecked Mr. Pipp and his malapropian wife (Kate Denin Wilson), who storms about her home issuing orders through a megaphone, have risen too quickly from the lowest blue-collar ranks into fabulous fortune. Mrs. Pipp has decided that no American is good enough for their daughters (Janet Beecher and Marion Draughn) and has forced her cowed husband to move to England, where there are so many "legible" noblemen ready to beg for the girls' hands. Mrs. Pipp has her heart set on roping in a count and a duke, blithely unable to see that both are bogus. The count is not above plotting to poison Mr. Pipp, so that he can wed the widow and thus get his claws on all the money. A riding master, who is really an

English lord stooping to conquer, and an American businessmen are far more gentlemanly suitors. By evening's end Mrs. Pipp has received an education in the snares of snobbery, and Mr. Pipp has learned how to stand up to his wife. The tiny, unctuous Bell and an excellent supporting cast turned the play into droll fun.

Most critics found H. A. Du Souchet's farce **Who Goes There?** (2-20-05, Princess) equally droll, but playgoers did not seem interested. Some commentators suggested the public had been sated by too many farces; other offered the theory that a lack of a star hurt the play's chances. Several officers, about to sail for Cuba, risk court-martial to sneak off base and marry their sweethearts before they embark. They meet at a nearby boardinghouse, where they find Lieutenant George Washington Newman, who is there for the same purpose but who has permission. He is conned into telling each of the girls' fathers that he is the groom. The other officers trust this will avoid problems, but naturally it merely leads to three acts of them.

A fine star could do nothing to save a weak play, so Forbes-Robertson's run in H. V. Esmond's **Love and the Man** (2-20-05, Knickerbocker) was brief. He played a rising politician in love with a woman unhappily married to a querulous invalid. The invalid's convenient death allows the lovers to consider marrying. The star quickly brought back his admired *Hamlet.*

Two Hal Reid melodramas converged on New York that same evening. The titular heroine of **Nobody's Darling** (2-20-05, 14th St.) was a waif found by a greedy Italian and set to hard labor in a cordage factory. The waif is the illegitimate daughter of a fallen woman, who persists in trying to get her seducer to wed her. His response is to enlist the Italian's snarling son to kidnap her, drag her to a "death pit" under the East River, and let the pit become flooded. The waif appears in time to save her mother. The seducer eventually is tied to a tree and forced to marry his victim, but the woman is no sooner satisfied than a former victim of the seducer rushes in and stabs him to death. The waif looks to marry an inventor she had saved from a fire.

For Fame and Fortune (2-20-05, Windsor) starred the celebrated prizefighter Terry McGovern. McGovern played a worker at a lumberyard along the East River. He has adopted a waif named Grasshopper and is in love with a beautiful girl, Grace. The villain is the waif's father, who has murdered his wife, hopes to kill Grasshopper, abduct and murder Grace, whom he knows to be an heiress, and present his scheming cohort (she, too, wears the villainess's red dress) as the real Grace in order to claim her fortune. The hero has to jump into the river to pull out Grasshopper after the malefactors have thrown her in; Grasshopper in turn saves Grace from being poisoned. The hero also is slated to fight an English champion, but the murderous husband and his girl, hoping to prevent the match, put dynamite in his medicine ball and attempt to inject Grace with chloral. When these ploys fail, they attempt to shoot the hero during the match. But like all such heroes, he is unstoppable.

Al H. Wilson, a singing comedian, was the star of Sidney Ellis's **The Watch on the Rhine** (2-20-05, Metropolis), playing a German who had been abducted and brought to America while still a child. Now a grown, prosperous man, he returns to find his mother. They identify each other by singing old songs. The ending recalled the Fritz plays, which J. K. Emmet had scored in during the 1870s.

Although some reviewers still retained reservations about Grace George's abilities as an actress, her warm, sparkling performance accounted for much of the popularity of Kellett Chambers's **Abigail** (2-21-05, Savoy). Abigail is a prim and proper New Englander who has come to New York to make her own way in the city. She has taken a room in a bohemian boardinghouse and refused her New York relatives' invitation to live with them. She has fallen in love with John "Booby" Kent (Conway Tearle), who saved her from being run over in the street, and when she receives some violets with his scribbled notation "I love you," she decides she is standing at the gates to Paradise. John is reluctant to tell her the violets were meant for someone else. By the time John realizes he prefers Abigail, she has been informed that she has inherited twelve million 1905 dollars. Fearing that Abigail will now conclude he loves her for her money, he sails to South America. While he is away Abigail is courted by several other men, among them a handsome, care-free English duke (Joseph Coyne). In the end, of course, John and Abigail recognize they were made for each other.

Critics admired the accurate recreation of bohemian life, especially a dance held in a high-ceilinged artist's studio, its almost rustic balcony crammed with unfinished paintings. They also applauded the performance of Louise Closser as a levelheaded artist who maintains a platonic friendship with John. Some critics felt she all but stole the show.

Mrs. James A. Herne was the producer of her daughter Julie's play **Richter's Wife** (2-27-05, Manhattan). The production was something of a family affair since Julie's sister, Chrystal, also had a principal role. Its story told of a famous conductor (John E. Kellerd) whose wife (Chrystal Herne) becomes insanely jealous of the attentions he pays to his youthful protégée (Julie Herne). Despairing of preventing a romance from blossoming, the wife takes poison and dies. With *Leah Kleschna* still holding the boards in the evenings and on Saturday matinees, the play was given for five successive weekday matinees. Considering the highly flattering notices it received, the drama could have been expected to move to another theatre for a regular run, even taking into account the relative lateness of the season. Yet for some reason, nothing happened. Not only did the play not move, but Julie Herne never again had another play on Broadway.

If Henri Dumay's **Mademoiselle Marni** (3-6-05, Wallack's) bore some uncanny resemblances to recent plays, that was purely coincidental, since Dumay, a professor in St. Louis, was known to have written the piece years earlier. In the first act his Fabienne Marni (Amelia Bingham) shows her humaneness by bringing a waif to a colorful dance at the studio of some bohemians (shades of *Abigail*) and auctioning off flowers to provide for the girl. Her business acumen is shown again in the rest of the play, but more chillingly, as she corners stocks in the Bourse in order to destroy her father, a baron (Frederic de Belleville) who refuses to acknowledge his paternity and stands in the way of her romance. The play ran exactly one month, as did a more genuinely French comedy that opened the same night.

That comedy was William Boosey and Cosmo Gordon Lennox's **The Prince Consort** (3-6-05, New Amsterdam), based on Léon Xanrof and Jules Chancel's Paris hit. Headlines detailing problems encountered by Holland's young Queen Wilhelmina after her marriage, when her consort balked at constraints imposed on him, were the source of the plot, but the authors diplomatically set the action in an imaginary kingdom. The roles of the Queen of Corconia and Prince Cyril were in the hands of two excellent London players, Ellis Jeffreys and Ben Webster. For many the most humorous performance was Henry E. Dixey's, as the consort's deposed father (actually the ex–Belgian king) looking for an easy berth. His scrapbook with photographs of beautiful chorus girls causes raised eyebrows among the stiff-necked Corconian courtiers.

Some disappointments followed. Elizabeth Lee Shepard's **The Red Carnation** (3-13-05, Yorkville) was a jumbled melodrama about adventures that befall a young lady who attempts to save Marie Antoinette from the guillotine.

In **Nancy Stair** (3-15-05, Criterion), which Paul M. Potter dramatized from Elinor Macartney Lane's novel, the poet Robert Burns (T. Daniel Frawley) helps the girl (Mary Mannering) he loves marry another man (Robert Loraine). A number of Burns's songs were sung during the evening.

Murray Carson and Nora Keith's English play **The Trifler** (3-16-05, Princess), in which a count bests a lady spy, was soundly thrashed by the critics and withdrawn after four performances.

Richard Mansfield brought a little excitement to a waning season when he opened a four-week stand at the New Amsterdam on the 20th. His first three weeks were devoted to revivals of past favorites, and not until his closing week did he appear in a role new to him.

Three days later an unusual entry received some extended attention. St. Petersburg actors who had been exiled for their anticzarist stance presented a special matinee at the Herald Square of Eugen Tschirikoff's study of Russian anti-Semitism, **The Chosen People.** The performance was praised (though great Russian ensemble playing would remain unknown to New York for nearly twenty more years). One actress "of wonderful temperamental and technical quality" was singled out. She was listed on programs as "Mme. A. Nasimoff." Shortly, as Alla Nazimova, she would become a major American stage and film artist. She and her fellow players popped up later in the season, presenting **The Karamasoff Brothers** and **The Misery of Misfortune.**

The freedom with which some players jumped from one play to another was demonstrated when the curtain rose on Mrs. Vance Thompson and Lena R. Smith's **The Lady Shore** (3-27-05, Hudson). The ineptly retold history of how Richard, Duke of Gloucester (John Blair), turned Edward IV against Jane Shore (Virginia Harned) and engineered her death featured Robert Loraine as the king. Just two weeks earlier Loraine had opened in *Nancy Stair,* but he left almost immediately after its first night. Both plays closed on the same evening, two weeks later.

The evening of *The Lady Shore*'s premiere also saw Ibsen's **When We Dead Awake** (3-27-05, Knickerbocker) begin a twenty-seven-performance stand. The play had been seen earlier in the month at a series of special matinees, and the surprising move was made despite tepid notices. Frederick Lewis was Rubek, Florence Kahn was Irene, and Dorothy Donnelly, the best-received of the players, was Maia.

A local stock company with some exceptionally fine performers brought out A. E. Lancaster's dramatization of **Anna Karenina** (3-27-05, Fifth Ave.). Isabelle Evesson had the title role, Henry Woodruff was Count Vronsky, and Theodore Roberts played Alexis.

Touring houses also displayed new wares. James J. Corbett was starred in Edmund Day's **Pals** (3-27-05, American). His role was that of a recent Harvard graduate whose former roommate loves the same girl he does. The roommate, sensing he is losing, turns nasty and pushes the hero off a cliff. The hero grabs a projecting branch, and when he is brought up somewhat dazed, all his girl can say is "Speak to me, Jim." The loser's persistence brings on the awaited fisticuffs, and "everything in sight [is] reduced to smithereens," including the unwanted suitor.

M. J. Fielding's **In the Shadow of Darkness** (3-27-05, Star) featured a country bumpkin "of the Sis Hopkins variety" as its heroine. Her guardian learns she is an heiress and employs a string of wicked plans to gain her money. Of course, he fails.

The year's special matinees continued to hold unusual interest. Many served to give New Yorkers a taste of great foreign writers; others gave playgoers an opportunity to see promising performers. Some combined both. In February, Margaret Wycherly had starred in a bill of William Butler Yeats's one-acters. On March 28 and 31, she headed the cast in Yeats's full-length **The Countess Cathleen** at the Madison Square.

Lord Drinkwell, Lord Playmore, Lady Speakill, and Lady Tattle were some of the Restoration and 18th-century character names resurrected for Stanislaus Stange's **The School for Husbands** (4-3-05, Wallack's), a comedy whose only connection to Molière was its title. Lady Belinda Manners (Alice Fischer) bristles when her husband (Joseph Kilgour) turns their home into a veritable gambling den and tavern, so after she comes into a handsome inheritance she shows him how to live on a truly grand scale. She simultaneously fosters a romance between an Indian prince and a lady friend. Bedecked with beautiful period costumes and settings, and played blithely as a comic opera without music, the play enjoyed a prosperous run.

Conversely, Kellett Chambers's **A Case of Frenzied Finance** (4-3-05, Savoy) folded after a single week. William A. Brady mounted it to replace Chambers's earlier *Abigail* on the same stage. It did little for Chambers's reputation but aided Douglas Fairbanks in catching New York's eye. Fairbanks was Bennie Tucker, a brash bellhop at the swank Vanbillion Hotel. He loves Daisy Johnson, daughter of Arizona copper magnate J. W. Johnson, and assures her he will not long be a bellhop but will make his fortune in watered stocks. When a J. W. Johnson (William J. Ferguson) registers at the hotel, Bennie assumes he is Daisy's father and fast-talks him into investing "fifty" in a stock on which he has had a tip. He orders $50,000 worth of shares. In fact, this J. W. Johnson is merely a boozy Yonkers undertaker who thinks he has gambled with $50. However, his name obviates the need for a down payment. The arrival of Daisy's father unleashes complications, and the appearance of his implacable foe, Bat Scranton, adds a touch of melodrama. In the end Bennie makes more than a million on his deal, and the flabbergasted magnate consents to his marrying his daughter. For the next decade Fairbanks would be one of Broadway's most promising actors.

. . .

Douglas Fairbanks [né Julius Ulman] (1883–1939) The handsome, virile, and athletic performer was born in Denver. He made his stage debut in Richmond, V., in 1900 as Florio in *The Duke's Jester*. His New York debut came two years later with a small part in *Her Lord and Master*. A season of touring and more small parts in New York followed before he landed his assignment in *A Case of Frenzied Finance*.

. . .

The flux of fashion was touched on in reviews of Liebler and Co.'s revival of *London Assurance* at the Knickerbocker on the 3rd, which featured many of the English players who had performed in *The Prince Consort*. One commentator observed, "The Dazzle of 1840 has been submerged by the equally absurd Razzle Dazzle of the present. Meddle was supplanted long ago by Marks the Lawyer, in 'Uncle Tom's Cabin,' and Marks survives only by subsisting on turnips on the country circuits." (The writer apparently considered Manhattan's combination houses, where *Uncle Tom's Cabin* still played every season, as being in the country.) For the most part, however, critics were regaled by the performances (Eben Plympton as Harcourt, Ellis Jeffreys as Lady Gay, Ben Webster as Charles, Ida Conquest as Grace, and Joseph Wheelock, Jr., as Dolly Spanker), so the play ran on merrily for one month.

Hal Reid's touring melodrama **The Gypsy Girl** (4-3-05, Star) pleased less demanding audiences with its saga of a young girl and her little brother who are living among a band of gypsies. They are menaced by the usual rogue and his female crony, who know the girl is an heiress. The little brother, Freckles, is killed, but the girl survives to see her tormentors carted off to jail.

If *Uncle Tom's Cabin* still found a regular berth on stages of the city's combination houses, so did other old plays all season long. One of the more noteworthy was a revival of Frank Mayo's bygone vehicle, *Davy Crockett*, which starred yet another of the many prizefighters supplementing their incomes by acting. In this case the star at the American was the heavyweight champion, James J. Jeffries.

Paul Armstrong enjoyed his first success when he resorted to an increasingly popular subject for his **The Heir to the Hoorah** (4-10-05, Hudson). The lateness of the comedy's arrival precluded a long stand, but if a return engagement in September is added to its tally the play had a presentable run of ten weeks. Armstrong's subject was the contempt of the polished East for the rough and ready West. The young proprietor (Guy Bates Post) of the Hoorah mine marries an impressionable girl who is under the thumb of her snooty mother. Mama is so annoyed at the gaucheries of her son-in-law and his buddies that his wife persuades him to go to Europe for a personal veneer job. The birth of a baby, not the European trip, brings about a happy ending. The play was so loosely knit that one critic called it a series of "clothesline studies." One act was devoted primarily to a group of uncouth miners ill at ease in white tie and tails. Elsewhere a Japanese valet set aside the story to perform a "Jiu-Jitsu" turn.

Israel Zangwill's **Jinny, the Carrier** (4-10-05, Criterion) unveiled the saga of a poor girl who drives a cart to help support her family. Even Annie Russell's appeal could not induce a run.

Neither Armstrong's nor Zangwill's plays attracted most first-string critics. Their interest was piqued by Richard Mansfield's lone novelty of the season—a novelty not because the play was new (it was 240 years old) but because Mansfield had never attempted a similar role. Made up to mirror drawings of Molière, the star came forth as Alceste in **The Misanthrope** (4-10-05, New Amsterdam). A few vociferous dissenters aside, Mansfield's witty, incisive performance was deemed one of his best. Sumptuous white-and-gold settings and colorful period costumes embellished the mounting. However, Molière was not for the vast majority of playgoers, so Mansfield rarely returned to him in the few years the star had left.

When Mansfield moved on, another old comedy took over the New Amsterdam's stage on the 17th, one more to the theatregoers' liking. *She Stoops to Conquer* enlisted some of the best players of the day, with Eleanor Robson displaying her versatility as Kate and Kyrle Bellew his "pulchritudinous" elegance as Marlow.

The hero of Daniel L. Hart's **At Old Point Comfort** (4-17-05, Murray Hill) was a detective sent to arrest a moonshiner. When he falls in love with the moonshiner's sister, he is torn between affection and duty. At first duty wins, but then a pardon for the imprisoned moonshiner allows the detective's sweetheart to forgive him.

An observant detective might have forestalled the comic problems a young wife (Hilda Spong) causes when she lies about her flirtations and her gambling in Willis Steell's **The Firm of Cunningham** (4-18-05, Madison Square). During the last week of the month-long run, H. H. Morrell and E. G. Malyon's **Mrs. Battle's Bath** (5-9-05) was added to the bill. A lady (Dorothy Donnelly) about to take a bath, and her suitor (Hassard Short) in his pajamas, are embarrassed to be locked accidentally in her room.

Marie Tempest closed her season in Cosmo Gordon Lennox's **The Freedom of Suzanne** (4-19-05, Empire) as a lady no happier when she is divorced than when she is married. She settles for wedlock.

Charles Cartwright and Cosmo Hamilton's **The Proud Laird** (4-24-05, Manhattan) ran a single week. During that time that young laird (Robert Loraine) and his American fiancée (Dorothy Donnelly), both reluctant to confess their feelings, were brought together by the ploys of the laird's family. A castle's leaky roof provided some comic moments.

A Friend of the Family (4-24-05, Murray Hill), which R. N. Skinner adapted from a German play by Robert Pohl, detailed the farcical developments that ensue after a woman, newly wed and immediately widowed, discovers her son-in-law is her old flame.

Touring plays and revivals comprised the remainder of the season. In Charles E. Blaney and Howard Hall's **The Millionaire Detective** (5-1-05, 14th St.), a wealthy stockbroker leads a double life by moonlighting as a sleuth. He bests a wicked lady manipulator who tries to ruin another broker. In one scene he is locked in a trunk, but when the trunk is opened he has escaped. Later his adversary poisons him, but an "electric homo-resuscitator" restores him to life.

George Fawcett brought many of his Baltimore players, including his wife, Percy Haswell, to the American on the same night in *Romeo and Juliet.* The troupe also performed *The Liars* and *The Merchant of Venice.*

A classier revival saw Ethel Barrymore impersonate Nora to Bruce McRae's Torvald and Edgar Selwyn's Dr. Rank in *A Doll's House* at the Lyceum on the 2nd. Critics were delighted with Miss Barrymore's ability to deal artfully with a play of more substance than the froth she customarily appeared in. It provided a glimpse of things to come.

Two nights earlier the plebeian Murray Hill Theatre had offered its patrons *The Master Builder.* The *Times,* betraying a certain surprise, noted that it lured in "an audience that apparently looked upon Ibsen at 50 cents a head as a great bargain and manifested its very obvious enjoyment in much applause."

Revivals also continued to keep the New Amsterdam lit. The latest was *Trilby,* on the 8th, with much of the original 1895 cast brought together again, most notably Lackaye as Svengali and Virginia Harned in the title role.

George Fawcett's players briefly rekindled interest in the faltering season when they revived *Fedora* on the 22nd. It was not the play that compelled dedicated theatre-lovers to rush to the American on 42nd Street, but the "new" star Fawcett hired, Bertha Kalish. To Jews on the Lower East Side she was hardly new, for she was the beautiful reigning queen of Second Avenue theatre, sometimes referred to as "the Yiddish Duse." The evening proved "a triumph little short of sensational" for the "tall, supple, gypsy-looking artiste, speaking the fascinating, exotic English of a Modjeska." Unlike Jacob Adler, Miss Kalish soon was shuttling back and forth between Yiddish theatre and Broadway. (Her name was sometimes transliterated as Kalich or Kalisch.)

At the 14th Street Theatre, Tully Marshall and E. J. Ratcliffe were featured in a series of revivals that began on June 5 with *The Ticket-of-Leave Man* and then moved on to *The Octoroon.* At the same time, devoted Shakespeareans, who had seen Hamlets ranging from the sublime (Forbes Robertson's return) to the ridiculous (Aldora Shem), could head for Harlem for yet another mounting, in this case with a lady (Adelaide Seim) as the prince. Her interpretation was scarcely thrilling, but critics did find it intelligent and interesting. She played it only for one week before turning to *Young Mrs. Winthrop.*

1905–1906

The new season brought with it a tremendous smash hit that had no major stars, and its remarkable success may well have alerted both dramatists and producers to the now obvious conclusion that good drama on its own could provide eminently satisfying and profitable theatre. Ibsenites might claim that their idol long ago had put the matter to rest as far as modern drama was concerned, but their opponents would have rebutted that, in America at least, Ibsen's plays still required a star such as Mrs. Fiske to give them currency. In any case, the 1906–07 season would introduce no fewer than two superb works that truly required no star (though both had them) and thus would initiate a decade in which native dramatists and native plays would beat a path to smooth the way for the American theatrical renaissance that ultimately emerged. Meanwhile, the 1905–06 season can now be seen as a prologue to the decade or as an epilogue to the last six years.

Once again, combination houses relit first. A show with "Belle" in its title suggested a musical to contemporary playgoers, but Sydney R. Toller's **The Belle of Richmond** (7-24-05, 58th St.) even dispensed with vaudeville turns so common to touring plays. Billed as a comedy-drama, it recounted how a slick villain convinces a lady her fiancé is unworthy, robs a bank, implicates an innocent man, and is finally exposed. The few critics who bothered to review it thought the play got the season off to a disappointing start.

A similar do-no-gooder made trouble in Edward Locke's **Fighting Fate** (8-14-05, Star). Determined to wrest away the heroine's legacy and that of her brother, he first loosens the bridle on a horse the brother will ride in a race. When that fails, he has more tricks up his sleeve. Unlike most writers of such lower-class shows, Locke eventually would enjoy at least one Broadway success.

The author of **Zorah** (8-14-05, Fifth Ave.) was Edwin Arden, a respected actor and an occasional dramatist. His play was set in Russia, where a Jewess is persecuted by a bigoted governor. When a rabbi (Arden) comes to her defense, he, the girl, and her father are sent to Siberia to work in a silver mine. A mine explosion (the play's sensation scene) blinds Zorah. Since he is reputed to have curative powers, the rabbi is summoned home to save the governor's dying little daughter. He agrees to come on two conditions: that Zorah and her father accompany him, and that all three will be allowed to emigrate if he succeeds. He succeeds.

A French kept woman is set up regally by her lover, not in Paris but in Harlem. When she marries a man she loves (he also is French), her provider naturally is angry. He tries to kill the husband. Instead the woman shoots him, but not before he has stabbed her. The husband rushes in to aid the dying woman, and she confesses her past. His reaction? "Now die!" Ostensibly set in 1869, Lawrence Marston's **A Woman's Sacrifice** (8-14-05, 58th St.) featured 1905 dresses and other modernities.

Equally absurd were the players' French accents, comical when they were not atrocious.

First-class houses began to reopen when Arthur Sidman's **York State Folks** (8-19-05, Majestic) came to town after several seasons on the road. One reviewer thought it "noteworthy for having no deep-eyed villain or sobbing lady with a black past and a black gown." An organ builder, Myron Cooper, and a rich wagon maker, Simon Martin, have fallen out over bringing a railroad to their town, so Simon insists his son, Frank, cannot marry Jennie Cooper. Her father lends the youngsters money to wed, money actually belonging to the village. Old Man Martin threatens to send both his son and Cooper to jail, but after he learns that Frank had convinced the railroad to come into town, his anger melts away. A final tableau, a "dream scene," showed Cooper asleep in a chair, with a red spotlight on him, while behind a scrim the rest of the cast sang a hymn at church, accompanied on an organ Cooper had built. The play remained a month but was always more popular on the road.

A few critics implied that *York State Folks* might have been better served at a combination house, but this ignored the fact that such rustic dramas lacked the mile-a-minute excitement so dear to galleryites. That sort of excitement was supplied by Hal Reid's **A Runaway Boy** (8-19-05, Metropolis). Young Joseph Santley was supposed to be its star, but an accident kept him out of the cast during this engagement. Little Harry Reynolds will not inherit $1,000,000 if his greedy uncle can prevent it. The uncle is abetted by an adventuress and her obsequious admirer, a "Hindoo man." Their initial attempt to murder the boy is bungled, and he runs away, joining a circus. They pursue him and cut the ropes of a trapeze on which he performs. Later they gloat over their apparent success at having Harry mugged, but his sudden reappearance results in a melee fatal to the uncle and the women. Clichés abounded, even in costuming. The adventuress's first entrance in a red dress immediately characterized her, just as a black dress signaled a remorseful lady with a past.

It remained a regular practice for the previous season's successes to make brief late-summer returns before heading out on the road. When *Mrs. Leffingwell's Boots* returned it was accompanied by Alfred Sutro's one-acter **A Maker of Men** (8-21-05, Lyceum), in which a wife (Margaret Illington) consoles a husband (Ernest Lawford) for his failure to win a promotion.

There were murders galore in Jay Hunt's **Hearts of Gold** (8-21-05, American), whose action spanned some twenty-five years. A woman jilts her betrothed to marry a rich man. The jilted man marries another woman. But one husband shoots the other, then commits suicide by throwing himself in a river. Years afterwards their children fall in love, only to find their own romance doomed by inadvertent fratricide. In one scene a brother knocks out his unrecognized sibling with a hammer, locks him in a cotton pen, and sets the pen on fire. A sister saves the unconscious man, but the would-be killer is shot by the police. Earlier another man is killed in a ruined church. However, light streaming through a stained glass window allows a witness to identify the killer. It was all very confusing.

But then so was Hal Reid's **Custer's Last Fight** (8-21-05, Star), since Custer's battle occupied only the final act, while the other three dealt with Buffalo Bill. Cody's mother is scalped by an embittered Indian, and Cody spends two more acts hunting the murderer and besting him in hand-to-hand combat.

There was more bloodshed in Fessler and Rae's **The Life That Kills** (8-21-05, Thalia). The fiendish villain of the new play is a bigamist not above murdering, or trying to murder, his wives when they stand in his way. His methods range from simple strangulation to substituting metal polish for cough medicine. The Thalia, of course, was the historic old Bowery, which for years had been used by Yiddish players.

Last season Francis Wilson and Digby Bell had deserted the ranks of musical theatre clowns to try their luck in straight plays. Now Raymond Hitchcock joined them. Hitchcock was "a lanky, raspy-voiced comic with sharp features and straw-colored hair that he brushed across his forehead." His vehicle was Edward E. Kidder's **Easy Dawson** (8-22-05, Wallack's). Many critics suggested it was a rehash of materials that long had served the late Sol Smith Russell, ignoring its resemblance to *York State Folks*. Replacing the organ builder was a fireman and boozy inventor, Ripley Royal Dawson, whose daughter, Rose (Julie Herne), loves Bruce Grierson (Earle Browne), son of the village's wealthiest man (Scott Cooper). The elder Grierson dislikes the seemingly shiftless Dawson and tries to get Dawson's equally bibulous buddy, Henry Titus (John Bunny), to steal Dawson's new idea for a cream separator. Naturally, he also tries to stop Bruce's marrying Rose. Both plots fail. Since there was so little story, Kidder filled the evening with colorful eccentrics. Hitchcock's wife, Flora Zabelle, portrayed a village flirt, while Jeffreys Lewis was cast as Mrs. Churchill-Churchill-Brenton, a latter-day Lady Gay Spanker, who adores automobiles as much as Lady Gay cared for horses. Songs were

interspersed throughout the comedy, which ran two months.

The season got under way in earnest the first Monday in September. Two of three new American entries were star vehicles provided accommodatingly by leading playwrights. The lesser of the pair was Augustus Thomas's **De Lancey** (9-4-05, Empire), in which John Drew impersonated a gentleman who falls in love with his best friend's fiancée. The friend is also a gentleman, so he finds another romance elsewhere.

Ravishingly beautiful Maxine Elliott was the star of Clyde Fitch's **Her Great Match** (9-4-05, Criterion). She played Jo Sheldon, who falls in love with Crown Prince Adolph of Eastphalia (Charles Cherry) while on a visit to England. The Grand Duchess of Hohenhetstein (Mathilde Cottrelly), assigned by the prince's father to prevent the marriage, is an old sentimentalist who does her best to abet the romance. On the other hand, Jo's unethical mother makes trouble by promising their host, an upstart brewer anxious for a title, that she can assure him one after the marriage if he will lend her a large sum. She does not tell him she needs that sum to avoid imprisonment as a swindler. At first Jo is offered a morganatic marriage, but when she rejects such an arrangement, Adolph renounces his claim to the throne. Once again, Fitch's clever stagecraft constantly whetted interest. The opening scene was a colorful charity bazaar at which Jo and Adolph meet when Jo reads his palm in a fortune-telling booth. Matter turned melodramatic after Jo's wrongful implication in her mother's swindling. Miss Elliott, modeling a succession of gorgeous gowns, was given a run for her money by Miss Cottrelly's droll duchess, while Cherry was an ideal leading man. With everything falling into place so delightfully, the comedy chalked up ninety-three showings.

Yet a starless comedy by a young unknown ran longer, 106 performances. Edward Peple's **The Prince Chap** (9-4-05, Madison Square) also focused on an American in England. His American was not a man who traveled in a moneyed, opulent world, but one who struggled in an artist's garret. (The struggle did not prevent his keeping a loyal servant, albeit the servant's pay was three months and eleven days in arrears.) William Musgrave Bakerville Peyton (Cyril Scott), for all his lack of money, has a loving heart. When Phoebe Puckers, his building's bedraggled little maid, tells his servant (Thomas A. Wise), "A 'ot brick in a cold cellar is *the* most comfortin' thing in life. It's 'eavenly!," Peyton gives her his own blanket. But Peyton's goodness is tested to the full when a former model dies in his arms after asking him to care for her five-year-old daughter. He takes the child, Claudia, under his wings, telling her to call him "Daddy." He is so kind to her that she asks, "Daddy . . . are you somebody's momma, with—trousers on?" Peyton not only shelters, feeds, and clothes her, he relates a story about a young man who came to London to make his way in the world. Claudia wants to know if the man was a prince, and Peyton agrees he may have been a prince of a chap, who left Princess Alice weeping on the dock at New York.

Three years pass. The real Alice (Grace Kimball), no princess, arrives at Peyton's studio. She is shocked by Claudia's presence, refusing to believe she is not the child of an indiscretion, and she demands Peyton throw out Claudia. Alice uses his refusal as a pretext for marrying another man. Ten more years elapse. Claudia is now a lovely girl of eighteen. A number of men are in love with her, including Peyton's friend, Jack Rodney, the Earl of Huntington (Cecil de Mille), another artist. Jack proposes, but Claudia's rejection alerts him to the true state of things. He leaves, handing Peyton his monocle and hinting that Peyton cannot see what is happening before his eyes. Peyton does see. He proposes and is accepted. Claudia was played by a different actress in each act. That might have seemed like an impediment to a comedy so often mushy and maudlin, yet somehow it all worked like a charm. Even extraneous touches delighted. Thus Puckers reappears in the last act. She is now herself a young woman, if not a young lady. She is cheaply, gaudily dressed, she works in a circus, and her visit is to invite Claudia and Peyton to her wedding. She is marrying one of her fellow performers: "A arry-nort. A hartist wot goes hup in a *bal*-loon, an' comes a-floatin' down in a parrot-shoot."

A new English drama, Hall Caine's **The Prodigal Son** (9-4-05, New Amsterdam), had the shortest run of the evening's openings, just over a month. It told of a selfish, ruthless younger brother (Aubrey Boucicault) who commits all manner of wrongs but later repents and returns home to beseech forgiveness.

The next evening ushered in another importation, but this was one of the season's biggest hits and one of four London plays seen during the season that are still performed today. Shaw's **Man and Superman** (9-5-05, Hudson) debated the uneven duel between men and women, with Robert Loraine starred as John Tanner. Tanner is witty, glib, and self-impressed. He spouts on and on about a "life force" that governs our existence. Before he realizes it, he is confronting that force in the person of a lady named Ann who is determined to allow him to talk

himself into marrying her. Having achieved her aim, she urges him, "Go on talking." A superb supporting cast included Fay Davis as Ann, Clara Bloodgood as Violet, and Edward Abeles as Henry Straker. The comedy ran for six months.

By contrast, W. W. Jacobs and Louis N. Parker's **Beauty and the Barge** (9-6-05, Lyceum) survived a mere week and a half, despite Nat Goodwin's presence as star. A young lady running away from an unwanted marriage takes refuge on a barge captained by an "haffable" cockney womanizer. She finds romance, but the captain sails away emptyhanded.

Edith Ellis Baker's **Mary and John** (9-11-05, Manhattan) was equally short-lived. Underlying its plot was an argument antithetical to Shaw's. Before her marriage Mary (Sadie Martinot) was a successful artist and a believer in suffragette principles. She leaves her husband, John (John Mason), when their views on marriage clash. But she soon discovers that her paintings had been purchased by a man who liked her and never opened his packages, or by her neighbors who had been given the purchase price by her father. She returns humbly to John.

That same evening Arnold Daly began a series of revivals of Shaw plays he had mounted in previous seasons. Not until the end of his stand at the Garrick did he offer new Shaw works.

Good things did not come in threes for George Ade. Following the hits he enjoyed with *The County Chairman* and *The College Widow,* he tripped clumsily with **The Bad Samaritan** (9-12-05, Garden). Uncle Ike (Richard Golden), a dealer in hides and tallow, leaves his business to his nephew and goes off to a fishing village. But his nephew is under the thumb of an ungrateful wife, so Ike is pleased to learn that because of a legal technicality his business and his fortune are still his own. He takes his newfound fishing friends to a posh hotel, renting a suite that he calls "a chambermaid's dream." (The suite was described variously in reviews as "decorated a la scrambled eggs with tomato trimmings" and looking like "spaghetti with tomato sauce.") But the friends turn out to be spongers, so Ike settles down with a kindly housekeeper at an inn whose autumn garden is filled with pumpkins. As in Ade's earlier plays, subsidiary characters provided much of the fun. For example, Samuel Reed won laughs as a crabbed hotel proprietor, while Jacques Kruger was an inventor determined to concoct an appliance to eliminate the need for Negroes to beat carpets. Besides the hotel suite and the inn, one striking setting showed the boardwalk at Nirvana-by-the-Sea. Whatever its virtues, the comedy folded after two weeks.

Three touring pieces made brief appearancs the

next Monday night. Daniel Hart's **Marching Through Georgia** (9-18-05, 14th St.), by virtue of where it was booked, was considered a notch above the others, but it simply replayed the old story of lovers on opposing sides during the Civil War. A northern officer is wounded protecting a southern mansion and the daughter of the house. She treats his wounds and comes to admire him, but a villainous overseer, "who wears flaring black whiskers, always sneers, and carries a whip," makes difficulties. A black slave provided comic relief.

In Alicia Ramsay and Rudolph De Cordova's **The Shadow Behind the Throne** (9-18-05, Murray Hill) the evil genius behind the Boxer Rebellion was seen to be a renegade American, but he was not the principal figure. Instead the usual rivalry of two men, one good, one wicked, for the same woman brought them to the forefront. The woman was the daughter of the American minister in Peking, and the rivals were two attachés. With wires cut, the girl and her fiancé attempt to get a letter through to the American army, but all their efforts are thwarted until they dress a young boy as a Chinese peasant woman. He gets through. Meanwhile, kidnappings, killings, and the dynamiting of the viceroy's palace (by the suicidal, repentant renegade) provided thrills.

Comedy held sway in Mark Swan's **The Great Jewel Mystery** (9-18-05, American), in which stolen jewels passed from hand to hand until they were restored to the rightful owner. The chase moved from a posh hotel to Madison Square Park, an East Side street, a palm garden, a grocery store used by fences, and finally a luxurious apartment. The Russell brothers, female impersonators, starred as Nolan and Dolan, a porter and engineer at the hotel, who don disguises to help in the hunt.

J. Hartley Manners and Henry Miller's **Zira** (9-21-05, Princess) was not a totally new play but a reworking of Clara Morris's old success *The New Magdalen*. Some critics thought it wasn't even a good reworking, and a few held reservations about Margaret Anglin's gesturing, such as kissing the hem of a dress as an act of contrition. In most reviews, however, her performance was regarded as a triumph. The *Times* noted, "In her eyes charged with lightning, in her vibrant, convulsive frame, in the spasms of her voice, and in the ringing changes from a high-pitched melodious clearness to a rasping guttural hoarseness, the element of despair was sounded clearly and unerringly. It was not surprising that the audience rose in transport."

. . .

Margaret Anglin (1876–1958) was born in Ottawa. Her father was speaker of the Canadian House of Commons, and her brother later became the country's chief justice. She trained at the acting school run by Charles Frohman in conjunction with the Empire Theatre. Impressed by her work, Frohman offered her a major role in *Shenandoah*, in which she made her New York debut in 1894. She then toured with James O'Neill and E. H. Sothern and played Roxanne (the program's spelling) to Mansfield's Cyrano. She returned for a time to Frohman's company but soon joined with Henry Miller.

. . .

The new star's reviews helped the play chalk up 128 performances.

Alfred Sutro, whose one-acter *A Maker of Men* had been poorly received a few weeks earlier, scored a major success with his full-length **The Walls of Jericho** (9-25-05, Savoy), in which a self-made man (James K. Hackett) rebels against the coldness and hypocrisy of English high society. Hackett's wife, Mary Mannering, was co-starred.

Charles H. Fleming's **The Way of the Transgressor** (9-25-05, Murray Hill) was a melodrama with a difference, or at least with something not seen in melodrama for some decades. To gain a girl's inheritance, her tormentor kills her father and subjects her to numerous indignities. He tries drowning her, tying her to railroad tracks, and abducting her to a secluded mansion. Each time she is rescued by her sweetheart, her cousin, and a detective given to protean disguises, all three acting in conjunction with Charlie, Leo, and Zip. Charlie, Leo, and Zip were dogs. Of course, trained dogs and their "dog dramas" had been standard fare on the Bowery half a century earlier. However, by 1905 animal acts were usually confined to vaudeville.

To a small extent George Ade compensated for *The Bad Samaritan* debacle with **Just Out of College** (9-27-05, Lyceum), but he never again was to know successes such as his first two. His problem remained the same. "As long as the entertainment consisted of character studies and contests of wit there was no fault to be found," the *Dramatic Mirror* observed, "but just as soon as the plot began to develop beyond the simple point of caricature there was a painful drop from originality." Edward Worthington Swinger (Joseph Wheelock, Jr.) asks permission of Septimus Pickering, a pickle manufacturer, to marry his daughter, Caroline. Septimus does not think much of Edward, so he consents if Edward will try his hand at a business venture and report some success after three months. He also lends him $20,000, considering the money well lost if it rids him of the pest. Edward is so successful that in three months the trust offers to buy him out, and Septimus, surprised, can raise no further objections. What business did Edward go into? He opened a rival pickle factory. Of course, there were complications along the way. Caroline becomes jealous of Edward's partner, N. W. Jones, a go-getting "female businessman." Later Edward is abashed when, after telling Jones his money came from a legacy from his late Aunt Julia, Aunt Julia appears. The play's settings—the pickle factory office, a "pure food" exhibition (Teddy Roosevelt was lobbying for the Pure Food and Drug Act), and a railway station—allowed for the introduction of amusing if extraneous characters. The comedy ran two months.

Poppycock lives of real and famous people continued to have a certain appeal. Theodore Burt Sayre's **Edmund Burke** (10-2-05, Majestic) was a vehicle for Chauncey Olcott, and its appeal rested mainly with Irish playgoers away from Broadway. Burke loses a comfortable situation after his benefactor catches him wooing the benefactor's daughter. She agrees to flee with him to Ireland to "live in a cottage as sweet as a lump of sugar, and about the same size." But she is kidnapped by the Prince of Wales. To discover her whereabouts, Burke promises the girl's maid any wish if she will help him find her. The girl is found, but the maid's wish is for Burke's promise of marriage. Fortunately, the maid turns out to be married, and the prince becomes Burke's friend by the final curtain. There were scenes of courting in a garden and in a garret, and "a scene in the same garret with a noble and angry father storming about, and the girl . . . hidden in a high-backed chair around which she peeps coquettishly while she bestows ecstatic little pats upon Mr. Olcott, standing joyously by the chair." Any Olcott vehicle had its quota of Irish songs, but those in this show were unexceptional.

The heroine of the anonymous **She Dared Be Right** (10-2-05, American) had been rescued as a child from a shipwreck by a tender-hearted Jew, who then raised her. She lands in hot water when a baby is left in her room and she is accused of abduction and possible murder. The Jew helps exculpate her, upon which she discovers that she is the long-lost sister of the baby's socially prominent mother.

Although Henry E. Dixey never was to latch on to a runaway success such as his *Adonis* of twenty years before, he enjoyed a pleasing success with Grace Livingston Furniss's dramatization of Harold Mac-Grath's novel **The Man on the Box** (10-3-05, Madison Square). Lt. Robert Worburton returns from a tour of duty and decides to surprise his sister by substituting for her coachman when she leaves a ball. After she alights from the carriage he kisses her, then discovers he has picked up the wrong lady (Carlotta Nillson). His kiss lands him in jail (where the comedy begins), but at his trial the lady pays his fine and hires him as her coachman. This affords him the opportunity not only to save her father when the nearly broke old man proposes to sell secret army plans to the Russians, but to court and win the lady. Dixey's nimble grace, his expressive face, and superb diction all made a mediocre comedy seem better than it was, while Miss Nillson revealed unexpected comic skills.

Joseph Jefferson, the most popular of all 19th-century American comedians, had died the previous spring, but his *Rip Van Winkle* was not to be laid to rest, at least not if his son could help it. As it turned out, Thomas Jefferson possessed none of his father's gifts (one critic called his accent a cross between Harvard and Louis Mann), and the production he arrived in at Wallack's on the 9th was driven away by dismissive notices after two weeks.

Shaw's delightfully glib analysis of the Irish question, **John Bull's Other Island** (10-10-05, Garrick), also ran two weeks. The cast included Arnold Daly as Larry Doyle, Dodson Mitchell as Broadbent, George Farren as Father Keegan, and Mary Shaw as Nora. The play's run had been limited in advance, so divided notices had little effect on business.

Sothern and Marlowe returned on the 16th to begin a month's stand at the Knickerbocker, presenting *The Taming of the Shrew, The Merchant of Venice, Twelfth Night,* and *Romeo and Juliet.* The mountings were elaborate and, as such, costly. Miss Marlowe's wardrobe for her shrew—three dresses and accessories—alone cost nearly $1500. Those accessories included red satin shoes ($38) and a gold-embroidered cap ($50). (Figures are from the Sothern-Marlowe account books, not from publicity releases.) For all the expense and effort, critical reaction was mixed in the extreme. Yet even naysayers had to acknowledge the pair's growing reputation as well as the ever blossoming give and take of their art. It was their interpretations they sometimes questioned. Thus Miss Marlowe's Katherine was no longer the born scold but a girl frustrated by attention accorded her not very bright, insinuatingly kittenish sister. Critical complaints could not discourage playgoers, so business was excellent. The couple returned late in May to the larger Academy of Music, at which time they restored *Much Ado About Nothing* to the bill.

Martha Morton's plays usually found berths at first-class theatres. Not so **The Truth Tellers** (10-16-

05, Grand Opera), in which five orphans disconcert their high-bred aunt. The kilted youngsters rode ponies to a bagpipe accompaniment, but nothing could kindle interest.

The following Monday brought in two of the season's most memorable productions. The native entry was Edwin Milton Royle's **The Squaw Man** (10-23-05, Wallack's), "a good, true play," a "thoroughly American play, quick beating with the red heart-blood of manly sincerity and self-sacrifice." Yet its hero was an Englishman. Captain James Wynnegate (William Faversham) loves his cousin's wife, Lady Diana (Selene Johnson), so when he discovers that his cousin has stolen funds from a charity, Wynnegate offers to emigrate to America. That will make it appear he is the culprit. His purpose is not martyrdom. Rather, he tells his craven cousin, "Man, it's her happiness we both are fighting for—I can't give her that but at least I can spare her the shame." Two years later he is a successful, high-principled cowboy, calling himself Jim Carston. At the Long Horn Saloon he comes to the aid of an Indian girl, Nat-u-ritch (Mabel Morrison), when he learns that his foe, the cattle-rustling Cash Hawkins (W. S. Hart), is attempting to cheat Nat-u-ritch's father, the Ute chief, Tabby-wana (Theodore Roberts).

Jim: Drop that, Hawkins.
Cash: (*falling back*)—What's that? (*Jim's boys rise. Cash utters an exclamation of rage and starts to pull his gun.*) Say, look here, son, ain't you kind of courtin' disaster, interferin' in my private business?
Jim: Do you call it "business," robbing Indians when they're drunk and insulting women?
Cash: Don't you accuse me of insultin' women. She ain't a woman—she's a squaw.

Jim gets the drop on Cash, who slinks away, threatening to return and kill Jim. But when Cash does return he is shot by Nat-u-ritch. Jim shields her from the authorities and takes her to live with him. Thus he becomes a squaw man, ostracized by many in the area. They have a son. However, when Lady Diana comes to tell Jim that his cousin is dead, and that his own innocence has been established and he is now Earl of Kerhill, Nat-u-ritch understands that she is in his way. She kills herself to allow her husband and young son a chance for a better life.

Real Utes, in minor roles, employed their own speech and sign language to add local color. The scenery helped, too. The sumptuous English estate gave way to the saloon with its long bar and gambling tables and with railroad cars seen behind its double doors. The last two acts showed Carston's

Utah ranch, its adobe stable and house on one side, a log cabin on the other, and the Uintah Mountains in the distance. Faversham's performance was a high-water mark in his career. He proved "much here beside the matinee hero," displaying "fine emotional power and straight strokes of sincerity direct from the heart." Liebler and Co.'s production ran for 222 performances. The drama was revived frequently until as late as 1921. It also provided the source for an important silent film and for the failed 1927 musical *The White Eagle.*

Bertha Kalish had made a brief appearance the previous season in English-speaking theatre. Now she came forth in Harrison Grey Fiske's production of Maurice Maeterlinck's **Monna Vanna** (10-23-05, Manhattan). She portrayed the wife of the commander (Henry Kolker) of a besieged city who is willing to sacrifice her reputation to spare her city. She goes to spend the night with the besieger (Henry Jewett). Nothing happens, but her husband refuses to believe that, and when he captures the besieger he orders him put to death. Giovanna, recognizing the captive's inherent goodness, tricks her husband into giving her the key to the dungeon. The equivocal ending allowed the audience to decide for itself whether the pair escape or die together. One headline, "A PLAY TOO GREAT FOR ITS ACTORS," summed up critical judgment. But Miss Kalish's performance was hardly dismissed. She was deemed regal and moving, if uneven. Many playgoers were not dissuaded by the critics' carping, so the play ran for fifty performances.

At the Garden, Robert Mantell came in with a repertory that offered the Cibber-Shakespeare *Richard III, Othello, Hamlet, Macbeth, King Lear,* and *Richelieu.*

In Daniel L. Hart's **A Rocky Road to Dublin** (10-23-05, Metropolis), the hero assumes blame for the peculations of his sweetheart's brother at a bank. To repay the money, he borrows from a supposed friend, who immediately calls in the loan. It seems the supposed friend also loves the hero's sweetheart, and this is his way of getting both his rival and the girl's brother out of his hair. What he fails to bargain for is the arrival of a wealthy man whose life once had been saved by the hero's father. The man pays the debt, tricks the villain into confessing, and buys the bank, putting the hero in charge.

On the 30th Ben Greet's company opened a stand at Mendelssohn Hall, presenting a schedule that included *Henry V, Macbeth, Much Ado About Nothing, The Merchant of Venice,* and *Julius Caesar.* His arrival meant that New Yorkers had a choice of three competing Shakespearean ensembles. But many New Yorkers had something more interesting on their minds, the opening that night of the season's most provocative play, Shaw's look at English prostitution, **Mrs. Warren's Profession** (10-30-05, Garrick). The play centered on Mrs. Warren's attempt to explain and to justify her position as a brothel-keeper to the world, to herself, and, most of all, to her daughter. A mere explanation, given public morality at the time, might have seemed scandalous enough, but to justify her income was too much. The play's notoriety had preceded it. Newspapers reported that thousands were turned away from the box office and that scalpers were getting $30 a ticket. Reviews were scathing: "the limit of stage indecency" (*Herald*); "unspeakable" (*Sun*); "It belongs to the moral clinics" (*World*). The few papers that approved of the play, such as the *Press,* were outshouted. Two leading players, Arnold Daly and Mary Shaw, were hauled into court, where they were promptly acquitted. However, by that time Daly's booking had finished, so the play's record for its first New York stand was a single performance.

Occasionally alloyed outrage swiftly gave way to occasionally modified rapture when what so far has proved the season's most durable work premiered. James M. Barrie's **Peter Pan** (11-3-05, Empire) told, as its rarely used subtitle revealed, of a "boy who wouldn't grow up." His flying nighttime visit to a Bloomsbury household confronts its children with comically menacing Indians and pirates, the latter led by a pirate chief who bears a remarkable resemblance to their father (Ernest Lawford). The title role gave Maude Adams the greatest part of her career, the sweet, whimsical, hoydenish characterization in which she has passed into theatrical legend. Not every aging critic was enchanted. A few railed against the play's treacliness, and a few even claimed to find the star no more than acceptable. But a second theatrical legend, that the play and its star initially were not received mostly with huzzas, is just that. Thus *Theatre* allowed, "There was not a flaw in her performance of the title role. She was, in turn, elfish, wistful, tender, joyous, sad. She danced and tripped, whistled and sang as gaily as the rest of the children, and invested the part with so much charm, poetry and atmosphere that it would be difficult to conceive of the part being better played." *Peter Pan* ran out the season. Maude Adams revived it regularly until her retirement in 1915, and since she left the stage others have flown happily to Never Land.

Charles Frohman's production was followed, a week apart, by two other major successes, but before they came in, lesser houses brought out several novelties. On the 13th at the Fifth Avenue, its great days behind it, J. Comyns Carr's version of **Oliver Twist** featured Amelia Bingham, her best days also gone by, as Nancy, and J. E. Dodson as Fagin.

Combination houses offered a variety of plays that same night. Langdon McCormick and Lawrence Marston's melodrama **When the World Sleeps** (11-13-05, Star) was inordinately complicated. Reduced to essentials, a woman picks up a bloody knife while she is sleepwalking, and her suitor confesses to the murder she is then accused of. Although they know he is innocent, a grab-bag of villains encourages the idea that he is guilty. The sensation scene saw the woman trapped in a burning mill, and the play ended with moonlight shining down on the reunited lovers and the ruined mill.

Carroll Fleming's **The Parson's Wife** (11-13-05, Metropolis) was billed as "a play with songs," but the *Dramatic Mirror* assured its readers that it was a melodrama, albeit a "domesticated" one, with "not a trace of bloodshed" and with scenery not "cajoled into doing wonderful tricks." A minister and a singer are in love, but an unscrupulous broker, who holds the mortgage on the singer's home, employs all sorts of nefarious devices to have her marry him instead. The heroine was played by Mabel McKinley, niece of the late president. She had been injured in a recent hotel fire and performed on crutches. Even making allowances for her handicap, critics felt she was not a good actress.

For several seasons baskets of roses had graced the sides of the proscenium at the Belasco. Audiences arriving for the first night of Belasco's **The Girl of the Golden West** (11-14-05, Belasco) immediately noticed one change. Roses had given way to cactus plants. Nor was the introductory music the kind they might have expected, for Belasco had replaced the traditional pit orchestra with a small band consisting of a concertina, "bones," and a banjo, which set the mood with "Camptown Races," "Pop Goes the Weasel," and "Rosalie, the Prairie Flower." After the house lights dimmed and the curtain rose, playgoers saw what seemed to be a show-curtain depicting a lonely cabin atop Cloudy Mountain. The curtain was actually a panorama, and as it moved upwards it took audiences down the precipitous, craggy slope to the small, shabby main street of a California mining camp and the façade of the Polka Saloon. Footlights were lowered briefly, stage lights came on, and the saloon's interior was disclosed as the last of the panorama quietly headed for the flies.

The saloon is run by the only white woman

(Blanche Bates) in the area. She is popular with all the miners. Most of them are good, honest men, even if their sheriff, Jack Rance (Frank Keenan), is not. He proposes to marry the Girl, hoping she and the others will not discover he has a wife in New Orleans. At the moment, however, his main interest is tracking down a highwayman known as Ramerrez. Back at her cabin, the Girl, whose name is Minnie, offers shelter to a handsome stranger as a snowstorm begins. The storm starts to howl, and the snow falls hard, icing up the cabin's windows and drifting through its cracks, but Minnie remains oblivious to it while the man speaks beguilingly of a better world beyond the mountains. He tells her his name is Dick Johnson (Robert Hilliard). With night falling, she offers him her curtained bed and prepares to sleep in front of the fire. Just then a posse arrives, searching for Ramerrez. One of the men notes a half-smoked cigar but, out of sympathy for Minnie, furtively pockets it. The posse leaves. Furious at Johnson's deception, Minnie orders him out into the storm. A shot is heard, and Johnson stumbles back in, wounded. Minnie's sympathies instantly are enlisted, so she leads him to the cabin's loft. He is no sooner hidden than a glowering Rance appears and demands Minnie turn over the thief. She convinces him that no one has entered the cabin, and, momentarily forgetting his pursuit, Rance tries to resume his ugly courtship. She rejects him. Rance goes to wipe his face with his large, white handkerchief, but as he does some drops of blood fall from the loft and land on it. "I'm talking to Jack Rance, gambler, now," Minnie quickly responds. She offers to play poker with him, with Johnson as the stakes. She wins the first hand, the sheriff the second. ("One could have heard a pin drop," a notice reported.) Fearful of losing, Minnie distracts the sheriff and pulls a pair of aces from her petticoat. The sheriff leaves, sulking. Johnson later is captured, but the men agree to allow him and Minnie a final interview. The pair use it to escape, trusting to find the better life Johnson had spoken of.

Not only were both the play and Belasco's brilliant mounting, especially the storm, extolled by critics, but so was the cast. Hilliard made a handsome, virile, and creditable hero. Miss Bates, in what many felt was the peak of her career, gave "breadth, variety, strength and a soul" to the Girl. But well-played villainy often commands the most attention, and Keenan's Rance was riveting. One commentator noted, "Mr. Keenan's mastery of repose, of minute and subtle stage business, amounts to something very like genius. He lights a cigar, and the spectator watches the match as he would watch the fuse of a dynamite bomb; he comes in out of the blizzard, and, standing motionless in the centre of the stage, warms an index finger by boring the tip of it into the palm of his other hand, and for some mysterious reason you are thrilled in every fiber . . . [The blood begins to seep from the loft.] In the glare of the spot-light the dark spot can be seen by every one in the audience. The sheriff slowly looks down, then up. He is tall and gaunt, all in black, face white as death. His gaze fixes itself on the rafters and then, in the silence, on the white handkerchief, drop—drop—drop falls the blood. The situation has the bite of theatrical genius, and Mr. Keenan fairly eats it alive." The drama ran out the season and played several profitable return engagements. It provided the source for Puccini's opera, which premiered at the Metropolitan Opera in 1910.

The season's biggest hit was Charles Klein's **The Lion and the Mouse** (11-20-05, Lyceum). With *The Music Master* heading for new records a few blocks away on Broadway, its success made Klein suddenly America's most promising dramatist. It was a promise never kept.

. . .

Charles Klein (1867–1915) was born in London and emigrated to America at the age of fifteen. He acted juvenile roles before turning playwright. His early efforts, in which he often was a silent partner, included *Heartsease* (1897) and *The Auctioneer* (1901). Although his new play was produced by Henry B. Harris, he worked closely with Charles Frohman, serving as his playreader and dying with him on the *Lusitania*. His brother, Manuel, was a popular composer.

. . .

The play was perceived as a thinly veiled, fictionalized account of Ida Tarbell's battle against John D. Rockefeller. Shirley Rossmore (Grace Elliston) returns home from Europe to learn that her father, a judge whose decisions have angered the trust, has been reduced to poverty and is threatened with removal from the bench through the machinations of the monopolists, led by John Burkett "Ready Money" Ryder. She vows to clear her father's name. Aboard ship Ryder's son, Jefferson (Richard Bennett), had fallen in love with her, but when he comes to propose marriage she turns down both his proposal and the idea of using him to unmask the elder Ryder. Some time passes. Shirley, using the name Sarah Green has written a best-selling novel, *The Great American Octopus,* whose leading figure has been patterned after Ryder. Ryder (Edmund Breese) is so impressed by the accuracy of the picture that he summons Miss Green to his mansion, a mansion where bodyguards are stationed everywhere. At first Miss Green rejects his invitations, but after Ryder meets her conditions, she comes. Her explanations of the parallels between her central figure and Ryder impress the man. Why, for example, did she make her protagonist afraid of death? "Most men who amass money are afraid of death," she tells him, "because death is about the only thing that can separate them from their money." When Ryder asks her to write an authorized biography of him and offers to open his files to her, she accepts, seeing an opportunity to exonerate her father. She finds incriminating letters in his files, which she leaks to the press, and she stiffens Jefferson's resolve not to marry the girl his father has ordered him to marry. Angry words lead to the revelation of who she really is. Sensing that the tide of public opinion has gone totally against him and that even his family has become alienated, Ryder capitulates: "I'm going to Washington on behalf of your father because I—I want you to marry my son. Yes, I want you in my family, close to me; I want your respect, my girl. I want your love. I want to earn it. I know I can't buy it. There's a weak link in every man's chain and that's mine, I always want what I can't get. I can't get your love unless I earn it."

Although three principals went on to distinguished careers, particularly Bennett, none at this time was a true star. Yet even without major names, and despite such flaws as its stagey coincidences, the play immediately was made welcome. Excellent characterizations, crisp dialogue, and pertinency were all in its favor. In a Sunday followup the *Times* observed, "The fact of the matter is, 'The Lion and the Mouse' is so much in advance of what most of our American dramas contain that its purposefulness was in most cases overlooked." Playgoers had plenty of time to dwell on its merits, for the play not only ran out the season but continued for most of the following season as well. A typographical error in *Best Plays of 1899–1909*, recording that its run was 686 performances, has led to the drama being considered the longest-running play of the decade, but contemporary sources agree the engagement ended after 586 showings. That probably means the record being compiled at the time by *The Music Master* was not soon surpassed.

Hal Reid's **Lured from Home** (11-20-05, Thalia) had to be content with a combination house's customary one-week booking. The play focused on an artist too much given to drink. The villain attempts to lure away the artist's unhappy wife, while Reid's umpteenth adventuress, knowing the artist is heir to a fortune, sinks her claws into him. Everyone realized the artist would reform in time

for a pleasing ending and that the conspirators would receive their just desserts. What mattered were the dramatic situations, which came one after the other in "cyclonic" fashion. At one point, the hero, recognizing the villain's villainy, declaims, "If there is any man here who loves his wife let him lend me a pistol." A pistol is produced at once. The play's big sensation scene saw the conspirators attempting to throw the artist's daughter from a tenement window into the gaping hole left by excavations for what was to become Penn Station. A derrick stands just outside the tenement, and the hero's friend, in a neighboring tenement, "catches hold of the beam of the derrick, swings across the stage, grabs the child in the nick of time and swings back again to safety." One scene set in a music hall allowed for the requisite specialties.

Harry McRae Webster's **Lieut. Dick, U.S.A.** (11-20-05, Murray Hill) told of an army officer in Wyoming who is ordered to ferret out a brother officer who runs a gambling den. Not even the kidnapping of his sweetheart daunts the purposeful soldier.

Its own weaknesses and not its potent competition confined the run of **The Marriage of William Ashe** (11-21-05, Garrick), which Margaret Mayo drew from Mrs. Humphrey Ward's novel. Before she dies, the eccentric behavior and published memoirs of a wife (Grace George) nearly destroy her husband's (H. Reeves-Smith) career. William A. Brady gave his own wife's vehicle a handsome production, especially a gaudy, lively Venetian carnival scene, although comic mishaps bedeviled the scene on opening night.

No more successful was Clyde Fitch's **The Toast of the Town** (11-27-05, Daly's), which was merely a rewriting, for Viola Allen, of *Mistress Betty*, which Modjeska had offered ten years earlier.

Two French plays had even shorter stays. In Pierre Berton's **La Belle Marseillaise** (11-27-05, Knickerbocker), the wife (Virginia Harned) of Napoleon's would-be assassin (J. H. Gilmour), who must pretend to be dead but really has gone into hiding, marries one of Napoleon's captains (William Courtenay) to prove her husband truly is dead. When she falls in love with her new husband, her first husband conveniently dies. By contrast, in Paul Hervieu's **The Labyrinth** [*Le Dédale*] (11-27-05, Herald Square), the illness of their child reunites a formerly married couple (Olga Nethersole and Hamilton Revelle), leaving the woman's second husband in the lurch. Afterwards the two men fight it out, both dying in a fall from a cliff. There were gasps at the end of one act, when the wife and her former husband head off to bed together as the curtain falls, but none of the legal problems Miss Nethersole and Revelle had encountered when he carried her to her bedroom in *Sapho*. In fact, when *The Labyrinth* was withdrawn after two weeks, the pair revived the Fitch-Daudet drama. They subsequently played *Carmen* and *Magda*. The *Dramatic Mirror,* assessing both French novelties in tandem, alluded to the recent, aborted moves in Congress when it remarked, "If these are to be considered average examples of European importations the native playwright will need no protective tariff to sustain him."

One "native" playwright (despite his foreign birth) was Theodore Kremer, and his latest sensation-melodrama, **Secret Service Sam** (11-27-05, American), led critics to ask again if he weren't writing tongue-in-cheek. A wealthy old man (the character was named Rockfeller) is murdered, and the killer tries to foist blame on the man's niece. Sam is called into the case, and he turns out to be something of a Houdini. He and the heroine are handcuffed and locked in a metal cage, but when the cage is opened they are gone. Later they are tied to chairs, draped with flags, and shot. The flags are pulled off—and no one is underneath. In one scene Sam disguises himself as a dentist and gives the villain, his patient, enough gas to keep him quiet for a while. At the end the ghost of the murdered man appears, bathed in an eerie green light, to force a confession from the killer.

After so rich a month, December was an anticlimax. It began dully enough with Henry Blossom's **A Fair Exchange** (12-4-05, Liberty). Although it was billed as a comedy, critics found it laughable only in its ineptitude. One disgruntled reviewer suggested the plot was better suited to touring melodrama. Cliffe Austin prevents a failing, unprincipled broker from succeeding at a series of deceptive ploys—one ploy per act. In Act I, Cliffe throws in a winning poker hand so that the broker will not win a pot from Cliffe's friend, Bob. In Act II, he takes the helm of Bob's yacht and causes the broker to lose a bet on a yacht race. The last act sees Cliffe thwart the scoundrel's attempt to involve Cliffe's family in his peculations.

Views of the Harlem Bridge at midnight and the lobby of the new Astor Hotel, along with characters such as Abe Liv-en-Ease and Ragtime Kate, embellished Henry Belmer's **New York by Night** (12-4-05, Metropolis). The plot, which recounted the efforts of a man to do away with a girl who is supposed to share an inheritance with him, trafficked in the expected shootings and abductions.

Lillian Mortimer's **No Mother to Guide Her** (12-4-05, Star) spotlighted a shop girl lured into a mock marriage by a bank robber. When she attempts to run away, he has her abducted by a band of gypsies lorded over by a fiendish gypsy queen. Miss Mortimer played the heroine's friend with the odd name of Bunco ("bunco" meant scam in period parlance), who sometimes shares her harrowing experiences and eventually frees her.

On the 11th at the Lyric "the Divine Sarah" opened another New York visit. For starters she showed how Sardou's *La Sorcière* should be performed. The remainder of her stand was devoted to old favorites Bernhardt fans never tired of, although she did give a few performances of Hugo's rarely done **Angelo,** the tale of a doomed actress. She returned again in June with more favorites. Critics raved, but both stands were of the briefest duration, part of a prebooked cross-country tour that frequently saw her performing in tents, outdoor arenas, and convention halls. By now, huge grosses as much as defiance of the Trust prompted such bookings.

Leo Ditrichstein found favor with **Before and After** (12-12-05, Manhattan), which he freely Americanized from Alfred Hennequin and Albert Milhaud's *La Poudre de l'escampette*. Pandora's box of farcical troubles opens after an inventor tests out a powder designed to make grouches merry.

E. S. Willard had begun a three-week engagement on the same night that Bernhardt had returned. Most of his bills, like hers, consisted of tested standbys, but he did present a single novelty, Kinsey Peile's one-act dramatization of Kipling's **The Man Who Was** (12-18-05, New Amsterdam). A British officer held captive for twenty years after the Crimean War returns to his regiment. He is little more than an animal, his knowledge of English and even of his own name erased by his harsh confinement. But the presence of his cruel Russian jailer, who now is being fêted by the regiment, restores his memory.

A wily Jewish peddler with the obvious name of Izzy Abrahams was the real hero of Jay Hunt and Hal Reid's **A Crown of Thorns** (12-18-05, 14th St.). A stock dastardly villain has imprisoned his own widowed sister-in-law in an insane asylum and hopes to marry his niece, the woman's daughter, so as to inherit his brother's vast estates. The mother escapes, and when the villain shows up to drag her back, the Jew dons her garment, so is confined in her stead. He escapes, too, and learns that the villain, unable to force his niece to marry him, plans to drown the girl in a millrace. She grabs onto the revolving millwheel and clings for dear life until the

Jew and the girl's sweetheart rescue her. After the girl and her fiancé are married, the Jew photographs their marriage certificate. The villain steals and destroys the original, but the Jew shows him the copy, telling him "a little Jewish bird from a Yiddisher Heaven" gave it to him. More perils and rescues follow before a happy ending. Critics might sneer, but not the playgoers, who loved this sort of hokum. One trade sheet reported, "The applause was as vociferous as if there had been a football game or a prize fight on the stage. The gallery yelled like Indians, whistled like street Arabs, and hissed like a thousand deadly serpents."

First-nighters had three choices on Christmas, only one American. The Rev. John M. Snyder's **As Ye Sow** (12-25-05, Garden) was deemed by some a staged sermon, by others a sensation-melodrama, with its sensation scenes taking place offstage. A minister (Frank Gillmore) returns to Cape Cod from a long sojourn in Europe and immediately proposes to a lady (Charlotte Walker), who turns him down on the grounds that she is a widow. He waves away her reservations, and they are married. They are welcomed by the minister's little adopted daughter. But no sooner are they all ensconced in the manse than the woman's supposedly dead husband appears. He is an evilly disposed man who had deserted his wife and taken their baby with him. His very arrival on the scene is owing to the minister's joining a rescue party and saving passengers in a shipwreck. But he has no gratitude and sets about making trouble. He can do this since he not only is the lady's husband, but turns out to be the minister's long-lost brother and the father of the minister's adopted daughter. His death in the Spanish-American War resolves matters. The convolutions of the plot were not the play's sole oddities. Critics pointed to such curious features as the Cape Cod town crier's being played as a black (of course, by a white in dark greasepaint).

Henrietta Crosman's starring vehicle **Mary, Mary, Quite Contrary** (12-25-05, Garrick) was simply Sardou's *Les Pattes de mouche*—or *A Scrap of Paper*—reworked and reset in 1905 America. Its cool reception goaded the star into adding a second piece, Mrs. W. K. Clifford's **Madeline** (1-5-06), in which an actress kills herself after spurning an infatuated diplomat (Guy Standing). Miss Crosman's forte was comedy, not tragedy, so the addition was no help.

The third of Christmas night's openings, a double bill from the start, was its best and most popular. Both plays were by James M. Barrie, and they featured all three young Barrymores, although only two appeared in each play. The main offering was **Alice Sit-by-the-Fire** (12-25-05, Criterion). Bruce McRae and Ethel Barrymore (who was twenty-six) played a middle-aged couple returning from years in India to be reunited with their children. The daughter, weaned on modern problem plays, overhears her mother accept an innocent invitation to the apartment of a handsome young bachelor (John Barrymore) and thereupon sets out to save her mother from scandal. In **Pantaloon,** Clown (John Barrymore), resentful that Harlequin has eloped with Pantaloon's daughter, Columbine, whom Clown himself had hoped to marry, attempts to oust Pantaloon (Lionel Barrymore) from the pantomime quartet. Some reviewers quibbled about Ethel's makeup, but all the Barrymores won laurels for their lively comic capering. They capered for two and a half months.

Even though one of the two plays arriving on the first night of 1906 outran the Barrie double bill, neither new entry was much to cheer about. As such they were harbingers of the mediocrity that overwhelmed the last half of the season. The hit was **Julie Bonbon** (1-1-06, Fields'), which Clara Lipman wrote as a starring vehicle for herself and her husband, Louis Mann. (Lipman had played a character called Julie Bonbon in the 1896 musical *The Girl from Paris*.) The new play's story was elementary. A pretty Frenchwoman, who runs a millinery shop, and a Knickerbocker scion have fallen in love during an Atlantic crossing. The man's snooty mother and the lady's boozy, boorish father (Mann) throw obstacles in their way, but romance wins. Settings provided color and cues for comedy and drama. The first act took place in the shop, filled with salesgirls and with costumers trying on the latest in hats. The second act showed the Van Brunt mansion, where Julie's father wears out his welcome by pilfering cigars and knickknacks. In the third act, the suitor, his mother's warnings abuzz in his ears, finds Julie dancing atop a table in a music hall and storms out. Matters are concluded satisfactorily in Julie's apartment. Miss Lipman was applauded for her vivacious comedy, but Mann, dropping his usual Dutch accent for a French one, again was assailed for laying on both his accent and his comedy too thickly.

The Crossing (1-1-06, Daly's), which Louis Evan Shipman and Winston Churchill adapted from Churchill's novel, told of a young man resolved to wreak vengeance on his faithless mother and the man who lured her away. Critically panned, the play folded after a single week.

Playgoers entering the theatre on the first night of

Thomas Dixon, Jr.'s **The Clansman** (1-8-06, Liberty) had a pamphlet, couched as an open letter to the playwright and called "As to the Leopard's Spots," pressed on them by a black who claimed to be a professor at Howard University. Its purpose was "to express the attitude and feeling of 10,000,000 of your fellow-citizens toward the evil propagandism of race animosity to which you have lent your literary powers." The professor and his assistants soon were hauled away by the police. Dixon's story, taken from his novel of the same name and from a second novel, *The Leopard's Spots,* recounted how carpetbaggers abet a black rabble-rouser (Holbrook Blinn) who prods his fellow blacks into seizing power and creating mayhem in a southern town. It takes the Ku Klux Klan to restore order. A Klan gathering, with menacing green lights illuminating it from the wings, was a high point of the evening. Many critics professed indignation at Dixon's story, but enough playgoers ignored them to give the play a passable run. Less than a decade later the same story would serve as the basis for an early American film masterpiece, *Birth of a Nation.*

Lottie Blair Parker's **The Redemption of David Corson** (1-8-06, Majestic) was a two-week dud. Its hero (William Courtleigh), a Quaker minister, falls irrationally in love with the gypsy wife (Emma Dunn) of a quack medicine man, Dr. Aesculapius. He follows them on their wanderings and attempts to estrange them, but he later repents, helping the quack in the charlatan's dying hours and finding a secure berth for the gypsy. He then picks up an axe and heads off to hew a lonely path to redemption.

A second dramatization of Shaw's *Cashel Byron's Profession,* this one by Stanislaus Stange, opened the same night at Daly's. This time the title role was taken by James J. Corbett.

Robert Sidney's **The German Gypsy** (1-8-06, 14th St.) bore no relation to *The Gypsy German* of six seasons before, although it, too, was one of those fence-straddlers, part romantic comedy, part musical. A young man who has been raised by gypsies hopes to ask his fiancée for her hand but feels he must first acquire permission from the girl's mother. The mother thinks she herself is being offered a proposal and accepts. This angers the man's uncle, who has been courting the mother. To make matters worse, a gypsy girl appears and announces that she and the man were wed when they were babies and that the gypsies still consider that marriage binding. A solution is found just before eleven o'clock. The play's star and a "gypsy trio" broke out in song at intervals.

Another of those starry-eyed groups that emerge periodically on Broadway promoting the cause of superior theatre suffered the fate of most such groups. It died virtually aborning. But in its fleeting existence the Progressive Stage Society offered the American premiere of Maeterlinck's misty tragedy **The Death of Tintaglies** (1-8-06, Berkeley Lyceum), coupled with Villiers d'Isle Adam's **The Revolt.**

Another double bill opened the next evening. The longer work was W. A. Tremayne and I. L. Hall's **The Braisley Diamond** (1-9-06, Madison Square). To cover her gambling debts, a wife secretly pawns a valuable jewel and substitutes a paste imitation. Later the husband loses the replacement, not knowing it is fake. The pair spend the evening trying to deceive each other and retrieve the original. The play was harshly received. However, the real attraction of the evening was the shorter work, H. Heijermans's **A Case of Arson,** in which seven people are interviewed by a magistrate after a factory burns down under suspicious circumstances. All seven interviewees were played by the Dutch actor Henri de Vries. His remarkable tour de force kept the box office humming for the one-month stand.

The story of Lincoln J. Carter's **Bedford's Hope** (1-15-06, 14th St.) was singularly uncomplicated for this sort of sensation-melodrama. A miner is tricked into selling shares in his supposedly worthless mine. No sooner has the trickster left than the mine is discovered to be the richest in the West. How to stop the trickster? Luckily the miner's son, just back from the East, owns a snazzy new red car. The son and his sister, the miner's daughter, jump in and head off to catch the speeding train carrying the villain and his ill-gotten shares. The car was on a treadmill with small bushes at its rear. Behind that a miniature train chugged along, and behind the train the customary panorama. At first the train seems unbeatable. But slowly the car, its occupants' hair and hats blown by a wind machine in the wings, gains on and finally passes the train.

Critics saw other virtues in the play. The *Dramatic Mirror* praised it for its cleanness, for omitting "the conventional Yiddish and Irish types of downtown melodrama" and substituting "human beings speaking sensible and intelligible English," and for its avoidance of hackneyed phrases—"There was not a single 'My God!' heard during the entire evening." Did this mean that Carter could change his style and tone when given a chance to play a first-class house—albeit a fast-fading one? Enthusiastic notices kept the play at the 14th Street for seven weeks, after which it immediately embarked on a tour of Manhattan's neighborhood houses.

Henry Miller suffered a quick failure when he presented himself in H. V. Esmond's English play **Grierson's Way** (1-18-06, Princess), in which a man marries a girl to protect her honor after another man (Guy Standing) has seduced her, and then commits suicide to warn her against returning to her unprincipled lover when the lover is widowed.

By contrast, Richard Harding Davis and Raymond Hitchcock combined their talents to make a popular success of **The Galloper** (1-22-06, Garden), which some commentators took as Davis's tongue-in-cheek sendup of himself. Copeland Schuyler (Hitchcock) is so smitten by Grace Whitney (Nanette Comstock) that he follows her to the battlefield when she becomes a Red Cross nurse in the 1897 Greco-Turkish War. To be with her he poses as a famous war correspondent, Kirke Warren. Like the central figure in *The Earl of Pawtucket,* he learns to his dismay that the real Warren is saddled with personal problems. Warren's ex-wife, a vaudevillian who performs as "the Human Fly," comes seeking tardy alimony payments. A wealthy Newark widow arrives to demand Warren keep his promise to marry her. And members of the French Foreign Legion demand a duel to satisfy their honor over a supposed snub. Meanwhile, the real Warren (Edgar L. Davenport) snoops about in disguise, seeking news stories. At one point the group is captured by the Turks. Among the snippets especially delicious to 1906 audiences was this dialogue between Blanche, "the Human Fly," and her ex-husband.

Blanche: How did you *like* the new act?
Warren: Made me laugh.
Blanche: Laugh! It isn't meant to make you *laugh.* When you see a woman turn four somersaults in the air and strike on the back of her neck, does that make you laugh?
Warren: It does, if I'm paying her alimony.

And then Schuyler, mistaken by some excited Greeks for Warren, who once had fought on their side, and forced to speak to them, shouts, "Men of Athens! Remember Marathon! (*Applause.*) Remember Thermopylae! (*Wild applause.*) Remember Andrew Jackson! (*Shrieks and roars of applause.*) What has the Republican party ever done for Greece? (*Thunderous outburst of enthusiasm.*)" Davis's amusing pictures of newspaper rivalry, of the sometimes polite absurdities of 1906 warfare, and of Americans responding to foreign mores were brought home to good advantage by Hitchcock's occasionally obstreperous but essentially homespun style.

When the curtain rose on Channing Pollock's **The Little Gray Lady** (1-22-06, Garrick), audiences saw the backyard of a Washington boardinghouse. A fence is at the rear (with a very live cat scampering across it); a hammock runs from the porch to a nearby tree. Anna Gray (Julia Dean) is lolling in the hammock. She is a sweet girl, dreaming of the day Perriton Carlyle (John W. Albaugh, Jr.) will marry her. But Carlyle has fallen in love with their landlady's brash, selfish daughter, Ruth Jordan (Dorothy Donnelly). Carlyle works at the Treasury Department, and he helps support himself by stealing bills. After Anna catches on and protects him, he not only promises to reform but recognizes with which girl his best interests lie. The play's month-long run was unprofitable, but a subsequent road company, with Pauline Lord in the leading role, proved more successful.

Alfred Sutro's **The Fascinating Mr. Vanderveldt** (1-22-06, Daly's) elicited laughs for the saga of a bounder (Frank Worthing) who craftily woos but nonetheless loses an attractive widow (Ellis Jeffreys).

Whether or not the 14th Street Theatre was still looked upon as a first-class house is uncertain, but it assuredly was a notch or so above combination houses. Having tasted success there with his *Bedford's Hope,* Lincoln J. Carter now had to reconcile himself to returning once again to a more lowly playhouse. Perhaps he consoled himself by recalling the Thalia's history. His melodrama **The Eye Witness** (1-22-06, Thalia), which had been touring for a year, was less restrained than his previous effort. It centered on a blackguard's attempt to deprive his cousin of an inheritance. The cousin's wife is chloroformed and left in a burning building; later she is sandbagged and dumped in the Chicago River. Of course, she is rescued both times. The villain also attempts to prevent his cousin from outracing him back to where some crucial documents are hidden. To this end he bribes a man to open a drawbridge just as the hero attempts to cross it in his car. But the car leaps over the opened span. The villain appears set to obtain the papers until a cyclone wrecks the house he is in and kills him.

The differences between sensation-melodrama and some plays offered at first-class houses were often of degree, not kind, as James K. Hackett demonstrated when he presented Herman Knickerbocker Viele's **The House of Silence** (1-23-06, Savoy). Apparently Hackett had tired of swashbuckling heroes and longed for a stab at darker, crueler figures. His Victor, a gardener "who talks like a menacing thunderstorm and strides across the stage as if clad in seven-league boots," murders his French master by pushing him off a cliff and then blackmails the murdered man's wife (Mary Mannering) into silence. His perverted thinking allows him to believe she will eventually come to accept him as a husband. Instead she falls in love with an American painter, Paul Gregory (Edward Arden), so Victor decides to choke Gregory to death. He almost does, but a bolt of lightning puts an end to his murderous ways. Breton settings and costumes gave the play a certain visual charm, but they were of no real help. Like most touring plays at combination houses, the drama had to be content with a single week's run.

February got off to a dismal start. In Sidney Bowkett's London comedy **Lucky Miss Dean** (2-5-06, Madison Avenue), a secretly married couple, about to be evicted from their flat for arrears, spread the word that the wife has inherited a fortune. Instead of getting their landlord off their backs, the lie brings a horde of avaricious relatives and other problems. Walter E. Grogan's **A Daughter of the Tumbrils** (2-5-06) preceded the longer play, telling of a lower-class ragamuffin who, during the French Revolution, hopes to be avenged on a nobleman by whom she once had been seduced but finds an old vow prevents her carrying out her scheme. Neither play was much thought of. The drama was withdrawn after one week (replaced by a "miniature musical comedy") and the comedy a week later.

Nor was William L. Roberts's **Big-Hearted Jim** (2-5-06, Third Ave.) any better, although one critic did admit the touring melodrama was "loaded to the muzzle with gun-play and local color." Local color included a comic "Chinaman" and angry Indians in Medicine Lodge, Mont., while virtually all the characters participated in the gunplay. As the heroine informs the audience in a long soliloquy, she has come west after she was deserted by a man who had only pretended to marry her, after her parents died of broken hearts, and after her baby had succumbed to a mysterious illness. She now teaches school and is courted by Jim, the town's strapping sheriff. Who should appear but the lady's ex. He is not looking for a reconciliation. Instead he's looking to kidnap an Indian girl he has heard is in line for a large fortune. He threatens to reveal the heroine's past if she stands in his way. His kidnapping of the girl provokes a Blackfoot riot. Jim captures the culprit but, thinking the schoolmarm loves him, is prepared to allow him to escape (echoes of *In Mizzoura*). The ingrate turns on Jim and tries to shoot him, only to be shot by the Indian girl.

A short-lived attempt to establish a repertory company devoted not to art drama but to solidly commercial plays began promisingly enough with David Gray's **Gallops** (2-12-06, Garrick). A young man, Jack Hemingway (Charles Richman), comes to visit friends on Long Island, where he is mistaken for his cousin, a celebrated steeplechase rider. Hoping to impress Nell Colfax (Frances Starr), whom he had met the year before while on a tour of Italy, he goes along with the error and agrees to ride in an important race. Nell's nasty suitor, Randolph Gordon, tries to make it appear that Jack has fouled him. An observant groom throws the lie in Randolph's face, so Jack and Nell announce their engagement at the cotillion following the race. The race was not shown. Instead spectators atop a large coach described the run. However, a horse introduced as "the leader of the cotillion" did come onstage, and on opening night it knocked over a large table. The comedy ran two months, but whether its title was confused with *The Galloper* and thus hurt chances for a longer run is unknown.

The only other American play to premiere that night at a first-class playhouse was Clay M. Greene's one-acter **For Love's Sweet Sake** (2-12-06, Princess). When a father returns from a long trip abroad, he is told his son (Thomas H. Ince) is a forger. He suggests to his son that they both commit suicide to save the family's honor. The son then confesses that the actual forger is the husband of the girl he had loved and that the shock of learning the truth might kill her, since she is pregnant. All the father can say is, "Jim, you're a bigger man than I am!" Critics dismissed the piece as an inane trifle. It was coupled with a revival of *The Bishop's Move*, whose title had been shortened to *The Bishop*. The double bill vanished after eight performances.

Two foreign works were more successful at finding an audience. R. C. Carton's **Mr. Hopkinson** (2-12-06, Savoy), like *The Fascinating Mr. Vanderveldt*, tickled theatregoers' funnybones with the comic saga of an unpleasant man. Only this time it was moot if he got his comeuppance. No sooner does a small-town clerk come into a fortune than he jilts his sweet fiancée and becomes engaged to a titled lady. His absurd airs—constantly polishing his new patent leather shoes and demanding everyone admire the diamond necklace he purchased as his wife's wedding gift—help drive his betrothed into a more suitable match. Through some clever blackmail the girl he jilted forces him to change his mind. Mr. Hopkinson was played by Dallas Welford, a small, pudgy puffball of a man with a repulsively smug, prissy mien. Critics predicted stardom and a long stay in America for the newcomer. He did remain here, but stardom proved elusive. However, the comedy ran out the season.

Henri Lavedan's **The Duel** (2-12-06, Hudson), translated by Louis N. Parker, didn't run quite that long, but then it was a more somber evening. A doctor (Guy Standing) falls in love with the wife (Fay Davis) of a dying patient, but his own brother (Otis Skinner), a priest who argues that religion and morality supersede science and expediency, stands in his way. The patient's death ends the argument. The play, in large measure a stirring debate, won high praise, as did most of the performances. But Skinner was brought to task for some florid bits of emoting as well as for employing a French accent when the rest of the cast did not.

The lone novelty on a combination-house stage that night was Owen Davis's **At the World's Mercy** (2-12-06, Star). Like *The Duel*, the play centered on the struggle between two brothers. Only in this case the struggle was not confined to high-flown words. The brothers love the same girl and also have been entrusted with raising a young heiress. The evil brother is a doctor. In league with a corrupt Jewish pawnbroker and an amoral Negro (referred to as "a bad nigger" in one review), he plots to turn his good brother into a drug addict and a drunkard, to kill the heiress, and to wed the girl. The action moved from New York, including the Lower East Side pawnshop, to the mountains, where the heroine and the heiress are imprisoned in a mine, which the villains attempt to blow up. The pawnbroker is eventually killed by a bolt of lightning, and the vicious doctor inadvertently drinks poison meant for his brother.

The producers of Edmund Day's **Behind the Mask** (2-19-06, West End) may have been trying to capitalize on the fame of a Broadway hit when they billed it as "a play of the golden West." Its hero, a miner, has married the daughter of a partner he thought he had killed in self-defense. Actually, the partner has not died, and he now returns in disguise, or, more accurately, a series of disguises. These disguises are a cover for his criminal ways. A jewel theft and a train robbery follow. Just before the final curtain the ex-partner's gang is rounded up, but for the sake of his wife the hero lets her father, who has promised to reform, wander off scot-free.

Two American failures arrived the next evening. Rupert Hughes's **The Triangle** (2-20-06, Manhattan) gave much of its plot away in its title. Under pressure from her mother, a young lady (Charlotte Walker) has spurned an ineligible bachelor (William Morris), whom she loves, and wed a weak but rich man (Ferdinand Gottschalk). When the husband discovers that the wife still sees the bachelor, he goes to kill him. His courage fails. At dinner he tells his wife what happened and adds, "I was too weak to strike him, but I'm not too weak for you!" He stabs her. A butler enters, and the dying wife says to him,

"Remember this. Mr. Enslee and I had a quarrel, and I stabbed myself. Remember this." The curtain falls with the husband groveling at his wife's feet. A novel first-act setting showed golf links at a country club. The other sets were elegant interiors.

In Winston Churchill's **The Title Mart** (2-20-06, Madison Square), an English nobleman (Frank Gillmore) comes to America posing as a commoner to find a suitable girl. He wins the very girl audiences knew he would halfway through the first act, even though she was depicted as something of a hellion.

The season's last show to have a reasonably long run—three months or more—was Rida Johnson Young's **Brown of Harvard** (2-26-06, Princess). Mrs. Young was a cleverly self-promoting Baltimorean who would write several successful plays but would be best recalled for her librettos to *Naughty Marietta* and *Maytime*. Her play seemed clearly indebted to both *The College Widow* and *Strongheart*. Tom Brown (Henry Woodruff) is a rich, handsome Harvard undergraduate, seemingly out just for a good time. On the quiet, he is serious and responsible. When a representative of the students' Lend-a-Hand Club asks him for a donation to assist a poor southerner, Gerald Thorne, through college, Brown agrees to provide a weekly allowance so long as its source remains anonymous. He also writes out a check for a boozy, gambling classmate, only to have the boy steal some blank checks when Brown's back is turned. (For reasons now lost, the character was originally called Wilton Amos, but a few weeks later the name was changed to Wilfred Kenyon, the name in the printed text.) Brown is equally considerate of public reputation. Thorne's sister, Marian, who loves Wilfred but worries about his behavior, comes to Brown's rooms to consult with him about how to reform her fiancé. She inadvertently closes the door, so Brown, unobserved by her, opens it again. Brown himself has reason to be concerned since he loves Wilfred's sister, Evelyn (Laura Hope Crews). Hearing her heading toward his digs with her mother and some other friends, he asks Marian to go into the next room. Then he concocts a ruse to have all the newcomers hide for a time in a third room, so he can sneak Marian out of the dorm. But before he can do that Wilfred returns, very drunk. Brown hides Wilfred in a large chest.

For all his caution Evelyn sees both Marian and Wilfred and angrily leaves. Harvard's big race against a selected team of British oarsmen is coming up, and Thorne is expected to be an important part of the Harvard team. A gambler to whom Wilfred is heavily in debt forces him to pretend to elope with

Marian, knowing that news of the elopement will so upset Thorne that he will not race. The trick almost works, but Brown takes his place and wins. However, Thorne has unearthed one of Brown's stolen checks, which Wilfred had forged and which makes it seem that Brown provided money for the elopement. He comes to Brown's room with a gun, but Wilfred's appearance brings out the truth. Nevertheless, Brown manages to regain Evelyn's affections without exposing her brother's slip to her.

The action moved from Brown's posh rooms to Harvard Yard to the boathouse and back to Brown's rooms. Typical of the play's humor was Brown's response to a student who boasts an 85 in geometry: "Who sat next to you?" The printed text gives some interesting glimpses of period staging. What sort of pacing allowed the boys to stop the action in the second act to sing six college-style songs in succession? Each act was also followed by a carefully planned series of curtain calls. The first, and sometimes the second, curtain call served as miniature epilogues. Thus at the end of Act III the first curtain showed everyone cheering the Harvard victory; the second showed Brown carried on his classmates' shoulders and even included additional dialogue. The picture was retained for the third and fourth calls, after which bows were awarded in a prescribed order. The ninth and final curtain call gave Brown a solo bow. (William Gillette was to put an end to this practice a few years down the road.) The play was the first starring vehicle for Woodruff. He was a strikingly handsome, boyish-looking actor, in his mid-thirties in 1906 and Harvard-educated; some critics felt he was always too self-conscious. Like so many others raised to stardom in this period, he was not a star for long.

With more affluent, sophisticated playgoers being regaled by *The Galloper*, less well heeled, less demanding patrons could enjoy a not too dissimilar story in Charles E. Blaney's **The Boy Behind the Gun** (2-26-06, American). The hero is a young reporter who is sent to cover the Russo-Japanese War. His friends, in true theatrical style, all manage to accompany him. Prominent among these are the girl who loves him—who disguises herself as a lady correspondent and later as a geisha—and his sister, who is lusted after by an abusive Russian count. The count has the girl kidnapped to Port Arthur, with the rest of the principals hot on her trail. They all escape and board a Japanese warship, where, during the Battle of the Sea of Japan, the hero mans a gatling gun to help the Japanese.

The evening on which these plays premiered also saw Joe Weber unveil his spoof *The Squawman of the Golden West* and was to have seen the opening of a play in which Indians were the only characters. Backstage difficulties delayed the opening a few nights, but William A. Brady's production of Donald MacLaren's **The Redskin** (3-1-06, Liberty) finally raised its curtain. Realizing that he is going blind, Lonawanda (Tyrone Power), the aging chief of the Ockotchees, announces he will relinquish his position to whichever warrior his daughter, Adulola (Katherine Gray), selects to marry. She prefers Niatawa (Edwin Arden), but he is not a true warrior, happy instead to wander dreamily through the forest. After his father, Matawagnon, furiously denounces Adulola as illegitimate, Lonawanda accidentally kills Matawagnon. Lashota (Bijou Fernandez), the faithless wife of the chief's adviser, Sheanaugua (Albert Bruning), covets Niatawa for herself. She moves to be rid of her husband and win the young man by telling him her husband, not the chief, was the real killer. When the truth comes out, Niatawa challenges Lonawanda to single combat. Sheanaugua insists on taking the chief's place. Sensing no good can come of all this, Niatawa allows himself to be slain. With his dying breath he begs Adulola not to commit suicide. The forlorn maiden boards a "phantom" canoe and carries her beloved's body across the Lake of Death.

The *Times* began its notice, "The American Indian has been subjected to a great many indignities in his time, but it remained for Donald MacLaren to inflict the final blow." The critic had no kind words for anything else in the production either. Indeed, few reviewers liked the play. They jumped on cardboard, stereotyped characterizations and on such supposed Indian circumlocutions as "bright day's regalia" for sunrise, as well as such un-Indian expressions as "methinks" and "in sooth." But most did welcome Brady's fine mounting, with its realistic teepees and gorgeously feathered Indians, its rousing war dance, and its final, poetic picture. They also hailed Power, whose resonant performance "evoked memories of the old-school tragedians now wrapt in lasting slumber." The play held the boards only until another producer readied a second vehicle for the star.

Several plays throughout the season had called to mind *The Earl of Pawtucket*, which Augustus Thomas had written for Lawrence D'Orsay, but none more than **The Embassy Ball** (3-5-06, Daly's), which Augustus Thomas had written for Lawrence D'Orsay. Once again D'Orsay played a silly Englishman visiting America, where his efforts to be more American than Americans prove ludicrous. And once again he was courting a girl he had met in

Europe but does not recognize. It seems he and the young lady had signed some sort of certificate in Paris, and the certificate turned out to be a marriage license. Luckily for the girl, she signed the name of a friend, and it is that friend the Englishman weds in the last act. Like all too many followups, the new play was a disappointment.

Neither producer Al Woods nor author Owen Davis had yet savored the joy of having a play in a first-class house, but their latest effort, **Chinatown Charlie** (3-5-06, American), pleased the audiences for whom it was intended. The play opens with the titular hero, remorseful about his addictions to drugs and alcohol, about to jump in the river. A pretty lady athlete saves him. This annoys his wicked cousin and a poolroom proprietress who are conspiring to make the wicked cousin the hero's heir. They employ a bagful of mean tricks to undo the hero and his savior. At one moment the hero, who has learned telegraphy, saves himself from death by tapping out a message on a water pitcher to alert a detective. Afterwards the girl is rescued from an opium den to which she has been abducted. Her rescuers are her fellow lady athletes, and they form a human bridge from the roof of the den to a neighboring roof. More troubles are in store before the cousin is shot and the poolroom proprietress led away in handcuffs.

James Kyrle MacCurdy's **The Old Clothes Man** (3-5-06, Third Avenue) began with the murder of a miserly Jewish millionaire and the pinning of the murder on the dead man's son by the villain, who then tricks the daughter of the dead man's cousin, the dealer in old clothes, into marriage. The son is abducted to the usual opium den, from which he is rescued by the girl. He subsequently takes the place of an Irish boxer the villain has drugged and wins the match. He also wins the girl. Somehow the author managed to get all his principals to a music hall, to permit the expected vaudeville turns. The leading role of the old-clothes man, Solomon Levi, "the standard comedy Jew," was taken by none other than the playwright, MacCurdy.

Francis Wilson, gradually winding down his career and apparently determined to end it away from the comic opera stages on which he had made his name, found a two-month success in **The Mountain Climber** (3-6-06, Criterion), which was adapted from Kurt Kraatz's German farce. The vain but craven Montague Sibsey had written home while on vacation detailing his mountain-climbing adventures, feats of daring he never dared but instead cribbed from a book he came across. On his return home he is horrified to learn that his letters have

been published in book form and that he is expected to show his climbing skills. A mountain never before mastered has been selected, and a photographer is to accompany him. To add to his woes, the author of the book he stole from comes to town. He eventually bribes the two men into silence by offering them his stepdaughters in marriage and, with feigned reluctance, promises his hysterical wife never again to go scaling peaks. The show was all Wilson. "To recount his troubles with the photographer whose dreadful camera he sought to avoid, . . . to follow him to the mountain inn at which his ghost appeared; and to attempt to indicate all the sinuosities of the lively two-step progress he was forced to make through the action, would be to make a motion picture by means of type," one critic observed. The final curtain call was interesting. Sibsey and his family are happily and "safely" reunited at home. Serenaders are heard outside. "The stage was darkened for a moment. Then with a quick change, the audience saw directly in front of them the [neoclassic] exterior of the house, with the characters bowing and smiling and laughing and waving their handkerchiefs" at the supposed serenaders, the audience.

Well into the run, Austin Strong and Lloyd Osborne's **The Little Father of the Wilderness** (4-16-06) was added as a curtain raiser. It represented a total change of pace for Wilson. Now old and bent, Père Marlotte has returned to France after proselytizing for years to Canadian Indians. Imagine his thrill when Louis XV (William Lewers) summons him to court, and imagine his crestfallen reaction after the king tells him he merely wants the good father to settle a bet about how high Niagara Falls is. The father tells Louis that the king has lost his bet. Louis turns away abruptly, and the courtiers ridicule the poor priest. A band of Indians is brought in. Seeing Père Marlotte, they kneel, hailing him as the Little Father of the Wilderness. Louis is so moved that he makes the priest an archbishop.

There was some fine music played both onstage and off in Ivy Ashton Root's **The Greater Love** (3-19-06, Madison Square). The music was Mozart's, since this loosely constructed, episodic drama purported to depict incidents in the composer's life. The incidents were strung together on a thin story line, which disclosed how the treacherous Schikaneder nearly sabotages the Prague premiere of *Don Giovanni* by persuading a prima donna not to appear. Another prima donna, La Mandini, who earlier had gotten Mozart out of a similar fix, rushes to his aid again. In gratitude the composer (Howard Kyle) tells her that any music he writes thereafter will have her as its inspiration. He then sits down to start on his last requiem. The final tableau, showing the composer's death, replicated a picture hanging at the time in New York's Metropolitan Museum. Critics were sharply divided on the play, calling it everything from a libel on Mozart to the season's most underrated drama. In the face of such disparate notices, the play ran one month.

Two old plays also returned the same evening. At the Manhattan, *Charley's Aunt* began a ten-week stand, with Etienne Giradot once more Lord Fancourt Babberley. At the New Amsterdam, Richard Mansfield came in for a three-week visit. His opening attraction was new to his repertory but not unknown to dedicated playgoers, Schiller's *Don Carlos*. He offered only a few performances of the work, for the rest of his engagement hastily running through the gamut of his old standbys.

For some years a tall, slim, craggy-faced man named Benjamin Chapin had been roaming Lyceum circuits, giving a one-man show about Lincoln. Perhaps inevitably, he turned his knowledge and experience into a play, with himself as star. Like *The Greater Love,* **Lincoln** (3-26-06, Liberty) was highly episodic. It unfolded almost entirely in the White House, starting with the firing on Fort Sumter and ending with the president leaving for a night out at the theatre. In between, besides touching on war matters, it depicted Lincoln's home life and told of the courtship of a niece of Mrs. Lincoln (Maude Granger) by a Confederate spy. The play was warmly received but failed to find a large audience.

Farcical turns of plot kept interest alive in Edgar Selwyn's **It's All Your Fault** (4-2-06, Savoy) and won it a month's run. To ensure himself a place in his uncle's will, Howard Beasley (Selwyn) tells his obese uncle that the Beasley son has been given the uncle's name, Caxton. The problem is that Beasley has no son. When the uncle comes to visit, Beasley is hard pressed. At that moment, Archibald (Master Pincus), a runaway from a home for difficult boys, climbs through the window. He is drafted to impersonate the nonexistent Caxton. Before the evening is over the uncle, Howard, and Howard's friend, Jack, who has posed as the boy's tutor, are all saddled with the lad's paternity. The boy turns out to be the son of a governess the uncle has employed. Master Pincus was revealed to be a former newsboy, Pincus Lekosky. One reviewer noted he "provided a touch of vulgar realism and translated the patois of the streets to the Savoy stage."

The Curse of Drink (4-9-06, American) was a temperance melodrama centering on a drunken locomotive engineer. His daughter is kidnapped by four villains and tied to the tracks over which his train is about to come hurtling. The chief villain's embittered "wife in the sight of heaven" and her Irish friend rush to free the girl, but they, too, are set upon and tied and gagged. After the Irishman succeeds in removing the wife's gag, she bites free of her ropes. The pair are struggling to save the girl as the lights of the train strike the track. On board the engine is a young man who is at one and the same time the heroine's lover, the son of the railroad's president, and the train's fireman. As the engine comes in sight from the wings, he is seen on the cowcatcher. He reaches down and grabs the girl in his arms. Her grateful father raises his hands skyward and vows never again to touch liquor. At a party celebrating the rescue and the couple's betrothal, a man appears in a Santa Claus costume. He is really the chief villain. He removes a package from his pocket and pours its contents into the fruit punch, exclaiming, "Strychnine! Now die like dogs." But his wife exposes him, and he runs out and shoots himself. In the era's topsy-turvy world of sensation-melodrama, the villain and his cronies were played by men who also constituted the "Electric Comedy Four." In this guise they participated in the variety turns, leading one critic to muse, "Before they have finished the first number one can understand what it was that drove [the engineer] to drink."

William Crane's latest vehicle was Charles T. Dazey and George Broadhurst's **The American Lord** (4-16-06, Hudson). Crane had been touring in the comedy all season. He played John Breuster, a North Dakotan who inherits vast estates in England. Breuster hurries over but is greeted with rampant anti-Americanism. A neighboring lord is especially antagonistic and takes his new neighbor into court. Matters are resolved after Breuster's daughter elopes with the lord's son and Breuster settles the property on the young couple. He also finds romance with an Irish widow (Hilda Spong). The comedy ran a month.

Edward A. Parry and Frederick Mouillot's English farce **What the Butler Saw** (4-16-06, Garrick) ran half as long. Its initial situation was much like *The American Lord*'s. In this instance a London cabby (Frank Gillmore) inherits an estate and a title, but no money, so he converts the estate into a health spa, where an odd assortment of guests provide the complications.

Tyrone Power discarded his warpaint and feathers to assume a totally different role in Alice M. Smith and Charlotte Thompson's **The Strength of the Weak** (4-17-06, Liberty). He portrayed a man whose son (Eugene Ormonde) falls in love with and proposes to marry the young mistress (Florence Roberts) his father has maintained. Since the man has used a false name in his relationship with the girl, she does not realize her dilemma (or theirs) until father and son meet in her presence. Her reaction is to commit suicide. Florence Roberts was a beautiful woman and San Francisco's leading actress. Although she was accorded highly laudatory notices, one comparing her to Mrs. Fiske, she rarely played New York, preferring the security of her West Coast stardom. Neither she nor Power could make a success of what many saw as a repulsive drama.

Arnold Daly's revival of *Arms and the Man* that night at the Lyric proved more acceptable, running six weeks, with *How He Lied to Her Husband* added on for the final fortnight.

Sydney Rosenfeld's brightly titled **The Optimist** (4-23-06, Daly's) limped away after a single dismal week. In that short time it recounted the tale of Jack (Wallace Eddinger), who has been jilted by Phyllis (Kathryn Browne) and is taken under the wing of the perenially sunny Norman (J. H. Gilmour). Norman assures Jack things will turn out for the best. They do, in a way. Phyllis comes crawling back to Jack, and he has the pleasure of bidding her good-bye.

Nor could Amelia Bingham find takers for Lawrence Marston and R. E. H. Greene's **Jeanne D'Arc** (4-23-06, Fifth Ave.). One critic saw the part as "entirely beyond her grasp."

A house afire, and the hero and his antagonist battling themselves splash into the river, were the sort of ingredients almost certain to excite less critical audiences at Edwin M. Simmonds's **The Man of Her Choice** (4-23-06, Murray Hill). Like his sensation scenes, Simmonds's basic plot was old hat—a rich heroine courted by a man who genuinely loves her and by another who wants her for her money and will stop at little to get it.

The second one-week failure in as many weeks was Frederick Paulding's **Cousin Louisa** (4-30-06, Daly's). Paulding, good-looking and well connected, had aspired twenty years earlier to a stardom his limited abilities denied him. Now middle-aged, he was forced to accept small supporting roles and hope fame would come as a playwright. Here, too, his skills were sadly wanting. Paulding's play apparently was a satire on greed. His heroine (Mary Van Buren) is a widow whose late husband has left it to her to distribute his estate. She visits her relatives, many of whom she has never met before, incognito and sees them for what they are. She also meets her first husband (Charles Cherry), whom she had divorced because he was so poor a provider. When he refuses to remarry her because of her money,

Louisa, now all too aware of the price of greed, gives most of her money away.

Not all touring plays were sensation-melodramas. Edward E. Rose's **A Square Deal** (4-30-06, 14th St.) was billed as a "political comedy drama." Its title apparently was borrowed from Teddy Roosevelt, and, according to some commentators, its plot was lifted from *The County Chairman*. Its hero is Hannibal Hawkins, a Kansan who has helped educate a promising lawyer. When Hannibal learns that the young man is courting the same schoolmarm that Hannibal has thought about marrying, he gallantly steps aside. His feelings change when the lawyer begins to rise in politics, forgets his promise to give his constituents a square deal, and aligns himself with corrupt legislators. Hannibal thereupon runs for office himself, exposes and defeats his protégé, and weds the teacher. An election-night scene, the stage filled with a hundred supers, many carrying placards and torches, was hailed for its verisimilitude. And the scene in which the repentant lawyer rushes into the Senate chamber to denounce his own bill won cheers from the gallery.

Critical cheers were more muted for Louis K. Anspacher's **The Embarrassment of Riches** (5-14-06, Wallack's), but even several reviewers who could find little to cheer about suggested the young playwright showed promise. That promise would be fulfilled once, a decade on. Meanwhile, Anspacher's offering, which mixed social comedy with farcical touches, had its compensations. Elizabeth Holt (Charlotte Walker) is a rich, beautiful girl who is so preoccupied with helping the poor that she has little time for an English duke who comes courting. Instead she busies herself at a Lower East Side settlement house run by John Russell (Bruce McRae), although, from a certain reluctance to place herself in the spotlight, she pretends to be her own secretary. The building next door is supposed to be a synagogue but actually is a gambling house. When it is raided, many of the gamblers, who are revealed as Elizabeth's social friends, try to escape by climbing into the settlement house's windows. One window drops shut, trapping a lady. But the police, unable to differentiate between escapees and social workers, arrest everyone in sight. After they are bailed out, Elizabeth realizes she loves John. A subplot concerned Elizabeth's cousin, who is blackmailed by a former employee of the settlement house. This girl's lover is a crook working at the gambling house. Both Miss Walker and McRae were praised for their light, charming comic touch, but the evening's honors went to fat, pasty-faced John Bunny as a loud-mouthed, know-it-all ward heeler.

(It was a small role, and earlier in the evening Bunny had portrayed a thick-brogued Irish servant.)

The Lower East Side was also the setting for Charles E. Blaney's **Old Isaacs from the Bowery** (5-14-06, American), which rehashed material from innumerable plays, most obviously *The Auctioneer.* Old Isaacs has won a measure of respectability and fortune running a pawnshop, but his beloved daughter has run off with a worthless Christian. Before the pair eloped they not only stole jewels from the shop but also sold him worthless mining stock. He is reduced to beggary and hustled away by his daughter to an insane asylum. The old man's son and a girl whom he has adopted remain loyal, entrap his scheming son-in-law, and effect a reconciliation between father and now wiser daughter. The worthless stock turns out to be worth hundreds of thousands.

Fast-changing notions of dramatic credibility led some commentators to scoff at the very notion of building a plot around a changeling. Apparently Jane Maudlin Feigl's **The Girl Patsy** (5-26-06, Savoy) lacked even a well-told plot. Its heroine (Mary Ryan) had been secretly exchanged years before for another baby. Patsy has grown up poor; the other girl has been raised in comfort. But after this second young lady elopes with her family's groom, a young artist who adores Patsy is able to show Patsy is the real heiress.

It was still customary at this time for programs to characterize figures in plays. The playbill for Robert Crookes's **The Goldfields of Nevada** (6-4-06, American) informed its readers that the hero, who had come west after a scapegrace existence in the effete East, was "fighting for lost ground," and that the lady he loved was "a true-hearted girl." Unfortunately, her father is determined that she marry another man and is blind to the fact that this man is a scoundrel only after the girl's money. The scoundrel blows up a safe containing the hero's cash, but the girl's quick-thinking, tomboyish maid, who witnessed the robbery, switches valises, leaving the man to run off with a suitcase filled with old newspapers.

This hardly deters him. Fortunately, the hero and heroine have a steadfast friend in a noble Indian, who is resolved to help them any way he can and who "explains this carefully to the audience in approved Wild West gutturals, ejaculations and grunts."

Neil Twomey's "rural comedy-drama" **The Postmaster's Daughter** (6-11-06, Grand Opera) brought down the curtain on the season. The heroine is the daughter of a Maine grocer and postmaster and of his Arizona-born wife. Having been raised at times in both states, she is a curious mixture of New England yokel and western hoyden. But that does not prevent a wealthy New Yorker from marrying her. His family looks down upon her for her Down East and Wild West upbringing, and her continuing impetuosity (she drenches the hero's uncle with a hose) ultimately leads to a split. But a reconciliation follows, with the couple heading for Europe to give the heroine some polish. Of course, there were dramatic moments. The heroine's rejected New England suitor goes after the hero with an axe, which the heroine grabs, telling the suitor her father needs it to chop kindling. And the hero's snobbish brother intercepts the hero's letters offering to kiss and make up.

No purpose would be served by underscoring that this last play was American or that its theme was the same as that of the great new American play that would provide a sort of theatrical breakthrough in the next season. Most, possibly all, theatrical revolutions are seen in retrospect merely as evolutions. Nor would much be achieved by pointing out that the very type of designed-for-touring play *The Postmaster's Daughter* represented belonged to a moribund genre. Films would write *finis* to it before the next great scene of American drama was over. For the next eight years a new, true, modern American style of dramaturgy would flex its muscles, preparing the way for the brilliant outpouring that would appear on American stages just as Europe became enbroiled in World War I.

ACT FIVE
1906–1914

The Advance Guard
of the New Drama

1906–1907

Given the lofty perspective that comes with twenty years' hindsight, one pioneering American theatrical historian, Arthur Hobson Quinn, saw the 1906–07 season as seminal, ushering in, with a remarkable succession of plays, "the advance guard of the new drama" and offering in a single theatrical year "about as many permanent additions to our dramatic literature as in the five years previous." Another sixty-odd years on, scholars might question the number of permanent additions with which the season enriched our stage, but most would agree, albeit no doubt with personal qualifications, on its significance as a breakaway year. Appropriately, what many of the more progressive critics saw as its best and most interesting play was entitled *The Great Divide*. In retrospect several other developments would prove critical to the future of American drama. Some months earlier, in 1905, George Pierce Baker had initiated his playwriting course at Harvard. Out of it would come many of our finest dramatists. The Society of Dramatic Authors was founded in 1906. It soon disappeared, as had such predecessors as the 1878 American Dramatic Authors' Society and the 1891 American Dramatists Club, but it again called attention to the need of playwrights not only to attain better financial treatment but to exert more artistic independence. Although decline would not become evident for many years, the season also marked the apogee for the American road. The burgeoning, irresistible rise of films would see to it that never again would so many companies of so many plays move from city to city for so many weeks between any August and any succeeding June. One by one small towns lost their lone source of live entertainment, as did many blue-collar areas in larger cities. Each season the count of defecting houses swelled. To the extent that patrons lost were largely ignorant, backwater yokels and equally unlettered newsboys, factory girls, or the plumber and his date (to whom George M. Cohan insisted he played), playhouses could hope to find themselves left with more enlightened audiences. The hope was not always realized, and much of the fun demanded by and often provided by a riotous gallery vanished from the American theatre.

Contemporaries, denied hindsight, naturally took a somewhat different view of the season. As usual, because of varying approaches, they could not even agree how many productions Broadway had seen. *Variety,* in a count made some years later, recorded 67 new plays, 34 new musicals, and 28 revivals, for a total of 129. *Theatre* listed 124 new plays and musicals. The *Dramatic Mirror,* the most comprehensive of chroniclers, tallied 238 new plays and musicals, with 116 of them in first-class (or "producing") houses, 67 at combination houses, 17 at stock theatres, and 38 at other venues. The paper devoted more than a full page—four elongated columns of minuscule print—to its list of "Old Plays and Revivals" but didn't stop to add them up.

As with the number game, newspapers and trade sheets offered end-of-season assessments displaying varying shades of opinion. To the degree that there was a consensus, it emerged on three salient points. The first and least important was the ongoing vogue for dramatized novels, a practice virtually all commentators decried. Second, observers rued what they saw as a lamentable, disproportionate number of failures. Unfortunately, none of the writers made clear whether he was speaking of artistic or commercial failure. By the standards of eight or more decades later, theatrical economics in 1906 seem almost utopian. Many a show that found no welcome in New York and left the Rialto in the red subsequently cleaned up on the road. Producers often willingly took a loss on a forced, extended New York run in order to advertise a lengthy Broadway stay in the hinterlands. But even if writers were referring to artistic shortfalls, and even if there were a dismaying number of disappointments, it was in one respect a wonderful season. Critics and public alike understood that American drama truly had begun to find itself. *Theatre*'s summation was headed "Past Season a Triumph for the American Playwright." Of the seven straight plays to run over 200 performances, six were native efforts. Of course, history relishes its ironies. None of the fascinating American hits of the 1906–07 season has had a major revival for half a century. (Nor, for that matter, has the season's long-running English hit.) Only Shaw's then controversial plays have held the stage.

Pauline Phelps and Marion Short's **Sweet Clover** (7-16-06, 125th St.) had been offered in numerous cities around the country for the past four or five seasons and was new only to Manhattan. Its genre was equivocal. The trade sheet hedged by calling it a "semi-rural comedy-drama." Its heroine, raised in ignorance of her mother's elopement with a married man, falls in love with an artist who turns out to be the man's son. She breaks off her engagement and weds another suitor. The spurned artist tries to talk her into eloping, and her new husband threatens to kill the artist, but all ends happily. The 125th Street Theatre, once Hammerstein's Harlem Opera House, had recently been taken over by two vaudeville giants, Keith and Proctor, who alternated seasons of variety and stock. Combination houses, those theatres devoted to touring productions, began to relight at month's end. Two reopened on the same night.

In Al Woods's production of Owen Davis's **The Gambler of the West** (7-28-06, American) an attractive heiress from the East Coast arrives at a rough-and-tumble mining camp in search of her long-lost father and brother. The villain, abetted by several unsavory cronies, covets the girl's money and attempts to force her into marriage. He is opposed by the latest of countless melodramatic heroes named Jack—more specifically in this instance, Lucky Jack. Jack is "a square gambler," that is, an honest one. He helps the heroine learn the fate of her father (scalped by the Indians) and her brother (raised by the red men as once of their own), and he ends up marrying the girl. Big moments included the holdup of a stage, the heroine tied to a tree as "red devils throw big knives so they stick in the bark close to her side and head," a "vivid" prairie fire, and a trained horse pulling a rope that raises an American flag to the top of a pole (the signal to effect the heroine's final rescue). Comedy relief was provided by the character of a Jewish Indian, with additional lighter moments supplied by the expected specialty acts. The applause for all this reportedly was "ear-splitting."

Davis's turns of plot were simplicity itself compared with the wild convolutions in Finley Pauley's **The King of Diamonds** (7-28-06, Third Ave.). At the Church of St. Mary the Virgin in New York, a young girl marries a rich old man. The bride really prefers a handsome fellow her own age, but she has agreed to the wedding to save her father from bankruptcy. A villain (with an identifying oiled and pointed mustache) and his adventuress-cohort (in a finger-pointing red dress) enter, bent on making trouble. He hopes to have the heroine for himself, and his sidekick wants to avenge the groom's dismissal of her. Also on the scene is a feisty reporter from an East Side Jewish newspaper. He prevents the bride and the adventuress from slashing each other as the first-act curtain falls. The next act finds all the principals on a western ranch, where the heroine proclaims, "I love John Hampton, but with God's help I will be faithful to my marriage vows," and where the villains murder the groom, then pin the killing on the heroine's true love. He is sentenced to prison. So is the newspaperman, for allegedly stealing a donkey. The two befriend a third prisoner, who dies after revealing to them the whereabouts of a diamond mine. The hero and the reporter escape. The fourth act takes place two years later. The heroine has returned to New York and works in Mrs. Osborne's famous dress shop (carefully replicated onstage). She is kidnapped by the villains and placed on a subway train hurtling toward Long Island. A man known as Dick Downing, King of Diamonds, hires a second train and, in the tunnel, rescues the heroine. Dick proves to be John Hampton. He has found the lost mine and now is rich. What's more, the newspaperman belatedly discloses that he has a photograph showing who really committed the murder two years before. The reporter was played by an actor who performed several specialties, which were "encored repeatedly." Two interesting sidelights. The refurbished playhouse was rechristened officially Dixon's Third Avenue Family Theatre, suggesting the audience it was seeking. However, it remained generally known by its shorter, older name. Yet even the families that attended this popular-priced house must have had some money to spare; the *Dramatic Mirror* reported the presence of ticket speculators in front of the theatre.

The Harlem stock company that had given New York its first, belated taste of *Sweet Clover* did the same for another play that had been produced around the country for several seasons, **Drusa Wayne** (8-6-06, 125th St.). The playwright was Franklyn Fyles, for so long drama critic on the *Sun*. Fyles's heroine had been violated while she was unconscious and has vowed to find the culprit and be avenged. A need for nurses during the Spanish-American War prompts her to set aside her quest temporarily. Of course, the badly wounded officer from the Rough Riders whom she is tending turns out to be the very man she has sought. Despite the machinations of the usual villainous duo—a malevolent thief and the heroine's jealous, scheming rival—Drusa's hate gives way to love and forgiveness and, in time, a wedding band.

Villainous scheming of sorts was responsible for the season's initial production at a first-class house.

With Bertha Kalish under contract to him, Harrison Grey Fiske announced that he would star her in an English version of her Yiddish success, Jacob Gordin's **The Kreutzer Sonata.** For all the publicity Yiddish plays and players had been receiving lately, their uptown reception had been modest, so there was little reason to think further about the matter. Broadwayites in the know were startled to read that Lincoln A. Wagenhals and Collin Kemper, two rising young producers who had taken over the lease for the soon to open Astor Theatre, had added another English version to their schedule for the new playhouse. They promised the offering as a late-season attraction. Probably hoping to forestall their production, Fiske let it be known his mounting would premiere September 10. A firm date was all the young go-getters needed to discover. In cahoots with William A. Brady, Wagenhals and Kemper rushed their effort into secret rehearsals and announced abruptly on Friday, August 10, that they would have it ready for critical inspection at the Manhattan the very next Monday, the 13th. Booking the Manhattan must have been like rubbing salt into Fiske's wounded pride, since the theatre had been home base for Fiske and his wife until a few months earlier. And open it did—to a critical shellacking.

The drama, which was assailed as "morbid," "unsavory," and "a picture . . . of Jewish Life . . . as libelous as it is scandalous," focused on a wealthy Russian Jew's daughter, pregnant by a Christian officer. His family's outrage at his offer to marry the girl drives the soldier to suicide. The girl's father persuades a corrupt, mercenary musician to wed her and take her to America. Her father, mother, and sister eventually follow the couple, but before long the sister has connived to involve her brother-in-law in an affair with her. The older girl, driven to distraction by her own and her family's misfortunes, kills her husband and her sluttish sister.

The critics cared no more for the production than they did for the play. Apart from Blanche Walsh, a fine actress uncomfortably miscast in the leading role of Miriam Friedlander (called Hattie in this redaction), the performers were not of the first rank. Nor were the sets, the costumes, or the direction. By the time Fiske brought in Langdon Mitchell's superior translation to the Lyric on September 10, the competing version had departed, and Miss Walsh was spotted watching from a box. Most reviewers, while not appreciably softening their stance on the play, found much to admire in the production, especially Bertha Kalish's intuitive, warm portrayal of Miriam. Yet the hordes of playgoers swarming through the theatre district

nightly were not interested. The Fiske-Kalish version closed after only nineteen performances.

No fewer than four novelties appeared at Manhattan's combination houses the same evening. One was not entirely new, for Theodore Kremer's **Bertha, the Sewing Machine Girl** (8-13-06, American) used the same title and the same basic story as had Charles Foster's 1871 dramatization of the *New York Weekly*'s all but forgotten serial. Of course, names were changed to protect both the innocents and their oppressors, and to avoid legal haggles; since titles cannot be copyrighted, that presented no problem. Not surprisingly, advertisements carried no acknowledgments of the play's antecedents. On the other hand, few reviewers recalled—or, if they did, thought it worthwhile to mention—that Foster's melodrama and older copycat versions had been among the most popular of early touring plays. Kremer's Bertha, whose surname is Sloane, comes to New York with her blind sister, Jessie, and with two noble purposes in mind. She intends to earn enough money to provide Jessie with a sight-restoring operation, and she hopes to locate her long-missing father. The sisters are unaware their father has been murdered. His killer's son and the son's hard-mouthed girl await Bertha and Jessie's arrival at Grand Central, determined the youngsters shall not lay claim to their father's wealth. Bertha is chloroformed, placed in a red automobile, and carried off to "an uncharted cave in Central Park," then thrown into a lake. She is rescued by a young man (who soon falls in love with Jessie), while the villains are held at bay by a German lady (Mrs. Katzenkopf, who keeps the boardinghouse where the girls plan to stay) and a young fireman (who quickly becomes Bertha's protector and suitor). Since all this occurs early in the first of four acts, the villains escape to commit more mayhem. Among other trials, Bertha is tossed on a moving belt heading for two huge, dovetailing wheels and later falsely accused of murder. Jessie is cast into irons and also trapped in a burning building. Although it usually falls to Mrs. Katzenkopf and the girls' admirers to come to the rescue, Bertha rides up to the fire-engulfed building at the wheel of a fire engine ("an extremely shaky fire engine," wrote one critic, which "thoroughly destroyed the realism of the scene").

An increasingly popular young Joseph Santley was credited with Walter Woods as co-author of **Billy the Kid** (8-13-06), Star), his latest starring vehicle. In this retelling of the famous saga, Billy's mother and stepfather are killed by the villain, who is none other than Billy's natural father, and Billy vows to live an outlaw life until he can avenge the deaths. Plots and counterplots follow hectically (if not fast enough for some). In one scene the murderer and his buddies are playing cards at a ranch as they await an opportunity to seize the hero. Billy fools them by appearing as a waitress and removing their guns while he pretends to serve wine. Then, "throwing off his dress and wig, he keeps them all at bay until he can break through a window and reach his horse outside." After the villain is killed and mistakenly identified as Billy, since he is wearing Billy's hat and coat, the hero renounces outlawry and walks peacefully away, hand in hand with his sweetheart. Although critics assailed the play as "superpuerile bravado" and faulted the production for not being "played fast enough to keep the audience in the state of excitement demanded by patrons of this type of drama," the melodrama toured all season.

There was no villain in Charles E. Blaney's **A Child of the Regiment** (8-13-06, 14th St.). At worst, a gentlemanly colonel comes to blows with an impudent Englishman, fatally strangles him, then loses all memory of the incident. A reformed gambler, who loves the colonel's daughter and who serves under him, assumes the blame. Before he can be shot for a murder he did not commit, he escapes, trailed closely by the cute, adoring regimental mascot, a blonde, curly-headed tot known as "the Little Major." The pair suffer through a blizzard ("a very good stereoptican blizzard indeed, with plenty of wind and waving trees"), an Indian attack, and other vicissitudes before the little lassie helps clear the hero's name and unite him with his beloved.

By contrast, there was never a shortage of villains or villainy in San Francisco's Chinatown, as Fred Summerfield and Della Clarke's **On Dangerous Ground** (8-13-06, Thalia) reminded playgoers. Its heroine is the usual sweet, smiling, moralizing innocent who elects to go slumming for the fun of it. At a Chinese music hall she is forced to konk a slimy "Chink" over the head with a music stand. Later she is drugged, then saved from a burning building when the hero carries her from one roof to another, "walking on what is meant to suggest a clothes line but is evidently a board." Inevitably the Chinese get their comeuppance, and "when the hero delivered a tirade against the Chinese population the applause of the audience was unmistakably spontaneous and sincere." The Thalia, by the way, once better known as the Bowery, was New York's oldest playhouse, celebrating its eightieth year.

The next Monday combination houses changed, or in some cases simply traded, bills. *On Dangerous Ground* switched stages with *Billy the Kid*. A new

version of *Dr. Jekyll and Mr. Hyde*, this one by Oscar Dane, took over the Third Avenue. Two more genuine novelties also appeared. The lesser of the two was John Oliver's **Ruled Off the Turf** (8-20-06, 14th St.), in which a young jockey (his name is Jack) is subjected to all manner of tribulations after he refuses his boss's order to throw a race. Described by one reviewer as "a racing drama . . . interrupted by songs, dances and revolver shots," it could also be perceived as a stage documentary, recreating on canvas settings of contemporary interest. Besides a stable and a yacht, the action unfolded on Union Square and in or in front of such new attractions as the Hippodrome and the Astor Hotel (where a song and dance by two pink-gowned girls preceded the revolver shots of a rescue scene in a hotel corridor).

Owen Davis's second touring melodrama of the season held far more interest. **The Power of Money; or, In the Clutches of the Trust** (8-20-06, American) was the latest theatrical attack on the growing trusts. Its hero has obtained a formula for manufacturing firebrick cheaply, but he rejects the monopolists' insultingly low offer and so brings upon himself all the genre's traditional escapades. He is reduced to poverty, evicted with his poor mother from their home, and gouged in the eye, and his arm is nearly crushed in a letter-press. Time and again he is saved by the last-minute arrival of his fiancée, who is the chief monopolist's daughter, and a friendly, comic black named Shiny (played, as was still the custom, by a white in blackface). The play's striking finale introduced two figures who had taken no part in the action but who appeared to urge on the hero. They were actors impersonating a cigar-smoking William Randolph Hearst and a toothy President Roosevelt. Unlike *The Lion and the Mouse* or similar dramas slated for a more sophisticated audience, *The Power of Money* made no attempt to find a middle ground for any of its characters, painting all of them either totally evil or good. Clearly Davis knew what his lower-class audiences, "aroused to mighty enthusiasm," sought. On its subsequent tour the play's title was changed to *From Tramp to Millionaire*.

If trusts were coming under increasing attack, so was the rigid public morality that allowed playwrights of Davis's stamp to depict people as extreme, unshaded examples. St. John Hankin's **The Two Mr. Wetherbys** (8-23-06, Madison Square) represented a newer, more enlightened, or at least more tolerant, school of thought. Richard Wetherby (William F. Hawtrey) is something of a scapegrace. His wife, Constantia (May Tully), has left him, but he meets her once a year to consider a reconciliation. Richard's brother, James (Hall McAllister), is a paragon of virtue, bridling under the restraints his goodness imposes on him. Richard persuades him to have a night on the town. This almost leads to a split between James and his wife, Margaret (Mabel Cameron). Richard's reasoning averts a crisis and even aids him in effecting a reunion of sorts with Constantia. If the ending was equivocal, it was not irrational. Hankin, a fine second-string English playwright now neglected, pleaded against "happy" endings, arguing they were essentially false. This comedy marked his American debut as well as that of Hawtrey, Charles's brother. Neither man was to win much popularity in America. *The Two Mr. Wetherbys* ran just three weeks.

A second importation from London, Michael Morton's farce **The Little Stranger** (8-27-06, Hackett), which the author derived from Edward S. Van Zile's *Clarissa's Troublesome Baby,* proved no more successful. One reviewer dismissed it as a "freak" play. To cure his wife of her infatuation for a fake miracle man and to expose the charlatan, a husband substitutes a midget for his baby. When the "baby" smokes, drinks whiskey, and even woos mama, consternation ensues. Critics enjoyed the performance of the seventeen-year-old English midget, who was billed as Master Edward Garratt, but they had small praise for the farce itself, the rest of the cast, or the mishap-plagued opening night.

While London shows threatened to usurp Manhattan's first-class stages, American hacks provided combination houses with a continuing flow of attractions. In Charles E. Blaney's second offering of the season, **A Bad Man from Mexico** (8-27-06, American), a duplicitous count attempts to appropriate a Mexican mine belonging to his American ward, but an old friend of the girl's parents—he was called Easy Lead—rights matters by summoning the U.S. Army. A spurned mistress puts an end to the count's misery with a well-placed bullet.

Owen Davis was equally prolific. His third opus of the still young season was **Secrets of the Police** (8-27-06, Thalia), written in collaboration with Arthur J. Lamb. Their story crossed more borders than did Blaney's. Since an American detective loves an English heiress whom a French baron pays Russian nihilists to kidnap, the action speeds from New York to London to Paris and finally to Moscow. Before the expected denouement in a spooky "Den of the Red Ring," hero and heroine undergo similarly expected harrowings. Their rescue often comes at the hands of a clownish Hebrew tramp known as Alias, who apparently needs no passport or tickets. In one minor departure, one of the villains, not the hero, was named Jack.

But convention was honored on another stage that night. The hero of Jay Hunt's **The Master Workman** (8-27-06, 14th St.) was named Jack Mitchell. He is a mill foreman who adores the sweet daughter of his greedy, capitalistic boss. The boss's treacherous nephew connives to have Jack convicted of murder and sent to Sing Sing, but Jack's union helps clear his name. One critic observed, "The play is filled with lines upholding the rights of the laboring man, and depends upon this feature for the measure of success it achieved." Of course, its more thrilling moments did not go for naught, and like all such plays it relied heavily on specialties. The same reviewer reported that the actor who played the office boy was the most popular member of the cast, and his interpolated parodies were encored."

Hilda Spong's first outing as a star was ill-fated. Harold Heaton's **Lady Jim** (8-29-06, Weber's) recounted the misadventures that befall a well-meaning woman after she pries into the private life of her niece's groom-to-be.

An oldtimer, William H. Crane, depended on the large following he had developed over the years for his modest run in Alfred Sutro's London drama **The Price of Money** (8-29-06, Garrick). He portrayed a financially hard-up editor of a small magazine. For a short while, he succumbs to his acquisitive brother's offer of a chance to make a large sum unethically by helping to obtain the deed to a mine, but he ultimately shreds the instrument and resigns himself to genteel poverty. Crane was at his best depicting shrewd, big-hearted blusterers, so this role gave him few opportunities to appear in top form.

Another English drama, Henry Arthur Jones's **The Hypocrites** (8-30-06, Hudson), became the season's first smash hit and undoubtedly confounded prognosticators by turning out to be the season's only English play to fall into that select category. Because it was presented to New York before being offered to London (where it flopped), a tenuous argument could be offered branding it American by adoption. A rich young man (Richard Bennett), about to make a most profitable marriage, is careless enough to render a working girl (Doris Keane) pregnant. His pretentious, arrogant parents (J. H. Barnes and Jessie Millward) are prepared to stop at nothing to brush the scandal under a rug, but the local curate (Leslie Faber) determines that the truth must come out, especially since the parents often have railed cruelly and publicly about poor people in the same predicament. He prods the boy into a confession.

Critics admitted that the play was almost dangerously melodramatic, but they added that Jones's intelligent observations and dialogue and, more to the point, superb playing kept the evening free of excess. Young Bennett's carefully nuanced performance gave his career a vigorous leg up. Miss Millward was showered with compliments as the hateful mother. And the relatively unknown Doris Keane "revealed unsuspected strength" as the girl.

The next evening Broadway welcomed a still bigger, unquestionably American hit, James Forbes's slangy, sharp-tongued look at backstage life, **The Chorus Lady** (9-1-06, Savoy). Patricia O'Brien (Rose Stahl), who has taken work as a chorus girl to help support her family and gain herself a measure of independence, returns home when the show she has been in folds. It really wasn't a very good show: "I never noticed anyone laff themselves to death. The comedians was a couple of morgues. The best joke in the show was the star, one of them hand-made blondes. She was in the original 'Black Crook' company an' she had a daughter at school *then*." Home for Pat has been a small house by the racing stables where her father is a trainer. The owner, Dan Mallory (Wilfred Lucas), has been courting her. Pat's sister, Nora (Eva Dennison), longs for Pat's freedom and pocket money. She is not above placing secret bets to provide herself a small income, although such betting could jeopardize her father's position if it became known. Unfortunately for Nora, her betting has put her in debt. When Dick Crawford (Francis Byrne), a handsome young man, buys part interest in the stables from the financially pinched Dan, she confesses her problem, and he agrees to pay the debt.

Nora's persistence finally prods Pat into allowing Nora to join her in the chorus of a new musical. Dressing-room talk is an odd mixture: gossipy, ill-informed, starry-eyed, egocentric, and bitchy. Pat mentions she has seen Mrs. Leslie Carter buying spangles at Macy's.

Inez: Did you see her close to?
Pat: I could a touched her. I rubbered to beat the band. Don't you just love Carter?
Inez: You bet.
Pat: Honest, I think that woman's got the most emotional hair in the business. . . . You know, Carter's a whole lot on my style.
Simpson: I hadn't noticed it.
Pat: Well, you know you're near-sighted.

To Pat's chagrin, she learns that Nora has gambled with the girls' money and lost heavily. Moreover, Nora has signed their father's name to a note Crawford demanded in return for paying the latest debts. Nora has gone to Crawford to ask him for the note back when Pat appears, ready for a confronta-

tion. With the equally unexpected arrival of Dan and Mrs. O'Brien (Alice Leigh), Pat is hurried into the same room where Crawford has hidden Nora. "*Pat rushes into the room, slamming the door behind her. An instant's pause, then Pat's voice is heard in heartbroken surprise exclaiming* 'Nora.' " Rather than destroy her sister's reputation, Pat makes it appear that she herself is having an affair with Crawford. Dan is outraged until he recognizes the true situation. He buys out Crawford and convinces Pat to leave the theatre to marry him. She accepts, remarking, "Dan, we'll settle down like a couple of Reubens. Us an' the cows."

Critics were delighted with both the comedy ("the most characteristic American play produced so far this season, and more vivid and real in many respects than any other") and with the star ("Probably no other American actress could so cleverly personify this individual type."). The role of Pat was seen as presenting "a character that is practically new to the stage." Such rave notices propelled both the meteoric career of the leading lady and the somewhat longer career of the playwright.

· · ·

Rose Stahl (1870–1955) was born in Montreal and made her acting debut with a Philadelphia stock company. She moved to other stock troupes and played minor roles on Broadway before turning to vaudeville, where she caused a stir in Forbes's skit "The Chorus Girl," on which her new play was based. Many contemporaries perceived a striking physical resemblance in the thin-faced, tousle-haired actress to a young Sarah Bernhardt. However, her nasal voice and her "breezy and crudely wholesome style" with its "unstudied and spontaneous zest" marked her as a breed apart.

· · ·

James Forbes (1871–1938) was, like his newfound star, Canadian-born. He moved to America to try his hand at acting, then worked as a press agent and a drama critic for the *Pittsburgh Dispatch* and the *New York World*. Writing for magazines and vaudeville proved most congenial. Indeed, his new hit started as a magazine story, then was adapted for the two-a-day stage. Forbes directed this and all his subsequent plays, besides staging works of other dramatists.

· · ·

The Chorus Lady ran out the season. Afterwards, with Miss Stahl always as star, it toured for four more years.

No such longevity awaited Harry D. Cottrell and Oliver Morosco's **The Judge and the Jury** (9-1-06, Wallack's), which was roundly panned and disappeared after little more than two weeks. During that time it recounted the plight of an orphan (Ida Conquest), grown to maturity in a wild New Mexican town, who is torn between her love for a local miner (William Desmond) and a visiting sophisticate (Walter Hale), and who is protected by the miner when she is falsely accused of shooting the visitor. (In his autobiography Morosco says the play had been a huge hit in Los Angeles, where it was first mounted, doing "land-office business.")

Two nights later Arthur Wing Pinero's **His House in Order** (9-3-06, Empire) opened to laudatory reviews and embarked on a four-month run. Pinero's story centered on a man who has idolized his late wife and after her death and his own remarriage has allowed the dead woman's narrow, selfish family to rule his affairs. A chance discovery opens his eyes to the dead woman's true nature and permits him to cast off his imperious in-laws. John Drew was starred. His seemingly effortless gifts for high comedy long had been taken for granted, but critics were pleased to observe how tellingly he handled the play's more serious moments.

The lawless West continued to be a preferred setting for touring melodramas, the latest of which was Harry D. Carey's **Montana** (9-5-06, Third Ave.). The hero is a ranch foreman who loves the rancher's daughter; the villain is a half-breed Indian who also loves the girl, kills her father, implicates the hero for the crime, kidnaps the girl, attempts to blow up the cabin her rescuers take her to, and, after uncounted stabbings and shooting, meets his proper end. The playwright, who went on to become a Hollywood favorite, doubled in brass by assuming the role of the hero.

Inglis Allen's **The Dear Unfair Sex** (9-10-06, Liberty) premiered on the same evening that saw Bertha Kalish offer her interpretation of *The Kreutzer Sonata*. With elegant Ellis Jeffreys in the leading role, the novelty described how a catty, domineering wife is finally put in her place. Broadway admired the star but not the play.

One reviewer observed that H. Grattan Donnelly's **Carolina** (9-10-06, American) "contained the usual stock characters which go to make up the so-called Southern drama, the old Colonel, the darky, the Boston visitor, a Northern hero and a Southern heroine." He might have added that the play also followed common practice by having a heroine (actually one of two in the play) named after her state. Whether two heroines gave the drama a certain originality or merely made for confusion is moot. A carpetbagging counterfeiter joins forces with a Carolina moonshiner. At the same time, he tricks one southern belle into marrying him and sets about to deprive the other belle of her plantation. A handsome northerner (his surname was Harvard) rushes forward to save the estate and to assist the Secret Service in locking up the counterfeiter.

Two minority groups, who usually figured in touring melodramas as either comics or villains, made up virtually the entire cast of characters in Howard Cooper's **A Midnight Escape** (9-10-06, Star). The hero and heroine are young Jews who come to grief at the hands of the girl's uncle, a banker on the verge of insolvency from his soured speculations, and the uncle's shyster lawyer. Because the heroine is rich, the men kidnap her to a Harlem houseboat, then, failing to get her to assign them her money, dump her into the river. She is fished out and conveyed to a hiding place by her fiancé, so the men tell the Black Hand that the boy has seduced and abandoned an Italian girl. This time both lovers are abducted. They are placed in a dungeon where a diabolical machine will shower them with rifle bullets precisely at midnight. Just as the clock is about to strike, the very girl the hero is supposed to have seduced enters and saves the pair. Besides the houseboat and dungeon, settings afforded playgoers such other glimpses of the world of Joe Mendel, Rosebelle Bloom, and Antoinette Pollotti as a fish market beneath the Williamsburg Bridge, a pawnbroker's shop, a Wall Street office, and a Fifth Avenue mansion.

Earlier in the season William A. Brady had lent Wagenhals and Kemper a helping hand with their ill-fated production of *The Kreutzer Sonata*. The pair returned the favor by signing over to him the rights to Avery Hopwood and Channing Pollock's **Clothes** (9-11-06, Manhattan) so that Brady could bring it out as a vehicle for his wife, Grace George. She played Olivia Sherwood, who loves the good life and is prodded by her friends to marry a man rich enough to maintain her in so glittering a world. She takes aim at Richard Burbank (Robert T. Haines). The money she will need to buy the clothes with which to ensnare Burbank comes, she believes, from the meager income her father left her. Actually it comes from her lawyer, Arnold West (Frank Worthing), an unhappily married man who looks on his secret payments as loans and someday hopes to collect on the debt by marrying Olivia. In time Olivia finds she has fallen genuinely in love with Burbank and proposes to him at a fancy dress ball. However, before the young sweethearts can enjoy the prospect of a wedding, West appears. He announces he is celebrating his wife's death, which means Olivia will not have to marry Burbank for his money but can wed him instead. Furious, Olivia shoves West away. He falls down a flight of stairs but is not seriously hurt. Burbank, however, believes Olivia has been deceiving and using him, and he stalks off. Later, realizing she does love him, he taps at her window. She lets him in, and they snuggle together in the windowsill for their reconciliation.

Critics found both men somewhat stiff and occasionally inaudible, but the star's charm came to the rescue and turned the play into a success. That success marked the beginning of a long, quick climb for Hopwood, who became reputedly the richest playwright of his day.

· · ·

[James] **Avery Hopwood** (1882–1928) was born in Cleveland and educated at the University of Michigan. After graduation he worked for a time as a newspaperman. He supposedly wrote *Clothes* after reading *Sartor Resartus*. The producers called in Channing Pollock, who revised the work without Hopwood's knowledge, but the young author was not offended, recognizing the improvements. Throughout his career he made no claim to artistic excellence, seeking only commercial success. However, on his death he left his alma mater money to establish a playwriting award.

· · ·

The new season was hardly two months old when Owen Davis had a fourth new touring melodrama ready for his followers. **The Burglar's Daughter** (9-17-06, Star) is Meg of Mulberry Bend. She has befriended a blind orphan girl who is an heiress but who stands at risk of her life since her vicious stockbroker guardian is resolved to have her fortune for himself. The man he hires to do away with his ward is none other than Meg's father. In the most exciting moment of the drama, the blind girl is tied to a speeding trolley car hurtling across a bridge. Meg climbs on the car's roof and shoots it out with the villains, who are riding on the platform. "The mechanism was so well managed," one reviewer wrote approvingly, "that it was well nigh impossible to believe that the car was standing still and that the scenery was doing the actual hustling." Later the guardian attempts to throw his blind ward from a yacht heading for the Battery, but Meg and her now reformed father save the girl, the father at the cost of his own life.

Hal Reid was heard from on the same night with **The Girl and the Gambler** (9-17-06, West End), his latest vehicle for Florence Bindley. Singer, dancer, showgirl, and overgrown tomboy, the star was afforded opportunities to demonstrate her numerous talents. She played the younger daughter of a rich old man, whom the villain and villainess persuade to disown his family. She stopped the show and the action singing several songs, one of which she performed in the "diamond dress" that had become a sort of trademark.

Sara MacDonald, the author of **Adrift in New York** (9-17-06, Third Ave.) played her own heroine, a girl who must support her drunken father and her tiny crippled brother. (The brother was portrayed by an actress listed on the program as Little Priscella.) The heroine's artist-lover must come to her rescue when her father's criminal buddy abducts her.

Another player, Stanley Dark, suffered an ignominious failure on a first-class stage when his **Man and His Angel** (9-18-06, Hackett) was withdrawn after a single week. Dark's story told of a warpedminded hunchback (Holbrook Blinn) who nearly destroys the love life of a prima donna (Frances Ring) who once had rescued him from possible imprisonment. The deep-voiced Blinn's brooding performance alone won praise.

William F. Hawtrey and Hilda Spong fared somewhat better when they appeared in Alicia Ramsey and Rudolph de Cordova's **John Hudson's Wife** (9-20-06, Weber's). At her avaricious family's urging, a young lady marries a wealthy man she does not love. She eventually comes to love him, and when her father and brother steal important papers and place her husband in a compromising position, she turns against them.

Just as Klaw and Erlanger had opened their New Amsterdam Theatre with a mounting of *A Midsummer Night's Dream* in 1903, so Wagenhals and Kemper elected to use the same comedy as the opening attraction at their new Astor Theatre, on Broadway and 45th Street. Plans originally called for a September 17th first night, and in fact the overture had been performed when fire marshals, citing firelaw violations, ordered the show stopped and the auditorium evacuated. Not until the 21st could audiences return to see a complete enactment. Critics found the production, which included "an electric-eyed owl with flapping wings," unexceptional and the cast no better. Only two players stood out: Annie Russell as a Puck whose merrymaking was tinged with sadness, and John Bunny as a fat, unctuous Bottom. The revival chalked up thirty-four performances.

Religious themes dominated openings the following Monday. With some magnificent spectacle to boot, **The Prince of India** (9-24-06, Broadway) enjoyed a two-month run as part of a lengthy transcontinental tour that had begun the preceding season. The play, much of it in blank and sometimes rhymed verse, was adapted by J. I. C. Clarke from General Lew Wallace's novel. The poetry ran to the order of:

Princess of the Morning Light
Lean sparkling from thy throne of mist,
The valley roses wait thee to be kissed.

Spectacle included an interior of Sancta Sophia showing arches, columns, and golden dome in perspective ("than which nothing more impressive and beautiful has ever been seen on our stage"), a palace with green and purple marble and multihued mosaics, a storm on the Bosphorus, and the sacking of Constantinople. The story focused on the Wandering Jew, who, as the Prince of India (Emmett Corrigan), attempts to spread the idea of religious tolerance and succeeds in bringing about the wedding of a Christian princess (Adelaide Keim) and Moslem prince (William Farnum). But the Jew finds his goodness brings him no respite. He lifts his arms skyward and cries, "Life! Life again! The centuries dead behind me, the centuries ever before me. Lord of Israel, how long?" By the time the show reached New York, all the original principals had been replaced except Farnum, whose striking good looks, full-throated delivery and vigor, made him the center of attention.

Ella Wheeler Wilcox and Luscombe Searelle's **Mizpah** (9-24-06, Academy of Music), a blank-verse retelling of the story of Asasueras (Charles Dalton), Esther (Elizabeth Kennedy), Haman (Frank Losee), and Queen Vashti (Lillian Lamson), found far less favor and vanished after a few weeks.

Langdon McCormick's **The Burglar and the Lady** (9-24-06, American) seemed satisfied with a typical period title when it might have called itself, more invitingly, *Raffles and Sherlock Holmes.* Copyright considerations apparently did not stop the dramatist from telling of an encounter between the famed gentleman-thief and the great English sleuth (on a visit to America). To whet interest further, Raffles was played by the famed boxer-turned-actor James J. Corbett. In pusuit of his loot, Raffles falls in love with his victim's beautiful niece. Time and again he and his newfound lady elude the police, led by the ever resourceful Holmes. The final curtain finds the lovers escaping on a Europe-bound ship. Some notices complained that the actor who portrayed Holmes was too combative, lacking the showily insouciant confidence expected in the part, but Corbett, as star, walked off with favorable assessments. (For what it's worth, Sherlock Holmes also made a brief appearance that same evening a few blocks away when Fred Stone impersonated him in a comic scene in Victor Herbert's musical *The Red Mill.*)

At a paunchy, graying forty-nine, Nat Goodwin might seem too old to impersonate the "young, healthy American type" hero suggested by the description in the printed text of William C. and Cecil B. de Mille's **The Genius** (10-1-06, Bijou), but such discrepancies rarely bothered contemporary playgoers, weaned on older ideas of casting. Besides, Goodwin was a very skilled and popular comedian, and critics felt the new comedy needed all the help it could get. The star portrayed Jack Spencer, a socialite who fears he will never win over art-mad Josephine Van Dusen (Louise Randolph) unless he can pass for a true artist. He goes to a studio shared by several impecunious bohemians. They are so poor that the painter (Robert Paton Gibbs) among them paints the remains of a breakfast on a plate so a visitor will not realize they have not eaten. Jack asks them to teach him, but they retort it might be easier if he were to pose as a genius who actually taught all three their varying arts. Together they hoodwink an absurdly effeminate but important reviewer (H. G. Lonsdale). His articles make Jack so famous that he hasn't a moment to call his own. Rebelling, he confesses the hoax, but nobody will believe him. In despair he hands Josephine to the critic and runs off with the sweet, unpretentious model (Edna Goodrich) whom the artists had adopted. With its echoes of *Trilby, The Music Master,* and other recent successes, and with jokes that had seemed funnier when they were used initially in other comedies, the play was dismissed as "cheap odds and ends, clumsily tacked together." However, Goodwin remained a strong enough draw to keep it going for a month.

Competing with Goodwin's first night was George M. Cohan's maiden effort for the nonmusical stage, **Popularity** (10-1-06, Wallack's). Cohan's time-tested plot was straightforward. Robert Rand (Thomas W. Ross), a matinee idol, falls in love with Gertrude Fuller (Adelaide Manola), daughter of the millionaire stove-polish czar (Frederic de Belleville). Naturally papa disapproves, and a nefarious rival for Gertrude's hand, Donald Burnside (Edgar Selwyn), gives him further, if spurious, reasons for objecting. Rand is so upset that he announces he will not perform, but Gertrude rushes backstage to his dressing room to plead that he change his mind. He does, and when in short order Donald is tricked into confessing his own treachery, the curtain falls on the beaming lovers. However trite his basic story was, Cohan added some effective touches. Thus after Rand heeds his fiancée's plea, the scene blacks out, and a moment later Rand is seen standing in front of the theatre's actual curtain, apologizing to the real audience as if it were the audience that he had kept waiting in the play. A program note urged audiences to "holler for Rand when the lights go out," and according to Cohan's biographer, they did, goaded on by "plants." Even more unusual, Cohan depicted his hero as having "the breeding of a newsboy" and "unmitigated impudence beyond the limit of endurance," charges sometimes leveled at Cohan himself. For Cohan still had not won many critics' acceptance, and they came down hard on his new play. It ran only three weeks but enjoyed a longer life as Cohan's 1909 musical *The Man Who Owns Broadway*. It would be several years before Cohan would prove his remarkable versatility outside the musical field.

· · ·

George M[ichael] Cohan (1851–1942) was born in Providence, R.I., just possibly on July 4, as he was wont to boast. His parents were vaudevillians, and when he and his sister came of age they joined their parents to constitute the Four Cohans, one of the best vaudeville acts of its day. Young George also appeared in such plays as *Peck's Bad Boy*. His earliest musicals were expansions of sketches the Four Cohans played in two-a-day. Real success followed with *Little Johnny Jones, Forty-five Minutes from Broadway,* and *George Washington, Jr.* These hits, with their still popular songs, made Cohan the first enduring figure of our modern musical comedy stage.

· · ·

Snootier playgoers betook themselves to the New Amsterdam, where H. B. Irving (the great Henry's son) and Dorothea Baird (H. B.'s wife and London's original Trilby) began a repertory engagement the same day. The couple opened with Stephen Phillips's poetic **Paolo and Francesca,** the latest recounting of Francesca da Rimini's sad story, then moved on to brief stands with such older plays as *King René's Daughter, The Lyons Mail,* and *Charles I.* Two other novelties were W. L. Courtney's **Markheim** (on October 22), based on Robert Louis Stevenson's tale of a murderer who turns himself in to the police, and **Mauricette** (on October 25), which Irving adapted from André Picard's *Jeunesse* and which told of the romantic upheavals brought about by a young girl's arrival at the home of a childless couple. Irving's performances were favorably received for the most part, although he never was accorded the adulation that had greeted his father. His wife's acting was less admired.

Harry Thaw had shot and killed the architect Stanford White on June 25, during a performance of *Mamzelle Champagne* on the Madison Square Garden Roof. The events were recreated in Hal Reid's **A Millionaire's Revenge** (10-1-06, West End). Names were altered, but only slightly. White became Black, and the killer Harold Daw. The lady in question, Evelyn Nesbit, was rechristened Emeline Hudspeth. The play opened with an orgy in Black's studio and Emeline stepping out of a huge pie; it ended somewhat inconclusively, with Daw justifying his behavior to his mother.

If Reid patently drew on recent headlines, Jesse Lynch Williams did, too, only less obviously. Critics could point to no specific source for **The Stolen Story** (10-2-06, Garden), but civic corruption was so endemic that Williams needed no single instance. A few years down the road Williams would become the first playwright awarded a Pulitzer Prize for Drama, but in 1906 the Illinois-born, Princeton-educated writer was better known as an author of short stories (on one of which his new play was based) and as a newspaperman (which provided colorful background for his tale). A "star" reporter, Billy Woods (James Lee Finney), is assigned to find out why the respected General Cunningham (R. Peyton Carter) is cavorting with known City Hall grafters. A romantic interest in the general's daughter (Dorothy Tennant), the machinations of a professional rival, and maneuvering by worried politicos all conspire to prevent Billy's getting his story. As a result he is fired. Shortly afterwards another paper hires him, and he succeeds in ferreting out the truth: the general is offering land for waterfront parks, and the grafters hope to use the land for their own greedy ends. Billy rushes to his desk and begins to pound away at his story, but in his excitement and confusion he doesn't realize he has returned to the paper that fired him. His old boss and his old associates keep his new employers and politicians at bay while he finishes his exposé. Critics, all newspapermen themselves, lauded the uncommonly accurate replication of a noisy, paper-cluttered newsroom. Beyond that they could discern little to praise. The play folded after two weeks.

The next evening, a Wednesday, brought in another pair of openings. Beautiful, charming Eleanor Robson had scored a huge hit in Israel Zangwill's *Merely Mary Ann.* Now she scored again in the playwright's equally airy, sentimental **Nurse Marjorie** (10-3-06, Liberty), playing a duchess's daughter who nurses an ultraliberal M.P. (H. B. Warner) back to health after an operation to cure a squint. Very English snobberies and political considerations stand in the way of a happy ending for nearly four acts. The tall, elegant, and good-looking Warner, son of the London actor Charles Warner, was warmly applauded in his New York debut. Good notices and Miss Robson's growing appeal kept the box office humming for two months.

The evening's other opening not only capped a busy week and ran far longer, but it proved the best American drama of the season and soon was perceived as a pivotal piece of American dramaturgy. The play was William Vaughn Moody's **The Great Divide** (10-3-06, Princess). Moody, the Harvard-educated son of a Mississippi riverboat captain, abandoned teaching to devote himself to poetry and drama. None of his early works, all blank-verse dramas, was ever produced on Broadway. He was in his late thirties by the time *The Great Divide* reached New York.

Moody's play opens in an Arizona desert, "intensely colored, and covered with the uncouth shapes of giant cacti, dotted with bunches of gorgeous blooms." Ruth Jordan (Margaret Anglin) shares a cabin with her brother, Philip (Charles Wyngate), and Philip's dissatisfied wife, Polly (Laura Hope Crews). The Jordans are New Englanders and have come west to recruit the family fortune by developing cactus fibers. When Ruth exclaims, "I think I shall be punished for being so happy," Polly can only see the "simon-pure New Englander" in her. Since Philip is accompanying Polly to the train station, an all-night ride away, Ruth is left alone for the evening. Just as she is preparing to go to bed, three ruffians force their way into the cabin. They would clearly abuse her, but she pleads with the most decent-looking to chase out the others, offering him "her life" in return. The man she has rested her hopes on is Stephen Ghent (Henry Miller). With money and a necklace of gold nuggets, he persuades his buddies to leave. To Ruth's horror, Ghent insists she keep her part of the bargain and come away with him. He tries to tell her he is not conscienceless or cynical: "I used to feel sometimes, before I went to the bad, that I could take the world . . . and tilt her over. And I can do it, too, if you say the word! I'll put you where you can look down on the proudest. I'll give you the kingdoms of the world and the glory of 'em." Reluctantly, she accompanies him.

Time has passed, and Ghent has prospered. He has brought a contractor and an architect to build a new home high in the Cordilleras. But two things disrupt his idyll. Philip appears, finally having learned Ruth's whereabouts. More shattering, Ghent learns that Ruth has been selling her weaving at a nearby hotel; when he asks her why, she tells him it is so that she can earn enough to repay him for the cash and gold he expended on "buying" her. She begs her brother to take her back to New England. Once she has returned there, all the life seems drained out of her. One day Ghent appears. The family learns that he has saved the cactus fiber operation that Philip had been forced to abandon, and that he has done so at the risk of losing his own mining interests. He pleads with the listless Ruth to leave behind her stilted, life-denying eastern ways, return with him, and be rejuvenated. There is no longer a moral issue involved, he insists, "because the first time our eyes met, they burned away all that was bad in our meeting, and left only the fact that we *had* met—pure good—pure joy—a fortune of it—for both of us!" But when Ruth responds that the wages of sin is death, Ghent acknowledges, "You've fought hard for me, God bless you for it,—but it's been a losing game with you from the first!—You belong here, and I belong out yonder—beyond the Rockies, beyond—the Great Divide!" His conclusion brings Ruth to her senses. She tells Ghent she now sees in herself "a woman in whose ears rang night and day the cry of an angry Heaven to us both—'Cleanse yourselves!' And I went about doing it the only way I knew . . . the only way my fathers knew—by wretchedness, by self-torture, by trying blindly to pierce your careless heart with pain." She agrees to go back to Arizona.

Most of New York's critics instantly appreciated the drama's worth. Typically, the *Sun* called it "so bold and vital in theme, so subtly precious and unaffectedly strong in the writing, that it is very hard . . . to speak of it in terms at once of justice and of moderation." Moody's inherently native theme, the immense barrier separating the rigidity of an aging eastern culture from the larger and freer, if more brutal, impulses of the frontier, was not totally new to the American stage, but it never before had been presented onstage so powerfully or poetically. Both principals gave what critics called "the performances of their careers." Miller, casting aside the polished man of the world that audiences had come to expect from him, gave a remarkable study of a man whose conditioned savagery warred with his basic decency. Of Miss Anglin the *Dramatic Mirror* observed, "While her emotional power was as great as ever, she acted with a restraint and at times even a lightness which she has never shown before." The play ran out the season, reopened after a summer hiatus for another three months, then embarked on a long, successful tour.

The next week saw four new plays arrive: two French comedies at first-class houses and two American touring melodramas. None did its theatre proud. Of major interest was Lillian Russell's first major foray into nonmusical theatre, **Barbara's Millions** (10-8-06, Savoy), which Paul Potter derived from Francis de Croisset's *Le Bonheur, mesdames.* Still beautiful, but lacking the airy comic flair required for her part, the star portrayed a rich American whose marriage to a Frenchman (H. Reeves-Smith) is nearly destroyed by absurd misunderstandings and who pretends to obtain an American divorce in order to save the marriage. Condemned for its "barren waste of dialogue and meaningless situations," the comedy was hurriedly shown the stage door.

An amazingly prolific Owen Davis had a fifth play ready for judgment with his pretentiously labeled "sceno-drama" **$10,000 Reward** (10-8-06, American). Its heroine is a young American girl who happens to know the whereabouts of a hidden treasure looted from a Burmese temple. A Burmese Svengali and some equally despicable Americans unite to wrest the secret from the girl. She loves a dashing soldier of fortune with the ultimate touring-melodrama-hero name, Jack Fearless. Her father won't hear of her wedding a poor man and insists that Jack must first earn $10,000. When the villains kidnap the girl and her father offers a $10,000 reward for her return, the rest is obvious. Only the oddball nature and settings of some of the expected trials and tribulations were of interest. These included a Bolivian mine and army camp, imprisonment on a pirate ship and rescue by an American battleship, a submarine, and a Burmese temple where dancing girls put on quite a show. With "consistency, plausibility and . . . heart interest . . . utterly disregarded," it was no wonder "the audience . . . laughed itself into tears over the crudities of the piece."

But the uncredited **For Her Sake** (10-8-06, Third Ave.) was no better. It concerned itself with the devious ploys used by a nihilist-turned-police-spy to prevent a Russian prince from marrying a commoner.

The Love Letter (10-9-06, Lyric) was adapted from Victorien Sardou's *La Piste* by Ferdinand Gottschalk, who was playing opposite Lillian Russell down near Herald Square. A fragment of a love note leads a volatile husband (William Courtenay) to suspect his wife (Virginia Harned) of infidelity, and she must scurry around to prove her innocence.

Cape Cod Folks (10-15-06, Academy of Music) was Earl W. Mayo's dramatization of Sarah P. McLean Greene's twenty-five-year-old novel. Just as the girl in *David Harum* had left New York City to teach in a small upstate town and thus escape an unhappy situation, so Emily Hungerford (Sarah Perry) comes from Boston to teach in a fishing village and avoid having to meet David Rollins (E. J. Ratcliffe), whom a will demands she marry or both youngsters must forfeit their inheritance. David follows her, but he is no sooner in the village than he seduces short-skirted, pigtailed Becky Cradlebow (Bessie Barriscale). Becky is loved by George Oliver (Charles Mackay), a fisherman, and Emily soon finds she is being courted by Becky's brother, Luther (Earle Browne), the village's best whaler and cranberry picker. David's seduction of Becky might seem to bode trouble, but when George is caught at sea in a storm, David rushes to his rescue, only to be drowned. Luther also rows to the rescue. The wrecked ship's mast lights bob up and down in the violent sea. In flashes of lightning and periodic beams from a nearby lighthouse, Luther is seen struggling in a trough until he reaches George and pulls him to safety. Comic relief was provided by a drunken black, Lucius Dionysius Smith (Harry Montgomery), who is about to be railroaded out of town when the villagers realize his vote will break a tied election. The Democrats' $10 bribe to Lucius proves persuasive. Although Lucius was played by a white in blackface, at least one of Emily's schoolchildren was reportedly a real black.

For the second time in less than a month Raffles burgled on a combination-house stage, only this time it was **The Girl Raffles** (10-15-06, 14th St.). The play was by Charles E. Blaney and starred his wife, Cecil Spooner, as a waif who has been raised in a life of crime by a fence operating an antique shop. She eventually learns that her father is a rich English lord and that she must crack a safe if she is to obtain the papers proving her lineage. Naturally the villains do everything possible to prevent her laying her hands on the papers, and just as inevitably they fail in the last act.

Such was William Gillette's reputation that his **Clarice** (10-16-06, Garrick) overrode generally derisive notices and enjoyed a profitable ten-week stand, after touring much of the prior season. Gillette's story was not complicated. Dr. Carrington loves his ward, Clarice (Marie Doro), but tells her she must wed his rival, Dr. Denbeigh (Francis Carlyle), after Denbeigh deceives Carrington into believe that he, Carrington, has tuberculosis. Heartbroken when Clarice does not wave to him from the train supposedly taking her to Denbeigh, Carrington takes poison. Denbeigh and Clarice rush in; Clarice assures Carrington of her love; and Denbeigh, after confessing his trickery, gives Carrington a life-saving injection.

The winsome Miss Doro won rave reviews, while

the same critics noted that Gillette was, as always, niggardly in expression and staccato in delivery. His "even, metallic utterance, and the trick of repeating, in preoccupied fashion, the same thought"—so effective in his earlier performances—were perceived here as annoying mannerisms. Strangely, while most disliked the play, they could not agree on why. "The sentiment drops into sentimentality," "impossible melodrama," and "[a basic theme] so ugly, so unreasonable and so entirely unsuited to dramatic treatment" were samples of their condemnation.

Nor could critics wax excited about **Sam Houston** (10-16-06, Garden), for which Clay Clement served as producer, star, and co-author with John McGovern and Jesse Edson. The play was episodic. Act I sees Houston alienate and leave his snobbish wife (Kathleen Kerrigan) when she bristles at his friendship with Indians. In the next act the hero convinces his followers that it is futile to attempt to save the Alamo and instead encourages them to declare Texas independent. The third act finds Sam avenging the Alamo but protecting Santa Anna from a lynch mob. His sadness at Texas's decision to secede from the Union at the outbreak of the Civil War is the focal point of the final act.

A number of fledgling playwrights had been introduced to theatregoers during the season. No one could know how tragically curtailed William Vaughn Moody's career would be or how disappointingly unproductive Jesse Lynch Williams's was to prove. Nor could anyone foresee the long, brilliant road ahead for Rachel Crothers.

. . .

Rachel Crothers (1878–1958) was born in Bloomington, Ill., daughter of two physicians. She began writing plays while still in her teens and, after graduating from the State Normal School of Illinois, studied acting at the Stanhope-Wheatcroft School and elsewhere. She abandoned acting when her earliest works were mounted by amateur and stock companies. These were both full-length and one-act plays, but none was successful. Later she directed most of her own plays.

. . .

Like Moody's *The Great Divide,* Rachel Crothers's **The Three of Us** (10-17-06, Madison Square) opens in the world of hardscrabble mining country, this time in Nevada. Rhys Macchesney (Carlotta Nillson) and her two brothers, thirteen-year-old Sonnie (Master George Clarke) and nineteen-year-old Clem (John Westley), have been bequeathed the Three of Us mine by their late father. The trio are barely eking out a living, but the resourceful, determined Rhys has resolved to keep the family together until the mine

proves productive. Two local men, Louis Berresford (Henry Kolker) and Stephen Townley (Frederick Truesdell), both court Rhys. Townley learns that their neighbor's property contains a rich lode, and he passes the information on to Rhys before arranging for the land's purchase. Clem, who is fed up with struggling and wants to run away, overhears the conversation and informs Berresford of it. When Berresford buys the mine, circumstances make it seem to Townley that Rhys has betrayed him. But he later learns better.

Most critics were delighted with the play. The *Times*'s man concluded, "Miss Crothers has gone straight ahead without any resort to the commonplace trickery of the stage. Her people have hearts and she gets to these hearts. They have brains and minds; they act on natural and not fictitious impulse." The critic for *Theatre* cooed, "Miss Crothers has the eyes of love for human nature." The finicky small talk and eddies of trivial incidents with which she filled the gaps between major scenes were tactfully overlooked. But only the *Dramatic Mirror* addressed what, depending on one's viewpoint, would develop as Miss Crothers's salient strength or weakness when it noted, "Her character delineation is best in the pictures she gives of the women." Her perception of men was and remained shallow and somewhat jaundiced. Thus her two principal males are the unprincipled, manipulative Berresford and the untrusting, truculent Townley. The brothers are ably limned, but the remaining male characters are either clowns or nonentities. The memorable figures are the stalwart maid, Maggie (Eva Vincent), the kindly, homesick neighbor, "Bixie" (Jane Peyton), and, of course, Rhys. Fortunately, Carlotta Nillson's vital yet restrained performance brought out all the richness of the playwright's study, and the rest of the cast was strong. Good notices and word of mouth allowed the play to run out the season.

A second aspiring lady playwright was not embraced very warmly. Cora Maynard's **The Measure of a Man** (10-20-06, Weber's) was a clichéd bit of muckraking. A young man, Arnold King (Robert Drouet), buys the rights to a process that will substantially reduce the cost of steelmaking. For money he approaches the rich-as-Croesus Christopher Guthrie (E. M. Holland), father of his fiancée, Ruth (Percy Haswell). Together the men conspire not only to wreck their competition but to cheat their own stockholders of dividends. Ruth gets wind of the plan and walks out on King, prompting him to make a public confession of his chicanery. In period parlance, the mounting was a "frost," vanishing after two weeks.

The next Monday evening offered the carriage trade two major openings. One was Clyde Fitch and Edith Wharton's stage version of Mrs. Wharton's **The House of Mirth** (10-22-06, Savoy), the saga of an ambitious young lady whose quest for a rich marriage leads her to reject her unmonied suitor and eventually drives her to suicide. From the start Fitch had his doubts about the workability of an essentially psychological tale, which, in his words, ran against "every rule of the drama," so he was not surprised by the dismal reception. However, for the highly admired, American-born Fay Davis, who assumed the leading role, the play's quick closing represented the last straw in a frustrating New York career. She spent the next quarter of a century in important roles in the West End.

By contrast, the month-long run of *Cymbeline,* which opened at the Astor the same evening, was as much as anyone could expect for one of Shakespeare's less well known, more difficult plays. Even his most popular works no longer were revived as regularly as they had been just a generation ago. Such a lack of revivals led many to agree with the critic who bemoaned, "The correct reading of blank verse has become almost a lost art." The art was certainly not lost on lovely Viola Allen, whose "refined sensibility and expressive sympathy" perfectly fitted her for the role of Imogen, "a womanly woman." The often massive, stark scenery created the requisite primitive air: "Great, rough stone walls with rude hangings, and such barbaric elegance as marked the period, represent the palace of Cymbeline. The ceilings are of crudely carved wood, supported by hewn stone columns, the landscapes seen through the openings are stretches of uncultivated meadow, dotted with druidical monuments." Only the star's supporting players let her down. One of the most severely criticized—for his inept handling of a sword, his unintelligible mumblings, and his clumsiness with blank verse—was Jefferson Winter, who played Posthumus and who was the son of brahmin William Winter.

Melodrama gave way briefly to farce at one combination house with **The Arrival of Kitty** (10-22-06, West End). Norman Lee Swartout's door-slammer was set in an Atlantic City hotel. The hero must resort to all manner of comic subterfuge, including dressing as a girl, to persuade his sweetheart's guardian to consent to their marrying. His problem is that the guardian's sister has offered her brother a small fortune if he prefers the hero's rival. The appearance of a glamorous actress, the Kitty of the title, provides complications. Songs and dances interpolated into the piece won more than the usual praise.

The Shulamite (10-29-06, Lyric) was dramatized by Edward Knoblauch and Claude Askew from Askew's novel of the same name. It recounted how a brutal, wife-beating old Boer is killed by his English overseer and how the overseer and the farmer's young widow escape punishment for the killing. The main attraction of the evening was the brilliant performance of one of England's finest and most promising actresses, Lena Ashwell.

An overseer was also the central figure in *The Shulamite*'s lowly American competition, Hal Reid's touring melodrama **The Cow Puncher** (10-29-06, West End). The hero must defend himself, the lady he works for, and his drunken brother from a band of holdup men and cattle rustlers. One rescue was novel. The hero is saved from certain death by a bear—who turns out to be not a real animal but a friend in disguise.

Some enthusiastic reviews—"one of the best plays seen in New York this season," "far above the ordinary"—greeted another American melodrama, Edward Peple's **The Love Route** (10-30-06, Lincoln Square). A complete change in tone and style from Peple's earlier hit, *The Prince Chap,* it set its love story against a railroad's right to seize land it wants. As in *The Cow Puncher,* the landowner is a lady, Allene Houston (Odette Tyler). She and her superintendent use force to keep the railroad's builders off her property, in the process shooting John Ashby (Guy Standing), the young engineer in charge of construction. Shocked by the shooting, Allene nurses John back to health and, in doing so, falls in love with him. When he is able to stand on his feet again, she leads him to the window, opens the curtain, and shows him the rail line, which she herself helped to complete. The scene in which two dozen men lay the line across the stage and bring on the first rail car was so realistically done that it provoked a rare standing ovation and several curtain calls. But the new Lincoln Square Theatre, on Broadway near 66th Street, was apparently much too far uptown for many playgoers (by 1909 it was a film house). The production did disappointing business and was withdrawn after six weeks—by no means a total failure, but far from the hit many reviews predicted it would be.

A rival opening ran no longer, but it remains the only play of the season still regularly revived. **Caesar and Cleopatra** (10-30-06, New Amsterdam) was Shaw's tongue-in-cheek "history" of how his latest antiheroic superman of destiny took and trained the kittenish young Egyptian queen. He had written the play expressly for the man he called "the classic actor of our day," Forbes-Robertson, and Forbes-

Robertson, with his wife, Gertrude Elliott, as the queen, offered the comedy to America before presenting it to London. The *Dramatic Mirror* noted, "There are in the lines such shiftings from burlesque to tragedy, from whimsical humor to serious philosophy . . . that the most artistic versatility is required. No matter what the situation Forbes Robertson is always Caesar. His speech to the Sphinx in the first act and his sermon against war are two splendid bits of elocution. His acting throughout is strong and convincing." Oddly (as with Jones's *The Hypocrites*), its initial reception in the West End was far cooler than in New York.

November began on a down note with a two-week failure, Arthur Conan Doyle's **Brigadier Gerard** (11-5-06, Savoy), in which Napoleon (A. G. Poulton) entrusts an officer (Kyrle Bellew) with retrieving important documents from a countess (Ida Conquest) before they fall into the hands of Talleyrand (Henry Harmon). Gerard succeeds—unwittingly.

Plump May Irwin's vehicles generally teetered precariously between one-woman musical and farce, and her latest was no exception. In George V. Hobart's **Mrs. Wilson, That's All** (11-5-06, Bijou), she played a lady who has dutifully waited seven years for the husband who deserted her immediately after their wedding to be declared legally dead. At the stroke of midnight she observes a minute or two of mourning, then pushes ahead with plans for her second marriage, only to have her first husband (John E. Hazzard) turn up alive. However, the discovery that he is a bigamist solves Mrs. Wilson's problems. To her loyalists' delight the star found occasion, if not excuse, to sing no fewer than six songs. Early in the nearly two-month run the play's title was changed to *Mrs. Wilson-Andrews*.

The evening of the 5th also saw Robert Mantell begin a stand at the Academy of Music in a hidebound repertory that included *Richard III, Hamlet, King Lear, Othello, Macbeth, The Merchant of Venice, Julius Caesar,* and *Richelieu*. Mantell's own hidebound style still appealed to admirers of a bygone day, but it drew snickers and more audible laughter from some resolute modernists. In the spring he repeated many of these plays during a short engagement at the more prestigious New Amsterdam.

Theodore Kremer named **A Woman of Fire** (11-5-06, American) after his "fashionably gowned villainess," a lady given to pouring kerosene on her victims and cremating them. Her base of operation is an opium den where she works in league with several sinister Chinese and Negroes, and her highest hope is to turn the heroine's handsome

young husband into her slave by making him an opium addict. Somehow the denouement to all this occurs in a battle between two submarines.

Critics gave Henry Miller (as producer and director) and Mrs. LeMoyne and Mabel Taliaferro (as Ottima and Pippa) high marks for courage when Browning's "unactable" *Pippa Passes* was staged at the Majestic on the afternoon of the 12th. Nine matinees sufficed to assuage the limited demand.

Despite the rapidly growing lure of films, there was still a large demand for touring melodramas. One of their leading scribes, Lincoln J. Carter, had announced amid April's excitement about the San Francisco earthquake that his next offering would feature the calamity. The result was **While 'Frisco Burns** (11-12-06, Star). The hero—the umpteenth Jack in the genre—is an heir, an inventor, and the suitor of a lovely girl. Unfortunately for Jack, his prospective father-in-law is a knave who attempts to steal his invention, deprive him of his inheritance, and marry the heroine to a treacherous confederate. At one point a drugged Jack is thrown from the balcony of the Cliff House into the sea (but he is rescued by a "comedy quartette"); later a bound Jack is nearly dynamited (until "the comedy Jew" comes to his aid). The *Dramatic Mirror* described the staged quake, which occurred midway in the play: "People run across from right first entrance [downstage] to left first entrance, plaster pours down from among the sky borders, the back drop falls, disclosing a wrecked building with a woman inside, and 'profiles' of ruins are pushed on from right and left."

A different sort of Wild West was depicted in **The Girl from the Ranch** (11-12-06, Third Ave.), for which no author took credit. Set during the Indian wars and peopled with colorful soldiers and cowboys, it told how an innocent officer is convicted of murder on the testimony of another officer, his rival for the heroine. The perjurer's deathbed confession absolves the hero.

Although many critics still held serious reservations about Ibsen as a playwright, most tripped over themselves reaching for laudatory phrases to embrace his latest interpreter, Alla Nazimova, who made her English-speaking debut in *Hedda Gabler* at the small Princess on the 13th.

. . .

Alla Nazimova (1879–1945) The Russian-born actress studied both in Switzerland and in her homeland before becoming a leading lady in St. Petersburg. Her American debut was in 1905 at Orlenoff's Russian Lyceum, where she called herself to the attention of Henry Miller, who urged her to learn English and then presented her in her English-speaking debut.

. . .

Her dark, sultry beauty, her rich, heavily accented voice, her supple movements, and her intelligent readings all thrilled reviewers. Yet a few worried aloud that her tendency to strike dramatic poses was a danger signal. One of her admirers described her Hedda's reaction to learning of Lovberg's suicide: "She was seated, the long, black, snaky body held erect, on her pale face the morbid exaltation of believing that he had killed himself 'beautifully'— that is to say, through the heart. Then came Brack's rasping: 'Not in the heart—in the bowels.' At the word, the erect torso, softly strong, snapped shut like a jack-knife and her pale hands clutched convulsively an imagined wound." As he did with his mounting of *Pippa Passes,* Henry Miller offered this revival only at matinees. However, the acclaim attracted enough playgoers to keep the production going for forty performances.

Despite short arid spells, the season moved swiftly from triumph to triumph. The latest was its best American comedy, which, had it been written in Europe, might still be revived regularly at least on native stages. Langdon Mitchell's **The New York Idea** (11-19-06, Lyric) had been fashioned expressly for Mrs. Fiske, and the author was careful to obey her stricture not to write any star parts—not even for her. The result was a beautifully balanced, exceptionally literate, and deliciously amusing high comedy that on further consideration was discovered to have probed knowingly below its shiny surface. Since Cynthia (Fiske) and John Karslake (John Mason) apparently have been divorced, there would seem to be little reason why Cynthia should not marry Judge Philip Phillimore (Charles Harbury). She is not deterred by the fact that the judge's snooty family "couldn't have received me with more warmth if I'd been a mulatto." Only the judge's ministerial brother seems to be tolerant, surprisingly so, of the circumstances: "There is nothing final in Nature, not even Death;—so then if Death is not final—why should marriage be final?" Cynthia explains that her first marriage was a love match. This one will be different: "I wanted a friend. Philip was ideal as a friend—for months. Isn't it nice to bind a friend to you?" Nor is Cynthia daunted when Philip's ex appears. Vida (Marion Lea) is a showy, conniving poseur, but Cynthia reassures her, "If people in our position couldn't meet, New York society would soon come to an end." This remark prompts Vida to announce that another person in

their position is about to enter the room, Cynthia's ex, John.

It soon becomes obvious that Vida has her sights set on John, who is clearly not averse to a fling. But John makes it equally clear that he still loves Cynthia, who had walked out on him because he would not accompany her to the races, and he continues to believe that underneath everything Cynthia still loves him. Enter a dapper English roué, Sir Wilfrid Cates-Darby (George Arliss), who wouldn't mind walking away with either of the ladies, even though he professes, "There's only one good reason for marrying, and that is because you'll die if you don't." After some time alone with Vida he adds, "They say your gals run to talk and I have seen gals here that would chat life into a wooden Indian! That's what you Americans call being clever. All brains and no stuffin'! In fact, some of your American gals are the nicest boys I ever met." Despite this, he invites Cynthia to put off her wedding and come with him to the races. She accepts, telegraphing Philip that she will be a little late. The delay and the family's reaction to it convince Cynthia she has made a mistake. She rushes to John's home after hearing that John and Vida are to wed, only to learn a wedding has taken place. Dismay turns to relief when she discovers the bride and groom are Vida and Sir Wilfrid. John tells Cynthia that their divorce is not legal because of a technicality, and he offers her the wedding ring she once had returned to him.

The mounting was exceptional, with the settings purportedly employing genuine Louis XV furnishings, rare paintings, and expensive silks. All the players were warmly received, with Mrs. Fiske's spirited, ultimately self-confident Cynthia and Arliss's droll Englishman perhaps edging out the others. Only prior commitments kept the comedy from running longer than sixty-six performances, and Mrs. Fiske returned to it on several occasions in later years.

The astonishing success of *The Music Master* and *The Lion and the Mouse* raised great expectations for Charles Klein's latest opus, **The Daughters of Men** (11-19-06, Astor). A few critics and playgoers felt expectations were realized; most did not. Klein's story spotlighted John Stedman (Orrin Johnson), a young labor lawyer whose fiancée, Grace Crosby (Effie Shannon), is the sister of a prominent capitalist. The pleadings of Grace's brother and the treacherous schemes of Grace's rival, Louise Stolbeck (Dorothy Donnelly), daughter of a union stalwart, nearly wreck the romance. Many playgoers, confronted by so large a list of more certifiably entertaining plays during this fine season, elected to ignore the new work. It was withdrawn after less than two months.

Haddon Chambers's **Sir Anthony** (11-19-06, Savoy), in which the titular figure never appears, lasted only a fortnight, during which time it unfolded the comic tale of a young clerk (William Morris) who puts on airs and claims friendship with an ex-cabinet member after a brief meeting.

Combination houses were also busy with new offerings. Hal Reid's **For a Human Life** (11-19-06, Star) found the standard villain and villainess killing a rich mine owner, framing his prospective son-in-law for the murder, and attempting to kill the dead man's daughter. She evades their clutches, puts on a series of disguises, and finally tricks their superstitious hireling into spilling the beans.

Travers Vale's **The Girl of the Sunny South** (11-19-06, Third Ave.) was a melodrama of "the familiar husband lost-in-the-war, old homestead mortgaged, stolen will variety." During the Civil War a shell-shocked captain is tricked into signing over his property by his superior officer. The treacherous colonel lets the captain's wife believe she is a widow and attempts to wed her. Then an odd tramp named Seedy Punkin appears. Of course, Seedy eventually turns out to be the missing husband, but he and his wife cannot resume their happy marriage until they have undergone more adventures, including his exile in Australia. One critic was amused that the southern mansion in the last act was the scene of a full-blown northern blizzard.

An uncredited **The Four Corners of the World** (11-19-06, American) delivered on the promise implicit in its title, taking audiences on a whirlwind global spree. Action rushed from New York to the Sierra Madre to Japan, Arabia, and a floating iceberg as the hero dashed to rescue his sweetheart and her banker-father from the inexhaustible wiles of the villain. The hero was named Jack, while the heroine shared the same given name as heroines in *The Girl of the Sunny South* and *Daughters of Men*—Grace.

Eleanor Robson and her latest leading man, H. B. Warner, were seen in a second offering, a double bill of Eugene W. Presbrey's **Susan in Search of a Husband,** taken from a Jerome K. Jerome story, and Clothilde Graves's one-acter **A Tenement Tragedy** (11-20-06, Savoy). The comedy had Miss Robson playing an American girl who has been deserted after her wedding and comes to England to serve as a chambermaid. She discovers the groom she believed to be an ordinary sailor is actually an English

lord. All is made happy by the final curtain. In the shorter piece the star played a waif rescued by a coster from a cruel organ grinder (Frederic de Belleville). When the old Italian attempts to reclaim her, the waif stabs him to death. Critics felt the weak drama did not give Miss Robson a chance to demonstrate her abilities in a more serious part, yet they found occasion to praise Emily Rigl—briefly, years before, a star herself—in the very tiny part of the organ grinder's wife. The double bill was short-lived.

Not so **The Rose of the Rancho** (11-27-06, Belasco), which David Belasco rewrote from Richard Walton Tully's California play, *Juanita*. Juanita (Frances Starr) is the half-American daughter of long-established landowners in California. Over her family's objections she has fallen in love with Kearney (Charles Richman), a young man sent by Washington to investigate murderous landgrabbing by some brutal, unscrupulous Americans. Juanita's own homestead is menaced by a vicious Nebraskan, Kinkaid (John W. Cope), and when he makes it appear that Kearney is in league with him, Juanita feels alienated. However, Kearney manages to save her land from Kinkaid and prove his own affection.

Theatre commented, "The plot, as may be inferred, is exceedingly thin. It is chiefly as spectacle that the piece pleases and holds the interest." What made the show so big a hit was Belasco's impeccable mounting. The *Dramatic Mirror* described the opening, set in the 1850s in "the mission garden at San Juan Bautista, in the late afternoon of a hot summer day. Padre Antonio, superior of the mission, is dozing over his missal and bottle of wine, on the porch of the mission house. On the bench under a rose tree Don Luis de la Torre . . . is sleeping away the afternoon. Pico, the water carrier, comes drowsily through the gate, a sleepy paroquet perched on her brown arm, languidly fills her water jar at the fountain, and passes out again to the hot, dusty street. Sunol, the muleteer, drives up to the gate with a carload of girls, stops and climbs down to gather oranges for his charges, leaves a coin in the Padre's hand, and drives on again." Belasco's picture-painting was just as vivid in the remaining two acts. The second took place on the patio of Juanita's home, framed by adobe galleries. Colorful, torrid Spanish dances enlivened the scene. The final setting was the roof of the house, near dawn, as the figures wait to see if help will arrive before Kinkaid's men seize the place. The chill of dawn mingled with the chill of fear. Along with his magnificently detailed settings (by Ernest Gros and William

Buckland), Belasco presented his newest discovery, Frances Starr.

· · ·

Frances [Grant] Starr (1881–1973) was born in Oneonta, N.Y., and spent many years in stock, including the old Murray Hill Company, after making her debut in 1901. Spotting her, Belasco hired her to replace Minnie Dupree in *The Music Master,* then advanced her to stardom. With her light hair and soft blue eyes, many considered her the most beautiful of Belasco's leading ladies.

· · ·

Everything came together so brilliantly that *The Rose of the Rancho* played out the season, took a summer vacation, then returned for eleven more weeks, compiling a run of 327 performances. But the day had dawned when newer writers such as William Vaughn Moody and Rachel Crothers would begin to alert an increasingly large number of critics and playgoers to Belasco's contrivances. His remarkable skill rested primarily in a form of theatrical sleight-of-hand, dressing high-class melodrama so sumptuously that it almost passed for something noble.

There was no pretense of nobility in touring melodramas that raised their curtains the following Monday. In Langdon McCormick's **How Hearts Are Broken** (12-3-06, American), a man kills the child of the girl he has pretended to marry. As he is leaving he bumps into a blind fiddler, who innocently shakes his hand. The mother is brought to trial for the murder of her child by a venal district attorney who offers to drop the case if she will sleep with him. Her own fiancé is a lawyer. He defends her by having the fiddler shake hands with the murderer and incriminate him. Before he is led away the killer murders a second time—killing the district attorney.

In his autobiography Oliver Morosco claimed co-authorship with Harry Cottrell for their Los Angeles hit *In South Car'liney.* By the time a revised, enlarged version reached New York as **A Southern Vendetta** (12-3-06, Star), Morosco was credited only as producer, and Cottrell was listed as the sole author. Whatever the precise relationship of the two men, the project represented a step down for both of them, since *The Judge and the Jury* at least had been given a first-class house. The story centered on a feud between two families in South Carolina moonshine country, a feud finally resolved when the son of one house wins the daughter of the second. Of course, perfidy abounded before the all-smiles ending.

The difference between these touring plays and the type of melodrama Belasco and others offered to Broadway was a difference more of degree than kind, but it was a large degree. And the fates of the plays varied greatly, too. Although the better touring shows often circulated for many seasons, changing homes weekly, that appears to have been their history. The best first-class melodramas enjoyed long runs in major cities, sent out several road companies, and subsequently were revived for years at the best stock houses. Even literate, affluent playgoers were eager for superior escapism. The day when so many theatres would go dark because of nose-in-the-air critics and equally destructive, self-aggrandizing intellectuals was still decades away.

George Broadhurst's **The Man of the Hour** (12-4-06, Savoy), the season's biggest hit, was another excellent instance of a play that left much to be desired as high art but nonetheless was gripping theatre. One critic branded it "a virile melodrama," while another, less pleased with its construction and depth, suggested, "The success of the play is in its characters." Charles Wainwright (James E. Wilson), a crafty, rapacious financier—"A lion would hunt much more successfully if he did not roar so loudly"—and Richard Horigan (Frank MacVicars), the arrogant local political boss, set out to obtain a perpetual monopoly on their city's public transit. To this end they push through the election of young Alwyn Bennett (Frederick Perry) as mayor. Bennett has been little more than a playboy, so the men feel he will be tractable. They take no heed of his warning to them, "If I am elected I shall keep my oath of office." When Bennett vetoes the franchise, the men use every means to destroy him. Bennett's problem is compounded by the fact that he loves Wainwright's niece, Dallas (Lillian Kemble), whose fortune is tied to the franchise's success. On Bennett's side are James Phelan (George Fawcett), a maverick alderman, and Henry Thompson (Geoffrey Stein), Wainwright's private secretary, who unbeknownst to Wainwright is the son of a man Wainwright drove to suicide. Together they frustrate the monopolists while saving Dallas's money.

The story unfolded excitingly, even though Broadhurst's writing was not without its weaknesses. There were theatrically convenient coincidences such as Thompson entering unseen by the other characters to overhear Dallas ask, "What is the real story about Mr. Garrison?" Thompson, whose actual name is Garrison, knows she is asking about his father. He *"grips his hands and sets his teeth. Then he stands, breathless, listening."* There was also the inevitable speechifying. And, as usual in muckraking tales, too many characters were preposterously black or white. Thus Bennett, on learning that his father had been guilty of cheating, insists on making the facts public and personally paying back the amount his father stole. On the other hand, some of the characters are more humanely drawn. Phelan is depicted as a crass politician opposing Horigan simply because Horigan has the power he himself craves, yet he throws large picnics not merely to placate voters but because he enjoys seeing underprivileged women and children made carefree: "It's a happy day when I down a man who's agin' me, it's a happy day when I help a man who's *for* me, but the *happiest* days *for me* are my picnic days." Even the unscrupulous Horigan is given his moment when he defends grafting by showing how the most respectable professions and institutions have their forms of graft: "Churches and colleges accept money they know has been obtained by fraud and oppression—graft!" One of the most entertainingly drawn characters was Dallas's empathetic if know-it-all-at-twenty-one brother, Perry. His light comic touch in the part gave a further boost to the rising Douglas Fairbanks. *The Man of the Hour* ran for more than a year, compiling a record of 479 performances.

Clyde Fitch's second play of the season, **The Girl Who Has Everything** (12-4-06, Liberty), ran one-tenth as long but nonetheless gave beguiling Eleanor Robson and skillful H. B. Warner their best roles of the season so far. Sylvia Lang has taken the post of housekeeper to her widowed brother-in-law (Earle Browne), although she knows his dissolute ways drove her sister to an early grave. Her hope is to bring up her nephews and nieces as properly as possible. But difficulties arise when the brother-in-law claims his wife left a second will leaving her money not to the children but to him. He and his corrupt lawyer (Reuben Fax) claim to have evidence that the woman had been unfaithful and changed her will in remorse. Sylvia's beau is a young lawyer, Philip Waring, who complicates matters by believing the false charges and advising Sylvia to drop the case. She finds another lawyer and wins, yet for some reason (shades of *The Three of Us*) still loves Philip. The tiny nephews and nieces provided the "cute" touches at which Fitch was so adept.

Faroff times or faraway places provided the settings for the next spate of openings. The only first-class offering was by Martin V. Merle, a young man who was still studying at a Jesuit seminary. His **The Light Eternal** (12-10-06, Majestic) employed blank verse as stilted as his title to tell how an early Christian (Edward Mackay) endures myriad persecutions by his fellow Romans. He succeeds in converting a princess (Edythe Chapman), but even she cannot save him from being fed to the lions. A high moment came when he was ordered to kneel and pray before a statue of Jupiter. The sky darkened abruptly, a flash of lightning rent the statue, and a luminous cross appeared in its place. The kindest thing critics could say about the play was that it might have been better suited to a combination house.

But combination houses were occupied with more stereotypical melodramas. In Al Woods's production of Owen Davis's sixth new play of the season, **A Marked Woman** (12-10-06, West End), the lady in question is the daughter of the American minister to China. She is kidnapped by a Chinese prince, but when she refuses to marry him he also abducts her boyfriend, a naval officer. That brings the navy in to rescue the pair. The final act depicted the successful defense of the American consulate during the Boxer uprising. Woods claimed the handsome costumes had been designed and sewn in China, but no one took the claim seriously.

The White Chief (12-10-06, Star) offered more of the same, only this time the adventures unfolded in a paint-and-canvas Arabia. Thirty years before the play's action begins, a lady had misplaced her baby boy while traveling in the desert. Now that her foster daughter has reached marriageable age, she has returned, hoping to find him and effect an alliance. Her deceitful lawyer has other plans—to kill the old gal and marry the young girl. He stabs the lady and is about to flee, taking the protesting girl with him, when a dashing Arab chieftain dashes onstage and stops him. The lady dies in the chieftain's arms, but not before she recognizes him as the baby she left behind thirty years earlier. The lawyer escapes, and a three-act chase ensues. At one point the attorney seems to gain the upper hand, when his mercenaries capture the chieftain and bind him to stakes in the desert, hoping he will bake to death. Since the leading role was played by one Montgomery Irving, a strongman who had been billed in vaudeville as "the original Sandow," few doubted he would tear himself loose and persist until the villain is led to prison and he and his newfound sweetheart can take the next steamer for America. Four live camels, a horse, and "a knowing donkey" provided some verisimilitude for a drama that needed all it could get.

Two old novels that had been refitted for the stage several times before were offered in fresh redactions. At the demodé 14th Street Theatre Mary J. Holmes's *Lena Rivers,* the story of a young woman whose ignorance of who is her father precipitates crises, was presented on the 16th in a version by Beulah Poynter. More important, four nights later at the Manhattan, William A. Brady brought out *Les Misérables* under the title **The Law and the Man.** Wilton Lackaye was the dramatizer, director, and star. Lackaye and such capable supporting players as Jeffreys Lewis and Melbourne MacDowell resorted to some good, old-fashioned emoting to add fire to an already heated story. The production was lavish, although cumbersome scene changes sometimes slowed the action. A divided press, playgoers who either preferred to read the book or to avoid an unpleasant story, and a bad case of the grippe, which forced Lackaye to miss many performances, cut down on attendance. The New York engagement lasted only until the beginning of February. Making her Broadway debut first as Fantine, whom Valjean rescues from the accusatory Javert, and then as Cosette, Fantine's illegitimate daughter, was a young actress billed as Josephine Sherwood. Decades on she would become a stage favorite under her married name, Josephine Hull.

Another lady who would move on to fame and fortune under her married name stumbled badly on her first outing. Inverting her married and maiden names, and probably trying to hide her womanhood, she offered her play, **The Double Life** (12-24-06, Bijou), under the nom de plume Rinehart Roberts. It was designed as a vehicle for the protean Dutch performer Henri de Vries, who played Frank Van Buren. Frank loses all memory of his past after he is grazed by a bullet in a robbery. Adopting the name Joseph Hartmann, he accepts work as a miner in the very mine of which he is part owner, but the father and son who hold the other two-thirds are banking on his not regaining his memory before the law hands over his share to them. He serves as a leader of the miners until the sight of his daughter in the arms of one of the mine owners shocks him into recalling the past. A confrontation and resolution follow. Apart from quibbling about his sometimes too heavily accented English, most critics admired the way the star differentiated between the carefree Van Buren and his more somber, intense persona as Hartmann. The same critics were all but unanimous in condemning the play, one of them branding it "an amateurish, poorly constructed melodrama." This led De Vries to take it upon himself to rewrite the play, and when Mrs. Rinehart learned of his changes she exercised her option to close the show. Her stand for artistic independence was deemed "an act of folly" by *Theatre.*

Lillian Mortimer's **A Man's Broken Promise** (12-24-06, 14th St.) was probably as poorly constructed as Mrs. Rinehart's melodrama, but since it was aimed at another sort of audience it was judged by other standards, when it was judged at all. "There is not a dull moment in the play and climax follows climax in hair-raising successions," one of its few reviewers observed. The man who broke his promise to marry the heroine did more than that. He tried to drown her, attempted to burn her true sweetheart alive, planned to kill his own half-brother to gain his wealth, and gloated over other dastardly deeds before meeting his just end.

By the early twentieth century many a show meant for New York folded after "dogging it" for a time on the road. However, a few first-class productions were designed solely for touring. One was Kellett Chambers's **The Butterfly** (12-24-06, Chestnut St., Philadelphia), which served Lillian Russell as a replacement for her failed *Barbara's Millions.* She played the widow of a man "who gathered up a great many millions by stealing railroads and invested a few thousand in salvation by supporting a church." His will has stipulated that if she remarries it must be to someone American-born. So when she falls in love with an English lord (Fred J. Tiden), she enters into a marriage of convenience with a personable American composer (Eugene Ormonde), intending to divorce him promptly thereafter. Audiences could immediately surmise that the English lord soon would be given the heave-ho.

The old year went out with a bang. Six novelties arrived on New Year's Eve. Half of them were hits and enjoyed sizable runs. The longest run was awarded to Beulah Marie Dix and Evelyn Greenleaf Sutherland's comedy-fantasy **The Road to Yesterday** (12-31-06, Lyric). Chaperoned by her Aunt Harriet (Alice Gale), Elspeth Tyrell (Minnie Dupree) comes to England to visit an artist, Will Leveson (Wright Kramer), and to see the sights. After an exhausting day of touring, she comes back to Will's studio, where Will's friend, Jack Greatorex (Robert Dempster), is posing for Will in a 17th-century costume. Will's wife, Malena (Helen Ware), jokes that the knife Jack is holding looks familiar and that it probably belonged to her when she was a gypsy in a previous life. Fatigued from sightseeing, Elspeth falls asleep and dreams she has traveled back to the 17th century. Aunt Harriet is now Goody Phelps, the scolding mistress of an inn, and she herself is Lady Elizabeth, who is fleeing from her libidinous guardian. All the people she has met in Will's studio reappear in new (or older) guises, but none more prominently than Jack. He is something of an outcast, eating his food with his knife and calling for help at the first sign of danger. But after varied trials he does manage to slay the wicked guardian, just as Elspeth awakens from her reverie. Elspeth is not slow to understand that she has found the man of her dreams.

Critics could not agree on how successful the play was as a satire on recent swashbucklers, but most confessed to enjoying themselves. A surprising number compared the play's fantastic touches to those in *Peter Pan* and found the American ladies need not take a back seat. Many of the same reviewers pulled out two of their favorite adjectives, "charming" and "winsome," to describe Miss Dupree and her acting. Photographs show settings were largely painted rather than architectural. Thus the inn's jugs and baskets, and even the niche in which they were stored over the door, were all the scene painter's handiwork. The show ran until July heat closed it. In 1924 it provided the source for Victor Herbert's last musical, *The Dream Girl*.

Two more mundane comedies, which opened the same night, were also musicalized eventually. Coincidentally, both shows ran just over twenty weeks. One was William Collier and Grant Stewart's **Caught in the Rain** (12-31-06, Garrick). The curtain rose on a Denver street scene—a Chinese laundryman hurries by, a barber closes his shop to attend a funeral, small boys rush back and forth, and a colored nurse pushes a baby carriage. Once the passing show has moved on, we learn that money-mad James Maxwell (George Nash) and his partner, woman-hating Dick Crawford (Collier), own a profitable copper mine. Maxwell is determined to force their neighboring mine owner, Mason (John Saville), to sell and to that end is prepared to foreclose on a mortgage he holds. After Maxwell has gone, a thunderstorm breaks loose, so Crawford takes refuge under the barbershop awning, not caring that a pretty girl (Nanette Comstock) has taken refuge there, too. A fierce thunderclap prompts the girl to grab Crawford for protection. The terrified girl and the startled, deadpan Crawford sink down side by side on the barbershop bench as the rain pours in torrents and the curtain falls. It develops that Mason's only chance for saving his mine is to marry off his daughter, and he asks his old buddy, Crawford, to be the groom. Out of duty Crawford consents, but then, remembering the girl he met in the rain, he attempts to back out. Naturally Mason's daughter and the girl in the rain are one and the same, but Crawford doesn't know that. Mistaken identities and misunderstandings pile upon each other until just before the final curtain. Collier—"calm, impudent, dry, perky and embarrassed"—dominated his own comedy, but Nash's conscienceless, pushy vulgarian gave him a

run for his money. In 1920 the comedy was set to music as *Pitter Patter.*

None of the evening's other openings has proved as long-lived or adaptable as **Brewster's Millions** (12-31-06, New Amsterdam), which Winchell Smith and Byron Ongley took from George Barr McCutcheon's novel. Subsequently it was made into two musicals that closed before reaching New York (*Zip Goes a Million* and *Bubbling Over*), a hit London musical (also called *Zip Goes a Million*), and several films. Montgomery Brewster (Edward Abeles) has been left $1 million by his grandfather, but Monty's uncle, who hated the old man, also dies, and leaves him $7 million provided he spends the grandfather's million within a year without explaining his action to anyone, without giving a cent to charity, and without marrying and thus giving the million to his wife. Monty sets about meeting the stipulations only to have all his plans backfire. He invests in a hopeless comic opera; it becomes a smash hit. He puts his money into plunging stocks; they suddenly turn around and skyrocket. He bets on the longest of long shots; the horse wins. So he takes his friends aboard a yacht for a world cruise. Even that cannot use up the million. A storm arises. The captain urges heading for port. Instead Monty blows the whistle to summon salvagers, knowing their charges will eat up his remaining fortune. Just as the year runs out and Monty thinks he is home free (and broke), a friend appears. This man (George Probart) had lost $35,000 of Monty's money and run off in shame. Now he has recouped his losses and comes to present Monty with a check. Calculating frantically, Monty figures out that $35,000 is precisely the amount the executors will require for handling his uncle's will. He hands over the check, proves he is penniless, and wins the $7 million. Of course, he also wins a lovely young lady, Peggy Gray (Mary Ryan). The comedy introduced a new playwright to Broadway, one who would go on to considerable fame.

. . .

Winchell Smith (1872–1933) was born in Hartford, Conn. He came to New York and took work as an usher at the Herald Square Theatre, where his off-hours mimickry of Richard Mansfield caught Mansfield's eye. The actor encouraged him to take up performing, and he made his debut in 1896 as the telegraph operator in *Secret Service.* He later became Arnold Daly's silent partner in the first American mounting of *Candida.* In afteryears he not only wrote plays but became a sought-after director and, most important, the leading play doctor of his era. He is wrongly credited with introducing the name George Spelvin to hide an actor's identity, but there is agreement that he did popularize the name, which he first employed in this play.

. . .

The last first-class opening needed no musicalization since it was laced with song and dance. Billed as a "farce with a song now and then," I. N. Morris's **Matilda** (12-31-06, Lincoln Square) was one of the period's many entertainments that straddled the fence between genres. In fact, since two minor figures were credited with lyrics and music, the piece arguably belongs in the roster of the lyric theatre. Like *Brewster's Millions,* it involved a preposterous stage will and took all its characters out on a yacht. In this instance the heroine (Amy Ricard) and an English lord (Lionel Walsh) are required by the will to marry. If either demurs, the other receives the entire estate. Matilda hires an actor friend, Rod Archer (Alfred Hickman), to impersonate her and make her seem so objectionable that the lord will back out. Her plan works. The setting on the yacht, with Manhattan's harbor and skyscrapers in the distance, won a round of applause. An even bigger showstopper was a song, "Wow-Yip-Po," in which the false Matilda celebrates the exploits of an Indian, Big Chief Husky Bear.

Originality was rarely a hallmark of touring melodramas, so, with renewed interest in *Bertha, the Sewing Machine Girl,* there was little reason why Owen Davis should not call his seventh play of the season **Nellie, the Beautiful Cloak Model** (12-31-06, West End). Al Woods again was Davis's producer. And Davis's story, like his title, covered well-trod grounds. Nellie had been separated from her mother in infancy. She has come to New York to earn a living, unaware her mother is now rich and seeking her. Her nefarious cousin is also hunting her down, hoping to dispose of her. In his autobiography Davis tells what happened next: "In the first act he pushed her under a descending elevator in the basement of a department store. In Act II he threw her off the Brooklyn Bridge and in the third he bound her to the tracks of the elevated railroad just as a train came thundering along. In the fourth act he climbs in her bedroom window at an early hour of the morning and when both modesty and prudence force her to shrink away from him he looked at her reproachfully and said: 'Why do you fear me, Nellie?' " In case all that failed to move playgoers, a little crippled brother hobbled pathetically across the stage from time to time.

But *Nellie* was straightforward and logical compared with Lem B. Parker's **The Phantom Detective** (12-31-06, American). An American general on a visit to India had stolen a potentate's sacred, bejeweled crown. In return the potentate had kidnapped the general's daughter and raised her, but she had escaped and returned to America. She has taken employment as housekeeper with the general, although neither recognizes the other. The Indian potentate comes to America, kills the general, and allows suspicion to fall on the housekeeper. The general's cruel adopted daughter and her lover, a forger, plot to run off with the general's money. A young detective, who loves the housekeeper, takes it upon himself to put all matters to rights, though that means everyone must somehow go to the Solomon Islands and the detective must rescue his girl from a lion's den.

At the beginning of 1907, Clyde Fitch occupied a unique place in his theatrical world. While not as prolific as several mass producers of touring melodramas, he was far more productive than any other writer for first-class stages. Yet this astonishing output did not prevent his being considered America's leading dramatist, even if it did lead many critics to question how much better a writer he might be would he devote more time to each work. Inevitably, some commentators felt that speed was not his problem, but rather that his own artistic limitations were. They argued he wrote as well as he could, and if "his fingers itched for his box of tricks," that was because he was incapable of creating any other way. His third and fourth plays of the season premiered on the same January evening, one across the street from the other in the heart of Times Square—renamed from Longacre Square less than three years before. Neither appeared to be a success. The less interesting, at least artistically, ran five weeks; the other ran only three plus a series of ten special matinees before embarking on tour.

Several reviewers prophesied that the more scandalous theme of **The Straight Road** (1-7-07, Astor) might help it commercially. An heiress (Dorothy Dorr) who does social work assists Mary O'Hara (Blanche Walsh), a Skid Row floozy, to rehabilitate herself. When the reformed girl comes to understand that the heiress's beau (Howard Estabrook) is merely a fortune hunter, she risks her restored reputation to show up the suitor for what he is. One critic claimed Fitch was suffering from "Kremeritis," resorting to the cheap ploys of touring melodramas. In the first act the heiress proves the floozy's worth to both herself and the floozy by placing a little crippled boy (Cornelia Flood) in the arms of the flustered girl. The mutual affection that springs up instantly told all and turned out to be one of the play's high moments. Afterwards, when Mary has arranged to meet the heiress's suitor in her room and has invited the innocent heiress to visit moments later, plans go awry with the unexpected arrival of Mary's own beau (Charles Dalton), a saloonkeeper. He misconstrues the scene and angrily casts off Mary, whose peace of mind and confidence are saved only as she glances at a portrait of the Virgin hanging on the wall.

A major critical complaint against **The Truth** (1-7-07, Criterion) was that it suffered from too much talk and too little action. Interest was maintained to a large extent because subsidiary, comic characters took over during the last half of the play. Early in the first act Becky Warder (Clara Bloodgood) insists, "I never told a malicious lie in my life. I never told a fib that hurt anyone but myself!" Unfortunately, Becky is a habitual liar, and the ironic truth of her comment soon comes to haunt her. A dear friend, Mrs. Lindon (Mrs. Sam Sothern), has separated from her philandering husband and has poured her heart out to Becky, hoping she can help rekindle the husband's affection. Although Becky truly loves her own husband (William J. Kelly), her response is to meet with the separated Lindon (George Spink) every day and carry on an innocent flirtation, all the while sincerely attempting to direct the man's attentions back to his wife. When confronted by Mrs. Lindon and her own husband, Becky glibly denies everything, even when the findings of a detective hired by Mrs. Lindon are placed before her. Becky promises Mr. Warder not to lie anymore, then immediately breaks her promise. This is too much for Warder, who leaves the house. Frightened, Becky rushes to Baltimore, where her gambler-father (William B. Mack) lives by his wits in a boardinghouse run by the pretentious, coarse-grained Mrs. Crespigny (Zelda Sears). (Part of Fitch's catty description of her on her first entrance reads: *"She has innumerable bracelets and bangles, and an imitation jewelled chain flaunts a heavy pair of lorgnettes, like a gargoyle hanging over a much-curved bust. Enormous wax pearls in her ears are in direct contrast to the dark beginnings of her otherwise russet-gold hair."*) The old man owes months of back rent to his landlady, whom he keeps putting off with promises of marriage, for, like his daughter, he lies perpetually. He convinces Becky the only way to bring back her husband is to wire him that she is dangerously ill. Sure enough, Warder hurries to her bedside. But Becky balks at her father's scheme, crying, "If I can't win his love back by the truth, I'll never be able to keep it, so what's the use of getting it back at all?" Whether or not Warder believes her latest promise never to lie again, he responds, "We don't love people because

they are perfect. . . . We love them because they are themselves."

Most reviewers gave Miss Bloodgood's performance their qualified approval, perhaps liking her more in her lighter moments than in her emotive ones. The critic for the *Dramatic Mirror* gave special mention to her "assumption of an unmistakable Baltimore accent." Followup notices were more flattering than were morning-after reviews, but by the time they appeared the damage had been done. Fitch could take some consolation from the fact that *The Truth* was subsequently a major success in London, running there for 170 performances, and all across the rest of Europe. But even that success was marred by a ghastly footnote, especially in the light of critical praise for Miss Bloodgood's "Baltimore accent." On the post-Broadway tour the star was found dead, a suicide, in her Baltimore hotel. Fitch strenuously denied the widely bruited rumor that her suicide had been prompted by his dedicating the play's published text to its London star, Marie Tempest.

Three combination houses offered novelties the same evening. Charles H. Fleming's **The Blackthorn** (1-7-07, Third Ave.) had been touring the hinterlands for several seasons with its story of a cad who proposes that a happily married woman elope with him. When she refuses, he sets in motion all the stock contrivances of the genre: locking the couple's child in a burning building, falsely accusing the wife of infidelity, driving the husband to drink. Moments before the last curtain, a will discovered in a blackthorn cane makes the reunited couple very rich. The other two openings, Langdon McCormick's **Our Friend Fritz** (1-7-07, 14th St.) and Robert Sidney's **Metz in the Alps** (1-7-07, Metropolis), were alike in that their German-accented heroes warbled a number of songs while helping others overcome obstacles thrown in their paths by their plays' antagonists. Both clearly stemmed from Emmet's *Fritz* plays and as such might be considered half-hearted musicals.

Great as Nazimova's November triumph had been in *Hedda Gabler,* it paled beside the acclaim accorded her Nora when Henry Miller presented *A Doll's House* at the Princess on January 14. Her ruthless, calculating, seemingly statuesque Hedda gave way to a petite, spontaneous, and girlish doll-wife whose awakening inner awareness finally uncovered her iron resolve. One awed reviewer remarked, "An apparent change in stature, gesture, voice and soul . . . made the audience wonder if this could be the same woman acting." Her performance prodded another aisle-sitter to observe, "She promises to become a figure in the theatre of every country which has a drama worth the name." The production moved to the Bijou for a month's stand, and a few weeks later *Hedda* was returned for a thirty-two-performance run at the Princess.

Eleanor Robson and H. B. Warner capped their up-and-down season with Paul Armstrong's **Salomy Jane** (1-19-07, Liberty), which was based on Bret Harte's story "Salomy Jane's Kiss" and was called that on some early programs. When Salomy realizes that the handsome young cowboy (Earle Browne) she loves is too craven to kill her unwanted but persistent suitor, she is at a loss until the menacing pest is shot by a horse thief who is only a step ahead of a posse. Although the killer (Warner) admits he killed the man for personal reasons and not to help Salomy, she kisses him and helps him escape. He is caught, but she again helps him to flee, this time with her at his side. The play was seen as an effective romantic melodrama, filled with such interesting minor figures as a good-hearted gambler (Holbrook Blinn), a fire-eating Kentucky Colonel (Reuben Fax), and a youngster (Donald Gallaher) under the spell of dime novels. The play ran for 122 performances before riding out to the road.

E. H. Sothern and Julia Marlowe, year by year adding to their reputation as America's premiere acting couple (although Sothern was still married to Virginia Harned), began their season with Sudermann's "turgid," "ponderous," "uninspired" retelling of the story of **John the Baptist** (1-21-07, Lyric). Miss Marlowe was, of course, Salome. Salomes or Salomys seemed to be voguish this season. The very next night, the Metropolitan Opera presented the American premiere of Strauss's then controversial *Salome.* Two months later, a German translation of Wilde's *Salome* was presented at the Irving Place.

For the last several seasons, stars of the musical stage had been trying their luck in nonmusical offerings. The latest to switch allegiance was frizzly-haired Lulu Glaser. Her vehicle was Sydney Rosenfeld's **The Aero Club** (1-28-07, Criterion). She played Myrtle Webb, who overhears her prospective mother-in-law's unkind comments about her and runs off to sail in a balloon. The balloon is becalmed, and Myrtle and the pilot, Jack Chandler (Orme Caldara), look to spend the night up in the air. They remove their hats, coats, and shoes, hoping the loss of that little weight will nudge the balloon. It does—right into a tree. Some additional complications follow, such as Jack's being found with the picture of a married woman in his pocket. However, before long Jack and Myrtle decide they would make a happy couple. The balloon was never

shown onstage. At most, the second act began with the balloon's anchor smashing through the window of a vacation cottage (owned by the husband of the woman whose picture is discovered in Jack's pocket). The anchor rips out the sash and carries it skyward.

Despite the number of superior and highly successful American plays produced during the season, nearly a century later only George Bernard Shaw's English comedies are regularly revived, although their initial American receptions were mixed and their runs (to a large degree because of prior bookings) short. **Captain Brassbound's Conversion** (1-28-07, Empire) may not be staged as regularly as *Caesar and Cleopatra,* but it does hold the boards. The comedy centers on an outspoken, uncrushable English lady whose unconventional attitudes win over wild Arabs, her snooty brother-in-law, and his piratical nephew. Ellen Terry, for whom the role was written, was America's first Lady Cicely Waynflete, and James Carew, soon to be her husband, was Brassbound.

The month ended with Sothern and Marlowe's second presentation, Percy MacKaye's blank-verse tragedy **Jeanne d'Arc** (1-29-07, Lyric). Percy was the late, pathblazing Steele MacKaye's son. The younger MacKaye was hardly a trailblazer, but he was in the vanguard of American dramatists who had allied themselves with England's Stephen Phillips and similarly minded Continental writers determined to restore poetry to the stage. His Jeanne tells a wounded soldier of the angelic voices she has heard and of her martial visions:

Out there—beyond: in the wide world beyond!
And there were thousands flashing in the sun
Beneath dark walls and mighty battlements,
And all their shining limbs were stiff with steel;
And rank by rank they rattled as they marched.

A shepherd's staff held high in her hands becomes a gleaming cross. At court she is not to be fooled; she immediately points out the disguised king. She leads the soldiers into battle and crowns the dauphin. But the tide turns against her, and she is condemned to death. Apart from Jeanne the most important figure was the cynical if honest Duc d'Alençon (Sothern), who comes both to believe in the maid and to fall in love with her. In her cell they renew each other's faith, and Jeanne's last words to him are "Be not afraid." The production caught the color and pageantry of the late middle ages but often illustrated what later might have been left to the imagination. For example, a winged St. Michael, flaming sword in hand, entered to protect the maiden from d'Alençon before the soldier's conversion. No critic objected, though some felt the actresses who played the saints in Jeanne's visions did not bring sufficient poetry to their readings. Succeeding weeks saw the company perform *The Sunken Bell, Hamlet, Romeo and Juliet,* and *The Merchant of Venice.*

That willing suspension of disbelief so often necessary in the theatre was particularly needed at combination houses. Arthur Nelson's **The Governor's Pardon** (2-4-07, Third Ave.) was a case in point. Years before the action of the play was supposed to begin, the heroine's mother had quarreled with her husband and run off to become mistress to an Indian chief. That wicked redskin had farmed out the woman's daughter—the heroine—with the idea that when she came of age he would reclaim her, marry her, and inherit her fortune. He now learns the grown young lady has fallen in love with a chauffeur. Audiences might not foresee that the villain would be named White Hawk and the heroine Margie, but even with their limited educations, they probably could make an educated guess about the hero's name—Jack, Jack Winton. Jack is to race his automobile against one owned by White Hawk and a crooked associate, Giovanna—who, despite the name, was a man. The miscreants plan to tamper with Jack's car, but Isaac Eichoch, a detective posing as a Jewish peddler, gets wind of the scheme and foils it. So White Hawk abducts Margie, chased by Jack, Isaac, and Tom Watson, a man escaped from prison, where he was sent on White Hawk's perjured testimony. At first White Hawk hides Margie in a mill, but when her friends draw close he places her in his car and hurries off. The automobile chase that followed, using two treadmills and a fast-moving panorama, was the evening's high point. Margie is rescued, but White Hawk escapes and alerts the police to Watson's presence. They are about to rearrest him when Jack dashes in with the governor's pardon. Isaac shoots White Hawk; Jack and Margie embrace. That the pardoning of a secondary figure should provide the play's title made little sense, but then so did the rest of the play.

Yet another instance of how fundamentally close first-class melodrama could be to touring melodrama was apparent in **Genesee of the Hills** (2-11-07, Astor), taken from Marah Ellis Ryan's *Told in the Hills* by Ryan and McPherson Turnbull. His story echoed *John Ermine of Yellowstone.* "Genesee" Jack Stewart (Robert Drouet), a white scout, is held in contempt by many of his neighbors because he was raised by Indians and remains friendly with them. Jack rescues Rachel Hardy (Chrystal Herne) from a snowstorm and allows her to spend the evening in his cabin. As a result, when he is accused of stealing horses on the same night, he can provide no alibi without unfairly damaging Rachel's reputation. He escapes from prison on learning the army plans to attack his Indian friends. The Indians seem to be surrounded, but Jack shows them an escape path. During the skirmish a young chieftain is killed and Jack is inadvertently shot by the Indians. Rachel promises to nurse him back to health. The production had some awkward moments. A grieving Jack is supposed to pick up the dead body of the young chieftain, but the scene drew snickers when audiences realized the "dead man" was a dummy.

Ernest Denny's fetching London fluff, **All-of-a-Sudden Peggy** (2-11-07, Bijou), starred Henrietta Crosman as the daughter of a deceased American entomologist. Her mother (Ida Waterman) pushes her to marry an English lord (Ernest Stallard), another spider-enthusiast, but she lands his younger brother (Frank Gillmore) and mates mama and the lord—thus becoming her own mother's sister-in-law. The star's exuberant gifts allowed audiences to overlook that she was nearer fifty than the twenty-five Peggy was supposed to be.

Ellen Terry closed out her short season with a double bill. Her audiences were familiar with *Nance Oldfield,* but Hermann Heijermans's **The Good Hope** (2-11-07, Empire) was new to them. Miss Terry played an old woman who has lost her husband and two sons to the sea and now must face the loss of her last two sons, who are drowned after sailing on a ship its owner knew was unseaworthy. Most critics, ignoring its small debt to *Pillars of Society,* admired the play, but not a few complained that the actors, good as they were, were too English to seem Dutch.

The lone play to open the next night ran for seventy-three performances, longer than all three of its immediate predecessors combined. Admittedly Arthur Schnitzler's **The Reckoning** (2-12-07, Berkeley Lyceum) was performed in a tiny auditorium, but it told a sad tale and had no major players to act as lures. An impressionable young girl learns that the man she thought loved her has been unfaithful and has been shot in a duel with a humiliated husband. She is warned that, if she goes to the cemetery to mourn him, she will not be the only distressed woman at his grave. Surprisingly, the drama enjoyed a successful tour and ran three weeks at the larger Madison Square Theatre the following season.

A combination house offered the only novelty to premiere the next week, Walter Montague's **Slaves of Passion** (2-18-06, Third Ave.). The villain is a music hall proprietor who kidnaps and tortures pretty girls as a sideline. His mistake is to attempt to kidnap the sweetheart of the hero (monicker: Jack Stirling). The usual outrages and escapes pile up before the villain accidentally swallows a poisoned drink his crony had meant for the heroine.

To all too many American dramatists, the Civil War still meant the touchy romance of a Confederate belle and a Union officer. Louis Evan Shipman broke no new ground with **On Parole** (2-25-07, Majestic). His one original touch seemed to be having Constance Pinckney (Charlotte Walker), who serves as a spy or courier, first disguise herself as the daughter of white trash, then later reappear as her ladylike self. When Major Dale (Vincent Serrano) comments on the resemblance, she airily denies it. Serrano's gentlemanly major won more critical praise then did Miss Walker's sometimes too studiedly posed heroine, though most critics acknowledged her charm. However, the man from the *Times* grumbled that the actors impersonating servants used "too much burnt cork . . . for realism."

The most glittering opening of the evening was not a new American play but an old Norwegian one done for the first time in America. Ibsen's **Peer Gynt** (2-25-07, New Amsterdam) was presented in William and Charles Archer's translation, with a number of cuts made by the producer-star, Richard Mansfield. Grieg's famous music served as background and for entr'actes. Even with Mansfield's cuts and with intermissions kept purposely short, the play ran for more than three and a half hours. A few anti-Ibsen diehards, such as the *Tribune*'s William Winter, were unforgiving, but a majority of critics, while faulting the play or the mounting here and there, advised their readers that, all in all, Mansfield had provided a compelling evening. At first his hero was "strong and lithe of limb, with a strange dark face, the sensitiveness of which is emphasized in full rich lips and black slanting brows." He pitched his voice high and moved with what appeared to one reviewer "near effeminacy." In middle age he was a dapper materialist "with white spats and English accent." The star pulled out every trick in his book as Peer Gynt aged—his hair growing white, his face twitching, his movements enfeebled. Emma Dunn's Ase also won applause.

After three weeks Mansfield reverted to a repertory of his older vehicles for his final week. These were his last New York appearances. His tour had begun in October and was to continue through the spring, but an attack of what was first diagnosed as peritonitis forced its cancellation two days after the New York visit ended. Mansfield never recovered

and died during the summer. In a way Mansfield could be seen as a bridge between the centuries. His acting tended to be broad, with eccentricities or "dramatic externals" developed in lieu of characterization. His delivery reverberated with ample hints of an older, declamatory mode, yet he also moved insistently toward a more natural style. Most significant, while he sometimes embraced a dusty, outmoded dramaturgy, he also pioneered with Shaw and Ibsen. He was not, like Booth and so many other 19th-century stars, locked into an ossified program.

Three combination houses brought out novelties the same evening, and one was of special interest. Liebler and Co. had become a major Broadway producer and Channing Pollock a promising playwright, yet the managers offered the dramatist's **In the Bishop's Carriage** (2-25-07, Grand Opera) to New York for a single week as part of a cross-country tour of lesser theatres. The play was based on a novel by Miriam Michaelson. Its story told of a young Philadelphia lawyer who takes an interest in a girlish thief, sets out to reform her, frustrates the plans of her old buddy to keep her enmeshed in crime, and marries her. Clearly the story resembled that in *Leah Kleschna*. In his autobiography Pollock provides an interesting history of the show and his own version of who borrowed from whom. He also says the show never played Broadway, which is correct if he is referring to New York's first-class houses. He fails to mention that the role of the lawyer's mother was taken by Rose Eytinge, a downbeat farewell for a once esteemed actress.

By a curious coincidence, Charles E. Blaney and Will H. Vedder's **Kidnapped for Revenge** (2-25-07, American) told a not dissimilar tale, albeit this time the reforming crook is a young man and his parade of adventures more in keeping with thrill-a-minute touring shows. The man's name is simply Prince, and he flees from his crooked mentors, taking a crippled waif with him to spare her a life of crime. He decides he must commit one more robbery in order to be financially independent, but the man he robs turns out to be his long-lost father, who immediately embraces him. Prince warns his newfound daddy, "a millionaire banker," that two of the banker's supposed friends are none other than husband-and-wife Fagins who directed the boy's criminal activity. When they are confronted with the charge, the couple kidnap the banker's daughter, then dump her from a ferry into the river. The show's scenery earned special praise, starting with the backyard of an East Side tenement and moving on to an East River pier, the library of a Park

Avenue mansion, the criminals' apartment, a ferry slip with the ferry pulling out, a pawnshop, and a bank. As customary, songs, dances, and other variety turns dotted the action.

According to one notice, Hal Reid's **The Avenger** (2-25-07, Thalia) contained "enough avenges to supply a dozen ordinary plays." The plot detailed the murderous villain's stratagems to marry a girl he alone knows is an heiress and her beau's untiring rush to her aid.

Riveting courtroom scenes were still a comparative rarity onstage, but George Broadhurst's **The Mills of the Gods** (3-4-07, Astor) began with one. James Clarke (Robert Drouet) and Frederick Payton (Edgar Selwyn) are on trial for embezzling from the grocery firm that employed them. The lawyers' thrusts and parries make it difficult to guess how a jury will decide. Then Clarke is handed a telegram notifying him of his sister's death. He breaks down, admitting he stole to pay for the consumptive girl's treatment, and he implicates Payton. The men are sentenced to five years. The rest of the play, while melodramatic, was anticlimactic, too. Clarke escapes from prison, moves far away, and succeeds in rising to manager of a glass company. The vengeful Payton, now released, comes seeking Clarke and attempts to blackmail him. Clarke discloses his true history to his employer (Frank Sheridan) and his sweetheart (Florence Rockwell). The employer promises to ask the governor for a pardon, and the girl promises to wait if a pardon is not forthcoming. One good act was not enough, so *The Mills of the Gods* ran little more than a month—one-tenth the run of Broadhurst's earlier *The Man of the Hour.*

Ben Greet's company of English Shakespeareans received surprisingly scant attention during their month's visit, which began at the Garden on the 4th. The plays, staged in quasi-Elizabethan fashion, included *The Merchant of Venice, Macbeth, As You Like It, Julius Caesar, Much Ado About Nothing,* and *Twelfth Night,* plus two works from other epochs, *Everyman* and Reade and Taylor's *Masks and Faces.* One notice singled out for praise the young unknown who played Nerissa, Sybil Thorndike. And what would later generations have given to see some of the other as yet unheralded players in the troupe, such as Fritz Leiber, Percy Waram, or Sydney Greenstreet?

Hal Reid's fertile—some might say febrile—brain was responsible for **The Shoemaker** (3-4-07, 14th St.). The daughter of a kindly Jewish shoemaker is lured from home by an unprincipled Christian scalawag, who has driven his own wife to drink. The old man's search to recover his daughter and rehabilitate the wronged wife takes everyone from the Bowery to a Rocky Mountain mining town. The shoemaker was played by Joe Welch, a popular dialect comedian in two-a-day.

Two more Shaw plays arrived back to back. For all his growing fame, or notoriety, producers were still wary of the playwright. As a result, the Shuberts offered **Widowers' Houses** (3-7-07, Herald Square), Shaw's look at slum landlords, for a limited series of sixteen matinees. Herbert Kelcey was Cokane; Effie Shannon, Blanche; and Henry Kolker, Trench. Two nights later *Mrs. Warren's Profession* was revived at the Manhattan. Mary Shaw again was Mrs. Warren, but this time she and her fellow actors encountered none of the harassment she had met with two years before. The revival ran three weeks.

The Alaska Gold Rush provided the background for the short-lived **The Spoilers** (3-11-07, New York), which Rex Beach and James MacArthur adapted from Beach's novel. Roy Glenister (Ralph Stuart) helps smuggle Helen Chester (Evelyn Vaughan) into the territory, unaware she is carrying papers that will help some unethical politicians deprive him of his mine. She herself is unaware of the papers' import. When Roy's mine is taken from him, he not only turns against Helen, believing she knew what she was doing, but joins a band of other disgruntled citizens who are out to lynch the most crooked of the politicians. Orders for the arrest of the crooks arrive from San Francisco in time to prevent a spate of hangings. Helen, understanding she has innocently caused Roy such anguish, hands him papers that would ensure long prison terms for the politicians, but since one of them is Helen's beloved uncle, Roy tears up the evidence.

Despite the violence implicit in the story, there was no shooting. One critic observed, "As soon as a gun appears in one man's hands another man takes it way from him." The reviewer, apparently disappointed, added, "Maybe the actors are afraid of the noise." Another aisle-sitter thought a calendar advertising Cuban steamship lines was an inappropriate hanging for a Nome law office. He also was amused by the amount of bright daylight above the Arctic Circle on Christmas Day.

One of the season's finest plays received an unwarranted cold shoulder, even if its leading lady did not. In John Galsworthy's **The Silver Box** (3-18-07, Empire), a rich man's son (Harry Redding) and a scrubwoman's husband (Bruce McRae) both steal the same purse, and the poor man is sent to prison for the theft while the wealthy boy walks away scot-free. The men in Charles Frohman's production were not the center of attention. Instead all eyes fell on Ethel

Barrymore in a stunning departure from the light, elegant roles she generally had played. As the scrubwoman she appeared as an old-before-her-time young woman who once must have been beautiful. Her hair was matted; her hands grimy; her clothes cheap, drab, and a little threadbare. One reviewer, seeing her performance as a revelation, remarked, "Her voice, which in 'straight' parts sounds masked and throaty, is well suited to character work and her mannerisms . . . seem to vanish. Few actresses could have better suggested the hopeless pathos of the character. Miss Barrymore's future lies in character parts, however much many of her young woman admirers may revolt at that thought." But they did revolt, so *The Silver Box* was withdrawn after less than three weeks, and the star resumed touring in *Captain Jinks,* following some brief revivals to fill out the booking.

The same evening witnessed the American debut of the great Italian actor Ermete Novelli. In his four weeks at the Lyric, he offered a staggeringly comprehensive repertory of eighteen plays ranging from Greek tragedy (*Oedipus Rex*) to modern comedy, with no fewer than six Shakespearean works among them for good measure. Novelli was an exceptionally large, tall man with a high voice and an impassioned style. But however much thought he brought to his interpretations, they were perceived as too idiosyncratic for American tastes. What's more, his supporting cast was weak and his mountings tacky. His approach branded him as the sort of superstar (like Salvini, Bernhardt, Irving, or Booth) whose day, unbeknownst to him, had passed by. Critics reported his audiences drew heavily from Italian-Americans.

Touring melodramas usually were written from scratch, however overused and unoriginal their stock situations may have become. Deriving such plays from popular novels was the exception. One such departure was **Parted on Her Bridal Tour** (3-18-07, American), which Laura Jean Libbey and James R. Garey dramatized from Libbey's *Miss Middleton's Lovers.* The new title speaks volumes for the nature of such plays. The drama's bad man murders his uncle and forges a will in which the uncle leaves him all his money and orders his own daughter, left penniless, to marry the nephew. The obedient girl does. But the nephew is arrested for the killing and sent to prison. Later he is reported to have died in an explosion. The heroine remarries, after which her first husband immediately reemerges, very much alive. The girl's troubles are resolved when the villain, besides being a killer and a forger, is shown to be a bigamist.

By April the season began to wind down. Cool receptions greeted all the month's earlier entries. Leo Ditrichstein and Percival Pollard's **The Ambitious Mrs. Alcott** (4-1-07, Astor) related how an elder brother (Ditrichstein) manages to prevent his younger sibling (Charles Cherry) from wedding a widow (Dorothy Dorr) with a past, then heads off to court the same lady himself. The production's scenery was elegant, especially a setting depicting a library.

Another library served as background for much of the action in **A Marriage of Reason** (4-1-07, Wallack's), J. Hartley Manners's adaptation of Mrs. Arthur Kennard's *The Second Lady Delcombe,* in which a marriage of convenience grows into a genuine love match. Kyrle Bellew was starred, but neither he nor his scenery could help a weak play.

Weakest of all was Beulah Marie Dix and Evelyn Greenleaf Sutherland's **The Lilac Room** (4-3-07, Weber's), which further dimmed the fast-fading career of Amelia Bingham. She played an American woman who comes to England (like the heroine in the authors' earlier play) and shows her hosts that their guest room is not haunted but rather is the hideaway of a counterfeiter. Reviews were so scathing that Miss Bingham made a curtain speech saying she hoped audiences would pack the playhouse simply to see how bad the comedy was. What she confronted instead was an injunction from the writers, who, like Mary Roberts Rinehart a few weeks before, were upset by unauthorized revisions.

One commentator judged Rida Johnson Young's **The Boys of Company B** (4-8-07, Lyceum) "another sweetly sentimental, mid-Victorian play of exuberant youth, cut to the same pattern as her Brown of Harvard." He also noted how compartmentalized its construction was, plot and humorous incident alternating from beginning to end. That plot focused on an up-and-coming lawyer, Tony Allen (Arnold Daly), whose attempt to court Eileen MacLane (Frances Ring) is blocked by her mother (Jennie A. Eustace). Mrs. MacLane wants Eileen to marry Arthur Stabler (Roy Fairchild), since Arthur's father helped the MacLanes through some tough times. Tony knows Arthur is a cad, so he proposes to Eileen over her mother's warnings and finally succeeds in getting Mrs. MacLane to agree that she will consent if he can have his uncle settle $50,000 on him within twelve months and if he can demonstrate his own ability to earn $20,000 a year. Misunderstandings arise, such as when Eileen sees Tony kissing the lisping Madge Blake (Florence Nash), but Tony inveigles his uncle (Verner Clarges) into giving him $50,000 by promising to relieve him of the burdens of his paramilitary obligations and lands a law partnership assuring him of $20,000 per. Settings included the sun-parlor gymnasium of a Fifth Avenue mansion and a paramilitary encampment on the Hudson. The settings allowed for displays of boxing, fencing, and drilling and for some songs as well. With something pleasant for almost everybody, the comedy ran out the season. Late in its run John Barrymore replaced Daly.

In Theodore Kremer's **The Outlaw's Christmas** (4-8-07, Thalia), a spurned siren implicates the latest hero-named-Jack in a murder she committed. Taking his wife and child with him, Jack, with the law and the siren in hot pursuit, scurries from New York to the Klondike to Colorado to the Rio Grande and back to New York before a mortally wounded accomplice of the siren confesses all to the police and the villainess, attempting to flee, is gunned down in a "fusillade of shots." At a high point, a horse carrying Jack, his wife, and their little girl jumps into the Rio Grande and swims to safety. Two nine-year-old tots who alternated as Jack's daughter, "the wordiest part of any," won the affection of critics and audiences alike.

Nazimova also won over reviewers and playgoers when she showed her remarkable versatility by dropping her Ibsen repertory and turning to a modern Italian comedy, Roberto Bracco's **Comtesse Coquette** (4-12-07, Bijou), in which a countess forces her husband to keep the bargain he made before their wedding—that she may continue with her harmless flirtations after their marriage.

Not long ago a spate of revivals often signaled a season's end, but this tradition had been waning in recent years. Only one major revival appeared in April, William A. Brady's restoration of Sardou's *Divorçons* at Wallack's on April 15, with Grace George, Frank Worthing, and Robert T. Haines as the principals. Yet even here change was in the air, for the revival used a "modern" adaptation by Margaret Mayo, providing the story with a more up-to-date setting.

The foster daughter of Irish lighthouse keepers and a poor farm boy fall in love, suffer numerous tribulations, and finally learn they are long-missing heirs to huge fortunes. Such was the basic story of Hal Reid's **Sweet Molly O** (4-15-07, Star). The heroine's struggles to reach the lighthouse during a storm were a highlight of the evening. With this, his seventh play of the season, Reid's output ran neck and neck with Owen Davis's.

Having competently adapted French comedy, Margaret Mayo turned her hand to an American novel and, working with its author, Upton Sinclair,

dramatized **The Jungle** (4-22-07, Fifth Ave.). In the process, what had been a conscience-shaking novel about the meat-packing industry became a standard melodrama in which a workingman's boss lusts for the workingman's wife and brings hardships on the pair when the wife will not succumb to his blandishments. Songs and dances were interpolated. The play had been touring lesser theatres all season, but this Manhattan presentation was staged by Keith and Proctor's stock company.

Far uptown, a second Keith and Proctor stock company offered another new play by another young playwright. Eugene Walter's **The Undertow** (4-22-07, Harlem Opera) told a tale not unlike *The Man of the Hour* but with a different ending. Walter's hero, an alcoholic newspaperman, battles the political bosses led by the newspaper owner for whom he once worked. He helps elect a reform mayor, then goes on an extended binge, during which time the machine manages to blackmail the new mayor into signing a franchise bill. When the reporter sobers up, there is little he can do but dress down his old boss. At most, the newspaperman's daughter, her eyes opened to his corruption, refuses her father's present. The play came and went quickly, but Walter soon would be looked upon as a major hope of native theatre.

No one would ever consider Langdon McCormick anything but a hack compiler of touring melodramas, even though, long after the genre supposedly had faded from the scene, he would have two of his plays done on Broadway and one would be a sizable hit. His latest was **The Women Who Dare** (4-22-07, Star), which employed a plot device reminiscent of the long-popular *The New Magdalene,* one woman pretending to be another. Of course, appropriate changes were made. One reviewer noted, "For the benefit of melodrama audiences the playwright introduces a villainous couplet of detective [with tell-tale black mustache] and lawyer, a noble and reforming young gambler [named Jack], a small cripple, a blind veteran, a comedy youth and an equally comedy maiden . . . and a trained automobile." Settings included the drugstore in the new Times Building, Delancey Street, and one showing the dressing rooms and stage of a vaudeville house, where several popular vaudevillians were hired to repeat their two-a-day turns.

The roster of rising young playwrights, expanded so impressively during the season, grew by one when Bayard Veiller presented his own play **The Primrose Path** (5-6-07, Majestic). His heroine, Joan Treghenna (Margaret Wycherly [Mrs. Veiller]) elopes to Paris with a young artist, Ned Templeton (Sheldon Lewis), and supports him through thick and thin, only to have him jilt her when his painting *The Primrose Path* is bought by a rich man and the patron's daughter (Sarah Whiteford) falls in love with him. Joan appeals to the girl, who selflessly tells Ned that he owes Joan his love. But Joan, realizing that she will only stand in the way of the pair's happiness and that Ned will never again truly love her, returns to her Devon roots. For some reason, many critics saw Ibsen's influence in the writing. Ibsen's archfoe, William Winter, yowled, "I can only suggest to Mr. Veiller that he take the filthy thing and bury it in the stench of the mud flats of Jersey from which he evidently took it." Veiller closed the play after two weeks, losing his whole investment in the process.

Some real Ibsen followed. Danish actress Oda Neilsen, who performed under the billing Madame Oda, gave New Yorkers their first taste of **Little Eyolf** (5-13-07, Carnegie Lyceum), which examined an unhappy couple's response to the drowning of their crippled boy. Even critics favorable to Ibsen could find almost nothing kind to say about the acting, so the engagement was cut short after the second playing.

The last novelty to play a first-class house during the season was Marion Fairfax's **The Builders** (5-20-07, Astor), which centered on Roger Grant (William Ingersoll), a young man who has served time for a murder committed while he was drunk. On his release he moves to Arizona, designs irrigation projects, shoulders aside a blackmailer, local opposition, and a fair-weather sweetheart, and finally finds both true love and success.

Another first-class house also offered a change of bill on the 20th, but the attraction at the Majestic was *Uncle Tom's Cabin*. The ending alone was novel, with Abraham Lincoln's signing of the Emancipation Proclamation replacing the customary "Apotheosis of Little Eva." This production of the old warhorse was not the only one to play Manhattan during the season. A few weeks earlier, two rival companies had competed for patrons on 125th Street. *The Two Orphans* also had visited combination houses, while this very week *Blue Jeans* again was thrilling playgoers at the once fashionable Fifth Avenue Theatre. The next week would see *Fanchon the Cricket* at the Metropolis. Nonetheless, each season fewer and fewer 19th-century favorites retained their hold on the boards. The tradition of incessant revival of popular old plays was disappearing as fast as had the tradition of special stars traveling in a repertory of "the legitimate."

Occasionally an old play would appear in a new guise. Thus Franklin Fyles and Ralph Stuart's **At the Rainbow's End** (5-20-07, Yorkville) was simply a reworking of Fyles's 1901 *Kit Carson*. The lone genuine novelty at a combination house was Clement Osgood's **The Great Wall Street Mystery** (5-20-07, American), although many observers would insist there was precious little that was original about any touring melodrama at this late date. In Osgood's saga a forger tricks a clerk into handing over a large sum of cash and then frames the clerk for embezzlement. It takes three more acts to bring the forger to court and convict him.

The Kalich Theatre was given over primarily to plays done in Yiddish, but at the close of the 1906–07 season it offered a few productions in English. Two were translations of plays presented in Yiddish earlier at the house. Julius Hopp's **The Friends of Labor** (5-21-07) dealt with the fatal attempt by a union agitator to cause trouble for a street railway company. In Z. Lubin's **Her Past** (6-5-07), a heartbroken wife dies in her husband's arms after being trapped into what might seem infidelity.

The Lincoln Square had opened its doors initially a few months before as a first-class playhouse, but its location instantly told against it. Charles E. Blaney, a leading writer and producer of touring melodramas and also, unlike such competitors as Davis, Kremer, or Reid, an important theatre owner and leaser, soon took it over. With J. Searle Dawley he wrote **The Dancer and the King** (5-27-07, Lincoln Square). The "comedy-drama," recounting the romance of Lola Montez and Ludwig (here called Louis) of Bavaria, was a vehicle for hoydenish Cecil Spooner, who sang, danced, showed her skill as a swordswoman, and coyly hid in a huge clock case. The play was the sixth for which Blaney took at least partial writing credit during the season. If his record fell one short of Davis's or Reid's, his multifarious activities no doubt were his excuse.

1907–1908

Given the preceding season's pulsating brilliance, few if any expected the new theatrical year to provide so exciting a sequel. But the new season, although not a total write-off, proved so bleak that even habitual pessimists were left stunned. End-of-season assessments agreed on the depth of the disappointment, although they could not agree on or pinpoint an overriding cause. One trade sheet noted, as if by way of consolation, that both quality and business had taken a marked plunge on stages the world over. At least New York—and therefore America—was not alone in its gloom. The *Dramatic Mirror,* the era's leading trade paper, ran articles all season long attempting to record and explain the slide. It could not decide if the financial panic, which began in October and was over by year's end, seriously affected the plunge. In no small measure, it suggested, the box-office decline simply reflected a decline in good theatrical offerings. However, when, in more than one instance, a play the paper and others admired fell by the wayside, the trade sheet was thrown for a loss. Only in a single category could it offer a confident explanation: the reason for the noticeable drop in attendance at combination houses could be summed up in two words—motion pictures.

Neither combination houses nor first-class theatres inaugurated the season. That distinction fell to a stock company in what once was a leading playhouse. Edna May Spooner's ensemble presented Ullie Akerstrom's **The Gypsy Sorceress** (7-1-07, Fifth Ave.). Miss Akerstrom, in her younger days a popular performer in New England backwaters, told a story that would have suited any combination-house stage. An heiress is kidnapped and raised by gypsies. She falls in love with a stalwart captain, but a perfidious marquis uses her dagger to frame her for her own father's murder and also implicates her lover about to be tortured, she consents to marry the marquis. A turnabout in the final act allows virtue to triumph. During intermissions motion pictures "helped to while away the time." The same troupe had a not dissimilar drama ready two weeks later, Samuel Lewis's **His Majesty and the Maid** (7-15-07, Fifth Ave.). This time the heroine was a princess reared in ignorance of her true position. She wins her rightful place in court only after foiling a plot to overthrow her father, the king. The plot has been hatched by the new queen, the heroine's wicked stepmother.

On a scorchingly hot Saturday night just short of a fortnight later, two combination houses relit for the new term. Last year's successful team of producer Al Woods and playwright Owen Davis supplied **The King and Queen of Gamblers** (7-27-07, American). Davis's heroine is "a poor, small, blue-eyed girl with yellowish golden braid down her back, her big childish eyes crying innocence and her hand holding as tightly as possible to the diagram of a mine." An archvillain, who looked like "a cross between a frog and a bad tragedian playing Richard III," the villain's assistant, and the "tall and stately and very spangly" Queen of the Gamblers resolve to get the map. A handsome, dapper, and appropriately named Jack Diamond, King of the Gamblers, sides with the teary-eyed blonde. To settle matters the "king" and "queen" play a game of poker. Neither is a model of honesty. The queen, like the Girl of the Golden West, manages to sneak a high card from her stocking, but the king goes one better, furtively substituting a new deck and dealing himself four aces. Afterwards, the queen discovers the girl is her long-lost daughter and switches allegiances. As a result, the remaining two villains abduct both women. At a deserted army post, the men place the heroine in a cannon and shoot it off, but the girl lands in the arms of the conveniently arrived hero. Pistols and cannons made noise throughout the evening, but not always as frighteningly as they were meant to. At times, one critic reported, "they snapped with a wheezy little apostrophe when they should have gone off with an exclamation."

Woods was the producer of the evening's other premiere, John Oliver's **A Race Across the Continent** (7-27-07, Thalia). Oliver's heroine, like Davis's, was named Sylvia. She and her brother are in the Klondike when they learn that they are heirs to millions, provided they can claim them at a New York bank before a specified date. Two impostors attempt to impede the pair and claim the inheritance for themselves. Shootings, stabbings, an abduction in a balloon, and a second abduction to a thieves' den are among the harrowings brother and sister must endure before a happy ending. Word quickly leaked out that John Oliver was merely a pen name for Davis. By whatever name, the playwright and his producer would briefly seem to grab a monopoly in their field.

Their third presentation was **A Chorus Girl's Luck in New York** (8-3-07, 14th St.). The heroine sported another name popular in the genre, Grace. She comes to New York to find and rehabilitate her fallen sister, hoping to support herself during her search by taking a job as a chorus girl. She is unaware that her sister has been debased by the very man she herself now approaches for help. Luckily, a young Klondike millionaire with the touring melodrama's favorite name, Jack, sets himself up as her defender. At one point Grace is tricked into coming to the villain's "secret chamber," where she is "chloroformed and put into a large clothes hamper. [Jack] swings across the airshaft on a rope from an opposite window, but is shot before he can rescue the girl. [Two of his friends], climbing the fire escape, arrive in time to rescue him from a demonically devised torture." In the last act the villain blows up the ship on which they all have been sailing. Hero, heroine, and villain find themselves floating on top of a cabin until the hero tosses the villain overboard. The lovers are saved when "a revenue cutter, containing the entire chorus from the Casino, arrives." The play's theatrical background allowed Woods to announce that he had imported such specialties as the Eight See Saw Girls from London to add songs and dances to the entertainment.

It was Woods and Oliver (Davis) again a few nights later with **Convict 999** (8-5-07, Thalia). For this thriller their hero was a dashing captain, and his sweetheart was a judge's daughter. But an adventuress, whom the captain has spurned, and a corrupt district attorney, who hates the hero for no good reason except that the villain must hate the hero, conspire to have him sent to prison for a murder actually committed by the D.A. The heroine provides the files that allow the hero to saw his way out of his cell, then "other convicts scale the walls in approved zouave fashion, slide along telegraph wires, and swing [the hero], now wounded by a guard, from one to the other and to safety." "Trick scenery" supplied added interest, with an old mill and a stone wall changing before audiences' eyes into a cornfield.

The fifth consecutive Woods-Davis collaboration, this time under Davis's real name, was **The Great Express Robbery** (8-12-07, American). Real horses and a miniature train passing across a distant canyon were scenic features in yet another tale of an attempt to seize a mine and, so as not to belie the title, rob a gold-bearing train. Set entirely in or near a California mining camp, the tale tied its hero to a post in a burning building and strapped its heroine to railroad tracks. One can imagine Woods and Davis hurrying from rehearsal to rehearsal. But with this production launched, they apparently decided they deserved a rest. They would not be heard from again for two weeks.

Their competitor Charles E. Blaney certainly was no slouch, producing plays he wrote and often presenting them at theatres he either owned or leased. Such was the case with **The Hired Girl's Millions** (8-12-07, Lincoln Square). Its heroine, an orphan, works as a salesgirl at Cooper-Macy's. Her inheritance has been withheld by her venal lawyer, who operates in cahoots with the duplicitous store manager. Luckily, the heroine has befriended two porters. Since the porters were played by the Russell brothers, popular female impersonators, audiences had a good idea of what would follow. The action moved from the department store, where the villains

attempt to kidnap the heroine during the push and shove of a bargain sale, to an East Side tenement to a posh Long Island summer resort, where the lawyer is disguised as a hotel manager and the store manager is disguised as a bartender, and finally to a courtroom, where the Russell brothers emerged as "modern Portias." The piece was larded with even more than the customary number of specialty turns. A small chorus line placed the show atop a genre-straddling fence.

The actress-heroine in Langdon McCormick's **The Life of an Actress** (8-12-07, Star), a play billed as the "Greatest Sensation Drama of Modern Times," is framed for a murder and barred from returning to the embrace of her family. She wanders to a mining camp, where she saves another girl from a cruel death at the hands of the villain (who becomes the victim of his own bomb) and in turn is saved from a train wreck by the hero (who, though gagged and bound, uses his brains and his chin to tap out a warning telegraph message). Throughout all this the audience received no hint of her professional repertory and only the smallest clues about her histrionic abilities.

McCormick had a second play ready the next Monday night. The heroine of **Jessie Left the Village** (8-19-07, 14th St.) is snubbed by her neighbors when she returns after an unexplained absence. What she had been doing was abetting the escape of a friend who had been wrongfully imprisoned for a murder. Later the real killers—a band of counterfeiters—kidnap the heroine and the young sheriff who has been courting her. The pair are bound and placed aboard a ship, which the villains plan to scuttle. But the hero "stumbles over to the furnace, bends and twists over it until he has opened the door, then into the fire he plunges his hands and burns away the rope which holds his wrists. Freed, he confronts Villain One, who rushes at him with an ax. . . . Then quick to the rescue of Jessie: A plunge overboard, and the ship having stood the strain as long as it could, goes to pieces with a thundering report." The title failed to lure in playgoers, so was changed shortly to *The Convict and the Girl*.

In Joseph Byron Totten's **The Cowboy and the Squaw** (8-19-07, Star), the cowboy was named Bronco Bob. Bob loves a girl named Ruth, who is abducted by Bob's rival. A pretty squaw, who is called Silver Heels and who loves Bob, rushes to rescue Ruth, but in the final shootout the poor little squaw is killed.

All summer long, first-class theatres had been offering new musicals (including Ziegfeld's earliest

1907–1908

Follies), but they played home to no new straight plays until Charles Frohman brought in Charles Marlowe's London hit **When Knights Were Bold** (8-20-07, Criterion) with Francis Wilson as star. Like *The Road to Yesterday* it used a dream to transport its contemporary figures back to olden times and comic misadventures. The play chalked up a profitable 100-performance run. Marlowe was the pen name of Harriet Jay.

Two American plays also began good runs when they opened during the following week. The longer run, 155 performances, went to Edmund Day's **The Round Up** (8-26-07, New Amsterdam), which arrived first. Day's plot was hardly original, but it sufficed. Jack Payson (Orme Caldara) marries Echo Allen (Florence Rockwell) without letting Echo learn that the man she loves most, Jack's best friend, Dick Lane (Wright Kramer), has returned after a two-year absence. Before he leaves again, Dick returns some money Jack has lent him, and this money leads to the suspicion that Jack is covering up a murder. When he tells Echo the true source of the cash, she demands he go out into the desert and find Dick. He does, but the men are attacked by Indians, and Dick is killed before soldiers can rescue them. However, Dick's death allows Jack to return to Echo with a reasonably clear conscience.

What made the show a hit was not its story but its spectacle and one stellar performance. Act III is set in a canyon with ledged cliffs on both sides. Dawn breaks. Some horsemen ride by, then mounted Indians in war paint appear on the ledges and ride off into the valley. The two principals are seen on the canyon floor beside a dried-up spring. The Indians reappear, this time without horses, and attack the men. One Indian is shot and falls with his head and arms hanging over a precipice. Others fall in less dramatic positions. Soon the hatted army men (more than thirty, according to photographs) arrive, carrying rifles and at least one machine gun, and rout the redskins. The stellar performance was Maclyn Arbuckle's. The hefty comedian enacted Sheriff "Slim" Hoover, who accepts that "nobody can love a fat man," with such naturalness and warmth that he all but stole the show.

Combination houses were busy on the same night. A refreshed Al Woods and Owen Davis, the latter again reverting to his pen name of John Oliver, presented their successor to *Bertha, the Sewing Machine Girl* and *Nellie, the Beautiful Cloak Model*. **Edna, the Pretty Typewriter** (8-26-07, American) works for her cousin, a callous importer. His tone changes when he learns Edna's father has left her the deed to a rich mine. It changes again

when she rebuffs his advances. The expected harassments follow. Edna is locked in a safe, dangled at the top of a long flight of stairs, nearly choked, shot at, and rescued in an automobile chase. A high point comes when she jumps from a roof onto the top of a passing elevated train.

Blaney also had a new offering: **His Terrible Secret; or, The Man Monkey** (8-26-07, Metropolis). The hero is heir to a gold mine, but he is also heir to a serious problem. While she was carrying him, his mother was terrified by a gorilla, and so he was born with an ape's body and face, if a man's mind. He loves the heroine, but when the normal, handsome man she loves is framed for murder by the villains, the man monkey accepts the blame. His condition makes him exempt from punishment. Deeding over the mine to the girl and her husband-to-be, he heads off to live alone in the jungle. Settings included a rain forest in the midst of a thunderstorm and the "oriental splendor" of a Cairo courtroom.

Hal Reid entered the lists for the first time this season with **The Singing Girl from Killarney** (8-26-07, 14th St.). The warbler is ordered killed by her prospective father-in-law, who wants his son to marry an heiress, and is nearly poisoned by laced chocolate creams offered her by a "scarlet gowned" adventuress, who eventually turns out to be her long-lost mother. Later some villains try to abduct her, until she flings hot pepper in their eyes, and her own father, angry that she will not support his debauchery, steals away with her newborn. Since the girl at one time must earn her keep by singing in a music hall, the standard touring melodrama specialty turns could be brought in conveniently. This singing girl was a close relation to the hired girl, since a "chorus of bright young colleens" again suggested how close many such plays veered toward musical comedy.

The season's second steamy jungle was depicted in William C. de Mille and Margaret Turnbull's **Classmates** (8-29-07, Hudson), which starred sober-faced Robert Edeson. Critics saw the play as a skillful bit of commercial hackwork in the tradition of *Brown of Harvard* and *The Boys of Company B*. Its action begins at West Point, where upperclassmen are hazing plebes. One cadet, Duncan Irving, is engaged to Sylvia Randolph (Flora Juliet Bowley), but a sneaky plebe, Bert Stafford (Wallace Eddinger), sets out to win Sylvia for himself. All three are from the same North Carolina town, but the Randolphs and the Staffords belong to the town's elite. The Irvings do not. When Bert insults Duncan, Duncan strikes him, leaving him temporarily blind. Duncan is expelled; Bert resigns because of his impaired sight. Bert goes on an expedition in the Amazon and is soon reported lost. Duncan tells Sylvia he is going to South America to find Bert. Having earlier misunderstood the battle between the men, Sylvia had broken her engagement to Duncan and accepted Bert's proposal. Her reaction to Duncan's offer is startling. She angrily tells him that nothing he can do will make her change her mind or love him again, and she gives him a message of her undying affection to deliver to Bert. Duncan promises to do so. In the jungle, "great trees rise out of the impenetrable underbush and tangles of vines. Stafford, fever-crazed, almost exhausted, wanders along, trailing a rusty gun, and talking to himself." Duncan and his buddies soon appear and save Bert. Back home, a grateful Sylvia accedes to Duncan's request to help him gain readmission to the academy. However, when Bert attempts to take the credit, Sylvia realizes which of the two men is truly the better one.

Edeson's manly Duncan won praise, as did Eddinger's "splendid restraint and . . . convincing surety" in a role so conducive to overacting. But for the second time in three nights, an impressively pudgy actor stole the limelight portraying a likable, comic fat man. His Bubby Dumble, Duncan's loyal pal, gave a healthy boost to Frank McIntyre's career. The play ran three months, then toured.

The only first-class entry of the week not to compile a respectable run was Harry and Edward Paulton's farce **The Other House** (8-30-07, Empire), in which a debt-ridden inventor (Richard Golden) decides to sell his soul to the devil and mistakes a manufacturer (Edwin Mordant), eager to buy an invention, for Beelzebub.

The week's final arrival was John Drew's vehicle for the new season and ran into the early winter. **My Wife** (8-31-07, Empire) was adapted by Michael Morton from Paul Gavault and Robert Charvay's *Mademoiselle Josette, ma femme*. Because the man she loves is abroad for a year, and she will lose a large inheritance if she does not wed before then, Beatrice "Trixie" Dupré is pressed by her avaricious family to marry the man of their choice. Instead she persuades a charming confirmed bachelor, Gerald Eversleigh, to marry her and then divorce her when her fiancé returns. All manner of comic complications intrude before Trixie and Gerald recognize that they have fallen in love. Their worries evaporate after the fiancé returns and announces he has married someone else. The play, a London hit, and Drew, an old hand at such roles, were both well received. Critics were more reserved in their judg-

ment of Drew's newest leading lady, petite, pugnosed, redheaded Billie Burke.

. . .

Billie [Mary William Ethelbert Appleton] **Burke** (1885–1970) was born in Washington, D.C., but raised in England, where her father was a popular clown. She played in several English musicals and with Charles Hawtrey before Charles Frohman brought her back to America. In 1914 she would become Mrs. Florenz Ziegfeld.

. . .

Augustus Thomas suffered a disappointment when **The Rangers** (9-2-07, Wallack's) was withdrawn after a few weeks. His hero, Captain Esmond (Dustin Farnum), rides from Arizona into Mexico in pursuit of two desperadoes. He is no sooner there than a native insurrection endangers all Americans, and Esmond agrees to dash sixty miles for relief. A number of other threads were woven into this basic plot, such as Esmond's romance with the daughter (Mary Boland) of an American who holds vast Mexican mining interests. Farnum demonstrated his skill on horseback as far as a constricting stage would allow, but there seemed no limits on the incessant gunshots, which sent acrid odors through the theatre. It was openly known that the producer, Charles Frohman, had successfully urged Thomas to modify the play's original virulently anti-Mexican stance. In assessing blame for the show's failure, many critics saw Thomas's capitulation as a salient problem.

A dramatization (by several hands) of **Anna Karenina** (9-2-07, Herald Square) received generally negative notices—"tedious," "depressing," "very depressing"—although its leading players, Virginia Harned, Robert Warwick (Vronsky), and especially John Mason (Alexis), often won high praise. For some reason the Shuberts forced a modest run, forty-seven showings.

Several of touring melodrama's big guns were heard from that same evening. Hal Reid's contribution was **From Broadway to the Bowery** (9-2-07, American), which starred Chuck Connors. Connors was a Bowery bum, originally from a respectable Irish family, who had caught the attention of several newspapermen. These writers dubbed him "the Mayor of Chinatown" and regularly reported on his outrageous grammar and exaggerated New York dialect. His philosophy was said to be "Work? Aah, fergit it!" He played himself with surprising energy in his new vehicle, regularly coming to the aid of the hapless heroine. Because she has refused to marry the villain, her father is bankrupted and turned into an alcoholic, her lover is framed for embezzling, and she is fired from her job (the villain must buy the factory to do so) and later abducted to an opium den.

Similar harrowings befell **Lottie, the Poor Saleslady** (9-2-07, Star), which Charles E. Blaney wrote and produced. A first cousin to Bertha and Nellie and Edna, Lottie is coveted by the owner of the department store where she works. Never mind that he is a married man, or that his wife proves to be Lottie's long-lost sister. Of course, everything turns out just fine.

With business at these combination houses falling away, fewer new playwrights were offering works. One who did was Paul Gilmore. His **Dublin Dan** (9-2-07, Yorkville) was a young detective who must rescue his sweetheart from her counterfeiting guardian and the guardian's equally nefarious allies.

Two flops finished out the week. Martha Morton's **The Movers** (9-3-07, Hackett) was perceived as an inferior rehashing of Fitch's *The Climbers*. Marion Manners (Dorothy Donnelly) learns that she and her husband (Vincent Serrano) have lived beyond their means and are about to lose everything. Moreover, Mr. Manners also has lost money entrusted to him by others. He commits suicide. To Marion's horror, she discovers her sister (Nellie Thorne) and brother-in-law (Malcolm Duncan) have not profited from their experience and are headed stubbornly in the same direction. But Marion refuses to marry the rich climber (Joseph Kilgour) who could solve her family's problems. Instead she marries a faithful old family friend (Robert Conness). Some reviewers claimed that the players, particularly Serrano and Miss Donnelly, emoted so frantically that they became unbelievable, thus adding to the drama's woes.

In Grace Livingston Furniss's **The Man on the Case** (9-4-07, Madison Square), a bankrupt (Neil Moran) fakes a jewel theft and calls in a detective (Charles Lamb) so as to seem genuinely victimized. Carroll Dempsey (Jameson Lee Finney) arrives, hoping to court the bankrupt's daughter (Elsie Leslie), but is mistaken for the sleuth. Following the expected confusions, Dempsey manages not only to win the girl but to retrieve the jewels and thus save his future father-in-law's reputation. Had this been a musical, the audience might well have walked out humming the scenery, notably the last act's. It pictured the garden of a summer resort with marshes, winding inlets, and the sea in the distance. Far out at sea two lighthouses were working away. One commentator added, "The illusion of a sultry evening, with mosquitoes 'for the first time this Summer,' is painfully realistic." So, apparently, was

the windstorm and drenching rain that came next. The curtain fell with the lovers, their hats blown off by the wind, standing helplessly under a tree. For Elsie Leslie the comedy represented another unsuccessful comeback attempt.

None of the season's dramas enjoyed the year-long run some recent American plays had been accorded. What's more, the season's longest run—a little more than eight months—went to an Englishman's translation of a French play: Haddon Chambers's adaptation of Henri Bernstein's **The Thief** (9-9-07, Lyceum). The play, which had catapulted its author to fame in Paris earlier in the year, told of a wife who steals to keep herself in fine clothes. When an admirer jumps in to take the blame for the thefts, she lets him. But her husband finally learns the truth, and the couple go off to exile in Brazil. Critics split in their assessment of Margaret Illington's performance. However, the play was virtually actor-proof.

Combination houses were busy that same night with new wares. Hal Reid had his third and fourth creations of the season ready, while Al Woods and Owen Davis (again as John Oliver) brought out their seventh new offering—and it was still only the second week of September. Reid's plays were **The Little Organ Grinder** (9-9-07, 14th St.) and **The Blackmailers of New York** (9-9-07, Star). In the former the heroine refuses to marry the hero (named Jack) until she can determine who her real mother and father are. Naturally a villain tries to keep the truth from her. But she borrows a monkey and disguises herself as an organ grinder to ferret out the facts. Before she can solve the mystery, her Jack must fight a sword duel with the villain in what one facetious reviewer called "the jungles of Staten Island." In Reid's other offering two brothers, German immigrants, establish a successful pretzel factory in America. Thanks to a mustachioed meany, they are unaware that they are heirs to a vast German fortune. The villain is also unkind to a lovely girl the bakers have befriended. Of course, virtue triumphs at about eleven o'clock, at which time the girl can embrace the handsome young man who had saved her from the path of two onrushing Third Avenue trolleys and whom she adores. One guess what the hero's name was.

"A boxing match, two dope fiends, a choice assortment of villains, and an attempted murder on a steamship that did *not* look like the *Lusitania*" helped make the Woods-Oliver **Broadway After Dark** (9-9-07, Thalia) "a lively affair." The critic who noted this got the incidents reversed; the villains and drug addicts attempt to throw the orphaned heroine overboard shortly after the first curtain, and the hero does not box with the chief malefactor until much later. Afterwards, all the characters find themselves in "a subterranean Canal Street dive" and on the grounds of a fashionable insane asylum before the hero and heroine can breathe easily.

Two favorites of the Yiddish theatre, dramatist Samuel Shipman and actor David Kessler, tested Broadway's waters and found them unwelcoming. Shipman's play was **The Spell** (9-16-07, Majestic). Kessler portrayed Benjamin Miller, a banker whose attractive wife (Ida Conquest) has fallen in love with a bank employee (Walter D. Greene). The wife is prepared to divorce her loving husband until she discovers that her supposed lover has caused a run on the bank and will not accept her without her husband's money. The immigrant banker saves both his marriage and his bank. "Crude" was an adjective that appeared in review after review, although many granted that the relatively tall, broad, peasant-necked Kessler excelled at high-pitched emotionalism: "Gusts of emotion come forth in tones scarcely above a whisper, and these are followed by outbursts of overpowering passion." The mounting survived a mere two weeks.

A different school of acting and writing was offered that evening on 42nd Street when James O'Neill, so rarely granted a first-class stage, opened at the Lyric in a revival of *Virginius*. An enthusiastic audience greeted a performance "at once florid and mellow." In his curtain speech O'Neill remarked, "It is the desire of my life that when I shall retire a few years hence there may be those who shall say: 'He could at least play other parts besides dear old Monte Cristo.' " Sure enough, three weeks later, on October 7, the star had returned to his old warhorse. Some critics complimented him on how young he was able to seem in the early scenes. His travel-worn scenery was another matter. Playing his son was his real son, James Junior.

Ramsay Morris, who had scored an isolated success with *The Ninety and Nine,* returned to the ranks of touring melodramatists with **Under Suspicion** (9-16-07, American). *The Ninety and Nine*'s big moment was a train ride through a blazing forest; *Under Suspicion*'s climax was suspiciously similar. Morris's hero had spent time in prison for allegedly picking pockets. Released, he has moved to a country town, earned a good reputation, and fallen in love. The very thief whose perjured testimony had sent the hero to jail reappears and again attempts to frame the innocent man for the thief's own breakins. The hero flees, but his sweetheart chases after him and persuades him to come back to

defend himself. Their ride home is on a motorcycle and takes them through a raging prairie fire. Once back, the hero tricks the villain into a confession. By coincidence, *The Ninety and Nine* was making the rounds of combination houses that very month.

The stock of both Ibsen and Nazimova rose appreciably with a splendid revival of *The Master Builder* at the Bijou on the 23rd, despite quibbles here and there. The star was helped by generally fine performances from such rising players as Walter Hampden (Solness), H. Reeves-Smith (Dr. Heryal), and Warner Oland (Ragnar). The result was an unexpectedly long run of sixty-five performances.

Edwin Milton Royle's "modern morality play" **The Struggle Everlasting** (9-26-07, Hackett) intrigued many critics but not a larger public. A college student, Mind (Arthur Byron), leaves his fraternity house and wanders in the woods, where he meets Body (Florence Roberts), a natural spirit. Years pass; Body has encountered and destroyed many men. Finally Mind and his brother, Soul (De Witt Jennings), show the dying Body the road to salvation. "In her death she grasps in one hand a book of Daily Life [or "Divine Light"] and in the other a rouge paw [the brush she had used to apply makeup]." The settings were contemporary, as were most of the costumes. Mind spent the evening in a tuxedo; only Body was dressed incongruously in medieval garments. One critic suggested some careless staging also hurt the play: "When you fill a stage with badly rouged Broadway supers singing the 'Stein Song,' it is not youth's fragrance the audience feels."

Nor did playgoers care for another view of religion, Henry Arthur Jones's **The Evangelist** (9-30-07, Knickerbocker), in which an itinerant revivalist (Howard Kyle) saves the marriage of an erring wife and a rigidly moral husband, but at great pain to everyone.

Two experienced hands provided the evening's novelties at combination houses. In conjunction with William J. McKiernan, Charles E. Blaney wrote **Dion O'Dare** (9-30-07, Lincoln Square) for Fiske O'Hara, who was being positioned as a rival to Chauncey Olcott. As a result, audiences knew precisely what to expect—a story of a handsome young Irishman, in this instance a sculptor, who wins the hand of a lovely girl despite some half-hearted feints by a not very villainous villain. And, of course, the young Irishman had so fine a tenor voice that he could not resist breaking out in song at least once in each of the four acts. The second-act setting amused one critic, who complained that what was listed in the program as "golf links" turns out to be "the garden wall of a baronial castle with the exterior of the mansion just on the other side."

In her 1905 melodrama *No Mother to Guide Her*, Lillian Mortimer had played Bunco, the heroine's friend. Her new thriller, **Bunco in Arizona** (9-30-07, American), gave the girl center stage. Bunco is an orphaned heiress who had been raised by kind if rough-hewn miners. In defending her from villains, her lover narrowly avoids being dynamited and burned at the stake. In the former case he has been knocked unconscious, "and a dynamite bomb with a lighted fuse is placed by him. The bridge leading across a chasm is cut down and he is left to die. But Bunco finds him, crawls over the abyss on an ore conveyor, seizes the bomb and throws it away in time to have it explode under Black Hawk [one of the villains], who is blown up." Action often still occurred in the curtain calls that followed each act. Thus, having rescued her lover for a second-act curtain, Bunco was immediately seen rushing off to save her foster father, trapped in a mine.

Touring plays provided the only nonmusical novelties for the first half of October. Of course, almost all touring shows continued to insert occasional musical turns. Some, such as **At Yale** (10-7-07, Yorkville), for which no author came forward, even had a few numbers written especially for them, but they still were not looked on as musicals. Instead *At Yale* was looked on as something of a steal from *Brown of Harvard*. The comedy-drama had toured cross-country the preceding season. Its hero, a poor boy at school on a scholarship, is selected to replace an irresponsible rich student on the crew for the Yale-Harvard race. The rich boy vows vengeance, especially since both men are courting the same girl. The hero is kidnapped but escapes and helps row the team to victory.

Joseph Le Brandt's **Through Death Valley** (10-7-07, American) resuscitated anti-Mormon sentiments to frame its adventures. A mining family decides to break with the church and head for California, but a band of "destroying angels," headed by the play's antagonist, sets out to stop them. The hero loves the family's beautiful daughter and does everything in his power to help the escape. In the play's sensation scene (an expression disappearing from the critical lexicon), "the hero is tied to four stakes on the desert and tortured by an Indian with fiendish ingenuity. The red man captures a huge rattlesnake and places it just out of striking distance of the prostrate form of the man on the ground. A leather thong holds the reptile. In a few minutes a rainstorm comes up, and the water stretches the leather. The enraged snake endeavors to strike . . . and every

moment brings it closer. . . . Just as it seems as if the rattler will bury its fangs in his trembling flesh a member of the hero's party comes up the trail in time to shoot the rattlesnake. . . . The wriggling of the snake is so real that only a slight effort of the imagination is necessary for the spectator to think the reptile might be alive. A shower of real water adds to the vividness of the scene." If that was not enough, a "Sioux Indian quartette" sang songs in English and German.

The turbulent West was also the setting for a second work for which no author accepted credit, **Fighting Bill, Sheriff of Silver Creek** (10-7-07, Thalia). The play's big moment was hardly original, with the sheriff-hero tied by the villain, his rival for the hand of the heroine, to a belt moving toward a spinning buzz saw.

The hero and heroine of Lem B. Parker's **Little Heroes of the Street** (10-7-07, Star) are sorely put upon by their "sworn enemy" and his female accomplice. For a time it appears the hero will be electrocuted in a wired chair the villains have constructed for him. But a Jewish detective and his Jewish girlfriend (Abie and Rebecca) are assisted by the play's titular "little heroes," children named Specks and Bobsey, in scurrying to the rescue.

Mines and dastardly doings were often as popular on first-class stages as in touring houses, but not in the case of Edward Peple's **The Silver Girl** (10-14-07, Wallack's). Jefferson Hunter (George Fawcett) has made a fortune with his Silver Girl mine and has brought his family to New York to give them polish and let them enter society. But Mrs. Hunter (Jane Oaker) falls in love with an unprincipled lawyer, Nathan Hargrave (George Nash), who attempts to steal both the mine and Mrs. Hunter. Hunter confronts him, hands him one of two guns, and announces, "Shoot when the clock strikes." The clock strikes. Hargrave shoots, while Hunter makes no attempt to return the fire. However, Hargrave's shot misses. Hunter asks, as his frenzied wife rushes in, "Man, why didn't you shoot straight?" Hunter goes back to Nevada, where he prepares to regain both his mine and his wife. This last act sent the aroma of real bacon cooking and real coffee brewing out into the auditorium.

Just two years earlier, Charles Klein was being hailed in some quarters as the great hope for American dramaturgy. Since then his stock had slipped, and he came badly a cropper with **The Stepsister** (10-14-07, Garrick). As the review in *Theatre* noted, he was in good company, since Augustus Thomas, Henry Arthur Jones, Edwin Milton Royle, and other respected writers had suffered equally ignominious failures during the season. In Klein's Cinderella variation, Doris Chapin (Chrystal Herne) works as a drudge for her cruel stepsister (Grace Filkins), who runs a dressmaker's shop, until a millionaire (Bruce McRae) woos and wins her. Never mind that Prince Charming turns out to be not nearly as rich as he was reputed to be.

Critical favor or disfavor probably meant little to Hal Reid, who had two more melodramas ready the same evening. In 1902 Reid's *The Peddler* had been scorched as a ripoff of *The Auctioneer*. Now **The Money Lender** (10-14-07, West End) was waved away as a rewrite of *The Peddler*. Its leading figure is a wealthy pawnbroker whose daughter is lured away by an unprincipled "swell." By the end of Act IV the kindly old Jew has overcome this and other tribulations. Reid's second offering was **A Child Shall Lead Them** (10-14-07, 14th St.). Belle Jeanette, a child actress making her debut as "a juvenile star," portrayed a young girl who fends off all the terrible plots her wicked uncle devises to discomfit her family.

The next evening Arnold Daly, a Japanese tragedienne named Hanako, and their respective "companies" began a two-month stay at the Berkeley Lyceum with a series of one-act plays. In mid-December, with the series over, Daly revived *Candida* for a month.

By 1907 criteria, a show that ran for 149 showings was almost assuredly a commercial success. Yet in a season so far replete with disappointments, the 149-performance stand of **A Grand Army Man** (10-16-07, Stuyvesant) also marked a falling off, for in this instance it represented the least successful of the Belasco-Warfield collaborations. Belasco rewrote the play from an original by Pauline Phelps and Marion Short, and he used the production to open his new theatre (later rechristened the Belasco and still standing, albeit usually dark). The plot eschewed complications so beloved by many lesser contemporary dramatists. Wes Bigelow (Warfield) has adopted and raised Robert (William Elliott), son of a comrade killed fighting beside him during the Civil War. He has spoiled the boy. When Robert is entrusted with $1000 raised for charity and asked to deposit it in the bank, the young man, hoping to prove his maturity and initiative, gambles it at the behest of a sharper who runs a bucket shop and loses it all. When the truth is discovered, Wes is at first furious. He had been a stagecoach driver and runs for his old whip to flog the boy, but after the very first blow he breaks into sobs, takes the boy in his arms, and promises to raise the money to repay the loss and, he hopes, allow Robert to avoid prosecu-

tion. Although Wes does raise the money, Robert is brought before a judge (Howard Hall) who not only holds a grudge against Wes for the oldtimer's political opposition but also is angry that Robert has been courting his daughter, Hallie (Antoinette Perry). Robert is sent to prison, but Wes and Hallie agree to await his release and move on with their lives as if nothing had happened. For all of Belasco's artistry, the evening clearly belonged to Warfield. Critics celebrated the simplicity and seeming honesty with which he achieved his ends. Walter Prichard Eaton, the *Sun*'s new critic, insisted, "No acting on our stage to-day can compare with Mr. Warfield's for immediate emotional effect."

Eaton and his colleagues were not nearly so happy with Percy MacKaye's blank-verse tragedy **Sappho and Phaon** (10-21-07, Lyric). "Let us not think that all verse is poetry—much of Mr. MacKaye's isn't," Eaton lamented. He found "the humble sitting room of *Wes Bigelow's* house, sleeping in the warm sunlight to the drowsy tick of the clock," far more poetic, if in a Whittier-like way. Harrison Gray Fiske gave the production eye-filling settings, particularly a promontory overlooking the Aegean, with a massive temple in the foreground. But the story of the siren Sappho's doomed love for the fisherman-slave (Henry Kolker) had no appeal to modern audiences, and Bertha Kalish's odd diction—"unintelligible," "obscure"—made matters worse. Bad blank verse, like off-target satire, closes on Saturday night. *Sappho and Phaon* did.

Walter Woods's **The Girl of the Eagle Ranch** (10-21-07, 14th St.) provided another example of touring melodrama's incessant rehashing. This girl, like the Girl of the Golden West, runs a bar and falls in love with a man being hunted as a criminal. Actually he is taking the blame for the real thief, his brother. A kidnapping, a dynamiting, and lots of shooting occur before peace is restored.

The evening of the 21st also witnessed the premiere of the season's most enduring stage piece. But it was a musical—*The Merry Widow*. The musical began a craze for Viennese operetta, which threatened to sweep American song-and-dance entertainments off the stage but fortunately had no effect on American comedies and dramas.

With **Artie** (10-28-07, Garrick), George Ade joined the growing list of established playwrights who seemed unable to get their act together during the season. In fact, a major fault of the comedy was its disjointed attempt to twit too many things. But it had most of its fun at the expense of naive initiative and real-estate speculation. Its optimistic, aggressive, and not entirely truthful young hero (Lawrence

Wheat) borrows way beyond his means to buy up land along what he believes will be the route of a new elevated line. Before he is proven right and rakes in gobs of money, he bounces from one comic misadventure to another. Highly praised settings included a union hall, a row of frame houses, a real estate office, and, most of all, a new suburban town. There are no houses yet in this swampy development, but all the fancy street signs are in place.

By the time Al Woods offered Owen Davis's **Since Nellie Went Away** (10-28-07, American), the pair may well have lost count of their presentations during the season. (Counters could have told them this was number eight.) Nellie, a country girl, runs off to New York to marry, but an "adventurer" and a society lady do all in their power to prevent the wedding.

Blaney was also heard from that same evening, but only as a producer. His mounting, **From Sing Sing to Liberty** (10-28-07, Star), was the work of his brother, Henry Clay Blaney. The hero—named Jack—was played by a performer billed as "Mr. Cunning, the Jail Breaker," a vaudevillian famed as both a strongman and an escape artist. So naturally the villains see to it that he is framed for murder and sent first to prison (where he escapes from his cell) and then to an insane asylum (where he escapes from his straitjacket). Both Jack and his girl, Nellie, endure other indignities before the final curtain.

In **The Right of Way** (11-4-07, Wallack's), Eugene W. Presbrey's adaptation of Sir Gilbert Parker's novel, a scoundrel (Guy Standing) marries a woman he does not love simply to prove he can win her away from the man who does love her. Later he loses his memory as the result of a brawl, goes off, and marries another girl. An operation restores his memory, and he promises to make good to both women.

A season so underscored with disappointment suffered yet another when Rachel Crothers, who had made such a promising debut a year earlier, brought out **The Coming of Mrs. Patrick** (11-6-07, Madison Square). Mrs. Patrick (Laura Nelson Hall) is a nurse attending a wealthy woman. When she realizes that the woman's children are about to enter into disastrous marriages, she sacrifices her own reputation and career to deter them. Her place and good name are saved when the truth comes out, and her reward is a proposal from a doctor she long has loved. The play's tone was set at the start: "The curtain rose on a darkened room—the melancholy front parlor of an old-fashioned New York house. Through the gloom the audience discerned black-walnut furniture upholstered in shabby red plush; an ancient square piano, which must never be opened because the invalid's room was just overhead; two large chromo landscapes in heavy frames; a fireplace mantel, iron, apparently, and painted and grained an atrocious brown to represent marble; upon it two statuettes of the pre-Rogers period. Outside, the stage wind whistled deliciously; occasional bits of sleet slapped the window-pane. Obviously, little 'joy of living' here."

Some playgoers may have been confused when *The Coming of Mrs. Patrick* was followed five nights later by the coming of Mrs. Patrick Campbell. The great London actress appeared in a repertory that consisted of *The Second Mrs. Tanqueray*, *The Notorious Mrs. Ebbsmith*, *Magda*, and *Hedda Gabler*.

Competing with Mrs. Campbell was the season's second morality play, **The Christian Pilgrim** (11-11-07, Liberty), which James MacArthur drew from Bunyan's *Pilgrim's Progress*. Christian was portrayed by Henrietta Crosman, while Tyrone Power assumed such parts as Beelzebub, Apollyon, Lord Hategood, and Giant Despair. New Yorkers would not buy it, although spectacle, including a Celestial City with white lights shining out into the audience, and ballet embellished the evening.

The string of short-lived disppointments was broken when Anne Warner's **The Rejuvenation of Aunt Mary** (11-12-07, Garden) achieved a modest success with May Robson as star. And Miss Robson was the sole attraction, since neither the play nor the supporting cast was highly thought of. She was seen as a peppery spinster who must save her scapegrace nephew from a blackmailing adventuress and marry him off to the right girl. She does this by going to the wicked city, which she finds is not so wicked after all. In fact, it's fun. She returns home a confirmed smoker and poker player. With such a role there was little call for subtlety, and the star reached into her bag of burlesque tricks to provoke laughs.

A small turnaround began when Augustus Thomas made up for the failure of *The Rangers* and gave playgoers the drama most observers considered the season's finest, **The Witching Hour** (11-18-07, Hackett). The play dealt with a dangerous subject, telepathy. With a theme so closely related to mesmerism, it might have been turned into a florid, *Trilby*-like melodrama. Instead, though even mesmerism was touched on in the play, Thomas wrote a gripping, theatrically believable drama. The action begins in the somber but elegant library of Jack Brookfield (John Mason), a professional gambler whose Louisville neighbors often have been startled by his ability to convey his thoughts telepathically.

Long ago Jack was rejected by Helen Whipple (Jennie A. Eustace), but he remains loyal and loving enough to approve the engagement of her son, Clay (Morgan Conan), to his niece, Viola Campbell (Janet Dunbar). When Clay is convicted of murdering a man who taunted him about his strange fear of cat's-eye jewels, Jack arranges a retrial. He knows that Clay has been railroaded by Frank Hardmuth (George Nash), a rival for Viola's hand, so Jack releases to the newspapers materials showing Hardmuth's complicity in a governor's murder. Jack is convinced that the readers' sympathy will be passed on by telepathy to the jurors. Clay is acquitted, and a furious Hardmuth comes gunning for Jack:

Hardmuth: (*Entering, rushes down toward dining-room and turns back to Jack who is under the lamp with his hand on its button.*) You think you'll send me to the gallows, but damn you, you'll go first yourself. (*Thrusts a derringer against Jack's body.*)
Jack: Stop! (*The big light flashes on above Hardmuth's eyes. . . . A pause.*) You can't shoot— that—gun. You can't pull the trigger. (*Pause.*) You can't—even—hold—the—gun. (*Pause. The derringer drops from Hardmuth's hand.*) Now, Frank, you can go.

Concluding that his curious psychic powers give him an ungentlemanly edge in his gambling, Jack resolves to quit. He cures Clay of his unreasonable fear and even helps Hardmuth escape across state lines.

The *Times,* speaking for a critical majority, called the work "a really remarkable play" and hoped carpers would not find the crucial scene implausible. It also had equally high praise for Mason's acting, "with its vigorous and dominating masculinity, its suggestiveness of the mental processes, and its superb authority and poise." The production ran out the season.

Charles Frohman imported W. J. Locke's **The Morals of Marcus** (11-18-07, Criterion) from the West End. It told of a scholarly cynic (C. Aubrey Smith) who adopts a waif (Marie Doro) and falls in love with her. Smith had played the role of Sir Marcus in England.

Probably most first-nighters at *The Witching Hour* or *The Morals of Marcus* were unaware that Owen Davis's ninth play of the season was premiering on the same night. For some reason, however, It's **Never Too Late to Mend** (11-18-07, Star) was not mounted by Woods but by a minor producer. The play was unexceptional. All the customary outrages are inflicted on the heroine, an heiress kidnapped while still a child and raised in ignorance of her true position, and the hero, a sailor, prior to the crime-does-not-pay finale.

America had nothing like England's tradition of Christmas pantomimes, but producers often brought out shows that might attract children during the preholiday season. Charles Frohman found a rare nonmusical example in **The Toymaker of Nuremberg** (11-25-07, Garrick), which was written by Austin Strong, Robert Louis Stevenson's stepgrandson. The son (Leo Herbert White) of the toymaker (W. J. Ferguson) loves the daughter (Consuelo Bailey) of the toymaker's boss (Frank Wunderlee), but the boss will not hear of his daughter wedding an apprentice who does nothing but paint eyelashes. After all, you cannot "support a wife on eyelashes." As it stands, even the boss is having trouble supporting the standard his family has become accustomed to, since the American market for Nuremberg dolls has collapsed. The youngsters' plan to elope is thwarted. Enter a stranger (Harrison Armstrong) driving a spanking-new and expensive automobile. He turns out to be the toymaker's older son. He has gone to America and become rich. How? By driving Nuremberg dolls off the market. You see, he is America's teddy-bear king. It develops that he has secretly purchased the boss's shop, so he is rich enough to make for happy endings all around. The play ran until Christmas and went into the records as an "almost success."

Any Chauncey Olcott vehicle swung between musical and drama. Theodore Burt Sayre's latest bit of Irish romantic fluff, **O'Neill of Derry** (11-25-07, Liberty), was no exception, although it was given a better stage than Olcott was accustomed to playing on and, whether this was cause or effect, was treated a jot more seriously by some reviewers. But the story hardly differed from what had served the star so well before. The play was set in Cromwell's day. Bryan O'Neill (Olcott) must help his friend, Lawrence Desmond (Edwin Carewe), retrieve Desmond's beloved (Rose Curry) from the lecherous Governor of Londonderry (Leonard Shepherd).

Lem B. Parker's **Shadowed by Three** (11-25-07, 14th St.) had a typical touring-melodrama plot but was enhanced by some marvelous curtains. The basic story told of a wicked woman who murders her husband. When a waif whom the murdered man had adopted discovers by tattoo marks that the wife's lover is her long-lost father, she impetuously attempts to take the blame for the killing. But one of the three men determined to protect her (their given names are Tom, Dick, and Harry) rides his red automobile through the bow window of the home in which the action has taken place, grabs the girl from the clutches of arresting officers, and rides off. Curtain. The end of Act II showed a locomotive rushing away from an attempted robbery. At the close of the third act, the stage was supposed to represent the stage of a town hall where a magician is performing. He draws the murdered husband's head out of a hat, and the head accuses the wife of murder. The wife, sitting in the rear of the actual theatre, screams, rushes down the aisle pursued by detectives, hurdles the footlights, and disappears into the wings. Just before the final curtain, the wife's lover suffers a blow on the head, which helps him recall he is not only the heroine's father but the murdered man's long-lost brother. So he, too, turns against the villainess.

Ermete Novelli began his second and final American visit on December 2 at the Lyric. The actor's repertory and his reception were much the same as they had been the preceding season. And once again Italian-Americans comprised a large portion of his audience. He remained only a fortnight.

Bucking the season's chain of reverses, Belasco batted two for two when he brought out William C. de Mille's **The Warrens of Virginia** (12-3-07, Belasco). Superficially it was merely another Civil War saga in which a southern belle finds herself at odds with her northern beau. The belle is Agatha Warren (Charlotte Walker), and she is stopped from passing through the lines to bring a basket of food to her father, General Warren (Frank Keenan), by her recent suitor, Union officer Lieutenant Burton (Charles D. Waldron). When Burton is brash enough to ask permission to call on her, she angrily refuses. Later the ailing general is furloughed and, meeting Burton, invites him to pay a visit. Burton's superiors learn of this and order him to carry some false dispatches, which they feel sure will be uncovered by the Confederates and prompt the enemy to move its troops to the wrong battle area. Agatha melts on seeing Burton again and even agrees to conceal his dispatch in her shoe. But when the papers are found and acted upon, and when the Warrens understand the trickery involved, Agatha once more spurns Burton. He is even at risk of being shot as a spy. Lee's surrender saves Burton's life. Five years pass. The Warrens have been impoverished. Burton appears, still anxious to court Agatha. The general rushes for his shotgun but changes his mind when he hears Agatha dismiss Burton and realizes the young man's true feelings. Instead of shooting him, he invites him to come back soon.

Most critics agreed that the play was no great shakes but that Belasco's consummate staging raised it to something approaching high theatrical art. The piece began in a deceptively idyllic setting, a wooded dell with a stream trickling down over rocks shaded by huge willow trees. Only a broken gun carriage hints all is not well. The second and third acts took place in the Warrens' home. While the general and his wife (Emma Dunn) have a grown son and daughter, they also have two youngsters, whose toys are much in evidence. The final act showed the garden beside the Warrens' rundown home. Performances were as excellent as the settings, with most praise going to Keenan for the "finish, subtlety, naturalness and power of expression" he brought to the role of General Warren. Some critics found space for kind words about two players in lesser roles: Cecil B. de Mille as the Warrens' grown son and golden-haired Mary Pickford, in her Broadway debut, as the Warrens' little girl. The play ran out the season.

Rida Johnson Young and J. Hartley Manners' **The Lancers** (12-3-07, Daly's), a quick flop, turned out to be a new translation of the same German comedy Daly had presented in 1881 as *The Passing Regiment*. Only this time some songs and showgirls were added, making it a borderline musical.

In **The Secret Orchard** (12-16-07, Lyric), Channing Pollock's dramatization of Agnes and Egerton Castle's novel, a young girl (Josephine Victor) asks the very duke (William Courtenay) who has seduced her how she should respond to his cousin's (Burke Clarke) proposal of marriage. A happy solution is found. The play received excellent notices but closed after one month. In his autobiography Pollock blamed the failure on an abrupt transferral from one theatre to another.

Far down in the Bowery, a new comedy-melodrama, J. Edwin Owen's **The Original Cohen** (12-16-07, Thalia), regaled playgoers. The Original Cohen and the Only Levi are rival secondhand clothes dealers on Baxter Street, but their children are determined to marry over their fathers' objections. Cohen's son changes his father's mind by hinting that the shock of a Levi marrying a Cohen might kill Levi. Hoping to have his rival out of the way, Cohen consents to the marriage. The lovers soon encounter additional touring-melodrama problems, but even these were presented in a humorous way. The refreshing slant prompted one critic to proclaim, "Let us have some more like The Original Cohen."

Christmas week was a busy one. It began with one of the season's most popular plays, Margaret Mayo's **Polly of the Circus** (12-23-07, Liberty). As with *The Warrens of Virginia,* reviewers saw little commendable in the play itself: "The plot is weak and the story hackneyed," one big scene "gets nowhere," another "missed fire." But the production as a whole, with its colorful, often ingenious settings and its bright young leading lady, was a different matter. Villagers are publicly shocked, though many are privately delighted, when a circus sets up alongside the home of the town's minister, the Rev. John Douglass (Malcolm Williams). They are further outraged when a pretty bareback rider, Polly (Mabel Taliaferro), injured in a fall, is given a room in the minister's house in which to convalesce. A year passes, during which Polly and the minister have fallen in love. The more sanctimonious members of his congregation demand that he send the girl on her way. He refuses, but he does attempt to persuade Polly to finish her education at a distant school. This leads Polly to think he doesn't love her, so when the circus reappears for its annual visit, she returns to it. Yet somehow she is not the fine rider she once had been. She has grown careless. When the minister comes seeking her out, he learns from the circus boss that Polly will probably be fired. The scene switches to inside the circus. Typically, bareback riders, trapeze artists, and clowns are all performing at once. Polly enters on a white horse and goes into her act. Then she spots the minister, loses her balance, and, luckily, falls into his arms. They acknowledge their love for each other, and the setting blacks out. When the lights come on again, the minister and Polly are standing alone, arm in arm, in a dark, empty field. In the distance the lights of the circus wagons can be seen retreating down a winding road. Although professional scuttlebutt at the time sometimes credited either Frederick Thompson (Miss Taliaferro's husband and the play's producer) or Winchell Smith with writing the play, her name on the program boosted Margaret Mayo's stock.

. . .

Margaret Mayo [née Lilian Clatten] (1882–1951) was born in Brownsville, Ill. She made her debut as an actress in 1896 and continued to perform until 1903, when she decided to devote herself to playwriting. Among her earlier works were two adaptations of novels: *The Marriage of William Ashe* (1905) and *The Jungle* (1907).

. . .

An American millionaire was the central figure in Alfred Sutro's London hit **John Glayde's Honor** (12-23-07, Daly's), which James K. Hackett imported as a vehicle for himself. But New Yorkers would not accept the play, in which the hero, finding his wife (Miss Darragh) has been unfaithful and lied about it when he confronted her, simply hands his wife over

to her lover (William Sauter) and wishes them good luck.

Al Woods was once again Owen Davis's producer when the latter's tenth play of the season, **Deadwood Dick's Last Shot** (12-23-07, 14th St.), premiered. The basic story and the sensation scenes were old hat. An orphan arrives in Monterey to establish her claim to her late father's mine and promptly falls into the hands of some murderous scoundrels. But Deadwood Dick, "an honest faro bank dealer," befriends her, routs the villains, and promises never again to gamble or shoot people if the heroine will marry him. One critic observed, "Every important speech was punctuated properly with the point of a gun, and the climaxes were all accented by an unlimited display or discharge of glittering revolvers."

In order to obtain papers that will help him gain control of a railroad, one of the line's officers attempts to have its president stabbed to death and the president's daughter kidnapped. The railroad's handsome superintendent, who loves his boss's daughter, helps send the schemer to jail. Such were the stock turns of plot in Robert Williams's **The Rocky Mountain Express** (12-23-07, American).

Only Ethel Barrymore's charm and popularity saved Clyde Fitch and Cosmo Gordon Lennox from being added to the all too long roster of admired playwrights who disappointed their audiences during this season. What was almost certainly a Fitch touch opened **Her Sister** (12-25-07, Hudson): a view of an exotic Temple of Isis, with Madam Isis reading futures. The temple turns out to be a room in a Bond Street fortune-telling shop, and Madam Isis is revealed to be Eleanor Alderson, a girl resolved to support herself until Mr. Right comes along. She latches on to a seeming Mr. Right (Charles Hammond), only to have a vicious-tongued troublemaker (Lucile Watson) cause her to be confused with a sister who has been named in a scandalous American divorce. At that point Mr. Right and his family show their true colors, so Eleanor settles for a better man (Arthur Byron). The play ran two months.

Henry Esmond's London trifle **Under the Greenwood Tree** (12-25-07, Garrick) was almost as popular, thanks in large measure to Maxine Elliott. She played a fabulously rich girl who runs away from society, poses as a gypsy, and finds true love with a country squire.

Tremendous advance ballyhoo promised a major new American playwright in Owen Johnson, a thirty-year-old novelist. "Have We an Ibsen amongst Us?" the banner of a full-page article in *Theatre* asked. When his **The Comet** (12-30-07, Bijou) opened, it quickly became obvious that he at least had read Sudermann's *Magda*. Lona, a famous actress, returns after many years to her home town bent on destroying the man who had ravished and deserted her. By chance she meets his son (Brandon Tynan), so she sets out to destroy him instead. When the father (Dodson Mitchell) comes to plead for his son, she reveals that she once had a son by the older man and that the baby died of starvation. The young man overhears this story and shoots himself. His father, crazed with fear, rushes out, leaving Lona by herself. The sound of horses and carriage bells let her know it is time to depart. Her emotions drained, she mechanically begins to put on her coat and gloves and hat, as the curtain falls.

Critics divided fiercely in their judgments of the play. The often Winteresque *Theatre,* ignoring its own puffery, branded it "incomprehensible and indefensible and reprehensible," while the *Dramatic Mirror* called it a work "that engenders thought. It has great truths." Critics were more of a mind about the star, Nazimova. Several stated she was probably not what the playwright had envisioned, but agreed that she was electrifying. In his *Sun* review Eaton, who always was to consider her a little too exotic for his tastes, called her Lona "a strange, fantastic vampire out of the realms of unreality." Primarily because of Nazimova's growing allure, the drama ran nearly two months. But Johnson would do little on Broadway, and whatever fame clings to him does so because of his 1911 novel *Stover at Yale*.

Another great actress was responsible for a genuinely European work's running thirty performances. Abetted by such fine players as Bruce McRae (Rosmer) and George Arliss (Brendel), Mrs. Fiske (Rebecca West) brought forth her version of Ibsen's *Rosmersholm* at the Lyric on the 30th. By underplaying until her confession in the third act, the star gave an overpowering performance. She made a poisonous figure understandable and believable if not likable. Acton Davies in the *Evening Sun* called the mounting "a superb achievement," a conclusion that accorded with many of his colleagues'.

Not many critics bothered any longer to review touring melodramas, but these clinkers still found a welcoming if dwindling audience. **Tony the Bootblack** (12-30-07, Metropolis) was Owen Davis's eleventh offering of the season and the tenth produced for him by Al Woods. Because the hero and heroine were played by performers popular as a song-and-dance team in vaudeville, the play was advertised as a "musical melodrama" and had more musical turns than the average touring play. Perhaps the alteration also reflected the fight to keep patrons

out of cheaper film houses. For all that, the story offered little new. Tony is really the heir apparent of an American banker, but he was kidnapped as a baby by the Black Hand and raised by them as a poor urchin in Little Italy. Now the gangsters plan to kidnap his sister, and though Tony does not know who he really is and so is unaware of his relationship to the girl, he and his sweetheart take her side and fight to rescue her.

Lem B. Parker had been heard from earlier in the season, but in no way could he catch up with Davis's record. His **The Card King of the Coast** (12-30-07, American) spotlighted a gentlemanly gambler from Kentucky (surname, Boone) who comes to the Klondike and rescues a lovely lady from a blackguard ready to frame her for a murder he himself committed. The villain was played by one of the few actors in the field who went on to better things, Noah Berry, Jr.

The new year got off to a languid start. A typically preposterous stage will precipitate the mysterious doings in **The House of a Thousand Candles** (1-6-08, Daly's), which George Middleton derived from Meredith Nicholson's novel. A rich uncle pretends to die and leaves his fortune to his nephew (Stephen Grattan) on condition that he live in the uncle's spooky mansion for a year. Secret passages, eerie noises, a duplicitous executor (William Hazeltine), a butler (E. M. Holland) who is not all he seems to be, and a sweet young lady (Mabel Roebuck) provide complications. The drama survived only two weeks in New York but proved a major success on the road and in stock.

There was one interesting twist in Joseph Le Brandt's touring melodrama **The Mysterious Burglar** (1-6-08, Star). The hero and heroine are time and again placed in jeopardy by a miscreant who has blinded the heroine's father, an old Klondike prospector, and appropriated important papers. In this case the hero steals the papers and frames the villain for the theft.

Theodore Kremer's waning talents were evident in **A Fighting Chance** (1-13-08, American), whose story owed much to *Leah Kleschna*. As in that earlier, superior play, the heroine is forced by her father not just to steal but to participate in robbing the good man she loves of gems, in this case from his jewelry store. The store owner helps rehabilitate her after the expected touring-melodrama agonies.

When *The Reckoning* was revived nearly a year after its premiere, it was paired with a second Schnitzler piece, **The Literary Sense** (1-13-08, Madison Square), in which a woman (Amy Ricard) given to writing poetry destroys her work, which would reveal her former amours, on the eve of her marriage to a philistine.

Maude Adams remained America's most beloved actress, so whatever profit Miguel Zamacoïs's **The Jesters** (1-15-08, Empire) reaped in its seven-week run probably was to her credit. In Paris, Bernhardt had triumphed in the play, but a number of reviewers felt the role of a prince who disguises himself as a hunchbacked fool to court a beautiful princess was unsuited to Miss Adams's more gentle, wistful art. One critic raised another objection: "Many of her quickly rippled phrases were almost unintelligible at the back of the house, and her habit of changing vowels into curious diphthong sounds— 'All my luck, I claim' into 'Ool my luck, I cle-e-em'—did not add to the effect."

Early in the first act of Paul Armstrong's **Society and the Bulldog** (1-18-08, Daly's), an effete east-erner enters a mining camp dressed in snazzy green riding togs and carrying his golf clubs. The absurd contrast set the tone for the comedy's clash of eastern and western ideals. Against that background the play's primary plot pitted ambitious if un-schooled figures against high-society snobs. Bill Farley (William Farnum) is a rich, self-made miner resolved to see his daughter, Genevieve (Catherine Proctor), establish herself among the Four Hundred. The *American*'s tongue-in-cheek Alan Dale professed to be amused by all the bit actresses parading about in "dekkletey." He dismissed the work as "archly preposterous" and quoted "Wall Street is the home of the quick or the dead" as an instance of its misfiring comedy, but he was pleased that "society got it in the neck." Some other critics, still basking in the steadfast glow of *The Great Divide,* seemed to resent the attempt to treat such fundamental themes as a comedy. The play was quickly withdrawn.

Better writing, fine acting, and laudatory notices could not save Anthony P. Wharton's London drama **Irene Wycherley** (1-20-08, Astor), in which a dutiful wife (Viola Allen) strives to no avail to save her marriage to a selfish cad (Edwin Arden). The husband is finally shot by his mistress's husband, who then commits suicide. The important part of the wife's loyal friend and would-be suitor was played by Walter Hampden.

A French farce fared better. **Twenty Days in the Shade** (1-20-08, Savoy) was Paul Potter's adaptation of a Hennequin and Veber original. Its central figure is a count (Richard Bennett) sentenced to twenty days in jail for a minor altercation. He persuades a friend (Charles Dickson) to take his place while he takes his family on vacation in Italy. When he

returns he finds his friend has invited his jailmate to visit. The jailmate, as played by pudgy, rubber-faced Dallas Welford, walked off with the show.

Graustark (1-20-08, Harlem Opera) was Grace Hayward's theatricalization of George Barr Mc-Cutcheon's 1901 best-seller. Several other versions had been done outside New York, but none, apparently, in Manhattan. This Harlem stock company's version followed the novel's basic story closely. Two Americans come to Edelweiss in search of a woman who they soon learn is Princess Yetive. They also learn she is in grave danger. With sword, gun, and cunning they fight to save her, and one of the men sits on the throne beside her by the final curtain. If it didn't already, the title would soon signify a special brand of swashbuckling romance set in an imaginary European land.

Sothern and Marlowe had parted temporarily, and by all accounts amicably, so Sothern's 1907 engagement found him utilizing other, lesser leading ladies. His choice for an opener at the Lyric on the 27th was surprising but in no way unwelcome, for he resurrected his father's favorite vehicle, *Our American Cousin.* His makeup as Dundreary was a little less outré than his father's had been, but the famous old hop, stammer, and vacuous laugh were all retained. The consensus was that the comedy, for all its age, was still very viable indeed. After fifty-one showings, Sothern brought out *Hamlet* and *If I Were King* before presenting two novelties.

In Anthony E. Wills's **The Lost Trail** (1-27-08, West End) a Colorado holdup man is reformed by a loving, loyal woman, the victim of one of his stagecoach robberies. He marries her after taking the blame for a crime her brother is supposed to have committed and after she learns her suitor, an army lieutenant, is a married man.

Religious drama now and then added variety to combination-house programs. Of course, these touring dramas had a healthy quota of sensations, but then so did many religious plays designed for first-class theatres. Eugene Thomas's **A Soldier of the Cross** (2-5-08, West End) centered on a Roman with pro-Christian leanings. His long-missing daughter is a convert to the new religion. The hero saves the life of a Roman princess lost in a cave, and she in gratitude promises to spare the Christians. She reneges when she learns that the hero's daughter is loved by the prince she herself is enamored of. The newly converted hero and his co-believers are subject to mistreatment until the eruption of Vesuvius buries the pagans but spares the Christians. The earthquake, eruption, and crumbling of Pompeii made for an exciting finale.

Olga Nethersole, always capable of providing her own brand of excitement, began a three-week stand, opening with **The Awakening** (2-10-08, Daly's), Sydney Grundy's translation of Paul Hervieu's play. She portrayed a married woman whose furtive romance with the heir apparent to the throne is scotched by his father's clever trickery. On the 20th she appeared in a double bill consisting of Hervieu's **The Enigma,** in which husbands determined to learn which one of their wives has been unfaithful discover all the spouses have been cheating, and Charles H. E. Brookfield's **I Pagliacci,** a redaction of the opera with incidental music from the same work. The rest of her repertory consisted of old favorites: *Adrienne Lecouvreur, Carmen, Magda, Sapho, Camille,* and *The Second Mrs. Tanqueray.*

Mrs. Patrick Campbell, herself closely identified with *The Second Mrs. Tanqueray,* was another actress guaranteed to raise eyebrows. She raised some by throwing a tantrum that delayed the first-night curtain when she presented a double bill featuring Arthur Symons's translation of Hugo von Hofmannsthal's version of Sophocles's **Electra** (2-11-08, Garden). With "her fluid, richly mellifluent speech, ductile as drawn silver," she quickly won forgiveness as an Electra as powerful and poetic as she was haunting: "face pallid as marble and a figure undulating rhythmically." Regrettably, her opening-night tantrum may have been a warning. At the beginning of the second week she suffered a nervous breakdown, and what might have been Broadway's most successful Greek revival in many years was closed abruptly. Accompanying the older tragedy was another, shorter one: a translation of Robert D'Humiere's transcription of a 16th-century Japanese play, **The Flower of Yamato,** in which a wife switches beds with her husband so that her murderous former lover will kill her instead of her spouse.

Another lady with a mind of her own was the central figure in David Graham Phillips's **The Worth of a Woman** (2-12-08, Madison Square). Phillips had been making a name for himself as a muckraker and as an advocate for the "new woman," but many observers felt he sold out in the last act of this, his first play. His heroine, Diana Merivale (Katherine Grey), learns she is pregnant and frantically wires her lover, Julian Burroughs (Robert Warwick), of her plight. He dutifully appears at the Merivale home, but his attitude is so evasive that Diana realizes he does not love her. Under the circumstances she will not hear of their marrying, and to Julian's further astonishment she tells her whole family of her situation and decision. Her father (Frank Young) comes to her support.

But in the final act, "in the limelight of the moon," Julian returns and confesses that her brave stand showed him how much he did, in fact, love her. They agree to wed. Phillips's morality bothered many critics. The more progressive ones suggested the last act cheapened the play; the more tradition-bound writers thought some punishment should have been in order for the lovers. The public seems not to have cared either way.

In outline **The Honor of the Family** (2-17-08, Hudson) might well have been mistaken for a touring melodrama. But this play, translated by Paul M. Potter from Émile Fabre's dramatization of Balzac's *La Rabouilleuse,* was more than the tale of a scheming woman (Percy Haswell) and her lover (Francis Carlyle), who attempt to dupe an old man (A. C. Andrews). For suddenly, and briefly, a figure, mustachioed and curly-headed, is seen swaggering past the window. A battered high hat sits cockily aslant his head, a greatcoat is bundled tightly about him, and he swings his cane with the air of a majordomo. Moments later he has entered, banged his cane on the table, ordered the schemers out, and lit his cigar. He is Colonel Philippe Bridau, the old man's nephew. The schemers are not so easily daunted. They try every ploy; at one point the woman even professes she has come to love him. But just as the scene reaches a pitch of high passion, Bridau quietly tells the lady he sees through her. Eventually Bridau kills her lover in a duel, saves the old man, and tells the vanquished woman she can wait for him in Paris. The honor of the family has been saved. And so was a piece of romantic hokum, thanks largely to Otis Skinner's brilliant tour de force. Once again in a season of disappointing plays, a star had turned a competent vehicle into a magical hit.

Henry Ludlowe had none of Skinner's panache. He was a Philadelphia dramatic coach with lofty ideas, so he bought sets once used by the late Richard Mansfield, hired a company, and presented himself at the Bijou for two weeks beginning February 17 in *The Merchant of Venice* and *Richard III,* after which he disappeared into theatrical annals.

The Irish National Theatre, later to be better known as the Abbey, was first seen in New York when Charles Frohman presented Yeats's **A Pot of Broth** (2-18-08, Savoy) in conjunction with the ongoing *Twenty Days in the Shade.* W. G. Fay portrayed the beggar who makes a couple (Bridget O'Dempsay and F. J. Fay) believe a stone has extraordinary properties. A week later, the Fays, with Dudley Digges and J. M. Kerrigan assisting them, supplanted the Yeats piece with Lady Gregory's **The Rising of the Moon** (2-24-08, Savoy), in which an outlaw escapes from the police by disguising himself as a ballad singer. Neither the plays nor the players created much excitement—at least not this time around.

The Four Mortons—one of vaudeville's most popular family acts—were starred in George V. Hobart's **The Big Stick** (2-24-08, West End). To save his son from going bankrupt in Wall Street, a father gives up the $5,000 he had squirreled away to start a business. Later the family's home is found to be standing in the path of a new railway tunnel, and the money they obtain for the house sets them once again on the road to prosperity.

Eugene Walter fulfilled the promise he had shown last season in *The Undertow* when he offered **Paid in Full** (2-25-08, Astor). Outwardly Joseph Brooks (Tully Marshall) seems an attractive man. But he is not what he seems. He is selfish, bitter, and unprincipled. As one friend remarks about his politics, "If Joe had got his ten-dollar raise today he'd be howling for capital. There are lots of such socialists." But Joe hasn't gotten a raise. He lives with his wife, Emma (Lillian Albertson), a girl who came from a higher level of society, in a rundown Harlem flat. On $18 a week they cannot even hire help, so Joe must share in cleaning the dishes. His mother-in-law (Hattie Russell) and his stern boss, Captain Williams (Frank Sheridan), who once had been Joe's late father-in-law's partner, visit the couple, but the visit only exacerbates Joe's bitterness. So does the realization that he cannot afford to treat his wife to a theatre party. As a result, he steals some of the money handed over to him in his position of collector for Captain Williams's steamship company. When Joe learns that Williams is aware of the theft, he orders Emma to go to Williams and plead for him, suggesting that if necessary she should be willing to prostitute herself for him. Williams's office is an unusual place for a supposedly hardhearted man. It is filled with memorabilia. A ship's wheel is above the door, and a capstan serves as a table. The old man recognizes the shamelessness of Joe's behavior, writes a letter exculpating him, then reads Emma the riot act. When Emma returns home, Joe is prepared to berate her for doing what he asked of her. She hands him the letter, tells him her eyes have been opened, and walks out.

A few critics complained that the promise of a psychological study of a weak, self-serving young man, implicit in the first act, was sacrificed for the sake of theatrically effective incidents, but virtually every reviewer acknowledged, as one concluded, that Walter had "told an interesting story in an uncommonly interesting way." There was also general agreement in praise of the acting and staging. So the play ran well into the summer. Its success lifted Walter fleetingly into the ranks of our most promising dramatists.

. . .

Eugene Walter (1874–1941) was born in Cleveland, Ohio. He held positions on newspapers in his home town, Cincinnati, Detroit, Seattle, and New York and served as a theatrical advance agent before turning to playwriting. His first drama was known variously as *Boots and Saddles* and *Sergeant James* and was inspired by his experiences as a cavalryman in the Spanish-American War. It never reached New York.

. . .

Much like the Four Mortons, Will Cressy and his wife, Blanche Dayne, were primarily vaudevillians. Cressy was famous for his rube act revolving about a goateed New Hampshire lawyer given to tough words and soft deeds. With the help of James Clarence Harvey, Cressy tried legitimate waters in **The Village Lawyer** (2-29-08, Garden). His Squire Tappan has two nephews. One is good and the other bad. The bad one borrows money from his brother, rewrites the check to make the figure ten times what the brother inked in, and causes other problems, which the kindly squire must solve. The first and last acts showed the exterior of the lawyer's office on the left, the village green in the middle, and his clapboard home on the right. The second act took place in a general store so realistic it "made one think that he had been transplanted into the very heart of a New Hampshire village." Act III had nothing to do with the rest of the show, being a series of vaudeville turns, with most of the time devoted to Cressy and Dayne's popular two-a-day skit "Billy Biffin's Baby." Playgoers were not necessarily vaudeville fans, so *The Village Lawyer* moved out after two weeks.

George Ade, like Augustus Thomas some months before, was able to redeem his failure earlier in the season with a success, albeit his **Father and the Boys** (3-2-08, Empire) was a more modest hit. Happily the play also served to give William H. Crane the sort of congenial role he had not had since *David Harum*. Lemuel Morewood, a wool broker, has a simple, practical desk in the middle of his office. His two sons have more elaborate desks. Bill's is elegant—cluttered with cigarette cases, a silver tea service, and photographs in fancy frames, and backed by a wall hung with hunting scenes—and

Tom's is laden with Indian clubs, boxing gloves, and other gym paraphernalia, for Bill (Forrest Orr) is devoted to high society and Tom (Robert MacKay) is a sport. Neither has much time for the business. So when Lemuel's lawyer (Percy Brooke) tells him a long-sought merger has finally gone through, Lemuel can only muse, "Waited years for this day to come—a dozen big jobbing concerns—all tails to my kite. And now—It's no fun to fly the kite." Bill throws a posh dinner party, prompting Lemuel to take himself out to a simple restaurant. Returning home, he learns that Bill is heavily in debt and reluctantly signs a check to cover the loss. But then he meets Bessie Brayton (Margaret Dale), an actress Bill has hired to entertain his society friends. She and Lemuel's lawyer tell Lemuel he must stop living for his boys and live for himself. That is probably the only way to bring his sons to their senses. Lemuel agrees. He goes upstairs, dons his evening clothes, returns, and takes his place at the roulette table Bill has set up. With Bessie's help, he breaks the bank—and the banker, who is none other than the man (Fred W. Sidney) to whom the check had to be made out. Then he heads out for a night on the town with Bessie.

Later Lemuel and Bessie win big at the races, but their noisy behavior offends Bill's society friends. Bill, his eyes at last opening, is furious at the snobs, not at his father. But Lemuel learns that Bessie is about to be bilked out of mining stock she owns by the very crook who had hoodwinked Bill. The old man and the young girl take the first train for Nevada. Lemuel's sons, his lawyer, and the two girls Lemuel hopes his sons will marry take the next train, fearing the old man is eloping. In Nevada, at a makeshift hotel with no comforts, Lemuel gives the villain the boot and reunites Bessie with her long-lost sweetheart. Bill and Tom, embracing their girls, promise to roll up their sleeves hereafter.

The play's humor was well distributed, and many of Ade's barbs at hoity-toity society fell to Lemuel's housekeeper (Adele Clarke). In a line that calls to mind a similar joke in *Mrs. Wiggs of the Cabbage Patch,* she speaks of a New York society leader with a hyphenated name as "the lady that wears a link in her name." When Bill insists the family hire a butler, she reacts, "Can't have much respect for a man that's around a house doin' woman's work." And of the new, late dinner hour she remarks, "Dinner at eight o'clock! I can remember when they had it at noon. After awhile they'll have it at two o'clock in the morning." As Lemuel, Crane found a perfect down-home, slap-on-the-back sort of role in which he thrived. Eaton observed, "The under note of

country sincerity, of a warm, generous nature, is never lacking in his performance; and the dry humor of the character, the comic perplexities, the efforts to master slang, to call himself a 'Six Cylinder Kid' without self-consciousness, and, above all, the unctuous abandonment to juvenile revels, are all denoted surely, easily, and with delightful effect." The show ran until mid-May and then, alternating with *David Harum,* toured for two full seasons.

Another popular comedian, Nat Goodwin, was not so fortunate. His career had been faltering, and the two-week debacle of George Broadhurst's **The Easterner** (3-2-08, Garrick) merely made matters worse. So did the fact that the play, reminiscent of the superior *In Mizzoura,* was a slipshod melodrama that required Goodwin to swing back and forth between serious and comic moments. Goodwin played an easterner who comes to mining country and is appointed a deputy sheriff. In that capacity he must rescue a young man (Wallace McCutcheon, Jr.) falsely accused of murder. The young man turns out to be the brother of the girl (Edna Goodrich) the sheriff wants to marry. Goodwin used comic routines to break the tension. He sent hand signals to a friend, then pretended they were simply attempts to swat a mosquito when they were misconstrued; he also mimicked a very French French waiter.

A very much admired Russian actress, Vera Komisarzhevsky, failed to thrill New York when she opened at Daly's on the 2nd for a three-week visit. The adjective "competent" appeared in notice upon notice. Her repertory mixed the relatively familiar with the totally unknown: Ibsen's *A Doll's House* and *The Master Builder,* Sudermann's *The Fires of St. John* and *The Battle of the Butterflies,* Ostrovsky's *A Child of Nature* and *The Dowerless Bride,* Gorky's *The Children of the Sun,* and Maeterlinck's *Sister Beatrice* and *The Miracle of St. Anthony.*

Byron Ongley's **The Rector's Garden** (3-3-08, Bijou) ran only a week after a critical drubbing for its mawkish sentiments and flowery prose. Dustin Farnum was starred as a minister who once had contemplated a career as a train robber. His romance with an heiress (Grace Elliston) who has purchased a neighboring property is nearly wrecked by a hot-headed West Point graduate (William Courtenay). Among other critical complaints was one that rose bushes in the first act sprouted azaleas later on.

Because less than a decade earlier Richard Mansfield had failed when he appeared in a dramatization of *Crime and Punishment,* E. H. Sothern's decision to star in Laurence Irving's version, with the unwieldy title **The Fool Hath Said "There Is No God"** (3-9-08, Lyric), gave many playgoers pause. Neither Irving's stagepiece nor Sothern's Rodion elicited the sort of enthusiasm that prompts playgoers to line up for tickets. The play was hurriedly withdrawn.

Toddles (3-16-08, Garrick), Clyde Fitch's translation of Tristan Bernard and André Godfernaux's *Triplepatte,* ran twice as long—two weeks. It featured John Barrymore as an indecisive English lord who must choose among three women: the five-year-old (Virginia Smith) to whom his family has engaged him, a rich old widow (Olive Temple), or the attractive daughter (Pauline Frederick) of a pushy climber (Isabel Richards). He spent much of the time in pajamas and red slippers before making the obvious selection.

Leo Ditrichstein's **Bluffs** (3-19-08, Bijou) could not even survive a full two weeks, although it had garnered oodles of publicity when it had premiered a month earlier in Plainfield, N.J. The reason for the attention was not the play itself but the news that Senator Robert La Follette's daughter, Fola, was making her stage debut and that a who's who of important Washington figures, including daddy, had entrained to the opening. The farce told of a famous actor, Carl Himmelhoch (Ditrichstein), who assumes the name of a supposedly dead friend so that he and his bride (Miss La Follette) can honeymoon incognito. When the dead friend (Alfred Kappeler) turns up very much alive, complications set in. Despite its abrupt closing, the play later toured with some success as *Sham Battles.*

The next Monday's busy roster was headed by one of the season's most interesting dramas, Charles Rann Kennedy's **The Servant in the House** (3-23-08, Savoy). Kennedy was the English-born grandson of a famous classical scholar. In his last years he would mount an annual festival of Greek plays, but not before a long career first as an actor and then as a writer of religious dramas. Although he divided this play into five acts, its action was continuous. The Reverend Wiliam Symthe (Charles Dalton), his haughty wife, "Auntie" (Edith Wynne Matthison), and his niece, Mary (Mabel Moore), are certain they have seen their new butler, Manson (Walter Hampden), somewhere before. But where? Manson is an odd man, almost embarrassingly humble and wise, who dresses in ancient Eastern garb. The vicar's more pressing problems include the need to repair his dilapidated church and the expected visits on this very same day of three people. First will be his wife's brother, the all-but-deaf-and-blind and openly worldly Bishop of Lancashire (Arthur Lewis). The bishop is coming in order to meet the vicar's brother

Joshua, a man who supposedly has served in a very distant see. Hasn't he been the Bishop of Benares or some such place? The third arrival will be another long-unseen brother, Robert (Tyrone Power), who took to drink after his own wife's death and lives as a common laborer. The vicar and his wife want nothing to do with him, but they have raised his daughter in ignorance of her father's history. It takes Manson's quiet charity and sense to bring the family closer together and teach them the true meaning of their religion. As the family sits down to dinner, they cannot account for the missing brother. Manson, moving flowers "to a more communal position" in the center of the table, remarks, "Perhaps you'd like to know, the Bishop of Benares is here."

Vicar: What, already! Let's have him in at once!
Manson: (deliberates with flowers before he speaks) He is here.
Vicar: What do you mean? Where is he?
Manson: (looks at him over the flowers) Here.
Vicar: (steps back, gazing at him. After a moment he gasps.) In God's name, who are you?
Manson: In God's name—your brother. (*He holds out his hand. The Vicar takes it, sinking to his knees and sobbing as one broken yet healed.*)

Eaton called the play "not a sermon or a tract, but a statement of applied or ethical religion in terms of the drama, a play with its own dramatic appeal and human significance." Arthur Ruhl, a less well known critic, delighted in its easily accessible allegory, exemplified by the characterization of the Bishop of Lancashire: "Every time the Servant addresses him and he irritably reaches for the ear-trumpet and squeaks, 'What's that, what's that?' Every time he squints and tries to see, or bumps into a table or chair, each spectator, according to his own experience and fervor, sees the deafness and blindness and bigotry and blundering of the modern fashionable church." The dramatic appeal kept the play on the boards until the hot weather forced it to close. It reopened for six more weeks in the fall, then toured. It also become a stock favorite and was revived several times on Broadway until the mid-1920s. Under Henry Miller's direction, the acting was "a near approach to perfection," with Power's gruff yet humane drainman and Hampden's spiritual yet human Manson accorded pride of place.

· · ·

Walter Hampden [Dougherty] (1879–1955) The tall, slim, aristocratic actor was born in Brooklyn and studied at the Brooklyn Polytechnic Institute and at Harvard. He apprenticed in England under F. R. Benson, learning numerous Shakespearean roles. He first came to Broadway's attention in 1907 when Henry Miller hired him to play opposite Alla Nazimova.

. . .

In later years many a commentator pointed to the pounding steam pipes in Clyde Fitch's **Girls** (3-23-08, Daly's) as a vividly remembered example of Fitch's preoccupation, for better or worse, with minutiae. Contemporaries also noticed the pipes but viewed (or heard) them simply as a legitimate bit of real life amusingly employed. Three girls, Pamela (Laura Nelson Hall), Violet (Ruth Maycliffe), and Kate (Amy Ricard), share an uncomfortable walkup furnished spartanly with a folding cot, a couch, and a morris chair that has seen better days. They also share an abiding mistrust of men. But one evening a man bursts into their apartment and asks them to help him escape from an irate husband who has returned home unexpectedly. They grudgingly provide a board that allows him to reach another window across an airshaft. Then, fighting their thoughts about the handsome gentleman and their steam pipes' percussive symphony, they go to sleep. Eventually Pamela obtains work in a law office. She is unhappy and about to resign when the junior partner, who has been away on vacation, returns. He is Edgar Holt (Charles Cherry), the man she helped escape. Violet has taken a job in the same office, where she spars verbally with the woman-hating Frank Lott (Leslie Kenyon). After just enough time for the expected misunderstandings, the girls and men are all paired happily. A program note stated, "The author wishes to acknowledge an indebtedness to a play by Hugo Holtz," but the actual source seems to have been Alexander Engel and Julius Horst's *Die Welt ohne Männer.* Whatever its basis, it proved the only Fitch play of the season to make money.

Hours before these shows premiered, some rising young players, bankrolled by George D. Ford, gave a special matinee to introduce New Yorkers to Ibsen's **Love's Comedy** (3-23-08, Hudson). Although other Ibsen plays had begun to gain national acceptance, this early work never was to please Americans.

The next evening *Marta of the Lowlands* was revived at the Garden. Its revival was noteworthy since it starred Bertha Kalish. Ashton Stevens devoted most of his *Evening Journal* review to her, proclaiming her "a unique artist" and continuing, "Her speech, as it soars from mood to mood, from low, passionate throbs to the very altissimo of grief or job, covers a greater scale than that of any contemporary actor."

William C. de Mille joined forces with his brother, Cecil B., to write **The Royal Mounted** (4-6-08, Garrick). Critics could find no high art in their work but agreed its commercial future looked bright. Victor O'Byrne (Cyril Scott) of the Mounties is assigned to solve a murder at a lumber camp. If he solves it he will be promoted to captain and written back into his father's will. O'Byrne quickly realizes that Sam Larabee (Charles Lane) is the killer. The trouble is that Sam is the brother of Rosa Larabee (Clara Blandick), the woman O'Byrne loves. So when Sam claims he killed the man while defending Rosa, O'Byrne allows him to escape. O'Byrne is then arrested for dereliction of duty. However, it soon is discovered that the man Sam killed was a wanted outlaw with a price on his head.

Sothern's second novelty of his season was Paul Kester's stage version of **Don Quixote** (4-8-08, Lyric). That it ran nearly four hours on opening night may partially explain its disdainful reception and very short stay.

Combination houses, busy hosting established plays, had not presented novelties for some weeks. For much of the nation, even Gordon Kean's **We Are King** (4-13-08, Metropolis) was hardly new, since Walker Whiteside, never a Manhattan idol, had toured with it for several seasons. Its arrival in New York came about only because another attraction the theatre had booked folded suddenly in Philadelphia. The play was little better than a parody on *The Prisoner of Zenda,* with a touch of Gilbert for good measure. A London newspaperman comes to Kahnburg to do some research. The prime minister immediately spots his remarkable resemblance to Kahnburg's increasingly insane king and talks him into replacing the institutionalized monarch. A romance soon blossoms with the princess of nearby Beronia. Just when the fraud is threatened with exposure, it is learned that the mad king and the newspaperman were switched secretly as babies, so the fraud is no fraud at all.

While Thomas, Ade, and Fitch had all scored varying degrees of success after failing earlier in the season, Eugene Walter went the other way. Not that **The Wolf** (4-18-08, Bijou) was a flop, but it in no way sparked the enthusiasm and excitement *Paid in Full* had provoked. Its run of eighty-one performances was terminated only by the onslaught of a heat wave, but how much of its run was forced is a matter no trade sheet addressed. Before the action of the play begins, Andrew McTavish's brutality has driven off his wife, so he has taken their daughter into the Hudson Bay region and raised her in innocence of the ways of the world. Hilda (Ida Conquest) grows into a beautiful young woman, whose golden hair hangs far down her back. She is loved by one of her few neighbors, a French-Canadian, Jules Beaubien (William Courtenay). An unscrupulous surveyor, William MacDonald (Walter Hale), comes on the scene. He lusts after Hilda and, sensing that McTavish (Thomas Findlay) is slightly off his rocker and very greedy, he proposes to take Hilda back to civilization with him and leaves McTavish with some vague promise of tremendous riches to come. Jules gets wind of this and persuades Hilda to flee with him. They have reached the end of their portage, a copse exploding in autumnal reds and yellows, when Jules becomes convinced MacDonald is on their trail. He tells a friend to move on with Hilda; he will join them after disposing of MacDonald. He will shoot his rifle twice to signal victory. Jules is left alone as night falls. Only the glow of a campfire lights the scene. MacDonald comes down the trail, sees Jules, shoots, and misses. Jules grabs MacDonald; they tussle, rolling over logs and underbrush. Knives glisten suddenly in the firelight. A scream is heard. One man stands up and lights a match. The man is Jules. He fires his signals, a shot is heard in reply, and the curtain falls.

Ridicule was the lot of Edward Vroom when he played the lead in his own romantic comedy **The Luck of MacGregor** (4-20-08, Garden). One despairing critic summed it up: "The plot is as conventional as a platitude, the characters as familiar as the footlights themselves, and the construction as crude as a comic supplement drawing." That platitudinous plot centered on a British soldier stationed at Fort George during the Revolution. He loves a girl (Katherine Mulkins) whose father is a spy for the Americans. In short order he is accused of treason, but his trial is disrupted by Mad Anthony Wayne's attack. The war over, he marries his beloved.

According to Thomas H. Sewell, **Kate Barton's Temptation** (4-20-08, Thalia) was a very run-of-the-mill touring-melodrama villain. Once she leaves her Bowery home and falls into his clutches, he kills her father, implicates her in a robbery he committed, disguises himself first as a woman, then as a Chinaman, and imprisons Kate and her blind sister in an opium den. It takes the arduous efforts of the good man Kate should have stuck with in the first place to save her.

One oddity was an **Untitled Play** (4-20-08, Harlem Opera), attributed to the combined talents of Mrs. C. A. Doremus, Beatrice Morgan, and Henry C. Colwell. A barmaid loves a young Irish lad but is lured away to London by a duke's promise to make her a leading lady at the Haymarket. Once they are in London, the duke gives the girl the choice of becoming his mistress or having the Irish lad hanged. She becomes the duke's mistress, which causes her to lose the lad's affections until the duke pays her £10,000 not to publish her memoirs. The play survived a single week, and one week later the Harlem Opera House was converted to films.

Guy Fletcher Bragdion and William Postance's **The Governor and the Boss** (4-27-08, Lincoln Square) was hardly a typical touring melodrama. Some saw it as a cheap-priced ripoff of *The Man of the Hour*. To his surprise an independent candidate for governor is endorsed by the Republican boss, a vindictive man out to settle some scores with his Democratic rivals. The Democrats aren't very nice, either. They persuade a girl to bring false charges of indecent behavior against the independent. His future seems hopeless, and even the Republican boss has second thoughts. Then the boss discovers that the daughter he long ago had abandoned and lost track of is the candidate's fiancée. By the final curtain the hero has won both the election and the girl.

The season's last novelty offered at a first-class house was Jean Aicard's **Papa Lebonnard** (4-28-08, Bijou), which Novelli initially had offered to New Yorkers more than a year earlier in Italian. Now the title role fell to a comedian whose heyday had slipped away, Henry E. Dixey. The fading star played a rich inventor who must confront his snooty wife and son with the son's illegitimate birth before they will acquiesce in permitting the inventor's daughter marrying a doctor with plebeian roots. Critics complained that Dixey was more interested in milking laughs than in probing the clockmaker's character, but Dixey's shrinking coterie of fans gave the play a modest run.

Romantic folderol set in the early 16th century was not common to lesser stages, but Carina Jordan's **The Lily and the Prince** (5-4-08, Yorkville) was just that, telling how a brave princess risks the rack to save her father from death and how she convinces her suitor-prince that she has not been unfaithful.

The next week the same house featured more typical fare, Matthew Barry's **The Provider** (5-11-08, Yorkville). The heroine is a schoolteacher; the hero, a bank clerk; the villain, the owner of the bank. Since he, too, loves the heroine, he successfully frames the hero for embezzlement, convinces even the heroine of the young man's guilt, and marries the girl. After years of suffering (luxurious suffering on the heroine's part), the truth comes out, the villain is shot dead, and the hero and heroine take up as if nothing had happened.

Few touring shows received the attention or the praise bestowed on Charles E. Blaney and J. Searle Dawley's **The Girl and the Detective** (5-11-08,

Lincoln Square). Little Tykie is a waif who hangs around Newspaper Row. When Henry Tanner, a fine young reporter, seems unable or willing to give his paper a detailed account of the murder of a visiting English lord, Tykie somehow obtains the material. She also falls in love with Tanner and believes he has fallen in love with her, until she finds him talking intimately to a beautiful lady. Thinking Tanner has played her false, she is not reluctant to inform Detective Haggerty that Tanner has a gun suspiciously like the one believed to have been used in the murder. Then Tykie learns the beautiful woman was not only the murdered man's wife but Tanner's sister. For the rest of the play, Tykie must keep Tanner from falling into Haggerty's hands. At one point she steals the policeman's automobile coat and goggles, giving them to Tanner to facilitate his escape. Eventually she helps track down and arrest the real killer, a gun manufacturer who hoped to marry the dead man's widow.

Just how superior the play truly was is moot, but its theatricality was enhanced by its star, Cecil Spooner. She was considered by many as one of the brightest lights of the cheap playhouses. The *Times,* which rarely reviewed touring plays at length, gave her latest vehicle an extended notice and concluded. "It is an everlasting pity that Cecil Spooner was not discovered by a Daly or a Belasco many years ago. . . . She is an unusually fine little artiste and, at the price, a decided bargain for the theatregoer." Unfortunately for her, she was strongly tied to the touring-melodrama tradition—a tradition now on its last legs—since in private life she was Mrs. Blaney.

Another rare costume drama was Theodore Kremer's pseudo-historical **The Triumph of an Empress** (5-18-08, Yorkville), in which Catherine the Great was shown fighting a duel, saving her sick baby poisoned by a wicked countess, and narrowly missing assassination herself.

Before a few stragglers wrote *finis* to the season at combination houses, the *Dramatic Mirror* ran a series of articles examining the slump in ticket sales. One of the more interesting was a lengthy interview with Howard Hall, who had written and starred in some of the long-lived touring vehicles. He put much of the blame for the poor ticket sales in combination houses on the shoddy goods offered. His fellow dramatists, he suggested, held their audiences in contempt and wrote to the cry "Get down to their level." This simply alienated the more intelligent among the poorer playgoers. Since they could not pay the $2 top that applied at most first-class theatres and would not sit through trash, they satisfied their craving for theatre by reluctantly plunking down fifty or seventy-

five cents for a first-class gallery seat. But a much larger, less intelligent group had also deserted, and their desertion could be attributed to just one thing, the bugaboo repeatedly mentioned in these articles— "the motion pictures."

Matthew Barry's **A Paradise of Lies** (6-1-08, Yorkville) opened with a prologue in which a man is seen weeping by a lily pond in which his child has drowned. As if by a miracle, another baby floats across the pond to him. He picks her up and adopts her. Years pass. The baby has grown into a lovely young woman, and the man has written two operas. The villain steals the operas, presents them as his own, and allows the old man to die of grief. He then courts the young woman. But she learns he is the father who abandoned her when she was a baby, so she heads off with an attractive actor.

There weren't many critical huzzas when Cecil Spooner was starred in Blaney and C. T. Dazey's **The Girl from Texas** (6-1-08, Lincoln Square). A simple Texas girl finds she is heir to a fine Irish castle. She also finds romance with the castle's current occupant. The play had toured without much success a few seasons earlier, but this was its New York premiere.

Bringing up the rear was another Blaney production, J. Searle Dawley's **A Daughter of the People** (6-8-08, Lincoln Square). A mill owner, for business and political reasons, has shut down his operation, bringing hardship on his employees. The daughter of one of them pleads with him to reopen the works, and he agrees, if she will marry him. She consents unhappily and later learns her marriage was a sham. Rejected by her family, she attempts to kill herself by falling into the plant's machinery. The mill owner comes to her aid and, realizing the consequences of his hypocrisy, reforms. The poverty of the employees, "supping off empty dishes," was contrasted with the showy luxury of the mill owner's home. Playgoers not angered by the contrast may have been touched by the character of the idiot boy who shares the home of the heroine and her father. The final setting, showing the engine room of the mill, won applause.

1908–1909

Broadway rebounded handsomely in the new season. The count of novelties offered in first-class theatres rose. More important, so did their quality.

And the stream of good or interesting stage works persisted from the season's start to its waning months. The lone exception was the continuing decline of touring melodrama and the concurrent falling away of combination houses from the ranks of legitimate theatre, a decline and falling away that became more unmistakable and alarming with each passing month. One by one new theatres and venerable old ones deserted the field of live drama.

Before the season got under way Bronson Howard died, lauded in his obituaries as "Dean of American Dramatists." Late in the theatrical year Modjeska passed away. (In France, Sardou and the great Coquelin preceded her by a few months.) These giants of another era, indeed another century, were widely mourned, but all through 1908–09 an impressive array of young playwrights and performers ensured that no one despaired of the American theatre's future, even if some traditionalists rued the end of antiquated styles.

Either oblivious to the drift or stubbornly determined to buck it, Charles E. Blaney leased one of the doomed combination houses and launched the season with his own play, **The Sheriff of Angel Gulch** (8-1-08, Third Ave.). Each evening, just before the final act, an announcer (for this first week it was the actor who played the chief villain) stepped in front of the footlights to advise playgoers, "Charles E. Blaney, the king of melodrama, will hereafter manage this house, and it is his determination to produce such plays that the young and old can enjoy alike; plays whose subjects can be discussed in the parlor as well as in the street. And it is the intention of the management to make the Third Avenue Theatre a meeting place for this great public of the great East Side." Who made the announcement in subsequent weeks is not known, nor is it certain for how many weeks the little speech was offered, but by January the theatre was a film house. Meanwhile, back at Angel Gulch, the hero must retrieve the deed to a mine from a villainous colonel who had killed the hero's father to steal it. You knew the colonel was no good since he "wore a black hat, a black mustache, a white tie, a black coat, and white trousers. If he wanted to live an upright life he would never have worn such things." Compounding the hero's difficulties is his love for the colonel's daughter. He kills the colonel only after learning the heroine was not really the colonel's child. Blaney must have sensed the move away from cheap melodrama. To lure in patrons on opening night, the drama was followed by an hour's worth of amateurs from the audience, brought onstage to demonstrate their talent—or lack of it.

A second Blaney work opened at a second doomed house nine evenings later. The heroine of **Tess of Tennessee** (8-10-08, 14th St.) is "a mountain waif" who has risen to become "Queen of the Moonshiners." She loves a man whose property contains a rich deposit of iron. Conspirators attempt to seize the land. They throw Tess and her sweetheart into a stream—but the lovers escape by climbing up a millwheel—and attempt to dynamite a train. All to no avail. An old fortune teller discloses that Tess's long-lost mother is the fallen woman the girl has befriended, and a happy ending follows quickly. So did an abbreviated title, *Tennessee Tess*.

In William G. Beckwith and Joseph Santley's **Lucky Jim** (8-10-08, Grand St.), which starred young Santley, the hero is the son of a Wall Street broker who has lost his fortune through the machinations of a deceitful associate. To win back the money and do in the deceiver, Jim takes the route so common to heroes of the period: he goes west to strike it rich in a mine. Naturally his nemesis dogs his footsteps and hires a notorious "greaser" to kill the lad. A final shootout leaves the two troublemakers dead and Jim embracing a pretty girl. The rising Santley was praised for his fine voice, his excellent delivery, and, most of all, "his modest, unassuming manner."

The same evening that welcomed these two touring melodramas also marked the start of the new play season at first-class houses. And what a start it was! Two of the year's best American plays and one of its most interesting importations premiered in quick succession. James Forbes's **The Traveling Salesman** (8-10-08, Liberty) arrived first. The curtain rises on the waiting room of a backwater train depot, a once whitewashed room now grimy with soot. Local characters saunter in and out. They include middle-aged Mrs. Babbit (Sarah McVicker), who is awaiting a train, and the baggage man, Crabb (R. C. Turner).

Mrs. Babbit: Say Mr. Crabb, when's the train due?
Crabb: What train? Think I'm a mind reader?
Mrs. Babbit: Train for Bird-in-Hand!
Crabb: Bird-in-Hand? 'Leven fifty-three.
Mrs. Babbit: When's it due?
Crabb: Seven minits afore twelve.
Mrs. Babbit: Ain't you the cute little smart Aleck? That joke was old when my grandfather was alive.
Crabb: Your *grand*father? Must be a darned old joke!

The Grand Crossing depot is run by young Beth Elliott (Gertrude Coghlan). Local folk agree she is "jest as smart as a steel trap," but she actually is naive enough to hope that no one will bid against her when her family's property is auctioned off for back taxes. Bob Blake (Frank McIntyre), a traveling salesman, detrains, depressed at being alone in the boondocks on Christmas Day. Beth offers to share her lunch with him, and the two shortly are taken with one another. Later, at his seedy hotel, Bob plays cards with other men in the trade, drinking booze from a teapot brought by the bellhop, and learns that some sharpies are resolved to buy the Elliott property, knowing a new rail track will be built across it. Bob quietly pays the Elliotts' back taxes, but the crooks make it seem he has cheated Beth out of the land. By the time she realizes that Bob is innocent, she has accepted the crooks' check, thereby apparently sealing a deal. Bob is told that no married woman in the state can execute a deed without her husband's signature. He sees an instant, happy way out. Phoning the desk clerk, Bob requests, "Send up one minister and two witnesses, quick!"

The earlier acts were crammed with vignettes of contemporary small-town life. The plot developed at what now might seem a painfully slow pace. But 1908 audiences loved it. So did most critics, although they hastily added quibbles. One observed, "It is the dialogue that makes *The Traveling Salesman* the success it has already become. The story is trite enough, and the characters, good as they are, are not unusual." Another reviewer echoed, "This may not be particularly good drama . . . but it is pretty good fun when the lines are as bright as these happen to be, and when the principal figure, as here, is in good hands." Those pudgy hands belonged to bulky Frank McIntyre, a skilled comedian who had won raves the previous season in *Classmates* but who would rarely, if ever again, have so good a role. He played Blake for the comedy's 280-performance run on Broadway and then for two full seasons on tour.

Booth Tarkington and Harry Leon Wilson's **The Man from Home** (8-17-08, Astor) was an even bigger hit, chalking up a New York run of 496 performances. In fact, it had been packing in audiences on the road during the 1907–08 season and arrived in New York with a lengthy Chicago stand to its credit. Yet in many ways it was very similar to *The Traveling Salesman*. Although set in a snooty Italian hotel, it was a comedy of conspicuously homespun American humor. Its story was simple and hardly original. Its star was another rising young comedian who never again would find so gratifying a role. And it received much the same yes/no reviews from critics. Daniel Voorhees Pike (William Hodge) is a straight-spoken, amiable lawyer from Kokomo, Ind., who

has come to Sorrento to visit his ward, Ethel Granger-Simpson (Madeline Louis). His skills are manifold: "I put a Pierce-Arrow together once after it had been run over by four Fords at the State Fair Grounds," he explains. Nor can his patriotism or his perceptions of American society be faulted:

Pike: Well, sir, of course, I know you've got some mighty fine historical architecture and public buildings over here, but when you come right down to it, Colonel, I wouldn't trade our new State Insane Asylum for the worst ruined ruin in Europe—not for hygiene and real comfort.
Le Blanc: And your people?
Pike: Well, we kind o' like each other.
Le Blanc: But you have no leisure class.
Pike: No leisure class? We've got a pretty good-sized colored population.

Pike is horrified to discover that Ethel has become engaged to Almeric St. Aubyn (Echlin P. Gayner), the spoiled son of an even more worthless English earl (Herbert McKenzie). By exposing this unsavory pair he not only wins Ethel's hand but extricates her brother, Horace (Hassard Short), from an equally distasteful alliance. Speaking for most of his fellow critics, Walter Prichard Eaton wrote, "We think it a pleasant and popular piece of extremely parochial jingo. We should call it an excellent bad play." Tall, reddish-blond, freckled, slightly gawky and sharp-featured, yet nonetheless attractive, Hodge was a comedian of the new "naturalistic," easygoing school, so natural and easygoing that more than one reviewer claimed he mumbled many of his lines and urged him to speak up. Coming after the success of his *Monsieur Beaucaire*, the play promised that the Indiana-born Tarkington, then in his late thirties and better known as a novelist, would find a place in the theatre as well.

Howard Hall, who the previous May had given an interview condemning the decline of cheap melo-drama, offered his remedy as producer, author, and star of **The Wall Street Detective** (8-17-08, 14th St.). His answer seemed to be to create a cliché-riddled piece and save it by assigning himself a protean role. He played a detective whose fiancée is pushed by her father into a marriage with a treacherous French count. The count, possessor of a magnificent cha-teau overlooking Manhattan-sur-Hudson, is in real-ity an adventurer in league with an adventuress posing as a German countess. They throw all manner of obstacles in the detective's path, and he is forced to disguise himself as an English lord and as a menacing member of the Black Hand to save his girl from the vicious pair.

The next evening New Yorkers were introduced to the best Continental playwright of the early 20th century, Ferenc Molnár. But it was an odd introduction indeed. The play, rather appropriately titled under the circumstances, was **The Devil** (8-18-08, Belasco and Garden). Legal loopholes and a bit of chicanery resulted in two versions premiering on the same night. The one at the Garden was mounted by Col. Henry W. Savage, a theatrically shrewd scoundrel who, at the time, was raking in huge profits from *The Merry Widow*. His adaptation, which reset the story in Germany, was by the popular humorist Oliver Herford and starred Edwin Stevens in the title role. Harrison Grey Fiske's presentation used a translation by Alexander Konta and William Trowbridge Larned, retained the original Hungarian setting, and starred George Arliss.

The story told of a portrait painter persuaded by the devil's subtle cajoling to steal his childhood sweetheart away from the prosperous banker she has wed. Stevens's performance was skillful if broad. Designed as a crowd-pleaser, it proved so popular that within a few weeks he handed over his role to Henry Dixey (who played it for the rest of the eleven-week New York run) and embarked with a second company on a two-season tour. Arliss's more subtle, lightly sardonic interpretation was aimed patently at the cognoscenti. First seen in dapper morning dress, with his "smooth, well-oiled hair, running back from his forehead, the ears lying close to the head, and the eyes that look out through narrow slits from underneath the delicately penciled, slanting eyebrows," he conveyed "absolutely the spirit of evil incarnate." His performance helped this version of the comedy run five months on Broadway and then briefly tour major cities. The reviews he received made him a star.

· · ·

George Arliss [Augustus George Arliss-Andrews] (1868–1946) was born in London, where his father was a printer and publisher. He began his stage career in 1886 and made his American debut fifteen years later in support of Mrs. Patrick Campbell. He rose rapidly, first under the aegis of Belasco, then of the Fiskes.

· · ·

Another up-and-coming player, Douglas Fairbanks, was raised to stardom somewhat prematurely in Rupert Hughes's **All for a Girl** (8-22-08, Bijou). That girl, Antoinette Hoadley (Adelaide Manola), is very, very rich (worth $10,000,000 in 1908) and is resolved to be loved for herself and not her wealth, so she takes herself and an older friend (Harriet Otis Dellenbaugh) off to the country and assumes a fictitious name. The friend secretly advises her nephew, Harold Jepson (Fairbanks), of the situation, but he nobly refuses to take advantage of it. He does, however, visit his aunt. He appears just as she and a young girl are leaving on a holiday. Harold concludes the young girl is Antoinette. Thus he thinks no more about her when he spies another pretty girl at the farm. She, of course, is Antoinette. The two instantly fall in love and just as quickly marry. But after the marriage Antoinette is led to believe that Harold knew she was rich all the while he was courting her. This rift is healed when, first, Harold agrees not to touch a penny of her money, and, second, a stock deal makes Harold wealthy. Fairbanks was praised as a fine example of "the new generation of speak-easy-and-move-smoothly actors." The play, like the season's two established American hits, was seen as threadbare in story but redeemed by bright lines and situations. For example, the couple's tiny apartment contained "plenty of rooms, but no room." As a result, furniture had to do double duty, a buffet swiveling to become a bookcase. Yet for all the complimentary notices, playgoers would not buy tickets, so the comedy closed after one month.

A month's run was also all that George Broadhurst's **The Call of the North** (8-24-08, Hudson) could muster. Broadhurst took his play from Stewart Edward White's *Conjuror's House* but could not make it work as a stage piece. It told of a Canadian trapper (Robert Edeson) who is sentenced to die for trespassing but wheedles his judge's daughter (Marjorie Wood) into aiding him to escape.

Matters brightened appreciably when Charles Frohman offered his newest star, Billie Burke, in **Love Watches** (8-27-08, Lyceum), which Gladys Unger derived from Robert de Flers and Gaston de Caillavet's comedy. She played an innocent young wife who believes her husband (Cyril Keightley) is not totally faithful and so decides to flirt with another man (Ernest Lawford) in order to make her husband jealous. Neither she nor the ridiculously bookish man she alights on quite know how to carry it off. Comic complications ensue. Long years later, after she had retired, Miss Burke would look back on the comedy as "the best play I was ever in," but many a critic felt she was better than her vehicle—"so whimsical, so earnest, so convincing, so artless and yet so full of artifice, so charming in person, with so many resources, that her performance is unique." Star and play settled in for a five-month run before touring.

Last season's busiest touring-melodrama factory, that remarkable combination of producer Al Woods and playwright Owen Davis, was heard from rather belatedly in this new season. Nor was their offering anything to cheer about. **The Prince of Spendthrifts** (8-31-08, Grand St.) is a young man so careless or generous with his wealth that he nearly loses it all to his treacherous secretary and the secretary's female accomplice. It requires four acts with seventeen scenes of stock situations before the hero and the heroine, who is the villainess's good cousin, can contemplate a peaceful marriage.

The Regeneration (9-1-08, Wallack's), Walter Hackett and Owen Kildare's dramatization of Kildare's *My Mamie Rose,* was a hodgepodge of combination-house melodrama, treacly sentimentality, society play, and muckraking. A young lady, Marie Deering (Jessie Izett), is abducted by Bowery hoods and taken to a seedy resort where, by coincidence, some of her uptown friends have gone slumming. A young tough, Owen Conway (Arnold Daly), forces his buddies to release the girl, and she, despite warnings by her friends, gratefully invites him to her home, so that she may educate and reform him. He duly comes, and she teaches him the alphabet and the Lord's Prayer. In short order he has left the Bowery behind and obtained work as a watchman in a settlement house. But when one of his old cronies, Skinny (Roy Fairchild), appears and pleads for Conway to hide him from the police, Conway acquiesces. The police arrive, as does Marie. Conway denies complicity, but Marie spots Skinny's cap. Marie, not abandoning hope for Conway, attempts to take the blame, but Conway will not allow her to, and he is led away by the police. The re-creation of the Bowery dive—called Chicory Hall in an obvious sneer at the demodé Chickering Hall—with its mixture of battling roughnecks, coarse entertainers, and cavalier aristocrats, won more admiration than did the play.

Hubert Henry Davies's London comedy **The Mollusc** (9-1-08, Garrick) found far more favor. It described how an Englishman (Joseph Coyne), after a long, invigorating stay in America, returns home to force his lazy sister (Alexandra Carlisle) to get up off her buttocks. Coyne had just spent a year in the West End as London's original Danilo in *The Merry Widow* (and some critics thought he could not jettison his musical comedy mannerisms), while Miss Carlisle was a highly touted English actress. Neither would have the sort of career, at least in America, in store for two performers in a one-acter that accompanied the longer play. Wilfred T. Coleby's trifle **The Likes O' Me** told how a beggar-boy (Doris Keane) so touchingly recounts his own sad history that a young lord (George Clark), no

older than the beggar, invites him to visit his palace. In a very minor role Dudley Digges again earned commendatory notices. But after a month this one-actor was replaced by another, George Ade's **Mrs. Peckham's Carouse** (9-29-08). May Irwin starred as a militant teetotaler who stops at nothing to keep her husband and his buddies from swigging from a bottle of forty-year-old rye. When her exertions cause her to faint, she herself is given a swig—and she proves she is not totally inhuman. One or two reviews took notice of the fact that the Garrick had replaced the traditional pit orchestra with something new, an organ.

Throughout the season the popular monthly *Theatre* ran a series of articles on new and potential stars. Women dominated, and sometimes monopolized, these features. The explanation for this, the magazine suggested, was that men "are not decorative, and the decorative is desirable." Yet roomy as the 1908–09 theatre was, it could not do justice to every talented young lady. Many fell very quickly by the wayside. One attractive, deft performer whose career faded almost as soon as it peaked was Carlotta Nillson. The same magazine may have had a small share in greasing the skids for her, since it took a crotchety view of new school acting and ranked her among its disciples: "That means softness, choking down sobs, suppressing emotion, to be a lady in any and all possible imaginable human circumstances, never to be visibly surprised at anything, to speak easily and to move softly." In Cicely Hamilton's London comedy **Diana of Dobson's** (9-5-08, Savoy), she played a shopgirl who comes into a small inheritance, uses it for a fling at a posh resort, is courted by a fortune-hunting guardsman, but finds true love with him after both bare their souls. It was not Broadway's cup of tea.

Lillian Russell's career also was fading fast, but she had been Broadway's darling for a quarter of a century. George Broadhurst and George V. Hobart had written **Wildfire** (9-7-08, Liberty) especially for her, and she had packed theatres with it in a cross-country tour during 1907–08. Once more acknowledging both her age and her glamor, she again was cast as a widow still capable of interesting attractive men. Mrs. Henrietta Barrington has been left a racing stables by her late husband but cannot publicly admit to ownership without jeopardizing the marriage of her sister (Ellen Mortimer) to the son (Joseph Tuohy) of a minister (John D. O'Hara) who heads the antiracing movement. She is banking on her horse, Wildfire, winning a big race, but a man (Franklyn Roberts) who pretends to be the stable's owner has convinced Wildfire's not-too-bright Negro jockey to watch him and, if he fails to wave his handkerchief, to throw the race. Henrietta learns of the plan and during the race sidles up to the man, grabs his hand holding the handkerchief, and frantically waves it. The horse wins. The truth about her ownership comes out. However, the marriage goes on, as does Henrietta's to a handsome young breeder (Thurston Hall). Miss Russell's Paris outfits included "a snowy white satin automobile duster, lined with pale blue silk and edged at the throat and cuffs with scarlet. With this also went a white Panama hat lined with pale blue silk and trimmed with purple and dahlia-colored peonies." Making his New York debut (in blackface as the jockey) was Ernest Truex. The comedy ran eight weeks.

Although it, too, had toured profitably during the preceding season, Rida Johnson Young's **Glorious Betsy** (9-7-08, Lyric) ran only three weeks in New York, during which time it played free and loose with the romance of Elizabeth Patterson (Mary Mannering) and Napoleon's brother, Jerome (George W. Howard). At Sweet Sulphur Springs, Jerome has disguised himself as a tutor to woo Betsy away from the likes of Henry Clay (Addison Pitt) and John C. Calhoun (Charles Clary). Betsy accompanies Jerome when he is ordered back to France, and it takes Napoleon (Claude Brooke) to persuade her to give up his brother. Betsy returns alone to America, but before long Jerome is standing on her doorstep. The third act took place on a ship off the foggy coast of France. On opening night machinery designed to create fog went haywire, and playgoers in the first few rows were sent coughing and weeping up the aisles.

Three novelties premiered at combination houses that same evening. Taylor Granville's **The Star Bout** (9-7-08, 14th St.) was doubly unusual, having been derived from a popular two-a-day sketch and centering on the seamy world of boxing. The hero (played by the author) is asked to throw a fight with another boxer, whose gambling debts have landed him in hot water. Naturally the hero has no time for the boxer's venal manager ("That man is so crooked he could hide behind a corkscrew"), so he refuses. For his pains he is drugged (in the moonlight alongside Grant's Tomb), dumped in a deep well, and must tap telegraphic signals to alert the heroine to his whereabouts. The pair then commandeer an automobile and hurry down Riverside Drive (only to be stopped for speeding). But of course they reach the Olympian Boxing Club in time for the match, which the hero wins, dukes up.

Those few critics who reviewed Walter Lawrence's **The Creole Slave's Revenge** (9-7-08, Grand St.) lavished praise on producer Al Woods for heeding "the call for a better class of melodrama." In synopsis the difference is impossible to discern. A Creole, betrayed many years earlier by a famous judge, learns that the judge is seeking his long-lost granddaughter and makes mischief by substituting another Creole slave for the girl. Curtain drops depicting a cotton plantation and a southern city were applauded, as was a real Negro chorus, although one aisle-sitter added, "Someone has made the mistake of lining up the members of this chorus and drilling them to move in unison. The effort to make this particular chorus appear artistic or fascinating only serves to make it appear ludicrous."

Whether or not Robert Norton's **False Friends** (9-7-08, Third Ave.) also heeded the call for better melodrama, in a slumping theatrical market it brazenly advertised itself as "advanced." Reviewers were hard put to detect the advances. Norton's story featured an American mining engineer who works in South America and falls in love with the daughter of the American consul. A sneaky Englishman and a corrupt police chief (named Castro) try to steal the mine and make trouble for the lovers until an erupting volcano separates the bad from the good.

A great star, a fine comedy, a marvelous new leading lady, and just about everything else playgoers could ask for came together to make a hit of Charles Frohman's production of Somerset Maugham's **Jack Straw** (9-14-08, Empire). John Drew had a field day as a bewhiskered waiter who agrees to court the daughter (Mary Boland) of a family of rude upstarts. He courts her as the elegant Archduke of Pomerania, who, it turns out, he really is. Rose Coghlan, a star when an older order of acting reigned, played the heroine's mother. The comedy ran for more than three months, then headed out on a prearranged tour.

Incessant touring was the lot of Lillian Mortimer's **A Girl's Best Friend** (9-14-08, 14th St.). As she so often did, the playwright served as her own star, portraying a girl raised in a tiny Virginia village unaware she is actually a kidnapped heiress. In one scene a detective who comes searching for her is dumped into a well and must employ telegraphic taps to alert her to his plight. Were these the same taps playgoers had heard at the same theatre a week before under similar circumstances?

James Hackett arrived for a month's visit at his Hackett Theatre on the 21st, but he offered nothing new, content to revive *The Prisoner of Zenda* and *The Crisis*.

Thomas Morris's **In the Nick of Time** (9-21-08, 14th St.) starred one of the touring circuit's most popular entertainers, Florence Bindley. She was seen as a pretty flower vendor who is seduced and abandoned by the smirking villain. He had won her by paying for her mother's funeral. The girl strays to New York, where she soon becomes a star at Hammerstein's (then New York's leading vaudeville house). The bad man's good brother spots her there and falls in love. Naturally the villain would prove difficult. He meets his death not at the hands of the hero or heroine but from the gun of a man whose sister he had betrayed. A replication of Hammerstein's, showing the stage and some boxes, earned cheers and also served to allow the star and selected vaudevillians to present their turns. The villain's assassination also took place in the box. Real vaudeville, coupled with films, took over at the old 14th Street Theatre when *In the Nick of Time* closed.

Belasco found another moneymaker in William J. Hurlbut's **The Fighting Hope** (9-22-08, Stuyvesant). The play, with its unmistakable echoes of *The Lion and the Mouse* and *Paid in Full*, had very patent weaknesses. One reviewer noted, "Many of the incidents put a strain upon one's credulity; it is hard to believe in a succession of coincidences such as brings about the climax." On the other hand, another critic observed, "Its finely arranged series of surprises was enough to keep the audience in the theatre some time after the curtain fell last night calling for the author and the star." Anna Granger (Blanche Bates) is the wife of Robert Granger (Howell Hansel), a bank cashier who has been sent to prison for approving a fraudulent overdraft. In his trial Granger insisted he did so on orders from the president of the bank, Burton Temple (Charles Richman), and newspapers have taken up his charge. Anna, using the name Miss Dale, takes employment as Temple's stenographer in hopes of finding evidence against the banker. She is abetted by the stern, puritanical Mrs. Mason (Loretta Wells), an old friend of Anna's and Temple's housekeeper. Anna no sooner arrives at Temple's house than she broadcasts her vindictiveness and her soppy sentimentality:

It's nothing to him to ruin our home—spoil Robert's life—disgrace my boys—send them into the world dishonored—Oh, nothing to him—if he can save his name, his honor! But he shall suffer—he shall pay—I'll sit here and write his letters—my eyes on his secret thoughts! I'll do his bidding—my hands rifling his desk. I'll sneak, I'll lie, I'll thieve, I'll watch him! Track him! Hound him! . . . Oh, Mrs. Mason, I wonder if you can understand all it means when my boys ask me where their father's gone—"When's papa coming home? Where is

he?"—and I have to look into their little faces and lie to them. When they give me their morning kiss I lie to them. When they say their evening prayers I lie to them. I even let those little tots lie to God.

But Anna soon discovers she has been lying to herself. She finds proof that her husband was guilty, and she also learns that he was prepared to spend the huge sum he was paid for his complicity on another woman. She burns the evidence. Meanwhile, Temple, knowing her only as Miss Dale, has fallen in love with her and proposes. She confesses what she has done, and Temple is forgiving. Then Granger suddenly appears, telling Anna he has been paroled. She is prepared to overlook all he has done until he implies that Temple's and Anna's relationship had not been all that pure. Anna, looking skyward, cries, "Oh, God, what a thing you've made in your likeness and called a man!" When the police surround the house, Anna realizes that Granger has not been paroled but has escaped. He is shot running from the building. Anna, *in a voice almost childlike,* whimpers that she wants her boys, and Temple assures her he will fetch them. Blanche Bates, dropping the more picturesque roles she had played, won praise for her simplicity and intensity. The drama ran into the spring, its single setting and unusually small cast augmenting profits.

In Edgar Selwyn's short-lived **Father and Son** (9-24-08, Majestic), Arthur Welby (George C. Staley), grown rich by monopolizing New Jersey silk mills, refuses to permit Billy Filkins (John Westley) to court his niece, Grace (Madeleine Louis). A strike breaks out at the mills, and Billy is one of its leaders. Peace is restored, and Billy and Grace are engaged, only after "Doc" Filkins (William Norris), the local philosopher—who is given to spouting sage saws he attributes to an imaginary friend, and who has raised Billy—discloses that Welby and Billy are father and son. Critics enjoyed the acting, especially Norris's Herne-like philosopher, but thought less of the play and less still of some of the scenery, such as Welby's drawing room, which was done up in a ghastly combination of chocolate and dark green.

Five-character plays were, according to one commentator, becoming "the fashion of the day." The commentator apparently felt that it took only two plays to create a fashion (and made no mention that both plays employed only one set apiece), but, unlike *The Fighting Hope,* Percy MacKaye's prose-comedy **Mater** (9-25-08, Savoy) failed to appeal to the public. Mater (Isabel Irving) is a startlingly beautiful and young-looking widow who is given to fantastic metaphors. She describes her late husband, a senator, as a black-swan dragon who carried her off. Her son, Michael (Frederick Lewis), is an unyielding radical politician; his twin sister, Mary (Hazel Mac-Kaye), is engaged to a man named Rudolf Verbeck (John Junior). Arthur Cullen (Charles A. Stevenson), a cynical politician, is willing to throw the winning votes Michael's way for a price, but Michael disdainfully rejects the idea. Cullen then turns to Mater. Awed by her beauty and mistaking her for her own daughter, he promises to help Michael win if she will agree not to marry Rudolf and will consider his proposal instead. Mater instantly agrees not to marry Rudolf. Michael wins, after which Mater helps Cullen distinguish fantasy from reality.

The Offenders (9-28-08, Hudson), Elmer Blaney Harris's crudely wrought bit of muckraking, also spotlighted some disreputable politicians. Klif King (Robert Edeson), an ex-convict, is caught by Helen Street (Katherine Grey) attempting to rob her husband's safe. She agrees not to say anything if he will help her expose abuses against child labor laws. King discovers that none other than Mrs. Street's husband (John Flood), a political boss, heads efforts to subvert the laws. Mrs. Street divorces her husband, but King dies of consumption before any romance can blossom. The show was the second failure for Edeson in a still young season. Although he would remain in the theatre for another dozen or so years, his star would continue to fall, and he would become one of the earliest Broadway names to devote much of his time to silent films.

By contrast, Douglas Fairbanks, who would desert the stage permanently in a few years, found himself in a smash hit when producers William A. Brady and Joseph Grismer transferred him from their failed *All for a Girl* to Harrison Rhodes and Thomas A. Wise's **A Gentleman from Mississippi** (9-29-08, Bijou). But Fairbanks did not have the play to himself; one of the co-authors was also his co-star. Once again, as in the last two openings, political scheming figured importantly in the story. William H. Langdon (Wise), newly elected as Mississippi's junior senator, is a greenhorn. You can tell that immediately by the hotel he picks, a hotel where a friend of his had stayed thirty years before and which has long since gone to seed. In its rundown lobby he meets "Bud" Haines (Fairbanks), a brash but savvy reporter come to interview him. When Haines tells Langdon that he is from New York, Langdon is courteous enough to let him know he has heard of "the Vicksburg of the North." The men quickly hit it off, and Langdon is sufficiently perspicacious to understand that Haines can be of help to him. He takes on the reporter as his private

secretary. But Langdon's senior colleague, along with a senator from Pennsylvania and even some members of Langdon's own family, is involved in shady dealings—assisting a steel company in taking over some Mississippi coastal property and pushing the navy to build a base there. Haines sniffs out the plot, but the plotters realize this and for a time turn Langdon and Haines against each other. In the end, however, Haines and Langdon see that right prevails. Haines also wins one of Langdon's daughters, but not the one he thought he loved at first.

Marvelous side touches embellished the plot. A down-and-out G.A.R. veteran (Frederick Bock) is being thrown out of the hotel by a colored bellhop (played in blackface by a white) when Langdon takes pity on him. They soon discover they fought on opposite sides in the same Civil War battle, and they set about recreating it with hats, canes, chairs, and potted palms. Afterwards Langdon gives the man money to return home.

Wise—heavy, slow, and avuncular—and Fairbanks—lithe, buoyant, and charming—made perfect foils. Some critics were pleased that none of the players attempted a southern accent. And with its generous quota of "bright lines, tender sentiment, and genuine local color," the play delighted New York for a full year.

Just as the next plays were premiering, the *Dramatic Mirror* ran a series of articles on "The Business Outlook" across the nation. The reports agreed that business in general was perky, so managers were assuming box offices also would be busy. The sole exception in every part of the country was what the trade sheet called the "middle-priced" attraction. This meant touring shows, since a city's cheapest seats were those offered by some local stock company. The fate of these touring shows was becoming inescapable. In area after area, the paper reported, "the middle-price attraction has been abolished entirely, for the class of people who have heretofore patronized such attractions find what they want in the moving pictures."

For the moment, first-class attractions arriving in New York were not faring much better. Even Maxine Elliott found no excuse to extend her announced four-week stand when she opened in Rachel Crothers' **Myself—Bettina** (10-5-08, Daly's). She played a New England girl who has grown selfish and conceited after spending four years studying music in Paris. Bettina shocks her home town by offering to perform Salome. She appears in costume at a reading in her family's home and starts to do the infamous dance before she is stopped. In her anger at the townsfolk's puritanical stance, she apparently seduces her own sister's fiancé (Eric Maturin). However, she eventually is brought to comprehend how arrogant she has been, while the villagers recognize that they have been too rigid.

McKee Rankin, one of the last survivors of an older school, presented his protégée, Nance O'Neil, in George Cameron's **Agnes** (10-5-08, Majestic) but found no success despite many encouraging notices. The star was cast as a woman who has been tricked by her calculating mother (Adelaide Stanhope Wheatcroft) into marrying a man (Cuyler Hastings) she does not love. After mother and husband seemingly are lost in a yacht sinking (the first act ends with Agnes dutifully trying to haul her unconscious husband up the sharply listing cabin stairs), she discovers that her mother had withheld from her love letters sent by the brain surgeon (Robert Drouet) Agnes really loved. She marries the doctor, and some years pass. A man, who has not been right since he was rescued from the sea long before, is brought in for an operation. Agnes realizes the man is her supposedly dead husband. She is terrified lest her whole story come out. But the man dies on the operating table.

That many critics who welcomed the newer school of acting could still be tolerant of Miss O'Neil's old style was seen in such remarks as, "In the second act where Agnes discovers Brent's old letters she discloses the sort of emotional acting that has brought her an enthusiastic following in the West and in some cities, too, in the East, particularly Boston. . . . [She] deserved the many curtain calls she received."

An English comedy, **His Wife's Family** (10-6-08, Wallack's), by George Egerton [Mrs. R. Golding Bright] enlisted no support for its tale of a likable but irresponsible Irish clan who stumble into an inheritance.

Two melodramas opened the next Monday evening, but only the one at a combination house admitted its lowly classification. The other, **Pierre of the Plains** (10-12-08, Hudson), which Edgar Selwyn adapted from Sir Gilbert Parker's *Pierre and His People,* was billed more pretentiously as a drama. Set in a remote part of Canada, the play offered druggings, hairbreadth escapes, treacherous shootings, and, very much like last season's *The Wolf,* a hand-to-hand combat with knives in a firelit woods. Selwyn played the lead, portraying a superstitious, half-breed gambler who helps the heroine's brother (Richard Sterling) escape from the Mounties. Later, when Pierre himself is caught and arrested, the grateful heroine (Elsie Ferguson) convinces her Mountie sweetheart (Clifford Stork) to allow Pierre to get away.

The touring melodrama was Charles H. Fleming's **Messenger Boy No. 42** (10-12-08, Grand St.). It was dismissed as infantile and old hat. Telling of an adventurer who tries to trick a rich girl into marrying him, it featured a particularly nasty villain: "He soaks his wife in coal oil and sets her ablaze; he burns buildings recklessly; he attempts to chop up the heroine in a corn cutting machine and to burn out her father's eyes with a red hot iron, and when accused of these atrocities he leans idly against a crimson rose growing prominently on the wall of the manor and with fingers between his teeth curses everything." A "loudly gowned" adventuress moves in tandem with him. But a young, blond messenger boy is there to foil them.

There were plenty of melodramatic moments in the play that marked Jules Eckert Goodman's debut as a Broadway dramatist, **The Man Who Stood Still** (10-15-08, Circle). At first it seemed Goodman was writing about an immigrant watchmaker (Louis Mann), whose old-world habits prevent him from making a success in the Bowery. However, the story soon took another turn. Krauss's daughter, Marie (Edith Browning), becomes pregnant by and elopes with a neighborhood ne'er-do-well (H. A. LaMotte). To get money for the elopement, the groom robs Krauss's shop. Nor does he really marry Marie, who is later reconciled with her father. By that time Krauss has lost his shop and works for a rising young Jew (Geoffrey Stein) once employed by him. The Jew's touchy courtship of a Christian girl (Emily Ann Wellman) furnished a subplot. Critics and playgoers long since had taken sides on Mann's merits. Most considered him a good dialect comedian whose more serious ambitions left much to be desired. A few vociferously hailed him as a second David Warfield. Goodman was deemed a most promising playwright, although time would prove him no more than a skilled technician.

Henri Bernstein's latest play to reach Broadway, **Samson** (10-19-08, Criterion), was not as well received as *The Thief* and had a shorter run, although five months was nothing to sneer at in 1908. Bernstein's financier sets out to destroy the fortune of his wife's lover. He succeeds but wrecks his own fortune in the process. Constance Collier and Arthur Byron, who played the wife and her lover, were accorded laudatory notices, but most critics felt that William Gillette's showy style of acting—his clipped speech, his theatrical pauses, his playing to the audience—made believing in or accepting the hero difficult.

Frederick Paulding was Gillette's contemporary, but the traditions and styles he embodied harked back to an earlier stage. He long ago had abandoned his attempts to become a star and had settled for writing plays, such as **The Great Question** (10-26-08, Majestic), that were perceived as "hopelessly outmoded" and "old-style." In this newest work, set "during the Cleveland administration," a Supreme Court justice, a southerner (A. H. Stuart), is being blackmailed into rendering a favorable decision in a case involving some western railroads, or else having the public learn that his daughter (Jessie Bonstelle) is his child by an octoroon. The daughter discovers the scheme and demands her father not capitulate. But she also tells the man (Julius McVicker) to whom she has been engaged that she cannot marry him lest their children also be tainted with Negro blood. Although Jessie Bonstelle received very encouraging notices, her career took her away from Broadway to run major stock companies elsewhere and eventually be dubbed "the Maker of Stars." The play was shunted hastily into cheap combination houses.

The insistence of those few critics who deigned to review touring melodramas that the genre was lifting itself up by its bootstraps simply may have been an attempt to give a badly needed boost to a faltering genre. Certainly in Al Wood's production of Owen Davis's **On Trial for His Life** (10-26-08, Grand Street) one cliché remained—the hero was named Jack, Lt. Jack Royal. He is falsely accused of murder by a fellow officer and spends the next eleven scenes vindicating himself. Big moments included the rescue of the hero from the roof of a burning prison and the rescue of the heroine by soldiers scaling a perpendicular rock wall. Among the villains were a band of beady-eyed Mexicans and a Japanese spy. One of the hero's helpers was a Jewish private who is captured by the Mexicans and alerts his buddies to his whereabouts by leaving a trail of scraps from a New York yellow-journal newspaper just then running a series called "Follow the Clue!"

"Melodrama of the crudest kind" and "melodrama of not much novelty" typified critical verdicts on Paul Armstrong and Winchell Smith's **Via Wireless** (11-2-08, Liberty), but these same reviews went on to predict success for the play largely because of two spectacular sensation scenes. The play was produced by Frederick W. Thompson, who had suggested the story to the playwrights and who had created both Coney Island and the mammoth Hippodrome Theatre, so playgoers' expectations were whetted when critics extolled the two scenes as worthy of anything at the resort or on the Hippodrome's stage. The play's hero was Lieutanant Sommers, U.S.N. (Edwin Arden), who has invented a new type of naval gun and who loves Frances Durant (Vera McCord), daughter of the gun foundry's owner. Edward Pinkney (J. E. Miltern), the foundry's manager, also loves Frances. He purposely miscasts the gun so that it will explode on testing, hoping its failure will alienate the lovers. Sommers and a Secret Service man board Durant's yacht in an effort to uncover the cause of the explosion. The yacht hits a reef and begins to sink. Sommers wires an SOS. The scene changes to a transatlantic steamship. Its radio operator picks up the signals and the ship rushes to the yacht's position. When they bring the rescued passengers and crew aboard from the lifeboats, they realize two are missing. One, of course, is Sommers, who has remained on the yacht to send the distress calls; the other is whoever is keeping the dynamo working, thereby permitting transmission. A head count shows that person to be Frances. They are saved, and the truth of Pinckney's chicanery is exposed.

The gun explosion and the sinking yacht were not the play's sensations. The forging of the gun and the scene in the radio office were. The foundry setting was praised for its suggestion of "intense heat, glowing furnaces and fervid activity." A white-hot cone of iron is removed from a furnace on one side of the room, gently transported across a space by a giant triphammer, and fed into the jaws of a second furnace. The third act showed a cross-section of the steamship's upper decks. The lower right is a brightly lit radio room; to its left are dimly lit passageways, and above it is the top deck with lifeboats on davits. "The elements are raging. Thunder crashes and peals, forked lightning plays across the inky sky. Sailors rush to and fro and the Captain shouts his orders as the vessel heaves and tosses with the waves running mountains high over the sides." The play ran eleven weeks, then toured.

The World and His Wife (11-2-08, Daly's) also ran eleven weeks, but a subsequent tour was not well received. The play was not truly new but merely Charles Frederic Nirdlinger's translation of Echegaray's *El Gran Galeoto*, which New York first had seen nine years earlier. The Spanish Nobel laureate never was to win American acceptance. In this revival William Faversham and his wife, Julie Opp, were starred.

Blue Grass (11-9-08, Majestic), Paul Armstrong's second play in as many weeks, was a compilation of threadbare motifs. A southern gentleman (Robert McWade, Jr.), so on his uppers that he hasn't enough money to provide dinner for his guests, hopes his horse, Blue Grass, will ride to victory and replenish his bank account. An unscrupulous gambler (Wayne Arey) hopes otherwise. An attractive young northerner (Regan Hughston) thwarts the gambler's villainy and claims the southerner's daughter as his reward. George Marion, better known as a stager of musicals (including *The Merry Widow*), directed the play and assumed the blackface role of Old Folks, the loyal old retainer. One much applauded setting showed a simple brick clubhouse with light refreshments being served on its covered porch. A balustraded stairs and ramp led from one end of the porch to an adjoining stables. The play proved more welcomed on the road than in New York.

Somerset Maugham's second play of the season was also his second hit. **Lady Frederick** (11-9-08, Hudson) recounted the problems befalling a woman with a misunderstood past; her quiet, generous actions ultimately win over a former suitor (Bruce McRae). Some critics carped that the star, Ethel Barrymore, had grown "stouter" or that her new-style, naturalistic acting sometimes seemed like mere indifference, but even carpers allowed that her performance was superb. In one scene she appeared in dishabille to convince an importunate swain that the seemingly loveliest of women can be unattractive without a careful toilette.

The next Monday evening was reserved for two touring melodramas. Langdon McCormick's **Wanted by the Police** (11-16-08, Metropolis) opens with the villain committing a murder in a busy railroad station and making it appear that the heroine is the killer. Just as the police come to arrest her, the hero grabs her and takes off in a conveniently waiting engine. The police commandeer a second engine, and a chase is on. "Amid clouds of steam, the clanging of bells and the shrieking of whistles the two engines are seen speeding through a forest" until the hero shoots the pursuing engineer, who somehow drops from the cab onto the cowcatcher as the curtain falls. But the heroine's troubles are far from over. She is kidnapped and hidden in an Italian's East Side thieves' den, and her swain is nearly dynamited.

Olive Harper's **Jack Sheppard, the Bandit King** (11-6-08, Grand St.) had some nice twists. The hero is a sort of Robin Hood, stealing from the rich and providing for the poor. He shows his gratitude for the heroine's kindnesses to him (such as giving him a glass of cool water on a hot day) by robbing her uncle and giving her half the loot. Then the uncle learns that the heroine has come into an immense fortune, so he plots to obtain it. He calls in the Secret Service to arrest Jack, but the man turns out to be Jack's long-lost brother. Jack promises to mend his ways.

The next evening a new playwright burst on the Broadway scene with a remarkable drama about the very sort of people who, until recently, might have patronized the galleries of combination houses. The very youthful author was Edward Sheldon.

· · ·

Edward [Brewster] **Sheldon** (1886–1946) was the son of wealthy Chicagoans and was educated at Harvard, where he was one of George Pierce Baker's first important pupils. His earliest play was rejected by Alice Krauser, a major play agent, but she encouraged him to work on an idea he offered, and that became his new work. Within a short time he was considered the most promising of American playwrights. Then he was attacked by a debilitating illness. Even after he was virtually totally paralyzed and could no longer write, he was revered and consulted by aspiring playwrights and established actors.

· · ·

Sheldon's play was **Salvation Nell** (11-17-08, Hackett). The scene is Sid McGovern's seedy Empire Bar on Tenth Avenue. The long bar is on the left; in the middle is a small free-lunch buffet. Sitting beside the buffet is a one-legged fiddler who has placed his cap, into which a few patrons throw coins, beside him on the floor. At right is a small, slightly fancier room with tables. The patrons are "a motley array of wrecks and muckers." Nell Saunders (Mrs. Fiske), her apron and clothes ragged and stained, her hands and arms red from hard work, is the bar's scrub-woman. She is loved by the besotted, ne'er-do-well Jim Platt (Holbrook Blinn). When Al McGovern (John Dillon) makes advances to Nell, Jim grabs him and kills him. As he is being led away by the police, Jim curses Nell: "Ye dam' tart, ye! Youse the one's done all this! You secondhand, cracked piece o' damaged goods!" Myrtle (Hope Latham), a brassy prostitute who has sought refuge at the bar after her brothel has been raided, seeks to enlist Nell into her ranks, but Nell instinctively gravitates to the born-again Hallelujah Maggie (Mary Madison), a Salvation Army disciple—especially after Myrtle has rather meanly told Nell about Jim's infidelities: "Yer easy meat, Nell! He's been hangin' around with that Keeney woman. I've watched him from my winder." Eight years pass. Nell has come under the influence of the organization's Major Williams (David Glassford). Sustained by her newfound fervor, she waits with her young son Jimmy (Antrim Short) for Jim's release from prison. But on his arrival he is concerned only with how he can pull off a robbery to earn some quick money. When she draws back in horror, he storms out. Nell falls on her knees to pray for him. Her prayers are answered as she addresses an Army meeting in the tenement district. A humbled Jim confesses, "I need ye—I need yer help!" Nell responds, "Wait fer me, Jim. I'll meet ye here. I want ye to take me home."

The last act took place on "one of the best street sets even seen on the stage." It showed one street, lined with tall tenements, that ended as it joined in a cross-street at the rear of the stage. Thus tenements could be seen on both sides and across the back wall of the stage. Some have stores on the ground floor, others simply stoops with trash alongside, now neatly put out, more often thrown helter-skelter. One of the tenements at the back is slightly shorter than the others, disclosing a small glimpse of sky. Laundry hangs from many of the fire escapes, children play and tussle (the cast had more than fifty players), a peddler pushes a cart down the street, other people come and go.

Writing in Fiske's *Dramatic Mirror*, Walter Prichard Eaton observed that Blinn "played as even this fine actor has never played before. The 'tough' vernacular never descended into caricature, yet never deserted him. . . . He lived out the part he was playing, and lived it so vividly that the mere picture of him became impressive." Noting that Mrs. Fiske also "has never been better," he continued, "In the first act it was almost painful to see and feel her in such an uncouth, unmoral, gutter-bred female, slopping up a barroom. Yet in the other two acts . . . she somehow, by an almost marvelous delicacy of suggestion, managed to convey the impression that this new Nell was merely the old Nell with the good brought out." Her famous bit, cradling Jim's head for several minutes all the while not saying a word, was singled out for attention in many notices. And of course, though reviewers espied gaucheries, which they attributed to inexperience, Sheldon was hailed. Charles Darnton of the *World* summed up his opinion by labeling *Salvation Nell* "a Divine Comedy of the Slums." The play sold out for virtually all of its nine-week booking, but prior commitments would not allow an extension.

William Collier and his collaborator, J. Hartley Manners, struck paydirt with their farce **The Patriot** (11-23-08, Garrick). Sir Augustus Plantagenet Armitage (Collier) despairs of finding a profitable lode at his gold mine in Bull Frog, Nev. Advised that he has come into a large inheritance, he returns to England. There he learns that he will only come into the money if he weds a particularly dislikable lady (Helena Collier-Garrick), so he returns to Bull Frog, uncovers an exceedingly rich vein, and marries the nice American (Helen Hale) he preferred anyway.

John Valentine's **The Stronger Sex** (11-23-08, Weber's) proved less acceptable. Its story was not unlike *The Patriot*'s. An American heiress (Annie Russell) weds a penniless Englishman (Oswald Yorke) but discovers he has only married her for her money. She sets about using her wealth and power to make life so miserable for him that by turns he comes to respect and finally to love her.

A group called the Sicilian Dramatic Company began a month-long visit that same evening at the Broadway. Best known among their repertory was *Cavalleria Rusticana*. The *Times* headlined its first notice of the troupe "Astonishing Exhibition of Unbridled Primitive Emotion."

Combination houses also had novelties to offer on that busy Monday. The hero of Lem B. Parker's **Sure-Shot Sam** (11-23-08, Grand Street) comes to Kentucky to arrest some counterfeiters, but moonshiners think he is on their trail. So for four acts Sam and the girl he loves are subjected to all kinds of touring-melodrama indignities. Down on Maple Farm, the site of Ullie Akerstrom's **Aunt Cynthy's Homestead** (11-23-08, Yorkville), the dear old spinster, taking time out from baking pies and sputtering homey adages, must stop a villain from bringing a railroad through her property and must restore the good name of her falsely maligned niece. A cross between *The Old Homestead* and *The County Fair,* the play reportedly delighted the fast-dwindling number of regulars at combination houses.

The Winterfeast (11-30-08, Savoy), Charles Rann Kennedy's stilted, pretentious, and nearly four-hour-long look at 11th-century Iceland, pleased virtually no one, despite some very fine acting and stage pictures that evoked images of old tapestries. The return of her lover (Walter Hampden) after twenty years in exile leads Herdisa (Edith Wynne Matthison) to the discovery that she was tricked into marriage with his weak brother (Frank Mills). Vengeance and countervengeance bring about the slaying of all but two old men. Typical of Kennedy's speeches was the returning Bjorn's taunt of his despised brother: "What hast thou been to her this long while, eh? Dost thou deem thyself fit mate for Herdisa? *Thou!* Thou! When she had once known *me!*"

At the other extreme, **The Blue Mouse** (11-30-08, Lyric), Clyde Fitch's fluffy Americanization of Alexander Engel and Julius Horst's German original, was so vastly entertaining that it ran out the season. The private secretary (Jameson Lee Finney) to the president (Harry Conor) of a railway hires a notorious dancer (Mabel Barrison) in hopes that the girl can inveigle his skirt-chasing boss into promoting him. Inevitably the wrong people pop up at the wrong times and precipitate complications.

Aging Henry E. Dixey, still looking vainly for another *Adonis,* came up with a very minor success in Edith Ellis's **Mary Jane's Pa** (12-3-08, Garden). He played Hiram Perkins, who many years earlier had answered the call of the wanderlust, leaving behind his pregnant wife and young daughter. When he returns home he finds his wife (Ann Sutherland) running a small-town newspaper to support her two girls. She is also running for office. At first she is reluctant to take back Hiram, especially since the townsfolk might not understand. She finally agrees to take him in in the guise of a cook. But her political opponents get wind of the situation and create problems that canot be solved until just before curtain time. A fine setting depicted the large room housing the office and the counter of the newspaper on the right, the printing press on the left, and a view of the town's main street beyond the windows and the door.

Turnaway business greeted a gripping drama about the eternal conflict between those who have achieved riches and jealous have-nots, Cleveland Moffett's **The Battle** (12-21-08, Savoy). John J. Haggleton (Wilton Lackaye) is a multimillionaire whose wife, appalled at his graspiness, had walked out years before, taking their young son with them. Haggleton learns that his son, Phillip (H. B. Warner), is now a grown man, living in a squalid tenement, one of many tenements Haggleton himself owns. He arranges to meet him under an assumed name and quickly finds out he is dealing with an angry young man.

Phillip: I'd like to tell Haggleton a few things about tenement improvements.
Haggleton: What?
Phillip: I'd tell him he owns blocks and blocks on the lower East Side, which are in such lovely state that he might as well be running a factory for turning out—What's the use?
Haggleton: Go on. A factory for turning out—what?
Phillip: Thieves and—drunkards and—wrecks of women.

Intrigued, Haggleton identifies himself. He insists Phillip has a one-sided, highly distorted view of life, and he makes him an offer. Haggleton will come to live in the tenement without any money. "I'm going to show you," he tells Phillip, "what I would do if I had to hustle in a tenement without a dollar." Sure enough, before long Haggleton is again on his way to prosperity. Slowly the men begin a reconciliation. Then a crazed socialist attempts to shoot Haggleton.

Phillip jumps in front of his father and is seriously wounded. During his recuperation, Phillip is completely reconciled with Haggleton, and the old man promises to use much of his fortune to improve the slum holdings. Phillip also finds romance with a pretty nurse (Josephine Victor). Lackaye's strong, broad methods contrasted with Warner's newer style to underscore the generation gap. Critics agreed the play was superb entertainment, beautifully acted, but little else. One complained that Moffett "neglected to prove anything," but another observed that, along with *Salvation Nell,* the play "made poverty interesting and not revolting."

Producer Al Woods and playchurner Owen Davis (the latter using his nom de plume John Oliver) gave some truly less affluent New Yorkers **Opium Smugglers of 'Frisco; or, Crimes of a Beautiful Opium Fiend** (12-21-08, Grand St.). The Svelte leader of an opium ring and her Chinese cohorts kidnap the daughter of a Secret Service agent who is on their trail. It requires the U.S. Navy, especially one dashing lieutenant, and a Jewish detective to rescue the heroine each time she is abducted.

December's biggest hit was a Charles Frohman importation, James M. Barrie's **What Every Woman Knows** (12-23-08, Empire). With Maude Adams, Broadway's most charming and popular actress, as Maggie Shand preaching Barrie's thesis on the potency of charm and secretly helping her ridiculously conceited husband climb the political ladder, it was hailed, appropriately, as "one of his most engagingly whimsical and insistently charming works." The comedy packed in audiences for six months. The rising Richard Bennett played Maggie's husband, John.

A week after Woods and Davis offered East Side playgoers their latest collaboration, one of their most successful rivals offered his. Lincoln J. Carter's **The Indian's Secret** (12-28-08, Third Ave.) begins when a young girl, her aunt, and their colored servant arrive in Nevada to seek the aunt's long-missing husband and son, who had gone prospecting for gold twenty years earlier. The women's efforts are hindered by the usual villains and some warlike Indians. But one handsome young brave befriends and helps them. They learn the fate of the men and also that they are heirs to a fabulously rich mine. Then the Indian reveals his secret: he is really a white man and so can marry the heroine. The colorful production added to the play's appeal, presenting "fantastic Indian ceremonies; a Sioux burying ground with the body of a chief laying high up from the ground on a rude bier of boughs, while his dog howls dismally at his feet in the moonlight;

[and] a flight across the sun-baked rocks of the Nevada wilderness."

The last show of 1908 was the premiere attraction at a newly opened, tiny (725 seats) jewel box of a theatre (paid for by J. P. Morgan). And naturally the opening attraction, Marion Fairfax's **The Chaperon** (12-30-08, Maxine Elliott's), was a vehicle for the house's namesake. The popular beauty was cast as a woman who has returned to America to divorce her European husband (Thomas Thorne). While she is chaperoning some youngsters in the Adirondacks, her old flame (Julian L'Estrange) comes by and invites her to go canoeing. The canoe hits a snag and is punctured, so the pair have to spend the night together in the woods. The next morning her husband appears and is happy to misconstrue the situation. To make matters worse for the chaperon, she returns to the lodge to discover that several of her charges have decided to become engaged to their suitors and that the servants have disappeared along with the silverware. Critics were too busy describing the lovely new playhouse to give any details of stage pictures, but a large public still adored Miss Elliott, so the play did good business for the eight weeks she agreed to play it.

The first entry of 1909 was a quick flop. George Broadhurst's **An International Marriage** (1-4-09, Weber's) told of the daughter (Christine Norman) of a millionaire Omaha laundryman and of her engagement to a Middle European duke. To avoid having to make a morganatic marriage she agrees to first wed a count (John Daly Murphy), divorce him, then marry as a titled woman. No, she doesn't fall in love with the count. Instead she decides all Europeans are merely fortune hunters, so she settles for her childhood sweetheart, a fine American lad (John Sainpolis). Ostensibly the star of the show was a favorite of the musical stage, Digby Bell, who played the laundryman. But everything about the comedy was so out of kilter that even he could do nothing.

There was little anyone could do about S. A. Judson's mediocre touring melodrama **Sold Into Slavery** (1-11-09, Grand Street). Its plot begins when a sweet, innocent girl is tricked into supposed wedlock by a villain who leads her to believe her father is a counterfeiter. Among the secondhand sensations was the villainess's attempt to gouge out the father's eyes with a red-hot iron—a bit used recently at the same house in *Messenger Boy No. 42*. Jaded critics pooh-poohed the whole affair, but blue-collar playgoers, lured in by "marrow-freezing lithographs," were satisfied. As one reporter noted, this sort of audience did not "delve deeply for psychological motives underlying everyday emotions. While the curtain is up it sympathizes or denounces—while it is down it eats its orange or 'crackerjack' and joins with the orchestra in 'Please Don't Take Me Home' or 'When I Marry You.' "

Just before the next major play arrived, the *Times* offered a midseason assessment. Given the general excellence of the past five months, it was a surprisingly gloomy one. It observed that "writing of plays in England has apparently been going downhill for several years" and noted that, since "the opening of the regular season, scarcely a week has passed without the production of one or more native plays." Yet after listing the plays, it concluded, "Of these more than half were outright failures, and of the others less than half a dozen could be called plays even by courtesy." Although its list included *The Traveling Salesman*, *The Man from Home*, *The Fighting Hope*, *A Gentleman from Mississippi*, and *Salvation Nell*, these works were either summarily dismissed or waved away as proving nothing. And the *Times* was not alone in longing for some absurdly roseate past or dreaming of an equally unrealistic, utopian future.

Edward Childs Carpenter's **The Barber of New Orleans** (1-15-09, Daly's) did nothing for American drama and only proved that William Faversham was having a hard time finding the right vehicle. He played a French immigrant who fights to keep plotters from preventing a full American takeover of Louisiana and who also wins the love of a beautiful girl—though he must buy her when a scoundrel puts her up for sale as a slave.

Nor did Edgar Allan Woolf and George Sylvester Viereck unleash much cheering with **The Vampire** (1-18-09, Hackett). Paul Hartleigh (John E. Kellerd), whose door-knocker is in the shape of a bat, insists he cannot help it if he gains fame and glory by depriving other artists of their inspirations. He is, after all, an Overman—or what others would call a Superman. In this he believes he is not different from Caesar or Napoleon or most artistic geniuses of the past. So with his "long ghost fingers" clutching at their brains, he drains the souls of a sculptor (Warner Oland), a painter (Katherine Florence), and a poet (John Westley). Critics felt sorry for such skilled players trapped in such an inanity. One wrote of Kellerd that he "is able to get through the long speeches, full of rounded periods, by the exercise of elocutionary strength, carrying many of the passages by the sheer force of his voice. He almost makes the part plausible."

But the next play gave American drama a powerful shot in the arm, although a few reviewers thought the injection was a dose of poison. The arrival was Belasco's mounting of Eugene Walter's **The Easiest Way** (1-19-09, Stuyvesant). Belasco's longtime advocate, puritanical William Winter, about to end forty-five years as critic for the *Tribune,* was shocked and indignant that the producer "should have lent his great reputation to the support of the vicious play which now disgraces his Stuyvesant Theatre. . . . We do not want to see in the theatre the vileness that should be shunned; we want to see the beauty that should be emulated and loved!" More progressive reviewers disagreed, hailing the play as one of "tremendous power," "a painful masterwork," and "almost perfect." Certainly the Frou-Frous and Irises of old had not been so unsparingly exposed. Laura Murdock (Frances Starr), a beautiful slip of a girl, has had an unhappy childhood and a disastrous marriage to a drunkard, who finally killed himself. Her attempts to support herself as an actress were getting nowhere until rich Willard Brockton (Joseph Kilgour) took her under his wing and paid to get her good roles—in return for obvious favors. But now Laura has spent a summer in Denver stock, where she has met and fallen in love with a young, penniless reporter, John Madison (Edward H. Robins). Brockton, who has come to Denver to escort her back to New York, scoffs when she tells him of their hopes to wed.

Will: What are you going to live on—the extra editions?
Laura: No, we're young, there's plenty of time. I can work in the meantime, and so can he; and then with his ability and my ability it will only be a matter of a year or two when things will shape themselves to make it possible.
Will: Sounds well—a year off.

Will consents to meet John; though their first few minutes together are touchy, the men reach an understanding. John agrees to notify Will if Laura leaves him, and Will promises to make Laura write to John if she goes back to Will. Six months later Laura, again in New York, is broke. She lives in the cheapest of theatrical boardinghouses and has pawned all her jewels, but she refuses to write John of her straits. Echoing Will's earlier sentiments, an old friend, Elfie (Laura Nelson Hall), asks, "What does he think you're going to live on?—asphalt croquettes with conversation sauce?" But Elfie, it soon turns out, has been sent by Will to bring Laura's discomfort and poverty home to her and to ease her into seeing Will again. Elfie quickly succeeds. However, Will first demands that Laura write John, telling him she has gone back to her old

ways. Laura does write the letter but burns it as soon as Will has left. Laura is living again in luxury when John suddenly reappears. He has made a fortune and is ready to marry her. Will's arrival reveals the truth. Will, feeling deceived, since Laura naturally never told him she burned the letter, stalks out. John tells her, "Laura, you're not immoral, you're just unmoral, kind o' all out of shape, and I'm afraid there isn't a particle of hope for you." He, too, leaves. Left alone, she tells her maid, Annie (Emma Dunn, in blackface), to help her dress: "I'm going to Rector's to make a hit, and to hell with the rest!"

These last, once famous lines were quoted repeatedly in reviews and reminiscences of the play. In fact, they are not the last lines. A hurdy-gurdy from the street below is heard grinding out "Bon-Bon Buddie, My Chocolate Drop," and Walter's stage directions read: *"There is something in this ragtime melody which is particularly and peculiarly suggestive of the low life, the criminality and prostitution that constitute the night excitement of that section of New York City known as the Tenderloin. The tune—its association—is like spreading before Laura's eyes a panorama of the inevitable depravity that awaits her."* After a moment Laura responds, "(*With infinite grief, resignation, and hopelessness.*) O God—O my God. (*She turns and totters toward the bedroom. The hurdy-gurdy continues, with the negress accompanying it.*)" Whether Belasco cut this ending or whether commentators, so intrigued with the Rector line, neglected it and all its implications is probably forever lost in history.

As usual, Belasco gave the production an added boost. The first act took place on a veranda overlooking the Colorado mountains, and the men's final dialogue coincided with the sun's setting, leaving only the light of a cigar as the curtain fell. The second-act setting was one of Belasco's most famous. He reputedly bought the contents of an actual boardinghouse room—right down to the soiled, peeling wallpaper—and duplicated it onstage. Frances Starr, beautiful, slim, and soft, made a totally believable and therefore not unsympathetic heroine, and her supporting cast also won kudos. The play ran out the season.

Mrs. Leslie Carter, who had been Belasco's first star and whom he had discarded when she eloped without alerting him of her plans, tried to salvage a fast-sinking career with a play by another of Belasco's former collaborators, John Luther Long. In **Kassa** (1-23-09, Liberty) a princess who has become a postulant at a nunnery is allowed out for one day. She is drugged, forced into a marriage, and deserted by the prince (Charles A. Millward).

She confronts several related problems before her mind snaps, and she returns to the nunnery believing she has been away only for a chaste twenty-four hours: "I am still in time—the bells have not rung." The scenery, "stupendous in its massiveness," showed the grounds near the convent in early morning and evening light, and a heavily ornamented Hungarian reception hall, but it was no help.

Mrs. Frances Hodgson Burnett's **The Dawn of a Tomorrow** (1-25-09, Lyceum) gave American playwrights yet one more hit. Sir Oliver Holt (Fuller Mellish), overhearing his physicians say that his lassitude is a sign of terminal illness, decides to buy some shabby clothes and a gun and commit suicide anonymously in a London slum. The scene changes to a fogbound Apple Blossom Court. Dim lights come from some windows and street lamps. Ruffians scuffle; children rush about; vendors hawk their wares. Sir Oliver is seen lurking in the background, slowly raising a pistol to his temples. But a bundle of rags on the forestage seemingly explodes, turning into a "red-headed, white-faced elf" named Glad. She grabs his arm and tells him he ought to be "thinkin' 'bout sompin' else." Before long he is under her spell. In gratitude he offers her money, and she no sooner takes it than a neighborhood tough grabs it. Oblivious to his own supposed weakness, Sir Oliver dodges garbage cans and vendors to chase down the thief and retrieve the money. He goes back with Glad to her room, hears her sad history, and finally helps her exonerate her beau, Dandy (Henry Stanford), of criminal charges—at the same time teaching his own caddish son (Aubrey Boucicault) a lesson in truthfulness. The *Dramatic Mirror* welcomed the play as "a little Sunday school lesson in the power of prayer" and added of its Glad, "Miss Robson is a delightful instructor." But this was the beautiful Eleanor Robson's last Broadway appearance, since she retired on marrying August Belmont III and became a leading socialite and philanthropist. However, she and the play did attract audiences into June.

For all practical purposes the touring melodrama, like William Winter, the doddering critic, and Miss Robson, still in the first bloom of her beauty, would disappear from the American theatrical scene by year's end. So there was an unintentional irony in the title of William Jossey's **The End of the Trail** (1-25-09, Grand St.). There was also little that was novel in this late, humdrum example. The heroine, "a plump blonde," confesses on returning to her father's New Mexico ranch that she had been tricked into a phoney marriage while a student in Boston. Her fiancé is forgiving. But her Boston seducer soon

turns up, bent on now seducing the heroine's sister and creating a grab-bag of other problems.

The rave reviews Charles Klein's **The Third Degree** (2-1-09, Hudson) received brought a temporary end to the slippage his reputation was suffering and gave him a taste of the success he had known a few years earlier. But unlike his earlier hits, which ran a year or more, *The Third Degree* had to be satisfied with a five-month run. Klein's story begins when Howard Jeffries, Jr. (Wallace Eddinger), a boozy wastrel disinherited by his father for marrying a waitress, arrives at the rooms of Robert Underwood (Francis Byrne), a shady art dealer in financial trouble, to ask for repayment of an old loan. Jeffries gulps down several drinks and passes out just as his new stepmother (Grace Filkins) comes to call. She has come in reply to a letter from Underwood, who once had been her fiancé, threatening to commit suicide. She denounces his ploy and storms out, upon which Underwood dashes into the adjoining room and shoots himself. The police, summoned to the apartment, have found a shaky Jeffries about to leave. Captain Clinton (Ralph Delmore), a harsh officer determined to wrap up the case, badgers the weak young man into a confession of murder, even though the police doctor has told the captain the death almost certainly was a suicide.

Jeffries's father (John Flood) will have nothing to do with his son, but the son's wife (Helen Ware), convinced of his innocence, wears down the family's attorney (Edmund Breese) by her stubborn but polite persistence, and he agrees to help though it means the senior Jeffries will no longer be his client. At his office the lawyer confronts the captain with medical records, the captain's own history of unjust accusations, and the threat to reveal that the captain uses the glint of a revolver to hypnotize suspects. All this, coupled with the wife's willingness to pretend she was the woman who visited Underwood and thus spare her mother-in-law, leads to a happy ending.

Read today, the play seems clumsy and singularly preposterous, but contemporary critics and theatregoers thought differently. Along with Klein, Helen Ware received the highest praise for her performance as the young wife, Annie—"unlettered and unpolished, but with sterling traits of honesty and unselfishness." The scene in which she forces herself to laugh though driven to tears was deemed a high point.

The Girl from Rector's (2-1-09, Weber's) did more than echo the celebrated line from *The Easiest Way*. Paul M. Potter's Americanization of Pierre Veber's farce, *Loute*, was one of the season's most notorious sensations. Trenton police, goaded by some noisy religious prigs, had raided the tryout. The publicity prompted several thousand potential playgoers to attempt to push their way in on opening night, and this time management had to call in the police. And what was the fuss all about? A little tale of some staid but not stay-at-home citizens of Battle Creek, Mich., who assume different names when they arrive in New York for a fling. The farce ran into July, giving Al Woods his first huge hit in the Big Time.

In John Grosvenor Wilson's **A Royal Divorce** (2-1-09, Yorkville), mounted by Manhattan's last surviving stock company, Josephine remains loyal to Napoleon after their divorce and saves her successor from an outraged mob.

Not many New Yorkers were smitten with the light-as-air English humor of Jerome K. Jerome's **The New Lady Bantock** (2-8-09, Wallack's), though the star was Fannie Ward, an American girl who had won popularity in London. The play was known there as *Fanny and the Servant Problem*. An English lord (John W. Dean) marries a music hall singer, having been led to believe she is a well-connected American, only to discover she is actually related to his entire serving staff.

Owen Davis and Al Woods joined forces again for **The Millionaire and the Policeman's Wife** (2-9-09, Grand St.). The millionaire wants the cop's wife "at any price." Helping him is his "blonde accomplice . . . who has a sort of mixed ale voice and a dimpled back." Together they force the policeman to jump from a ferry and duel underwater with another crony to retrieve some valuables. Later the policeman is nearly blown up crossing the old Tarrytown Bridge, chased around the tower of the new Singer Building, and forced to rescue his wife from a burning building and a Chinatown opium den. Siding with the goodies was the genre's now all but inevitable comic Jew, here called Moses Notmuchsky.

Another touring piece, Sidney R. Ellis's **When Old New York Was Dutch** (2-9-09, Metropolis), was seen as a hodgepodge of romantic historical drama, musical comedy, Hoytian farce, and Blaney melodrama. Its German hero is forced by scandal to flee to colonial America immediately after his wedding. He soon finds himself in trouble in the New World, but his wife, who has immigrated in search of him, falls in love with him all over again albeit she does not recognize him, and she helps extricate him. Anachronisms, such as the show's star giving his imitation of Harry Lauder, failed to bother an uncritical audience.

"Shakespeare, the managers say, is dead," one commentator wrote, and just such thinking may have been in part responsible for the temporary breakup of Sothern and Marlowe. But Marlowe's solo vehicle, Mary Johnston's **The Goddess of Reason** (2-15-09, Daly's), was a turgid blank-verse tragedy that made the most leaden of Shakespeare seem lively. Only the star's lure kept it on the boards for a little more than a month. She played a country girl who falls in love with a baron in late 18th-century France, joins the revolutionists when he spurns her, later repents and tries to save him, and finally goes to her death arm in arm with him. Critics complained that the characters and the plot were never fully developed, that Miss Marlowe's speeches were so long and dominating that the play was little better than a monologue, and that the poetry was bad. One example of the writing:

> They dream of woodland gods and castles high,
> Of faun and Pan and of the round table,
> Of dryad trees and of a maiden dark—

David and Milton Higgins had not been heard from for some time, and, with the market for cheap-priced plays about to be swept away, Milton would disappear from the scene and David devote himself to acting in other men's plays. So their **Captain Clay of Missouri** (2-15-09, Metropolis) marked an unintentional farewell. David himself played the captain, who is impoverished but still refuses to allow his fleet steed to be raced after he discovers his fiancée opposes his gaming proclivities. A young neighbor steals the horse, races it, and quietly turns over his winnings to the captain. A forged check and other difficulties make the captain's road bumpier still, but he wins the girl, swears off gambling, and decides to run for Congress. Horses that figured prominently in plots often gave their names to their plays' titles—witness Wildfire and Blue Grass earlier in the season. Captain Clay's horse was named Missouri.

The police raid of *The Girl from Rector's* was not the only sign of a resurgence of rigid conservatism. Divorce had come under feverish attack. As one report noted, "Ministers are preaching against it, legislatures are taking steps to curtail its frequency." But Thompson Buchanan, a newspaperman who was the son of a Kentucky clergyman, took a different tack, writing **A Woman's Way** (2-22-09, Hackett), a delicious comedy holding divorce up to ridicule. Howard Stanton (Frank Worthing), his arm in a sling, sits in his drawing room surrounded by newspapers with headlines crying "Divorce," Divorce Scandal," and "Family Conference." Stanton knows full well yesterday's automobile accident has brought on the headlines, since he was riding with an unidentified woman. His wife, Marion (Grace George), attempting to be rid of a particularly pestiferous reporter, tells the man she was the lady in question. The reporter leaves, remarking, "Then allow me to congratulate you, Mrs. Stanton, on your splendid recovery. The lady in the car broke her leg—good-day." Marion is resolved not to destroy her marriage. She tells her mother (Ruth Benson), "We fight to get our husbands—why not fight to hold them?" But as far as Mr. Stanton is concerned, she pretends divorce is hardly out of the question. She tells him that when he remarries he and his new wife can decorate the room, and he can put his new crest up—"crossed hearts above an automobile rampant." And she even invites the lady involved, Mrs. Blakemore (Dorothy Tennant), to dinner at the Stanton home, along with some male friends and relations of the Stantons. It soon becomes apparent to Mr. Stanton that Mrs. Blakemore has had friendly relations with all the men invited. He has been only the latest on her list. She is sent packing, and the Stantons are reunited.

Buchanan's career would span twenty years, but he would have few successes. By contrast, Avery Hopwood's twenty-year career would make him Broadway's biggest money machine. However, his **This Woman and This Man** (2-22-09, Maxine Elliott's) gave little hint of his future. This woman is Thelka Mueller (Carlotta Nillson), who finds herself pregnant by her employer's son, Norris Townsend (Milton Sills). She refuses to consider putting up the child for adoption, and when Norris in turn refuses to consider marrying her, she forces him to agree at gunpoint. Like the husband in *The Stronger Sex,* he eventually comes to love her for her strength and decency. The play folded after three weeks. Subsequently it toured for two years, bringing Hopwood $12,000 in royalties. Wanting more, Hopwood hereafter wrote mostly farces and comedies.

March was busy, if not especially rewarding. Three soon forgotten failures premiered on its first evening. "The play of situations brought about by transparent and fortuitous incidents and circumstances is at an end," *Theatre's* critic observed at the start of his review of Louis Anspacher's second play to reach Broadway, **A Woman of Impulse** (3-1-09, Herald Square). The incidents and circumstances are precipitated when a hotheaded prima donna (Kathryn Kidder) attempts to prevent a notorious rake (Charles Wyngate) from seducing her sister (Jane Marbury). Before she can intervene, the sister stabs the rake. "You did right to kill him. You are a brave little sister," the prima donna says consolingly. But the rake is apparently not dead. The prima

donna's jealous husband (Cuyler Hastings) enters the room, thinks the rake has been after his wife, and slugs him. This time the rake is dead. All three confess to the police. But the authorities, aware of the lothario's reputation, list his death as accidental.

Jewish-Christian antagonism—a subject rarely dwelled upon for long in contemporary American drama but touched on briefly in October in *The Man Who Stood Still*—was the theme of Thomas Addison's **Meyer and Son** (3-1-09, Garden). However, Addison chose to minimize his risks by falling back on the stock motif of the theme. More than religious differences have come between Nathan Meyer (William Humphrey) and Major Gray (George C. Staley), for the men are on opposing sides of a struggle to obtain a telephone monopoly. Exacerbating matters is the fact that Meyer's son, Max (Franklin Ritchie), is courting Gray's daughter, Doris (Irene Moore). The opponents are reconciled only after the elder Meyer discreetly helps Gray's dissolute son (Kenneth Hill) out of a scrape. For the most part, notices were highly encouraging, but the play did not appeal to 1909 audiences. Both *A Woman of Impulse* and *Meyer and Son* closed after two weeks.

The Richest Girl (3-1-09, Criterion), Michael Morton's West End rendering of Paul Gavault's Paris farce, *La Petite Chocolatière,* ran a week longer. Marie Doro was starred as the daughter of a chocolate tycoon. After the young lady's car breaks down, she takes shelter at the home of an attractive young man, inadvertently causes him to lose his fiancée and his job, and finally marries him.

Lamentations over Shakespeare's declining popularity were muted briefly when Robert Mantell began a three-week stand at the New Amsterdam on the 8th, opening bravely with one of the poet's least popular works, *King John.* One critic spoke for many when he pegged the star as "a conscientious, uninspired actor"; another critic summed up the consensus when he assessed the production as "noble, impressive and adequate," with sometimes ragged scenery often more memorable than the acting. After a week the play gave way to *Macbeth, Hamlet, The Merchant of Venice, Romeo and Juliet, King Lear,* and two non-Shakespearean works, *Louis XI* and *Richelieu.* During later visits at the Academy of Music and elsewhere, Mantell brought out *Othello, Richard III, The Lady of Lyons,* and *The Marble Heart.*

In Clyde Fitch's **The Bachelor** (3-15-09, Maxine Elliott's), a broker (Charles Cherry) falls in love with his stenographer (Ruth Maycliffe), a girl whose family lost everything in the San Francisco earthquake and who works under an assumed name. The trip to the altar is detoured for a time when comments by the girl's brother (Ralph Morgan) are misunderstood. Cherry, another of many players hastily pushed to stardom, received good notices, but Miss Maycliffe was assailed as "affected" and "unconvincing." The most glowing notices went to Janet Beecher as a young Swedish housemaid. Fitch had written the play for Ethel Barrymore but had turned it over to the Shuberts after Frohman had rejected it. Its modest success—a two-month run— was the last Fitch would live to enjoy.

The competing opening had been rejected by all Broadway's major producers, so it fell to the Actors' Society of America, a never strong union now on its last legs, to mount it. Elizabeth Robins's English play **Votes for Women** (3-15-09, Wallack's) was deemed more a suffragette tract than a proper play. It focused on an embittered woman, beautifully played by Mary Shaw, who becomes a rabid advocate of women's rights and only softens a bit when the man who once jilted her agrees to support her cause.

If the plot of *Votes for Women* struck critics as "wan, lost [and] hysterical," the story of Lee Wilson Dodd's **The Return of Eve** (3-17-09, Herald Square), and certainly its trappings, were seen as ridiculous, or at best a clever idea wasted. Two orphans, Adam and Eve, are raised by a foster father in a West Virginia village called Eden. When they grow up, Adam (Richard Buhler) remains in the dreary backwater, while Eve (Bertha Galland) heads for New York. Neither can find happiness. Then Eve returns to Eden, where she learns that she and Adam are not brother and sister. The pair look at each other with new eyes.

Major Guy Du Maurier's **An Englishman's Home** (3-22-09, Criterion), which fantasized unpleasantly about what might happen if an unspecified foreign army invaded an unprepared England, had caused a furor in Britain but held little interest for Americans.

Many of these same Americans were intrigued by **A Fool There Was** (3-24-09, Liberty), which Porter Emerson Browne developed as a modern morality play from a suggestion in Kipling. The Husband (Robert Hilliard) is a devoted family man and an important diplomat. His loving family comes to see him off as he is about to sail on a mission to England. They are witnesses to a horrifying incident. A young man (Howard Hull), spurned by The Woman (Katharine Kaelred), shoots himself and falls dead at her feet. She laughs and sprinkles rose petals on the body. When the body is removed and the blood wiped away, she asks that her deck chair

be placed on the same spot. The Husband is fascinated and instantly falls under her sway. She tells him there are two kinds of love, one as pallid as a white rose, the other as impassioned as a red rose. His family soon hears about his degradation and tries to draw him back, but when he curses The Woman she responds, "Kiss me, my fool," and he does. He loses his family and his position; his now servantless home is a shambles. In one last, desperate effort to free himself, he attempts to choke The Woman. But the excitement is too much; he drops dead. She laughs and throws rose petals on his body.

Hilliard, acting with unexpected reserve, and Miss Kaelred, tall, dark-eyed, and voluptuous, were perfectly mated. And since Frederick Thompson was producer, the scenery was spectacular. The deck of the huge liner, with its presailing hustle and bustle, won tremendous applause, as had the ship setting in his November mounting of *Via Wireless*. On opening night, following the last-act curtain, the curtain rose again to reveal Hilliard and Miss Kaelred in a tableau replicating a Burne-Jones painting on a similar theme. But the tableau, sneered at by critics, was dropped after the first night. The drama ran until the hot weather killed business, then toured for several seasons.

Earlier in the season Henrietta Crosman had played briefly in some of Manhattan's second-class houses, offering a repertory of her old hits. The tour must have been a failure, for immediately thereafter she and her producer-husband declared bankruptcy. So there was a touch of irony when she appeared in Geraldine Bonner and Elmer Blaney Harris's **Sham** (3-17-09, Wallack's), playing Katherine Van Riper, a full-time spendthrift and sometime sponger, who has gotten head over heels in debt. To solve her problem her aunts select a rich mine owner for her to marry, but she prefers a struggling engineer (Paul Dickey). Typical misunderstandings arise before the aunts, to save the family's name, agree to pay Katherine's debts, and Katherine prepares to struggle along with her engineer. The play ran two months and apparently made some money. At least Miss Crosman did not have to file for bankruptcy again.

In **The Conflict** (3-29-09, Garden), freely adapted by Maurice V. Samuels from Balzac's *La Peau de chagrin,* a man (Robert Drouet) obtains a magical skin that will grant any wish, but it will shrink each time a wish is granted and will not prevent the owner's health from deteriorating. The skin brings the man unhappiness until he realizes his wishes must not be selfish ones. The play was one of many during the season to survive a mere fortnight.

That same evening E. H. Sothern came into

Daly's with a schedule consisting of *Richelieu, Our American Cousin, Hamlet,* and *If I Were King*. He remained three weeks to disappointing business, after which he announced that he and Julia Marlowe would tour together again.

A two-week hiatus followed in which no new plays opened, but then four premiered on the same Monday. One, Edward Locke's **The Climax** (4-12-09, Weber's), got a beat on the others by starting out with a matinee performance. In fact, it was only booked for a handful of matinees until a surprisingly enthusiastic critical reception turned it into a whopping hit, allowing it to span the hot weather and run well into the next season. Praise ran on the order of "an interesting sentimental comedy in a fresh and charming vein" and "Such delicate pathos and homely humor have not been found this year or in past years." Curiously, a number of critics compared it with *The Music Master* while none saw it as a reversed *Trilby*.

The story unfolded in a single, simple setting and involved only four characters. Adelina von Hagen (Leona Watson), a half-German, half-Italian girl from Azalia, Ohio, comes to New York to study singing with her mother's brother, Luigi (Albert Bruning). She shares her uncle's small apartment with her cousin, Pietro (Effingham A. Pinto), helping with the dishes and other household chores whenever necessary. Pietro falls in love with his cousin, composing fervent "soul songs" for her, but Adelina is absorbed in her study. Her hometown suitor, Dr. John Raymond (William Lewers), appears on the scene just as Adelina learns she will need some minor throat surgery. The operation is a success, but Raymond, in an effort to have Adelina abandon her plans and marry him, hypnotizes her into losing her voice. "There is one chance in a thousand that you will ever sing again," he advises discouragingly. Gloomily accepting his conclusion, Adelina agrees to the wedding. On the wedding day Raymond confesses his deception. Adelina's voice returns at once. But an equivocal ending leaves the audience to imagine whether she forgives Raymond, takes a second look at Pietro, or ditches both men to pursue her career.

All the performances were admired, even if one critic couldn't resist writing of Bruning that he "makes the old music master a wonderful composite, who looks like Warfield's Von Barwig, and talks Italian macaroni with Spanish trimmings and a Houston Street Hungarian accent." The play became a stock favorite and was revived on Broadway as late as the 1930s.

Paul Armstrong and Rex Beach's **Going Some** (4-12-09, Belasco) ran three months, missing by a mere four showings that charmed circle of plays that run 100 or more performances. Yet it, too, received sunny reviews, and since it was a farce, it could have been expected to hurdle the summer more readily than did *The Climax*. Perhaps its large cast—sixteen principals plus supers—made it economically difficult. Its hero was J. Wallingford Speed (Lawrence Wheat), a Yale man whose surname has gone to his very swelled (and very blond) head. Arriving for vacation at a New Mexico ranch, he agrees to represent the ranch in a crucial race. Knowing he really cannot win, he secretly wires a buddy, a champion in the 100-yard dash, to come and take his place. Then Speed discovers that the champion is in jail and also that, if he himself runs and loses, some mercurial cowhands are likely to shoot him. He is relieved when the champion wires that he is out of jail and on his way, but Speed's joy turns sour when the champ arrives on crutches. Speed's only recourse is to bribe his opponent, Skinner (William Harrigan). Speed is such a slow, clumsy runner that Skinner has trouble throwing the race, but he does. The race scene, played out in front of a comically stop-and-start panorama, with Skinner's ludicrously patent attempts at stumbling, was the laugh-filled culmination of a farce that had built skillfully from its first curtain.

The evening's third success, J. Hartley Manners's **The House Next Door** (4-12-09, Gaiety), was derived from Leo Walther Stein and Ludwig Weller's *Die Von Hochsatte*, reset in England, and reiterated the same motifs played out a few weeks earlier in *Meyer and Son*. England is "a small country entirely surrounded by Jews," barks a moneyless aristocrat, Sir John Cotswold (J. E. Dodson), resentful of the success of his neighbor, the newly knighted Sir Isaac Jacobson (Thomas Findlay), and furious that his son and daughter love Sir Isaac's daughter and son. Disclosure of how Sir Isaac secretly helped the Cotswold family alters the old man's attitudes. The play had "humor," "charm," and "taste," but most of all it had Dodson's remarkable performance of a cantankerous lord whose good breeding and inherent decency finally tell. Dodson had been a respected supporting player since he first came to America thirty years before and even had a brief fling at artificially proclaimed stardom. With this bright feather in his cap, he retired from the stage although he was still in his early fifties and destined to live on for twenty-two years.

The evening's lone, unhappy failure was Clyde Fitch's **The Happy Marriage** (4-12-09, Garrick). The comedy was completed with Grace George in mind, but she turned it down. Its relatively uncomplicated story centered on an unreasonably jealous wife (Doris Keane). She misconstrues the relationship between her husband (Edwin Arden) and another woman, so prepares to run away with a handsome rake (Milton Sills). The husband catches them, pretends to accept their feeble disclaimers, and tactfully takes back his contrite wife. Playing the part of the couple's very young son was a future award-winning playwright, Albert Hackett.

The season's shortest-lived flop so far on a first-class stage was **The Gay Life** (4-19-09, Daly's), which Roy L. McCardell dramatized from his sketches of Gotham's bohemian life in the *Evening World*. The comedy ran a single week. Lulu Lorrimer (Consuelo Bailey), an Altoona waitress who has come to New York to try her luck on the stage, takes a room at a theatrical boardinghouse run by plump, feisty Mama De Branscombe (Katherine De Barry), an ex-burlesque queen. Lulu falls in love with rich William Thorton, Jr. (Schuyler Ladd). Thorton's father (Frank Currier) refuses to hear of his son's wedding a onetime waitress (shades of *The Third Degree*) and attempts to buy her off. Mistakenly he buys off the wrong boarder. Matters come to a head when everyone gathers at a bohemian eatery (supposedly a replica of a real contemporary resort) and Lulu, annoyed by the elder Thorton's sentiments, jumps on a table and does a skirt dance. Woven in and out of the story was one of McCardell's best-liked characters, Dopey McKnight (Thomas Thorner), who writes sad songs and who looks absurdly dapper in his hand-me-downs. Typical of McCardell's humor was one flirtatious boarder telling her dismayed suitor, "When you was away all last summer, George, I was true to you. I never drank anything but your wine, no matter who I was with."

April's offerings had echoed the Christian-Jewish conflict and the reactionary-father–liberal-son conflict of the season's earlier presentations. The month's last mounting, continuing "the present passion for contemporary sociological subjects in the drama," returned to the slum tenements. That play was William J. Hurlbut's second of the season, **The Writing on the Wall** (4-26-09, Savoy). Hurlbut, in the year's most undisguised bit of muckraking, went after the Trinity Church Corporation, which exposés had shown to be one of New York's most notorious slum landlords. As a reformer (Robert T. Haines) tells Barbara Lawrence (Olga Nethersole), wife of a man (William Morris) who is both a member of the corporation and the owner of numerous unsafe tenements himself, "Their clergy sprinkle rose water, but their deeds smell to heaven" and "In the

very shadow of the church there are tenements where men and women live in squalor and disease and worse, but the stained-glass windows shut out the view." (The lines were singled out by many critics). Barbara is shown through the buildings and made aware of safety violations such as fire escapes unable to hold the legal weight. She begs her husband to make changes, and he promises her he will do so, but he simply orders the fire escapes repainted. Barbara sends their young son (J. R. Wallace) to a tenement party, a fire breaks out, and he is unable to escape. The loss of his son leads Lawrence to reform.

Two problems beset the production. One was the play's "air of insincerity" and its concessions to easy theatricality in a story "needlessly complicated and confused with a secret love affair of the husband, a love affair between the wife and the reformer, and a trite episode concerning a confusion of Christmas gifts." Worse, the star, Miss Nethersole, seemed burned out, "incapable of exhibiting anything but the monotonous parade of affectations, posturings and falsities." The play gave up after a month's forced run.

Another estranged father, one of those " 'get-rich-anyhow' and 'business is business' characters that infest our latter-day native drama," was the central figure in **The Great John Ganton** (5-3-09, Lyric), which a productive J. Hartley Manners dramatized from Arthur J. Eddy's novel. Ganton (George Fawcett) is finally reconciled to his son (A. H. Van Buren) through the efforts of the son's fiancée, May Keating (Laurette Taylor), daughter of the elder Ganton's old enemy. Labor problems and a troublesome Chicago matron (Jane Payton) figured in subplots. Critics saw the play as a watered-down *Lion and the Mouse*, saved largely by Fawcett's powerful acting. Those critics who didn't ignore her saw nothing unique in Miss Taylor.

The next Monday night brought in William Collier in a revival of *The Man from Mexico*, which ran for two months at the Garrick.

Two failures brought May and the fading season to a close, at least as far as novelties were concerned. The implicit immorality of Federico Mariani's **The Game of Love** (5-24-09, Wallack's) bothered some straitlaced commentators. Mariani's hero (E. J. Ratcliffe) is an artist so embittered at losing the girl he loved to a rich man that he sets out to wreck all his friends' marriages and flirt with their wives and sisters. He ends up marrying one of the newly divorced women. As one reviewer noted sourly, Mariani had been the son-in-law of Cleveland's mayor until he divorced the mayor's daughter.

John Montague's **The Narrow Path** (5-31-09, Hackett) was perceived as an even worse play, "a pale reflex, not only of 'The Easiest Way,' but of several other plays that have been inveighed against in the last season on account of their presentation of certain so-called seamy sides of life." Its heroine is Bertha Clark (Ida Conquest), a manicurist who is resolved to walk the straight and narrow, who loves a poor journalist (Frederick Perry), and who resists the allurements of an unscrupulous married man (George Parsons). But when she learns that the villain has left one of her co-workers pregnant, she goes to his apartment to force him to take care of the girl. The man's wife (Dorothy Rossmore) and Bertha's poor journalist both misinterpret the check she is given until the pregnant girl (Irene Osher) appears and sets matters aright. A last-minute substitution, Miss Osher did not know her lines on opening night. She had no chance to learn them, since opening night and closing night were the same for the play.

At the Academy of Music that same evening, a reunited Sothern and Marlowe raised the curtain on a summer season of Shakespeare that consisted of *Romeo and Juliet, Hamlet, The Merchant of Venice, Twelfth Night,* and *The Taming of the Shrew.* But their visit was merely a prelude of more exciting things to come for them a few months down the road.

Almost as an afterthought, *The Mollusc* was revived briefly at the Empire on June 7 to allow New Yorkers to see it with its original London stars, Charles Wyndham and Mary Moore.

A few weeks earlier, the *Dramatic Mirror* had presented its annual summary of the just finished season. By the trade sheet's commercial standards, it had been an excellent season. Rising costs had meant that an unfortunate number of failures had not repaid their investments, but the number of failures and the magnitude of their losses, though money is never cheap, were small by later yardsticks. The good news was that theatrical business in New York and around the country had prospered. The number of hits, especially the number and percentage of American plays to make the grade, was heartening. In only one category was the news unremittingly bleak. The paper reported, "During the year seven combination houses [in Manhattan alone] ceased to be of importance to producers." Two of these had gone over to Yiddish theatre; one had introduced a cheap-priced stock company—a policy that soon collapsed. The other four houses had converted to films or to a mixture of films and vaudeville. Among the latter was the historic 14th Street Theatre. A mere half-dozen years had passed since Edwin S. Porter's one-reeler *The Great Train Robbery* had caught the public's fancy. Hollywood had only begun to be home to film makers. D. W. Griffith, Cecil B. de Mille, Thomas Ince, and others had yet to make their classic films or their mark. Yet in a way the *Dramatic Mirror*'s announcement was premature. Had it waited only a few months until the new season got under way, it could have noted that in the new theatrical year not a single Manhattan playhouse remained devoted to touring melodramas and that, for all practical purposes, no touring melodramas toured.

1909–1910

A season of exceptional, sustained interest rarely is followed by an equally exciting season. If 1909–10 was hardly as brilliant as its prececessor, it was by no means a weak one. Its theatrical comings and goings were constantly newsworthy. Among the goings—for all practical purposes, among the gones—was the all but total disappearance of touring melodrama, along with the conversion to films, or in a few cases to other purposes, of theatres which once had hosted them. Touring melodramas had evolved slowly and naturally from the need to entertain the lower classes; they disappeared quickly but just as naturally when these same playgoers found cheaper and in some ways better diversions. The plays never had added anything to dramatic literature. Like the silent films that superannuated them, they were essentially visual. Their stories leaped from sensation to sensation; their characterizations were elementary and again often visual—like the villainess's traditional red dress. After all, they were designed for audiences consisting of immigrants who frequently had no understanding of English, the least literate of native Americans, and galleries full of noisemakers.

The most notable coming could not have been more different. Although it had been talked about for years, it appeared abruptly and seemingly full grown. Its creation was anything but natural—the handiwork of a committee. And it was designed for an elite of pretentious socialites and dedicated intellectuals. It was what was called in its day an "endowed theatre"—a theatre subsidized by the same rich families who underwrote opera, museums, and similarly suitable cultural institutions. But it would be several months before the magnificent new house would be ready to open its doors. Meanwhile, the more firmly rooted commercial theatre got under way.

The season's first drama used a setting that would become increasingly popular, the Tenderloin. It also printed in its program a pivotal line from the play, "Being on the square with a pal is the only law we know." **The Only Law** (8-2-09, Hackett) was the work of George Bronson Howard, the late playwright's dandyish son, and Wilson Mizner, a wit and jack-of-many-trades, whose biographer characterized him as a rogue. Their play centered on a Tenderloin denizen, a Casino chorus girl named Jean (Mabel Cameron), who lives with a ne'er-do-well parasite—a "Broadway rounder" in the period's jargon—named MacAvoy (Forrest Winant). Bannister (George S. Christie), a Wall Street broker, admires Jean and gives her $1000, which she turns into $18,000 by following Bannister's suggestion for investment. Jean tries to persuade MacAvoy to buy a farm in California with her, but MacAvoy steals the money and attempts to flee to Europe with another chorus girl. Spider (Ben Johnson), a crook with some decent instincts who admires Jean, fingers MacAvoy for the police and pushes a wiser Jean into Bannister's arms. "No Good Served By Year's First Play," the *World*'s banner warned, while the *Time*'s headline dismissed the drama as "Vulgar and Crude." Although pummeled with unfavorable notices, the drama held on for six weeks.

A comedy that opened on the same evening used another setting that would be seen over and over again, the deck of a ship. **Billy** (8-2-09, Daly's) was written by Mrs. Sidney Drew using the name George Cameron. She based the play on a sketch she and her husband had performed in vaudeville. (Sidney was John's younger, probably illegitimate brother.) To get accustomed to his new false teeth away from home, Billy (Drew) sails to Havana on the S.S. *Florida*. He is dismayed to find his sweetheart (Marian Chapman) on board. Just as he starts to explain his behavior to her, a careless deck steward bumps into him, knocking out his teeth. The search for them, his attempt to purloin replacements, and his repurchase of them at a ship's auction provided laughs. The comedy survived for two months. Late in the run a curtain raiser was added. Robert B. Kegerreis's **The Tell-Tale Heart** (9-18-09) was based on Poe's famous story of a servant who murders his master and whose guilty conscience leads him to hear the dead man's heartbeats. The author himself impersonated the demented, doomed killer.

The next Monday evening again brought in one drama and one comedy—both of which ran approximately a month. Olive Porter's **The Ringmaster** (8-9-09, Maxine Elliott's) was not a circus play but rather the latest example of what Broadway had come to label "Wall Street drama." As such, playgoing regulars could have outlined the basic plot. At his mother's urging, John LeBaron, Jr. (Arthur Byron), has renounced the ways of his late father, whose ruthless methods made him a multimillionaire. The younger John lives a quiet, largely idle life until he falls in love with Eleanor Hillary (Laurette Taylor), daughter of the most successful and vicious man on Wall Street, Richard Hillary (George Howell). Hillary's associates refer to him as "the Ringmaster." Eleanor demands that John prove his business abilities, so John buys a controlling interest in the very railroad Hillary is seeking. A battle ensues, and Eleanor for a time is led to believe that John is the one whose actions are unscrupulous. Of course, truth and goodness triumph. For the second week in a row, first-nighters could gaze on an attractive ship setting, in this instance the sumptuous yacht *Nomadic*, with its fine paneling and wicker deck furniture. Regrettably, on opening night "the apparatus which was supposed to cause the yacht to float lazily up and down upon a moonlit sea" broke down with an ominous thump.

Nor was the plot of **The Florist Shop** (8-9-09, Liberty), which Oliver Herford derived from Alexander Engel and Julius Horst's *Glück bei Frauen*, all that new. Two brides believe their new husbands' pasts to be precisely the opposite of what they really are, and the men feel obliged to humor the misconceptions.

Before the next new plays appeared, William Winter resigned huffily from the *Tribune* after more than forty years as its critic. He quit because, while confessing that "my articles relative to indecent and reprehensible plays have been, and are, framed for the purpose of doing . . . injury to the business of the persons exploiting them," he was angry when his most intemperate assaults had been blue-penciled. Long out of touch with modern ideas and too frequently belligerent, he was not much missed, but other, younger Jeremiahs hurried in to fill his shoes.

Two Monday nights after the last pair of openings, another, rather similar pair of plays arrived. The more serious work was George Broadhurst's **The Dollar Mark** (8-23-09, Wallack's), the season's second "Wall Street drama" and its third play set in part at sea. James Gresham (Robert Warwick), an idealistic mine owner and banker, and Carson Baylis (Cuyler Hastings), a greedy monopolist, both love Alice Chandler (Frances Ring), and the men are also battling over control of a mine. Baylis invites Gresham to sail with him on his yacht, hoping to destroy him by creating a run on Gresham's bank while they are away. Gresham learns of the plot and forces Baylis at gunpoint to return to shore. He not only avoids a panic, he wins Alice.

Michael Morton's **Detective Sparkes** (8-23-09, Garrick) served as a vehicle for Hattie Williams when she moved from musical comedy to straight stages. The detective does not exist, but Athole Forbes (Miss Williams) poses as him and as several other people in an attempt to prevent the discovery that her married sister had gone on a balloon ride with another man.

Is Matrimony a Failure? (8-24-09, Belasco) was taken by Leo Ditrichstein from Oskar Blumenthal and Gustav Kadelburg's *Die Thur in Freie* and was the season's first big hit (183 performances). It also marked one of David Belasco's rare sallies at the time into the field of comedy. Some badgered or henpecked husbands learn that their marriages, thanks to a technicality, were not legal. They leave home until their wives agree to give them more freedom. But they soon find second bachelorhood has its own drawbacks.

Francis de Croisset and Maurice Leblanc's **Arsene Lupin** (8-26-09, Lyceum) was France's answer to Raffles. The gentlemanly thief (William Courtenay) always advises his victims of his plans in advance. On this occasion he poses as a duke and courts a rich girl (Virginia Hammond) before robbing her father (Charles Harbury). A knowing detective (Sidney Herbert) closes in but is not unhappy when the resourceful scoundrel makes a daring, last-minute escape along with his real beloved (Doris Keane). The play ran 144 performances, then set out on an extended tour.

Audiences were taken to sea again in Charles Frohman's importation of Major W. P. Drury and Leo Trevor's London hit **The Flag Lieutenant** (8-30-09, Criterion), which began aboard a British warship and later offered glimpses of British encampments during a Cretan insurrection. The story told of a carefree officer (Bruce McRae) who is accused of cowardice after he gallantly credits a wounded friend (Francis Carlyle) with his own daring dash for aid. The play failed to interest Americans and was quickly withdrawn.

Some of *The Flag Lieutenant*'s motifs and more exciting scenes once had been the stock in trade of touring melodramas. The genre's sad fate was summed up in the first sentence of a review of **The Queen of the Secret Seven** (8-30-09, Court, Brooklyn), which diehard Al Woods presented across the

river: "If one wishes to indulge in a taste for popular priced melodrama in the greater city he must make his way across one of the bridges." Its web of romances and vengeful, spurned lovers was waved away as "hackneyed and time-worn." Among similar plays Brooklyn saw during the late summer or fall were **The Workingman's Wife** (8-23-09), Sedley Brown's **A Navaho's Love** (9-20-09), in which an Indian and a Wall Street speculator vie for the hand of a heroine whose father is in danger of going bankrupt, Hal Reid's *Human Hearts* (9-28-09), which found its blacksmith-hero falsely accused by an adventuress, **The River Pirates** (9-28-09), and **The Clansman** (10-4-09). The plays received increasingly smaller notices, and by spring the houses where they had played were showing films.

At heart there was precious little difference between the old American touring melodramas and London's Drury Lane melodramas. Broadway was offered a recent example of the latter in Cecil Raleigh and Henry Hamilton's **The Sins of Society** (8-31-09, New York). Sensation scenes follow swift and sure after a bankrupt English lady attempts to pawn a fake tiara, poison the pawnbroker, and steal the fake lest it implicate her. Settings included the clubhouse at Longchamps, the rhododendron garden at Windsor, a waterfall (into which the comedian jumps "at the end of an ostensibly invisible wire"), a ship sinking in a fog at sea, and a church. Americans either had had enough of such spectacles or simply realized that silent films could present them more dramatically, so the play failed.

In retrospect Channing Pollock attributed the modest 103-performance run of his **Such a Little Queen** (8-31-09, Hackett) to a brutal September heat wave, ignoring the longer runs—sometimes much longer—of other late August and early September entries. The truth was, his comedy was pleasant but unexceptional and fell apart artistically after its second act. With European royalty apparently still safely ensconced on their thrones, a program note explained the comedy's premise: "The author begs to admit having manufactured history for Bosnia and Herzogovina. Also, to recall instances of monarchs who have experienced poverty in exile; among the number, Napoleon III, Louis Philippe, and Theodore I of Corsica." Pollock's exiled, impoverished queen is Anna (Elsie Ferguson), a Herzogovinian whom political plotters have chased across the Atlantic. She lives in a cheap Harlem walkup at St. Nicholas Avenue and 138th Street. She holds court in her kitchen. Never having seen a refrigerator, she uses it for a wardrobe. She cooks her own potatoes, mashing them with her scepter.

An American admirer (Francis Byrne) obtains work for her at the Broadway offices of a meat packer. Later, when Stephen IV (Frank Gillmore), the Bosnian to whom she was engaged in childhood, appears, having been exiled by the same plotters, he, too, is given work, which he does reluctantly and indifferently. For a brief time it looks as if Stephen will be accused of stealing money from incoming mail, but that charge is disproved just as the plotters admit they cannot govern without Stephen. However, they refuse to allow Anna to return. Stephen insists he will not go back alone, so Anna's American admirer helps bribe the plotters to change their demands. Whatever delights the comedy provided for 1909 audiences, its later charm came from the period pictures it inadvertently painted. Thus we see Anna amazed at the workings of a self-locking door, and there is this bit of dialogue:

Queen: (*A trumpet sounds in the courtyard. The Queen runs to the window.*) Is that the President?
Trainor [the American admirer]: No. A scissors-grinder.

Ever changing standard usage was evident—a girl is referred to as a "typist" rather than a "typewriter"—while more evanescent slang was abundant in such exchanges as:

Queen: A Queen must marry a King.
Trainor: Not on this side of the wet! Over here a woman marries the man she loves.

But some theatrical practices were not evolving so rapidly. Each act was followed by curtain calls with their own small narratives. At the close of Act II her boss, Mr. Lauman (Ralph Stuart), shows Anna the bills he believes Stephen has stolen and tells her the man is "a loafer, a no-good, a failure!" But Anna, having spotted some kingly qualities in Stephen's actions, scoffs and storms out. The curtain was followed by "*SECOND CURTAIN: Lauman stands stupified, looking after her*" and *THIRD CURTAIN: He throws the bills furiously into the waste basket, and exits into his office, slamming the door behind him.*" In 1913 the comedy was musicalized as *Her Little Highness*.

The season's biggest hit but one (345 performances) was Winchell Smith's **The Fortune Hunter** (9-04-09, Gaiety). "It is necessary to hark back to George Ade's 'County Chairman' to find a suitable comparison for [this] breezy and wholesome little comedy of American village life," *Theatre* proclaimed. And it did spin an engagingly fresh yarn. Nathaniel Duncan (John Barrymore) was spoiled rotten by a rich father. Unfortunately old man

Duncan died broke, and Nat has been unable to earn a living. Nat's friend, Henry Kellogg (Hale Hamilton), points out a possible solution. The brightest, most ambitious country boys come to the city to make good, leaving the best country girls to languish at home. "All you have to do," Kellogg suggests, "is to select some small country town, far enough away from the city, where you can content yourself to settle down to the simple life for a while, and make yourself solid in the community by your exemplary habits, combined with good clothes and polite manners. There are always country heiresses just waiting to be asked for by such a chap—they may even do the proposing themselves."

With a stake from his buddy, Nat heads for a small town in far-off Pennsylvania and takes work in a rundown drugstore. He promptly sets about revitalizing the store at the same time he begins his pursuit of the richest girl in the village, Josie Lockwood (Eda Bruna). That pursuit turns sour when another suitor accuses Nat of being an embezzler sought by the police. Happily, Nat has found true romance with the druggist's daughter, Betty Graham (Mary Ryan). The lovers plight their troth in the bower in front of the girl's home, oblivious to a sudden downpour. Mr. Graham (Forrest Robinson) comes to their aid with a huge umbrella. The play called playgoers' attention to pretty, talented Mary Ryan. More important, it consolidated Barrymore's fast-growing celebrity.

. . .

John [Sydney Blythe] **Barrymore** (1882–1942) was the younger son of Maurice and Georgiana Drew Barrymore and the brother of Lionel and Ethel. He was born in Philadelphia and made his stage debut in 1903 in Chicago in *Magda*. For the next six years he moved swiftly from role to role, performing in drama, comedy, and even in musicals. His handsome aquiline profile soon became a sort of trademark.

. . .

In 1925 the comedy was musicalized unsuccessfully by Jerome Kern as *The City Chap*.

Superb sets were not enough to attract audiences to Rupert Hughes's **The Bridge** (9-4-09, Majestic), the latest in the swelling list of plays that coupled labor-management strife with romance. Although settings such as the sumptuous Gothic balcony of a hotel ballroom elicited praise, the second act's view of a bridge under construction garnered the most attention: "The steel structure of a great bridge [is shown] reaching into the flies and apparently spanning a wide river. A horde of workmen throng the narrow girders, hammering, riveting, swinging aloft on beams." These workmen have threatened to strike for higher wages. The young engineer (Guy Bates Post) in charge of the project, coming as he does from a working-class background, is sympathetic to their demands. He is also courting the daughter (Katherine Emmet) of the president (Albert Gran) of the railroad building the bridge. The president sends out armed men to disperse the workers but eventually agrees to remove them if the engineer will give up seeing his daughter. To save the men, the engineer accepts—but love is not to be put down. The *American*'s acerbic Alan Dale was among many naysayers, writing, "*The Bridge* shows a good deal of weakness. Some of its arches are a bit shaky. It is a bridge that won't stand much. In fact, common sense gives it a jolt."

The English playwright Israel Zangwill offered **The Melting-Pot** (9-6-09, Comedy), his highly charged look at a facet of American life, to Americans first. London would not see it for several years. David (Walker Whiteside) is a young musician, an immigrant still haunted by the sight of his family being killed in a pogrom. He lives with his loving but fanatically orthodox grandmother (Louise Muldenar) and his uncle (Sheridan Block), a man who ekes out his sustenance by giving music lessons and playing in the pit orchestras of cheap theatres. Vera (Chrystal Herne), a young immigrant woman from the settlement house, comes to ask David to give a concert. He pours out his fragile yet blazing hope to her in one of the play's innumerable speeches (some critics called them "preachments"): "America is God's Crucible, the great Melting-Pot where all races of Europe are melting and reforming! Here you stand, good folk, think I, when I see them at Ellis Island, here you stand in your fifty groups, with your fifty languages and histories, and your fifty blood hatreds and rivalries. But you won't be long like that, brothers, for these are the fires of God you've come to—these are the fires of God." Vera learns that David has written a symphony, so she brings a rich playboy (Grant Stewart) and his personal concertmaster (Henry Vogel) to discuss performing it.

The playboy is outraged when he discovers that David is Jewish, so the concertmaster quits and offers to perform the work at the settlement house. Vera had fled Russia rather than face imprisonment for her revolutionist leanings. Now her father (John Blair) and stepmother (Leonora von Ottinger) appear, seeking her. The stepmother is even more anti-Semitic than the playboy, and so, it would seem, is the father. David recognizes him as the officer who headed the pogrom. Moved by his daughter's pleadings, he hands his pistol to David

and tells him to shoot him. Naturally David cannot. Later, after his symphony is performed triumphantly, David, still shaken by all the continuing hatred he has seen, asks Vera to help restore his faith in the melting pot.

The drama had been highly successful on much of its tour the previous season, but Broadway was less welcoming. Half the critics "slated" it; the other half admired it with reservations. It ran four months at the tiny new house. Its published text was dedicated to Theodore Roosevelt.

A well-worn device served Kellett Chambers's **An American Widow** (9-6-09, Hudson) poorly. The terms of her late husband's will require that his widow (Grace Filkins) must marry an American. Since she has her eyes on the coronet of an English earl (Thomas Thorne), she plots to marry "in name only" a charming young composer (Frederick Perry), divorce him, and then be free to wed whomever she chooses. Audiences knew the outcome early on.

Charles Richman's **The Revellers** (9-7-09, Maxine Elliott's) found few takers. Jack Randolph (Richman) is a potentially great lawyer frittering his life away in nightly debauches in the Tenderloin. Dorothy Dean (Ida Conquest) latches onto him and sets him back on the right path. In gratitude he marries her. Then Henry Van Cleve (George Nash), a man Randolph once nearly had killed in a barroom brawl, appears and announces he is Dorothy's husband. He is about to shoot Randolph when he learns that Randolph, like him, is a Mason. (This "turn of events was almost too much for the risibilities of Tuesday night's audience," the *Dramatic Mirror* reported.) A contrite Van Cleve confesses the marriage was a fraud and leaves the couple to live out their lives in peace. For the rest of his career, Richman confined himself to acting in other writers' plays.

Still beautiful Lillian Russell was the only reason for seeing Edmund Day's **The Widow's Might** (9-13-09, Liberty): Lillian Russell in a shopping outfit of gray satin trimmed with silver lace and lynx and with a cockade hat; Lillian Russell in a rhinestone-studded gown of clinging white satin with a pleated skirt; Lillian Russell in a blue and gold brocaded ballroom gown; and Lillian Russell in a white carriage dress and a turban of moonlight blue. All these outfits were worn by a widow whose admirers deceive her into thinking she has been paying for the clothes with money left by her late husband. That poor man actually died broke. The widow's uncle attempts to steal the money and bankrupt the most attractive of the suitors, but the widow overhears him gloating, rips up his power of attorney, and sends him on his way.

In **The Awakening of Helen Ritchie** (9-20-09, Savoy), which Charlotte Thompson took from Margaret Deland's novel, the heroine (Margaret Anglin) has fled to a small town, Old Chester, to escape an unhappy marriage. When her husband dies, the man (Eugene Ormonde) she thought would marry her turns out only to be interested in an affair. Helen has come to be fond of a local orphan (Raymond Hackett), but when she attempts to adopt him the townsfolk object, citing her uncertain past. The local doctor (John Findlay) brings her a letter from her lover, and he is anxious to see how she will respond. She responds by burning it unread. Pleased, the doctor carries in a bundle and deposits it on the sofa. The bundle proves to be the orphan. Swaying crinolines and long-out-of-fashion wallpapers of the 1860s, in which the play was set, added a period charm. Such sweet sentimentality still attracted a large number of playgoers, so the comedy-drama ran fifteen weeks.

Somerset Maugham's **The Noble Spaniard** (9-20-09, Criterion) went back a decade earlier to set its slight comic plot against an 1850 background. An impetuous Spaniard (Robert Edeson) pursues a Scottish widow (Gertrude Coghlan) so feverishly that, in order to fend him off, she claims to be married. The Spaniard's persistence finally wins out. Late in the run a curtain raiser was added. J. F. J. Archibald's **The Outpost** (10-11-09) took place in the Philippine jungles, where two American soldiers have lost their way. Both have loved the same girl back home. She has been writing to Billy (Macey Harlam), but Jeff (Edeson) has been intercepting the letters and stashing them away in his gear. Feeling guilty, he lights a match so he can locate them and give them to Billy; the match alerts the Spaniards to their whereabouts, and a bullet kills Billy. Not realizing Billy is dead, he starts to read one of the letters to him and thus learns that Billy and the girl have married secretly. Jeff has little time to absorb this news, for a second shot kills him.

Inconstant George (9-21-09, Empire) was Gladys Unger's blue-penciled version of de Flers and de Caillavet's *L'Âne de Buridan,* brought out as a vehicle for John Drew. His George, in bed and clad in blue pajamas, is confronted by a friend who has learned that George has been having affairs both with his wife and his cousin (mistress, in the French), and he demands that George choose one or the other. George selects neither. Instead he falls in love with his friend's orphaned ward (Mary Boland), whose wild behavior he finds irresistible. One

kindly, accepting critic observed that Drew's "annual impersonations of himself have an unchangeable quality compared to which most other national institutions seem shifting and unreliable" and that as a result the star had become "as beneficent as he has long been well beloved." The comedy played eleven weeks before heading out on tour.

The only other American premiere of the week was a quick flop. The farcical complications in Thompson Buchanan's **The Intruder** (9-22-09, Bijou) stemmed from an unlikely source. The daughter (Adelaide Manola) of a divorced man (Arthur Byron) makes problems for his new wife (Janet Beecher), whom she considers an interloper.

September's last premiere was **The White Sister** (9-27-09, Daly's), which Walter Hackett and F. Marion Crawford, who had died shortly before opening night, derived from the novelist's bestseller. Sister Giovanna (Viola Allen), who had taken the veil after hearing that her lover, Giovanni Severi, had died in battle, discovers he (William Farnum) is still alive. He tricks her into coming to his rooms and, despite her tearful protestations, forces her to sign a petition asking the pope to absolve her of her vows. But she is so distressed that he kills himself in remorse. She is cradling the dying Giovanni in her arms when Monsignore Saracinesca (James O'Neill) enters. At first he misconstrues the scene, but after the nun explains the situation he offers her what small consolation he can. In the original novel the lapsed nun and the soldier had married, but the dramatists changed the ending so as not to displease numerous Catholic playgoers. What critics thought of the drama was another matter. But they conceded that the mounting was eye-filling and the acting superb. Farnum made a handsome, ardent lover; O'Neill as dignified a prelate as his patent unhappiness with the role would allow. Miss Allen, whose pallid face was all her habit allowed audiences to see, brought warmth, intelligence, and credibility to her part. After a month and a half, the play went on tour.

The first two American offerings for October were deemed wholly unsatisfactory and disappeared almost as soon as they arrived. Several critics suggested that H. H. Boyd's **A Citizen's Home** (10-4-09, Majestic) might have prospered a few years earlier on the touring-melodrama circuit. A corrupt political boss (Thomas MacLarnie) kidnaps the heroine (Sara Biala), a girl who has rebuffed him and whose guardian (Adolphe Lestina) is a maverick. The boss subjects the girl to numerous indignities until he is killed by one of his cronies—the girl's long-lost father, an Italian named Donovan (Sheldon Lewis)!

Act Five : 1906–1914

In Cosmo Hamilton's **The Master Key** (10-4-09, Bijou) the heir (Orrin Johnson) to an ironworks troubled by labor strife disguises himself as a worker in order to understand his employees' thinking and bring about an equitable solution. At the same time, he finds romance with a schoolmarm (Frances Ring) who supports the workers.

Hedwig Reicher, a young German actress with a more famous actor-father, made her American debut in **On the Eve** (10-4-09, Hudson), Martha Morton's adaptation of a Leopold Kampf drama. She portrayed a dedicated revolutionary whose lover (Frederick Lewis) has drawn the straw that means he must throw the bomb killing himself and the czar's hated chief of police (Frank Keenan). She is to give the signal. She does, then commits suicide. For the most part, Miss Reicher received warm, encouraging notices, but her American career was never to take off.

Far and away the evening's biggest hit was Jerome K. Jerome's **The Passing of the Third Floor Back** (10-4-09, Maxine Elliott's). Forbes-Robertson starred as a Christ-like stranger whose short stay transforms a cheap London boardinghouse from a place of petty jealousies, petty thieveries, and petty gossip to one of hope, decency, and charity. If the witty nastiness of the first act, before the stranger's arrival, was the best part of the play, the star's luminous performance made the whole evening praiseworthy and justified its six-month run.

Joseph Medill Patterson, scion of a Chicago newspaper empire and future founder of the *New York Daily News,* collaborated with Harriet Ford to write a riveting, successful newspaper drama, **The Fourth Estate** (10-6-09, Wallack's). As presented on opening night, it told of Walter Brand (Charles Waldron), crusading editor of the *Advance,* who has been fighting civic corruption with telling effect and now is determined to bring down a venal judge, Donald Bartelmy (Charles A. Stevenson). He tricks the judge into coming to his office and accepting a bribe, just as photographers' bulbs flash. The judge's attractive daughter, Judith (Pauline Frederick), appears and pleads for Brand to kill the exposé. Then his boss, Michael Nolan (Thomas Findlay), pushed by his socially ambitious wife and daughter, orders him not to print the material. Brand disobeys the order, sets the presses going, locks himself in his office, and blows his brains out. The scene blacks out, the curtain falls, and the paper's lead article, including Brand's announcement of his own suicide, is projected on the drop. Many playgoers and critics decried the ending, and, in a sign of how audience-oriented and pliable

1909 theatre was, within a week a "happy ending" had been introduced, with Brand's offer of marriage accepted by Judith. One remarkable thing that remained unchanged was the last act's set showing a cross-section of a newspaper plant. On the right a spacious glassed-in office at the rear looks down on banks of Mergenthaler linotype machines, all in use. On the left are more makeshift offices and standup desks serving various functions. A photograph of the scene shows nineteen workers busily at their jobs.

The Debtors (10-11-09, Bijou), a two-week dud, was Margaret Mayo's translation of Franz von Schönthan's dramatization of incidents from Dickens's *Little Dorritt.* The play covered William Dorritt's prison stay, with Digby Bell as Dorritt.

Walter Prichard Eaton wrote that, since *The Witching Hour,* "Mr. Thomas's sudden preoccupation with subtle things, with immaterial forces, seemed to breed in him a new gift of imagination and a new capacity for style. . . . He has created an American drama of ideas, and into the artificial atmosphere of the theatre brought the tonic of a real psychology and the magic of mysterious things." The new Augustus Thomas play that prompted these laurels was **The Harvest Moon** (10-18-09, Garrick). Most of the more discerning critics agreed, although they chose to ignore the sometimes implausible twists and coincidences Thomas retained from an older school. All her life Dora (Adelaide Nowak) has been warned by her Aunt Cornelia (Margaret Sayres) and her supposed father, Professor Fullerton (Stephen Wright), that she must beware of following in the footsteps of her mother, who deserted her husband and died in Paris, where she had gone to learn acting. Her family's fears are realized when Dora insists on going on the stage. These ambitions are encouraged by a visitor to the Fullertons' Massachusetts home, Monsieur Vavin (George Nash), a famous French writer. By simple suggestion Vavin deceives a well man into believing he is sick, then remarks that, if he can do that to a grown man, how susceptible must a young girl be. He drives home his point after Dora and her playwright-suitor, Graham Winthrop (Thomas Russell), quarrel, by setting them to rehearsing a love scene while moonlight streams through the window. When they are reconciled and gone, he stands silhouetted in the same window, holding up a glass of wine that flashes like a prism, and says to his servant, "It is a droll God, Henri, with His vintage and His children and His harvest moon." As many playgoers no doubt suspected early on, Vivan turns out to be Dora's real father, having married her mother when Fullerton divorced her. Whether critics liked the play or not, to a man they admired Nash's brilliant yet not patently showy performance as the warm, understanding Vavin. The play, like *The Fourth Estate,* ran three months.

Refugees from the defunct touring-melodrama circuits surfaced at two houses the same evening. Henry D. Carey—later Harry Carey of Hollywood—was author, producer, and star of **Two Women and That Man** (10-18-09, Majestic), dismissed by one critic as "a conventional melodrama, conventionally done." Neil McLain's wife, Kate (Lucy Milliken), a former San Francisco music hall singer, has grown weary of life in Alaska and so is easily sweet-talked by Dave Kirke (Hector Dunn) into running off with him. The next thing Neil hears is that Kate is dead, so he marries the appropriately named Alaska (Fern Foster). Kate reappears, realizes Neil no longer cares for her, and kills herself. Neil is brought up on murder charges but acquitted. A snowstorm scene won applause, but audiences were less accepting of an auditorium doused with pine fragrance for effect.

Amelia Weed Holbrook's **The Little Terror** (10-18-09, Lincoln Square) was produced by Charles E. Blaney as a vehicle for his wife, Cecil Spooner. It centered on the hoyden of Poverty Gulch. She meets a New Yorker who is hunting nearby, and he is so impressed that he pays to have her educated in New York. In time she discovers that her benefactor is her long-lost daddy. The Lincoln Square had been serving since September as part of the subway circuit, housing plays fresh from Broadway. This was the only exception and apparently no solution to the theatre's problem. At the beginning of November the house reverted to films.

Booth Tarkington and Harry Leon Wilson had at best a squeak-by success with **Springtime** (10-19-09, Liberty), which they took from a short story by George Bronson Howard. In 1815 a very sheltered young Louisiana girl (Mabel Taliaferro) of French extraction is betrothed by her family to her cousin. Immediately afterwards she falls in love with a young American (Earle Browne), who goes off to fight with "Andy" Jackson. The boy is reported killed, and the girl goes insane. News that he is still alive restores her sanity and convinces her family to waive its objections. Although Howard Pyle was a celebrated illustrator, his sets and costumes were passed over by the critics with no more than perfunctory compliments. More attention was given to Harry Rowe Shelley's music, "which gurgles quite merrily whenever Madeleine appears, trembles whenever she is unhappy, and rumbles quite fiercely whenever there is the least allusion to a soldier." In a hint of things to come, critics

reported that the actors refused to participate in midplay curtain calls.

Probably cognizant of what happened to *The Fourth Estate,* producer Charles Frohman ordered the end of Henri Bernstein's **Israel** (10-25-09, Criterion) altered before its Broadway opening, but weakened as it was the play still packed a punch. Bernstein's look at French anti-Semitism focused on a young clubman (Graham Browne), a notorious Jew-baiter, who is so incensed that an elderly Jewish banker (Edwin Arden) has been admitted to his club that he purposely provokes an argument, which must lead to a duel. His distraught mother (Constance Collier), a duchess, sees no way out but to tell the son the truth—the Jew is his father. In the original the son puts a bullet in his own head; on Broadway he finds a distracting romance with a pretty girl (Christine Norman). The softened version ran nine weeks.

A second Frohman importation, brought in the next night, ran little more than half as long. Alfred Sutro's **The Builder of Bridges** (10-26-09, Hudson) dealt a blow to its bridge-building hero (Kyrle Bellew) with the revelation that the woman (Gladys Hansen) he is courting has let him woo her in hopes he would prevent her thieving brother (Eugene O'Brien) from going to prison.

Another English play, Stephen Phillips's blank-verse drama **Herod** (10-26-09, Lyric), drew a raft of ecstatic notices but few ticket buyers. Sumptuously mounted with a huge cast and more than fifty supers, the play recounted how Herod (William Faversham) loses the love of his wife (Julie Opp) after he has killed her brother, and how he himself goes mad after her death. While united in praise of the tragedy, many critics felt Faversham did not have the breadth and dynamics to convey a truly heroic picture.

Roy Horniman's **Idols** (11-1-09, Bijou), based on a novel by W. J. Locke, was the season's third look at Jewish-Gentile relationships. A Christian (Orlando Daly) has secretly wed a Jewish girl (Leonore Harris), whose fear of being disinherited has prompted the secrecy. When her father (Sheldon Lewis) is approached by her husband to see how amenable the old man might be, he tells the Christian he would rather see his daughter dead than married outside the faith. Shortly afterwards the old man is murdered, and suspicion falls on the husband. At his trial his wife refuses to clear up matters by stating factually that her husband was with her at the time of the murder, so the wife of his attorney, whose life the accused once had saved, perjures herself and claims he was with her at the time. The last-act setting was a splendid recreation of a paneled, Tudor-style English courtroom, peopled with more than fifty jurors, spectators, lawyers, and, of course, a bewigged judge. But weaknesses in the telling and accusations of a tinge of anti-Jewish leanings hurt the play's chances.

One week later, November 8, the New Theatre opened, ostensibly the major social and theatrical event of the season. In answer to cries for an endowed (read subsidized) theatre that would be above the pressures of commercial Broadway, many of New York's richest, most socially prominent families had joined forces to erect and underwrite the magnificent beaux arts building, which ran along Central Park West from 62nd to 63rd streets. Some of the house's physical problems became evident on its first night. It was situated snobbishly far above the main cluster of playhouses. Its seating capacity of 2300 branded it a throwback to the huge auditoriums of a century earlier, auditoriums now being replaced by more intimate playhouses. Acoustics were not the best, and the problem was aggravated by a noisy ventilating system. Many of the seats at the rear or in the upper reaches were squintingly far from the stage. And a horseshoe of boxes proclaimed its social pretensions. A "permanent" company of good but not top-flight players had been enlisted, to be supplemented in some offerings by stars. Since the opening attraction was most certainly a special occasion, Sothern and Marlowe were signed on to offer *Antony and Cleopatra*. A chorus of complaints exploded and would become louder as the season progressed. Most commentators saw the theatre as beautiful but unwieldly. By consensus, the first mounting was a disaster. Sothern's "pale and drooping" style was all wrong for the vibrant, reckless Antony, just as Miss Marlowe's flowery air of sweet ingenuousness ran counter to Shakespeare's young queen. Curiously, the honor of having opened the doomed theatre gave the team a cachet they never were to lose.

With far less ballyhoo, the season's biggest hit came in two nights later. One totally pleased critic called it "as amusing a farce as Broadway has seen for a long, long time," adding happily that it was paced at a "smart, rattling clip." Mary Roberts Rinehart and Avery Hopwood's **Seven Days** (11-10-09, Astor) was based on a story by Mrs. Rinehart. A burglar (William Eville) is seen prowling through the drawing room of a home on Riverside Drive. He hurries behind a fireplace screen as two men enter. One is James Wilson (Herbert Corthell), an artist who owns the house; the other is Dallas Brown (Allan Pollock). They are joined shortly by Dallas's

wife, Anne (Florence Reed), and Jim's new friend, Kit McNair (Georgia O'Ramey). They are about to go to dinner when a telegram arrives announcing that Jim's Aunt Selina is coming to visit him and his wife, Bella. Aunt Selina, who supports Jim generously, does not know Jim has been divorced. The couples decide this news calls for some stiff drinks. When Selina (Lucille LaVerne) appears, she thinks Kit is Bella, and they all decide to play along. Meanwhile, Jim's valet has been rushed to a hospital. Bella (Hope Latham), passing by, sees the ambulance and, thinking it might be Jim who is ill, also enters. So does an irate policeman (Jay Wilson), who tells the visitors that they and he are quarantined in the house for a week since the valet, whom he had helped remove, has smallpox.

The rest of the evening dealt with the attempts to keep Bella and Selina apart, with various frustrated escape ploys, and with a tipsy Anne's sallies into spiritualism. Supposedly alone in the room, Anne sees the firpelace screen and the cloth-covered table move seemingly of their own accord, and she is convinced this means her "control," and not the comically desperate burglar, is there, too. The first of Bella's attempts to flee lands her in a coalhole from which she emerges covered with soot. On her second attempt she is caught in a window and released only by Jim and Kit's tugging her loose, but not before she is scratched by a nail. She asks Jim if he has any peroxide. His response: "Not since you left, Bella." The play ran a year and left Hopwood, who kept careful records, $110,000 richer.

The expatriate Edward Knoblauch's **The Cottage in the Air** was the New Theatre's second offering, on November 11. It was based on a novel, *Princess Priscilla's Fortnight*, and told a story not unlike *Such a Little Queen*. A Graustarkian princess (Olive Wyndham) runs away to try to lead a simple life in England. The play was dismissed as too talky and too fey, although the author in his autobiography suggested another, probably equally valid reason for its failure: "To play a slight, light comedy, like my adaptation, in the columned huge theatre would, I felt, spell nothing but disaster. . . . A village set in the Second Act with houses and roadway leading off to the backcloth proved to be sixty feet deep. It is a well-known fact that comedy 'evaporates' in big sets." To underscore his point, Knoblauch noted that a revised version (by the novelist) succeeded when played in a small London theatre.

Just six nights later, on the 17th, the New Theatre presented a better, more powerful albeit still foreign work, John Galsworthy's **Strife.** As a concession to critical grousing about the un-American nature of the repertory, this saga of a labor leader (Albert Bruning) and a capitalist (Louis Calvert) who find they both must compromise was reset along the Ohio River.

For the second time in the month, a W. J. Locke novel was transferred unsuccessfully to the stage. Philip Littell was the dramatizer of **Septimus** (11-22-09, Hackett). George Arliss abandoned his suave, subtly sinister villains to impersonate a sweet, loving, eccentric English inventor, who agrees to marry his neighbor (Emily Stevens) after she discloses that she is pregnant by a lover who has eloped with another woman. They assume that they will eventually divorce, and, indeed, Septimus is packing to spend some years abroad when Emmy reveals how much she has grown to love him. Lines such as "Roses somehow smell sweeter on the days when letters do not come" set the tone. "Every lovable quality in Mr. Locke's creation has been grasped by Mr. Arliss," one critic rejoiced, but such praise could not whet playgoers' interest. The play went on tour after a month of disappointing trade.

Lawrence Mulligan's **His Name on the Door** (11-22-09, Bijou) folded after two weeks. A young lawyer (Wilson Melrose), who has not understood that the law firm he works with is in cahoots with the insurance company it represents to defraud policyholders, has his eyes opened when an actress (Ethel Clayton) he has befriended is cheated out of payments. His superiors try to frame him after the firms are brought into court, but shorthand notes taken by the actress's maid (Lida Hall), who has been studying to become a secretary, exonerate him.

Divorce (11-29-09, Lyric) was Stanislaus Stange's translation from the French of Paul Bourget and André Cury. The play was mounted at matinees on the same stage where Stange's American libretto for *The Chocolate Soldier* was being performed in the evenings. A good reception, it was hoped, would prompt a move to another house for a regular run. But critics savaged the work as a talky, one-sided diatribe against divorce, so a handful of matinees sufficed.

December was unusually busy and unusually productive, beginning with the only American play offered at the New Theatre during its first season. Edward Sheldon's **The Nigger** (12-4-09) opens at the pillared mansion of Philip Morrow (Guy Bates Post). He is a southern gentleman who serves his community as sheriff. Like any good southern gentleman he hates "niggers," but when one of them, crazed by liquor, commits the "usual crime," he attempts to save him from a lynch mob. (Also "usual" was the assigning of the role of the Negro to

a white man). Morrow's conniving cousin, Clifton Noyes (Ben Johnson), the president of a distillery, hopes to push Morrow into the governorship. Accordingly he advises him not to stand in the mob's way. The black is killed. Morrow has his doubts about southern justice, but his fiancée, Georgiana Byrd (Annie Russell), consoles him by pointing out "he is only a Negro." Morrow wins the governorship and almost immediately is confronted by a race riot sparked by some drunken rowdies. As a result he is sympathetic to a prohibition bill vehemently opposed by Noyes. When he tells Noyes he must sign the bill, Noyes reveals a letter suggesting that Morrow's grandmother was a slave girl. He brings in Jinny (Beverly Sitgreaves), the long-dead girl's now aged sister. At first she is vague about what happened, but on hearing the letter read she is overcome by emotion and corroborates its contents. Morrow tells Georgiana the news, and she backs away from him in shock and revulsion. Later she repents, saying she will be loyal and loving, but Morrow tells her that she cannot marry a "nigger" and that he must spend the rest of his days attempting to better the lot of his fellow blacks. He goes off to make his disgrace public.

The best thing about the play, critics agreed, was its fine stage pictures. But then, excellent if sometimes overly elaborate settings had been the New Theatre's most highly praised achievement so far. The acting was seen as good but sometimes diminished by the vastness of the house. Reviewers disagreed on the play's merits, most conceding that its melodramatic moments (Georgiana's distaste when Morrow pleads with her and tries to kiss her; Jinny's slowly flaming hysterics) were well received. The lynch scene, in which Sheldon tries to see the good and bad in both sides, must have been harrowingly effective. Even allowing for period hyperbole, Sheldon's description of the rapist's first appearance suggests the power and terror of the episode: "The negro crawls from a gap in the shrubbery. He is a huge, very black young African, his lips gray with terror, the whites of his eyes rolling. He is still panting and exhausted. His miserable clothing is torn and muddy. He does not try to rise, but crouches down near the driveway, his head bent—a horrible picture of bestial fear."

Many probably silently agreed with *Theatre*, which said that a character who pleads for more racial unity "should have had more sense" since "the fact that the negroes in the South outnumber the whites [would mean] the disappearance of the whites in the black quicksand." Critics and first-nighters doubtless were unaware of the peculiar southern dialect Sheldon wrote into his script, such as Morrow's reaction to the news that a black sympathizer would run for governor: "Senatoh Long fo' Gove'noh? The man that has da'kies at his dinnahtable? Why, you don't mean 'The White Niggah?' " How closely the players attempted to follow Sheldon's writing is not known, but at least one morning-after review reported Georgiana's first-act curtain line as "it was only a nigger." The drama was given twenty-four times as part of the repertory.

Rida Johnson Young's more commercial farce, **The Lottery Man** (12-6-09, Bijou), ran six months. Jack Wright (Cyril Scott), a newspaperman on his uppers, convinces his paper to run a lottery—at $1 a shot—with Jack himself as the prize. No sooner is the lottery under way than Jack falls in love with a pretty, well-to-do girl, Helen Heyer (Janet Beecher), who is not amused by his ploy. But Jack is so handsome that when his picture is published $300,000 pours in, his clothes are shredded by a band of lovesick maidens, and Helen herself must admit she is not unattracted by him. Unfortunately the winner would appear to be a scrawny, dour spinster (Helen Lowell). Luckily it comes to light that she found the winning ticket, which actually had been purchased by an already engaged cook. Jack consents to give them a substantial share of the lottery earnings and walks away happily with Helen. Critics welcomed the delightful escapism so deftly played by the capable Scott and the increasingly knowing Miss Beecher.

Marie Tempest, by contrast, had learned the tricks of her trade long ago, and she was still youthful and beautiful. Yet she was not able to do much with Somerset Maugham's **Penelope** (12-13-09, Lyceum), in which a young wife wins back her straying husband by looking the other way, in the face of tepid notices for the play and chillier ones for her supporting cast.

St. Elmo (12-13-09, Academy of Music), which Willard Holcomb took from Mrs. Augusta Evans's novel, was a touring melodrama, "a typical play for the masses," as one trade sheet said. Set against backgrounds such as an old blacksmith's rundown shop in the woods, a rectory garden and nearby chapel, and a dilapidating cemetery, the play recounted how the cynical hero comes to love the orphan girl who hides him from the police after a duel. The company that played New York was one of only three criss-crossing the country.

St. Elmo was not representative of the more lurid, sensation-packed touring melodramas, which, until the previous season, regularly had entertained less affluent, less demanding playgoers in cheaper houses. They were gone from Manhattan, and only Al Woods's Brooklyn theatre continued the struggle locally. But they still toured the backwaters and occasional big cities. Thus Al Woods's *Broadway After Dark* troupe was in Baltimore during the week and his *King of the Bigamists* in Philadelphia. In the hinterlands two companies of *Kidnapped for a Million* were touring Iowa and Nebraska; three companies of *The Girl from the U.S.A.* were making the rounds of Nebraska (two troupes) and Indiana. *In Wyoming* was hoping to thrill playgoers in Oregon and Washington. Three companies each of *Lena Rivers* and *Graustark,* both deemed of a slightly higher order, were playing one-night stands from Indiana to California. There were numerous others. But first-class successes were doing better. For example, five road companies of *The Climax,* three of *Paid in Full,* and three of *The Traveling Salesman* were among many attractions generally enjoying handsome business.

Two nights after the Maugham opening and *St. Elmo*'s New York appearance, the New Theatre brought out the once almost annual *School for Scandal* on the 16th. Grace George's Lady Teazle was applauded, though not wildly so. Skilled players such as Rose Coghlan and E. M. Holland had relatively minor roles and acquitted themselves well. But all in all, the consensus was the mounting represented a sad falling-off from the stylish performances of a generation earlier.

Booth Tarkington and Harry Leon Wilson's **Cameo Kirby** (12-20-09, Hackett), which starred Dustin Farnum, began the new week disappointingly. Set colorfully in 1832 New Orleans, it cast its spotlight on Eugene Kirby, a professional riverboat gambler given to wearing not only the customary frilled shirts and precious stones but, more singularly, cameos. Fleeing from a duel in which he has killed his rival, he takes refuge in a home where there are other guests. One is Adele Randall (May Buckley), who falls in love with Kirby; the other is Adele's brother, Tom (Gordon Johnstone), who recognizes Kirby as the gambler reputed to have bankrupted their father at the card table and driven him to suicide. Things look black for Kirby until he proves that the man he has just killed in the duel was the man who actually destroyed their father and that he himself, without even knowing Adele or her brother, had attempted to retrieve their father's losses. The play, originally slated for Nat Goodwin, was perceived as "watery" and "hopelessly out of date." One critic wrote that Farnum "has the definite charm of a romantic personality and plays the role with the ingratiating smile, the sweeping gesture, and the grace of manner which such a hero might be supposed to have," only to add, "He does not vary much, if any, from role to role." Another reviewer described him as "Chesterfieldian."

In *The Fortune Hunter* a character had spoken of the best country boys going off to try their luck in the city. The play that arrived the night following *Cameo Kirby's* premiere gave one idea of such men's fate. It also echoed other earlier plays of the season, as when it confronted its hero with a dark secret from his family's past. But these reverberations were ignored by 1909 critics and playgoers because **The City** (12-21-09, Lyric) was not only Clyde Fitch's last play—he had died suddenly in France during the summer, after an operation for a ruptured appendix—but was one that had made headlines during its New Haven tryout. "New Fitch Drama Makes Woman Faint," and "Daring Profanity in Play" were among the *Times*'s banners. Unlike most Fitch plays, this one's interest was meant to center on its men, and did. George Rand (A. H. Stuart) is a small-town banker who has discouraged his family from moving to the city. His daughter, Teresa (Lucile Watson), has gone to the city and traveled abroad, and what has it gotten her but an engagement to a worthless bounder, Gordon Van Vranken (Edward Emery)? His other daughter, Cicely (Mary Nash), and his son, George junior (Walter Hampden), also plead to be allowed to live in town but are sternly rebuffed. Since old man Rand has not answered his recent letters, George Frederick Hannock (Tully Marshall) barges in. He demands money, or he will reveal that Rand supported his mother for many years until her death and has even sent him checks. Rand responds, "I kept on giving to you, till I found out you were a sot and a degenerate blackguard—a drug fiend and a moral criminal." When Rand persists in his refusal, Hannock pulls out a pistol and threatens to kill himself. Fearing scandal, Rand gives him a check. After the man has left, he confides a long-kept secret to his son: Hannock is his illegitimate son and therefore George junior's brother. Overwhelmed with emotions, the elder Rand collapses and dies. George, shocked by the revelations and his father's death, nonetheless cries out triumphantly, "The City!"

Several years elapse. George lives in New York, is engaged to Eleanor Vorhees (Helen Holmes), and is to be nominated for governor. Then his world crumbles. Teresa and Gordon are about to embark on a nasty, public divorce, which through devious promises he gets them to postpone until after the election. Hannock, high on drugs or booze, appears.

He has been retained by George out of charity as a secretary; now, fearing to lose his post, he attempts to blackmail George by disclosing some of George's questionable business dealings. George is hardly moved, but then he learns from Cicely that she and Hannock were married that morning. He says that they must never consummate the marriage. When Hannock refuses to listen to his pleas, in an anguished but controlled voice, George reveals, "Cicely is your *sister!*"

Hannock: [*With a cry.*] Cicely is *what?*
George: Your sister!
Hannock: [*Sees 'red,' and nearly goes mad.*] You're a God damn liar!

It was this oath that caused the sensation in the theatre. In Fitch's subsequent directions Hannock is "*out of his mind, with an insane laugh,*" and "*sits in a chair mumbling to himself incoherently every other minute, working his hands, his mouth and his chin wet with saliva.*" In this state he kills Cicely. George understands that his political ambitions are ruined, but he is more stunned when Eleanor tells him she cannot marry a man who was not on the up and up. George's mother (Eva Vincent), who had sympathized with her children's wish to leave their small town, wails, "Oh, what the City has done for the whole of us!" And Teresa and Gordon decide to leave town and attempt a reconciliation away from New York's madness. But George exclaims, "*No! You're all wrong! Don't blame the City. It's not her fault! It's our own! What the City does is to bring out what's strongest in us. If at heart we're good, the good in us will win! If the bad is strongest, God help us!*" He vows to make good his wrongs, and this stance wins back Eleanor.

"The workmanship of this play is so fine that it would seem that he [Fitch] had reached the perfection of his artistic growth," one critic rejoiced. Another called it "the most important play that Clyde Fitch ever wrote," while a third thought that Fitch "had surpassed himself." Marshall's performance all but stole the show: "In view of the audience he administers a hypodermic injection of morphine to brace himself for the ordeal he is about to go through with George Rand. His face has the sickly pallor of the victim of dope. His hands twitch nervously and his eyes shift uneasily. He is brazen and ugly-tempered." The same critic was less complimentary about Hampden, who was to have a much longer, more distinguished career. The reviewer noted "a slight awkwardness of pose, an over-emphasis of tone and an excessive gravity of manner"—flaws that would remain with Hampden to the end. No doubt regret at Fitch's passing prompted some of the hyperbolic notices. Certainly today *The City* does not read as well as some other Fitch plays. But the notices helped the play run out the season.

David Belasco added one more success to his seemingly unbreakable parade of hits when he offered his adaptation of Pierre Wolff and Gaston Leroux's **The Lily** (12-23-09, Stuyvesant). A puritanical if selfish martinet (Charles Cartwright) has forced his elder daughter (Nance O'Neil) to renounce her suitor and become his own housekeeper, but when he attempts to interfere in the life of his younger daughter (Julia Dean), the older girl joins her in a passionate rebellion. (In Parisian slang a lily was a girl forced to remain celibate.) Under Belasco's knowing direction, Miss O'Neil used "a simple economy of means" rare for her, but with "her full, clear, bell-like voice" she made her big moment "eloquent of genuine emotion." As a result she received the sort of old-fashioned acknowledgment that must have thrilled her: "The curtain was raised again and again in response to the shouts of 'brava' that rewarded her effort."

The next Monday afternoon **Know Thyself** (12-27-09, Berkeley Lyceum), Algernon Boyesen's translation of Paul Hervieu's *Connais-toi*, began a series of matinee performances (nine in all), telling a story not unlike that of *The Lily*. A despotic old general (Arnold Daly) takes a young second wife (Muriel Hope). He is soon accusing her and also her friend (Louise Rutter) of infidelity. The wife must point out that her friend's seducer is the general's own son (Norman Thorp) and that his own absurd rigidity has driven her into another man's arms. The old man is forced to accept the truth of what he has been told. Hervieu, like so many other fine Continental playwrights, never was to be accorded much acceptance in America.

Four plays premiered that evening, but only one was a hit. (Coincidentally, the other three each ran for twenty-four showings.) The long run went to **The Bachelor's Baby** (12-27-09, Criterion), an inconsequential farce Francis Wilson wrote as a vehicle for himself. His Thomas Beech was an inveterate, open child-hater who abruptly inherits an orphan (Baby Davis) his late twin brother had adopted. She cannot tell the difference and thinks he is her daddy. Bit by bit Beech is won over, buying a carriage for the tot's rag doll, panicking when he thinks she has appendicitis, and washing out his own mouth with soap after he inadvertently uses a naughty word in front of her.

Reviews for Charles Klein's **The Next of Kin** (12-27-09, Hudson) evinced a growing disenchantment with the playwright. One commentator suggested his villains "ne'er existed on sea or land, and his politer characters generally, in their more offhand colloquial moments, seem to be quoting from bad editorials." Another went further, questioning the depth and sincerity of Klein's muckraking and asking whether he was not simply a "playmaker seizing on 'timely' themes." In this work a covetous uncle (Harry Davenport) hires a venal, well-connected lawyer (Frank Sheridan) to disinherit his niece (Hedwig Reicher). In turn the lawyer hires a mesmerist (Edwin W. Morrison) to make the girl appear insane. The plan almost succeeds, but the uncle's playboy stepson (Wallace Eddinger) falls in love with the girl, has a change of heart, and helps win her case.

For their second play of the season, **A Little Brother of the Rich** (12-27-09, Wallack's), Joseph Medill Patterson and Harriet Ford took Patterson's talked-about novel as their source. Their hero was a weakish society man (Vincent Serrano) who loves one girl (Ida Conquest) but is tricked by a scheming woman (Hilda Spong) into a compromising position and forced to marry. The wife soon runs off with another man (Henry C. Mortimer). The pair are killed in an automobile accident, so the hero is free to court his real love again. A backstage setting was praised by some as almost equal to the newspaper room in *The Fourth Estate*.

An officer's wife (Gertrude Dallas) puts on his uniform and goes out to avert a meeting between her lover (Charles Lane) and a blackmailer (Robert T. Haines). Before she arrives the blackmailer kills the lover. Suspicion falls on the woman's husband. At least one critic thought Theodore Burt Sayre's **The Commanding Officer** (12-27-09, Savoy) represented a new wave in melodrama, one in which "the heroine does not wear white, the red-costumed 'villainess' is absent, and the unities of time, place and action are fairly well followed." Most other critics simply thought the play mediocre.

Three foreign entries closed out the year. The first was Arthur Conan Doyle's **The Fires of Fate** (12-28-09, Liberty), in which an English officer (Hamilton Revelle), told he has only a year to live, goes on a trip down the Nile. His party is captured by a marauding band, and he is left for dead after a blow on the head. He regains consciousness and signals for help. The party is rescued, and the officer learns that the blow he received cured his illness. Good acting and "remarkably realistic" settings showing the banks of the Nile with palm trees, dunes, and small ruins could not substitute for a disappointing drama.

Not yet two months old, the New Theatre was coming in for growingly dyspeptic criticism. Its new double bill failed to still the clamor. Frederick Fenn and Richard Pryce's **Liz the Mother** (12-30-09) told of a cockney girl (Annie Russell) who refuses to trade her illegitimate baby for a dead one, although it might mean her baby would receive a better upbringing. The outcry against the play was so vociferous that it was pulled after its first performance. The bill's longer offering was Rudolph Besier's **Don**. Its title figure was a quixotic young man (Matheson Lang)—thus his nickname and the title—who jeopardizes his own marriage plans by innocently spending the night with a young lady (Thais Lawton) whom he is helping flee an abusive husband. The play's reception was courteous but not enthusiastic.

Booth Tarkington and Harry Leon Wilson's third play of the season was 1910's first hit, albeit a modest one. Walter Prichard Eaton, speaking for many of his fellow critics, tagged **Your Humble Servant** (1-3-10, Garrick) as "fluff" and "spun-sugar," but fortunately for everyone it had been written as a vehicle for a larger-than-life player, Otis Skinner. Skinner portrayed "an actor of the old bad school," Lafayette Towers, whose barnstorming troupe is playing *The Bandit's Bride* in Weedsport. They are playing it to a virtually empty house because a burlesque troupe had preceded them and gobbled up the tank town's small ration of theatre money. A sheriff has seized the company's trunks (but not without being drafted into replacing a disabled player in a bit part) after the troupe's manager, Isidore Blum (A. G. Andrews), absconds with the meager takings. Towers has been grooming his lovely leading lady, Margaret Druce (Izetta Jewell), for stardom. He loves her but has a potent rival in Dick Prentice (Alfred Hudson, Jr.), a handsome, rich young man testing theatrical waters over his family's opposition. Prentice abandons the troupe when hard times prove more than he can take. After the company folds, Towers and Margaret accept work performing at a society party. The party turns out to be at the Prentice home. Margaret discourages any further advances of Prentice by telling him she loves Towers. Towers overhears, forcing Margaret to say she made the statement merely to rebuff Prentice. Blum, a big winner at the races, stars Margaret in a Broadway show. She is a hit. Blum's quiet recitation of all Towers has done for her makes the girl realize she does love him after all.

Eaton noted of Skinner, "There was always the touch of the barn-stormer of the comic cuts and popular tradition in his speech and attitude, but never did he quite let go a suggestion of underlying sincerity and even poetry." Thus, sent out by his fellow lodgers to make a small purchase, "he put on his rusty frock-coat and pot hat, he stuck a paper flower in his button-hole, he swung a cane under his arm, drew himself up erect and remarked, 'As for Lord Roseberry's policies, I care not for them. If Lady Huntington calls, say that I have gone on a yachting trip to the Solent. In the meantime, do not be surprised to receive a packet from Third Avenue'; and he strutted out." Later, forced to accept a bit part in a road company, he rationalizes that he would rather paint a perfect miniature than a tasteless large canvas.

Laurence Irving found less favor when he offered his translation of Eugène Brieux's *Les Hannetons* as **The Affinity** (1-3-10, Comedy). The play, which dealt with two unsuited people attempting to live together, had been offered some months earlier at special matinees under the less appealing title *The Incubus*.

Playgoers, apparently agreeing with the critic who complained that "too many plays of the Frozen North have seen production," stayed away in droves from **The Barrier** (1-10-10, New Amsterdam), which Eugene W. Presbrey dramatized from a Rex Beach novel. John Gale (Theodore Roberts) has a daughter named Necia (Florence Rockwell), who believes she is a half-breed and therefore cannot marry Captain Burrell (James B. Durkin). Gale is forced to tell her the truth. Gale had once loved a woman who married another man, Dan Stark. Stark (W. S. Hart) abused her, killed her, and pinned the murder on Gale. Gale was forced to flee to Alaska, taking the Starks' baby with him. Stark's convenient appearance and confession resolve matters. Whatever critics thought of the play, they admired Roberts's performance. One wrote, "If the character were one that we could respect, Mr. Theodore Roberts' acting would count as the most distinguished achievement of his career." But poor Roberts, so universally acclaimed, never was to find the key to major stardom. *The Barrier* was removed after three weeks.

The next Monday night, the 17th, the Ben Greet Players began a three-month stand at the Garden. Their repertory ranged from Shakespeare and Marlowe to Goldsmith, Sheridan, and Gilbert, with two new works thrown in for good measure. The first, Katrina Trask's **The Little Town of Bethlehem** (1-17-10, Garden), set the love story of a Roman lady and a Greek poet against a background of the Nativity. The second, **Three Wonder Tales** (3-28-10), was

Act Five : 1906–1914

Rose Meller O'Neil's theatricalization of Hawthorne's *The Wonder Book.*

The following night a second dramatized novel was offered. **A Lucky Star** (1-19-10, Hudson) was C. N. and A. M. Williamson's *The Motor Chaperon* reworked by Anne Crawford Flexner. Ronald Lester Starr (William Collier), a young American painter, invites two pretty girls to join him cruising Dutch canals in a houseboat he has rented. They accept, providing he brings along a chaperone. He tells them he will wire his Scottish aunt, and when she proves unavailable he advertises for any woman who speaks English with a Scottish burr. He is swamped with applicants, finally taking on a nice, gray-haired, bespectacled lady (Marjorie Wood). Starr's guests turn out to have two irresistible male suitors. However, just as Starr is most despondent the fake aunt pulls off her wig, removes her glasses, and reveals herself as quite a beauty. The "crisp, dry humor of the comedian and the snappy manner in which he turns the dialogue to his advantage" elicited laughs, especially "with Mr. Collier in his funniest vein teaching the bogus aunt to speak with a Scotch burr, horrifying her at the thought of the awful meaning of the words 'hoot Mon' . . . [and] trying to dislodge the unwelcome guests from their chairs beside the girls." Collier's skill propelled the comedy into a three-month run.

One of the season's shortest runs—13 performances—went to one of the season's most interesting plays, William Vaughn Moody's **The Faith Healer** (1-19-10, Savoy). Henry Miller had tried out the play nearly a year earlier, at which time it had been a complete failure. However, he knew that Moody was dying and felt he owed the playwright a New York hearing. He himself assumed the role of Ulrich Michaelis, a faith healer who travels with a mute Hopi Indian boy named Lazarus (James Hagan), whom he had restored to life. He comes to the "decayed" home of skeptical Matthew Beeler (Harold Russell) and makes Matthew's crippled wife, Mary (Mabel Bert), walk again. He also falls in love with the Beelers' niece, Rhoda (Jessie Bonstelle): "All my life long I have known you, and fled from you. I have heard you singing on the hills of sleep and have fled from you into the waking day. I have seen you in the spring forest, dancing and throwing your webs of sunlight to snare me; on moonlit mountains, laughing and calling; in the streets of crowded cities, beckoning and disappearing in the crowd—and everywhere I have fled from you, holding above my head the sign of God's power in me, my gift and my mission." But now that he has found her, his gifts seemingly

have deserted him. A cynical young doctor (Edward See), not unhappy at Michaelis's failure, is willing to rationalize the healer's success and subsequent loss of ability. A local minister (Theodore Friebus) is less understanding or forgiving. Then Rhoda confesses she has had an affair with the doctor. On Easter morning Michaelis wrestles with himself and comes to recognize he can love Rhoda regardless of her past lapses. The realization restores his power, and he saves the dying baby of a mother (Laura Hope Crews) who has come to plead with him. He tells Rhoda, "You needed what the whole world needs—healing, healing, and as I rose to meet that need, the power that I had lost poured back into my soul." Critics praised the players but were unusually harsh on the play. Moody died the following October.

Since Frederic Arnold Kummer's **Mr. Buttles** (1-20-10, Weber's) opened one night later and closed on the same evening as *The Faith Healer,* only twelve audiences saw the resourceful butler (Henry E. Dixey) turn his impecunious master's home into a hostelry.

Trial matinees were a commonplace of the era, but one of the few to merit special notice here was **The Wishing Ring** (1-20-10, Daly's). The Shuberts produced the work, which, with its story of an impoverished pastor's daughter who marries a wealthy young man, was looked on as a Cinderella-ish fairy tale. What made the event of interest was that it was the first time an Owen Davis play was offered on a first-class stage. Although it later enjoyed a moderately successful road tour, its star, Marguerite Clark, and its director, Cecil B. de Mille, were soon heading west to filmland.

Legend has it that Paul Armstrong wrote **Alias Jimmy Valentine** (1-21-10, Wallack's) at the suggestion of George Tyler of Liebler and Co., that he wrote it in a single weekend, and that it was on the boards two weeks later. True or not, this dramatization of O. Henry's "A Retrieved Reformation" was one of the decade's most memorable successes. Jimmy Valentine, a notorious safecracker, had once saved Rose Lane (Laurette Taylor) from an abusive stranger on a train, and she in turn had later helped get him out of Sing Sing, where he was serving time for a crime he insisted he had not committed. Of course, he had. But on his release he had taken the name of Lee Randall (H. B. Warner) and sincerely determined to reform. Rose has obtained work for him at her father's bank as a cashier and fallen in love with him. However, Detective Doyle (Frank Monroe) has been relentlessly pursuing Valentine for a Massachusetts burglary. He confronts Randall, who glibly and skillfully provides a seemingly irrefutable alibi. The detective has just begun to leave when a hysterical watchman (Earle Browne) runs in, announcing that the banker's younger daughter Kitty (Alma Sedley), has locked herself in the bank's new vault and the combination has not been set. Unless the massive door can be opened soon, the tot will die.

Randall is caught in a dilemma. Deciding that the youngster's life is worth more than his freedom, he rushes to open the safe. "One of the tensest situations imaginable is produced when the scene magically changes to the cellar of the bank, and Randall accompanied by the bank watchman is seen in a state of feverish excitement working in the semi gloom to open the combination by the phenomenal sense of feeling with which nature has endowed him. From an open door the sleuth is seen watching the efforts of his prey, while in another door, contemplating the scene, stands Rose." Having opened the vault and saved the child, Randall resignedly walks toward the detective to surrender. But Doyle snarls, "For the sake of my self-respect, I hope you didn't think I fell for that alibi story of yours," and he turns and walks out of Randall's life. The producers elevated the suavely handsome Warner to stardom for his playing, a stardom he would cling to without much distinction until he left the stage with the coming of sound films. However, more than one review contained a line such as "But he had to divide honors with Laurette Taylor, who was charming." The play ran out the season.

Audiences had not seen a good shipboard setting since the houseboat in *A Lucky Star,* nearly a week before. But the deck and interior of a yacht, the *Firefly,* were magnificently recreated in Frank Stanton's comedy **The Inferior Sex** (1-24-10, Daly's). Charles Winslow (Arthur Byron) specializes in writing books showing why women are indisputably the weaker sex. He writes them on his yacht, on which no weak creature is allowed. He is reluctant to make an exception even when a woman is spotted unconscious in a lifeboat. He finally accedes to his crew's protestations and brings her aboard. She turns out to be Eva Addison (Maxine Elliott). Winslow will not head back to land for her nor make any concessions. His rudeness finally leads her to goad the crew into mutiny, but when they soon turn against her she tricks them into going below, then secures the hatches against them. At this point Winslow is incapacitated by the flu. She runs the ship, with some help from Winslow's valet (O. B. Clarence), until an ocean liner comes alongside to pick her up. As she leaves, Winslow asks for her address.

Miss Elliott's vehicle ran eight weeks; Billie Burke's ran nine. Somerset Maugham's third play of the season, **Mrs. Dot** (1-24-10, Lyceum), was a "rippling, shallow but peculiarly entertaining" comedy about a pretty, rich widow who lures the man (Julian L'Estrange) she loves away from a young girl he once foolishly promised to marry. Some reviewers thought Miss Burke's pert, redheaded good looks exceeded her talents, but playgoers couldn't have cared less.

Sothern and Marlowe, smarting from their failure in *Antony and Cleopatra,* had resigned from the New Theatre, so the house's second Shakespeare mounting, *Twelfth Night,* brought out on the 26th, was cast with some lesser players. Only Annie Russell as Viola and possibly Oswald Yorke as Malvolio were superior, and yet they, too, had their drawbacks. Miss Russell, for example, was extolled for her grace and sweetness but seen to lack a contagious sprightliness and gift for poetry. As usual, the settings were opulent, even overwhelming, beginning with a seacoast of Illyria that depicted a moonlit sky reflected on waters seen between "frowning rocks in the darkness."

A low-budget play, Cora Maynard's **The Watcher** (1-27-10, Comedy), discovered cheap running costs to be no help in the face of slighting notices. The watcher, never seen, was the dead mother of Vivian Kent (Percy Haswell), whose unhappy sister-in-law (Cathrine Countiss) had once spurned Vivian's suitor (Thurlow Bergen) in favor of Vivian's brother (John Emerson) and now, finding that her husband is a worthless drunkard and gambler, attempts to compromise her old suitor and prevent his marrying Vivian. The dead mother's presence is felt, and things veer toward a happy solution.

Frank Keenan, like Theodore Roberts, was a widely admired actor who many thought never reached the heights his fine character acting entitled him to. He was elevated briefly to stardom in a play appropriately called **The Heights** (1-31-10, Savoy), the maiden work of William Anthony McGuire, who would become a dependable hack on Broadway and write one superior comedy. With its "extraordinarily realistic" snowstorm and its scene in which a boulder rolls down and wrecks a mountain hut, the new play recalled many a beloved 19th-century melodrama. Curiously, the "star" did not appear until the second act. In the first act a girl (Willette Kershaw) refuses to accept that men can be importunate, and so runs away. She runs to the Alps, where she finds shelter in the hut of an embittered recluse (Keenan). When he proves no different from other men and attempts to make love to her, she threatens to kill herself. He later tells her that her virtue has restored his faith in humanity, and when her lover (Frank Mills) comes seeking her, the hermit joins their hands and wishes them a happy life. The drama lasted only two weeks.

Most critics lauded the brilliant craftsmanship in Pinero's **Mid-Channel** (1-31-10, Empire) but questioned whether theatregoers would find its unpleasantness palatable. They did, thanks in good measure to Ethel Barrymore. "Her art," one reviewer observed, "like her figure, has rounded out, and both show marked improvement. Her Zoë Blundell has sparkle and charm, the charm of the old young Ethel Barrymore, combined with a nervous intensity, a fire, a pathos, which, though it may have been latent, has not been called forth before." Zoë and her husband (Charles Waldron) have reached "the shoals of mid-channel" in their marriage, so they separate, and he and she both have flings. But while she forgives his, he will not forgive hers. Zoë jumps off a balcony. The Frohman production did three months of excellent business as part of an extended tour of major cities.

Another great producer had less to be happy about. *Theatre* began its notice of Eugene Walter's **Just a Wife** (2-1-10, Belasco) noting, "The theatregoer has grown so accustomed to Belasco triumphs that when that clever producer fails to hit the bull's-eye squarely in the center the disappointment is looked upon almost in the light of a personal injury." Some critics saw a literary value—"literary dignity," one called it—lacking in Walter's earlier works but nonetheless lamented a falling away in theatricality. John Emerson (Edmund Breese) married a poor but respectable southern girl, Mary Ashby (Charlotte Walker), to cover up his long affair with the widowed Eleanor Lathrop (Amelia Gardner). Emerson first met Eleanor when he was an insignificant clerk, and he credits her with pushing him to the top of the business ladder. After his marriage he still spent most of his time at his office or with Eleanor. Now Eleanor senses that her hold on Emerson is slipping, so she comes to his house for a facedown. However, it is Mary who forcefully, but not without compassion, tells her that she must pay the price of aging. Mary then sends Emerson packing, saying, "Come to me, John, when you have time to be something more than a man of business cares and responsibilities and can meet me with love in your heart. I won't say that I shall be waiting for you, but your chance will be as good as any other man's."

Those "infinite Belascan touches that make even the commonplace seem interesting and the artificial seem lifelike" included the intermittent "off-stage

chug-chug of an automobile" during much of one act. Additional laudatory notices went to Miss Walker, Walter's first wife. Walter himself came in for special praise two months later when Laurence Irving addressed a dinner given in honor of Forbes-Robertson at the Lotos Club. He placed Walter on a par with "Rostand in France, and Shaw in England," hailing their infusion of fresh blood into playwriting. We must, he told his audience, "keep close to life, and we must examine the dark corners before we can illuminate the lighter ones." By that time, however, *Just a Wife* was limping to the end of its ten-week run.

Henry W. Savage had a much bigger hit when he presented Alexandre Bisson's Paris hit *La Femme X* as **Madame X** (2-2-10, New Amsterdam), translated by John N. Raphael and then "Americanized" by William Henry Wright. The so-called Americanization still retained the play's original Parisian setting. Dorothy Donnelly starred as a degenerate woman brought to trial for her lover's murder. It soon develops that the judge (Robert Drouet) is the husband who years before disowned her because she had an affair and that the young prosecuting attorney is her son (William Elliott). The play was a real tearjerker: "Never was there such snivelling. Even the men got the habit and were asking for their handkerchiefs back before the final curtain." Both Miss Donnelly and Elliott (soon to be Belasco's son-in-law) received rave notices, too. But oddly enough, though it was only the beginning of February, this was the season's last hit. Till now the season had been almost as good as, possibly equal to, the prior season. Suddenly the theatrical world seemed to collapse. There would be a few interesting, worthwhile mountings during the remaining four months, but only one play would pull within an appreciable distance of the 100-performance mark.

In Ernest Poole's short-lived **None So Blind** (2-3-10, Hackett), the hero (John Mason) is a bridge builder who has lost his sight and left the Rockies to have an eye operation in the East. Learning that his wife (Mabel Roebuck) has come under the seductive influence of a "literary man" (Walter Hale), he pretends on his return that the operation has been a failure. The final act "discloses a magnificent view of the snow-capped crests of the Rocky Mountains, bathed in a flood of light from the rising sun, with the foreground veiled in the mists of early dawn. The mists disperse slowly and disclose John Howe seated like a statue on a high rock gazing intently into the distance." He has come there to avoid seeing his wife run away with her new friend. But the wife, her own eyes having been opened, climbs the rock and rejoins her husband.

Paul Gavault and Robert Charvay's *L'Enfant du miracle* was bowdlerized for Broadway by Maurice Campbell as **Where There's a Will** (2-7-10, Weber's). Farcical complications arise after a widow (May Buckley) learns she cannot inherit her late husband's estate unless she produces an heir. Campbell, who served as his own producer, was the husband of Henrietta Crosman, but neither she nor any other top-drawer player was cast for the piece, which nevertheless ran eight weeks.

That same evening saw Sothern and Marlowe open a month-long stand at the Academy of Music. Their repertory included *Romeo and Juliet, The Taming of the Shrew, The Merchant of Venice, Hamlet, As You Like It,* and, perhaps somewhat tactlessly, *Twelfth Night,* which meant they were in direct competition with the mounting at the New Theatre, so recently and so abruptly deserted by them. But business was good enough to warrant a two-week return in late March.

Rachel Crothers's **A Man's World** (2-8-10, Comedy) was a very superior play, too forthright to win more than a modicum of success (nine weeks). It came to New York after a four-month tour, pleading one of Miss Crothers's favorite themes—the need to abolish a double standard. Frank Ware (Mary Mannering), a young lady who lives in a Greenwhich Village boardinghouse and writes novels about life on the East Side, has told newspaperman Malcolm Gaskell (Charles Richman) that he is "the one man" in her life, so he is relieved to learn that the little illegitimate boy (Master Mark Short) she has raised is not her child. He could not have forgiven her for that: "Man sets the standard for woman. He knows she's better than he is and he demands that she be—and if she isn't she's got to suffer for it. That's the whole business in a nut shell—and you know it." But events soon disclose that Gaskell himself is the boy's father. Gaskell sees nothing wrong in that, thus infuriating Frank.

Frank: Oh, I want to forgive you. If you could only see. If your soul could only see. Oh, dear God! Malcolm, tell me, tell me you know it was wrong—that you'd give your life to make it right. Say that you know this thing was a crime.

Gaskell: No! Don't try to hold me to account by a standard that doesn't exist. Don't measure me by your theories. If you love me you'll stand on that and forget everything else.

Frank: I can't. I can't.

Gaskell: I'm not a man to beg, Frank. Do you want me to go? Is that it? Is this the end?

Frank: There's nothing else.

The awkwardly long arm of coincidence—Frank had adopted the boy after his mother had died in her arms in Paris—bothered some critics, but, that flaw aside, most were unstinting in their praise of the play. They lauded "its searching truth of feminine psychology, its air of quiet but studied realism, its obvious significance as a comment on the feminist movement of the day." They also admired the playwright's skilled delineation of secondary figures. There was the mercurial, embittered singer (Ruth Holt Boucicault), who warns, "You can't stir up any man's life. You're lucky if it looks right on top." And, most touching, there was the pathetic, talentless painter (Helen Ormsbee), whose exhibition no one came to: "No man has ever asked me to marry him. I've never had a beau—a real beau—in my life. I—I've always been superfluous and plain. Absolutely superfluous. I'm not necessary to one single human being. I'm just one of those everlasting women that the world is full of. There's nobody to take care of me and I'm simply not capable of taking care of myself. . . . Oh, I can't bear it, Frank. I can't bear it! I often wish I were pretty and bad and could have my fling and die."

There were fewer takers for the latest addition to the New Theatre's repertory, H. Wiers-Jenssen's **The Witch** (2-14-10). Although a Danish work, it used the background of witch-hunting Salem for its gloomy tale of a young wife (Bertha Kalish) who falls in love with her elderly husband's son (Guy Bates Post).

Some idea of how vital 1910 theatre was could be gauged by an article appearing on the same page of the *Dramatic Mirror* as its review of *The Witch.* Its headline announced that producer William A. Brady had twelve new plays either in rehearsal or about to go into production. Not all of these plays reached Broadway. One or two may even have been a press agent's fantasy. But the article could not have had credibility had it not hewed closely to contemporary theatrical realities.

Except for working on musical librettos, that gadfly of bygone seasons, Sydney Rosenfeld, had not been heard from for several years. The consensus was that his latest work, **Children of Destiny** (2-21-10, Savoy), wasn't worth the wait. It told of a girl (Laura Nelson Hall) who learns she is illegitimate and so loses her fiancé. She runs off to lead a debauched life in Monte Carlo only to find redemption there in love.

Mr. and Mrs. Daventry (2-23-10, Hackett) was bruited to have been the brainchild of Oscar Wilde, written to a lesser or greater extent by Frank Harris after Wilde accepted that the scandal attached to him made presentation of any new work by him impossible. It told of a philandering husband (Arthur Maude) who has refused to grant his wife (Constance Crawley) a divorce, hoping for a reconciliation, but who kills himself after learning she is pregnant by her lover (Edwin August). The play closed after five performances.

"One should never give a woman anything she can't wear in the evening" and "Nothing ages like happiness" were famous Wilde epigrams, but they were heard again in the play rushed in to fill the stage left empty by the sudden departure of *Mr. and Mrs. Daventry.* On opening night playwright Preston Gibson read a prepared statement confessing that some of the lines in **The Turning Point** (2-28-10, Hackett) had been lifted from Wilde but insisting they amounted to no more than fifty words. The epigrams filched by the socially prominent young author found their way into a story detailing how a villainous promoter (Cuyler Hastings), straight out of the now defunct touring melodrama, connives but fails to take over a rich Virginia mine. Just before the play closed, Gibson added a one-acter to the bill, **The Vacuum** (3-24-10), which he based on Balzac's "La Grande Bretêche." In his modernized version an inventor realizes his wife's lover has hidden himself in a vacuum closet, so he lets out the air, thereby killing the man.

The New Theatre's next entry was its second Danish novelty in a row, Sophus Michaelis's **A Son of the People** (2-28-10). John Mason recently had been enlisted in the company, and he portrayed a leader of the French Revolution who knowingly betrays his cause and sacrifices his life to allow a newlywed nobleman to escape.

No one was given credit, or blame as it turned out, for the adaptation of Gustav Kadelburg's **The Girl He Couldn't Leave Behind Him** (3-9-10, Garrick) in which a young man (Vincent Serrano) brings an evening's worth of problems on himself by promising a seductive Spanish dancer (Hattie Williams) that he will devote one day every year to her even after his forthcoming marriage. William Collier, who served as producer and director, could not inject fun into the affair, nor could the attractive Miss Williams's musical comedy savvy help. The best notices went to Zelda Sears as the battle-axe mother-in-law.

A double bill was the latest in the increasingly telltale outpouring of mountings at the New Theatre. The curtain raiser was the fourth act of Ibsen's **Brand** (3-14-10), in which the hero (Lee Baker) forces his wife (Annie Russell) to give their dead child's clothes to save a gypsy's baby. The sacrifice breaks the wife's heart. In the main offering,

Maurice Maeterlinck's **Sister Beatrice,** the Virgin Mary takes the place of a nun (Edith Wynne Matthison) who has left her convent to enjoy the world. The translation was by Edward Knoblauch.

Manhattanites who wanted to see a touring play not destined for Broadway had only to take a subway to Brooklyn to watch Robert M. Baker's **Beverly** (3-14-10, Grand, Brooklyn), taken from George Barr McCutcheon's *Beverly of Graustark.* Its heroine, an American girl visiting Graustark, falls into the hands of outlaws led by an exiled prince. She later saves the prince's life, and when he is recalled to court he marries her. Neither the players nor settings were Broadway caliber, but they were apparently good enough to please less demanding audiences.

Henri Bernstein's Paris hits seemed to many playgoers to suffer a sea change. This certainly held true when his *La Rafale* was presented to Americans as **The Whirlwind** (3-23-10, Daly's), which marked the English-speaking debut of a petite, slightly dumpy actress with brownish-red hair, Marietta Olly, a Viennese favorite. She played an unfaithful wife whose desperate attempt to save her lover from bankruptcy and disgrace is forestalled by his suicide. Neither the play nor the debutante was accorded much of a welcome.

A revival of Ibsen's *Pillars of Society* at the Lyceum on the 28th clearly had limited appeal, but it was greatly to the liking of most discerning critics, thanks primarily to Mrs. Fiske and Holbrook Blinn. A few gently chastised Blinn for being "too dignified, too urbane," but there was little to fault in Mrs. Fiske's interpretation of Lona, a relatively secondary role. Walter Prichard Eaton especially rejoiced at the actors' joint playing in Bernick's last-act confession: "Here the better and more convincing was the acting of Mr. Blinn, of course the more convincing became the by-play of Mrs. Fiske. She sat quite still, on her face the joy of her spiritual victory over his baser nature writing itself out most marvellously and finally expressing itself in a little smothered sob of triumphant love which no other American actress would have invented, or could have executed if she had."

Whether financial or aesthetic considerations prompted it, the troubled New Theatre closed its season by discarding its penchant for heavy settings and offering *A Winter's Tale,* also on the 28th, with only a few platforms and some curtains as scenery. The theatre thus stumbled on what many considered its finest achievement. Put on their mettle, the players, including Edith Wynne Matthison (Hermione), Leah Bateman-Hunter (Perdita), E. M.

Holland (Old Shepherd), Ferdinand Gottschalk (Clown), Henry Kolker (Leontes), and Albert Bruning (Autolycus), showed what fine ensemble work they were capable of. But it would be some years before the idea of truly simplifying Shakespearean mountings caught on.

The story of **The Lady from Lobster Square** (4-4-10, Weber's), a sanitized version of Feydeau's *Un Fil à la patte,* turned inside out the plot of *The Girl He Couldn't Leave Behind Him.* In this case problems arise when a young man (Fritz Williams) about to be married attempts to dissociate himself from a music hall singer (Georgia Caine). Miss Caine was a favorite in musical comedy, and Lobster Square was a pet name for Times Square, with all its lobster houses, but neither lyric-theatre favorites nor fashionable nicknames could lure audiences.

The lone late-season play to come anywhere near a 100-performance run—chalking up 88 showings— was Porter Emerson Browne's **The Spendthrift** (4-11-10, Hudson). It did so by taking an unpleasant theme and treating it lightly. Frances Ward (Thais Magrane) is a selfish, irresponsible wife, refusing to have children and spending so freely that she drives her husband, Richard (Edmund Breese), to the verge of bankruptcy. To avert humiliation she borrows from a notorious rake, Suffern Thorpe (Robert Cain), the money needed to save her husband. At first Ward believes his wife has accepted the money from her millionaire aunt (Mattie Ferguson), but when he discovers the truth he enters his wife's bedroom late at night, wakes up the frightened woman, and demands she have Thorpe come over immediately. He confronts Thorpe with a pistol, but after Thorpe confesses he lent Mrs. Ward money in a losing gamble on her virtue, Ward merely shoots into the rug and leaves. The furious wife walks out on her husband, but a reconciliation follows. Typical of Browne's approach was his characterization of the aunt, whom many saw as patterned after the infamous Hetty Green. But whereas the celebrated rich miser was generally detested, Browne made the aunt thoughtful and amusing.

Few plays received as much advance ballyhoo as René Fauchois's French success **Beethoven** (4-11-10, New)—all to no avail. A huge cast of good but not top-drawer players, sumptuous settings, and a symphony orchestra behind the scenes failed to interest playgoers in this episodic recreation of the composer's life. Among the incidents recalled were his rededication of his Third Symphony and his alleged romance with Countess Guicciardi. A Ziegfeldian touch had his nine symphonies represented by nine beautiful showgirls. The production was not part of the New Theatre's regular program but was mounted with the hopes of keeping the expensive theatre lit until the hot weather. Instead the play was withdrawn after three weeks.

Mrs. Fiske concluded her brief New York season with a revival of Hauptmann's *Hannele* at the Lyceum on the 11th. Amazingly, the star elected to play the child who is the central figure; perhaps more amazing, critics felt she carried it off triumphantly. (Coincidentally, two groups, the American Dramatic Guild and the Socialist Dramatic Movement, co-presented the New York premiere of Hauptmann's *Einsame Menschen* as **Lonely Lives** (4-10-10, Hackett) for a single performance.) Coupled with *Hannele* was Arthur Schnitzler's **The Green Cockatoo,** a Pagliacci-like story set against the French Revolution.

Two adaptations from the French followed. Laurence Irving was both translator and star of Eugène Brieux's **The Three Daughters of Monsieur Dupont** (4-13-10, Comedy), the story of a scheming bourgeois who, having written off one daughter as a religious spinster and a second as an outcast, forces his last child into an unhappy marriage.

Lulu's Husbands (4-14-10, Maxine Elliott's), which Thompson Buchanan took from Maurice Soulié and Henri de Gorsse's *Le Mari de Loulou,* ran twice as long, forty-two performances. Lulu (Mabel Barrison), a music hall star, answers the ad of a man (Edward Heron) seeking a bride by sending him her own name but the picture of a married friend (Fanchon Campbell), unaware that the friend is eloping with her lover (Robert Dempster). With the friend's perturbed husband (Harry Conor) in pursuit, the characters embark on a gay merry-go-round of a chase.

New York's fast-swelling ranks of new playhouses grew a bit larger with the addition of a tiny theatre virtually next door to Maxine Elliott's. At the start it was known as Nazimova's 39th Street Theatre. Fittingly, Nazimova was starred in its opening attraction on the 18th, a revival of Isben's *Little Eyolf.* Her performance thrilled most critics. In the first act she perfectly conveyed Rita's repressed, feline sexuality. She delivered her speech about Allmers's not tasting champagne "lying prone on a couch, with her figure quivering, her nostrils dilating, her fingers twitching, and nervous twinges playing about her mouth . . . a picture of desire not soon to be forgotten." And she "formed a thrilling picture of transfixed horror as she stood by the curtained door, on realizing that little Eyolf has been drowned." But her later remorse was equally well done, leading to the memorable final scene: "Standing on the cliff in the moonlight, filled with a soft joy that she is to keep her husband as well as the joy of finding a work in the world to make her forget, or to atone for, the 'great staring eyes,' she slowly lifted her face and then her hand to the heavens; and the curtain descended on her deep, sweet voice speaking the one word of thanks and on a picture that expressed to the eye with wonderful clarity the mood of the conclusion." The revival ran for six weeks.

In contrast to the small, dark, exotic Nazimova, little Mabel Taliaferro had "the big, wondering, child-eyes and the serious voice and old-fashioned ways that built a vast following for Maggie Mitchell years ago." But whatever following the younger actress had built, it would not support her when she appeared in Edward Peple's **The Call of the Cricket** (4-19-10, Belasco)—a title that obviously brought Maggie Mitchell back to mind. Rosalie is a child of nature from Kentucky horse country who comes to New York to visit her socialite friend, Fannie Marsh (Lillian Thatcher), and falls in love with Fannie's brother, Norman (Everett Butterfield). This last development displeases Norman's reptilian fiancée, Rena (Norma Mitchall). After rescuing Rosalie, who has fallen overboard on a yachting trip (which allowed for another of the season's voguish ship settings), Norman finds he reciprocates her feelings. They are married. After a time, however, Norman begins to miss the more scintillating Rena, and the marriage heads for the rocks. Rosalie's Uncle Ben (Joseph Brennan) comes to take her home. The realization that he will lose her shocks Norman into changing his mind, and he promises to be loyal. Rosalie's initial response is to reject Norman's plea, but after he sinks into a chair and buries his head in his hands she comes and strokes him on the temples. He looks up, very much suprised, and the youngsters fall into each other's arms. The star not only had to deal with thumbs-down notices for her vehicle but to read review upon review singling out William Harrigan for special praise. He played a young man courting Fannie and wildly endeavoring to come up with an invention that will make him rich enough to win her family's approval. With all this, Broadway cognoscenti smiled knowingly when the play closed after two weeks, ostensibly because of the star's sudden illness.

Not long ago Broadway seasons regularly concluded with a series of revivals. That practice had all but withered, but the current season did welcome two old plays in its waning weeks. And welcome is the word. The absurdly faddist notion that last year's success is old hat this year had not yet taken hold. The first to arrive was Charles Frohman's loving resurrection of Robertson's *Caste* at the Empire on the 25th. A sterling cast included Marie Tempest as Polly, Elsie Ferguson as Esther, Edwin Arden as George, and G. P. Huntley as Eccles. The play ran into June.

Not so **The Girl with the Whooping Cough** (4-25-10, New York), taken by Stanislaus Stange from a mercifully unidentified French play and unmercifully damned by the critics. It focused on a girl (Valeska Suratt) who spreads her germs to every man she kisses—and she kisses many of them. The girl is hauled into court in the last act, and since Miss Suratt was better known on vaudeville and musical stages the courtroom served as a showcase for her turns. The play's run was brief—three weeks—but it confirmed Al Woods's position as a producer of first-class attractions.

Alongside the *Dramatic Mirror*'s review of the farce was its weekly listing of current attractions. The list bore witness to how many playhouses that Woods, and even more prestigious producers, had once used had gone over to films. No fewer than seven were showing silent films, including the venerable 14th Street Theatre and the relatively new Savoy, so recently the home of so many Broadway hits.

The season's last yacht, a luxurious one with a richly paneled main salon, gave its name to Edward Peple's "melodramatic comedy" **The Spitfire** (4-25-10, Lyceum). Bruce Morson (Charles Cherry), a young gem collector, has learned that thieves who stole some of his rarest jewels have gotten aboard the yacht by deceiving its owner (C. D. Herman) and his hot-tempered daughter, Valda (Ruth Maycliffe), so he arranges to be thrown overboard from a tug and picked up by the yacht. But before he can unmask the crooks the yacht hits a rock and is wrecked. On a "sandy beach under the cliffs, with the nose of the *Spitfire* high in the air among the rocks," Morson makes coffee over a driftwood fire, confounds the thieves, and wins Valda. In the face of dispiriting reviews, the comedy struggled along for five weeks.

Another comedy opened to the sort of "money notices" theatre folk dream about but ran only a little longer, its promising career apparently nipped in the bud by hot weather. The author of **Her Husband's Wife** (5-9-10, Garrick) was A. E. Thomas, a newspaperman recently appointed drama critic of the *Sun*. He wrote about a young wife (Laura Hope Crews) who learns she is dying and sets out to select her own successor. She chooses the former fiancée (Grace Elliston) of her brother (Robert Warwick). The girl seems to be dumpy and dowdy, but when she learns she has been singled out just because of her unprepossessing appearance and nature, she transforms herself into a chic charmer. The wife becomes eaten up with jealousy. In the end the wife learns she will not die after all, and her rival-successor once again finds the brother attractive. Henry Miller, who was the play's director and, with Klaw and Erlanger, its producer, assumed the small but important role of the wife's wise old uncle.

The second end-of-season revival and the year's last nonmusical offering was *Jim, the Penman,* which William Brady brought out with a superb cast headed by Wilton Lackaye at the Lyric on the 10th. "There was no end of enthusiasm at the Lyric last night," one notice began, and by all accounts the enthusiasm persisted throughout the play's one-month stand.

The next Sunday the *Times*'s critic, Adolph Klauber, offered his look at the just concluded season. His lists of plays he admired and plays he disliked were about the same as any that the other better aisle-sitters might have compiled. Among his more interesting conclusions was that "overproduction, too many theatres, and a resultant overcompetition have served to reduce profits, while leading to a condition of unrest and dissatisfaction on the part of many people directly concerned with the business of 'giving the public what the public wants.' " But this glut of theatres and the need to keep them lit, he felt, had benefited American playwrights, and therefore American playgoers, by making producers more receptive to their works.

1910–1911

The new season began on a down note, with two more venerable theatres making sad headlines. The trouble-plagued Herald Square, which had suffered a nasty fire some months earlier, was sold to developers, who planned to replace it with a high-rise office building. The once aristocratic Academy of Music was leased to Corse Payton, who boasted he was "the World's Best Bad Actor." For many years he had successfully run a ten-twent'-thirt' playhouse in Brooklyn—a theatre that put on popular revivals for two performances a day and whose ticket prices ranged from ten cents for the balcony to a thirty-cent top. Payton's Manhattan

gamble soon proved a disappointment. Within a few seasons the theatre joined the ranks of film houses.

There was other bad news. In a full-page editorial the *Dramatic Mirror* bewailed that the economy never fully had recovered from the 1907 crash, and that not only films but "the automobile craze" was accountable for a 25 percent falling-off of trade in larger cities and an even uglier drop in smaller stands. In a way it seemed as if any excuse could be offered, for while lamenting the loss of older playhouses the editorial also blamed "the unwise multiplying of theatres in the large cities, in New York in particular." This rash of theatre construction in the face of lessening business was attributed to the desperate rivalry between the increasingly weak Trust and the rising Shubert brothers.

Yet by season's end a months-long parade of hits and other plays of discernible merit blew away much of the gloom.

The season began pleasantly with **The Cheater** (6-29-10, Lyric), which the popular dialect comedian Louis Mann adapted from Wilhelm Jacoby and Arthur Lippschitz's *Der Doppelmensch* as a vehicle for himself. He was cast as Godfried Plittersdorf, a successful if financially pressed politician who has risen to office on the strength of his ardent prohibitionism. His black-sheep half-brother, owner of the town's biggest saloon, dies, having willed the saloon to Plittersdorf. The politician must find a way of having the best of both worlds. In one escapade he attends a costume ball at the saloon disguised as a burglar, only to be mistaken for the real thing. Many critics once had found Mann heavy-handed but over the years had come to accept and welcome him. So had a sizable public, thereby allowing the comedy to span the hot weather.

As yet, A. E. Matthews, a forty-year-old London comedian, had no American following. He made his American debut in **Love Among the Lions** (8-8-10, Garrick), Winchell Smith's adaptation of F. Anstey's novel. Matthews was seen as a timid tea-taster whose fiancée (Jane Oaker) insists they be married in a cage filled with lions. That's too much for the milquetoast. He faints, and his place is taken by a liontamer (J. E. Miltern) in love with the coward's fiancée. But the liontamer's own girl (May Blayney) switches places with the other girl. All ends happily. The cage and its lions were never shown.

For **The Brass Bottle** (8-11-10, Lyceum) Anstey served as his own adaptor. His story told of a young man (Richard Bennett) who buys a battered Oriental lamp, rubs it, finds he has an obliging genie (Edwin Stevens) at his service, and discovers that having all one's wishes answered leads to farcical problems. One real problem was that some critics felt Bennett, a generally fine actor, was no farceur.

The season's first hit, James Forbes's **The Commuters** (8-15-10, Criterion), didn't send the critics dancing into the streets, either, but many recognized its likely appeal to playgoers. The play focused on a group until now largely ignored in non-musical attractions: suburbanites regulating their lives around train schedules and beset with servant problems. Larry Brice (Orrin Johnson) brings home his friend, Sammy Fletcher (Taylor Holmes), a playboy New York bachelor, and forgets about him in his rush to the train the next morning. A hungover, disheveled Fletcher wobbles downstairs later in the morning as Hetty Brice (May de Sousa) is entertaining her lady friends. When the men take themselves for another night out after Hetty has run from neighbor to neighbor borrowing the wherewithal for a hurriedly prepared dinner, Hetty explodes. She tells one friend (Amy Lesser) she is going to "do something *devilish*."

Hetty: Devilish. Sitting home here since half-past nine, ruining my digestion eating chocolates and worrying. Why, if I go in to a matinee I have to leave before the play's half over, so afraid dear Larry might get home first and be anxious.
Mrs. Colton: It's terrible. I haven't seen an emotional actress die since I've been married. . . . (*An auto siren is heard in the distance*) Oh, there's Salome. (*Rises*)
Hetty: Salome?
Mrs. Colton: I call the car Salome cause it wiggles.

The men return and are furious to find Hetty gone. They insist what's sauce for the gander is not sauce for the goose. Larry vacillates between being angry at Hetty's possibly cheating on him and frightened that some accident has befallen her. Peace reigns only after she returns home safe, sound, and certifiably innocent. Sammy finally leaves with an invitation to "come out soon and spend the day," but when the Brices are out of sight he rejoices, "Oh, you Broadway!" The comedy, somewhat underrated, ran twenty weeks and toured.

Just as her husband, Louis Mann, had served as adaptor of his most recent vehicle, so Clara Lipman was the translator of hers. She took **The Marriage of a Star** (8-15-10, Hackett) from the French of Alexandre Bisson and Georges Thurner. Its story revolved around an actress's sudden realization that her daughter's very social young man (Albert Parker), who has given the girl an engagement ring over his snooty parents' protestations, has fallen out

of love with the girl and in love with her. Mama sees to it a sensible rapprochement follows.

Two weeks after he presented Broadway with his dramatization of one novel, Winchell Smith had a second ready. **Bobby Burnit** (8-22-10, Republic) was taken from a popular work by George Randolph Chester. It centered on a rich playboy (Wallace Eddinger) who is convinced he is a brilliant businessman and, despite obvious evidence to the contrary, bumbles his way to success. Broadway preferred to read about and see his adventures in its mind's eye rather than onstage, so the play's run was brief.

Margaret Mayo's **Baby Mine** (8-23-10, Daly's) was one of the season's biggest, most memorable hits, provoking "perfect cyclones of laughter" and running well into the spring. Its many touring companies scarcely had taken their last bows when Jerome Kern musicalized it in the 1918 *Rock-a-Bye Baby*. As the curtain rises Zoie Hardy (Marguerite Clark) is whimpering to Jimmy Jinks (Walter Jones) about her falling-out with her husband, Alfred (Ernest Glendinning), who considers Jimmy his best friend:

Zoie: Alfred has *found out* that I lied about the luncheon.
Jimmy: What luncheon?
Zoie: Our luncheon, yesterday.
Jimmy: Why did you lie?
Zoie: I didn't know he *knew.*
Jimmy: Knew what?
Zoie: That I'd eaten with a man.
Jimmy: He couldn't object to your eating with me?
Zoie: Oh, *couldn't* he? If there's anything he doesn't object to I haven't found it out yet.
Jimmy: (*Annoyed*) Well, why did you *lunch* with me if you thought he wouldn't like it?
Zoie: I was hungry.

Actually, Zoie was far from home and reluctant to eat alone in a restaurant and be stared at censoriously, so she grabbed at Jimmy's invitation. No matter. Alfred stalks in, packs his bag, and stalks out again. But Jimmy and his wife, Aggie (Ivy Troutman), come up with a plan to win back Alfred. They will wait a few months, then wire him that Zoie has had a baby. The baby will be adopted from a children's home. The time comes, and there's Zoie in her rose-and-white negligée in her rose-and-white bedroom with a rose-and-white crib nearby. Complications start when Alfred returns prematurely, while Jimmy is still dickering about the baby. He brings back a baby boy, only to learn the mother has reconsidered. He immediately heads out to find another infant as Alfred comes in, sees the baby, and starts to fawn over it, to Zoie's chagrin and disgust.

Before long there are three "borrowed" babies in the bedroom and Alfred euphorically believes he has fathered triplets. Of course, Alfred eventually learns the truth and is forgiving, although Zoie gives no indication she will never not be dishonest (or, overlooked in the fun, that she could have any love for a toddler).

Bad luck brought Sewell Collins's **Miss Patsy** (8-29-10, 39th St.) to Broadway in *Baby Mine*'s wake. The play was waved away as an amiable if second-rate farce about a kindly busybody (Gertrude Quinlan) whose meddling sends members of a touring stock company spinning. By the play's end Miss Patsy realizes she'll be happier as a farmer's wife. The theatrical milieu allowed for the insertion of a few specialty turns.

Margaret Mayo's husband, Edgar Selwyn, provided August's last hit, **The Country Boy** (8-31-10, Liberty). Its thesis was essentially that of Clyde Fitch's in *The City,* but its homespun, comic approach was worlds apart. Hiram Belknap (G. C. Staley) will not allow his daughter, Jane (Edith Lyle), to marry Tom Wilson (Forrest Winant), whom he considers a ne'er-do-well, even though the Belknaps and the Wilsons have been friends in their small town for years. To prove his worth, Tom heads for New York, but there his naive belief that good things will simply come his way, and his flirtation with a selfish young actress (Willette Kershaw), lead to his downfall. Just as he is about to be evicted from his boardinghouse, Tom is made an intriguing offer by Fred Merkel (Robert McWade, Jr.), a grouchy newspaperman who is a fellow boarder and has watched Tom's struggle with a certain interest. Fred has lent money to a third boarder, a Jewish ticket speculator named Joe Weinstein (Arthur Shaw), and Joe, an inveterate gambler, has struck it big. The three men decide to go to Tom's home town and found a newspaper. The newspaper succeeds. But when Jane learns that the paper is about to expose her father's shady dealings, she comes to plead with Tom. Even though Jane is supposedly engaged to another man, Tom acquiesces. Tom and Jane, dismissing her supposed fiancé, embrace and swear undying love.

The play had flaws, especially in its largely unattractive delineation of Jane and its uncreditable ending, but even those critics who most sharply complained agreed with their colleague who praised it as "a real play, with real characterizations and a real plot." Those characterizations included the slang-spouting, knife-tongued Joe and the archetypical hot-cold New York landlady, Mrs. Bannon (Mrs. Stuart Robson). Joe, stuck in a dull, unreceptive

tank town, asks, "Ain't you lonesome for the big lane [Broadway]?" And when a local bigot tells him they don't have or want Jews in the village, he responds, "That's why its a village." Mrs. Bannon is not above drinking her tenants' beer and apologizing when the ice cream she purposely forgot to order doesn't arrive in time for dessert, but she does lend a helping hand to troubled boarders when no one is looking.

The published edition brings out an interesting point about contemporary theatre when it suggests that the Belknaps' maid in the first act and the boardinghouse maid in the second and third acts could be played by the same actress. Audiences would not be confused, since the New York maid was a black and would have been performed in blackface and with a kinky black wig. The comedy ran into January.

September's first entry, Tom Barry's faux-Shavian **The Upstart** (9-1-10, Maxine Elliott's), was a four-performance flop, despite some encouraging notices. Its maverick hero (John Westley) advocates divorce for unhappily married couples but finds himself stranded on a road beside a broken-down automobile after persuading a minister's wife (Jane Cowl) to run off with her chauffeur (Francis Byrne).

By contrast, Somerset Maugham's **Smith** (9-5-10, Empire) delighted audiences during its three-and-a-half-month run and long post-Broadway tour. It starred the always dependable, always-the-same John Drew as an English expatriate who returns to London, rejects the society of his peers, and asks his family's maid (Mary Boland)—the Smith of the title—to marry him and help him farm in South Africa. An excellent supporting cast included Hassard Short as a sponging playboy and two fine West End players, Lewis Casson and his wife, Sybil Thorndike, in minor roles.

Jules Eckert Goodman's tearjerker **Mother** (9-1-10, Hackett) outran the costlier Maugham comedy, compiling 133 showings, thanks in some measure to an affecting performance by tiny Emma Dunn in the title role. Her Mrs. Wetherill was a widow with six children. A gold-digging actress has taken the eldest Wetherill boy (Frederick Perry) for all he's worth, so he forges his mother's signature to a large check. She keeps silent, even though it means her daughter will have to leave college and the youngest children, twin boys, may have to go to bed hungry. When a second actress (Jane Corcoran) makes eyes at son number two (Albert Latscha), mother sends her packing. Taking the good with the bad, she joins her babes in their bedtime prayers. Critics were full of quibbles. Some objected to a college-educated girl resorting to such slang as "Well, it beats everything, don't it?" and "Looks like he has a case on her!" Nor was the staging found faultless. One commentator sneered, "The mother, with what was apparently intended as engaging homeliness, came in from mixing pie-crust in the kitchen to brush her flour-covered fingers on the parlor carpet."

An unnamed German farce was the source of George V. Hobart's **Welcome to Our City** (9-12-10, Bijou), which critics greeted with Bronx cheers and which left town hurriedly after just two weeks. Hefty Maclyn Arbuckle was starred as a southern colonel whose visit to a big city goes comically awry.

An "all-star" cast helped a revival of Sardou's *Diplomacy* enjoy a month of good business at Maxine Elliott's beginning on the 13th. Charles Richman was Henry; Milton Sills, Julian; Thurlow Bergen, Orloff; Effingham Pinto, Algie; Theodore Roberts, Stein; Florence Roberts, Zicka; Chrystal Herne, Dora; and Mrs. LeMoyne, the marquise. Since contemporary critics were not as anxious as later ones to perceive their parents' favorites as dated, the play was seen to "hold its own with anything that went before or has come after it."

For the second time in less than a month, George Randolph Chester stories served as the springboard for a play, this time for a long-remembered smash hit, George M. Cohan's **Get-Rich-Quick Wallingford** (9-19-10, Gaeity). Personable, beefy J. Rufus Wallingford (Hale Hamilton) and his slimmer but equally suave crony, Horace "Blackie" Daws (Edward Ellis), jump from town to town, selling stocks in companies they claim they are setting up, then absconding before the bubble bursts. Daws is first to approach the "boobs," professing amazement at their ignorance of Wallingford's celebrity: "What! never heard of J. Rufus Wallingford, the president of the Mexican Rio Grande Rubber Company—owner of the San Diego Blood Orange Plantation company? The man who controls the Locos Lead Development company? Never heard of J. Rufus Wallingford!" A favorite Wallingford ploy is to walk into a hotel when he first comes to town and, as he signs the register, whisper a plea to the desk clerk not to sell his autograph. The pair arrive in Battlesburg ("Fourteen thousand people and nine automobiles!"), and at the start their plans to set up a factory to manufacture cloth-covered carpet tacks seem to go smoothly. Wallingford has trouble resisting importuning would-be investors, such as the young man, Edward Lamb (Grant Mitchell), who has saved $11,000.

Wallingford: Better not invest it all at once. Ten thousand will be sufficient.
Lamb: Yes, I might need the other thousand.
Wallingford: I'm sure of that. But understand—your promise not to talk. This is to be our little secret.
Lamb: Honest!
Wallingford: Would you swear to that on your bended knees?
Lamb: (*Gets down on both knees and raises his right hand.*) On my word of honor!
Wallingford: (*Shakes his hand and lifts Lamb to his feet.*) I believe you, my boy. Of course, the quicker the money is placed, the quicker the returns.
Lamb: I'll go and get it right away.
Wallingford: One thing more, my boy. I don't want you to keep thanking me for this. Once I've invested your money, forget it.
Lamb: I'll try, Colonel.
Wallingford: Do you promise?
Lamb: On my—(*Starts to kneel.*)
Wallingford: (*Stops him from kneeling.*) No, never mind kneeling again—I'll take your word.

Then the plans happily turn sour. The company succeeds, and Battlesburg prospers. Wallingford looks to become richer than he ever dreamed and even wins the hand of Fannie Jasper (Frances Ring), a stenographer who saw through him yet believed in him. When a detective (Spencer Charters) appears, one who long had been the men's nemesis, he realizes they've genuinely reformed and done much good, so like his colleague in *Alias Jimmy Valentine*, he decides to let them alone. But Daws and Wallingford aren't certain they can stay reformed, and they conclude they must ask the detective to keep an eye on them. Cohan (in conjunction with Sam Forrest) not only staged the laugh-filled comedy at his expected breakneck speed but filled the evening with knowing tricks. A brass band played a rousing Cohan march, and his effect of a brightly lit trolley car crossing the stage in the distance won a big hand. All in all the show was, as one critic joyously reported, "a knockout." It ran a year in New York and soon had two more companies regaling the road.

Hattie Williams and G. P. Huntley, for all their comic skills, could only keep **Decorating Clementine** (9-19-10, Lyceum) on the boards for six weeks. Gladys Unger derived the farce from de Caillavet and de Flers's *Le Bois sacré*, telling of an authoress's misfiring attempts to win herself the Legion of Honor.

Another French farce, *Théodore et Cie.*, was the

source of Oliver Herford's **Con & Co.** (9-20-10, 39th St.), in which a young American (Harry Stone) who lives in Berlin off the generosity of friends and relations must prevent a duel by finding someone who resembles the woman in a photograph a jealous husband has uncovered, which the husband is certain is a photograph of his wife.

Robert Peyton Carter and Anna Alice Chapin's **The Deserters** (9-20-10, Hudson) was viewed by critics as "old-school melodrama" and "popular fiction set to scenery," yet it lured in playgoers for two months and subsequently did well on the road. A prologue, performed behind a gauze scrim, showed two army officers arguing over their affections for the wife of a third man. One man shoots the other and, believing he has killed him, flees. The husband then appears and finishes off the wounded man. The play proper begins in a San Francisco music hall, where Madge Summers (Helen Ware) supposedly sings and dances. Actually, Madge is the daughter of an old army man and is a sometime detective, now seeking the deserter, James Craig (Orme Caldara). She does not know he is wanted for murder. She succeeds in arresting him and having him held for court-martial but in the process falls in love with him. She also comes to believe in Craig's innocence. At his trial her questioning tricks the real killer into an inadvertent confession. The production marked Miss Ware's elevation to stardom, but her nights of glory were to be few although she remained on Broadway for twenty more years.

Percy MacKaye's **Anti-Matrimony** (9-22-10, Garrick) proved caviar to the general and so became the latest in Henrietta Crosman's growing list of disappointments. The Rev. Elliott Grey (Walter Greene) and his wife, Mildred (Crosman), are aghast that Grey's brother, Morris (Gordon Johnstone), and Mildred's sister, Isabelle (Grace Carlyle), both fallen hopelessly under the spell of modern playwrights, insist on living together without benefit of clergy, even though they have a baby. Isabelle's telling list of exemplars includes Cleopatra, Candida, Magda, Rebecca West, Nora, Ann Whitefield, and Rautendelein. Morris's own new play centers on an artist named Hosmer, whose genius is being sapped by an unhappy marriage. Enter Amorata, "the psychic emanation of the oversoul, the embodied spirit of Anti-Matrimony. She enters palely beautiful, wearing a swarm of bees." She restores Hosmer's art, leaving both free to jump to their deaths in a millrace. But not before they have dealt with some other characters—"a morphine patient, an inebriate pastor, a suicidal doctor, a tubercular poet, a kleptomaniac" heading the parade. Mildred

listens to all this bosh good-humoredly and decides to show the couple their absurdity by playing along with their ridiculous ideas. Her scheme works.

American audiences were not beguiled by Monckton Hoffe's London comedy **The Little Damozel** (9-24-10, Comedy). The girl (May Buckley) of the title plays in a café band, dressed as an Austrian Hussar. Her soldier-lover (George Graham), jilting her for a more socially acceptable lady, pays a poor, handsome young man (Cyril Keightley) to court her. A romance blossoms, and not even the abrupt discovery of the true situation can prevent a blissful ending. Some deft comic playing was not enough to save a slim comedy, which cried out for musicalization.

"I am a good woman if God did make me look like Upper Broadway," says Mabel (Anne Sutherland), an ex-convict trying to keep to the straight and narrow. She and her friend, Edith (Mary Carter), are the central figures in **My Man** (9-27-10, Bijou), which Forrest Halsey theatricalized from his own story "The Quality of Mercy." Edith is also a former convict, and she has violated her parole by removing her young son from the home to which the law sent him. She supports herself by painting shells and eventually remarries. Circumstances lead both women to steal again, and they are unmasked, but their obviously sincere yearning to be good allows everyone to look the other way. Critics felt neither the writing nor acting realized the play's potential. "It is not invidious," *Theatre* observed, "to prophesy that had Belasco put the piece on and selected its cast, another 'Easiest Way' would have gone on record." As it was, the record shows the play ran only fifteen performances.

For months commentators had pontificated about the troubled New Theatre. A few, belatedly recognizing the wisdom of the late Clyde Fitch and others who had argued that its haughty, absurd disdain for commercial realities would doom it from the start, suggested the project be abandoned. The proud trustees disagreed, but when the magnificent playhouse—it was still merely that and not a full-fledged acting company—began its second season they did, for a time, allow it to discard the costly repertory system. Unchanged were the casting of generally second-rank players, an almost total reliance on foreign plays at a time when new American dramatists were being hailed left and right, and the promise of eye-filling productions. The season's opener was Maurice Maeterlinck's **The Blue Bird** (10-1-10). Its story of how Tyltyl (Gladys Hulette) and Mytyl (Irene Brown), the son and daughter of a woodchopper, are guided by "a hooked nosed and humped back" Fairy Berylune (Louise Closser

Hale) in their search for the blue bird of happiness, was sumptuously mounted. Some settings, such as the woodchopper's hut, had a "Rembrandtesque" realism, but others consisted of arches or pillars so austerely simple that they would seem modern a century later. A few costumes were also realistic; a few were odd, such as the Cat, with his whiskered nose and his tail, cavorting in the suit of an 18th-century gentleman. Most outfits were merely drapey. Many critics felt the show would please children more than adults, and some dared to suggest that even children would do better imagining the events in their minds' eyes while reading a printed version. Yet for all the critical reservations, the show was a success, running a month at the New and then transferring to a nearby playhouse for two additional months.

Another show with a marked appeal to youngsters was **Rebecca of Sunnybrook Farm** (10-3-10, Republic), which Kate Douglas Wiggin and Charlotte Thompson based on Wiggin's 1903 novel. Sunnybrook Farm never was seen on the stage. Instead, early in Act I, a stagecoach is heard rattling over a wooden bridge. A whip is cracked, urging horses up a hill, and the coach comes in view with kindly Jeremiah Cobb (Archie Boyd) on the box and Rebecca (Edith Taliaferro) as one of the passengers. Rebecca wears a faded calico dress and carries a pink parasol. She is coming to Riverboro to live in the brick house owned by her aunts, the dour, puritanical Miranda (Marie L. Day) and the vacillating Jane (Eliza Glassford). Rebecca tells Cobb that she must be careful with her beloved parasol: "I never put it up when the sun shines—pink fades dreadfully, and I only carry it to meeting on cloudy Sundays." Cobb is understanding, but Miranda is not. She throws away the flowers Rebecca has brought and in every way makes the child so unhappy that Rebecca, undaunted by a violent thundershower, runs away to Cobb's house. He gently convinces her to return. Before long Rebecca has found a way to help her less fortunate friends, to prevail on an unmarried couple to wed, and to win not only the grudging affection of Miranda but the more open admiration of handsome, rich Adam Ladd (Ralph Kellerd).

Even the most stonyhearted critics capitulated to the charms of the play and its superb mounting and cast. Edith Taliaferro, a slim brunette and Mabel's tinier younger sister, was nearly seventeen, so it required little stretching to see her as a thirteen-year-old (sixteen in the last act). After all, this season Henrietta Crosman and John Drew had played figures half their own ages—or less. The

comedy remained on Broadway for more than six months, and Miss Taliaferro was almost twenty before she permanently relinquished the role.

A third hit followed in quick succession when David Belasco presented Herman Bahr's **The Concert** (10-4-10, Belasco) in an adaptation by Leo Ditrichstein. It told of a self-centered, randy pianist (Ditrichstein) who runs off to a Catskills retreat with one of his pupils (Jane Grey) but is brought to his senses after his wife (Janet Beecher) and the pupil's husband (William Morris) appear on the scene pretending to a romance of their own. The curtain falls with his wife lovingly bleaching some of the pianist's fading locks. Belasco's stage picture showed a luxurious Catskills "cottage," with hunting trophies in a richly paneled room, replete with heavy draperies and stained glass windows. But the evening's triumphs, and the real reasons the comedy ran well into May, were the adaptation and acting of Ditrichstein. He brilliantly conveyed the mercurial pianist's changing moods—his arrogance, his genuine talent, his childishness and insecurity, his absurd vanity.

. . .

Leo [James] Ditrichstein (1865–1928) was the son of a count and the grandson of a famous Austrian novelist. Heavy-set, round-faced, and gruffly handsome, he apprenticed in Berlin before arriving in America in 1890. His first appearances here were with the German-speaking theatre in New York. He made his English-speaking debut on tour in *Mr. Wilkinson's Widows*.

. . .

A rash of failures followed the three hits. Robert H. Davis's **The Family** (10-11-10, Comedy), which ran less than a full week, described the varying reactions of a father (Sam Edwards), mother (Mabel Bert), and brother (John Westley) to the news that their daughter/sister (Julie Herne) had run off with and been deserted by a member of a minstrel troupe.

To some reviewers Al Wood's mounting of William J. Hurlbut's **New York** (10-17-10, Bijou) smacked of the lurid touring melodramas Woods so recently had been presenting. A staid father (Orrin Johnson) must find a way of exculpating his young bride-to-be (Laura Nelson Hall) after she stabs to death his dissolute, illegitimate son (Mortimer Weldon) while "preserving her honor."

A Parisian hit, Henri Bataille's **The Scandal** (10-17-10, Garrick), failed to titillate Manhattan with its tale of a wife (Gladys Hanson) who strays but is forgiven by her husband (Kyrle Bellew). Like *New York*, it survived a mere fortnight.

But that was half a week more than Butler Davenport's **Keeping Up Appearances** (10-20-10, Comedy) could muster, despite some laudatory notices. A callous husband (J. Harry Benrimo) allows his wife (Amelia Gardner), two selfish daughters (Pamela Gaythorne and Mabel Moore), and a more altruistic son (A. Hylton Allen) to struggle in relative penury while he maintains a mistress (Gertrude Dallas). The wife learns that his illegitimate child by the mistress has suddenly died, and she tries to be compassionate, but her overtures are rebuffed, so she concludes divorce is the only solution. The best reviews went to Zelda Sears for the comic relief she provided in the role of a dressmaker who usually talks with pins clamped in her teeth.

Fred Terry—Ellen's brother—reputedly had performed Baroness Orczy and Montague Barstow's **The Scarlet Pimpernel** (10-24-10, Knickerbocker) more than 2000 times in England before bringing it to America. Although Terry was not showered with the encomiums that regularly greeted his sister, this lavish staging recounted many of the highlights of the baroness's popular novel about an Englishman risking his own life to rescue innocent victims of the Revolution. The spectacle, part of a two-play repertory, ran a prearranged forty showings.

Three more failures, including one that opened the same night as *The Scarlet Pimpernel,* raised their curtains in short order. Edward E. Rose's **The Rosary** (10-24-10, Garden) centered on a parish priest (Harrington Reynolds) who saves a girl from a vengeful suitor, then saves the marriage of the suitor, whose wife is the girl's sister.

Thomas Jefferson's close resemblance to his famous father, Joseph, in both looks and mannerisms was seen as a disadvantage to him when he made a grab for stardom in George Totten Smith's farce **The Other Fellow** (10-31-10, Bijou). But then, the feeble farce was no help either. Wilton Smith (Jefferson) and his buddy, Dr. Button (Gerald Harcourt), agree to allow a Hindu swami (Fred W. Peters) to set their souls free temporarily. Unfortunately, the swami afterwards finds he can't get the right soul into the right body, leaving Smith to wander around behaving as if he were Button. Somehow the usual, foreseeable complications did not prove very amusing.

Nor could William Gillette's **Electricity** (10-31-10, Lyceum) generate the exciting currents its title promised. Its heroine (Marie Doro) is a rich young lady who has become a dedicated socialist and vowed to marry a member of the proletariat. Her brother's wealthy college roommate (Shelley Hull) falls in love with her and, in order to court her, changes places with an electrician (Francis D. McGinn) who is rewiring her family's home. Complications arise when the young lady calls at the home of the real electrician and learns he is engaged to another girl.

A third show opening the same evening allowed October to end as it began, with a hit. In fact, most reviews for Charles Klein's **The Gamblers** (10-31-10, Maxine Elliott's) were so enthusiastic that Broadway might have expected the drama to equal the runs of his earliest successes. It didn't, though it did run profitably for six months. A group of bankers who have been playing fast and loose with their depositors' money become aware that they are about to be hauled into court. They decide to draw cards, with the loser taking the blame for all the others. The ill lot falls to an elderly banker, but his son, Wilbur Emerson (George Nash), quietly agrees to take his place. Emerson learns that the incriminating papers are at the home of the district attorney, James Darwin (Charles Stevenson), and he goes there at night, entering on a ruse. He is caught rummaging through Darwin's files by Darwin's wife, Catherine (Jane Cowl), who once had been in love with him. She grabs the papers and refuses to give them to Emerson. Darwin appears suddenly. Not only does he misconstrue his wife's behavior, but his questioning of her is so callous that she turns against him. She gives the papers to Emerson, but he is still convicted. Catherine has come to realize that Emerson, while guilty of serious peculation, is a decent man doing what "everybody else is doing," while her husband is vicious, unscrupulous, and hate-filled. She tells Emerson she will wait for his release, divorcing Darwin in the meantime.

Jane Cowl's "impressive" performance garnered the most flattering reviews: "Her facial expression and gradual breaking down under the questionings of her husband and her final explosion were so well done that she was accorded an extra round of applause." William B. Mack, as the craven banker who turns against his colleagues, also won a big hand.

Two nights after he closed in his failed *The Scandal,* Kyrle Bellew reappeared on November 1 at the Gaiety, recreating his old role in *Raffles.*

A booking mixup was blamed for the short, one-month run of Thompson Buchanan's **The Cub** (11-1-10, Comedy) in the face of surefire money notices for both the comedy-drama and its leading man, Douglas Fairbanks. Buchanan had begun his career as a newspaperman in Kentucky, so some aisle-sitters discerned autobiographical hints in his scared cub reporter, Steve Oldham, sent to cover a blazing mountain-family feud. He is taken in by one of the sides, then complicates his own situation by falling in love with a schoolteacher (Millicent Evans) belonging to the enemy faction. Despite comically unnerving turns of events, Oldham arranges a truce, which is celebrated by dancing some reels and passing jugs from hand to hand. The jugs marked "For Men" purportedly contain moonshine; those labeled "For Women," lemonade. Oldham's reward for ending the feud is, first, his paper's skepticism that the hatreds could ever be resolved and, then, its fury that he may have killed what promised to be an ongoing story. But, of course, Oldham does have his girl. Fairbanks was praised for "the breeziness, the sauciness, the good humor to make every point tell," and "his virility and his masculinity, which remain dominant traits in spite of the suggested timidity."

May Irwin stopped by for a limited engagement in a written-to-order vehicle, Booth Tarkington and Harry Leon Wilson's **Getting a Polish** (11-7-10, Wallack's). She played Mrs. Jim, a miner's widow who runs a boardinghouse until a big strike is found in her husband's claim. Then she takes herself to Paris, where she squirms uncomfortably in the latest fashions and is pursued by fortune hunters. She settles for one of them but is jilted at the altar after the groom-to-be is bribed by the rough-and-ready miner (George Fawcett) who loves her for herself. As always, the star inserted several of her lusty songs, but not as many as usual.

R. C. Carton's London hit **Mr. Preedy and the Countess** (11-7-10, 39th Street) was cold-shouldered in New York. With Weedon Grossmith as star, it detailed the comic plight of a timid man whose senior partner (John Clulow) forces him to act as chaperon overnight to the partner's prospective bride (Charlotte Granville). Naturally the junior partner's fiancée (Sheila Heseltine) and her relatives show up and misconstrue the situation. Largely ignored by the critics in her inauspicious American debut was a slim, feline young English actress named Lynn Fontanne.

The New Theatre's second offering of the season was the last of the evening's openings. But the return of true repertory with the mounting of *The Merry Wives of Windsor* was no occasion for handclapping. The interpretation was dismissed with such damning descriptions as "dull," "weak," "disappointing," and "not very merry." Five nights later the playhouse brought out Pinero's **The Thunderbolt** (11-12-10), in which a family greedily makes plans for spending the money it seems likely to inherit from an estranged brother, only to discover that he left it all to an illegitimate daughter.

At a more commercially minded theatre, the Lyceum, *The Importance of Being Earnest* began a comfortable six-week stand on the 14th with Hamilton Revelle as Jack, A. E. Matthews as Algernon, and Jane Oaker as Gwendolen.

No other producer of the era seemed to possess David Belasco's knack for shepherding hits onto the stage. His latest, and his second comedy in a row, was Avery Hopwood's **Nobody's Widow** (11-15-10, Hudson). A crucial scene early in its first act must have reminded inveterate first-nighters of one in Wilde's comedy. Roxana (Blanche Bates) arrives at the Palm Beach home of her friend, Betty (Adelaide Prince), for a visit, and she arrives in widow's weeds, forlornly mourning her husband, "Mr. Clayton," who, she reports, died of "enlargement of the heart" almost immediately after the wedding. She has scarcely had time to tell of her sorrow when her supposedly dead husband appears bright-eyed on the scene in his true identity, the Duke of Moreland (Bruce McRae). "I buried you, remain dead!" she growls at him. Roxana, it seems, is an independently minded young lady. She had gone for a whirl in Europe, fallen in love with the duke and married him, then stormed out after finding him kissing a pretty little thing named Suzette. She knew full well the duke was very much alive, but she had wired her family and friends of his death. The duke is resolved to win her back, and he all but has when Betty throws herself on him and kisses him just as Roxana walks into the room. Similar misunderstandings plague the couple until just before eleven o'clock.

Delicious performances by Miss Bates, McRae, and their supporting cast glossed over any weaknesses in the script, and the comedy played happily for more than six months. After touring with the show, Miss Bates fell out with Belasco, apparently over her marrying without his permission, much as Mrs. Leslie Carter had years earlier. She left Belasco's roster, and her career soon sagged. Coincidentally Mrs. Carter, whose fate had been much the same, would make one of her futile attempts at a comeback two weeks on.

There were few takers for Arthur Conan Doyle's dramatization of his **The Speckled Band** (11-21-10, Garrick), in which an Anglo-Indian villain (Edwin Stevens) uses a snake to commit his killings until he is brought to justice by Sherlock Holmes (Charles Millward).

Anne Caldwell's **The Nest Egg** (11-22-10, Bijou) gave Zelda Sears, the young actress then being hailed as "the Greatest of Stage Old Maids," a juicy role as a spinster who writes a sentimental poem, along with her address and the date, on one of the eggs she sells to a huge marketing concern. Three years later she receives a telegram from a man who has purchased the egg; he advises her he is coming to visit. She jumps to the conclusion that he wants to marry her. In no time her house is decorated with orange blossoms and a huge floral bell over the door. Her neighbors come bearing wedding gifts—and when she discovers each and every one has brought a cream pitcher, she remarks she could use a cow. But the caller turns out to be not a suitor but a pure-food-and-drug fanatic who wants to sue the company that kept the egg in cold storage for three years. So Hetty Gandy ruefully goes off on her honeymoon alone, only to stumble on a real prospective husband at the hotel. The play was a modest success, but Miss Caldwell would win her real fame as a lyricist and librettist for the period's musicals.

Weddings that failed to materialize were becoming a cliché of the season. In Edgar Selwyn and William Collier's **I'll Be Hanged If I Do** (11-28-10, Comedy), the potential hangee is Percival Kelly (Collier). The play opens with his father, his bride, her mother and brother arriving at his apartment to find him enjoying his tub and contemplating a scrumptious breakfast, totally unconcerned that a minister and a churchload of guests have been kept waiting. The bride cancels the wedding, and Percival is packed off to Nevada for hardening. There he is mistaken for a stagecoach robber. He keeps pursuers at bay with a jewel-studded pistol he bought at Tiffany's and minimizes the risk of his being hanged by buying up all the rope in town—and all the twine. Finally brought to trial, he is confronted by a jury that includes a German barmaid who doesn't understand English and a foreman who is the real robber and determined to convict him. Not only is he acquitted, but he strikes it fabulously rich and returns home to marry the girl he really preferred. Fans of Collier's sharp, dry humor kept the comedy on the boards for ten weeks.

Fred Terry and his wife, Julia Neilson, closed their visit with William Devereux's **Henry of Navarre** (11-28-10, Knickerbocker), in which Henry thwarts the sinister machinations of his enemies at the court of Charles IX.

In **Two Women** (11-29-10, Lyric), which Rupert Hughes took from an unidentified Italian drama, the wife of a titled but impoverished painter (Robert Warwick) dies in his arms, leaving the picture he was painting of her unfinished. The artist learns that a famous and notorious music hall dancer is supposedly the very image of his dead wife. He meets her and somehow convinces her to give up her wild ways

and live with him, until a misunderstanding sends her back to her lover's luxurious apartment. A duel ensues in which the artist is blinded, but the girl, just about to walk out on him, hears the artist's protestations of love and returns. Both women were played by Mrs. Carter in a performance that delighted most critics. A first-act death scene, a dance in the music hall, moments of romantic passion, and a comic bit involving going off to milk the artist's cow while dressed in men's clothes gave the star ample opportunity to show her diverse skills, and she did. All she lacked was a creditable vehicle. But her allure was still potent enough to keep the play on the boards for a slightly forced six weeks.

A parade of stars launched December, led off by Sarah Bernhardt in her second "farewell tour." Her repertory ranged from such old standbys as *La Dame aux camélias* and *La Tosca* to new plays recently seen on Broadway in English versions, such as *Les Bouffons* (done with Maude Adams as *The Jesters*) and *La Femme X* (which Dorothy Donnelly had offered as *Madame X*). Bernhardt's latest leading man was Lou Tellegen, an Adonis with wavy blond hair, blue eyes, a physique so magnificent that Rodin had employed him as a model, a heavy Dutch accent, and precious little acting ability. He remained in America for some years, trading on his matinee-idol appeal, then, finding his vogue fading, grabbed final headlines with a ghastly suicide. The troupe lingered in New York at the Globe for a month, starting on December 5.

That same evening saw two Sherlock Holmeses in Manhattan. The second was the best of all, Gillette, who began an extended stand at the Empire in his most famous vehicle. Later in the engagement he brought out *The Private Secretary, Secret Service, Too Much Johnson,* and *Held by the Enemy.* In all these plays he "was able to give to the most trivial things an air of mystery and importance."

If Gillette made much of minor material, some critics rued that Sothern and Marlowe, for all their prestige and dedication, continued to overreach, especially Sothern. "One sometimes feels," a commentator noted, "that here is a light comedian lost to make a somewhat indifferent interpreter of tragedy. The weight of Shakesperian tradition hangs heavy on him." The pair offered nothing new for their appearances, which started at the Broadway, also on the 5th, content to redo *As You Like It, Hamlet, Macbeth,* and *Romeo and Juliet.*

The evening's lone novelty was Maeterlinck's **Mary Magdalene** (12-5-10, New), which Paris had yet to see. The theatre's immensity led to problems again. Critics complained that Olga Nethersole, brought in with actors of her own choosing for the mounting, grotesquely overplayed. One distressed critic observed, "There was no part of the stage which she left untouched during the course of an act. Her hands were constantly busy, now held high in the air with tense fingers, now pressed against her shoulder with fingers relaxed. . . . She contrived to give the simplest speeches something which robbed them of all their simplicity." The "Russian Symphony Orchestra" provided accompaniment.

Two comedies premiered the next evening. Neither was a rousing success. The better of the two was James Montgomery's **The Aviator** (12-6-10, Astor), which featured yet one more of the season's many timid heroes. In this case the man is Robert Street (Wallace Eddinger), who has written a best-selling book on how to fly although he himself never has been up in an "aeroplane." His bluff is called when he is challenged to a race by a French ace (Frederick Paulding). Street takes a few hasty lessons from an expert (Edward Begley), who also never has flown— since he is too fat to permit a plane to get off the ground. They use chairs for a fuselage, Street's hat for the steering mechanism, and two friends to pose as wings. The race is finally run, with telegrams advising nearby spectators of the incredible maneuvers the incompetent, flustered Street is inadvertently performing. Then the goggled Street is seen briefly flying through the clouds in what was purported to be a genuine Blériot. Street wins both the race and a pretty girl (Christine Norman). In 1917 the comedy was successfully musicalized as *Going Up*.

Albert Chevalier, a popular English music-hall star, made his American debut in **Daddy Dufard** (12-6-10, Hackett), a comedy he and Lechmere Worrall derived from an unidentified French piece. The clown, most famous as a cockney costermonger, portrayed a faltering French actor determined to give his daughter (Violet Heming) a leg up on the stage.

The New Theatre's next offering, on the 19th, was an odd choice, brought forth ostensibly "in accordance with the policy of holding occasional revivals of noteworthy modern plays." Many critics agreed that *Old Heidelberg* was not the modern play most deserving a rehearing, so they gave the mounting short shrift.

Nor were they elated with **The Foolish Virgin** (12-19-10, Knickerbocker), which Rudolph Besier translated from Henri Bataille's play. Even Mrs. Patrick Campbell could not elicit interest in this story of a devoted wife's attempt to save her callous, philandering husband (Robert Drouet) from scandal.

Annie Russell, so fine an actress, so regularly plagued with hard luck, fared no better in Leonard Merrick and Michael Morton's **The Imposter** (12-20-10, Garrick), playing a destitute young lady who finds romance with a Canadian farmer (Charles Richman) after his English parents and his dissolute cousin have been cruel to her.

Louis N. Parker's **Pomander Walk** (12-20-10, Wallack's) has several tenuous claims to being called an American play, even though its French-born playwright was a British subject. First, it was performed in America before the West End saw it. It ran longer here. And its setting so delighted a New York developer that he recreated part of it on a New York side street. The setting showed a glimpse of winding river on the left with the rest of the stage occupied by a miniature crescent of five tiny Queen Anne houses. Four have dark green woodwork, but the one on the far right, the heroine's house, is painted white. Played out in this idyllic view of 1805 England was the story of a father (Yorke Stephens) who sets about to break up the romance of his son (Edgar Kent) and a young resident (Dorothy Parker) of the crescent until he realizes that the girl's mother (Sybil Carlisle) once was his own sweetheart. A 1922 musical version was called *Marjolaine*, after the heroine.

Preston Gibson's **Drifting** (12-21-10, 39th St.) told of Hortense Harrison (Edith Luckett), a naive wife, and her husband, Henry (Walter Hale). Their marriage is nearly destroyed by Althea Anderson (Mrs. Sam Sothern), an adventuress apparently brought over from some defunct touring melodrama, and William Worthington (Frank Goldsmith), a caddish man-about-town. At least one other character also had an alliterating name. A report that the "actors were not as bad as the play" may account for the ten-performance run.

Billie Burke was seemingly the only reason for seeing **Suzanne** (12-26-10, Lyceum), which Haddon Chambers adapted from Frantz Fonson and Fernand Wicheler's Belgian comedy *Le Mariage de Mlle. Beulemans,* but her feathery charms kept it afloat for two months. As Suzanne she not only helped her father's troubled bottling business but made the man (Conway Tearle) she was engaged to break the engagement and marry a poor girl by whom he had fathered a child. She then found herself a better mate (Julian L'Estrange). Exactly a month later, what the *American* called "about the briefest work that has ever appeared in a theatre," E. Harcourt Williams's dramatization of Anthony Hope's **The Philosopher,** was added to the bill. It took no more than fifteen minutes for a young lady (Miss Burke) to make an unworldly dreamer

(Lumsden Hare) understand that he ought to love her as she loved him.

Henry Arthur Jones's **We Can't Be as Bad as All That** (12-30-10, 39th St.) really wasn't, if many contemporary reviews can be trusted, yet it proved a dismal failure both in America and later in England. It recounted how a woman with a past (Katharine Kaelred) foils attempts by a snobbish society to hurt her.

"Why should it be assumed that a few years would relegate a good play to the refuse-heap of old-fashioned frumpery?" *Theatre* asked of 1911's initial offering, thereby reaffirming that the trend toward believing only today's work is worthwhile was already spreading its contagion along Broadway. The offering was a revival of *Trelawny of the Wells* at the Empire on January 1, with Ethel Barrymore, "charming with her own simplicity," as star and such fine players as Lawrence D'Orsay, Constance Collier, Charles Walcot, and George C. Boniface in support. The revival chalked up a six-week stand.

The new year's first big hit arrived the next evening. As the curtain rose on Philip H. Bartholomae's **Over Night** (1-2-11, Hackett), a steamboat's whistle blasted through the auditorium and the enclosed deck of Albany Day Line's S.S. *Hendrik Hudson* was revealed, with wooded banks beyond its Poughkeepsie pier seen in the distance. Among the passengers are timid, lisping little Richard Kettle (Herbert A. Yost) and his amazon suffragette of a bride, Georgina (Jean Newcombe). There is no question who will be boss in this marriage. Richard's Yale classmate, tall, rugged Percy Darling (Robert Kelly), and his petite new wife, Elsie (Margaret Lawrence), also are embarking on their honeymoon. Just as the ship is about to sail the couples realize that some of their luggage is missing, so Georgina and Percy march off together in search of it. The boat sails without them. Richard and Elsie are mistaken for husband and wife and decide it would be best not to correct the error. Elsie is also mistaken for a suffragette and pressed into giving a rousing "Votes for Women" speech, after which she breaks down and cries on Richard's shoulder. They put up that evening at the Rip Van Winkle Inn, again signing the register as man and wife. Fast on the heels of further complications come the irate, upset Georgina and Percy, demanding explanations. But Richard's experiences have turned a mouse into a man overnight, and when he barks at Georgina to sit down and shut up, she does. The comedy ran twenty weeks. In 1915, with the hero's name changed, it reappeared as a Jerome Kern musical, *Very Good Eddie*.

During the previous season a play called *These Are My People* and billed as a sequel to *The Squaw Man* was tried on the road, where it failed. Similarly, another play by Edwin Milton Royle, **The Silent Call** (1-2-11, Broadway), was also announced as a sequel to the same play. Those critics who reviewed it insisted it was no sequel but the original article, perhaps touched up ever so slightly. Within days the better-known name was restored, and the worked played out its two-week booking apparently to satisfactory trade.

The fast-collapsing New Theatre's next effort was **Vanity Fair** (1-7-11, New), a dramatization Robert Hichens and Cosmo Gordon Lennox had made for London about the same time Mrs. Fiske was presenting Langdon Mitchell's transcription to New York. The West End star had been Marie Tempest [Mrs. Cosmo Gordon Lennox], and it was to allow her a two-week guest appearance that this version was put on. The star's "charm, grace and piquancy" were welcomed, but most reviewers, even when they were not explicit, made it clear they thought Mitchell's the better adaptation and Mrs. Fiske's the more memorable Becky.

Broadway's less nose-in-the-air critics instantly greeted Paul Armstrong and Wilson Mizner's **The Deep Purple** (1-9-11, Lyric) as a zinger of a crook-play, and it quickly became one of the season's big money-makers, running nineteen weeks before heading out on a prolonged tour. A suave crook (James Lee Finney) has lured an attractive young girl (Catherine Calvert) away from her family, ostensibly to marry her but actually to use her to decoy rich, blackmailable men. One of the potential victims is a wealthy mining engineer (Richard Bennett), who catches on to the scheme, recognizes the innocent girl's plight, and shoots the crook. Technically the engineer should be arrested and brought to trial, but the police, aware of both men's reputations, look the other way. Although Bennett and Finney won high praise, Miss Calvert was dismissed as "artificial," while Ada Dwyer walked away with rave notices as the crook's hardnosed landlady.

As far as more higher-browed critics were concerned, the evening's best opening was H. S. Sheldon's **The Havoc** (1-9-11, Bijou), which was produced by and starred the man many considered Broadway's most responsible actor-manager, Henry Miller. Even they granted the play's premise was farfetched. A husband discovers his wife (Laura Hope Crews) is having an affair with their boarder (Francis Byrne). He demands a divorce but also insists that the boarder shall marry the woman and that he himself shall remain in the house as a lodger.

The new husband turns out to be an embezzler and runs away, leaving the wife saddled with debts. The first husband takes her on as his secretary. Critics admired not only the intelligent writing but the fine playing as well, especially Miller's "intense, almost saturnine husband." Yet though its cast of four made *The Havoc* a low-budget drama, it could muster only half the run of *The Deep Purple*.

C. M. S. McLellan's latest drama, **Judith Zaraine** (1-16-11, Astor), ran only a fortnight. Curiously, while several plays by English and French writers had been done in America this season before being unveiled in their homelands, this American play previously had been done in London as *The Strong People*. Lena Ashwell, the fine English actress with a "lyric quality of voice and speech," played the title role of a woman who helps lead a band of disgruntled workers in Minetown against the United Mining Company. At one point she threatens to use a stiletto on the colonel (John E. Kellerd) sent to put down the rebellious men. She also falls in love with a young man (Charles Waldron) posing as a reporter but in reality an executive of the mining combine. In time she brings him to see her viewpoint and to help arrange a fair settlement.

Boyishly handsome William Faversham was just the right actor to pop out of a huge urn of geraniums with only the barest covering for his torso and nothing to hide his tiny horns and pointed ears as he made his first appearance in the title role of Edward Knoblauch's **The Faun** (1-16-11, Daly's). The faun saves a bankrupt lord (Martin Sabine) from suicide and, in return for a promise to pick winners at the racetrack, is given entry into society as a supposed prince. He sets about righting society's more correctable wrongs but in the end, like Adonis and Galatea and so many others before him, decides to return to his orginal condition. The fantasy remained for six weeks, then returned to the road.

The central figure in the next play to appear also opted to return to his original state. Unfortunately, Percy MacKaye's **The Scarecrow** (1-17-11, Garrick) lacked a star with Faversham's box-office appeal. Its Broadway run was only twenty-three performances. But *The Scarecrow*, which MacKaye called "a Tragedy of the Ludicrous," remains possibly the most viable of all this season's American plays, and while Broadway has neglected it shamefully, it has received its due with some regularity in college theatres and regional playhouses and even enjoyed one superb off-Broadway mounting. The story reputedly was suggested by Hawthorne's "Feathertop."

Goody Rickby (Alice Fischer) is a blacksmith and a witch in late 17th-century New England. Years earlier Gilead Merton had seduced her, then deserted her and her baby, which soon died. Now Merton (Brigham Royce) is a justice who has threatented to execute her for witchcraft, and she plots vengeance. While working on a metal scarecrow, which will outlast straw and cloth ones, she uses her tongs to pull a goatishly bearded devil, Dickon (Edmund Breese), from her forge. Together they conspire to turn the scarecrow into a real man (Frank Reicher), whom they name Lord Ravensbane and whom they plan to palm off on Merton's niece, Rachel (Fola La Follette). One problem they face is that Ravensbane must smoke a pipe to stay alive. Rachel is smitten with the young man, going so far as to reject her betrothed, Richard (Earle Browne). To further their scheme, Dickon has presented himself to Merton as Mr. Dickonson, Ravenbane's tutor, and indulged in some gentle blackmail. However, Goody has sold Rachel a magic mirror, which shows the beholder his or her real self. Rachel and Richard see only themselves in the glass, but Ravensbane sees a grotesque scarecrow. At first he thinks it a demon and rushes at it with his sword. Then he understands what it truly represents. Shattered, he breaks his pipe:

Ravensbane: Oh, Rachel, could I have been a man—! (*He sways, staggering.*)
Rachel: Richard! Richard! support him. (*She draws the curtain of the mirror, just opposite which Ravensbane has sunk upon the floor. At her cry, he starts up faintly and gazes at his reflection, which is seen to be a normal image of himself.*) Look, look: the glass!
Ravensbane: (*His face lighting with an exalted joy, starts to his feet, erect, before the glass.*) A man! (*He falls back into the arms of the two lovers.*) Rachel!
Richard: (*Bending over him.*) Dead!
Rachel: (*With an exalted look.*) But a man!

Although Breese was the cast's best-known player, and the staging was thus tilted in his favor, Reicher grabbed many of the most gratified notices. The *Times* observed, "He made [Ravensbane's] foppish imitation of manners both quaint and amusing, at the same time emphasizing with very sympathetic skill the pathos at the bottom of the subterfuge."

When the box office opened to sell tickets for Louis N. Parker's translation of Edmond Rostand's **Chantecler** (1-23-11, Knickerbocker), the line began on Broadway near 38th and extended all along 38th Street over to Sixth Avenue. So unusual was it that many newspapers sent photographers rushing to record the scene. The play was not the reason for the line; rather, it was Charles Frohman's daring casting of Maude Adams in the leading role, a role designed for the late Coquelin and played virtually everywhere by a man. This third fantasy in just over a week detailed the awakening to reality of a rooster who believes the whole world depends on and revolves about him. All the characters were animals, mostly the barnyard variety and costumed accordingly. Opening night brought about another awakening, demonstrating that America's most popular actress had rigidly marked limitations. She could not suggest the rugged masculine ego or the palpable male sex appeal Chantecler required. Thanks largely to a huge advance sale and to assertive publicity, the play ran three months, but its heavy initial outlays and high running costs meant it closed in the red.

A play Frohman produced the next evening also failed commercially and was removed after a single month. Like *Chantecler,* Henri Lavedan's **Sire** (1-24-11, Criterion) was brought out in Louis N. Parker's translation. Mlle. De Saint-Salbi (Mabel Bert), a senescent aristocrat, is convinced the dauphin who might have become Louis XVII was not killed and is living somewhere in obscurity. She sets out to find him. Fearing for her sanity, her family hires a strolling player (Otis Skinner) to impersonate the dead prince and mollify the woman. It provided the sort of ripe, fruity role Skinner thrived on, but he could not carry so lackluster a play alone. In his autobiography Skinner gives the play merely passing mention, just enough to imply it was better than many thought.

In that same book Skinner acknowledged that he prodded Josephine Preston Peabody to write **The Piper** (1-30-11, New), then refused to star in it. So the theatre assigned Edith Wynne Matthison his role, leading Walter Prichard Eaton to howl, "There is no more reason why Miss Matthison should have been assigned to the part than why Miss Adams should have played Rostand's rooster." To make matters worse: "Constantly through 'The Piper' she has as distinct a sob in her voice as Caruso in the famed finale to Act I of 'Pagliacci.'" At least this retelling of the Pied Piper legend was, as were all New Theatre productions, sumptuously mounted. The first and last acts showed Hamelin's market square, surrounded by steep-roofed houses and a dark church. The second act took place in a gigantic cave, where the piper makes a rainbow to ease the children's fears. The third depicted a crossroads, with a neglected shrine and a weather-worn figure of Christ. Here "the procession of priests and villagers from Hamelin is heard approaching, swinging censers and chanting. The Piper softly pipes, and the

gravest of them, all the pilgrims, begin to dance their way back home in confusion." Inevitably the blank-verse drama's theme meant matinees were crowded, but evening performances were not. Like *Judith Zaraine,* this American play had been performed in England before Broadway saw it; there it had won the coveted Stratford Prize.

Edward Sheldon's **The Boss** (1-30-11, Astor) was probably the season's most gripping new American drama. James Griswold (Henry Weaver) and his son, Donald (Howard Estabrook), two grain contractors who consider themselves gentlemen, reluctantly confess they have been driven to the wall since Michael Regan, an "Irish tough of an ex-barkeep[,] has come along and swindled and blackjacked and knifed his way up." They have agreed to meet Regan at their home to discuss a resolution to the problem. When Regan (Holbrook Blinn) arrives, he is seen to be a thirtyish Irishman who obviously has come into money and power but doesn't yet know how to handle his new position gracefully. The Griswolds are cautiously surprised to learn that Regan will work out a compromise even though he knows the elder Griswold is a director of the banks that have lent the Griswold firm money: "D'ye think a jury o' reformed porch climbers is goin' t' believe them securities was any better when ye gave 'em than they are now? Hear me laugh! Ha! Ha! No, ye was a director an' ye used the bank's funds to float yer own business an' ye got left. That's how it'll look on the front page o' the one-cent daily!" But the key demand of Regan's outrages the men: the Griswold daughter, Emily (Emily Stevens), in marriage. Emily is a beautiful young woman who spends much of her free time working with the poor in the very ward out of which Regan rose. She agrees, to her family's consternation, to accept Regan—not so much to save her father and brother as to spare the many workers who would lose everything if the Griswolds' default led to bank failures. But she, too, has a condition: "I'll marry you. But if I do, it's with the understanding that everything stops at the church door. I won't really be your wife." Regan agrees.

Time passes. The vengeful younger Griswold has persuaded Regan's employees to strike, persuaded the workers' archbishop to back him, and thwarted an attempt of Regan to bring in new help. Regan's answer is to plan to move his operations out of the country, bankrupt the city, and, before even that can happen, foreclose on the mortgages of his striking employees. He also gets his henchmen to attack Donald, who is rushed to the hospital in serious condition. His actions bring about a showdown between him and Emily, who shouts that she is his wife. Regan replies:

"My wife! That's a good one, that is! . . . Ye've built a wall round yerself t' keep me out, an' gee! it done the job. Why, I seen ye crack a smile at the butler there an' talk t' him almost like he was human! But me! Say, have ye ever done any more than that t' me? No, by Gawd, ye let me live here in the house with ye day after day, ye let me lie alone there in my bed night after night, thinkin' o' the locked door between us an' sufferin' through the black hours like I didn't know a man could suffer. . . . Ye say ye feel sorry for them strikers. Well, lemme tell ye right here, there's not one of 'em that ain't got more'n me! I don't care if he's cold an' his stummick's empty an' the window's busted an' the roof's leakin'! *He's got someone t' love him,* so I guess he'll see it through!"

After Regan is carted off to jail and news comes that Donald will pull through, Emily and Regan meet and realize how much they have come to love each other. Regan abandons his plans to run away, and he hands over the mortgages to Emily.

Neither the coarse, brutally grasping Regan (reputedly suggested by a contemporary Buffalo politician) nor the sometimes fuzzily liberal Emily was a character likely to appeal to the more affluent playgoers needed to keep the box office humming. Yet Blinn's "unimpeachably fine" performance succeeded in making Regan comprehensible, even at times likable, while the slim, flaxen-haired Miss Stevens, who was Mrs. Fiske's niece, brought her growing experience and credibility to Emily. The play ran eleven weeks.

February began with another of the season's many one-week flops. The growing count of such fiascos suggested that theatrical economics, while uncommonly healthy by late 20th-century standards, could still be harsh, although numerous such shows hurried back out on the road. In Walter Hackett's **Our World** (2-6-11, Garrick) a doctor (Campbell Gollan), ignoring the fact that he himself is a reformed drunkard and his son (Malcolm Duncan) is showing signs of incipient alcoholism, demands that his prospective daughter-in-law (Doris Keane) prove that she can behave herself in society better than her mother (Amelia Gardner), a woman with a past, had. When the girl nearly falls for the wiles of the same conscienceless roué (Vincent Serrano) who once had seduced her mother, mama storms into the man's apartment to save her.

February's biggest hit was Rupert Hughes's **Excuse Me** (2-13-11, Gaiety), a farce made additionally

memorable by its remarkable replication of entire Pullman cars. In one act the sleeping car is made up for the evening; in the last act it is seen by day. The second act shows the lounge and observation car. Just as the train is about to pull out, Harry Mallory (John Westley) and Marjorie Newton (Ann Murdock) dash aboard. Harry has been called to army duty in the Philippines. The couple had hoped to marry and have a brief honeymoon before he left, but their taxi broke down on the way to the minister, so they board the train still unwed. They hope against hope that a minister may be on board. Actually one is, but the Rev. Walter Temple (John Findlay) has doffed his clerical garb, put on a sporting red cravat, and embarked with his wife (Lottie Alter) on a long-dreamt-of spree. He refuses to acknowledge his calling. Another couple on board are in a similar position to Harry and Marjorie, so they have wired ahead for a minister to meet and marry them in Ogden. But there the train starts to pull out as the clergyman finishes his first service. Harry tries to stop him and is left holding the hurriedly departed minister's jacket for his pains. Then two masked men attempt to hold up the train. The holdup discloses the presence of the disguised clergyman. Harry grabs one of the holdup men's guns, forces both men to surrender, and then turns the pistol on the minister—who performs the marriage.

Besides the principal characters, the train was filled with interesting minor figures, such as a fat man who can't stop eating, a long-suffering conductor, a flirtatious divorcée, and, best of all according to contemporary commentators, a porter deliciously played in blackface by Willis Sweatnam, who decades earlier had been a famous minstrel. The farce regaled New Yorkers for twenty weeks. In 1918 it became a Jerome Kern musical, *Toot-Toot!*

The evening's three other openings all had foreign tinges. **Nobody's Daughter** (2-13-11, New) was an English play by George Paston (the pen name for a British lady). American audiences were not interested in the attempts of two well-born Londoners to interfere in the life of their illegitimate daughter. Nor were they entertained by **The Zebra** (2-13-11, Garrick), Paul Potter's Americanization of a French farce by Paul Armont and Marcel Nancey in which two husbands attempt to take a holiday without their wives. And, *Trelawny of the Wells* having run its course, Ethel Barrymore appeared in a revival of *Alice Sit-by-the-Fire* coupled with a Barrie one-acter, **The Twelve-Pound Look** (2-13-11, Empire). Its slight story told of a woman who has left home and supported herself rather than live with an insufferable husband (Charles Dalton) and who finds herself called on to be his temporary secretary. In afteryears the playlet served as a favorite vehicle for Miss Barrymore's vaudeville appearances.

Another farce, this time of Hungarian origin, had a modest success thanks in large part to one young actress. Ferenc Herczeg's **Seven Sisters** [*Gyurkovics lányok* (*The Gyurkovics Girls*)] (2-20-11, Lyceum) recounted the comic difficulties a mother (Clara T. Bracy) has in marrying off her daughters in order of their age, especially after the one daughter who was thought to present no problem, having been consigned to a convent, is sent back home following a wild midnight fling. Of the actress who played that daughter, one critic noted, "Miss Laurette Taylor, with limited opportunities, was, in fact, the shining light of the performance. To begin with, she is an actress with a most engagingly fresh and different personality. To this she adds the values of a method of playing unlike anyone else. In her hands Mici became a fascinating little hoyden, arch, saucy, irresponsible, and yet always delightfully feminine and appealing."

By the criteria of seven decades later, no success of the 1910–11 season is more baffling than that of Walter Browne's morality play **Everywoman** (2-27-11, Herald Square). In an inexplicable hodgepodge of rhymed couplets, blank verse, and prose, Browne unfolded the saga of Everywoman (Laura Nelson Hall), her true and false friends, and her hangers-on such as Youth (Patricia Collinge), Beauty (Aurora Platt), Conscience (Wilda Bennett), and Wealth (Frederic de Belleville). Everywoman's search for Love leads her to become an actress, to entertain lavishly in a sumptous dining room, to witness the passing away of Youth amid Broadway's bright lights and skyscrapers, and finally to discover that Love (Edward Mackay) has been awaiting her all the time right at home. Costumes were also an outlandish melange, ranging from modern gowns and tails through Puritan garb, medieval clothing, and Greek drapery. Typical of Browne's writing was the entrance of Youth, Beauty, and Modesty (Juliette Day):

Born of a sunbeam's purity
Beauty, Youth and Modesty.
Three little winsome maidens we,
Each of sunshine savors.

And then there was the entrance of Flattery (Frank Lacy):

No stranger, I. When not on active duty,
    Attending my lord and master, King Love the
    First,

Within the magic of a maiden's mirror
I make my home.

Despite such nonsense, headlines on the order of "Everyone, Everywhere, Will Like 'Everywoman' " attracted sufficient patronage to keep the play running for 144 performances.

The settings and costumes for Mary Austin's **The Arrow Maker** (2-27-11, New) were even more magnificent. The first set—The Chisera's Wickiup, Valley of Sagharawite—showed the bottom of a deep canyon whose rocky walls ascended into the flies; the second act—The Camp of Sagharawite—depicted a small Indian village crammed onto a mesa ledge, with the desert stretching endlessly into the distance below; another high-walled mountain pass—The Top of Toorape—was the setting for the last act. Indian costumes with gaudy beads, colorful fabrics, and feathery spectacle added to the picture, as did war dances staged by one Chief Red Eagle, a man reputed to be half Winnebago and half Piute. Only the "lethargic" play was unsatisfactory. It centered on an Indian medicine woman, a Chisera (Edith Wynne Matthison), who loves Simwa (Frank Gillmore), an arrow maker. For all his fine craftsmanship, he cannot match the magic arrow she gives him: "However far and feebly it is shot, it flies straight to the mark, over hills and high mountains, in the dark or light, and death rides upon its shaft." When she finds that Simwa has been unfaithful and has agreed to marry the daughter of the tribe's chief, the Chisera brings famine and plague on her village. She claims she has lost the power to do good, but after Simwa is slain just as he himself was about to kill her with the magic arrow, the power returns.

At a time when several exciting new playwrights were emerging each season, one voice from the past continued to come across loud and clear. More than one critic hailed Augustus Thomas's **As a Man Thinks** (3-13-11, 39th St.) as the author's best work. Two stories were skillfully interwoven. One told of a famous publisher, Frank Clayton (John Flood), who learns that his wife (Chrystal Herne) has gone to visit another man, Benjamin De Lota (Walter Hale), in his apartments and so demands a divorce, even though he himself had been caught twice being unfaithful to Mrs. Clayton. In the second story a young Jewish girl, Vedah Seelig (Charlotte Ives), discovers that her betrothed, the same De Lota, is a notorious philanderer and so agrees to wed Julian Burrill (Vincent Serrano), even though her deeply religious parents will object to her marrying a Christian. Tying the two stories together was Vedah's father, Dr. Seelig (John Mason), a compassionate physician who overcomes both his friends' and neighbors' anti-Semitism and his own prejudice against mixed marriages.

A number of contrivances—such as a phone conveniently left off the hook at a crucial moment—strained credulity. And some of Seelig's arguments might not be accepted by later generations. Thus Seelig addresses Mrs. Clayton, who is furious at her husband's double standard: "Men work for the children because they believe the children are—their own—*believe*. Every mother *knows* she is the mother of her son or daughter. Let her be however wicked, no power on earth can shake that knowledge. Every father believes he is a father only by his faith in the woman. Let him be however virtuous, no power on earth can strengthen in him a conviction greater than that faith. There is a double standard of morality because upon the golden basis of woman's virtue rests the welfare of the world." Yet for all the play's faults, the elegance of its writing gave immediate theatrical acceptability to Thomas's intricate artificialities. Moreover, fine performances, especially that of Mason—"simple and quiet and authoritative in his manner"—augmented its appeal. The play ran until hot weather stifled it.

Many a critic gleefully advised (or warned) his readers that the James Halleck Reid listed as the author of **The Confession** (3-13-11, Bijou) was none other than the Hal Reid of the recently jettisoned touring melodramas. His story was hardly new, and his writing, while discarding the multiple cliff-hanging curtains of the old school, betrayed his history. A priest (Orrin Johnson) who has heard the confession of a murderer (Theodore Roberts) must remain silent when his own brother (Harold Vosbrugh) is accused of the crime, tried, convicted, and sentenced to be hanged. The killer's last-minute confession spares the innocent man. Mixed in with this for comic relief were such old touring-melodrama standbys as a slang-spouting waif and a clownish Irishman. The parts were actors' delights, and "Theodore Roberts never was in better shape than when, in a great scene, he decides that the hangman's noose was too uncomfortable to consider and that he preferred to let the innocent man hang, all of which he expressed to the priest by sign manuals, guttural utterances, wicked leers of triumph and other manifestations of deviltry known only to people of supreme deviltry who know how to act. As a bit of acting it is worth seeing." Contemporary audiences clearly relished such carryings-on. Another reviewer reported that the drama's pathetic moments "kept the majority of women in tears for fully half of the playing time." With such responses

it was small wonder the play did seven weeks of good late-season business in New York and prospered on tour.

The next afternoon saw the premiere at a special matinee of a play by Reid's most prolific erstwhile rival, Owen Davis. **Lola** (3-14-11, Lyceum) begins as Dr. Barnheim (Sheldon Lewis) reveals to his shocked prospective son-in-law, John Dorris (Shelley Hull), that he has perfected an instrument to restore dead people to life. Dorris protests, fearing that, while the doctor might make the heart beat again, he could not restore the soul. The matter is put to the test almost at once when the doctor's daughter, Lola (Laurette Taylor), dies suddenly. Sure enough, the girl who had been so sweet and docile is now seen as selfish and vicious. There is a happy ending when the whole affair turns out to be a dream. Critics slapped the writing and scoffed at the increasingly clichéd use of a green spotlight on an odd scientific experiment, but once again they sang paeans to Miss Taylor.

Only a sumptuous mounting of **Thaïs** (3-14-11, Criterion), which Paul Wilstach dramatized from Anatole France's novel and which starred Tyrone Power as the anchorite and Constance Collier as the seductress, came between the Reid and Davis plays and another work by a onetime touring melodramatist. But Theodore Kremer's *The Triumph of an Empress,* which opened a month's run at the Garden on the 20th, was not new. It first had been done on the road in 1903 and had played at the Yorkville Theatre in May of 1908.

That same evening saw a more worthwhile revival at the Lyceum, where Mrs. Fiske reappeared in *Becky Sharp,* with Henry E. Dixey as Steyne and Henry Stephenson as Rawdon Crawley. New York's most dogged playgoers were thereby afforded a chance to compare this fine American version with the London redaction offered at the New Theatre earlier in the season.

That struggling playhouse had a new bill ready the following week—if only for a single matinee—when it offered **Noah's Flood** and **Nice Wanton** (3-27-11, New), two medieval mystery or morality plays, accompanied by a lecture from Brander Matthews.

A brace of novelties ushered in April. One was among the season's best plays—and its last hit. The play was Harry James Smith's **Mrs. Bumpstead-Leigh** (4-3-11, Lyceum) with Mrs. Fiske in the title role. Contemporary critics, however, were not bowled over by the work, although they disagreed on its flaws. One, for example, thought the basic premise preposterous; another claimed the play lacked a consistency of tone, moving back and forth among burlesque, farce, and high comedy.

The de Salles—mama (Florine Arnold), married daughter, Adelaide (Mrs. Fiske), and eligible younger daughter, Violet (Kathleen MacDonell)—have come to Long Island hoping to finalize plans for Violet's marriage to Anthony Rawson (Douglas J. Wood). It is soon obvious that Adelaide—Mrs. Bumpstead-Leigh—is in charge. She is quick, clever, and haughty, and though she admits to having been born in Washington, she professes to know little about America, having been brought up in the best European circles. Her English marriage suggests as much. She tells Anthony and his maiden aunt (Kate Lester) that America sometimes both baffles and frightens her:

Adelaide: Am I correctly informed, Anthony, that in certain of your institutions of learning for young women, the students meet regularly in football contests with antagonists of the opposite sex?
Anthony: I question it.
Adelaide: Ça me donne les frissons!—yet why? Only because, in imagination, I seem to see our girls so engaged. And the thought comes; has not the American young woman inherited many of the best traits of the Indian women—what was the scientific term for them? Papooses?—that preceded her?
Miss Rawson: (Horrified but impressed) Of course, there is no actual blood-relationship between them.
Adelaide: Surely not! Oh, surely not! And yet family, here in America, impresses us English as being such an odd, tangled sort of affair!

Actually, Mrs. Bumpstead-Leigh should have no difficulty understanding American ways, for she was born and raised in Missionary Loop, Ind., home base for her father as he traveled about the country peddling Sayle's Favorite Stomach Elixir and Sissapoola Indian Herb Remedies. But hiding her past is not Mrs. Bumpstead-Leigh's only problem, for Violet is having doubts about marrying Anthony—especially after meeting his younger, more carefree brother, Geoffrey (Malcolm Duncan). Adelaide warns her sister about all men:

Adelaide: Not one man in a dozen is what a nice woman would like to think him. He's selfish, he's greedy, he's egotistical; and the more he fiddle-diddles about the beauty and sacredness of love, the more you'd better look out for him!
Violet: (With dismay) Oh! How can you bear to live!
Adelaide: (With buoyant conviction) Oh, I decided

quite a long time ago—just as you are going to decide—that there's something—very—well—worth—living for—after all! (Measuring each word)
Violet: Yes?
Adelaide: To strike—the best bargain—with the world—you can!

A third problem crops up suddenly and ominously in the figure of a tombstone salesman, Peter Swallow (Henry E. Dixey), who had been Adelaide's beau in her Missionary Loop days. Adelaide skillfully bluffs her way through their meeting, only to have Violet, upset at Anthony, explode the whole charade. The de Salles are ordered to leave at once, but by threatening to tell all to a waiting newspaperman, Adelaide convinces the Rawsons to accept Violet and Geoffrey's engagement and to allow her and her mother to remain until they can make a more graceful exit.

Whatever reservation aisle-sitters had about the play, most were laudatory about the star. "Mrs. Fiske," exclaimed one delighted reviewer, "has never played anything with more delicious drollery and naturalness. Politely suave in her company manners, she has the raucous voice of the old days when she commands her mother or lays down the law to her younger sister." He might have added that she reinforced some of her edicts with an elbow in the ribs. An eight-week New York engagement was part of a highly profitable cross-country tour. Besides being the Fiskes' biggest money-maker in many a season, it served to introduce another playwright of great promise— one who, like several other of his equally promising contemporaries, would have his career tragically cut short.

. . .

Harry James Smith (1880–1918) was born in New Britain, Conn., studied biology at Williams College and Harvard, then taught at Oberlin. He left teaching to take a position as an associate editor of the *Atlantic Monthly* in 1906. At the same time he started to write plays, but none was produced until *Mrs. Bumpstead-Leigh*.

. . .

Having dealt successfully with a gentleman from Mississippi, Harrison Rhodes and Thomas A. Wise turned their attention to **An Old New Yorker** (4-3-11, Daly's), but this time their luck ran out on them. Wise was starred as Samuel Beekman, who turns over the business he has run along old-fashioned lines for many years to his late partner's son (William Rosell). The young man overreaches and nearly destroys the company until Beekman returns to set matters right again.

A revival of *The Dictator,* at the Comedy on the 13th, with William Collier recreating his original role, enjoyed good business for six weeks.

Two days later a new theatre opened. The bandbox Playhouse was to be William A. Brady's flagship for many years, and he opened it on the 15th for two special performances—matinee and evening—of Geraldine Bonner and Hutcheson Boyd's **Sauce for the Goose.** Mrs. Brady—Grace George—was starred. Perhaps naturally, perhaps tellingly, most reviews gave far more space to the theatre than to the play, which they perceived as a trite rehashing of *Divorçons.* With no cry for it to be held over, the comedy's first two performances were its last.

Mildred Holland, reputedly a great favorite in smaller towns across America, braved New York in a vehicle that had served her well for several seasons, Carina Jordan's *The Lily and the Prince* (4-17-11, Garden). She played a girl who comes to the Borgias to seek their help in freeing her father, falsely accused of treason. A prince (Jack Standing) who had been courting Lucretia Borgia (Dorothy Rosemore) falls in love with her, thereby angering the family. After a week Miss Holland switched to *Camille.*

Robert Mantell, increasingly viewed as limited in artistry and superannuated in style, came into Daly's on the 17th. He began with *King Lear,* then moved on swiftly to *As You Like It, The Merchant of Venice, Hamlet, Othello, Richard III, Macbeth, Romeo and Juliet, Julius Caesar,* and two non-Shakespearean works, *Richelieu* and *Louis XI.*

An all-star revival of *The Lights o' London* arrived at the Lyric on May 1 and did good business for its four-week engagement. Stars included William Courtenay, Charles Richman, Holbrook Blinn, Thomas A. Wise, Douglas Fairbanks, Lawrence D'Orsay, Thomas Q. Seabrooke (a musical-stage favorite), and Doris Keane.

Two foreign plays closed the season. Both were seven-performance failures. No doubt Doris Keane and William Courtenay were too busy with *The Lights o' London* to see Charles Recht's translation of Jaroslav Kvapil's **The Clouds** (5-15-11, Bijou). The intriguing question is, did Edward Sheldon, who was then courting Miss Keane, see it before he sailed for his European vacation that same month? For *The Clouds* told of a beautiful young actress (Sara Biala) who returns to her hometown and finds that the young man (Harry L. Fraser) she has loved since childhood is studying for the priesthood. He

falls madly in love with her again, but, sensing that she would stand in the way of his calling, she lets him believe she has been trifling with him and returns to the stage.

Youth (6-8-11, Bijou), Herman Bernstein's translation of Max Halbe's drama, told a not unrelated story. A young girl (Louise Woods) in the first throes of womanhood is slated for a convent. But she decides to run away with her childhood sweetheart (Pell Thorton) instead. Her idiot half-brother (David Manning), aiming to kill the young man, kills the girl by mistake. Many critics agreed with their colleague who saw possibilities in the play but rued that "the translation was very bad, and the acting with few exceptions was worse."

However disappointing the season's end was, most commentators took a rosy view of the year as a whole. "The past season," one wrote, "has distinction in the very high quality of some of the new and notable plays produced, and in its marked tendency in the progressive development of new ideas, and in the new treatment of old ideas." Admittedly some of the most highly praised works failed at the box office, while less admired plays thrived. But that is always the case. Another writer, taking a more commercial stance, noted, "Of the ninety-nine new plays [including musicals]—and this means new to New York—twenty-three were pronounced successes. That is not such a bad record." The same observer added that thirty-three more shows, although they had failed to recoup their costs on Broadway, seemed likely to reap handsome profits on the road. Yet there were a few depressing notes. Business on the road, albeit good, was still feeling the impact of films. In New York the highly touted New Theatre threw in the towel. Renamed the Century, it was leased to commercial interests for the coming season.

1911–1912

Optimism abounded as the new season got under way. *Theatre*'s lead article in September was a survey of forthcoming months, framed by miniature photographs of thirty starred players, from such oldtimers as Sothern and Drew to such youngsters as Grace George, Alla Nazimova, and Billie Burke. The article branded the new term as "unusually promising" and went on to assert, "The challenge for native plays of superior merit has been answered

690

by every American dramatist of promise"—a pronouncement no one would have dared to make a decade earlier. By season's end many of the brightest promises were viewed as woefully tarnished; still, the year as a whole was very good indeed.

Actually the season had begun long before *Theatre*'s September issue appeared on newsstands. On June 19, Sarah Bernhardt, concluding a strenuous cross-country tour, came into the Globe for four performances before sailing home. If her trek had exhausted the sixty-seven-year-old actress, she gave no sign of it. She offered *Sister Beatrice* and *Jean Marie* on her first night, *L'Aiglon* the following evening, *La Femme X* at a matinee, and *La Dame aux camélias* for her farewell the same night.

A heat wave and negative reviews doomed the season's first American play, Thomas T. Railey's **Baxter's Partner** (6-27-11, Bijou). Railey, himself a lawyer, told of the courtroom clash between two attorneys. Dan Huntley (Robert Ellis) has killed a man in self-defense, then fled rather than involve the lady who was with him at the time. He is caught and brought to trial, where he is defended by Howard MacFarland (Robert Ober), who loves the woman Huntley is believed to be shielding. MacFarland was also formerly a partner of Benjamin Baxter (Charles Reigle), now the prosecutor in the case. Baxter's blistering examination of the defendant brings out the identity of the woman Huntley really is protecting—Baxter's own wife.

The same heat wave cut short Sothern and Marlowe's engagement at the Broadway, which began on July 3 and, after Miss Marlowe became ill, closed on July 4. They hurried aboard an ocean liner and spent the summer in England, where they were married. When they returned in the fall they came into the huge Manhattan Opera House in November, offering the repertory they had promised in July: *Macbeth, The Taming of the Shrew, Hamlet, The Merchant of Venice, Romeo and Juliet, Twelfth Night,* and, for added measure, *As You Like It.*

"With a personality of compelling charm, a comic technic unsurpassed on the stage to-day, Miss Henrietta Crosman is persistently unfortunate in the selection of the mediums for the display of her admirable art. Here is a comedienne whose methods are as magnetic, as buoyant and as artlessly convincing as those of Ellen Terry. She should be a veritable fixture in the metropolis, yet her visits are short and far between, and all for want of a good, suitable vehicle." According to most critics, the beautiful, matronly actress didn't stumble on one in Catherine Chisholm Cushing's **The Real Thing** (8-10-11, Maxine Elliott's). She played a widow who finds her sister (Minnie Dupree) is so preoccupied with her children and so house-proud that she is neglecting and losing her husband (Frank Mills). She puts her sister back on the path to a happy marriage and wins herself a new husband (Albert Brown) in the process. Despite the play's critical drubbing, Miss Crosman's followers were numerous enough to keep the comedy on the boards for two months before it set out on tour.

Another summer heat wave was responsible in part for quickly finishing off a more interesting venture. With temperatures approaching ninety, John E. Kellerd took over the old, and of course unair-conditioned, Irving Place Theatre, New York's major home to German-language productions, to offer what was billed as the first New York performance in English of Sophocles' *Oedipus Rex.* George Riddle had presented some performances in the 1880s, but he had spoken in Greek while the rest of the cast used an English translation. Critics reviewing Kellerd's premiere on August 21 were enthusiastic, praising the mounting's simplicity and honesty and suggesting Kellerd frequently conveyed Sophocles' tragic exultation. Some, however, quibbled that playing the drama through without an intermission was foolish, especially in light of the heat. *Hamlet, Macbeth,* and *The Merchant of Venice* were also part of Kellerd's short-lived repertory. They caused no stir at the time, although Kellerd's Dane would shortly enter theatrical history.

A younger, more widely popular actor had better luck with a lesser work, a comic treatment of the increasingly voguish crook play. **A Gentleman of Leisure** (8-24-11, Playhouse) was dramatized by John Stapleton and P. G. Wodehouse from Wodehouse's story of New York high life. Its playboy hero agrees, on a bet, to burglarize a house. That house happens to be home to New York's tough, crooked deputy chief of police, "Big Phil" Creedon (George Fawcett), and Creedon's very pretty daughter, Mollie (Ruth Shepley), whom, by farcical coincidence, the hero had met and mooned over during a recent transatlantic crossing. Two acts of complications and one of happy resolution followed. The hero was played "with zest and swirling vitality" by Douglas Fairbanks, "his eyes shining like black brilliants, out of a strong-featured, sun-bronzed face." Critics thought the play didn't quite come off, but it ran ten weeks. When it was done two years later in Chicago as *A Thief for a Night,* it starred another rising young player, John Barrymore.

In late 1911 Rose Stahl, who many felt resembled a young Bernhardt in appearance, was bigger box office than either Fairbanks or Barrymore, and

Charles Klein, the author of her newest vehicle, **Maggie Pepper** (8-31-11, Harris), still stood tall in the front ranks of American dramatists. The new vehicle was something of a change for Klein, a heart-tugging comedy. His curtain rose on the oak-paneled stockroom of Holbrook and Co., a dry-goods store. The store is not flourishing since the third-generation Holbrook, Joe (Frederick Truesdell), is too busy cavorting around Europe. He has turned operations over to the haughty, nepotic Mr. Hargen (Grant Stewart), to whose niece, Ethel (Jean Horton), he is engaged. As one disgruntled employee remarks, goods at the store are "as new as a cold-storage egg" (echoes of last season's *The Nest Egg*). There is one bright live wire in the store, Maggie Pepper, who should be in line for promotion to buyer but is passed over by Hargen in favor of his niece's friend. To make matters worse, Maggie's own niece (Beatrice Prentice) and her sister-in-law (Beverly Sitgreaves), the daughter and widow of Maggie's late brother, are arrested in the store for shoplifting. The sister-in-law has come under the influence of a professional crook, Jim Darkin (J. Harry Benrimo), so with the help of a sympathetic store detective, the mannish Mrs. Thatcher (Eleanor Lawson), Maggie arranges to send the older woman off to prison and take the fourteen-year-old under her own tutelage. Upset by the commotion and by being unfairly passed over, Maggie pours her heart out to a stranger who saunters into the stockroom and asks Maggie what she would do to improve sales: "What would I do? I'd turn things upside down—We're overstocked—we sell old goods—and we don't advertise as we ought—We're behind the times—It's old mildewed methods that are ruining Holbrook and Company—Why it's like a morgue here—We ought to have music—life—gayety—I've got an idea for an escalator to go all around the store—you know how tired fat women get, chasing different departments." Luckily for Maggie, the man she tells all this to is Joe, and he puts her in charge.

A year passes, and the store is prospering. Only Hargen and Ethel are unhappy at how close Joe and Maggie have grown. Why, they have even been seen dining together in a restaurant (echoes now of *Baby Mine*)! Hargen and Ethel contrive to make Maggie think Joe desires her resignation. A tipsy Joe, who has learned of the trickery, comes to Maggie's apartment to reassure her, but he is shot by Darkin, who has come in search of his wife (paroled and living with Maggie) and his stepdaughter. Maggie nurses Joe back to health, and Joe realizes he really loves her. In subplots Darkin blackmails Maggie

over her wish to retain her niece, and Maggie is courted by a comic Jewish peddler (Lee Kohlmar).

It was Miss Stahl's performance that made a no more than competent play the season's first hit. Although she played a sharp, strong girl, her initial entrance—when Maggie is weighed down by rumors she is to be passed over—gave proof of her art. "People came and went [in the stock room] uttering the jargon of their trade. Suddenly there was a hush in the audience. Something had happened on the stage to focus the divided interest. A woman had crept in from the first entrance [downstage], a crushed, crouching, tired little figure in rusty black, with a worn sad face and hopeless eyes. For five minutes she said not a word, merely glancing in a frightened way from one to the other, her eyes travelling from stern faces to angry ones, from angry to indifferent. But one forgot all the other figures on stage, and saw only hers." She and the play were so well received that she performed it for nearly five months in New York and then on tour for three full seasons. A 1922 musical version was called *Letty Pepper*. No one could know that this was the last success either she or Klein would enjoy. Klein, his career itself sinking fast, was lost on the *Lusitania;* Miss Stahl, although she lived to a very ripe old age, faded after her failure to discover other suitable vehicles.

At least in New York, Hubert Henry Davies's London comedy **A Single Man** (9-4-11, Empire) was almost as successful, chalking up a three-month run. But then, virtually any play with the incomparably polished John Drew as star was ensured some success. Drew played a middle-aged writer who decides it is time for him to wed and must choose among three prospects (Mary Boland, Thais Lawton, and Carroll McComas).

Three plays that fell short of success by varying degrees followed. Frank McIntyre, "who has the figure of President Taft and almost as large a popular following," was the main attraction in George Bronson Howard's **Snobs** (9-4-11, Hudson). As Henry Disney, a milkman with a route covering 142 families, he suddenly learns that he is heir to a dukedom and $70,000,000. His attempts to be certain that people like him for himself and not for his position or wealth provided the laughs. In time he wins the hand of a rich pickle manufacturer's daughter (Willette Kershaw).

As unusual set was the best thing about Elmer Harris's short-lived, four-character comedy **Thy Neighbor's Wife** (9-5-11, Lyceum). The curtain rose to disclose two adjoining, semi-detached suburban cottages, with small, neat lawns out front. Their porched lower floors have quarry-stone walls; their second stories have eaved, shingled roofs. Mrs. Robins (Pamela Gaythorne) loves all-night parties and hates housekeeping; her husband, John (Arthur Byron), is a quiet stay-at-home. Next door the situation at the Millers' (Frederick Tiden and Alice Johns) is just the opposite. So the couples decide to exchange partners but end by concluding their first choices were better. A sign of how healthy theatrical economics were at the time was the show's prompt taking to the road after a dismal two weeks on Broadway.

If the scene as the curtain rose on *Thy Neighbor's Wife* was its best moment, many critics selected the quiet seconds before the final curtain at Lee Wilson Dodd's **Speed** (9-9-11, Comedy) as its high point. To keep up with their other suburban neighbors, Edwin and Victoria Wise (Orrin Johnson and Oza Waldrop) buy an automobile they can scarcely afford. It soon drives them to distraction and near-bankruptcy; then their chauffeur (Larry Broder) wrecks it during a joy ride. A more sensible young couple might have left bad enough alone, but the Wises immediately order a new car. As soon as it is delivered, they hurry out to test it. Their little son (Thomas R. Tobin, Jr.), forgotten in the excitement, stands forlornly by the living-room window, watching them drive away.

Much publicity was accorded the fact that the Isaac Landman who wrote **A Man of Honor** (9-14-11, Weber's) was a rabbi. But his play had little to do directly with religion, focusing instead on a judge (Edmund Breese) who refuses to be swayed in trying a case by blackmailers ready to reveal his son (Hans Robert) is an embezzler. The play was dismissed as platitudinous and preachy.

First-string critics that same night found more satisfaction in a British play, Haddon Chambers's **Passers-by** (9-14-11, Criterion). A rich young man (Richard Bennett), prompted by his valet (Julian Royce), takes in some homeless Londoners. One (Louise Rutter) turns out to be the girl he had loved and, unknown to him, had a child by but of whom he had lost track. They are happily reunited only after the youngster (Master Davis) is taken away temporarily by the other homeless guest (Ernest Lawford).

Its programs called Thompson Buchanan's **The Rack** (9-15-11, Playhouse) "a play of social inquisition," leading one waggish critic to observe, "Slow torture would describe it more tersely and directly." That curious bugaboo of the era opens the play: a wife (Katherine Grey) is found by her mercurial husband (Milton Sills) dining publicly with another man (Conway Tearle). Shots ensue, and the man falls dead. The husband thinks the wife fired the gun; the wife believes her husband did it. A courtroom scene brings out that neither was the actual killer. The play ran a week and a half.

Harrison Rhodes's **Modern Marriage** (9-16-11, Bijou), taken from the German, ran a week longer. It told how a young suitor (Cyril Scott) brings all manner of comic complications on himself by pretending to be the author of a book on marriage, which his fiancée (Emily Stevens) uses as a guide.

Two of the season's biggest hits followed on two successive evenings. The first was a play about an English prime minister, written to order by an English dramatist for an English-born star. However, since that star, George Arliss, had become an American by adoption, and since the play was done in America five years before the West End saw it, Louis N. Parker's **Disraeli** (9-18-11, Wallack's) has some precarious claim to being considered American. When Sir Michael Probert (Herbert Standing), the short-sighted, anti-Semitic head of the Bank of England, refuses to lend Disraeli the money he needs to purchase controlling interest in the Suez Canal, the prime minister turns to a fellow Jew, a rich banker, Hugh Meyers (Oscar Ayde). But Disraeli must also contend with Mrs. Travers (Margaret Dale), a clever adventuress in the pay of the Russians, who also covet the canal. To this end he wins over a snobbish young bigot, Charles, Viscount Deeford (Ian Maclaren), hoping at the same time to make Charles more acceptable to the charming Lady Clarissa Pevesney (Elsie Leslie), who loves Charles but has refused his proposal because she objects to his haughty, hate-filled comments. Mrs. Travers has sent her husband to Cairo to outbid the English, but Disraeli sees to it that Charles gets there first and wins. His triumph is short-lived, for Mrs. Travers has conspired to bankrupt Meyers, meaning the check the English have offered the Egyptians is worthless. Disraeli summons Probert and demands the bank help. Probert insolently refuses, shouting, "You cannot touch the Bank!"

Disraeli: I'll smash the Bank! Parliament granted the Bank its charter; Parliament can withdraw it.
Probert: Good God!
Disraeli: And shall withdraw it at my bidding! Your board of directors will be swept away; your shareholders bankrupt, the Bank ruined and you disgraced. I am Prime Minister! I *can* do this, and if you don't sign, by God, I *will!*
Probert: (*After some hesitation, crosses to the table and signs*) There, take your paper. I have signed it. I've signed it to save the Bank. It is outrageous

that a man like you should have such power! (*Exit*)

Clarissa: (*Coming to him with joyous enthusiasm*) Oh, Mr. Disraeli, thank God you have such power!

Disraeli: (*Whimsically*) I haven't, dear child; but he doesn't know that.

With the deal concluded, Victoria made Empress of India, and honors handed out all around, there is general forgiving and good will at a celebratory ball. Some side conversations in the play suggest that the more things change, the more they remain the same. Thus Charles tells a duke (Charles Carey) and duchess (Leila Repton) of his plans to build model cottages for the peasantry.

Duke: D'ye know what yer happy peasantry'll do, Deeford? They'll sell yer drain pipes for old lead; use yer staircase for fire-wood and keep pigs in yer pantry.

Charles: Then I shall turn them out.

Duke: Ay—and be held up to public execration as a harsh landlord.

Arliss's makeup defined Disraeli's appearance for two generations of Americans. And his performance, a few dissensions about his "staccato utterance" aside, won high praise. Walter Prichard Eaton wrote, "Dizzy was something of a fop . . . and Mr. Arliss catches this suggestion. But he was a brilliant man besides, with a Shavian gift of epigram, and Mr. Arliss tosses off those epigrams as brilliantly and spontaneously as could be desired. Disraeli, too, was Prime Minister of England, in the face of opposition, and that meant crafty power and iron will behind the suave, dandified ways and the bantering, sharp-edged epigrams. Not the least effective feature of Mr. Arliss's impersonation is his constant suggestion of this power and will, a suggestion made without our being conscious of the method. Merely, he dominates the scene when he is present." In the face of such enthusiastic notices, Arliss and the play enjoyed five full years of excellent business, including this eight-month New York stand.

William C. de Mille's **The Woman** (9-19-11, Republic) was a gripping, muckraking melodrama. "The public makes me sick," Jim Blake (John W. Cope) snarls contemptuously. Blake and his son-in-law, Mark Robertson (Edwin Holt), are corrupt congressmen, wheeling and dealing at the moment to push through a bill legalizing railway overcapitalization. They are being fought tooth and nail by a young maverick, Matthew Standish (Cuyler Has-

tings), and their only hope for victory is to find the identity of the woman with whom Standish once spent the night at a hotel. Standish is a married man, and the woman, though registered as Mrs. Standish, was not his wife. They decide to try to trick Standish by letting him think they know the lady's name and hoping he will rush to phone her. At first the ploy seems to work. Standish goes to the hotel's telephone operator, Wanda Kelly (Mary Nash)—her open booth is in the lobby—gives her a number, and speaks to the woman. Immediately afterward Robertson comes up to Wanda. He is determined to ingratiate himself with Wanda in order to wheedle the number from her. But first he tells the girl he wants to call his wife, Grace (Jane Peyton). The number he gives her is the same number Standish has just called. (This first-act curtain brought gasps from the audience.) Wanda is later interrogated by Robertson and Blake but steadfastly refuses to reveal the number Standish called. She also pulls the plug when the congressmen attempt to phone some malicious material about Standish to the newspapers. Her efforts not only result in the bill being killed and Mrs. Robertson's reputation preserved, but they win for her the love of Blake's more idealistic son, Tom (Harold Vosburgh).

Although the woman of the title was clearly meant to be Mrs. Robertson, for many playgoers the girl of the evening was dark-haired, dark-eyed Mary Nash. The young beauty's performance as Wanda deftly and tastefully mixed humor, determination, and pathos and earned her a reputation that would bring her important roles for more than a decade. But, as usually happened with any show in which he had a hand, David Belasco was looked on by critic after critic as the real genius behind the mounting's success. Not only did he elicit fine performances from all his players, but his knowing touches were everywhere and became for a time the talk of the town. In the case of *The Woman* a bit of telltale dialogue was heard before the curtain rose on each act. For example, as the lights dimmed at the start of Act I, Wanda was heard working her switchboard. And, of course, his physical production was memorable. "In this play," one critic reported, "he gives a section of hotel lobby that is complete in its illusive reproduction, with its marble walls, its telephone switchboard [fenced in by brass railings], the political 'Amen Corner,' its upholstered furniture, its telephone booths, in which the electric bulb indicates use; its uniformed boys paging guests, and every minute, essential details." The critic neglected to mention the elevator, which whirred on its way up and down and whose gate clicked realistically, or the night view, from the lobby window, of the Capitol with the House wing lit and the Senate wing dark. The drama ran a little more than seven months.

Arab bazaars crowded with real Arabs (whose nightly promenade from their rooms to the stage door became one of Broadway's most interesting sights for a while), palm trees, and even a genuine camel added a touch of verisimilitude to Edgar Selwyn's **The Arab** (9-23-11, Lyceum). The swarthily handsome author served as his own star, playing Jamil Abdullah Azam, "the best dragoman in the world." Jamil has been converted to Christianity four times—each in order to receive the gifts promised by missionaries. But when he falls in love with Mary Hilbert (Edna Baker), an American, his conversion seems more sincere, and he proves his sincerity by foiling an attempt of his Islamic brothers to massacre the Christians. He is dissuaded from sailing to America with Mary by the warning that Americans would not give a fig for his rank, so he extracts a promise from her that she will one day return and become his wife. Playgoers were left to end the romance as they chose. Selwyn's desert song was only moderately successful, playing two months before embarking on tour.

What the Doctor Ordered (9-20-11, Astor) in A. E. Thomas's farce was that a quarreling husband (Fritz Williams) and wife (Virginia Hammond) keep their distance from one another. They communicate by writing on their child's blackboard and by throwing dishes until the inevitable last-act reconciliation. The play closed after two and a half weeks but soon reappeared on vaudeville stages in a much shortened version.

The season's longest-running hit (431 performances) was George Broadhurst's **Bought and Paid For** (9-26-11, Playhouse). Its heroine, like the girl in *The Woman*, is a telephone operator. Her name is Virginia Blaine (Julia Dean). While she and her sister, Fanny (Marie Nordstrom), and blowhard brother-in-law-to-be, Jimmy Gilley (Frank Craven), are waiting for Robert Stafford (Charles Richman) to arrive at his swank apartment to join them in the dinner he has invited them to, she tells them how she met Stafford: "I was at my desk in the hotel about three months ago and he came and wanted a trunk call—I think it was Washington. There was some trouble getting his number and, as people will, we got into conversation about it." Thereafter Stafford found excuses for making a lot of calls from the hotel. Fanny and Jimmy hope Stafford will use the dinner to propose and will put them as well as Virginia on easy street. After all, Stafford has made himself one of the biggest men in "the City of Big

Things." Sure enough, he asks Virginia to marry him, but she is reluctant to decide. As they sit down to dinner she tells Fanny, "I haven't promised." Stafford overhears and raises his glass. "No, dear, but you will! To the future Mrs. Stafford."

Stafford always gets what he wants, and a year and a half later the Staffords are living in luxury. He has been a good brother-in-law, giving Jimmy a salary far beyond his value and even buying a car for the Gilleys. Virginia has fine clothes, jewels, and a box at the opera. But there is a dark side to all this. Stafford can be a mean drunk. When he comes home quite tipsy, Virginia refuses his embraces. He barks at her, "Who were you till I married you—nobody! And now who are you? You're Mrs. Robert Stafford; and what are you—you're the wife of one of the richest men in the country—and how did he get his wife? He bought you and he paid for you." Virginia rushes into her bedroom and locks the door. Stafford grabs a poker from the fireplace, smashes a hole in the door with it, puts his arm through the hole, unlocks the door, and enters the bedroom. Virginia leaves him. She, her sister, and Jimmy struggle along in a small apartment on 176th Street until Jimmy phones Stafford and leads him to believe that Virginia is repentant. Jimmy's ruse is quickly exposed, but Virginia and Stafford realize they love each other and Stafford swears off drink.

This time the telephone operator had the show stolen from her by Craven's likeably pushy shipping clerk. Jimmy has mixed feelings about his newfound good life. He loves his opera duds, but as to opera itself—"Fancy paying five a throw to hear a sawed-off Italian let go a few top notes, when you can have the same seat in a vaudeville theater and get Eva Tanguay and a whole bunch of good acts for a dollar! Five a throw to hear a dago yodel something I don't even understand." The play also offered one interesting sidelight at a time when critics, albeit less than formerly, were complaining about the use of slang in plays. In *Disraeli* Lady Clarissa was relieved to escape the stilted polite conversation of the drawing room and lapse into some refreshing slang. In *Bought and Paid For* the upstarts Fanny and Jimmy make a comic point of avoiding slang, or at least trying to. Later in the season, in *Lady Patricia* and *The Rainbow*, oldsters bridle on hearing a younger generation's slang. Parenthetically, in this and several other of the season's plays, "telephone" becomes " 'phone" in print.

September's last entry, Rida Johnson Young's **Next** (9-28-11, Daly's), was a quick flop. It centered on a barber who arrives to set up shop in the wildest of Wild West towns. What is unusual about the barber, whose surname is Brush, is that her given name is Sophie (Helen Lowell). The tough hombres in the town at first sneer, but when she singlehandedly captures a long-sought thief, gives the town madam her comeuppance, and in other ways shows her spunk, the men change their tone. Despite its short run, the Shuberts felt they had a savable property on their hands. A little more than a year later it resurfaced, again with the bug-eyed Miss Lowell in the lead, as a Jerome Kern musical, *The Red Petticoat*.

October began with a charming English comedy, A. E. W. Mason's **Green Stockings** (10-2-11, 39th St.), which had been done in London as *Colonel Smith*. It starred Margaret Anglin as an eldest sister who, because her spinsterhood is standing in the way of her youngest sister's marrying, announces she is engaged to an officer who has sailed to fight in Somaliland. She later pretends the soldier has been killed, only to have a real colonel (H. Reeves-Smith) of the same name appear on her doorstep. According to the play, green stockings were worn by old-maid sisters at their siblings' weddings. Among the excellent supporting players was Maude Granger as a spunky aunt from Chicago. For all its charms, the play held limited interest to New Yorkers.

But Broadway had no time at all for **Rebellion** (10-3-11, Maxine Elliott's), which Joseph Medill Patterson dramatized from his own novel of the same name. It starred Maxine Elliott's sister, Gertrude, as a poor Irish girl trapped by her church's refusal to free her from a marriage to a worthless drunkard.

Nor was there a warmer welcome for **The Great Name** (10-4-11, Lyric), James Clarence Harvey's adaptation of a German comedy by Victor Léon and Leo Feld. Its hero is a famous composer (Henry Kolker) of popular songs who attempts to help an unsuccessful friend (Russ Whytal) by presenting the friend's symphony as his own and then, after its acclaimed premiere, disclosing the truth. A hint of international polarization seeping into the arts could be read in one notice, which remarked, "It ill becomes us who have laughed so heartily over so many German plays to call a piece Teutonic, thereby expecting to dispose of it."

The short hop from Berlin to Paris was represented by **The Runaway** (10-1-11, Lyceum), which Michael Morton took from Pierre Veber and Henri de Gorsse's *La Gamine*. To escape her strait-laced aunts, who would wed her to a boorish neighbor, an orphan runs away to Paris and finds romance with a handsome artist who had befriended her. The play did two months of profitable business before heading out for the road. Many critics felt the role of Colette,

the orphan, was the best Billie Burke had been given to date and credited her, along with a fine supporting cast headed by suave C. Aubrey Smith, for the play's popularity. But Miss Burke passed over the work in silence in her autobiography.

Another short hop took playgoers to Scotland, by way of the London stage, of course. Yet the *Tribune* greeted Graham Moffat's **Bunty Pulls the Strings** (10-1-11, Comedy) by claiming, "There is not a stagey thing about it." The *Herald* called it "delightfully naive," and the *Times*, its grammar slipping a bit, hailed it as "the freshest and most wholesome thing that the theatres in New York has housed since the days of 'Peter Pan.'" The principal roles were played mostly by genuine Scots. Bunty (Molly Pearson) is a just-about-perfect little girl who gets her wayward brother (Edmond Beresford) on the right track and finds a potential bride (Margaret Nybloc) for him, exposes as a crook a mean-spirited spinster (Jean Cadell) who is trying to trap Bunty's father (Campbell Gullan) into marriage, and sees to it the widowed man weds a decent woman (Amy Singleton). The simple but touchingly effective comedy ran almost a full year.

The play that followed had to settle for a fortnight's engagement. George Beban, popular in vaudeville as a delineator of Italian immigrants, expanded his two-a-day sketch into a full-length piece, **The Sign of the Rose** (10-11-11, Garrick), taking the leading role of a delivery man who is mistaken for a rich child's kidnapper. A setting depicting a Fifth Avenue florist shop won more praises from some than did the play.

Tearjerkers seemed to be the order of the month. The third in a row was Winchell Smith's **The Only Son** (10-16-11, Gaiety), in which a scapegrace son (Wallace Eddinger) remains loyal to his mother (Louise Randolph) after she confesses to an affair and is shown the door by her husband (Claude Gillingwater). He eventually brings about a reconciliation between his parents, thereby winning the hand of the girl (Olive Wyndham) who had spurned him because of his dissolute ways. The play ran one month, instantly overshadowed by the great tearjerker that opened one night later.

With David Warfield as its star, David Belasco's **The Return of Peter Grimm** (10-17-11, Belasco) was one of the era's most admired and successful productions. It all took place somewhere in New York State, in "an old cottage, wainscoted with oak and with oak beams in the ceiling, hung with ancient Dutch portraits, and dominated by an old Dutch chimney piece full of niches and covered with crockery, pipes and a hundred suitable relics. In one corner stands a whatnot bearing bowls of sprouting bulbs. By the fireplace are bundles of shoots wrapped up in sacking—precious plants which have been the source of the Grimm fortune, and really ought to be out in the moist greenhouse or store room! There is an old-fashioned square piano."

For seven generations Grimm's Botanic Gardens and Nurseries have flourished here. You can see more hints of them by looking out the windows, where there is even an old windmill amid all the plantings and greenhouses. But Peter Grimm is an old man, and though he doesn't know it, his weak heart is failing. His only heir is his nephew, Frederik (John Sainpolis), a trimmer who unbeknownst to Peter has resolved to sell the nurseries as soon as Peter has died. Peter has also adopted and raised Kathrien (Janet Dunbar), and he hopes she and Frederik will marry. Furthermore, he has taken under his wing a little boy named William (Percy Helton), the grandson of his housekeeper. William's mother had run away without disclosing who the boy's father was. When Dr. MacPherson (Joseph Brennan) pays a call, he and Peter are soon on MacPherson's favorite topic, the notion that the dead can return and speak to the living. Peter rejects the idea but, to humor his friend, agrees to a compact stipulating whoever dies first will attempt to return and communicate with the other.

A circus clown (Tony Bevan) appears at the window and announces the arrival of a one-ring circus—"Only one ring. No confusion." Peter sends William to buy tickets, reminds Kathrien of her promise to marry Frederik, sits down to smoke his pipe, and quietly dies. William returns just as the family has realized what has occurred. "He can't be dead," he blurts out, "I've got his ticket to the circus." On Kathrien's wedding evening Peter is seen watching the goings-on. Having "crossed over," since there is really no such thing as death, he has crossed back briefly to participate in the festivities.

But little is festive. Kathrien is marrying the contemptible Frederik only because she had promised Peter she would; she loves a better man (Thomas Meighan). Frederik is frantically trying to sell the business. And William is dying of a fever. Peter tries talking to Kathrien, Frederik, and MacPherson. They can neither see nor hear him. At best they sense something odd is happening and respond accordingly. Only William sees and hears Peter, and through him Peter brings out that Frederik is William's father, thus releasing Kathrien from her promise. He also realizes William's condition, though, and consoles the boy: "Like little moon moths,—they look in at the windows; they

beat at the panes; they see the lights of happy firesides—the lights of home, but they never get in. You are one of these wanderers, William. And so it is well for you that before your playing time is over—before your man's work begins,—you're going to know the great secret. Happy boy!" In the dimming light, the circus music is heard in the distance, as are the hawkings and barkings and clownings of the circus people. Peter picks up William and carries him to wherever they will "cross over" together.

Critics rejoiced that Belasco eschewed "the theatrical artifices of colored lights and gauzes" to create his effects, depending instead on Warfield's "tremendously appealing, tender and natural performance," with its "directness, simplicity, understanding, and the economy of means which in combination spell the great art of acting." Warfield had been touring with the play since the previous January and, after running out the current season in New York, continued on the road for two more full seasons. He also revived the play successfully a decade later, shortly before his retirement.

Robert Hichens and Mary Anderson's **The Garden of Allah** (10-21-11, Century) ran the least bit longer on Broadway, or, more accurately, on Central Park West. But the play itself, with its tale of a monk (Lewis Waller) who leaves his monastery, has an affair with a beautiful girl (Mary Mannering), and is persuaded by her to return to his cell, was far from the main reason for the run. Long before the play opened, excited publicity alerted playgoers that Mary Anderson, still "beloved by us all in the memory of her public life as an actress," was co-author. Waller was ballyhooed as England's best romantic actor and its handsomest. And the Century, formerly the New, assured audiences of eye-filling spectacle on its huge stage. No wonder hundreds of eager patrons filled the lobby despite a torrential downpour and fought to obtain tickets for the opening performance. The promised spectacle included a prologue showing an extended caravan with numerous horses and camels slowly traversing a seemingly limitless desert. Among other settings were a luxurious, palm-courted hotel and an elaborate dance hall, with slithering dancing girls reputedly imported from the Near East, even if most of the play's "Arabs" were admittedly Americans with stained faces. A sandstorm added to the thrills. In a cutdown version, the play toured for several seasons. The large Manhattan Opera House served as home to a 1918 revival.

Rave notices helped **The Million** (10-23-11, 39th St.), taken from Georges Berr and Marcel Guillemaud's farce, enjoy a lengthy, prosperous run. Broadway scuttlebutt credited Leo Ditrichstein with the adaptation. The girlfriend of one of a group of bohemians gives his overcoat to a burglar who is escaping from the police. She is unaware the coat contains a lottery ticket. After the ticket is found to be worth $1,000,000, the bohemians chase all over town trying to track down the burglar and the coat.

By contrast, dismissive reviews swept Gretchen Dale and Howard Estabrook's **Mrs. Avery** (10-23-11, Weber's) off the stage after a single week, during which time it recounted the dilemma facing a wife (Dale) who receives a large sum of money from an admirer and debates whether to give it to her husband (Estabrook) to help promote his invention.

Reviews for Anne Caldwell and James O'Dea's **Uncle Sam** (10-30-11, Liberty) weren't that much better, but since Thomas A. Wise and John Barrymore were starred, the comedy eked out a six-week stand. Wise played Col. Sam Gunnison, a Nevada mine owner, who sails to Germany to lure his nephew, Robert Hudson (Barrymore), back to the States and, he hopes, unto marriage with Amy Wright (Marjorie Wood). Hudson insists he prefers his carefree bachelor life. To discourage his Uncle Sam, he pretends to be a very effeminate fop. At first Sam is repelled, but with the help of Amy's aunt (Ida Darling) everything works out just fine. Sam even decides to marry the aunt.

Robert Edeson's faltering career was given no help by **The Cave Man** (10-30-11, Fulton), which Gelett Burgess dramatized from his own novel *Lady Méchante*. Foreshadowing Shaw's *Pygmalion*, but with the sexes reversed, it described what happens when a socialite (Grace Elliston) decides to amuse herself at the expense of her snobbish friends by passing off a coal heaver (Edeson) as a gentleman.

An even more dismal reception awaited May Robson and Charles T. Dazey's **The Three Lights** (10-31-11, Bijou). Written as a vehicle for the down-to-earth clowning of Miss Robson, it allowed her to portray a young-after-her-time "granmum" who gets into all sorts of comic scrapes in order to prove her two grandsons are decent young men. One week and it was gone.

By the beginning of November, *Bought and Paid For* was unmistakably the season's biggest hit, yet some critics thought George Broadhurst might have surpassed himself with his second play of the season, **The Price** (11-1-11, Hudson). The widow (Jessie Ralph) of a dead artist takes a position as housekeeper with the artist's former secretary (Helen Ware) and the secretary's new husband (Harrison Hunter). The widow is convinced that the secretary

had been the artist's mistress and that she knew her breaking off the relationship would kill the artist (Warner Oland), who suffered from a weak heart. The widow first manages to make the husband aware that his wife is seeing yet another man and then tricks her into revealing her relationship with the dead man. The husband, unable to trust his wife, leaves her. For all their enthusiastic praise, some critics held reservations about the drama's ability to catch on. *Theatre*, for example, noted how unsympathetically all the characters were drawn, and the *Times* questioned the play's lack of comic relief. Their caution proved justified. The drama was withdrawn after ten weeks, while the more commercially slanted *Bought and Paid For* ran on and on.

The same evening saw a group of good, dedicated, but not especially glamourous performers, who had banded together under the name of the Drama Players, open a short stay at the Lyric in an interesting repertory. Beginning with Broadway's first mounting of Ibsen's **The Lady from the Sea,** in which a woman is almost seduced away from a comfortable marriage by a sailor she once had loved, the troupe quickly added Molière's *Les Femmes savantes* (billed as *The Learned Ladies*) and Pinero's *The Thunderbolt*. Excellent reviews could not entice playgoers, so the company moved on to Chicago and oblivion.

The Best of Plays of 1909–1919 lists H. M. Horkheimer and Lucile Sawyer's *The Strugglers* as opening at the Bijou on the 6th and running for eight performances. Contemporary newspapers tell a different story. Sunday theatre sections on the 5th gave some idea of the plot: a young man stakes out a mining claim and then begins to gamble it away but the duenna of the gambling house recognizes him as her long-lost son and sets out to cure his addiction to wagering. No advertisements appeared in Monday's papers and no reviews on Tuesday's drama pages. Most papers passed over the play in silence, but the *American* notified its readers that the drama had been "indefinitely postponed." Broadway is still waiting for a new opening date.

The growth of large producing organizations had brought with it the concurrent inflation of press agentry. Witness Lieber and Co.'s astute promoting of *The Garden of Allah*. Al Woods, although still relatively new to first-class stages, apparently had retained an equally effective P.R. department from his days as a leader of cheap touring melodrama. Long before Edward Peple's **The Littlest Rebel** (11-14-11, Liberty) reached Manhattan, New Yorkers were regaled with stories of its Chicago triumph; of how the production brought together brothers Dustin and William Farnum in their first joint stardom; of how, though she appeared only in one act, "it was necessary to pay a large salary to an actress of Miss [Percy] Haswell's standing for only forty minutes work"; and of the search for a tot, at once attractive and talented, to play the title role. The littlest rebel is sweet-faced, blonde-tressed Virgie Cary (Mary Miles Minter), who remains at home in her family's pillared colonial house with her mother (Miss Haswell) and slaves while her father (William Farnum) serves as a Confederate scout. He visits them briefly, pursued by Union soldiers under the command of Lieutenant Colonel Morrison (Dustin Farnum). To Morrison's fury one of his men sets fire to the house. He returns two months later, still seeking Cary, to find that Mrs. Cary has died and that Virgie lives alone, with only a rag doll for company, in one of the plantation's less damaged buildings. He also discovers Cary hiding in the loft. But when he learns that Cary has come merely to attempt to take Virgie to safety across Union lines, he agrees to help. The three are attacked by both Confederate and Union troops and finally brought before a cigar-chomping General Grant (William B. Mack), who is prepared to hang Morrison as a traitor and Cary as a spy. Only Virgie's plea softens the general's heart. The men are pardoned.

The dialogue was "written in a somewhat operatic style, with, now and then, an aria of sentimental appeal, an idyll of child-talk, or a recitative of warlike patriotism." Morrison says to Cary:

Do you know, Cary, this war for us—the men—may be a hell; but what is it for those we leave at home? The women! who wait—and wait! *We* have the excitement of it. The rush! Our battles—no matter if we win or lose. We live—and *know!* We—the brothers of one nation and one land— who make our loved ones' lives a deeper hell than ours. They watch and listen—with hunger in their hearts—month in, month out, and often without a word. They starve on crusts of hope! Waiting— waiting—hunting the papers for the one thing they dread to find: a name!—among the missing! A name among the dead!

Peple's curtains presented almost soppily theatrical pictures. At the end of the second act, after Morrison has agreed to help Cary and Virgie, "*Cary turns to him. The hands of the two men go out and meet across the fallen door, Virgie standing between them. Just as the hands of Morrison and Cary meet, the sunlight is shot through the hole in the wall, falling on them, while the orchestra changes from the plaintive air it has been playing to the 'Star Spangled Banner.'*"

For all Woods's preopening publicity, *The Littlest Rebel* ran only seven weeks, though it did well on tour. With its essentially cinematic scenes—the house burning, horses riding by, the battles—it was a natural for Hollywood, which filmed it in 1935 with Shirley Temple as star.

The Wife Decides (11-14-11, Weber's), Thomas McKean's adaptation of his own novel, related how a faithful wife (Jane Wheatly) forgives a husband (Elwood F. Bostwick) who nearly killed her in the mistaken suspicion of infidelity. Theatregoers decided the play wasn't for them.

Some less educated, less mannered playgoers decided another play shouldn't have been staged, but since these playgoers were hot-headed Irishmen and the work in question was J. M. Synge's **The Playboy of the Western World,** history repudiated their booing and potato-hurling. Synge's comedy, which tells of a shiftless young man who briefly becomes a hero to his fellow villagers when they believe his boast that he has killed his father, was but one of more than a dozen works presented by the Irish Players of the Abbey Theatre at Maxine Elliott's beginning on November 20th. Even those critics who professed to like the play suggested they would prefer to wait for a less troubled performance before making a final judgment. Lady Gregory, Yeats, St. John Ervine, Lennox Robinson, and Shaw were among the writers represented in the repertory, which was performed by, among others, Arthur Sinclair, Sara Allgood, Cathleen Nesbitt, J. M. Kerrigan, and Una O'Connor. Many observers were disappointed by the highly touted ensemble, with the *Times*'s lofty Adolph Klauber putting down the actors as "merely indifferent amateurs." The expression "talented amateurs" appeared in Walter Prichard Eaton's comments, but he admired their "simplicity of gesture and movement, the emphasis on text." Rioting in the theatre and controversy in the newspapers helped build attendance, but some of the finest, if most uncompromising, dramas, such as Synge's **Riders to the Sea,** pulled meager houses.

Louis N. Parker's **The Lady of Coventry** (11-21-11, Daly's) might have been aided by some controversy, but in 1911 no retelling of the Lady Godiva legend would dare parade its heroine, particularly as played by the prim Viola Allen, nude across the stage. The play folded after two weeks.

Two squeak-by hits closed out November. William Collier and James Montgomery's **Take My Advice** (11-27-11, Fulton) was a piece of such gossamer fluff that one reviewer observed, "The Collier clientèle gets a fair $2.00 worth of nothing." Collier was seen as William Ogden, who can inherit a California lemon ranch and $1,000,000 if he refrains from gambling or drinking for a year. He also will inherit the right to marry Diana Kardly (Dorothy Unger)—"Diana of the perpetual headaches." Ogden soon recognizes that the advisers the will saddled him with are all hypocrites, so he drops them, tells Diana he hopes she'll "get well—or something," and goes out to earn a fortune on his own and marry a better girl (Paula Marr).

Martha Morton's **The Senator Keeps House** (11-27-11, Garrick) begins with Sam (William W. Jefferson, a white playing in blackface) attempting to serve breakfast to the widowed Senator Larkin (William H. Crane) and the senator's nephew-secretary, Patrick (Jack Devereaux), since the latest in a long line of housekeepers has left in a huff. Eva Flower (Lorraine Frost) appears and applies for the job. The senator rejects her as too young, but Patrick falls instantly in love with her. Eva then suggests her mother (Mabel Bert) could handle the work, and after an interview the senator agrees. What he doesn't know is that a corrupt New York congressman, Adolphus Judson (Harry Harwood), has planted her there. Judson is attempting to push through a sincere but worthless claim of Mrs. Flower's, hoping to make some "honest graft" in the process. Naturally Larkin gets wind of Mrs. Flower's claim and suspects her motives for working for him. But all ends happily, with Patrick and Eva, and the senator and Mrs. Flower, all making plans for the altar. Crane's amiable bluster, in scenes such as the one where Mrs. Flower plants a smelly cigar by the senator in her drive to have him give up smoking, still had wide appeal. Like Collier, he kept his admirers pleased for ten weeks.

Dolley Madison's early years were the subject of Charles Nirdlinger's **The First Lady in the Land** (12-4-11, Gaiety). As the widowed Mrs. Todd (Elsie Ferguson), she runs a Philadelphia boardinghouse, where Aaron Burr (Frederick Perry) is both her tenant and her suitor. He makes the mistake of introducing her to his friend James Madison (Lowell Sherman), and he further alienates her by failing to keep his promise not to shoot Alexander Hamilton. The beautiful Miss Ferguson was "coquettishly demure," but Perry's vivacious, charming Burr nabbed many of the best adjectives. The play kept the Gaiety's footlights glowing for eight weeks.

In A. E. W. Mason's second play of the season, **The Witness for the Defense** (12-4-11, Empire), a wife (Ethel Barrymore) who has murdered her brutish husband (W. L. Abingdon) in self-defense is acquitted in a trial after a former lover (A. E. Anson) perjures himself. Her past comes back to haunt her when she remarries. The play had been a West End success, but most Broadway critics were unimpressed. Only their praise for the star's warm, telling acting, and her growing host of admirers, accounted for another eight-week run.

Yet a third eight-week run went to **The Marionettes** (12-5-11, Lyceum), which Gladys Unger translated from the French of Pierre Wolff. It starred Nazimova as a mousy, convent-bred bride who turns a marriage of convenience into a love match. Assisting her in putting over the play were Frank Gillmore as the husband, Kate Meek as a sharp-tongued, crabby grande dame, and gorgeous gowns that brought ahs and oohs from the ladies in the audience each time a new one appeared.

Sadly, the best play of the week had its shortest run. Charles Kenyon's highly praised **Kindling** (12-5-11, Daly's) was simply too uncompromising for fun-seeking Broadway, despite the play's "happy" ending. Maggie Schultz (Margaret Illington), a pregnant girl from the roughest of tenements, fears her embittered husband (Byron Beasley) will keep his promise to kill any baby she has. After a neighbor describes the warmer and more carefree life in far-away Wyoming, she dreams of living there. When, at almost the same time, she learns that a strike will mean her husband is about to lose his paycheck and that the matron, Mrs. Burke Smith, who has offered her work, owns the tenement, she succumbs to the blandishments of her worthless neighbor, Steve (George Probert), and agrees to help him rob Mrs. Burke Smith's house. She pawns the jewelry Steve has given her for her aid. Later she has qualms. Mrs. Burke Smith's niece, Alice (Anne Meredith), a social worker, learns of Maggie's plight, retrieves the jewels, and contrives to exonerate the girl. A grateful Maggie is left with only the wan hope that there are roses in Wyoming. Critics applauded the star and her new husband, Major Edward J. Bowes, for bringing the play to Broadway, and most praised Miss Illington's ability to convey the variegated but strong emotions of the heroine. However, a few naysayers carped that her accent was far too ladylike to suggest the low-class tenement girl.

Charles T. Dazey said farewell to Broadway with **The Stranger** (12-21-11, Bijou), a melodrama many critics condemned as hopelessly old-fashioned all the while they agreed it was not ineffective. Its hero had been raised in a poorhouse and sneered at, especially by one cruel, snobbish rich boy, who accused him of being illegitimate. Now a grown man and a traction magnate, John Marshall (Wilton Lackaye), the once penniless lad, returns to Virginia, where he bests his ancient taunter, Howard Carter (Malcolm Williams), in business, wins the hand of the girl, Mary Washington (Muriel Starr), that both men have courted, and discovers not only that Carter was born out of wedlock but that he himself is actually legitimate. At least one critic complained that "the whole cast . . . talk with a Lambs' Club 'Southern' accent that would hardly pass muster below Mason and Dixon's line," but most reviewers commended Lackaye for humanizing a cardboard figure.

Two nights later *Ben Hur,* advertising "Thirteenth Year of Continued Popularity," came into the New Amsterdam for an extended return. There were no topflight names in the cast; the play drew on its own reputation.

The old year ended with a colorful Christmas present. The expatriate American Edward Knoblauch had peddled a bit of romantic Orientalia around New York and London theatrical offices for several seasons without a nibble. Only after Oscar Asche mounted it in London with undreamed-of success did Harrison Fiske and his onetime enemies, Klaw and Erlanger, grab **Kismet** (12-25-11, Knickerbocker) for New York. Otis Skinner was starred. Eaton reported happily, "For once the right part has come to the right player, the right play to the right producer, and unlimited financial resources have been wisely and well used, not squandered in sham and tinsel."

Even before the curtain rose, dancers, jugglers, and flute players entertained in the aisles and on the stage's apron. Exotic Near Eastern perfumes wafted through the auditorium. They were the perfumes of Baghdad, where the beggar, Hajj, plies his trade by the door of the Mosque of Carpenters. Caught stealing, he is brought before the Wazir Mansur (Hamilton Revelle), who agrees not to chop off Hajj's right hand if Hajj will slay the caliph. Hajj does not know that the caliph (Fred Eric), disguised as a gardener, has been courting Hajj's daughter, Marsinah (Rita Jolivet). But Hajj's attempt to plunge his dagger into the caliph's heart is thwarted by the coat of mail the caliph wears under his white robes. Hajj is thrown into prison. There he murders his cellmate (Sheridan Block), who is about to be released, and dons his clothes to escape. By now he realizes how perfidious the Wazir is, so he secretly enters the wazir's high ceilinged, Moorish-arched harem, where lovely maidens ("undressed" according to one reviewer) bathe in the pool, and Hajj drowns the wazir in the same pool. The caliph appears, and though he reveals his true identity to Marsinah and announces his intention of marrying her, he orders Hajj to leave Baghdad forever by sunrise. As night falls, Hajj resumes his place in front of the mosque, pleading, "Alms, for the love of Allah; for the love of Allah, alms," then falls asleep in the silver moonlight.

Among the highly praised settings was "the gorgeous view of the Caliph's Palace, with a far-reaching effect of opalescent sky, against which stand forth the towers and mosques bathed in sunlight." But it was Skinner's magnificent performance that capped the evening: "His impersonation is consistently the beggar. . . . Never for an instant is he anything else, be his borrowed robes ever so grand. It is lit with a grim, masculine humor [such as spitting on his enemies' possessions], it is touched with tenderness for his daughter and with fierce passions of revenge. But humor, tenderness, passion, are all held in the key of romantic fable, and so while he counts the bubbles that arise from the drowning Wazir there is no horror in the episode, and when he goes to sleep again at last in his beggar's rags there is no sorrow—only a half smile for the round-the-circle logic of it, and the pleasant finish to a good tale told." Skinner, "swathed in a few scraps of thin rags, my feet, legs, arms and chest with no covering but a wash of brown paint," did not always find playing what would be his best-remembered role so pleasant. Nevertheless, he and the show ran out not only this season but nearly two more as well. The playwright claimed in his autobiography that the New York run was cut short after the *Titanic* sinking soured business, but whether the last two months of the stand were indeed forced cannot be determined. Skinner is silent on the matter in his own memoirs. In 1953 a musical version, starring Alfred Drake, was equally successful.

The year's end prompted some interesting midseason assessments. One account, noting that almost half the sixty productions to reach Broadway since June had paid off their investments, concluded, "In no other profession is mediocrity so often rewarded with success." At the same time, it renewed the old cry that "theatrical business has been bad financially," pointing out how many shows that folded on the road were not included in the count and how many theatres were dark for weeks at a time. Year-end theatrical advertisements suggested there was not much cause for gloom. William A. Brady's advertisement listed four companies each of *Baby Mine* and *Over Night* traipsing around the country, two companies of *Mother,* a company of *Way Down East* ("17th year"), and numerous other productions. Klaw and Erlanger boasted of fifteen different shows in New York or on tour, including Henry

Miller in last season's *The Havoc* and Robert Hilliard in the older *A Fool There Was*. Henry Savage pointed to three companies of *Excuse Me* and two of *Everywoman*. Producers also announced a plethora of new mountings "in preparation."

The pair of plays that ushered in 1912 gave little reason for cheering. Each ran only three weeks. Louis Evan Shipman's **The Grain of Dust** (1-1-12, Criterion) starred James K. Hackett as a rising young lawyer who jilts his rich fiancée (Pauline Neff) and marries his secretary (Izetta Jewel), though she is not sure she loves him. When the jilted girl's father (Frazer Coulter) sets out to hurt the attorney's career, the attorney fights back brutally and effectively until his wife, who has decided she does care for him, urges him to be compassionate. Many of the actors were old-school, with Hackett's Zenda-like "succession of mouthings and leerings and posturings" receiving a critical hosing. The kindest words were reserved for another relative oldtimer, E. M. Holland, who put across the role of a fellow lawyer "with sly winks and wise pauses, ever aided by the absorbing contortions of two wonderfully expressive hands."

Earlier in the season Grace George had abandoned two shows on the road, including a stab at Shakespeare's Beatrice. The play she did elect to bring to New York proved no more attractive. Cicely Hamilton's **Just to Get Married** (1-1-12, Maxine Elliott's) spotlighted a young lady who regrets she listened to her family's entreaties to marry a bashful young man (Lyn Harding), decides to run away, then is talked out of it by her new husband when he meets her, soaked from a downpour, at their small-town railroad station, where she was waiting for her train.

In the mid-1940s the leading ladies of the two plays that opened the following Monday would both be enjoying comeback successes in the same drama—Laurette Taylor scoring her most memorable triumph in the original company of *The Glass Menagerie* and Pauline Lord heading the road company. In Marion Fairfax's **The Talker** (1-8-12, Harris), Miss Lord played Ruth Lenox, an impressionable lady who comes under the sway of her sister-in-law (Lillian Albertson), a militant women's rights advocate. Ruth elopes with a married man, is deserted by him, but returns a sadder, wiser, and forgiven girl. Neither of the ladies was the drama's leading player; that role fell to Tully Marshall as Ruth's understanding brother. A small, well-written play, beautifully acted (Miss Lord's breathy, jerky mannerisms had not yet become evident), *The Talker* ran into May.

At least in New York, Richard Walton Tully's **The Bird of Paradise** (1-8-12, Daly's) did not last quite as long, its stay cut short at 112 performances in part by its high running costs but more by disagreements between its producer, Oliver Morosco, and New York's theatre owners. Tully's story centered on a beautiful, superstitious Hawaiian princess, Luana (Taylor). A promising scientist, Paul Wilson (Lewis S. Stone), gives up his career to marry her, but the marriage plays havoc with his ambition. Neither an attempt by fellow Americans to foment a revolution, which would make Luana queen, nor a move back to civilization dispels Wilson's lethargy. When Kilauea begins to rumble, Luana believes it is a sign that the gods are angry with her and demand a human sacrifice. To appease the gods and to give Wilson a second chance, she throws herself into the flaming crater. A subplot balanced the main story by recounting the regeneration of a beachcomber, "Ten Thousand Dollar" Dean (Guy Bates Post). The Hawaiian settings were magnificent, starting with the garden in front of both Luana's thatched hut and a neighboring cave, a palm-framed view of the sea in the background, and ending with the volcano's crater, "ingenious in its suggestions of molten rock, broken by jets of steam and flame."

A few critics complained about Miss Taylor's peculiar barefoot walk, which she replied she learned from Italian peasants who must carry heavy loads on their heads. But by and large her notices were ecstatic. *Theatre*, proclaiming her performance one of "real genius," went on to say, "It is an impersonation that for beauty of treatment, sensuous grace and charm, innate dignity, feminine coquetry and poignant pathos deserves a place among the ambitiously great accomplishments of the modern stage."

. . .

Laurette [Cooney] **Taylor** (1884–1946) was born in New York and began her stage career in vaudeville as "La Belle Laurette." As a slim young lady with red hair and large hazel-blue eyes, she played in stock and in touring melodramas, some of which were written by her first husband, Charles A. Taylor. She won critical notices in small parts before performing in *Alias Jimmy Valentine* (1910). Although some accused her of playing, however winningly, too obviously to her audiences, Theresa Helburn of the Theatre Guild later said, "Her inner radiance fell like moonlight on an audience without the use of any stage tricks that I could detect. In my day there has been no such radiant personality as hers."

. . .

But good as Taylor's performance was, it was not crucial, for Morosco soon had numerous road companies traversing the country for several years. In 1930 the play was musicalized as *Luana*.

A gripping if not very original courtroom scene accounted for the six-month run of an English play, Edward G. Hemmerde and Francis Neilson's **A Butterfly on the Wheel** (1-9-12, 39th St.). The butterfly was a neglected wife (Madge Titheradge) whose careless flirtations land her in a divorce court.

In October, Mme Simone, a round-faced, big-nosed, chestnut-haired French actress, had met with disappointment when she played—in English—her versions of *The Thief* and *The Whirlwind*. She enjoyed a better reception when she reappeared in Maurice Donnay's **The Return from Jerusalem** (1-10-12, Hudson), playing a converted Jewess who steals a Christian husband from his Christian wife only to find that their upbringings make them incompatible.

Another French play, Gustave Guiches and Pierre Barthélemy Gheusi's *Chacun sa vie,* had the week's shortest run—twelve performances—as **The Right to Happiness** (1-11-12, Bijou). The third opening in a row centering on marital malaise, it told how a betrayed husband (Wilton Lackey), much like the husband in last season's *The Havoc,* forces his wife's lover (Wedgwood Nowell) to agree to marry the woman (Adelaide Keim) after the husband divorces her.

Another Arabian Nights story grabbed Broadway's attention, but this was one with a major difference—for **Sumurun** (1-16-12, Casino) was Max Reinhardt's Deutsches Theater production of Friedrich Freska's "wordless" play. The pantomime was imported by one of New York's most venturesome new producers, Winthrop Ames. Even if they hadn't been lured into the playhouse by the pre-opening publicity, audiences knew just how different this saga of the intrigues of a hunchback, a sheik and his son, a cloth merchant, and others for the loves of some harem and dancing girls would be when the cast made its first appearance running down a ramp from the rear of the theatre, over the heads of the playgoers and onto the stage. The settings, like much else in the play, were highly stylized. A skyline of mosques and minarets was silhouetted against a deep-blue, cloudless sky and given perspective by a high ecru wall in the foreground; later a spiral staircase was "bathed in shadow." The production alerted Broadway to the ferment rising on European stages and signaled that the day of the scene painter and the careful realism of his flats was about to give way to the more imaginative architecture and lighting of the set designer. Equally, it gave notice that the plots and construction of a century of well-made plays were about to be questioned. The production ran two months and toured.

A far more traditional play, **Elevating a Husband** (1-22-12, Liberty), which Samuel Shipman and Clara Lipman wrote as a vehicle for Miss Lipman's husband, Louis Mann, became the fifth in January's swelling list of hits. Mann portrayed Charlie Sample, owner of a growing chain of five-and-dimes. His proposal of marriage is accepted by Letty (Emily Ann Wellman), who lives in the same boardinghouse as he does. During intermission he builds her a baronial mansion, where Mrs. Sample can entertain her rich hangers-on and inculcate Charlie with the pleasures of fine painting and great music, instead of the sports news he relishes. Herbert Duncan (Conway Tearle), a former suitor of Letty's, is taken on as Sample's manager, but he is not grateful. He courts Letty on the sly and ruins Sample by speculating with Sample's funds. Sample, who already has told Letty, "I would prefer a child to your Schopenhauer philosophy and swell people," now tells Duncan to kill himself or be exposed. Not surprisingly, Duncan refuses both choices, so Sample kicks Duncan, Letty, and her haughty spongers out of the house he no longer can afford. As he prepares to start over again, he learns a repentant Letty will help him.

A pair of dramatized novels failed to interest New Yorkers, although both productions did well on the road—before and after. **White Magic** (1-24-12, Criterion), which Roi Cooper Megrue took from David Graham Phillips's book, began more or less as *Just to Get Married* had ended, with the heroine finding true love after taking refuge from a downpour. In this instance the heroine (Gertrude Elliott) is a very rich girl who stumbles into the studio of a poor artist (Julian L'Estrange).

Eugene Walter's adaptation of John Fox's **The Trail of the Lonesome Pine** (1-29-12, New Amsterdam) recorded how John Hale (Berton Churchill) comes west to work the mines and help build a railroad, how he falls in love with a mountain girl, June (Charlotte Walker), and how he wins her despite the enmity of her moonshining father (W. S. Hart) and her cousin (Willard Robertson), who has loved her since childhood. Miss Walker was seen as far too elegant for a mountain girl, but the mountains themselves, painted with old-fashioned realism, won high praise.

Two other plays that opened the same evening as the Walter adaptation fared better. A marvelous little cast—just Ethel Barrymore, John Barrymore, and Hattie Williams—had fun with J. M. Barrie's burlesque **A Slice of Life** (1-29-12, Empire), which spoofed playwriting clichés. A prankish maid (Miss

Williams) sends both a husband and wife identical telegrams, telling them to leave town at once since all is discovered. The couple, after reading the cables, confess to each other that they had both lied about their pasts, making themselves seem far more wicked than they really had been. After a series of preposterous asides and absurdly theatrical posturings, a reconciliation is achieved. The short piece was coupled with a revival of *Cousin Kate* in which neither John nor Miss Williams appeared.

January's longest-running novelty—if only by one performance—was Augustin MacHugh's **Officer 666** (1-29-12, Gaiety). Travers Gladwin (Wallace Eddinger) secretly returns home from Europe after picking up hints that someone may be planning to steal his art collection. At lunch at the Ritz, he had spotted a beautiful blonde eating a grapefruit but had not been able to learn more about her, though he had fallen instantly in love. To his amazement the girl, Helen (Ruth Maycliffe), appears at his door, telling him she has come to meet Gladwin and elope with him once Gladwin has removed some of his paintings. Gladwin realizes the girl has been duped by the would-be robber. He convinces a policeman (Francis D. McGinn) to change clothes with him. When the policeman asks what all this means, Gladwin responds:

Gladwin: It means I'm going outside to wait for myself—and if I find myself, I'll arrest myself—if both myself and I have to go to jail for it—now do you understand?
Phelan: No, I'm damned if I do!
Gladwin: Damned if I do, either!

The crook (George Nash), accompanied by Gladwin's perfidious butler (Charles K. Gerard), arrives. So do two separate contingents of police and Helen's aunt (Camilla Crume), with a warrant for Gladwin's arrest. Mistaken identities, handcuffings, abrupt escapes and chases, and other confusions (such as the police almost arresting one of their own) follow before the kindhearted Gladwin helps the crook escape and wins Helen's somewhat baffled admiration.

Gladwin: Try to keep on liking Travers Gladwin, won't you?
Helen: I can't comprehend it—it seems just as if it couldn't happen except in a play.
Gladwin: Believe me, dear, it couldn't.

Since George M. Cohan was co-producer (with his partner, Sam Harris) and director, audiences could be sure the melodramatic farce would be played at high speed and in the broadest possible style—not

quite fist-on-the-forehead, but as close to it as 1912 sensibilities would allow.

Like January, February got off to a sluggish start. Needing a vehicle to replace *Green Stockings*, Margaret Anglin had pressed Henry Arthur Jones to rush **Lydia Gilmore** (2-1-12, Lyceum) to completion. The hasty writing was patent at the premiere. Jones's story showed the plight of a woman who agrees to perjure herself at her husband's trial for murder in order to spare their little boy the shame of having a convict for a father.

Some of the profits William A. Brady was reaping from *Bought and Paid For* and his other hits went down the drain on two different Monday nights. Both plays folded the Saturday after they opened. An explosion breaking up a logjam, snow blowing through the chinks of a log cabin, and several poorly staged fights were supposedly among the scenic and dramatic high points of Owen Davis's **Making Good** (2-5-12, Fulton). Davis's hero, Tom Lawrence (William Courtenay), is a rich New Yorker, disinherited by his father after he refuses to marry the girl his father has selected for him. He goes west, buys a general store serving a lumber camp, wins the "good girl" of the camp, Deronda Deane (Doris Keane), away from a villainous lumberjack (John Willard), and eventually saves his father from bankruptcy. As David noted, "The title of this play turned out to be a god-send to the New York critics," who refused to see any improvement over the dramas Davis once had mass-manufactured for blue-collar theatres.

Brady's next mounting was by a young man who soon would move on to become one of Brady's principal rivals and one of Broadway's most thoughtful producers. But Arthur Hopkins's **The Fatted Calf** (2-19-12, Daly's), which told of a girl (Margaret Greene) who believes someone is trying to poison her parents (Frank Hatch and Ann Warrington) and of their misfiring attempts to reassure her, was dismissed as an inept, unfunny comedy.

Only one of the trio of plays that opened the next Monday was American. Set in a cluttered, paper-strewn newspaper office—there are more sheets on the floor than in the racks along the wall—Hayden Talbot's **The Truth Wagon** (2-26-12, Daly's) followed the adventures of a young newspaperman resolved to tell nothing but the truth.

The setting for much of Rudolph Besier's **Lady Patricia** (2-26-12, Empire) was even more unusual: the deck of a luxurious tree house. The story centered on a married couple (Mrs. Fiske and Leslie Faber). Each believes he or she must remain loyal to a loving mate, although each also believes a new, younger, and truer love has appeared. The new "affinities" (Maud Gilbert and Shelley Hull) soon find they prefer each other, leaving the husband and wife to effect their own, flowery reconciliation. The absurdly sentimental heroine had been written especially for Mrs. Patrick Campbell, who played the role in England. Mrs. Fiske—dressed in gorgeous pre-Raphaelite gowns—did the best she could to enrich the play's "thin humor." One critic wrote, "There was no suggestion of tedium while she was on stage. The distinctness of her diction was such last night that none of Besier's wit lost its value." Even so, the play went down in the books as a failure.

On the other hand, a new mounting of *Oliver Twist,* in a version by J. Comyns Carr, did turnaway business after it opened at the New Amsterdam on the same evening. A first-rate cast included Marie Doro as Oliver, Nat Goodwin as Fagin, Constance Collier as Nancy, and Lyn Harding as Bill Sykes.

Arthur Wing Pinero's feather-light comedy **Preserving Mr. Panmure** (2-27-12, Lyceum) found few takers with its tale of a portly old gentleman (William McVey) who, in a moment of excited gratitude, kisses his maid (Gertrude Elliott) and, when news of the maid's having been kissed spreads throughout the house, must keep a straight face as he leads the search to uncover the kisser.

Nor did a Parisian hit find favor. Edmond Rostand's *La Princesse lointaine* was offered to New Yorkers in Louis N. Parker's translation as **The Lady of Dreams** (2-28-12, Hudson), with Mme Simone as star. She played a princess of renowned beauty who awaits the coming of a poet (A. E. Anson) who has written verses for her. Mistaking the poet's friend (Julian L'Estrange) for the poet, she falls in love with the wrong man.

The week's biggest hit was Paul Armstrong and Wilson Mizner's **The Greyhound** (2-29-12, Astor). Like *Officer 666,* it took what one critic called a "lurid" theme and made it into what a second review termed "One Long Laugh." When Louis Fellman's wife, Claire (Louise Woods), urges him to give up his crooked ways, he feeds her some poison and leaves her for dead. Fellman (Henry Kolker) is an oily, sleek gambler known as "the Greyhound." With his cronies, the crude "Pale Face Kid" (Jay Wilson), suave "Whispering Alex" (Douglas J. Wood), and flamboyant "Deep Sea Kitty" (Elita Proctor Otis), he boards the *Mauretania,* looking for easy victims. Fellman latches on to a rich lady (Jennie Eustace), who pays him $50,000 to keep a poor boy from marrying her daughter (Bernice Golden). What the crooks fail to reckon with is the presence aboard ship of McSherry (Robert Mc-

Wade, Jr.), a reformed crook who long has loved Claire and who found her in time to save her. He has smuggled her onto the ship. One by one he confounds the villains (his poker game with "Pale Face" was deemed by many the evening's most comic scene). He leaves Fellman for last, but when he confronts the Greyhound with his supposedly dead wife, Fellman jumps overboard. At first the play did excellent business, but the careful line it drew between shipboard ugliness and fun was destroyed in mid-April when the *Titanic* sank. Weekly grosses plummeted. The play held on a few weeks, hoping the revulsion would pass over. When business continued to sag, the play had to be withdrawn.

March roared in belatedly. Not until midmonth did the parade of premieres resume, but then a single evening unveiled three productions that had critics throwing their hats in the air, and it also witnessed the preview of a fine play that held off its official opening until the next night.

Overjoyed critics hailed A. E. Thomas's **The Rainbow** (3-11-12, Liberty) as not only a play of "unparalleled charm" but as "a sheer advance in the presentation and development of the native American drama." Like the central figure in *The Greyhound,* that in the new play was a gambler. But Neil Sumner (Henry Miller) is an honorable, compassionate gentleman. Unfortunately, he once broke a promise to his wife (Edith Baker) not to play cards with his brother-in-law. The brother-in-law's losses in a subsequent game drove him to attempt suicide, and that in turn prompted Ruth Sumner to leave Neil and to take their young daughter with her. Ruth has believed the money she receives regularly comes from her brother. She does not know that her brother, a real scoundrel, has frittered away all her savings and that it is Neil who secretly supports her. When the play begins the daughter, Cynthia (Ruth Chatterton), has just come of age and has insisted on meeting her father. There is instant and deep affection on both sides. Sumner even tries to keep his less socially acceptable friends at arm's length, but when some persist in visiting him, Ruth and Neil's sister, the sharp-tongued but warm-hearted Betsy (Laura Hope Crews), persuade him to walk out of Cynthia's life. A later meeting, in Europe, proves that father and daughter remain as fond of each other as ever, and when Ruth discovers the source of her income, Cynthia has no trouble bringing about a reunion.

Cynthia: I love you both! I want you both! I can't— be happy without you both! (*Sinks into chair, sobbing, Ruth and Neil go to her hurriedly to comfort her)*

Ruth: Oh Cynthia, darling, don't please don't.

Neil: Oh don't, don't—my little maid—don't—(*He raises her out of chair, his arm around her, turns to Ruth*) And I love you both! I want you both!—I can't be happy without you both! (*Extending his hand to Ruth*) Ruth— (*Ruth turns to him. With one arm about his little maid, his other draws her mother to his breast. The final curtain falls.*)

Fine settings—Sumner's cramped New York apartment, his spacious, old-fashioned home in Port Washington, and Ruth's French villa—and a superb cast all garnered excellent notices. But it was the petite, beautiful Miss Chatterton, in what some reviewers mistakenly took for her New York debut, who most forcefully called attention to herself, even if most of her lines were mere gush. ("What an idea! I wonder if any other girl's daddy ever says such nice things"; "Oh, please, please, daddy. It would make her so happy"; "Oh, you dearest daddy in all the world, don't be a silly or you'll have me crying in a minute.") Despite such nonsense, one critic hailed her as "a natural ingenue. An exquisite little person, who knows how to express feeling and to radiate charm, she is so far without a trace of affectation." With everything falling into place, *The Rainbow* ran until summer.

Florence Reed was an even better actress, who also would soon be a major star, but in Menyhert Lengyel's Hungarian drama **The Typhoon** (3-11-12, Fulton) she played second fiddle to Walker Whiteside's villain-hero. Whiteside (who produced the play) cast himself as a Japanese spy in Germany, where he is seduced and taunted by a prostitute (Miss Reed). Her taunts so enrage him that he kills her. Since he is too valuable to Japan, embassy officials arrange for another man to confess in his place. However, the excitement proves too much, and the spy keels over, dead.

Lewis Waller, continuing his prolonged American visit, revived the late Richard Mansfield's successs *Monsieur Beaucaire* at Daly's and kept it on the boards for two months.

The play that held off its official opening for a night was John Galsworthy's **The Pigeon** (3-12-12, Little). One reason for the delay was that the play's producer owned the new theatre in which it was being shown and wanted to make certain both play and playhouse received proper attention. Winthrop Ames had briefly managed the doomed New Theatre and had attributed its failure in important measure to its outlandish size. His own auditorium was the tiniest first-class theatre in New York, seating fewer than 500.

. . .

Winthrop Ames (1870–1937) was born in North Easton, Mass., son of a wealthy old New England family. After graduating from Harvard, he first decided on a career in art and architecture, then switched to the theatre. He leased Boston's venerable Castle Square Theatre in 1904, running it as a stock company. He then toured European theatres extensively, returning home to be appointed manager of the grand auditorium being erected in Central Park West.

. . .

Galsworthy's latest work was welcomed, but not quite as enthusiastically as was the bandbox playhouse. Perhaps echoing *Passers-by,* it recounted what happens when an artist (Russ Whytal), a perennial soft touch, takes in three of what a later generation would call "street people." The play left behind one memorable line: "There is nothing that gives more courage than to see the irony of things."

On and off during the season a band of Russian actors led by Paul Orleneff, who had come to America with Alla Nazimova, had presented revivals of such plays as *Brand, Ghosts,* and *The Chosen People* in first-class houses. Their only novelty apparently was Dmitri Mereshkovsky's **Czar Paul I** (3-18-12, Garrick), which reputedly had been banned in Russia. It told how the cruel czar was assassinated by his own officers, to be replaced by his more humane son.

The same evening, Mme Simone concluded her season with a week-long revival of *Frou-Frou* at the Hudson.

Putting his new theatre to the fullest use, a week after *The Pigeon* opened Winthrop Ames began a series of matinee performances of an unusual double bill. The afternoon started with **The Flower of the Palace of Han** (3-19-12, Little), a medieval Chinese drama adapted by Louis Laloy as *Chagrin dans le palais de Han* then anglicized by Charles Rann Kennedy. It told of a girl (Edith Wynne Matthison) who drowns herself to prevent her emperor (Frank Reicher) from going to war with the Tartars over her. Next came Kennedy's **The Terrible Meek,** in which a Roman captain (Sidney Valentine) on duty at the Crucifixion is converted to Christianity after listening to Jesus' mother (Matthison) speak. Although Kennedy had adopted America as his home, his characters, such as a cockney soldier and the obviously university-bred captain, remained steadfastly English, a fact underscored by the English-born players assigned the roles. The short drama was performed in virtual darkness until the last moment. Then "a wonderfully impressive tableau of the Crucifixion left the audience at the Little Theatre stunned and dazed. . . . The effect was remarkable. The usual applause was omitted, women put on their hats and wraps without a word, and all the men in the audience, if they talked at all, did so in whispers and muffled tones."

The quick failure of *The Right to Happiness* earlier in the season could not discourage Kellett Chambers from calling his newest play **The Right to Be Happy** (3-26-12, Hudson). But its reviews discouraged playgoers, and the play's month-long run was somewhat forced. Just who had a right to be happy wasn't clear. To save her brother (George Le Guere) from being charged with embezzlement, Janet Van Roof (Dorothy Donnelly) becomes the mistress of James Morehouse (Edmund Breese), head of an international rubber cartel. Then she falls head over heels in love with John Forrester (Leslie Faber), an idealistic inventor whose discovery of a synthetic rubber threatens the cartel. Morehouse would destroy the romance by making public his own relationship with Janet, but Forrester is too idealistic to care about her past.

The season faded away early, with the coming of spring. Only two major openings occurred in April. Warner Oland, later famous as Charlie Chan in films, co-produced and played the leading role in **The Father** (4-19-12, Berkeley Lyceum), Strindberg's study of a man driven insane by his wife (Rosalind Ivan) in their fight for dominance over their daughter (Helen Pullman). Most critics felt Oland was not up to the part, and they singled out for praise Louise Dempsey, who played the nurse. Whether they liked Strindberg or not, most also granted that the drama was a powerful, disturbing piece of theatre. In the face of such highly qualified notices, the production nonetheless survived a month at the tiny auditorium.

Dear Old Charlie (4-15-12, Maxine Elliott's), Charles H. Brookfield's translation of Delacour and Labiche's *Célimare le bien-aimé*, ran a month at a somewhat larger house thanks in part to a third Charlie, its star, Charles Hawtrey. In London, Brookfield had been scolded for banning more lofty works in his position as play censor while turning a blind eye to his own saga of a roué's attempt to conceal his amours from his wife, his parents, and his lady friends' husbands.

New York also mirrored London's lukewarm response to Somerset Maugham's **The Explorer** (5-7-12, Daly's), in which the hero (Waller) nearly wrecks his chance for marital happiness when he

resolutely keeps his pledge not to reveal the cowardly way the brother (Reginald Dane) of his fiancée (Constance Collier) died during their African expedition. In a futile attempt to boost business, a curtain raiser was added during the show's second week. W. Cronin Wilson's **The Great Game** (5-16-12) was set in a cellar where a burglar (Frank Woolfe) and his buddy (Lewis Broughton) are caught by a cleverly disguised detective (James Finlayson).

Few if any other plays in years had received such disdainful notices as Joseph Noel's **The Marriage— Not** (5-12-12, Maxine Elliott's). The *Times* began its review, "In the second act of 'The Marriage—Not' a supposedly soulful poet plays the violin very badly, while his audience on stage stretch their arms and yawn. And for once an audience had the satisfaction of knowing that actors were undergoing a share of the misery provided for those who sat in front." The few ticket buyers who saw the play during its week's run sat through a story of a marriage dashed on the rocks after the wife (Oza Waldrop) flirts with a notorious cad (Fritz Williams). For the time being Noel hurried back to his newspaper job in California; his producer and director, Cecil B. de Mille, soon headed west permanently.

1912–1913

Rumblings overseas grew a little louder and a little more ominous during the new season, but Broadway blithely went its own way, rarely attempting to look at the gathering storm or to scratch beneath the surface of domestic problems. Relying comfortably on romance and farce, the theatre was busy providing the simple escapist entertainment most ticket buyers sought. *Variety*'s count indicated the number of productions climbed sharply to 162, up from 140 in the preceding year. That the count of American hits dropped slightly while the number of successful foreign plays rose a bit probably is meaningless. Curiously, a few of the foreign plays dared to tackle subjects American writers still held at arm's length. Yet none, or at most one, of the foreign works continues to be revived with any regularity. The record of major revivals for the American offerings is no better, but several retained the affection of a generation of playgoers only now disappearing from the scene.

The season's first play, George Broadhurst and Mark Swan's **Just Like John** (8-12-12, 48th St.), opened Broadway's newest playhouse but nonetheless went into the records as a sixteen-performance flop. Its hero, a supposed Secret Service man named John Endicott (Walter Jones), is photographed with his arm around a pretty nihilist. His explanation that he must have a double doesn't sit well with his wife (Helene Lackaye). The authors' inability to provide laugh-provoking complications necessitated the introduction of vaudeville turns, in the manner of bygone farce-comedies and touring melodramas.

Chicago, much of the rest of the country, and even London had embraced James Montgomery's **Ready Money** (8-19-12, Maxine Elliott's) before New York had a chance to see it. New Yorkers quickly concurred. Its central figure was a young, handsome, well-bred, but down-at-the-heels socialite, Stephen Baird (William Courtenay), who seems about to lose his last piece of property, the Sky Rocket mine. An acquaintance, Jackson Ives (Joseph Kilgour), offers him a life-saving $20,000 for a part share in the mine, pays him with twenty $1000 bills, then reveals the bills are counterfeit. Stephen is aghast, so Ives makes his point—"If you've got money you don't have to *spend* it, all you have to do is *show* it. It *takes money to get money.*" Sure enough, Baird's friends now fight among themselves to invest in his mine, and his fiancée, Grace Tyler (Margaret Greene), and harridan mother-in-law-to-be (Ida Darling) cast off all their doubts. The arrival of some Secret Service agents is no problem. His friends think they are actors hired by Baird as an excuse for refusing their money. A series of lucky mixups sees to it that, each time the agents examine some bills, the bills turn out to be genuine. Then Baird receives a telegram from the engineer in charge of the mine—"Have just opened richest pay streak ever discovered in this section"— and his worries are over. Drearily as the play reads today, it delighted New Yorkers until shortly before Christmas and in 1918 reappeared as the musical *Oh, Look!*

The shopworn yet recurring saga of a weak man torn from his loyal wife by a temptress was played out again in Edgar James's **The Master of the House** (8-22-12, 39th St.). In this case the temptress is a beautiful woman named Bettina (Florence Reed), whom Frederick Hoffman (Malcolm Williams) hires to be a companion to his wife, Anna (Grace Reals). Bettina first goes after the Hoffmans' son, Harry (Ralph Morgan), but drops him when she realizes his father would disinherit him. She then seduces the elder Hoffman only to leave him for a young violinist-composer (Pedro De Cordoba). Critics had commented about the violinist in last season's *The*

Marriage—Not, but they ignored the fiddling in the new play, although Bettina had a line reading, "Did I not tell you he had an inspiration?" Despite unflattering notices, the play ran eleven weeks.

So did Philip Bartholomae's **Little Miss Brown** (8-29-12, 48th St.), which took a not dissimilar theme and played it for laughs. A married man (William Morris) spends the night in his hotel suite unaware that a lost young lady, Miss Brown (Madge Kennedy), mistakenly has been told to take a bed in the suite. The next morning the husband has some explaining to do to his wife (Olive Harper Thorne), as well as to the lawyers he and his wife call in to settle the matter, since both lawyers (George Pauncefort and John Bowers) have been courting the girl. One critic questioned how innocent Miss Brown was in light of her "free use of hotel conveniences, her staggering order of Manhattan cocktails for the sake of the glacéd cherries in them, [and] her calm appropriation of the candy Dennison has brought his wife." But reviewers agreed that Madge Kennedy was a comedienne to watch. They also extoled Ned Sparks as a grouchy, bored-to-death hotel clerk— the sort of sourpuss role he would play for the rest of his life. In 1926 Bartholomae helped turn the comedy into the musical *Kitty's Kisses.*

Augustus Thomas suffered a major disappointment with the quick closing of his **The Model** (8-31-12, Harris), which critics condemned as hopelessly talky. Duncan Coverly (Frederick Perry), an American artist living in Paris, is urged by his somewhat older friend, Emile Bergeret (William Courtleigh), not to abandon his model, Louise (Gail Kane), upon marrying Adele Witherspoon (Catherine Calhoun). Finding Adele resentful of Louise, Coverly agrees to break off the engagement. He marries Louise instead, at which point Emile discovers Louise is his long-lost daughter. Courtleigh won the best notices, praised for "the volatility, the lightness, the humor, and the breadth of view" of his playing. Miss Kane was seen as beautiful enough to be a real model but not talented enough to play one. One critic thought Perry looked "as if he was drawn by James Montgomery Flagg," while a second thought he "seemed especially desirous of soaring into the rhetorical empyrean."

September began modestly enough. In **The Ne'er-Do-Well** (9-2-12, Lyric), which Charles Klein dramatized from a Rex Beach novel, a wealthy but dissolute college athlete (Hale Hamilton) is drugged and placed on board a Panama-bound ship with a ticket that carries a criminal's name in his pocket. He is befriended by an unhappily married woman (Katharine Kaelred) and, when her husband is murdered, is accused of the crime. The boy's father (DeWitt C. Jennings) comes to his rescue by disguising the crew of his yacht as U.S. Marines and by bribing local officials. Father, son, and widow sail home together. Even critics who disliked the play praised the scenery. Among the settings they singled out were three decks of an ocean liner seen from the ship's stern; a sumptuous dining room with elegant moldings, wallpaper, and drapes but with wicker chairs; a distant view of canal operations; and a sunlit square in Colón. The play ran five weeks.

Alfred Sutro's **The Perplexed Husband** (9-2-12, Empire) ran twice as long, almost entirely on the box-office power of John Drew. Nearly sixty, the bug-eyed, large-nosed, but suave matinee idol could still win his loyal audiences' sympathies as he impersonated a husband who returns home from a long trip to find his wife (Nina Sevening) has become a slogan-spouting suffragette. He enlists the aid of a beautiful girl (Mary Boland) given to Grecian ideals to bring his wife back to sanity.

The English actor Lewis Waller opened his second New York season with **Discovering America** (9-7-12, Daly's), by the expatriate Edward Knoblauch. Knoblauch's hero was himself an American raised in Italy, where he has fallen in love with a married princess (Miriam Clements). The loss of his wealth forces him to return to New York to try to recoup his fortune. At an ordinary boardinghouse he finds a new love interest (Madge Titheradge) and, in her father's machine to sew on buttons, a key to his future prosperity. The sudden appearance of the princess, now widowed, presents only a temporary dilemma.

September's second week brought in three successive hits. Arthur Wing Pinero's **The "Mind-the-Paint" Girl** (9-9-12, Lyceum) detailed how a musical comedy chorus girl (Billie Burke) wins the hand of a viscount (William Raymond). For audiences' delectation the charming star was handed two Jerome Kern songs to sing.

In later years, commentators discussing Belasco's theatrical realism time and again chose his mounting of Alice Bradley's **The Governor's Lady** (9-10-12, Republic) as an exemplar, for better or worse. The play long since has been forgotten, and so has the fact that a majority of critics hailed it as a strong, honest, and moving drama. However, one setting has entered theatrical legend. Daniel S. Slade (Emmett Corrigan) is a self-made man whose homebody wife (Emma Dunn) doesn't share his social and political ambitions, so Slade determines to divorce her and marry the beautiful, ambitious Katherine Strickland (Gladys Hanson). A meeting

of the two women opens Mary Slade's eyes to her husband's behavior, but at the same time Katherine is so touched by Mary's goodness and innocence that she walks out of Slade's life. Mary, bitter at her treatment, divorces Slade and moves to New York. After Slade is elected governor, he comes to New York to find her.

The curtain rose on the epilogue to reveal a Childs' restaurant. On the right is the large window, giving onto the street. Passers-by can be seen scurrying along, a few stopping, then entering the double doors just to the rear of the window. In the window is a griddle-cake cooker (audiences could smell the pancakes being made). Along the rear wall by the doors is the cashier's stand, and further left is a long counter with a coffee urn, stacks of dishes and cups, and hot trays. A clock and several signs, one advertising the recently opened Childs' in Atlantic City, hang on the white walls beyond. In front are five or six oblong, marble-topped tables, each with four or six bentwood, rattan chairs. There are diners scattered through the room and white-aproned waiters watching to serve them. A scrubwoman is cleaning the tile floor. (Belasco announced that all the equipment was supplied by the Childs' Restaurant Equipment Company.) One of the diners is Mary. A dapper, white-tied Slade enters, comes to Mary's table, and begs her to return. She refuses, but Slade can sense that she still loves him. When she uses her unfamiliarity with his new friends as an excuse, he responds, "I'll introduce you to them after we're married." He picks her up and carries her off, in search of a parson.

The week's biggest hit, and the second-longest-running play of the season, was Bayard Veiller's **Within the Law** (9-11-12, Eltinge), a rousing, novel variation on the crook-play. That it arrived, at another new house, just as New York was embroiled in its latest scandal about police and bought justice (or injustice) helped whet interest. Edward Gilder (Dodson Mitchell), the owner of the Emporium, thinks nothing of using his influence to avoid a speeding ticket and readily looks the other way when a socially prominent lady is picked up in his store for shoplifting, but when Mary Turner (Jane Cowl), one of his salesgirls, is arrested for taking merchandise—found in her locker—he demands she be made an example of, even though everyone tells him the girl is probably as innocent as she claims she is. She confronts him and, still insisting she did not steal anything, tells him she is not surprised that someone did, since "an honest girl can't live decently on six dollars a week." She warns him she will be revenged: "You're going to pay me."

Four years later, out of prison, Mary has an apartment on Gramercy Park, where she works with some other former jailbirds, profiting from shady deals always just "within the law." She takes time out from her enterprises to marry Gilder's son, Dick (Orme Caldara), and when Gilder arrives to protest, she gloats, "Four years ago you took away my name and gave me a number. Now I've given up that number and I've got your name."

The elder Gilder has secretly bought some stolen, illegally imported art, and the police, annoyed at being foiled by Mary's schemes, use another ex-con to goad Mary's cronies into robbing the house. Their plan is to let Mary learn of the robbery; she will run to stop it and be caught with the others. The plan nearly works. But Dick, who has appeared unexpectedly, still hoping to make Mary love him, finds himself being arrested after one of the crooks is shot. The police try to twist matters to make Mary seem guilty. However, the real killer (William B. Mack) confesses, and the police's interception of a letter from the girl who actually had stolen the merchandise Mary had been accused of taking, a letter they recognize they cannot hide, leads to a happy ending.

Miss Cowl's marvelous change from a pale, teary girl in a shabby black dress to the self-assured, richly garbed woman of the later acts, and her high voltage in the most dramatic scenes, skyrocketed her to stardom.

. . .

Jane Cowl (1884–1950) was born in Boston. After studying at Columbia, she worked for Belasco, playing small parts in numerous plays from *Sweet Kitty Bellairs* on. She left his company in 1910. The slim, dark-haired beauty had dark eyes "so black, so limpid, it was a wonder they didn't dissolve and run down her cheeks."

. . .

The play's success also called attention to its author.

. . .

Bayard Veiller (1869–1943) was born in Brooklyn. He combined his earlier experiences as a police reporter and a theatrical press agent to create this, the first in a series of superior thrillers.

William Boden's **Honest Jim Blunt** (9-16-12, Hudson) threw its spotlight on a character who got his nickname by returning a lost glass eye to its owner. In short, Jim (Tim Murphy) is not the most honest of men, and his plans—such as to make a killing on Wall Street and to sell the Great Salt Lake for a salt mine—have a way of backfiring on him.

But he's such a likable fellow his friends and relations forgive him—provided he takes the next boat for Argentina and doesn't come back. Tim Murphy, a cornpone comedian, was more popular on the road than in bigger cities, so the comedy was hustled off to the hinterlands after a mere two weeks, despite money notices.

The capacious Manhattan Opera House played home to Orestes Bean's **An Aztec Romance** beginning on the 16th. Its story unfolded the saga of a temptress (Minnie Tittell Brune) assigned to vamp and destroy the son (Robert Warwick) of an Aztec high priest; she disobeys her orders after she falls in love with him. The *American*'s Alan Dale, resorting to a favorite comic misspelling of his, noted that the hero stalked about in "dekkletey and seemed very proud of his chest." He added that the settings' "primary colors" soon became nerve-wracking. Incidental music was becoming increasingly rare in most plays, but this "romantic spectacular play" had a full score by Harold Orlob, a second-rater best recalled in musical history as the composer who sold the melody for "I Wonder Who's Kissing Her Now" to the man who took credit for it.

In the printed preface to his **Fanny's First Play** (9-16-12, Comedy), George Bernard Shaw branded the piece a "potboiler." Although the comedy is rarely revived, contemporary critics relished it, and playgoers gave it the longest run—256 performances—of any first mounting of a Shaw play in America. Shaw's prologue and epilogue had fun twitting certain West End critics; the body of the work satirized British morality by showing how two engaged middle-class youngsters (Gladys Harvey and Quentin Tod) change their attitudes after becoming involved in scrapes and spending time in jail.

A second British entry ran almost as long. Arnold Bennett and Edward Knoblauch's **Milestones** (9-17-12, Liberty) spanned fifty-two years and presented three generations of a single family, always liberal in their younger years but always ossifying and turning against the liberalism of their own children.

Some very reserved notices for **The Attack** (9-19-12, Garrick), George Egerton's translation of Henri Bernstein's *L'Assaut,* failed to totally quash interest. Its 100-performance run edged it into the hit column. Observers later attributed much of that success to John Mason, who played the elderly French politician battling ugly stories about his youthful embezzling (long since paid back) and fending off the lovesick approaches of his daughter's closest friend (Martha Hedman). The long recitation with which the politician gently turns down the girl "showed how broad and polished" Mason's art was. Miss Hedman was a beautiful Swedish blonde. Much was expected of her, but that promise never was fulfilled, although she had a long, variegated Broadway career.

Following the rash of foreign hits, the next week opened with an American success, George M. Cohan's **Broadway Jones** (9-23-12, Cohan). The *Times* reported that the comedy kept audiences "laughing all the time, laughing for the most part frankly, unreservedly and hilariously" and attributed this to Cohan's "keen faculty for observing things." Given a few days more to consider matters, *Theatre* dismissed Cohan's story as "almost juvenile" but, echoing the *Times,* concluded: "Mr. Cohan is a true observer of men and conditions, and applies the little comic and pathetic touches of life in a way which makes his completed fabric something distinctly vital and real."

Jackson "Broadway" Jones (Cohan) returns home at dawn to his posh New York apartment, waves to his friends who are crooning the "Wedding March" in the street below, tipsily hands his hat and coat to his butler, and does his own bemused song and dance. Whether he has much to celebrate is questionable. Jones some while back abandoned his "jay" Connecticut hometown for the pleasures of the Great White Way. Now, having gone through his own fortune and $50,000 in debt, he has been accepted by a mean, homely, but very rich widow (Ada Gilman). Word comes that his uncle has died and left him the family chewing-gum business. Jones hurries to Connecticut hoping to sell the company and thus recruit his back account. But the company's pretty secretary, Josie Richards (Myrtle Tannehill), explains that the townsfolk will be left jobless since the competitors who would purchase the plant will do so only to shut it down. Nor can she see the appeal of Broadway.

Josie: What is Broadway?
Jones: Broadway?
Josie: A street?
Jones: Sure, it's the greatest street in the world.
Josie: Some people say it's terrible.
Jones: Philadelphia people.

Both quickly agree that it is terrible and wonderful and, most of all, "a mystery." Before long "Broadway" has fallen in love with Josie, given the widow her walking papers, and settled in among the "jays" to marry Josie and save the chewing-gum plant.

Chicago had been all agog over novelist Henry Kitchell Webster's **June Madness** (9-25-12, Fulton), but Broadway snubbed it. The play had been mounted in Chicago as part of the repertory of the

Drama Players, a group that had been seen briefly on Broadway. Some of that now defunct company headed the cast. Twenty-two years before the story unveiled in the play proper began, a young, loveless girl had enjoyed a fling, given birth to a baby girl, and intentionally lost sight of the father. The mother has become Mrs. Thornborough (Hedwig Reicher), the $12,000-a-year secretary to a railroad magnate (Edward Emery), who praises her, not without irony, as "one of the two best railroad men in the country." Her daughter, June (Renee Kelly), is engaged to the magnate's son (A. Hylton Allen), but the magnate's troublemaking wife (Helen Tracy) learns that Mrs. Thornborough is unmarried and demands that the engagement be broken off and that the secretary quit or be fired. The unexpected appearance of June's father (Charles Waldron)—to court the magnate's daughter (Adelaide Nowak)—and his willingness to lie to save Mrs. Thornborough's good name brings about a happy if unbelievable ending.

A past action comes home to haunt the heroine of Graham Moffat's **A Scrape o' the Pen** (9-26-12, Weber's), which some had prophesied would repeat the success of *Bunty Pulls the Strings*. It didn't, albeit its ten-week run was respectable enough considering how esoteric the play and the players' Scottish dialects were. Young lovers (Lila Barclay and Leopold Profeit) sign a pact to marry when the man returns from a long stay in Africa. During that time the girl learns how badly he has behaved, and she adopts his illegitimate daughter, whose mother has died. She also marries another suitor (W. G. Robb). The man returns, prepared to make trouble, but the sight of the youngster in her bed prompts him to burn the agreement.

Another worthless man provided the title for John T. McIntyre's **Steve** (9-28-12, Harris). In order to obtain money to marry Molly (Josephine Victor), who lives in the same tenement as he does, Steve (Arnold Daly) resorts to a variety of scams to trick his brother (Alphonz Ethier) into forking over some of the brother's hard-earned savings. The ploys fail, serving only to expose Steve's vicious nature. Molly goes off with the brother, who loved her all along. The play, which ran one week, served inauspiciously for Arthur Hopkins's debut as producer, a debut he conveniently forgot in his autobiography.

September concluded with three revivals. At the Hudson, Robert Loraine brought back *Man and Superman*. Lewis Waller was praised for his dashing portrayal in *Henry V* at Daly's, but his supporting cast was colorless and his production, according to several notices, shockingly dirty and threadbare.

Some critics looked back longingly to Rignold and Mansfield's splendid mountings. The Manhattan Opera House once more played host to Sothern and Marlowe, who also reappeared on the 30th. During their month-long visit at the huge barn of a theatre, they offered the same plays they had presented a season earlier, with nothing as venturesome as Waller's *Henry*.

Although Edward Locke was credited as author of **The Case of Becky** (10-1-12, Belasco), even Locke acknowledged that crucial rewriting had been the work of the play's producer-director, David Belasco. Reviews and a ninety-five-performance run, just short of the golden century mark, testified that Belasco's singular artistry increasingly was wearing thin for some critics and perhaps, too, for some playgoers. Walter Prichard Eaton noted, "It is sometimes Mr. Belasco's triumph to make us forget the essential triteness of his themes in the magic of his narration. Here we do not feel that he has succeeded." Part of the problem this time was the play's rather fantastic premise and coincidences; another difficulty was that Becky was not truly the central figure, and therefore neither was the star who portrayed her.

Dr. Emerson (Albert Bruning) is a distinguished physician who uses hypnotism as a tool; Professor Balzamo (Charles Dalton) is a charlatan who employs hypnotism to evil ends. Years before the play begins, Balzamo had seduced Dr. Emerson's wife into leaving her husband and traveling with him. Now the good doctor is absorbed by a particularly intriguing case. He is treating a young lady (Frances Starr) with a markedly split personality. As Dorothy she is sweet and docile; as Becky, vicious and rebellious. Her treatment seems to be progressing rapidly until Balzamo makes a sudden appearance at the doctor's home, claiming Dorothy is his daughter. He "summons" her, and after some moments Dorothy comes slowly down the doctor's spiral staircase and into the living room. The doctor, realizing the sinister nature of the man, invites the professor into his laboratory. He purposely boasts about his marvelous new equipment, and Balzamo scoffs, so the doctor suggests he try some on the professor. In no time the professor is under his power and discloses that Dorothy is actually the doctor's daughter. Waking from his trance, the professor finds he has lost his hypnotic powers.

Belasco, remembering Mansfield's brilliant Jekyll-Hyde transformations, eschewed theatrical tricks in turning Dorothy into Becky and back again: "Miss Starr changes from Dorothy to Becky on a fully lighted stage. She is seated, reading a book, the gift of the youth whom she loves, and as she reads she hums the air of a pretty little song. Gradually the smile fades from her face, her lips contract, her mouth grows thin and hard, her features are drawn, and the color fades away, leaving an ashy pallor. The voice that has been pleasant now grows raucous, and the movements, as she tosses the book aside with an ugly pout, are quick and angular, in contrast to Dorothy's liquid graceful gesture."

Inevitably Belasco's physical production drew extended comment: "The last act shows the doctor's laboratory at night, a fascinating piece of Belascan realism, with white walls and strange machines, such as the lullaby instrument which croons like the wind and sings on three sweet notes, and the static machine with its crackling, leaping spark, and that curious machine, of which we know not the name, which seems to be composed of a small electric fan blade, brilliantly illuminated, into which the subject looks as it revolves till the hypnotic sleep comes."

Good writing and fine acting could not save Frederic Arnold Kummer's oddly titled **The Brute** (10-8-12, 39th St.). A young couple (Ernest Glendinning and Ruth Shepley) move from their simple Harlem flat to a luxurious Fifth Avenue apartment after the wife is bequeathed a fortune by the rich man with whom she planned to elope but who suddenly died. When the husband learns he has become a laughingstock, he takes the couple's child and returns to the old Harlem rooms. The wife comes to recover the child and plead with the husband to be sensible. Instead the husband tears off her jewels and orders her to learn her place. She does, but not before accusing him of being brutish.

In the dreamy dusk, against a background of opalescent clouds, a sailboat garlanded with flowers sails slowly down a river, two occupants intoning an eerie Oriental melody. Thus begins **The Daughter of Heaven** (10-12-12, Century), translated by George Egerton from the French of Pierre Loti and Judith Gautier. One spectacular scene followed another in this tale of Manchurian emperor (Basil Gill) and a Ming empress (Viola Allen) who commit suicide when they cannot reconcile their warring nations. Not all of the spectacle worked. Dead soldiers falling from the walls were all too obviously padded dummies. A four-hour running time, with long waits for scene changes, didn't help. Still, the mounting ran twelve weeks.

First-nighters moved from the huge Century to Broadway's loveliest intimate playhouse for what was billed as "a sequence of episodes," although its translator, Granville Barker, had called it "a series of dialogues." Episodes or dialogues, Arthur

Schnitzler's **The Affairs of Anatol** (10-14-12, Little) journeyed with its roué hero (John Barrymore) from one romance to another—five in all (although Schnitzler actually wrote more). Marguerite Clark and Doris Keane were among the courted ladies. Critics disagreed on Barrymore's performance: "Mr. Barrymore plays here with charming variety and plenty of the right sort of humor"; "The monotony of his voice and gesture helped to foil his good attempts."

Except for a last-act scene in the Plumfield apple orchard, all of **Little Women** (10-12-12, Playhouse) unfolded in what was advertised as a precise recreation of the Alcott living room at Concord, Mass., as it had been restored by local clubwomen in 1912. Jessie Bonstelle (who conceived and co-directed the production) and Marian de Forest dramatized Louisa May Alcott's popular novel. The play kept as much of the story as time and the limitations of a stage would allow. With Alice Brady as Meg, Gladys Hulette as Beth, Beverly West as Amy, and Marie Pavey as Jo, William A. Brady's mounting ran until spring.

Basil Macdonald Hastings's English play **The New Sin** (10-16-12, Wallack's) had that rarity, an all-male cast. It had an unusual story to tell. It also had little dramatic effectiveness and no staying power. The story concerned a young man (Cyril Keightley) whose father's will prevents his brothers and sisters from inheriting anything so long as he lives. He decides to commit suicide, but when his deranged brother (O. P. Heggie) kills a man, he quickly accepts responsibility for the murder. Clever questioning by a friend (Julian L'Estrange) exonerates him. The play led a parade of failures that continued into November.

In Jules Eckert Goodman's **The Point of View** (10-25-12, 48th St.), Myra Dimsley (Emily Stevens) is taken under the wing of Frances Lawton (Lucile Watson), a society girl who is unaware her brother (Howard Estabrook) has violated Myra, although Myra is engaged to another man (Robert Kelly). Myra's fiancé persuades everyone to forgive and forget. The "febrile, nervous, vital playing" of Miss Stevens, who had controlled her tendency to bite her lips at dramatic moments, added sparks to a drama that badly needed some.

Cosmo Hamilton's West End drama **The Blindness of Virtue** (10-28-12, 39th St.) debated how much parents should tell their children about the world's wicked ways. With a title as dissuasive as its subject, the play closed after a fortnight.

For years the Metropolis, at 143rd Street and Third Avenue, had been home to lurid touring melodramas. When films killed the market in such plays, Charles E. Blaney, who had written and produced many of them, and who had built a chain of theatres with his profits from them, set up the theatre as home base for his wife, Cecil Spooner, and her stock company. Most of their mountings were tested Broadway favorites, but now and then an original play was offered. They only hinted at the thrill-a-minute style of the bygone pieces and seem not to have toured much, if at all. One example was Blaney and J. H. Shepard's **My Indian Love** (10-28-12, Metropolis), in which Miss Spooner took on the role of a daughter of the governor of New Amsterdam who falls in love with an Indian chief. Both families are horrified by the prospect. Reviews imply a happy ending without specifying how interracial difficulties were resolved. **The Man Who Dared** and **The Adventures of Polly** were among the other novelties the Blaneys offered their loyal, but shrinking and changing, clientele.

"Emotional female stars have had hard times these days in securing suitable mediums for the display of their talents. Helen Ware is no exception." So *Theatre* opened its review of Elmer Harris's **The Trial Marriage** (10-29-12, Hudson), which supposedly was written expressly for the actress and which critics took delight in shredding. They pointed out, for example, that the "trial marriage" was no marriage—no wedding had taken place—but merely a "well-hidden liaison." At least the setting was novel, a Maine hunting lodge. There Blair Thomas (Harrison Hunter) brings Marie Louise Ridgeway, suspects her of having a fling with his best friend, Alexander Prince (Charles Stevenson), and at first seems unsympathetic when her mother (Karra Kenwyn) is outraged at the situation. However, Marie's anguish and tears finally bring him to present her with a wedding ring.

A newlywed (Ralph Herz) and his bachelor buddies encountered some unfunny situations in Jackson D. Haag and James Montgomery's **Bachelors and Benedicts** (11-2-12, Criterion). A not too dissimilar story propelled Frank Mandel and Helen Kraft's **Our Wives** (11-4-12, Wallack's). Frank Bowers (Henry Kolker), a librettist, has watched with a mixture of gloom and contempt as one by one his cronies have walked down the aisle. Then, suddenly, he meets a composer whom he had known only as Wilson. Wilson turns out to be a beautiful girl (Pamela Gaythorne). The pair pledge to work together and ignore that they are members of different sexes. They find they can't ignore those differences, but all ends harmoniously. The comedy was at best a modest success, faring better when it was made into a Victor Herbert musical, *The Only Girl,* two years later.

Four other plays opened the same evening as *Our Wives.* Not just its novelty sent critics out praising George C. Hazleton and J. Harry Benrimo's **The Yellow Jacket** (11-4-12, Fulton). A colorful, careful production, and a curious combination of story and presentation, made for gripping, touching theatre. Benrimo, who was also an actor and director (he directed this mounting), grew up in San Francisco and was familiar with that city's Chinese playhouses. He and Hazelton reputedly used several genuine if unidentified Chinese dramas to create this new one, staged in as pure a Chinese tradition as possible. That meant an almost Shakespearean simplicity, with only curtains and props, with an Oriental orchestra twanging away on a small balcony just above and behind the playing area, and with a dour, chain-smoking, noncommittal Property Man (Arthur Shaw) to provide minimal scenic elements, such as a bamboo pole to suggest a tree, a handful of white confetti thrown to represent a snowstorm, or a ladder offered to help a character ascend to heaven. It also meant each important character, as he or she first appeared, addressed the audience by way of a flowery introduction.

And so Due Jung Fah (Grace Valentine), walking with mincing steps and holding a fan before her face, bows and says, "Gentle listeners, here in my garden, with ceremonial bow, I tell you, I am Due Jung Fah, most unhappy of ladies. I am the second wife of Wu Sin Yin, the Great. There would be music in my heart if it were not for the first wife. The butterflies and bees and humming-birds do not come to my garden. They fly to make hers beautiful." So she plots to have her rival and the rival's young son killed. But the man assigned to kill them knows how good they are. He kills a wicked woman instead and disguises the corpse so no one can tell the difference. The spared woman dies a natural death and leaves the boy to the man who spared her. The boy grows up and, as Wu Hoo Git (George Relph), determines to assume his rightful place. His half-brother, Wu Fah Din (Schuyler Ladd), an absurdly effeminate man known as "the Daffodil," throws various snares in his path. But Wu Hoo Git triumphs and dons the yellow jacket, which symbolizes power and status.

The play ran ten weeks—the longest run of any of the evening's openings—yet all apparently was not well. One critic, writing a few weeks after the opening, pleaded for playgoers to rush to the Fulton to help a worthy drama "struggling for survival." A 1916 revival ran far longer, and the play retained a certain popularity through the 1920s.

There were no urgent pleas for James Bernard Fagan's **Hawthorne of the U.S.A.** (11-4-12, Astor), but the play toured for an entire season after what apparently was a satisfactory nine-week run in New York. Its action unfolded in "Oberon, the small capital of Borrovina, a small independent state somewhere in the mess of Southeastern Europe." There, in a once elegant garden—now going to seed, with its stonework dilapidating—Anthony Hamilton Hawthorne (Douglas Fairbanks), an American who has just broken the bank at Monte Carlo, spots a gorgeous girl and falls hopelessly in love with her. Then he learns to his dismay that she is Princess Irma Augusta Elizabeth Overitch (Irene Fenwick) and that she is being forced to marry Prince Vladimir (Martin Alsop). He also discovers that Vladimir is treacherously plotting to kill the king and assume the throne.

Hawthorne pulls the rug out from under Vladimir's plans. He tells the mob assembled to demand the king's abdication to persist in their demand, if they choose, "but before the year is out, you will find that you are making a great big mistake." And he continues, "Do you know who I am? Do you know what my business is? Making money. Do you know why I left America and came over here to Borrovina? I've been keeping this under cover but I'll tell you now—simply because I knew that there were greater possibilities here than in my own land." With a few well-placed bribes, he quells the revolution. Within a year he has turned the bankrupt country into a very prosperous place and won himself a bride. Fairbanks, "that young man with a smile that invites confidence and muscles that enforce it," boosted ticket sales with his "rollicking good nature, dramatic fire and true American hurrah!"

The least successful of the evening's novelties was James Forbes's **A Rich Man's Son** (11-4-12, Harris), in which Ralph Morgan played a spoiled offspring who rebels when his father (Paul Everton) demands he marry a drab socialite (Lillian Sinnott). He prefers his father's secretary (Louise Rutter) and whisks her away in a show of determination.

Four weeks was not much of a run for a new play like Forbes's, but it was a commendable stand for a Shakespearean revival. The mounting was William Faversham's vision of *Julius Caesar* at the Lyric, with Faversham as Antony, Tyrone Power as Brutus, Frank Keenan as Cassius, and Fuller Mellish as Caesar. Settings of chromatic realism were done in the style of Alma Tadema, and costumes were equally colorful—"Antony's delicate raspberry peplum . . . the scarlet-banded toga of the Senator."

Different critics praised (or censured) different players, but the consensus was that this was a very good revival indeed.

Winthrop Ames's policy of keeping his new theatre lit as often as possible saw him bring out Jessie Graham White's version of **Snow White and the Seven Dwarfs** (11-7-12, Little) for matinees. Marguerite Clark, who was seen in the evenings on the same stage as one of Anatol's ladies, made a fetching Snow White. Elaine Inescort was lauded for her wicked queen, who broke the magic mirror when she was told she was no longer the fairest in the land and, losing her orange, gold, and green gown, metamorphosed before the audience's eyes into an ugly, shabbily dressed hag. The demand for seats was so great that the production lasted for seventy-two showings.

Exactly a week after his *Hawthorne of the U.S.A.* premiered, James Bernard Fagan had a second offering ready. **Bella Donna** (11-11-12, Empire) was his dramatization of Robert Hichens's popular novel. But what small favor was accorded to this story of a vampirish wife (Alla Nazimova) who attempts to poison her husband's coffee and run off with another man, only to eventually have both men shut their doors to her, came from its exotic settings (a magnificent yacht and lush views of the Middle East), the star's glamorous gowns, and Nazimova's tigerish emoting.

Broadway marked Frederic Chapin's **C.O.D.** (11-11-12, Gaiety) "return to sender." Three men, all with the initials C.O.D., are heading to meet their wives in the Adirondacks when their train is wrecked and they find themselves taking refuge at a farmhouse where there are three pretty farmer's daughters. The men pretend they are widowers. As might be expected in farce, the wives suddenly appear at the farm. They arrive arm in arm with three young men to whom they have pretended they are widows. The rest can be imagined.

The same evening brought forth another more interesting venture. "Annie Russell," one commentator observed, "is like the scent of lavender. She is a reminder of rare old lace, or the strain of a sweet, old-fashioned ballad of love. She is girlhood embodied in imperishable manner. Quaintness, sweetness and youth [she was pushing fifty] that persist are the three attributes that give her unlikeness to anyone else on the American stage." Though most critics long had admired the doleful-eyed actress, she had never achieved widespread success or popularity. Tellingly, when she organized her Old English Comedy Company and leased the 39th Street Theatre, she "secured subscriptions from her faithful patrons, fine old relics of the Knickerbocker age in New York, persons who do not go to the theatre any more save when Annie Russell plays, because her presence is to them a guaranty against vulgarity." The troupe opened with a tasteful presentation of *She Stoops to Conquer* and later moved on to equally tasteful revivals of *Much Ado About Nothing* and *The Rivals*. Her performances with her company marked her last regular appearances before her retirement.

Some of the vulgarity missing in Annie Russell's presentations probably contributed to the fun at W. H. Post and William Collier's **Never Say Die** (11-12-12, 48th St.). Dionysius Woodbury (Collier), learning he has only a year or two to live, agrees to marry his friend's girl (Paula Marr) and leave her a rich widow, whom the friend (John Junior) could then marry. (Just why he couldn't leave his money directly to his friend went unsaid.) When Dionysius learns the diagnosis was a mistake, he dutifully tries all manner of ways to commit suicide but survives each attempt. He and the girl finally decide they have come to love one another, so the friend must look elsewhere. Not only did the comedy change from a somewhat sombre first act to fast-paced farce in the last two acts, it made no effort to adhere to its principal story, content to filch laughs from Collier's endeavor to eat asparagus with a fork and spoon in one hand and from his confrontation with a dog saddled on him by a precocious neighbor (William Collier, Jr.). For all its faults, and possible vulgarities, the comedy ran five months.

The title of Rupert Hughes's **What Ails You?** (11-18-12, Criterion) suggested it might tell a similar story, but it didn't. However, it did resemble Hughes's far more successful *Excuse Me* with its penchant for athletics. The play begins in a posh restaurant where a drunken playboy (Shelley Hull) is told he can change his ways and win the girl of his dreams by a regimen of calisthenics. The scene then switches to a gymnasium where a preposterously tall man is swinging at and missing his near-midget sparring partner, a fat man is trying futilely to touch his toes, and a scrawny woman and a grotesquely obese one look equally ridiculous in tight jerseys. Of course, the hero eventually wins out. However, his road to success was not funny enough to keep the show on the boards for long.

The same evening saw John Kellerd and his company reappear, at the Garden Theatre. Most critics gave his revival of *Hamlet* no more than a skimpy paragraph or two. They remarked on the simplicity and appropriateness of the scenery and costumes, praised the vigorous, intelligent acting, and rued how few playgoers attended. Yet this mounting has gone down in history books for supposedly breaking Booth's record of 100 consecutive performances, closing after its 102nd playing. The record is open to serious question, since from the start Kellerd had announced a repertory that would also include *The Merchant of Venice* and *Oedipus Rex*. It takes three full months of eight-performance weeks to achieve 100 performances, but Shakespeare's comedy was on the boards by January 20, and the Greek tragedy was brought out at the beginning of February. In any case, for a brief time in November three Shakespearean mountings—*Julius Caesar, Hamlet,* and *Much Ado About Nothing*—held the boards simultaneously, while Waller's *Henry V* and Sothern and Marlowe had only recently left. Broadway was welcoming Shakespeare more heartily than it had in years.

Broadway, and especially the post-Broadway hinterlands, also welcomed Edward Sheldon's **The High Road** (11-19-12, Hudson), allowing Mrs. Fiske, who starred in the play and produced and directed it in collaboration with her husband, to recoup the losses incurred with *Lady Patricia*. Critics pointed to Sheldon's *The Nigger* and to plays such as *Mrs. Dane's Defense* and *The Man of the Hour* to suggest that there was little original about the new drama. But if young Sheldon broke no new ground, he still wrote with an admirable perceptiveness and integrity. Some commentators used the occasion to highlight what they perceived were becoming Sheldon's salient virtues. One saw these as "a certain grace in writing, and a feeling for a romantic note underneath the commonplaces of life." A second extolled "the 'big scenes' which Mr. Sheldon handles with a skill excelled by no one."

Mary Page (Mrs. Fiske), a sweet girl in simple calicos and sunbonnets, leaves the home of her narrow, flinty father (Charles Fisher), furious at his confinement of her and at his bilking of a young lawyer, Winfield Barnes (Frederick Perry). For a while she becomes a kept woman; rebelling against that sort of life, too, she takes up the cause of abolishing child labor. In time her efforts bring her to the attention of the new governor—Barnes. He reveals he long had loved her, and even her confession of her previous life cannot deter him from marrying her. However, when Barnes is nominated to run for the presidency, an unscrupulous newspaper owner, John Stephen Maddock (Arthur Byron), whose other enterprises employ child labor, threatens to expose her past. Mary confronts him, and her fiery righteousness shames him into silence.

Another kind of melodrama, the spectacular Drury Lane variety, was becoming increasingly rare on Broadway, but a rip-roaring example was provided by Cecil Raleigh and Henry Hamilton's **The Whip** (11-22-12, Manhattan Opera House). "The Whip" is a racehorse the villains conspire to prevent from running in the big race. Their plan is overheard by its trainer, posing in Madame Tussaud's as a wax model of a famous murderer. Audiences watched the horse being loaded into a railway car, the train leave the station, and one of the villains creep along the running board of the coaches to uncouple the horse's car. Lights revolving behind the train conveyed an impression of speed, while a moving panorama took the train from woodlands into a tunnel. There the separated car is in danger of being smashed by an oncoming engine. But the horse is rescued in the nick of time (the smashup was another roof-raising effect) to run (on treadmills) and win the race. The thriller packed the enormous auditorium for five months.

Producers were increasingly unwilling to keep heavily panned shows going. An embarrassing instance was the removal of Augustus Thomas's **Mere Man** (11-25-12, Harris), which opened on Monday and closed on Saturday, marking his second abrupt failure of the season. Despite its title, its central figure was neither male nor wholly earthbound but a lady astrologist (Chrystal Herne), who is brought to trial as a charlatan and as a woman with a past (she doesn't, it turns out, have a wicked one). Thomas attempted to use her misadventures for some misfiring jabs at the campaign to allow women to vote.

A competitive entry, Edith Sessions Tupper's **The Road to Arcady** (11-25-12, Berkeley), was almost as short-lived, illuminating during its week-and-a-half stand Antoinette "Tony" Gerard's falling in love with a man (Frank Ritchie) who was her partner at a Harvard dance. But Tony (Lily Cahill) has an ambitious mother (Helen Tracy), who tries to force her to marry a richer boy (Wilson Hummel) by claiming the Gerards are bankrupt and the marriage will save the family. Tony's brother (Albert Latscha) exposes the mother's chicanery.

Mme Simone, winding down her failed attempt to establish an American following, was the star of the evening's third flop, **The Paper Chase** (11-25-12, Wallack's), derived by Louis N. Parker from Henry Montoy's novel *The Minister of Police*. In the bewigged, rococo elegance of Marie Antoinette's world, her lady-in-waiting contrives to keep a scurrilous manuscript from falling into the hands of the Duke of Richelieu (Edgar Kent).

Likewise, December's first arrival was also its first

departure. **The Indiscretion of Truth** (12-3-12, Harris) was merely the latest theatricalization of Wilkie Collins's *Man and Wife*. Its author, J. Hartley Manners, would provide playgoers with a far more memorable stage piece later in the month.

News of the to-do it had caused in London preceded the Broadway opening of Stanley Houghton's **Hindle Wakes** (12-9-12, Maxine Elliott's). It dealt more directly and more honestly with a subject touched on in *June Madness*. In this instance a poor young girl (Emelie Polini), resolving to live by her own standards and her own ideas of what represents a sensible reality for her, firmly rejects the notion that she and the rich mill owner's son (Roland Young) who had seduced her must right the wrong by marrying. Just a few seasons back such a theme would have evoked howls of outrage, but 1912 reviewers greeted the drama with everything from quiet respect to yawns. It lasted one month.

In recent years the Grand Opera House, at 23rd Street and Eighth Avenue, had served as home to post-Broadway touring attractions and to films. Its days of regularly presenting novelties was long past. But one new play was offered with **Freckles** (12-16-12, Grand Opera), Neil Twomey's dramatization of Gene Stratton-Porter's novel. Milton Noble, Jr., son of the famous touring star of yesteryear, played the title role of an Irish lad who comes to a lumber camp, thwarts Black Jack (Robert A. Wessell), makes good, and marries the appropriately named Angel (Ruth Gray). The *Dramatic Mirror* saw the scenery as better than expected for a traveling show. In particular it noted a forest "with birds twittering in branches of the trees had real moments of charm." However, *Freckles* was designed for tank towns and lesser neighborhoods, so after playing out its single-week booking it moved on, stopping now and then at once proud theatres not unlike the Grand.

Some once bright (or at least very promising) performers, such as Edwin Arden, Robert T. Haines, and Olive May, could do nothing for Sherman Dix's **The Question** (12-19-12, Daly's). A Southern "dry," whose gentlemanly colonel-father is a boozer, objects to his sister marrying a northern distillery owner. When the father gets his daughter drunk, even the northerner consents to campaign for—well, moderation? The drama, branded "The Season's Worst" in one headline, lasted half a week.

The season's runaway hit was Manners's **Peg o' My Heart** (12-20-12, Cort), which was the author's "betrothal present" to his star, and opened yet another new playhouse. The snooty Chichesters—mama (Emilie Melville), son Alaric (Hassard Short),

and daughter Ethel (Christine Norman)—have learned that a bank failure has left them fundless. The empty-headed Alaric responds, "Don't worry, Mater. (*Buttons his coat determinedly.*) I'll go down and tell 'em just what I think of 'em. They can't play the fool with me. Don't you care, Mater. You've got a son, thank God. And one no bank can take liberties with." Ethel's response is to seriously consider running away with a married man, Christian Brent (Reginald Mason).

They are locked in an embrace when a girl appears on the threshold—"*a beautiful girl of eighteen, shabbily but cleanly dressed in a simple print dress, a wide-brimmed cheap straw hat from under which hangs a profusion of short, natural curls of gleaming reddish hair. She is carrying a bag and a paper parcel somewhat the worse for wear under one arm, and under the other arm is a shaggy unkempt, and altogether disgraceful looking Irish terrier.*" She is consigned haughtily to the kitchen when the embarrassed lovers can get nothing from her but such strange remarks as "The gentleman said to me, he said, 'You go to the place that's written down on the card, and you sit down at the house, and you wait, and that's all you do—just wait.'"

The gentleman turns out to be the family lawyer (Clarence Handyside), who advises the Chichesters that the girl is a niece, the daughter of a cast-out and now deceased sister of Mrs. Chichester. The will of Mrs. Chichester's late brother will give them enough money to keep afloat if they will take the girl in and teach her mannerly ways. Her real name is Margaret O'Connell, but she prefers to be called Peg (Laurette Taylor). Indeed, her ne'er-do-well father, who has remained in America, has always referred to her as "Peg o' My Heart." A fight ensues at once, when Peg is ordered to get rid of her dog. She refuses, pointing to the pampered little poodle Ethel carries—"I thought it was her knitting until it moved." A month's trial is agreed upon. However, matters do not go smoothly. There are numerous clashes. Peg's only ally seems to be a neighbor who has been a soldier, read for a career in law, and now has a nearby farm. He introduces himself to her only as Jerry (H. Reeves-Smith). The two quickly fall in love, although she is alarmed later to learn that he is really Sir Gerald and her uncle's executor. After Peg spurns proposals of marriage from both Alaric and the lawyer, and after her quick thinking prevents Ethel from ruining her life by eloping with Brent, the family discovers that the bank has been saved after all and that Peg and Jerry will wed. "Sure," she tells Jerry, "there's nothing half so sweet in life as love's young dream."

Although critics applauded the play as charming, they fell in line with their colleague who suggested that "when Miss Taylor is off the stage the curtain might as well be down." The original production played 604 performances in New York, after which the star took the play to London. As late as 1914–15 no fewer than eight complete companies were lighting up American stages. Posters for some of these companies supposedly featured Miss Taylor's name in large print above the name of the actress who played Peg, leading many to believe they had seen Miss Taylor when they actually had not. The play has been musicalized several times, never successfully.

Compared to *Peg o' My Heart*'s year-and-a-half stand, the 153-performance run of John Roberts's **The Conspiracy** (12-21-12, Garrick) was insignificant, but it represented more typically the run of the period's hits. The play was the sort of hokum that, when grippingly done, usually finds a place in a healthy theatre. A writer (John Emerson) of mysteries tricks his secretary (Jane Grey) into confessing that she is the wanted murderess of the chief of a band of white slaves. He tricks her by dictating a story describing the killing and killer in great detail. However, he also helps her clear her name.

The 1912 theatre understood that it must build for the future by allowing children to cultivate the habit of playgoing. *Little Women* and *Snow White and the Seven Dwarfs* were both profiting from large numbers of youngsters in the audience. A tiny, unused auditorium atop the troubled Century Theatre was converted into a playhouse designed specifically for children and opened with Frances Hodgson Burnett's **Racketty-Packetty House** (12-23-12, Children's). A ramshackle doll house, long neglected in favor of a more elegant one built to resemble a turreted castle, is about to be consigned to the fire, but its little denizens come to life and work to save it. The come-to-life dolls were all portrayed by children. Among the older players was Maude Granger in the important role of the old nurse. As if three shows all meant to lure in children were not enough, *Racketty-Packetty House*'s opening coincided with the return of Maude Adams as *Peter Pan* at the Empire.

Githa Sowerby's **Rutherford and Son** (12-24-12, Little), a London hit, was by no means for children. It depicted a ruthless, narrow businessman (Norman McKinnel), willing to destroy his own family to attain his ends, who finally is put in his place by an equally ruthless but more humane daughter-in-law (Thyrza Norman). McKinnel, one of the most admired West End actors of the time, made his only important American appearance in this play. "He is notably effective," one critic wrote, "in conveying a suggestion of the man's grim cynicism. The smile that curls about the corner of his mouth is far more cruel, far more disconcerting than words of bitterness." But his fine acting, along with that of Leo G. Carroll in his American debut, could not make the play a hit.

Another play that opened the same night and two that premiered the next all scored much longer runs. Harriet Ford and Harvey J. O'Higgins's **The Argyle Case** (12-24-12, Criterion), "written in co-operation with William J. Burns," the city's most famous detective, was Broadway's latest crook-play. One review noted of the genre, "They have the novelty and the merit of being innocuous. In them crime is incidental. . . . Most are as harmless as peep shows." This one centered on Asche Kayton (Robert Hilliard), called in to solve a millionaire's murder. Suspicion falls on the dead man's adopted daughter, Mary (Stella Archer). But since Kayton has fallen in love with her, he and the audience know she is innocent. He slyly gets all the other suspects to supply him with their fingerprints and sits by stolidly as they nervously talk themselves out of or into suspicion. When he arrests the real killer, he proposes to Mary and is accepted by her. Time had taken its toll on Hilliard, and no one still called him the handsomest man on the stage, but with his years of experience behind him he played the detective with convincing suavity and ease.

Some more experienced old hands helped a pair of young playwrights enjoy a hit. Fanny and Frederic Hatton were a husband and wife who had worked together for some time at newspapers in Mrs. Hatton's native Chicago. (Mr. Hatton had been born in Peru, Ill., and had studied chemistry at the University of Wisconsin and at Princeton.) Their maiden effort was **Years of Discretion** (12-25-12, Belasco) and was produced and directed by no less than Belasco himself.

A greying, socially confined New England widow, Mrs. Farrell Howard (Effie Shannon), fed up with life in Brookline, Mass., and with her holier-than-thou son (Grant Mitchell), flees to New York, dyes her hair, hires a dressmaker and a French maid, and sets out to have some fun on the town. Before long she is courted by a brash Irish politician (Bruce McRae), a parlor socialist and notorious philanderer (Herbert Kelcey), and the gentlemanly Christopher Dallas (Lyn Harding). She decides to accept Dallas's proposal but realizes she must first confess she is not as young as she has pretended to be. To her astonishment he confesses he isn't exactly as chipper as he has let on. They agree to abandon their plans for a gay life abroad and settle back into a sensible old age. Obvious as the comedy was, superior acting and staging kept it on the boards in New York for six months.

Yet another crook-play-cum-farce, Carlyle Moore's **Stop Thief** (12-25-12, Gaiety), settled in for five months. The curtain rises as a wedding is about to take place at the Carr home. Papa Carr (Frank Bacon) is in a dither, knowing how absent-minded he is and wondering what important matter he has forgotten to attend to. James Cluney (Percy Ames), soon to be his son-in-law, tells him not to worry. After all, every one of us has some sort of failing. Cluney thinks his own is that he may be a kleptomaniac. Suddenly valuables such as jewels and bonds turn up missing, only to be found in Cluney's pockets. At the same time, the Carrs' maid (Mary Ryan) secretly has let in her fiancé, Jack Doogan (Richard Bennett), a professional thief. Mayhem and the police also arrive in short order. The police are headed by Joseph Thompson (James C. Marlowe), "the best detective in the state of Rhode Island," but that doesn't prevent him from having his pocket picked, misplacing his warrant, or slamming a door on his own coat, which he is wearing at the moment. By the time matters are resolved, Doogan and the maid join Cluney and Madge Carr (Louise Woods) in standing side by side before the minister.

Much of the play was performed in the "rapid-fire style" so befitting the sort of farce that mustn't give audiences time to think, although the *Times*'s notice reported, "There was one portion of the third act in which for almost five minutes nothing happened except that the whole bridal party was being watched by a squad of policemen, and yet the ensemble acting was such that the audience kept laughing for the whole period."

There was a hint of the crook-play in Mary Roberts Rinehart's **Cheer Up** (12-30-12, Harris), which the authoress called "an optimistic comedy in two clouds and a silver lining." But there was also more than a hint of her recent hit *Seven Days*. In that comedy the characters found themselves quarantined in a house; in her new piece the characters were snowbound in a sanitarium. Its owner has died and bequeathed it to his grandson, Dickie Carter (Effingham Pinto), but Dickie is loathe to reveal himself since his new bride, Dorothy (Fayette Perry), would have to learn that he once had been sued for breach of promise by a gold-digging actress, Julia Summers (Lotta Linthicum), who is now a patient there. Dickie's reluctance to come forward

allows an impostor, Alan Pierce (Walter Hampden), to create problems. But then, so do a convenient assortment of other figures. Trivia buffs might want to know that the play was produced and directed by Cecil B. de Mille.

In Ethelyn Emery Keays's **His Wife by His Side** (12-30-12, Berkeley Lyceum), the "pouting 'baby wife' " (Nanette Comstock) of a young physician (Frank Ritchie) demands he cling to her and fire his nurse (Elsie Esmond), of whom the wife is unreasonably jealous. The doctor's bachelor friend (Robert Drouet) clears up the problem, which bothered them and audiences for a mere two weeks.

Short as the run of the Keays comedy was, it survived far longer than Rutherford Mayne's dangerously titled London play **The Drone** (12-30-12, Daly's). When the play was withdrawn after its second performance, the reason given offered a novel twist on an old excuse: the theatre, not the play, was being shut for repairs. The comedy's story related how a perennial nonachiever, a would-be inventor (Whitford Kane), saves his brother (Robert Forsyth) from a breach-of-promise suit by selling the plaintiff (Margaret O'Gorman) the rights to one of his worthless inventions.

The final crook play of 1912, Joseph Byron Totten's **Alibi Bill** (12-31-12, Weber's), didn't do much better. It ran three performances. Critics looked on it—sneered at it might be more accurate—as an atrociously acted and miserably written ripoff of such plays as *Alias Jimmy Valentine* and *Within the Law*. "Alibi" Bill Harrison (Ralph Stuart) is a reformed crook who has joined the Secret Service. He exposes the felonious carryings on of the D.A., G. Fouler Carlton (Lionel Adams), and wins Elsie Davis (Millicent Davis), whom both men had wooed.

One crook play having closed 1912, another was the first theatre piece to arrive in 1913. However, Harry James Smith's **Blackbirds** (1-6-13, Lyceum) held a special interest, being Smith's first play since his noteworthy debut with *Mrs. Bumpstead-Leigh*. Like that play, and even more like *Years of Discretion*, it focused on impostors. But these were impostors operating on the wrong side of the law. Nevil Trask (H. B. Warner) is the fortune-hunting, resentful, illegitimate son of a British nobleman; Leonie Sobatsky (Laura Hope Crews) is an international smuggler posing as a Polish grande dame. On shipboard each tries to gull the other until they realize they ply kindred trades. They then combine their talents, fend off attempts to expose or rehabilitate them, and ship out to foreign parts to continue their escapades. Smith wrote a friend that critics had "pounced" on the play "in the most wantonly ferocious, bloodthirsty manner, tearing it into shreds and laughing as the feathers flew." But those same critics could not agree whether the play treated a serious theme too lightly, was not funny enough, or simply failed to establish a consistent tone. Belasco, who was to have his own hit two nights later, originally had optioned the work but released it to Henry Miller. For all his astuteness, Miller could not find the answer to the play's difficulties. The birds fluttered out of sight after two weeks. By April the drama had been trimmed into a short one-act play for vaudeville.

It was only a small jump as far as titles went from *Blackbirds* to Eugene Walter's **Fine Feathers** (1-7-13, Astor), but it was a somewhat larger jump from the crook-play to this muckraking drama, a type the newer kind of thriller seemed to have supplanted. John Brand (Wilton Lackaye), a cynical contractor, argues that the dam he is building does not need the expensive concrete stipulated in the specifications. He urges Bob Reynolds (Robert Edeson), the project inspector, to approve a cheaper substitute. At first Reynolds balks, but, goaded by his wife (Lolita Robertson), who hankers after a better life than she has found in their Staten Island bungalow, he agrees. Between the wife and the strong-willed, unprincipled builder, Reynolds is led into further shady transactions. When the dam bursts, causing the loss of many lives, Reynolds snaps. He goes to the phone, announces his intention of shooting himself, turns out the light, and fires the gun. Most reviewers concurred that, while *Fine Feathers* was intelligently written, it could not compare for dramatic power with some of Walter's earlier plays—especially *Paid in Full* and *The Easiest Way*. They could not, on the other hand, find common ground about the acting. Some said Lackaye and Rose Coghlan (as a busybody neighbor) belonged to an older acting school unsuited to such modern drama; others thought they were just right. Right or wrong, they helped *Fine Feathers* run ten weeks.

Belasco's third hit of the season was **A Good Little Devil** (1-8-13, Republic), "a fairy-tale for grown-ups" adapted by Austin Strong from the play by Rosemonde Gerard (Mme Edmond Rostand) and her son Maurice. Moving between the real world and a world of vivid childish imaginations, it told of how little Charles MacLance (Ernest Truex) is put upon by his witchlike aunt (William Norris) and her mean cohorts, Old Nick, Sr. (Edward Connelly), and Old Nick, Jr. (Etienne Girardot), He almost forgets his sweet, blind girlfriend, Juliet (Mary Pickford), but remembers her in time and returns to

wed her after the fairies have restored her sight. As always, Belasco's stage pictures won the highest praise. Typically, in the first act the lights faded in Charles's room "to show the star-gemmed night sky, and then the angels floating in and standing about the bed in a faint golden radiance, like a moonlit fresco by Fra Angelico."

The cast was also lauded. The twenty-three-year-old Truex made a believable youngster, and with his small stature and boyish looks he would be trapped in similar roles for years. Norris had a field day in drag as Mrs. MacMiche. But many of the best notices were reserved for Mary Pickford, who, according to *Theatre,* already was the most popular actress in films. The same magazine noted in its review of the play, "If Mary Pickford . . . is a product of the movies, then commend us to the photo-play posing as a school for acting. Contrary to expectations, her facial expression was restrained rather than overemphatic [what does this say about judging contemporary stage performances by film acting?] and her diction was rarely fine. But both these qualities and her winsome prettiness are as nothing compared with the spirituality, the sweet childish simplicity with which she played her part." Another up-and-coming film actress, Lillian Gish, took a small role.

Three nights later, the 11th, the Century opened its doors and its huge stage to another spectacle, Louis N. Parker's **Joseph and His Brethren.** Lavish, gigantic settings recreated the Pyramids, the wells of Dothan, the garden and exteriors of Potiphar's home. A flock of real sheep was herded across the stage. Brandon Tynan, a handsome, deep-voiced actor many felt would have been a great romantic actor had he been born a generation earlier, played Joseph. James O'Neill, a romantic actor who many felt could have been a great tragedian had he not sold out to *Monte Cristo,* played both Jacob and Pharoah. The beautiful Pauline Frederick was Potiphar's baleful wife. In the tiny roles of Asher and Ranofer was a man Hollywood later would typecast as a prissy comic, Franklyn Pangborn. Critics appreciated the writing, staging, and casting, so the mounting ran fifteen weeks at the big theatre, then went on extended tour.

Henri Kistemaeckers's Paris hit *La Flambée* was offered to New Yorkers in Peter Le Marchant's translation as **The Spy** (1-13-13, Empire). A man (Cyril Keightley) kills a spy, not in self-defense, but in defense of his country. At his trial he is defended by the lover (Julian L'Estrange) of his wife (Edith Wynne Matthison). Wife and lover recognize that country comes before self-interest; they break off their liaison. A play that roused French patriotism found only a lukewarm response on this side of the Atlantic.

Frederick Lonsdale's **The Woman of It** (1-14-13, 39th St.), first done in London as *The Best People*, told a story similar to last season's *Thy Neighbor's Wife* but set in posher surroundings. The husbands and wives who traded off were the Bayles (Cyril Scott and Janet Beecher) and Lord and Lady Emsworth (Dallas Anderson and Josephine Brown). By coincidence, the new play ran exactly as long as last season's—fifteen performances.

An opening night spooked by technical mishaps failed to deter most critics from delighting in Eleanor Gates's sugary **The Poor Little Rich Girl** (1-21-13, Hudson). Gwendolyn (Viola Dana) is a darling child whose social-climbing mother (Laura Nelson Hall) and business-oriented father (Boyd Nolan) are so busy that they have turned her rearing over to a reptilian governess (Grace Griswold) and a two-faced nurse (Gladys Fairbanks). Her request to attend school and be privately tutored is waved aside. The result, as Gwendolyn tells a friendly doctor (Howard Hall) is:

Gwendolyn: I think Pretend friends are awfully nice. I go paddling in the water with them, and we make mud-pies, and they come into my nursery whenever I want them.
Doctor: Ah! And when you don't want them, raus mit 'em! Eh? (*He makes a gesture of ejecting some one.*)
Gwendolyn: I have so many of them. First of all, there's father, and mother . . .
Doctor: Father and mother! *Pretend* friends?
Gwendolyn: Oh, father and mother are the Dearest Pretend! At night, when I'm in bed, I pretend that father sits on one side, and mother on the other. And father holds this hand (*She puts out her left.*) and says, "Good night, little daughter." And mother kisses me (*She puts out her right hand.*) and sings—Would you like to hear me sing?

In order to have a date with a policeman (Joseph Bingham) who is "heels over head" in love with her, the nurse gives Gwendolyn a strong sleeping potion and leaves. Before long Gwendolyn finds herself in the Tell-Tale Forest, where "no matter what a person *pretends* to be, the moment he enters these woods, he changes. . . . Instantly, without knowing it, he appears as he really is." And so the policeman soon comes in walking on his head, and Gwendolyn's father appears dressed in a suit made of large dollar bills. The governess has become a snake, and the nurse does have two faces. In reality the nurse

unintentionally has given her charge a near-fatal overdose.

When Gwendolyn awakens, in her fourposter bed laden with teddy bears and toy soldiers, she is told her father and mother have decided to live simply and she can go to public school. (That father's poor investments have left the family virtually broke was something probably only adults in the audience fully understood.) The play ends with father drawing the curtains, the bedroom darkening, and mother singing "Sweet and Low." Then, in a touch reminiscent of *A Good Little Devil*, "*as the orchestra takes up the melody, the back of the nursery becomes transparent. Through it, across the bed where a little form lies sleeping,—watched on either side by a quiet figure— can be seen a grassy, wooded slope, and Father with a fishing pole; Mother in a simple outdoor dress . . . and* Gwendolyn,—*at her side, Rover.*" With its mature subtext adding its appeal to older playgoers, the fantasy ran out the season. The play later served as the source of a Shirley Temple film.

In his sometimes evasive autobiography, Arthur Hopkins claims this play marked his debut as producer. It didn't, but it did provide the first major milestone in a distinguished career.

. . .

Arthur [Melanchthon] **Hopkins** (1878–1950) was born in Cleveland and spent time as a newspaperman before turning to the theatre. He became a vaudeville agent, a writer of vaudeville playlets, and an unsuccessful dramatist. He also worked with Irene and Vernon Castle. His first production, *Steve* (1912), was a failure.

. . .

Some notices implied that Charles Frohman had gone to his warehouse for the sets of **The New Secretary** (1-23-13, Lyceum), Cosmo Gordon Lennox's adaptation of Francis de Croisset's comedy *Le Coeur dispose*. His prudence proved justified, for the tale of a penniless secretary (Charles Cherry) who wins his rich boss's haughty, defiant daughter (Marie Doro) failed to find a large public.

Two and a half weeks after Edwin Milton Royle's **The Unwritten Law** (2-7-13, Fulton) opened, the playwright had little to show for it but a fistful of reviews, which lauded the drama but warned readers that the play was unremittingly stark. Potential patrons obviously heeded the warnings. A former district attorney, John Wilson (George Farren), has become such a forlorn alcoholic that he can no longer care for his wife (May Buckley) and little son (Tommy Tobin). Mrs. Wilson takes up with Larry McCarthy (Frank Sheridan), a smooth but scoundrelly ward heeler. When she realizes McCarthy is merely using her, she stabs him to death. Wilson staggers in just as the killing takes place. He assumes blame for it. However, at his trial a hypnotist elicits the truth. An understanding jury refuses to indict Mrs. Wilson.

New Yorkers interested in seeing a new drama intended primarily for touring could have attended the single Saturday night showing of Hutcheson Boyd's **The Hundredth Man** (2-18-13, Wallack's), in which a beachcomber kills the recluse he finds living on a South Sea island, assumes the dead man's identity, then learns the dead man is wanted for murder. The same producers followed a similar path when they unveiled Elizabeth G. Crane's **The Necken** (4-15-13, Lyceum), a play in rhymed verse about a young girl's nearly tragic romance with a water sprite. Coupled with this was Robert H. Davis's **The Guilty Conscience**, a one-acter a punster labeled "a crook playlet." It recounted how a detective, who believes he is up on all the latest psychological tricks, is convinced he has gotten a lady to hand over to him some stolen jewels, when she has merely given him paste imitations and escaped.

Apart from some of the Irish Players' revolving repertory, the next week brought only one new play. But that play was Edward Sheldon's **Romance** (2-10-13, Maxine Elliott's). It may say something about the nature of playgoing fashions that, for all the seeming dominance at the time of crook-plays and farces, the season's two works that held the boards longest over the years were two that would be perceived primarily as love stories—*Peg o' My Heart* and this play. Of course, both were also well-limned character studies of intriguing women.

In his comfortable 1913 library on Washington Square, the aged Bishop Armstrong (William Courtenay) is approached by his grandson, Harry (William Raymond), whose family is shocked at his desire to marry an actress. Harry is not certain his grandfather can put himself in a similar situation, but he asks his advice anyway. Bishop Armstrong assures Harry he can empathize and tells him of events forty years ago, when the diva Cavallini was all the rage. Back then, Tom Armstrong had just become the rector of St. Giles. At a gala ball given by one of his wealthy parishioners, Cornelius Van Tuyl (A. E. Anson), he meets a dark-haired, brown-eyed foreigner (Doris Keane). At first he is distant, but he quickly comes to enjoy her company and tells her carelessly, "I thought that you were one of those Italian opera singers!" She merely laughs, but when he mentions Cavallini she confides:

Rita: You 'ave not miss much vhen you miss La Cavallini. She is of a fatness—(*With a gesture.*) Oh, like dat!
Tom: You're sure?
Rita: (*Nodding.*) She eat tvelve poun' of spaghetti every day!
Tom: No!
Rita: (*Enthusiastically*) An' ugly—oh, Madonna!— 'ow dat vomans is ugly! Jus' to look at 'er give vone de nose-bleed.

Of course, she is Cavallini. The two fall in love with one another and soon are neglecting their careers to be with each other. Van Tuyl, whose mistress Cavallini has been, tries to counsel both. They will not listen. Finally Tom gives her his mother's prized jewels and proposes. He is even prepared to abandon his calling, until he learns of Cavallini's relationship with Van Tuyl—the only part of her past she felt necessary to conceal from him. He demands she leave:

Rita: (*After trying once or twice to find her voice.*) Meestaire—Meestaire Tom—(*He shudders at the sound. She goes to the mirror, takes off his mother's earrings and necklace, kisses the locket, and lays them on the mantelpiece. Then she puts on her coat, picks up her muff and monkey* [a real one, whom Cavallini cattily names "Adelina Patti"] *from the chair where she left them earlier in the act. Softly to the monkey.*) Basta—basta—poverina mia! (*She stands looking at Tom. He makes no sign. Then at last, very simply.*) T'ank you for 'aving loved me. (*She drops her veil and goes out. As he hears the door close . . . he breaks into silent convulsive sobs. From far away comes the sound of the little hand-organ. It is still playing the old waltz.*)

With Cavallini about to sail for home, Tom appears at her suite, hysterically begging her to repent, to reform, and to love him. This time it is her turn to dismiss him: "Go avay! My 'eart it vill go vit' you alvays, but I don' care—jus' so you let me keep my soul!"

When Harry leaves the bishop, having decided to marry the actress regardless of anyone's advice, the bishop's granddaughter (Louise Seymour) arrives to read from the newspaper to him. She has not heard the men's conversation, so she is unaware of how meaningful to the bishop is the news of Cavallini's death. The diva's obituary recounts the good deeds she did late in life and notes that she never married. Left alone, the bishop puts on an old Cavallini recording and from his pocket removes a handkerchief and some violets she had given him decades ago.

The passing of time and some things' abilities to transcend it were themes subtly and beautifully played throughout the drama. Early on, Van Tuyl speaks of some Greek vases: "By Jove, they breathe a fragrance of eternal youth—and the hand that made them has been dust two thousand years." Later Van Tuyl confesses to Cavallini that he still has a soft spot in his heart for a girl who died before he could tell her he loved her. When he begs the singer to forget the clergyman, she replies, "I t'ink I vill not forget 'im—or if I do it take a long, long time!"

Critics also suggested that the characters were the most believable Sheldon had created, that they did not need a Mrs. Fiske to give them credence. Nonetheless, there was no question how much Doris Keane brought to the role, portraying Cavallini "with a bewitching accent, with infectious fun, with delicious capriciousness, with true tenderness, too." The play ran out the season, toured for two more years, then went to England, where Miss Keane played it for more than 1000 times. She revived the work in the early 1920s. In the late 1940s a charming Sigmund Romberg operetta version, *My Romance,* failed.

The swelling roster of successful crook plays grew by one with the opening of Daniel D. Carter's **The Master Mind** (2-17-13, Harris). The master mind (Edmund Breese) had a brother who was sent to the electric chair on what he believes were trumped-up charges. He has vowed to get the district attorney responsible. That man is Courtland Wainwright (Elliot Dexter), and over the years he has received mysterious notes on colored paper, which warn him that when a note comes on black paper his time is up. Meanwhile, the master mind has seen to it that Wainwright has fallen in love with Lucene Blount (Katherine LaSalle), unaware that she and her supposed family, all gathered together by the master mind, are actually convicted felons. Learning that Wainwright plans to run for governor, the master mind prepares to spring his trap. But he, too, has fallen in love with Lucene. "Love," Wainwright tells him, "is the only thing that is greater than hate." Seeing the truth of the remark, the master mind relents. Some special styles were becoming associated with crook plays. Critics observed that they were played more broadly and more sweepingly than ordinary dramas, in a way closer to how farce was played. And they noted the tendency of the crooks to pose "in angles, obtuse or acute, according to the relative intensity of the situation," while the honest folk usually stood up straight.

Thompson Buchanan's sometimes up but mostly down career suffered another down with **The Bridal Path** (2-18-13, 39th St.). Some critics were at a loss to figure out why the author mixed comedy and drama so indiscriminately in his story of a girl (Ann Murdock) who finds a husband (Robert Warwick) by scanning the most scandalous society sheets for a prospect and then settles into a rocky marriage until an old black family retainer (Mrs. Charles G. Craig) shows the couple how to live happily ever after.

Any play with blonde, buxom, and brassy May Irwin had to have a few jaunty songs interpolated, but once Miss Irwin was through with Catherine Chisholm Cushing's **Widow by Proxy** (2-24-13, Cohan) it generally was offered as a straight farce. Critics generally agreed with their colleague who dismissed the piece as "of no magnitude," but most also sang Miss Irwin's praises—"great fun," "always comic." The star was cast as Gloria Grey, who has taken in Dolores Pennington (Clara Blandick) and spent her last penny nursing the young lady back to health ever since news of Jack Pennington's death reached her. Now Dolores has been told she will inherit money from Jack's estate, but she refuses to go to Jack's home and claim it, remembering how Jack's snobbish relations had snubbed her because she was an actress. Gloria decides to go in Dolores's stead. She meets Jack's cousin, Steven (Orlando Daly), and they realize they are affinities. She consents to marry Steve but fears what will happen when he learns she is not Dolores. Her fears are made worse when news arrives that Jack is not dead. And then Jack (Lynn Pratt) enters. When Gloria explains that she was concerned merely to prevent the real Dolores from starving, all is forgiven. Much of the humor was tough or snarly, with bits of theatrical topicality thrown in. Gloria ekes out a living teaching singing, and she has just finished a hopeless lesson:

Gloria: (*Shaking fist in direction of departed pupil*) Can I get blood from a stone? Can I make a nightingale out of a crow? A Svengali himself couldn't teach her to chirp.
Dolores: It's a downright shame.
Gloria: (*Throwing up hands and gazing heavenward*) Who would believe that existence were purchased at such a price? (*Then explosively as if overcome with the tragedy of it, rises*) Good Lord! With all the money in the world, why can't a little fall my way? (*Then crossing melodramatically, hands outstretched à la Beggar in Kismet"* "Alms—for the love of Allah—alms." That's

what I'll be doing next—chaperoned by a mangy dog at the end of a string.

Some of the humor inevitably derived from the situations in the play, as when Gloria, learning Jack still lives, worries to Dolores about how "*our* husband" will react. The comedy played eleven weeks, during part of which time the star revived *Mrs. Peckham's Carouse* to form a double bill. It then headed for the road, where Miss Irwin was always as welcome as she was in New York.

The season began to run downhill with the coming of March—an even earlier retreat than in the previous year. Paul Dickey and Charles W. Goddard's **The Ghost Breaker** (3-3-13, Lyceum) found its hero, a Kentucky gentleman (H. B. Warner), taking refuge from the Spanish police in the castle of a lady (Katherine Emmett). He overcomes her alarm and soon wins her love, but not before besting a suit of armor that suddenly comes to life and seems impervious to modern bullets. Critics slammed the play as slapdash and heard nothing southern in Warner's English accent nor anything Spanish in Miss Emmett's American intonations. As it so often did at a time when the theatre was relatively healthy economically, the public made up its own mind and patronized the play for nine weeks.

Conversely, for all the warm notices it received, **The Five Frankfurters** (3-13-13, 39th St.) ran only two weeks longer. The play, Basil Hood's English-language version of Carl Rossler's German original, told of the rise of the Rothschilds in the wake of the Battle of Waterloo. Its outstanding performance was that of Mathilde Cottrelly as the family grande dame, who discourages her son, Solomon (Frank Losee), from arranging a match between his daughter (Alma Belwin) and a Christian duke (Edward Mackay).

Florence Reed's equally praised performance could not save Frederic Arnold Kummer's **The Painted Woman** (3-5-13, Playhouse) from going down in the record books as an ignominious two-performance flop. Luxuriously set in 1670 Jamaica, it recounted the attempts of a pale, wistful-eyed beauty to find true love away from the pirate world she so long has been a part of. The play marked John Cromwell's debut as a director.

Late-season revivals, so old a tradition, began with *Everyman* at the Children's on the 10th and *Liberty Hall* at the Empire on the 11th.

The month's most interesting entries premiered on the same evening. On 39th Street, between Broadway and Sixth Avenue, New York's newest and smallest playhouse, the 299-seat Princess, opened under the aegis of Holbrook Blinn as a theatre devoted to bills of one-act plays from both native and foreign authors. Good notices kept playgoers coming until the hot weather chased them away, but none of the short pieces seems noteworthy in retrospect, nor has any endured. One example would be William C. de Mille's **Food** (4-13-13), which programs called "a tragedy of the future." In the 1960s the Food Trust has succeeded in increasing the cost of all comestibles beyond belief. The meager foodstuffs most families can obtain are guarded in safes provided with screeching burglar alarms. A New York couple (Edward Ellis and Fanny Hartz) are sharing their cracker and droplets of milk when the wife informs her husband that doctors have said she must have an egg if she is to live. The husband responds that buying an egg would drive them too deeply into debt. After the husband discovers the wife has obtained an egg by offering herself to an officer (John Stokes) of the Food Trust, he hurls the egg to the floor.

Even Eugène Brieux's **Damaged Goods** [*Les Avariés*] (3-14-13, Fulton) no longer is revived, although it unquestionably was one of the most powerful and most controversial dramas of its era. A generation earlier William Winter and his tribe probably would have made production of such a play impossible. As it was, Brieux had written *Les Avariés* some ten years before. Moreover, Richard Bennett, in conjunction with Wilton Lackaye, moved cautiously, booking the play initially for a single matinee and enlisting the support of the *Medical Review of Reviews,* John D. Rockefeller, and New York's mayor. A minister made a speech before the curtain rose. Brieux's story told of George Dupont (Bennett), who has contracted syphilis but who refuses to heed the warning of his doctor (Lackaye) not to marry. A shorter, not uninteresting story took place outside the theatre. One newspaper, after mentioning that the production was mounted under the auspices of the medical journal and its Sociological Fund, added, "Although efforts had been made to limit the seats to those who would be properly interested in the performance, the omnipresent speculator was in evidence on the sidewalk and offered his wares without apparent interference." The play's reception prompted a second matinee and then a modest run of eight weeks.

For all Broadway's newfound willingness to broach once unmentionable topics, some subjects and treatments and playwrights were still kept at arm's length—none more so than Strindberg, whose treatment of his themes often was deemed psychopathic. As a result a double bill of his **The Stronger** and **Pariah** (3-18-13, 48th St.), which was produced by actor Warner Oland and included Walter Hampden in the cast, was brought out for a single matinee, while his play more commonly called *Miss Julie* was given three matinees at the same theatre in late April and early May under the title **Countess Julia.**

A waif (Olive Wyndham) lives with her wicked "uncle" (J. D. O'Hara) in a Chesapeake Bay fishing village. Her only real friend is a peg-legged fisherman (E. M. Kimball). A smooth-talking city slicker (Joseph Manning) lures her to the big city and, when she refuses to submit to him, frames her for theft. A nice young man (Frank Underwood) comes to her defense. Eventually it is shown that the uncle is no uncle at all, that the waif's real mother is still alive, and that the girl is an heiress. If all this sounds a little old-fashioned, well, the play billed itself as "old-fashioned"; and if the plot smacks of the now departed cheap touring melodrama, that could be because it was the plot of Owen Davis's **What Happened to Mary** (3-24-13, Fulton). Like *The Ghost Breaker*, it overcame thumbs-down reviews to eke out a moderate run.

Ernest Poole's **A Man's Friends** (3-24-13, Astor) had an even more modest run, but then its reviews were hardly encouraging. Perhaps as a muckraking drama in a season of crook-plays it was a bit behind times. It spotlighted a number of figures involved in passing bribes to flout building codes. Tom Whalen (George Fawcett), the political boss, is behind the bribes, but his hirelings are convicted and imprisoned. The play ends with the district attorney (Frederick Burton) vowing that someday he'll get Whalen.

Francis Wilson suffered the worst failure of his career when, for a single week, he starred in his own play **The Spiritualist** (3-24-13, 48th St.). He portrayed a man who at first is appalled at his own ability to use occult forces but happily employs them to save the child of the widow (Edna Burns) he hopes to marry from poisoning by an evil doctor (Wright Kramer). A few reviewers with long memories suggested the evening's funniest scene, a seance with a floating table and the ghostlike dance of some curtains, had been appropriated from *Our Goblins,* a farce-comedy that had helped launch Wilson's career more than thirty years earlier.

Another player, Lucille LaVerne, was also the author of the play in which she appeared (albeit did not star), and it, too, ran just one week. **Ann Boyd** (3-31-13, Wallack's) was derived from William Nathaniel Harben's novel and detailed how a decent woman (Nance O'Neil) turns the tables on her

vicious, small-town neighbors, who are prodded by the venomous Jane Hemmingway (LaVerne).

Aside from one novelty, April was given over to revivals. The first three were presented by William A. Brady and strongly suggested that he and his audiences preserved a loyalty to bygone theatricals. Brady's wife, Grace George, was starred in his remounting of *Divorçons* at the Playhouse on the 1st. At the Lyric on the 18th, Lester Wallack's fifty-year-old *Rosedale* was the attraction. Some reviewers reported that the audience occasionally laughed at situations meant to be taken seriously and that some of the writing "creaks with age," but they also acknowledged how effective a stage piece the play remained. A fine cast included Charles Cherry as Elliott Grey, Frank Gillmore as Matthew Leigh, Robert Warwick as Miles McKenna, Jobyna Howland as Lady Florence May, Alice Fischer as Tabitha, and Della Fox as Sarah Sykes. Miss Howland and Miss Fox were both better known for their work on musical stages, although the latter died a few days after this revival closed. Dustin and William Farnum, Crystal Herne, and Elsie Ferguson were the leads in Brady's revival of *Arizona* at the Lyric on the 28th. That same evening saw Charles Frohman contribute to the parade of revivals with *The Amazons* at the Empire. Billie Burke was starred.

April's lone novelty was Elizabeth Jordan's **The Lady from Oklahoma** (4-2-13, 48th St.). Jessie Bonstelle, who already had begun to carve her niche in theatrical history with her celebrated stock companies, served as producer, co-director, and leading lady. She was seen as the drab wife of a newly elected senator (William K. Harcourt). In no time he is being vamped by some very attractive Washington ladies, so Mrs. Dixon decides to remold herself. She visits a beauty parlor, buys some ultra-fashionable new clothes, takes a few lessons in speech and deportment, and routs the sirens. The replication of a typical period beauty parlor was a Belasco-like touch that earned a hearty round of applause but was not enough to save an otherwise weak show from failure. Nor, according to one critic, was Miss Bonstelle's un-New York style: "Her method is that of popular stock where it is deemed necessary to 'pound home' all the points. And the sort of insistent over-emphasis and underlining in which she indulges are frequently apparent in the acting of the others."

May's small shower of flops closed the season. Margaret Townsend's four-performance dud, **The Passing of the Idle Rich** (5-1-13, Garden), was suggested to her by Frederick Townsend Martin's articles on social problems. The problem for the heroine (Ethel Valentine) is that she is forced by her social-climbing family into a titled marriage. She runs off and doesn't return until the marriage has been declared invalid. The problem for audiences was that the staging was as "thoroughly amateurish" as the writing. On opening night actors assigned to later scenes walked blankly onstage in the midst of the heroine's emotional scene, requiring it to be started over again.

A French innkeeper (Walter Jones) on a busman's holiday walks into the wrong room, upsets a strange lady (Millicent Evans), and precipitates three acts of farcical contretemps in **The Gentleman from Number 19** (5-1-13, Comedy), Mark Swan's version of *Le No. 18* by Henri Kéroul and Albert Barré. Broadway was not amused, so the work was pulled after four performances. But so ignominious a run did not seal the play's fate. A week later it was back out on the road, hoping to regale playgoers in Newark, Boston, and possibly elsewhere.

The evening's third premiere, which also served to open yet one more new theatre, had an only slightly better run—twelve showings. William J. Hurlbut and Frances Whitehouse's **Are You a Crook?** (5-1-13, Longacre) was conceived as a sendup of the popular crook-plays. Amy Herrick (Marguerite Clark) has seen so many of the voguish plays that she decides she can be a crook, too. She dresses up as a boy and steals a pearl necklace at gunpoint. She does not know the necklace is a fake; the real one is safe in a vault. Quick as a wink she is being pursued by real and fake detectives, while the real and fake pearls change hands almost as fast. It was a cute idea that didn't work, so the play itself was soon sent up to Cain's Warehouse.

The comically inept attempt of a lady (Laura Hope Crews) to act as lawyer in her friend's divorce trial provided the matter for C. W. Bell's **Her First Divorce** (5-5-13, Comedy). The comedy was one of the season's many one-week failures and led one reviewer to observe, "In these days of vital competition the 'fairly good' has little chance of enduring success." It was a cry that would grow louder as the decades rushed by.

1913–1914

The pat optimism that had prevailed for so long in so many seasonal forecasts was missing in a number of late summer articles crystal-balling prospects for the new theatrical year. Whether a restive sense of doom or merely a swelling list of projected entries crowded out the old complacency is uncertain. What was certain was that readers had to look harder to find it.

At the beginning of autumn, *Life* issued a "War Number," which featured a large cartoon of flag-carrying, gun-toting masses aligned in the shape of a snake. Beneath the picture was the ominous remark, "The trail of the serpent of war still follows the path of progress." On the other hand, *Theatre* discounted the conversion of old playhouses to film theatres by observing, "The old-fashioned theatre, with its huge stage, cavernous-like auditorium, bad acoustics, is rapidly becoming an institution of the past. The tendency among modern theatre-builders to erect small houses is growing more apparent every day. . . . The little theatres are of a benefit to [more artistic] plays, and consequently to playwrights. It gives wider opportunities and serves the public at the same time."

That public was not well served by the season's first entry, Edward Locke's **The Silver Wedding** (8-11-13, Longacre), a rustic drama of a superannuated school, which one critic branded a "long drawn out essay on sentimentality." Ludwig Koehler (Thomas A. Wise), a Pennsylvania Dutch saddler, hears his prospective son-in-law (Calvin Thomas) speak of "a pigheaded Dutchman," concludes the young man is talking about him, and withdraws his consent to the marriage of his daughter (Cecile Breton). His wife (Alice Gale) does her best to smooth over matters, but only when Koehler can sit down in his rocking chair and croon a German lullaby to his new grandchild is he fully reconciled. Critics disliked not only the play but the seemingly spurious Pennsylvania Dutch dialects of both the playwright and the players.

For a time early in the season, plays about white slavers threatened to supplant crook-dramas as the latest vogue. In a sense such stories were simply extensions of those told in crook-plays. But in the eyes of many, and—more important, in the eyes of the law—they went too far. First to arrive was a play by a former Secret Service agent, George Scarborough's **The Lure** (8-14-13, Maxine Elliott's). A touch of futuristic drama was seen in the program, where characters were listed as merely The Girl (Mary Nash), The Madam (Dorothy Dorr), or The Special Agent (Vincent Serrano). Of course, they have names in the play. The Girl's is Sylvia, and she badly needs money to support her ailing mother. She remembers a woman who gave her a card offering "extra work for girls in the evening." So she goes to the elegant sky-blue-and-gold home of the woman. By the time she realizes the nature of the extra work, she is in debt to The Madam, who will not let her leave. The Special Agent at first questions Sylvia's innocence, but when he recognizes it he supports her in escaping, then clamps down on The Madam and the politicians behind her. The play was powerfully written and compellingly acted. Even some of the most prudish reviewers joined in hailing it. But it worried New York's police, although they waited until a second white-slave play came before springing into action.

Meanwhile, a play of far less merit established itself as the season's first smash hit. Montague Glass's **Potash and Perlmutter** (8-16-13, Cohan) was based on Glass's stories in the *Saturday Evening Post*. Charles Klein gave an important, uncredited assist. A. H. Woods, coming up quickly in the world of first-class theatre, was producer. Featured were squat, baldish, slightly cross-eyed Barney Bernard as Abe Potash and the taller, curly-haired, better-looking Alexander Carr as Mawruss Perlmutter. Potash and Perlmutter are mediocre dressmakers, fighting to stay afloat and hounded by an unscrupulous lawyer, Feldman (Joseph Kilgour). A top designer, Ruth Snyder (Louise Dresser), takes pity on them and helps them prosper. But after Boris Andrieff (Albert Parker), their bookkeeper and the fiancé of Abe's daughter, Irma (Marguerite Anderson), is sought for extradition by the Russian government on dubious charges, Abe puts up the company's $20,000 as bail and, on mistaken advice, urges Boris to flee to Canada. The company faces bankruptcy. Boris is cleared and returns in time to allow the partners to retrieve their money. Ruth accepts Mawruss's proposal of marriage.

The dialogue was hardly brilliant. Mawruss dictates a letter to their firm's talentless designer: "Dear Sir: Your contract with us expires next week, and you can expire with it."

Potash: Expire—what do you mean expire? Why don't you speak English?
Perlmutter: Expires—goes out!
Potash: You mean we discharge him?
Perlmutter: No, we are firing him.

There were more amusing glimpses of the tight-fistedness of the businessmen and of the closeness and nepotism in the trade. Potash explodes when he reads one salesman's expense account: "Twenty-two dollars for sleeping cars, and he was recommended as a wide-awake salesman." The salesman's short-lived successor tells the partners: "Me and Ed Mendelberger married cousins; that is to say, my wife's mother's sister is a sister-in-law to a brother of Ed Mendelberger's wife's mother." Whatever the

play's flaws, it was rib-tickling enough to chalk up a run of 441 performances, spurred in part no doubt by the patronage of the very cloak-and-suiters it poked fun at.

Far away from the garment district, academia was displaying a growing interest in theatre, and nowhere more than at Harvard under George Pierce Baker's tutelage. The excitement there prompted John Blair, the actor-director of Boston's Castle Square stock company, to offer a prize each season for a Harvard student's play. One winner was Frederick Ballard's **Believe Me Xantippe** (8-19-13, 39th St.), the latest "wager play," with a story revolving around a bet. In this instance the bet is the brainchild of George MacFarland (John Barrymore), who is disgusted with the police's inaction following a robbery. He bets a friend that he can commit a forgery and evade the law for a whole year. As McGinnis, the forger, he heads west, but luck seems to run against him. Hungry and footsore, he almost comes a cropper when a rambunctious sheriff (Theodore Roberts) and the sheriff's pretty daughter, Dolly (Mary Young), put two and two together after reading an A.P.B. But his luck turns again after he rescues Dolly from Simp Calloway (Frank Campeau) in a fistfight. The suave Mac-Farland-McGinnis manages to talk himself out of arrest until the year is up. Naturally he also talks himself into marriage with Dolly. In one trick scene the hero allows himself to be photographed with a flash camera. After the blinding flash, the whole stage is dark for a second. When the lights come on again MacFarland-McGinnis is nowhere in sight.

While the comedy might have been insubstantial, it was clever, short, and "acted with lightning speed." Many a reviewer credited Barrymore with carrying the night and welcomed him as one of the stage's most accomplished farceurs. It was a label that the fast-rising actor claimed to resent. In interviews he insisted he was determined to get his teeth into meatier roles. At the same time, onstage he was beginning to show signs of the cavalier irresponsibility that marked his later years. Roberts and he had a scene in which Roberts was to bring home a point by poking his finger repeatedly into Barrymore's chest. One evening Barrymore took off his hat and hung it on Roberts's finger. The play lingered ten weeks, then toured—without Barrymore.

Just as his erstwhile producer, A. H. Woods, was savoring success in the first-class arena, so, at last, was Owen Davis.

. . .

Owen Davis (1874–1956) was born in Portland, Me., and educated at Harvard. He first tried his hand at writing blank-verse tragedy, but the need to support his family made him abandon the effort and begin churning out touring melodramas. For many years, until the genre's swift downfall, he was probably its most prolific exponent. His initial efforts to provide material for first-class theatres met with disappointment, but he soon learned to satisfy more demanding audiences.

. . .

The producer of Davis's **The Family Cupboard** (8-21-13, Playhouse) was not Woods but William A. Brady. The two would work in tandem often and successfully in coming years. In Davis's story a neglected husband (William Morris) has taken on a mistress (Irene Fenwick) but discards her in an attempt to save his sagging marriage. To avenge her abrupt throwing-over, the girl sets out to seduce her ex-lover's wastrel son (Forrest Winant) and almost succeeds in destroying both the boy and his father's home. Although critics insisted Davis still was unable to rid himself totally of his melodramatic touches and speeches, they concurred that *The Family Cupboard* was his best play to date. They admired both his handling of his principal characters and the way they were acted. However, bit parts pleased them even more. The mistress's pathetic father (Frank Hatch) was a cab driver, who excuses the way his daughter earns the better things in life by pointing to how dog-eat-dog cab driving is. A backwater vaudevillian (Franklyn Ardell) likewise made a colorful, memorable figure.

Philip Bartholomae's **Kiss Me Quick** (8-26-13, 48th St.) recounted the misadventures of a movie company on location, especially after a neighborhood spinster (Helen Lowell) develops a crush on the leading man (Arthur Aylesworth). The quickest thing about the comedy was its exit.

In Mark E. Swan's **Her Own Money** (9-1-13, Comedy), a wife (Julia Dean), fearful of embarrassing her cash-short husband (Sidney Booth) by lending him some of her savings, arranges to use a neighbor (George Hassell) as an intermediary. The neighbor's wife (Beverly Sitgreaves) witnesses the transaction—from a window across a narrow passageway—and misconstrues it. So does the strapped husband. Wife and husband separate, and the little woman proves she is no mean business-woman when she enters the chicken market. A reconciliation follows.

Two revivals appeared on the same evening. The more important was *Much Ado About Nothing* at the Empire—noteworthy, first of all, for its not-too-many-expenses-barred mounting by Charles Frohman. Noteworthy, too, was its pairing of sixty-year-

old John Drew as Benedick with the Beatrice of twenty-seven-years-younger Laura Hope Crews. Mary Boland was Hero. The critical consensus was that the production was pleasant and skillful but not especially memorable. It remained before the footlights for three weeks.

The engagement of *The Old Homestead* at the vast Manhattan Opera House also was for three weeks. Edward L. Snader, a player better known on the road than in New York, appeared in the role made famous by the late Denman Thompson.

In afteryears much confusing material was published about Bayard Veiller's **The Fight** (9-2-13, Hudson). The *Best Plays* lists it as having been produced first at the Fulton on October 31, 1912, by Joseph Gaites and running for four performances. If it was, no advertisements were placed in major newspapers, and no major source seems to have reviewed it. In his memoirs Veiller recalls the play running just four showings but says William Harris was the producer. Harris did produce the 1913 mounting. Veiller also says the play was originally done out of town as *Big Sister*, but old papers show its first public title was *Standing Pat*. In any case, the drama's 1913 production did precipitate a brouhaha. Its story centered on Jane Thomas (Margaret Wycherly), who heads the Colorado bank founded by her late father. However, Jane is not content with her comfortable berth. She sets out to become mayor and to abolish child labor and white slavery. Her quest for political prominence might only have amused her opponents, but her programs infuriate them. They determine to engineer her defeat and to ruin the bank in the process. They fail to consider her shrewdness and resolve, so they are ruined in the end.

The *Dramatic Mirror,* perhaps reflecting New York's relentless chauvinism, sneered that "Circassian walnut panelings" were probably unheard of in real Colorado banks and that the "immaculate attire of every one of the female characters" was equally implausible. But these were minor objections compared to one others found far more disturbing. An act took place in "a disorderly house" with dialogue "brutally frank, but not salacious." This scene and a similar one in *The Lure* were too much for the politically ambitious Chief Magistrate McAdoo, who issued warrants allowing the police to close both plays on the 9th. The producers (the Shuberts for *The Lure*) responded by insisting the plays were moral and designed to expose the cruelties of white slavery. However, both plays were allowed to continue only after the bordello settings were dropped and some of the more offending lines expunged. *The Lure* ran for 132 performances; *The Fight* for 80.

Ferenc Molnár's **Where Ignorance Is Bliss** (9-3-13, Lyceum), in a translation by Philip Littell, ran a single week. It told of an actor (William Courtleigh) who tests the fidelity of his wife (Rita Jolivet) by pretending to be a dashing soldier. Some critics blamed the play's failure on the stifling heat wave; some on sluggish emoting; some on the fact that the whole concept was alien to Americans. This last group was proved wrong a decade later when the Lunts resurrected the play as *The Guardsman*.

Leo Ditrichstein, another Austro-Hungarian, fared better as adaptor and star of **The Temperamental Journey** (9-4-13, Belasco), which was taken from André Rivoire and Yves Mirande's *Pour vivre heureux* and was brought out, with all his customary panache, by Belasco. Ditrichstein appeared as Jacques Dupont, a painter belittled by critics and unloved by his wife (Isabel Irving). The critics reconsider after he fakes a suicide, and his wife takes to selling fake Duponts to add to her bank account. He discloses he is still alive and weds his loyal, loving model (Josephine Victor).

The Temperamental Journey and Edgar Selwyn's **Nearly Married** (9-4-13, Gaiety) opened one night apart and closed on the same evening, sixteen weeks later. The leading figures in Selwyn's farce are Harry and Betty Lindsay (Bruce McRae and Jane Grey). They have been driven to obtain a divorce by Betty's hot-tempered, busybody brother, Dick (John Westley). Later Betty spots Harry having tea at a posh Fifth Avenue hotel with the attractive woman who acted as co-respondent, Hattie King (Virginia Pearson). But when Harry confesses to Betty that he still loves her, they run off to an inn up along the Hudson. The irate brother, the suddenly jilted Hattie (soaked from her long ride in a leaky taxi), a baffled justice of the peace, and other characters appear at the inn, where people run in and out of doors, mistaken identities and misunderstandings run rampant, and a wily innkeeper (Schuyler Ladd) runs a little blackmail operation on the side. Harry and Betty decide to head off somewhere else. No matter that it is pouring, or that the leaky cab they grab, the one Hattie arrived in and forgot to discharge, has a meter showing $27.

Richard Harding Davis's **Who's Who?** (9-11-13, Criterion) had a novel opening scene. A Wild West bar and dance hall, the White Hope Saloon, presents flickers to stimulate trade. As the play begins, one of the films is being projected on a sheet in the rear while a tinny-voiced soprano sings "When You Were Sweet Sixteen." Lester Ford (William Collier) sits in the foreground in his cowboy togs, oblivious to all this. He has come west under an assumed name, been sorely put upon by more knowing, hardboiled men around him, and now is being offered the chance to escape by returning to civilization and pretending to be a lawyer (who himself has come west in disguise). He accepts, but his latest false identity merely brings him more problems. Reviewers condemned the play as disorganized and illogical and concluded that without Collier it wouldn't have even gotten on the boards.

Madam President (9-15-13, Garrick), a Maurice Hennequin and Pierre Veber farce translated by José G. Levy, found its fun by allowing a pretty actress to be mistaken for the stodgy wife of a small-town magistrate. The fun lasted sixteen weeks.

Paul Armstrong's **The Escape** (9-20-13, Lyric) earlier had been submitted as a possibility for the New Theatre's repertory and rejected by the theatre's board shortly before the theatre itself was rejected by the public. Critics were not hard put to see why the play had been turned down. It was disjointed and crude, patently designed to exploit the public's fascination with low life. But it was not without its better moments. Armstrong's play focused on May Joyce (Catherine Calvert), who escapes from her shabby tenement and the prospect of marriage to a brutal hood (Harry Mestayer) by taking work with a senator (George Farren). The senator proves more sophisticated but no less corrupt. (Honest senators were becoming a rarity on the stage.) May's sister (Anne McDonald) marries the hood but dies after he abuses her, while May's brother (Charles Mylott) is railroaded into prison. May is given a modicum of hope when she falls in love with a young doctor (Jerome Patrick). The play disappeared after two weeks.

Seven Keys to Baldpate (9-22-13, Astor), George M. Cohan's dramatization of an Earl Derr Biggers novel, was the season's second smash hit. Critics mostly conceded that the play was sure to be a crowd-pleaser, but openly or implicitly they seemed to feel it was too "ingenious" and "a trick." Perhaps because of this several rather meanly gave away the ending in their reviews.

The action unfolds in the two-storied lobby of the Baldpate Inn. A balcony of white-painted woodwork gives access to the rooms. It is nearly midnight, and a snowstorm is raging outside. William Hallowell Magee (Wallace Eddinger), author of "wild, thrilling tales for the tired businessman's tired wife; shots in the night; chases after fortunes; Cupid busy with his arrows all over the place," has come to "the lonesomest spot on earth . . . a summer resort in winter." He has bet the inn's owner that if left alone he can turn out a thriller in twenty-four hours. In turn the owner has handed over to Magee what he assures the writer is the only key to the inn. The caretaker (Edgar Halstead) tells Magee that, except when some venal politicians once tried to hide some illegal money in the hotel during the winter, nothing has ever happened off season. He also remarks that a nearby hermit sometimes dons sheets and pretends to be a ghost.

Magee is left alone and settles down to write. Before long no fewer than eight people, employing five more keys, enter. Seven are after $200,000, which a local businessman had hoped to hand over secretly to the mayor for his help in pushing through a bill. The eighth is the hermit. Each key holder assumed his or her key was unique, and all refuse to say where they obtained their keys. The police arrive but seem just as interested as the others in securing the money for their own illicit ends. One of the figures, a young woman, is shot dead. Then the owner appears, using the seventh key to enter, and tells Magee it was all a joke. The visitors are actors he has hired, and he produces the supposedly dead girl, very much alive, to prove his point. The lights go out.

In the epilogue Magee informs the caretaker that he has finished his story. He is surprised to hear the caretaker mention some names he used in the story and thought were his own invention. Then the owner calls. Magee gets on the phone and tells the man, "I'm going to collect that five thousand from you, old pal. . . . And say, Hal, listen; I've got you in the story." Audiences were left to decide if the events in the main part of the play actually occurred or simply represented the story Magee is writing. No poll of playgoers seems to have been taken, although there were plenty of opportunities. The play ran out the season, and several companies toured first-class venues for three more seasons. The play remained a favorite—reputedly Cohan's biggest money-maker—in summer stock and on amateur stages until well after the Second World War.

September's second Beatrice and Benedick resumed their feuding when Sothern and Marlowe reappeared at the Manhattan Opera House. By now most critics—and no doubt many playgoers—had come to take the stars for granted. And there also seemed to have been something vaguely déclassé about playing the huge house. Most reviews were little more than extended notices rather than critiques, and when there was real criticism it often took the form of trying to excuse an absence of genuine fire or greatness in Sothern. Marlowe was far more easily admired. One critic noted that the audience resembled markedly the playgoers who a week before had been sitting on the edge of the seats at the same theatre rapt in *The Old Homestead.* Aside from their standard Shakespearean repertory, the stars also offered *If I Were King* during their five-week engagement.

In Canada, where it had been done as *Deborah,* William Legrand's **The Smoldering Flame** (9-23-13, 48th St.) provoked both animated debate and threats of censorship. In New York its fate was swifter and more brutal. The play centered on a frustrated old maid (Fernanda Eliscu), who employs a ruse to supplant her niece (Ethel Gray Terry) in a tryst and have a child by the niece's none-the-wiser lover (Conway Tearle). Two old-maid sisters (Maud Sinclair and Marie Day), who live together in a home where the blinds are always drawn, were also prominent characters. Unfortunately for the play, so were two children. Authorities goaded the Gerry Society—as if that group ever needed much goading—to petition to close the play, and the petition was granted. There was no second night for *The Smoldering Flame.*

An English crook play, Dion Clayton Calthrop and Cosmo Gordon Lennox's **Shadowed** (9-24-13, Fulton), at least finished out the week, telling in its brief visit of a failed attempt to swindle a bank.

An English double bill—Stanley Houghton's **The Younger Generation** and James M. Barrie's **Half an Hour** (9-25-13, Lyceum)—had a somewhat warmer reception. Houghton's drama dealt with the need for hidebound parents to bend a bit to the changing mores of their children. In Barrie's play an unhappily married woman (Grace George) must return to her vicious husband (H. E. Herbert) after the lover (Nigel Barry) with whom she would have eloped is killed in an accident.

On the 27th Holbrook Blinn's Princess Players began their second season of one-acters. Although some English and French playlets were offered, most entries were native. Among the authors were C. M. S. McLellan, William Hurlbut, and George Jean Nathan.

Two nights later Forbes-Robertson came into the brand-new Shubert Theatre for a three-month stand that signaled the beginning of a two-and-a-half-year farewell tour. The newly knighted actor opened with his much admired *Hamlet,* then moved on to *The Merchant of Venice, Othello,* and his non-Shakespearean successes: *Caesar and Cleopatra, The Light That Failed, Mice and Men, The Passing of the Third Floor Back,* and *The Sacrament of Judas.*

Competing with the English actor for first-nighters were players from the recent revival of *Much Ado About Nothing*—John Drew, Laura Hope Crews, and Mary Boland—joining forces in a revivial of *The Tyranny of Tears* at the Empire. Chambers's play was coupled with the second new Barrie one-acter in four nights, **The Will.** The little play covered three reigns. In Victoria's time a poor but loving young couple (Drew and Miss Boland) come to a solicitor's office to draw up a will. The wife is tearily grateful that the husband leaves what little he has to her. In Edward's day the wife, now older and richer, comes to make sure that any new will the husband might draw leaves his vast fortune to her. By George's day the disgruntled old husband, a widower whose children have not turned out well, cynically leaves his money to his former competitors, knowing they haven't been able to enjoy what money they possess and so won't get any pleasure from what they inherit.

September closed with a three-month revival of *The Auctioneer* at the Belasco beginning on the 30th. David Warfield recreated his original role, then took both this revival and *The Return of Peter Grimm* back out on the road.

The production of **Evangeline** (10-4-13, Park) was not a revival of the popular musical burlesque but a straightforward attempt to put Longfellow's poem on a stage. Critics lauded the beautiful scenery and acknowledged the enterprise's serious intent but found the affair deadly dull. It languished for two weeks.

Many of the same critics assailed **To-day** (10-6-13, 48th St.) as "an indecent, vicious play," "offensive," or "reprehensible"—the very sort of pejorative terms to prompt playgoers to pack the theatre for eight months. What shocked critics and delighted audiences was the story of a wife (Emily Stevens) who bridles at the inability of her husband (Edwin Arden)—once rich but now bankrupt—to provide her with the luxuries she feels she is entitled to. To earn herself the wherewithal to buy gems and furs, she takes work at the latest of the season's many disorderly houses. The husband comes there on business for the property's landlord. Realizing how low his wife will stoop, he walks out on her. The play's history was interesting. Its co-author, Abraham S. Schomer, was a popular Yiddish playwright, and the drama initially and been produced in Yiddish on the Lower East Side. Schomer collaborated with George Broadhurst to make the play acceptable to uptown audiences.

Some more old-fashioned, more preposterous material was more to the critics' liking and almost as popular with the public. George Scarborough's second hit of the season, **At Bay** (10-7-13, 39th St.), brought Aline Graham (Crystal Herne) to the home of a venal lawyer, Judson Flagg (Mario Majeroni). He attempts to blackmail her with a letter she wrote, one which is actually quite innocent but appears incriminating. He also takes a flash photo of her before she realizes what he is doing. Flagg then demands she either pay him for both the letter and the photo or else become his mistress. As he moves toward her, she picks up a file from his desk and stabs him. Enter Aline's suitor, Capt. Lawrence Holbrook (Guy Standing), who destroys the letter and the photo. An autopsy shows Flagg died of a heart attack seconds before he was stabbed.

Playgoers interested in seeing James M. Barrie's third new playlet of the season, **The Censor and the Dramatists** (10-14-13, Globe), had to buy tickets to the musical *The Doll Girl,* into which the one-acter had been interpolated. It described how a censor overlooks all questionable situations in a new work but bans it on the grounds that the setting is architecturally implausible.

A play by another Englishman, Arnold Bennett, was given the honor of opening Broadway's newest playhouse. **The Great Adventure** (10-16-13, Booth), like *The Temperamental Journey* a month earlier, told of an artist (Lyn Harding) who feigns death in order to see his work recognized. Playgoers preferred Belasco's production to Winthrop Ames's highly praised mounting.

Hardly anyone preferred Anna Steese Richardson and Edmund Breese's **The Love Leash** (10-20-13, Harris), in which a doting, mothering wife (Grace Filkins) overhears her husband (Elliott Dexter) say he wants his freedom and gives it to him. Within a year the couple are back together. A string quartet played between acts. This group became something of a rage during the season, moving from theatre to theatre.

In the season's next entry, Mona Fitzgerald (Florence Reed) has inherited the Eagles, a baseball team, from her father and has vowed to win a pennant in his memory. But the team's manager and his equally shady buddy (Tully Marshall and Malcolm Williams) are determined the team will lose, so that a discouraged Mona will put it up for sale. In the ninth inning the Eagles seem about to go down to defeat by one run, but a young benchwarmer, Copley Reeves (William Courtenay), is called in to pinch-hit. He wins the game and Mona. The play opened with Mona being introduced to her players in a fenced-off area overlooking the team's hometown. The crucial game took place offstage. It was recounted by some ejected players and reinforced by a changing scoreboard. The names of the players—Cy Dobb, Hans Flagner, etc.—skewered famous names of the day. No one was too surprised that a lady was co-author of this baseball comedy. After all, she was an established playwright. But Rida Johnson Young's collaborator on **The Girl and the Pennant** (10-23-13, Lyric) was Christy Mathewson, who undoubtedly helped make the baseball talk seem authentic.

Augustus Thomas's string of disappointments continued with **Indian Summer** (10-27-13, Criterion). Thomas's story centered on the courtship of a much younger girl (Martha Hedman) by an aging artist (John Mason), who for many years has pretended to be the father of the girl's illegitimate brother (Creighton Hale). The boy is now a sailor, and he is fleeing from the police after shooting a man who insulted his mother. The play's most theatrical moment came when the sailor, after a chase on the roof, drops into the artist's studio through a skylight. His pursuers follow him and shoot him.

The ever adventurous Winthrop Ames enjoyed a modicum of success when he offered New Yorkers Laurence Housman and Granville Barker's verse-drama **Prunella; or, Love in a Garden** (10-27-13, Little). It followed the elopement of the naive, confined Prunella (Marguerite Clark) and the worldly mummer, Pierrot (Ernest Glendinning), the falling apart of their marriage, and its restoration when they return to the simple, austere delights of her old home.

What success **Tante** (10-28-13, Empire), Haddon Chambers's dramatization of Ann Douglas Sedgwick's novel, enjoyed was attributed to the box-office pull of Ethel Barrymore, who courageously assumed the role of a thoroughly detestable woman. Her Madame Okraska was a mean, self-obsessed artist who selfishly wrecks the lives of anyone not flattering her ego.

Anne Crawford Flexner's **The Marriage Game** (10-29-13, Comedy) had a droll, winning first act and some striking sets. The charms were enough to seduce most reviewers into extolling the comedy and win for it a modest run. The play's action moved from the deck of a magnificent yacht to its luxurious "saloon," with doors leading off to each of its cabins, to a last act that showed both the saloon and the deck above. The Frosts (William Sampson and Josephine Lovett) have stayed together in a crabbed, joyless marriage; the Packards (George W. Howard and Alison Skipworth) remain married legally but live separate lives; the newly wedded Updegraffs (Charles Trobridge and Vivian Martin) show ominous signs of falling away early in the game. So Mrs. Updegraff's brother, Nevil Ingraham (Orrin Johnson), invites them for a trip on his yacht, hoping the closeness and sea air will turn the marriages around. Jim Packard misunderstands the invitation, does not realize his wife has been asked, and brings along his mistress, Mrs. Oliver (Alexandra Carlisle). The wives quickly turn against the sophisticated widow, but by her example and her somewhat tedious last-act lecturings she shows them how to evoke again their earlier ardor. Many of the best one-liners were given to the Frosts: "When a man's at his club you never know *where* he is!"; "What a woman doesn't know, she suspects,"; and, echoing Barrie, "Charm! Unless a woman wants something she has no business to get, she has no *need* of charm!"

Some critics also thought the first act was the best thing about William C. and Cecil B. de Mille's **After Five** (10-29-13, Fulton), which opened the same night and generally got the short end of the stick. Ted Ewing (Forrest Winant) has speculated away not only his own money but that of his ward and fiancée, Nora Hildreth (Ivy Troutman). To rectify matters he arranges with a member (Bruno Schwartz) of the Black Hand, who has come to dun him for an overdue debt, to kill him after he has taken out a large insurance policy. Ted's attempts at suicide and his subsequent attempts to stop his own murder after his stocks rebound occupy most of the evening. Of course, everything ends happily.

November's first opening was a one-week failure that heralded a drab month. In Albert Lee's **Miss Phoenix** (11-3-13, Harris), a wife (Ann Murdock) disobeys the injunction of her husband (Conway Tearle) against visiting a turkish bath. While she is there the building catches fire, and she is carried out in only a towel to a bachelor apartment nearby. The requisite complications ensue. Miss Murdock was widely touted as another Billie Burke, but her career went nowhere.

A revival of *The Second in Command* at Wallack's on the 3rd served to reintroduce Cyril Maude to American audiences. By 1913 the elfin, still youthful-looking actor had become one of London's most popular comedians, and few remembered that his very first stage appearances were in America thirty years earlier. His return marked the beginning of his extended transatlantic shuttling.

Almost lost in the good-sized cast of **General John Regan** (11-10-13, Hudson) was a player who had been a star when Cyril Maude was in kneepants. But by 1913 Oliver Doud Byron was reduced to the minor role of a priest in Ballymoy (some programs listed the setting as Ballyway), and the *Times*'s critic carelessly referred to him as Bryan (perhaps confusing him with a John N. O'Brien, also in the cast). Ballymoy is a somnolent Irish village until an American (Frederick Burton) decides to revitalize it by inventing one General Regan, trumpeting him as the saviour of Bolivia, and claiming Ballyway as his birthplace. The townsfolk, led by their young doctor (Arnold Daly), set about creating a history of the fictitious general and raising a statue to his honor. The author of the play, listed as George A. Birmingham, actually was the Rev. Cannon Hannay, dean of St. Patrick's, Dublin.

That evening's American offering, Edward Childs Carpenter's **The Tongues of Men** (11-10-13, Harris), was less welcomed and marked another failure for the so often unfortunate Henrietta Crosman. In a way it represented a twisted retelling of *Romance*. The Rev. Penfield Sturgis (Frank Gillmore) fulminates against a famous actress, preaching that if she plays a wicked woman she must be one. The actress, Jane Bartlett (Crosman), confronts him and says he is unfair and prejudiced. In short order he has fallen in love with her and is even prepared to break off his own engagement to marry her. She sends him back to his fiancée a wiser, more charitable man.

In the last few seasons most of David Belasco's productions had been receiving shorter and shorter runs, though they all were at least moderately profitable. But these shorter runs hinted that the once infallible producer was slowly losing his grip. With Roland Burnham Molineux's **The Man Inside** (11-10-13, Criterion), he suffered his first failure in many years. Of course, a sixty-three-performance run was no disgrace, but it was not the sort of stand once associated with the producer. From the start Belasco may have understood he was walking on thin ice. The play Molineux brought him was hardly a play, merely "a lot of words." Belasco whipped it into shape, no doubt hoping the playwright's notoriety would help sell tickets. Molineux, son of a prominent New York family, had spent time on Sing Sing's death row after being convicted for murder but was acquitted and freed following a retrial. When still fresh, the events were depicted in a 1902 touring melodrama, *The Great Poison Mystery*. By the time this drama was produced, he was showing early signs of the paresis that would lead to his death in a mental institution in 1917. The result of Belasco's labors divided the critics. Some agreed with their associates who hailed the play's "depth" and "absolute sincerity"; many more fell in line with the man who regretted the lack of Belasco's customary "pyrotechnical brilliancy."

Molineux's play centered on an assistant district attorney, Richard Gordon (Milton Sills), who visits a thieves' den in order to study criminals and learn what it is inside a man that makes him break the law. He befriends the forger "Red" Mike (A. E. Anson), his daughter, Annie (Helen Freeman), and Mike's accomplice, the man to whom Annie is engaged, "Big" Frank (Edward H. Robins). When the "bulls" (the period equivalent of "pigs") raid the den, Gordon unwittingly allows Annie to swallow the check that would convict her father. For a time Gordon appears to be in hot water. But his honesty and goodness impress not only the rather cynical D.A. (Charles Dalton) but Annie and her menfolk, too. Annie tells Frank she will be loyal while he serves his term. One of the play's delights was its cameo depictions of various criminals, such as "Old 'Pop' Olds" (John Cope). "Pop" had been a hellion in his day, but now, aged and frail, he makes a crooked living painting sparrows yellow and selling them as canaries.

Rachel Crothers's **Ourselves** (11-12-13, Lyric) also looked at a seamy side of life, but more honestly, more intelligently, and with fewer theatrical sops. As a result its run was quite short. There was no "disorderly house" in the play but rather the next stop for some prostitutes and other ladies of the streets—a reformatory. The girls there have had varying experiences and have reacted variously to them. One young immigrant, seduced as soon as she got off the boat, seems not to fully comprehend what has happened. Another pines for her abusive lover, remembering him longingly as someone to come home to. A socialite, Beatrice Barrington (Jobyna Howland), visits the reformatory and takes one of its girls, Molly (Grace Elliston), under her wing. Things go well until Beatrice's attractive artist brother, Bob (Thurlow Bergen), appears and seduces Molly. When Bob's wife (Selene Johnson) and Beatrice confront him, he dismisses his actions by saying that Molly meant nothing to him and that men, being different from women, must be permitted to relieve their stronger sexual drives. Bob's wife points out that women have similar instincts but have spent generations mastering them. Although she is pregnant, she leaves Bob. Molly, her eyes fully opened, tells Beatrice she will go out in the world and teach other girls how to protect themselves.

Cyril Maude's second offering was a double bill consisting of a revival of *Beauty and the Barge* and a one-act curtain raiser, W. W. Jacobs and Charles Rock's **The Ghost of Jerry Bundler** (11-13-13, Wallack's), in which a practical joker disguises himself as a ghost and is shot dead by the people he meant to scare.

The Strange Woman (11-17-13, Lyceum) in William Hurlbut's comedy was not unlike Mrs. Oliver in *The Marriage Game.* She (Elsie Ferguson) was an American who had been married once and spent much of her life in Paris. But Inez, who has resolved to have no more church weddings, has fallen in love with John Hemingway (Charles D. Waldron), and he has insisted on their receiving his mother's blessing. So the pair entrain for Delphi, Iowa. There Inez shoots down one by one the gossipy, malicious townswomen, but Mama Hemingway (Sara von Leer) cajoles her into heading for the altar.

Cyril Maude hit paydirt when he came out in Horace Hodges and T. Wigney Percyval's **Grumpy** (11-19-13, Wallack's). The story told of a retired criminal lawyer, a "dear old man" who wavers between grouchiness and warmheartedness. He solves the mystery after a valuable diamond is stolen from the fiancé (Edward Combermere) of his granddaughter (Margery Maude). Maude played the part in New York until the spring, then took the play to London. Over the next few years he portrayed "Grumpy" Bullivant nearly 2000 times.

Paul Dickey and Charles Goddard, who had written *The Ghost Breaker* last season, also had an offering that ran into spring with **The Misleading Lady** (11-25-13, Fulton). When an actress (Inez Buck) toys with a man's affections by getting him to propose, then turning him down, he (Lewis Stone) throws a cloak over her, carries her to his car, and drives to his Adirondacks retreat. There he chains one of her feet and starts to teach her lessons in good manners. They are interrupted by an escapee (Frank Sylvester) from a lunatic asylum—a man who thinks he is Napoleon—and other oddly assorted people, including the actress's gun-toting fiancé. Eventually the loony is led away while everyone sings the "Marseillaise," and the actress decides she has come to prefer her abductor.

Neither the past nor the present, as seen in December's first two offerings, held much interest for playgoers. The "Marseillaise" was sung on a New York stage for the second time in just over a week in Carina Jordan's **Rachel** (12-1-13, Knickerbocker). This half-fictitious stage biography began with the little street singer selling a stolen umbrella to pay for a copy of Racine and awing passersby with her readings from the dramatist. Intrigues and rocky amours cannot hold her back from her seemingly predestined theatrical glory. George Sand, Alfred de Musset, Chopin, and Saint Aulaire all cross her path, for better or worse. But Bertha Kalish's poetry

and ardor could not invest the tritely written, loosely episodic play with a compelling theatricality.

Children of To-day (12-1-13, Harris) was created by Clara Lipman and Samuel Shipman as a vehicle for Miss Lipman's husband, Louis Mann. The authors cast the star as the middle-aged suitor of an attractive widow (Maude Turner Gordon). The suitor's main obstacles are the widow's spoiled, intrusive children (Emily Ann Wellman and Lorin Raker). He overcomes this hurdle by proving to the son and daughter that their own suitors are merely a pair of fortune hunters.

The two failures were followed a week later by the month's biggest hit, Laurence Eyre's **The Things That Count** (12-8-13, Maxine Elliott's). Done originally in Philadelphia as *Mrs. Xmas Angel,* the play was produced by William A. Brady and gave his daughter, Alice, one of her first major assignments. The story was simple enough. Mean Mrs. Hennaberry (Florine Arnold) and her henpecked husband (Albert Reed) disown their son after he marries an actress (Miss Brady). The son dies, leaving his wife and young child (Grace Dougherty) in poverty. Suspicious of her husband's regular disappearances, Mrs. Hennaberry trails him and discovers he is trying to help his daughter-in-law and grandchild. Mrs. Hennaberry's heart melts, and she becomes a fairy godmother. For a time the daughter-in-law rebels against their belated interest, but she, too, has a change of heart. Underscoring the main plot were the comings and goings of the daughter-in-law's volatile, bickering neighbors—a theatrical potpourri of Italians, Irish, Jews, and Scandinavians. The slim, sentimental comedy ran out the season.

The New Henrietta (12-22-13, Knickerbocker) was Bronson Howard's old favorite, updated by Winchell Smith and Victor Mapes. Twenty-six years after the original delighted Broadway, William H. Crane was back as Nicholas Van Alstyne, but the role of his underestimated son, Bertie, remembered by so many playgoers for the late Stuart Robson's unique performance, was assumed by a totally different sort of actor, Douglas Fairbanks. One critic noted that, where Robson had been "droll and dry," Fairbanks was "unctuously humorous." The character of the spoiled, uncaring Nicholas junior was drastically changed, and his death scene was omitted. Time promoted some other changes. Figures mentioned in the original had to be doubled or more in the light of a quarter of a century's inflation; and Crane was given a comic scene in which Van Alstyne tries to keep up with the younger set by learning how to smoke a cigarette.

Belasco added another hit to his record with

his production of Henri Bernstein's **The Secret** (12-23-13, Belasco). Its heroine, Gabrielle Jannelot (Frances Starr), seems to be a sweet, affectionate thing, with a "propensity to climb all over the furniture like a playful kitten." She loves her husband (Basil Gill) and does everything she can to promote the marriage of her friend, Henriette (Marguerite Leslie), to Denis le Guern (Frank Reicher), in the face of Denis's worry that Henriette is withholding an unpleasant story from him. Only after the marriage does Gabrielle bring the matter to a head by inviting Henriette's former lover (Robert Warwick)—the secret Henriette has withheld from Denis—to join the others at dinner. The explosions that ensue force the men to take pragmatic measures and Gabrielle to promise with tearful contrition that she hereafter will control her viperish other self.

Diantha Kerr (Bessie Barriscale), the heroine of Eleanor Gates's **We Are Seven** (12-24-13, Maxine Elliott's), is a charity worker teaching eugenics to Lower East Side immigrants. Since the nice young man who accompanies her is deaf and dumb, she thinks nothing of talking out loud to herself about her dreams for a perfect mate and their seven children. Of course, the man isn't really deaf or dumb at all. The play ended quirkily with his pointing to the shadows of their seven dream children silhouetted on a window shade, "stepladder fashion." Effie Ellsler, so long absent from the New York stage, won applause as Diantha's comic aunt.

Two importations from England brought down the curtain on 1913. In Somerset Maugham's **The Land of Promise** (12-25-13, Lyceum), a young girl (Billie Burke), forgotten in her late employer's will and abused by her Canadian brother (Lumsden Hare) and sister-in-law (Lillian Kingsbury), impetuously weds a hired man (Shelley Hull) and goes to live with him in his shack. The marriage is tempestuous—at one point the wife fires a rifle at the husband, only to discover it is not loaded—but eventually the girl comes to recognize the wisdom of her choice.

Two women (Ernita Lascelles and Mary Lawton) who appear to have difficulty making their choice are central figures in Shaw's **The Philanderer** (12-30-13, Little). Charles Maude had the title role in this sendup of Ibsen's vogue among a certain set. The comedy ran three months at the tiny house.

"Advanced women" were also the center of attention in 1914's first American entry. That the girls were delicately twitted was somewhat surprising in light of the fact that Rachel Crothers was the author of **Young Wisdom** (1-5-14, Criterion). Her approach proved how broad-minded, in both senses of the word, the playwright was. Victoria Claffenden (Mabel Taliaferro) returns home from college to attend the wedding of her younger sister, Gail (Edith Taliaferro), to the contentedly conventional Peter Van Horn (Richard Sterling). Victoria is filled with notions of what a modern woman should be, and in no time she has convinced Gail of the absurdity of marriage. Gail in turn convinces the baffled but compliant Peter that they should have a trial marriage. With Victoria and Victoria's beau, Christopher Bruce (Hayward Ginn), in tandem they head for a farmhouse, which an artist friend, Max Norton (Regan Houston), uses as a studio. The sensible Norton promptly drives them all back home. When they return in the wee hours the girls' exasperated father (Aubrey Beattie), a conservative judge, phones a minister to hurry over and marry them. Resigned to marriage, but still craving some modern excitement, the girls rush out to elope—Victoria with Christopher and Gail with Max. Their dutiful chauffeur: Peter Van Horn. Mabel Taliaferro's usual "honey-flavored sweetness" and Edith's "gingery vivacity" had earned them the labels of "dramatic sugar" and "dramatic spice." To everyone's delight the sisters switched types in this comedy, but for all the play's money notices—"one of the most agreeable plays of the season," "a very satisfying evening," "a charming and delightful comedy"—it ran only seven weeks. Rachel Crothers's intelligence and skill were as yet not very marketable.

On the other hand, a beloved English playwright and America's favorite actress—for whom he often had written—scored a much bigger success, although critical opinion held the play "so thin in idea and texture as to be practically no play at all." The nonplay was Barrie's **The Legend of Leonora** (1-5-14, Empire) and the star, of course, Maude Adams. Barrie's story told of a woman on trial for murder—for pushing a man from a speeding train after he refused to close a window and thus stop the draft that would give her baby a cold. Barristers, judge, jury, and gleefully perjuring witnesses turn the law topsy-turvy to acquit her. One equally prejudiced reviewer wrote that the star "never played with finer touches of delicate and ingratiating humor, or richer glimpses of real womanliness and tenderness, so that the general adoration seems the most natural thing imaginable."

The next evening brought in one of the season's oddities, Percy MacKaye's blank-verse retelling of the Turandot tale, **A Thousand Years Ago** (1-6-14, Shubert). The Shuberts had tried out a version of Schiller's drama on the road, withdrawn it, and asked MacKaye to come up with a free reworking. In MacKaye's telling the princess (Rita Jolivet) is not a heartless woman. She asks her unanswerable riddles to ward off suitors since she has fallen in love with a beggar whom she once saw in her garden and subsequently lost track of. The beggar was Calaf, Prince of Astrakhan (Jerome Patrick). He refuses to reveal the fact when he appears in the guise of another prince and answers all her riddles. He then says she need not marry him if she can find out his real name. As he waits to see what will happen, he broods (in a foreshadowing of Puccini's "Nessun dorma"),

O endless, awful night, you are like thought—
Hollow, unanswering and full of echoes!
And like my heart you, too, are sleepless,
    yearning
With dim and palpitating mystery.

MacKaye injected into this Oriental story a band of commedia dell'arte characters—Scaramouche, Punchinello, Pantaloon, and Harlequin—headed by the appropriately named Capocomico (Henry E. Dixey). It is this wily clown who sees through both lovers' facades and engineers the happy denouement. The physical production and staging were done in Reinhardt's stylized manner, with one whole scene—Turandot's dream—performed in pantomime. The aging emperor was played by Frederick Warde, who not long before had been a major touring star. Playgoers were not necessarily turned off by the mounting's more unusual aspects, so the play stayed eleven weeks.

A more conventional comedy, William Collier and Grant Stewart's **A Little Water on the Side** (1-6-14, Hudson), ran only eight weeks. Its action moved from a cracker-barrel store and post office (the cracker barrel was milked for laughs throughout the first act) to a luxurious yacht called the *Limit* (as in "That yacht's the limit!"). The movement reflected the rise of the hero (Collier), who returns from Europe to save his family's failing little emporium but finds there is more money to be made by developing some seashore property he owns ("a little water on the side"). That the father (Henry Weaver) of his sweetheart (Paula Marr) also covets the property provided what small dramatic tension the comedy required.

The month's biggest hit (278 performances) was Catherine Chisholm Cushing's sentimental comedy **Kitty Mackay** (1-7-14, Comedy). Kitty McNab (Molly McIntyre) is a foundling who has been lovingly raised by the penniless Sandy McNab (Ernest Stallard) and his wife (Carrie Lee Stoyle).

Sandy is a darkly religious man, convinced he will be sent to a heaven filled with goats. This so bothers Kitty and her friend Mag (Margaret Nybloc) that they set about to rewrite the Bible.

Mag: How about the Garden of Eden tale? Will you tamper with that?
Kitty: Well, we must leave something spicy, or the book'll never get read.

Without much warning, the family who abandoned her back to London, where, as Kitty Mackay, she falls in love with Lt. Davis Graham (Eugene O'Brien). Graham backs away when he is led to believe she is his half-sister, and Kitty returns to Scotland. News that as a baby she was switched for the half-sister who had died allows for a joyous ending. A 1920 musical version, *Lassie,* failed.

H. V. Esmond's London comedy **Eliza Comes to Stay** (1-7-14, Garrick) stayed only a week and a half. The author played a man who "inherits" what he presumes to be a toddler but turns out to be a young cockney (Eva Moore). He and his friends take charge of her metamorphosis into a lady. (Shaw's *Pygmalion* had been written but not yet mounted in England, so the similarities were probably coincidental. For what it is worth, in Esmond's comedy Eliza is made to change her name to Dorothy, since Eliza is considered too plebeian a name—"it sounds like dust-pans.")

With Richard Walton Tully's **Omar, the Tentmaker** (1-13-14, Lyric), beautifully mounted exotica overcame disdainful notices to achieve a minor success. A prologue showed how Omar (Guy Bates Post) wins "one dear bought hour of love" with a girl (Jane Salisbury) betrothed to the Shah. Years pass. Omar adopts and rears a little girl, but only when she has come of age does he learn she (again Salisbury) is his daughter of the long-ago night. Meanwhile, he faces other trials and tribulations. Post was a technically accomplished player, but he lacked that special charisma to light up this sort of romantic role.

Walter Hackett's **Don't Weaken** (1-14-14, Maxine Elliott's) lacked the strength to survive a full week. Billed as "an optimistic comedy," it revealed how its hero (Earle Browne), urged on by his college buddies who "recite in chorus their creed of 'Don't Weaken,'" rises by sheer gumption from a penniless lad to a position of wealth and prestige. It went without saying that he also won himself a bride (Renee Kelly).

Maria Rosa (1-19-14, 39th St.) was a foreign play that required several translations before reaching Broadway. Written in Catalan by Angel Guimera, it was translated into Spanish by José Echegaray and then into English by Guido Marburg and Wallace Gillpatrick. The story told of a peasant (Lou Tellegen) who contrives to have the husband of the woman (Dorothy Donnelly) he loves convicted and executed for someone else's crimes. On their wedding day the drunken peasant blurts out the truth and is stabbed to death by the widow. Tellegen, in his first English-speaking role, garnered divided notices. One critic felt, "His was an impersonation of fine distinction. . . . His poses were beautifully plastic, his calm impressive, his passion finely stirring." A dissenting reviewer wrote, "His method was florid, and his acting . . . always of a rather obvious sort." His accent coupled with the wildly diverse accents of the rest of the cast jarred some aisle-sitters. In his outlandishly vain autobiography Tellegen noted, "As an addition to my make-up for the rôle, I made little round curls on each cheek. Women quickly copied these things, which became known as 'spit-curls'—of all things."

Broadway gave a quick heave-ho to **The House of Bondage** (1-19-14, Longacre), a dramatization by Joseph Byron Totten of Reginald Wright Kauffman's novel. The gist of most dismissals was that playgoers (read critics) were tired by plays touching on prostitution—or, as they were somewhat inaccurately branded, white-slavery plays.

That specious argument was disproved the very next night by Michael Morton's **The Yellow Ticket** (1-20-14, Eltinge). The play was produced by A. H Woods, to whom its sensationalism no doubt appealed. But it was in a class far removed from the potboilers the producer had brought out years before. In Russia a yellow ticket was given to prostitutes to allow them to ply their trade. Marya Varenka (Florence Reed) is a Jewish girl who sees prostitution as the only way to help support her dying father. (Remember, the heroine in *The Lure* took to prostitution to help her dying mother.) Marya's yellow ticket allows her to roam freely beyond the areas to which Jews are normally confined. A baron (John Mason) who heads the secret police tricks her into coming to his apartment, tries to seduce her, and is stabbed to death with her hairpin for his pains. It takes the resourcefulness and persistence of an American newspaperman (John Barrymore), who has fallen in love with her, to bring about her release. Dark-haired, dark-eyed Miss Reed imbued Marya with gentle dignity. For Barrymore the role of the rather buoyant, flippant reporter marked a step away from comedy toward more serious assignments.

In Margaret Turnbull's **The Deadlock** (1-20-14,

Maxine Elliott's), a man (Thomas J. Carrigan) who became a priest after being told his wife was dead is about to officiate at the dedication of his new church. His parishioners have invited a famous opera star to sing for the occasion. She turns out to be the supposedly dead wife (Edith Wynne Matthison), and she has brought along their ten-year-old son (Master Norris Millington).

H. V. Esmond and his wife, Eva Moore, having failed to delight New Yorkers with their first offering, tried again with his **The Dear Fool** (1-26-14, Garrick). Second time around brought no better luck with this saga of a young widow who nearly ruins her reputation by quoting Omar Khayyam and running off for a one-night fling with a man half her age.

Change (1-27-14, Booth), J. O. Francis's prize-winning English drama, took a hard look at Welsh life and its rebellious younger generation. Performed by Welsh actors, the show was withdrawn after one week, but a vociferous, sustained outcry by a coterie of advocates prompted its revival for a few additional showings in March.

Rida Johnson Young's **Shameen Dhu** (2-1-14, Grand Opera) was a vehicle for Chauncey Olcott, who inevitably inserted a few Irish songs into her text. By 1914 Olcott was in his mid-fifties, neither his voice nor his looks what they once were. But that could not stop him from portraying the dashing Dare O'Donnell, who lets himself enter into an engagement of convenience with a widow (Beth Franklyn) in order to help her out of a scrape, then discovers his selflessness nearly wrecks his plans for wedding a lovely colleen (Constance Molineaux).

William Faversham's lavish revival of *Othello*, which began a two-week stand at the Lyric on the 9th, was notable chiefly for the star's novel approach to Iago, whom he saw as "a humorist." R. D. MacLean gave Othello "a certain slow-witted dignity," while Cecilia Loftus was a "colorless" Desdemona.

In Jack Lait's **Help Wanted** (2-11-14, Maxine Elliott's) a rich manufacturer (Charles Richman), disdainful of the unsophisticated girl (Lois Meredith) his son (Charles Ruggles) would marry, makes a pass at her. Matters are smoothed over, although the old man remains unrepentant.

With the ten-week run of **The Rule of Three** (2-16-14, Harris), Guy Bolton began to make a name for himself as a playwright.

. . .

Guy [Reginald] **Bolton** (1884–1979) was born in England to American parents. He studied to be an architect and practiced for a time before changing callings. Although he would become better known as a librettist, he would continue to place interesting comedies and dramas before audiences for the next forty years.

. . .

In this early play a couple (Francis Byrne and Katherine Grey) head off to a honeymoon in Vermont. But their anticipated pleasures are abruptly set in abeyance when the bride's first two husbands (George Hassell and Orrin Johnson) appear. She must find eligible ladies for her exes. A comic bellboy (Will Archie) garnered many of the laughs, as did the wife's daughter (Vivian Tobin) by differentiating among the men in her mother's life. Number one she calls "father," number two "daddy," and number three "papa." The high-ceilinged, false-Tudor lobby of the Mountain View House and its comfortable wicker furniture added eye appeal to the evening.

Henry W. Savage hoped his production of Holman Day's **Along Came Ruth** (2-23-14, Gaiety) might have a different sort of appeal. His advertisements promised a comedy "as wholesome as your grandmother's gingerbread." Programs noted that the play was derived from a French work (it was actually Belgian—*La Damoiselle de màgasin*), but the piece that reached Broadway was so Down East Yankee that critics were hard put to see any influences. Critics labeled the heroine (Irene Fenwick) a "Puritan Maggie Pepper" and a "Pine Tree Bunty"; this little lass who comes to stodgy, tradition-bound Old Port, Me., takes a job in blue-blooded Israel Putnam Hubbard's furniture store, and brings the town to life.

February saved its best for last. The curtain of Frank Craven's **Too Many Cooks** (2-24-14, 39th St.) rose to show a suburban building lot with only the foundation of a small house on it. The house will someday be a snuggery for Albert Bennett (Craven) and his bride-to-be, Alice Cook (Inez Plummer). Alice is so proud and happy that she invites her entire family to look at the plot. And the Cooks come en masse—her battle-axe mother, her belligerent unionist father, her two equally distasteful sisters, her towering hulk of a brother, her consumptive brother, and her haughty if vulgar aunts. Tagging along is Alice's acid-tongued friend, Ella (Eva Gordon). Their suggestions for improving the house seem more like orders to Albert and bode ill.

By the second act the framework for the house is largely up. Albert's rich uncle and employer (Edward McWade) enters, decides he likes what he sees, and tells the young lovers he will take a room in the house. In minutes the Cooks and Uncle George are at war. Alice and Albert are sucked into the battle—on opposing sides—so Alice angrily gives back her engagement ring and storms out. Her father orders the builders to go on strike.

The last act shows the house's exterior finished. The finish is not the best, since Albert and some helpers had to do the work themselves. Among other disappointments the shingling is crooked. Albert has also planted a small garden, and one rose is blooming. But, lonely as he is, Albert is seen putting up a For Sale sign. Alice has been just as unhappy. Her unhappiness prompts her to return to look at the house. She plucks the rose, then sees Albert. There are apologies and forgiveness on both sides.

Alice: And you love me enough to forgive me for the way I behaved?
Albert: I love you enough to forgive you if you were your mother.

The whole Cook clan and Uncle George barge in but are politely sent on their way. Alice and Albert resolve that the house will be for them and them alone. A distant train whistle is heard.

Alice: There goes the train to the city with the folks.
Albert: That's my idea of many happy returns.

The headline of Walter Prichard Eaton's notice read "A Victory of Unpretentiousness," and Eaton himself concluded, " 'Too Many Cooks' is funny, it is wholesome, it is true—and, best of all, it is unconsciously and thoroughly American." Craven, with his "stubbornly homey face" and his similarly homey style, entertained Broadway for nearly seven months and for a time headed one of the comedy's several road companies. In 1922 the show returned successfully in musical guise as *Up She Goes*.

. . .

Frank Craven (1875–1945) The Boston-born son of actors, he made his first appearance alongside them in 1887 in *The Silver King*. His Broadway debut came in 1908 in *Artie*. Not until he played Jimmy Gilley, the heroine's brash, sponging brother, in *Bought and Paid For* in 1911 did he call attention to himself. He was a small, slightly jowly man.

. . .

March's first two openings survived a mere fortnight. Both were by men still raking in money from earlier hits. Augustin MacHugh's **What Would You Do?** (3-2-14, Hudson) was a crook play, although his crook was a bungling but lucky amateur. George Scarborough's **The Last Resort** (3-2-14, Longacre) was a muckraking drama produced when muckraking was beginning to bore audiences.

In MacHugh's play a wealthy man (Richie Ling) talks a weak-willed husband (Milton Sills) into embezzling some money, hoping to court the man's wife (Bessie Barriscale) after he is caught and jailed. But the husband parlays his crooked money into a small fortune. Although he comes home to find his wife and the rich man in each other's arms, he eventually forgives her. His money is turned over to a charity for crippled children. Scarborough's story followed attempts by corrupt politicians to silence a rising, idealistic young attorney (Wilson Melrose). A spunky newspaperwoman (Olive Wyndham) determines to help the lawyer and silence the grafters. He becomes governor, and she becomes the governor's lady.

A power-mad union may have stopped the building of a house in *Too Many Cooks,* but fortunately unions had not yet got a serious foothold into the theatre in 1914. As a result, when the cast of *Peg o' My Heart* wanted to relieve the tedium of hundreds of repetitions they had no trouble mounting a series of special matinees, which presented a series of one-act plays J. Hartley Manners had written for them. **Just As Well** (3-6-14, Cort) told of a pair of doubting lovers (Laurette Taylor and Hassard Short), both with speech defects, who decide to go ahead with their marriage after all. **Happiness** told how a humble shopgirl (Miss Taylor) finds contentment. In **The Day of Dupes** Miss Taylor played a courtesan who says farewell to her lovers before entering a convent.

The brahmin Margaret Anglin was accorded divided but generally favorable notices when she came into the Hudson on the 16th in a repertory of *As You Like It, The Taming of the Shrew,* and *Twelfth Night.* Her set designer, Livingston Platt, received a far more enthusiastic reception: "There is Oriental splendor in the palace of Orsino and in the garden of Olivia, the loveliness of rose-rinted blossoms, green cypresses, and tawny walls rising against a far and hazy sky." After just two weeks she switched to a revival of *Lady Windermere's Fan,* which ran out the season.

Whatever reception Laurette Taylor won with her bill of short plays, the season of one-acters at the other end of the theatre district had limped to a halt. In its place came Washington Pezet and Bertram Marburgh's farce **Marrying Money** (3-18-14, Princess), which saw its hero (William Roselle), possessed of a champagne name and beer purse, decide to marry the heroine (Nan Campbell) for her money, unaware her family has just lost its fortune. Love triumphs over bank accounts. Newspapers reported that one of the playwrights was, in fact, Don

Alfonso Washington Pezet, son of the Peruvian minister, but that news failed to spur ticket sales.

Edward Peple's **A Pair of Sixes** (3-20-14, Longacre) might be perceived as a waspish *Potash and Perlmutter,* and the fact that it ran only half as long conceivably says something about 1914 New York playgoers, since, at least on paper, it is far better motivated and filled with funnier business and considerably more humorous lines. Certainly critics thought so, welcoming it as "an unintermittingly laughable farce," "hilarious," and "uproarious fun."

Everybody at the Eureka Digestive Pill Company seems to snap at each other, even the office help.

Jimmy: Aw, how many tings does yer want me to be doin' at the same time? I ain't no orty-me-bile truck!
Sally: (*Rather amused*) No, you're a noisy little runabout that needs more spanking than you do cranking.

But the real problem is that Eureka's two partners, George B. Nettleton (George Parsons) and T. Boggs Johns (Hale Hamilton), can't get along. Nettleton, for instance, is unhappy that Johns has used violet coloring to coat "the little pill that fills the bill." Their arguments become so heated and so frequent that their attorney, Thomas J. Vanderholt (Fritz Williams), has them play a game of poker, with the loser to stay away from the business for a year and serve, instead, as the winner's butler. Vanderholt's ploy is not entirely disinterested, since he is Johns's rival for pretty Florence Cole (Ann Murdock). Johns loses, and since he will have to forfeit his share of the business if he fails to keep his part of the bargain, all sorts of obstacles and annoyances are thrown in his path. Among other things, Nettleton tells him he's discontinued the violet coating: "I've changed it to a polka dot." Florence urges Johns to play up to Mrs. Nettleton (Ivy Troutman), thereby making Nettleton suspicious and jealous. The trick works. Florence also points out that the whole arrangement was illegal, since it was based on a game of chance. The partners shake and make up.

The published text, like that of *Too Many Cooks,* details the curtain calls after each act. Those in *Too Many Cooks* seemingly are simple bows, but in *A Pair of Sixes* the older practice of tableaux that in effect continue the action sometimes is stipulated. One way or another, the practice would be discontinued within a few seasons. In 1926 *A Pair of Sixes* was turned into the hit musical *Queen High.*

A careful look at the passing record demonstrates how quickly popular themes and popular players could find new attractions or new vehicles. Three weeks after he opened in the failed *What Would You Do?* Milton Sills was the leading man in Monckton Hoffe's **Panthea** (3-28-14, Booth). The producer's strange choice for Sills's leading lady was Olga Petrova, who, despite her name, was an English girl heretofore better known in vaudeville and musical comedy. Both she and Sills soon went on to fame in silent films. In the play they took the parts of lovers who meet a tragic end after he learns she has allowed herself to be seduced so that his opera might be presented. This time Sills found employment for ten weeks.

To replace the failed *Land of Promise* for the remainder of Billie Burke's season, Charles Frohman brought out Catherine Chisholm Cushing's **Jerry** (3-28-14, Lyceum). The play unfolded in an attractive Main Line mansion, its wide glass doors offering a glimpse of the rolling country that makes up so much of Philadelphia's suburbs. A road winds through the hills. It is twilight, and "the black body and gleaming headlights of an automobile can be seen approaching along the distant road. It is seen crossing and recrossing the landscape, growing larger and larger, and finally drawing up at the door with a sudden blaze of its lights and the bang of a blow-out. Enter Jerry."

Jerry is a very young lady, not merely up-to-date but "an hour ahead of time." She has long loved Montagu Wade (Shelley Hull), even though he is many years her senior and engaged to her aunt (Gladys Hanson). To win him away, she causes the aunt and her fiancé to quarrel, sends an announcement of her aunt's engagement to another man to a Philadelphia newspaper, and even feigns suicide (looking very lovely in her pink pajamas).

On the afternoon of the 30th, the same day Margaret Anglin presented *Lady Windermere's Fan,* the Lyceum, where *Jerry* had premiered two nights before, played host to a second revival. The play was Thomas Heywood's 300-year-old *A Woman Killed with Kindness.* It was offered only for a single matinee, but that it was offered at all suggested that Broadway was becoming willing not only to explore new styles of plays but to remount neglected masterworks from the past. Curiously coupled with this Elizabethan tragedy was Ridgely Torrence's **Granny Maumee** (3-30-14, Lyceum), in which Dorothy Donnelly, in blackface, portrayed a 100-year-old former slave who miraculously regains her eyesight to see that her new great-great-grandchild has white blood.

The season's last hit was yet another variant of the crook-play. **The Dummy** (4-3-14, Hudson), Harriet Ford and Harvey O'Higgins's reshaping of material from O'Higgins's short stories. Its hero was a resourceful and determined sixteen-year-old Bowery scamp, still of an age to wear knickers. He is Barney Cook (Ernest Truex), and he is resolved to be a detective. To his surprise and delight, on applying at a detective agency for a position, he is asked to pose as a deaf-and-dumb scion of a Chicago fortune and allow himself to be abducted by the same kidnappers who are holding a little girl (Joyce Fair), then to rescue the girl. When his new, elegantly spoken little mate inquires what a detective is, he replies in his thick Bowery accent, "He's de guy dat does de woik de cop gets paid for." Later, when she keeps on nodding off he suggests that she has put the "nap" in "kidnap." The first part of the scheme, at a shuttered gambling house, works very well until the main detective is caught lurking about. Then the kidnappers take Barney and the girl to a secluded mountain retreat. There Barney himself nods off in a chair and babbles revealingly in his sleep. Awakened, he is quick-witted enough to talk his way out of danger, and he finally rescues the girl. His reward is to be made an honest-to-goodness detective. He also is given a second reward, the $10,000 offered for the girl's return. Asked what he will do with the money, he replies laconically, "Count it." Years down the road the little girl who played the first kidnap victim would carve careers for herself in the theatre and elsewhere—but under the name Clare Booth Luce. Meanwhile, the comedy's 200-performance run gave a major boost to her rescuer.

. . .

Ernest Truex (1889–1973) was born in Rich Hill, Mo., and made his debut as a child prodigy there in 1894. The tiny, raspy-voiced actor first appeared in New York in 1908. His smallness and boyish looks allowed him to play characters much younger than he actually was for many years. Eventually his stage career spanned more than seven decades.

. . .

The Governor's Boss (4-14-14, Garrick) was part crook-play (if politicians can be considered crooks), part muckraking drama, and part dramatized tabloid. Written by James S. Barcus, a former senator with no other experience at playwriting, it offered a thinly disguised retelling of the Sulzer Affair. Aided by corrupt political bosses, William Sulzer was elected governor of New York in 1912. He promptly turned against the very backroom wheelers and dealers who elected him, apparently hoping to become another Teddy Roosevelt. Not unexpectedly, the politicians turned against him, had him impeached, and removed from office.

In Barcus's play the governor was named Lancelot Shackleton (John E. Kellerd); the leader of his promoters-turned-enemies, Hiram Tally (George Fawcett). For obvious box-office reasons, Barcus gave his drama a happy ending, with the boss exposed for what he is by hidden motion picture cameras and dictographs. Although Kellerd was still basking in the afterglow of his long run as Hamlet, critics had few kind words for him, virtually to a man preferring Fawcett's rugged, forceful acting. No one liked the play.

Grace George, looking especially fetching in a white gown with gold lace and a girdle of peacock blue gems, headed the cast of a revival of Clyde Fitch's *The Truth* at the Little on the 14th. Her support included Conway Tearle, Ferdinand Gott-schalk, and (from the original) Zelda Sears. The small role of the messenger was taken by Guthrie McClintic. Since its initial, unsuccessful Broadway stand the play had won acclaim in London and on the Continent. New York's critics thought the play had aged well or hadn't aged at all. A fine production and critical praise allowed the revival to enjoy excellent business for its limited seven-week stand, which, in any case, was longer than its 1907 engagement.

Myra Wiren's **Vik** (4-29-14, Wallack's) attempted to recount the first triumph of Christianity over paganism in Switzerland but was hooted off the stage after five showings.

William A. Brady's production of Sydney Rosen-feld's **The Charm of Isabel** (5-5-14, Maxine Elliott's) apparently wasn't much better. It tallied seven performances. One critic described it as "an advanced first act French farce grafted on to two acts of New England stock, of the 'Way Down East' variety." Isabel (Marie Nordstrom) is an American widow vacationing in Paris. When her French suitor (Albert Brown) climbs through her window to press his suit, she shields herself with her sheets and pillows, promises him an answer later in the day, then rushes to take the first boat back to America. The suitor follows her to her home in Salem but has to settle for one of Isabel's friends, since Isabel has decided to wed a minister (Felix Krembs). Her charms also cure a cantankerous invalid (Ned Sparks). But Miss Nordstrom's charms were no-where in evidence, and critic after critic ruled that she was sadly miscast.

The season's last offering was Charles Frohman's all-star revival of Sardou's *A Scrap of Paper* at the Empire on the 11th. John Drew, Ethel Barrymore, Mary Boland, Ernest Glendinning, Charles Dalton, and Mrs. Thomas Whiffen were the best-known names in the cast.

There is some reason to believe that President Wilson attended a Washington performance of the play prior to making his "scrap of paper" speech. But before that occurred, and before the next season really got under way, all hell broke loose in Europe. On June 29, Archduke Francis Ferdinand and his wife were assassinated at Sarajevo. Ultimatums flew back and forth. Then, on July 29, Austria-Hungary declared war on Serbia, and Germany declared war on Russia and France. Days later guns started firing, and World War I was on.

The war brought an end to an era, an era that would soon be looked on as an age of innocence, even though common sense demonstrates no era is innocent. The theatre was quickly hurt, with many of its fine, young European talents drafted into battle and no small number of them killed. The attitude toward theatre and plays also changed. A harsher, sometimes less romantic view, while not new, gained wider currency.

Of course, the theatre, like almost everything else, is constantly in flux, and someone who had first gone to the theatre forty-five years earlier, during Daly's first season, and who had remained a faithful playgoer ever since would have seen countless changes—although he or she might not have noticed the more gradually evolving ones. Over those years the growing ethnic diversity and the ever increasing population meant an end to the long years of loyalty to English plays and stage traditions. It also meant not only more plays to fill a swelling number of theatres, but a greater variety in playwriting styles to please more disparate tastes, especially in New York. On the road, beginning in the 1870s, burgeoning railroads brought more and better theatre to communities whose choices had been severely restricted or that had enjoyed no theatre at all. But tastes away from Broadway were also in flux.

If Shakespeare and English comedy began to wane in appeal, melodrama, whose antecedents seemed more Continental than English, flourished. It thrived in no small measure because more and more less moneyed, less educated audiences were attending the theatre both in large cities and in small towns. Many were immigrants who had difficulty with the language but not with the stage pictures. Indeed, the language itself was less flowery, more mundane—since vernacular prose was swiftly replacing ornate blank verse (a change sweeping European stages every bit as much as American ones). By contrast, Robertson's refined new "cup and saucer" comedies had appealed to a smaller elite and, in effect, created a separate, more sophisticated theatre.

This newer, more intimate type of play needed a

new, more intimate type of theatre, and Americans, slowly at first, then more rapidly, started to erect just such playhouses (as the West End and other European theatrical centers werre doing). This newfound intimacy in turn altered notions of acting, for bringing players and playgoers closer together vividly demonstrated how ludicrously, if sometimes necessarily, overblown older mannerisms were. It also furthered the death knell for huge wing-and-drop settings and clearly favored box sets.

The coming of electrification in the 1880s served to further these changes. Scene painters and costumers were able to abandon primary colors for more subtle tones. At the same time, even the best painted sets often appeared to have an unfortunate air of unintended unreality about them, and this gave rise to cries for an end to realism, for stylized and suggestive scenery. Within a few years Appia, Craig, Reinhardt, and others were experimenting in Europe, and Robert Edmond Jones would alert his fellow Americans to the artistic possibilities of set design early in 1915. Similarly, the brighter new footlights, especially in the new smaller houses, helped modify acting styles. They also doomed the old practice of fifty- and sixty-year-old performers playing youngsters.

A decade or so after the electrification of theatres, the first primitive films were shown. In short order they killed lower-class theatres by usurping their audiences, reinforced the realization of how unnatural some older acting techniques were, and even changed Americans' ideas of what a beautiful leading lady or handsome leading man should look like.

If melodrama disappeared from American stages, shortly after the turn of the century, it left behind several descendants. Certainly the crook play was a more restrained, polished version of the old blood-and-thunder cliff-hangers, while the who-dunit evolved almost ineluctably from the crook-play. And the crook-play itself would be reinvigorated a few years on with the coming of Prohibition and bootlegging. Quite possibly the great muckraking plays of the turn of the century belong to the same family. When muckraking, with its eye on specific local wrongdoings, faded, the protest drama, dealing with vaster social problems, would take over. Of course, there were less spectacular, smaller dramas, which possibly could look back to Scribe's well-made play as a progenitor. And these provided much of the more serious entertainment theatregoers sought.

French traditions of vaudeville and farce were the inspiration for much American comedy, even if turn-of-the-century puritans wanted nothing to do with them. But Americans also loved homespun comedies. Very early on, when theatres were still confined to a handful of American cities, they dwelt on the humor to be found there, at most introducing a bumpkinish country cousin for contrast. But as theatre spread to smaller towns, and as Americans raised in rural areas moved to towns but often looked back longingly, rural settings served to frame many of the best American comedies, although by the outbreak of World War I sunny rural comedies were being supplanted by jaundiced looks at suburbia.

Whether comedy or drama, more and more plays were American. The early pleas for more native theatre were being largely answered. Now the cry became a wail against the often slapdish, blatantly commercial thrust of indigenous writing. That cry was not to fade away. Still, all but the most unreasonably demanding whiners were even now beginning to find cause for cheers.

So someone who had been going to the theatre for forty-five years had seen lots of changes by mid-1914. If he or she could hang on for another decade or two, the changes would continue to startle.

APPENDIX

Abbey's Theatre Broadway and 38th Street.

Academy of Music 14th Street and Irving Place.

American Theatre 42nd Street and Eighth Avenue.

Astor Theatre Broadway at 45th Street.

Belasco Theatre For a time between 1902 and 1910 the Republic Theatre on 42nd Street just west of Seventh Avenue bore the name. A second play-house, initially called Belasco's Stuyvesant, was opened in 1907 on 44th Street between Broadway and Sixth Avenue. In 1910, after the Republic reverted to its original name, its name was shortened to Belasco

Berkeley Lyceum 44th Street just west of Fifth Avenue.

Bijou Theatre Broadway at 30th Street.

Booth Theatre 45th Street west of Broadway.

Booth's Theatre 23rd Street and Sixth Avenue. Built in 1869 by Edwin Booth and soon lost, it was home to some of his most memorable mountings. Demolished in 1882.

Bowery Theatre Built just south of Canal Street, it opened in 1826 and survived until 1929. In our period it was in decline. Not to be confused with the later New Bowery Theatre, erected a few blocks away and destroyed by fire in 1866.

Broadway Theatre The name given to numerous playhouses. In the years covered by this volume it applied briefly to a theatre at 728 Broadway and, after 1888, to a one on Broadway at 41st Street.

Carnegie Lyceum A small playhouse situated at Seventh Avenue and 57th Street in the same building that houses Carnegie Hall.

Century Theatre See New Theatre.

Circle Theatre Broadway at Columbus Circle.

Cohan Theatre 43rd Street at Broadway. Officially called George M. Cohan's Theatre.

Columbus Theatre 125th Street between Lexington and Fourth Avenues.

Comedy Theatre The name given briefly in 1889–90 to a theatre on 8th Street, between Broadway and Fourth Avenue. From 1909, a playhouse on 41st Street between Sixth and Seventh Avenues.

Cort Theatre 48th Street between Sixth and Seventh Avenues.

Criterion Theatre One of the auditoriums in the Olympia complex built by Oscar Hammerstein on Broadway, between 44th and 45th Streets.

Daly's Theatre See Wood's Museum.

Eagle Theatre Sixth Avenue between 32nd and 33rd Streets. Later called the Standard.

Eltinge Theatre 42nd Street between Seventh and Eighth Avenues.

Empire Theatre Broadway just below 40th Street.

Fifth Avenue Theatre The first theatre was on 24th Street west of Broadway, just behind the Fifth Avenue Hotel. After it burned in 1873 it was replaced by another theatre with the same name at 28th and Broadway. In the interim a theatre at 728 Broadway briefly was utilized and called the New Fifth Avenue. Until 1899 all these playhouses were home to Augustin Daly's ensembles.

Forty-eighth Street Theatre 48th Street between Sixth and Seventh Avenues.

Fourteenth Street Theatre 14th Street just west of Sixth Avenue. Also known at times as the Théâtre Français, the French Theatre, the Lyceum, and Haverly's or Haverly's Lyceum. It was demol-ished in 1938, after serving as home to the Civic Repertory Theatre during the late 1920s and early 1930s.

French Theatre See Fourteenth Street Theatre.

Fulton Theatre 46th Street west of Broadway.

Gaiety Theatre Broadway at 45th Street.

Garden Theatre Madison Avenue at 27th Street, part of the Madison Square Garden complex.

Garrick Theatre 35th Street just east of Sixth Avenue.

Grand Opera House 23rd Street and 8th Avenue. It survived until destroyed by fire in the 1960s.

Grand Street Theatre Grand and Chrystie Streets.

Appendix

Hackett Theatre 42nd Street between Seventh and Eighth Avenues. Later called the Harris.

Harlem Opera House 125th Street between Seventh and Eighth Avenues.

Harris Theatre See Hackett Theatre.

Haverly Lyceum See Fourteenth Street Theatre.

Herald Square Theatre Broadway and 35th Street.

Herrmann's Theatre Built as the San Francisco Minstrel Hall on Broadway between 28th and 29th Streets. It had numerous other names.

Hoyt's Theatre See Madison Square Theatre.

Hudson Theatre 44th Street between Broadway and Sixth Avenue.

Knickerbocker Theatre See Abbey's Theatre.

Liberty Theatre 42nd Street between Seventh and Eighth Avenues.

Lina Edward's Theatre Broadway at 8th Street.

Lincoln Square Theatre Broadway between 65th and 66th Streets.

Little Theatre 44th Street west of Broadway.

Longacre Theatre 48th Street west of Broadway.

Lyceum Theatre Although several other playhouses, such as the Fourteenth Street Theatre, briefly carried this name, the two most important auditoriums to use it were one on Fourth Avenue between 23rd and 24th Streets (from 1885 to 1902) and one on 45th Street just east of Broadway (from 1903 to the present).

Lyric Theatre 42nd Street between Seventh and Eighth Avenues.

Madison Square Theatre 24th Street west of Fifth Avenue, on the site of Daly's first Fifth Avenue Theatre.

Majestic Theatre Eighth Avenue and 58th Street.

Manhattan Opera House On 34th Street between Eighth and Ninth Avenues. Still standing in 1992.

Manhattan Theatre The first was on 34th Street between Broadway and Seventh Avenue. Opened in 1892, it soon became Koster and Bial's Music Hall. From 1897 to 1909 the old Standard Theatre was given this name.

Maxine Elliott's Theatre 39th Street between Broadway and Sixth Avenue.

Mendelssohn Hall 113 West 40th Street.

Metropolitan Opera House Broadway between 39th and 40th Streets.

Metropolis Theatre 143rd Street and Third Avenue.

Mount Morris Theatre Third Avenue and 130th Street.

Mrs. Osborne's Playhouse See Berkeley Lyceum.

Murray Hill Theatre Lexington Avenue between 41st and 42nd Streets.

New Theatre Central Park West between 62nd and 63rd Streets.

New Amsterdam Theatre 42nd Street between Seventh and Eighth Avenues.

New York Theatre Part of Hammerstein's Olympia complex on Broadway between 44th and 45th Streets. Formerly the Olympia Music Hall.

Niblo's Broadway and Prince Streets, part of the Metropolitan Hotel. Already in decline in the period covered.

Olympia Music Hall Broadway between 44th and 45th Streets.

Olympic Theatre 624 Broadway. Already in decline in the period covered.

Palmer's Theatre See Wallack's Theatre.

Park Theatre Broadway between 21st and 22nd. It was built in 1874 and was destroyed by fire in 1882. A later theatre of the same name stood at 35th and Broadway. After 1911, the Majestic Theatre at Columbia Circle used the name for a time.

Peoples Theatre 199 Bowery.

Playhouse, The 48th Street between Sixth and Seventh Avenues.

Princess Theatre Broadway between 28th and 29th Streets, the playhouse had numerous other names, including Herrmann's Theatre. Demolished in 1907. A new playhouse with the same name was built subsequently on 39th Street between Broadway and Seventh Avenue and opened in 1913.

Republic Theatre 42nd Street just west of Seventh Avenue.

Savoy Theatre 34th Street just west of Broadway.

Shubert Theatre   44th Street west of Broadway.

St. James Theatre   In 1878 an auditorium at 23rd Street west of Sixth Avenue briefly used the name. A later theatre with this name was on 28th Street, west of Broadway.

Standard Theatre   See Eagle Theatre.

Star Theatre   Broadway and 13th Street. See Wallack's Theatre. This playhouse was demolished in 1901. Another theatre with the same name was opened in 1902 at Lexington Avenue and 107th Street.

Stuyvesant Theatre   44th Street east of Broadway. After 1910 known as the Belasco.

Thalia Theatre   See Bowery Theatre.

Third Avenue Theatre   Third Avenue between 30th and 31th Streets.

Thirty-Ninth Street Theatre   39th Street just east of Broadway.

Tony Pastor's Theatre   Until 1881 at 585 Broadway. Thereafter on 14th Street between Irving Place and Fourth Avenue.

Twenty-third Street Theatre   23rd west of Sixth Avenue. Also known as the St. James, and home to Salmi Morse's *Passion Play.*

Union Square Theatre   14th Street, opposite the Square, between Broadway and Fourth Avenue.

Victoria Theatre   42nd Street and Seventh Avenue.

Wallack's Theatre   Wallack's first house during the period was at Broadway and 13th Street. It was renamed The Star after Wallack sold it in 1881 and opened Wallack's in 1882 at Broadway and 30th. This second theatre was later renamed Palmer's.

West End Theatre   125th Street and St. Nicholas Avenue.

Windsor Theatre   43 Bowery.

Wood's Museum   Broadway at 30th. Later Daly's.

Yorkville Theatre   Lexington Avenue and 86th Street.

INDEX

The index is divided into two major sections. The first covers the plays discussed in the book; the second, the people.

PLAYS The Play index lists the plays treated in the book and has a subsection that lists the sources (foreign plays, foreign and domestic novels, poems or short stories) for many of the plays. Most works are given their English language titles. However, if a major overseas star—such as Bernhardt or Salvini—performed the work in its original language, the original title is usually—but not always—given. As a result a foreign title may be repeated in the Sources subsection of the Plays index. Not all sources are provided. In some instances a play's title or subtitle, such as *Wolfert's Roost; or, A Legend of Sleepy Hollow* reveals the source. The few plays that were later revised and retitled by their playwrights appear under both titles, but not in the Sources subsection. Some plays mentioned only in passing and musicals derived from plays discussed are not indexed.

PEOPLE Playwrights and writers whose works served as sources are listed in the People index, as are producers, directors, and designers, but, because listing all performers mentioned would have made the index excessively large, only those players found on six or more pages are included. However, celebrated foreigners, players best known in other fields (musicals, vaudeville, films), some players who were road favorites but rarely appeared in New York, a handful with family connections, and a very few deemed particularly interesting for one reason or another have been included in spite of the six-or-more rule. Exceptions have also been made for certain old timers whose careers came to a halt early on in the chronicle and for some younger players whose careers were more or less just starting at the close of the time frame. Critics per se have not been indexed; they appear only if they also wrote or worked on plays dealt with in this volume. Composers and adjunct figures mentioned in passing have been ignored. Page numbers in bold print indicate mini-biographies.

PLAYS

747

Index

Plays

Index

Plays

Plays

Index

Plays

Plays

Index

Plays

759

Index

Plays

Index

Plays

Plays

Plays

Index

Plays

Index

SOURCES

Index

People

PEOPLE

Index

Index

Index

Index

People

Gill, William, 180, 185, 195, 204, 216, 235, 281, 409, 474, 545
Gillette, William, **165**, 169, 211, 240, 241, 271, 281, 299, 311, 333, 347, 372, 399, 433, 450, 451, 452, 463, 475, 495, 525, 573, 592, 593, 639, 679, 681
Gillingwater, Claude, 696
Gillmore, Frank, 349, 568, 572, 575, 605, 655, 687, 700, 725, 733
Gillpatrick, Wallace, 737
Gilmore, Barney, 400
Gilmore, Paul, 615
Gilmour, J. H., 242, 270, 274, 276, 291, 299, 311, 449, 511, 523, 566, 576
Giradot, Etienne, 354, 355, 417, 436, 522, 575, 720
Giroux, Paul, 276
Gish, Lillian, 720
Glaser, Lulu, 604
Glass, Montague, 727
Glendinning, Ernest, 674, 712, 732, 741
Go-Won-Go-Mohawk, 290, 472
Goatcher, Philip, 221, 232, 245, 246, 252, 253, 270, 272, 290
Goddard, Charles W., 724, 734
Godfernaux, André, 628
Godfrey, G. W., 180, 183
Goethe, Johann Wolfgang, 119, 120
Golden, Richard, 281, 549, 560, 614
Golden William Echard, 327
Goldoni, Carlo, 344, 393
Goldsmith, Oliver, 20, 665
Gollan, Campbell, 395, 399, 476, 541, 686
Gondinet, Edmond, 182, 409
Goodall, William Richard, 378
Goodman, Jules Eckert, 639, 675, 713
Goodwin, Nat C., 173, 179, 184, 202, 203, 278, 307, 325, 338, **352**, 353, 385, 386, 415, 431, 432, 454, 457, 479, 503, 522, 545, 546, 560, 589, 627, 662, 705
Gordin, Jacob, 446, 583
Gorky, Maxim, 627
Görner, C. A., 324
Gotthold, J. Newton, 191, 206, 257
Gottschalk, Ferdinand, 362, 392, 408, 452, 572, 592, 671, 741
Grandin, Elmer, 367, 419
Grangé, Eugène, 57
Granger, Maude, 60, 67, 76, 82, 89, 105, 118, 120, 127, 135, 143, 147, 155, 188, 189, 190, 204, 210, 279, 444, 494, 575, 696, 718
Grant, Robert, 475
Granville, Taylor, 636

Granville-Barker (*see* Barker, Harley Granville)
Grau, Maurice, 262
Graves, Clothilde, 343, 597
Gray, David, 571
Gray, William B., 492
Greenbaum, J. L., 543
Greene, Clay M., 112, 125, 179, 236, 254, 266, 300, 322, 343, 369, 379, 397, 400, 471, 514, 571
Greene, R. E. H., 576
Greene, Sarah P. McLean, 592
Greenstreet, Sidney, 607
Greet, Ben, 500, 532, 563, 607, 665
Gregory, Lady, 626, 699
Grenet-Dancourt, Ernest, 215
Grismer, Joseph, 343, 375, 421, 438, 638
Grogan, Walter E., 571
Gros, Ernest, 408, 458, 470, 476, 597
Grossmith, Weedon, 248, 499, 680
Grove, F. C., 160
Grover, Leonard, 98, 104, 105, 180, 189, 205, 233, 270, 281, 319, 379
Grundy, Sydney, 134, 189, 199, 244, 254, 262, 291, 293, 303, 306, 322, 359, 371, 375, 403, 416, 435, 452, 455, 484, 490, 625
Grute, Nain, 496, 543
Guiches, Gustave, 703
Guillemaud, Marcel, 697
Guimera, Angel, 521, 736
Gunter, Archibald Clavering, 155, 156, 162, 175, 191, 197, 238, 266, 244, 255, 259, 274, 307, 345, 400
Gurney, Edward S., 346
Gyp (Marie-Antoinette, Comtesse de Martel de Janville), 552

Haag, Jackson D., 713
Habberton, John, 117, 156
Hackett, Albert, 651
Hackett, James H., 14, 15, 106, 459, 523
Hackett, James K., 384, 402, 405, 407, 418, 437, 438, **459**, 481, 502, 510, 523, 535, 547, 561, 570, 622, 636, 702
Hackett, Walter, 635, 657, 686, 736
Hading, Jane, 274, 359, 450
Haggard, Rider, 263
Haines, Genevieve Greville, 495, 549
Haines, Robert T., 463, 472, 483, 487, 495, 504, 549, 587, 609, 651, 664, 717
Halbe, Max, 690
Hale, Frederick, 253
Hale, Louise Closser, 554, 677

Halévy, Ludovic, 18, 127, 145, 266, 415, 424
Hall, A. Oakey, 92
Hall, Arthur D., 418, 426
Hall, Howard, 444, 453, 460, 480, 492, 518, 532, 557, 618, 631, 633, 721
Hall, Irving L., 526, 569
Hall, Josephine,
Hall, Laura Nelson, 619, 629, 645, 669, 678, 687, 721
Hall, Thurston, 539, 636
Halliday, Andrew, 15, 59, 64, 107
Halsey, Forrest, 677
Hamilton, Cicely, 635, 702
Hamilton, Cosmo, 557, 658, 713
Hamilton, Hale, 655, 676, 708, 739
Hamilton, Henry, 195, 245, 388, 417, 434, 435, 654, 716
Hamilton, Theodore, 75, 98, 108, 190
Hammerstein, Oscar, 308, 309, 467
Hampden, Walter, 616, 624, **628,** 642, 663, 719, 725
Hanford, Edwin, 336
Hankin, St. John, 584
Hannan, Charles, 502
Hannay, Rev. Cannon, 733
Harben, Nathaniel, 725
Harcourt, William, 371, 400, 426, 523, 526, 725
Hardenberg, Frank, 65, 70, 71, 82, 111, 123, 130, 133, 141, 165
Harding, Lyn, 702, 705, 718, 731
Hardy, Thomas, 174, 181
Hare, John, 390, 404, 470
Harkins, D. H., 13, 24, 27, 32, 36, 39, 52, 54, 56, 57, 60, 62, 65, 71, 72, 80, 89, 91, 113, 117, 131, 133, 198, 258, 296, 314, 334, 473, 494
Harkins, James W., Jr., 371, 389, 390, 409, 492, 495, 516
Harned, Virginia, 317, 334, 371, 378, 379, 398, 407, 426, 429, 450, 460, 466, **488**, 498, 530, 535, 555, 557, 566, 592, 604, 614
Harper, Olive, 641
Harrigan, Edward, 87, 152, 179, 187, 227, 235, 238, 288, 380, 444, 483, 507, 518, 650, 672
Harris, Augustus, 164, 173, 265, 315, 351, 392
Harris, Dr. F., 129
Harris, Elmer Blaney, 638, 649, 692, 713
Harris, Frank, 669
Harris, Hamilton, 426
Harris, Henry B., 565
Harris, Sam, 482, 485, 517, 704
Harris, William, 345, 728
Harrison, Duncan Bradley, 273, 298, 299

Index

People

Lotta (*see* Crabtree, Charlotte)
Loti, Pierre, 712
Lovell, G. W., 20
Lowell, Helen, 357, 395, 538, 662, 696, 728
Lubin, Z., 610
Lubormirski, Prince, 119
Luce, Clare Booth, 740
Lumley, Ralph R., 288, 396
Lytell, Bert, 505

MacArthur, James, 483, 607
MacCurdy, James Kyrle, 574
MacDonald, Ronald, 499
MacDonald, Sara, 588
MacDonough, Glen, 341, 371, 501, 544
MacGrath, Harold, 562
MacHugh, Augustin, 704, 738
MacKaye, Percy, 95, 294, 604, 618, 684, 735, 736
MacKaye, Steele, **43,** 44, 90, 91, 94, 114, 115, 133, 134, 146, 149, 150, 151, 164, 208, 220, 221, 227, 228, 231, 255, 264, 265, 271, 284, 286, 294, 604
MacLaren, Donald, 573
Mack, Andrew, 329, 463, 480, 509, 544
Mack, William B., 518, 520, 544, 547, 548, 603, 679, 699, 710
Mackay, F. F., 55, 56, 58, 60, 65, 71, 77, 83, 143, 204, 231, 243, 350, 388, 402
Macquet, Auguste, 129
Maddern, Minnie, 29, 35, 176, 208, 226, 227, 228, 232, 242, 257, 281 (*see also* Mrs. Fiske)
Madison, Marie, 313
Maeder, Clara Fisher, 35
Maeder, Frederick G., 35, 38, 58, 277, 297
Maeterlinck, Maurice, 491, 563, 569, 627, 670, 677, 681
Magnus, Julian, 95, 128, 370
Major, Charles, 473, 527
Mallefille, Félicien, 80
Malyon, E. G., 557
Mandel, Frank, 713
Manley, Charles, 428
Mann, Louis, 324, 448, 464, 482, 508, 545, 562, 568, 639, 673, 674, 703, 734
Mannering, Mary, 402, 405, 407, 418, 430, 435, 452, 457, 460, 471, 495, 501, 529, 555, 561, 570, 636, 669, 697
Manners, J. Hartley, 506, 561, 608, 621, 642, 650, 651, 717, 739

Manning, William, 515
Manola, Marion, 342, 344, 346
Mansfield, Richard, **184,** 185, 198, 201, 228, 238, 252, 256, 258, 260, 264, 267, 270, 289, 290, 291, 292, 293, 295, 296, 306, 314, 318, 323, 324, 336, 355, 356, 368, 371, 385, 389, 402, 403, 414, 424, 428, 452, 468, 469, 488, 503, 521, 532, 549, 555, 556, 561, 575, 601, 606, 625, 706, 712
Mantell, Robert B., 194, 209, 221, **248,** 252, 267, 292, 314, 324, 329, 335, 526, 546, 563, 595, 648, 690
Mapes, Victor, 481, 525, 734
Marble, Ed, 165
Marble, Scott, 319, 347, 365, 374, 389, 397, 400, 401, 416, 428, 429, 430, 433
Marburg, Guido, 737
Marburgh, Bertram, 739
Marbury, Elisabeth, 325, 428
Marc-Michel, 149
Marchmont, Arthur, 530
Mariani, Federico, 651
Marion, George, 641
Marlowe, Charles, 389, 613 (*see also* Jay, Harriet)
Marlowe, Julia, 154, **264,** 266, 292, 313, 394, 407, 409, 420, 437, 448, 449, 473, 504, 536, 543, 562, 604, 624, 647, 650, 652, 660, 667, 669, 681, 691, 712, 730
Marryat, Captain Frederick, 521
Mars, Anthony, 408
Marsden, Blanche, 351
Marsden, Frederick, 72, 95, 99, 102, 127, 185, 189, 191, 230, 239, 281
Marshall, Frank, 54
Marshall, Harry (*see* Maur, Harry St.)
Marshall, Robert, 438, 464, 465, 477, 480, 485, 497, 508, 539
Marshall, Tully, 557, 626, 663, 702, 731
Marston, John Westland, 233
Marston, Lawrence, 256, 317, 335, 401, 415, 488, 490, 500, 505, 542, 558, 564, 576
Marston, Richard, 52, 55, 65, 67, 69, 83, 94, 112, 117, 134, 161, 171, 177, 212, 217, 222, 231, 232, 373, 393, 406, 409, 488
Martin, Édouard, 549
Martin, Frederick Townsend, 725
Martin, Gabriel, 437
Martinot, Sadie, 187, 209, 221, 300, 338, 365, 381, 426, 489, 560
Martyn, Edward, 462
Mason, A. E. W., 483, 696, 700

Mason, John B., 215, 221, 234, 243, 342, 344, 346, 453, 460, 471, 472, 508, 539, 547, 548, 560, 596, 614, 619, 668, 670, 687, 688, 710, 732, 737
Mason, Reginald, 717
Massinger, Philip, 14
Masson, Michel, 134
Mather, Margaret, 229, 233, 234, 249, 268, 277, 305, 319, 329, 343, 406
Mathews, Charles, 13, 33, 40, 41, 45, 46, 68, 105
Mathews, Frances Aymar, 161, 421, 511, 513
Mathewson, Christy, 732
Matthews, A. E., 673, 680
Matthews, Brander, 116, 252, 278, 342, 346, 394, 447, 688
Matthison, Arthur, 189
Matthison, Edith Wynne, 500, 532, 628, 642, 670, 685, 687, 706, 720
Maude, Cyril, 732, 733, 734
Maugham, Somerset, 636, 641, 657, 662, 667, 675, 707, 735
Maurey, Max, 435
Mawson, Harry P., 316, 461
Mawson, Jean, 427
May, Olive, 361, 456, 717
Mayer, Charles G., 108
Maynard, Cora, 593, 667
Mayne, Rutherford, 719
Mayo, Earl W., 592
Mayo, Edwin F., 278, 342
Mayo, Frank, 26, 40, **60,** 61, 72, 80, 86, 125, 131, 149, 222, 273, 275, 278, 321, 379, 556
Mayo, Margaret, 566, 609, 621, **622,** 658, 674, 675
Mayor, Annie, 284, 292, 299
McAuley, Bernard, 130, 167, 216
McCann, John Ernest, 315, 369
McCardell, Roy L., 651
McCarthy, Dan, 363
McCarthy, Justin Huntley, 274, 288, 384, 418, 484, 521
McClintic, Guthrie, 741
McCloskey, James J., 30, 37, 49, 87, 177, 338, 356, 406, 460, 514, 515
McComas, Carroll, 692
McCormick, Langdon, 532, 564, 589, 603, 609, 612, 641
McCullough, John, 36, **74,** 77, 78, 87, 106, 159, 170, 182, 189, 193, 203, 206, 241, 249, 272, 348, 428
McCutcheon, George Barr, 601, 624, 670
McCutcheon, John T., 544
McDonald, George F., 166
McGovern, John, 593

Index

Index

Index